District Gazetteers of India Series 97

GAZETTEER
OF THE
BOMBAY PRESIDENCY

District Gazetteers of India Series 97

GAZETTEER
OF THE
BOMBAY PRESIDENCY

27 VOLUMES (IN 35 BINDINGS)
VOLUME I. PART I.

HISTORY OF GUJARAT.

EDITED BY
JAMES M. CAMPBELL

GYAN

Published by

Gyan Publishing House
5, Ansari Road
Daryaganj, New Delhi-110002
Phone: 011-47034999, 9811692060
E-mail: books@gyanbooks.com

Distribution Network
gyanbooks.com
India, USA, Canada, UK, Australia, France

ISBN: 978-81-212-8560-5 (Set) 27 Volumes (In 35 Bindings)
978-81-212-8344-1 (PB)
First Published, 1896

2nd Impression 2024

Printed at: Gyan Press, Delhi.

GAZETTEER OF THE BOMBAY PRESIDENCY (VOL. I, PART I)
Editor: JAMES M. CAMPBELL

LIST OF VOLUMES

S. NO.	ISBN NO.	VOLUME	TITLE	AUTHOR	PRICE	PAGES
			ASSAM DISTRICT GAZETTEERS			
1	9788121285926	1st	Cachar	B. C. Allen	600	300
2	9788121285919	2nd	Sylhet	B. C. Allen	750	378
3	9788121285902	3rd	Goalpara	B. C. Allen	400	203
4	9788121285896	4th	Kamrup	B. C. Allen	675	344
5	9788121285889	5th	Darrang	B. C. Allen	725	364
6	9788121285872	6th	Nowgong	B. C. Allen	560	280
7	9788121285865	7th	Sibsagar	B. C. Allen	675	343
8	9788121285858	8th	Lakhimpur	B. C. Allen	690	347
9	9788121285841	9th	Naga Hills and Manipur	B. C. Allen	580	294
10	9788121285834	10th	The Khasi And Jaintia Hills, The Garo Hills And The Lushai Hills	B. C. Allen	675	363
11	9788121285827	11th	The Sadiya and Balipara Frontier Tract	B. C. Allen	375	190
			BENGAL DISTRICT GAZETTEERS			
12	9788121218672	1st	Angul	L. S. S. O'Malley	340	168
13	9788121259637	2nd	Bakarganj	J. C. JACK	970	194
14	9788121218696	3rd	Balasore	L. S. S. O'Malley	450	228
15	9788121259590	4th	Bankura	L. S. S. O'Malley	1000	199
16	9788121218375	5th	Bhagalpur	J. Byrne	390	194
17	9788121218290	6th	Birbhum	L. S. S. O'Malley	300	150
18	9788121259651	7th	Eastern Bengal and Assam - Bogra	J. N. Gupta	940	188
19	9788121218351	8th	Burdwan	J. C. K. Peterson	450	227
20	9788121259538	9th	Calcutta District Gazetteer - Statistics, 1901 - 02		340	68
21	9788121218313	10th	Champaran	L. S. S. O'Malley	410	205
22	9788121259613	11th	Eastern Bengal District Gazetters - Chittagong	L. S. S. O'Malley	1080	216
23	9788121259552	12th	Chota Nagpur Tributary		130	26
24	9788121259415	13th	The Cooch Behar Gazette: Statistics		1460	292
25	9788121218412	14th	Cuttack	L. S. S. O'Malley	490	248
26	9788121261357	15th	Eastern Bengal District Gazetteers Dacca	B. C. Allen	400	207
27	9788121218436	16th	Darbhanga	L. S. S. O'Malley	360	180
28	9789362089335	17th	Darjeeling	L. S. S. O'Malley	500	248
29	9788121259453	18th	Eastern Bengal District Gazetteers - Dinajpur	F. W. Strong	890	178
30	9788121259392	19th	Faridpur	L. S. S. O'Malley	700	140
31	9788121218474	20th	Gaya	L. S. S. O'Malley	540	270
32	9788121214032	21st	Bihar and Orissa District Gazetteer: Hazaribagh	E. Lister	715	234
33	9788121218337	22nd	Hooghly	L. S. S. O'Malley	680	340
34	9788121218191	23rd	Bengal District Gazetteer Howrah	L. S. S. O'Malley	390	199
35	9788121259293	24th	Eastern Bengal and Assam - Jalpaiguri	John F. Gruning	890	178
36	9788121259279	25th	Jessore	L. S. S. O'Malley	960	192
37	9788121259231	26th	Khulna	L. S. S. O'Malley	1100	220
38	9788121259217	27th	Malda	G. E. Lambourn	670	134
39	9788121267854	28th	Manbhum	H. Coupland	600	313
40	9788121218498	29th	Midnapore	L. S. S. O'Malley	500	252
41	9788121218597	30th	Monghyr	L. S. S. O'Malley	560	280
42	9788121259156	31st	Murshidabad	L. S. S. O'Malley	1250	250
43	9788121259576	32nd	Bengal District Gazetteers - Muzaffarpur	L. S. S. O'Malley	940	188
44	9788121259132	33rd	Mymensingh	F. A. Sachse	960	192
45	9788121259118	34th	Nadia	J. H. E. Garrett	1070	214
46	9788121259095	35th	Eastern Bengal and Assam - Noakhali	J. E. Webster	580	115
47	9788121218450	36th	Feudatory States of Orissa	L. E. B. Cobdenramsay	790	395
48	9788121259071	37th	Pabna	L. S. S. O'Malley	710	142
49	9788121218511	38th	Palamau	L. S. S. O'Malley	380	190
50	9788121218634	39th	Patna	L. S. S. O'Malley	500	250
51	9788121218535	40th	Puri	L. S. S. O'Malley	650	328
52	9788121218757	41st	Purnea	L. S. S. O'Malley	440	220
53	9788121258937	42nd	Rajshahi	L. S. S. O'Malley	1080	216
54	9788121256681	43rd	Bihar and Orissa District Gazetteers: Ranchi	M. G. Hallett	1350	278
55	9788121258913	44th	Eastern Bengal and assam - Rangpur	J. A. Vas	890	178
56	9788121218559	45th	Sambalpur	L. S. S. O'Malley	480	242
57	9788121214056	46th	Santal Parganas	L. S. S. O'Malley	940	308
58	9788121218610	47th	Saran	L. S. S. O'Malley	380	190
59	9788121218658	48th	Shahabad	L. S. S. O'Malley	380	190
60	9788121256704	49th	The Gazetteer of Sikhim	H. H. Risley	960	481
61	9788121218573	50th	Singhbhum, Saraikela And Kharsawan	L. S. S. O'Malley	560	280
62	9788121259439	51st	Eastern Bengal District Gazetteers - Tippera	J. E. Webster	730	146
63	9788121259033	52nd	24 Parganas	L. S. S. O'Malley	1420	284

S. NO.	ISBN NO.	VOLUME	TITLE	AUTHOR	PRICE	PAGES
			CENTRAL PROVINCES DISTRICT GAZETTEERS			
64	9789362081728	1st, Vol. A	Akola (Descriptive)	A. E. Nelson, C. Brown	870	436
65	9789362085481	2nd, Vol. A	Amraoti (Descriptive)	S. V. Fitzgerald, A. E. Nelson	1050	524
66	9789362089267	3rd,Vol. A	Balaghat (Descriptive)	R. V. RUSSELL	430	216
67	9789362083494	4th, Vol. A	Betul (Descriptive)	R. V. RUSSELL	610	306
68	9789362085146	5th, Vol. A	Bhandara (Descriptive)	R. V. RUSSELL	580	292
69	9789362088390	6th, Vol. A	Bilaspur (Descriptive)	R. V. RUSSELL	870	434
70	9789362086044	7th, Vol. A	Buldana (Descriptive)	A. E. Nelson	1090	543
71	9789362089014	8th, Vol. B	Chanda (Descriptive)	R. V. RUSSELL	470	234
72	9789362086938	9th	Chhattisgarch Feudatory State	E. A. De Brett	880	440
73	9789362082961	10th	Chhindwara (Descriptive)	R. V. RUSSELL	550	274
74	9789362089342	11th, Vol. A & B	Damoh (Descriptive and Statistical Tables 1891-1901)	R. V. RUSSELL	830	414
75	9789362081230	12th, Vol. A	Durg (Descriptive)	A. E. Nelson	460	232
76	9789362086037	13th, Vol. A	Hoshangabad (Descriptive)	R. V. RUSSELL	860	430
77	9789362086792	14th, Vol. A	Jubbulpore (Descriptive)	A. E. Nelson	950	474
78	9789362089663	15th, Vol. A & B	Mandla (Descriptive and Statistical Tables 1891-1901)	R. V. RUSSELL	370	186
79	9789362086419	16th, Vol. A	Nagpur (Descriptive)	R. V. RUSSELL	790	394
80	9789362080646	17th, Vol. A	Narsinghpur (Descriptive)	R. V. RUSSELL	510	257
81	9789362084835	18th, Vol. A	Nimar (Descriptive)	R. V. RUSSELL	600	299
82	9789362087737	19th, Vol. A	Raipur (Descriptive)	A. E. Nelson	790	396
83	9789362080264	20th, Vol. A	Saugor (Descriptive)	R. V. RUSSELL	570	285
84	9789362081117	21st, Vol. A	Seoni (Descriptive)	R. V. RUSSELL	460	232
85	9789362084965	22nd, Vol. A	Wardha (Descriptive)	R. V. RUSSELL	600	302
86	9789362083401	23rd, Vol. A	Yeotmal (Descriptive)	R. V. RUSSELL	550	277
87	9789362080325	24th, Vol. I, Pt. I	Gwalior (Text and Tables)	R. V. RUSSELL	980	489
88	9789362087133	24th, Vol. I, Pt. II	Gwalior (Maps)	R. V. RUSSELL	400	198
89	9789362086341	24th, Vol. I, Pt. III	Gwalior (Village List)	R. V. RUSSELL	810	406
90	9789362085467	24th, Vol. I, Pt. IV	Gwalior (Photos)	R. V. RUSSELL	1400	698
91	9789362087393	25th, Vol. II	Indore (Text and Tables)	C. E. Luard	1050	524
92	9789362084422	26th, Vol. III	Bhopal (Text and Tables)	C. E. Luard	540	272
93	9789362086815	27th, Vol. IV	Rewah (Text and Tables)	C. E. Luard	500	250
94	9789362087584	28th, Vol. V, Pt. A	Western States - Malwa (Text)	C. E. Luard	1520	762
95	9789362087300	29th, Vol. VI, Pt. A	Eastern States - Bundelkhand (Text)	C. E. Luard	930	463
96	9789362082169	30th, Vol. VI, Pt. B	Eastern States - Bundelkhand (Tables)	C. E. Luard	830	417
			GAZETTEER OF THE BOMBAY PRESIDENCY:			
97	9788121283441	1st, Part I	History of Gujarat	Ed.: James M. Campbell	3220	644
98	9788121285582	1st, Part II	History of the Konkan Dakhan and Southern Maratha Country	Ed.: James M. Campbell	4200	840
99	9788121285568	2nd	Gujarat, Surat and Broach	Ed.: James M. Campbell	2990	598
100	9788121285544	3rd	Kaira and Panch Mahals	Ed.: James M. Campbell	1690	339
101	9788121285520	4th	Ahmedabad	Ed.: James M. Campbell	1860	372
102	9788121285506	5th	Cutch, Palanpur, and Mahi Kantha	Ed.: James M. Campbell	2390	478
103	9788121285483	6th	Rewa Kantha, Narukot, Cambay, and Surat States	Ed.: James M. Campbell	1450	290
104	9788121285469	7th	Baroda	Ed.: James M. Campbell	3260	652
105	9788121285445	8th	Kathiawar	Ed.: James M. Campbell	3790	758
106	9788121285421	9th, Part I	Gujarat Population - Hindus	Ed.: James M. Campbell	3170	636
107	9788121285407	9th, Part II	Gujarat Population - Musalmans and Parsis	Ed.: James M. Campbell	1520	304
108	9788121285384	10th	Ratnagiri and Savantvadi	Ed.: James M. Campbell	2500	501
109	9788121285360	11th	Kolaba and Janjira	Ed.: James M. Campbell	2550	513
110	9788121285346	12th	Khandesh	Ed.: James M. Campbell	3190	638
111	9788121285322	13th Part I	Thana	Ed.: James M. Campbell	2050	413
112	9788121285308	13th Part II	Thana	Ed.: James M. Campbell	1770	357
113	9788121285285	14th	Thana - Places of Interest	Ed.: James M. Campbell	3290	659
114	9788121285261	15th Part I	Kanara	Ed.: James M. Campbell	2340	348
115	9788121285247	15th Part II	Kanara	Ed.: James M. Campbell	1740	348
116	9788121285223	16th	Nasik	Ed.: James M. Campbell	3490	698
117	9788121285209	17th	Ahmadnagar	Ed.: James M. Campbell	3860	772
118	9788121285186	18th Part I	Poona	Ed.: James M. Campbell	2930	586
119	9788121285162	18th Part II	Poona	Ed.: James M. Campbell	2680	537
120	9788121285148	18th Part III	Poona	Ed.: James M. Campbell	2500	503
121	9788121285124	19th	Satara	Ed.: James M. Campbell	3450	692
122	9788121285100	20th	Sholapur	Ed.: James M. Campbell	2730	547
123	9788121285087	21st	Gazetteer of the Bomaby Presidency: Belgaum	Ed.: James M. Campbell	2570	514
124	9788121285063	22nd	Dharwar	Ed.: James M. Campbell	4200	841
125	9788121285049	23rd	Gazetteer of the Bombay Presidency:Bijapur	Ed.: James M. Campbell	3550	712
126	9788121285025	24th	Kolhapur	Ed.: James M. Campbell	2250	450

S. NO.	ISBN NO.	VOLUME	TITLE	AUTHOR	PRICE	PAGES
127	9788121285001	25th	Botany	Ed.: James M. Campbell	2040	408
128	9788121284981	26th, Part I	Materials Towards a Statistical Account of the Town and Island of Bombay - History	Ed.: James M. Campbell	2500	504
129	9788121284967	26th, Part II	Materials Towards a Statistical Account of the Town and Island of Bombay - Trade and Fortifications	Ed.: James M. Campbell	2690	538
130	9788121284943	26th, Part III	Materials Towards a Statistical Account of the Town And Island of Bombay - Administration	Ed.: James M. Campbell	2450	702
131	9788121284929	27th	General Index	Ed.:R. E. Enthoven	2190	428
			MADRAS DISTRICT GAZETTEERS			
132	9788121258814	1st	Anantapur	W. Francis	1140	227
133	9788121258555	2nd	Malabar	C. A Innes & F. B Evans	3010	602
134	9788121258791	3rd	Bellary	W. Francis	1890	377
135	9788121258777	4th	Statistical Appendix For Chingleput		280	56
136	9788121258753	5th	Coimbatore	K. N. Krishnaswami Ayyar	3420	628
137	9788121232814	6th	Madras District Gazetteers District Gazetteer Cuddapah	C. F. Brackenbury	1120	285
138	9788121258715	7th	Statistical Appendix For Ganjam		370	73
139	9788121256766	8th, Vol. 1st	Godavari District Gazetteer	F. R. Hemingway	650	320
140	9788121256803	8th, Vol. 2nd	Godavari District Gazetteer	F. R. Hemingway	160	83
141	9788121258678	9th	Statistical Appendix For Kistna		640	127
142	9788121258654	10th	Statistical Appendix For Kurnool		270	54
143	9788121258616	11th	Madura	W. Francis	1900	379
144	9788121258579	12th	Statistical Appendix For Madura		740	148
145	9788121258630	13th	The Nilgiris	W. Francis	2190	437
146	9788121234276	14th	Madras District Gazetteers Gazetteer Of The Nellore District Brought Upto 1938		1150	386
147	9788121258517	15th	North Arcot		590	118
148	9788121258494	16th, Vol. 1, Part I	Salem	F. J. Richards	1710	343
149	9788121258593	16th, Vol. 1, Part II	Salem	F. J. Richards	1800	360
150	9788121258456	17th	South Arcot	W. Francis	2400	480
151	9788121258470	18th	Statistical Appendix For South Canara		400	80
152	9788121258432	19th, Vol. 1st & 2nd	Tanjore: Main Volume and Statistical Appendix		2070	401
153	9788121258395	20th	Tinnevelly	H. R. Pate	2740	547
154	9788121258418	21st	Statistical Appendix For Tinnevelly		320	64
155	9788121258371	22nd, 1st & 2nd	Trichinopoly: Main Volume and Statistical Appendix	F. R. Hemingway	2440	487
156	9788121241953	23rd	Vizagapatam District Gazetteer	W. Francis	760	385
			PUNJAB DISTRICT GAZETTEERS			
157	9788121255943	1st	Ambala District 1883-84		620	124
158	9788121255967	2nd	Amritsar		1180	236
159	9788121255981	3rd	Delhi		1300	260
160	9788121256001	4th	Ferozepore		950	188
161	9788121256025	5th	Faridkot		350	70
162	9788121256049	6th	Gujranwala 1893-94		1270	254
163	9788121256063	7th	Gujrat	C. E. Luard	1140	228
164	9788121256087	8th	Gurdaspur 1891-92		1260	252
165	9788121256100	9th	Gurgaon 1883-4		1020	203
166	9788121256124	10th	Hazara	H. D. Watson	2290	458
167	9788121256148	11th	Hissar district and Lohar State		1840	367
168	9788121256162	12th	Hoshiarpur		1420	283
169	9788121256186	13th	Jhang		1070	213
170	9788121256209	14th	Jhelam		1010	202
171	9788121256223	15th	Jalandhar District 1883-84		540	108
172	9788121256247	16th, Vol. XIV-A	Jullundur District, with maps and Kapurthala		1990	398
173	9788121256261	17th, Pt. I	Kangra (Proper)		1450	290
174	9788121256285	17th, Pt. II	Kangra (Kulu, Lahual, Spiti)		1800	357
175	9788121256308	18th	Karnal		1930	386
176	9788121256322	19th	Kohat		1540	307
177	9788121256346	20th	The Lahore District 1883-84		1220	244
178	9788121256384	21st	Ludhiana and Maler Kotla		1680	335
179	9788121256407	22nd	Lyallpur		735	147
180	9788121256421	23rd	Mianwali		1170	234
181	9788121256445	24th	Montgomery	P. J. Fagan	1590	318
182	9788121258364	25th	Multan (1901-02)	E. D. Maclagan	2400	480
183	9788121258708	26th	The Rohtak District 1883-84		980	196
184	9788121258746	27th, Vol. III A	Dujana State 1904		500	16
185	9788121256483	28th	Shahpur District		1780	356
186	9788121256506	29th	Simla District		800	159

S. NO.	ISBN NO.	VOLUME	TITLE	AUTHOR	PRICE	PAGES
187	9788121256520	30th	The Chamba State		2040	408
188	9788121256544	31st	The Chenab Colony 1904		1550	310
189	9788121256568	32nd	Kalsia State		270	53
190	9788121256582	33rd	Suket and Mandi		770	154
191	9788121256605	34th	Phulkian States, Patiala Jind And Nabha 1904		2070	414
192	9788121256643	35th	Simla Hill States		2220	443
193	9788121256667	36th	Sirmur		920	183
			RAJPUTANA DISTRICT GAZETTEERS			
194	9789362088994	1st, Vol. I-A & B	Ajmer-merwara (Text and Statistics Tables)	C. C. Watson	1230	246
195	9789362080882	2nd. Vol. II-A & B	Mewar Residency (Text and Statistics Tables)	K.D. Erskine	1700	339
196	9789362088444	3rd, Vol. III-A & B	The Western Rajputana States Residency And The Bikaner Agency	K.D. Erskine	3590	718
			UNITED PROVINCES OF AGRA AND OUDH DISTRICT GAZETTEERS			
197	9789362087560	Vol. I	Agra	H. R. Nevill	2260	452
198	9789362082466	Vol. II	Aligarh	H. R. Nevill	1300	260
199	9789362089779	Vol. III	Allahabad	H. R. Nevill	2050	409
200	9789362081346	Vol. IV	Almora	H. G. Walton	1670	333
201	9789362085658	Vol. V	Azamgarh	D. L. Drake Brockman	1750	349
202	9789362080547	Vol. VI	Bahraich	H. R. Nevill	1410	281
203	9789362085214	Vol. VII	Ballia	H. R. Nevill	1750	350
204	9789362084668	Vol. VIII	Banda	D. L. Drake Brockman	1750	349
205	9789362086518	Vol. IX	Bara Banki	H. R. Nevill	1720	344
206	9789362084101	Vol. X	Bareilly	H. R. Nevill	1640	327
207	9789362086631	Vol. XI	Basti	H. R. Nevill	1610	321
208	9789362083814	Vol. XII	Benares	H. R. Nevill	2290	458
209	9789362086105	Vol. XIII	Bijnor	H. R. Nevill	1820	363
210	9789362081674	Vol. XIV	Budaun	H. R. Nevill	1890	378
211	9789362086891	Vol. XV	Bulandshahr	H. R. Nevill	2100	419
212	9789362081520	Vol. XVI	Cawnpore	H. R. Nevill	2210	442
213	9789362088031	Vol. XVII	Dehra Dun	H. G. Walton	1710	342
214	9789362088710	Vol. XVIII	Etah	E. R. Neave	1600	320
215	9789362082992	Vol. XIX	Etawah	D. L. Drake Brockman	1390	277
216	9789362082220	Vol. XX	Farrukhabad	E. R. Neave	1620	324
217	9789362083869	Vol. XXI	Fatehpur	H. R. Nevill	1890	377
218	9789362085962	Vol. XXII	Fyzabad	H. R. Nevill	1700	339
219	9789362087997	Vol. XXIII	Garhwal	H. G. Walton	1270	254
220	9789362089892	Vol. XXIV	Ghazipur	H. R. Nevill	1600	320
221	9789362085436	Vol. XXV	Gonda	H. R. Nevill	1650	330
222	9789362080271	Vol. XXVI	Gorakhpur	H. R. Nevill	1890	378
223	9789362086129	Vol. XXVII	Hamirpur	D. L. Drake Brockman	1390	277
224	9789362087638	Vol. XXVIII	Hardoi	H. R. Nevill	1680	336
225	9789362081636	Vol. XXIX	Jalaun	D. L. Drake Brockman	1180	236
226	9789362084309	Vol. XXX	Jaunpur	H. R. Nevill	1750	350
227	9789362084187	Vol. XXXI	Jhansi	D. L. Drake Brockman	1960	391
228	9789362089168	Vol. XXXII	Kheri	H. R. Nevill	1650	330
229	9789362086778	Vol. XXXIII	Lucknow	H. R. Nevill	1760	352
230	9789362088635	Vol. XXXIV	Mainpuri	H. R. Nevill	1740	348
231	9789362080424	Vol. XXXV	Meerut	H. R. Nevill	2170	434
232	9789362081087	Vol. XXXVI	Mirzapur	D. L. Drake Brockman	2430	486
233	9789362085443	Vol. XXXVII	Moradabad	H. R. Nevill	1900	380
234	9789362082763	Vol. XXXVIII	Muttra	D. L. Drake Brockman	2140	428
235	9789362089915	Vol. XXXIX	Muzaffarnagar	H. R. Nevill	2260	451
236	9789362086143	Vol. XL	Naini Tal	H. R. Nevill	1890	377
237	9789362086761	Vol. XLI	Partabgarh	H. R. Nevill	1560	312
238	9789362081124	Vol. XLII	Pilibhit	H. R. Nevill	1570	314
239	9789362084453	Vol. XLIII	Rai Bareli	H. R. Nevill	1610	322
240	9789362088284	Vol. XLIV	Rampur	H. R. Nevill	1170	234
241	9789362083654	Vol. XLV	Saharanpur	H. R. Nevill	2190	438
242	9789362083142	Vol. XLVI	Shahjahanpur	H. R. Nevill	1510	302
243	9789362083623	Vol. XLVII	Sitapur	H. R. Nevill	1590	317
244	9789362089939	Vol. XLVIII	Sultanpur	H. R. Nevill	1330	266
245	9789362080851	Vol. XLIX	Unnao	H. R. Nevill	1530	305

GAZETTEER

OF THE

BOMBAY PRESIDENCY

VOLUME I. PART I.

HISTORY OF GUJARÁT.

UNDER GOVERNMENT ORDERS.

BOMBAY:
PRINTED AT THE GOVERNMENT CENTRAL PRESS.
1896.

Bombay Castle, 14th February 1902.

In further recognition of the distinguished labours of Sir James McNabb Campbell, K.C.I.E., and of the services rendered by those who have assisted him in his work, His Excellency the Governor in Council is pleased to order that the following extract from Government Resolution No. 2885, dated the 11th August 1884, be republished and printed immediately after the title page of Volume I, Part I, of the Gazetteer, and published in every issue:

"His Excellency the Governor in Council has from time to time expressed his entire approval of the Volumes of the Gazetteer already published, and now learns with much satisfaction that the remaining Statistical Accounts have been completed in the same elaborate manner. The task now brought to a close by Mr. Campbell has been very arduous. It has been the subject of his untiring industry for more than ten years, in the earlier part of which period, however, he was occasionally employed on additional duties, including the preparation of a large number of articles for the Imperial Gazetteer. When the work was begun, it was not anticipated that so much time would be required for its completion, because it was not contemplated that it would be carried out on so extensive a scale. Its magnitude may be estimated by the fact that the Statistical Accounts, exclusive of the general chapters yet to be reprinted, embrace twenty-seven Volumes containing on an average 500 pages each. Mr. Campbell could not have sustained the unflagging zeal displayed by him for so long a period without an intense interest in the subjects dealt with. The result is well worthy of the labour expended, and is a proof of the rare fitness of Mr. Campbell on the ground both of literary ability and of power of steady application for the important duty assigned to him. The work is a record of historical and statistical facts and of information regarding the country and the people as complete perhaps as ever was produced on behalf of any Government, and cannot fail to be of the utmost utility in the future administration of the Presidency.

"2. The thanks of Government have already been conveyed to the various contributors, and it is only necessary now to add that they share, according to the importance of their contributions, in the credit which attaches to the general excellence of the work."

The whole series of Volumes is now complete, and His Excellency in Council congratulates Sir James Campbell and all associated with him in this successful and memorable achievement.

H. O. QUIN,
Secretary to Government,
General Department.

THE earliest record of an attempt to arrange for the preparation of Statistical Accounts of the different districts of the Bombay Presidency is in 1843. In 1843 Government called on the Revenue Commissioner to obtain from all the Collectors as part of their next Annual Report the fullest available information regarding their districts.[1] The information was specially to include their own and their Assistants' observations on the state of the cross and other roads not under the superintendence of a separate department, on the passes and ferries throughout the country, on the streets in the principal towns, and on the extension and improvement of internal communications. As from Collectors alone could any knowledge of the state of the district be obtained, the Collectors were desired to include in their Annual Reports observations on every point from which a knowledge of the actual condition of the country could be gathered with the exception of matters purely judicial which were to be supplied by the Judicial Branch of the Administration. Government remarked that, as Collectors and their Assistants during a large portion of the year moved about the district in constant and intimate communication with all classes they possessed advantages which no other public officers enjoyed of acquiring a full knowledge of the condition of the country, the causes of progress or retrogradation, the good measures which require to be fostered and extended, the evil measures which call for abandonment, the defects in existing institutions which require to be remedied, and the nature of the remedies to be applied. Collectors also, it was observed, have an opportunity of judging of the effect of British rule on the condition and character of the people, on their caste prejudices, and on their superstitious observances. They can trace any alteration for the better or worse in dwellings clothing and diet, and can observe the use of improved implements of husbandry or other crafts, the habits of locomotion, the state of education particularly among the higher classes whose decaying means and energy under our most levelling system compared with that of preceding governments will attract their attention. Finally they can learn how far existing village institutions are effectual to

[1] Secretary's Letter 4223 to the Revenue Commissioner dated 30th December 1843. Revenue Volume 1854 of 1843.

their end, and may be made available for self-government and in the management of local taxation for local purposes.

In obedience to these orders reports were received from the Collectors of Ahmedábád Broach Kaira Thána and Khándesh. Some of the reports, especially that of Mr. J. D. Inverarity, contained much interesting information. These five northern reports were practically the only result of the Circular Letter of 1843.

The question of preparing District Statistical Manuals was not again raised till 1870. In October 1867 the Secretary of State desired the Bombay Government to take steps for the compilation of a Gazetteer of the Presidency on the model of the Gazetteer prepared during that year for the Central Provinces. The Bombay Government requested the two Revenue Commissioners and the Director of Public Instruction to submit a scheme for carrying into effect the orders of the Secretary of State. In reply the officers consulted remarked that the work to be done for the Bombay Presidency would be of a multifarious character; that the article on the commerce of Bombay would require special qualifications in the writer; that again special qualifications would be required for writing accounts of the sacred cities of Násik and Pálitána, of the caves of Ajanta and Ellora, of the histories of Sindh Gujarát and Ahmednagar, and of the Portuguese connection with Western India. The Committee observed that a third form of special knowledge would be required to write accounts of Pársis Khojás and other castes and tribes; that in short the undertaking would be one of much wider scope and greater difficulty than the preparation of the Gazetteer of the Central Provinces. Much thought would be required before the general plan could be laid down, and after the plan was fixed all sorts of questions as to arrangement and treatment of particular parts would be sure to arise. In the Committee's opinion local revenue officers could not as a rule find time to devote to work of this description without neglecting their ordinary duties; but they could correct and amplify such information as a special officer could compile from the published and unpublished records of Government.

In January 1868 the Bombay Government decided that the general supervision and direction of the work should be placed in the hands of a Committee consisting of the Revenue Commissioners, the Director of Public Instruction, and the Commissioner of Customs, and that an Editor should be appointed with a small copying establishment to act under the directions of the Committee. The Editor was to give his entire time to the work and was expected to finish it in about a year. He was to collect and arrange in alphabetical order all recorded information regarding the towns and other places of interest in each Collectorate, and to send printed on half margin each draft when completed to the local officers for verification, additions, and alterations. When the drafts were returned and corrected by the Editor, they were to be laid before the Committee. To enable the Editor to meet such expenses as a fair remuneration for articles contributed by qualified persons, and also to pay for the printing of the work with small accompanying maps, an amount not exceeding Rs. 12,000 was sanctioned for the total expense of the Gazetteer including the payment of the Editor. At the outset it was decided to place a portion of the sum sanctioned not exceeding Rs. 2000, at the disposal of the Commissioner in Sindh to secure the preparation of articles referring to Sindh. The Committee were requested to meet at Poona in June 1868 and to report to Government on the best mode of preparing and editing the Gazetteer and supervising its publication. The Collectors and Political Officers were in the meanwhile requested to ascertain what records in their possession were likely to be useful for the preparation of a Gazetteer and what papers in the possession of others and likely to be useful for the purpose were obtainable within their charge. Collectors and Political Officers were requested to send their replies direct to the Director of Public Instruction who would collect them on behalf of the Committee.

In August 1868 the Bombay Gazetteer Committee, composed of Messrs. A. F. Bellasis Revenue Commissioner N. D. Chairman, Mr. W. H. Havelock Revenue Commissioner S. D. and Sir Alexander Grant, Director of Public Instruction, submitted a report recommending the following arrangements :

(1) That Mr. W. H. Crowe, C. S., then Acting Professor in the Dakhan College, be appointed Editor of the Gazetteer with a monthly remuneration of Rs. 200 out of the Rs. 12,000 sanctioned for the expense of the Gazetteer and that he should at the same time be attached as an Assistant to the Collector of Poona ;

(2) That Mr. Crowe be allowed an establishment not exceeding Rs. 50 a month chargeable to the grant of Rs. 12,000, and such contingent charges as may be passed by the Committee ;

(3) That Professor Kero Luxman Chhatre be requested to assist Mr. Crowe on various questions both local and mathematical, and that on the completion of the work a suitable honorarium be granted to Professor Kero ;

(4) That agreeably to the suggestions of Major Prescott and Colonel Francis, Mr. Light should be directed to compile for the different districts all information in the possession of the Survey Department in communication

with the Editor of the Gazetteer who was to work under the Committee's orders ;

(5) That the above appointments be made at present for one year only, at the end of which from the Committee's progress report, it would be possible to state with approximate definiteness the further time required for the completion of the Gazetteer.

These proposals were sanctioned on the 11th September 1868. Towards the close of 1868 Mr. (now Sir) J. B. Peile took the place of Sir A. Grant on the Committee and Colonel Francis was added to the list of the members. Adhering as far as possible to the arrangement followed in the Gazetteer of the Central Provinces, which had met with the approval of the Secretary of State, Mr. Crowe drew out the following list of subjects which was forwarded to all Collectors Sub-Collectors and Survey Superintendents :

I.—GENERAL DESCRIPTION.
- (a) Latitude and Longitude.
- (b) Locality.
- (c) Boundaries.
- (d) Aspect.
- (e) Water-supply.
- (f) Rivers.
- (g) Mountains.
- (h) Area.
- (i) Altitude.

II.—CLIMATE, SEASONS.
- (a) Rainfall.
- (b) Health.
- (c) Prevailing Diseases.

III.—GEOLOGY.
- (a) Soils.
- (b) Minerals.
- (c) Scientific Details.

IV.—HISTORY.

V.—ADMINISTRATION.
- (a) Judicial.
- (b) Revenue.
- (c) Miscellaneous.

VI.—REVENUE.
- (a) Imperial.
- (b) Local.

VII.—POPULATION.
- (a) Census.
- (b) Description of Inhabitants.
- (c) Castes.

VIII.—SUB-DIVISIONS.
- (a) Names of Tálukás.
- (b) Names of Towns.

IX.—PRODUCTION.
- (a) Agriculture.
- (b) Forest.
- (c) Animals.
- (d) Minerals.
- (e) Manufactures.

X.—TRADE AND COMMERCE.

XI.—COMMUNICATIONS.
- (a) Roads.
- (b) Railways.
- (c) Telegraphs.
- (d) Post.

XII.—REVENUE SYSTEM AND LAND TENURES.

XIII.—EDUCATION.
- Schools.
- Instruction.

XIV.—LANGUAGE.

XV.—ARCHITECTURAL REMAINS AND ANTIQUITIES.

XVI.—PRINCIPAL TOWNS AND VILLAGES.

In 1869 the draft articles prepared by Mr. Crowe were submitted to Mr. (now Sir) W. W. Hunter of the Bengal Civil Service who expressed his satisfaction at the progress made. The Committee adopted certain suggestions made by Sir W. Hunter for the arrangement of the work and for obtaining fuller district figures from the Marine, Irrigation, Cotton, and Survey Offices. In March 1870 a further extension of one year was accorded. The Bombay Government directed that each Collector should choose one of his Assistants to correspond with the Editor and obtain for him all possible information from local records. All Heads of Offices were also desired to exert themselves zealously in aiding the prosecution of the work. In 1871 Mr. Crowe's draft article on the Dhárwár District was sent to Mr. Hunter for opinion who in addition to detailed criticism on various points made the following general remarks :

"My own conception of the work is that, in return for a couple of days' reading, the Account should give a new Collector a comprehensive, and, at the same time, a distinct idea of the district which he has been sent to administer. Mere reading can never supersede practical experience in the district administration. But a succinct and well conceived district account is capable of antedating the acquisition of such personal experience by many months and of both facilitating and systematising a Collector's personal enquiries. The Compiler does not seem to have caught the points on which a Collector would naturally consult the Account. In order that the Editor should understand these points it is necessary that he should have had practical acquaintance with district administration and that he should himself have experienced the difficulties which beset an officer on his taking charge of a district or sub-division. The individual points will differ according to the character of the country. For example in deltaic districts the important question is the control of rivers ; in dry districts it is the subject of water-supply. But in all cases a District Account besides dealing with the local specialties should furnish an historical narration of its revenue and expenditure since it passed under the British rule, of the sums which we have taken from it in taxes, and of the amount which we have returned to it in the protection of property and person and the other charges of civil government."

Sir William Hunter laid much stress on the necessity of stating the authority on the strength of which any statement is made and of the propriety of avoiding anything like libels on persons or classes. In 1871 Sir W. Hunter was appointed Director General of Statistics to the Government of India. In this capacity he was to be a central guiding authority whose duty it was to see that each of the Provincial Gazetteers contained the materials requisite for the comparative statistics of the Empire. As some of the Bombay District Accounts were incomplete and as it was thought advisable to embody in the District Accounts the results of the general Census of 1872, it was decided, in October 1871, that pending the completion of the census the Gazetteer work should be suspended and that when the results of the census were compiled and classified a special officer should be appointed for a period of six months to revise and complete the drafts. In October 1871, pending the compilation of the census returns, Mr. Crowe was appointed Assistant Collector at Sholápur and the Gazetteer records were left in a room in the Poona Collector's Office. In September 1872 the whole of the Gazetteer records, including thirty-one articles on British Districts and Native States, were stolen by two youths who had been serving in the Collector's Office as peons. These youths finding the Gazetteer office room unoccupied stole the papers piece by piece for the sake of the trifling amount they fetched as waste paper. Search resulted in the recovery in an imperfect state of seven of the thirty-one drafts. The youths were convicted and sentenced to a year's imprisonment in the Poona Reformatory.

In 1873 Mr. Francis Chapman then Chief Secretary to Government took the preparation of the Gazetteer under his personal control. And in June 1873 Mr. James M. Campbell, C.S., was appointed Compiler. An important change introduced by Mr. Chapman was to separate from the preparation of the series of District Manuals certain general subjects and to arrange for the preparation of accounts of those general subjects by specially qualified contributors. The subjects so set apart and allotted were :

No.	General Contributors, 1873.	
	Subject.	Contributor.
1	Ethnology	Dr. J. Wilson.
2	Meteorology...	Mr. C. Chambers, F.R.S.
3	Geology	Mr. W. Blandford.
4	Botany	Dr. W. Gray.
5	Archæology	Dr. J. Burgess.
6	Manufactures and Industry.	Mr. G. W. Terry.
7	Trade and Commerce ...	Mr. J. Gordon.

These arrangements resulted in the preparation of the following papers each of which on receipt was printed in pamphlet form :

I. Ethnology ; II. Meteorology ; III. Geology ; and IV. Botany.

Of these papers it has not been deemed advisable to reprint Dr. J. Wilson's Paper on Castes as it was incomplete owing to Dr. Wilson's death in 1875. Reprinting was also unnecessary in the case of Mr. Blandford's Geology and of the late Mr. Chambers' Meteorology, as the contents of these pamphlets have been embodied in works specially devoted to the subject of those contributions. Dr. Burgess never prepared his article on the Archæology of the Presidency, but the materials supplied by the late Pandit Bhagvánlal Indraji prevented the evil effect which this failure would otherwise have caused. Dr. Bhagvánlal also ably supplied the deficiency caused by Dr. G. Bühler's failure to contribute an article on the Early History of Gujarát. The notices of the manufactures in the more important industrial centres to some extent supply the blank caused by the absence of Mr. Terry's contribution. Nothing came of the late Mr. Gordon's Account of the Trade of the Presidency.

On the important subject of Botany besides Dr. W. Gray's original contribution, a valuable paper On Useful Trees and Plants was prepared by Dr. J. C. Lisboa, and a detailed account of Kaira field trees by the late Mr. G. H. D. Wilson of the Bombay Civil Service. These three papers together form a separate Botany Volume No. XXV.

The general contributions on History contained in Vol. I. Parts I. and II. are among the most valuable portions of the Gazetteer. Besides the shorter papers by Mr. L. R. Ashburner, C.S.I., on the Gujarát Mutinies of 1857, by Mr. J. A. Baines, C.S.I., on the Maráthás in Gujarát, by Mr. W. W. Loch, I.C.S., on the Musalmán and Marátha histories of Khándesh and the Bombay Dakhan, and by the late Colonel E. W. West, I. S. C., on the modern history of the Southern Marátha districts, there are the Reverend A. K. Nairne's History of the Konkan which is specially rich in the Portuguese period (A.D. 1500-1750), the late Colonel J. W. Watson's Musalmáns of Gujarát with additions by Khán Sáheb Fazl Lutfullah Farídi of Surat, and the important original histories of the Early Dakhan by Professor Rámkrishna Gopál Bhandárkar, C.I.E., Ph.D., and of the Southern Marátha districts by Mr. J. F. Fleet, I.C.S., C.I.E., Ph.D. With these the early history of Gujarát from materials supplied by the late Pandit Bhagvánlál Indraji, Ph.D., is perhaps not unworthy to rank. The work of completing Dr. Bhagvánlál's history was one of special difficulty. No satisfactory result would have been obtained had it not been for the valuable assistance received from Mr. A. M. T. Jackson, M.A., of the Indian Civil Service.

The importance and the interest of the great subject of Population have added several contributions to the Reverend Doctor J. Wilson's original pamphlet of twenty-three pages. Most of these contributions appear in different District Statistical Accounts especially Dr. John Pollen's, I.C.S., accounts in Khándesh, Mr. Cumine's, I.C.S. in Bijápur, Mr. K. Raghunáthji's in Thána and Poona, Assistant Surgeon Shántárám

Vináyak's in Sholápur, Mr. P. F. DeSouza's in Kánara, and the late Ráo Bahádur Trimalrao's in Dhárwár. Except the valuable articles contributed in the Statistical Account of Kachh by Major J. W. Wray, Mr. Vináyakráo Náráyan and Ráo Sáheb Dalpatrám Pránjivan Khakhar, in the Account of Káthiawár by the late Colonel L. C. Barton, and in the Account of Rewa Kántha by Ráo Bahádur Nandshankar Tuljáshankar the early date at which the Gujarát Statistical Accounts were published prevented the preparation of detailed articles on population. This omission has now been supplied in a separate volume No. IX. The chief contributions to this volume are Ráo Bahádur Bhimbhái Kirpárám's Hindus, Khán Sáheb Fazl Lutfullah Farídi's Musalmáns, and Messrs. Kharsetji N. Servai and Bamanji B. Patel's Pársis.

Besides to these general contributors the series of Statistical Accounts owes much of their fullness and practical usefulness to District Officers especially to the labours of the District Compilers who in most cases were either Collectors or Assistant Collectors. The most important contributors of this class were for Ahmeda'ba'd Mr. F. S. P. Lely, C. S.; for Kaira Mr. G. F. Sheppard, C. S.; for the Panch Maha'ls Mr. H. A. Acworth, C. S.; for Tha'na Messrs. W. B. Mulock, C. S., E. J. Ebden, C. S., W. W. Loch, C. S., and A. Cumine, C. S.; for Kola'ba Mr. E. H. Moscardi, C. S.; for Ratna'giri Mr. G. W. Vidal, C. S.; for Kha'ndesh Mr. W. Ramsay, C. S., Dr. John Pollen, C. S., and Mr. A. Crawley-Boevey, C. S.; for Na'sik Messrs. W. Ramsay, C. S., J. A. Baines, C. S., and H. R. Cooke, C. S.; for Ahmednagar Mr. T. S. Hamilton, C. S.; for Poona Messrs. J. G. Moore, C. S., John MacLeod Campbell, C. S., G. H. Johns, C. S., and A. Keyser, C. S.; for Sa'ta'ra Mr. J. W. P. Muir-Mackenzie, C. S.; for Shola'pur Mr. C. E. G. Crawford, C. S.; for Belgaum Mr. G. McCorkell, C. S.; for Dha'rwa'r Messrs. F. L. Charles, C. S., and J. F. Muir, C. S.; for Bija'pur Messrs. H. F. Silcock, C. S., A. Cumine, C. S., and M. H. Scott, C. S.; and for Ka'nara Mr. J. Monteath, C. S., and Colonel W. Peyton. Of the accounts of Native States, the interesting and complete Gazetteer of Baroda is the work of Mr. F. A. H. Elliott, C. S. The chief contributors to the other Statistical Accounts of Native States were for Kachh Colonel L. C. Barton; for Ka'thia'wa'r Colonel J. W. Watson and Colonel L. C. Barton; for Pa'lanpur Colonel J. W. Watson; for Mahi Ka'ntha Colonels E. W. West and P. H. LeGeyt; for Rewa Ka'ntha Colonel L. C. Barton and Ráo Báhádur Nandshankar Tuljáshankar; for Sa'vantva'di Colonel J. F. Lester; for Ja'njira Mr. G. Laroom; for Kolha'pur Colonels E. W. West and W. F. F. Waller and

Ráo Bahádur Yeshvant M. Kelkar. The names of numerous other contributors both in and out of Government service who gave help in compiling information connected with their districts have been shewn in the body of each District Statistical Account. Of these the learned and most ungrudging assistance received from Dr. J. Gerson DaCunha of Bombay requires special recognition.

The third main source of preparation was the Compiler's head-quarters office. Through the interest which Mr. Francis Chapman took in the Gazetteer the Compiler was able to secure the services as Assistant of Ráo Báhádur Bhimbhái Kirpárám who was Head Accountant in the Kaira Treasury when the Statistical Account of Kaira was under preparation in 1874. Mr. Bhimbhái's minute knowledge of administrative detail, his power of asking for information in the form least troublesome to district establishments, and of checking the information received, together with his talent for directing the work at head-quarters formed one of the most important elements in the success of the Gazetteer arrangements. Besides to the interest taken by Mr. Francis Chapman the Gazetteer owed much to the advice and to the support of Sir W. W. Hunter, who, in spite of the delay and expense which it involved, secured the full record of the survey and other details in which the Bombay revenue system is specially rich.

In addition to Ráo Bahádur Bhimbhái, the members of the Compiler's office whose work entitles them almost to a place among contributors are: Ráo Sáheb Krishnaráo Narsinh, who drafted many of the Land Revenue and Survey Histories; the late Mr. Ganesh Bhikáji Gunjikar, B.A., who drafted many of the Political Histories; the late Mr. Vaikunthrám Manmathrám Mehta, B.A., and Ráo Bahádur Itchárám Bhagvándás, B.A., who drafted many articles on Description, Production, Agriculture, Capital, and Trade; Mr. K. Raghunáthji who prepared many of the fullest caste accounts; Mr. Ratirám Durgárám, B.A., who drafted many papers on places of interest; and Messrs. Yeshvant Nilkanth and Mahádev G. Nádkarni who drafted many of the sections on Population, Agriculture, Capital, and Trade.

Other officers of Government who have had an important share in the satisfactory completion of the Gazetteer are: Mr. J. Kingsmill the former and Mr. Frámroz Rustamji the present Superintendent of the Government Central Press and Mr. T. E. Coleman the Head Examiner, whose unfailing watchfulness has detected many a mistake. Mr. Waite the late Superintendent of the Photozincographic Press and Mr. T. LeMesurier the present Superintendent have supplied a set of most handy, clear, and accurate maps.

A further means adopted for collecting information was the preparation of papers on the different social, economic, and religious subjects which had proved of interest in preparing the earliest District Statistical Accounts. Between 1874 and 1880 forty-nine question papers which are given as an Appendix to the General Index Volume were from time to time printed and circulated. The answers received to these papers added greatly to the fullness and to the local interest of all the later Statistical Accounts.

The Statistical Accounts of the eighteen British districts and eighty-two Native States of the Bombay Presidency, together with the Materials towards a Statistical Account of the Town and Island of Bombay extend over thirty-three Volumes and 17,800 pages. In addition to these Statistical Accounts 475 articles were prepared in 1877-78 for the Imperial Gazetteer.

JAMES MACNABB CAMPBELL.

Bombay Customs House,
29th May 1896.

HISTORY OF GUJARÁT.

This Volume contains the Articles named below :

I.—EARLY HISTORY OF GUJARÁT (B.C. 319 - A.D. 1304). — From materials prepared by the late Pandit Bhagvánlál Indraji, Ph.D., completed with the help of A. M. T. Jackson, Esquire, M.A., of the Indian Civil Service.

II.—HISTORY OF GUJARÁT, MUSALMÁN PERIOD (A.D. 1297 - 1760).—Prepared by the late Colonel J. W. Watson, Indian Staff Corps, former Political Agent of Káthiáváḍa, with additions by Khán Sáheb Fazlullah Lutfulláh Farídi of Surat.

III.—HISTORY OF GUJARÁT, MARÁTHA PERIOD (A.D. 1760 - 1819).—By J. A. Baines, Esquire, C.S.I., Late of Her Majesty's Bombay Civil Service.

IV.—DISTURBANCES IN GUJARÁT (A.D. 1857 - 1859).—By L. R. Ashburner, Esquire, C.S.I., Late of Her Majesty's Bombay Civil Service.

APPENDICES :

I.—The Death of Sultán Bahádur.

II.—The Hill Fort of Mándu.

III.—Bhinmál or Shrimál.

IV.—Java and Cambodia.

V.—Arab References.

VI.—Greek References.

JAMES M. CAMPBELL.

29th May 1896.

CONTENTS.

EARLY HISTORY OF GUJARÁT.

THE KINGDOM OF ANAHILAVÁDA (A.D. 720-1300).

MUSALMAN PERIOD (A.D. 1297-1760).

MARÁTHA PERIOD (A.D. 1760-1819).

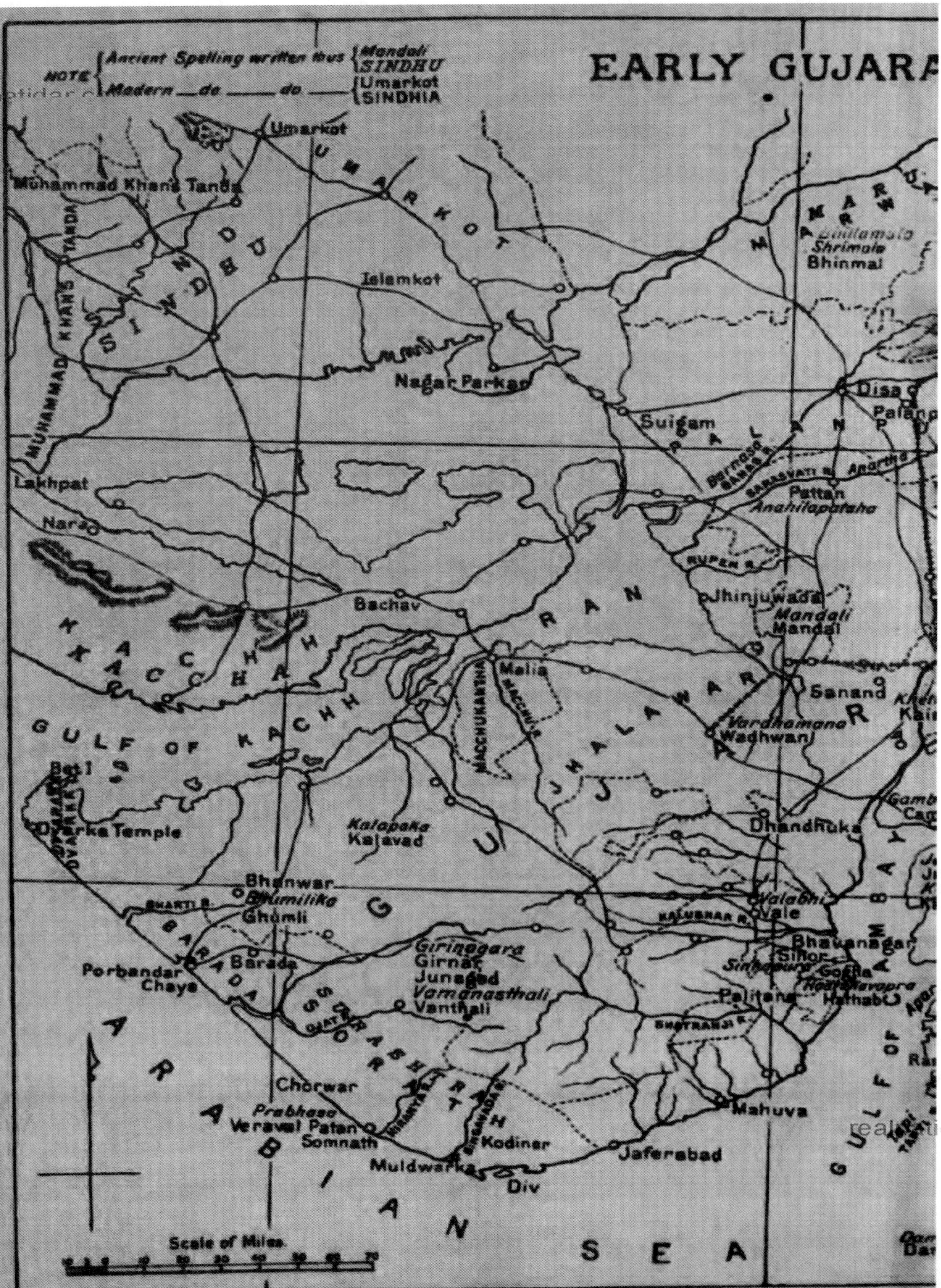

Govt Photozinco Office, Poona, 1896.

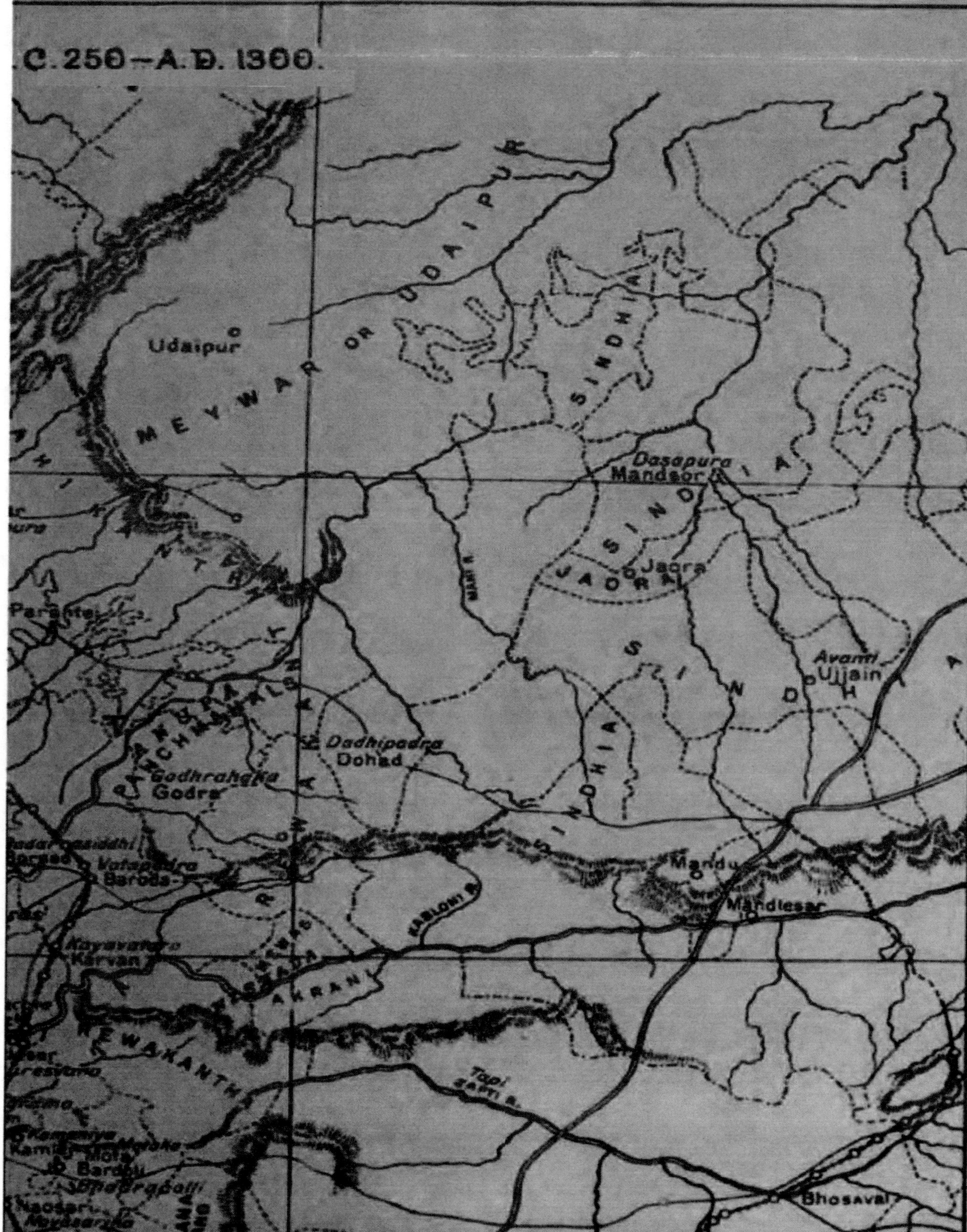
.C. 250—A.D. 1300.
Udaipur
MEYWAR OR UDAIPUR
SINDHIA
Dasapura
Mandsor
Jaora
JAORA
Avanti
Ujjain
Dadhipadra
Dohad
Godhrahaka
Godra
Vatapadra
Baroda
Mandu
Mandlesar
Karvan
REWAKANTHA
Tapi
SAPTI R.
Bhosaval
Naosari
Bardoli

GUJARÁT DISTURBANCES (A.D. 1857-1859).

APPENDICES.

ERRATA.

Page 3 note 5:

For about thirty miles north-east of Ábu
Read about fifty miles west of Ábu.

Page 140 note 5 and page 145 top line of notes:

For Aldjayháni *read* Aljauhari.

EARLY HISTORY OF GUJARÁT.

CHAPTER I.

BOUNDARIES AND NAME.

Chapter I.

Boundaries.

The portion of the Bombay Presidency known as Gujarát fills the north-east corner of the coast of Western India.

On the west is the Arabian Sea; on the north-west is the Gulf of Cutch. To the north lie the Little Ran and the Mevád desert; to the north-east Ábu and other outliers of the Arávali range. The east is guarded and limited by rough forest land rugged in the north with side spurs of the Vindhyas, more open towards the central natural highway from Baroda to Ratlám, and southwards again rising and roughening into the northern offshoots from the main range of the Sátpudás. The southern limit is uncertain. History somewhat doubtfully places it at the Tápti. Language carries Gujarát about a hundred miles further to Balsár and Párdi where wild forest-covered hills from the north end of the Sahyádri range stretch west almost to the sea.

The province includes two parts, Mainland Gujarát or Gurjjara-ráshtra and Peninsular Gujárat the Sauráshtra of ancient, the Káthiá-váḍa of modern history. To a total area of about 72,000 square miles Mainland Gujarát with a length from north to south of about 280 miles and a breadth from east to west varying from fifty to 150 miles contributes 45,000 square miles; and Peninsular Gujarát with a greatest length from north to south of 155 miles and from east to west of 200 miles contributes about 27,000 square miles. To a population of about 9,250,000 Mainland Gujarát contributes 6,900,000 and the Peninsula about 2,350,000.

The richness of Mainland Gujarát the gift of the Sábarmati Mahi Narbada and Tápti and the goodliness of much of Sauráshtra the Goodly Land have from before the beginning of history continued to draw strangers to Gujarát both as conquerors and as refugees.

By sea probably came some of the half-mythic Yádavas (B.C. 1500-500); contingents of Yavanas (B.C. 300 - A.D. 100) including Greeks Baktrians Parthians and Skythians; the pursued Pársis and the pursuing Arabs (A.D. 600 - 800); hordes of Sanganian pirates (A.D. 900 - 1200); Pársi and Naváyat Musalmán refugees from Khulagu Khán's devastation of Persia (A.D. 1250 - 1300); Portuguese and rival Turks (A.D. 1500 - 1600); Arab and Persian Gulf pirates (A.D. 1600 - 1700); African Arab Persian and Makran soldiers of fortune (A.D. 1500 - 1800); Armenian Dutch and French traders (A.D. 1600 - 1750); and the British (A.D. 1750 - 1812). By land from the north

Chapter I. THE NAME.

have come the Skythians and Huns (B.C. 200 - A.D. 500), the Gurjjaras (A.D. 400 - 600), the early Jádejás and Káthis (A.D. 750 - 900), wave on wave of Afghan Turk Moghal and other northern Musalmáns (A.D. 1000 - 1500), and the later Jádejás and Káthis (A.D. 1300 - 1500) : From the north-east the prehistoric Aryans till almost modern times (A.D. 1100 - 1200) continued to send settlements of Northern Bráhmans ; and since the thirteenth century have come Turk Afghan and Moghal Musalmáns : From the east have come the Mauryans (B.C. 300), the half - Skythian Kshatrapas (B.C. 100 - A.D. 300), the Guptas (A.D. 380), the Gurjjars (A.D. 400 - 600), the Moghals (A.D. 1530), and the Maráthás (A.D. 1750) : And from the south the S'átakarnis (A.D. 100), the Chálukyas and Ráshtrakuṭas (A.D. 650 - 950), occasional Musalmán raiders (A.D. 1400 - 1600), the Portuguese (A.D. 1500), the Maráthás (A.D. 1660 - 1760), and the British (A.D. 1780 - 1820).

Gujars.

The name Gujarát is from the Prákrit Gujjara-ratta, the Sanskrit of which is Gurjjara-ráshtra that is the country of the Gujjaras or Gurjjaras. In Sanskrit books and inscriptions the name of the province is written Gurjjara-maṇḍala and Gūrjjara-des'a the land of the Gurjjaras or Gūrjjaras. The Gurjjaras are a foreign tribe who passing into India from the north-west gradually spread as far south as Khándesh and Bombay Gujarát. The present Gujars of the Panjab and North-West Provinces preserve more of their foreign traits than the Gujar settlers further to the south and east. Though better-looking, the Panjab Gujars in language dress and calling so closely resemble their associates the Játs or Jats as to suggest that the two tribes entered India about the same time. Their present distribution shows that the Gujars spread further east and south than the Játs. The earliest Gujar settlements seem to have been in the Panjab and North-West Provinces from the Indus to Mathurá where they still differ greatly in dress and language from most other inhabitants. From Mathurá the Gujars seem to have passed to East Rajputána and from there by way of Kotah and Mandasor to Málwa, where, though their original character is considerably altered, the Gujars of Málwa still remember that their ancestors came from the Doab between the Ganges and the Jamna. In Málwa they spread as far east as Bhilsa and Saharanpur. From Málwa they passed south to Khándesh and west probably by the Ratlam-Dohad route to the province of Gujarát.

Like the modern Ahirs of Káthiáváḍa the Gujars seem to have been a tribe of cattle-rearers husbandmen and soldiers who accompanied some conqueror and subsequently were pushed or spread forwards as occasion arose or necessity compelled. In the absence of better authority the order and locality of their settlements suggest that their introduction into India took place during the rule of the Skythian or Kushán emperor Kanerkes or Kanishka (A.D. 78 - 106) in whose time they seem to have settled as far east as Mathurá to which the territory of Kanishka is known to have extended. Subsequently along with the Guptas, who rose to power about two hundred years later (A.D. 300), the Gujars settled in East Rajputána, Málwa, and Gujarát, provinces all of which were apparently subjugated by the Guptas. It seems probable that in reward for their share in the Gupta conquests the leading Gujars were allotted fiefs and territories which in the declining power of their Gupta overlords they afterwards (A.D. 450 - 550) turned into independent kingdoms.

Chapter I.
THE NAME.

The earliest definite reference to a kingdom of North Indian Gujars is about A.D. 890 when the Kashmir king S'ankaravarman sent an expedition against the Gurjjara king Alakhána and defeated him. As the price of peace Alakhána offered the country called Takkades'a. This Takkades'a[1] appears to be the same as the Tsehkia of Hiuen Tsiang[2] (A.D 630 - 640) who puts it between the Biyás on the east and the Indus on the west thus including nearly the whole Panjab. The tract surrendered by Alakhána was probably the small territory to the east of the Chináb as the main possessions of Alakhána must have lain further west between the Chináb and the Jehlam, where lie the town of Gujarát and the country still called Gujar-des'a the land of the Gujars.[3]

Northern Gurjjara Kingdom.
Hiuen Tsiang's Kiu-che-lo, A.D. 620.

As early as the sixth and seventh centuries records prove the existence of two independent Gurjjara kingdoms in Bombay Gujarát one in the north the other in the south of the province. The Northern kingdom is mentioned by Hiuen Tsiang in the seventh century under the name Kiu-che-lo. He writes: 'Going north from the country of Valabhi 1800 li (300 miles) we come to the kingdom of Kiu-che-lo. This country is about 5000 li in circuit, the capital, which is called Pi-lo-mo-lo, is 30 li or so round. The produce of the soil and the manners of the people resemble those of Saurásthtra. The king is of the Kshatriya caste. He is just twenty years old.'[4] Hiuen Tsiang's Kiu-che-lo is apparently Gurjjara, the capital of which Pi-lo-mo-lo is probably Bhilmál or Bhinmál, better known as S'rimál.[5] Though Hiuen Tsiang calls the king a Kshatriya he was probably a Gujar who like the later Southern Gujars claimed to be of the Kshatriya race.

---

[1] Rája Tarangini (Calc. Edition), V. 150, 155; Cunningham's Archæological Survey, II. 8. An earlier but vaguer reference occurs about the end of the sixth century in Bána's Sriharshacharita, p. 274, quoted in Ep. Ind. I. 67ff, where Prabhákaravardhana of Thánesar the father of the great S'ri Harsha is said to have waged war with several races of whom the Gurjaras are one.

[2] Beal's Buddhist Records of the Western World, I. 165 note 1.

[3] Cunningham's Archæological Survey, II. 71.

[4] Beal's Buddhist Records, II. 270.

[5] This identification was first made by the late Col. J. W. Watson, I.S.C. Ind. Ant. VI. 63. Bhinmál or Bhilmál also called S'rimál, is an old town about thirty miles north-east of Abu, north latitude 25° 4′ east longitude 71° 14′. General Cunningham (Ancient Geography of India, 313) and Professor Beal (Buddhist Records, II. 270) identify Pi-lo-mo-lo with Bálmer or Bádamera (north latitude 71° 10′ east longitude 26° 0′) in the Jodhpur State of West Rájputána. This identification is unsatisfactory. Bálmer is a small town on the slope of a hill in an arid tract with no vestige of antiquity. Hiuen Tsiang notes that the produce of the soil and the manners of the people of Pi-lo-mo-lo resemble those of Suráshtra. This description is unsuited to so arid a tract as surrounds Bálmer; it would apply well to the fertile neighbourhood of Bhilmál or Bhinmál. Since it is closely associated with Juzr that is Gurjjara the Al Bailáiman of the Arabs (A.D. 750, Elliot's History, I. 442) may be Bhilmal. A Jain writer (Ind. Ant. XIX. 233) mentions Bhilmál as the seat of king Bhímasena and as connected with the origin of the Gadhia coinage. The date Bhinmál in a M.S. of A.D. 906 (Ditto, page 35) suggests it was then a seat of learning under the Gurjjaras. The prince of S'rimál is mentioned (Rás Málá, I. 58)

Chapter I.
THE NAME.
Southern Gurjjara Kingdom, A.D. 589 - 735.

The Southern Gurjjara kingdom in Gujarát, whose capital was at Nándipuri, perhaps the modern Nándod the capital of the Rájpipla State, flourished from A.D. 589 to A.D. 735.[1] The earlier inscriptions describe the Southern Gurjjaras as of the Gurjjara Vans'a. Later they ceased to call themselves Gurjjaras and traced their genealogy to the Puránic king Karṇa.

From the fourth to the eighth century the extensive tract of Central Gujarát between the North and South Gurjjara kingdoms was ruled by the Valabhis. The following reasons seem to show that the Valabhi dynasty were originally Gujars. Though it is usual for inscriptions to give this information none of the many Valabhi copper-plates makes any reference to the Valabhi lineage. Nor does any inscription state to what family Senápati Bhaṭárka the founder of the dynasty belonged. Hiuen Tsiang describes the Valabhi king as a Kshatriya and as marrying with the kings of Málwa and Kanauj. The Valabhi king described by Hiuen Tsiang is a late member of the dynasty who ruled when the kingdom had been greatly extended and when the old obscure tribal descent may have been forgotten and a Kshatriya lineage invented instead. Intermarriage with Málwa and Kanauj can be easily explained. Rajputs have never been slow to connect themselves by marriage with powerful rulers.

The establishment of these three Gujar kingdoms implies that the Gurjjara tribe from Northern and Central India settled in large numbers in Gujarát. Several Gujar castes survive in Gujarát. Among them are Gujar Vániás or traders, Gujar Sutárs or carpenters, Gujar Sonis or goldsmiths, Gujar Kumbhárs or potters, and Gujar Saláts or masons. All of these are Gujars who taking to different callings have formed separate castes. The main Gujar underlayer are the Lewás and Kaḍwás the two leading divisions of the important class of Gujarát Kaṇbis. The word Kaṇbi is from the Sanskrit Kuṭumbin, that is one possessing a family or a house. From ancient times the title Kuṭumbin has been prefixed to the names of cultivators.[2] This practice still obtains in parts of the North-West Provinces where the peasant proprietors are addressed as Gṛihasthas or householders. As cattle-breeding not cultivation was the original as it still is the characteristic calling of many North Indian Gujars, those of the tribe who settled to cultivation came to be specially known as Kuṭumbin or householders. Similarly Deccan surnames show that many tribes of wandering cattle-owners settled as householders and are now known as Kunbis.[3] During the last

---

as accompanying Múla Rája Solankhi (A.D. 942 - 997) in an expedition against Sorath. Al Biruni (A.D. 1030, Sachau's Edn., I. 153, 267) refers to Bhillamála between Multán and Anhilaváda. As late as A.D. 1611 Nicholas Ufflet, an English traveller from Agra to Ahmadádád (Kerr's Voyages, VIII. 301) notices "Beelmahl as having an ancient wall 24 *kos* (36 miles) round with many fine tanks going to ruin." The important sub-divisions of upper class Gujarát Hindus who take their name from it show S'rímál to have been a great centre of population.

[1] Indian Antiquary, XIII. 70 - 81. Bühler (Ind. Ant. VII. 62) identifies Nandipuri with a suburb of Broach.

[2] Bombay Gazetteer, Násik, page 604. Bombay Arch. Survey Sep. Number X. 38.

[3] Among Deccan Kunbi surnames are Jádhav, Chuhán, Nikumbha, Parmár, Selár, Solké. Cf. Bombay Gazetteer, XXIV. 65 note 2, 414.

twenty years the settlement as Kunbis in Khándesh of tribes of wandering Wanjára herdsmen and grain-carriers is an example of the change through which the Gujarát Kanbis and the Deccan Kunbis passed in early historic times.

Chapter I.
The Name.

Gujars.

Besides resembling them in appearance and in their skill both as husbandmen and as cattle-breeders the division of Gujarát Kanbis into Lewa and Kadwa seems to correspond with the division of Málwa Gujars into Dáha and Karad, with the Lewa origin of the East Khándesh Gujars, and with the Lawi tribe of Panjáb Gujars. The fact that the head-quarters of the Lewa Kanbis of Gujarát is in the central section of the province known as the Charotar and formerly under Valabhi supports the view that the founder of Valabhi power was the chief leader of the Gujar tribe. That nearly a fourth of the whole Hindu population of Gujarát are Lewa and Kadwa Kanbis and that during the sixth seventh and eighth centuries three Gujar chiefs divided among them the sway of the entire province explain how the province of Gujarát came to take its name from the tribe of Gujars.[1]

---

[1] Though the identification of the Valabhis as Gurjjaras may not be certain, in inscriptions noted below both the Chávadás and the Solankis are called Gurjjara kings. The Gurjjara origin of either or of both these dynasties may be questioned. The name Gurjjara kings may imply no more than that they ruled the Gurjjara country. At the same time it was under the Chávadás that Gujarát got its name. Though to Al Biruni (A.D. 1020) Gujarát still meant part of Rájputána, between A.D. 750 and 950 the name Gurjjaras' land passed as far south as the territory connected with Anhilváḍa and Vaḍnagara that is probably as far as the Mahi. As a Rástrakuta copperplate of A.D. 888 (S. 810) (Ind. Ant. XIII. 69) brings the Konkan as far north as Variáv on the Tápti the extension of the name Gujarát to Láṭa south of the Mahi seems to have taken place under Musalmán rule. This southern application is still somewhat incomplete. Even now the people of Surat both Hindus and Musalmáns when they visit Pattan (Anhilváḍa) and Ahmadabad speak of going to Gujarát, and the Ahmadábád section of the Nágar Bráhmans still call their Surat caste-brethren by the name of Kunkaṇás that is of the Konkaṇ.

CHAPTER II.

ANCIENT DIVISIONS.

Chapter II.
ANCIENT DIVISIONS.
A'nartta.

FROM ancient times the present province of Gujarát consisted of three divisions Ánartta, Suráshtra, and Láṭa. Ánartta seems to have been Northern Gujarát, as its capital was Ánandapura the modern Vaḍanagara or Chief City, which is also called Ánarttapura.[1] Both these names were in use even in the times of the Valabhi kings (A.D. 500-770).[2] According to the popular story, in each of the four cycles or *yugas* Ánandapura or Vaḍanagara had a different name, Chamatkárapura in the first or Satya-yuga, Ánarttapura in the second or Tretá-yuga, Ánandapura in the third or Dvápara-yuga, and Vriddha-nagara or Vaḍanagar in the fourth or Káli-yuga. The first name is fabulous. The city does not seem to have ever been known by so strange a title. Of the two Ánarttapura and Ánandapura the former is the older name, while the latter may be its proper name or perhaps an adaptation of the older name to give the meaning City of Joy. The fourth Vriddha-nagara meaning the old city is a Sanskritized form of the still current Vadnagar, the Old or Great City. In the Girnár inscription of Kshatrapa Rudradáman (A.D. 150) the mention of Ánartta and Suráshtra as separate provinces subject to the Pahlava viceroy of Junágadh agrees with the view that Ánartta was part of Gujarát close to Káthiáváḍa. In some Puránas Ánartta appears as the name of the whole province including Suráshtra, with its capital at the well known shrine of Dwáriká. In other passages Dwáriká and Prabhás are both mentioned as in Suráshṭra which would seem to show that Suráshṭra was then part of Ánartta as Káthiáváḍa is now part of Gujarát.

Suráshṭra.

Suráshṭra the land of the Sus, afterwards Sanskritized into Sauráshṭra the Goodly Land, preserves its name in Sorath the southern part of Káthiáváḍa. The name appears as Suráshṭra in the Mahábhárata and Páṇini's Gaṇapáṭha, in Rudradáman's (A.D. 150) and Skandagupta's (A.D. 456) Girnár inscriptions, and in several Valabhi copper-plates. Its Prákrit form appears as Suratha in the Násik inscription of Gotamiputra (A.D. 150) and in later Prákrit as Suraṭhṭha in the Tirthakalpa of Jinaprabhásuri of the thirteenth or fourteenth century.[3] Its earliest foreign mention is perhaps Strabo's (B.C. 50 - A.D. 20) Saraostus and Pliny's (A.D. 70) Oratura.[4] Ptolemy

---

[1] See Nagarakhaṇḍa (Junagadh Edition), 13, 32, 35, 185, 289, 332, 542.

[2] The Alina grants (Indian Antiquary, VII. 73, 77) dated Valabhi 330 and 337 (A.D. 649-656) are both to the same donee who in the A.D. 649 grant is described as originally of Ánarttapura and in the A.D. 656 grant as originally of Ánandapura.

[3] Girnára-Kalpa, *Atthi Suraṭhṭha vesaé Ujjinto náma pavvao rammo.* In the Suraṭhṭha district is a lovely mountain named Ujjinto (Girnár).

[4] Hamilton and Falconer's Strabo, II. 252 - 253 ; Pliny's Natural History, VI. 20.

Chapter II.

ANCIENT DIVISIONS.

the great Egyptian geographer (A.D. 150) and the Greek author of the Periplus (A.D. 240) both call it Surastrene.[1] The Chinese pilgrim Hiuen Tsiang (A.D. 600-640) mentions Valabhi then large and famous and Surásh̤tra as separate kingdoms.[2]

Láṭa.

Láṭa is South Gujarát from the Mahi to the Tápti. The name Láṭa does not appear to be Sanskrit. It has not been found in the Mahábhárata or other old Sanskrit works, or in the cave or other inscriptions before the third century A.D., probably because the Purános include in Aparánta the whole western seaboard south of the Narbada as far as Goa. Still the name Láṭa is old. Ptolemy (A.D. 150) uses the form Larike[3] apparently from the Sanskrit Láṭaka. Vátsyáyana in his Káma-Sutra of the third century A.D. calls it Láṭa; describes it as situated to the west of Málwa; and gives an account of several of the customs of its people.[4] In Sanskrit writings and inscriptions later than the third century the name is frequently found. In the sixth century the great astronomer Varáhamihira mentions the country of Láṭa, and the name also appears as Láṭa in an Ajanta and in a Mandasor inscription of the fifth century.[5] It is common in the later inscriptions (A. D. 700-1200) of the Chálukya Gurjara and Ráshṭrakúṭa kings[6] as well as in the writings of Arab travellers and historians between the eighth and twelfth centuries.[7]

The name Láṭa appears to be derived from some local tribe, perhaps the Lattas, who, as *r* and *l* are commonly used for each other, may possibly be the well known Ráshṭrakúṭas since their great king Amoghavarsha (A.D. 851-879) calls the name of the dynasty Ratta. Laṭṭalura the original city of the Raṭṭas of Saundatti and Belgaum may have been in Láṭa and may have given its name to the country and to the dynasty.[8] In this connection it is interesting to note that the country between Broach and Dhár in Málwa in which are the towns of Bágh and Tánda is still called Ráṭha.

---

[1] Bertius' Ptolemy, VII. 1; McCrindle's Periplus, 113. The Periplus details regarding Indo-Skythia, Surastrene, and Ujjain are in agreement with the late date (A.D. 247) which Reinaud (Indian Antiquary of Dec. 1879 pp. 330-338) and Burnell (S. Ind. Pal. 47 note 3) assign to its author.

[2] Hiuen Tsiang's Valabhi kingdom was probably the same as the modern Gohilváda, which Jinaprabhásuri in his S'atrunjaya-kalpa calls the Valláka-Visaa.

[3] Bertius' Ptolemy, VII. 1.

[4] Vátsyáyana Sutra, Chap. II.

[5] Arch. Sur. of Western India, IV. 127. The Mandasor inscription (A.D. 437-38) mentions silk weavers from Láṭavishaya. Fleet's Corpus Ins. Ind. III. 80. The writer (Ditto, 84) describes Láṭa as green-hilled, pleasing with choice flower-burdened trees, with temples *vihäras* and assembly halls of the gods.

[6] Ind. Ant. XIII. 157, 158, 163, 180, 188, 196, 199, 204.

[7] Elliot's History, I. 378.

[8] Compare Lassen in Ind. Ant. XIV. 325.

CHAPTER III.

LEGENDS.

Chapter III.

LEGENDS.

A'nartta the First Puránic King of Gujarát.

THE oldest Puránic legend regarding Gujarát appears to be that of the holy king Ánartta son of S'aryáti and grandson of Manu. Ánartta had a son named Revata, who from his capital at Kuśasthali or Dwáriká governed the country called Ánartta. Revata had a hundred sons of whom the eldest was named Raivata or Kakudmi. Raivata had a daughter named Revati who was married to Baladeva of Kus'asthali or Dwáriká, the elder brother of Krishṇa. Regarding Revati's marriage with Baladeva the Puránic legends tell that Raivata went with his daughter to Brahmá in Brahma-loka to take his advice to whom he should give the girl in marriage. When Raivata arrived Brahmá was listening to music. As soon as the music was over Raivata asked Brahmá to find the girl a proper bridegroom. Brahmá told Raivata that during the time he had been waiting his kingdom had passed away, and that he had better marry his daughter to Baladeva, born of Vishnu, who was now ruler of Dwáriká.[1] This story suggests that Raivata son of Ánartta lost his kingdom and fled perhaps by sea. That after some time during which the Yádavas established themselves in the country, Raivata, called a son of Revata but probably a descendant as his proper name is Kakudmi, returned to his old territory and gave his daughter in marriage to one of the reigning Yádava dynasty, the Yádavas taking the girl as representing the dynasty that had preceded them. The story about Brahmá and the passing of ages seems invented to explain the long period that elapsed between the flight and the return.

The Yádavas in Dwáriká.

The next Puránic legends relate to the establishment of the Yádava kingdom at Dwáriká. The founder and namegiver of the Yádava dynasty was Yadu of whose family the Puránas give very detailed information. The family seems to have split into several branches each taking its name from some prominent member, the chief of them being Vrishṇi, Kukkura, Bhoja, S'átvata, Andhaka, Madhu, S'urasena, and Daśárha. S'átvata was thirty-seventh from Yadu and in his branch were born Devaki and Vasudeva, the parents of the great Yádava hero and god Krishṇa. It was in Krishṇa's time that the Yádavas had to leave their capital Mathurá and come to Dwáriká. This was the result of a joint invasion of Mathurá on one side by a

[1] The Vishnu Purána (Anśa iv. Chap. i. Verse 19 to Chap. ii. Verse 2) gives the longest account of the legend. The Bhágavata Purána (Skanda ix. Chap. iii. Verse 16-36) gives almost the same account. The Matsya Purána (Chap. xii. Verse 22-24) dismisses the story in two verses. See also Harivanśa, X.

legendary Deccan hero Kálayavana and on the other by Jarásandha the powerful king of Magadha or Behar, who, to avenge the death of his brother-in-law[1] Kansa killed by Krishna in fulfilment of a prophecy, is said to have invaded the Yádava territory eighteen times.

According to the story Kálayavana followed the fugitive Krishna and his companions as far as Suráshtra where in a mountain cave he was burnt by fire from the eye of the sleeping sage Muchakuṇḍa whom he had roused believing him to be his enemy Krishṇa. According to the Harivansa the fugitive Yádavas quitting Mathurá went to the Sindhu country and there established the city of Dwáriká on a convenient site on the sea shore making it their residence.[2] Local tradition says that the Yádavas conquered this part of the country by defeating the demons who held it.

The leading Yádava chief in Dwáriká was Ugrasena, and Ugrasena's three chief supporters were the families of Yadu, Bhoja, and Andhaka. As the entire peninsula of Káthiáváḍa was subject to them the Yádavas used often to make pleasure excursions and pilgrimages to Prabhás and Girnár. Krishṇa and Baladeva though not yet rulers held high positions and took part in almost all important matters. They were in specially close alliance with their paternal aunt's sons the Pándava brothers, kings of Hastinápura or Delhi. Of the two sets of cousins Krishṇa and Arjuna were on terms of the closest intimacy. Of one of Arjuna's visits to Káthiáváḍa the Mahábhárata gives the following details: 'Arjuna after having visited other holy places arrived in Aparánta (the western seaboard) whence he went to Prabhás. Hearing of his arrival Krishṇa marched to Prabhás and gave Arjuna a hearty welcome. From Prabhás they came together to the Raivataka hill which Krishna had decorated and where he entertained his guest with music and dancing. From Girnár they went to Dwáriká driving in a golden car. The city was adorned in honour of Arjuna; the streets were thronged with multitudes; and the members of the Vrishṇi, Bhoja, and Andhaka families met to honour Krishṇa's guest.'[3]

Some time after, against his elder brother Baladeva's desire, Krishṇa helped Arjuna to carry off Krishṇa's sister Subhadrá, with whom Arjuna had fallen in love at a fair in Girnár of which the Mahábhárata gives the following description: 'A gathering of the Yádavas chiefly the Vrishṇis and Andhakas took place near Raivataka. The hill and the country round were rich with fine rows of fruit trees and large mansions. There was much dancing singing and music. The princes of the Vrishṇi family were in handsome carriages glistening with gold. Hundreds and thousands of the people of Junágadh with their families attended on foot and in vehicles of various kinds. Baladeva with his wife Revati moved about attended by many Gandharvas. Ugrasena was there with his thousand queens and musicians. Sámba and Pradyumna attended

---

[1] Compare Máhábh. II. 13,594ff. Jarásandha's sisters Asti and Prápti were married to Kansa.

[2] Hari-vansa, XXXV. - CXII. [3] Mahábhárata Ádiparva, chaps. 218 - 221.

Chapter III.
LEGENDS.
The Yádavas.

in holiday attire and looked like gods. Many Yádavas and others were also present with their wives and musicians.'

Some time after this gathering Subhadrá came to Girnár to worship and Arjuna carried her off. Eventually Vasudeva and Baladeva consented and the runaways were married with due ceremony. The large fair still held in Mágh (February - March) in the west Girnár valley near the modern temple of Bhavanáth is perhaps a relic of this great Yádava fair.

The Yádava occupation of Dwáriká was not free from trouble. When Krishṇa was at Hastinápura on the occasion of the Rájasúya sacrifice performed by Yudhishṭhira, S'álva king of Mṛittikávati in the country of S'aubha led an army against Dwáriká. He slew many of the Dwáriká garrison, plundered the city and withdrew unmolested. On his return Krishṇa learning of S'álva's invasion led an army against S'álva. The chiefs met near the sea shore and in a pitched battle S'álva was defeated and killed.[1] Family feuds brought Yádava supremacy in Dwáriká to a disastrous end. The final family struggle is said to have happened in the thirty-sixth year after the war of the Mahábhárata, somewhere on the south coast of Káthiáváḍa near Prabhás or Somnáth Pátan the great place of Bráhmanical pilgrimage. On the occasion of an eclipse, in obedience to a proclamation issued by Krishṇa, the Yádavas and their families went from Dwáriká to Prabhás in state well furnished with dainties, animal food, and strong drink. One day on the sea shore the leading Yádava chiefs heated with wine began to dispute. They passed from words to blows. Krishṇa armed with an iron rod[2] struck every one he met, not even sparing his own sons. Many of the chiefs were killed. Baladeva fled to die in the forests and Krishṇa was slain by a hunter who mistook him for a deer. When he saw trouble was brewing Krishṇa had sent for Arjuna. Arjuna arrived to find Dwáriká desolate. Soon after Arjuna's arrival Vasudeva died and Arjuna performed the funeral ceremonies of Vasudeva Baladeva and Krishṇa whose bodies he succeeded in recovering. When the funeral rites were completed Arjuna started for Indraprastha in Upper India with the few that were left of the Yádava families,

---

[1] Mahábhárata Vanaparva, Chap. xiv. - xxii. Skanda x. Mṛittikávati the capital of S'álva cannot be identified. The name of the country sounds like S'vabhra in Rudradáman's Girnár inscription, which is apparently part of Charotar or South Ahmadabad. A trace of the old word perhaps remains in the river Sábhramati the modern Sábarmati. The fact that S'álva passed from Mṛittikávati along the sea shore would seem to show that part of the seaboard south of the Mahi was included in S'álva's territory. Dr. Bühler (Ind. Ant. VII. 263) described Pandit Bhagvánlál's reading of S'vabhra as a bold conjecture. A further examination of the original convinced the Pandit that S'vabhra was the right reading.

[2] The following is the legend of Krishṇa's iron flail. Certain Yádava youths hoping to raise a laugh at the expense of Viśvámitra and other sages who had come to Dwáriká presented to them Sámba Krishṇa's son dressed as a woman big with child. The lads asked the sages to foretell to what the woman would give birth. The sages replied: 'The woman will give birth to an iron rod which will destroy the Yádava race.' Obedient to the sage's prophecy Sámba produced an iron rod. To avoid the ill effects of the prophecy king Ugrasena had the rod ground to powder and cast the powder into the sea. The powder grew into the grass called *eraka* Typha elephantina. It was this grass which Krishna plucked in his rage and which in his hands turned into an iron flail. This *eraka* grass grows freely near the mouth of the Hiranya river of Prabhás.

Chapter III.
LEGENDS.
The Yádavas.

chiefly women. On the way in his passage through the Panchanada[1] or Panjab a body of Ábhíras attacked Arjuna with sticks and took several of Krishṇa's wives and the widows of the Andhaka Yádava chiefs. After Arjuna left it the deserted Dwáriká was swallowed by the sea.[2]

---

[1] This suggests that as in early times the Great Ran was hard to cross the way from Káthiáváḍa to Indraprastha or Delhi was by Kachch and Sindh and from Sindh by Multán and the Lower Panjáb. According to the Bhágavata Purána Krishna took the same route when he first came from Indraprastha to Dwáriká. On the other hand these details may support the view that the head-quarters of the historic Krishṇa were in the Panjáb.

[2] So far as is known neither Gujarát nor Kathiáváḍa contains any record older than the Girnár rock inscription of about B.C. 240: The Great Kshatrapa Rudra Dáman's (A.D. 139) inscription on the same rock has a reference to the Maurya Rája Chandragupta about B.C. 300. No local sign of Krishna or of his Yádavas remains.

In the Journal of the Royal Asiatic Society, XX. XXI. and XXII. Mr. Hewitt has recently attempted to trace the history of Western India back to B.C. 3000 perhaps to as early as B.C. 6000. The evidence which makes so far-reaching a past probable is the discovery of Indian indigo and muslin in Egyptian tombs of about B.C. 1700 (J. R. A. S. XX. 206); and the proof that a trade in teak and in Sindhu or Indian muslins existed between Western India and the Euphrates mouth as far back as B.C. 3000 or even B.C. 4000 (J. R. A. S. XX. 336, 337 and XXI. 204). According to Mr. Hewitt the evidence of the Hindu calendar carries the historical past of India into still remoter ages. The moon mansions and certain other details of the Hindu calendar seem to point to the Euphrates valley as the home of Hindu lunar astronomy. As in the Euphrates valley inscriptions of the Semitic king Sargon of Sippara prove that in B.C. 3750 moon-worship was already antiquated (J. R. A. S. XXI. 325), and as the precession of the equinoxes points to about B.C. 4700 as the date of the introduction of the sun zodiac (Sayce's Hibbert Lectures, 398) the system of lunar mansions and months, if it came from the Euphrates valley, must have reached India before B.C. 4700. The trade records of the black-headed perhaps Dravidian-speaking Sumris of the Euphrates mouth prove so close relations with the peninsula of Sinai and Egypt as to make a similar connection with Western India probable as far back as B.C. 6000. (Compare Sayce's Hibbert Lectures, 33: J. R. A. S. XXI. 326.) Of the races of whose presence in Gujarát and the neighbourhood Mr. Hewitt finds traces the earliest is the same black-headed moon-worshipping Sumri (Ditto). Next from Susiana in south-east Persia, the possessors of a lunar-solar calendar and therefore not later than B.C. 4700 (J. R. A. S. XXI. 325, 327, 330), the trading Sus or Saus, in Hindu books known as Suvarnas, entered India by way of Baluchistán and settled at Pátala in South Sindh. (J. R. A. S. XXI. 209.) With or soon after the Sus came from the north the cattle-herding sun-worshipping Sakas (J. R. A. S. XXII. 332). The Sus and Sakas passed south and together settled in Surashtra and West Gujarát. At a date which partly from evidence connected with the early Vedic hymns (J. R. A. S. XXII. 466) partly from the early Babylonian use of the Sanskrit Sindhu for India (J. R. A. S. XXI. 309), Mr. Hewitt holds cannot be later than B.C. 3000 northern A'ryas entered Gujarát and mixing with the Sus and Sakas as ascetics traders and soldiers carried the use of Sanskrit southwards. (J. R. A. S. XX. 343.) Of other races who held sway in Gujarát the earliest, perhaps about B.C. 2000 since their power was shattered by Parasuráma long before Mahábhárata times (J. R. A. S. XXI. 209 - 266), were the snake-worshipping perhaps Accadian (Ditto, 265) Haihayas now represented by the Gonds and the Haihayas' vassals the Vaidarbhas (Ditto, 209) a connection which is supported by trustworthy Central Indian Uraon or Gond tradition that they once held Gujarát (Elliott's Races, N. W. P., I. 154). Next to the Haihayas and like them earlier than the Mahábhárata (say B.C. 1500 - 2000) Mr. Hewitt would place the widespread un-Aryan Bhárats or Bhárgavs (J. R. A. S. XXI. 279 - 282, 286) the conquerors of the Haihayas (Ditto, 288). In early Mahábhárata times (say between B.C. 1000 and 800, Ditto 197 and 203) the Bhárats were overcome by the very mixed race of the Bhojas and of Krishna's followers the Vrishnis (Ditto, 270). Perhaps about the same time the chariot-driving Gandharvas of Cutch (Ditto, 273) joined the Sus and Sakas, together passed east to Kosala beyond Benares, and were there established in strength at the time of Gautama Buddha (B.C. 530) (Ditto). To the later Mahábhárata times, perhaps about B.C. 400 (Ditto, 197 - 271), Mr. Hewitt would assign the entrance into Gujarát of the Ábhíras or Ahirs whom he identifies with the northern or

Chapter III.

LEGENDS.
The Yádavas.

Skythian Abárs. Mr. Hewitt finds the following places in Gujarát associated with those early races. Pátála in South Sindh he (J. R. A. S. XXI. 209) considers the head-quarters of the Sus and Sakas. Another Su capital Prágjyotisha which is generally allotted to Bengal he would (XXI. 206) identify with Broach. With the Vaidarbhas the vassals of the Haihayas he associates Surparika, that is Sopara near Bassein, which he identifies (Ditto, 206) with the modern Surat on the Tapti. He connects (Ditto, 266) the Baroda river Vis'vámitra and Vaidurga the hill Pávágad with the same tribe. He finds a trace of the Bhárats in Baroda and in Bharati an old name of the river Mahi (Ditto, 286) and of the same race under their name Bhárgav in Broach (Ditto, 289). The traditional connection of the Bhojas with Dwárka is well established. Finally Kárpásika a Mahábhárata name for the shore of the Gulf of Cambay (Ditto, 209) may be connected with Kárván on the Narbada about twenty miles above Broach one of the holiest Shaiv places in India. Though objection may be taken to certain of Mr. Hewitt's identifications of Gujarát places, and also to the extreme antiquity he would assign to the trade between India and the west and to the introduction of the system of lunar mansions, his comparison of sacred Hindu books with the calendar and ritual of early Babylonia is of much interest.

CHAPTER IV.

MAURYAN AND GREEK RULE

(B.C. 319–100.)

Chapter IV.

The Mauryas, B.C. 319 - 197.

After the destruction of the Yádavas a long blank occurs in the traditional history of Gujarát. It is probable that from its seaboard position, for trade and other purposes, many foreigners settled in Káthiáváḍa and South Gujarát; and that it is because of the foreign element that the Hindu Dharmasástras consider Gujarát a Mlechchha country and forbid visits to it except on pilgrimage.[1] The fact also that Aśoka (B.C. 230) the great Mauryan king and propagator of Buddhism chose, among the Buddhist Theras sent to various parts of his kingdom, a Yavana Thera named Dhamma-rakhito as evangelist for the western seaboard,[2] possibly indicates a preponderating foreign element in these parts. It is further possible that these foreign settlers may have been rulers. In spite of these possibilities we have no traditions between the fall of the Yádavas and the rise of the Mauryas in B.C. 319.

Gujarát history dates from the rule of the Mauryan dynasty, the only early Indian dynasty the record of whose rule has been preserved in the writings of the Bráhmans, the Buddhists, and the Jains. This fulness of reference to the Mauryas admits of easy explanation. The Mauryas were a very powerful dynasty whose territory extended over the greater part of India. Again under Mauryan rule Buddhism was so actively propagated that the rulers made it their state religion, waging bloody wars, even revolutionizing many parts of the empire to secure its spread. Further the Mauryas were beneficent rulers and had also honourable alliances with foreign, especially with Greek and Egyptian, kings. These causes combined to make the Mauryans a most powerful and well remembered dynasty.

Inscriptions give reason to believe that the supremacy of Chandragupta, the founder of the Mauryan dynasty (B.C. 319), extended over Gujarát. According to Rudradáman's inscription (A.D. 150) on the great edict rock at Girnár in Káthiáváḍa, a lake called Sudarśana[3] near the edict rock was originally made by Pushyagupta of the Vaiśya caste, who is described as a brother-in-law of the Mauryan king Chandragupta.[4] The language of this inscription leaves no doubt that Chandragupta's sway extended over

[1] Mahábhárata Anuśásanaparvan 2158-9 mentions Láṭas among Kshatriya tribes who have become outcastes from seeing no Bráhmans. Again, Chap. VII. 72. ib. couples (J. Bl. As. Soc. VI. (1) 387) thievish Báhikas and robber Suráshtras. Compare Vishnu Purána, II. 37, where the Yavanas are placed to the west of Bháratavarsha and also J. R. A. S. (N. S.) IV. 468; and Brockhaus' Prabodha Chandrodaya, 87. The *s'loka* referred to in the text runs: He who goes to Anga, Vanga, Kalinga, Sauráshṭra, or Magadha unless it be for a pilgrimage deserves to go through a fresh purification.

[2] Turnour's Mahávanso, 71.

[3] Bombay Branch Royal Asiatic Society Journal, 1891, page 47.

[4] It is interesting to note that Chandragupta married a Vaiśya lady. Similarly while at Sánchi on his way to Ujjain Aśoka married Deví, the daughter of a Setthi. Turnour's Mahávanso, 76; Cunningham's Bhilsa Topes, 95.

Chapter IV.
THE MAURYAS.
B.C. 319-197.

Girnár as Pushyagupta is simply called a Vaiśya and a brother-in-law of king Chandragupta and has no royal attribute, particulars which tend to show that he was a local governor subordinate to king Chandragupta. The same inscription[1] states that in the time of Aśoka (B.C. 250) his officer Yavanarája Tusháspa adorned the same Sudarśana lake with conduits. This would seem to prove the continuance of Mauryan rule in Girnár for three generations from Chandragupta to Aśoka. Tusháspa is called Yavanarája. The use of the term *rája* would seem to show that, unlike Chandragupta's Vaiśya governor Pushyagupta, Tusáshpa was a dignitary of high rank and noble family. That he is called Yavanarája does not prove Tusháspa was a Greek, though for Greeks alone Yavana is the proper term. The name Tusháspa rather suggests a Persian origin from its close likeness in formation to Kersháshp, a name still current among Bombay Pársis. Evidence from other sources proves that Aśoka held complete sway over Málwa, Gujarát, and the Konkan coast. All the rock edicts of Aśoka hitherto traced have been found on the confines of his great empire. On the north-west at Kapurdigiri and at Shabazgarhi in the Baktro-Páli character; in the north-north-west at Kálsi, in the east at Dhauli and Jaugada; in the west at Girnár and Sopára, and in the south in Maisur all in Maurya characters. The Girnár and Sopára edicts leave no doubt that the Gujarát, Káthiáváḍa, and North Konkan seaboard was in Aśoka's possession. The fact that an inland ruler holds the coast implies his supremacy over the intervening country. Further it is known that Aśoka was viceroy of Málwa in the time of his father and that after his father's death he was sovereign of Málwa. The easy route from Mandasor (better known as Daśapur) to Dohad has always secured a close connection between Málwa and Gujarát. South Gujarát lies at the mercy of any invader entering by Dohad and the conquest of Káthiáváḍa on one side and of Upper Gujarát on the other might follow in detail. As we know that Káthiáváḍa and South Gujarát as far as Sopára were held by Aśoka it is not improbable that Upper Gujarát also owned his sway. The Maurya capital of Gujarát seems to have been Girinagara or Junágadh in Central Káthiáváḍa, whose strong hill fort dominating the rich province of Sorath and whose lofty hills a centre of worship and a defence and retreat from invaders, combined to secure for Junágadh its continuance as capital under the Kshatrapas (A.D. 100–380) and their successors the Guptas (A.D. 380-460). The southern capital of the Mauryas seems to have been Sopára near Bassein in a rich country with a good and safe harbour for small vessels, probably in those times the chief centre of the Konkan and South Gujarát trade.

Buddhist and Jain records agree that Aśoka was succeeded, not by his son Kunála who was blind, but by his grandsons Daśaratha and Samprati. The Barábar hill near Gayá has caves made by Aśoka and bearing his inscriptions; and close to Barábar is the

---

[1] Probably from some mistake of the graver's the text of the inscription अशोकस्य ते यवनराजेन yields no meaning. Some word for governor or officer is apparently meant.

Nágárjuna hill with caves made by Daśaratha also bearing his inscriptions. In one of these inscriptions the remark occurs that one of the Barábar caves was made by Daśaratha 'installed immediately after.' As the caves in the neighbouring hill must have been well known to have been made by Aśoka this 'after' may mean after Aśoka, or the 'after' may refer solely to the sequence between Daśaratha's installation and his excavation of the cave. In any case it is probable that Daśaratha was Aśoka's successor. Jaina records pass over Daśaratha and say that Aśoka was succeeded by his grandson Samprati the son of Kunála. In the matter of the propagation of the Jain faith, Jain records speak as highly of Samprati as Buddhist records speak of Aśoka.[1] Almost all old Jain temples or monuments, whose builders are unknown, are ascribed to Samprati who is said to have built thousands of temples as Aśoka is said to have raised thousands of *stupas*. In his Pátaliputra-kalpa Jinaprabhasuri the well known Jaina Áchárya and writer gives a number of legendary and other stories of Pátaliputra. Comparing Samprati with Aśoka in respect of the propagation of the faith in non-A'ryan countries the Áchárya writes: 'In Pátaliputra flourished the great king Samprati son of Kunála lord of Bharata with its three continents, the great Arhanta who established *vihâras* for Sramaṇas even in non-Áryan countries.'[2] It would appear from this that after Aśoka the Mauryan empire may have been divided into two, Daśaratha ruling Eastern India, and Samprati, whom Jaina records specially mention as king of Ujjain, ruling Western India, where the Jain sect is specially strong. Though we have no specific information on the point, it is probable, especially as he held Málwa, that during the reign of Samprati Gujarát remained under Mauryan sway. With Samprati Mauryan rule in Gujarát seems to end. In later times (A.D. 500) traces of Mauryan chiefs appear in Málwa and in the North Konkan. The available details will be given in another chapter.

After Samprati, whose reign ended about B.C. 197, a blank of seventeen years occurs in Gujarát history. The next available information shows traces of Baktrian-Greek sway over parts of Gujarát. In his description of Surastrene or Surashtra the author of the Periplus (A.D. 240) says: 'In this part there are preserved even to this day memorials of the expedition of Alexander, old temples, foundations of camps, and large wells.'[3] As Alexander did not

---

[1] Hemachandra's Parisishta Parva. Merutunga's Vichâraśreni.

[2] The text is '*Kundlasûnustrikhandabharatádhipah Paramárhanto Anáryadeśeshvapi Pravarttitaśramaṇa-vihárah Samprati Mahárája Sohábhavat*' meaning 'He was the great king Samprati son of Kunâla, sovereign of India of three continents, the great saint who had started monasteries for Jain priests even in non-Aryan countries.'

[3] McCrindle's Periplus, 115. The author of the Periplus calls the capital of Surastrene Minnagara. Pandit Bhagvanlál believed Minnagara to be a miswriting of Girinagara the form used for Girnár both in Rudradáman's (A.D. 150) rock inscription at Girnár (Fleet's Corpus Ins. Ind. III. 57) and by Varáha-Mihira (A.D. 570) (Brihat-Samhitá, XIV. 11). The mention of a Minagara in Ptolemy inland from Sorath and Monoglossum or Mangrul suggests that either Girnar or Junagaḍh was also known as Minnagara either after the Mins or after Men that is Menander. At the same time it is possible that Ptolemy's Agrinagara though much out of place may be Girinagara and that Ptolemy's Minagara in the direction of Ujjain may be Mandasor.

Chapter IV.
THE GREEKS.
B.C. 180 - 100.

come so far south as Káthiáváḍa and as after Alexander's departure the Mauryas held Káthiáváḍa till about B.C. 197, it may be suggested that the temples camps and wells referred to by the author of the Periplus were not memorials of the expedition of Alexander but remains of later Baktrian-Greek supremacy.

Demetrius, whom Justin calls the king of the Indians, is believed to have reigned from B.C. 190 to B.C. 165.[1] On the authority of Apollodorus of Artamita Strabo (B.C. 50 - A.D. 20) names two Baktrian-Greek rulers who seem to have advanced far into inland India. He says: 'The Greeks who occasioned the revolt of Baktria (from Syria B.C. 256) were so powerful by the fertility and advantages of the country that they became masters of Ariana and India....... Their chiefs, particularly Menander, conquered more nations than Alexander. Those conquests were achieved partly by Menander and partly by Demetrius son of Euthydemus king of the Baktrians. They got possession not only of Pattalene but of the kingdoms of Saraostus and Sigerdis, which constitute the remainder of the coast.'[2] Pattalene is generally believed to be the old city of Pátál in Sindh (the modern Haidarábád), while the subsequent mention of Saraostus and Sigerdis as kingdoms which constitute the remainder of the coast, leaves almost no doubt that Saraostus is Suráshtra and Sigerdis is Ságaradvípa or Cutch. The joint mention of Menander (B.C. 126) and Demetrius (B.C. 190) may mean that Demetrius advanced into inland India to a certain point and that Menander passed further and took Sindh, Cutch, and Káthiáváḍa. The discovery in Cutch and Káthiáváḍa of coins of Baktrian kings supports the statements of Justin and Strabo. Dr. Bhagvanlál's collecting of coins in Káthiáváḍa and Gujarát during nearly twenty-five years brought to light among Baktrian-Greek coins an obolus of Eucratides (B.C. 180 - 155), a few drachmæ of Menander (B.C. 126 - 110), many drachmæ and copper coins of Apollodotus (B.C. 110 - 100), but none of Demetrius. Eucratides was a contemporary of Demetrius. Still, as Eucratides became king of Baktria after Demetrius, his conquests, according to Strabo of a thousand cities to the east of the Indus, must be later than those of Demetrius.

As his coins are found in Káthiáváḍa Eucratides may either have advanced into Káthiáváḍa or the province may have come under his sway as lord of the neighbouring country of Sindh. Whether or not Eucratides conquered the province, he is the earliest Baktrian-Greek king whose coins have been found in Káthiáváḍa and Gujarát. The fact that the coins of Eucratides have been found in different parts of Káthiáváḍa and at different times seems to show that they were the currency of the province and were not merely imported either for trade or for ornament. It is to be noticed that these coins are all of the smallest value of the numerous coins issued by Eucratides. This may be explained by the fact that these small

---

[1] Justin's date is probably about A.D. 250. His work is a summary of the History of Trogus Pompeius about A.D. 1. Watson's Justin, 277; Wilson's Ariana Antiqua, 231.

[2] Hamilton and Falconer's Strabo, II. 252 - 253.

coins were introduced by Eucratides into Káthiáváḍa to be in keeping with the existing local coinage. The local silver coins in use before the time of Eucratides are very small, weighing five to seven grains, and bear the Buddhist symbols of the Svastika, the Trident, and the Wheel. Another variety has been found weighing about four grains with a misshapen elephant on the obverse and something like a circle on the reverse.[1] It was probably to replace this poor currency that Eucratides introduced his smallest obolus of less weight but better workmanship.

The end of the reign of Eucratides is not fixed with certainty: it is believed to be about B.C. 155.[2] For the two Baktrian-Greek kings Menander and Apollodotus who ruled in Káthiáváḍa after Eucratides, better sources of information are available. As already noticed Strabo (A.D. 20) mentions that Menander's conquests (B.C. 120) included Cutch and Suráshtra.[3] And the author of the Periplus (A.D. 240) writes: 'Up to the present day old drachmæ bearing the Greek inscriptions of Apollodotus and Menander are current in Barugaza (Broach).'[4] Menander's silver drachmæ have been found in Káthiáváḍa and Southern Gujarát.[5] Though their number is small Menander's coins are comparatively less scarce than those of the earliest Kshatrapás Nahapána and Chashṭana (A.D. 100 - 140). The distribution of Menander's coins suggests he was the first Baktrian-Greek king who resided in these parts and that the monuments of Alexander's times, camps temples and wells, mentioned by the author of the Periplus[6] were camps of Menander in Suráshtra. Wilson and Rochette have supposed Apollodotus to be the son and successor of Menander,[7] while General Cunningham believes Apollodotus to be the predecessor of Menander.[8] Inferences from the coins of these two kings found in Gujarát and Káthiáváḍa support the view that Apollodotus was the successor of Menander. The coins of Apollodotus are found in much larger numbers than those of Menander and the workmanship of Apollodotus' coins appears to be of a gradually declining style. In the later coins the legend is at times undecipherable. It appears from this that for some time after Apollodotus until Nahapána's (A.D. 100) coins came into use, the chief local currency was debased coins struck after the type of the coins of Apollodotus. Their use as the type of coinage generally happens to the coins of the last king of a dynasty. The statement by the author of the Periplus that in his time (A.D. 240) the old drachmæ of Apollodotus and Menander were

---

[1] These small local coins which were found in Hálár Gondal were presented to the Bombay Asiatic Society by the Political Agent of Káthiáwár and are in the Society's cabinet. Dr. Bhagvanlál found the two elephant coins in Junágadh.

[2] Wilson's Ariana Antiqua, 266. Gardner's British Museum Catalogue, 26, brings Eucratides to after B.C. 162.

[3] See above page 15.

[4] McCrindle's Periplus, 121.

[5] The Bombay Asiatic Society possesses some specimens of these coins of bad workmanship found near Broach with the legend incorrect, probably struck by some local governor of Menander. Two were also found in Junágaḍh.

[6] McCrindle's Periplus, 115.

[7] Numismatic Chronicle (New Series), X. 80; Wilson's Ariana Antiqua, 288.

[8] Numismatic Chronicle (New Series), X. 80.

Chapter IV.
The Greeks.
B.C. 180-100.

current in Barugaza, seems to show that these drachmæ continued to circulate in Gujarát along with the coins of the Western Kshatrapas. The mention of Apollodotus before Menander by the author of the Periplus may either be accidental, or it may be due to the fact that when the author wrote fewer coins of Menander than of Apollodotus were in circulation.

The silver coins both of Menander and Apollodotus found in Gujarát and Káthiáváda are of only one variety, round drachmæ. The reason that of their numerous large coins, tetradrachmæ didrachmæ and others, drachmæ alone have been found in Gujarát is probably the reason suggested for the introduction of the obolus of Eucratides, namely that the existing local currency was so poor that coins of small value could alone circulate. Still the fact that drachmæ came into use implies some improvement in the currency, chiefly in size. The drachmæ of both the kings are alike. The obverse of Menander's coins has in the middle a helmeted bust of the king and round it the Greek legend ΒΑΣΙΛΕΩΣ ΣΩΤΗΡΟΣ ΜΕΝΑΝΔΡΟΥ Of the king the Saviour Menander. On the reverse is the figure of Athene Promachos surrounded by the Baktro-Páli legend Mahárájasa Trádátasa Menandrasa that is Of the Great king the Saviour Menander, and a monogram.[1] The drachmæ of Apollodotus have on the obverse a bust with bare filleted head surrounded by the legend ΒΑΣΙΛΕΩΣ ΣΩΤΗΡΟΣ ΑΠΟΛΛΟΔΟΤΟΥ Of the king the Saviour Apollodotus. Except in the legend the reverse with two varieties of monogram[2] is the same as the reverse of the drachmæ of Menander. The legend in Baktro-Páli character is Mahárájasa Rájátirájasa Apaladatasa that is Of the Great king the over-king of kings Apaladata. During his twenty-five years of coin-collecting Dr. Bhagvánlál failed to secure a single copper coin of Menander either in Gujarát or in Káthiáváda. Of the copper coins of Apollodotus a deposit was found in Junágadh, many of them well preserved.[3] These coins are of two varieties, one square the other round and large. Of the square coin the obverse has a standing Apollo with an arrow in the right hand and on the top and the two sides the Greek legend ΒΑΣΙΛΕΩΣ ΣΩΤΗΡΟΣ ΚΑΙ ΦΙΛΟΠΑΤΟΡΟΣ ΑΠΟΛΛΟΔΟΤΟΥ that is Of the King Saviour and Fatherlover Apollodotus. On the reverse is the tripod of Apollo with a monogram[4] and the letter *drí* in Baktro-Páli on the left and the legend in Baktro-Páli characters Mahárájasa Trádátasa Apaladatasa. The round coin has also, on the obverse, a standing Apollo with an arrow in the right hand; behind is the same monogram as in the square coin and all round runs the Greek legend ΒΑΣΙΛΕΩΣ ΣΩΤΗΡΟΣ ΑΠΟΛΛΟΔΟΤΟΥ. On the reverse is the tripod of Apollo with on its right and left the letters *di* and *u* in Baktro-Páli and all round the Baktro-Páli legend Mahárájasa Trádátasa Apaladatasa.

[1] Wilson's Ariana Antiqua, Plate XXII. Number 41. Gardner's British Museum Catalogue, Plate XI. Number 8.

[2] Wilson's Ariana Antiqua, Plate XXII. Number 66, shows one variety of this monogram.

[3] These coins are said to have been found in 1882 by a cultivator in an earthen pot. Two of them were taken for Pandit Bhagvánlál and one for Mr. Vajeshankar Gaurishankar Naib Diván of Bhávnagar. The rest disappeared.

[4] Ariana Antiqua, Plate XXII. Number 47.

Chapter IV.

The Greeks.

B.C. 180-100.

The reason why so few copper coins of Apollodotus have been found in Gujarát perhaps is that these copper coins were current only in the time of Apollodotus and did not, like his silver drachmæ, continue as the currency of the country with the same or an imitated die. The date of the reign of Apollodotus is not fixed. General Cunningham believes it to be B.C. 165-150,[1] Wilson and Gardner take it to be B.C. 110-100.[2] Though no Indian materials enable us to arrive at any final conclusion regarding this date the fact that Apollodotus' coins continued to be issued long after his time shows that Apollodotus was the last Baktrian-Greek ruler of Gujarát and Káthiáváḍa. After Apollodotus we find no trace of Baktrian-Greek rule, and no other certain information until the establishment of the Kshatrapas about A.D. 100. The only fact that breaks this blank in Gujarát history is the discovery of copper coins of a king whose name is not known, but who calls himself Basileus Basileon Soter Megas that is King of Kings the Great Saviour. These coins are found in Káthiáváḍa and Cutch as well as in Rájputána the North-West Provinces and the Kábul valley, a distribution which points to a widespread Indian rule. The suggestion may be offered that this king is one of the leaders of the Yaudheyas whose constitution is said to have been tribal, that is the tribe was ruled by a number of small chiefs who would not be likely to give their names on their coins.[3]

---

[1] Numismatic Chronicle (New Series), X. 86.

[2] Ariana Antiqua, 288; Gardner and Poole's Catalogue of Indian Coins, xxxiii.

[3] Wilson (Ariana Antiqua, 332-334) identifies the coins marked Basileus Basileon Soter Megas with a king or dynasty of Indian extraction who reigned between Azes and Kadphises (B.C. 50-25), chiefly in the Panjáb. Gardner (British Museum Catalogue, 47) says: The Nameless king is probably cotemporary with Abdagases (A.D. 30-50): he may have been a member of the Kadphises dynasty. Cunningham (Ancient Geography, 245) places the coins of the tribal Yaudheyas in the first century A.D. The remark of Prinsep (Jour. Bengal Soc. VI. 2, 973) that in the Behat group of Buddhist coins some with Baktro-Páli legends have the name Yaudheya in the margin seems to support the suggestion in the text. But the marked difference between the Stag coins of the Yaudheyas (Thomas' Prinsep, I. Plate V.) and the Nameless king's coins (Gardner, Plate XIV. 1-6) tells strongly against the proposed identification. Of the Yaudheyas details are given below.

CHAPTER V.

THE KSHATRAPAS

(B.C. 70 – A.D. 398.)

Chapter V.

THE KSHATRAPAS, B.C. 70 - A.D. 398.

WITH the Kshatrapas (B.C. 70) begins a period of clearer light, and, at the same time, of increased importance, since, for more than three centuries, the Kshatrapas held sway over the greater part of Western India. Till recently this dynasty was known to orientalists as the Sáh dynasty a mistaken reading of the terminal of their names which in some rulers is Simha Lion and in others, as in Rudra Sena (A.D. 203-220) son of Rudra Simha, Sena Army.[1]

Two Dynasties.

The sway of the rulers who affix the title Kshatrapa to their names extended over two large parts of India, one in the north including the territory from the Kábul valley to the confluence of the Ganges and the Jamná ; the other in the west stretching from Ajmir in the north to the North Konkan in the south and from Málwa in the east to the Arabian

---

[1] Journal Bengal Asiatic Society (1835), 684; (1837), 351; (1838), 346; Thomas' Prinsep's Indian Antiquities, I. 425 - 435, II. 84 - 93; Thomas in Journal Royal Asiatic Society (Old Series), XII. 1 - 72; Wilson's Ariana Antiqua, 405 - 413; Journal B. B. R. A. S. VI. 377, VII. 392; Burgess' Archæological Report of Káthiáwár and Kachh, 18 - 72; Journal B. B. R. A. S. XII. (Proceedings), XXIII.; Indian Antiquary, VI. 43, X. 221 - 227.

The dynasty of the Kshatrapas or Mahákshatrapas of Sauráshtra was known to Prinsep (J. R. A. S. Bl. VII. - I. (1837), 351) to Thomas (J. R. A. S. F. S. XII. 1 - 78), and to Newton (Jl. B. B. R. A. S. IX. 1 - 19) as the Sah or Sâh kings. More recently, from the fact that the names of some of them end in Sena or army, the Kshatrapas have been called the Sena kings. The origin of the title Sah is the ending *siha*, that is *simha* lion, which belongs to the names of several of the kings. *Siha* has been read either *sáh* or *sena* because of the practice of omitting from the die vowels which would fall on or above the top line of the legend and also of omitting the short vowel *i* with the following *anusvára*. Sáh is therefore a true reading of the writing on certain of the coins. That the form Sáh on these coins is not the correct form has been ascertained from stone inscriptions in which freedom from crowding makes possible the complete cutting of the above-line marks. In stone inscriptions the ending is *siha* lion. See Fleet's Corpus Inscriptionum Indicarum, III. 36 note 1. Mr. Fleet (Ditto) seems to suggest that with the proof of the incorrectness of the reading Sáh the evidence that the Kshatrapas were of Indo-Skythian origin ceases. This does not seem to follow. In addition to the Parthian title Kshatrapa, their northern coinage, and the use of the Śaka (A.D. 78) era, now accepted as the accession of the great Kushán Kanishka, the evidence in the text shows that the line of Káthiaváda Kshatrapas starts from the foreigner Chashṭana (A.D. 130) whose predecessor Naháпana (A.D. 120) and his Śaka son-in-law Ushavadatta are noted in Násik inscriptions (Násik Gazetteer, 538 and 621) as leaders of Śakas, Palhavas, and Yavanas. Further as the limits of Ptolemy's (A.D. 150) Indo-Skythia (McCrindle, 136) agree very closely with the limits of the dominions of the then ruling Mahákshatrapa Rudradáman (A.D. 150) it follows that Ptolemy or his informer believed Rudradáman to be an Indo-Skythian. There therefore seems no reasonable doubt that the Kshatrapas were foreigners. According to Cunningham (Num. Chron. VIII. 231) they were Śakas who entered Gujarát from Sindh. The fact that the Kushán era (A.D. 78) was not adopted by the first two of the Western Kshatrapas, Chashṭana and Jayadáman, supports the view that they belonged to a wave of northerners earlier than the Kushán wave.

Chapter V.

THE KSHATRAPAS, B.C. 70 - A.D. 398.

The Name.

Sea in the west. The former may be called the Northern the latter the Western Kshatrapas.

Besides as Kshatrapa, in the Prákrit legends of coins and in inscriptions the title of these dynasties appears under three forms Chhatrapa,[1] Chhatrava,[2] and Khatapa.[3] All these forms have the same meaning namely Lord or Protector of the warrior-race, the Sanskrit Kshatra-pa.[4] It is to be noted that the title Kshatrapa appears nowhere as a title of any king or royal officer within the whole range of Sanskrit literature, or indeed on any inscription, coin, or other record of any Indian dynasty except the Northern and the Western Kshatrapas. According to Prinsep Kshatrapa is a Sanskritized form of Satrapa, a term familiar to the Grecian history of ancient Persia and used for the prefect of a province under the Persian system of government. As Prinsep further observes Satrapa had probably the same meaning in Ariana that Kshatrapa had in Sanskrit, the ruler feeder or patron of the *kshatra* or warrior class, the chief of a warlike tribe or clan.[5] Prinsep further notes the Persian kings were often in need of such chiefs and as they entrusted the chiefs with the government of parts of their dominions the word came to mean a governor. So during the anarchy which prevailed on the Skythian overthrow of Greek rule in Baktria[6] (B.C. 160) several chiefs of Malaya, Pallava, Ábhíra, Meda, and other predatory tribes came from Baktria to Upper India, and each established for himself a principality or kingdom. Subsequently these chiefs appear to have assumed independent sovereignty. Still though they often call themselves *rájás* or kings with the title Kshatrapa or Mahákshatrapa, if any Baktrian king advanced towards their territories, they were probably ready to acknowledge him as Overlord. Another reason for believing these Kshatrapa chiefs to have been foreigners is that, while the names of the founders of Kshatrapa sovereignty are foreign, their inscriptions and coins show that soon after the establishment of their rule they became converts to one or other form of the Hindu religion and assumed Indian names.[7]

---

[1] The Taxila plate in Journal R. A. S. (New Series), IV. 487; the Baktro-Páli on Nahapána's coins also gives the form Chhatrapa.

[2] Chhatrava appears in an unpublished Kshatrapa inscription from Mathurá formerly (1888) in Pandit Bhagvánlál's possession.

[3] Khatapa appears in the inscription of Nahapána's minister at Junnar (Bombay Gazetteer, XVIII. Pt. III. 167) and in some coins of the Northern Kshatrapa kings Pagamasha, Rájavula, and Sudása found near Mathurá. Prinsep's Indian Antiquities, II. Pl. XLIV. Figs. 12, 20, 21.

[4] Kshatrampátíti Kshatrapah.

[5] Thomas' Prinsep, II. 63 and 64.

[6] Malaya or Malava, Pallava, Ábhíra, Meva or Meda, and Mihira or Mehr appear to be the leading warlike tribes who came to India under these chiefs. These tribes formed the Kshatras whose lords or Kshatrapas these chiefs were.

[7] The explanation of the word Kshatrapa started by Prinsep and accepted by Pandit Bhagvánlál is of doubtful accuracy. The title is well known in Greek literature in the form σατραπης, and in the form Kshatrapávan occurs twice (B.C. 520) in connection with the governors of Baktria and Arachosia in the great Behistan inscription of Darius (Rawlinson's Herodotus, I. 329; Spiegel's Altpersische Keilinschriften, 24-26). The meaning of Kshatrapávan in old Persian is not "protector of the Kshatra race" but "protector of the kingdom," for the word *kshatram* occurs in the inscriptions of the Achæmenidæ with the meaning of "kingship" or "kingdom" (Spiegel, Altpersische Keilinschriften, 215). As is well known Satrap was the official title of the ruler of a Persian province. That the name continued in use with the same meaning under the Greek kings of Baktria

Chapter V.

Northern Kshatrapas, B.C. 70 - A.D. 78.

According to inscriptions and coins Northern Kshatrapa rule begins with king Maues about B.C. 70 and ends with the accession of the Kushán king Kanishka about A.D. 78. Maues probably belonged to the Śaka tribe of Skythians. If the Maues of the coins may be identified with the Moga of the Taxila plate the date of king Patika in the Taxila plate shows that for about seventy-five years after the death of Maues the date of his accession continued to be the initial year of the dynasty. From their connexion with the Sakas, arriving in India during the reign of the Saka Maues and for nearly three quarters of a century accepting the Śaka overlordship, the Kshatrapas, though as noted above their followers were chiefly Malayas, Pallavas, Ábhíras, and Medas, appear to have themselves come to be called Sakas and the mention of Saka kings in Puránik and other records seems to refer to them. After lasting for about 150 years the rule of the Northern Kshatrapas seems to have merged in the empire of the great Kushán Kanishka (A.D. 78).

Though recently found inscriptions and coins show that the Kshatrapas ruled over important parts of India including even a share of the western seaboard, nothing is known regarding them from either Indian or foreign literary sources. What little information can be gleaned is from their own inscriptions and coins. Of the Northern Kshatrapas this information is imperfect and disconnected. It shows that they had probably three or four ruling branches, one in the Kábul valley, a second at Taxila near Attak on the North-West Panjab frontier, a third at Behát near Sahåranpur or Delhi, and a fourth at Mathurá. The last two were perhaps subdivisions of one kingdom; but probably those at Kábul and at Taxila were distinct dynasties. An inscription found

---

(B.C. 250-100) is known from Strabo, who says (XI. 11) "the Greeks who held Baktria divided it into satrapies (σατραπειας) of which Aspionus and Touriva were taken from Eukratides (B.C. 180) by the Parthians." It is to be presumed that the Baktro-Grecians introduced the same arrangement into the provinces which they conquered in India. The earliest occurrence of the title in its Indian form is on the coins of a Rajabula or Ranjabola (Gardner, B. M. Cat. 67), who in his Greek legend makes use of the title "King of kings," and in his Indian legend calls himself "The unconquered Chhatrapa." His adoption for the reverse of his coins of the Athene Promachos type of Menander and Apollodotus Philopator connects Rajabula in time with those kings (B.C. 126-100) and we know from an inscription (Cunningham Arch. Rep. XX. 48) that he reigned at Mathurá. He was probably a provincial governor who became independent about B.C. 100 when the Greek kingdom broke up. The above facts go to show that Kshatrapa was originally a Persian title which was adopted by the Greeks and continued in use among their successors: that it originally denoted a provincial governor; but that, when the Greek kingdom broke up and their provincial chiefs became independent, it continued in use as a royal title. That after the Christian era, even in Parthia, the title Satrapes does not necessarily imply subjection to a suzerain is proved by the use of the phrase σατραπης των σατραπων Satrap of Satraps, with the sense of King of Kings in Gotarzes' Behistan inscription of A.D. 50. See Rawlinson's Sixth Monarchy, 88 n. 2 and 260 n. 1.—(A. M. T. J.)

The Pandit's identification of the Malavas or Malayas with a northern or Skythian tribe is in agreement with Alberuni (A.D. 1015), who, on the authority of the Báj Purána (Sachau's Text, chap. 29 page 150-155) groups as northern tribes the Pallavas, Śakas, Mallas, and Gurjars. In spite of this authority it seems better to identify the Mallas, Malavas, or Malayas with Alexander the Great's (B.C. 325) Malloi of Multan (compare McCrindle's Alexander's Invasion of India, Note P). At the same time (Rockhill's Life of Buddha, 132, 133, 137) the importance of the Mallas in Vaisáli (between Patná and Tirhút) during the lifetime of Sákya Muni (B.C. 580) favours the view that several distinct tribes have borne the same or nearly the same name.

Chapter V.

NORTHERN KSHATRAPAS, B.C. 70 - A.D. 78.

in Mathurá shows a connection either by marriage or by neighbourhood between the Behát and Mathurá branches. This is a Baktro-Páli inscription recording the gift of a stúpa by Nandasiriká daughter of Kshatrapa Rájavula and mother of Kharaosti Yuvarája. Kharaosti is the dynastic name of the prince, his personal name appears later in the inscription as Talama (Ptolemy ?). From his dynastic name, whose crude form Kharaosta or Kharaottha may be the origin of the Prakrit Chhaharáta and the Sanskritised Kshaharáta, this Talama appears to be a descendant of the Kshatrapa Kharaosti whose coins found at Taxila call him Artaputa that is the son of Arta apparently the Parthian Ortus.

The same Baktro-Páli Mathurá inscription also mentions with special respect a Kshatrapa named Patika,[1] who, with the title of Kusulaka or Kozolon, ruled the Kábul valley with his capital first at Nagaraka and later at Taxila.

The same inscription further mentions that the stúpa was given while the Kshatrapa Sudása son of the Mahákshatrapa Rájavula was ruling at Mathurá. The inference from the difference in the titles of the father and the son seems to be that Sudása was ruling in Mathurá as governor under his father who perhaps ruled in the neighbourhood of Delhi where many of his coins have been found. While the coins of Sudása have the legend in Nágarí only, Rájavula's coins are of two varieties, one with the legend in Báktro-Páli and the other with the legend in Nágarí, a fact tending to show that the father's territories stretched to the far north.

Though Kharaosti is mentioned as a Yuvarája or prince heir-apparent in the time of his maternal uncle Sudása, the inscription shows he had four children. It is curious that while the inscription mentions Nandasiriká as the mother of Kharaosti Yuvarája, nothing is said about her husband. Perhaps he was dead or something had happened to make Nandasiriká live at her father's home.

WESTERN KSHATRAPAS, A.D. 70 - 398.

Another inscription of Sudása found by General Cunningham at Mathurá is in old Nágarí character. Except that they have the distinctive and long continued Kshatrapa peculiarity of joining *ya* with other letters the characters of this inscription are of the same period as those of the inscriptions of the great Indo-Skythian or Kushán king Kanishka. This would seem to show that the conquest of Mathurá by Kanishka took place soon after the time of Kshatrapa Sudása. It therefore appears probable that Nahapána, the first Kshatrapa ruler of Gujarát and Káthiáváḍa, the letters of whose inscriptions are of exactly the same Kshatrapa type as those of Sudása, was a scion of the Kharaosti family, who, in this overthrow of kingdoms, went westwards conquering either on his own account or as a general sent by Kanishka. Nahapána's[2] advance seems to have lain through East Rajputána by Mandasor[3]

---

[1] Patika was apparently the son of the Liako Kujulako of the Taxila plate. Dowson in Jour. R. A. S. New Series. IV. 497 mistranslates the inscription and fails to make out the name Patika.

[2] Compare Specht. Jour. Asiatique. 1883. t. II. 325. According to Chinese writers about A.D. 20 Yen-kao-tchin-tai or Kadphises II. conquered India (Thientchou) and there established generals who governed in the name of the Yuechi.

[3] Pandit Bhagvánlál found two of his copper coins at Mandasor in 1884.

Chapter V.
Western Kshatrapas, A.D. 70-398.

in West Málwa along the easy route to Dohad as far as South Gujarát. From South Gujarát his power spread in two directions, by sea to Káthiáváḍa and from near Balsár by the Dáng passes to Násik and the Deccan, over almost the whole of which, judging from coins and inscriptions, he supplanted as overlord the great Ándhra kings of the Deccan. No evidence is available to show either that East Málwa with its capital at Ujjain or that North Gujarát formed part of his dominions. All the information we have regarding Nahapána is from his own silver coins and from the inscriptions of his son-in-law Ushavadáta at Násik and Kárle and of his minister Ayama (Sk. Áryaman) at Junnar. Nahapána's coins are comparatively rare. The only published specimen is one obtained by Mr. Justice Newton.[1] Four others were also obtained by Dr. Bhagvánlál from Káthiáváḍa and Násik.

Kshatrapa I. Nahapána, A.D. 78-120.

The coins of Nahapána are the earliest specimens of Kshatrapa coins. Though the type seems to have been adopted from the Baktrian-Greek, the design is original and is not an imitation of any previous coinage. The type seems adopted in idea from the drachma of Apollodotus (B.C. 110-100). On the obverse is a bust with a Greek legend round it and on the reverse a thunderbolt and an arrow probably as on the reverse of the coins of Apollodotus[2] representing the distinctive weapons of Athene Promachos and of Apollo. In addition to the Báktro-Páli legend on the Apollodotus drachma, the reverse of Nahapána's coin has the same legend in Nágarí, since Nágarí was the character of the country for which the coin was struck. The dress of the bust is in the style of the over-dress of Nahapána's time. The bust, facing the right, wears a flat grooved cap and has the hair combed in ringlets falling half down the ear. The neck shows the collar of the coat. The workmanship of the coins is good. The die seems to have been renewed from time to time as the face altered with age. Of Dr. Bhagvánlál's four coins one belongs to Nahapána's youth, another to his old age, and the remaining two to his intervening years. In all four specimens the Greek legend is imperfect and unreadable. The letters of the Greek legend are of the later period that is like the letters on the coins of the great Skythian king Kadphises I. (B.C. 26). One of the coins shows in the legend the six letters LLODO-S. These may be the remains of the name Apollodotus (B.C. 110-100). Still it is beyond doubt that the letters are later Greek than those on the coins of Apollodotus. Until the legend is found clear on some fresher specimen, it is not possible to say anything further. In three of the coins the Báktro-Páli legend on the reverse runs:

रञो छहरातस नहपानस.
Raño Chhaharátasa Nahapánasa.
Of king Chhaharáta Nahapána.

The fourth has simply रञो छहरातस
Raño Chhaharátasa.
Of king Chhaharáta.

[1] This is a bad specimen with the legend dim and worn.
[2] Some coins of Apollodotus have on the reverse Apollo with his arrow; others have Athene Promachos with the thunderbolt.

The old Nágarí legend is the same in all :

रञो क्षहरातस नहपानस

Raño Kshaharátasa Nahapánasa.

Of king Kshaharáta Nahapána.

The Chhaharáta of the former and the Kshaharáta of the latter are the same, the difference in the initial letter being merely dialectical. As mentioned above Kshaharáta is the family name of Nahapána's dynasty. It is worthy of note that though Nahapána is not styled Kshatrapa in any of his coins the inscriptions of Ushavadáta at Násik repeatedly style him the Kshaharáta Kshatrapa Nahapána.[1]

Ushavadáta, A.D. 100 - 120.

Ushavadáta was the son-in-law of Nahapána being married to his daughter Dakhamitá or Dakshamitrá. Ushavadáta bears no royal title. He simply calls himself son of Dínika and son-in-law of Nahapána, which shows that he owed his power and rank to his father-in-law, a position regarded as derogatory in India, where no scion of any royal dynasty would accept or take pride in greatness or influence obtained from a father-in-law.[2] Násik Inscription XIV. shows that Ushavadáta was a S'aka. His name, as was first suggested by Dr. Bhau Dáji, is Prákrit for Rishabhadatta. From the many charitable and publicly useful works mentioned in various Násik and Kárle inscriptions, as made by him in places which apparently formed part of Nahapána's dominions, Ushavadáta appears to have been a high officer under Nahapána. As Nahapána seems to have had no son Ushavadáta's position as son-in-law would be one of special power and influence. Ushavadáta's charitable acts and works of public utility are detailed in Násik Inscriptions X. XII. and XIV. The charitable acts are the gift of three hundred thousand cows; of gold and of river-side steps at the Bárnása or Banás river near A'bu in North Gujarát; of sixteen villages to gods and Bráhmans; the feeding of hundreds of thousands of Bráhmans every year; the giving in marriage of eight wives to Bráhmans at Prabhás in South Káthiáváḍa; the bestowing of thirty-two thousand cocoanut trees in Nanamgola or Nárgol village on the Thána seaboard on the Charaka priesthoods of Pinḍitakávaḍa, Govardhana near Násik, Suvarṇamukha, and Rámatírtha in Sorpáraga or Sopára on the Thána coast; the giving of three hundred thousand cows and a village at Pushkara or Pokhar near Ajmir in East Rajputána; making gifts to Bráhmans at Chechina or Chichan near Kelva-Máhim on the Thána coast; and the gift of trees and 70,000 *kárshápaṇas* or 2000 *suvarṇas* to gods and Bráhmans at Dáhánu in Thána. The public works executed by Ushavadáta include rest-houses and alms-houses at Bharu Kachha or Broach, at Daśapura or Mandasor in North Málwa, and gardens and wells at Govardhana and Sopára; free ferries across the Ibá or Ambiká, the Paráda or Pár, the Damaná or Damanganga, the Tápi or Tápti, the Karabená or Káveri, and the Dáhánuká or Dáhánu river. Waiting-places and steps were also built on both banks of each of these rivers. These charitable and public works of Ushavadáta savour much of the Bráhmanic religion. The only

[1] Bom. Gaz. XVI. 571ff.

[2] A well known Sanskrit saying is श्वशुरख्यातोऽधमाधम : A man known through his father-in-law is the vilest of the vile.

Chapter V.
WESTERN KSHATRAPAS, A.D. 70 - 398.
Ushavadáta, A.D. 100 - 120.

Buddhist charities are the gift of a cave at Násik; of 3000 *kárshápanas* and eight thousand cocoanut trees for feeding and clothing monks living in the cave; and of a village near Kárle in Poona for the support of the monks of the main Kárle cave. Ushavadáta himself thus seems to have been a follower of the Bráhmanical faith. The Buddhist charities were probably made to meet the wishes of his wife whose father's religion the Buddhist wheel and the Bodhi tree on his copper coins prove to have been Buddhism. The large territory over which these charitable and public works of Ushavadáta spread gives an idea of the extent of Nahapána's rule. The gift of a village as far north as Pokhara near Ajmir would have been proof of dominion in those parts were it not for the fact that in the same inscription Ushavadáta mentions his success in assisting some local Kshatriyas. It is doubtful if the northern limits of Nahapána's dominions extended as far as Pokhar. The village may have been given during a brief conquest, since according to Hindu ideas no village given to Bráhmans can be resumed. The eastern boundary would seem to have been part of Málwa and the plain lands of Khándesh Násik and Poona; the southern boundary was somewhere about Bombay; and the western Káthiáváḍa and the Arabian sea.

Nahapána's Era.

Nahapána's exact date is hard to fix. Ushavadáta's Násik cave Inscriptions X. and XII. give the years 41 and 42; and an inscription of Nahapána's minister Ayáma at Junnar gives the year 46. The era is not mentioned. They are simply dated *vase* Sk. *varshe* that is in the year. Ushavadáta's Násik Inscription XII. records in the year 42 the gift of charities and the construction of public works which must have taken years to complete. If at that time Ushavadáta's age was 40 to 45, Nahapána who, as Inscription X. shows, was living at that time, must have been some twenty years older than his son-in-law or say about 65. The Junnar inscription of his minister Ayáma which bears date 46 proves that Nahapána lived several years after the making of Ushavadáta's cave. The bust on one of his coins also shows that Nahapána attained a ripe old age.

Nahapána cannot have lived long after the year 46. His death may be fixed about the year 50 of the era to which the three years 41, 42, and 46 belong. He was probably about 75 years old when he died. Deducting 50 from 75 we get about 25 as Nahapána's age at the beginning of the era to which the years 41, 42, and 46 belong, a suitable age for an able prince with good resources and good advisers to have established a kingdom. It is therefore probable that the era marks Nahapána's conquest of Gujarát. As said above, Nahapána was probably considered to belong to the Śaka tribe, and his son-in-law clearly calls himself a Śaka. It may therefore be supposed that the era started by Nahapána on his conquest of Gujarát was at first simply called Varsha; that it afterwards came to be called Śakavarsha or Śakasamvatsara; and that finally, after various changes, to suit false current ideas, about the eleventh or twelfth century the people of the Deccan styled it Śáliváhana Saka mixing it with current traditions regarding the great Śátavahana or Śáliváhana king of Paithan. If, as mentioned above, Nahapána's conquest of Gujarát and the establishment of his era be taken to come close after the conquest of Mathurá by

Nahapána's Era.

Kanishka, the Gujarát conquest and the era must come very shortly after the beginning of Kanishka's reign, since Kanishka conquered Mathurá early in his reign. As his Mathurá inscriptions[1] give 5 as Kanishka's earliest date, he must have conquered Mathurá in the year 3 or 4 of his reign. Nahapána's expedition to and conquest of Gujarát was probably contemporary with or very closely subsequent to Kanishka's conquest of Mathurá. So two important eras seem to begin about four years apart, the one with Kanishka's reign in Upper India, the other with Nahapána's reign in Western India. The difference being so small and both being eras of foreign conquerors, a Kushán and a Śaka respectively, the two eras seem to have been subsequently confounded. Thus, according to Dr. Burnell, the Javanese S'aka era is A.D. 74, that is Kanishka's era was introduced into Java, probably because Java has from early times been connected with the eastern parts of India where Kanishka's era was current. On the other hand the astrological works called Karaṇa use the era beginning with A.D. 78 which we have taken to be the Western era started by Nahapána. The use of the S'aka era in Karaṇa works dates from the time of the great Indian astronomer Varáha Mihira (A.D. 587). As Varáha Mihira lived and wrote his great work in Avanti or Málwa he naturally made use of the S'aka era of Nahapána, which was current in Málwa. Subsequent astronomers adopted the era used by the master Varáha Mihira. Under their influence Nahapána's A.D. 78 era passed into use over the whole of Northern and Central India eclipsing Kanishka's A.D. 74 era. On these grounds it may be accepted that the dates in the Násik inscriptions of Ushavadáta and in Ayáma's inscription at Junnar are in the era founded by Nahapána on his conquest of Gujarát and the West Deccan. This era was adopted by the Western Kshatrapa successors of Nahapána and continued on their coins for nearly three centuries.[2]

---

[1] Cunningham's Arch. Sur. III. Plate 13. Inscriptions 2 and 3.

[2] The author's only reason for supposing that two eras began between A.D. 70 and 80 seems to be the fact that the Javanese Śaka era begins A.D. 74, while the Indian Śaka era begins A.D. 78. It appears, however, from Lassen's Ind. Alt. II. 1040 note 1, that the Javanese S'aka era begins either in A.D. 74 or in A.D. 78. The author's own authority, Dr. Burnell (S. Ind. Pal. 72) while saying that the Javanese Śaka era dates from A.D. 74, gives A.D. 80 as the epoch of the Saka era of the neighbouring island of Bali, thus supporting Raffle's explanation (Java, II. 68) that the difference is due to the introduction into Java of the Muhammadan mode of reckoning during the past 300 years. The Javanese epoch of A.D. 74 cannot therefore be treated as an authority for assuming a genuine Indian era with this initial date. The era of Kanishka was used continuously down to its year 281 (Fergusson Hist. of Ind. Architecture, 740) and after that date we have numerous instances of the use of the S'akanṛipakála or Sakakála down to the familiar S'aka of the present day. It seems much more likely that the parent of the modern S'aka era was that of Kanishka, which remained in use for nearly three centuries, than that of Nahapána, who so far as we know left no son, and whose era (if he founded one) probably expired when the Kshaharáta power was destroyed by the Andhrabhṛityas in the first half of the second century A.D. We must therefore assume A.D. 78 to be the epoch of Kanishka's era. There remains the question whether Nahapána dates by Kanishka's era, or uses his own regnal years. There is nothing improbable in the latter supposition, and we are not forced to suppose that Nahapána was a feudatory of the Kushán kings. It has been shown above that the use of the title Kshatrapa does not necessarily imply a relation of inferiority. On the other hand (*pace* Oldenburg in Ind. Ant. X. 213) the later Kshatrapas certainly seem to have used Kanishka's era: and Nahapána and the Kushán dynasty seem to have been of the same race: for Heraus, who was certainly a Kushán, apparently calls himself Saka on his coins (Gardner B. M. Cat. xlvii.): and it is highly probable that Nahapána, like his son-in-law Ushavadáta, was a Saka. Further, the fact that Nahapána does not call himself Mahárája but Rája goes to show that he was not a paramount sovereign. —(A. M. T. J.)

Chapter V.

Western Kshatrapas, A.D. 70-398.

The Málava Era, B.C. 56.

The question arises why should not the dates on the Western Kshatrapa coins belong to the era which under the incorrect title of the Vikrama era is now current in Gujarát and Málwa. Several recently found Málwa inscriptions almost prove that what is called the Vikrama era beginning with B.C. 56 was not started by any Vikrama, but marks the institution of the tribal constitution of the Málavas.[1] Later the era came to be called either the era of the Málava lords[2] or Málava Kála that is the era of the Málavas. About the ninth century just as the S'aka era became connected with the S'aliváhana of Paithan, this old Málava era became connected with the name of Vikramáditya, the great legendary king of Ujain.

It might be supposed that the Málavas who gave its name to the Málava era were the kings of the country now called Málwa. But it is to be noted that no reference to the present Málwa under the name of Málavadeśa occurs in any Sanskrit work or record earlier than the second century after Christ. The original Sanskrit name of the country was Avanti. It came to be called Málava from the time the Málava tribe conquered it and settled in it, just as Káthiáváḍa and Meváḍa came to be called after their Káthi and Meva or Meda conquerors. The Málavas, also called Málayas,[3] seem like the Medas to be a foreign tribe, which, passing through Upper India conquered and settled in Central India during the first century before Christ. The mention in the Mudrárákshasa[4] of a Málaya king among five Upper Indian kings shows that in the time of the Mauryas (B.C. 300) a Málaya kingdom existed in Upper India which after the decline of Maurya supremacy spread to Central India. By Nahapána's time the Málavas seem to have moved eastwards towards Jaipur, as Ushavadáta defeated them in the neighbourhood of the Pushkar lake: but the fact that the country round Ujain was still known to Rudradáman as Avanti, shows that the Málavas had not yet (A.D. 150) entered the district now known as Málava. This settlement and the change of name from Avanti to Málava probably took place in the weakness of the Kshatrapas towards the end of the third century A.D. When they established their sway in Central India these Málavas or Málayas like the ancient Yauddheyas (B.C. 100) and the Káthis till recent times (A.D. 1818) seem to have had a democratic constitution.[5] Their political system seems to have proved unsuited to the conditions of a settled community. To put an end to dissensions the Málava tribe appears to have framed what the Mandasor inscription terms a *sthiti* or constitution in honour of which they began a new era.[6] It may be asked, Why may not Nahapána have been the head of the Málavas who under the new constitution became the first Málava sovereign and his reign-dates be those of

---

[1] Jour. B. B. R. A. S. XVI. 378; Ind. Ant. XV. 198, 201, XIII. 126; Arch. Sur. X. 33.

[2] Cunningham's Arch. Sur. XIII. 162. Cf. Kielhorn in Ind. Ant. XIX. 20ff.

[3] Cunningham's Arch. Sur. X. 33-34. Numerous Western India inscriptions prove that *ya* and *va* are often intermixed in Prákrit.

[4] Vide Telang's Mudrárákshasa, 204. Mr. Telang gives several readings the best of which mean either the king of the Málaya country or the king of the Málaya tribe.

[5] Macmurdo (1818) notices the democratic constitution of the Káthis. Trans. Bom. Lit. Soc. I. 274.

[6] Compare Fleet's Corpus Ins. Ind. III. 87, 152, 158 from the (supremacy of) the tribal constitution of the Málavas. Prof. Kielhorn has however shown that the words of the inscription do not necessarily mean this. Ind. Ant. XIX. 56.

The Málava Era, B.C. 56.

the new Málava era? Against this we know from a Násik inscription of Ushavadáta[1] that Nahapána was not a Málava himself but an opponent of the Málavas as he sent Ushavadáta to help a tribe of Kshatriyas called Uttamabhadras whom the Málavas had attacked. Further a chronological examination of the early ruling dynasties of Gujarát does not favour the identification of the Kshatrapa era with the Málava era. The available information regarding the three dynasties the Kshatrapas the Guptas and the Valabhis, is universally admitted to prove that they followed one another in chronological succession. The latest known Kshatrapa date is 310. Even after this we find the name of a later Kshatrapa king whose date is unknown but may be estimated at about 320. If we take this Kshatrapa 320 to be in the Vikrama Samvat, its equivalent is A.D. 264. In consequence of several new discoveries the epoch of the Gupta era has been finally settled to be A.D. 319. It is further settled that the first Gupta conqueror of Málwa and Gujarát was Chandragupta II.[2] the date of his conquest of Málwa being Gupta 80 (A.D. 399). Counting the Kshatrapa dates in the Samvat era this gives a blank of (399 − 264 =) 135 years between the latest Kshatrapa date and the date of Chandragupta's conquest of Gujarát to fill which we have absolutely no historical information. On the other hand in support of the view that the Kshatrapa era is the S'aka era the Káthiáváḍa coins of the Gupta king Kumáragupta son of Chandragupta dated 100 Gupta closely resemble the coins of the latest Kshatrapa kings, the workmanship proving that the two styles of coin are close in point of time. Thus taking the Kshatrapa era to be the S'aka era the latest Kshatrapa date is 320 + 78 = A.D. 398, which is just the date (A.D. 399) of Chandragupta's conquest of Málwa and Gujarát. For these reasons, and in the absence of reasons to the contrary, it seems proper to take the dates in Ushavadáta's and Ayáma's inscriptions as in the era which began with Nahapána's conquest of Gujarát, namely the S'aka era whose initial date is A.D. 78.

Kshatrapa II. Chashṭana, A.D. 130.

After Nahapána's the earliest coins found in Gujarát are those of Chashṭana. Chashṭana's coins are an adaptation of Nahapána's coins. At the same time Chashtana's bust differs from the bust in Nahapána's coins. He wears a mustache, the cap is not grooved but plain, and the hair which reaches the neck is longer than Nahapána's hair. In one of Chashtana's coins found by Mr. Justice Newton, the hair seems dressed in ringlets as in the coins of the Parthian king Phraates II. (B.C. 136 - 128).[3] On the reverse instead of the thunderbolt and arrow as in Nahapána's coins, Chashṭana's coins have symbols of the sun and moon in style much like the sun and moon symbols on the Parthian coins of Phraates II., the moon being a crescent and the sun represented by eleven rays shooting from a central beam. To the two on the reverse a third symbol seems to have been added consisting of two arches resting on a straight line, with a third arch over and between

---

[1] Inscription 10 lines 3 - 4. Bom. Gaz. XVI. 572.
[2] Details are given below under the Guptas.
[3] Burgess' Archæological Report of Káthiáwár and Cutch, 55; Numismata Orientalia, I. Pl. II. Fig. 8.

Chapter V.

WESTERN KSHATRAPAS, A.D. 70 - 398.

Chashtana's Coins, A.D. 130.

the two arches, and over the third arch an inverted semicircle. Below these symbols stretches a waving or serpentine line.[1]

The same symbol appears on the obverse of several very old medium-sized square copper coins found in Upper India. These coins Dr. Bhagvánlál took to be coins of Aśoka. They have no legend on either side, and have a standing elephant on the obverse and a rampant lion on the reverse. As these are the symbols of Aśoka, the elephant being found in his rock inscriptions and the lion in his pillar inscriptions, Dr. Bhagvánlál held them to be coins of Aśoka. The arch symbol appears in these coins over the elephant on the obverse and near the lion on the reverse but in neither case with the underlying zigzag line.[2] So also a contemporary coin bearing in the Aśoka character the clear legend वटस्वक Vaṭasvaka shows the same symbol, with in addition a robed male figure of good design standing near the symbol saluting it with folded hands. The position of the figure (Ariana Antiqua, Plate XV. Fig. 30) proves that the symbol was an object of worship. In Chashṭana's coins we find this symbol between the sun and the moon, a position which suggests that the symbol represents the mythical mountain Meru, the three semicircular superimposed arches representing the peaks of the mountain and the crescent a *Siddha-śilá* or Siddhas' seat, which Jaina works describe as crescent-shaped and situated over Meru. The collective idea of this symbol in the middle and the sun and moon on either side recalls the following śloka:

यावद्वीचीतरङ्गान्वहति सुरनदी जान्हवी पूर्णतोया ।
यावच्चाकाशमार्गे तपति दिनकरो भास्करो लोकपालः
यावद्वज्रेन्दुनीलस्फटिकमणिशिला वर्तते मेरुशृङ्गे ।
तावत्त्वं पुत्रपौत्रैः स्वजनपरिवृतो जीव शम्भोः प्रसादात् ॥

Mayest thou by the favour of S'ambhu live surrounded by sons grandsons and relations so long as the heavenly Ganges full of water flows with its waves, so long as the brilliant sun the protector of the universe shines in the sky, and so long as the slab of diamond moonstone lapis lazuli and sapphire remains on the top of Meru.

Dr. Bird's Kanheri copperplate has a verse with a similar meaning regarding the continuance of the glory of the relic shrine of one Pushya, so long as Meru remains and rivers and the sea flow.[3] The meaning of showing Meru and the sun and moon is thus clear. The underlying serpentine line apparently stands for the Jáhnaví river or it may perhaps be a representation of the sea.[4] The object of repre-

---

[1] The meaning of this symbol has not yet been made out. It is very old. We first find it on the punched coins of Málwa and Gujarát (regarded as the oldest coinage in India) without the serpentine line below, which seems to show that this line does not form part of the original symbol and has a distinct meaning.

[2] Compare Wilson's Ariana Antiqua, Plate XV. Fig. 26 - 27.

[3] Cave Temple Inscriptions, Bombay Archæological Survey, Extra Number (1881), 58.

[4] Ariana Antiqua, Plate XV. Fig. 29. Some imaginary animals are shown under the serpentine line.

senting these symbols on coins may be that the coins may last as long as the sun, the moon, mount Meru, and the Ganges or ocean. Against this view it may be urged that the coins of the Buddhist kings of Kuninda (A.D. 100), largely found near Sahāranpur in the North-West Provinces, show the arch symbol with the Buddhist trident over it, the Bodhi tree with the railing by its side, and the serpentine line under both the tree and the symbol, the apparent meaning being that the symbol is a Buddhist shrine with the Bodhi tree and the river Niranjana of Buddha Gaya near it. The same symbol appears as a Buddhist shrine in Andhra coins[1] which make it larger with four rows of arches, a tree by its side, and instead of the zigzag base line a railing. This seems a different representation perhaps of the shrine of Mahábodhi at Buddha Gaya. These details seem to show that popular notions regarding the meaning of this symbol varied at different times.[2]

Chapter V.

WESTERN KSHATRAPAS, A.D. 70-398.

Çhashṭana's Coins, A.D. 130.

Such of the coins of Chashṭana as have on the reverse only the sun and the moon bear on the obverse in Báktro-Páli characters a legend of which the four letters रञो जिमो Raño jimo can alone be made out. An illegible Greek legend continues the Báktro-Páli legend. The legend on the reverse is in old Nágarí character :

राज्ञो क्षत्रपस य्समोतिकपुत्र [सच] ष्टनस.[3]

Rájño Kshatrapasa Ysamotikaputra(sa Cha)shṭanasa.

Of the king Kshatrapa Chashṭana son of Ysamotika.

The variety of Chashṭana's coins which has the arch symbol on the reverse, bears on the obverse only the Greek legend almost illegible and on the reverse the Báktro-Páli legend चटनस Chaṭanasa meaning. Of Chashṭana and in continuation the Nágarí legend :

राज्ञोमहाक्षत्रपस य्समोतिकपुत्रस चष्टनस

Rájño Mahákshatrapasa Ysamotikaputrasa Chashṭanasa.

Of the king the great Kshatrapa Chashṭana son of Ysamotika.

Chashṭana's Father.

The name Zamotika is certainly not Indian but foreign apparently a corruption of some such form as Psamotika or Xamotika. Further the fact that Zamotika is not called Kshatrapa or by any other title, would seem to show that he was an untitled man whose son somehow came to authority and obtained victory over these parts where (as his earlier coins with the sun and the moon show) he was at first called a Kshatrapa and afterwards (as his later coins with the third symbol show) a Mahákshatrapa or great Kshatrapa. We know nothing of any connection between Nahapána and Chashṭana. Still it is clear that Chashṭana obtained a great part of the territory over which

[1] Jour. B. B. R. A. Soc. XIII. 303.

[2] The variations noted in the text seem examples of the law that the later religion reads its own new meaning into early luck signs.

[3] This letter य्स in both is curiously formed and never used in Sanskrit. But it is clear and can be read without any doubt as य्स. Pandit Bhagvánlál thought that it was probably meant to stand as a new-coined letter to represent the Greek Z which has nothing corresponding to it in Sanskrit. The same curiously formed letter appears in the third syllable in the coin of the fourth Kshatrapa king Dámajadaśri.

Chapter V.

WESTERN KSHATRAPAS, A.D 70-398.

Chashṭana, A.D. 130.

Nahapána previously held sway. Though Chashṭana's coins and even the coins of his son and grandson bear no date, we have reason to believe they used a nameless era, of which the year 72 is given in the Junágad inscription of Chashṭana's grandson Rudradáman.[1] Though we have no means of ascertaining how many years Rudradáman had reigned before this 72 it seems probable that the beginning of the reign was at least several years earlier. Taking the previous period at seven years Rudráman's succession may be tentatively fixed at 65. Allowing twenty-five years for his father Jayadáman and his grandfather Chashṭana (as they were father and son and the son it is supposed reigned for some years with his father[2]) Chashṭana's conquest of Gujarát comes to about the year 40 which makes Chastana contemporary with the latter part of Nahapána's life. Now the Tiastanes whom Ptolemy mentions as having Ozene for his capital[3] is on all hands admitted to be Chashṭana and from what Ptolemy says it appears certain that his capital was Ujjain. Two of Chashṭana's coins occur as far north as Ajmir. As the Chashṭana coins in Dr. Gerson DaCunha's collection were found in Káthiáváḍa he must have ruled a large stretch of country. The fact that in his earlier coins Chashṭana is simply called a Kshatrapa and in his latter coins a Mahákshatrapa leads to the inference that his power was originally small. Chashtana was probably not subordinate to Nahapána but a contemporary of Nahapána originally when a simple Kshatrapa governing perhaps North Gujarát and Málwa. Nor was Chashṭana a member of Nahapána's family as he is nowhere called Kshaharáta which is the name of Nahapána's family. During the lifetime of Nahapána Chashṭana's power would seem to have been established first over Ajmir and Mewád. Perhaps Chashṭana may have been the chief of the Uttamabhadra Kshatriyas, whom, in the year 42, Ushavadáta went to assist when they were besieged by the Málayas or Málavas[4]; and it is possible that the Málavas being thus driven away Chashṭana may have consolidated his power, taken possession of Málwa, and established his capital at Ujjain.

Deccan Recovered by the Andhras, A.D. 138.

On Nahapána's death his territory, which in the absence of a son had probably passed to his son-in-law Ushavadáta, seems to have been wrested from him by his Ándhra neighbours, as one of the attributes of Gautamiputra S'átakarni is exterminator of the dynasty of Khakharáta (or Kshaharáta). That North Konkan, South Gujarát, and Káthiáváḍa were taken and incorporated with Ándhra territory appears from Gautamíputra's Násik inscription (No. 26) where Suráshṭra and Aparánta are mentioned as parts of his dominions. These Ándhra

---

[1] The text of the inscription is रुद्रदाम्नो वर्षे that is in the year of Rudradáman. That this phrase means 'in the reign of' is shown by the Gunda inscription of Rudradáman's son Rudrasiṃha, which has रुद्रसिंहस्य वर्षे त्र्युत्तरशते that is in the hundred and third year of Rudrasiṃha. Clearly a regnal year cannot be meant as no reign could last over 103 years. So with the year 72 in Rudradáman's inscription. The same style of writing appears in the inscriptions at Mathurá of Huvishka and Vasudeva which say 'year —— of Huvishka' and 'year —— of Vasudeva' though it is known that the era is of Kanishka. In all these cases what is meant is 'the dynastic or era year —— in the reign of ——'.

[2] See below page 34. [3] McCrindle's Ptolemy, 155. [4] See above page 29.

Chapter VI
WESTERN KSHATRAPAS, A.D. 70-398.

conquests seem to have been shortlived. Chashtana appears to have eventually taken Káthiáváḍa and as much of South Gujarát as belonged to Nahapána probably as far south as the Narbada. Meváḍ, Málwa, North and South Gujarát and Káthiáváḍa would then be subject to him and justify the title Mahákshatrapa on his later coins.

The Mevas or Meḍas.

The bulk of Chashṭana's army seems to have consisted of the Mevas or Meḍas from whose early conquests and settlements in Central Rajputána the province seems to have received its present name Meváḍa. If this supposition be correct an inference may be drawn regarding the origin of Chashṭana. The Mathurá inscription of Nandasiriká, daughter of Kshatrapa Rájavula and mother of Kháraosti Yuvarája, mentions with respect a Mahákshatrapa Kuzulko Patika who is called in the inscription Mevaki that is of the Meva tribe. The inscription shows a relation between the Kharaostis (to which tribe we have taken Kshaharáta Nahapána to belong) and Mevaki Patika perhaps in the nature of subordinate and overlord. It proves at least that the Kharaostis held Patika in great honour and respect.

The Taxila plate shows that Patika was governor of Taxila during his father's lifetime. After his father's death when he became Mahákshatrapa, Patika's capital was Nagaraka in the Jallálábád or Kábul valley. The conquest of those parts bý the great Kushán or Indo-Skythian king Kanishka (A.D. 78) seems to have driven Patika's immediate successors southwards to Sindh where they may have established a kingdom. The Skythian kingdom mentioned by the author of the Periplus as stretching in his time as far south as the mouths of the Indus may be a relic of this kingdom. Some time after their establishment in Sindh Patika's successors may have sent Chashṭana, either a younger member of the reigning house or a military officer, with an army of Mevas through Umarkot and the Great Ran to Central Rajputána, an expedition which ended in the settlement of the Mevas and the change of the country's name to Meváḍa. Probably it was on account of their previous ancestral connection that Nahapána sent Ushavadáta to help Chashṭana in Meváḍa when besieged by his Málava neighbours. That Ushavadáta went to bathe and make gifts[1] at Pushkara proves that the scene of the Uttamabhadras' siege by the Málayas was in Meváḍa not far from Pushkara.

Chashṭana is followed by an unbroken chain of successors all of the dynasty of which Chashṭana was the founder. As the coins of Chashṭana's successors bear dates and as each coin gives the name of the king and of his father they supply a complete chronological list of the Kshatrapa dynasty.

Kshatrapa III. Jayadáman, A.D. 140-143.

Of Chashṭana's son and successor Jayadáman the coins are rare. Of three specimens found in Káthiáváḍa two are of silver and one of copper. Both the silver coins were found in Junágadh[2] but they are doubtful specimens as the legend is not complete. Like Chashṭana's

[1] See above page 25.

[2] Of these coins Dr. Bhagvánlál kept one in his own collection. He sent the other to General Cunningham. The Pandit found the copper coin in Amreli in 1863 and gave it to Dr. Bhau Dáji.

Chapter V.
WESTERN KSHATRAPAS, A.D. 70-398.
Kshatrapa III. Jayadaman, A.D. 140-143.

coins they have a bust on the obverse and round the bust an incomplete and undecipherable Greek legend. The reverse has the sun and the moon and between them the arched symbol with the zigzag under-line. All round the symbols on the margin within a dotted line is the legend in Báktro-Páli and Devanágari. Only three letters रञो छ त्र of the Báktro-Páli legend can be made out. Of the Nágari legend seven letters राज्ञो क्षत्रपस ज Rájno Kshatrapasa Ja can be made out. The remaining four letters Dr. Bhagvánlál read यदामस Yadámasa.[1] The copper coin which is very small and square has on the obverse in a circle a standing humped bull looking to the right and fronting an erect trident with an axe. In style the bull is much like the bull on the square hemidrachmæ of Apollodotus (B.C. 110-100). Round the bull within a dotted circle is the legend in Greek. It is unfortunate the legend is incomplete as the remaining letters which are in the Skythian-Greek style are clearer than the letters on any Kshatrapa coin hitherto found. The letters that are preserved are STRXY. The reverse has the usual moon and sun and between them the arched symbol without the zigzag under-line. All round within a dotted circle is the Nágarí legend:

राज्ञो क्षत्र पस] जयदामस.

Rájno Kshatra(pasa) Jayadámasa.

Of the king Kshatrapa Jayadáman.

Though the name is not given in any of these coins, the fact that Chashṭana was Jayadáman's father has been determined from the genealogy in the Gunda inscription of Rudrasimha I. the seventh Kshatrapa,[2] in the Jasdhan inscription of Rudrasena I. the eighth Kshatrapa,[3] and in the Junágadh cave inscription[4] of Rudradáman's son Rudrasimha. All these inscriptions and the coins of his son Rudradáman call Jayadáman Kshatrapa not Maháksbatrapa. This would seem to show either that he was a Kshatrapa or governor of Káthiáváḍa under his father or that his father's territory and his rank as Mahákshatrapa suffered some reduction.[5] The extreme rarity of his coins suggests that Jayadáman's reign was very short. It is worthy of note that while Zamotika and Chashṭana are foreign names, the names of Jayadáman and all his successors with one exception[6] are purely Indian.

Kshatrapa IV. Rudradáman, A.D. 143-158.

Jayadáman was succeeded by his son Rudradáman who was probably the greatest of the Western Kshatrapas. His beautiful silver coins, in style much like those of Chashṭana, are frequently found in Káthiáváḍa. On the obverse is his bust in the same style of dress as Chashṭana's and

---

[1] Except that the ज is much clearer the Nágari legend in the silver coin obtained for General Cunningham is equally bad, and the Baktro-Pali legend is wanting.

[2] Ind. Ant. X. 157.

[3] Journal B. B. R. A. Soc. VIII. 234-5 and Ind. Ant. XII. 32ff.

[4] Dr. Burgess' Archæological Report of Káthiáwár and Cutch, 140.

[5] The explanation of the reduction of Jayadáman's rank is probably to be found in the Násik Inscription (No. 26) of Gautamíputra Sáṭakarṇi who claims to have conquered Suráshṭra, Kukura (in Rajputána), Anúpa, Vidarbha (Berar), Akara, and Avanti (Ujein). (A. M. T. J.)

[6] See below page 39.

Chapter V.

Western Kshatrapas, A.D. 70-398.

Kshatrapa IV. Rudradáman, A.D. 143-158.

round the bust is the Greek legend incomplete and undecipherable. The reverse has the usual sun and moon and the arched symbol with the zigzag under-line. The old Nágarí legend fills the whole outer circle. None of Rudradáman's coins shows a trace of the Báktro-Páli legend. The Nágarí legend reads:

राज्ञो क्षत्रपस जयदामपुत्रस राज्ञो महाक्षत्रपस रुद्रदामस.

Rájno Kshatrapasa Jayadámaputrasa
Rájno Mahákshatrapasa Rudradámasa.

Of the king the great Kshatrapa Rudradáman son of the king the Kshatrapa Jayadáman.

None of Rudradáman's copper coins have been found. Except Jayadáman none of the Kshatrapas seem to have stamped their names on any but silver coins.[1]

An inscription on the Girnár rock gives us more information regarding Rudradáman than is available for any of the other Kshatrapas. The inscription records the construction of a new dam on the Sudars'ana lake close to the inscription rock in place of a dam built in the time of the Maurya king Chandragupta (B.C. 300) and added to in the time of his grandson the great Ásoka (B.C. 240) which had suddenly burst in a storm. The new dam is recorded to have been made under the orders of Suvishákha son of Kulaipa a Pahlava by tribe, who was 'appointed by the king to protect the whole of Ánarta and Suráshtra.' Pahlava seems to be the name of the ancient Persians and Parthians[2] and the name Suvishákha as Dr. Bhau Dáji suggests may be a Sanskritised form of Syávaxa.[3] One of the Kárle inscriptions gives a similar name Sovasaka apparently a corrupt Indian form of the original Persian from which the Sanskritised Suvishákha must have been formed. Sovasaka it will be noted is mentioned in the Kárle inscription as an inhabitant of Abulámá, apparently the old trade mart of Obollah at the head of the Persian Gulf. This trade connection between the Persian Gulf and the Western Indian seaboard must have led to the settlement from very early times of the Pahlavas who gradually became converted to Buddhism, and, like the Parsis their modern enterprising representatives, seem to have advanced in trade and political influence. Subsequently the Pahlavas attained such influence that about the fifth century a dynasty of Pallava kings reigned in the Dekhan, Hindu in religion and name, even tracing their origin to the great ancient sage Bháradvája.[4]

Sudarśana Lake, A.D. 150.

The statement in Rudradáman's Sudarśana lake inscription, that Ánarta and Suráshṭra were under his Pahlava governor, seems to show

---

[1] Several small mixed metal coins weighing from 3 to 10 grains with on the obverse an elephant in some and a bull in others and on the reverse the usual arched Kshatrapa symbol have been found in Málwa and Káthiáváḍa. The symbols show them to be of the lowest Kshatrapa currency. Several of them bear dates from which it is possible as in the case of Rudrasiṃha's and Rudrasena's coins to infer to what Kshatrapa they belonged. Lead coins have also been found at Amreli in Káthiáváḍa. They are square and have a bull on the obverse and on the reverse the usual arched Kshatrapa symbol with underneath it the date 184.

[2] Compare however Weber, Hist. of Indian Lit. 187-8.

[3] Jour. B. B. R. A. S. VII. 114.

[4] Ind. Ant. II. 156; V. 50, 154 &c.

Chapter V.
WESTERN KSHATRAPAS, A.D. 70-398.
Kshatrapa IV. Rudradáman, A.D. 143-158.

that Rudradáman's capital was not in Gujarát or Káthiáváda. Probably like his grandfather Chashṭana Rudradáman held his capital at Ujjain. The poetic eulogies of Rudradáman appear to contain a certain share of fact. One of the epithets 'he who himself has earned the title Mahákshatrapa' indicates that Rudradáman had regained the title of Mahákshatrapa which belonged to his grandfather Chashṭana but not to his father Jayadáman. Another portion of the inscription claims for him the overlordship of Ákarávanti,[1] Anúpa,[2] Ánarta, Suráshtra, Śvabhra,[3] Maru,[4] Kachchha,[5] Sindhu-Sauvíra,[6] Kukura,[7] Aparánta,[8] and Nisháda;[9] that is roughly the country from Bhilsa in the east to Sindh in the west and from about Ábu in the north to the North Konkan in the south including the peninsulas of Cutch and Káthiáváda. The inscription also mentions two wars waged by Rudradáman, one with the Yaudheyas the other with Śátakarṇi lord of Dakshinápatha. Of the Yaudheyas the inscription says that they had become arrogant and untractable in consequence of their having proclaimed their assumption of the title of Heroes among all Kshatriyas. Rudradáman is described as having exterminated them. These Yaudheyas were known as a warlike race from the earliest times and are mentioned as warriors by Pánini.[10]

The Yaudheyas.

Like the Málavas these Yaudheyas appear to have had a democratic constitution. Several round copper coins of the Yaudheyas of about the third century A.D. have been found in various parts of the North-West Provinces from Mathurá to Sahâranpur. These coins

---

[1] Akarávanti that is Akara and Avanti are two names which are always found together. Cf. Gotamiputra's Násik inscription (No. 26). Avanti is well known as being the name of the part of Málwa which contains Ujjain. Akara is probably the modern province of Bhilsa whose capital was Vidiśa the modern deserted city of Besnagar. Instead of Ákarávanti Bṛihatsaṃhitá mentions Ákaravenávantaka of which the third name Vená Pandit Bhagvánlal took to be the country about the Sagara zilla containing the old town of Eraṇ, near which still flows a river called Vená. The adjectives east and west are used respectively as referring to Ákara which is East Málwa and Avanti which is West Málwa. Compare Indian Antiquary, VII. 259; Bombay Gazetteer, XVI. 631.

[2] Anúpa is a common noun literally meaning well-watered. The absence of the term *nívrit* or 'country' which is in general superadded to it shows that Anúpa is here used as a proper noun, meaning the Anúpa country. Dr. Bhagvánlál was unable to identify Anúpa. He took it to be the name of some well-watered tract near Gujarát.

[3] See above page 10 note 1. The greater part of North Gujarát was probably included in Śvabhra.

[4] Maru is the well known name of Marwár.

[5] Kachchha is the flourishing state still known by the name of Cutch.

[6] Sindhu Sauvíra like Ákarávanti are two names usually found together. Sindhu is the modern Sind and Sauvíra may have been part of Upper Sind, the capital of which is mentioned as Dáttámitrí. Alberuni (I. 300) defines Sauvíra as including Multan and Jahráwár.

[7] Nothing is known about Kukura and it cannot be identified. It was probably part of East Rajputána.

[8] Aparánta meaning the Western End is the western seaboard from the Mahi in the north to Goa in the south. Ind. Ant. VII. 259. The portion of Aparánta actually subject to Rudradáman must have been the country between the Mahi and the Damanganga as at this time the North Konkan was subject to the Ándhras.

[9] Nishada cannot be identified. As the term Nishada is generally used to mean Bhils and other wild tribes, its mention with Aparánta suggests the wild country that includes Bánsda, Dharampur, and north-east Thána.

[10] Grammar, V. iii. 117.

The Yáudheyas.

which are adapted from the type of Kanishka's coins[1] have on the obverse a standing robed male figure extending the protecting right hand of mercy. On the reverse is the figure of a standing Kártikasvámi and round the figure the legend in Gupta characters of about the third century:

यौधेय गणस्य

Yáudheya Gaṇasya.

Of the Yaudheya tribe.[2]

That the Girnár inscription describes Rudradáman as the exterminator of 'the Yaudheyas' and not of any king of the Yaudheyas confirms the view that their constitution was tribal or democratic.[3]

The style of the Yaudheya coins being an adaptation of the Kanishka type and their being found from Mathurá to Sahâranpur where Kanishka ruled is a proof that the Yaudheyas wrested from the successors of Kanishka the greater part of the North-West Provinces. This is not to be understood to be the Yaudheyas' first conquest in India. They are known to be a very old tribe who after a temporary suppression by Kanishka must have again risen to power with the decline of Kushán rule under Kanishka's successors Huvishka (A.D. 100-123) or Vasudeva (A.D. 123-150?) the latter of whom was a contemporary of Rudradáman.[4] It is probably to this increase of Yaudheya power that Rudradáman's inscription refers as making them arrogant and intractable. Their forcible extermination is not to be understood literally but in the Indian hyperbolic fashion.

The remark regarding the conquest of Śátakarni lord of Dakshinápatha is as follows: 'He who has obtained glory because he did not destroy Śátakarni, the lord of the Dekhan, on account of there being no distance in relationship, though he twice really conquered him.'[5] As Sátakarni is a dynastic name applied to several of the Ándhra kings, the question arises Which of the Sátakarnis did Rudrádaman twice defeat? Of the two Western India kings mentioned by Ptolemy one Tiastanes with his capital at Ozene or Ujjain[6] has been identified with Chashṭana; the other Siri Ptolemaios or Polemaios, with his royal seat at Baithana or Paithan,[7] has been identified with the Pulumáyi Vásishṭhíputra of the Násik cave inscriptions. These statements of

---

[1] Compare Gardner and Poole's Catalogue, Pl. XXVI. Fig. 2 &c.

[2] Another variety of their brass coins was found at Behat near Saharánpur. Compare Thomas' Prinsep's Indian Antiquities, I. Pl. IV. Figs. 11B 12B and Pl. XIX. Figs. 5, 6, 9. General Cunningham, in his recent work on The Coins of Ancient India, 75ff, describes three chief types, the Behat coins being the earliest and belonging to the first century B.C., the second type which is that described above is assigned to about A.D. 300, and the third type, with a six-headed figure on the obverse, is placed a little later. General Cunningham's identification of the Yaudheyas with the Johiya Rajputs of the lower Sutlej, seems certain, Rudradáman would then have "uprooted" them when he acquired the province of Sauvíra.

[3] Mr. Fleet notices a later inscription of a *Mahárája Mahásenápati* "who has been set over" the 'Yaudheya gaṇa or tribe' in the fort of Byána in Bharatpur. Ind. Ant. XIV. 8, Corp. Insc. Ind. III. 251ff. The Yaudheyas are also named among the tribes which submitted to Samudragupta. See Corp. Insc. Ind. III. 8.

[4] Huvishka's latest inscription bears date 45 that is A.D. 123 (Cunningham's Arch. Sur. III. Pl. XV. Number 8).

[5] Ind. Ant. VII. 262. [6] McCrindle's Ptolemy, 152. [7] McCrindle's Ptolemy, 175.

Chapter V.
WESTERN KSHATRAPAS, A.D. 70-398.
Kshatrapa IV. Rudradáman, A.D. 143-158.

Ptolemy seem to imply that Chashṭana and Pulumáyi were contemporary kings reigning at Ujjain and Paithan. The evidence of their coins also shows that if not contemporaries Chashṭana and Pulumáyi were not separated by any long interval. We know from the Násik inscriptions and the Puránas that Pulumáyi was the successor of Gautamíputra Śátakarni and as Gautamíputra Śátakarni is mentioned as the exterminator of the Kshaharáta race (and the period of this extermination has already been shown to be almost immediately after Nahapána's death), there is no objection to the view that Chashṭana, who was the next Kshatrapa after Nahapána, and Pulumáyi, who was the successor of Gautamíputra, were contemporaries. We have no positive evidence to determine who was the immediate successor of Pulumáyi, but the only king whose inscriptions are found in any number after Pulumáyi is Gautamíputra Yajña Śrí Śátakarni. His Kanheri inscription recording gifts made in his reign and his coin found among the relics of the Sopára stúpa built also in his reign prove that he held the North Konkan. The Sopára coin gives the name of the father of Yajñaśrí. Unfortunately the coin is much worn. Still the remains of the letters constituting the name are sufficient to show they must be read चतुरपन Chaturapana.[1] A king named Chaturapana is mentioned in one of the Nánághát inscriptions where like Pulumáyi he is called Vásishṭhíputra and where the year 13 of his reign is referred to.[2] The letters of this inscription are almost coeval with those in Pulumáyi's inscriptions. The facts that he was called Vásishṭhíputra and that he reigned at least thirteen years make it probable that Chaturapana was the brother and successor of Pulumáyi. Yajñaśrí would thus be the nephew and second in succession to Pulumáyi and the contemporary of Rudradáman the grandson of Chashṭana, whom we have taken to be a contemporary of Pulumáyi. A further proof of this is afforded by Yajñaśrí's silver coin found in the Sopára stúpa. All other Ándhra coins hitherto found are adapted from contemporary coins of Ujjain and the Central Provinces, the latter probably of the S'ungas. But Gautamíputra Yajñaśrí Śátakarni's Sopára coin is the first silver coin struck on the type of Kshatrapa coins; it is in fact a clear adaptation of the type of the coins of Rudradáman himself which proves that the two kings were contemporaries and rivals. An idea of the 'not distant relationship' between Rudradáman and Yajñaśrí Śátakarni mentioned in Rudradáman's Girnár inscription, may be formed from a Kanheri inscription recording a gift by a minister named Satoraka which mentions that the queen of Vásishṭhíputra Śátakarni was born in the Kárdamaka dynasty and was connected apparently on the maternal side with a Mahákshatrapa whose name is lost. If the proper name of the lost Vásishṭhíputra be Chaturapana, his son Yajñaśrí Śátakarni would, through his mother being a Mahákshatrapa's granddaughter, be a relative of Rudradáman.

Rudradáman's other epithets seem to belong to the usual stock of

[1] Jour B. B. R. A. Soc. XV. 306.

[2] Jour. B. B. R. A. Soc. XV. 313, 314. See also Ind. Ant. XII 272, where Bühler suggests that the queen was a daughter of Rudradáman, and traces the syllables Rudradá . . . in the Kanheri inscription.

Chapter V.

WESTERN KSHATRAPAS, A.D. 70-398.

Kshatrapa IV. Rudradáman, A.D. 143-158.

Indian court epithets. He is said 'to have gained great fame by studying to the end, by remembering understanding and applying the great sciences such as grammar, polity, music, and logic.' Another epithet describes him as having 'obtained numerous garlands at the Svayamvaras of kings' daughters,' apparently meaning that he was chosen as husband by princesses at several *svayamvaras* or choice-marriages a practice which seems to have been still in vogue in Rudradáman's time. As a test of the civilized character of his rule it may be noted that he is described as 'he who took, and kept to the end of his life, the vow to stop killing men except in battle.' Another epithet tells us that the embankment was built and the lake reconstructed by 'expending a great amount of money from his own treasury, without oppressing the people of the town and of the province by (exacting) taxes, forced labour, acts of affection (benevolences) and the like.'

As the Kshatrapa year 60 (A.D. 138) has been taken to be the date of close of Chashṭana's reign, and as five years may be allowed for the short reign[1] of Jayadáman, the beginning of the reign of Rudradáman may be supposed to have been about the year 65 (A.D. 143). This Girnár inscription gives 72 as the year in which Rudradáman was then reigning and it is fair to suppose that he reigned probably up to 80. The conclusion is that Rudradáman ruled from A.D. 143 to 158.[2]

Kshatrapa V. Dámázada or Dámájadaśri, A.D. 158-168.

Rudradáman was succeeded by his son Dámázaḍa or Dámájaḍaśrí regarding whom all the information available is obtained from six coins obtained by Dr. Bhagvánlál.[3] The workmanship of all six coins is good, after the type of Rudradáman's coins. On the obverse is a bust in the same style as Rudradáman's and round the bust is an illegible Greek legend. Like Rudradáman's coins these have no dates, a proof of their antiquity, as all later Kshatrapa coins have dates in Nágarí numerals. The reverse has the usual sun and moon and between them the arched symbol with the zigzag under-line. Around them in three specimens is the following legend in old Nágarí:

राज्ञो महाक्षत्रपस रुद्रदामपुत्रस[4] राज्ञः क्षत्रपस दामाय्सडस

Rájño Maháksbatrapasa Rudradámaputrasa Rájñaḥ Kshatrapasa Dámáysaḍasa.

Of the king the Kshatrapa Dámázaḍa[5] son of the king the Kshatrapa Rudradáman.'

---

[1] See above page 34.

[2] It seems doubtful whether the Pandit's estimate of fifteen years might not with advantage be increased. As his father's reign was so short Rudradáman probably succeeded when still young. The abundance of his coins points to a long reign and the scarcity of the coins both of his son Dámázaḍa and of his grandson Jivadáman imply that neither of his successors reigned more than a few years. Jivadáman's earliest date is A.D.178 (S.100). If five years are allowed to Jivadáman's father the end of Rudradáman's reign would be A.D. 173 (S.95) that is a reign of thirty years, no excessive term for a king who began to rule at a comparatively early age.—(A. M. T. J.)

[3] Two specimens of his coins were obtained by Mr. Vajeshankar Gavrishankar Náib Diwán of Bhávnagar, from Káthiáváḍa, one of which he presented to the Pandit and lent the other for the purpose of description. The legend in both was legible but doubtful. A recent find in Káthiáváḍa supplied four new specimens, two of them very good.

[4] Apparently a mistake for रुद्रदाम्नः पुत्रस.

[5] As in the case of Zamotika the father of Chashṭana, the variation द्स for ज proves that at first द्स and afterwards ज was used to represent the Greek Z.

Chapter V.

WESTERN KSHATRAPAS, A.D. 70 - 398.

Kshatrapa V. Dámázada or Dámájadaśrí, A.D. 158 - 168.

The legend on the other three is:

राज्ञो महाक्षत्रपस रुद्रदाम्न: पुत्रस राज्ञ: क्षत्रपस दामाजडश्रिय:

Rájño Mahákshatrapasa Rudradámnahputrasa Rájñah
Kshatrapasa Dámájadas'riyah.

Of the king the Kshatrapa Dámájadaśrí son of the king
the great Kshatrapa Rudradáma.

Dámázada and Dámájadaśrí seem to be two forms of the same name, Dámázada with स्स for Z being the name first struck, and Dámájadaśrí, with the ordinary ज for Z, and with Srí added to adorn the name and make it more euphonic, being the later form. It will be noted that, except by his son Jivadáman, Dámázada or Dámájadaśrí is not called a Mahákshatrapa but simply a Kshatrapa. His coins are very rare. The six mentioned are the only specimens known and are all from one find. He may therefore be supposed to have reigned as heir-apparent during the life-time of Rudradáman, or it is possible that he may have suffered loss of territory and power. His reign seems to have been short and may have terminated about 90 that is A.D. 168 or a little later.

Kshatrapa VI. Jivadáman, A.D. 178.

Dámázada or Dámájadaśrí was succeeded by his son Jivadáman. All available information regarding Jivadáman is from four rare coins obtained by Pandit Bhagvánlal, which for purposes of description, he has named A, B, C, and D.[1] Coin A bears date 100 in Nágarí numerals, the earliest date found on Kshatrapa coins. On the obverse is a bust in the usual Kshatrapa style with a plump young face of good workmanship. Round the bust is first the date 100 in Nágarí numerals and after the date the Greek legend in letters which though clear cannot be made out. In these and in all later Kshatrapa coins merely the form of the Greek legend remains; the letters are imitations of Greek by men who could not read the original. On the reverse is the usual arched symbol between the sun and the moon, the sun being twelve-rayed as in the older Kshatrapa coins. Within the dotted circle in the margin is the following legend in old Nágarí:

राज्ञो महाक्षत्रपस दामश्रिय: पुत्रस राज्ञो महाक्षत्रपस जीवदाम्न[:]

Rájño Mahákshatrapasa Dámasriyahputrasa Rájño
Mahákshatrapasa Jivadámnah.

Of the king the great Kshatrapa Jivadáman son of the king
the great Kshatrapa Dámasrí.

Coin B has the bust on the obverse with a face apparently older than the face in A. Unfortunately the die has slipped and the date has not been struck. Most of the Greek legend is very clear but as in coin A the result is meaningless The letters are K I U I U Z K N S Y L perhaps meant for Kuzulka. On the reverse are the usual three symbols, except

---

[1] The oldest of the four was found by the Pandit for Dr. Bhau Dáji in Amreli. A fair copy of it is given in a plate which accompanied Mr. Justice Newton's paper in Jour. B. B. R. A. S. IX, page 1ff. Plate I. Fig. 6. Mr. Newton read the father's name in the legend Dámasri, but it is Dámájadaśrí, the die having missed the letters ज and ड though space is left for them. This is coin A of the description. Of the remaining three, B was lent to the Pandit from his collection by Mr. Vajeshankar Gavrishankar. C and D were in the Pandit's collection.

Chapter V.

WESTERN KSHATRAPAS, A.D. 70 - 398.

Kshatrapa VI. Jivadáman, A.D. 178.

that the sun has seven instead of twelve rays. The legend is:

राज्ञो महाक्षत्रपस दामजडस पुत्रस राज्ञो महाक्षत्रपस जीवदामस

Rájño Mahákshatrapasa Dámajaḍasaputrasa Rájño Mahákshatrapasa Jivadámasa.

Of the king the great Kshatrapa Jivadáman son of the king the great Kshatrapa Dámajaḍa.

Coin C though struck from a different die is closely like B both on the obverse and the reverse. Neither the Greek legend nor the date is clear, though enough remains of the lower parts of the numerals to suggest the date 118. Coin D is in obverse closely like C. The date 118 is clear. On the reverse the legend and the symbols have been twice struck. The same legend occurs twice, the second striking having obliterated the last letters of the legend which contained the name of the king whose coin it is:

राज्ञो महाक्षत्रपस दामजडस पुत्रस

Rájño Mahákshatrapasa Dámajaḍasaputrasa.

Of the son of the king the great Kshatrapa Dámájaḍa.

In these four specimens Dámaśrí or Dámájaḍa is styled Mahákshatrapa, while in his own coins he is simply called Kshatrapa. The explanation perhaps is that the known coins of Dámaśrí or Dámajaḍa belong to the early part of his reign when he was subordinate to his father, and that he afterwards gained the title of Mahákshatrapa. Some such explanation is necessary as the distinction between the titles Kshatrapa and Mahákshatrapa is always carefully preserved in the earlier Kshatrapa coins. Except towards the close of the dynasty no ruler called Kshatrapa on his own coins is ever styled Mahákshatrapa on the coins of his son unless the father gained the more important title during his lifetime.

The dates and the difference in the style of die used in coining A and in coining B, C, and D are worth noting as the earliest coin has the date 100 and C and D the third and fourth coins have 118. If Jivadáman's reign lasted eighteen years his coins would be common instead of very rare. But we find between 102 and 118 numerous coins of Rudrasimha son of Rudradáman and paternal uncle of Jivadáman. These facts and the difference between the style of A and the style of B, C, and D which are apparently imitated from the coins of Rudrasiṃha and have a face much older than the face in A, tend to show that soon after his accession Jivadáman was deposed by his uncle Rudrasiṃha, on whose death or defeat in 118, Jivadáman again rose to power.

Kshatrapa VII. Rudrasiṃha I. A.D. 181 - 196.

Rudrasimha the seventh Kshatrapa was the brother of Dámajaḍaśrí. Large numbers of his coins have been found. Of thirty obtained by Dr. Bhagvánlál twenty have the following clearly cut dates: 103, 106, 108, 109, 110, 112, 113, 114, 115, 116, and 118. As the earliest year is 103 and the latest 118 it is probable that Rudrasimha deposed his nephew Jivadáman shortly after Jivadáman's accession. Rudrasiṃha appears to have ruled fifteen years when power again passed to his nephew Jivadáman.

Chapter V.
WESTERN KSHATRAPAS.
Kshatrapa VII. Rudrasiṃha I. A.D. 181 - 196.

The coins of Rudrasiṃha are of a beautiful type of good workmanship and with clear legends. The legend in old Nágarí character reads :

राज्ञो महाक्षत्रपस रुद्रदामपुत्रस राज्ञो महाक्षत्रपस रुद्रसिंहस

Rájño Maháksbatrapasa Rudradámaputrasa Rájño Mahákshatrapasa Rudrasiṃhasa.

Of the king the great Kshatrapa Rudrasiṃha son of the king the great Kshatrapa Rudradáma.

Rudrasiṃha had also a copper coinage of which specimens are recorded from Málwa but not from Káthiáváḍa. Pandit Bhagvánlál had one specimen from Ujjain which has a bull on the obverse with the Greek legend round it and the date 117. The reverse seems to have held the entire legend of which only five letters रुद्रसिंहस (Rudrasiṃhasa) remain. This coin has been spoilt in cleaning.

To Rudrasiṃha's reign belongs the Gunda inscription carved on a stone found at the bottom of an unused well in the village of Gunda in Halár in North Káthiáváḍa.[1] It is in six well preserved lines of old Nágarí letters of the Kshatrapa type. The writing records the digging and building of a well for public use on the borders of a village named Rasopadra by the commander-in-chief Rudrabhúti an Ábhíra son of Senápati Bápaka. The date is given both in words and in numerals as 103, 'in the year' of the king the Kshatrapa Svámi Rudrasiṃha, apparently meaning in the year 103 during the reign of Rudrasiṃha. The genealogy given in the inscription is : 1 Chashṭana ; 2 Jayadáman ; 3 Rudradáman ; 4 Rudrasiṃha, the order of succession being clearly defined by the text, which says that the fourth was the great grandson of the first, the grandson of the second, and the son of the third. It will be noted that Dámájaḍasrí and Jívadáman the fifth and sixth Kshatrapas have been passed over in this genealogy probably because the inscription did not intend to give a complete genealogy but only to show the descent of Rudrasiṃha in the direct line.

Kshatrapa VIII. Rudrasena, A.D. 203 - 220.

The eighth Kshatrapa was Rudrasena, son of Rudrasiṃha, as is clearly mentioned in the legends on his coins. His coins like his father's are found in large numbers. Of forty in Dr. Bhagvánlál's collection twenty-seven bear the following eleven[2] dates, 125, 130, 131, 132, 133, 134, 135, 136, 138, 140, 142. The coins are of the usual Kshatrapa type closely like Rudrasiṃha's coins. The Nágarí legend reads :

राज्ञो महाक्षत्रपस रुद्रसिंहस पुत्रस राज्ञो महाक्षत्रपस रुद्रसेनस

Rájño Mahákshatrapasa Rudrasiṃhasa putrasa Rájño Mahákshatrapasa Rudrasenasa.

Of the king the great Kshatrapa Rudrasena son of the king the great Kshatrapa Rudrasiṃha.

Two copper coins square and smaller than the copper coins of

[1] This inscription which has now been placed for safe custody in the temple of Dwárkánáth in Jamnagar, has been published by Dr. Bühler in Ind. Ant. X. 157 - 158, from a transcript by Áchárya Vallabji Haridatta. Dr. Bhagvánlál held that the date is 103 *tryuttaraśate* not 102 *dvyuttaraśate* as read by Dr. Bühler ; that the name of the father of the donor is Bápaka and not Bahaka ; and that the name of the *nakshatra* or constellation is Rohiní not Śravaṇa.

[2] Several coins have the same date.

Chapter V.

WESTERN KSHATRAPAS, A.D. 70-398.

Kshatrapa VIII. Rudrasena, A.D. 203-220.

Rudrasimha have been found in Ujjain[1] though none are recorded from Káthiáváda. On their obverse these copper coins have a facing bull and on the back the usual symbols and below them the year 140, but no legend. Their date and their Kshatrapa style show that they are coins of Rudrasena.

Besides coins two inscriptions one at Muliyásar the other at Jasdan give information regarding Rudrasena. The Muliyásar inscription, now in the library at Dwárka ten miles south-west of Muliyásar, records the erection of an upright slab by the sons of one Vánijaka. This inscription bears date 122, the fifth of the dark half of Vaishákha in the year 122 during the reign of Rudrasimha.[2] The Jasdan inscription, on a stone about five miles from Jasdan, belongs to the reign of this Kshatrapa. It is in six lines of old Kshatrapa Nágarí characters shallow and dim with occasional engraver's mistakes, but on the whole well-preserved. The writing records the building of a pond by several brothers (names not given) of the Mánasasa *gotra* sons of Pranáthaka and grandsons of Khara. The date is the 5th of the dark half of Bhádrapada 'in the year' 126.[3] The genealogy is in the following order:

Mahákshatrapa Chashṭana.
Kshatrapa Jayadáman.
Mahákshatrapa Rudradáman.
Mahákshatrapa Rudrasimha.
Mahákshatrapa Rudrasena.

Each of them is called Svámi Lord and Bhadramukha Luckyfaced.[4] As Rudrasena's reign began at least as early as 122, the second reign of Jivadáman is narrowed to four years or even less. As the latest date is 142 Rudrasena's reign must have lasted about twenty years.

Kshatrapa IX. Prithivísena, A.D. 222.

After Rudrasena the next evidence on record is a coin of his son Prithivísena found near Amreli. Its workmanship is the same as that of Rudrasena's coins. It is dated 144 that is two years later than the last date on Rudrasena's coins. The legend runs:

राज्ञो महाक्षत्रपस रुद्रसेनस पुत्रस राज्ञः क्षत्रपस पृथिवीसेनस

Rajño Mahakshatrapasa Rudrasenasa putrasa Rájñaḥ Kshatrapasa Prithivísenasa.

Of the king the Kshatrapa Prithivísena son of the king the great Kshatrapa Rudrasena.

As this is the only known specimen of Prithivísena's coinage; as the earliest coin of Prithivísena's uncle the tenth Kshatrapa Sanghadáman is dated 144; and also as Prithivísena is called only Kshatrapa he seems to have reigned for a short time perhaps as Kshatrapa of Suráshtra or Káthiáváda and to have been ousted by his uncle Sanghadáman.

Kshatrapa X. Sanghadáman, A.D. 222-226.

Rudrasena was succeeded by his brother the Mahákshatrapa Sanghadáman. His coins are very rare. Only two specimens have been

---

[1] One is in the collection of the B. B. R. A. Society, the other belonged to the Pandit.

[2] An unpublished inscription found in 1865 by Mr. Bhagvánlál Sampatrám.

[3] The top of the third numeral is broken. It may be 7 but is more likely to be 6.

[4] The Jasdan inscription has been published by Dr. Bháu Dáji, J. B. R. A. S. VIII. 234ff, and by Dr. Hoernle, Ind. Ant. XII. 32ff.

Chapter V.
WESTERN KSHATRAPAS, A.D. 70-398.
Kshatrapa X. Sanghadáman, A.D. 222-226.

obtained, of which one was in the Pandit's collection the other in the collection of Mr. Vajeshankar Gavrishankar.[1] They are dated 145 and 144. The legend in both reads:

राज्ञो महाक्षत्रपस रुद्रसिंहस पुत्रस राज्ञो महाक्षत्रपस संघदाम्न [:]

Rájño Mahákshatrapasa Rudrasimhasa putrasa Rájño Mahákshatrapasa Sanghadámna.

Of the king the great Kshatrapa Sanghadáman son of the king the great Kshatrapa Rudrasimha.

These two coins seem to belong to the beginning of Sanghadáman's reign. As the earliest coins of his successor Dámasena are dated 148 Sanghadáman's reign seems not to have lasted over four years.[2]

---

[1] Five have recently been identified in the collection of Dr. Gerson daCunha.

[2] His name, the fact that he regained the title Mahákshatrapa, and his date about A.D. 225 suggest that Sanghadáman (A.D. 222-226) may be the Sandanes whom the Periplus (McCrindle, 128) describes as taking the regular mart Kalyán near Bombay from Saraganes, that is the Dakhan Satakarnis, and, to prevent it again becoming a place of trade, forbidding all Greek ships to visit Kalyán, and sending under a guard to Broach any Greek ships that even by accident entered its port. The following reasons seem conclusive against identifying Sanghadáman with Sandanes: (1) The abbreviation from Sanghadaman to Sandanes seems excessive in the case of the name of a well known ruler who lived within thirty years of the probable time (A.D. 247) when the writer of the Periplus visited Gujarát and the Konkan: (2) The date of Sanghadáman (A.D. 222-226) is twenty to thirty years too early for the probable collection of the Periplus details: (3) Apart from the date of the Periplus the apparent distinction in the writer's mind between Sandanes' capture of Kalyán and his own time implies a longer lapse than suits a reign of only four years.

In favour of the Sandanes of the Periplus being a dynastic not a personal name is its close correspondence both in form and in geographical position with Ptolemy's (A.D. 150) Sadaneis, who gave their name, Ariake Sadinôn or the Sadins' Aria, to the North Konkan, and, according to McCrindle (Ptolemy, 39) in the time of Ptolemy ruled the prosperous trading communities that occupied the sea coast to about Semulla or Chaul. The details in the present text show that some few years before Ptolemy wrote the conquests of Rudradáman had brought the North Konkan under the Gujarát Kshatrapás. Similarly shortly before the probable date of the Periplus (A.D. 247) the fact that Sanghadáman and his successors Dámasena (A.D. 226-236) and Vijayasena (A.D. 238-249) all used the title Mahákshatrapa makes their possession of the North Konkan probable. The available details of the Káthiáváda Kshatrapas therefore confirm the view that the Sadans of Ptolemy and the Sandanes of the Periplus are the Gujarát Kshatrapas. The question remains how did the Greeks come to know the Kshatrapas by the name of Sadan or Sandan. The answer seems to be the word Sadan or Sandan is the Sanskrit *Sádhana* which according to Lassen (McCrindle's Ptolemy, 40) and Williams' Sanskrit Dictionary may mean agent or representative and may therefore be an accurate rendering of Kshatrapa in the sense of Viceroy. Wilford (As. Res. IX. 76, 198) notices that Sanskrit writers give the early English in India the title Sádhan Engrez. This Wilford would translate Lord but it seems rather meant for a rendering of the word Factor. Prof. Bhándárkar (Bom. Gaz. XIII. 418 note 1) notices a tribe mentioned by the geographer Varáhamihira (A.D. 580) as Sántikas and associated with the Aparántakas or people of the west coast. He shows how according to the rules of letter changes the Sanskrit Sántika would in Prákrit be Sándino. In his opinion it was this form Sandino which was familiar to Greek merchants and sailors. Prof. Bhandárkar holds that when (A.D. 100-110) the Kshatrapa Nahapána displaced the Sátaváhanas or Ándhrabhrityas the Sántikas or Sandino became independent in the North Konkan and took Kalyán. To make their independence secure against the Kshatrapas they forbad intercourse between their own territory and the Dakhan and sent foreign ships to Barygaza. Against this explanation it is to be urged; (1) That Násik and Junnar inscriptions show Nahapána supreme in the North Konkan at least up to A.D. 120; (2) That according to the Periplus the action taken by the Sandans or Sadans was not against the Kshatrapas but against the Sátakarnis; (3) That the action was not taken in the time of Nahapána but at a later time, later not only than the first Gautamíputra the conqueror of Nahapána or his son-in-law Ushavadáta (A.D. 138), but later than the second Gautamiputra, who was defeated by the Kathiaváda Kshatrapa Rudradáman some time before A.D. 150; (4) That if the Santikas were solely a North

Chapter V.

Western Kshatrapas, A.D. 70-398.

Kshatrapa XI. Dámasena, A.D. 226-236.

Sanghadáman was succeeded by his brother Dámasena, whose coins are fairly common, of good workmanship, and clear lettering. Of twenty-three specimens eleven have the following dates: 148, 150, 153, 155, 156, 157, 158. The legend runs:

राज्ञो महाक्षत्रपस रुद्रसिंहस पुत्रस राज्ञो महाक्षत्रपस दामसेनस

Rájño Maháksliatrapasa Rudrasiṃhasa putrasa Rájño Maháksliatrapasa Dámasenasa.

Of the king the great Kshatrapa Dámasena son of the king the great Kshatrapa Rudrasiṃha.

Dámasena seems to have reigned ten years (148-158) as coins of his son Víradáman are found dated 158.

Kshatrapa XII. Dámájadaśri II. A.D. 236.

Dámájadaśrí the twelfth Kshatrapa is styled son of Rudrasena probably the eighth Kshatrapa. Dámájadaśrí's coins are rare.[1] The legend runs:

राज्ञो महाक्षत्रपस रुद्रसेनपुत्रस राज्ञः क्षत्रपस दामाजडश्रियः

Rájño Maháksliatrapasa Rudrasenaputrasa Rajñaḥ Kshatrapas Dámájadaśriyaḥ.

Of the king the Kshatrapa Dámájadaśrí son of the king the great Kshatrapa Rudrasena.

Five specimens, the only specimens on record, are dated 154.[2] As 154 falls in the reign of Dámasena it seems probable that Dámájadaśrí was either a minor or a viceroy or perhaps a ruler claiming independence, as about this time the authority of the main dynasty seems to have been much disputed.

Konkan tribe they would neither wish nor be able to send foreign ships to Broach. The action described in the Periplus of refusing to let Greek ships enter Kalyán and of sending all such ships to Broach was the action of a Gujarát conqueror of Kalyán determined to make foreign trade centre in his own chief emporium Broach. The only possible lord of Gujarát either in the second or third century who can have adopted such a policy was the Kshatrapa of Ujjain in Málwa and of Minnagara or Junagadh in Káthiáváda, the same ruler, who, to encourage foreign vessels to visit Broach had (McCrindle's Periplus, 118, 119) stationed native fishermen with well-manned long boats off the south Káthiáváda coast to meet ships and pilot them through the tidal and other dangers up the Narbada to Broach. It follows that the Sandanes of the Periplus and Ptolemy's North Konkan Sádans are the Gujarát Maháksliatrapas. The correctness of this identification of Sadan with the Sanskrit Sádhan and the explanation of Sádhan as a translation of Kshatrapa or representative receive confirmation from the fact that the account of Kálakácharya in the Bharaheśwara Vritti (J. B. B. R. A. S. IX. 141-142), late in date (A.D. 1000-1100) but with notable details of the Śaka or Śáhi invaders, calls the Śaka king Sádhana-Simha. If on this evidence it may be held that the Kshatrapas were known as Sádhanas, it seems to follow that Śántika the form used by Varáhamihira (A.D. 505-587) is a conscious and intentional Sanskritizing of Sádan whose correct form and origin had passed out of knowledge, a result which would suggest conscious or artificial Sanskritizing as the explanation of the forms of many Puránic tribal and place names. A further important result of this inquiry is to show that the received date of A.D. 70 for the Periplus cannot stand. Now that the Kanishka era A.D. 78 is admitted to be the era used by the Kshatrapas both in the Dakhan and in Gujarát it follows that a writer who knows the elder and the younger Śátakarnis cannot be earlier than A.D. 150 and from the manner in which he refers to them must almost certainly be considerably later. This conclusion supports the date A.D. 247 which on other weighty grounds the French scholar Reinaud (Ind. Ant. Dec. 1879. pp. 330, 338) has assigned to the Periplus.

[1] The Pandit's coin was obtained by him in 1863 from Amreli in Káthiáváda. A copy of it is given by Mr. Justice Newton who calls Sanghadáman son of Rudrasiṃha (Jour. B. B. R. A. S. IX. Pl. I. Fig. 7). The other specimen is better preserved.

[2] One of these coins was lent to the Pandit by Mr. Vajeshankar Gavrishankar.

Chapter V.
WESTERN KSHATRAPAS, A.D. 70 - 398.

After Dámasena we find coins of three of his sons Víradáman Yaśadáman and Vijayasena. Víradáman's coins are dated 158 and 163, Yaśadáman's 160 and 161, and Vijayasena's earliest 160. Of the three brothers Víradáman who is styled simply Kshatrapa probably held only a part of his father's dominions. The second brother Yaśadáman, who at first was a simple Kshatrapa, in 161 claims to be Mahákshatrapa. The third brother Vijayasena, who as early as 160, is styled Mahákshatrapa, probably defeated Yaśadáman and secured the supreme rule.

Kshatrapa XIII. Víradáman, A.D. 236-238.

Víradáman's coins are fairly common. Of twenty-six in Pandit Bhagvánlál's collection, nineteen were found with a large number of his brother Vijayasena's coins. The legend reads:

राज्ञो महाक्षत्रपस दामसेनस पुत्रस राज्ञो क्षत्रपस वीरदाम्नः

Rájño Mahákshatrapasa Dámasenasa putrasa Rájñah Kshatrapasa Víradámnaḥ.

Of the king the Kshatrapa Víradáman son of the king the great Kshatrapa Dámasena.

Of the twenty-six ten are clearly dated, six with 158 and four with 160.

Kshatrapa XIV. Yaśadáman, A.D. 239.

Yaśadáman's coins are rare. Pandit Bhagvánlál's collection contained seven.[1] The bust on the obverse is a good imitation of the bust on his father's coins. Still it is of inferior workmanship, and starts the practice which later Kshatrapas continued of copying their predecessor's image. On only two of the seven specimens are the dates clear, 160 and 161. The legend on the coin dated 160 is:

राज्ञो महाक्षत्रपस दामसेनस पुत्रस राज्ञः क्षत्रपस यशदाम्नः

Rájño Mahákshatrapasa Dámasenasa putrasa Rájñah Kshatrapasa Yaśadámnaḥ.

Of the king the great Kshatrapa Yaśadáman son of the king the great Kshatrapa Dámasena.

On the coin dated 161 the legend runs:

राज्ञो महक्षत्रपस दामसेनस पुत्रस राज्ञो महाक्षत्रपस यशदाम्नः

Rájño Mahákshatrapasa Dámasenasa putrasa Rájño Mahákshatrapasa Yaśadámnaḥ.

Of the king the great Kshatrapa Yaśadáman son of the king the great Kshatrapa Dámasena.

Kshatrapa XV. Vijayasena, A.D. 238-249.

Vijayasena's coins are common. As many as 167 were in the Pandit's collection. Almost all are of good workmanship, well preserved, and clearly lettered. On fifty-four of them the following dates can be clearly read, 160, 161, 162, 163, 164, 165, 166, 167, 168, 170, and 171. This would give Vijayasena a reign of at least eleven years from 160 to 171 (A.D. 238-249). The legend reads:

राज्ञो महाक्षत्रपस दामसेनपुत्रस राज्ञो महाक्षत्रपस विजयसेनस

Rájño Mahákshatrapasa Dámasenaputrasa Rájño Mahákshatrapasa Vijayasenasa.

Of the king the great Kshatrapa Vijayasena son of the king the great Kshatrapa Dámasena.

---

[1] One specimen in the collection of Mr. Vajeshankar bears date 158.

In two good specimens of Vijayasena's coins with traces of the date 166 he is styled Kshatrapa. This the Pandit could not explain.[1]

Chapter V.
Western Kshatrapas, A.D. 70-398.

Kshatrapa XVI. Dámájadaśrí, A.D. 250-255.

Vijayasena was succeeded by his brother Dámájaḍaśrí III. called Mahákshatrapa on his coins. His coins which are comparatively uncommon are inferior in workmanship to the coins of Vijayasena. Of seven in the Pandit's collection three are dated 174, 175, and 176.

After Dámájaḍaśrí come coins of Rudrasena II. son of Víradáman, the earliest of them bearing date 178. As the latest coins of Vijayasena are dated 171, 173 may be taken as the year of Dámájaḍasrí's succession. The end of his reign falls between 176 and 178, its probable length is about five years. The legend on his coins reads :

राज्ञो महाक्षत्रपस दामसेनपुत्रस राज्ञो महाक्षत्रपस दामाजडश्रियः

Rájño Mahákshatrapasa Dámasenaputrasa Rájño Mahákshatrapasa Dámájaḍasriyaḥ.
Of the king the great Kshatrapa Dámájaḍas'rí son of the king the great Kshatrapa Dámasena.

Kshatrapa XVII. Rudrasena II. A.D. 256-272.

Dámájaḍasrí III. was succeeded by Rudrasena II. son of Dámájaḍasrí's brother Víradáman the thirteenth Kshatrapa. Rudrasena II.'s coins like Vijayasena's are found in great abundance. They are of inferior workmanship and inferior silver. Of eighty-four in Dr. Bhagavánlál's collection eleven bore the following clear dates: 178, 180, 183, 185, 186, 188, and 190. The earliest of 178 probably belongs to the beginning of Rudrasena's reign as the date 176 occurs on the latest coins of his predecessor. The earliest coins of his son and successor Viśvasimha are dated 198. As Viśvasiṃha's coins are of bad workmanship with doubtful legend and date we may take the end of Rudrasena II.'s reign to be somewhere between 190 and 198 or about 194. This date would give Rudrasena a reign of about sixteen years, a length of rule supported by the large number of his coins. The legend reads :

राज्ञो क्षत्रपस वीरदामपुत्रस राज्ञो महाक्षत्रपस रुद्रसेनस

Rájño Kshatrapasa Víradámaputrasa Rájño Mahákshatrapasa Rudrasenasa.
Of the king the great Kshatrapa Rudrasena son of the king the Kshatrapa Víradáma.

Kshatrapa XVIII. Vis'vasiṃha, A.D. 272-278.

Rudrasena was succeeded by his son Viśvasiṃha. In style and abundance Viśvasimha's coins are on a par with his father's. They are carelessly struck with a bad die and in most the legend is faulty often omitting the date. Of fifty-six in the Pandit's collection only four bear legible dates, one with 198, two with 200, and one with 201. The date 201 must be of the end of Viśvasimha's reign as a coin of his brother Bharttṛidáman is dated 200. It may therefore be held that Viśvasimha reigned for the six years ending 200 (A.D. 272-278). The legend reads :

राज्ञो महाक्षत्रपस रुद्रसेनपुत्रस राज्ञः क्षत्रपस विश्वसिंहस.

Rájño Mahákshatrapasa Rudrasenaputrasa Rájñaḥ Kshatrapasa Vis'vasiṃhasa.
Of the king the Kshatrapa Vis'vasimha son of the king the great Kshatrapa Rudrasena.

---

[1] One of them was lent by Mr. Vajeshankar Gavrishankar.

Chapter V.

WESTERN KSHATRAPAS, A.D. 70-398.

It is not known whether Viśvasimha's loss of title was due to his being subordinate to some overlord, or whether during his reign the Kshatrapas suffered defeat and loss of territory. The probable explanation seems to be that he began his reign in a subordinate position and afterwards rose to supreme rule.

Kshatrapa XIX. Bharttridáman, A.D. 278-294.

Viśvasimha was succeeded by his brother Bharttṛidáman.[1] His coins which are found in large numbers are in style and workmanship inferior even to Viśvasimha's coins. Of forty-five in the Pandit's collection seven bear the dates 202, 207, 210, 211, and 214. As the earliest coin of his successor is dated 218, Bharttṛidáman's reign seems to have lasted about fourteen years from 202 to 216 (A.D. 278-294). Most of the coin legends style Bharttṛidáman Maháksbatrapa though in a few he is simply styled Kshatrapa. This would seem to show that like his brother Viśvasimha he began as a Kshatrapa and afterwards gained the rank and power of Mahákshatrapa.

In Bharttṛidáman's earlier coins the legend reads:

राज्ञो महाक्षत्रपस रुद्रसेनपुत्रस राज्ञः क्षत्रपस भर्तृदाम्नः

Rajño Mahákshatrapasa Rudrasenaputrasa Rajñaḥ
Kshatrapasa Bhartṛidámnaḥ.

Of the king the Kshatrapa Bharttṛidáman son of the king
the great Kshatrapa Rudrasena.

In the later coins the legend is the same except that महाक्षत्रपस the great Kshatrapa takes the place of क्षत्रपस the Kshatrapa.

Kshatrapa XX. Viśvasena, A.D. 294-300.

Bharttṛidáman was succeeded by his son Viśvasena the twentieth Kshatrapa. His coins are fairly common, and of bad workmanship, the legend imperfect and carelessly struck, the obverse rarely dated. Of twenty-five in Dr. Bhagvánlál's collection, only three bear doubtful dates one 218 and two 222. The legend reads:

राज्ञो महाक्षत्रपस भर्तृदामपुत्रस राज्ञः क्षत्रपस विश्वसेनस,

Rájño Mahákshatrapasa Bhartṛidáma putrasa Rájñaḥ
Kshatrapasa Viśvasenasa.

Of the king the Kshatrapa Viśvasena son of the king the
Mahákshatrapa Bharttṛidáman.

It would seem from the lower title of Kshatrapa which we find given to Viśvasena and to most of the later Kshatrapas that from about 220 (A.D. 298) the Kshatrapa dominion lost its importance.

A hoard of coins found in 1861 near Karád on the Krishna, thirty-one miles south of Sátára, suggests[2] that the Kshatrapas retained the North Konkan and held a considerable share of the West Dakhan down to the time of Viśvasena (A.D. 300). The hoard includes coins of the six following rulers: Vijayasena (A.D. 238-249), his brother Dámájaḍaśrí III. (A.D. 251-255), Rudrasena II. (A.D. 256-272) son of Víradáman, Viśvasimha (A.D. 272-278) son of Rudrasena, Bharttṛidáman (A.D. 278-294) son of Rudrasena II., and Viśvasena (A.D. 296-300) son of Bharttirdáman. It may be argued that this Karád hoard is of no historical value being the chance importation of some Gujarát pilgrim to the Krishna. The following considerations favour the

[1] This name has generally been read Atridáman. [2] Jour. B. B. R. A. S. VII. 16.

Chapter V.

WESTERN KSHATRAPAS, A.D. 70-398.

Kshatrapa XX. Viśvasena, A.D. 294-300.

view that the contents of the hoard furnish evidence of the local rule of the kings whose coins have been found at Karád. The date (A.D. 238-249) of Vijayasena, the earliest king of the hoard, agrees well with the spread of Gujarát power in the Dakhan as it follows the overthrow both of the west (A.D. 180-200) and of the east (A.D. 220) Śátakarnis, while it precedes the establishment of any later west Dakhan dynasty: (2) All the kings whose coins occur in the hoard were Mahákshatrapas and from the details in the Periplus (A.D. 247), the earliest, Vijayasena, must have been a ruler of special wealth and power: (3) That the coins cease with Viśvasena (A.D. 296-300) is in accord with the fact that Viśvasena was the last of the direct line of Chashṭana, and that with or before the close of Viśvasena's reign the power of the Gujarát Kshatrapas declined. The presumption that Kshatrapa power was at its height during the reigns of the kings whose coins have been found at Karád is strengthened by the discovery at Amrávati in the Berars of a hoard of coins of the Mahákshatrapa Rudrasena (II. ?) (A.D. 256-272) son of the Mahákshatrapa Dámájadaśrí.[1]

Kshatrapa XXI. Rudrasiṃha, A.D. 308-311.

Whether the end of Chashṭana's direct line was due to their conquest by some other dynasty or to the failure of heirs is doubtful. Whatever may have been the cause, after an interval of about seven years (A.D. 300-308) an entirely new king appears, Rudrasimha son of Jívadáman. As Rudrasiṃha's father Jívadáman is simply called Svámi he may have been some high officer under the Kshatrapa dynasty. That Rudrasiṃha is called a Kshatrapa may show that part of the Kshatrapa dominion which had been lost during the reign of Viśvasena was given to some distant member or scion of the Kshatrapa dynasty of the name of Rudrasimha. The occurrence of political changes is further shown by the fact that the coins of Rudrasiṃha are of a better type than those of the preceding Kshatrapas. Rudrasiṃha's coins are fairly common. Of twelve in Dr. Bhagvánlál's collection five are clearly dated, three 230, one 231, and one 240. This leaves a blank of seven years between the last date of Viśvasena and the earliest date of Rudrasiṃha. The legend reads:

स्वामिजीवदामपुत्रस राज्ञः क्षत्रपस रुद्रसिंहस

Svámi Jívadáma putrasa Rajñaḥ Kshaṭrapasa Rudrasiṃhasa.

Of the king the Kshatrapa Rudrasiṃha son of Svámi Jívadáman.

Kshatrapa XXII. Yaśadáman, A.D. 320.

Rudrasiṃha was succeeded by his son Yaśadáman whose coins are rather rare. Of three in Dr. Bhagvánlál's collection two are dated 239, apparently the first year of Yaśadáman's reign as his father's latest coins are dated 240. Like his father Yaśadáman is simply called Kshatrapa. The legend reads:

राज्ञः क्षत्रपस रुद्रसिंहपुत्रस राज्ञः क्षत्रपस यशदाम्नः

Rájñaḥ Kshatrapasa Rudrasiṃhaputrasa Rájñaḥ Kshatrapasa Yaśadámnaḥ.

Of the king the Kshatrapa Yasadáman son of the king the Kshatrapa Rudrasiṃha.

---

[1] See below Chapter VI. page 57.

Chapter V.
WESTERN KSHATRAPAS, A.D. 70-398.
Kshatrapa XXIII. Dámasiri, A.D. 320.

The coins found next after Yaśadáman's are those of Dámasiri who was probably the brother of Yaśadáman as he is mentioned as the son of Rudrasiṃha. The date though not very clear is apparently 242. Only one coin of Dámasiri's is recorded. In the style of face and in the form of letters it differs from the coins of Yaśadáman, with which except for the date and the identity of the father's name any close connection would seem doubtful. The legend on the coin of Dámasiri reads:

राज्ञो महाक्षत्रपस रुद्रसिंहस पुत्रस राज्ञो महाक्षत्रपस दामसिरिस,

Rájño Mahákshatrapasa Rudrasiṃhasaputrasa Rájño Mahákshatrapasa Dámasirisa.

Of the king the great Kshatrapa Dámasiri son of the king the great Kshatrapa Rudrasiṃha.

It will be noted that in this coin both Rudrasiṃha and Dámasiri are called great Kshatrapas, while in his own coin and in the coins of his son Yaśadáman, Rudrasiṃha is simply styled Kshatrapa. It is possible that Dámasiri may have been more powerful than Yaśadáman and consequently taken to himself the title of Mahákshatrapa. The application of the more important title to a father who in life had not enjoyed the title is not an uncommon practice among the later Kshatrapas. The rarity of Dámasiri's coins shows that his reign was short.

After Dámasiri comes a blank of about thirty years. The next coin is dated 270. The fact that, contrary to what might have been expected, the coins of the later Kshatrapas are less common than those of the earlier Kshatrapas, seems to point to some great political change during the twenty-seven years ending 270 (A.D. 321-348).

Kshatrapa XXIV. Rudrasena, A.D. 348-376.

The coin dated 270 belongs to Svámi Rudrasena son of Svámi Rudradáman both of whom the legend styles Mahákshatrapas. The type of the coin dated 270 is clearly adapted from the type of the coins of Yaśadáman. Only two of Rudrasena's coins dated 270 are recorded. But later coins of the same Kshatrapa of a different style are found in large numbers. Of fifty-four in the Pandit's collection, twelve have the following dates 288, 290, 292, 293, 294, 296, and 298. The difference in the style of the two sets of coins and the blank between 270 and 288 leave no doubt that during those years some political change took place. Probably Rudrasena was for a time overthrown but again came to power in 288 and maintained his position till 298. Besides calling both himself and his father Mahákshatrapas Rudrasena adds to both the attribute Svámi. As no coin of Rudrasena's father is recorded it seems probable the father was not an independent ruler and that the legend on Rudrasena's coins is a further instance of a son ennobling his father. The legend is the same both in the earlier coins of 270 and in the later coins ranging from 288 to 298. It reads:

राज्ञो महाक्षत्रपस स्वामिरुद्रदामपुत्रस राज्ञो महाक्षत्रपस स्वामिरुद्रसेनस.

Rájño Mahákshatrapasa Svámi Rudradámaputrasa Rajño Mahákshatrapasa Svámi Rudrasenasa.

Of the king the great Kshatrapa Svámi Rudrasena son of the king the great Kshatrapa Svámi Rudradáman.

Chapter V.

Western Kshatrapas, A.D. 70-398.

Kshatrapa XXV. Rudrasena, A.D. 378-388.

After Rudrasena come coins of Kshatrapa Rudrasena son of Satyasena. These coins are fairly common. Of five in the Pandit's collection through faulty minting none are dated. General Cunningham mentions coins of Kshatrapa Rudrasena dated 300, 304, and 310.[1] This would seem to show that he was the successor of Rudrasena son of Rudradáman and that his reign extended to over 310. The legend on these coins runs:

राज्ञो महाक्षत्रपस स्वामिसत्यसेनपुत्रस राज्ञो महाक्षत्रपस स्वामिरुद्रसेनस.

Rájño Mahákshatrapasa Svámi Satyasenaputrasa Rájño Mahákshatrapasa Svámi Rudrasenasa.

Of the king the great Kshatrapa Svámi Rudrasena son of the king the great Kshatrapa Svámi Satyasena.

Of Rudrasena's father Satyasena no coin is recorded and as this Rudrasena immediately succeeds Rudrasena IV. son of Rudradáman, there is little doubt that Satyasena was not an actual ruler with the great title Mahákshatrapa, but that this was an honorific title given to the father when his son attained to sovereignty. General Cunningham records that a coin of this Rudrasena IV. was found along with a coin of Chandragupta II. in a *stúpa* at Sultánganj on the Ganges about fifteen miles south-east of Mongir.[2]

Kshatrapa XXVI. Simhasena.

With Rudrasena IV. the evidence from coins comes almost to a close. Only one coin in Dr. Bhagvánlál's collection is clearly later than Rudrasena IV. In the form of the bust and the style of the legend on the reverse this specimen closely resembles the coins of Rudrasena IV. Unfortunately owing to imperfect stamping it bears no date. The legend reads:

राज्ञो महाक्षत्रपस स्वामि रुद्रसेनस राज्ञो महाक्षत्रपस स्वस्रीयस्य स्वामिसिंहसेनस,

Rájño Mahákshatrapasa Svámi Rudrasenasa Rájño Mahákshatrapasa svasríyasya Svámi Siṃhasenasa.

Of the king the great Kshatrapa Svámi Siṃhasena, sister's son of the king the great Kshatrapa Svámi Rudrasena.

This legend would seem to show that Rudrasena IV. left no issue and was succeeded by his nephew Siṃhasena. The extreme rarity of Siṃhasena's coins proves that his reign was very short.

Kshatrapa XXVII. Skanda.

The bust and the characters in one other coin show it to be of later date than Siṃhasena. Unfortunately the legend is not clear. Something like the letters राज्ञो क्षत्रपस Rajno Kshatrapasa may be traced in one place and something like पुत्रस स्कन्द Putrasa Skanda in another place. Dr. Bhagvánlál took this to be a Gujarát Kshatrapa of unknown lineage from whom the Kshatrapa dominion passed to the Guptas.

Íśvaradatta, A.D. 230-250.

Along with the coins of the regular Kshatrapas coins of a Kshatrapa of unknown lineage named Íśvaradatta have been found in Káthiáváḍa. In general style, in the bust and the corrupt Greek legend on the obverse, and in the form of the old Nágarí legend

---

[1] Cunningham's Arch. Sur. X. 127; XV. 29-30.

[2] This coin of Rudrasena may have been taken so far from Gujarát by the Gujarát monk in whose honour the *stúpa* was built.

Chapter V.

WESTERN KSHATRAPAS, A.D. 70-398.

Kshatrapa XXVIII. Ísvaradátta, A.D. 230-250.

on the reverse, Ísvaradatta's coins closely resemble those of the fifteenth Kshatrapa Vijayasena (A.D. 238-249). At the same time the text of the Nágarí legend differs from that on the reverse of the Kshatrapa coins by omitting the name of the ruler's father and by showing in words Ísvaradatta's date in the year of his own reign. The legend is:

राज्ञो महाक्षत्रपस ईश्वरदत्तस वर्षे प्रथमे,

Rájño Mahákshatrapasa Ísvaradattasa varshe prathame.
In the first year of the king the great Kshatrapa Ísvaradatta.

Most of the recorded coins of Ísvaradatta have this legend. In one specimen the legend is

वर्षे द्वितीये.

Varshe dvitíye.
In the second year.

It is clear from this that Ísvaradatta's reign did not last long. His peculiar name and his separate date leave little doubt that he belonged to some distinct family of Kshatrapas. The general style of his coins shows that he cannot have been a late Kshatrapa while the fact that he is called Mahákshatrapa seems to show he was an independent ruler. No good evidence is available for fixing his date. As already mentioned the workmanship of his coins brings him near to Vijayasena (A.D. 238-249). In Násik Cave X. the letters of Inscription XV. closely correspond with the letters of the legends on Kshatrapa coins, and probably belong to almost the same date as the inscription of Rudrádaman on the Girnár rock that is to about A.D. 150. The absence of any record of the Ándhras except the name of the king Madharíputa Sirisena or Sakasena (A.D. 180), makes it probable that after Yajñaśrí Gautamíputra (A.D. 150) Ándhra power waned along the Konkan and South Gujarát seaboard. According to the Puránas the Ábhíras succeeded to the dominion of the Ándhras. It is therefore possible that the Ábhíra king Ísvarasena of Násik Inscription XV. was one of the Ábhíra conquerors of the Ándhras who took from them the West Dakhan. A migration of Ábhíras from Ptolemy's Abiria in Upper Sindh through Sindh by sea to the Konkan and thence to Násik is within the range of possibility. About fifty years later king Ísvaradatta[1] who was perhaps of the same family as the Ábhíra king of the Násik inscription seems to have conquered the kingdom of Kshatrapa Vijayasena, adding Gujarát, Káthiáváḍa, and part of the Dakhan to his other territory. In honour of this great conquest he may have taken the title Mahákshatrapa and struck coins in the Gujarát Kshatrapa style but in an era reckoned from the date of his own conquest. Ísvaradatta's success was shortlived. Only two years later (that is about A.D. 252) the Mahákshatrapa Dámájaḍasrí won back the lost Kshatrapa territory. The fact that Ísvaradatta's recorded coins belong to only two years and that the break between the regular

[1] Ísvaradatta's name ends in *datta* as does also that of Śivadatta the father of king Ísvarasena of the Násik inscription.

Chapter V.

WESTERN KSHATRAPAS, A.D. 70-398.

Kshatrapas Vijayasena and Dámájadaśrí did not last more than two or three years gives support to this explanation.[1]

The following table gives the genealogy of the Western Kshatrapas:

---

[1] Dr. Bhagvánlál's suggestion that Vijayasena (A.D. 238-249) was defeated by the Ábhír or Ahír king Íśvaradatta who entered Gujarát from the North Konkan seems open to question. First as regards the suggestion that Vijayasena was the Kshatrapa whose power Íśvaradatta overthrew it is to be noticed that though the two coinless years (A.D. 249-251) between the last coin of Vijayasena and the earliest coin of Dámájadaśrí agree with the recorded length of Íśvaradatta's supremacy the absence of coins is not in itself proof of a reverse or loss of Kshatrapa power between the reigns of Vijayasena and Dámájadaśrí. It is true the Pandit considers that Íśvaradatta's coins closely resemble those of Vijayasena. At the same time he also (Násik Stat. Acct. 624) thought them very similar to Víradáman's (A.D. 236-238) coins. Víradáman's date so immediately precedes Vijayasena's that in many respects their coins must be closely alike. It is to be noted that A.D. 230-235 the time of rival Kshatrapas among whom Víradáman was one (especially the time between A.D. 236 and 238 during which none of the rivals assumed the title Mahákshatrapa) was suitable to (perhaps was the result of) a successful invasion by Íśvaradatta, and that this same invasion may have been the cause of the transfer of the capital, noted in the Periplus (A.D. 247) as having taken place some years before, from Ozene or Ujjain to Minnagara or Junágadh (McCrindle, 114, 122). On the other hand the fact that Vijayasena regained the title of Mahákshatrapa and handed it to his successor Dámájadaśrí III. would seem to shew that no reverse or humiliation occurred during the coinless years (A.D. 249-251) between their reigns, a supposition which is supported by the flourishing state of the kingdom at the time of the Periplus (A.D. 247) and also by the evidence that both the above Kshatrapas ruled near Karád in Sátára. At the same time if the difference betweed Víradáman's and Vijayasena's coins is sufficient to make it unlikely that Íśvaradatta's can be copies of Víradáman's it seems possible that the year of Íśvaradatta's overlordship may be the year A.D. 244 (K. 166) in which Vijayasena's coins bear the title Kshatrapa, and that the assumption of this lower title in the middle of a reign, which with this exception throughout claims the title Mahákshatrapa, may be due to the temporary necessity of acknowledging the supremacy of Íśvaradatta. With reference to the Pandit's suggestion that Íśvaradatta was an Ábhíra the fact noted above of a trace of Kshatrapa rule at Karád thirty-one miles south of Sátára together with the fact that they held Aparánta or the Konkan makes it probable that they reached Karád by Chiplún and the Kumbhárli pass. That the Kshatrapas entered the Dakhan by so southerly a route instead of by some one of the more central Thána passes, seems to imply the presence of some hostile power in Násik and Khándesh. This after the close of the second century A.D. could hardly have been the Ándhras or Śátakarnis. It may therefore be presumed to have been the Ándhras' successors the Ábhíras. As regards the third suggestion that Kshatrapa Gujarát was overrun from the North Konkan it is to be noted that the evidence of connection between Íśvarasena of the Násik inscription (Cave X. No. 15) and Íśvaradatta of the coins is limited to a probable nearness in time and a somewhat slight similarity in name. On the other hand no inscription or other record points to Ábhíra ascendancy in the North Konkan or South Gujarát. The presence of an Ábhíra power in the North Konkan seems inconsistent with Kshatrapa rule at Kalyán and Karád in the second half of the third century. The position allotted to Aberia in the Periplus (McCrindle, 113) inland from Surastrene, apparently in the neighbourhood of Thar and Párkar; the finding of Íśvaradatta's coins in Káthiáváda (Násik Gazetteer, XIII. 624); and (perhaps between A.D. 230 and 240) the transfer westwards of the headquarters of the Kshatrapa kingdom seem all to point to the east rather than to the south, as the side from which Íśvaradatta invaded Gujarát. At the same time the reference during the reign of Rudrasimha I. (A.D. 181) to the Ábhíra Rudrabhúti who like his father was Senápati or Commander-in-Chief suggests that Íśvaradatta may have been not a foreigner but a revolted general. This supposition, his assumption of the title Mahákshatrapa, and the finding of his coins only in Káthiáváda to a certain extent confirm.

Chapter V.

The Kshatrapa Family Tree.

THE WESTERN KSHATRAPAS.

I.
NAHAPÁNA,
King, Kshaharáta, Kshatrapa
(A.D. 100 - 120 ?).

II.
Chashtana, son of Zamotika,
King, Mahákshatrapa
(A.D. 100 - 130).

III.
Jayadáman, King, Kshatrapa
(A.D. 130 - 140).

IV.
Rudradáman,
King, Mahákshatrapa
(A.D. 143 - 158 *circa*).

V.
Dámázada or Dámájadas'ri,
King, Kshatrapa
(A.D. 168 *circa*).

VI.
Jívadáman,
King, Mahákshatrapa
(A.D. 178, A.D. 196 *circa*).

VII.
Rudrasimha,
King, Mahákshatrapa
(A.D. 180 - 196 *circa*).

VIII.
Rudrasena,
King, Mahákshatrapa
(A.D. 200 - 220 *circa*).

X.
Sanghadáman,
King, Mahákshatrapa
(A.D. 222 - 226 *circa*).

XI.
Dámasena,
King, Mahákshatrapa
(A.D. 226 - 236 *circa*).

IX.
Prithivísena, King, Kshatrapa
(A.D. 222 *circa*).

XII.
Dámájadas'ri II. King, Kshatrapa
(A.D. 232 *circa*).

XIII.
Víradáman,
King, Kshatrapa
(A.D. 236, 238 *circa*).

XIV.
Yas'adáman II.
King, Kshatrapa
(A.D. 238, 239 *circa*).

XV.
Vijayasena,
King, Kshatrapa and
Mahákshatrapa
(A.D. 238 - 249 *circa*).

XVI.
Dámájadas'ri III.
King, Mahákshatrapa
(A.D. 251 - 255 *circa*).

XVII.
Rudrasena II.
King, Mahákshatrapa
(A.D. 256 - 272 *circa*).

XVIII.
Vis'vasimha,
King, Kshatrapa
(A.D. 272 - 278 *circa*).

XIX.
Bharttridáman,
King, Kshatrapa and
Mahákshatrapa
(A.D. 278 - 294 *circa*).

XX.
Vis'vasena,
King, Kshatrapa
(A.D. 296 - 300 *circa*).

XXI.
Rudrasimha son of
Svámi Jívadáman,
King, Kshatrapa
(A.D. 308, 309, 318 *circa*).

XXII.
Yas'adáman II. King, Kshatrapa
(A.D. 318 *circa*).

XXIII.
Dámasiri, King, Mahákshatrapa
(A.D. 320 *circa*).

XXIV.
Svámi Rudrasena III.
King, Mahákshatrapa
son of king Mahákshatrapa, Svámi Rudradáma,
(A.D. 348, 366 - 376 *circa*).

XXV.
Svámi Rudrasena IV.
King, Mahákshatrapa,
son of king Mahákshatrapa, Svámi Satyasena,
(A.D. 378 - 388 *circa*).

XXVI.
Svámi Simhasena
King, Mahákshatrapa,
sister's son of king Mahakshatrapa
Svámi Rudrasena (XXV).

XXVII.
Skanda——?

CHAPTER VI.

THE TRAIKÚṬAKAS

(A.D. 250-450.)

Chapter VI.

TRAIKUTAKAS, A.D. 250-450.

Two Plates.

THE materials regarding the Traikúṭakas, though meagre, serve to show that they were a powerful dynasty who rose to consequence about the time of the middle Kshatrapas (A.D. 250). All the recorded information is in two copperplates, one the Kanheri copperplate found by Dr. Bird in 1839,[1] the other a copperplate found at Párdi near Balsár in 1885.[2] Both plates are dated, the Kanheri plate 'in the year two hundred and forty-five of the increasing rule of the Traikúṭakas'; the Párdi plate in Saṃvat 207·clearly figured. The Kanheri plate contains nothing of historical importance; the Párdi plate gives the name of the donor as Dahrasena or Dharasena 'the illustrious great king of the Traikúṭakas.' Though it does not give any royal name the Kanheri plate expressly mentions the date as the year 245 of the increasing rule of the Traikúṭakas. The Párdi plate gives the name of the king as 'of the Traikúṭakas' but merely mentions the date as Saṃ. 207. This date though not stated to be in the era of the Traikúṭakas must be taken to be dated in the same era as the Kanheri plate seeing that the style of the letters of both plates is very similar.

The initial date must therefore have been started by the founder of the dynasty and the Kanheri plate proves the dynasty must have lasted at least 245 years. The Párdi plate is one of the earliest copper-plate grants in India. Neither the genealogy nor even the usual three generations including the father and grandfather are given, nor like later plates does it contain a wealth of attributes. The king is called 'the great king of the Traikúṭakas,' the performer of the *aśvamedha* or horse-sacrifice, a distinction bespeaking a powerful sovereign. It may therefore be supposed that Dahrasena held South Gujarát to the Narbáda together with part of the North Konkan and of the Ghát and Dakhan plateau.

Initial Date.

What then was the initial date of the Traikúṭakas? Ten Gujarát copper-plates of the Gurjjaras and Chalukyas are dated in an unknown era with Saṃ. followed by the date figures as in the Párdi plate and as in Gupta inscriptions. The earliest is the fragment from Sáṅkheḍá in the Baroda State dated Saṃ 346, which would fall in the reign of Dadda I. of Broach.[3] Next come the two Kaira grants of the Gurjjara king Dadda Praśántarága dated Saṃ. 380 and Saṃ. 385[4]; and the Sáṅkheḍá grant of Raṇagraha dated Saṃ. 391[5]; then the Kaira grant of the Chalukya king Vijayarája or Vijayavarman dated Saṃvatsara 394[6]; then the Bagumrá grant of the Sendraka chief Nikumbhalla-

---

[1] Cave Temple Inscriptions, Bom. Arch. Sur. Sep. Number XI. page 57ff.
[2] J. B. B. R. A. S. XVI. 346. [3] Epigraphia Indica, II. 19. [4] Ind. Ant. XIII. 81ff.
[5] Ep. Ind. II. 20.
[6] Ind. Ant. VII. 248ff. Dr. Bhandárkar (Early Hist. of the Deccan, 42 note 7) has given reasons for believing this grant to be a forgery.

Chapter VI.
TRAIKUTAKAS, A.D. 250-450.
Initial Date.

śakti[1]; two grants from Navsári and Surat of the Chalukya king Síláditya Sryáśraya dated 421 and 443[2]; two the Navsari and Kávi grants of the Gurjjara king Jayabhaṭa dated respectively Saṃ. 456 and Saṃ. 486[3]; and a grant of Pulakeśi dated Saṃvat 490.[4]

Of these the grant dated 421 speaks of Śíláditya Śryáśraya as Yuvarája or heir-apparent and as the son of Jayasiṃhavarmman. The plate further shows that Jayasiṃhavarmman was brother of Vikramáditya and son of Pulakeśi Vallabha 'the conqueror of the northern king Harshavardhana.' The name Jayasiṃhavarmman does not occur in any copperplate of the main line of the Western Chalukyas of the Dakhan. That he is called Mahárája or great king and that his son Síláditya is called Yuvarája or heir-apparent suggest that Jayasiṃhavarmman was the founder of the Gujarát branch of the Western Chalukyas and that his great Dakhan brother Vikramáditya was his overlord, a relation which would explain the mention of Vikramáditya in the genealogy of the copper-plate. Vikramáditya's reign ended in A.D. 680 (Saka 602).[5] Supposing our grant to be dated in this last year of Vikramáditya, Saṃvat 421 should correspond to Śaka 602, which gives Saka 181 or A.D. 259 as the initial date of the era in which the plate is dated. Probably the plate was dated earlier in the reign of Vikramáditya giving A.D. 250. In any case the era used cannot be the Gupta era whose initial year is now finally settled to be A.D. 319.

The second grant of the same Śíláditya is dated Saṃvat 443. In it, both in an eulogistic verse at the beginning and in the text of the genealogy, Vinayáditya Satyáśraya Vallabha is mentioned as the paramount sovereign which proves that by Saṃvat 443 Vikramáditya had been succeeded by Vinayáditya. The reign of Vinayáditya has been fixed as lasting from Śaka 602 to Śaka 618 that is from A.D. 680 to A.D. 696-97.[6] Taking Śaka 615 or A.D. 693 to correspond with Saṃvat 443, the initial year of the era is A.D. 250.

The grant of Pulakeśivallabha Janáśraya dated Saṃvat 490, mentions Mangalarasaráya as the donor's elder brother and as the son of Jayasiṃhavarmman. And a Balsár grant whose donor is mentioned as Mangalarája son of Jayasiṃhavarmman, apparently the same as the Mangalarasaráya of the plate just mentioned, is dated Śaka 653.[7] Placing the elder brother about ten years before the younger we get Saṃvat 480 as the date of Mangalarája, which, corresponding with Śaka 653 or A.D. 730-31, gives A.D. 730 minus 480 that is A.D. 250-51 as the initial year of the era in which Pulakeśi's grant is dated. In the Navsári plates, which record a gift by the Gurjjara king Jayabhaṭa in Saṃvat 456, Dadda II. the donor of the Kaira grants which bear date 380 and 385, is mentioned in the genealogical part at the beginning as 'protecting the lord of Valabhi who had been defeated by the great lord the illustrious Harshadeva.' Now the great Harshadeva or Harsha Vardhana of Kanauj whose court was visited by the Chinese pilgrim Hiuen

[1] Ind. Ant. XVIII. 265ff.
[2] J. B. B. R. A. S. XVI. 1ff. ; Trans. Vienna Or. Congress, 210ff.
[3] Ind. Ant. XIII. 70ff. and V. 109ff.
[4] Trans. Vienna Or. Congress, 210ff.
[5] Fleet's Kánarese Dynasties, 27.
[6] Fleet's Kánarese Dynasties, 27.
[7] Ind. Ant. XIV. 75 and Jour. B. B. R. A. S. XVI. 1ff.

Chapter VI.

TRAIKUTAKAS, A.D. 250-450.

Initial Date.

Tsiang between A.D. 629 and 645, reigned according to Reinaud from A.D. 607 to about A.D. 648. Taking A.D. 250 as the initial year of the era of the Kaira plates, Dadda II.'s dates 380 and 385, corresponding to A.D. 630 and 635, fall in the reign of Harshavardhana.

These considerations seem to show that the initial date of the Traikúṭaka era was at or about A.D. 250 which at once suggests its identity with the Chedi or Kalachuri era.[1] The next question is, Who were these Traikúṭakas. The meaning of the title seems to be kings of Trikúta. Several references seem to point to the existence of a city named Trikúṭa on the western seaboard. In describing Raghu's triumphant progress the Rámáyaṇa and the Raghuvaṃśa mention him as having established the city of Trikúṭa in Aparánta on the western seaboard.[2] Trikúṭakam or Trikúṭam, a Sanskrit name for sea salt seems a reminiscence of the time when Trikúṭa was the emporium from which Konkan salt was distributed over the Dakhan. The scanty information regarding the territory ruled by the Traikúṭakas is in agreement with the suggestion that Junnar in North Poona was the probable site of their capital and that in the three ranges that encircle Junnar we have the origin of the term Trikúṭa or Three-Peaked.

Their Race or Tribe.

Of the race or tribe of the Traikúṭakas nothing is known. The conjecture may be offered that they are a branch of the Ábhíra kings of the Puráṇas, one of whom is mentioned in Inscription XV. of Násik Cave X. which from the style of the letters belongs to about A.D. 150 to 200. The easy connection between Násik and Balsár by way of Peth (Peint) and the nearness in time between the Násik inscription and the initial date of the Traikúṭakas support this conjecture. The further suggestion may be offered that the founder of the line of Traikútakas was the Íśvaradatta, who, as noted in the Kshatrapa chapter, held the overlordship of Káthiáváḍa as Mahákshatrapa, perhaps during the two years A.D. 248 and 249, a result in close agreement with the conclusions drawn from the examination of the above quoted Traikúṭaka and Chálukya copperplates. As noted in the Kshatrapa chapter after two years' supremacy Íśvaradatta seems to have been defeated and regular Kshatrapa rule restored about A.D. 252 (K. 174) by Dámájaḍaśrí son of Vijayasena. The unbroken use of the title Mahákshatrapa, the moderate and uniform lengths of the reigns, and the apparently unquestioned successions suggest, what the discovery of Kshatrapa coins at Karád near Sátára in the Dakhan and at Amrávati in the Berárs seems to imply, that during the second half of the third century Kshatrapa rule was widespread and firmly established.[3] The conjecture may be offered that Rudrasena (A.D. 256-272) whose coins have been found in Amrávati in the Berárs spread his power at the expense of the Traikúṭakas driving them towards the Central Provinces where they established themselves at Tripura and Kálanjara.[4] Further that under Bráhman

---

[1] Mr. Fleet (Corp. Ins. Ind. III. 9) and Sir A. Cunningham (Arch. Sur. IX. 77) agree in fixing A.D. 250 as the initial date of the Chedi era. Prof. Kielhorn has worked out the available dates and finds that the first year of the era corresponds to A.D. 249-50. Ind. Ant. XVII. 215.

[2] Válmíki's Rámáyaṇa, Ganpat Krishnaji's Edition: Raghuvaṃśa, IV. 59.

[3] For details see above page 48.

[4] Tripura four miles west of Jabalpur; Kálanjara 140 miles north of Jabalpur.

Chapter VI.

TRAIKUTAKAS, A.D. 250-450.

Their Race or Tribe.

influence, just as the Gurjjaras called themselves descendants of Karṇa the hero of the Mahábhárata, and the Pallavas claimed to be of the Bháradvája stock, the Traikúṭakas forgot their Ábhíra origin and claimed descent from the Haihayas. Again as the Valabhis (A.D. 480-767) adopted the Gupta era but gave it their own name so the rulers of Tripura seem to have continued the original Traikúṭaka era of A.D. 248-9 under the name of the Chedi era. The decline of the Kshatrapas dates from about A.D. 300 the rule of Viśvasena the twentieth Kshatrapa son of Bharttṛidáman. The subsequent disruption of the Kshatrapa empire was probably the work of their old neighbours and foes the Traikúṭakas, who, under the name of Haihayas, about the middle of the fifth century (A.D. 455-6) rose to supremacy and established a branch at their old city of Trikúṭa ruling the greater part of the Bombay Dakhan and South Gujarát and probably filling the blank between A.D. 410 the fall of the Kshatrapas and A.D. 500 the rise of the Chálukyas.

About 1887 Pandit Bhagvánlál secured nine of a hoard of 500 silver coins found at Daman in South Gujarát. All are of one king a close imitation of the coins of the latest Kshatrapas. On the obverse is a bust of bad workmanship and on the reverse are the usual Kshatrapa symbols encircled with the legend:

महाराजेंद्रवर्मपुत्रपरमवैष्णवश्रीमहाराजरुद्रगण :

Mahárájendravarmaputra Parama Vaishnava
Srí Mahárája Rudragaṇa.

The devoted Vaishnava the illustrious king Rudragaṇa
son of the great king Indravarma.

At Karád, thirty-one miles south of Sátára, Mr. Justice Newton obtained a coin of this Rudragaṇa, with the coins of many Kshatrapas including Viśvasiṃha son of Bharttṛidáman who ruled up to A.D. 300. This would favour the view that Rudragaṇa was the successful rival who wrested the Dakhan and North Konkan from Viśvasiṃha. The fact that during the twenty years after Viśvasiṃha (A.D. 300-320) none of the Kshatrapas has the title Mahákshatrapa seems to show they ruled in Káthiáváḍa as tributaries of this Rudragaṇa and his descendants of the Traikúṭaka family. The Dahrasena of the Párdi plate whose inscription date is 207, that is A.D. 457, may be a descendant of Rudragaṇa. The Traikúṭaka kingdom would thus seem to have flourished at least till the middle of the fifth century. Somewhat later, or at any rate after the date of the Kanheri plate (245 = A.D. 495), it was overthrown by either the Mauryas or the Guptas.[1]

---

[1] That the era used by the Gurjjaras and Chalukyas of Gujarát was the Chedi era may be regarded as certain since the discovery of the Sáṅkhedá grant of Nirihullaka (Ep. Ind. II. 21), who speaks of a certain Saṅkaraṇa as his overlord. Palæographically this grant belongs to the sixth century, and Dr. Bühler has suggested that Saṅkaraṇa is the Chedi Saṅkaragaṇa whose son Buddharája was defeated by Mangaliśa some time before A.D. 602 (Ind. Ant. XIX. 16). If this is accepted, the grant shows that the Chedis or Kalachuris were in power in the Narbáda valley during the sixth century, which explains the prevalence of their era in South Gujarát. Chedi rule in the Narbádá valley must have come to an end about A.D. 580 when Dadda I. established himself at Broach. It being established that the Kalachuris once ruled in South Gujarát, there is no great difficulty in the way of identifying the Traikúṭakas with them. The two known Traikúṭaka grants are dated in the third century of their era, and belong palæographically to the fifth century A.D. Their era, therefore, like that of the Kalachuris, begins in the third century A.D.: and it is simpler to suppose that the two eras were the same than

that two different eras, whose initial points were only a few years apart, were in use in the same district. Now that the S'aka and the Vikrama eras are known to have had different names at different times, the change in the name of the era offers no special difficulty. This identification would carry back Kalachuri rule in South Gujarát to at least A.D. 455-6, the date of the Párdi grant: and it is worth noting that Varáhamihira (Bṛ. Saṃh. XIV. 20) places the Haihayas or Kalachuris in the west along with the Aparántakas or Konkanis.

Though the name Traikúṭaka means of Trikúṭa, the authorities quoted by Dr. Bhagvánlál do not establish the existence of a city called Trikúṭa. They only vouch for a mountain of that name somewhere in the Western Gháts, and there is no evidence of any special connection with Junnar. Further, the word Trikúṭakam seems to mean rock-salt, not sea-salt, so that there is here no special connection with the Western coast. Wherever Trikúṭa may have been, there seems no need to reject the tradition that connects the rise of the Kalachuris with their capture of Kálanjara (Cunningham's Arch. Surv. IX. 77ff), as it is more likely that they advanced from the East down the Narbádá than that their original seats were on the West Coast, as the Western Indian inscriptions of the third and fourth centuries contain no reference either to Traikúṭakas or to Junnar or other western city as Trikúṭa.

With reference to the third suggestion that the Traikúṭakas twice overthrew the Kshatrapas, under Ís'varadatta in A.D. 248 and under Rudragaṇa in A.D. 310-320, it is to be noted that there is no evidence to show that Ís'varadatta was either an Ábhíra or a Traikúṭaka and that the identification of his date with A.D. 248-250 seems less probable than with either A.D. 244 or A.D. 236. (Compare above Footnote page 53). Even if Ís'varadatta's supremacy coincided with A.D. 250 the initial date of the Traikúṭaka era, it seems improbable that a king who reigned only two years and left no successor should have had any connection with the establishment of an era which is not found in use till two centuries later. As regards Rudragaṇa it may be admitted that he belonged to the race or family who weakened Kshatrapa power early in the fourth century A.D. At the same time there seems no reason to suppose that Rudragaṇa was a Traikúṭaka or a Kalachuri except the fact that his name, like that of S'aṅkaragaṇa, is a compound of the word *gaṇa* and a name of S'iva; while the irregular posthumous use of the title Mahákshatrapa among the latest (23rd to 26th) Kshatrapas favours the view that they remained independent till their overthrow by the Guptas about A.D. 410. The conclusion seems to be that the Traikúṭaka and the Kalachuri eras are the same namely A.D. 248-9: that this era was introduced into Gujarát by the Traikúṭakas who were connected with the Haihayas; and that the introduction of the era into Gujarát did not take place before the middle of the fifth century A.D.—(A. M. T. J.)

CHAPTER VII.

THE GUPTAS

(G. 90–149; A.D. 410–470.)

Chapter VII.
THE GUPTAS, A.D. 410-470.

AFTER the Kshatrapas (A.D. 120-410) the powerful dynasty of the Guptas established themselves in Gujarát. So far as the dynasty is connected with Gujarát the Gupta tree is :

Gupta.
G. 1-12 (?)—A.D. 319-322 (?)
Petty N. W. P. Chief.
|
Ghaṭotkacha.
G. 12-29 (?)—A.D. 332-349 (?)
Petty N. W. P. Chief.
|
Chandragupta I.
G. 29-49 (?)—A.D. 349-369 (?)
Powerful N. W. P. Chief.
|
Samudragupta.
G. 50-75 (?)—A.D. 370-395.
Great N. W. P. Sovereign.
|
Chandragupta II.
G. 70-96—A.D. 396-415.
Great Monarch conquers Málwa.
G. 80 A.D. 400 and Gujarát G. 90 A.D. 410.
|
Kumáragupta.
G. 97-133—A.D. 416-453.
Rules Gujarát and Káthiáváḍa.
|
Skandagupta.
G. 133-149—A.D. 454-470.
Rules Gujarát Káthiáváḍa and Kachch.

According to the Puránas[1] the original seat of the Guptas was between the Ganges and the Jamna. Their first capital is not determined. English writers usually style them the Guptas of Kanauj. And though this title is simply due to the chance that Gupta coins were first found at Kanauj, further discoveries show that the chief remains of Gupta records and coins are in the territory to the east and south-east of Kanauj. Of the race of the Guptas nothing is known. According to the ordinances of the Smṛitis or Sacred Books,[2] the terminal *gupta* belongs only to Vaiśyas a class including shepherds

---

[1] Váyu Puráṇa, Wilson's Works, IX. 219n.

[2] Vishnu Puraṇa, III. Chapter 10 Verse 9: Burnell's Manu, 20. Mr. Fleet (Corp. Ins. Ind. III. Ins. 11 note 1) quotes an instance of a Bráhman named Brahmagupta.

cultivators and traders. Of the first three kings, Gupta Ghaṭotkacha and Chandragupta I., beyond the fact that Chandragupta I. bore the title of Mahárájádhirája, neither descriptive titles nor details are recorded. As the fourth king Samudragupta performed the long-neglected horse-sacrifice he must have been Bráhmanical in religion. And as inscriptions style Samudragupta's three successors, Chandragupta II. Kumáragupta and Skandagupta, Parama Bhágavata, they must have been Smárta Vaishnavas, that is devotees of Vishnu and observers of Vedic ceremonies.

The Founder Gupta, A.D. 319-322 (?).

The founder of the dynasty is styled Gupta. In inscriptions this name always appears as Śrí-gupta which is taken to mean protected by Śrí or Lakshmí. Against this explanation it is to be noted that in their inscriptions all Gupta's successors have a Śrí before their names. The question therefore arises; If Śrí forms part of the name why should the name Śrígupta have had no second Śrí prefixed in the usual way. Further in the inscriptions the lineage appears as Guptavaméa that is the lineage of the Guptas never Śríguptavaméa[1]; and whenever dates in the era of this dynasty are given they are conjoined with the name Gupta never with Śrígupta.[2] It may therefore be taken that Gupta not S'rígupta is the correct form of the founder's name.[3]

Ghaṭotkacha, A.D. 322-349 (?).

Gupta the founder seems never to have risen to be more than a petty chief. No known inscription gives him the title *Mahárájádhirája* Supreme Ruler of Great Kings, which all Gupta rulers after the founder's grandson Chandragupta assume. Again that no coins of the founder and many coins of his successors have been discovered makes it probable that Gupta was not a ruler of enough importance to have a currency of his own. According to the inscriptions Gupta was succeeded by his son Ghaṭotkacha a petty chief like his father with the title of Mahárája and without coins.

Chandragupta I. A.D. 349-369 (?).

Chandragupta I. (A.D. 349-369 [?]), the son and successor of Ghaṭotkacha, is styled Mahárájádhirája either because he himself became powerful, or, more probably, because he was the father of his very powerful successor Samudragupta. Though he may not have gained the dignity of "supreme ruler of great kings" by his own successes Chandragupta I. rose to a higher position than his predecessors. He was connected by marriage with the Lichchhavi dynasty of Tirhút an alliance which must have been considered of importance since his son Samudragupta puts the name of his mother Kumárádeví on his coins, and always styles himself daughter's son of Lichchhavi.[4]

---

[1] Fleet's Corp. Ins. Ind. III. Ins. 53 line 7.

[2] Compare Skandagupta's Junágaḍh Inscription line 15, Ind. Ant. XIV.; Cunningham's Arch. Sur. X. 118; Fleet's Corp. Ins. Ind. III. Ins. 59.

[3] Compare Mr. Fleet's note in Corp. Ins. Ind. III. Ins. 8.

[4] Fleet's Corp. Ins. Ind. III. 135. Mr. Fleet believes that the Lichchhavi family concerned was that of Nepál, and that they were the real founders of the era used by the Guptas. Dr. Bühler (Vienna Or. Journal, V. Pt. 3) holds that Chandragupta married into the Lichchhavi family of Páṭaliputra and became king of that country in right of his wife. The coins which bear the name of Kumáradevi are by Mr. Smith (J. R. A. S. (N. S.) XXI. 63) and others assigned to Chandragupta I., reading the reverse legend *Lichchhavayaḥ* The Lichchhavis in place of Dr. Bhagvánlál's *Lichchhaveyaḥ* Daughter's son of Lichchhavi. On the Kácha coins see below page 62 note 2.

The Lichchhavis claim to be sprung from the solar dynasty. Manu (Burnell's Manu,

Chapter VII.

THE GUPTAS, A.D. 410-470.

Samudragupta, A.D. 370-395.

Samudragupta was the first of his family to strike coins. His numerous gold coins are, with a certain additional Indian element, adopted from those of his Indo-Skythian predecessors. The details of the royal figure on the obverse are Indian in the neck ornaments, large earrings, and headdress; they are Indo-Skythian in the tailed coat, long boots, and straddle. The goddess on the reverse of some coins with a fillet and cornucopia is an adaptation of an Indo-Skythian figure, while the lotus-holding Ganges on an alligator and the standing Glory holding a flyflapper on the reverse of other coins are purely Indian.[1]

His Coins.

A noteworthy feature of Samudragupta's coins is that one or other of almost all his epithets appears on each of his coins with a figure of the king illustrating the epithet. Coins with the epithet *Sarva-rájochchhettá* Destroyer-of-all-kings have on the obverse a standing king stretching out a banner topped by the wheel or disc of universal supremacy.[2]

Coins[3] with the epithet *Apratiratha* Peerless have on the obverse a standing king whose left hand rests on a bow and whose right hand holds a loose-lying unaimed arrow and in front an Eagle or Garuda standard symbolizing the unrivalled supremacy of the king, his arrow no longer wanted, his standard waving unchallenged. On the obverse is the legend :

---

308) describes them as descended from a degraded Kshatriya. Beal (R. A. S. N. S. XIV. 39) would identify them with an early wave of the Yuechi or Kushâns; Smith (J. R. A. S. XX. 55 n. 2) and Hewitt (J. R. A. S. XX. 355-366) take them to be a Kolarian or local tribe. The fame of the Lichchhavis of Vaisáli or Passalæ between Patna and Tirhút goes back to the time of Gautama Buddha (B.C. 480) in whose funeral rites the Lichchhavis and their neighbours and associates the Mallas took a prominent share (Rockhill's Life of Buddha, 62-63, 145, 203. Compare Legge's Fa Hien, 71-76; Beal's Buddhist Records, II. 67, 70, 73, 77 and 81 note). According to Buddhist writings the first king of Thibet (A.D. 50) who was elected by the chiefs of the South Thibet tribes was a Lichchhavi the son of Prasenadjit of Kośala (Rockhill's Life of Buddha, 208). Between the seventh and ninth centuries (A.D. 635-854) a family of Lichchhavis was ruling in Nepal (Fleet's Corp. Ins. Ind. III. 134). The earliest historical member of the Nepál family is Jayadeva I. whose date is supposed to be about A.D. 330 to 355. Mr. Fleet (Ditto, 135) suggests that Jayadeva's reign began earlier and may be the epoch from which the Gupta era of A.D. 318-319 is taken. He holds (Ditto, 136) that in all probability the so-called Gupta era is a Lichchhavi era.

[1] The figure of the Ganges standing on an alligator with a stalked lotus in her left hand on the reverse of the gold coins of Samudragupta the fourth king of the dynasty may be taken to be the Sri or Luck of the Guptas. Compare Smith's Gupta Coinage, J. Beng. A. S. LIII. Plate I. Fig. 10. J. R. A. S. (N. S.) XXI. Pl. I. 2.

[2] The presence of the two letters क च that is *ka cha* on the obverse under the arm of the royal figure, has led the late Mr. Thomas, General Cunningham, and Mr. Smith to suppose that the coins belonged to Ghaṭotkacha, the last two letters of the name being the same. This identification seems improbable. Ghaṭotkacha was never powerful enough to have a currency of his own. *Sarvarájochchhettá* the attribute on the reverse is one of Samudragupta's epithets, while the figure of the king on the obverse grasping the standard with the disc, illustrating the attribute of universal sovereignty, can refer to none other than Samudragupta the first very powerful king of the dynasty. Perhaps the Kacha or Kácha on these coins is a pet or child name of Samudragupta. Mr. Rapson (Numismatic Chron. 3rd Ser. XI. 48ff) has recently suggested that the Kácha coins belong to an elder brother and predecessor of Samudragupta. But it seems unlikely that a ruler who could justly claim the title Destroyer-of-all-kings should be passed over in silence in the genealogy. Further, as is remarked above, the title *Sarvarájochchhettá* belongs in the inscriptions to Samudragupta alone: and the fact that in his lifetime Samudragupta's father chose him as successor is against his exclusion from the throne even for a time.

[3] Smith's Gupta Coinage in J. R. A. S. (N. S.) XXI. Pl. I. 10.

Chapter VII.

THE GUPTAS, A.D. 410 - 470.

Samudragupta, A.D. 370 - 395.

अप्रतिरथराजन्यकीर्ति (र) मम विजयते.

Apratirathárájanyakírti(r)mama vijáyate.[1]

Triumphant is the glory of me the unrivalled sovereign.

Coins with the attribute *Kritánta parašu* the Death-like-battle-axe have on the obverse a royal figure grasping a battle-axe.[2] In front of the royal figure a boy, perhaps Samudragupta's son Chandragupta, holds a standard. Coins with the attribute *Ásvamedhaparákramaḥ* Able-to-hold-a-horse-sacrifice have on the obverse a horse standing near a sacrificial post *yúpa* and on the reverse a female figure with a flyflap.[3] The legend on the obverse is imperfect and hard to read. The late Mr. Thomas restores it :

नवजमधः राजाधिराज पृथिवीं जियत्य.

Navajamadhaḥ rájádhirája prithivím jiyatya.

Horse sacrifice, after conquering the earth, the great king (performs).

Coins with the legend *Lichchhaveyaḥ*, a coin abbreviation for *Lichchhavidauhitra* Daughter's son of Lichchhavi (?), have on the obverse a standing king grasping a javelin.[4] Under the javelin hand are the letters *Chandraguptaḥ*. Facing the king a female figure with trace of the letters *Kumáradeví* seems to speak to him. These figures of his mother and father are given to explain the attribute Lichchhaveya or scion of Lichchhavi. This coin has been supposed to belong to Chandragupta I. but the attribute *Lichchhaveyaḥ* can apply only to Samudragupta.

His Allahábád Inscription.

A fuller source of information regarding Samudragupta remains in his inscription on the Allahábád Pillar.[5] Nearly eight verses of the first part are lost. The first three verses probably described his learning as what remains of the third verse mentions his poetic accomplishments, and line 27 says he was skilled in poetry and music, a trait further illustrated by what are known as his Lyrist coins where he is shown playing a lute.[6] The fourth verse says that during his lifetime his father chose Samudragupta to rule the earth from among others of equal birth. His father is mentioned as pleased with him and this is followed by the description of a victory during which several opponents are said to have submitted. The seventh verse records the sudden destruction of the army of Achyuta Nágasena and the punishment inflicted on a descendant of the Kota family.

Lines 19 and 20 record the conquest, or submission, of the following South Indian monarchs, Mahendra of Kosala, Vyághrarája of Mahá Kántára,[7] Mundarája of Kauráttá,[8] Svámidatta of Paishtapura Mahendra-Giri and Auṭṭura[9], Damana of Airaṇḍapallaka, Vishṇu of Káñchí, Nílarája S'ápávamukta,[10] Hastivarman of Veṅgí, Ugrasena of Pálaka,[11]

---

[1] Compare Wilson's Ariana Antiqua, Pl. XVIII. Fig. 8, which has the same legend with *me* for *mama*. [2] Smith J. R. A. S. (N. S.) XXI. Pl. I. 11, 12.

[3] Smith J. R. A. S. (N. S.) XXI. Pl. I. 4.

[4] Smith J. R. A. S. (N. S.) XXI. Pl. I. Mr. Smith reads *Lichchhavayaḥ* (the Lichchhavis) and assigns this type to Chandragupta I.

[5] Corpus Ins. Ind. III. 1. [6] Smith J. R. A. S. (N. S.) XXI. Pl. I. 5, 6.

[7] Apparently South Kosala, the country about Raipur and Chhattisgarh.

[8] Fleet reads Maṇṭarája of Keraḷa.

[9] Fleet divides the words differently and translates "Mahendra of Pishṭapura, Svámidatta of Koṭṭúra on the hill."

[10] Fleet reads "Nílarája of Avamukta." [11] Fleet reads Palakka or Pálakka.

Chapter VII.
THE GUPTAS, A.D. 410-470.
Samudragupta, A.D. 370-395.

Kubera of Daivaráshṭra, and Dhanamjaya of Kausthalapura. Line 21 gives a further list of nine kings of Áryávarta exterminated by Samudragupta:

Rudradeva.	Chandravarman.	Achyuta.
Matila.	Gaṇapatinága.	Nandin.
Nágadatta.	Nágasena.	Balavarmman.

As no reference is made to the territories of these kings they may be supposed to be well known neighbouring rulers. General Cunningham's coins and others obtained at Mathurá show that the fifth ruler Gaṇapatinága was one of the Nága kings of Gwálior and Narwár.[1] The inscription next mentions that Samudragupta took into his employ the chiefs of the forest countries. Then in lines 22 and 23 follows a list of countries whose kings gave him tribute, who obeyed his orders, and who came to pay homage. The list includes the names of many frontier countries and the territories of powerful contemporary kings. The frontier kingdoms are:[2]

Samataṭa. Ḍaváka. Kámarúpa. Nepála. Karttṛika.

The Indian kingdoms are:[3]

Málava.	Mádraka.	Sanakáníka.
Arjunáyana.	Ábhíra.	Káka.
Yauddheya.	Prárjuna.	Kharaparika.

Mention is next made of kings who submitted, gave their daughters in marriage, paid tribute, and requested the issue of the Garuḍa or Eagle charter to secure them in the enjoyment of their territory.[4] The tribal names of these kings are:[5]

Devaputra.	Saka.
Sháhi.	Muruṇḍa.
Sháhánusháhi.	Saiṃhalaka.

Island Kings.

---

[1] Arch. Surv. II. 310; J. B. A. S. 1865. 115-121.

[2] Samataṭa is the Ganges delta: Daváka may, as Mr. Fleet suggests, be Dacca: for Karttṛika Mr. Fleet reads Kartṛipura, otherwise Cuttack might be intended.

[3] For the Málavas see above page 24. The Arjunáyanas can hardly be the Kalachuris as Mr. Fleet (C. I. I. III. 10) has suggested, as Varáha Mihira (Bṛ. S. XIV. 25) places the Arjunáyanas in the north near Trigarta, and General Cunningham's coin (Coins of Ancient India, 90) points to the same region. The Yaudheyas lived on the lower Sutlej: see above page 36. The Mádrakas lived north-east of the Yaudheyas between the Chenáb and the Sutlej (Cunningham Anc. Geog. 185). The Ábhíras must be those on the south-east border of Sindh. The Prárjunas do not appear to be identifiable. A Sanakáníka Mahárája is mentioned (C. I. I. III. 3) as dedicating an offering at Udayagiri near Bhilsá, but we have no clue to the situation of his government. The name of his grandfather, Chhagalaga, has a Turkí look. Káka may be Kákúpur near Bithúr (Cunningham Anc. Geog. 386). Kharaparika has not been identified.—(A. M. T. J.)

[4] Mr. Fleet translates "(giving) Garuḍa-tokens, (surrendering) the enjoyment of their own territories."

[5] The first three names Devaputra, Sháhi, and Sháhánusháhi, belong to the Kushán dynasty of Kanishka (A.D. 78). Sháhánusháhi is the oldest, as it appears on the coins from Kanishka downwards in the form Sháhanáno Sháho (Stein in Babylonian and Oriental Record, I. 163). It represents the old Persian title Sháhansháh or king of kings. Sháhi, answering to the simple Sháh, appears to be first used alone by Vásudeva (A.D 128-176). The title of Devaputra occurs first in the inscriptions of Kanishka. In the present inscription all three titles seem to denote divisions of the Kushán empire in

Chapter VII.

THE GUPTAS, A.D. 410-470.

Samudragupta, A.D. 370-395.

The inscribed pillar is said to have been set up by the great Captain or Dandanáyaka named Tilabhaṭṭanáyaka.

This important inscription shows that Samudragupta's dominions included Mathurá, Oudh, Gorakhpur, Allahábád, Benares, Behár, Tirhut, Bengal, and part of East Rájputána. The list of Dakhan and South Indian kingdoms does not necessarily imply that they formed part of Samudragupta's territory. Samudragupta may have made a victorious campaign to the far south and had the countries recorded in the order of his line of march. The order suggests that he went from Behár, by way of Gayá, to Kosala the country about the modern Ráipur in the Central Provinces, and from Kosala, by Ganjam and other places in the Northern Circars, as far as Káñchí or Conjeveram forty-six miles south-west of Madras. Málwa is shown in the second list as a powerful allied kingdom. It does not appear to have formed part of Samudragupta's territory nor, unless the Śakas are the Kshatrapas, does any mention of Gujarát occur even as an allied state.

Chandragupta II. A.D. 396-415.

Samudragupta was succeeded by his son Chandragupta II. whose mother was the queen Dattádeví. He was the greatest and most powerful king of the Gupta dynasty and added largely to the territory left by Samudragupta. His second name Vikramáditya or the Sun of Prowess appears on his coins. Like his father Chandragupta II. struck gold coins of various types. He was the first Gupta ruler who spread his power over Málwa and Gujarát which he apparently took from the Kshatrapas as he was the first Gupta to strike silver coins and as his silver coins of both varieties the eastern and the western are modifications of the Kshatrapa type. The expedition which conquered Málwa seems to have passed from Allahábád by Bundelkhand to Bhilsá and thence to Málwa. An undated inscription in the Udayagiri caves at Vidiśá (the modern Besnagar) near Bhilsa records the making of a cave of Mahádeva by one S'ába of the Kautsa gotra and the family name of Vírasena, a poet and native of Pâṭaliputra who held the hereditary office of minister of peace and war *sandhivigrahika*, and who is recorded to have arrived with the king who was intent upon conquering the whole earth.[1] A neighbouring cave bears an inscription of a feudatory of Chandragupta who was chief of Sanakáníka.[2] The chief's name is lost, but the names of his father Vishnudása and of his grandfather Chhagalaga remain. The date is the eleventh of the bright half of

India. The title of Sháhi was continued by the Turks (A.D. 600 ?-900) and Bráhmans (A.D. 900-1000) of Kábul (Alberuni, II. 10) and by the Sháhis (Elliot, I. 138) of Alor in Sindh (A.D. 490 ?-631). Unless it refers to the last remnants of the Gujarát Mahákshatrapas the word S'aka seems to be used in a vague sense in reference to the non-Indian tribes of the North-West frontier. The Muruṇḍas may be identified with the Muruṇḍas of the Native dictionaries, and hence with the people of Lampáka or Lamghán twenty miles north-west of Jalálábád. It is notable that in the fifth century A.D. Jayanátha, Mahárája of Uchchakalpa (not identified) married a Muruṇḍadeví (Corp. Ins. Ind. III. 128, 131, 136).

The mention of the king of Siṃhala and the Island Kings rounds off the geographical picture. Possibly after the Chinese fashion presents from these countries may have been magnified into tribute. Or Siṃhala may here stand, not for Ceylon, but for one of the many Siṃhapuras known to Indian geography. Sihor in Káthiáváda, an old capital, may possibly be the place referred to. The Island Kings would then be the chiefs of Cutch and Káthiáváda.—(A. M. T. J.)

[1] Corp. Ins. Ind. III. Ins. 6. [2] Corp. Ins. Ind. III. Ins. 3.

Chapter VII.
The Guptas, A.D. 410-470.
Chandragupta II. A.D. 396-415.

Ashádha Samvatsara 82 (A.D. 401). From this Chandragupta's conquest of Vidiśá may be dated about Samvatsara 80 (A.D. 399) or a little earlier.

A third inscription is on the railing of the great Sáñchi stúpa.[1] It is dated the 4th day of Bhádrapada Samvat 93 (A.D. 412) and records the gift of 25 *dínáras* and something called Íśvaravásaka (perhaps a village or a field) to the monks of the great monastery of Kákanádabotaśrí for the daily maintenance of five *bhikshus* and the burning of a lamp in the *ratnagriha* or shrine of the Buddhist *triratna*, for the merit of the supreme king of great kings Chandragupta who bears the popular name of Devarája or god-like.[2] The donor a feudatory of Chandragupta named Ámrakárdava is described as having the object of his life gratified by the favour of the feet of the supreme ruler of great kings the illustrious Chandragupta, and as showing to the world the hearty loyalty of a good feudatory. Ámrakárdava seems to have been a chief of consequence as he is described as winning the flag of glory in numerous battles. The name of his kingdom is also recorded. Though it cannot now be made out the mention of his kingdom makes it probable that he was a stranger come to pay homage to Chandragupta. The reference to Chandragupta seems to imply he was the ruler of the land while the two other inscriptions show that his rule lasted from about 80 (A.D. 399) to at least 93 (A.D. 412). During these years Chandragupta seems to have spread his sway to Ujjain the capital of west Málwa, of which he is traditionally called the ruler. From Ujjain by way of Bágh and Tánda in the province of Ráth he seems to have entered South Gujarát and to have passed from the Broach coast to Káthiáváda. He seems to have wrested Káthiáváda from its Kshatrapa rulers as he is the first Gupta who struck silver coins and as his silver coins are of the then current Kshatrapa type. On the obverse is the royal bust with features copied from the Kshatrapa face and on the reverse is the figure of a peacock, probably chosen as the bearer of Kártikasvámi the god of war. Round the peacock is a Sanskrit legend. This legend is of two varieties. In Central Indian coins it runs:

श्री गुप्तकुलस्य महाराजाधिराज श्री चंद्रगुप्तविक्रमाङ्कस्य

Srí Guptakulasya Mahárájadhirája Srí Chandraguptavikramáñkasya.

(Coin) of the king of kings the illustrious Chandragupta Vikramáñka, of the family of the illustrious Gupta.[3]

In the very rare Káthiáváda coins, though they are similar to the above in style, the legend runs:

परमभागवत महाराजाधिराज श्री चन्द्रगुप्त विक्रमादित्य

Paramabhágavata Mahárájádhirája Srí Chandragupta Vikramáditya.

The great devotee of Vishnu the supreme ruler of great kings, the illustrious Chandragupta Vikramáditya.[4]

Several gold coins of Chandragupta show a young male figure behind the king with his right hand laid on the king's shoulder. This youthful figure is apparently Chandragupta's son Kumáragupta who may have acted as Yuvarája during the conquest of Málwa.

---

1 Corp. Ins. Ind. III. Ins. 5.

2 Mr. Fleet (Corp. Ins. Ind. III. Ins. 33) prefers to take Devarája to be the name of Chandragupta's minister.

3 J. R. A. S. (N. S.) XXI. 120.

4 J. R. A. S. (N. S.) XXI. 121.

Chandragupta II. A.D. 396 - 415.

The rareness of Chandragupta's and the commonness of Kumáragupta's coins in Káthiáváḍa, together with the date 90 (A.D. 409) on some of Kumarágupta's coins make it probable that on their conquest his father appointed Kumâragupta viceroy of Gujarát and Káthiáváḍa.

As the first Gupta was a chief of no great power or influence it is probable that though it is calculated from him the Gupta era was established not by him but by his grandson the great Chandragupta II.[1] This view is confirmed by the absence of dates on all existing coins of Chandragupta's father Samudragupta. It further seems probable that like the Málavas in B.C. 57 and the Kshatrapas in A.D. 78 the occasion on which Chandragupta established the Gupta era was his conquest of Málwa. The Gupta era did not remain long in use. After the fall of Gupta power (A.D. 470) the old Málava era of B.C. 57 was revived. The conjecture may be offered that, in spite of the passing away of Gupta power, under his title of Vikramáditya, the fame of the great Gupta conqueror Chandragupta II. lived on in Málwa and that, drawing to itself tales of earlier local champions, the name Vikramáditya came to be considered the name of the founder of the Málava era.[2]

Working back from Gupta Saṁvat 80 (A.D. 400) the date of Chandragupta's conquest of Málwa we may allot 1 to 12 (A.D. 319 - 332) to the founder Gupta: 12 to 29 (A.D. 332 - 349) to Gupta's son Ghaṭotkacha: 29 to 49 (A.D. 349 - 369) to Ghaṭotkacha's son Chandragupta I.: and 50 to 75 (A.D. 370 - 395) to Chandragupta's powerful son Samudragupta who probably had a long reign. As the latest known date of Chandragupta II. is 93 (A.D. 413) and as a Bilsad inscription[3] of his successor Kumáragupta is dated 96 (A.D. 416) the reign of Chandragupta II. may be calculated to have lasted during the twenty years ending 95 (A.D. 415).

---

[1] Mr. Fleet (Corp. Ins. Ind. III. Introd. 130ff) argues that the era was borrowed from Nepal after Chandragupta I. married his Lichchhavi queen. Dr. Bühler thinks there is no evidence of this, and that the era was started by the Guptas themselves (Vienna Or. Jl. V. Pt. 3).

[2] The further suggestion may be offered that if as seems probable Dr. Bhagvánlál is correct in considering Chandragupta II. to be the founder of the Gupta era this high honour was due not to his conquest of Málwa but to some success against the Indo-Skythians or Sakas of the Punjáb. The little more than nominal suzerainty claimed over the Devputras, Sháhis, and Sháhánusháhis in Chandragupta's father's inscription shows that when he came to the throne Chandragupta found the Saka power practically unbroken. The absence of reference to conquests is no more complete in the case of the Panjáb than it is in the case of Gujarát or of Káthiáváda which Chandragupta is known to have added to his dominions. In Káthiáváda, though not in Gujarát, the evidence from coins is stronger than in the Panjáb. Still the discovery of Chandragupta's coins (J. R. A. S. XXI. 5 note 1) raises the presumption of conquests as far north and west as Panipat and as Ludhiána (in the heart of the Panjáb). Chandragupta's name Devarája may, as Pandit Bhagvánlál suggests, be taken from the Saka title Devaputra. Further, the use of the name Vikramáditya and of the honorific Srí is in striking agreement with Beruni's statement (Sachau, II. 6) that the conqueror of the Sakas was named Vikramáditya and that to the conqueror's name was added the title Srí. Mr. Fleet (Corp. Ins. Ind. III. 37 note 2) holds it not improbable that either Chandragupta I. or II. defeated the Indo-Skythians. The fact that Chandragupta I. was not a ruler of sufficient importance to issue coins and that even after his son Samudragupta's victories the Sakas remained practically independent make it almost certain that if any subjection of the Sakas to the Guptas took place it happened during the reign of Chandragupta II.

[3] Corp. Ins. Ind. III. Ins. 10.

Chapter VII.
THE GUPTAS, A.D. 410-470.
Kumáragupta, A.D. 416-453.

Chandragupta II. was succeeded by his son Kumáragupta whose mother was the queen Dhruva-Deví. On Kumáragupta's coins three titles occur: Mahendra, Mahendra-Vikrama, and Mahendráditya. As already noticed the circulation of Kumáragupta's coins in Káthiáváḍa during his father's reign makes it probable that on their conquest his father appointed him viceroy of Káthiáváḍa and Gujarát. Kumarágupta appears to have succeeded his father about 96 (A.D. 416). An inscription at Mankuwár near Prayága shows he was ruling as late as 129 (A.D. 449) and a coin of his dated 130 (A.D. 450) adds at least one year to his reign. On the other hand the inscription on the Girnár rock shows that in 137 (A.D. 457) his son Skandagupta was king. It follows that Kumáragupta's reign ended between 130 and 137 (A.D. 450-457) or about 133 (A.D. 453).

None of Kumáragupta's four inscriptions gives any historical or other details regarding him.[1] But the number and the wide distribution of his coins make it probable that during his long reign he maintained his father's dominions intact.

Large numbers of Kumáragupta's coins of gold silver and copper have been found. The gold which are of various types are inferior in workmanship to his father's coins. The silver and copper coins are of two varieties, eastern and western. Both varieties have on the obverse the royal bust in the Kshatrapa style of dress. In the western pieces the bust is a copy of the moustached Kshatrapa face with a corrupted version of the corrupt Greek legend used by the Kshatrapas. The only difference between the obverses of the Western Gupta and the Kshatrapa coins is that the date is in the Gupta instead of in the Kshatrapa era. On the reverse is an ill formed peacock facing front as in Chandragupta II.'s coins. The legend runs:

परम भागवत महाराजाधिराज श्री कुमारगुप्त महेन्द्रादित्य.

Paramabhágavata Mahárájádhirája S'rí Kumáragupta Mahendráditya.

The great Vaishnava the supreme ruler of great kings, the illustrious Kumáragupta Mahendráditya.[2]

In Kumáragupta's eastern silver and copper coins the bust on the obverse has no moustache nor is there any trace of the corrupt Greek legend. The date is in front of the face in perpendicular numerals one below the other instead of behind the head as in the Kshatrapa and Western Kumáragupta coins. On the reverse is a well-carved peacock facing front with tail feathers at full stretch. Round the peacock runs the clear cut legend:

विजितावनिरवनिपति कुमारगुप्तो देवं जयति.

Vijitávaniravanipati Kumáragupto devaṃ jayati.

This legend is hard to translate. It seems to mean:

Kumáragupta, lord of the earth, who had conquered the kings of the earth, conquers the Deva.

---

[1] Corp. Ins. Ind. III. Ins. 8, 9, 10 and 11.

[2] J. R. A. S. (N. S.) XXI. 123.

Chapter VII.

The Guptas, A.D. 410-470.

Skandagupta, A.D. 454-470.

Probably the Deva whose name suggested the antithesis between the kings of the earth and the gods was one of tho Devaputra family of Indo-Skythian rulers.[1]

Kumáragupta was succeeded by his son Skandagupta. An inscription of his on a pillar at Bhitarí near Saidpur in Ghásipur bearing no date shows that on his father's death Skandagupta had a hard struggle to establish his power.[2] The text runs: "By whom when he rose to fix fast again the shaken fortune of his house, three months[3] were spent on the earth as on a bed," an apparent reference to flight and wanderings. A doubtful passage in the same inscription seems to show that he was opposed by a powerful king named Pushyamitra on whose back he is said to have set his left foot.[4] The inscription makes a further reference to the troubles of the family stating that on re-establishing the shaken fortune of his house Skandagupta felt satisfied and went to see his weeping afflicted mother. Among the enemies with whom Skandagupta had to contend the inscription mentions a close conflict with the Húnas that is the Ephthalites, Thetals, or White Huns.[5] Verse 3 of Skandagupta's Girnár inscription confirms the reference to struggles stating that on the death of his father by his own might he humbled his enemies to the earth and established himself. As the Girnár inscription is dated 136 (A.D. 456) and as Kumáragupta's reign ended about 134, these troubles and difficulties did not last for more than two years. The Girnár inscription further states that on establishing his power he conquered the earth, destroyed the arrogance of his enemies, and appointed governors in all provinces. For Suráshṭra he selected a governor named Parṇadatta and to Parṇadatta's son Chakrapálita he gave a share of the management placing him in charge of Junágaḍh city. During the governorship of Parṇadatta the Sudarsána lake close to Junágaḍh, which had been strongly rebuilt in the time of the Kshatrapa Rudradáman (A.D. 150), again gave way during the dark sixth of Bhádrapada of the year 136 (A.D. 456). The streams Palásiní Sikatá and Vilásiní[6] burst through the dam and flowed unchecked. Repairs were begun on the first of bright *Gríshma* 137 (A.D. 457) and finished in two months. The new dam is said to have been 100 cubits

---

[1] J. R. A. S. (N. S.) XXI. 126. That Kumáragupta's two successors, Skandagupta and Budhagupta, use the same phrase *devaṃ jayati* makes the explanation in the text doubtful. As Mr. Smith (Ditto) suggests *devaṃ* is probably a mistake for *devo*, meaning His Majesty. The legend would then run; Kumaraguptadeva lord of the earth . . . . . . is triumphant. Dr. Bhagvánlál would have preferred *devo* (see page 70 note 2) but could not neglect the *anusvára*.—(A. M. T. J.)

[2] Corp. Ins. Ind. III. Ins. 13.

[3] Mr. Fleet (Corp. Ins. Ind. III. 53, 55) reads "*nítá triyámá*" and translates "a (whole) night was spent." Dr. Bhagvánlál read "*nítás trimásáḥ*."

[4] Mr. Fleet finds that Pushyamitra is the name of a tribe not of a king. No. VI. of Dr. Bühler's Jain inscriptions from Mathurá (Ep. Ind. I. 378ff) mentions a Pushyamitriya-kula of the Váraṇagaṇa, which is also referred to in Bhadrabáhu's Kalpa-sútra (Jacobi's Edition, 80), but is there referred to the Cháraṇa-gaṇa, no doubt a misreading for the Váraṇa of the inscription. Dr. Bühler points out that Varaṇa is the old name of Bulandshahr in the North-West Provinces, so that it is there that we must look for the power that first weakened the Guptas.—(A. M. T. J.)

[5] See V. de St. Martin's Essay, Les Huns Blancs; Specht in Journal Asiatique Oct.-Dec. 1883 and below page 74.

[6] In Rudradáman's inscription the Palásiní is mentioned, and also the Suvarṇasikatás "and the other rivers." In Skandagupta's inscription Mr. Fleet translates Sikatávilásiní as an adjective agreeing with Palásiní.

Chapter VII.

The Guptas, A.D. 410-470.

Skandagupta, A.D. 454-470.

long by 68 cubits broad and 7 men or about 38 feet high. The probable site of the lake is in the west valley of the Girnár hill near what is called Bhavanátha's pass.[1] The inscription also records the making of a temple of Vishṇu in the neighbourhood by Chakrapálita, which was probably on the site of the modern Dámodar's Mandir in the Bhavanátha pass, whose image is of granite and is probably as old as the Guptas. A new temple was built in the fifteenth century during the rule of Mandalika the last Chuḍásamá ruler of Junágaḍh. At the time of the Musalmán conquest (A.D. 1484) as violence was feared the images were removed and buried. Mandalika's temple was repaired by Amarji Diván of Junágaḍh (1759-1784). It was proposed to make and consecrate new images. But certain old images of Vishṇu were found in digging foundations for the enclosure wall and were consecrated. Two of these images were taken by Girnára Bráhmans and consecrated in the names of Baladevji and Revatí in a neighbouring temple specially built for them. Of the original temple the only trace is a pilaster built into the wall to the right as one enters. The style and carving are of the Gupta period.

As almost all the Gupta coins found in Cutch are Skandagupta's and very few are Kumáragupta's, Skandagupta seems to have added Cutch to the provinces of Gujarát and Káthiáváḍa inherited from his father. In Káthiáváḍa Skandagupta's coins are rare, apparently because of the abundant currency left by his father which was so popular in Káthiáváḍa that fresh Kumáragupta coins of a degraded type were issued as late as Valabhi times.

Like his father, Skandagupta issued a gold coinage in his eastern dominions but no trace of a gold currency appears in the west. Like Kumáragupta's his silver coins were of two varieties, eastern and western. The eastern coins have on the obverse a bust as in Kumáragupta's coins and the date near the face. On the reverse is a peacock similar to Kumáragupta's and round the peacock the legend :

विजितावनिरवनिपति जयति देवं स्कन्दगुप्तो यं

Vijitávaniravanipati jayati devaṃ Skandagupto'yaṃ.

This king Skandagupta who having conquered the earth conquers the Deva.[2]

Skandagupta's western coins are of three varieties, one the same as the western coins of Kumáragupta, a second with a bull instead of a peacock on the reverse, and a third with on the reverse an altar with one upright and two side jets of water. Coins of the first two varieties are found both in Gujarát and in Káthiáváḍa. The third water-jet variety is peculiar to Cutch and is an entirely new feature in the western Gupta coinage. On the reverse of all is the legend :

परमभागवत महाराजाधिराज स्कन्दगुप्त क्रमादित्य

Paramabhágavata Mahárájadhirája Skandagupta Kramáditya.

The great Vaishnava the supreme ruler of great kings,
Skandagupta the Sun of Prowess.[3]

---

[1] Remains of the dam were discovered in 1890 by Khán Bahádur Ardesir Jamsetji Special Diván of Junágaḍh. The site is somewhat nearer Junágaḍh than Dr. Bhagvánlál supposed. Details are given in Jour. B. B. R. A. S. XVIII. Number 48 page 47.

[2] The reading *devo* is to be preferred but the *anusvára* is clear both on these coins and on the coins of his father. For these coins see J. R. A. S. (N. S.) XXI. Pl. IV. 4.

[3] J. R. A. S. (N. S.) XXI. Pl. IV. 6-7.

Chapter VII.

The Guptas, A.D. 410-470.

Bhudagupta, A.D. 485.

The beginning of Skandagupta's reign has been placed about Gupta 133 or A.D. 453: his latest known date on a coin in General Cunningham's collection is Gupta 149 or A.D. 469.[1]

With Skandagupta the regular Gupta succession ceases.[2] The next Gupta is Budhagupta who has a pillar inscription[3] in a temple at Eraṇ in the Saugor district dated 165 (A.D. 485) and silver coins dated Saṃvat 174 and 180 odd (A.D. 494 - 500 odd). Of Budhagupta's relation or connection with Skandagupta nothing is known. That he belonged to the Gupta dynasty appears from his name as well as from his silver coins which are dated in the Gupta era and are the same in style as the eastern coins of Skandagupta. On the obverse is the usual bust as in Skandagupta's coins with the date (174, 180 odd) near the face. On the reverse is the usual peacock and the legend is the same as Skandagupta's:

देवं जयति विजितावनिरवनिपति श्री बुधगुप्तो

Devaṁ jayati vijitávaniravanipati S'rí Budhagupto.

The king the illustrious Budhagupta who has conquered the earth conquers the Deva.[4]

Since the coins are dated Saṃvat 174 and 180 odd (A.D. 494 and 500 odd) and the inscription's date is 165 (A.D. 485) the inscription may be taken to belong to the early part of Budhagupta's reign the beginning of which may be allotted to about 160-162 (A.D. 480-482). As this is more than ten years later than the latest known date of Skandagupta (G. 149 A.D. 469) either a Gupta of whom no trace remains must have intervened or the twelve blank years must have been a time of political change and disturbance. The absence of any trace of a gold currency suggests that Budhagupta had less power than his predecessors. The correctness of this argument is placed beyond doubt by the pillar inscription opposite the shrine in the Eraṇ temple where instead of his predecessor's title of monarch of the whole earth Budhagupta is styled protector of the land between the Jamna (Kálindí) and the Narbádá implying the loss of the whole territory to the east of the Jamna.[5] In the west the failure of Gupta power seems still more complete. Neither in Gujarát nor in Káthiáváḍa has an inscription or even a coin been found with a reference to Budhagupta or to any other Gupta ruler later than Skandagupta (G. 149 A.D. 469). The pillar inscription noted above which is of the year 165 (A.D. 485) and under the rule of Budhagupta states that the pillar was a gift to the temple by Dhanya Vishṇu and his brother Mátṛi Vishṇu who at the time of the gift seem to have been local Bráhman governors. A second inscription on the lower part of the neck of a huge Boar or Varáha image in a corner shrine of the same temple records that the image was completed on the tenth day of Phálguna in the first year of the reign of

---

[1] The known dates of Skandagupta are 136 and 137 on his Girnár inscription, 141 in his pillar inscription at Kahaon in Gorakhpur, and 146 in his Indor-Khera copperplate. The coin dates given by General Cunningham are 144, 145, and 149.

[2] But see below page 73.

[3] Dr. Bhagvánlál examined and copied the original of this inscription. It has since been published as Number 19 in Mr. Fleet's Corp. Ins. Ind. III.

[4] J. R. A. S (N. S.) XXI. 134.

[5] It is now known that the main Gupta line continued to rule in Magadha. See page 73 below.

Chapter VII.

THE GUPTAS, A.D. 410-470.

Bhudagupta, A.D. 485.

Toramáṇa the supreme ruler of great kings and was the gift of the same Dhanya Vishṇu whose brother Mátṛi Vishṇu is described as gone to heaven.[1] Since Mátṛi was alive in the Budhagupta and was dead in the Toramáṇa inscription it follows that Toramáṇa was later than Budhagupta. His name and his new era show that Toramáṇa was not a Gupta. A further proof that Toramáṇa wrested the kingdom from Budhagupta is that except the change of era and that the bust turns to the left instead of to the right, Toramáṇa's silver coins are directly adapted from Gupta coins of the eastern type.

Certain coin dates seem at variance with the view that Toramáṇa flourished after Budhagupta. On several coins the date 52 is clear. As Toramáṇa's coins are copies of the coins of Kumáragupta and Skandagupta and as most of these coins have a numeral for one hundred the suggestion may be offered that a one dropped out in striking Toramáṇa's die and that this date should read 152 not 52. Accepting this view Toramáṇa's date would be 152 (A.D. 472) that is immediately after the death of Skandagupta.

The Gwálior inscription[2] mentions prince Mihirakula as the son of Toramáṇa and a second inscription from a well in Mandasor[3] dated Málava Saṃvat 589 (A.D. 533) mentions a king named Yas'odharman who was ruler of Málwa when the well was built and who in a second Mandasor inscription[4] is mentioned as having conquered Mihirakula. This would separate Mihirakula from his father Toramáṇa (A.D. 471) by more than sixty years. In explanation of this gap it may be suggested that the [1]52 (A.D. 472) coins were struck early in Toramáṇa's reign in honour of his conquest of the eastern Gupta territory. A reign of twenty years would bring Toramáṇa to 177 (A.D. 497). The Gwálior inscription of Mihirakula is in the fifteenth year of his reign that is on the basis of a succession date of 177 (A.D. 497) in Gupta 192 (A.D. 512). An interval of five years would bring Yaśodharman's conquest of Mihirakula to 197 (A.D. 517). This would place the making of the well in the twenty-first year of Mihirakula's reign.

Bhánugupta, A.D. 511.

After Budhagupta neither inscription nor coin shows any trace of Gupta supremacy in Málwa. An Eraṇ inscription[5] found in 1869 on a *liṅga*-shaped stone, with the representation of a woman performing *satí*, records the death in battle of a king Goparájá who is mentioned as the daughter's son of Śarabharája and appears to have been the son of king Mádhava. Much of the inscription is lost. What remains records the passing to heaven of the deceased king in the very destructive fight with the great warrior (*pravíra*) Bhánugupta brave as Pártha. The inscription is dated the seventh of dark Bhádrapada Gupta 191 in words as well as in numerals that is in A.D. 511. This Bhánugupta would be the successor of Budhagupta ruling over a petty Málwa principality which lasted till nearly the time of the great Harshavardhana the beginning of the seventh century (A.D. 607-650), as a Devagupta of Málwa is one of Rájyavardhana's rivals in the Śrīharshacharita. While Gupta power failed in Málwa

[1] Published by Mr. Fleet Corp. Ins. Ind. III. Ins. 36.
[2] Fleet Corp. Ins. Ind. III. Ins. 37.
[3] Fleet Corp. Ins. Ind. III. Ins. 35.
[4] Fleet Corp. Ins. Ind. III. Ins. 33.
[5] Fleet Corp. Ins. Ind. III. Ins. 20.

Chapter VII.

The Guptas, A.D. 410-470.

and disappeared from Western India a fresh branch of the Guptas rose in Magadha or Behár and under Naragupta Báláditya, perhaps the founder of the eastern branch of the later Gupta dynasty, attained the dignity of a gold coinage.[1]

The Pushyamitras, A.D. 455.

[Though the history of their last years is known only in fragments, chiefly from inscriptions and coins, little doubt remains regarding the power which first seriously weakened the early Guptas. The Bhitari stone pillar of Skandagupta[2] speaks of his restoring the fortunes of his family and conquering the Pushyamitras and also of his joining in close conflict with the Húṇas.[3] Unfortunately the Bhitari inscription is not dated. The Junágaḍh inscription, which bears three dates covering the period between A.D. 455 and 458,[4] mentions pride-broken enemies in the country of the Mlechchhas admitting Skandagupta's victory. That the Mlechchhas of this passage refers to the Huns is made probable by the fact that it does not appear that the Pushyamitras were Mlechchhas while they and the Huns are the only enemies whom Skandagupta boasts either of defeating or of meeting in close conflict. It may therefore be assumed that the Huns became known to Skandagupta before A.D. 455. As according to the Chinese historians[5] the White Huns did not cross the Oxus into Baktria before A.D. 452, the founding of the Hun capital of Badeghis[6] may be fixed between A.D. 452 and 455. As the above quoted inscriptions indicate that the Huns were repulsed in their first attempt to take part in Indian politics the disturbances during the last years of Kumáragupta's reign were probably due to some tribe other than the Huns. This tribe seems to have been the Pushyamitras whose head-quarters would seem to have been in Northern India. Some other enemy must have arisen in Málwa

---

[1] On Naragupta see below page 77, and for his coins J. R. A. S. (N. S.) XXI. note Pl. III. 11. [2] Fleet's Corp. Ins. Ind. III. Ins. 13 lines 10 and 15.

[3] The Pushyamitras seem to have been a long established tribe like the Yaudheyas (above page 37). During the reign of Kanishka (A.D. 78-93) Pushyamitras were settled in the neighbourhood of Bulandshahr and at that time had already given their name to a Jain sect.

The sense of the inscription is somewhat doubtful. Mr. Fleet (Corp. Ins. Ind. III. page 62) translates: Whose fame, moreover, even (his) enemies in the countries of the Mlechchhas . . . . . having their pride broken down to the very root announce with the words 'Verily the victory has been achieved by him.' Prof. Peterson understands the meaning to be that Skandagupta's Indian enemies were forced to retire beyond the borders of India among friendly Mlechchhas and in a foreign land admit that the renewal of their conflict with Skandagupta was beyond hope. The retreat of Skandagupta's Indian enemies to the Mlechchhas suggests the Mlechchhas are the Húṇas that is the White Huns who were already in power on the Indian border, whom the enemies had previously in vain brought as allies into India to help them against Skandagupta. This gives exactness to the expression used in Skandagupta's Bhitari inscription (Corp. Ins. Ind. III. Number 13 page 56) that he joined in close conflict with the Húṇas . . . . . . among enemies, as if in this conflict the Húṇas were the allies of enemies rather than the enemies themselves. For the introduction into India of foreign allies, compare in B.C. 327 (McCrindle's Alexander in India, 412) the king of Taxila, 34 miles north-west of Ráwalpindi, sending an embassy to Baktria to secure Alexander as an ally against Porus of the Gujarát country. And (Ditto, 409) a few years later (B.C. 310) the North Indian Malayaketu allying himself with Yavanas in his attack on Pátaliputra or Patna.

[4] Fleet's Corp. Ins. Ind. III. Ins. 14 line 4.

[5] T'oungtien quoted by Specht in Journal Asiatique for Oct. - Dec. 1883.

[6] Badeghis is the modern Badhyr the upper plateau between the Merv and the Herat rivers. The probable site of the capital of the White Huns is a little north of Herat. See Marco Polo's Itineraries No. I.; Yule's Marco Polo, I. xxxii.

Chapter VII.

THE GUPTAS, A.D. 410-470.

The Pushyamitras, A.D. 455.

since the terms of Parṇadatta's appointment to Suráshṭra in A.D. 455-6 suggest that country had been lost to the Gupta empire and re-conquered by Skandagupta which would naturally be the case if a rival state had arisen in Málwa and been overthrown by that king. So far as is known the Huns made no successful attack on the Gupta empire during the lifetime of Skandagupta whose latest date is A.D. 468-9. It is not certain who succeeded Skandagupta. His brother Pura(or Sthira-)gupta ruled in or near Magadha. But it is not certain whether he was the successor or the rival of Skandagupta.[1] That Skandagupta's inscriptions are found in the Patna district in the east[2] and in Káthiáváḍa in the west[3] suggests that during his life the empire was not divided nor does any one of his inscriptions hint at a partition. The probability is that Skandagupta was succeeded by his brother Puragupta, who again was followed by his son Narasiṁhagupta and his grandson Kumáragupta II.[4]

White Huns, A.D. 450-520.

Among the northerners who with or shortly after the Pushyamitras shared in the overthrow of Gupta power two names, a father and a son, Toramáṇa and Mihirakula are prominent. It is not certain that these kings were Húṇas by race. Their tribe were almost certainly his rivals' allies whom Skandagupta's Bhitari and Junágaḍh inscriptions style the one Húṇas the other Mlechchhas.[5] On one of Toramáṇa's coins Mr. Fleet reads[6] the date 52 which he interprets as a regnal date. This though not impossible is somewhat unlikely. The date of Mihirakula's succession to his father is fixed somewhere about A.D. 515.[7] In the neighbourhood of Gwálior he reigned at least fifteen years.[8] The story of Mihirakula's interview with Báláditya's mother and his long subsequent history[9] indicate that when he came to the throne he was a young man probably not more than 25. If his father reigned fifty-two years he must have been at least 70 when he died and not less than 45 when Mihirakula was born. As Mihirakula is known to have had at least one younger brother,[10] it seems probable that Toramáṇa came to the throne a good deal later than A.D. 460 the date suggested by Mr. Fleet.[11] The date 52 on Toramáṇa's coins must therefore refer to some event other than his own accession. The suggestion may be offered that that event was the establishment of the White Huns in Baktria and the founding of their capital Badeghis,[12] which, as fixed above between A.D. 452 and 455, gives the very suitable date of A.D. 504 to 507 for the 52 of Toramáṇa's coin. If this suggestion is correct a further identification follows. The Chinese ambassador Sungyun (A.D. 520)[13]

---

[1] See the Ghazipur Seal. Smith & Hœrnle, J. A. S. Ben. LVIII. 84ff. and Fleet Ind. Ant. XIX. 224ff. [2] Bihar Ins. Fleet's Corp. Ins. Ind. III. Ins. 12.

[3] Junagadh Inscrip. Fleet's Corp. Ins. Ind. III. Ins. 14. [4] See note 1 above.

[5] See above notes 1 and 2. [6] Ind. Ant. XVIII. 225.

[7] Fleet's Corp. Ins. Ind. III. Introdn. 12. [8] Fleet's Corp. Ins. Ind. Ins. 37 line 4.

[9] Beal's Buddhist Records, I. 169-172 and Rájataranginí, I. 289-326 quoted by Fleet in Ind. Ant. XV. 247-249.

[10] Beale's Hiuen Tsiang, I. 169-171. As Mr. Fleet suggests the younger brother is possibly the Chandra referred to in Corp. Ins. Ind. III. Ins. 32 line 5 and Introd. 12 and 140 note 1. [11] Ind. Ant. XIII. 230 and Corp. Ins. Ind. III. Introdn. 12.

[12] Specht in Journal Asiatique for Oct.-Dec. 1883. Histoire des Wei.

[13] Beal's Buddhist Records, I. c.-cii.

Chapter VII.

The Guptas, A.D. 410-470.

White Huns, A.D. 450-520.

describes an interview with the king of Gandhára whose family Sungyun notices was established in power by the Ye-tha, that is the Ephthalites or White Huns, two generations before his time.[1] Mihirakula is known to have ruled in Gandhára[2] and Sungyun's description of the king's pride and activity agrees well with other records of Mihirakula's character. It seems therefore reasonable to suppose that the warlike sovereign who treated Sungyun and the name of his Imperial mistress with such scant courtesy was no other than the meteor Mihirakula. If Sungyun is correct in stating that Mihirakula was the third of his line the dynasty must have been established about A.D. 460. Beal is in doubt whether the name Lae-lih given by Sungyun[3] is the family name or the name of the founder. As a recently deciphered inscription shows Toramáṇa's family name to have been Jaúvla[4] it seems to follow that Lae-lih, or whatever is the correct transliteration of the Chinese characters, is the name of the father of Toramáṇa. Sungyun's reference to the establishment of this dynasty suggests they were not White Huns but leaders of some subject tribe.[5] That this tribe was settled in Baktria perhaps as far south as Kabul before the arrival of the White Huns seems probable. The Hindu or Persian influence notable in the tribal name Maitraka and in the personal name Mihirakula seems unsuited to Húṇas newly come from the northern frontiers of China and proud of their recent successes.[6] Chinese records show[7] that the tribe who preceded the White Huns in Baktria and north-east Persia, and who about A.D. 350-400 destroyed the power of Kitolo the last of the Kusháns, were the Yuan-Yuan or Jouen-Jouen whom Sir H. Howorth identifies with the Avars.[8] To this tribe it seems on the whole probable that

---

[1] Beal's Buddhist Records, I. xcix.-c.

[2] Beal's Buddhist Records, I. 171. Hiuen Tsiang's statement (Ditto) that Mihirakula conquered Gandhára after his capture by Báláditya may refer to a reconquest from his brother, perhaps the Chandra referred to in note 10 on page 74.

[3] Beal's Buddhist Records (I. c.) suggests that Lae-lih is the founder's name: in his note 50 he seems to regard Lae-lih as the family name.

[4] Bühler. Ep. Ind. I. 238. Dr. Bühler hesitates to identify the Toramáṇa of this inscription with Mihirakula's father.

[5] Beal's Buddhist Records, I. xcix.-c. This is the kingdom which the Ye-tha destroyed and afterwards set up Lae-lih to be king over the country.

[6] Maitraka is a Sanskritised form of Mihira and this again is perhaps an adaptation of the widespread and well-known Western Indian tribal name Mer or Med. Compare Fleet's Corp. Ins. Ind. III. 326-327. It is to be remembered that the name of the emperor then (A.D. 450-500) ruling the White Huns was Khushnawáz, a Persian name, the Happy Cherisher..... The emperor's Persian name, Mihirakula's reported (Darmsteter Jl. Asiatique, X. 70 n. 3) introduction of Magi into Kashmir, and the inaptness of Mihirakula as a personal name give weight to Mr. Fleet's suggestion (Ind. Ant. XV. 245-252) that Mihirakula is pure Persian. The true form may then be Mihiragula, that is Sun Rose, a name which the personal beauty of the prince may have gained him. 'I have heard of my son's wisdom and beauty and wish once to see his face' said the fate-reading mother of king Báláditya (Beal's Buddhist Records, I. 169) when the captive Mihirakula was led before her his young head for very shame shrouded in his cloak.

[7] Specht in Jour. Asiatique 1883 II. 335 and 348.

[8] J. R. A. S. XXI. 721. According to other accounts (Ency. Brit. IX. Ed. Art. Turk. page 658) a portion of the Jouen-Jouen remained in Eastern Asia, where, till A.D. 552, they were the masters of the Tuhkiu or Turks, who then overthrew their masters and about ten years later (A.D. 560) crushed the power of the White Huns.

Chapter VII.
THE GUPTAS, A.D. 460-470.
White Huns, A.D. 450-520.

Lae-lih the father of Toramáṇa belonged.[1] At the same time, though perhaps not themselves White Huns, the details regarding Toramáṇa and Mihirakula so nearly cover the fifty years (A.D. 470-530) of Húṇa ascendancy in North India that, as was in keeping with their position in charge of his Indian outpost, the White Hun emperor Khushnáwaz, while himself engaged in Central Asia and in Persia (A.D. 460-500),[2] seems to have entrusted the conquest of India to Toramáṇa and his son Mihirakula. Of the progress of the mixed Yuan-Yuan and White Hun invaders in India few details are available. Their ascendancy in the north seems to have been too complete to allow of opposition, and Húṇas were probably closely associated with the Maitraka or Mehara conquest of Káthiáváḍa (A.D. 480-520). The southern fringe of the White Hun dominions, the present Saugor district of the Central Provinces, seems to have been the chief theatre of war, a debateable ground between the Guptas, Toramáṇa, and the Malwa chiefs. To the east of Saugor the Guptas succeeded in maintaining their power until at least A.D. 528-9.[3] To the west of Saugor the Guptas held Eraṇ in A.D. 484-5.[4] About twenty years later (A.D. 505)[5] Eraṇ was in the hands of Toramáṇa, and in A.D. 510-11 Bhánugupta[6] fought and apparently won a battle at Eraṇ.

Mihirakula, A.D. 512.

Mihirakula's accession to the throne may perhaps be fixed at A.D. 512. An inscription of Yaśodharman, the date of which cannot be many years on either side of A.D. 532-3, claims to have enforced the submission of the famous Mihirakula whose power had established itself on the tiaras of kings and who had hitherto bowed his neck to no one but Śiva.[7] In spite of this defeat Mihirakula held Gwalior and the inaccessible fortress of the Himálayas.[8] These dates give about A.D. 520 as the time of Mihirakula's greatest power, a result which suggests that the Gollas, whom, about A.D. 520, the Greek merchant Cosmas Indikopleustes heard of in the ports of Western India as the supreme ruler of Northern India was Kulla or Mihirakula.[9]

Yaśodharman of Málwa, A.D. 533-4.

Regarding the history of the third destroyers of Gupta power in Málwa, inscriptions show that in A.D. 437-8, under Kumáragupta, Bandhuvarman son of Vishnuvarman ruled as a local king.[10]

---

[1] The name Jouen-Jouen seems to agree with Toramáṇa's surname Jaúvla and with the Juvia whom Cosmas Indikopleustes (A.D. 520-535) places to the north-east of Persia. Priaulx's Indian Travels, 220.

[2] Rawlinson's Seventh Monarchy, 311-349.

[3] Fleet's Corp. Ins. Ind. III. Ins. 25 line 1.

[4] Fleet's Corp. Ins. Ind III. Ins. 19 line 2.

[5] Fleet's Corp. Ins. Ind. III. Ins. 36.

[6] Fleet's Corp. Ins. Ind. III. Ins. 20.

[7] Fleet's Corp. Ins. Ind. III. Ins. 33.

[8] Fleet's Corp. Ins. Ind. III. and Ind. Ant. XVIII. 219.

[9] Priaulx's Indian Travels, 222. Compare Yule's Cathay, I. clxx.; Mignes' Patr. Gr. 88 page 450. For the use of Kula for Mihirakula, the second half for the whole, compare Fleet's Corp. Ins. Ind. III. 8 note. As regards the change from Kula to Gollas it is to be noted that certain of Mihirakula's own coins (Ind. Ant. XV 249) have the form Gula not Kula, and that this agrees with the suggestion (page 75 note 6) that the true form of the name is the Persian Mihiragula Rose of the Sun. Of this Gollas, who, like Mihirakula, was the type of conqueror round whom legends gather, Cosmas says (Priaulx, 223): Besides a great force of cavalry Gollas could bring into the field 2000 elephants. So large were his armies that once when besieging an inland town defended by a water-fosse his men horses and elephants drank the water and marched in dry-shod.

[10] Fleet's Corp. Ins. Ind. III. Ins. 18.

Chapter VII.

THE GUPTAS, A.D. 460 - 470.

Yaśodharman of Málwa, A.D. 533-4.

Possibly Bandhuvarman afterwards threw off his allegiance to the Guptas and thereby caused the temporary loss of Suráshtra towards the end of Kumáragupta's reign. Nothing further is recorded of the rulers of Málwa until the reign of Yaśodharman in A.D. 533-4.[1] It has been supposed that one of Yaśodharman's inscriptions mentioned a king Vishnuvardhana but there can be little doubt that both names refer to the same person.[2] The name of Yaśodharman's tribe is unknown and his crest the *aulikara* has not been satisfactorily explained.[3] Mandasor[4] in Western Málwa, where all his inscriptions have been found, must have been a centre of Yaśodharman's power. Yaśodharman boasts[5] of conquering from the Brahmaputra to mount Mahendra and from the Himálayas to the Western Ocean. In the sixth century only one dynasty could claim such widespread power. That dynasty is the famous family of Ujjain to which belonged the well known Vikramáditya of the Nine Gems. It may be conjectured not only that Yaśodharman belonged to this family but that Yaśodharman was the great Vikramáditya himself.[6]

The difficult question remains by whom was the power of Mihirakula overthrown. Yaśodharman claims to have subdued Mihirakula, who, he distinctly says, had never before been defeated.[7] On the other hand, Hiuen Tsiang ascribes Mihirakula's overthrow to a Báláditya of Magadha.[8] Coins prove that Báláditya[9] was one of the titles of Narasimhagupta grandson of Kumáragupta I. (A.D. 417-453) who probably ruled Magadha as his son's seal was found in the Gházipur district.[10] If Hiuen Tsiang's story is accepted a slight chronological difficulty arises in the way of this identification. It is clear that Mihirakula's first defeat was at the hands of Yaśodharman about A.D. 530. His defeat and capture by Báláditya must have been later. As Skandagupta's reign ended about A.D. 470 a blank of sixty years has to be filled by the two reigns of his brother and his nephew.[11] This, though not impossible, suggests caution in identifying Báláditya. According to Hiuen Tsiang Báláditya was a feudatory of Mihirakula who rebelled against him when he began to persecute the Buddhists. Hiuen Tsiang notices that, at the intercession of his own mother, Báláditya spared Mihirakula's life and allowed him to retire to Kashmir. He further notices that Mihirakula and his brother were rivals and his statement suggests that from Kashmir Mihirakula defeated his brother and recovered Gandhára. The ascendancy of the White Huns cannot have lasted long after Mihirakula. About A.D. 560 the power of the White Huns was crushed between the combined attacks of the Persians and Turks.[12]—(A. M. T. J.)]

[1] Fleet's Corp. Ins. Ind. III. Ins. 33 - 35.
[2] Fleet's Corp. Ins. Ind. III. Ins. 35 line 5.
[3] Fleet's Corp. Ins. Ind. III. 151 note 4.
[4] N. Lat. 24° 3'; E. Long. 75° 8'.
[5] Fleet's Corp. Ins. Ind. III. Ins. 33 line 5.
[6] This has already been suggested by Genl. Cunningham, Num. Chron. (3rd Ser.), VIII. 41. Dr. Hœrnle (J. B. A. S. LVIII. 100ff) has identified Yaśodharman with Vikramáditya's son Śiláditya Pratápaśila.
[7] Fleet's Corp. Ins. Ind. III. Ins. 33 line 6.
[8] Beal's Buddhist Records, I. 169.
[9] Hœrnle in J. B. A. S. LVIII. 97.
[10] See Smith and Hœrnle J. B. A. S. LVIII. 84; and Fleet Ind. Ant. XIX. 224.
[11] Hœrnle makes light of this difficulty: J. B. A. S. LVIII. 97.
[12] Rawlinson's Seventh Monarchy, 420, 422.

CHAPTER VIII.

THE VALABHIS

(A.D. 509–766.)

Chapter VIII.

THE VALABHIS, A.D. 509-766.

Vaḷeh Town, 1893.

THE Valabhi dynasty, which succeeded the Guptas in Gujarát and Káthiáváḍa, take their name from their capital in the east of Káthiáváḍa about twenty miles west of Bhávnagar and about twenty-five miles north of the holy Jain hill of Satruñjaya. The modern name of Valabhi is Vaḷeh. It is impossible to say whether the modern Vaḷeh is a corruption of Valahi the Prakrit form of the Sanskrit Valabhi or whether Valabhi is Sanskritised from a local original Vaḷeh. The form Valahi occurs in the writings of Jinaprabhasuri a learned Jain of the thirteenth century who describes S'atruñjaya as in the Valáhaka province. A town in the chiefship of Vaḷeh now occupies the site of old Valabhi,[1] whose ruins lie buried below thick layers of black earth and silt under the modern town and its neighbourhood. The only remains of old buildings are the large foundation bricks of which, except a few new houses, the whole of Vaḷeh is built. The absence of stone supports the theory that the buildings of old Valabhi were of brick and wood. In 1872 when the site was examined the only stone remains were a few scattered Lingas and a well-polished life-size granite Nandi or bull lying near a modern Mahádeva temple. Diggers for old bricks have found copper pots and copperplates and small Buddhist relic shrines with earthen pots and clay seals of the seventh century.

The ruins of Valabhi show few signs of representing a large or important city. The want of sweet water apparently unfits the site for the capital of so large a kingdom as Valabhi. Its choice as capital was probably due to its being a harbour on the Bhávnagar creek. Since

---

[1] Mr. Vajeshankar Gavrishankar, Náib Diván of Bhávnagar, has made a collection of articles found in Valabhi. The collection includes clay seals of four varieties and of about the seventh century with the Buddhist formula *Ye Dhárma hetu Prabhavá*: a small earthen tope with the same formula imprinted on its base with a seal; beads and ring stones *nangs* of several varieties of *akik* or carnelian and *sphatik* or coral some finished others half finished showing that as in modern Cambay the polishing of carnelians was a leading industry in early Valabhi. One circular figure of the size of a half rupee carved in black stone has engraved upon it the letters *ma ro* in characters of about the second century.* A royal seal found by Colonel Watson in Vaḷeh bears on it an imperfect inscription of four lines in characters as old as Dhruvasena I. (A.D. 526). This seal contains the names of three generations of kings, two of which the grandfather and grandson read Ahivarmman and Pushyâṇa all three being called *Mahárája* or great king. The dynastic name is lost. The names on these moveable objects need not belong to Valabhi history. Still that seals of the second and fifth centuries have been discovered in Valabhi shows the place was in existence before the founding of the historical Valabhi kingdom. A further proof of the age of the city is the mention of it in the Kathásarit-ságara a comparatively modern work but of very old materials. To this evidence of age, with much hesitation, may be added Balai Ptolemy's name for Gopnáth point which suggests that as early as the second century Vaḷeh or Baleh (compare Alberuni's era of Balah) was known by its present name. Badly minted coins of the Gupta ruler Kumáragupta (A.D. 417 - 453) are so common as to suggest that they were the currency of Valabhi.

* The *ma* and *ra* are of the old style and the side and upper strokes, that is the *kána* and *mátra* of *ro* are horizontal.

Chapter VIII.

THE VALABHIS, A.D. 509 - 766.

the days of Valabhi's prime the silt which thickly covers the ruins has also filled and choked the channel which once united it with the Bhávnagar creek when the small Ghelo was probably a fair sized river.

Valabhi in A.D. 630.

In spite of the disappearance of every sign of greatness Hiuen Tsiang's (A.D. 640) details show how rich and populous Valabhi was in the early part of the seventh century. The country was about 1000 miles (6000 *li*) and the capital about five miles (30 *li*) in circumference. The soil the climate and the manners of the people were like those of Málava. The population was dense; the religious establishments rich. Over a hundred merchants owned a hundred *lákhs*. The rare and valuable products of distant regions were stored in great quantities. In the country were several hundred monasteries or *sanghárámas* with about 6000 monks. Most of them studied the Little Vehicle according to the Sammatiya school. There were several hundred temples of Devas and sectaries of many sorts. When Tathágata or Gautama Buddha (B.C. 560 - 480) lived he often travelled through this country. King As'oka (B.C. 240) had raised monuments or *stúpas* in all places where Buddha had rested. Among these were spots where the three past Buddhas sat or walked or preached. At the time of Hiuen Tsiang's account (A.D. 640) the king was of the Kshatriya caste, as all Indian rulers were. He was the nephew of S'íláditya of Málava and the son-in-law of the son of S'íláditya the reigning king of Kanyákubja. His name was Dhruvapaṭu (Tu-lu-h'o-po-tu). He was of a lively and hasty disposition, shallow in wisdom and statecraft. He had only recently attached himself sincerely to the faith in the three precious ones. He yearly summoned a great assembly and during seven days gave away valuable gems and choice meats. On the monks he bestowed in charity the three garments and medicaments, or their equivalents in value, and precious articles made of the seven rare and costly gems. These he gave in charity and redeemed at twice their price. He esteemed the virtuous, honoured the good, and revered the wise. Learned priests from distant regions were specially honoured. Not far from the city was a great monastery built by the Arhat Áchára ('O-che-lo), where, during their travels, the Bodhisattvas Gunamati and Sthiramati (Kien-hwni) settled and composed renowned treatises.[1]

Valabhi Copperplates.

The only historical materials regarding the Valabhi dynasty are their copperplates of which a large number have been found. That such powerful rulers as the Valabhis should leave no records on stones and no remains of religious or other buildings is probably because, with one possible exception at Gopnáth,[2] up to the ninth century all temples and religious buildings in Káthiáváḍa and Gujarát were of brick and wood.[3]

---

[1] As suggested by Dr. Bühler (Ind. Ant. VI. 10), this is probably the Vihára called Śrí Bappapádiyavihára which is described as having been constructed by Áchárya Bhadanta Sthiramati who is mentioned as the grantee in a copperplate of Dharasena II. bearing date Gupta 269 (A. D. 588). The Sthiramati mentioned with titles of religious veneration in the copperplate is probably the same as that referred to by Hiuen Tsiang. (Ditto).

[2] Burgess' Káthiáwár and Kutch, 187.

[3] Stories on record about two temples one at S'atruñjaya the other at Somanátha support this view. As regards the Sátruñjaya temple the tradition is that while the minister of Kumarapála (A.D. 1143 - 1174) of Anahilaváḍa was on a visit to S'atruñjaya to worship and meditate in the temple of Ádinátha, the wick of the lamp in the shrine was removed

Chapter VIII.
THE VALABHIS, A.D. 509-766.
Valabhi Copperplates.

The Valabhi copperplates chiefly record grants to Brahmanical temples and Buddhist monasteries and sometimes to individuals. All are in one style two plates inscribed breadthwise on the inner side, the earliest plates being the smallest. The plates are held together by two rings passed through two holes in their horizontal upper margin. One of the rings bears on one side a seal with, as a badge of the religion of the dynasty, a well-proportioned seated Nandi or bull. Under the bull is the word Bhaṭárka the name of the founder of the dynasty. Except such differences as may be traced to the lapse of time, the characters are the same in all, and at the same time differ from the character then in use in the Valabhi territory which must have been that from which Devanágarí is derived. The Valabhi plate character is adopted from that previously in use in South Gujarát plates which was taken from the South Indian character. The use of this character suggests that either Bhaṭárka or the clerks and writers of the plates came from South Gujarát.[1] The language of all the grants is Sanskrit prose. Each records the year of the grant, the name of the king making the grant, the name of the grantee, the name of the village or field granted, the name of the writer of the charter either the minister of peace and war *sandhivigrahádhikṛita* or the military head *baládhikṛita*, and sometimes the name of the *dútaka* or gift-causer generally some officer of influence or a prince and in one case a princess. The grants begin by recording they were made either 'from Valabhi' the capital, or 'from the royal camp' '*Vijayaskandhávára*.' Then follows the genealogy of the dynasty from Bhaṭárka the founder to the grantor king. Each king has in every grant a series of attributes which appear to have been fixed for him once for all. Except in rare instances the grants contain nothing historical. They are filled with verbose description and figures of speech in high flown Sanskrit. As enjoined in law-books or *dharmaśástras* after the genealogy of the grantor comes the name of the composer usually the minister of peace and war and after him the boundaries of the land granted. The plates conclude with the date of the grant, expressed in numerals following the letter *saṃ* or the letters *saṃva* for *saṃvatsara* that is year. After the numerals are given the lunar month and day and the day of the week, with, at the extreme end, the sign manual *svahasto mama* followed by the name of the king in the genitive case that is Own hand of me so and so. The name of the era in which the date is reckoned is nowhere given.

Period Covered.

So far as is known the dates extend for 240 years from 207 to 447. That the earliest known date is so late as 207 makes it pro-

---

by mice and set on fire and almost destroyed the temple which was wholly of wood. The minister seeing the danger of wooden buildings determined to erect a stone edifice (*Kumárapála Charita*). The story about Somanátha is given in an inscription of the time of Kumárapála in the temple of Bhadrakáli which shows that before the stone temple was built by Bhímadeva I. (A.D. 1022 - 1072) the structure was of wood which was traditionally believed to be as old as the time of Kṛishṇa. Compare the Bhadrakáli inscription at Somanátha.

[1] The correctness of this inference seems open to question. The descent of the Valabhi plate character seems traceable from its natural local source the Skandagupta (A.D. 450) and the Rudradáman (A.D. 150) Girnár inscriptions.—(A. M. T. J.)

Chapter VIII.

The Valabhis, A.D. 509-766.

Period Covered.

bable that the Valabhis adopted an era already in use in Káthiáváḍa. No other era seems to have been in use in Valabhi. Three inscriptions have their years dated expressly in the Valabhi Saṃvat. The earliest of these in Bhadrakáli's temple in Somnáth Pátan is of the time of Kumárapála (A.D. 1143-1174) the Solanki ruler of Anahiláváḍa. It bears date Valabhi Saṃvat 850. The second and third are in the temple of Harsata Devi at Verával. The second which was first mentioned by Colonel Tod, is dated Hijra 662, Vikrama Saṃvat 1320, Valabhi Saṃvat 945, and Siṃha Saṃvat 151. The third inscription, in the same temple on the face of the pedestal of an image of Krishṇa represented as upholding the Govardhana hill, bears date Valabhi S. 927. These facts prove that an era known as the Valabhi era, which the inscriptions show began in A.D. 319, was in use for about a hundred years in the twelfth and thirteenth centuries. This may be accepted as the era of the Valabhi plates which extended over two centuries. Further the great authority (A.D. 1030) Alberuni gives Śaka 241 that is A.D. 319 as the starting point both of the 'era of Balah' and of what he calls the Guptakála or the Gupta era. Beruni's accuracy is established by a comparison of the Mandasor inscription and the Nepál inscription of Aṃśuvarman which together prove the Gupta era started from A.D. 319. Though its use by the powerful Valabhi dynasty caused the era to be generally known by their name in Gujarát in certain localities the Gupta era continued in use under its original name as in the Morbí copperplate of Jáikadeva which bears date 588 "of the era of the Guptas."[1]

Valabhi Administration, A.D. 500-700.

The Valabhi grants supply information regarding the leading office bearers and the revenue police and village administrators whose names generally occur in the following order:

(1) *Áyuktaka,* } meaning appointed, apparently any superior
(2) *Viniyuktaka* } official.

(3) *Drángika,* apparently an officer in charge of a town, as *dranga* means a town.

(4) *Mahattara* or Senior has the derivative meaning of high in rank. *Mhátára* the Maráthi for an old man is the same word. In the Valabhi plates *mahattara* seems to be generally used to mean the accredited headman of a village, recognised as headman both by the people of the village and by the Government.

(5) *Cháṭabhaṭa* that is *bhaṭas* or sepoys for *chiṭas* or rogues, police mounted and on foot, represent the modern police *jamádárs havaldárs* and constables. The Kumárapála Charita mentions that Cháṭabhaṭas were sent by Siddharája to apprehend the fugitive Kumárapála. One plate records the grant of a village 'unenterable by *cháṭabhaṭas*.'[2]

(6) *Dhruva* fixed or permanent is the hereditary officer in charge of the records and accounts of a village, the Taláti and Kulkarni

[1] The era has been exhaustively discussed by Mr. Fleet in Corp. Ins. Ind. III. Introduction.

[2] Nepaul Inscriptions. The phrase *achâṭa-bhaṭa* is not uncommon. Mr. Fleet (Corp. Ins. Ind. III. page 98 note 2) explains *achâṭa-bhaṭa-praveśya* as "not to be entered either by regular (*bhaṭa*) or by irregular (*cháṭa*) troops."

Chapter VIII.
THE VALABHIS, A.D. 509-766.
Valabhi Administration, A.D. 500-700.

of modern times. One of the chief duties of the Dhruva was to see that revenue farmers did not take more than the royal share.[1] The name is still in use in Cutch where village accountants are called *Dhru* and *Dhruva*. *Dhru* is also a common surname among Nágar Bráhmans and Modh and other Vániás in Cutch Gujarát and Káthiáváḍa.

(7) *Adhikaraṇika* means the chief judicial magistrate or judge of a place.

(8) *Daṇḍapáśika* literally 'holding the fetters or noose of punishment,' is used both of the head police officer and of the hangman or executioner.

(9) *Chauroddharaṇika* the thief-catcher. Of the two Indian ways of catching thieves, one of setting a thief to catch a thief the other the *Pagi* or tracking system, the second answers well in sandy Gujarát and Káthiáváḍa where the Tracker or *Pagi* is one of the *Bárábalute* or regular village servants.

(10) *Rájasthániya*, the foreign secretary, the officer who had to do with other states and kingdoms *rájasthánas*. Some authorities take *rájasthániya* to mean viceroy.

(11) *Amátya* minister and sometimes councillor is generally coupled with *kumára* or prince.

(12) *Anutpannádánasamudgráhaka* the arrear-gatherer.

(13) *Śaulkika* the superintendent of tolls or customs.

(14) *Bhogika* or *Bhogoddharaṇika* the collector of the *Bhoga* that is the state share of the land produce taken in kind, as a rule one-sixth. The term *bhoga* is still in use in Káthiáváḍa for the share, usually one-sixth, which landholders receive from their cultivating tenants.

(15) *Vartmapála* the roadwatch were often mounted and stationed in *thánás* or small roadside sheds.[2]

(16) *Pratisaraka* patrols night-guards or watchmen of fields and villages.[3]

(17) *Vishayapati* division-lord probably corresponded to the present subáh.

(18) *Ráshṭrapati* the head of a district.

(19) *Grámakúṭa* the village headman.

Territorial Divisions.

The plates show traces of four territorial divisions: (1) *Vishaya* the largest corresponding to the modern administrative Division: (2) *Áhára* or *Áharaṇí* that is collectorate (from *áhára* a collection) corresponding to the modern district or zillah: (3) *Pathaka*, of the road, a sub-division, the place named and its surroundings: (4) *Sthalí* a petty division the place without surroundings.[4]

Land Assessment.

The district of Kaira and the province of Káthiáváḍa to which the Valabhi grants chiefly refer appear to have had separate systems

---

[1] Bühler in Ind. Ant. V. 205. [2] Ind. And. VII. 68. [3] Ind. Ant. VII. 68.

[4] Of the different territorial divisions the following examples occur: Of *Vishaya* or main division Svabhágapuravishaye and Súryapuravishaye: of *Áhára* or collectorate Kheṭaka-áhára the Kaira district and Hastavapra-áhara or Hastavapráharaṇí the Háthab district near Bhávnagar: of *Pathaka* or sub-division Nagar-panthaka Porbandar-panthaka (Pársis still talk of Navsári panthaka): of *Sthali* or petty division Vaṭasthalí, Loṇápadrakasthalí, and others.

Land Assessment.

of land assessment Kaira by yield Káthiáváḍa by area. Under the Káthiáváḍa system the measurement was by *pádávarta* literally the space between one foot and the other that is the modern *kadam* or pace. The pace used in measuring land seems to have differed from the ordinary pace as most of the Káthiáváḍa grants mention the *bhúpádávarta* or land pace. The Kaira system of assessment was by yield the unit being the *piṭaka* or basketful, the grants describing fields as capable of growing so many baskets of rice or barley (or as requiring so many baskets of seed). As the grants always specify the Kaira basket a similar system with a different sized basket seems to have been in use in other parts of the country. Another detail which the plates preserve is that each field had its name called after a guardian or from some tree or plant. Among field names are Kotilaka, Atimaṇa-kedára, Khaṇḍa-kedára, Gargara-kshetra, Bhíma-kshetra, Khagali-kedára, S'ami-kedára.

Religion.

The state religion of the Valabhi kings was S'aivism. Every Valabhi copperplate hitherto found bears on its seal the figure of a bull with under it the name of Bhaṭárka the founder of the dynasty who was a S'aiva. Except Dhruvasena I. (A.D. 526) who is called *Paramabhágavata* or the great Vaishṇava and his brother and successor Dharapaṭṭa who is styled *Paramádityabhakta* or the great devotee of the sun, and Guhasena, who in his grant of Sam. 248 calls himself *Paramopásaka* or the great devotee of Buddha, all the Valabhi kings are called *Parama-máheśvara* the great S'aiva.

The grants to Buddhist *vihâras* or monasteries of which there are several seem special gifts to institutions founded by female relatives of the granting kings. Most of the grants are to Bráhmans who though performing Vaidik ceremonies probably as at present honoured S'aivism. This S'aivism seems to have been of the old Páśupata school of Nakulíśa or Lakulíśa as the chief shrine of Lakulíśa was at Kárávana the modern Kárván in the Gáikwár's territory fifteen miles south of Baroda and eight miles north-east of Miyágám railway station a most holy place till the time of the Vághelá king Arjunadeva in the thirteenth century.[1] The special

[1] Kárván seems to have suffered great desecration at the hands of the Musalmáns. All round the village chiefly under pipal trees, images and pieces of sculpture and large *liṅgas* lie scattered. To the north and east of the village on the banks of a large built pond called Kaśikunda are numerous sculptures and *liṅgas*. Partly embedded in the ground a pillar in style of about the eleventh century has a writing over it of latter times. The inscription contains the name of the place Sanskritised as Káyávarohana, and mentions an ascetic named Vírabahadraráśi who remained mute for twelve years. Near the pillar, at the steps leading to the water, is a carved doorway of about the tenth or eleventh century with some well-proportioned figures. The left doorpost has at the top a figure of S'iva, below the S'iva a figure of Súrya, below the Súrya a male and female, and under them attendants or *gaṇas* of S'iva. The right doorpost has at the top a figure of Vishṇu seated on Garuḍa, below the seated Vishṇu a standing Vishṇu with four hands, and below that two sitting male and female figures, the male with hands folded in worship the female holding a purse. These figures probably represent a married pair who paid for this gateway. Further below are figures of *gaṇas* of S'iva. In 1884 in repairing the south bank of the pond a number of carved stones were brought from the north of the town. About half a mile north-west of the town on the bank of a dry brook, is a temple of Chámuṇḍá Deví of about the tenth century. It contains a mutilated life-size image of Chámuṇḍá. Facing the temple lie mutilated figures of the seven Mátrikás and of Bhairava, probably the remains of a separate altar

Chapter VIII.
The Valabhis, A.D. 509-766.
Religion.

holiness attached to the Narbádá in S'aivism and to its pebbles as *liṅgas* is probably due to the neighbourhood of this shrine of Kárván. The followers of the Nakulíśa-Páśupata school were strict devotees of S'aivism, Nakulíśa the founder being regarded as an incarnation of S'iva. The date of the foundation of this school is not yet determined. It appears to have been between the second and the fifth century A.D. Nakulíśa had four disciples Kuśika, Gárgya, Kárusha, and Maitreya founders of four branches which spread through the length and breadth of India. Though no special representatives of this school remain, in spite of their nominal allegiance to S'ankarácharya the Daśanámis or Atíts are in fact Nakulíśas in their discipline doctrines and habits—applying ashes over the whole body, planting a *liṅga* over the grave of a buried Atít, and possessing proprietary rights over S'aiva temples. The Páśupatas were ever ready to fight for their school and often helped and served in the armies of kings who became their disciples. Till a century ago these unpaid followers recruited the armies of India with celibates firm and strong in fighting. It was apparently to gain these recruits that so many of the old rulers of India became followers of the Páśupata school. To secure their services the rulers had to pay them special respect. The leaders of these fighting monks were regarded as pontiffs like the Bappa-páda or Pontiff of the later Valabhi and other kings. Thus among the later Valabhis S'íláditya IV. is called *Bávapádánudhyáta* and all subsequent S'íládityas *Bappapádánudhyáta* both titles meaning Worshipping at the feet of Bava or Bappa.

This Báva is the popular Prakrit form of the older Prakrit or *deśí* Bappa meaning Father or worshipful. Bappa is the original of the Hindustáni and Gujaráti Báva father or elder; it is also a special term for a head Gosávi or Atít or indeed for any recluse. The epithet *Bappa-pádánudhyáta*, Bowing at the feet of Bappa, occurs in the attributes of several Nepál kings, and in the case of king Vasantasena appears the full phrase:

Parama-daivata-bappa-bhaṭṭáraka-mahárája-S'rí-pádánudhyáta.

Falling at the illustrious feet of the great Mahárája Lord Bappa.

These Nepál kings were S'aivas as they are called *parama-máheśvara* in the text of the inscription and like the Valabhi seals their seals bear a bull. It follows that the term *Bappa* was applied both by the Valabhis and the Nepál kings to some one, who can hardly be the same individual, unless he was their

---

facing the temple with the *mátri-maṇḍala* or Mother-Meeting upon it. The village has a large modern temple of S'iva called Nakleśvara, on the site of some old temple and mostly built of old carved temple stones. In the temple close by are a number of old images of the sun and the boar incarnation of Vishnu all of about the tenth or eleventh century. The name Nakleśvara would seem to have been derived from Nakulíśa the founder of the Páśupata sect and the temple may originally have had an image of Nakulíśa himself or a *liṅga* representing Nakulíśa. Close to the west of the village near a small dry reservoir called the Kuṇḍa of Rájarájeśvara lies a well-preserved black stone seated figure of Chaṇḍa one of the most respected of S'iva's attendants, without whose worship all worship of S'iva is imperfect, and to whom all that remains after making oblations to S'iva is offered. A number of other sculptures lie on the bank of the pond. About a mile to the south of Kárván is a village called Lingthali the place of *liṅgas*.

Chapter VIII.

THE VALABHIS, A.D. 509-766.

Religion.

common overlord, which the distance between the two countries and still more the fact that his titles are the same as the titles of the Valabhi kings make almost impossible. In these circumstances the most probable explanation of the Bappa or Báva of these inscriptions is that it was applied to Shaivite pontiffs or ecclesiastical dignitaries. The attribute *Parama-daivata* The Great Divine prefixed to Bappa in the inscription of Vasantasena confirms this view. That such royal titles as *Mahárájádhirája, Paramabhaṭṭáraka,* and *Parameśvara* are ascribed to Bappa is in agreement with the present use of Mahárája for all priestly Bráhmans and recluses and of Bhaṭṭáraka for Digambara Jain priests. Though specially associated with Śaivas the title *bappa* is applied also to Vaishnava dignitaries. That the term *bappa* was in similar use among the Buddhists appears from the title of a Valabhi *vihára* Bappapádíyavihára The monastery of the worshipful Bappa that is Of the great teacher Sthiramati by whom it was built.[1]

Origin of the Valabhis.

The tribe or race of Bhaṭárka the founder of the Valabhi dynasty is doubtful. None of the numerous Valabhi copperplates mentions the race of the founder. The Chalukya and Ráshṭrakúṭa copperplates are silent regarding the Valabhi dynasty. And it is worthy of note that the Gehlots and Gohils, who are descended from the Valabhis, take their name not from their race but from king Guha or Guhasena (A.D. 559-567) the fourth ruler and apparently the first great sovereign among the Valabhis. These considerations make it probable that Bhaṭárka belonged to some low or stranger tribe. Though the evidence falls short of proof the probability seems strong that Bhaṭárka belonged to the Gurjara tribe, and that it was the supremacy of him and his descendants which gave rise to the name Gurjjara-rátra the country of the Gurjjaras, a name used at first by outsiders and afterwards adopted by the people of Gujarát. Except Bhaṭárka and his powerful dynasty no kings occur of sufficient importance to have given their name to the great province of Gujarát. Against their Gurjara origin it may be urged that the Chinese traveller Hiuen Tsiang (A.D. 640) calls the king of Valabhi a Kshatriya. Still Hiuen Tsiang's remark was made more than a century after the establishment of the dynasty when their rise to power and influence had made it possible for them to ennoble themselves by calling themselves Kshatriyas and tracing their lineage to Puranic heroes. That such ennobling was not only possible but common is beyond question. Many so-called Rájput families in Gujarát and Káthiaváḍa can be traced to low or stranger tribes. The early kings of Nándipurí or Nándod (A.D. 450) call themselves Gurjjaras and the later members of the same dynasty trace their lineage to the Mahábhárata hero Karṇa. Again two of the Nandod Gurjjaras Dadda II. and Jayabhata II. helped the Valabhis under circumstances which suggest that the bond of sympathy

[1] Compare Beal Buddhist Records, II. 268 note 76 and Ind. Ant. VI. 9. The meaning and reference of the title *Bappa* have been much discussed. The question is treated at length by Mr. Fleet (Corp. Ins. Ind. III. 186 note 1) with the result that the title is applied not to a religious teacher but to the father and predecessor of the king who makes the grant. According to Mr. Fleet *bappa* would be used in reference to a father, *báva* in reference to an uncle.

Chapter VIII.
The Valabhis, A.D. 509-766.
Origin of the Valabhis.

may have been their common origin. The present chiefs of Nándod derive their lineage from Karṇa and call themselves Gohils of the same stock as the Bhávnagar Gohils who admittedly belong to the Valabhi stock. This supports the theory that the Gurjjaras and the Valabhis had a common origin, and that the Gurjjaras were a branch of and tributary to the Valabhis. This would explain how the Valabhis came to make grants in Broach at the time when the Gurjjaras ruled there. It would further explain that the Gurjjaras were called *sámantas* or feudatories because they were under the overlordship of the Valabhis.[1]

History.

The preceding chapter shows that except Chandragupta (A.D. 410) Kumáragupta (A.D. 416) and Skandagupta (A.D. 456) none of the Guptas have left any trace of supremacy in Gujarát and Káthiáváḍa. Of what happened in Gujarát during the forty years after Gupta 150 (A.D. 469), when the reign of Skandagupta came to an end nothing is known or is likely to be discovered from Indian sources. The blank of forty years to the founder Bhaṭárka (A.D. 509) or more correctly of sixty years to Dhruvasena (A.D. 526) the first Valabhi king probably corresponds with the ascendancy of some foreign dynasty or tribe. All trace of this tribe has according to custom been blotted out of the Sanskrit and other Hindu records. At the same time it is remarkable that the fifty years ending about A.D. 525 correspond closely with the ascendancy in north and north-west India of the great tribe of Ephthalites or White Huns. As has been shown in the Gupta Chapter, by A.D. 470 or 480, the White Huns seem to have been powerful if not supreme in Upper India. In the beginning of the sixth century, perhaps about A.D. 520, Cosmas Indikopleustes describes the north of India and the west coast as far south as Kalliena that is Kalyán near Bombay as under the Huns whose king was Gollas.[2] Not many years later (A.D. 530) the Hun power in Central India suffered defeat and about the same time a new dynasty arose in south-east Káthiáváḍa.

First Valabhi Grant, A.D. 526.

The first trace of the new power, the earliest Valabhi grant, is that of Dhruvasena in the Valabhi or Gupta year 207 (A.D. 526). In this grant Dhruvasena is described as the third son of the Senápati or general Bhaṭárka. Of Senápati Bhaṭárka neither copperplate nor inscription has been found. Certain coins which General Cunningham Arch. Surv. Rept. IX. Pl. V. has ascribed to Bhaṭárka have on the obverse a bust, as on the western coins of

[1] Whether the Valabhis were or were not Gurjjaras the following facts favour the view that they entered Gujarat from Málwa. It has been shown (Fleet Ind. Ant. XX, 376) that while the Guptas used the so-called Northern year beginning with Chaitra, the Valabhi year began with Kártika (see Ind. Ant. XX. 376). And further Kielhorn in his examination of questions connected with the Vikrama era (Ind. Ant. XIX. and XX.) has given reasons for believing that the original Vikrama year began with Kártika and took its rise in Málwa. It seems therefore that when they settled in Gujarát, while they adopted the Gupta era the Valabhis still adhered to the old arrangement of the year to which they had been accustomed in their home in Málwa. The arrangement of the year entered into every detail of their lives, and was therefore much more difficult to change than the starting point of their era, which was important only for official acts. —(A. M. T. J.)

[2] Montfauçon's Edition in Priaulx's Indian Travels, 222-223. It seems doubtful if Cosmas meant that Gollas' overlordship spread as far south as Kalyán. Compare Migne's Patrologiæ Cursus, lxxxviii. 466; Yule's Cathay, I. clxx.

Chapter VIII.

The Valabhis, A.D. 509-766.

Kumáragupta, and on the reverse the Śaiva trident, and round the trident the somewhat doubtful legend in Gupta characters:

Rajño Mahákshatri Paramádityabhakta S'rí S'arvva-bhaṭṭárakasa.

Of the king the great Kshatri, great devotee of the sun, the illustrious S'arvva-bhaṭṭáraka.

This S'arvva seems to have been a Ráshtrakúṭa or Gurjjara king. His coins were continued so long in use and were so often copied that in the end upright strokes took the place of letters. That these coins did not belong to the founder of the Valabhi dynasty appears not only from the difference of name between Bhaṭṭáraka and Bhaṭárka but because the coiner was a king and the founder of the Valabhis a general.

Senápati Bhaṭárka, A.D. 509-520?

Of the kingdom which Senápati Bhaṭárka overthrew the following details are given in one of his epithets in Valabhi copperplates: 'Who obtained glory by dealing hundreds of blows on the large and very mighty armies of the Maitrakas, who by force had subdued their enemies.' As regards these Maitrakas it is to be noted that the name Maitraka means Solar. The sound of the compound epithet *Maitraka-amitra* that is Maitraka-enemy used in the inscription makes it probable that the usual form Mihira or solar was rejected in favour of Maitraka which also means solar to secure the necessary assonance with *amitra* or enemy. The form Mihira solar seems a Hinduizing or meaning-making of the northern tribal name Meḍh or Mehr, the Mehrs being a tribe which at one time seem to have held sway over the whole of Káthiáváḍa and which are still found in strength near the Barda hills in the south-west of Káthiáváḍa.[1] The Jethvá chiefs of Porbandar who were formerly powerful rulers are almost certainly of the Mehr tribe. They are still called Mehr kings and the Mehrs of Káthiáváḍa regard them as their leaders and at the call of their Head are ready to fight for him. The chief of Mehr traditions describes the fights of their founder Makaradhvaja with one Mayúradhvaja. This tradition seems to embody the memory of an historical struggle. The *makara* or fish is the tribal badge of the Mehrs and is marked on a Morbí copperplate dated A.D. 904 (G. 585) and on the forged Dhíníki grant of the Mehr king Jáíkádeva. On the other hand Mayúradhvaja or peacock-bannered would be the name of the Guptas beginning with Chandragupta who ruled in Gujarát (A.D. 396-416) and whose coins have a peacock on the reverse. The tradition would thus be a recollection of the struggle between the Mehrs and Guptas in which about A.D. 470 the Guptas were defeated. The Mehrs seem to have been a northern tribe, who, the evidence of place names seems to show, passed south through Western Rájputana, Jaslo, Ajo, Bad, and Koml leaders of this tribe giving their names to the settlements of Jesalmir, Ajmir, Badmer, and Komalmer. The resemblance of name and the nearness of dates suggest a connection between the Mehrs and the great Panjáb conqueror of the Guptas Mihirakula (A.D. 512-540?). If not them-

The Maitrakas, A.D. 470-509.

[1] The Mehrs seem to have remained in power also in north-east Káthiáváḍa till the thirteenth century. Mokheráji Gohil the famous chief of Piram was the son of a daughter of Dhan Mehr or Mair of Dhanduka. Rás Málá, I. 316.

Chapter VIII.
The Valabhis, A.D. 509-766.
The Maitrakas, A.D. 470-509.

selves Húṇas the Mehrs may have joined the conquering armies of the Húṇas and passing south with the Húṇas may have won a settlement in Káthiáváḍa as the Káthis and Jhádejás settled about 300 years later. After Senápati Bhaṭárka's conquests in the south of the Peninsula the Mehrs seem to have retired to the north of Káthiáváḍa.

The above account of the founder of the Valabhis accepts the received opinion that he was the Senápati or General of the Guptas. The two chief points in support of this view are that the Valabhis adopted both the Gupta era and the Gupta currency. Still it is to be noted that this adoption of a previous era and currency by no means implies any connection with the former rulers.[1] Both the Gurjjaras (A.D. 580) and the Chálukyas (A.D. 642) adopted the existing era of the Traikúṭakas (A.D. 248-9) while as regards currency the practice of continuing the existing type is by no means uncommon.[2] In these circumstances, and seeing that certain of the earlier Valabhi inscriptions refer to an overlord who can hardly have been a Gupta, the identification of the king to whom the original Senápati owed allegiance must be admitted to be doubtful.

All known copperplates down to those of Dharasena (A.D. 579 the great grandson of Bhaṭárka) give a complete genealogy from Bhaṭárka to Dharasena. Later copperplates omit all mention of any descendants but those in the main line.

Senápati's Sons.

Senápati Bhaṭárka had four sons, (1) Dharasena (2) Droṇásiṃha (3) Dhruvasena and (4) Dharapaṭṭa. Of Dharasena the first son no record has been traced. His name first appears in the copperplates of his brother Dhruvasena where like his father he is called Senápati. Similarly of the second son Droṇasiṃha no record exists except in the copperplates of his brother Dhruvasena. In these copperplates unlike his father and elder brother Dhruvasena is called *Mahárája* and is mentioned as 'invested with royal authority in person by the great lord, the lord of the wide extent of the whole world.' This great lord or *paramasvámi* could not have been his father Bhaṭárka. Probably he was the king to whom Bhaṭárka owed allegiance. It is not clear where Droṇasiṃha was installed king probably it was in Káthiáváḍa from the south-east of which his father and elder brother had driven back the Mehrs or Maitrakas.[3]

---

[1] All the silver and copper coins found in Valabhi and in the neighbouring town of Sihor are poor imitations of Kumáragupta's (A.D. 417-453) and of Skandagupta's (A.D. 454-470) coins, smaller lighter and of bad almost rude workmanship. The only traces of an independent currency are two copper coins of Dharasena, apparently Dharasena IV., the most powerful of the dynasty who was called *Chakravartin* or Emperor. The question of the Gupta-Valabhi coins is discussed in Jour. Royal As. Socy. for Jan. 1893 pages 133-143. Dr. Bühler (page 138) holds the view put forward in this note of Dr. Bhagvánlál's namely that the coins are Valabhi copies of Gupta currency. Mr. Smith (Ditto, 142-143) thinks they should be considered the coins of the kings whose names they bear.

[2] The three types of coins still current at Ujjain, Bhilsa, and Gwálior in the territories of His Highness Sindhia are imitations of the previous local Muhammadan coinage.

[3] As the date of Droṇasiṃha's investiture is about A.D. 520 it is necessary to consider what kings at this period claimed the title of supreme lord and could boast of ruling the whole earth. The rulers of this period whom we know of are Mihirakula,

Chapter VIII.

The Valabhis, A.D. 509-766.

Dhruvasena I. A.D. 526-535.

The third son Dhruvasena is the first of several Valabhis of that name. Three copperplates of his remain: The Kukad grant dated Gupta 207 (A.D. 526),[1] an unpublished grant found in Junágaḍh dated Gupta 210 (A.D. 529), and the Vaḷeh grant dated Gupta 216 (A.D. 535).[2] One of Dhruvasena's attributes *Parama-bhaṭṭáraka-pádánudhyáta*, Bowing at the feet of the great lord, apparently applies to the same paramount sovereign who installed his brother Droṇasiṃha. The paramount lord can hardly be Dhruvasena's father as his father is either called *Bhaṭárka* without the *parama* or more commonly *Senápati* that is general. Dhruvasena's other political attributes are *Mahárája* Great King or *Mahásámanta* Great Chief, the usual titles of a petty feudatory king. In the A.D. 535 plates he has the further attributes of *Mahápratihára* the great doorkeeper or chamberlain, *Mahádaṇḍanáyaka*[3] the great magistrate, and *Máhákártakritika* (?) or great general, titles which seem to show he still served some overlord. It is not clear whether Dhruvasena succeeded his brother Droṇasiṃha or was a separate contemporary ruler. The absence of 'falling at the feet of' or other successional phrase and the use of the epithet 'serving at the feet of' the great lord seem to show that his power was distinct from his brothers. In any case Dhruvasena is the first of the family who has a clear connection with Valabhi from which the grants of A.D. 526 and 529 are dated.

In these grants Dhruvasena's father Bhatárka and his elder brothers are described as 'great Máheśvaras' that is followers of Śiva, while Dhruvasena himself is called *Paramabhágavata* the great Vaishṇava. It is worthy of note, as stated in the A.D. 535 grant, that his niece Duḍḍá (or Lulá ?) was a Buddhist and had dedicated a Buddhist monastery at Valabhi. The latest known date of Dhruvasena is A.D. 535 (G. 216). Whether Dharapaṭṭa or Dharapaṭṭa's son Guhasena succeeded is doubtful. That Dharapaṭṭa is styled Mahárája and that a twenty-four years' gap occurs between the latest grant of Dhruvasena and A.D. 559 the earliest grant of

---

Yaśodharman Vishṇuvardhana, the descendants of Kumáragupta's son Puragupta, and the Gupta chiefs of Eastern Málwa. Neither Toramáṇa nor Mihirakula appears to have borne the paramount title of Parameśvara though the former is called Mahárájádhirája in the Eraṇ inscription and Avanipati or Lord of the Earth (= simply king) on his coins: in the Gwálior inscription Mihirakula is simply called Lord of the Earth. He was a powerful prince but he could hardly claim to be ruler of "the whole circumference of the earth." He therefore cannot be the installer of Droṇasiṃha. Taking next the Guptas of Magadha we find on the Bhitári seal the title of Mahárájádhirája given to each of them, but there is considerable reason to believe that their power had long since shrunk to Magadha and Eastern Málwa, and if Hiuen Tsiang's Báláditya is Narasiṃhagupta, he must have been about A.D. 520 a feudatory of Mihirakula, and could not be spoken of as supreme lord, nor as ruler of the whole earth. The Guptas of Málwa have even less claim to these titles, as Bhánugupta was a mere Mahárája, and all that is known of him is that he won a battle at Eraṇ in Eastern Málwa in A.D. 510-11. Last of all comes Vishṇuvardhana or Yaśodharman of Mandasor. In one of the Mandasor inscriptions he has the titles of Rájádhirája and Parameśvara (A.D. 532-33); in another he boasts of having carried his conquests from the Lauhitya (Brahmaputra) to the western ocean and from the Himálaya to mount Mahendra. It seems obvious that Yaśodharman is the Paramasvámi of the Valabhi plate, and that the reference to the western ocean relates to Bhaṭárka's successes against the Maitrakas.—(A.M.T.J.)

[1] Ind. Ant. V. 204. [2] Ind. Ant. IV. 104.

[3] In a commentary on the Kalpasútra Daṇḍanáyaka is described as meaning *Tantrapála* that is head of a district.

Chapter VIII.
The Valabhis, A.D. 509-766.

Guhasena favour the succession of Dharapaṭṭa. On the other hand in the A.D. 559 grant all Guhasena's sins are said to be cleansed by falling at the feet of, that is, by succeeding, Dhruvasena. It is possible that Dharapaṭṭa may have ruled for some years and Dhruvasena again risen to power.

Guhasena, A.D. 539-569.

Of Guhasena (A.D. 539?-569) three plates and a fragment of an inscription remain. Two of the grants are from Vaḷeh dated A.D. 559 and 565 (G. 240 and 246)[1]: the third is from Bhávnagar dated A.D. 567 (G. 248).[2] The inscription is on an earthen pot found at Vaḷeh and dated A.D. 566 (G. 247).[3] In all the later Valabhi plates the genealogy begins with Guhasena who seems to have been the first great ruler of his dynasty. Guhasena is a Sanskrit name meaning Whose army is like that of Kárttika-svámi: his popular name was probably Guhila. It appears probable that the Gohil and Gehlot Rajput chiefs of Káthiávaḍa and Rájputána, who are believed to be descendants of the Valabhis, take their name from Guhasena or Guha, the form Gehloti or Gehlot, *Guhila-utta*, being a corruption of Guhilaputra or descendants of Guhila, a name which occurs in old Rájpút records.[4] This lends support to the view that Guhasena was believed to be the first king of the dynasty. Like his predecessors he is called Mahárája or great king. In one grant he is called the great S'aiva and in another the great Buddhist devotee (*paramopásaka*), while he grants villages to the Buddhist monastery of his paternal aunt's daughter Duḍḍá. Though a S'aivite Guhasena, like most of his predecessors, tolerated and even encouraged Buddhism. His minister of peace and war is named Skandabhaṭa.

The beginning of Guhasena's reign is uncertain. Probably it was not earlier than A.D. 539 (G. 220). His latest known date is A.D. 567 (G. 248) but he may have reigned two years longer.

Dharasena II. A.D. 569-589.

About A.D. 569 (G. 250) Guhasena was succeeded by his son Dharasena II. Five of his grants remain, three dated A.D. 571 (G. 252),[5] the fourth dated A.D. 588 (G. 269),[6] and the fifth dated A.D. 589 (G. 270).[7] In the first three grants Dharasena is called Mahárája or great king; in the two later grants is added the title Mahásámanta Great Feudatory, seeming to show that in the latter part of his reign Dharasena had to acknowledge as overlord some one whose power had greatly increased.[8] All his copperplates style Dharasena II. *Parama-máheśvara* Great S'aiva. A gap of eighteen years occurs between A.D. 589 Dharasena's latest grant and A.D. 607 the earliest grant of his son S'íláditya.

S'íláditya I. A.D. 594-609.

Dharasena II. was succeeded by his son S'íláditya I. who is also called Dharmáditya or the sun of religion.

The S'atruñjaya Máhátmya has a prophetic account of one S'íláditya who will be a propagator of religion in Vikrama Saṃvat

---

[1] Ind. Ant. VII. 66; IV. 174.
[2] Ind. Ant. V. 206.
[3] Ind. Ant. XIV. 75.
[4] Kumárápála-Charita, Abu Inscriptions.
[5] Ind. Ant. VIII. 302, VII. 68, XIII. 160.
[6] Ind. Ant. VI. 9.
[7] Ind. Ant. VII. 90.
[8] This change of title was probably connected with the increase of Gurjara power, which resulted in the founding of the Gurjara kingdom of Broach about A.D. 580. See Chapter X. below.

S'íláditya I. A.D. 590 - 609.

477 (A.D. 420). This Máhátmya is comparatively modern and is not worthy of much trust. Vikrama Samvat 477 would be A.D. 420 when no Valabhi kingdom was established and no S'íláditya can have flourished. If the date 477 has been rightly preserved, and it be taken in the S'aka era it would correspond with Gupta 237 or A.D. 556, that is thirty to forty years before S'íláditya's reign. Although no reliance can be placed on the date still his second name Dharmáditya gives support to his identification with the S'íláditya of the Máhátmya.

His grants like many of his predecessors style S'íláditya a great devotee of S'iva. Still that two of his three known grants were made to Buddhist monks shows that he tolerated and respected Buddhism. The writer of one of the grants is mentioned as the minister of peace and war Chandrabhaṭṭi; the Dútaka or causer of the gift in two of the Buddhist grants is Bhaṭṭa Ádityayaśas apparently some military officer. The third grant, to a temple of S'iva, has for its Dútaka the illustrious Kharagraha apparently the brother and successor of the king.

S'íláditya's reign probably began about A.D. 594 (G. 275). His latest grant is dated A.D. 609 (G. 290).[1]

Kharagraha, A.D. 610 - 615.

S'íláditya was succeeded by his brother Kharagraha, of whom no record has been traced. Kharagraha seems to have been invested with sovereignty by his brother S'íláditya who probably retired from the world. Kharagraha is mentioned as a great devotee of S'iva.

Dharasena III. A.D. 615 - 620.

Kharagraha was succeeded by his son Dharasena III. of whom no record remains.

Dhruvasena II. (Báláditya) A.D. 620 - 640.

Dharasena III. was succeeded by his younger brother Dhruvasena II. also called Báláditya or the rising sun. A grant of his is dated A.D. 629 (G. 310).[2] As observed before, Dhruvasena is probably a Sanskritised form of the popular but meaningless Dhruvapaṭṭa which is probably the original of Hiuen Tsiang's T'u-lu-h'o-po-tu, as A.D. 629 the date of his grant is about eleven years before the time when (640) Hiuen Tsiang is calculated to have been in Málwa if not actually at Valabhi. If one of Dhruvasena's poetic attributes is not mere hyperbole, he made conquests and spread the power of Valabhi. On the other hand the Navsári grant of Jayabhaṭa III. (A.D. 706 - 734) the Gurjjara king of Broach states that Dadda II. of Broach (A.D. 620 - 650) protected the king of Valabhi who had been defeated by the great Srí Harshadeva (A.D. 607 - 648) of Kanauj.

Dharasena IV. A.D. 640 - 649.

Dhruvasena II. was succeeded by his son Dharasena IV. perhaps the most powerful and independent of the Valabhis. A copper-plate dated A.D. 649 (G. 330) styles him *Parama-bhaṭṭáraka, Mahárájádhirája, Parameśvara, Chakravartin* Great Lord, King of Kings, Great Ruler, Universal Sovereign. Dharasena IV.'s successors continue the title of *Mahárájádhirája* or great ruler, but none is called *Chakravartin* or universal sovereign a title which implies numerous conquests and widespread power.

---

[1] Ind. Ant. XI. 306.

[2] Ind. Ant. VI. 13.

Chapter VIII.
THE VALABHIS, A.D. 509-766.
Dharasena IV. A.D. 640-649.

Two of Dharasena IV.'s grants remain, one dated A.D. 645 (G. 326) the other A.D. 649 (G. 330). A grant of his father Dhruvasena dated A.D. 634 (G. 315) and an unpublished copperplate in the possession of the chief of Morbí belonging to his successor Dhruvasena III. dated A.D. 651 (G. 332) prove that Dharasena's reign did not last more than seventeen years. The well known Sanskrit poem Bhaṭṭikávya seems to have been composed in the reign of this king as at the end of his work the author says it was written at Valabhi protected (governed) by the king the illustrious Dharasena.[1] The author's application to Dharasena of the title *Narendra* Lord of Men is a further proof of his great power.

Dhruvasena III. A.D. 650-656.

Dharasena IV. was not succeeded by his son but by Dhruvasena the son of Derabhaṭa the son of Dharasena IV.'s paternal grand-uncle. Derabhaṭa appears not to have been ruler of Valabhi itself but of some district in the south of the Valabhi territory. His epithets describe him as like the royal sage Agastya spreading to the south, and as the lord of the earth which has for its two breasts the Sahya and Vindhya hills. This description may apply to part of the province south of Kaira where the Sahyádri and Vindhya mountains may be said to unite. In the absence of a male heir in the direct line, Derabhaṭa's son Dhruvasena appears to have succeeded to the throne of Valabhi. The only known copperplate of Dhruvasena III.'s, dated A.D. 651 (G. 332), records the grant of the village of Peḍhapadra in Vanthali, the modern Vanthali in the Navánagar State of North Káthiáváḍa. A copperplate of his elder brother and successor Kharagraha dated A.D. 656 (G. 337) shows that Dhruvasena's reign cannot have lasted over six years.

Kharagraha, A.D. 656-665.

The less than usually complimentary and respectful reference to Dhruvasena III. in the attributes of Kharagraha suggests that Kharagraha took the kingdom by force from his younger brother as the rightful successor of his father. At all events the succession of Kharagraha to Dhruvasena was not in the usual peaceful manner. Kharagraha's grant dated A.D. 656 (G. 337) is written by the Divirapati or Chief Secretary and minister of peace and war Anahilla son of Skandabhaṭa.[2] The Dútaka or causer of the gift was the Pramátṛi or survey officer Śríná.

Śíláditya III. A.D. 666-675.

Kharagraha was succeeded by Śíláditya III. son of Kharagraha's elder brother Śíláditya II. Śíláditya II. seems not to have ruled at Valabhi but like Derabhaṭa to have been governor of Southern Valabhi, as he is mentioned out of the order of succession and with the title Lord of the Earth containing the Vindhya mountain. Three grants of Śíláditya III. remain, two dated A.D. 666 (G. 346)[3] and the third dated A.D. 671 (G. 352).[4] He is called *Parama-bhaṭṭáraka* Great Lord, *Mahárájádhirája* Chief King among Great Kings, and *Parameśvara* Great Ruler. These titles continue to be applied to all

---

[1] *Kávyamidam rachitam mayá Valabhyám, S'rí Dharasena-narendra pálitáyám.*
[2] Ind. Ant. VII. 76.
[3] Journ. Beng. A. S. IV. and an unpublished grant in the museum of the B. B. R. A. Soc.
[4] Ind. Ant. XI. 305.

Chapter VIII.

The Valabhis, A.D. 509 - 766.

subsequent Valabhi kings. Even the name Śíláditya is repeated though each king must have had some personal name.

Śíláditya IV. A.D. 691.

Śíláditya III. was succeeded by his son Śíláditya IV. of whom one grant dated A.D. 691 (G. 372) remains.[1] The officer who prepared the grant is mentioned as the general Divirapati Srí Haragaṇa the son of Bappa Bhogika. The Dútaka or gift-causer is the prince Kharagraha, which may perhaps be the personal name of the next king Siláditya V.

Śíláditya V. A.D. 722.

Of Śíláditya V. the son and successor of Śíláditya IV. two grants dated A.D. 722 (G. 403) both from Gondal remain. Both record grants to the same person. The writer of both was general Gillaka son of Buddhabhaṭṭa, and the gift-causer of both prince Śíláditya.

Śíláditya VI. A.D. 760.

Of Śíláditya VI. the son and successor of the last, one grant dated A.D. 760 (G. 441) remains. The grantee is an Atharvavedi Bráhman. The writer is Śasyagupta son of Emapatha and the gift-causer is Gánjaśáti Srí Jajjar (or Jajjir).

Śíláditya VII. A.D. 766.

Of Síláditya VII. the son and successor of the last, who is also called Dhrúbhaṭa (Sk. Dhruvabhaṭa), one grant dated A.D. 766 (G. 447) remains.

Valabhi Family Tree.

The following is the genealogy of the Valabhi Dynasty:

VALABHI FAMILY TREE,
A.D. 509 - 766.

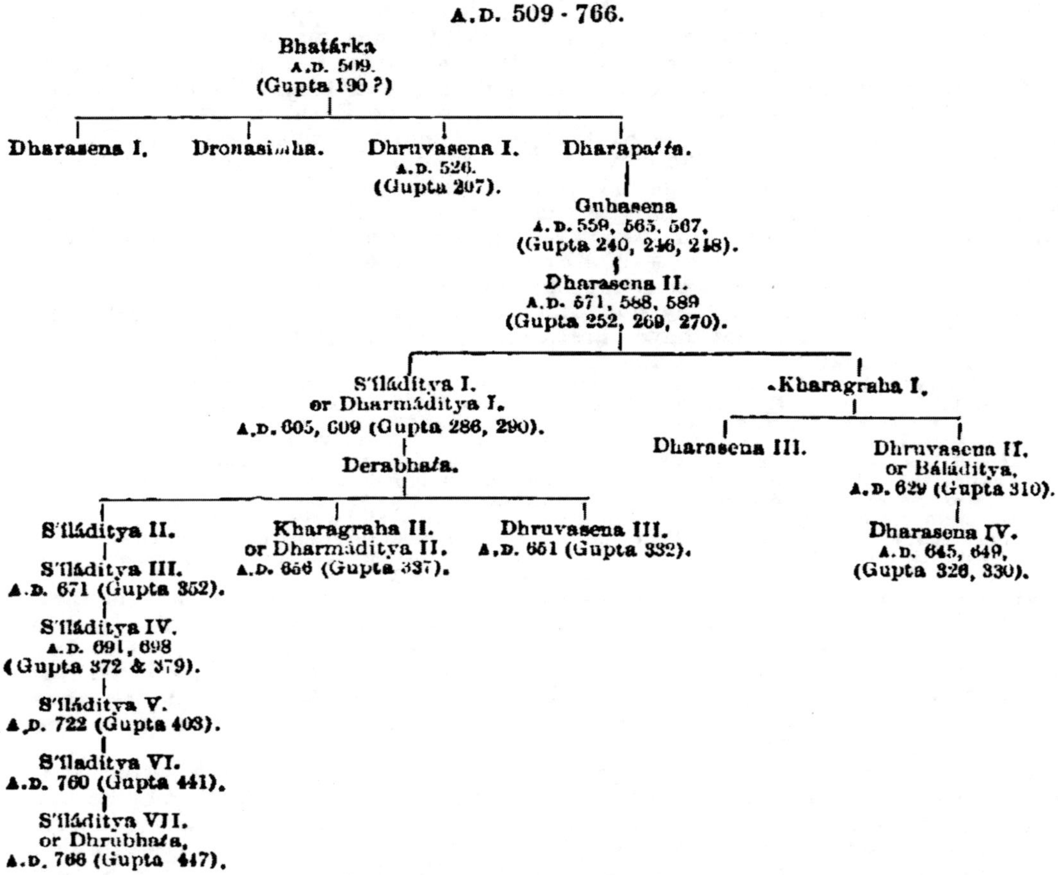

[1] Ind. Ant. V. 208.

Chapter VIII.

THE VALABHIS, A.D. 509-766.

The Fall of Valabhi, A.D. 750-770.

Of the overthrow of Valabhi many explanations have been offered.[1] The only explanation in agreement with the copperplate evidence that a Śíláditya was ruling at Valabhi as late as A.D. 766 (Val. Sam. 447)[2] is the Hindu account preserved by Alberuni (A.D. 1030)[3] that soon after the Sindh capital Mansúra was founded, say A.D. 750-770, Ranka a disaffected subject of the era-making Valabhi, with presents of money persuaded the Arab lord of Mansúra to send a naval expedition against the king of Valabhi. In a night attack king Valabha was killed and his people and town were destroyed. Alberuni adds: Men say that still in our time such traces are left in

---

[1] Since his authorities mention the destroyers of Valabhi under the vague term *mlechchhas* or barbarians and since the era in which they date the overthrow may be either the Vikrama B.C. 57, the Saka A.D. 78, or the Valabhi A.D. 319, Tod is forced to offer many suggestions. His proposed dates are A.D. 244 Vik. Sam. 300 (Western India, 269), A.D. 424 Val. Sam. 105 (Ditto, 51 and 214), A.D. 524 Val. Sam. 205 (Annals of Rájásthán, I. 83 and 217-220), and A.D. 619 Val. Sam. 300 (Western India, 352). Tod identifies the barbarian destroyers of Valabhi either with the descendants of the second century Parthians, or with the White Huns Getes or Káthis, or with a mixture of these who in the beginning of the sixth century supplanted the Parthians (An. of Ráj. I. 83 and 217-220; Western India, 214, 352). Elliot (History, I. 408) accepting Tod's date A.D. 524 refers the overthrow to Skythian barbarians from Sindh. Elphinstone, also accepting A.D. 524 as an approximate date, suggested (History, 3rd Edition, 212) as the destroyer the Sassanian Naushirván or Chosroes the Great (A.D. 531-579) citing in support of a Sassanian inroad Malcolm's Persia, I. 141 and Pottinger's Travels, 386. Forbes (Rás Málá, I. 22) notes that the Jain accounts give the date of the overthrow Vik. Sam. 375 that is A.D. 319 apparently in confusion with the epoch of the Gupta era which the Valabhi kings adopted.* Forbes says (Ditto, 24): If the destroyers had not been called *mlechchhas* I might have supposed them to be the Dakhan Chálukyas. Genl. Cunningham (Anc. Geog. 318) holds that the date of the destruction was A.D. 658 and the destroyer the Ráshṭrakúṭa Rája Govind who restored the ancient family of Sáuráshṭra. Thomas (Prinsep's Useful Tables, 158) fixes the destruction of Valabhi at A.D. 745 (S. 802). In the Káthiáwár Gazetteer Col. Watson in one passage (page 671) says the destroyers may have been the early Muhammadans who retired as quickly as they came. In another passage (page 274), accepting Mr. Burgess' (Arch. Sur. Rep. IV. 75) Gupta era of A.D. 195 and an overthrow date of A.D. 642, and citing a Wadhwán couplet telling how Ebhal Valabhi withstood the Iranians, Col. Watson suggests the destroyers may have been Iranians. If the Pársis came in A.D. 642 they must have come not as raiders but as refugees. If they could they would not have destroyed Valabhi. If the Pársis destroyed Valabhi where next did they flee to.

* Similarly S. 205 the date given by some of Col. Tod's authorities (An. of Ráj. I. 82 and 217-220) represents A.D. 524 the practical establishment of the Valabhi dynasty. The mistake of ascribing an era to the overthrow not to the founding of a state occurs (compare Sachau's Alberuni, II. 6) in the case both of the Vikrama era B.C. 57 and of the Sáliváhana era A.D. 78. In both these cases the error was intentional. It was devised with the aim of hiding the supremacy of foreigners in early Hindu history. So also, according to Alberuni's information (Sachau, II. 7) the Guptakála A.D. 319 marks the ceasing not the beginning of the wicked and powerful Guptas. This device is not confined to India. His Mede informant told Herodotus (B.C. 450 Rawlinson's Herodotus, I. 407) that B.C. 708 was the founding of the Median monarchy. The date really marked the overthrow of the Medes by the Assyrian Sargon.

[2] Tod (An. of Ráj. I. 231) notices what is perhaps a reminiscence of this date (A.D. 766). It is the story that Bappa, who according to Mewáḍ tradition is the founder of Gehlot power at Chitor, abandoned his country for Irán in A.D. 764 (S. 820). It seems probable that this Bappa or Saila is not the founder of Gehlot power at Chitor, but, according to the Valabhi use of Bappa, is the founder's father and that this retreat to Irán refers to his being carried captive to Mansúra on the fall either of Valabhi or of Gandhár.

[3] Reinaud's Fragments, 143 note 1; Mémoire Sur l'Inde, 105; Sachau's Alberuni, I. 193. The treachery of the magician Ranka is the same cause as that assigned by Forbes (Rás Málá, I. 12-18) from Jain sources. The local legend (Ditto, 18) points the inevitable Tower of Siloam moral, a moral which (compare Rás Málá, I. 18) is probably at the root of the antique tale of Lot and the Cities of the Plain, that men whose city was so completely destroyed must have been sinners beyond others. Dr. Nicholson (J. R. A. S. Ser. I. Vol. XIII. page 153) in 1851 thought the site of Valabhi bore many traces of destruction by water.

Chapter VIII.

The Valabhis, A.D. 509 - 766.

The Fall of Valabhi, A.D. 750 - 770.

that country as are found in places wasted by an unexpected attack.[1] For this expedition against Valabhi Alberuni gives no date. But as Mansúra was not founded till A.D. 750[2] and as the latest Valabhi copperplate is A.D. 766 the expedition must have taken place between A.D. 750 and 770. In support of the Hindu tradition of an expedition from Mansúra against Valabhi between A.D. 750 and 770 it is to be noted that the Arab historians of Sindh record that in A.D. 758 (H. 140) the Khalif Mansúr sent Amru bin Jamal with a fleet of barks to the coast of Barada.[3] Twenty years later A.D. 776 (H. 160) a second expedition succeeded in taking the town, but, as sickness broke out, they had to return. The question remains should the word, which in these extracts Elliot reads Barada, be read Balaba. The lax rules of Arab cursive writing would cause little difficulty in adopting the reading Balaba.[4] Further it is hard to believe that Valabhi, though to some extent sheltered by its distance from the coast and probably a place of less importance than its chroniclers describe, should be unknown to the Arab raiders of the seventh and eighth centuries and after its fall be known to Alberuni in the eleventh century. At the same time, as during the eighth century there was, or at least as there may have been,[5] a town Barada on the south-west coast of Káthiáváḍa the iden-

---

[1] Lassen (Ind. Alt. III. 533) puts aside Alberuni's Arab expedition from Mansúra as without historical support and inadmissible. Lassen held that Valabhi flourished long after its alleged destruction from Mansúra. Lassen's statement (see Ind. Alt. III. 533) is based on the mistaken idea that as the Valabhis were the Balharas the Balharas' capital Mánkir must be Valabhi. So far as is known, except Alberuni himself (see below) none of the Arab geographers of the ninth tenth or eleventh centuries mentions Valabhi. It is true that according to Lassen (Ind. Alt. 536) Masudi A.D. 915, Istakhri A.D. 951, and Ibn Háukal A.D. 976 all attest the existence of Valabhi up to their own time. This remark is due either to the mistake regarding Malkhet or to the identification of Bálwi or Balzi in Sindh (Elliot's History, I. 27 - 34) with Valabhi. The only known Musalmán reference to Valabhi later than A.D. 750 is Alberuni's statement (Sachau, II. 7) that the Valabhi of the era is 30 *yojanas* or 200 miles south of Anahilaváḍa. That after its overthrow Valabhi remained, as it still continues, a local town has been shown in the text. Such an after-life is in no way inconsistent with its destruction as a leading capital in A.D. 767.

[2] According to Alberuni (Sachau, I. 21) Al Mansúra, which was close to Bráhmanábád about 47 miles north-east of Haidarábád (Elliot's Musalmán Historians, I. 372 - 374) was built by the great Muhammad Kásim about A.D. 713. Apparently Alberuni wrote Muhammad Kásim by mistake for his grandson Amru Muhammad (Elliot, I. 372 note 1 and 442-3), who built the city a little before A.D. 750. Reinaud (Fragments, 210) makes Amru the son of Muhammad Kásim. Masudi (A.D. 915) gives the same date (A.D. 750), but (Elliot, I. 24) makes the builder the Ummayide governor Mansúr bin Jamhur. Idrísi (A.D. 1137 Elliot, I. 78) says Mansúra was built and named in honour of the Khalif Abu Jáfar-al-Mansur. If so its building would be later than A.D. 754. On such a point Idrísi's authority carries little weight.

[3] Elliot, I. 244.

[4] That the word read Barada by Elliot is in the lax pointless *shikasta* writing is shown by the different proposed readings (Elliot, I. 444 note 1) Narand, Barand, and Barid. So far as the original goes Balaba is probably as likely a rendering as Barada. Reinaud (Fragments, 212) says he cannot restore the name.

Though, except as applied to the Porbandar range of hills, the name Barada is almost unknown, and though Ghumli not Barada was the early (eighth-twelfth century) capital of Porbandar some place named Barada seems to have existed on the Porbandar coast. As early as the second century A.D., Ptolemy (McCrindle, 37) has a town Barda-xema on the coast west of the village *Kome* (probably the road or *kom*) of Sauráshtra; and St. Martin (Geographie Grecque et Latine de l'Inde, 203) identifies Pliny's (A.D. 77) Varetatæ next the Odomberæ or people of Kachh with the Varadas according to Hemachandra (A.D. 1150) a class of foreigners or *mlechchhas*. A somewhat tempting identification of Barada is with Beruni's Bárwi (Sachau, I. 208) or Baraous (Reinaud's Fragments, 121) 84 miles (14 *parasangs*) west of Somanátha. But an examination of Beruni's text shows that Bárwi is not the name of a place but of a product of Kachh the *bára* or bezoar stone.

Chapter VIII.

THE VALABHIS, A.D. 509-766.

The Fall of Valabhi, A.D. 750-770.

tification of the raids against Barada with the traditional expedition against Balaba though perhaps probable cannot be considered certain. Further the statement of the Sindh historians[1] that at this time the Sindh Arabs also made a naval expedition against Kandahár seems in agreement with the traditional account in Tod that after the destruction of Valabhi the rulers retired to a fort near Cambay from which after a few years they were driven.[2] If this fort is the Kandahár of the Sindh writers and Gandhár on the Broach coast about twenty miles south of Cambay, identifications which are in agreement with other passages, the Arab and Rajput accounts would fairly agree.[3]

The Importance of Valabhi.

The discovery of its lost site; the natural but mistaken identification of its rulers with the famous eighth and ninth century (A.D. 753-972) Balharas of Málkhet in the East Dakhan;[4] the tracing to Valabhi of the Rána of Udepur in Mewáḍ the head of the Sesodias or Gohils the most exalted of Hindu families[5]; and in later times the wealth of Valabhi copperplates have combined to make the Valabhis one of the best known of Gujarát dynasties. Except the complete genealogy, covering the 250 years from the beginning of the sixth to the middle of the eighth century, little is known of Valabhi or its chiefs. The

---

[1] Elliot, I. 445.

[2] Compare Tod (Annals, I. 83 and 217). Gajni or Gayni another capital whence the last prince Síláditya was expelled by Parthian invaders in the sixth century.

[3] Compare Reinaud (Fragments, 212 note 4) who identifies it with the Ain-i-Akbari Kandahár that is Gandhár in Broach. The identification is doubtful. Tod (Annals, I. 217) names the fort Gajni or Gayni and there was a fort Gajni close to Cambay. Elliot (I. 445) would identify the Arab Kandahár with Khandadár in north-west Káthiáváḍa.

Even after A.D. 770 Valabhi seems to have been attacked by the Arabs. Dr. Bhagvánlál notices that two Jain dates for the destruction of the city 826 and 886 are in the Vira era and that this means not the Mahávira era of B.C. 526 but the Vikram era of B.C. 57. The corresponding dates are therefore A.D. 769 and 829. Evidence in support of the A.D. 769 and 770 defeat is given in the text. On behalf of Dr. Bhagvánlál's second date A.D. 829 it is remarkable that in or about A.D. 830 (Elliot, I. 447) Músa the Arab governor of Sindh captured Bála the ruler of As Sharqi. As there seems no reason to identify this As Sharqi with the Sindh lake of As Sharqi mentioned in a raid in A.D. 750 (Elliot, I. 441: J. R. A. S. (1893) page 76) the phrase would mean Bála king of the east. The Arab record of the defeat of Bála would thus be in close agreement with the Jain date for the latest foreign attack on Valabhi.

[4] The identification of the Balharas of the Arab writers with the Chálukyas (A.D. 500-753) and Ráshṭrakúṭas (A.D. 753-972) of Málkhet in the East Dakhan has been accepted. The vagueness of the early (A.D. 850-900) Arab geographers still more the inaccuracy of Idrísi (A.D. 1137) in placing the Balharas capital in Gujarát (Elliot, I. 87) suggested a connection between Balhara and Valabhi. The suitableness of this identification was increased by the use among Rájput writers of the title Balakarai for the Valabhi chief (Tod An. of Ráj. I. 83) and the absence among either the Chálukyas (A.D. 500-753) or the Ráshṭrakúṭas (A.D. 753-972) of Málkhet of any title resembling Balhara. Prof. Bhandárkar's (Deccan History, 56-57) discovery that several of the early Chálukyas and Ráshṭrakúṭas had the personal name Vallabha Beloved settled the question and established the accuracy of all Masudi's (A.D. 915) statements (Elliot, I. 19-21) regarding the Balhara who ruled the Kamkar, that is Kamrakara or Karnáṭak (Sachau's Beruni, I. 202; II. 318) and had their Kánarese (Kiriya) capital at Mankir (Málkhet) 640 miles from the coast.

[5] After their withdrawal from Valabhi to Mewáḍ the Válas took the name of Gehlot (see below page 98), then of Aharya from a temporary capital near Udepur (Tod's An. of Ráj. I. 215), next of Sesodia in the west of Mewáḍ (Tod's An. of Ráj. I. 216; Western India, 57). Since 1568 the Rána's head-quarters have been at Udepur. Ráj. Gaz. III. 18. After the establishment of their power in Chitor (A.D. 780), a branch of the Gehlot or Gohil family withdrew to Kheir in south-west Márwár. These driven south by the Ráthods in the end of the twelfth century are the Gohils of Piram, Bhávnagar, and Rájpipla in Káthiáváḍa and Gujarát. Tod's Annals of Ráj. I. 114, 228.

Chapter VIII.

The Valabhis, A.D. 509 - 766.

The Importance of Valabhi, A.D. 750 - 770.

origin of the city and of its rulers, the extent of their sway, and the cause and date of their overthrow are all uncertain. The unfitness of the site, the want of reservoirs or other stone remains, the uncertainty when its rulers gained an independent position, the fact that only one of them claimed the title *Chakravarti* or All Ruler are hardly consistent with any far-reaching authority. Add to this the continuance of Maitraka or Mer power in North Káthiáváḍa, the separateness though perhaps dependence of Saurāshtra even in the time of Valabhi's greatest power,[1] the rare mention of Valabhi in contemporary Gujárat grants,[2] and the absence of trustworthy reference in the accounts of the Arab raids of the seventh or eighth centuries tend to raise a doubt whether, except perhaps during the ten years ending 650, Valabhi was ever of more than local importance.

Valabhi and the Gehlots.

In connection with the pride of the Sesodias or Gohils of Mewáḍ in their Valabhi origin[3] the question who were the Valabhis has a special interest. The text shows that Pandit Bhagvánlál was of opinion the Valabhis were Gurjjaras. The text also notes that the Pandit believed they reached south-east Káthiáváḍa by sea from near Broach and that if they did not come to Broach from Málwa at least the early rulers obtained (A.D. 520 and 526) investiture from the Málwa kings. Apart from the doubtful evidence of an early second to fifth century Bála or Valabhi three considerations weigh against the theory that the Valabhis entered Gujarát from Málwa in the sixth century. First their acceptance of the Gupta era and of the Gupta currency raises the presumption that the Valabhis were in Káthiáváḍa during Gupta ascendancy (A.D. 440 - 480): Second that the Sesodias trace their pedigree through Valabhi to an earlier settlement at Dhánk in south-west Káthiáváḍa and that the Válas of Dhánk still hold the place of heads of the Válas of Káthiáváḍa: And Third that both Sesodias and Válas trace their origin to Kanaksen a second century North Indian immigrant into Káthiáváḍa combine to raise the presumption that the Válas were in Káthiáváḍa before the historical founding of Valabhi in A.D. 526[4] and that the city took its name from its founders the Válas or Bálás.

Whether or not the ancestors of the Gohils and Válas were settled in Káthiáváḍa before the establishment of Valabhi about A.D. 526

---

[1] The somewhat doubtful Jáikadeva plates (above page 87 and Káthiáváḍa Gazetteer, 275) seem to show the continuance of Maitraka power in North Káthiáváḍa. This is supported by the expedition of the Arab chief of Sándhán in Kachch (A.D. 840) against the Medhs of Hind which ended in the capture of Mália in North Káthiaváḍa. Elliot, I. 450. Hiuen Tsiang (A.D. 630) (Beal's Buddhist Records, II. 69) describes Sauráshṭra as a separate state but at the same time notes its dependence on Valabhi. Its rulers seem to have been Mehrs. In A.D. 713 (Elliot, I. 123) Muhammad Kasim made peace with the men of Surasht, Medhs, seafarers, and pirates.

[2] The only contemporary rulers in whose grants a reference to Valabhi has been traced are the Gurjjaras of Broach (A.D. 580-808) one of whom, Dadda II. (A.D. 633), is said (Ind. Ant. XIII. 79) to have gained renown by protecting the lord of Valabhi who had been defeated by the illustrious Srí Harshadeva (A.D. 608 - 649), and another Jayabhaṭa in A.D. 706 (Ind. Ant. V. 115) claims to have quieted with the sword the impetuosity of the lord of Valabhi.

[3] Tod An. of Raj. I. 217: Western India, 269.

[4] Tod An. of Raj. I. 112 and Western India, 148: Rás Málá, I. 21. It is not clear whether these passages prove that the Sesodias or only the Válas claim an early settlement at Dhánk. In any case (see below page 101) both clans trace their origin to Kanaksen.

Chapter VIII.

The Valabhis, A.D. 509-766.

Valabhi and the Gehlots.

several considerations bear out the correctness of the Rájput traditions and the Jain records that the Gohils or Sesodias of Mewáḍ came from Bala or Valabhi in Káthiáváḍa. Such a withdrawal from the coast, the result of the terror of Arab raids, is in agreement with the fact that from about the middle of the eighth century the rulers of Gujarát established an inland capital at Anahilaváḍa (A.D. 746).[1] It is further in agreement with the establishment by the Gohil refugees of a town Balli in Mewáḍ ; with the continuance as late as A.D. 968 (S. 1024) by the Sesodia chief of the Valabhi title Śíláditya or Sail[2]; and with the peculiar Valabhi blend of Sun and S'iva worship still to be found in Udepur.[3] The question remains how far can the half-poetic accounts of the Sesodias be reconciled with a date for the fall of Valabhi so late as A.D. 766. The mythical wanderings, the caveborn Guha, and his rule at Idar can be easily spared. The name Gehlot which the Sesodias trace to the caveborn Guha may as the Bhávnagar Gehlots hold have its origin in Guhasena (A.D. 559-567) perhaps the first Valabhi chief of more than local distinction.[4] Tod[5] fixes the first historical date in the Sesodia family history at A.D. 720 or 728 the ousting of the Mori or Maurya of Chitor by Bappa or Sail. An inscription near Chitor shows the Mori in power in Chitor as late as A.D. 714 (S. 770).[6] By counting back nine generations from Sakti Kumára the tenth from Bappa whose date is A.D. 1038 Tod fixes A.D. 720-728 as the date when the Gohils succeeded the Moris. But

---

[1] Tod's Western India, 51. [2] Tod's An. of Raj. I. 230.

[3] The cherished title of the later Valabhis, Síláditya Sun of Virtue, confirms the special sun worship at Valabhi, which the mention of Dharapaṭṭa (A.D. 550) as a devotee of the supreme sun supports, and which the legends of Valabhi's sun-horse and sun-fountain keep fresh (Rás Málá, I. 14-18). So the great one-stone liṅgas, the most notable trace of Valabhi city (J. R. A. S. Ser. I. Vol. XIII. 149 and XVII. 271), bear out the Valabhi copperplate claim that its rulers were great worshippers of S'iva. Similarly the Rána of Udepur, while enjoying the title of Sun of the Hindus, prospering under the sun banner, and specially worshipping the sun (Tod's Annals, I. 565) is at the same time the Minister of S'iva the One Liṅg *Eklingakadiwán* (Ditto 222, Ráj. Gaz. III. 53). The blend is natural. The fierce noon-tide sun is Mahákála the Destroyer. Like S'iva the Sun is lord of the Moon. And marshalled by Somanátha the great Soul Home the souls of the dead pass heavenwards along the rays of the setting sun. [Compare Sachau's Alberuni, II. 168.] It is the common sun element in S'aivism and in Vaishnavism that gives their holiness to the sunset shrines of Somanátha and Dwárka. For (Ditto, 169) the setting sun is the door whence men march forth into the world of existence Westwards, heavenwards.

[4] This explanation is hardly satisfactory. The name Gehlot seems to be Guhila-putra from Gobhila-putra an ancient Bráhman gotra, one of the not uncommon cases of Rájputs with a Bráhman gotra. The Rájput use of a Bráhman gotra is generally considered a technical affiliation, a mark of respect for some Bráhman teacher. It seems doubtful whether the practice is not a reminiscence of an ancestral Bráhman strain. This view finds confirmation in the Aitpur inscription (Tod's Annals, I. 802) which states that Guhadit the founder of the Gohil tribe was of Bráhman race *Vipra-kula*. Compare the legend (Rás Málá, I. 13) that makes the first Śíláditya of Valabhi (A.D. 590-609) the son of a Bráhman woman Compare (Elliot, I. 411) the Bráhman Chách (A.D. 630-670) marrying the widow of the Sháhi king of Alor in Sindh who is written of as a Rájput though like the later (A.D. 850-1060) Shahiyas of Kabul (Alberuni, Sachau II. 13) the dynasty may possibly have been Bráhmans.* The following passage from Hodgson's Essays (J. A. Soc. Bl. II. 218) throws light on the subject: Among the Khás or Rájputs of Nepal the sons of Bráhmans by Khás women take their fathers' gotras. Compare Ibbetson's Panjáb Census 1881 page 236.

* In support of a Bráhman origin is Prinsep's conjecture (J. A. S. Bl. LXXIV. [Feb. 1838) page 93) that Divaij the name of the first recorded king may be Dvija or Twice-born. But Divaij for Deváditya, like Silaij for S'íláditya, seems simpler and the care with which the writer speaks of Chach as the Bráhman almost implies that his predecessors were not Bráhmans. According to Elliot (II. 426) the Pála of Kábul were Rajputs, perhaps Bhattias.

[5] Tod's Annals, I. 229-231. [6] Annals, I. 229.

the sufficient average allowance of twenty years for each reign would bring Bappa to A.D. 770 or 780 a date in agreement with a fall of Valabhi between A.D. 760 and 770, as well as with the statement of Abul Fazl, who, writing in A.D. 1590, says the Rána's family had been in Mewáḍ for about 800 years.[1]

The Válas of Káthiaváḍa.

The Arab accounts of the surprise-attack and of the failure of the invaders to make a settlement agree with the local and Rájputána traditions that a branch of the Valabhi family continued to rule at Vaḷeh until its conquest by Múla Rája Solaṇkhi in A.D. 950.[2] Though their bards favour the explanation of Vála from the Gujaráti *valvu* return or the Persian *válah*[3] noble the family claim to be of the old Valabhi stock. They still have the tradition they were driven out by the Musalmáns, they still keep up the family name of Selait or Śíláditya.[4]

The local tradition regarding the settlement of the Válas in the Balakshetra south of Valabhi is that it took place after the capture of Valabhi by Múla Rája Solaṇkhi (A.D. 950).[5] If, as may perhaps be accepted, the present Válas represent the rulers of Valabhi it seems to follow the Válas were the overlords of Balakshetra at least from the time of the historical prosperity of Valabhi (A.D. 526 - 680). The traditions of the Bábriás who held the east of Sorath show that when they arrived (A.D. 1200 - 1250) the Vála Rájputs were in possession and suggest that the lands of the Válas originally stretched as far west as Diu.[6] That the Válas held central Káthiáváḍa is shown by their possession of the old capital Vanthali nine miles south-west of Junágaḍh and by (about A.D. 850) their transfer of that town to the Chuḍásamás.[7] Dhánk, about twenty-five miles north-west of Junágaḍh, was apparently held by the Válas under the Jetwas when (A.D. 800 - 1200 ?) Ghumli or Bhumli was the capital of south-west Káthiáváḍa. According to Jetwa accounts the Válas were newcomers whom the Jetwas allowed to settle at Dhánk.[8] But as the Jetwas are not among the earliest settlers in Káthiáváḍa it seems more probable that, like the Chuḍásamás at Vanthali, the Jetwas found the Válas in possession. The close connection of the Válas with the earlier waves of Káthis is admitted.[9] Considering that the present

[1] Gladwin's Ain-i-Akbarí, II. 81 ; Tod's Annals, I. 235 and note*. Tod's dates are confused. The Aitpur inscription (Ditto, page 230) gives Śakti Kumára's date A.D. 968 (S. 1024) while the authorities which Tod accepts (Ditto, 231) give A.D. 1068 (S. 1125). That the Moris were not driven out of Chitor as early as A.D. 728 is proved by the Navsárí inscription which mentions the Arabs defeating the Mauryas as late as A.D. 738-9 (Sam. 490). See above page 56.

[2] Tod Western India 268 says Siddha Rája (A.D. 1094 - 1143) : Múla Rája (A.D 942 - 997) seems correct. See Rás Málá, I. 65.

[3] Káthiáwár Gazetteer, 672.

[4] The chronicles of Bhadrod, fifty-one miles south-west of Bhávnagar, have (Káth. Gaz. 380) a Selait Vála as late as A.D. 1554.

[5] Káthiáwár Gazetteer, 672. Another account places the movement south after the arrival of the Gohils A.D. 1250. According to local traditions the Válas did not pass to Bhadrod near Mahuva till A.D. 1554 (Káth. Gaz. 380) and from Bhadrod (Káth. Gaz. 660) retired to Dholarva.

[6] Káth. Gaz. 111 and 132. According to the Ain-i-Akbarí (Gladwin, II. 69) the inhabitants of the ports of Mahua and Tulája were of the Vála tribe.

[7] Káth. Gaz. 680.

[8] Káth. Gaz. 414.

[9] The Vála connection with the Káthis complicates their history. Col. Watson (Káth. Gaz. 130) seems to favour the view that the Válas were the earliest wave of Káthis who came into Káthiáváḍa from Málwa apparently with the Guptas (A.D. 450) (Ditto, 671). Col. Watson seems to have been led to this conclusion in consequence of the existence

Chapter VIII.
THE VALABHIS, A.D. 509 - 766.

(1881) total of Káthiáváḍa Vála Rájputs is about 900 against about 9000 Vála Káthis, the Válas,[1] since their loss of power, seem either to have passed into unnoticeable subdivisions of other Rájput tribes or to have fallen to the position of Káthis.

The Válas and Káthis.

If from the first and not solely since the fall of Valabhi the Válas have been associated with the Káthis it seems best to suppose they held to the Káthis a position like that of the Jetwas to their followers the Mers. According to Tod[2] both Válas and Káthis claim the title *Tata Multánka Rai* Lords of Tata and Multán. The accounts of the different sackings of Valabhi are too confused and the traces of an earlier settlement too scanty and doubtful to justify any attempt to carry back Valabhi and the Válas beyond the Maitraka overthrow of Gupta power in Káthiáváḍa (A.D. 470 - 480). The boast that Bhaṭárka, the reputed founder of the house of Valabhi (A.D. 509), had obtained glory by dealing hundreds of blows on the large and very mighty armies of the Maitrakas who by force had subdued their enemies, together with the fact that the Valabhis did and the Maitrakas did not adopt the Gupta era and currency seem to show the Válas were settled in Káthiáváḍa at an earlier date than the Mers and Jetwas. That is, if the identification is correct, the Válas and Káthis were in Káthiáváḍa before the first wave of the White Huns approached. It has been noticed above under Skandagupta that the enemies, or some of the enemies, with whom, in the early years of his reign A.D. 452-454, Skandagupta had so fierce a struggle were still in A.D. 456 a source of anxiety and required the control of a specially able viceroy at Junágaḍh. Since no trace of the Káthis appears in Káthiáváḍa legends or traditions before the fifth century the suggestion may be offered that under Vála or Bála leadership the Káthis were among the enemies who on the death of Kumáragupta (A.D. 454) seized the Gupta possessions in Káthiáváḍa. Both Válas and Káthis would then be northerners driven south from Multán and South

---

of the petty state of Kátti in west Khándesh. But the people of the Kátti state in west Khándesh are Bhils or Kolis. Neither the people nor the position of the country seems to show connection with the Káthis of Káthiáváḍa. Col. Watson (Káth. Gaz. 130) inclines to hold that the Válas are an example of the rising of a lower class to be Rájputs. That both Válas and Káthis are northerners admitted into Hinduism may be accepted. Still it seems probable that on arrival in Káthiáváḍa the Válas were the leaders of the Káthis and that it is mainly since the fall of Valabhi that a large branch of the Válas have sunk to be Káthis. The Káthi traditions admit the superiority of the Válas. According to Tod (Western India, 270: Annals, I. 112-113) the Káthis claim to be a branch or descendants of the Válas. In Káthiáváḍa the Válas, the highest division of Káthis (Rás Málá, I. 296; Káth. Gaz. 122, 123, 131, 139), admit that their founder was a Vála Rájput who lost caste by marrying a Káthi woman. Another tradition (Rás Málá, I. 296; Káth. Gaz. 122 note 1) records that the Káthis flying from Sindh took refuge with the Válas and became their followers. Col. Watson (Káth. Gaz. 130) considers the practice in Porbandar and Navanagar of styling any lady of the Dhánk Vála family who marries into their house Káthiáníbái the Káthi lady proves that the Válas are Káthis. But as this name must be used with respect it may be a trace that the Válas claim to be lords of the Káthis as the Jetwas claim to be lords of the Mers. That the position of the Válas and Káthis as Rájputs is doubtful in Káthiáváḍa and is assured (Tod's Annals, I. 111) in Rájputána is strange. The explanation may perhaps be that aloofness from Muhammadans is the practical test of honour among Rájputana Hindus, and that in the troubled times between the thirteenth and the seventeenth centuries, like the Jhálas, the Válas and Káthis may have refused Moghal alliances, and so won the approval of the Ránás of Mewáḍ.

[1] Káth. Gaz. 110 - 129.

[2] Western India, 207; Annals, I. 112 - 113.

Chapter VIII.

The Valabhis, A.D. 509-766.

Sindh by the movements of tribes displaced by the advance of the Ephthalites or White Huns (A.D. 440-450) upon the earlier North Indian and border settlements of the Yuan-Yuan or Avars.[1]

Descent from Kanaksen, A.D. 150.

The Sesodia or Gohil tradition is that the founder of the Válas was Kanaksen, who, in the second century after Christ, from North India established his power at Virát or Dholka in North Gujarát and at Dhánk in Káthiáváḍa.[2] This tradition, which according to Tod[3] is supported by at least ten genealogical lists derived from distinct sources, seems a reminiscence of some connection between the early Válas and the Kshatrapas of Junágaḍh with the family of the great Kushán emperor Kanishka (A.D. 78-98). Whether this high ancestry belongs of right to the Válas and Gohils or whether it has been won for them by their bards nothing in the records of Káthiáváḍa is likely to be able to prove. Besides by the Válas Kanaksen is claimed as an ancestor by the Chávaḍás of Okhámandal as the founder of Kanakapurí and as reigning in Krishna's throne in Dwárká.[4] In support of the form Kanaka for Kanishka is the doubtful Kanaka-Śakas or Kanishka-Śakas of Varáhamihira (A.D. 580).[5] The form Kanik is also used by Alberuni[6] for the famous Vihára or monastery at Pesháwar of whose founder Kanak Alberuni retails many widespread legends. Tod[7] says; 'If the traditional date (A.D. 144) of Kanaksen's arrival in Káthiáváḍa had been only a little earlier it would have fitted well with Wilson's Kanishka of the Raja Tarangini.' Information brought to light since Tod's time shows that hardly any date could fit better than A.D. 144 for some member of the Kushán family, possibly a grandson of the great Kanishka, to make a settlement in Gujarát and Káthiáváḍa. The date agrees closely with the revolt against Vasudeva (A.D. 123-150), the second in succession from Kanishka, raised by the Panjab Yaudheyas, whom the great Gujarát Kshatrapa Rudradáman (A.D. 143-158), the introducer of Kanishka's (A.D. 78) era into Gujarát, humbled. The tradition calls Kanaksen Kośalaputra and brings him from Lohkot in North India.[8] Kośala has been explained as Oudh and Lohkot as Lahore, but as Kanak came from the north not from the north-east an original Kushána-putra or Son of the Kushán may be the true form. Similarly Lohkot cannot be Lahore. It may be Alberuni's Lauhavar or Lahur in the Káshmir uplands one of the main centres of Kushán power.[9]

---

[1] It is worthy of note that Bálas and Káthiás are returned from neighbouring Panjáb districts. Bálas from Dehra Ismail Khán (Panjáb Census Report 1891 Part III, 310), Káthiá Rájputs from Montgomery (Ditto, 318), and Káthiá Játs from Jhang and Dera Ismail Khán (Ditto, 143). Compare Ibbetson's (1881) Panjáb Census, I. 259, where the Káthiás are identified with the Kathaioi who fought Alexander the Great (B.C. 325) and also with the Káthis of Káthiáváḍa. According to this report (page 240) the Válas are said to have come from Málwa and are returned in East Pánjab.

[2] Tod's Annals, I. 83 and 215; Elliot, II. 410; Jour. B. Br. A. S. XXIII.

[3] Annals, I. 215.

[4] Kath. Gaz. 589.

[5] Bṛihat-Saṁhitá, XIV. 21. The usual explanation (compare Fleet Ind. Ant. XXII. 180) Gold-Śakas seems meaningless.

[6] Sachau, II. 11. Among the legends are the much-applied tales of the foot-stamped cloth and the self-sacrificing minister.

[7] Western India, 213.

[8] Tod's Annals, I. 83, 215; Western India, 270-352.

[9] Sachau, I. 208, II. 341. For the alleged descent of the Sesodiás and Válas from Ráma of the Sun race the explanation may be offered that the greatness of Kanishka, whose power was spread from the Ganges to the Oxus, in accordance with the Hindu

Chapter VIII.
THE VALABHIS, A.D. 509-766.
Mewád and the Persians.

One further point requires notice, the traditional connection between Valabhi and the Ránás of Mewáḍ with the Sassanian kings of Persia (A.D. 250-650). In support of the tradition Abul Fazl (A.D. 1590) says the Ránás of Mewáḍ consider themselves descendants of the Sassanian Naushirván (A.D. 531-579) and Tod quotes fuller details from the Persian history Maaser-al-Umra.[1] No evidence seems to support a direct connection with Naushirván.[2] At the same time marriage between the Valabhi chief and Maha Banu the fugitive daughter of Yezdigerd the last Sassanian (A.D. 651) is not impossible.[3] And the remaining suggestion that the link may be Naushirván's son Naushizád who fled from his father in A.D. 570 receives support in the statement of Procopius[4] that Naushizád found shelter at Belapatan in Khuzistán perhaps Balapatan in Gurjaristán. As these suggestions are unsupported by direct evidence, it seems best to look for the source of the legend in the fire symbols in use on Káthiáváḍa and Mewáḍ coins. These fire symbols, though in the main Indo-Skythian, betray from about the sixth century a more direct Sassanian influence. The use of similar coins coupled with their common sun worship seems sufficient to explain how the Agnikulas and other Káthiáváḍa and Mewáḍ Rájputs came to believe in some family connection between their chiefs and the fireworshipping kings of Persia.[5]

Válas.

Can the Vála traditions of previous northern settlements be supported either by early Hindu inscriptions or from living traces in the present population of Northern India? The convenient and elaborate tribe and surname lists in the Census Report of the Panjáb, and vaguer information from Rajputána, show traces of Bálas and Válas among the Musalmán as well as among the Hindu population of Northern India.[6] Among the tribes mentioned in Varáha-Mihira's sixth century (A.D. 580)[7] lists the Váhlikas appear along with the dwellers on Sindhu's banks. An inscription of a king Chandra, probably Chandragupta and if so about A.D. 380-400,[8] boasts of crossing the seven mouths of the Indus to attack the Váhlikas. These references suggest that the Bálas or Válas are the Válhikas and that the Bálhikas of the Harivaṃśa (A.D. 350-500?) are not as Langlois supposed people then ruling

doctrine (compare Beal's Buddhist Records, I. 99 & 152; Rás Málá, I. 320; Fryer's New Account, 190) that a conqueror's success is the fruit of transcendent merit in a former birth, led to Kanishka being considered an incarnation of Ráma. A connection between Kanishka and the race of the Sun would be made easy by the intentional confusing of the names Kshatrapa and Kshatriya and by the fact that during part at least of his life fire and the sun were Kanishka's favourite deities.

[1] Gladwin's Ain-i-Akbari, II. 81: Tod's Annals, I. 235.

[2] The invasion of Sindh formerly (Reinaud's Fragments, 29) supposed to be by Naushirvan in person according to fuller accounts seems to have been a raid by the ruler of Seistán (Elliot, I. 407). Still Reinaud (Mémoire Sur l'Inde, 127) holds that in sign of vassalage the Sindh king added a Persian type to his coins.

[3] Compare Tod's Annals, I. 235-239 and Rawlinson's Seventh Monarchy, 576.

[4] Rawlinson Seventh Monarchy, 452 note 3.

[5] Compare Tod's Annals, I. 63; Thomas' Prinsep, I. 413; Cunningham's Arch. Survey, VI. 201. According to their own accounts (Rás Málá, I. 296) the Kathis learned sun-worship from the Vála of Dhánk by whom the famous temple of the sun at Thán in Káthiáváḍa was built.

[6] Válas Musalmán Játs in Lahor and Gurdaspur: Váls in Gujarát and Gujranwálá: Váls in Mozafarnagar and Dhera Ismael Khan. Also Válahs Hindus in Kángra. Panjáb Census of 1891, III. 162.

[7] Bṛihaṭ Saṃhitá, V. 80.

[8] Corp. Ins. Ind. III. 140-141.

in Balkh but people then established in India.[1] Does it follow that the Válhikas of the inscriptions and the Bálhikas of the Harivaṃśa are the Panjáb tribe referred to in the Mahábhárata as the Báhikas or Bálhikas, a people held to scorn as keeping no Bráhman rites, their Bráhmans degraded, their women abandoned?[2] Of the two Mahábhárata forms Báhika and Bálhika recent scholars have preferred Bálhika with the sense of people of Balkh or Baktria.[3] The name Bálhika might belong to more than one of the Central Asian invaders of Northern India during the centuries before and after Christ, whose manner of life might be expected to strike an Áryávarta Bráhman with horror. The date of the settlement of these northern tribes (B.C. 180 - A.D. 300) does not conflict with the comparatively modern date (A.D. 150 - 250) now generally received for the final revision of the Mahábhárata.[4] This explanation does not remove the difficulty caused by references to Báhikas and Bálhikas in Pánini and other writers earlier than the first of the after-Alexander Skythian invasions. At the same time as shown in the footnote there seems reason to hold that the change from the Bákhtri of Darius (B.C. 510) and Alexander the Great (B.C. 330) to the modern Balkh did not take place before the first century after Christ. If this view is correct it follows that

[1] The references are; Langlois' Harivaṃśa, I. 388-420, II. 178. That in A.D. 247 Balkh or Báktria was free from Indian overlordship (McCrindle's Periplus, 121), and that no more distant tribe than the Gandharas finds a place in the Harivaṃśa lists combine to make it almost certain that, at the time the Harivaṃśa was written, whatever their origin may have been, the Báhlikas were settled not in Báktria but in India.

[2] The passage from the Karṇa Parva or Eighth Book of the Mahábhárata is quoted in Muir's Sanskrit Texts, II. 482, and in greater fullness in St. Martin's Geog. Greque et Latine de l'Inde, 402-410. The Báhikas or Balhikas are classed with the Madras, Gandháras, Araṭṭas, and other Panjáb tribes. In their Bráhman families it is said the eldest son alone is a Bráhman. The younger brothers are without restraint Kshatriyas, Vaiśyas, Sudras, even Barbers. A Bráhman may sink to be a Barber and a barber may rise to be a Bráhman. The Báhikas eat flesh even the flesh of the cow and drink liquor. Their women know no restraint. They dance in public places unclad save with garlands. In the Harivaṃśa (Langlois, I. 493 and II. 178, 388, 420) the Bahlikas occur in lists of kings and peoples.

[3] Kern in Muir's Sanskrit Texts, II. 446. St. Martin (Geog. Greque et Latine de l'Inde, 149) takes Báhika to be a contraction of Báhlika. Reasons are given below for considering the Mahábhárata form Báhika a confusion with the earlier tribes of that name rather than a contraction of Báhlika or Bálhika. The form Báhika was also favoured by the writer in the Mahábhárata because it fitted with his punning derivation from their two fiend ancestors *Vahi* and *Hika*. St. Martin, 408.

[4] St. Martin Geog. Greque et Latine de l'Inde, 403, puts the probable date at B.C. 380 or about fifty years before Alexander. St. Martin held that the passage belonged to the final revision of the poem. Since St. Martin's time the tendency has been to lower the date of the final revision by at least 500 years. The fact noted by St. Martin (Ditto, page 404) that Jartika which the Mahábhárata writer gives as another name for Báhika is a Sanskritised form of Jat further supports the later date. It is now generally accepted that the Jats are one of the leading tribes who about the beginning of the Christian era passed from Central Asia into India.

[5] The name Valabhi, as we learn from the Jain historians, is a Sanskritised form of Valahi, which can be easily traced back to one of the many forms (Bálhika, Bálhika, Balhika, Bahlíka, Báhlika, Váhlíka, Vahlíka, Válhíka, Válhika, Valhika) of a tribal name which is of common occurrence in the Epics. This name is, no doubt rightly, traced back to the city of Balkh, and originally denoted merely the people of Baktria. There is, however, evidence that the name also denoted a tribe doubtless of Baktrian origin, but settled in India: the Emperor Chandra speaks of defeating the Váhlikas after crossing the seven mouths of the Indus: Varáha-Mihira speaks of the Válhíkas along with the people who dwell on Sindhu's banks (Bṛ. Saṃ. V. 80): and, most decisive of all, the Káśiká Vritti on Pāṇ. VIII. iv. 9 (A.D. 650) gives Bahlíka as the name of the people of the Sauvíra country, which, as Alberuni tells us, corresponded to the

Chapter VIII.
The Valabhis, A.D. 509-766.
Válas.

if the form Bahlika occurs in Páṇini or other earlier writers it is a mistaken form due to some copyist's confusion with the later name Bahlika. As used by Páṇini the name Báhika applied to certain Panjáb tribes seems a general term meaning Outsider a view which is supported by Brian Hodgson's identification of the Mahábhárata Báhikas with the Bahings one of the outcaste or broken tribes of Nepál.[1] The use of Báhika in the Mahábhárata would then be due either to the wish to identify new tribes with old or to the temptation to use a word which had a suitable meaning in Sanskrit. If then there is fair ground for holding that the correct form of the name in the Mahábhárata is Bálhika and that Bálhika means men of Balkh the question remains which of the different waves of Central Asian invaders in the centuries before and after Christ are most likely to have adopted or to have received the title of Baktrians. Between the second century before and the third century after Christ two sets of northerners might justly have claimed or have received the title of Baktrians. These northerners are the Baktrian Greeks about B.C. 180 and the Yuechi between B.C. 20 and A.D. 300. Yavana is so favourite a name among Indian writers that it may be accepted that whatever other northern tribes the name Yavana includes no name but Yavana passed into use for the Baktrian Greeks. Their long peaceful and civilised rule (B.C. 130 - A.D. 300 ?) from their capital at Balkh entitles the Yuechi to the name Baktrians or Báhlikas. That the Yuechi were known in India as Baktrians is proved by the writer of the Periplus (A.D. 247), who, when Baktria was still under Yuechi rule, speaks of the Baktrianoi as a most warlike race governed by their own sovereign.[2] It is known that in certain cases the Yuechi tribal names were of local origin. Kushán the name of the leading tribe is according to some authorities a place-name.[3]

---

modern Multán, the very country to which the traditions of the modern Válas point.

If the usual derivation of the name Bálhika be accepted,* it is possible to go a step further and fix a probable limit before which the tribe did not enter India. The name of Balkh in the sixth century B.C. was, as we learn from Darius' inscriptions, Bákhtri, and the Greeks also knew it as Baktra: the Avesta form is Bakhdhi, which according to the laws of sound-change established by Prof. Darmsteter for the Arachosian language as represented by the modern Pushtu, would become Bahli (see Chants Populaires des Afghans, Introd. page xxvii). This reduction of the hard aspirates to spirants seems to have taken place about the first century A.D.: parallel cases are the change from Parthava to Palhava, and Mithra to Mihira. It would seem therefore that the Bahlikas did not enter India before the first century A.D.: and if we may identify their subduer Chandra with Chandragupta I., we should have the fourth century A.D. as a lower limit for dating their invasion.

Unfortunately, however, these limits cannot at present be regarded as more than plausible: for the name Balhika or Valhika appears to occur in works that can hardly be as modern as the first century A.D. The Atharvaveda-pariśishtas might be put aside, as they show strong traces of Greek influence and are therefore of late date: and the supposed occurrences in Páṇini belong to the commentators and to the Gaṇapátha only and are of more or less uncertain age. But the name occurs, in the form Balhika, in one hymn of the Atharvaveda itself (Book V. 22) which there is no reason to suppose is of late date.

The lower limit is also uncertain as the identification of Chandra of the inscription with the Gupta king is purely conjectural.—(A. M. T. J.)

* There is a very close parallel in the modern Panjáb, where (see Census Report of 1881) the national name Baluch has become a tribal name in the same way as Bálhika.

[1] Hodgson's Essays on Indian Subjects, I. 405 Note.

[2] McCrindle's Periplus, 121. Compare Rawlinson's Seventh Monarchy, 79. The absence of Indian reference to the Yuechi supports the view that in India the Yuechi were known by some other name.

[3] According to Reinaud (Mémoire Sur l'Inde, 82 note 3) probably the modern

And it is established that the names of more than one of the tribes who about B.C. 50 joined under the head of the Kushāns were taken from the lands where they had settled. It is therefore in agreement both with the movements and with the practice of the Yuechi, that, on reaching India, a portion of them should be known as Báhlikas or Bálhikas. Though the evidence falls short of proof there seems fair reason to suggest that the present Rajput and Káthi Válas or Bálas of Gujarát and Rajputána, through a Sanskritised Váhlika, may be traced to some section of the Yuechi, who, as they passed south from Baktria, between the first century before and the fourth century after Christ, assumed or received the title of men of Balkh.

One collateral point seems to deserve notice. St. Martin[1] says : 'The Greek historians do not show the least trace of the name Báhlika.' Accepting Báhika, with the general sense of Outsider, as the form used by Indian writers before the Christian era and remembering [2] Pánini's description of the Málavas and Kshudrakas as two Báhika tribes of the North-West the fact that Pāṇini lived very shortly before or after the time of Alexander and was specially acquainted with the Panjáb leaves little doubt that when (A.D. 326) Alexander conquered their country the Malloi and Oxydrakai, that is the Málavas and Kshudrakas, were known as Báhikas. Seeing that Alexander's writers were specially interested in and acquainted with the Malloi and Oxydrakai it is strange if St. Martin is correct in stating that Greek writings show no trace of the name Báhika. In explanation of this difficulty the following suggestion may be offered.[3] As the Greeks sounded their *kh* (χ) as a spirant, the Indian Báhika would strike them as almost the exact equivalent of their own word βακχικος. More than one of Alexander's writers has curious references to a Bacchic element in the Panjáb tribes. Arrian[4] notices that, as Alexander's fleet passed down the Jhelum, the people lined the banks chanting songs taught them by Dionysus and the Bacchantes. According to Quintus Curtius[5] the name of Father Bacchus was famous among the people to the south of the Malloi. These references are vague. But Strabo is definite.[6] The Malloi and Oxydrakai are reported to be the descendants of Bacchus. This passage is the more important since Strabo's use of the writings of Aristobulus Alexander's historian and of Onesikritos Alexander's pilot and Bráhman-interviewer gives his details a special value.[7] It may be said Strabo explains why the Malloi and Oxydrakai were called Bacchic and Strabo's explanation is not in agreement with the proposed Báhika origin. The answer is that Strabo's explanation can be proved to be in part, if not altogether, fictitious. Strabo[8] gives two reasons why the Oxydrakai

---

Kochanya or Kashania sixty or seventy miles west of Samarkand. This is Hiuen Tsiang's (A.D. 620) Ki'uh-shwangi-ni-kia or Kushánika. See Beal's Buddhist Records, I. 34.

[1] Etude sur la Geographie Grecque et Latine de l'Inde, 147.

[2] McCrindle's Alexander in India, 350.

[3] The suggestion is made by Mr. A. M. T. Jackson.

[4] McCrindle's Alexander, 136. [5] McCrindle's Alexander, 252.

[6] Compare Strabo, XV. I. 8. The Oxydrakai are the descendants of Dionysus. Again, XV. I. 24 : The Malloi and the Oxydrakai who as we have already said are fabled to be related to Dionysus.

[7] See McCrindle's Alexander, 157, 369, 378, 398. Compare St. Martin Geog. Grecque et Latine de l'Inde, 102.

[8] Strabo, XV. I. 8 and 24, Hamilton's Translation, III. 76, 95.

Chapter VIII.
THE VALABHIS, A.D. 509-766.
Valas.

were called Bacchic. First because the vine grew among them and second because their kings marched forth *Bakkhikôs* that is after the Bacchic manner. It is difficult to prove that in the time of Alexander the vine did not grow in the Panjáb. Still the fact that the vines of Nysa near Jalálábád and of the hill Meros are mentioned by several writers and that no vines are referred to in the Greek accounts of the Panjáb suggests that the vine theory is an after-thought.[1] Strabo's second explanation, the Bacchic pomp of their kings, can be more completely disproved. The evidence that neither the Malloi nor the Oxydrakai had a king is abundant.[2] That the Greeks knew the Malloi and Oxydrakai were called Bakkhikoi and that they did not know why they had received that name favours the view that the explanation lies in the Indian name Báhika. One point remains. Does any trace of the original Báhikas or Outsiders survive? In Cutch Káthiáváḍa and North Gujarát are two tribes of half settled cattle-breeders and shepherds whose names Rahbáris as if Rahábaher and Bharváds as if Bahervâda seem like Báhika to mean Outsider. Though in other respects both classes appear to have adopted ordinary Hindu practices the conduct of the Bharvád women of Káthiáváḍa during their special marriage seasons bears a curiously close resemblance to certain of the details in the Mahábhárata account of the Báhika women. Colonel Barton writes:[3] 'The great marriage festival of the Káthiáváda Bharváds which is held once in ten or twelve years is called the Milkdrinking, *Dudhpíno*, from the lavish use of milk or clarified butter. Under the exciting influence of the butter the women become frantic singing obscene songs breaking down hedges and spoiling the surrounding crops.' Though the Bharváds are so long settled in Káthiáváḍa as to be considered aboriginals their own tradition preserves the memory of a former settlement in Márwár.[4] This tradition is supported by the fact that the shrine of the family goddess of the Cutch Rabáris is in Jodhpur,[5] and by the claim of the Cutch Bharváds that their home is in the North-West Provinces.[6]

---

[1] References to the vines of Nysa and Meros occur in Strabo, Pliny, Quintus Curtius, Philostratus, and Justin: McCrindle's Alexander in India, 193 note 1, 321, and 339. Strabo (Hamilton's Translation, III. 86) refers to a vine in the country of Musikanus or Upper Sindh. At the same time (Ditto, 108) Strabo accepts Megasthenes' statement that in India the wild vine grows only in the hills.

[2] The Kathaioi Malloi and Oxydrakai are (Arrian in McCrindle's Alexander, 115, 137, 140, 149) called independent in the sense of kingless: they (Ditto, 154) sent leading men not ambassadors: (compare also Diodorus Siculus and Plutarch, Ditto 287, 311): the Malloi had to chose a leader (Q. Curtius, Ditto 236).

[3] Káthiáwár Gazetteer, 138. [4] Káthiáwár Gazetteer, 137. [5] Cutch Gazetteer, 80.

[6] Cutch Gazetteer, 81.

CHAPTER IX.

THE CHÁLUKYAS

(A.D. 634-740.)

Chapter IX.

THE CHÁLUKYAS, A.D. 634-740.

THE Chálukyas conquered their Gujarát provinces from the south after subduing the Konkan Mauryas of Purí either Rájápurí that is Janjira or Elephanta in Bombay harbour. The fifth century Váda inscription of king Suketuvarmman proves that this Maurya dynasty[1] ruled in the Konkan for at least a century before they came into collision with the Chálukyas under Kírtivarmman.[2] They were finally defeated and their capital Purí taken by Chaṇḍadaṇḍa an officer of Pulakeśi II. (A.D. 610-640).[3] The Chálukyas then pressed northwards, and an inscription at Aihole in South Bijápur records that as early as A.D. 634 the kings of Láṭa, Málava, and Gurjjara submitted to the prowess of Pulakeśi II. (A.D. 610-640).

Jayasiṃhavarmman, A.D. 666-693.

The regular establishment of Chálukya power in South Gujarát seems to have been the work of Dháráśraya Jayasiṃhavarmman son of Pulakeśi II. and younger brother of Vikramáditya Satyáśraya (A.D. 670-680). A grant of Jayasiṃhavarmman's son Śíláditya found in Navsárí describes Jayasiṃhavarmman as receiving the kingdom from his brother Vikramáditya. As Jayasiṃhavarmman is called *Paramabhaṭṭáraka* Great Lord, he probably was practically independent. He had five sons and enjoyed a long life, ruling apparently from Navsárí. Of the five Gujarát Chálukya copperplates noted below, three are in an era marked Saṃ. which is clearly different from the Śaka era (A.D. 78) used in the grants of the main Chálukyas. From the nature of the case the new era of the Gujarát Chálukyas may be accepted as of Gujarát origin. Grants remain of Jayasiṃhavarmman's sons dated S. 421, 443, and 490.[4] This checked by Vikramáditya's known date (A.D. 670-680) gives an initial between A.D. 249 and 259. Of the two Gujarát eras, the Gupta-Valabhi (A.D. 319) and the Traikúṭaka (A.D. 248-9), the Gupta-Valabhi is clearly unsuitable. On the other hand the result is so closely in accord with A.D. 248-9, the Traikúṭaka epoch, as to place the correctness of the identification almost beyond question.

Jayasiṃhavarmman must have established his power in South Gujarát before A.D. 669-70 (T. 421), as in that year his son Śryáśraya made a grant as heir apparent. Another plate of Śryáśraya found in Surat shows that in A.D. 691-2 (T. 443) Jayasiṃhavarmman was still ruling with Śryáśraya as heir apparent. In view of these facts the establishment of Jayasiṃhavarmman's power in Gujarát must be taken at about A.D. 666. The copperplates of his sons and grandson do not say whom Jayasiṃhavarmman overthrew. Probably the defeated rulers were Gurjjaras, as about this time a Gurjjara dynasty held the Broach district with its capital at Nándípurí the modern Nándod in the Rájpipla State about thirty-five miles east of Broach. So far

---

[1] Bom. Gaz. XIV. 372. [2] Ind. Ant. VIII. 243. [3] Ind. Ant. VIII. 244.
[4] J. B. B. R. A. S. XVI. 1ff. : Proceedings VIIth Oriental Congress, 210ff.

Chapter IX.
THE CHÁLUKYAS, A.D. 634-740.
Jayasimhavarmman, A.D. 666-693.

as is known the earliest of the Nándod Gurjjaras was Dadda who is estimated to have flourished about A.D. 580 (T. 331).[1] The latest is Jayabhata whose Navsárí copperplate bears date A.D. 734-5 (T. 486)[2] so that the Gurjjara and Chálukya kingdoms flourished almost at the same time. It is possible that the power of the earlier Gurjjara kings spread as far south as Balsár and even up to Konkan limits. It was apparently from them that, during the reign of his brother Vikramáditya, Jayasimhavarmman took South Gujarát, driving the Gurjjaras north of the Tápti and eventually confining them to the Broach district, the Gurjjaras either acknowledging Chalukya sovereignty or withstanding the Chálukyas and retaining their small territory in the Broach district by the help of the Valabhis with whom they were in alliance.[3] In either case the Chálukya power seems to have hemmed in the Broach Gurjjaras, as Jayasimhavarmman had a son Buddhavarmman ruling in Kaira. A copperplate of Buddhavarmman's son Vijayarája found in Kaira is granted from Vijayapura identified with Bijápur near Párantij, but probably some place further south, as the grant is made to Bráhmans of Jambusar. Five copperplates remain of this branch of the Chálukyas, the Navsárí grant of S'ryáśraya S'íláditya Yuvarája dated A.D. 669-70 (T. 421); the Surat grant of the same Śíláditya dated A.D. 691-2 (T. 443); the Balsár grant of Vinayáditya Mangalarája dated A.D. 731 (S'aka 653); the Navsárí grant of Pulakeśi Janáśraya dated A.D. 738-9 (T. 490); the Kaira grant of Vijayarája dated Saṃvatsara 394; and the undated Nirpan grant of Nágavarddhana Tribhuvanáśraya.

Sryáśraya Síláditya (Heir Apparent), A.D. 669-691.

The first four grants mention Jayasiṃhavarmman as the younger brother of Vikramáditya Satyáśraya the son of Pulakeśi Satyáśraya the conqueror of Harshavarddhana the lord of the North. Jayasimhavarmman's eldest son was Sryáśraya Śíláditya who made his Navsárí grant in A.D. 669-70 (T. 421); the village granted being said to be in the Navasáriká Vishaya. S'ryáśraya's other plate dated A.D. 691-2 (T. 443) grants a field in the village of Osumbhalá in the Kármaneya Áhára that is the district of Kámlej on the Tápti fifteen miles north-east of Surat. In both grants S'íláditya is called Yuvarája, which shows that his father ruled with him from A.D. 669 to A.D. 691. Both copperplates show that these kings treated as their overlords the main dynasty of the southern Chálukyas as respectful mention is made in the first plate of Vikramáditya Satyáśraya and in the second of his son Vinayáditya Satyáśraya. Apparently S'ryáśraya died before his father as the two late grants of Balsár and Kheḍá give him no place in the list of rulers.

Mangalarája, A.D. 698-731.

Jayasimhavarmman was succeeded by his second son Mangalarája. A plate of his found at Balsár dated A.D. 731 (Saka 653) records a grant made from Mangalapurí, probably the same as Purí the doubtful Konkan capital of the Śiláháras.[4] As his elder brother was heir-apparent in A.D. 691-2 (T. 443), Mangalarája must have succeeded some years later, say about A.D. 698-9 (T. 450). From this it may be inferred that the copperplate of A.D. 731 was issued towards the end of his reign.

---

[1] See Chap. X. below. [2] Ind. Ant. XIII. 73. [3] Ind. Ant. XIII. 70.
[4] B. B. R. A. S. XVI. 5.

Chapter IX.

THE CHÁLUKYAS, A.D. 634-740.

Pulakeśi Janáśraya, A.D. 738.

Mangalarája was succeeded by his younger brother Pulakeśi Janáśraya. This is the time of Khalif Hashám (H. 105-125, A.D. 724-743) whose Sindh governor Junaid is recorded to have sent expeditions against Marmád, Mandal, Dalmaj (Kámlej ?), Bárus, Uzain, Máliba, Baharimad (Mevad ?), Al Bailáimán (Bhinmál ?), and Juzr. Though several of these names seem to have been misread and perhaps misspelt on account of the confusion in the original Arabic, still Marmád, Mandal, Barus, Uzain, Máliba, and Juzr can easily be identified with Márvád, Mandal near Viramgám, Bharuch, Ujjain, Málwa, and Gurjjara. The defeat of one of these raids is described at length in Pulakeśi's grant of A.D. 738-9 (T. 490) which states that the Arab army had afflicted the kingdoms of Sindhu, Kacchella, Sauráshtra, Chávotaka, Maurya, and Gurjjara that is Sindh, Kacch, the Chávaḍás, the Mauryas of Chitor,[1] and the Gurjjaras of Bhínmál.[2]

---

[1] For the Moris or Mauryas, described as a branch of Pramáras, who held Chitor during the eighth century compare Tod. Jr. R. A. S. 211 ; Wilson's Works, XII. 132.

[2] The text of the copperplate runs :

शरद्मसीरमुद्गरोद्धारिणि तरलतरतारतरवारिदा

[24] रितोदितसैन्धवकच्छेल्लसौराष्ट्र चावोटक मौर्यगुर्जरादिरा [ज्ये] निःशेष-
दाक्षिणात्याक्षितिपतिजि

[25] गीषया दक्षिणापथप्रवेश···············प्रथममेवनवसारिकाविषयप्र-
साधनायागते त्वरित

PLATE II.

[1] तुरगखरमुखरखुरोत्खातधरिणिधूलिधूसरितदिगन्तरे कुन्तप्रान्तानितान्ताव‍ि-
मर्द्यमानरभसाभिधावितो

[2] द्भटस्थलोदरविवरविनिर्गतांत्रप्रधुतररुधिरधारारंजितकवचभीषणवपुषि स्वा-
मिमहा

[3] सन्मानदानग्रहण ˇक्रयीकृतस्वशिरोभिरभिमुखमापतितैप्रदंषदशनाग्रदष्टोष्ट-
पुटकैरने

[4] कसमराजिरविवरवरिकरिकटितटहयविघटनाविशाल्तिघनरुधिरपटलपाट-
ल्तिपटुकृपाणपट्टैरपि महा

[5] योवैरलब्धपरभागैः विपक्षक्षपणाक्षेपक्षिप्रक्षिप्रतीक्ष्णक्षुरप्रप्रहारविलूनवैरि-
।शिर ˇकमलगलनालैरा

[6] हवरसरभसरोमांचकंचुकाच्छादिततनूभिरनेकैरपि नरेन्द्रवृंदवृदारकैरजित-
पुर्वै : व्यपगतमस्माक

[7] ग्रणमनेन स्वामिनः स्वशिर :प्रदानेनाद्यतावदेकजन्मीयामित्येवमिषोपजातप-
रितोषानन्तरप्रहतपट्टप

[8] टहरवप्रवृत्तकबन्धबद्धरासमण्डलीके समराशिरासि विजितेताजिकानिके शो-
य्यानुरागिणा श्रीवदत्रमनरें

[9] द्रेण प्रसादीकृतापरनामचतुष्टयस्तद्यथा दक्षिणापथसाधारणचलुक्किकुलालं-
कारपृथ्वीवदत्रमानिवर्त्तकनिव

[10] र्त्तयित्रवनिजनाश्रयश्रीपुलकेशिराजस्सर्वानेवात्मीयान्

Chapter IX.

THE CHÁLUKYAS, A.D. 634-740.

Pulakeśi was at this time ruling at Navsárí. It is uncertain how much longer this Chálukya kingdom of Navsárí continued. It was probably overthrown about A.D. 750 by the Gujarát branch of the Ráshṭrakúṭas who were in possession in A.D. 757-8.[1]

Buddhavarmman, A.D. 713 (?).

The Kaira grant dated 394 gives in hereditary succession the names Jayasimha, Buddhavarmman, and Vijayarája.[2] The grant is made from Vijayapura, which, as the late Colonel West suggested, may be Bijápur near Parántij though this is far to the north of the otherwise known Chálukya limits. The village granted is Pariyaya in the Káśákula division. If taken as Traikúṭaka the date 394 corresponds to A.D. 642-3. This is out of the question, since Vijayarája's grand-uncle Vikramáditya flourished between A.D. 670 and 680. Professor Bhandarkar considers the plate a forgery, but there seems no sufficient reason for doubting its genuineness. No fault can be found with the character. It is written in the usual style of Western Chálukya grants, and contains the names of a number of Bráhman grantees with minute details of the fields granted a feature most unusual in a forged grant. In the Gupta era, which equally with the Traikúṭaka era may be denoted by the word *Saṃ.* and which is more likely to be in use in North Gujarát the 394 would represent the fairly probable A.D. 713. Jayasimha may have conquered part of North Gujarát and sent his son Buddhavarmman to rule over it.

Nágavarddhana.

Jayasimha appears to have had a third son Nágavarddhana ruling in West Násik which was connected with South Gujarát through Balsár, Párdi, and Penth. The Nirpan grant of Nágavarddhana is undated,[3] and, though it gives a wrong genealogy, its seal, the form of composition, the *biruda* or title of the king, and the alphabet all so closely agree with the style of the Gujarát Chálukya plates that it cannot be considered a forgery.

Not long after A.D. 740 the Chálukyas seem to have been supplanted in South Gujarát by the Ráshṭrakúṭas.

Chálukya Tree.

CHÁLUKYA FAMILY TREE.

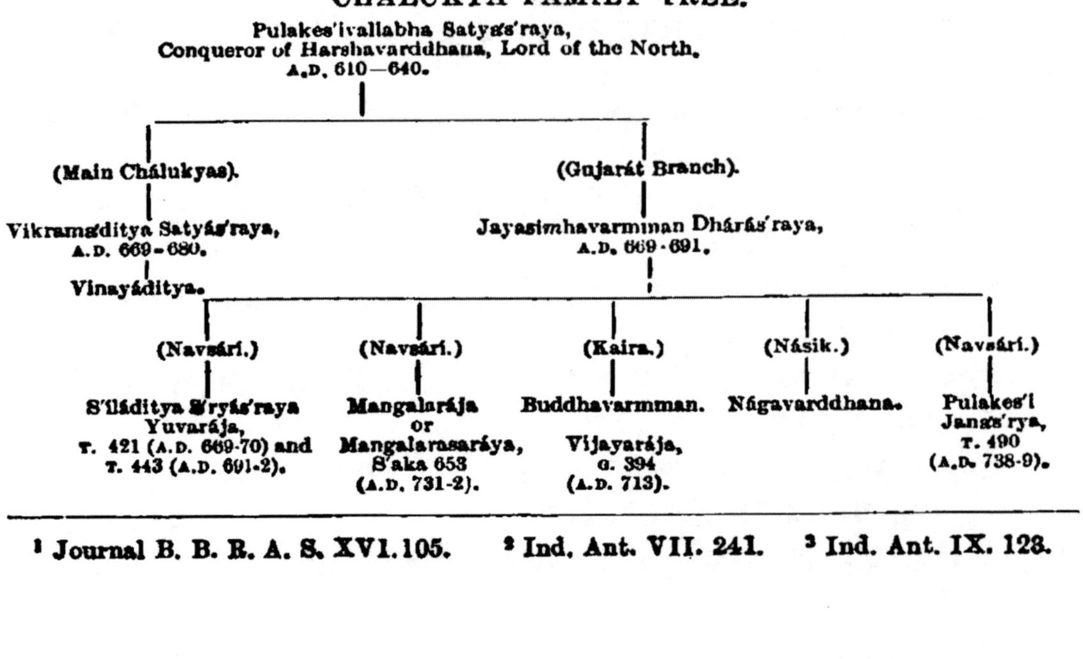

[1] Journal B. B. R. A. S. XVI. 105. [2] Ind. Ant. VII. 241. [3] Ind. Ant. IX. 123.

Chapter IX.

THE CHÁLUKYAS, A.D. 634 - 740.

Vijayarája's grant of the year 394 (A.D. 642-3) is the earliest trace of Chálukya rule in Gujarát. Dr. Bhagvánlál, who believed in its genuineness, supposes it to be dated in the Gupta era (G. 394 = A.D. 714) and infers from it the existence of Chálukya rule far to the north of Broach. But the most cursory comparison of it with the Khedá grants of Dadda II. (see Ind. Ant. XIII. 81ff) which are dated (admittedly in the [so-called] Traikúṭaka era) 380 and 385 respectively, shows that a large number of Dadda's grantees reappear in the Chálukya grant. The date of the Chálukya plate must therefore be interpreted as a Traikúṭaka or Chedi date.

A.D. 610 - 640.

This being so, it is clearly impossible to suppose that Vijayarája's grandfather Jayasiṃha is that younger son of Pulakeśi II. (A.D. 610 - 640) who founded the Gujarát branch family. It has been usually supposed that the Jayasiṃha of our grant was a younger brother of Pulakeśi II. : but this also is chronologically impossible : for Jayasiṃha can hardly have been more than ten years of age in A.D. 597-98, when his elder brother was set aside as too young to rule. His son Buddhavarmman could hardly have been born before A.D. 610, so that Buddhavarmman's son Vijayarája must have made his grant at the age of twelve at latest. The true solution of the question seems to be that given by Dr. Bhandárkar in his Early History of the Deccan (page 42 note 7), namely that the grant is a forgery. To the reasons advanced by him may be added the fact pointed out by Mr. Fleet (Ind. Ant. VII. 251) that the grant is a palimpsest, the engraver having originally commenced it "Svasti Vijayavikshepán Na." It can hardly be doubted that *Na* is the first syllable of Nándípurí the palace of the Gurjjara kings. Many of the grantees were Bráhmans of Jambusar and subjects of Dadda II. of Broach, whose grants to them are extant. It seems obvious that Vijayarája's grant was forged in the interest of these persons by some one who had Gurjjara grants before him as models, but knew very little of the forms used in the chancery of the Chálukyas.

Setting aside this grant, the first genuine trace of Chálukya rule in Gujarát is to be found in the grant of the Sendraka chief Nikumbhallaśakti, which bears date Saṃ. 406 (A.D. 654-5) and relates to the gift to a Bráhman of the village of Balisa (Wanesa) in the Treyaṇṇa (Ten) district. Dr. Bühler has shown (Ind. Ant. XVIII. page 265ff) that the Sendrakas were a Kánarese family, and that Nikumbhallaśakti must have come to Gujarát as a Chálukya feudatory, though he names no overlord. He was doubtless subordinate to the Chálukya governor of Násik.

The next grant that requires notice is that of Nágavarddhana, who describes himself distinctly as the son of Pulakeśi's brother Jayasiṃha, though Dr. Bhagvánlál believed this Jayasiṃha to be Pulakeśi's son. Mr. Fleet points out other difficulties connected with this grant, but on the whole decides in favour of its genuineness (see Ind. Ant. IX. 123). The description of Pulakeśi II. in this grant refers to his victory over Harshavarddhana, but also describes him as having conquered the three kingdoms of Chera, Chola, and Páṇḍya by means of his horse of the Chitrakauṭha breed, and as meditating on the feet of Śri Nágavarddhana. Now all of these epithets, except the reference to Harshavarddhana, belong properly, not to Pulakeśi II. but to his son Vikramáditya I. The conquest of the confederacy of Cholas, Cheras (or Keraḷas), and Páṇḍyas is ascribed to Vikramáditya in the inscriptions of his son Vinayáditya (Fleet in Ind. Ant. X. 134): the Chitrakaṇṭha horse is named in Vikramáditya's own grants (Ind. Ant. VI. 75 &c.) while his meditation upon the feet of Nágavarddhana recurs in the T. 421 grant of Śryáśraya Śíláditya (B. B. R. A. S. XVI. 1ff). This confusion of epithets between Pulakeśi II. and Vikramáditya makes it difficult to doubt that Nágavarddhana's grant was composed either during or after Vikramáditya's reign, and under the influence of that king's grants. It may be argued that even in that case the grant may be genuine, its inconsistencies being due merely to carelessness. This supposition the following considerations seem to negative. Pulakeśi II. was alive at the time of Hiuen Tsiang's visit (A.D. 640), but is not likely to have reigned very much longer. And, as Vikramáditya's reign is supposed to have begun about A.D. 669-70, a gap remains of nearly thirty years. That part of this period was occupied by the war with the three kings

Chapter IX.

THE CHÁLUKYAS, A.D. 634 - 740.

of the south we know from Vikramáditya's own grants: but the grant of Sryáśraya Śíláditya referred to above seems to show that Vikramáditya was the successor, not of his father, but of Nágavarddhana upon whose feet he is described as meditating. It follows that Nágavarddhana succeeded Pulakeśi and preceded Vikramáditya on the imperial throne of the Chálukyas whereas his grant could not have been composed until the reign of Vikramáditya.

Although the grant is not genuine, we have no reason to doubt that it gives a correct genealogy, and that Nágavarddhana was the son of Pulakeśi's brother Jayasiṃha and therefore the first cousin of Vikramáditya. The grant is in the regular Chálukya style, and the writer, living near the Northern Chálukya capital, Násik, had better models than the composer of Vijayarája's grant. Both grants may have been composed about the time when the Chálukya power succumbed to the attacks of the Ráshṭrakúṭas (A.D. 743).—(A. M. T. J.)

CHAPTER X.

THE GURJJARAS

(A.D. 580–808.)

Chapter X.

THE GURJJARAS, A.D. 580 - 808.

DURING Valabhi and Chálukya ascendancy a small Gurjjara kingdom flourished in and about Broach. As has been noticed in the Valabhi chapter the Gurjjaras were a foreign tribe who came to Gujarát from Northern India. All the available information regarding the Broach Gurjjaras comes from nine copperplates,[1] three of them forged, all obtained from South Gujarát. These plates limit the regular Gurjjara territory to the Broach district between the Mahí and the Narbadá, though at times their power extended north to Kheḍá and south to the Tápti. Like the grants of the contemporary Gujarát Chálukyas all the genuine copperplates are dated in the Traikúṭaka era which begins in A.D. 249-50.[2] The Gurjjara capital seems to have been Nándípurí or Nándor,[3] the modern Nándod the capital of Rájpipla in Rewa Kántha about thirty-four miles east of Broach. Two of their grants issue *Nándípurítaḥ*[4] that is 'from Nándípurí' like the *Valabhítaḥ* or 'from Valabhi' of the Valabhi copperplates, a phrase which in both cases seems to show the place named was the capital since in other Gurjjara grants the word *vásaka* or camp occurs.[5]

Copperplates.

Though the Gurjjaras held a considerable territory in South Gujarát their plates seem to show they were not independent rulers. The general titles are either *Samadhigata-panchamahásabda* 'He who has attained the five great titles,' or *Sámanta* Feudatory. In one instance Jayabhaṭa III. who was probably a powerful ruler is called *Sámantádhipati*[6] Lord of Feudatories. It is hard to say to what suzerain these Broach Gurjjaras acknowledged fealty. Latterly they seem to have accepted the Chálukyas on the south as their overlords. But during the greater part of their existence they may have been feudatories of the Valabhi dynasty, who, as

---

[1] Ind. Ant. V. 109ff; Ind. Ant. VII. 61ff.; Jour. R. A. S. (N. S.), I. 274ff.; Ind. Ant. XIII. 81 - 91; Jour. B. B. R. A. Soc. X. 19ff.; Ind. Ant. XIII. 115 - 119. Ind. Ant. XVII. and Ep. Ind. II. 19ff.

[2] See above page 107.

[3] That Nándor or Nándod was an old and important city is proved by the fact that Bráhmans and Vániás called Nándorás that is of Nándor are found throughout Gujarát. Mángrol and Chorvád on the South Káthiáváḍa coast have settlements of Velári betel-vine cultivators who call themselves Nandora Vániás and apparently brought the betel-vine from Nándod. Dr. Bühler, however, identifies the Nándípurí of the grants with an old fort of the same name about two miles north of the east gate of Broach. See Ind. Ant. VII. 62.

[4] Ind. Ant. XIII. 81, 88.

[5] Ind. Ant. XIII. 70.

[6] The fact that the Umetá and Iláo plates give their grantor Dadda II. the title of *Mahárájádhirája* Supreme Lord of Great Kings, is one of the grounds for believing them forgeries.

Chapter X.
THE GURJJARAS, A.D. 580-808.
Copperplates.

mentioned above were probably Gurjjaras who passed from Málwa to South Gujarát and thence by sea to Valabhi leaving a branch in South Gujarát.

The facts that in A.D. 649 (Valabhi 330) a Valabhi king had a 'camp of victory' at Broach where Raṇagraha's plate[1] shows the Gurjjaras were then ruling and that the Gurjjara king Dadda II. gave shelter to a Valabhi king establish a close connection between Valabhi and the Nándod Gurjjaras.

Their copperplates and seals closely resemble the plates and seals of the Gujarát Chálukyas. The characters of all but the forged grants are like those of Gujarát Chálukya grants and belong to the Gujarát variety of the Southern India style. At the same time it is to be noted that the royal signature at the end of the plates is of the northern type, proving that the Gurjjaras were originally northerners. The language of most of the grants is Sanskrit prose as in Valabhi plates in a style curiously like the style of the contemporary author Báṇa in his great works the Kádambarí and Harshacharita. From this it may be inferred that Báṇa's style was not peculiar to himself but was the style in general use in India at that time.

Gurjjara Tree.

The following is the Gurjjara family tree :

Dadda I. A.D. 580.
|
Jayabhaṭa I. A.D. 605.
|
Dadda II. A.D. 633.
|
Jayabhaṭa II. A.D. 655.
|
Dadda III. A.D. 680.
|
Jayabhaṭa III. A.D. 706-734.

A recently published grant[2] made by Nirihullaka, the chieftain of a jungle tribe in the lower valley of the Narbadá, shows that towards the end of the sixth century A.D. that region was occupied by wild tribes who acknowledged the supremacy of the Chedi or Kalachuri kings : a fact which accounts for the use of the Chedi or Traikúṭaka era in South Gujarát. Nirihullaka names with respect a king S'aṅkaraṇa, whom Dr. Bühler would identify with S'aṅkaragaṇa the father of the Kalachuri Buddhavarmman who was defeated by Mangalísa the Chálukya about A.D. 600.[3] S'aṅkaragaṇa himself must have flourished about A.D. 580, and the Gurjjara conquest must be subsequent to this date. Another new grant,[4] which is only a fragment and contains no king's name, but which on the ground of date (Sam. 346 = A.D. 594-5) and style may be safely attributed to the Gurjjara dynasty, shows that the Gurjjaras were established in the country within a few years of S'aṅkaragaṇa's probable date.

A still nearer approximation to the date of the Gurjjara conquest is suggested by the change in the titles of Dharasena I. of Valabhi, who

[1] Ep. Ind. II. 20. [2] Ep. Ind. II. 21. [3] Ind. Ant. VII. 162. [4] Ep. Ind. II. 19.

Chapter X.
THE GURJJARAS, A.D. 580-808.

in his grants of Samvat 252[1] (A.D. 571) calls himself Mahárája, while in his grants of 269 and 270[2] (A.D. 588 and 589), he adds the title of Mahásámanta, which points to subjection by some foreign power between A.D. 571 and A.D. 588. It seems highly probable that this power was that of the Gurjjaras of Bhínmál; and that their successes therefore took place between A.D. 580 and 588 or about A.D. 585.

Dadda I. c. 585-605 A.D.

The above mentioned anonymous grant of the year 346 (A.D. 594-95) is ascribed with great probability to Dadda I. who is known from the two Kheḍá grants of his grandson Dadda II. (c. 620-650 A.D.)[3] to have "uprooted the Nága" who must be the same as the jungle tribes ruled by Nirihullaka and are now represented by the Náikdás of the Panch Mahále and the Talabdas or Locals of Broach. The northern limit of Dadda's kingdom seems to have been the Vindhya, as the grant of 380 (A.D. 628-29) says that the lands lying around the feet of the Vindhya were for his pleasure. At the same time it appears that part at least of Northern Gujarát was ruled by the Mahásámanta Dharasena of Valabhi, who in Val. 270 (A.D. 589-90) granted a village in the *áhára* of Kheṭaka (Kheḍá).[4] Dadda is always spoken of as the *Sámanta*, which shows that while he lived his territory remained a part of the Gurjjara kingdom of Bhínmál. Subsequently North Gujarát fell into the hands of the Málava kings, to whom it belonged in Hiuen Tsiang's time (c. 640 A.D.).[5] Dadda I. is mentioned in the two Kheḍá grants of his grandson as a worshipper of the sun: the fragmentary grant of 346 (A.D. 594-95) which is attributed to him gives no historical details.

Jayabhaṭa I. Vítarága, c. 605-620 A.D.

Dadda I. was succeeded by his son Jayabhaṭa I. who is mentioned in the Kheḍá grants as a victorious and virtuous ruler, and appears from his title of Vítarága the Passionless to have been a religious prince.

Dadda II. Praśántarága, c. 620-650 A.D.

Jayabhata I. was succeeded by his son Dadda II. who bore the title of Praśántarága the Passion-calmed. Dadda was the donor of the two Kheḍá grants of 380 (A.D. 628-29) and 385 (A.D. 633-34), and a part of a grant made by his brother Raṇagraha in the year 391 (A.D. 639-40) has lately been published.[6] Three forged grants purporting to have been issued by him are dated respectively Śaka 400 (A.D. 478), Śaka 415 (A.D. 493), and Śaka 417 (A.D. 495).[7] Both of the Kheḍá grants relate to the gift of the village of Siríshapadraka (Sisodra) in the Akrúreśvara (Ankleśvar) vishaya to certain Bráhmans of Jambusar and Broach. In Raṇagraha's grant the name of the village is lost.

Dadda II.'s own grants describe him as having attained the five great titles, and praise him in general terms: and both he and his brother Raṇagraha sign their grants as devout worshippers of the sun. Dadda II. heads the genealogy in the later grant of 456 (A.D. 704-5),[8] which states that he protected "the lord of Valabhi who had been defeated by the great lord the illustrious Harshadeva." The event referred to must have been some expedition of the great Harshavardhana of Kanauj

[1] Ind. Ant. VII. 68, VIII. 302, XIII. 160, and XV. 187.
[2] Ind. Ant. VI. 9, VII. 70. [3] Ind. Ant. XIII. 81-88. [4] Ind. Ant. VII. 70.
[5] Beal's Buddhist Records, II. 266, 268. [6] Ind. Ant. XIII. 81-88, Ep. Ind. II. 19.
[7] On these forged grants see below page 117. [8] Ind. Ant. XIII. 70.

Chapter X.
THE GURJJARAS,
A.D. 580-808.
Dadda II.
Prasántarága,
C. 620-650 A.D.

(A.D. 607-648), perhaps the campaign in which Harsha was defeated on the Narbadá by Pulakeśi II. (which took place before A.D. 634). The protection given to the Valabhi king is perhaps referred to in the Kheḍá grants in the mention of "strangers and suppliants and people in distress." If this is the case the defeat of Valabhi took place before A.D. 628-29, the date of the earlier of the Kheḍá grants. On the other hand, the phrase quoted is by no means decisive, and the fact that in Hiuen Tsiang's time Dhruvasena of Valabhi was son-in-law of Harsha's son, makes it unlikely that Harsha should have been at war with him. It follows that the expedition referred to may have taken place in the reign of Dharasena IV. who may have been the son of Dhruvasena by another wife than Harsha's granddaughter.

To Dadda II.'s reign belongs Hiuen Tsiang's notice of the kingdom of Broach (C. 640 A.D.).[1] He says "all their profit is from the sea" and describes the country as salt and barren, which is still true of large tracts in the west and twelve hundred years ago was probably the condition of a much larger area than at present. Hiuen Tsiang does not say that Broach was subject to any other kingdom, but it is clear from the fact that Dadda bore the five great titles that he was a mere feudatory. At this period the valuable port of Broach, from which all their profit was made, was a prize fought for by all the neighbouring powers. With the surrounding country of Láṭa, Broach submitted to Pulakeśi II. (A.D. 610-640):[2] it may afterwards have fallen to the Málava kings, to whom in Hiuen Tsiang's time (A.D. 640) both Kheḍá (K'ie-ch'a) and Ánandapura (Vadnagar) belonged; later it was subject to Valabhi, as Dharasena IV. made a grant at Broach in V.S. 330 (A.D. 649-50).[3]

Knowledge of the later Gurjjaras is derived exclusively from two grants of Jayabhaṭa III. dated respectively 456 (A.D. 704-5) and 486 (A.D. 734-5).[4] The later of these two grants is imperfect, only the last plate having been preserved. The earlier grant of 456 (A.D. 704-5) shows that during the half century following the reign of Dadda II. the dynasty had ceased to call themselves Gurjjaras, and had adopted a Puránic pedigree traced from king Karṇa, a hero of the Bhárata war. It also shows that from Dadda III. onward the family were Śaivas instead of sun-worshippers.

Jayabhaṭa II.
C. 650-675 A.D.

The successor of Dadda II. was his son Jayabhaṭa II. who is described as a warlike prince, but of whom no historical details are recorded.

Dadda III.
Báhusaháya,
C. 675-700.

Jayabhaṭa's son, Dadda III. Báhusaháya, is described as waging wars with the great kings of the east and of the west (probably Málava and Valabhi). He was the first Śaiva of the family, studied Manu's works, and strictly enforced "the duties of the *varṇas* or castes and of the *áśramas* or Bráhman stages." It was probably to him that the Gurjjaras owed their Puránic pedigree and their recognition as true Kshatriyas. Like his predecessors Dadda III.

---

[1] Beal's Buddhist Records, II. 259. [2] Ind. Ant. VIII. 237.
[3] Ind. Ant. XV. 335. [4] Ind. Ant. V. 109, XIII. 70.

Chapter X.
The Gurjjaras, A.D. 580 - 808.

was not an independent ruler. He could claim only the five great titles, though no hint is given who was his suzerain. His immediate superior may have been Jayasimha the Chálukya, who received the province of Láṭa from his brother Vikramáditya (c. 669 - 680 A.D.)[1]

Jayabhaṭa III. c. 704 - 734 A.D.

The son and successor of Dadda III. was Jayabhaṭa III, whose two grants of 456 (A.D. 704-5) and 486 (A.D. 734-5)[2] must belong respectively to the beginning and the end of his reign. He attained the five great titles, and was therefore a feudatory, probably of the Chálukyas: but his title of Mahásámantádhipati implies that he was a chief of importance. He is praised in vague terms, but the only historical event mentioned in his grants is a defeat of a lord of Valabhi, noted in the grant of 486 (A.D. 734-5). The Valabhi king referred to must be either S'íláditya IV. (A.D. 691) or S'íláditya V. (A.D. 722). During the reign of Jayabhaṭa III. took place the great Arab invasion which was repulsed by Pulakeśi Janáśraya at Navsárí.[3] Like the kingdoms named in the grant of Pulakeśi, Broach must have suffered from this raid. It is not specially mentioned probably because it formed part of Pulakeśi's territory.

After A.D. 734-5 no further mention occurs of the Gurjjaras of Broach. Whether the dynasty was destroyed by the Arabs or by the Gujarát Ráshtrakúṭas (A.D. 750) is not known. Later references to Gurjjaras in Ráshṭrakúṭa times refer to the Gurjjaras of Bhínmál not to the Gurjjaras of Broach, who, about the time of Dadda III. (c. 675 - 700 A.D.), ceased to call themselves Gurjjaras.

A few words must be said regarding the three grants from Iláo, Umetá, and Bagumrá (Ind. Ant. XIII. 116, VII. 61, and XVII. 183) as their genuineness has been assumed by Dr. Bühler in his recent paper on the Mahábhárata, in spite of Mr. Fleet's proof (Ind. Ant. XVIII. 19) that their dates do not work out correctly.

Dr. Bhagvánlál's (Ind. Ant. XIII. 70) chief grounds for holding that the Umetá and Iláo grants (the Bagumrá grant was unknown to him) were forgeries were :

(1) Their close resemblance in palæography to one another and to the forged grant of Dharasena II. of Valabhi dated S'aka 400 ;

(2) That though they purport to belong to the fifth century they bear the same writer's name as the Kheḍá grants of the seventh century.

Further Mr. Fleet (Ind. Ant. XIII. 116) pointed out :

(3) That the description of Dadda I. in the Iláo and Umetá grants agrees almost literally with that of Dadda II. in the Kheḍá grants, and that where it differs the Kheḍá grants have the better readings.

To these arguments Dr. Bühler has replied (Ind. Ant. XVII. 183) :

(1) That though there is a resemblance between these grants and that of Dharasena II., still it does not prove more than that the forger of Dharasena's grant had one of the other grants before him ;

(2) That, as the father's name of the writer is not given in the Kheḍá grants, it cannot be assumed that he was the same person as the writer of the Iláo and Umetá grants ; and

---

[1] B. B. R. A. S. Jl. XVI. 1ff.

[2] Ind. Ant. V. 109, XIII. 70. The earlier grant was made from Káyávatára (Kárwán): the later one is mutilated.

[3] Before A.D. 738-9. See Chap. IX. above.

Chapter X.

THE GURJJARAS, A.D. 580 - 808.

(3) That genuine grants sometimes show that a description written for one king is afterwards applied to another, and that good or bad readings are no test of the age of a grant.

It may be admitted that Dr. Bühler has made it probable that the suspected grants and the grant of Dharasena were not all written by the same hand, and also that the coincidence in the writer's name is not of much importance in itself. But the palæographical resemblance between Dharasena's grant on the one hand and the doubtful Gurjjara grants on the other is so close that they must have been written at about the same time. As to the third point, the verbal agreement between the doubtful grants on the one hand and the Kheḍá grants on the other implies the existence of a continuous tradition in the record office of the dynasty from the end of the fifth till near the middle of the seventh century. But the Saṅkheḍá grant of Nirihullaka (Ep. Ind. II. 21) shows that towards the end of the sixth century the lower Narbadá valley was occupied by jungle tribes who acknowledged the supremacy of the Kalachuris. Is it reasonable to suppose that after the first Gurjjara line was thus displaced, the restorers of the dynasty should have had any memory of the forms in which the first line drew up their grants? At any rate, if they had, they would also have retained their original seal, which, as the analogy of the Valabhi plates teaches us, would bear the founder's name. But we find that the seal of the Kheḍá plates bears the name "Sámanta Dadda," who can be no other than the "Sámanta Dadda" who ruled from c. 585 - 605 A.D. It follows that the Gurjjaras of the seventh century themselves traced back their history in Broach no further than A.D. 585. Again, it has been pointed out in the text that a passage in the description of Dadda II. (A.D. 620 - 650) in the Kheḍá grants seems to refer to his protection of the Valabhi king, so that the description must have been written for *him* and not for the fifth century Dadda as Dr. Bühler's theory requires.

These points coupled with Mr. Fleet's proof (Ind. Ant. XVIII. 91) that the Śaka dates do not work out correctly, may perhaps be enough to show that none of these three grants can be relied upon as genuine.—(A. M. T. J.)

CHAPTER XI.

THE RÁSHṬRAKÚṬAS

(A.D. 743–974.)

Chapter XI.

The Ráshṭrakúṭas, A.D. 743-974.

The Ráshṭrakúṭa connection with Gujarát lasted from S'aka 665 to 894 (A.D. 743-974) that is for 231 years. The connection includes three periods: A first of sixty-five years from S'aka 665 to 730 (A.D. 743-808) when the Gujarát ruler was dependent on the main Dakhan Ráshṭrakúṭa: a second of eighty years between S'aka 730 and 810 (A.D. 808-888) when the Gujarát family was on the whole independent: and a third of eighty-six years S'aka 810 to 896 (A.D. 888-974) when the Dakhan Ráshṭrakúṭas again exercised direct sway over Gujarát.

Their Origin.

Information regarding the origin of the Ráshṭrakúṭas is imperfect. That the Gujarát Ráshṭrakúṭas came from the Dakhan in S'aka 665 (A.D. 743) is known. It is not known who the Dakhan Ráshṭrakúṭas originally were or where or when they rose to prominence. Ráthoḍ the dynastic name of certain Kanauj and Márwár Rajputs represents a later form of the word Ráshṭrakúṭa. Again certain of the later inscriptions call the Ráshṭrakúṭas Raṭṭas a word which, so far as form goes, is hardly a correct Prakrit contraction of Ráshṭrakúṭa. The Sanskritisation of tribal names is not exact. If the name Raṭṭa was strange it might be pronounced Ratta, Ratha, or Raddi. This last form almost coincides with the modern Kánarese caste name Reddi, which, so far as information goes, would place the Ráshṭrakúṭas among the tribes of pre-Sanskrit southern origin.

Their Name.

If Raṭṭa is the name of the dynasty *kúṭa* or *kúḍa* may be an attribute meaning prominent. The combination Ráshṭrakúṭa would then mean the chiefs or leaders as opposed to the rank and file of the Raṭṭas. The bardic accounts of the origin of the Ráthoḍs of Kanauj and Marwár vary greatly. According to a Jain account the Ráthoḍs, whose name is fancifully derived from the *raht* or spine of Indra, are connected with the Yavans through an ancestor Yavanaśva prince of Párlipur. The Ráthoḍ genealogies trace their origin to Kuśa son of Ráma of the Solar Race. The bards of the

Chapter XI.
THE RÁSHTRAKÚTAS, A.D. 743-974.
Their Name.

Solar Race hold them to be descendants of Hiranya Kaśipu by a demon or *daitya* mother. Like the other great Rájput families the Ráthods' accounts contain no date earlier than the fifth century A.D. when (A.D. 470, S. 526) Náin Pál is said to have conquered Kánauj slaying its monarch Ajipál.[1] The Dakhan Ráshtrakútas (whose earliest known date is also about A.D. 450) call themselves of the Lunar Race and of the Yadu dynasty. Such contradictions leave only one of two origins to the tribe. They were either foreigners or southerners Bráhmanised and included under the all-embracing term Rájput.

Early Dynasty, A.D. 450-500.

Of the rise of the Ráshtrakútas no trace remains. The earliest known Ráshtrakúta copperplate is of a king Abhimanyu. This plate is not dated. Still its letters, its style of writing, and its lion seal, older than the Garuda mark which the Ráshtrakútas assumed along with the claim of Yádava descent, leave no doubt that this is the earliest of known Ráshtrakúta plates. Its probable date is about A.D. 450. The plate traces the descent of Abhimanyu through two generations from Mánánka. The details are :

Mánánka.
|
Devarája.
|
Bhavishya.
|
Abhimanyu.

The grant is dated from Mánapura, perhaps Mánánka's city, probably an older form of Mányakheta the modern Málkhed the capital of the later Ráshtrákútas about sixty miles south-east of Sholápur. These details give fair ground for holding the Mánánkas to be a family of Ráshtrakúta rulers earlier than that which appears in the usual genealogy of the later Ráshtrakúta dynasty (A.D. 500-972).

The Main Dynasty, A.D. 630-972.

The earliest information regarding the later Ráshtrakútas is from a comparatively modern, and therefore not quite trustworthy, Chálukya copperplate of the eleventh century found by Mr. Wathen. This plate states that Jayasimha I. the earliest Chálukya defeated the Ráshtrakúta Indra son of Krishna the lord of 800 elephants. The date of this battle would be about A.D. 500. If historic the reference implies that the Ráshtrakútas were then a well established dynasty. In most of their own plates the genealogy of the Ráshtrakútas begins with Govinda about A.D. 680. But that Govinda was not the founder of the family is shown by Dantidurga's Elura Daśávatára inscription (about A.D. 750) which gives two earlier names Dantivarmman and Indra. The founding of Ráshtrakúta power is therefore of doubtful date. Of the date of its overthrow there is no question. The overthrow came from the hand of the Western Chálukya Tailappa in S'aka 894 (A.D. 972) during the reign of the last Ráshtrakúta Kakka III. or Kakkala.

---

[1] Tod's Annals of Rájásthán, I. 88; II. 2.

The following is the Ráshṭrakúṭa family tree:

Chapter XI.
The Ráshṭrakúṭas, A.D. 743 - 974.
Ráshṭrakúṭa Family Tree, A.D. 630 - 972.

- 1 Dantivarmman (about A.D. 630).
  - 2 Indra I. (about A.D. 655).
    - 3 Govinda I. (about A.D. 680).
      - 4 Kakka I. or Karka I. (about A.D. 705).
        - 5 Indra II. (about A.D. 730).
          - 6 Dantidurga, Dantivarmman (S'aka 675, A.D. 753).
        - Dhruva.
          - Govinda.
            - Kakka II. S'aka 669 (A.D. 747).
        - 7 Krishna (about A.D. 765).
          - 8 Govinda II. (about A.D. 780).
          - 9 Dhruva, Dhárávarsha, Nirupama, Dhora, (about A.D. 795).
            - 10 Govinda III. Prabhútavarsha Vallabhanarendra, Jagattunga Prithivívallabha, (S'aka 725, 728, 729, A.D. 803, 806, 807).
              - 11 Amoghavarsha S'arvva, Durlabha S'rívallabha; Lakshmívallabha, Vallabha Skanda, (S'aka 773, 799, A.D. 851, 877).
                - 12 Akálavarsha Krishna II. Kannara (about A.D. 880—911).
                  - Jagattunga (did not reign.)
                    - 13 Indra III. Prithivívallabha Raṭṭakandarpa, Kirttinaráyana Nityamvarsha (S'aka 836, A.D. 914).
                      - 14 Amoghavarsha.
                      - 15 Govindarája Sáhasánka Suvarnavarsha.
                    - 16 Baddiga.
                      - 17 Krishna (S'. 867, 878 A.D. 945, 956).
                      - 19 Kottiga.
                      - Nirupama.
                        - Kakkala or Karkarája (S'aka 894, A.D. 972).
            - I. Indra (founder of Gujarát Branch).
              - II. Karka (S'aka 734, 738, 743, A.D. 812, 816, 821).
                - Dantivarmman (?)
                  - VII. Akálavarsha-Krishna (S'aka 810, A.D. 888).
                - IV. Dhruva I. Dhárávarsha, Nirupama, (S'aka 757, A.D. 835).
                  - V. Akálavarsha S'ubhatunga, (A.D. 867).
                    - VI. Dhruva II. (S'aka 789, 793, A.D. 867, 871).
              - III. Govinda Prabhútavarsha, (S'aka 749. A.D. 827).

Copperplates.

The earliest Gujarát Ráshṭrakúṭa grant, Kakka's of S'aka 669 (A.D. 747), comes from Ántroli-Chároli in Surat. It is written on two plates in the Valabhi style of composition and form of letters, and, as in Valabhi grants, the date is at the end. Unlike Valabhi grants the era is the S'aka era. The grant gives the following genealogy somewhat different from that of other known Ráshṭrakúṭa grants:

- Kakka.
  - Dhruva.
    - Govinda.
      - Kakka II. (S'aka 669, A.D. 747).

Chapter XI.
The Ráshtrakútas, A.D. 743-974.
Kakka II. A.D. 747.

The plate notices that Kakka the grantor was the son of Govinda by his wife the daughter of the illustrious Nágavarmman. Kakka is further described by the feudatory title '*Samadhigatapanchmahâśabdaḥ*' Holder of the five great names. At the same time he is also called *Paramabhaṭṭáraka-Mahárája* Great Lord Great King, attributes which seem to imply a claim to independent power. The grant is dated the bright seventh of Áśvayuja, Śaka 669 (A.D. 747). The date is almost contemporary with the year of Dantidurga in the Sámangad plate (A.D. 753). As Dantidurga was a very powerful monarch we may identify the first Kakka of this plate with Kakka I. the grandfather of Dantidurga and thus trace from Dhruva Kakka's son a branch of feudatory Ráshṭrakúṭas ruling in Málwa or Gujarát, whose leaders were Dhruva, his son Govinda, and Govinda's son Kakka II. Further Dantidurga's grant shows that he conquered Central Gujarát between the Mahí and the Narbadá[1] while his Elura Daśávatára inscription (A.D. 750) shows that he held Láṭa and Málava[2] Dántidurga's conquest of Central Gujarát seems to have been signalised by grants of land made by his mother in every village of the Mátri division which is apparently the Mátar táluka of the Kaira district.[3] It is possible that Dantidurga gave conquered Gujarát to his paternal cousin's son and contemporary Kakka, the grantor of the Ántroli plate (A.D. 747), as the representative of a family ruling somewhere under the overlordship of the main Dakhan Ráshṭrakúṭas. Karka's Baroda grant[4] (A.D. 812) supports this theory. Dantidurga died childless and was succeeded by his uncle Kṛishṇa. Of this Kṛishṇa the Baroda grant says that he assumed the government for the good of the family after having rooted out a member of the family who had taken to mischief-making. It seems probable that Kakka II. the grantor of the Ántroli plate is the mischief-maker and that his mischief was, on the death of Dantidurga, the attempt to secure the succession to himself. Kṛishṇa frustrated Kakka's attempt and rooted him out so effectively that no trace of Kakka's family again appears.

Kṛishṇa and Govinda II. A.D. 765-795.

From this it follows that, so far as is known, the Ráshṭrakúṭa conquest of Gujarát begins with Dantidurga's conquest of Láṭa, that is South Gujarát between the Mahí and the Narbadá, from the Gurjjara king Jayabhaṭa whose latest known date is A.D. 736 or seventeen years before the known date of Dantidurga. The Gurjjaras probably retired to the Rájpipla hills and further east on the confines of Málwa where they may have held a lingering sway.[5] No Gujarát event of importance is recorded during the reign of Kṛishṇa (A.D. 765) or of his son Govinda II. (A.D. 780) who about

[1] Ind. Ant. XI. 112. [2] Bombay Arch. Sur. Separate Number, 10, 94.
[3] This verse which immediately follows the mention of Govinda's conquests on the banks of the Mahí and the Narbadá punningly explains the name of the Mátar táluka as meaning the Mother's táluka. [4] Ind. Ant. XII. 156.
[5] The Khándesh Reve and Dore Gujars of Chopdá and Raver in the east, and also over most of the west, may be a remnant of these Gujars of Broach who at this time (A.D. 740), and perhaps again about sixty years later, may have been forced up the Narbadá and Tápti into South Málwa and West Khándesh. This is doubtful as their migration is said to have taken place in the eleventh century and may have been due to pressure from the north the effect of Mahmúd Ghaznavi's invasions (A.D. 1000-1025).

A.D. 795 was superseded by his powerful younger brother Dhruva.[1]

Chapter XI. The Ráshṭrakúṭas, A.D. 743-974. Dhruva I. A.D. 795.

Dhruva was a mighty monarch whose conquests spread from South India as far north as Allahábád. During Dhruva's lifetime his son Govinda probably ruled at Mayúrakhandi or Morkhanda in the Násik district and held the Ghát country and the Gujarát coast from Balsár northwards. Though according to a Kapadvanj grant Govinda had several brothers the Rádhanpur (A.D. 808) and Van-Dindori (A.D. 808) grants of his son Govinda III. state that his father, seeing Govinda's supernatural Kṛishṇa-like powers, offered him the sovereignty of the whole world. Govinda declined, saying, The Kaṇṭhiká or coast tract already given to me is enough. Seeing that Mayúrakhandi or Morkhanda in Násik was Govinda's capital, this Kaṇṭhiká appears to be the coast from Balsár northwards.

Govinda III. A.D. 800-808.

According to Gujarát Govinda's (A.D. 827-833) Káví grant (A.D. 827), finding his power threatened by Stambha and other kings, Dhruva made the great Govinda independent during his own lifetime. This suggests that while Dhruva continued to hold the main Rashṭrakúṭa sovereignty in the Dakhan, he probably invested Govinda with the sovereignty of Gujarát. This fact the Káví grant (A.D. 827) being a Gujarát grant would rightly mention while it would not find a place in the Rádhanpur (A.D. 808) and Van-Dindori (A.D. 808) grants of the main Ráshṭrakúṭas. Of the kings who opposed Govinda the chief was Stambha who may have some connection with Cambay, as, during the time of the Anahilaváḍa kings, Cambay came to be called Stambha-tírtha instead of by its old name of Gambhútá. According to the grants the allied chiefs were no match for Govinda. The Gurjjara fled through fear, not returning even in dreams, and the Málava king submitted. Who the Gurjjara was it is hard to say. He may have belonged to some Gurjjara dynasty that rose to importance after Dantidurga's conquest or the name may mean a ruler of the Gurjjara country. In either case some North Gujarát ruler is meant whose conquest opened the route from Broach to Málwa. From Málwa Govinda marched to the Vindhyas where the king apparently of East Málwa named Márá S'arva submitted to Govinda paying tribute. From the Vindhyas Govinda returned to Gujarát passing the rains at S'ríbhavana,[2] apparently Sarbhon in the Ámod táluka of Broach, a favourite locality which he had ruled during his father's lifetime. After the rains Govinda went south as far as the Tungabhadra. On starting for the south Govinda handed Gujarát to his brother Indra with whom begins the Gujarát branch of the Ráshṭrakúṭas. Several plates distinctly mention that Indra was given the kingdom of the lord of Láṭa by (his brother) Govinda. Other Gujarát grants, apparently with intent to show that Indra won Gujarát and did not receive it in gift, after mentioning S'arvva Amoghavarsha as the successor of Govinda (A.D. 818), state that the king (apparently of Gujarát) was S'arvva's uncle Indra.

[1] Ind. Ant. VI. 65; Jour. B. A. Soc. V. 350. [2] Ind. Ant. VI. 65.

Chapter XI.
THE RÁSHTRAKÚTAS, A.D. 743 - 974.
Indra, A.D. 808 - 812.

As Govinda III. handed Gujarát to his brother Indra about S'aka 730 (A.D. 808) and as the grant of Indra's son Karka is dated S'aka 734 (A.D. 812) Indra's reign must have been short. Indra is styled the ruler of the entire kingdom of Látes'vara,[1] the protector of the *mandala* of Láṭa given to him by his lord. An important verse in an unpublished Baroda grant states that Indra chased the lord of Gurjjara who had prepared to fight, and that he honourably protected the multitude of Dakhan (Dakshiṇápatha) feudatories (*mahásámantas*) whose glory was shattered by S'rívallabha (that is S'arvva or Amoghavarsha)[2] then heir-apparent of Govinda. That is, in attempting to establish himself in independent power, Indra aided certain of the Ráshṭrakúṭa feudatories in an effort to shake off the overlordship of Amoghavarsha.

Karka I. A.D. 812 - 821.

Indra was succeeded by his son Karka I. who is also called Suvarṇavarsha and Pátálamalla. Karka reversed his father's policy and loyally accepted the overlordship of the main Ráshṭrakúṭas. Three grants of Karka's remain, the Baroda grant dated S'aka 734 (A.D. 812), and two unpublished grants from Navsárí and Surat dated respectively S'aka 738 (A.D. 816) and S'aka 743 (A.D. 821). Among Doctor Bhagvánlál's collection of inscriptions bequeathed to the British Museum the Baroda grant says that Karka's *svámi* or lord, apparently Govinda III., made use of Karka's arm to protect the king of Málava against invasion by the king of Gurjjara who had become puffed up by conquering the lords of Gauda and Vanga that is modern Bengal. This powerful Gurjjara king who conquered countries so distant as Bengal has not been identified. He must have been ruling north of the Mahí and threatened an invasion of Málwa by way of Dohad. He may have been either a Valabhi king or one of the Bhinmál Gurjjaras, who, during the decline of the Valabhis, and with the help of their allies the Chávaḍás of Aṇahilaváḍa whose leader at this time was Yog Rája (A.D. 806 - 841), may have extended their dominion as far south as the Mahí. As the Baroda plate (A.D. 812) makes no mention of Amoghavarsha-S'arvva while the Navsárí plate (A.D. 816) mentions him as the next king after Govinda III. it follows that Govinda III. died and Amoghavarsha succeeded between A.D. 812 and 816 (S'. 734 and 738). This supports Mr. Fleet's conclusion, on the authority of Amoghavarsha's Sirur inscription, that he came to the throne in S'aka 736 (A.D. 814). At first Amoghavarsha was unable to make head against the opposition of some of his relations and feudatories, supported, as noted above, by Karka's father Indra. He seems to have owed his

---

[1] The kingdom is not called Láṭa in the copperplate but Láṭesvara-maṇḍala. An unpublished Baroda grant has शास्ता प्रतापप्रथितः पृथिव्यां सर्वस्य लाटेश्वरमण्डलस्य The ruler famous by glory, of the whole kingdom of the king of Láṭa. Other published grants record Govinda's gift of Gujarát to Indra as तद्दत्तलाटेश्वरमण्डलस्य Of him (Indra) to whom the kingdom of the lord of Láṭa had been given by him (Govinda). Ind. Ant. XII. 162.

[2] Ind. Ant. XII. 160; unpublished Baroda grant. S'rívallabha appears to mean Amoghavarsha who is also called Lakshmívallabha in an inscription at Sirur in Dhárwár (Ind. Ant. XII. 215).

Karka I. A.D. 812-821.

subsequent success to his cousin Karka whom an unpublished Surat grant and two later grants (S'. 757 and S'. 789, A.D. 835 and 867) describe as establishing Amoghavarsha in his own place after conquering by the strength of his arm arrogant tributary Ráshtrakúṭas who becoming firmly allied to each other had occupied provinces according to their own will.

Karka's Baroda plates (S'. 734, A.D. 812) record the grant of Baroda itself called Vaḍapadraka in the text. Baroda is easily identified by the mention of the surrounding villages of Jambuvávika the modern Jámbuváda on the east, of Ankottaka the modern Ákotá on the west, and of Vagghláchchha perhaps the modern Vághodia on the north. The writer of the grant is mentioned as the great minister of peace and war Nemáditya son of Durgabhaṭṭa, and the Dútaka or grantor is said to be Rájaputra that is prince Dantivarmman apparently a son of Karka. The grantee is a Bráhman originally of Valabhi.

Karka's Navsárí grant (S'. 738, A.D. 816) is made from Kheḍá and records the gift of the village of Samípadraka in the country lying between the Mahí and the Narbadá. The grantee is a South Indian Bráhman from Bádámi in Bijápur, a man of learning popularly known as Paṇḍita Vallabharája because he was proficient in the fourteen Vidyás. The Dútaka of this grant is a South Indian *bhaṭa* or military officer named the illustrious Droṇamma.

Karka's Surat grant (S'. 743, A.D. 821) is made from the royal camp on the bank of the Vankiká apparently the Vánki creek near Balsár. It records the grant of a field in Ambápátaka village near Nágasárika (Navsárí) to a Jain temple at Nágariká (Navsárí). The writer of the grant is the minister of war and peace Náráyana son of Durgabhaṭṭa. As this is the first grant by a Gujarát Ráshṭrakúṭa of lands south of the Tápti it may be inferred that in return for his support Amoghavarsha added to Karka's territory the portion of the North Konkan which now forms Gujarát south of the Tápti.

Dantivarmman, Heir Apparent.

According to Karka's Baroda plate (S'.734, A.D.812) Karka had a son named Dantivarmman who is mentioned as the princely Dútaka of the plate. The fact of being a Dútaka implies that Dantivarmman was then of age. That Dantivarmman was a son of Karka is supported by Akálavarsha's Bagumrá plate (S'. 810, A.D. 888), where, though the plate is badly composed and the grammar is faulty, certain useful details are given regarding Dantivarmman who is clearly mentioned as the son of Karka. Karka had another son named Dhruva, who, according to three copperplates, succeeded to the throne. But as Dantivarmman's son's grant is dated S'aka 810 or seventy-six years later than the Baroda plate some error seems to have crept into the genealogy of the plate. Neither Dantivarmman nor Dhruva seems to have succeeded their father as according to Govinda's Kávi grant (A.D. 827) their uncle Govinda succeeded his brother Karka. The explanation may be that Dantivarmman died during his father's lifetime, and that some years later, after a great yearning for a son,[1] probably in Karka's old age, a second

[1] Several copperplates give Karka the epithet *Putriyataslasya* Son-yearning.

Chapter XI.
THE RÁSHTRAKÚTAS, A.D. 743-974.
Govinda, A.D. 827-833.

son Dhruva was born, during whose minority, after Karka's death, Govinda appears to have temporarily occupied the throne.

This Govinda, the brother and successor of Karka, was also called Prabhútavarsha. One plate of Govinda's Káví grant is dated Śaka 749 (A.D. 827). It gives no details regarding Govinda. The grant is made from Broach and records the gift of a village[1] to a temple of the Sun called Jayáditya in Kotipur near Kápiká that is Káví thirty miles north of Broach. The writer of the grant is Yogeśvara son of Avalokita and the Dútaka or grantor was one Bhaṭṭa Kumuda. As it contains no reference to Govinda's succession the plate favours the view that Govinda remained in power only during the minority of his nephew Dhruva.

Dhruva I. A.D. 835-867.

This Dhruva, who is also called Nirupama and Dhárávarsha, is mentioned as ruler in a Baroda grant dated S'aka 757 (A.D. 835).[2] He therefore probably came to the throne either on attaining his majority in the lifetime of his uncle and predecessor Govinda or after Govinda's death. Dhruva's Baroda grant (S'. 757, A.D. 835) is made from a place called Sarvvamangalá near Kheḍá and records the gift of a village to a Bráhman named Yoga[3] of Badarasidhi apparently Borsad. The writer of the grant is mentioned as the minister of peace and war, Náráyaṇa son of Durgabhaṭṭa, and the Dútaka or grantor is the illustrious Devarája. Dhruva seems to have abandoned his father's position of loyal feudatory to the main Ráshṭrakútas. According to a copperplate dated S'aka 832 (A.D. 910) Vallabha that is Amoghavarsha, also called the illustrious great Skanda, sent an army and besieged and burned the Kaṇthiká that is the coast tract between Bombay and Cambay. In the course of this campaign, according to Dhruva II.'s Bagumrá grant (S. 789, A.D. 867),[4] Dhruva died on the field of battle covered with wounds while routing the army of Vallabha or Amoghavarsha. This statement is supported by a Kanheri cave inscription which shows that Amoghavarsha was still alive in S'aka 799 (A.D. 877).

Akálavarsha, A.D. 867.

Dhruva was succeeded by his son Akálavarsha also called S'ubhatuṅga. A verse in Dhruva II.'s Bagumrá grant (S' 789, A.D. 867) says that Akálavarsha established himself in the territory of his father, which, after Dhruva's death in battle, had been overrun by the army of Vallabha and had been distracted by evil-minded followers and dependants.[5]

Dhruva II. A.D. 867.

Akálavarsha was succeeded by his son Dhruva II. also called Dhárávarsha and Nirupama. Of Dhruva II. two copperplates remain the published Bagumrá grant dated Śaka 789[6] (A.D. 867) and an

---

[1] All village and boundary details have been identified by Dr. Bühler. Ind. Ant. V. 148.
[2] Ind. Ant. XIV. 199.
[3] This donee is said to have been given the name of Jyotishika by the illustrious Govindarája apparently the uncle and predecessor of the granting king.
[4] Ind. Ant. XII. 179.
[5] Ind. Ant. XII. 184. The verse may be translated 'By whom before long was occupied the province handed down from his father which had been overrun by the forces of Vallabha and distracted by numbers of evil-minded followers.'
[6] Ind. Ant. XII. 179.

Dhruva II. A.D. 867.

unpublished Baroda grant dated S'aka 793 (A.D. 871).[1] Both plates record that Dhruva crushed certain intrigues among his relatives or *bandhuvarga,* and established himself firmly on the throne. Regarding the troubles at the beginning of his reign the Bagumrá plate states that on one side Vallabha the head of the Dakhan Ráshṭrakúṭas was still against him; on another side Dhruva had to face an army of Gurjjaras instigated by a member of his own family[2]; thirdly he was opposed by certain of his relatives or *bándhaváḥ*; and lastly he had to contend against the intrigues of a younger brother or *anuja.* It further appears from Dhruva II.'s Bagumrá plate that he checked an inroad by a Mihira king with a powerful army. This Mihira king was probably a chief of the Káthiáváḍa Mehrs who on the downfall of the Valabhis spread their power across Gujarát. In all these troubles the Bagumrá grant notes that Dhruva was aided by a younger brother named Govindarája. This Govindarája is mentioned as appointed by Dhruva the Dútaka of the grant.

Dhruva II.'s Bagumrá (A.D. 867) grant was made at Bhṛigu-Kachchha or Broach after bathing in the Narbadá. It records the gift to a Bráhman of the village of Páráhanaka, probably the village of Palsána[3] twelve miles south-east of Bagumrá in the Balesar sub-division of the Gáikwár's territory of Surat and Navsárí. Dhruva's Baroda grant (A.D. 871) was also made at Broach. It is a grant to the god Kapáles'vara Mahádeva of the villages Konvalli and Nakkabhajja both mentioned as close to the south bank of the Mahí. The facts that the Bagumrá grant (A.D. 867) transfers a village so far south as Balesar near Navsárí and that four years later the Baroda grant (A.D. 871) mentions that Dhruva's territory lay between Broach and the Mahí seem to prove that between A.D. 867 and 871 the portion of Dhruva's kingdom south of Broach passed back into the hands of the main Rashṭrakúṭas.

Akálavarsha-Krishṇa, A.D. 888.

The next and last known Gujarát Ráshtrakúṭa king is Akálavarsha-Krishṇa son of Dantivarmman. A grant of this king has been found in Bagumrá dated S'aka 810 (A.D. 888).[4] The composition of the grant is so bad and the genealogical verses after Karka are so confused that it seems unsafe to accept any of

---

[1] This plate was in Dr. Bhagvánlál's possession. It is among the plates bequeathed to the British Museum. Dr. Bhandárkar (B. B. R. A. S. Jl. XVIII. 255) mentions another unpublished grant of S'. 789 (A.D. 867) made by Dhruva's brother Dantivarmman.

[2] These may be either the Gurjjaras between Málwa and Gujarát, or the Bhínmál Gurjjaras north of the Mahí. It is also possible that they may be Chávaḍás as in this passage the term Gurjjara does not refer to the tribe but to the country. [There seems little reason to doubt the reference is to the Gurjjaras of Bhínmál or S'rímál, probably acting through their underlords the Chávaḍás of Anahilaváḍa whose king in A.D. 865 was the warlike Kshem Rája (A.D. 841-866). Census and other recent information establish almost with certainty that the Chávaḍás or Chávoṭakas are of the Gurjjara race.]

[3] The identification is not satisfactory. Except the Bráhman settlement of Mottaka, apparently the well known Motála Bráhman settlement of Motá, which is mentioned as situated on the west though it is on the north-east, none of the boundary villages can be identified in the neighbourhood of Palsána. In spite of this the name Palsána and its close vicinity to Bagumrá where the grant was found make this identification probable.

[4] Ind. Ant. XIII. 65.

Chapter XI.

THE RÁSHTRAKÚTAS, A.D. 743-974.

Akálavarsha-Kṛishṇa, A.D. 888.

its details except its date which is clearly Śaka 810 (A.D. 888). It seems also improbable that the son of Dantivarmman who flourished in Śaka 734 (A.D. 812) could be reigning in Śaka 810 (A.D. 888) seventy-six years later. Still the sixty-three years' reign of the contemporary Mányakheṭa Ráshṭrakúṭa Amoghavarsha (Ś. 736-799, A.D. 814-877) shows that this is not impossible.

The grant which is made from Anklesvar near Broach records the gift to two Bráhmans of the village of Kavithasádhi the modern Kosád four miles north-east of Surat, described as situated in the Variávi (the modern Variáv two miles north of Surat) sub-division of 116 villages in the province of Konkan. The grant is said to have been written by the peace and war minister the illustrious Jajjaka son of Kaluka, the Dútaka being the head officer *(mahattama-sarvádhikári)* the Bráhman Ollaiyaka.[1] This grant seems to imply the recovery by the local dynasty of some portion of the disputed area to the south of the Tápti. This recovery must have been a passing success. After Śaka 810 (A.D. 888) nothing is known of the Gujarát Ráshṭrakúṭas. And the re-establishment of the power of the Ráshṭrakúṭas of Mányakheṭa of the main line in south Gujarát in Śaka 836 (A.D. 914) is proved by two copperplates found in Navsárí which record the grant of villages near Navsárí, in what the text calls the Láṭa country, by king Indra Nityamvarsha son of Jagattuṅga and grandson of Kṛishṇa Akálavarsha.[2]

Main Line Restored, A.D. 888-974.

That Amoghavarsha's long reign lasted till Śaka 799 (A.D. 877) is clear from the Kanheri cave inscription already referred to. His reign can hardly have lasted much longer; about Śaka 800 (A.D. 878) may be taken to be its end.

Kṛishṇa Akálavarsha, A.D. 888-914.

Amoghavarsha was succeeded by his son Kṛishṇa also called Akálavarsha, both his names being the same as those of the Gujarát Ráshṭrakúṭa king of the same time (A.D. 888).[3] It has been noted above that, in consequence of the attempt of Karka's son Dhruva I. (A.D. 835-867) to establish his independence, Amoghavarsha's relations with the Gujarát Ráshtrakúṭas became extremely hostile and probably continued hostile till his death (A.D. 877). That Amoghavarsha's son Kṛishṇa kept up the hostilities is shown by Indra's two Navsárí plates of Śaka 836 (A.D. 914) which mention his grandfather Kṛishṇa fighting with the roaring Gurjjara.[4] Regarding this fight the late Ráshṭrakúṭa Kardá plate (Ś. 891, A.D. 973) further says that Kṛishṇa's enemies frightened by his exploits abandoned Khetaka, that is Kheḍá, with its Maṇḍala and its forepart that is the surrounding country. Probably this roaring Gurjjara or king of Gujarát, was a northern ally called in by some Ráshtrakúta of the

[1] Ind. Ant. XIII. 65-69.

[2] These were among Dr. Bhagvánlál's copperplates, and seem to be the same as the two grants published by Dr. Bhandárkar in B. B. R. A. S. Jl. XVIII. 253.

[3] See above page 127.

[4] The text is: उद्यद्दीधितिरत्नजालजटिलंव्याकृष्टमीदृग्धनुः। क्रुद्धेनोपरि वैरिवीरशिरसामेवं विमुक्ताः शराः। धारासारिणी सेन्द्रचापवलये यस्येत्थमब्दागमे गर्जद्गुर्जरसंगरव्यतिकरं जीर्णोजनः शंसति.

Chapter XI.

The Ráshtrakútas, A.D. 743-974.

Krishṇa Akálavarsha, A.D. 888-914.

Gujarát branch, perhaps by Krishṇa's namesake the donor of the A.D. 888 Bagumrá grant. The Dakhan Krishṇa seems to have triumphed over his Gujarát namesake as henceforward South Gujarát or Láṭa was permanently included in the territory of the Dakhan Ráshṭrakúṭas.[1]

At this time (A.D. 910) a grant from Kapadvanj dated S'. 832 (A.D. 910) and published in Ep. Ind. I. 52ff. states that a *mahásámanta* or noble of Krishṇa Akálavarsha's named Prachaṇḍa, with his *daṇḍanáyaka* Chandragupta, was in charge of a sub-division of 750 villages in the Kheḍá district at Harshapura apparently Harsol near Parántij. The grant gives the name of Prachaṇḍa's family as Bráhma-vaka (?) and states that the family gained its fortune or Lakshmí by the prowess of the feet of Akálavarsha, showing that the members of the family drew their authority from Akálavarsha. The grant mentions four of Prachaṇḍa's ancestors, all of whom have non-Gujarát Kánarese-looking names. Though not independent rulers Prachaṇḍa's ancestors seem to have been high Ráshṭrakúṭa officers. The first is called S'uddha-kkumbaḍi, the second his son Degaḍi, the third Degaḍi's son Rájahaṁsa, the fourth Rájahaṁsa's son Dhavalappa the father of Prachaṇḍa and Akkuka. The plate describes Rájahaṁsa as bringing back to his house its flying fortune as if he had regained lost authority. The plate describes Dhavalappa as killing the enemy in a moment and then giving to his lord the Maṇḍala or kingdom which the combined enemy, desirous of glory, had taken. This apparently refers to Akálavarsha's enemies abandoning Kheṭaka with its Maṇḍala as mentioned in the late Ráshṭrakúṭa Kardá plate (A.D. 973). Dhavalappa is probably Akálavarsha's general who fought and defeated the roaring Gurjjara, a success which may have led to Dhavalappa being placed in military charge of Gujarát.[2] The Kapadvanj (A.D. 910) grant describes Dhavalappa's son Prachaṇḍa with the feudatory title 'Who has obtained the five great words.' Dr. Bhagvánlál believed Prachaṇḍa to be a mere epithet of Akkuka, and took Chandragupta to be another name of the same person, but the published text gives the facts as above stated. The grantee is a Bráhman and the grant is of the village of Vyághrása, perhaps Vágrá in Broach.[3] The plate describes Akkuka as gaining glory fighting in the battle field. A rather unintelligible verse follows implying that at this time the Sella-Vidyádharas, apparently the North Konkan S'iláháras (who traced their lineage from the Vidyádharas) also helped Akálavarsha against his enemies,[4] probably by driving them from South Gujarát. The S'iláhára king at this time would be Jhanjha (A.D. 916).

---

[1] It will be noted that in S'aka 836 (A.D. 914) Krishṇa's grandson Indra re-grants 400 resumed villages many of which were perhaps resumed at this time by Krishṇa.

[2] It follows that none of Dhavalappa's three ancestors had any connection with Gujarát.

[3] Dr. Hultsch (Ep. Ind. I. 52) identifies Vyághrása with Vaghás, north-east of Kapadvanj. Dr. Bhagvánlál's account of the grant was based on an impression sent to him by the Mámlatdár of Kapadvanj.

[4] The text is: सेल्ल विद्याधरेणापि सेलु [हेलो] क्षालित तपानि पाणिना निहत्या शत्रून् समधे [रे] यशसाक्लमलंकृत. Dr. Hultsch takes the Sella-Vidyádhara here named to be another brother of Prachaṇḍa and Akkuka. The verse is corrupt.

Chapter XI.
The Ráshtrakútas, A.D. 743-974.
Indra Nityamvarsha, A.D. 914.

Krishna or Akálavarsha had a son named Jagattuṅga who does not appear to have come to the throne. Other plates show that he went to Chedi the modern Bundelkhand and remained there during his father's lifetime. By Lakshmí the daughter of the king of Chedi, Jagattuṅga had a son named Indra also called Nityamvarsha Raṭṭakandarpa. In both of Indra's Navsárí copperplates (A.D. 914) Indra is mentioned as *Pádánudhyáta*, Falling at the feet of, that is successor of, not his father but his grandfather Akálavarsha.[1] One historical attribute of Indra in both the plates is that "he uprooted in a moment the Mehr,"[2] apparently referring to some contemporary Mehr king of North Káthiáváḍa. Both the Navsárí plates of Śaka 836 (A.D. 914) note that the grants were made under peculiar conditions. The plates say that the donor Indra Nityaṃvarsha, with his capital at Mányakheta, had come to a place named Kuruṇḍaka for the *paṭṭabandha* or investiture festival. It is curious that though Mányakheṭa is mentioned as the capital the king is described as having come to Kuruṇḍaka for the investiture. Kuruṇḍaka was apparently not a large town as the plates mention that it was given in grant.[3] At his investiture Indra made great gifts. He weighed himself against gold or silver, and before leaving the scales he gave away Kuruṇḍaka and other places, twenty and a half lákhs of dramma coins, and 400 villages previously granted but taken back by intervening kings. These details have an air of exaggeration. At the same time gifts of coins by *lákhs* are not improbable by so mighty a king as Indra and as to the villages the bulk of them had already been alienated. The fact of lavish grants is supported by the finding of these two plates of the same date recording grants of two different villages made on the same occasion, the language being the same, and also by a verse in the late Ráshṭrakúṭa Kardá plate (Ś. 894, A.D. 972) where Indra is described as making numerous grants on copperplates and building many temples of Śiva.[4] The date of Indra's grants (Ś. 836, A.D. 914) is the date of his investiture and accession. This is probable as the latest known date of his grandfather Krishṇa is Śaka 833[5] (A.D. 911) and we know that Indra's father Jagattuṅga did not reign.[6] Umvará and Tenna, the villages granted in the two investiture plates, are described as situated near Kammaṇijja the modern Kámlej in the Láṭa province. They are probably the modern villages of Umra near Sáyan four miles west of Kámlej, and of Tenna immediately to the west of Bárdoli, which last is mentioned under the form Váraḍapalliká as the eastern boundary village. Dhruva II.'s Bagumra plate (Ś. 789, A.D. 867) mentions Tenna as granted

---

[1] The Khárepátan grant makes this clear by passing over Indra's father Jagattuṅga in the genealogy and entering Indra as the grandson and successor of Akálavarsha. Jour. B. B. R. A. Soc. I. 217.

[2] The text has *Helonmúlitameruṇá* to chime with the poetical allusion and figure about Indra. By Meru no doubt Mera or Mehr is meant.

[3] Kuruṇḍaka may be the village of Kurund in the Thána zilla seven miles north-east of Bhiwndi. It was a village given away in grant and cannot therefore be any large town. [Kurundvád at the holy meeting of the Krishna and Pañchganga in the Southern Marátha Country close to Narsoba's Vadi seems a more likely place for an investiture.] [4] J. R. A. S. III. 94. [5] Ind. Ant. XI. 109. [6] See above.

by Dhruva I. to a Bráhman named Dhoḍḍi the father of the Nennapa who is the grantee of Dhruva II.'s A.D. 867 Bagumrá grant, whose son Siddhabhaṭṭa is the grantee of Indra's A.D. 914 grant.[1] The re-granting of so many villages points to the re-establishment of the main Ráshṭrakúṭa power and the disappearance of the Gujarát branch of the Ráshṭrakúṭas.[2]

Though no materials remain for fixing how long after A.D. 914 Gujarát belonged to the Mányakheṭa Ráshṭrakúṭas, they probably continued to hold it till their destruction in S'aka 894 (A.D. 972) by the Western Chálukya king Tailappa. This is the more likely as inscriptions show that till then the neighbours of Gujarát, the North Konkan S'iláháras, acknowledged Ráshṭrakúṭa supremacy.

It is therefore probable that Gujarát passed to the conquering Tailappa as part of the Ráshṭrakúṭa kingdom. Further, as noted below in Part II. Chapter II., it seems reasonable to suppose that about S'aka 900 (A.D. 978) Tailappa entrusted Gujarát to his general Bárappa or Dvárappa, who fought with the Solanki Múlarája of Anahilaváḍa (A.D. 961-997).

[The text does not carry the question of the origin of the Ráshṭrakúṭas beyond the point that, about the middle of the fifth century A.D., two tribes bearing the closely associated names Ráthoḍ and Raṭṭa, the leaders of both of which are known in Sanskrit as Ráshṭrakúṭas, appeared the first in Upper India the second in the Bombay Karṇáṭak, and that the traditions of both tribes seem to show they were either southerners or foreigners Bráhmanised and included under the all-embracing term Rajput. The Sanskrit form Ráshṭrakúṭa may mean either leaders of the Ráshṭra tribe or heads of the territorial division named *ráshtra*. The closely related forms Ráshṭrapati and Grámakúṭa occur (above page 82) in Valabhi inscriptions. And Mr. Fleet (Kánarese Dynasties, 32) notices that Ráshṭrakúṭa is used in the inscriptions of many dynasties as a title equivalent to Ráshṭrapati. Such a title might readily become a family name like that of the Sáhi Játs of the Panjáb or the Maráthi surnames Patel, Nadkarni, and Desái. It may be noted that one of the Márwár traditions (Rajputána Gazetteer, III. 246) connects the word Ráthoḍ with Ráshṭra country making the original form Ráshṭravara or World-blessing and referring to an early tribal guardian Ráshṭras'yena or the World-Falcon. It is therefore possible that the origin of both forms of the name, of Ráthoḍ as well as of Ráshṭrakúṭa, is the title ruler of a district. At the same time in the case of the southern Ráshṭrakúṭas the balance of evidence is in support of a tribal origin of the name. The Raṭṭas of Saundatti in Belgaum, apparently with justice, claim descent from the former Ráshṭrakúṭa rulers (Belgaum Gazetteer, 355). Further that the Ráshṭrakúṭas considered themselves to belong to the Raṭṭa tribe is shown by Indra Nityamvarsha (A.D. 914)

---

[1] Though the name of the *gotra Lakshamaṇasa* and *Lákshâyaṇasa* differs slightly in the two grants, the identity of the name Nennapa the son of Dhoḍḍi and the father of Siddhabhaṭṭa the A.D. 914 grantee, suggests that the original grant of the village of Tenna by Dhruva I. (A.D. 795) had been cancelled in the interval and in A.D. 914 was renewed by king Indra Nityamvarsha. [Dr. Bhandárkar reads the name in Indra's Navsári grant (A.D. 914) as Vennapa.]

[2] That in A.D. 915 the Dakhan Ráshṭrakúṭas held Gujarát as far north as Cambay is supported by the Arab traveller Al Masúdi who (Prairies d'Or, I. 253-254) speaks of Cambay, when he visited it, as a flourishing town ruled by Bania the deputy of the Balhará lord of Mánkir. The country along the gulf of Cambay was a succession of gardens villages fields and woods with date-palm and other groves alive with peacocks and parrots.

Chapter XI.

THE RÁSHTRAKÚTAS, A.D. 743-974.

calling himself Raṭṭakandarpa the Love of the Raṭṭas. The result is thus in agreement with the view accepted in the text that Rashṭrakúṭa means leaders of the Raṭṭa tribe, the form Ráshṭra being perhaps chosen because the leaders held the position of Ráshṭrakúṭas or District Headmen. According to Dr. Bhandárkar (Deccan History, 9) the tribal name Raṭṭa or Rashṭra enters into the still more famous Dakhan tribal name Maharáṭha or Mahrátta. So far as present information goes both the Raṭṭas and the Great Raṭṭas are to be traced to the Rástikas mentioned in number five of Asoka's (B.C. 245) Girnár edicts among the Aparántas or westerners along with the Peteṇikas or people of Paithan about forty miles north-east of Ahmadnagar (Kolhápur Gazetteer, 82). Whether the Rástika of the edicts is like Peteṇika a purely local name and if so why a portion of the north Dakhan should be specially known as the country or Ráshṭra are points that must remain open.[1]

The explanation that Kúṭa the second half of Ráshṭrakúṭa, means chief, has been accepted in the text. This is probably correct. At the same time the rival theory deserves notice that the name Ráshṭrakúṭa is formed from two tribal names Kúṭa representing the early widespread tribe allied to the Gonds known as Koṭṭas and Koḍs in the Central Provinces North Konkan and Delhi (Thána Gazetteer, XII. Part II. 414). In support of this view it may be noticed that Abhimanyu's fifth century Ráshṭrakúṭa inscription (J. Bo. Br. R. As. XVI. 92) refers to the Koṭṭas though as enemies not allies of the Ráshṭrakúṭas. At the same time certain details in Abhimanyu's grant favour an early Ráshṭrakúṭa settlement in the Central Provinces, the probable head-quarters of the Koṭṭas. The grant is dated from Mánapura and is made to Dakshiṇa Śiva of Peṭhapaṅgaraka which may be the Great Śiva shrine in the Mahádev hills in Hoshangábád, as this shrine is under the management of a petty chief of a place called Pagára, and as Mánpur in the Vindhya hills is not far off. Against the tribal origin of the word Kúṭa is to be set the fact that the northern Raṭṭas are also called Ráshṭrakúṭas though any connection between them and the Koṭṭa tribe seems unlikely.

The question remains were the southern Raṭṭas or Ráshṭrakúṭas connected with the northern Ráthoḍs or Ráshṭrakúṭas. If so what was the nature of the connection and to what date does it belong. The fact that, while the later southern Ráshṭrakúṭas

---

[1] It seems doubtful whether the Kánarese *Raṭṭas* the Belgaum Radis and the Telugu Reddis could have been Rástikas or locals in the north Dakhan. The widespread Reddis trace their origin (Balfour's Encyclopædia of India, III. 350) to Rájamandri about thirty miles from the mouth of the Godávari. A tradition of a northern origin remains among some of the Reddis. The Tinnivelly Reddis (Madras J. Lit. and Science, 1887-88, page 136 note 96) call themselves Audh Reddis and assert that Oudh is the native country of their tribe. The late Sir George Campbell (J. R. As. Soc. XXXV. Part II. 129) has recorded the notable fact that the fine handsome Reddis of the north of the Kánara country are like the Játs. With this personal resemblance may be compared the Reddis' curious form of polyandry (Balfour's Encyclopædia, III. 330) in accordance with which the wife of the child-husband bears children to the adult males of the family, a practice which received theories (compare Mr. Kirkpatrick in Indian Ant. VII. 86 and Dr. Muir in Ditto VI. 315) would associate with the northern or Skythian conquerors of Upper India during the early centuries of the Christian era. In support of a northern *Ráta* element later than Asoka's Rástikas the following points may be noted. That the Kshaharáta or Khaharáta tribe to which the great northern conqueror Nahápana (A.D. 180) belonged should disappear from the Dakhan seems unlikely. Karaháṭaka the Mahábhárata name (As. Res. XV. 47, quoted in Wilson's Works VI. 178) for Karád on the *Krishna* suggests that Nahapána's conquest included Sátára and that the name of the holy place on the *Krishna* was altered to give it a resemblance to the name of the conqueror's tribe. That, perhaps after their overthrow by Gautamiputra Śátakarni (A.D. 140), the Khaharátas may have established a local centre at Kurandwád at the meeting of the Krishna and the Panchgangá may be the explanation why in A.D. 914, centuries after Mányakheta or Málkhet had become their capital, the *Ráshṭrakúṭa* Indra should proceed for investiture to Kuru*ndaka*, which, though this is doubtful, may be Kurand*wád*. The parallel case of the Khaharátas' associates the Palhavas, who passed across the southern Dakhan and by intermarriage have in the *Pállas* assumed the characteristics of a southern tribe, give a probability to the existence of a northern Khaharáta or Ráta element in the southern *Ráshṭrakúṭas* and *Raṭṭas* which the facts at present available would not otherwise justify.

Chapter XI.
The Ráshtrakútas A.D. 743-974.

call themselves Yádavas of the Lunar race, the northerners claim descent either from Kuśa the son of Ráma or from Hiraṇyakaśipu would seem to prove no connection did not Abhimanyu's fifth century grant show that in his time the southern Ráshṭrakúṭas had not begun to claim Yádava descent. That the Márwár Ráthoḍs trace their name to the *ráht* or spine of Indra (Tod's Annals, II. 2), and in a closely similar fashion the Ráth or Rattu Játs of the Sutlej (Ibbetson's 1881 Census, page 236) explain their name as stronghanded, and the Raṭṭas of Bijápur (Bijápur Stat. Account, 145) trace their name to the Kánarese *raṭṭa* right arm, may imply no closer connection than the common attempt to find a meaning for the name Raṭṭa in a suitable word of similar sound. A legend preserved in the Rájputána Gazetteer (III. 246), but not noted by Tod, tells how Sevji, after (A.D. 1139) the Musalmáns drove his father Jaichand out of Kanauj (Tod's Annals, I. 88) took Khergad from the Gehlots and went to the Karṇáṭak where the Ráthoḍs had ruled before they came to Kanauj. From the Karṇáṭak Sevji brought the image of the Ráhtoḍ Ráshṭraśyena which is now in the temple of Nágána in Meváḍ. The account quoted in the text from Tod (Annals, I. 88) that the Ráthoḍs who rose to power in Márwár in the thirteenth century belonged to a royal family who had held Kanauj since the fifth century has not stood the test of recent inquiry. It is now known that about A.D. 470 Kanauj was in the hands of the Guptás. That about A.D. 600, according to the contemporary Śríharshacharita it was ruled by the Maukhari Grahavarmán who was put to death by a Málwa chief and was succeeded by Harsha. About A.D. 750, according to the Rájátaraṅginí, Kanauj was held by Yaśovarmán, and, in the next century, as inscriptions prove by the family of Bhoja. It was not till about A.D. 1050 that Kanauj was occupied by the Gáhadavála or Gáharwála family from whom the Ráthoḍs of Márwár claim descent.[1] If the legendary connection of the Márwár Ráthoḍs with Kanauj must be dismissed can the Márwár Ráthoḍs be a branch of the southern Ráshṭrakúṭas who like the Maráthás some 800 years later spread conquering northwards? Such a northern settlement of the southern Ráshṭrakúṭas might be a consequence of the victories of the great Ráshṭrakúṭa Dhruva who according to received opinions about A.D. 790 conquered as far north as Allahábád. It is beyond question that southerners or Karṇáṭas were settled in North India between the seventh and the eleventh centuries. Still the latest information makes it improbable that Dhruva's conquests extended further north than Gujarát. Nor has any special connection been traced between the southern Ráshṭrakúṭas and the middle-age settlements of southerners or Karṇáṭas in North India.[2] Must therefore the North Indian tribe of Ráthoḍs be admitted to have its origin

---

[1] The eleventh century Kanauj Gáhadaválas are now represented by the Bundelas who about A.D. 1200 overthrew the Chándels in Bundelkhand. These Gáharwáls or Bundelas trace their origin to Benares or Kási and may, as Hœrnle suggests, have been related to the Pálas of that city who several times intermarried with the Dakhan Ráshṭrakúṭas. The Gáharwáls seem to have nothing to do with the district of Garhwál (Gadwál) in the Himálayas.—(A. M. T. J.)

[2] The Vatsarája defeated by Dhruva who has hitherto been identified with the Vatsa king of Kosambi is more likely to prove to be a Bachrája of the Gurjjaras of Bhinmál or Śrímál in north Gujarát. Among references to southern settlements in North India between A.D. 600 and 1000 may be noted the tradition (Wilson's Indian Caste, II. 143) of a Dravidian strain in the Kashmir Bráhmans and in the eleventh century also in Kashmir (Rajátarangini, VI. 337) the presence of a Śátaváhana dynasty bearing the same name as the early Śátaváhanas of Paithan near Ahmadnagar. Other instances which might seem more directly associated with the southern Ráshṭrakúṭas (A.D. 500-970) are the six Kárnátaka rulers of Nepál beginning with A.D. 889 (Ind. Ant. VII. 91) and the natives of Karnátadeśa in Máhmúd Ghasnavi's army (A.D. 1000-1025) who (Sachau's Alberuni, I. 173; II. 157) used the Karnáta alphabet. The presence of Karnáta rulers in Nepál in the ninth and tenth centuries remains a puzzle. But the use of the term Karnáta for Chálukyas of Kalyán in A.D. 1000 (Ep. Ind. I. 230) suggests that the Nepál chiefs were Chálukyas rather than Ráshṭrakúṭas: while Máhmúd Ghasnavi's Karnátas may naturally be traced to the mercenary remains of Bárappa's army of Kalyán Chálukyas whose general Bárappa was slain (Rás Málá, I. 61) and his followers dispersed in north Gujarát by Múla Rája Solanki at the close of the tenth century. The only recorded connection of the southern Ráshṭrakúṭas with Northern India during the middle ages (A.D. 750-1150) are their intermarriages

Chapter XI.
THE RÁSHTRAKÚTAS, A.D. 743-974.

as late as the twelfth century, and further is the North Indian name Ráthoḍ not tribal but derived from the title head of a district. Several considerations make both of these solutions unlikely if not impossible. First there is the remarkably widespread existence of the name Ráhtor, Ratha, or Ratti, and endless variations of these names, in almost all parts of the Panjáb, among all castes from the Bráhman to the Baluch, among all religions Musalmán, Sikh, Jain, and Bráhmanic.[1] No doubt the practice of a waning tribe adopting the name of a waxing tribe has always been common. No doubt also the fame of the name during the last 600 years must have tempted other classes to style themselves Ráthoḍ. Still it is to be noted: first that (Ibbetson, page 240) the Ráthoḍs of the Panjáb though widespread are not numerous: and second that the list of sub-caste names has this merit that with a few exceptions the holders of the sub-name are not known by it but by some general or craft name. The evidence of these sub-caste or tribal names seems therefore to support the view that some very large section of the Panjáb population represent an important tribe or nation of whom the least mixed remnant are perhaps the Ráthis or lower class Rájputs of Kángra and Chamba (Ibbetson, pages 219 and 251) and from some connection with whom the Márwár Ráthoḍs of the thirteenth century may have taken their name. Among other traces of northern Ráshṭras in the middle ages may be mentioned the twelfth and thirteenth century Ráshṭrakúṭas of Badaun in the North-West Provinces (Kielhorn in Epigraphia Indica, I. 61 and 63) and (A.D. 1150) in the Kumárapála-Charitra (Tod's Western India, 182) the mention of Ráshṭra-deśa near the Sawálak hills. Among earlier and more doubtful references are the Aratrioi whom probably correctly (since at that time A.D. 247 one main Roman trade route to Central Asia passed up the Indus) the author of the Periplus (McCrindle, 120) places between Abhiria or lower Sindh and Arachosia or south-east Afghanistán that is in north Sindh or south Panjáb. Another earlier and still more doubtful reference is Pliny's (A.D. 77) Oraturæ (Hist. Nat. VI. 23) whom Vivien de St. Martin (Geog. Greque et Latine de l'Inde, 203) identifies with the Ráthoḍs. The fact that while claiming descent from Ráma the Márwár Ráthoḍs (Tod's Annals, II. 2 and 5) preserved the legend that their founder was Yavanaśwa from the northern city of Paralipur supports the view that the tribe to which they belonged was of non-Indian or Central Asian origin, and that this is the tribe of whom traces remain in the Ráthi Rájputs of the Kángra hill country and less purely in the widely spread Ráts, Rattas, and Rátis of the Panjáb plains. The examples among Panjáb caste names Rora for Arora (Ibbetson's 1881 Census, page 297), Her for Ahir (Ditto, 230-275), and Heri for Aheri (Ditto, 310) suggest that the Panjáb Ráthors or Raṭṭas may be the ancient Araṭṭas whom the Mahábhárata (Chap. VII. Verse 44. J. Bl. Soc. VI. Pt. I. 337 and Vivien de St. Martin Geog. Greque et Latine de l'Inde, 149) ranks with Prasthalas, Madras, and Gandháras, Panjáb and frontier tribes, whose identification with the Báhikas (Karṇaparvan, 2063ff.) raises the probability of a common Central Asian origin. Remembering that the evidence (Kshatrapa Chapter, pages 22 and 33) favours the view that the Kshatrapa family who ruled the Panjáb between B.C. 70 and A.D. 78 were of the same tribe as Nahápana, and also that Sháhi is so favourite a prefix in Samudra Gupta's (A.D. 380) list of Kushán tribes, the suggestion may be offered that Kshaharáta is the earlier form of Sháharaṭṭa and is the tribe of foreigners afterwards known in the Panjáb as Araṭṭas and of which traces survive in the present widespread tribal names Ráta, Ratta, Batha, and Ráthor.]

---

with the Pálas of Benares (A.D. 850-1000) mentioned above (Page 132 Note 1), and, between A.D. 850 and 950, with the Kalachuris of Tripura near Jabalpur (Cunningham's Arch. Survey Report for 1891, IX. 80).

[1] The details compiled from the excellent index and tables in the Panjáb Census yield the following leading groups: 37 sub-castes named Ráthor, Rátor, and other close variants; 53 Rath and R this and 2 Rahtas; 50 Ratas, Batis, or other close variants. Compare Ráhti the name of the people of Mount Abu (Rajputána Gazetteer, III. 139) and the Raht tract in the north-west of Alvar (Ditto, 167).

CHAPTER XII.

THE MIHIRAS OR MERS.

A.D. 470–900.

Chapter XII.

The Mers, A.D. 470-900.

That the Guptas held sway in Káthiáváḍa till the time of Skandagupta (A.D. 454-470) is proved by the fact that his Sorath Viceroy is mentioned in Skandagupta's inscription on the Girnár rock. After Skandagupta under the next known Gupta king Budhagupta (Gupta 165-180, A.D. 484-499) no trace remains of Gupta sovereignty in Sorath. It is known that Budhagupta was a weak king and that the Gupta kingdom had already entered on its decline and lost its outlying provinces. Who held Suráshṭra and Gujarát during the period of Gupta decline until the arrival and settlement of Bhaṭkárka in A.D. 514 (Gupta 195) is not determined. Still there is reason to believe that during or shortly after the time of Budhagupta some other race or dynasty overthrew the Gupta Viceroy of these provinces and took them from the Guptas. These powerful conquerors seem to be the tribe of Maitrakas mentioned in Valabhi copperplates as people who had settled in Káthiáváḍa and established a *maṇḍala* or kingdom. Though these Maitrakas are mentioned in no other records from Suráshṭra there seems reason to identify the Maitrakas with the Mihiras the well-known tribe of Mhers or Mers. In Sanskrit both *mitra* and *mihira* are names of the sun, and it would be quite in agreement with the practise of Sanskrit writers to use derivatives of the one for those of the other. These Mhers or Mers are still found in Káthiáváḍa settled round the Barda hills while the Porbandar chiefs who are known as Jethvás are recognized as the head of the tribe. The name Jethvá is not a tribal but a family name, being taken from the proper or personal name of the ancestor of the modern chiefs. As the Porbandar chiefs are called the kings of the Mhers they probably belong to the same tribe, though, being chiefs, they try, like other ruling families, to rank higher than their tribe tracing their origin from Hanúmán. Though the Jethvás appear to have been long ashamed to acknowledge themselves to belong to the Mher tribe the founders of minor Mher kingdoms called themselves Mher kings The Porbandar chiefs have a tradition tracing their dynasty to Makaradhvaja son of Hanúmán, and there are some Puránik legends attached to the tradition. The historical kernel of the tradition appears to be that the Mhers or Jethvás had a *makara* or fish as their flag or symbol. One of the mythical stories of Makaradhvaja is that he fought with Mayúradhvaja. Whatever coating of fable may have overlaid the story, it contains a grain of history. Mayúradhvaja stands for the Guptas whose chief symbol was a peacock *mayúra*, and with them Makaradhvaja that is the people with the fish-symbol that is

Chapter XII.
THE MERS,
A.D. 470-900.

the Mhers had a fight. This fight is probably the historical contest in which the Mhers fought with and overthrew the Gupta Viceroy of Káthiáváḍa.

The Káthiáváḍa Mhers are a peculiar tribe whose language dress and appearance mark them as foreign settlers from Upper India. Like the Málavas, Játs, Gurjaras, and Pahlavas, the Mhers seem to have passed through the Punjáb Sindh and North Gujarát into Káthiáváḍa leaving settlements at Ajmír, Bádner, Jesalmír, Kokalmír, and Mherváḍa. How and when the Mhers made these settlements and entered Káthiáváḍa is not known. It may be surmised that they came with Toramáṇa (A.D. 470-512) who overthrew the Guptas, and advanced far to the south and west in the train of some general of Toramáṇa's who may perhaps have entered Suráshṭra. This is probable as the date of Toramáṇa who overthrew Budhagupta is almost the same as that of the Maitrakas mentioned as the opponents and enemies of Bhaṭárka. In the time of Bhaṭárka (A.D. 509-520 ?) the Mhers were firmly established in the peninsula, otherwise they would not be mentioned in the Valabhi grants as enemies of Bhaṭárka, a tribe or *maṇḍala* wielding incomparable power. As stated above in Chapter VIII. some time after the Mher settlement and consolidation of power, Bhaṭárka seems to have come as general of the fallen Guptas through Málwa and Broach by sea to East Káthiáváḍa. He established himself at Valabhi and then gradually dislodged the Mhers from Sorath until they retired slightly to the north settling eventually at Morbi, which the Jethvás still recognize as the earliest seat of their ancestors. At Morbi they appear to have ruled contemporarily with the Valabhis. In support of this it is to be noted that no known Valabhi plate records any grant of lands or villages in Hálár, Machhukántha, or Okhámandal in North Káthiáváḍa. As the northmost place mentioned in Valabhi plates is Venuthali known as Wania's Vanthali in Hálár it may be inferred that not the Valabhis but the Mhers ruled the north coast of Káthiáváḍa, probably as feudatories or subordinates of the Valabhis. On the overthrow of Valabhi about A.D. 770 the Mhers appear to have seized the kingdom and ruled the whole of Káthiáváḍa dividing it into separate chiefships grouped under the two main divisions of Bardái and Gohelvádia. About A.D. 860 the Mhers made incursions into Central Gujarát. A copperplate dated Śaka 789 (A.D. 847) of the Gujarát Ráshṭrakúṭa king Dhruva describes him as attacked by a powerful Mihira king whom he defeated.[1] At the height of their power the Mhers seem to have established their capital at the fort of Bhumli or Ghumli in the Bardá hills in the centre of Káthiáváḍa. The traditions about Ghumli rest mainly on modern Jethvá legends of no historical interest. The only known epigraphical record is a copperplate of a king named Jâchikadeva found in the Morbi district.[2] Unfortunately only the second plate remains. Still the fish mark on the plate, the locality where it was found, and its date

[1] Ind. Ant. XII. 179. [2] Ind. Ant. II. 257.

Chapter XII.

The Mers, A.D. 470-900.

leave little doubt that the plate belongs to the Makaradhvaja or Jethvá kings. The date of the grant is 585 Gupta era the 5th Phálguna Sudi that is A.D. 904, about 130 years after the destruction of Valabhi, a date with which the form of the letters agrees.

A similar copperplate in which the king's name appears in the slightly different form Jáikadeva has been found at Dhiniki in the same neighbourhood as the first and like it bearing the fish mark.[1] This copperplate describes the king as ruling at Bhúmiliká or Bhúmli in Sorath and gives him the high titles of Paramabhaṭṭáraka-Mahárájádhirája-Parameśvara, that is Great Lord Great King of Kings Great King, titles which imply wide extent and independence of rule. This grant purports to be made on the occasion of a solar eclipse on Sunday Vikrama Saṃvat 794 Jyeshṭha constellation, the no-moon of the second half of Kárttika. This would be A.D. 738 or 166 years before the Jáchika of the Morbí plate. Against this it is to be noted that the letters of this plate, instead of appearing as old as eighth century letters, look later than the letters of the tenth century Morbí plate. As neither the day of the week, the constellation, nor the eclipse work out correctly Dr. Bhagvánlál believed the plate to be a forgery of the eleventh century, executed by some one who had seen a fish-marked copperplate of Jáchika dated in the *Saka* era. It should however be noted that the names of ministers and officers which the plate contains give it an air of genuineness. Whether the plate is or is not genuine, it is probably true that Jáikadev was a great independent sovereign ruling at Bhúmli. Though the names of the other kings of the dynasty, the duration of the Bhúmli kingdom, and the details of its history are unknown it may be noted that the dynasty is still represented by the Porbandar chiefs. Though at present Bhúmli is deserted several ruined temples of about the eleventh century stand on its site. It is true no old inscriptions have been found; it is not less true that no careful search has been made about Bhúmli.

Early in the tenth century a wave of invasion from Sindh seems to have spread over Kacch and Káthiáváḍa. Among the invading tribes were the Jádejás of Kacch and the Chudásamás of Sorath, who like the Bhattis of Jesalmír call themselves of the Yaduvaṃśa stock. Doctor Bhagvanlál held that the Chúḍásamás were originally of the Ábhíra tribe, as their traditions attest connexion with the Ábhíras and as the description of Graharipu one of their kings by Hemachandra in his Dvyáśraya points to his being of some local tribe and not of any ancient Rájput lineage. Further in their bardic traditions as well as in popular stories the Chúḍásamás are still commonly called Áhera-ránás. The position of Aberia in Ptolemy (A.D. 150) seems to show that in the second century the Ahirs were settled between Sindh and the Panjáb. Similarly it may be suggested that Jádejá is a corruption of Jaudhejá which

[1] Ind. Ant. XII. 151.

Chapter XII.

The Mers, A.D. 470-900.

in turn comes from Yaudheya (the change of *y* to *j* being very common) who in Kshatrapa Inscriptions appear as close neighbours of the Ahirs. After the fall of the Valabhis (A.D. 775) the Yaudheyas seem to have established themselves in Kacch and the Ahirs settled and made conquests in Káthiáváḍa. On the decline of local rule brought about by these incursions and by the establishment of an Ahir or Chúḍásamá kingdom at Junágaḍh, the Jethvás seem to have abandoned Bhúmli which is close to Junágaḍh and gone to Srínagar or Káṇṭelun near Porbandar which is considered to have been the seat of Jethvá power before Porbandar.

A copperplate found at Haddálá on the road from Dholka to Dhandhuka dated A.D. 917 (Śaka 839) shows that there reigned at Vadhwán a king named Dharaṇívaráha of the Chápa dynasty,[1] who granted a village to one Mahesvarácharya, an apostle of the Ámardáka Śákhá of Saivism. Dharaṇívaráha and his ancestors are described as feudatory kings, ruling by the grace of the feet of the great king of kings the great lord the illustrious Mahípáladeva. This Mahípála would seem to be some great king of Káthiáváḍa reigning in A.D. 917 over the greater part of the province. Dr. Bhagvánlál had two coins of this king of about that time, one a copper coin the other a silver coin. The coins were found near Junágaḍh. The copper coin, about ten grains in weight, has one side obliterated but the other side shows clearly the words Ráná Śrí Mahípála Deva. The silver coin, about fourteen grains in weight, has on the obverse a well-executed elephant and on the reverse the legend Ráná Śrí Mahípála Deva. From the locality where the name Mahípála appears both in coins and inscriptions, and from the fact that the more reliable Chúḍásamá lists contain similar names, it may be assumed as probable that Mahípála was a powerful Chúḍásamá ruler of Káthiáváḍa in the early part of the tenth century.

After the fall of Valabhi no other reliable record remains of any dynasty ruling over the greater part of Gujarát. The most trustworthy and historical information is in connection with the Chávaḍás of Aṇahilapura. Even for the Chávaḍás nothing is available but scant references recorded by Jain authors in their histories of the Solaṅkis and Vághelás.

The Chúdásamás, A.D. 900-940.

[The modern traditions of the Chúḍásamá clan trace their origin to the Yádava race and more immediately to the Samma tribe of Nagar Thatha in Sindh.[2] The name of the family is said to have been derived from Chúḍáchandra the first ruler of Vanthalí

---

[1] The inscription calls Chápa the founder of the dynasty. The name is old. A king Vyághrarája of the Chápa Vamśa is mentioned by the astronomer Brahmagupta as reigning in Śaka 550 (A.D. 628) when he wrote his book called Brahma-Gupta Siddhánta. The entry runs "In the reign of Śrí Vyághramukha of the Śrí Chápa dynasty, five hundred and fifty years after the Śaka king having elapsed." Jour. B. B. R. A. Soc. VIII. 27. For Dharaṇívara's grant see Ind. Ant. XII. 190ff.

[2] Elliot's History, I. 266.

(Káthiáwár Gazetteer, 489). Traces of a different tradition are to be found in the Tuhfat-ul-Kirám (Elliot, I. 337) which gives a list of Chúḍásammá's ancestors from Nuh (Noah), including not only Krishṇa the Yádava but also Ráma of the solar line. In this pedigree the Musalmán element is later than the others: but the attempt to combine the solar and lunar lines is a sure sign that the Samma clan was not of Hindu origin, and that it came under Hindu influence fairly late though before Sindh became a Musalmán province. This being admitted it follows that the Sammas were one of the numerous tribes that entered India during the existence of the Turkish empire in Transoxiana (A.D. 560 - c. 750). In this connection it is noteworthy that some of the Jáms bore such Turkish names as Tamáchi, Tughlik, and Sanjár.

The migration of the Sammas to Kacch is ascribed by the Taríkh-i-Tahiri (A.D. 1621) to the tyranny of the Súmra chiefs. The Sammas found Kacch in the possession of the Cháwaras, who treated them kindly, and whom they requited by seizing the fort of Gúntrí by a stratagem similar to that which brought about the fall of Girnár.

The date of the Chúḍásamá settlement at Vanthalí is usually fixed on traditional evidence, at about A.D. 875, but there is reason to think that this date is rather too early. In the first place it is worthy of notice that Chúḍáchandra, the traditional eponym of the family, is in the Tuhfat-ul-Kirám made a son of Jádam (Yádava) and only a great-grandson of Krishṇa himself, a fact which suggests that, if not entirely mythical, he was at all events a very distant ancestor of Múlarája's opponent Grahári, and was not an actual ruler of Vanthalí. As regards Grahári's father Viśvavaráha and his grandfather Múlarája, there is no reason to doubt that they were real persons, although it is very questionable whether the Chúḍásamás were settled in Káthiáváḍa in their time. In the first place, the Morbí grant of Jáikadeva shows that the Jethvás had not been driven southwards before A.D. 907. Secondly Dharaṇívaráha's Vadhván grant proves that the Chápa family of Bhínmál were still supreme in Káthiáváḍa in A.D. 914: whereas the Taríkh-i-Tahiri's account of the Chúḍásamá conquest of Kacch implies that the Cháwaras, who must be identified with the Chápas of Bhínmál, were losing their power when the Chúḍásamás captured Gúntrí, an event which must have preceded the settlement at Vanthalí in Káthiáváḍa. Beyond the fact that Múlarája Solaṅki transferred the capital to Anahilaváḍa in A.D. 942, we know nothing of the events which led to the break-up of the Bhínmál empire. But it is reasonable to suppose that between A.D. 920 and 940 the Chápas gradually lost ground and the Chúḍásamás were able first to conquer Sindh and then to settle in Káthiáváḍa.—A. M. T. J.]

[Káthiáváḍa contains three peculiar and associated classes of Hindus, the Mers, the Jethvás, and the Jhálás. The Mers and the Jethvás stand to each other in the relation of vassal and lord. The Jhálás are connected with the Jethvás by origin history and alliance. The bond

Chapter XII.

The Mers, A.D. 470-900.

The Jethvás.

of union between the three classes is not only that they seem to be of foreign that is of non-Hindu origin, but whether or not they belong to the same swarm of northern invaders, that they all apparently entered Káthiáváḍa either by land or sea through Sindh and Kacch. So far as record or tradition remains the Mers and Jethvás reached Káthiáváḍa in the latter half of the fifth century after Christ, and the Jhálás, and perhaps a second detachment of Mers and Jethvás, some three hundred years later.[1] The three tribes differ widely in numbers and in distribution. The ruling Jethvás are a small group found solely in south-west Káthiáváḍa.[2] The Jhálás, who are also known as Makvánas, are a much larger clan. They not only fill north-east Káthiáváḍa, but from Káthiáváḍa, about A.D. 1500, spread to Rajputána and have there established a second Jhálávaḍa,[3] where, in reward for their devotion to the Sesodia Rája of Mewáḍ in his struggles with the Emperor Akbar (A.D. 1580-1600), the chief was given a daughter of the Udepur family and raised to a high position among Rájputs.[4] The Mers are a numerous and widespread race. They seem to be the sixth to tenth century Medhs, Meds, Mands, or Mins of Baluchistan, South-Sindh, Kacch, and Káthiáváḍa.[5] Further they seem to be the Mers of Meváḍa or Medapatha in Rajputána[6] and of Mairváḍa in Málava,[7] and also to be the Musalmán Meos and Minas of Northern India.[8] In Gujarát

---

[1] According to the Káthiáwár Gazetteer pages 110 and 278, the first wave reached about A.D. 650 and the second about 250 years later. Dr. Bhagvánlál's identification of the Mers with the Maitrakas would take back their arrival in Káthiáváḍa from about A.D. 650 to about A.D. 450. The Mers were again formidable in Gujarát in the late ninth and early tenth centuries. In A.D. 867 (see above Pages 127 and 130) the Ráshṭrakúṭa Dhruva II. checked an inroad of a Mihira king with a powerful army. Again in A.D. 914 the Ráshṭrakúṭa Indra in a moment uprooted the Mehr (Ditto).

[2] The Ain-i-Akbari (Gladwin, II. 69) notices that the sixth division of Sauráshṭra, which was almost impervious by reason of mountains rivers and woods, was (A.D. 1580) inhabited by the tribe Cheetore that is Jetwa.

[3] Of the Jhálás or Chalahs the Ain-i-Akbari (Gladwin, II. 64) has: Chaláwareh (in north-east Káthiáváḍa) formerly independent and inhabited by the tribe of Chálah.

[4] Tod's Annals of Rájasthán, II. 113.

[5] Elliot and Dowson, I. 114 and 519-531. It is noted in the text that to the Arab invaders of the eighth and ninth centuries the Medhs of Hind were the chief people of Káthiáváḍa both in Soráth in the south and in Mália in the north. They were as famous by sea as by land. According to Beláduri (A.D. 950) (Reinaud's Mémoire Sur l'Inde, 234-235) the Meyds of Saurásthra and Kacch were sailors who lived on the sea and sent fleets to a distance. Ibn Khurdadba (A.D. 912) and Idrisi (A.D. 1130), probably from the excellent Aldjayháni (Reinaud's Abulfeda, lxiii. and Elliot, I. 79), have the form Mand. Elliot, I. 14. The form Mand survives in a musical mode popular in Rajputána, which is also called Rajewári. The Mand is like the Central Asian Mus-tazad (K. S. Fazullah Lutfallah.)

[6] Indian Antiquary, VI. 191.

[7] Rajputána Gazetteer, I. 11.

[8] Rajputána Gazetteer, I. 66; North-West Province Gazetteer, III. 265; Ibbetson's Panjáb Census page 261. Some of these identifications are doubtful. Dr. Bhagvánlál in the text (21 Note 6 and 33) distinguishes between the Mevas or Medas whom he identifies as northern immigrants of about the first century B.C. and the Mers. This view is in agreement with the remark in the Rajputána Gazetteer, I. 66, that the Mers have been suspected to be a relic of the Indo-Skythian Meds. Again Tod (Annals of Rajasthán, I. 9) derives Meváda from *madhya* (Sk.) middle, and the Mer of Merwáda from *meru* a hill. In support of Tod's view it is to be noted that the forts Balmer Jesalmer Komalmer and Ajmer, which Pandit Bhagvánlál would derive from the personal names of Mer leaders, are all either hill forts or rocks (Annals, I. 11, and Note †). It is, on the other hand, to be noted that no hill forts out of this particular tract of country are called Mers, and that the similar names Koli and Malava, which with equal probability as Medh might be derived from Koh and Mala hill, seem to be tribal not geographical names.

The Mers.

their strength is much greater than the 30,000 or 40,000 returned as Mers. One branch of the tribe is hidden under the name Koli; another has disappeared below the covering of Islám.[1]

Formerly except the vague contention that the Medhás, Jhetvás, and Jhála-Makvánás were northerners of somewhat recent arrival little evidence was available either to fix the date of their appearance in Káthiáváḍa or to determine to which of the many swarms of non-Hindu Northerners they belonged.[2] This point Dr. Bhagvánlál's remarks in the text go far to clear. The chief step is the identification of the Mers with the Maitrakas, the ruling power in Káthiáváḍa between the decline of the Guptas about A.D. 470 and the establishment of Valabhi rule about sixty years later. And further that they fought at the same time against the same Hindu rulers and that both are described as foreigners and northerners favours the identification of the

[1] The tales cited in the Rás Malá (I. 103) prove that most of the Kolis between Gujarát and Kathiáváḍa are Mairs. That till the middle of the tenth century the south-east of Káthiáváḍa was held by Medhs (Káth. Gazetteer, 672) supports the view that the Kolis, whom about A.D. 1190 (Tod's Western India, I. 265) the Gohils drove out of the island of Piram, were Medhs, and this is in agreement with Idrisí (A.D. 1130 Elliot, I. 83) who calls both Piram and the Medhs by the name Mand. Similarly some of the Koli clans of Kacch (Gazetteer, 70) seem to be descended from the Medhs. And according to Mr. Dalpatram Khakkar three subdivisions of Brahmo-Kshatris, of which the best known are the Mansura Mers and the Pipalia Mers, maintain the surname Mair or Mer. (Cutch Gazetteer, 52 note 2.) Mera or Mehra is a common surname among Sindhi Baluchis. Many of the best Musalmán captains and pilots from Káthiáváḍa, Kacch, and the Makrán coast still have Mer as a surname. Mehr is also a favourite name among both Khojáhs and Memans, the two special classes of Káthiáváḍa converts to Islám. The Khojáhs explain the name as meaning Meher Ali the friend of Ali; the Memans also explain Mer as Meher or friend. But as among Memans Mer is a common name for women as well as for men the word can hardly mean friend. The phrase Merbaí or Lady Mer applied to Meman mothers seems to have its origin in the Rajput practice of calling the wife by the name of her caste or tribe as Kathianibaí, Meranibai. In the case both of the Khojáhs and the Memans the name Mer seems to be the old tribal name continued because it yielded itself to the uses of Islám. Mehr, Mihr, and Mahar are also used as titles of respect. The Khant Kolis of Girnar, apparently a mixture of the Maitrakas of the text and of a local hill tribe, still (Káthiawar Gazetteer, 142) honour their leaders with the name Mer explaining the title by the Gujarati *mer* the main bead in a rosary. Similarly in Málwa a Gurjjara title is Mihr (Rajputána Gazetteer, I. 80) and in the Panjáb Máhar (Gazetteer of Panjáb, Gujrát, 50-51). And in Kacch the headman among the Bharwáds, who according to some accounts are Gurjjarás, is called Mir (Cutch Gazetteer, 81). Similarly among the Rabáris of Kacch the name of the holy she-camel is Máta Meri. (Ditto, 80.) All these terms of respect are probably connected with Mihira, Sun.

[2] Compare Tod (Western India, 420): Though enrolled among the thirty-six royal races we may assert the Jethvás have become Hindus only from locality and circumstance. Of the Jhálás Tod says (Rajasthán, I. 113): As the Jhálás are neither Solar Lunar nor Agnikula they must be strangers. Again (Western India, 414): The Jhála Makvanás are a branch of Húṇas. Of the name Makvana (Káthiawár Gazetteer, 111; Rás Málá, I. 297) two explanations may be offered, either that the word comes from Mák the dewy tracts in Central Kacch (Cutch Gazetteer, 75 note 2) where (Káthiáwár Gazetteer, 420) the Jhálás stopped when the Mers and Jethvás passed south, or that Makvána represents Mauna a Puranic name for the Húṇas (Wilson's Works, IV. 207). Tod's and Wilford's (Asiatic Researches, IX. 287) suggestion that Makvána is Mahâhuna is perhaps not phonetically possible. At the same time that the Makvanas are a comparatively recent tribe of northerners is supported by the ascendancy in the fourteenth century in the Himálayas of Makvánis (Hodgson's Essays, I. 397; Government of India Selections XLVII. 54 and 119) who used the Indo-Skythian title Sah (Ditto). With the Nepal Makvánis may be compared the Makpons or army-men the caste of the chief of Baltistán or Little Tibet. Vigne's Kashmir, II. 258, 439.

Chapter XII.
THE MERS, A.D. 470-900.
White Húṇas.

power of the Maitrakas with the North Indian empire of the Epthalites, Yethas, or White Húṇas.[1]

Though the sameness in name between the Mihiras and Mihirakula (A.D. 508-530), the great Indian champion of the White Húṇas, may not imply sameness of tribe it points to a common sun-worship.[2]

That the Multán sun-worship was introduced under Sassanian influence is supported by the fact (Wilson's Ariana Antiqua, 357) that the figure of the sun on the fifth century Hindu sun coins is in the dress of a Persian king: that the priests who performed the Multán sun-worship were called Magas; and by the details of the dress and ritual in the account of the introduction of sun-worship given in the Bhavishya Purána.[3] That the Meyds or Mands had some share in its introduction is supported by the fact that the Purána names the third or Sudra class of the sun-worshippers Mandagas.[4] That the Meyds were associated with the Magas is shown by the mention of the Magas as Mihiragas.[5] The third class whom the Bhavishya Purána associates with the introduction of sun-worship are the Mânas who

---

[1] The evidence in support of the statement that the Maitrakas and Húṇas fought at the same time against the same Hindu rulers is given in the text. One of the most important passages is in the grant of Dhruvasena III. (Epig. Ind. I. 89 [A.D. 653-4]) the reference to Bhatárka the founder of Valabhi (A.D. 509-520) meeting in battle the matchless armies of the Maitrakas.

[2] Mr. Fleet (Epigraphia Indica, III. 327 and note 12) would identify Mihirakula's tribe with the Maitrakas. More recent evidence shows that his and his father Toromaṇa's tribe was the Jáuvlas. That the White Húṇas or other associated tribes were sun-worshippers appears from a reference in one of Mihirakula's inscriptions (Corpus Inscriptiorum Indicorum, III. 161) to the building of a specially fine temple of the sun; and from the fact that in Kashmír Mihirakula founded a city Mihirapura and a temple to Mihireshwar. (Darmsteter in Journal Asiatique, X. 70: Fleet in Indian Antiquary, XV. 242-252.) Mihirakula's (A.D. 508-530) sun-worship may have been the continuance of the Kushan (A.D. 50-150) worship of Mithro or Helios (Wilson's Ariana Antiqua, 357). At the same time the fact that Mihirakula uses the more modern form Mihir makes it probable (Compare Rawlinson's Seventh Monarchy, 284) that Mihirakula's sun-worship was more directly the result of the spread of sun-worship in Central Asia under the fiercely propagandist Sassanians Varahan V. or Behram Gor (A.D. 420-440), and his successors Izdigerd II. (A.D. 440-457), and Perozes (A.D. 457-483). The extent to which Zoroastrian influence pervaded the White Húṇas is shown by the Persian name not only of Mihirakula but of Kushnawaz (A.D. 470-490) the great emperor of the White Húṇas the overthrower of Perozes. That this Indian sun-worship, which, at latest, from the seventh to the tenth century made Multán so famous was not of local origin is shown by the absence of reference to sun-worship in Multán in the accounts of Alexander the Great. Its foreign origin is further shown by the fact that in the time of Beruni (A.D. 1020 Sachau's Edition, I. 119) the priests were called Maghas and the image of the sun was clad in a northern dress falling to the ankles. It is remarkable as illustrating the Hindu readiness to adopt priests of conquering tribes into the ranks of Bráhmans that the surname Magha survives (Cutch Gazetteer, 52 note 2) among Shrimáli Bráhmans. These Maghas are said to have married Bhoja or Rajput girls and to have become the Bráhman Bhojaks of Dwárka. Even the Mands who had Saka wives, whose descendants were named Mandagas, obtained a share in the temple ceremonies. Reinaud's Mémoire Sur l'Inde, 393.

[3] Wilson's Vishnu Purána Preface XXXIX. in Reinaud's Mémoire Sur l'Inde, 391. Details are given in Wilson's Works, X. 381-385.

[4] Reinaud's Mémoire Sur l'Inde, 393; Wilson's Works, X. 382.

[5] The name Mehiraga is explained in the Bhavishya Purána as derived from their ancestress a daughter of the sage Rigu or Rijvahva of the race named Mihira (Reinaud's Mémoire Sur l'Inde, 393; Wilson's Works, X. 382). The name Mihiraga suggests that the spread of sun-worship in the Panjáb and Sindh, of which the sun-worship in Multán Sindh Káthiáváda and Mewáḍ and the fire-worshipping Rajput and Sindh coins of the fifth and sixth centuries are evidence, was helped by the spread of Sassanian influence

Chapter XII.

The Mers, A.D. 470-900.

White Húṇas.

are given a place between the Magas and the Mands. The association of the Mânas with the Mihiras or Maitrakas suggests that Mâna is Mauna a Puránik name for the White Húṇas.[1] That the Multán sun idol of the sixth and seventh centuries was a Húṇa idol and Multán the capital of a Húṇa dynasty seems in agreement with the paramount position of the Rais of Alor or Rori in the sixth century. Though their defeat by Yesodharmman of Málwá about A.D. 540 at the battle of Karur, sixty miles east of Multán, may have ended Húṇa supremacy in north and north-west India it does not follow that authority at once forsook the Húṇas. Their widespread and unchallenged dominion in North India, the absence of record of any reverse later than the Karur defeat, the hopelessuess of any attempt to pass out of India in the face of the combined Turk and Sassanian forces make it probable that the Húṇas and their associated tribes, adopting Hinduism and abandoning their claim to supremacy, settled in west and north-west India. This view finds support in the leading place which the Húṇas and Hára-Húṇas, the Maitrakas or Mers, and the Gurjjaras hold in the centuries that follow the overthrow of the White Húṇa empire. According to one rendering of Cosmas[2] (A.D. 525) the chief of Orrhotha or Sorath in common with several other coast rulers owed allegiance to Gollas, apparently, as is suggested at page 75 of the text, to Gulla or Mihirgulla the Indian Emperor of the White Húṇas. These details support the view that the Maitrakas, Mihiras, or Mers who in Cosmas' time were in power in Káthiáváḍa, and to whose ascendancy during the seventh and eighth centuries both the Chinese pilgrim Hiuen Tsiang (A.D. 612-640) and the Arab historians of Sindh bear witness, were a portion of the great White Húṇa invasion (A.D. 480-530).[3] In the many recorded swarmings south from

---

into Baluchistán Kacch-Gandevi and other parts of western Sindh, through Sakastene the modern western Seistan near the lake Helmund. This Sakastene or land of the S'akas received its name from the settlement in it of one of the earlier waves of the Yuechi in the second or first century before Christ. The name explains the statement in the Bhavishya Purána that sun-worship was introduced by Magas into Multán from Sakadvipa the land of the S'akas. In this connection it is interesting to note that Darmsteter (Zend Avesta, xxxiv.) holds that the Zend Avesta was probably completed during the reign of Sháhpur II. (A.D. 309-379); that (lxxxix.) Zend was a language of eastern Persia an earlier form of Pashtu; and that (lxxxiv.) western Seistan and the Helmund river was the holy land of the Avesta the birth-place of Zoroaster and the scene of king Vishtasp's triumphs. A memory of the spread of this western or Sassanian influence remains in the reference in the Mujmalu-T-Tawáríkh in Elliot, I. 107-109, to the fire temples established in Kandabil (Gandevi) and Buddha (Mansura) by Mahra a general of Bahman that is of Varahran V. (A.D. 420-440). It seems probable that Mahra is Mehr the family name or the title (Rawlinson's Sassanian Monarchy, 224 note 4 and 312) of the great Mihran family of Persian nobles. The general in question may be the Mehr-Narses the minister of Varahran's son and successor Izdigerd II. (A.D. 440-457), who enforced Zoroastrianism in Armenia (Rawlinson, Ditto 305-308). Mehr's success may be the origin of the Indian stories of Varahran's visit to Málwá. It may further be the explanation of the traces of fire temples and towers of silence noted by Pottinger (1810) in Baluchistán (Travels, 126-127) about sixty miles west of Khelat.

[1] Wilson's Works, IX. 207.

[2] Compare Priaulx's Embassies, 222.

[3] The White Húṇas overran Bakhtria and the country of the Yuechi between A.D. 450 and 460. About a hundred years later they were crushed between the advancing Turks and the Sassanian Chosroes I. or Naushirván (A.D. 537-590). Rawlinson's Sassanian Monarchy, 420; Specht in Journal Asiatique (1883) Tom II. 349-350. The Húṇas supremacy in North India did not last beyond A.D. 530 or 540. The overthrow of their

Chapter XII.
THE MERS, A.D. 470-900.
White Húṇas.

Central Asia into Persia and India no feature is commoner than the leading of the conquered by certain families of the conquering tribe. Chinese authorities place it beyond doubt that when, towards the middle of the fifth century A.D., the White Húṇas crossed the Oxus they found in power a cognate tribe of northerners whose date of settlement on the Indian frontier was less than a century old. This preceding swarm was the Yuán-Yuán, Var-Var, or Avár, who, about the close of the fourth century (A.D. 380), had driven from Balkh southwards into the Kabul valley Kitolo the last ruler of the long established Yuetchi (B.C. 50 - A.D. 380).[1] It is known that in retreating before the Yuán-Yuán a division of the Baktrian Yuetchi, under the leadership of Kitolo's son, under the name of the Kidáras or Little Yuetchi, established their power in Gandhára and Peshávar.[2] This Kidára invasion must have driven a certain share of the people of the Kabul valley to the east of the Indus. The invasion of the White Húṇas a century later, who were welcomed as allies by some of the Panjáb chiefs,[3] would cause fresh movements among the frontier tribes. The welcome given to the Húṇas, and the show and dash which marked their century of ascendancy in India and Persia, make it probable that as leaders they conducted south as far as Káthiáváḍa and Málava large bodies of the earlier northern settlers. To which of the waves of earlier northerners the Medhs belonged is doubtful.[4] The view held by Pandit Bhagvánlál that one branch of the Medhs entered India in the first century before Christ among the tribes of which the great Yuechi were the chief is on the whole in agreement with General Cunningham's argument that Medus Hydaspes, Virgil's phrase for the Jhelum, proves that the Medhs were then (B.C. 40) already settled on its banks.[5]

---

supremacy perhaps dates from A.D. 540 the battle of Karur about sixty miles east of Múltán, their conqueror being Yasodharmman of Malwá the second of the three great Vikramádityas of Málwá. Of the Húṇas' position among Hindu castes Colonel Tod says: The Húṇas are one of the Skyths who have got a place among the thirty-six races of India. They probably came along with the Káthi, Bála, and Makvána of Sauráshṭra. Tod's Annals of Rajasthán, I. 110.

[1] Specht in Journal Asiatique (1883), II. 348.

[2] Specht in Journal Asiatique (1883), II. 349.

[3] Compare above Chapter VII. page 73 note 3.

[4] Dr. Bhagvánlál (Text, 33) traces one set of Medhs to the Mevas the tribe of Ysamotika the father of the Kshatrapa Chashtana (A.D. 130). He holds these Mevas entered India (21) with the Malayas, Palhavas, and Abhíras about B.C. 150 (?) At the same time he seems to have considered those early Mevas different from the fifth and sixth century Mihiras and from the seventh and eighth century Medhs.

[5] Arch. Report for 1863-64, II. 52. In support of this Cunningham cites Ptolemy's (A.D. 150) Euthymedia that is Sagala, sixty miles north-west of Lahor, and the Media of Peutinger's Tables (A.D. 400). This Euthymedia is a corruption of the original Euthydemia the name given to Sagala by Demetrios (B.C. 190) the great Græco-Baktrian in honour of his father Euthydemos (Compare Text page 16 and McCrindle's Ptolemy, 124). Of the cause of this change of name, which may be only a clerical error, two different explanations have been offered. Tod (An. of Rajn. I. 233) would make the new form Yuthi-media the Middle Yuchi. Cunningham (Arch. Surv. Rep. II. 53) would attribute it to the southward migration towards Sindh about B.C. 50 of the Kushán-pressed horde which under Moas or Mogha came from Little Tibet and entered the Panjáb either by way of Kashmír or down the Swát valley. According to General Cunningham (Ditto, 53) the followers of this Moas were Mandrueni called after the Mandrus river south of the Oxus. The two forms Medh and Mand are due to the cerebral which explains the Minnagaras of Ptolemy and the Periplus; Masudi's (A.D. 915) Mind and Ibn Khurdad-

Chapter XII.

The Mers, A.D. 470-900.

White Húṇas.

Dr. Bhagvánlál's view that the Jethvás are Medhs ennobled by long overlordship is somewhat doubtfully shared by Colonel Watson[1] and is not inconsistent with Tod's opinions.[2] Still though the Hindu ruler-worship, which, as in the case of the Marátha Siváji, explains the raising to the twice-born of leaders of successful early and foreign tribes makes it possible that the Jethvás were originally Mers, it seems on the whole probable that the Jethvás' claim to an origin distinct from the Mers is well founded. The evidence recorded by Colonel Tod and the name Jethva led the late Dr. John Wilson to trace the Jethvás to the Játs or Jits.[3] According to the bards the name of the Káthiáváḍa tribe Jethva is derived from Jetha No. 85 or No. 95 of the Porbandar list, who was probably so called because he was born under the Jyeshṭha constellation.[4] The common practice of explaining a tribal name by inventing some name-giving chief deprives this derivation of most of its probability.[5] In the present case it may further be noticed that the name Jethi is borne by two of the chiefs earlier than the Jetha referred to.[6] In the absence of any satisfactory explanation the name Jethva suggests an origin in Yetha the shortened Chinese form of Ye-ta-i-li-to or Ephthalite the name of the ruling class of the White Húṇas.[7] It is true that so good an authority as Specht[8] holds that the shortened form Yetha is peculiar to the Chinese and was never in use. But the form Tetal or Haital, adopted by

---

bha's (died A.D. 912) and Idrisi's (perhaps from Aldjayháni) Mand (Elliot, I. 14 and 79, Reinaud's Abulfeda, lxiii.); the present associated Mers and Mins in Rajputána (Ditto, 53); and perhaps the Musalmán Meos and Minas of the Panjáb (Ibbetson's Census, 261).

[1] The Jethvás are closely allied to the Medhs (Káth. Gaz. 138); they entered Káthiávada along with the Medhs (Ditto, 278).

[2] The passages are somewhat contradictory. Tod (Western India, 413) says: Jethvás marry with Káthis, Ahirs, and Mers. In the Káthiáwár Gazetteer (page 110) Colonel Barton seems to admit the Jethvás' claim to be of distinct origin from the Mers. In another passage he says (page 138): The Mers claim to be Jethvás: this the Jethvás deny. So also Colonel Watson in one passage (page 621) seems to favour a distinct origin while in another (page 279) he says: It seems probable the Jethvás are merely the ruling family Rájkula of the Mers and that they are all of one tribe. Two points seem clear. The Jethvás are admitted to rank among Káthiáváḍa Rajputs and they formerly married with the Mers. The further question whether the Jethvás were originally of a distinct and higher tribe remains undetermined.

[3] Bombay Administration Report for 1873. Colonel Tod made the same suggestion: Western India, 256. Compare Pottinger's (Travels in Baluchistán, 81) identification of the Jeths of Kacch-Gandevi north of Khelat with Játs or Jits.

[4] Tod's Western India, 413.

[5] Compare Buhler in Epigraphia Indica, I. 294. Like the Chálukyas and other tribes the Jethvás trace the name Jethva to a name-giving chief. Of the Jethvás Tod says (Annals of Rajasthán, I. 114): The Jethvás have all the appearance of Skythian descent. As they make no pretension to belong to any of the old Indian races they may be a branch of Skythians. In his Western India (page 412), though confused by his identification of Śankha-dwára with Sakotra instead of with Bet-Dwárka (compare Káth. Gaz. 619), Tod still holds to a northern origin of the Jethvás.

[6] Nos. 6 and 82 of Colonel Watson's List, Káthiáwár Gazetteer, 621. The Pandit's evidence in the text ascribes to the somewhat doubtful Jáikadeva a date of A.D. 738 (Vikram 794); to Jáchikadeva a date of about A.D. 904 (Gupta 585); and to the Gúmli ruins a probable eleventh century. Tod (Western India, 417) traces the Jethvás further back putting the founding of Ghúmli or Bhúmli at about A.D. 692 (S. 749) the date of a settlement between the Tuars of Delhi and the Jethvás (Ditto, 411). Col. Watson (Káth. Gaz. 278) gives either A.D. 650 or A.D. 900.

[7] The form Yetha is used by the Chinese pilgrim Sung-yun A.D. 519. Beal's Buddhist Records, I. xc.

[8] Journal Asiatique (1883), II. 319.

Chapter XII.
THE MERS, A.D. 470 - 900.
White Húṇas.

Armenian Musalmán and Byzantine historians,[1] makes probable an Indian Yethál or Jethál if not a Yetha or Jetha. Nor does there seem any reason why Yetha the Chinese form of the word should not be more likely to be adopted in India than the western and otherwise less correct form Tetal or Haithal. In any case the irregular change from a correct Yethál to an incorrect Yetha cannot be considered of much importance, if, as seems likely, the change was made in order to give the word an Indian meaning.[2] The *v* in Jethva would come to be added when the origin from a chief named Jetha was accepted.

Jhálás.

Another name for the White Húṇas, or for a section of the White Húṇa swarm, is preserved by Cosmas[3] in the form Juvia. This form, if it is not a misreading for Ounia or Húṇa, suggests Jáuvla the recently identified name of the tribe ennobled in India by the great Toramaṇa (A.D. 450 - 500) and his son Mihirakula (A.D. 500 - 540), and of which a trace seems to remain in the Jáwla and Jháwla divisions of Panjáb Gujjars.[4] This Jáuvla, under such a fire baptism as would admit the holders of the name among Hindus, might be turned into Jvála flaming and Jvála be shortened to Jhála. That Jhála was formerly punningly connected with flame is shewn by a line from the bard Chand, 'The lord of the Ranas the powerful Jhála like a flaming fire.'[5] That the Káthiáváḍa bards were either puzzled by the name Jhála or were unwilling to admit its foreign origin is shewn by the story preserved in the Rás Málá,[6] that the tribe got the name because the children of Hirpál Makvána, about to be crushed by an elephant, were snatched away *jhála* by their witch-mother. It has been noticed in the text that the break in Gujarát History between A.D. 480 and 520, agreeing with the term of Húṇa supremacy in North India, seems to imply a similar supremacy in Gujarát. The facts that up to the twelfth century Húṇas held a leading place in Gujarát chronicles,[7] and that while in Rajputána and other parts of Northern India the traces of Huns are fairly widespread in Gujarát they have almost if not altogether disappeared, support the view that the Húṇa strain in Káthiáváḍa is hid under the names Mera, Jethva, and Jhála.[8]

---

[1] Journal Asiatique (1883), II 314.

[2] Compare for the chief's name Jetha, Colonel Watson Káth. Gaz. 622 in the Jyeshṭha Nakshatra.

[3] Priaulx's Embassies, 220; Migne's Patrologiæ Cursus Vol. 88 page 98.

[4] Census of 1891. III 116. A reference to the Jhauvlas is given above page 75 note 4. General Cunningham (Ninth Oriental Congress, I. 228 - 244) traces the tribe of Jhauvla ruling in Sindh, Zabulistan or Ghazni, and Makran from the sixth to the eighth and ninth centuries.

[5] Tod's Western India, 194 Note ‡. Tod adds: Chand abounds in such jeu-de-mot on the names of tribes.

[6] Rás Málá, I. 302: Káthiáwár Gazetteer, III. [7] Tod's Annals of Rajasthán, I. 111.

[8] Among references to Húṇas may be noted: In the Váyu Purána (Sachau's Alberuni, I. 300) in the west between Karnaprávarna and Darva; in the Vishnu Purána Húṇas between the Saindhavas and the Salvás (Wilson's Works, VII. 133 and 134 Note †); in the eighth century Ungutsi lord of the Húṇas who helped Chitor (Tod's Annals, II. 457); in the Khichi bard Mogji, traditions of many powerful Húṇa kings in India (Tod's Annals, I. 111 Note †) among them the Húṇa chief of Barolli (Ditto, II. 705); and Rája Húṇa of the Pramára race who was lord of the Pathár or plateau of Central India (Ditto, II. 457).

In the Middle Ages the Húṇas were considered Kshatriyas and Kshatriyas married Húṇa wives (Wilson's Works, VII. 134 Note †). Of existing traces in the Panjáb may be noted Hon and Hona Rájputs and Gujjars, Hona Jats, Hon Labánas, Hon Lohárs, Honi Malis, Hon Mochis, Húṇa Barbers, and Haun Rabáris (Panjáb Census. 1891. III. pages 116, 139, 227, 233, 246, 265, 276, 305, 315). The only traces Colonel Tod succeeded in finding in Gujarát were a few Húṇa huts at a village opposite Umetha on the gulf of Cambay, a second small colony near Somanátha, and a few houses at Trisauli five miles from Baroda, (Western India, 247, 323.) Since 1825 these traces have disappeared.

PART II.

THE KINGDOM OF AṆAHILAVAḌA.

A.D. 720-1300.

CHAPTER I.

THE CHÁVADÁS

(A.D. 720—956.)

Chapter I.

The Chávadás, A.D. 720-956.

The history embodied in the preceding chapters is more or less fragmentary, pieced together from coins, stone and copperplate inscriptions, local traditions, and other similar sources. A history based on such materials alone must of necessity be imperfect, leaving blanks which it may be hoped fresh details will gradually fill.

The rise of the Aṇahilaváḍa kingdom (A.D. 720) marks a new period of Gujarát history regarding which materials are available from formal historical writings.[1] Though this section of Gujarát history begins with the establishment of Aṇahilaváḍa by the Chávaḍás (A.D. 720-956) the details for the earlier portions are very imperfect being written during the time of the Chálukya or Solaṅki (A.D. 957-1242) successors of the Chávaḍás. The chief sources of information regarding the earlier period of Chávaḍá rule are the opening chapters of the Prabandhachintámaṇi, Vichárasreṇi, Sukṛitasankírtana, and Ratnamálá.[2]

Pañchásar, A.D. 788.

Before the establishment of Aṇahilaváḍa a small Chávaḍá chiefship centred at Pañchásar, now a fair-sized village in Vadhiár between Gujarát and Kacch.[3] The existence of a Chávaḍá chiefship at Pañchásar is proved by the Navsárí grant dated Samvat 490 (A.D. 788-89) of the Gujarát Chálukya king Pulikeśí Janáśraya. This grant in recording the triumphant progress of an army of Tájikas or Arabs

---

[1] The following manuscript histories have been used in preparing Part II. Hemachandra's Dvyáśrayakávya, Merutunga's Prabhandhachintámaṇi, Merutunga's Vichárasreṇi, Jinaprabhasúri's Tírthakalpa, Jinamandanopádhyáya's Kumárapálaprabandha, Kṛishṇa-ṛishi's Kumárapálacharita, Kṛishṇabhaṭṭa's Ratnamálá, Someśvara's Kírtikaumudí, Arisiṇha's Sukṛitasankírtana, Rájaśekhara's Chaturvinśatiprabandha, Vastupálacharita, and published and unpublished inscriptions from Gujarát and Káthiaváḍa.

[2] The Prabhandhachintámaṇi is a short historical compilation; the Vichárasreṇi, though a mere list of kings, is more reliable; the Ratnamálá is a poetic history with good descriptions and many fables taken from the Prabandhachintámaṇi; the Sukṛitasankírtana is a short work largely borrowed from the Vichárasreṇi.

[3] This is apparently Vṛiddhi Áhára or the Vṛiddhi Collectorate, probably called after some village or town of that name.

Chapter I.
THE CHÁVAḌÁS, A.D. 720-956.
Pañchásar, A.D. 788.

from Sindh to Navsárí and mentioning the kingdoms "afflicted" by the Arabs, names the Chávoṭakas next after the kings of Kacch and Sauráshṭra. These Chávoṭakas can be no other than the Cháva̱ḍás of Pañchásar on the borders of Kacch. The Chávaḍás of Pañchásar do not appear to have been important rulers. At the most they seem to have held Vadhiár and part of the north coast of Káthiáváḍa. Whatever be the origin of the name Chávaḍá, which was afterwards Sanskritised into the highsounding Chápoṭkaṭa or Strongbow, it does not seem to be the name of any great dynasty. The name very closely resembles the Gujaráti Chor (Prakrit Chauṭá or Choraṭá) meaning thieves or robbers; and Jávaḍá, which is a further corruption of Chávaḍá, is the word now in use in those parts for a thief or robber. Except the mention of the Chávoṭakas in the Navsárí copperplate we do not find the Chávaḍás noticed in any known cotemporary Gujarát copperplates. For this reason it seems fair to regard them as unimportant rulers over a territory extending from Pañchásar to Aṇahilaváḍa.

Jayaśekhara, A.D. 696.

The author of the Ratnamálá (c. 1230 A.D.) says that in A.D. 696 (S. 752) Jayaśekhara the Chávaḍá king of Pañchásar was attacked by the Chaulukya king Bhuvaḍa of Kalyánakaṭaka in Kanyákubja or Kanoj and slain by Bhuvaḍa in battle. Before his death Jayaśekhara, finding his affairs hopeless, sent his pregnant wife Rupasundarí to the forest in charge of her brother Surapála, one of his chief warriors. After Jayaśekhara's death Rupasundarí gave birth to a son named Vanarája who became the illustrious founder of Aṇahilaváḍa. It is hard to say how much truth underlies this tradition. In the seventh century not Chaulukya but Pála kings flourished in Kanoj. No place of importance called Kalyánakaṭaka is recorded in the Kanoj territory. And though there was a southern Chálukya kingdom with its capital at Kalyán, its establishment at Kalyán was about the middle of the eleventh not in the seventh century. Further the known Dakhan Chálukya lists contain no king named Bhuvaḍa, unless he be the great Chálukya king Vijayáditya (A.D. 696 - 733) also called Bhuvanáśraya, who warred in the north and was there imprisoned but made his escape. The inference is that the author of the Ratnamálá, knowing the Solaṅkis originally belonged to a city called Kalyán, and knowing that a Chálukya king named Bhuvaḍa had defeated the Chávaḍás may have called Bhuvaḍa king of Kalyánkaṭaka and identified Kalyánkataka with a country so well known to Puránik fame as Kanyákubja. This view is supported by the absence in the Prabandhachintámaṇi and other old records of any mention of an invasion from Kanoj. It is possible that in A.D. 696 some king Bhuvaḍa of the Gujarát Chálukyás, of whom at this time branches were ruling as far north as Kaira,[1] invaded the Chávaḍás under Jayaśekhara. Since traces of a Chávoṭaka kingdom remain, at least as late as A.D. 720, it seems probable that the destruction of Pañchásar was caused not by Bhuvaḍa in A.D. 696, but in the Arab raid mentioned above whose date falls about A.D. 720.[2] About A.D. 720 may therefore be taken as the date

---

[1] See above page 108. [2] See above page 109.

Chapter I.
THE CHÁVADÁS, A.D. 720-956.

of the birth of Vanarája. Merutuṇga the author of the Prabandhachintámaṇi tells how Rupasundarí was living in the forest swinging her son in a hammock, when a Jain priest named S'ílaguṇasúri noticing as he passed royal marks on the boy bought him from his mother. The story adds that a nun named Víramatí brought up the boy whom the *sádhu* called Vanarája or the forest king. When eight years old, the priest employed Vanarája to protect his place of worship from rats. The boy's skill in shooting rats convinced the priest he was not fit to be a *sádhu* but was worthy of a kingdom. He therefore returned the boy to his mother. These details seem invented by the Jains in their own honour. No mention of any such story occurs in the Ratnamálá.[1]

Vanarája, A.D. 720-780 (?).

In the forests where Vanarája passed his youth lived his maternal uncle Surapála, one of Jayas'ekhara's generals, who, after his sovereign's defeat and death, had become an outlaw. Vanarája grew up under Surapála's charge. The Prabandhachintámaṇi records the following story of the origin of Vanarája's wealth. A Kanyákubja king married Mahánaká the daughter of a Gujarát king. To receive the proceeds of the marriage cess which the Gujarát king had levied from his subjects, a deputation or *panchkúla* came from Kanyákubja to Gujarát. The deputation made Vanarája their leader or *sellabhrit* to realize the proceeds of the cess. In six months Vanarája collected 24 *lákhs* of *Páruttha drammas*[2] and 4000 horse, which the deputation took and started for Kanyákubja. Vanarája waylaid and killed them, secured the money and horses, and remained in hiding for a year. With the wealth thus acquired Vanarája enrolled an army and established his power assuming the title of king. He fixed the site of a capital which afterwards rose to be the great city of Aṇahilapura. The story of the choice of the site is the usual story of a hunted hare turning on the hounds showing the place to be the special nurse of strength and courage. Vanarája is said to have asked a Bharváḍ or Shepherd named Aṇahila son of Sákhadá to show him the best site. Aṇahila agreed on condition that the city should be called by his name. Aṇahila accordingly showed Vanarája the place where a hare had attacked and chased a dog. Though much in this tradition is fabulous the city may have been called after some local chief since it was popularly known as Aṇahilaváḍa (Sk. Aṇahilaváta) that is the place of Aṇahila. In the Prabandhachintámaṇi Merutuṇga gives A.D. 746 (S. 802) as the date of the installation of Vanarája, while in his Vichárasreni the same author gives A.D. 765 (S. 821 Vaisakha Śukla 2) as the date of the foundation of the city. The discrepancy may be explained by taking A.D. 746 (S. 802) to refer to the date of Vanarája's getting money enough to fix the site of his capital, and A.D. 765 (S. 821) to refer to the date of his installation in the completed Aṇahilaváḍa. Local tradition connects the date A.D. 746 (S. 802) with an image of Ganpati which is said to be as old as the establishment of the city and

Founding of Aṇahilaváḍa, A.D. 746-765.

[1] In the Satyapurakalpa of his Tírthákalpa, Jinaprabhasúri tells an almost identical story of another king.

[2] This name often recurs in Jain works. These would seem to be Kshatrapa coins as Gadhaiya coins are simply called *drammas*.

Chapter I.
The Chávadás, A.D. 720-956.
Founding of Aṇahilaváḍa, A.D. 746-765.

to bear the date 802. But as the letters of the inscription on the image can be made out by ordinary readers they cannot have been inscribed at nearly so early a date as 802. A.D. 765 (S. 821), the year given in the Vichárasreni, seems the more probable date for the installation as the Prabandhachintámaṇi says that Vanarája got himself installed at Aṇahilapura when he was about fifty. This accords with the date fixed on other grounds. Placing Vanarája's birth at about A.D. 720 would make him 44 in A.D. 765 (Ś. 821) the date at which according to the Vicháraśreṇi he was formally installed as sovereign of Aṇahilaváḍa. Merutuṅga in both his works gives the length of Vanarája's life at 109 and of his reign at sixty years. The figure 60 seems to mark the length of his life and not of his reign. So long a reign as sixty years is barely possible for a sovereign who succeeded late in life, and the 109 years of his life can hardly be correct. Taking Vanarája's age at 45 when he was installed in A.D. 765 (S. 821) and allowing fifteen years more to complete the sixty years A.D. 780 (S. 836) would be the closing year of his reign.

Vanarája's Installation.

The Prabandhachintámaṇi narrates how generously Vanarája rewarded those who had helped him in his adversity. His installation was performed by a woman named Śrí Deví of Kákara village whom in fulfilment of an early promise Vanarája had taken to be his sister.[2] The story regarding the promise is that once when Vanarája had gone with his uncle on a thieving expedition to Kákara village and had broken into the house of a merchant he by mistake dipped his hand into a pot of curds. As to touch curds is the same as to dine at a house as a guest, Vanarája left the house without taking anything from it.[3] Hearing what had happened the merchant's sister invited Vanarája as a brother to dinner and gave him clothes. In return Vanarája promised if he ever regained his father's kingdom he should receive his installation as king at her hands.[4] Vanarája chose as minister a Bania named Jámba. The story is that while Vanarája was looting with two others he came across a merchant Jámba who had five arrows. Seeing only three enemies, Jámba broke and threw away two of the arrows, shouting 'One for each of you.' Vanarája admiring his coolness persuaded Jámba to join his band and found him so useful that he promised to make him minister. From the absence of any reference to him in these and similar tales it is probable that his uncle Surapála died before the installing of Vanarája. Vanarája is said to have built at Aṇahilváḍa a Jain temple of Pañchásará Párasnáth so called because the image was brought from the old settlement of Pañchásar. Mention of this temple continues during the Solaṅki and Vághelá times.

His Image.

Vanarája is said to have placed a bowing image of himself facing the image of Párasnáth. The figure of Vanarája is still shown at Sidhpur

---

1 The text is 'Pañchásatavarshadesyaḥ."

2 Probably Kákrej famous for its bullocks.

3 Stories of thieves refraining from plundering houses where they have accidentally laid their hands on salt or millet are common.

4 The making of the installation mark on the forehead is the privilege of the king's sister who gives a blessing and receives a present of villages.

Chapter I.
The Chávaḍás, A.D. 720 - 956.
Image of Vanarája.

and a woodcut of it is given by the late Mr. Forbes in his Rás Málá. It is clearly the figure of a king with the umbrella of state and a nimbus round the head and in the ears the long ornaments called *kundalas* noticed by Arab travellers as characteristic of the Balhara or Ráshtrakúṭa kings who were cotemporary with Vanarája.[1] The king wears a long beard, a short waistcloth or *dhoti*, a waistband or *kammarband*, and a shoulder garment or *uparna* whose ends hang down the back. Besides the earrings he is adorned with bracelets armlets and anklets and a large ornament hangs across the chest from the left shoulder to the right hip. The right hand is held near the chest in the act of granting protection: and the left hand holds something which cannot be made out. By his side is the umbrella-bearer and five other attendants. The statue closely resembles the lifesize figure of a king of the Solaṅki period lying in the yard of a temple at Máliá about twenty-four miles north of Somanátha Patan. At Somanátha Patan are similar but less rich cotemporary figures of local officers of the Solaṅkis. Another similar figure of which only the torso remains is the statue of Anrája the father of Vastupála in a niche in Vastupála's temple at Girnár. The details of this figure belong to the Solaṅki period.

Vanarája's Successors, A.D. 780 - 961.

The lists of Vanarája's successors vary so greatly in the names, in the order of succession, and in the lengths of reigns, that little trust can be placed in them. The first three agree in giving a duration of 196 years to the Chávaḍá dynasty after the accession of Vanarája. The accession of the Solaṅki founder Múlarája is given in the Vichárasreṇi at Samvat 1017 and in the Prabandhachintámaṇi at Samvat 998 corresponding with the original difference of nineteen years (S. 802 and 821) in the founding of the city. This shows that though the total duration of the dynasty was traditionally known to be 196 years the order of succession was not known and guesses were made as to the duration of the different reigns. Certain dates fixed by inscriptions or otherwise known to some compilers and not known to others caused many discrepancies in the various accounts.

Yogarája, A.D. 806 - 841.

According to the calculations given above Vanarája's reign lasted to about A.D. 780. Authorities agree that Vanarája was succeeded by his son Yogarája. The length of Yogarája's reign is given as thirty-five years by the Prabandhachintámaṇi and the Ratnamálá and as twenty-nine by the Vichárasreṇi. That is according to the Prabandhachintámaṇi and Ratnamálá his reign closes in A.D. 841 (S. 897) and according to the Vichárasreṇi in A.D. 836 (S. 891). On the whole the Prabandhachintámaṇi date A.D. 841 (S. 897) seems the more probable. The author of the Vichárasreṇi may have mistaken the 7 of the manuscripts for a 1, the two figures in the manuscripts of that date being closely alike. If A.D. 780 is taken as the close of Vanarája's reign and A.D. 806 as the beginning of Yogarája's reign an interval of twenty-six years is left. This blank, which perhaps accounts for the improbably long reign and life assigned to Vanarája, may have been filled by the forgotten reign of a childless elder brother of Yogarája.

[1] Elliot and Dowson, I. 11.

Chapter I.
THE CHÁVADÁS, A.D. 720 - 956.
Yogarája, A.D. 806 - 814.

Of Yogarája the Prabandhachintámaṇi tells the following tale. Kshemarája one of Yogarája's three sons reported that several ships were storm-stayed at Prabhása or Somanátha. The ships had 10,000 horses, many elephants, and millions of money and treasure. Kshemarája prayed that he might seize the treasure. Yogarája forbad him. In spite of their father's orders the sons seized the treasure and brought it to the king. Yogarája said nothing. And when the people asked him why he was silent he answered: To say I approve would be a sin; to say I do not approve would annoy you. Hitherto on account of an ancestor's misdeeds we have been laughed at as a nation of thieves. Our name was improving and we were rising to the rank of true kings. This act of my sons has renewed the old stain. Yogarája would not be comforted and mounted the funeral pyre.

Kshemarája, A.D. 841 - 880.

According to the Prabandhachintámaṇi in A.D. 841 (S. 898) Yogarája was succeeded by his son Kshemarája. The Vichárasʹreṇi says that Yogarája was succeeded by Ratnáditya who reigned three years, and he by Vairisiṃha who reigned eleven years. Then came Kshemarája who is mentioned as the son of Yogarája and as coming to the throne in A.D. 849 (S. 905). The relationship of Yogarája to Ratnáditya and Vairisiṃha is not given. Probably both were sons of Yogarája as the Prabandhachintámaṇi mentions that Yogarája had three sons. The duration of Kshemarája's reign is given as thirty-nine years. It is probable that the reigns of the three brothers lasted altogether for thirty-nine years, fourteen years for the two elder brothers and twenty-five years for Kshemarája the period mentioned by the Prabandhachintámaṇi. Accepting this chronology A.D. 880 (S. 936) will be the date of the close of Kshemarája's reign.

Chámuṇḍa, A.D. 880 - 908.

According to the Vichárasʹreṇi and the Sukṛitasankírtana Kshemarája was succeeded by his son Chámuṇḍa. Instead of Chámuṇḍa the Prabandhachintámaṇi mentions Bhúyada perhaps another name of Chámuṇḍa, as in the Prabandhachintámaṇi the name Chámuṇḍa does not occur. The Prabandhachintámaṇi notes that Bhúyada reigned twenty-nine years and built in Aṇahilaváḍa Patan the temple of Bhúyadeshvar. The Vichárasʹreṇi gives twenty-seven years as the length of Chámuṇḍa's reign an insignificant difference of two years. This gives A.D. 908 (S. 964) as the close of Chámuṇḍa's reign according to the Vichárasʹreṇi.

Ghaghaḍa, A.D. 908 - 937.

After Bhúyada the Prabandhachintámaṇi places Vairisiṃha and Ratnáditya assigning twenty-five and fifteen years as the reigns of each. The Vichárasʹreṇi mentions as the successor of Chámuṇḍa his son Ghaghaḍa who is called Ráhaḍa in the Sukṛitasankírtana. Instead of Ghaghaḍa the Prabandhachintámaṇi gives Sámantasiṃha or Lion Chieftain perhaps a title of Ghághaḍa's. The Vichárasʹreṇi gives Ghaghaḍa a reign of twenty-seven years and mentions as his successor an unnamed son who reigned nineteen years. The Sukṛitasankírtana gives the name of this son as Bhúbhaṭa. According to these calculations the close of Ghághaḍa's reign would be A.D. 936 (Saṃvat 965 + 27 = 992). Adding nineteen years for Bhúbhaṭa's reign brings the date of the end of the dynasty to A.D. 956 (Saṃvat

993 + 19 = 1012) that is five years earlier than S. 1017 the date given by the Vichárasreṇi. Until some evidence to the contrary is shown Merutuṅga's date A.D. 961 (S. 821 + 196 = 1017) may be taken as correct.

According to the above the Chávaḍá genealogy stands as follows:

Vanarája, born A.D. 720; succeeded A.D. 765; died A.D. 780.
|
Interval of twenty-six years.
|
Yogarája, A.D. 806 - 841.
|
Ratnáditya, A.D. 842. — Vairisiṃha, A.D. 845. — Kshemarája, A.D. 856.
|
Chámuṇḍa or Bhúyada (?), A.D. 881. (son of Kshemarája)
|
Ghágha'a or Ráhaḍa, A.D. 908.
|
Name Unknown, A.D. 937 - 961.

[The period of Chávaḍá rule at Aṇahilaváḍa is likely to remain obscure until the discovery of cotemporary inscriptions throws more light upon it than can be gathered from the confused and contradictory legends collected by the Solaṅki historians, none of whom are older than the twelfth century. For the present a few points only can be regarded as established:

(i) The Chávaḍás, Chávoṭakas, or Chápotkaṭas, are connected with the Chápas of Bhínmál and of Vadhván and are therefore of Gurjjara race. (Compare Ind. Ant. XVII. 192.)

(ii) They probably were never more than feudatories of the Bhínmál kings.

(iii) Though the legend places the fall of Pañchásar in A.D. 696 and the foundation of Anahilaváḍa in A.D. 746, the grant of Pulakeśi Janáśraya shows that a Chávaḍá (Chávoṭaka) kingdom existed in A.D. 728.

As regards the chronology of the dynasty, the explanation of the long life of 110 years ascribed to Vanarája may be that a grandson of the same name succeeded the founder of the family. The name of Chámuṇḍa has, as Dr. Bühler long ago pointed out, crept in through some error from the Solaṅki list. But when the same author in two different works gives such contradictory lists and dates as Merutuṅga does in his Prabandhachintámaṇi and his Vicharas'reni, it is clearly useless to attempt to extract a consistent story from the chroniclers.—A. M. T. J.]

CHAPTER II.

THE CHAULUKYAS OR SOLAṄKIS

(A.D. 961—1242.)

Chapter II.
THE CHAULUKYAS, A.D. 961 - 1242.
Authorities.

THE next rulers are the Chaulukyas or Solaṅkis (A.D. 964-1242) whose conversion to Jainism has secured them careful record by Jain chroniclers. The earliest writer on the Solaṅkis, the learned Jain priest Hemachandra (A.D. 1089-1173), in his work called the Dvyáśraya, has given a fairly full and correct account of the dynasty up to Siddharája (A.D. 1143). The work is said to have been begun by Hemachandra about A.D. 1160, and to have been finished and revised by another Jain monk named Abhayatilakagaṇi in A.D. 1255.[1] The last chapter which is in Prakrit deals solely with king Kumárapála. This work is a grammar rather than a chronicle, still, though it has little reference to dates, it is a good collection of tales and descriptions. For chronology the best guide is the Vicháraśreṇi which its author has taken pains to make the chief authority in dates. The Vicháraśreṇi was written by Merutuṅga about A.D. 1314, some time after he wrote the Prabandhachintamaṇi.

The Name Chaulukya.

According to the Vicháraśreṇi after the Chávaḍás, in A.D. 961 (Vaishakh Suddha 1017), began the reign of Múlarája the son of a daughter of the last Chávaḍá ruler. The name Chaulukya is a Sanskritised form, through an earlier form Chálukya, of the old names Chalkya, Chalikya, Chirîkya, Chálukya of the great Dakhan dynasty (A.D. 552-973), made to harmonise with the Puránik-looking story that the founder of the dynasty sprang from the palm or *chuluka* of Brahma. The form Chaulukya seems to have been confined to authors and writers. It was used by the great Dakhan poet Bilhaṇa (c. 1050 A.D.) and by the Aṇahilaváḍa chroniclers. In Gujarát the popular form of the word seems to have been Solaki or Solaṅki (a dialectic variant of Chalukya), a name till lately used by Gujarát bards. The sameness of name seems to show the Dakhan and Gujarát dynasties to be branches of one stock. No materials are available to trace the original seat of the family or to show when and whence they came to Gujarát. The balance of probability is, as Dr. Bühler holds, that Múlarája's ancestors came from the north.[2]

Múlarája, A.D. 961 - 996.

The Sukritasankírtana says that the last Chávaḍá king Bhúbhaṭa was succeeded by his sister's son Múlarája. Of the family or country of Múlarája's father no details are given. The Prabandhachintamaṇi calls Múlarája the sister's son of Sámantasiṁha and gives the following details. In A.D. 930 of the family of Bhuiyaḍa (who destroyed Jayaśekhara) were three brothers Ráji, Bija, and Daṇḍaka, who stopped at Aṇahilaváḍa on their way back from a pilgrimage to Somanátha in the guise of Kárpaṭika or Kápdi beggars. The three brothers attended a cavalry

---

[1] Ind. Ant. IV. 71 - 72 and VI. 180.

[2] Ind. Ant. VI. 180ff. The suggestion may be offered that the Kanyákubja which is mentioned as the seat of Múlarája's ancestors, is Karṇakubja, an old name of Junágaḍh. Compare Burgess' Káthiáwár and Kutch, 156.

Chapter II.

THE CHAULUKYAS, A.D. 961 - 1242.

Múlarája, A.D. 961 - 996.

parade held by king Sámantasimha. An objection taken by Ráji to some of the cavalry movements pleased Sámantasimha, who, taking him to be the scion of some noble family, gave him his sister Líládeví in marriage. Líládeví died pregnant and the child, which was taken alive from its dead mother's womb was called Múlarája, because the operation was performed when the Múla constellation was in power. Múlarája grew into an able and popular prince and helped to extend the kingdom of his maternal uncle. In a fit of intoxication Sámantasimha ordered Múlarája to be placed on the throne. He afterwards cancelled the grant. But Múlarája contended that a king once installed could not be degraded. He collected troops defeated and slew his uncle and succeeded to the throne in A.D. 942 (S. 998). The main facts of this tale, that Múlarája's father was one Ráji of the Chálukya family, that his mother was a Chávaḍá princess, and that he came to the Chávaḍá throne by killing his maternal uncle, appear to be true. That Múlarája's father's name was Ráji is proved by Dr. Bühler's copperplate of Múlarája.[1] Merutuṅga's details that Ráji came in disguise to Aṇahilaváḍa, took the fancy of Sámantasimha, and received his sister in marriage seem fictions in the style common in the bardic praises of Rájput princes. Dr. Bühler's copperplate further disproves the story as it calls Múlarája the son of the illustrious Ráji, the great king of kings *Mahárájádhirája*, a title which would not be given to a wandering prince. Ráji appears to have been of almost equal rank with the Chávaḍás. The Ratnamálá calls Ráji fifth in descent from Bhuvaḍa, his four predecessors being Karṇáditya, Chándráditya, Somáditya, and Bhuvanáditya. But the Ratnamálá list is on the face of it wrong, as it gives five instead of seven or eight kings to fill the space of over 200 years between Jayaśekhara and Múlarája.

Most Jain chroniclers begin the history of Aṇahilaváḍa with Múlarája who with the Jains is the glory of the dynasty. After taking the small Chávaḍá kingdom Múlarája spread his power in all directions, overrunning Káthiáváḍa and Kacch on the west, and fighting Bárappa of Láṭa or South Gujarát on the south, and Vigraharája king of Ajmir on the north. The Ajmir kings were called Sapádalaksha. Why they were so called is not known. This much is certain that Sapádalaksha is the Sanskrit form of the modern Sewálik. It would seem that the Chohâns, whom the Gujarát Jain chroniclers call Sapádalakshíya, must have come to Gujarát from the Sewálik hills. After leaving the Sewálik hills the capital was at Ajmir, which is usually said to have been first fortified by the Chohán king Ajayapála (A.D. 1174-1177).[2] This story seems invented by the Chohâns. The name Ajmir appears to be derived from the Mehrs who were in power in these parts between the fifth and the eighth centuries. The Hammíramahákávya begins the Chohán genealogy with Vásudeva (A.D. 780) and states that Vásudeva's fourth successor Ajayapála established the hill fort of Ajmir. About this time (A.D. 840) the Chohâns seem to have made settlements in the Ajmir country and to have harassed Gujarát. Vigraharája the tenth in suc-

[1] Ind. Ant. VI. 191ff.

[2] Kirtane's Hammíramahákávya, I.

Chapter II.
THE CHAULUKYAS, A.D. 961-1242.
Mularája, A.D. 961-996.

cession from Vásudeva is described as killing Múlarája and weakening the Gurjjara country.[1] The author of the Prabandhachintámaṇi gives the following details. The Sapádalaksha or Ajmir king entered Gujarát to attack Múlarája and at the same time from the south Mularája's territory was invaded by Bárappa a general of king Tailapa of Telingána.[2] Unable to face both enemies Múlarája at his minister's advice retired to Kanthádurga apparently Kanthkot in Cutch.[3] He remained there till the Navarátra or Nine-Night festival at the close of the rains when he expected the Sapádalaksha king would have to return to Ajmir to worship the goddess Śákambharí when Bárappa would be left alone. At the close of the rains the Sapádalaksha king fixed his camp near a place called Śákambharí and bringing the goddess Śákambharí there held the Nine-Night festival. This device disappointed Múlarája. He sent for his *sámantas* or nobles and gave them presents. He told them his plans and called on them to support him in attacking the Sapádalaksha king. Múlarája then mounted a female elephant with no attendant but the driver and in the evening came suddenly to the Ajmir camp. He dismounted and holding a drawn sword in his hand said to the doorkeeper 'What is your king doing. Go and tell your lord that Múlarája waits at his door.' While the attendant was on his way to give the message, Múlarája pushed him on one side and himself went into the presence. The doorkeeper called 'Here comes Múlarája.' Before he could be stopped Múlarája forced his way in and took his seat on the throne. The Ajmir king in consternation asked 'Are you Múlarája?' Múlarája answered 'I would regard him as a brave king who would meet me face to face in battle. While I was thinking no such brave enemy exists, you have arrived. I ask no better fortune than to fight with you. But as soon as you are come, like a bee falling in at dinner time, Bárappa the general of king Tailapa of Telingana has arrived to attack me. While I am punishing him you should keep quiet and not give me a side blow.' The Ajmir king said, 'Though you are a king, you have come here alone like a foot soldier, not caring for your safety. I will be your ally for life.' Múlarája replied 'Say not so.' He refused the Rája's invitation to dine, and leaving sword in hand mounted his elephant and with his nobles attacked the camp of Bárappa. Bárappa was killed and eighteen of his elephants and 10,000 of his horses fell into Múlarája's hands. While returning with the spoil Múlarája received news that the Sapádalaksha king had fled.

[1] The Chohâns of Ajmir were also known as the rulers of Śákambharí, the Sámbhar lake in Rajputána on the borders of Jaipur and Jodhpur. The corrected edition of the Harsha inscription published by Prof. Kielhorn in Epigraphia Indica II. 116ff. shows that their first historical king was Gúvaka, who reigned some time in the first half of the ninth century (c. 820 A.D.) The Chohâns are still very numerous in the neighbourhood of the Sewálik hills, especially in the districts of Ambálá and Karnál. Compare Ibbetson's Panjáb Census for 1881.

[2] It appears from the grant of Śaka 972 published by Mr. Dhruva in Ind. Ant. XII. 196 and from the Surat grant of Kírttirája dated Śaka 940, that this Bárapa was the founder of a dynasty who ruled Láṭa or South Gujarát as under-kings of the Dakhan Chálukyas until at least A.D. 1050. Bárappa was, as his name shows, a Southerner from the Kánarese country, but his descendants spell the family name Chaulukya in the same way as the dynasty of Anahilaváda.

[3] Dr. Bühler (Ind. Ant. XII. 123) sees a reference to this retirement in Múlarája's grant of Saṃvat 1043.

Chapter II.

The Chaulukyas, A.D. 961-1242.

Múlarája, A.D. 961-996.

This story of the author of the Prabandhachintámaṇi differs from that given by the author of the Hammírakávya who describes Múlarája as defeated and slain. The truth seems to be that the Ajmír king defeated Múlarája and on Múlarája's submission did not press his advantage. In these circumstances Múlarája's victory over Bárappa seems improbable. The Dvyás'raya devotes seventy-five verses (27-101) of its sixth chapter to the contest between Bárappa and Múlarája. The details may be thus summarised. Once when Múlarája received presents from various Indian kings Dvárappa[1] king of Látades'a sent an ill-omened elephant. The marks being examined by royal officers and by prince Chámuṇḍa, they decided the elephant would bring destruction on the king who kept him. The elephant was sent back in disgrace and Múlarája and his son started with an army to attack Láṭades'a and avenge the insult. In his march Múlarája first came to the Śvabhravatí or Sábarmatí which formed the boundary of his kingdom, frightening the people. From the Sábarmatí he advanced to the ancient Purí[2] where also the people became confused. The Láṭa king prepared for fight, and was slain by Chámuṇḍa in single combat. Múlarája advanced to Broach where Bárappa who was assisted by the island kings opposed him. Chámuṇḍa overcame them and slew Bárappa. After this success Múlarája and Chámuṇḍa returned to Aṇahilapura.[3]

The Dvyás'raya styles Bárappa king of Láṭades'a; the Prabandhachintámaṇi calls him a general of Tailapa king of Telingána; the Sukṛitasankírtana a general of the Kanyákubja king; and the Kírtikaumudí[4] a general of the Lord of Láṭa.

Other evidence proves that at the time of Múlarája a Chaulukya king named Bárappa did reign in Láṭades'a. The Surat grant of Kírtirája grandson of Bárappa is dated A.D. 1018 (Saka 940). This, taking twenty years to a king, brings Bárappa's date to A.D. 978 (Śaka 900), a year which falls in the reign of Múlarája (A.D. 961-996; S. 1027-1053). The statement in the Prabandhachintámaṇi that Bárappa was a general of Tailapa seems correct. The southern form of the name Bárappa supports the statement. And as Tailapa overthrew the Ráshṭrakúṭas in A.D. 972 (Śaka 894) he might well place a general in military charge of Láṭa, and allow him practical independence. This would explain why the Dvyás'raya calls Bárappa king of Látades'a and why the Kírtikaumudí calls him general of the Lord of Láṭa.

One of Múlarája's earliest wars was with Graharipu the Ábhíra or Chuḍásamá ruler of Sorath.[5] According to Múlarája's bards, the cause

---

[1] Apparently a Sanskrit form of Bárappa. [2] Broach according to the commentator.
[3] The Sukṛitasankírtana mentions this defeat of Bárappa who is said to be a general of the Kanyákubja or Kanoj king. The Prabandhachintámaṇi (Múlarája-prabandha) also mentions the invasion and slaughter of Bárappa; but there is no reference to it in the grant of Bárappa's descendant Trilochanapála (Ind. Ant. XII. 1966.) [4] Canto II. Verse 3.
[5] As Mr. Forbes rightly observed Graharipu the Planet-seizer is a made-up title based on the resemblance of the planet-seizer's name Ráhu to Rá the title of the Chudásamás of Junágaḍh. The personal name of the chief is not given and the list of the Junágaḍh Chudásamás is too incomplete to allow of identification.

Chapter II.
The Chaulukyas, A.D. 961-1242.
Múlarája, A.D. 961-996.

of war was Graharipu's oppression of pilgrims to Prabhása. Graharipu's capital was Vámanasthalí, the modern Vanthalí nine miles west of Junágadh, and the fort of Durgapalli which Graharipu is said to have established must be Junágadh itself which was not then a capital. Graharipu is described as a cow-eating Mlechha and a grievous tyrant. He is said to have had much influence over Lákhá son of king Phula of Kacch and to have been helped by Turks and other Mlechhas. When Múlarája reached the Jambumáli river, he was met by Graharipu and his army. With Graharipu was Lákhá of Kacch, the king of Sindh probably a Sumrá, Mewás Bhilas, and the sons of Graharipu's wife Nílí who had been summoned from near the Bhadar river by a message in the Yavana language.[1] With Múlarája were the kings of S'iláprastha,[2] of Márwár, of Kásí, of Arbuda or Abu, and of S'rímála or Bhínmál. Múlarája had also his own younger brother Gangámah, his friend king Revatímitra, and Bhils. It is specially mentioned that in this expedition Múlarája received no help from the sons of his paternal uncles Bíja and Dandaka. The fight ended in Graharipu being made prisoner by Múlarája, and in Lákhá being slain with a spear. After the victory Múlarája went to Prabhása, worshipped the *liṅga*, and returned to Anahilaváḍa with his army and 108 elephants.

According to the author of the Prabandhachintámaṇi Lákhá met his death in a different contest with Múlarája. Lákhá who is described as the son of Phuladá and Kámalatá daughter of Kírttirája a Parmár king, is said to have been invincible because he was under the protection of king Yas'ovarman of Málwa. He defeated Múlarája's army eleven times. In a twelfth encounter Múlarája besieged Lákhá in Kapilakot, slew him in single combat, and trod on his flowing beard. Enraged at this insult to her dead son Lákhá's mother called down on Múlarája's descendants the curse of the spider poison that is of leprosy.[3]

Mr. Forbes, apparently from bardic sources, states that on his wife's death Ráji the father of Múlarája went to the temple of Vishnu at Dwárká. On his return he visited the court of Lákhá Phuláni and espoused Lákhá's sister Ráyáji by whom he had a son named Rákháich. This marriage proved the ruin of Ráji. In a dispute about precedence Lákhá slew Ráji and many of his Rájput followers, his wife Ráyáji becoming a Satí. Bíja the uncle of Múlarája urged his nephew to avenge his father's death and Múlarája was further incited against Lákhá because Lákhá harboured Rákháich the younger son of Ráji at his court as a rival to Múlarája.

According to the Dvyáśraya, either from the rising power of his son or from repentance for his own rough acts, after Chámuṇḍa's victory over Bárappa Múlarája installed him as ruler and devoted himself to religion and charity. According to the Prabandhachintámaṇi Múlarája built in Aṇahilaváḍa a Jain temple named Múlavasatiká. But as the Nandi

[1] The mention of her name and of the language in which she wrote suggest something remarkable in the race and position of queen Nílí.

[2] Perhaps Sithá in Jhálávád.

[3] The same account appears in the Kumárapálacharita.

Chapter II.

THE CHAULUKYAS, A.D. 961-1242.

Múlarája, A.D. 961-996.

symbol on his copperplate shows that Múlarája was a devoted Śaivite, it is possible that this temple was built by some Jain guild or community and named after the reigning chief.[1] Múlarája built a Mahádeva temple called Múlasvámi in Aṇahilaváḍa, and, in honour of Somanátha, he built the temple of Múles'vara at Maṇḍali-nagara where he went at the bidding of the god.[2] He also built at Aṇahilaváḍa a temple of Mahádeva called Tripurushaprásáda on a site to which the tradition attaches that seeing Múlarája daily visiting the temple of Múlanáthadeva at Maṇḍali, Somanatha Mahádeva being greatly pleased promised to bring the ocean to Aṇahilaváḍa. Somanátha came, and the ocean accompanying the god certain ponds became brackish. In honour of these salt pools Múlarája built the Tripurushaprásáda. Looking for some one to place in charge of this temple, Múlarája heard of an ascetic named Kaṇthadi at Siddhapura on the banks of the Sarasvatí who used to fast every other day and on the intervening day lived on five morsels of food. Múlarája offered this sage the charge of the temple. The sage declined saying 'Authority is the surest path to hell.' Eventually Vayajalladeva a disciple of the sage undertook the management on certain conditions. Múlarája passed most of his days at the holy shrine of Siddhapura, the modern Sidhpur on the Sarasvatí about fifteen miles north-east of Aṇahilaváḍa. At Sidhpur Múlarája made many grants to Bráhmans. Several branches of Gujarát Bráhmans, Audíchyas Śrígauḍas and Kanojias, trace their origin in Gujarát to an invitation from Múlarája to Siddhapura and the local Puránas and Máhátmyas confirm the story. As the term Audíchya means Northerner Múlarája may have invited Bráhmans from some such holy place as Kurukshetra which the Audíchyas claim as their home. From Kanyákubja in the Madhyadeśa between the Ganges and the Yamuná another equally holy place the Kanojías may have been invited. The Śrí Gauḍas appear to have come from Bengal and Tirhut. Gauḍa and Tirhut Bráhmans are noted Tántriks and Mantrasástris a branch of learning for which both the people and the rulers of Gujarát have a great fondness. Grants of villages were made to these Bráhmans. Sidhpur was given to the Audíchyas, Simhapura or Sihor in Káthiáváḍa to some other colony, and Stambhatírtha or Cambay to the Śrí Gauḍas. At Siddhapura Múlarája built the famous temple called the Rudramahálaya or the great shrine of Rudra. According to tradition Múlarája did not complete the Rudramahálaya and Siddharája finished it. In spite of this tradition it does not appear that Múlarája died leaving the great temple unfinished as a copperplate of A.D. 987 (S. 1043) records that

---

[1] Compare the Lakshmí-Vihára Jain temple in Jesalmir built by the Jain Saṅgha and called after the reigning king Lakshmaṇa.

[2] Dr. Bühler's copperplate of Múlarája records a grant to this temple, said to be of Múlanáthadeva in Maṇḍali in the Vardhi zilla, apparently the modern Mándal near Pañchásar in the Vadhiár province near Jhinjhuváḍa. The grant is in Saṃvat 1043 and is dated from Aṇahilapura though the actual gift was made at Śrísthala or Sidhpur after bathing in the Sarasvatí and worshipping the god of the Rudramahálaya. The grant is of the village of Kamboika, the modern Kamboi near Modhera. Ind. Ant. VI. 192-193. The grant is said to have been written by a Káyastha named Káñchaṇa and ends with the words "of the illustrious Múlarája."

Chapter II.
THE CHAULUKYAS, A.D. 961-1242.
Múlarája, A.D. 961-996.

Múlarája made the grant after worshipping the god of the Rudramahálaya on the occasion of a solar eclipse on the fifteenth of the dark half of Mágha. It would seem therefore that Múlarája built one large Rudramahálaya which Siddharája may have repaired or enlarged. Múlarája is said while still in health to have mounted the funeral pile, an act which some writers trace to remorse and others to unknown political reasons. The Vicháras'reṇi gives the length of Múlarája's reign at thirty-five years A.D. 961-996 (S. 1017-1052); the Prabandhachintámaṇi begins the reign at A.D. 942 (S. 998) and ends it at A.D. 997 (S. 1053) that is a length of fifty-five years.[1] Of the two, thirty-five years seems the more probable, as, if the traditional accounts are correct, Múlarája can scarcely have been a young man when he overthrew his uncle's power.

Chámuṇḍa, A.D. 997-1010.

Of Mularája's son and successor Chámuṇḍa no historical information is available. The author of the Prabandhachintámaṇi assigns him a reign of thirteen years. The author of the Dvyáśraya says that he had three sons Vallabha Rája, Durlabha Rája, and Nága Rája. According to one account Chámuṇḍa installed Vallabha in A.D. 1010 (S. 1066) and went on pilgrimage to Benares. On his passage through Málwa Muñja the Málwa king carried off Chámuṇḍa's umbrella and other marks of royalty.[2] Chámuṇḍa went on to Benares in the guise of a hermit. On his return he prayed his son to avenge the insult offered by the king of Málwa. Vallabha started with an army but died of small-pox. The author of the Prabandhachintámaṇi gives Chámuṇḍa a reign of six months, while the author of the Vicháraśreṇi entirely drops his name and gives a reign of fourteen years to Vallabha made up of the thirteen years of Chámuṇḍa and the six months of Vallabha. This seems to be a mistake. It would seem more correct, as is done in several copperplate lists, to omit Vallabha, since he must have reigned jointly with his father and his name is not wanted for purposes of succession. The Vicháras'reṇi and the Prabandhachintámaṇi agree in ending Vallabha's reign in A.D. 1010 (S. 1066). The author of the Dvyáśraya states that Chámuṇḍa greatly lamenting the death of Vallabha installed Vallabha's younger brother Durlabha, and himself retired to die at S'uklatírtha on the Narbadá.

Durlabha, A.D. 1010-1022.

Durlabha whom the Sukṛitasankírtana also calls Jagatjhampaka or World Guardian came to the throne in A.D. 1010 (S. 1066). The Prabandhachintámaṇi gives the length of his reign at eleven years and six months while the Vicháraśreṇi makes it twelve years closing it in A.D. 1022 (S. 1078). The author of the Dyvás'raya says that along with his brother Nága Rája, Durlabha attended the Svayamvara or bridegroom-choosing of Durlabha Deví the sister of Mahendra the

[1] The difference between 1052 and 1053 is probably only a few months.

[2] The fight with Muñja must have taken place about A.D. 1011 (S. 1067). As Chámuṇḍa started just after installing Vallabha the beginning of the reign must be before A.D. 997 as Tailapa who fought with Muñja died in that year. This is proved by a manuscript dated A.D. 994 (S. 1050) which gives the reigning king as Muñja. That Bhoja Muñja's successor was ruling in A.D. 1014 (S. 1070) makes it probable that Muñja's reign extended to A.D. 1011 (S. 1067).

Chapter II.

The Chaulukyas, A.D. 961-1242.

Durlabha, A.D. 1010-1022.

Rája of Nadol in Márwár. The kings of Anga, Kásí, Avantí, Chedí, Kuru, Húṇa, Mathurá, Vindhya, and Andhra were also present.[1] The princess chose Durlabha and Mahendra gave his younger sister Lakshmí to Durlabha's brother Nága Rája. The princess' choice of Durlabha drew on him the enmity of certain of the other kings all of whom he defeated. The brothers then returned to Aṇahilaváḍa where Durlabha built a lake called Durlabhasarovara. The author of the Prabandhachintámaṇi says that Durlabha gave up the kingdom to his son (?) Bhíma.[2] He also states that Durlabha went on pilgrimage and was insulted on the way by Muñja king of Málwa. This seems the same tale which the Dvyás'raya tells of Chámuṇḍa. Since Muñja cannot have been a cotemporary of Durlabha the Dvyás'raya's account seems correct.

Bhíma I. A.D. 1022-1064.

Durlabha was succeeded by his nephew Bhíma the son of Durlabha's younger brother Nága Rája. The author of the Dvyás'raya says that Durlabha wishing to retire from the world offered the kingdom to his nephew Bhíma; that Bhíma declined in favour of his father Nága Rája; that Nága Rája refused; that Durlabha and Nága Rája persuaded Bhíma to take the government; and that after installing Bhíma the two brothers died together. Such a voluntary double death sounds unlikely unless the result was due to the machinations of Bhíma. The Prabandhachintámaṇi gives Bhíma a reign of fifty-two years from A.D. 1022 to 1074 (S. 1078-1130), while the Vichárasreṇi reduces his reign to forty-two years placing its close in A.D. 1064 (S. 1120). Forty-two years would seem to be correct as another copy of the Prabandhachintámaṇi has 42.

Two copperplates of Bhíma are available one dated A.D. 1030 (S. 1086) eight or nine years after he came to the throne, the other from Kacch in A.D. 1037 (S. 1093).

Bhíma seems to have been more powerful than either of his predecessors. According to the Dvyás'raya his two chief enemies were the kings of Sindh and of Chedí or Bundelkhand. He led a victorious expedition against Hammuka the king of Sindh, who had conquered the king of Sivasána and another against Karṇa king of Chedí who paid tribute and submitted. The Prabandhachintámaṇi has a verse, apparently an old verse interpolated, which says that on the Málwa king Bhoja's death, while sacking Dhárápuri, Karṇa took Bhíma as his coadjutor, and that afterwards Bhíma's general Dámara took Karṇa captive and won from him a gold *maṇḍapiká* or canopy and images of Ganes'a and Nílakaṇthes'vara Mahádeva. Bhíma is said to have presented the canopy to Somanátha.

When Bhíma was engaged against the king of Sindh, Kulachandra the general of the Málwa king Bhoja with all the Málwa feudatories, invaded Aṇahilaváḍa, sacked the city, and sowed shell-money at the gate where the time-marking gong was sounded. So great was the

[1] This Svayaṃvara and the list of attendant and rival kings seem imaginary. The Nadol chiefship was not important enough to draw kings from the countries named.

[2] The text has son but Bhíma was Durlabha's nephew not his son.

Chapter II.
THE CHAULUKYAS, A.D. 961-1242.
Bhíma I. A.D. 1022-1064.

loss that the 'sacking of Kulachandra' has passed into a proverb. Kulachandra also took from Aṇahilaváḍa an acknowledgment of victory or *jayapatra*. On his return Bhoja received Kulachandra with honour but blamed him for not sowing salt instead of shell-money.[1] He said the shell-money is an omen that the wealth of Málwa will flow to Gujarát. An unpublished inscription of Bhoja's successor Udayáditya in a temple at Udepur near Bhilsá confirms the above stating that Bhíma was conquered by Bhoja's officers.[2]

The Solaṅki kings of Aṇahilapura being S'aivites held the god Somanátha of Prabhása in great veneration. The very ancient and holy shrine of Prabhása has long been a place of special pilgrimage. As early as the Yádavas of Dwárká,[3] pilgrimages to Prabhása are recorded but the Mahábhárata makes no mention either of Somanátha or of any other S'aivite shrine. The shrine of Somanátha was probably not established before the time of the Valabhis (A.D. 480-767). As the Valabhi kings were most open-handed in religious gifts, it was probably through their grants that the Somanátha temple rose to importance. The Solaṅkis were not behind the Valabhis in devotion to Somanátha. To save pilgrims from oppression Múlarája fought Graharipu the A'bhíra king of Sorath.[4] Múlarája afterwards went to Prabhása and also built temples in Gujarát in honour of the god Somanátha. As Múlarája's successors Chámuṇḍa and Durlabha continued firm devotees of Somanátha during their reigns (A.D. 997-1022) the wealth of the temple must have greatly increased.

Mahmúd's Invasion, A.D. 1024.

No Gujarát Hindu writer refers to the destruction of the great temple soon after Bhíma's accession.[5] But the Musalmán historians place beyond doubt that in A.D. 1024 the famous tenth raid of

---

[1] By sowing cowries Kulachandra may have meant to show the cheapness of Aṇahilaváḍa. Bhoja's meaning was that as shells are money, to sow shells was to sow Málwa wealth in Gujarát. If Kulachandra had sown salt all would have melted, and no trace been left. [This seems a symbolic later-stage explanation. The sense seems to be shell-sowing keeps the Aṇahilaváḍa guardians in place since guardians can live in shells: salt-sowing scares the guardian spirits and makes the site of the city a haunt of demons. Bhoja saw that thanks to his general the Luck of Aṇahilaváḍa would remain safe in the shells.]

[2] The Prabandhachintámaṇi tells other stories of the relations between Bhíma and Bhoja. Once when Gujarát was suffering from famine Bhíma heard that Bhoja was coming with a force against Gujarát. Alarmed at the news Bhíma asked Dámara his minister of peace and war to prevent Bhoja coming. Dámara went to Málwa, amused the king by witty stories, and while a play was being acted in court degrading and joking other kings, something was said regarding Tailapa of Telingana. On this Damara reminded the king that the head of his grandfather Muñja was fixed at Tailap's door. Bhoja grew excited and started with an army against Telingana. Hearing that Bhíma had come against him as far as Bhímapura (?) Bhoja asked Dámara to prevent Bhíma advancing further. Dámara stopped Bhíma by taking him an elephant as a present from Bhoja. The Prabandachintámaṇi gives numerous other stories showing that at times the relations between Bhoja and Bhíma were friendly.

[3] See above page 9. [4] See above page 160.

[5] With this silence compare the absence (Reinaud's Mémoire Sur l'Inde, 67) of any reference either in Sanskrit or in Buddhist books to the victories, even to the name, of Alexander the Great. Also in modern times the ignoring of British rule in the many inscriptions of Jain repairers of temples on Satruñjaya hill who belong to British territory. The only foreign reference is by one merchant of Daman who acknowledges the protection of the Phirangi játi Puratakala Pátasáhi the king of the Firangis of Portugal. Bühler in Epigraphia Indica, II. 36.

Somanátha, A.D. 1024.

Mahmúd of Ghazni, ended in the destruction and plunder of Somanátha.[1]

Of the destruction of Somanátha the earliest Musalmán account, that of Ibn Asír (A.D. 1160-1229), supplies the following details: In the year A.D. 1024 (H. 414) Mahmúd captured several forts and cities in Hind and he also took the idol called Somanátha. This idol was the greatest of all the idols of Hind. At every eclipse[2] the Hindus went on pilgrimage to the temple, and there congregated to the number of a hundred thousand persons. According to their doctrine of transmigration the Hindus believe that after separation from the body the souls of men meet at Somanátha; and that the ebb and flow of the tide is the worship paid to the best of its power by the sea to the idol.[3] All that is most precious in India was brought to Somanátha. The temple attendants received the most valuable presents, and the temple was endowed with more than 10,000 villages.[4] In the temple were amassed jewels of the most exquisite quality and of incalculable value. The people of India have a great river called Ganga to which they pay the highest honour and into which they cast the bones of their great men, in the belief that the deceased will thus secure an entrance to heaven. Though between this river and Somanátha is a distance of about 1200 miles (200 *parasangs*) water was daily brought from it to wash the idol.[5] Every day a thousand Bráhmans performed the worship and introduced visitors.[6] The shaving of the heads and beards of pilgrims employed three hundred barbers.[7] Three hundred and fifty persons sang and danced at the gate of the temple,[8] every one receiving a settled daily allowance. When Mahmúd was gaining victories and demolishing idols in North India, the Hindus said Somanátha is displeased with these idols. If Somanátha had been satisfied with them no one could have destroyed or injured them. When Mahmúd heard this he resolved on making a campaign to destroy Somanátha, believing that when the Hindus saw their prayers and imprecations to be false and futile they would embrace the Faith.

So he prayed to the Almighty for aid, and with 30,000 horse besides volunteers left Ghazni on the 10th Sha'bán (H. 414, A.D. 1024).

---

[1] Elliot and Dowson, II. 468ff. Sir H. M. Elliot gives extracts for this expedition from the Tárikh-i-Alfí, Tabakát-i-Akbari, Tabakát-i-Náśiri, and Rauzatu-s-safá.

[2] Since the earliest times Hindus have held eclipse days sacred. According to the Mahabhárata the Yadavas of Dwárká came to Somanátha for an eclipse fair. Great fairs are still held at Somanátha on the Kártika and Chaitra (December and April) fullmoons.

[3] This old Indian idea is expressed in a verse in an inscription in Somanátha Pátan itself.

[4] Ten thousand must be taken vaguely.

[5] Compare Sachau's Alberuni, II. 104. Every day they brought Somanátha a jug of Ganges water and a basket of Kashmir flowers. Somanátha they believed cured every inveterate sickness and healed every desperate and incurable disease. The reason why Somanátha became so famous was that it was a harbour for those who went to and fro from Sofala in Zanzibar to China. It is still the practice to carry Ganges water to bathe distant gods.

[6] These must be the local Sompura Bráhmans who still number more than five hundred souls in Somanátha Patan.

[7] Shaving is the first rite performed by pilgrims.

[8] Dancers are now chiefly found in the temples of Southern India.

Chapter II.
THE CHAULUKYAS, A.D. 961-1242.
Somanátha, A.D. 1024.

He took the road to Multán and reached it in the middle of Ramzán. The road from Multán to India lay through a barren desert without inhabitants or food. Mahmúd collected provisions for the passage and loading 30,000 camels with water and corn started for Aṇahilaváḍa. After he had crossed the desert he perceived on one side a fort full of people in which place there were wells.[1] The leaders came to conciliate him, but he invested the place, and God gave him victory over it, for the hearts of the people failed them through fear. He brought the place under the sway of Islám, killed the inhabitants, and broke in pieces their images. His men carrying water with them marched for Aṇahilaváḍa, where they arrived at the beginning of Zílkáda.

The Chief of Aṇahilaváḍa, called Bhím, fled hastily, and abandoning his city went to a certain fort for safety and to prepare for war. Mahmúd pushed on for Somanátha. On his march he came to several forts in which were many images serving as chamberlains or heralds of Somanátha. These Mahmúd called Shaitán or devils. He killed the people, destroyed the fortifications, broke the idols in pieces, and through a waterless desert marched to Somanátha. In the desert land he met 20,000 fighting men whose chiefs would not submit. He sent troops against them, defeated them, put them to flight, and plundered their possessions. From the desert he marched to Dabalwárah,[2] two days' journey from Somanátha. The people of Dabalwárah stayed in the city believing that the word of Somanátha would drive back the invaders. Mahmúd took the place, slew the men, plundered their property, and marched to Somanátha.

Reaching Somanátha on a Thursday in the middle of Zílkáda Mahmúd beheld a strong fortress built on the sea-shore, so that its walls were washed by the waves.[3] From the walls the people jeered at the Musalmáns. Our deity, they said, will cut off the last man of you and destroy you all. On the morrow which was Friday the assailants advanced to the assault. When the Hindus saw how the Muhammadans fought they abandoned their posts and left the walls. The Musalmáns planted their ladders and scaled the walls. From the top they raised their war-cry, and showed the might of Islám. Still their loss was so heavy that the issue seemed doubtful. A body of Hindus hurried to Somanátha, cast themselves on the ground before him, and besought him to grant them victory. Night came on and the fight was stayed.

Early next morning Mahmúd renewed the battle. His men made greater havoc among the Hindus till they drove them from the town to the house of their idol Somanátha. At the gate of the temple the slaughter was dreadful. Band after band of the defenders entered the temple and standing before Somanátha with their hands clasped round their necks wept and passionately entreated him. Then they issued forth to fight and fought till they were slain. The few left alive took

[1] Mahmúd seems to have crossed the desert from Multán and Baháwalpur to Bikánír and thence to Ajmír.

[2] Apparently Delváda near Uná. Mahmúd's route seems to have been from Aṇahilaváḍa to Modhera and Mándal, thence by the Little Ran near Pátri and Bajána, and thence by Jhálávaḍ Gohelváḍ and Bábriaváḍ to Delváda.

[3] The waves still beat against the walls of the ruined fort of Somanátha.

Somanátha, A.D. 1024.

to the sea in boats but the Musalmáns overtook them and some were killed and some were drowned.

The temple of Somanátha rested on fifty-six pillars of teakwood covered with lead.[1] The idol was in a dark chamber. The height of the idol was five cubits and its girth three cubits. This was what appeared to the eye; two cubits were hidden in the basement. It had no appearance of being sculptured. Mahmúd seized it, part of it he burnt, and part he carried with him to Ghazni, where he made it a step at the entrance of the Great Mosque.[2] The dark shrine was lighted by exquisitely jewelled chandeliers. Near the idol was a chain of gold 200 *mans* in weight. To the chain bells were fastened. And when each watch of the night was over the chain was shaken and the ringing of the bells roused a fresh party of Bráhmans to carry on the worship. In the treasury which was near the shrine were many idols of gold and silver. Among the treasures were veils set with jewels, every jewel of immense value. What was found in the temple was worth more than two millions of *dinárs*. Over fifty thousand Hindus were slain.[3]

After the capture of Somanátha, Mahmúd received intelligence that Bhím the chief of Aṇahilaváḍa had gone to the fort of Khandahat,[4] about 240 miles (40 *parasangs*) from Somanátha between that place and the desert. Mahmúd marched to Khandahat. When he came before it he questioned some men who were hunting as to the tide. He learned that the ford was practicable, but that if the wind blew a little the crossing was dangerous. Mahmúd prayed to the Almighty and entered the water. He and his forces passed safely and drove out the enemy. From Khandahat he returned intending to proceed against Mansúra in central Sindh, whose ruler was an apostate Muhammadan. At the news of Mahmúd's approach the chief fled into the date forests. Mahmúd followed, and surrounding him and his adherents, many of them were slain, many drowned, and few escaped. Mahmúd then went

---

[1] This shows that the temple was a building of brick and wood. According to Alberuni (Sachau, II. 105) the temple was built about a hundred years before Mahmúd's invasion. An inscription at Patan states that Bhímadeva I. (A.D. 1022-1072) rebuilt the Somanátha temple of stone. In Dr. Bhagvánlal's opinion the first dynasty in Gujarát to make stone buildings were the Solaṅkis. Before them buildings and temples were of wood and brick.

[2] Of the fate of the great Liṅga Alberuni (Sachau, II. 103) writes: Prince Mahmúd ordered the upper part to be broken. The rest with all its coverings and trappings of gold jewels and embroidered garments he transported to Ghazni. Part of it together with the brass Chakravarti or Vishnu of Thánesvar has been thrown into the hippodrome of the town: part lies before the mosque for people to rub their feet on.

[3] The next paragraph relating to Mahmúd's return will be found on page 249 of the same volume of Sir H. Elliott's work.

[4] Khandahat which must have been on the coast has not been identified. The description suggests some coast island in the gulf of Kacch. By the Girnár route forty *parasangs* that is 240 miles would reach the Kacch coast. Kanthkot in Vágad in east Kacch suits well in sound and is known to have been a favourite resort of the Solaṅkis. But the ebb and flow of the tide close to it are difficult to explain. The identification with Kanthkot is favoured by Dr. Bühler. Colonel Watson (Káthiáwár Gazetteer, 80) prefers Gándhvi on the Káthiáváda coast a few miles north-east of Miáni. M. Reinaud and Dr. Weil suggest Gandhár in Broach on the left bank of the mouth of the Dhádhar river. Sir H. Elliot (I. 445 and II. 473) prefers Khandadar at the north-west angle of Káthiáváḍa.

Chapter II.
THE CHAULUKYAS, A.D. 961-1242.
Somanátha, A.D. 1024.

to Bhátiá, and after reducing the inhabitants to obedience, returned to Ghazni where he arrived on the 10th Safar 417 H. (A.D. 1026).

The Rauzatu-s-safá of Mirkhand supplements these details with the following account of Mahmúd's arrangements for holding Gujarát: 'It is related that when Sultan Mahmúd had achieved the conquest of Somanátha he wished to fix his residence there for some years because the country was very extensive and possessed many advantages among them several mines which produced pure gold. Indian rubies were brought from Sarandíp, one of the dependencies of the kingdom of Gujarát. His ministers represented to Mahmúd that to forsake Khurásán which had been won from his enemies after so many battles and to make Somanátha the seat of government was very improper. At last the king made up his mind to return and ordered some one to be appointed to hold and carry on the administration of the country. The ministers observed that as it was impossible for a stranger to maintain possession he should assign the country to one of the native chiefs. The Sultán accordingly held a council to settle the nomination, in concurrence with such of the inhabitants as were well disposed towards him. Some of them represented to him that amongst the ancient royal families no house was so noble as that of the Dábshilíms of whom only one member survived, and he had assumed the habit of a Bráhman, and was devoted to philosophical pursuits and austerity.'[1]

That Mahmúd should have found it necessary to appoint some local chief to keep order in Gujarát is probable. It is also probable that he would choose some one hostile to the defeated king. It has been suggested above that Bhíma's uncle Durlabha did not retire but was ousted by his nephew and that the story of Vallabha and Durlabha dying together pointed to some usurpation on the part of Bhíma. The phrase the Dábshilíms seems to refer either to Durlabhasena or his son. Whoever was chosen must have lost his power soon after Mahmúd's departure.[2]

---

[1] According to Ferishta (Bombay Persian Ed. I. 57, Briggs' Translation, I. 74) Mahmúd stayed and meant to make his capital at Aṇahilaváḍa not at Somanátha. That Mahmúd did stay at Aṇahilaváḍa the Martyr's Mound and the Ghazni Mosque in Patan are evidence. Still the mound was probably raised and the mosque may at least have been begun in honour of the capture of Aṇahilavaḍa on the journey south. Traces of a second mosque which is said to have had a tablet recording Mahmúd of Ghazni as the builder have recently (1878) been found at Munjpur about twenty-five miles south-east of Rádhanpur.

[2] Briggs' Ferishta, I. 75. This account of the Dábshilíms reads more like a tradition than an historical record. It is to be noted that the authors both of the 'Ain-i-Akbarí (A.D. 1583) and of the Mirat-i-Ahmadí (A.D. 1762) give Chámuṇḍa as king at the time of Mahmúd's invasion. Their statements cannot weigh against Ibn Asír's account. Compare Dr. Bühler's remarks in Ind. Ant. VI. 184. Of Mahmúd's return to Ghazni (A.D. 1026) the Tabakát-i-Akbarí says: 'When Mahmúd resolved to return from Somanátha he learned that Parama Dev, one of the greatest Rájás of Hindustán, was preparing to intercept him. The Sultán, not deeming it advisable to contend with this chief, went towards Multán through Sindh. In this journey his men suffered much in some places from scarcity of water in others from want of forage. After enduring great difficulties he arrived at Ghazni in A.D. 1029 (H. 417).' This Parama Dev would seem to be the Parmára king of A'bu who could well block the Ajmir-Gujarát route. The route taken by Mahmúd must have passed by Mansúra near Bráhmanábád, Bhátia, and Multán. It

Chapter II.

The Chaulukyas, A.D. 961-1242.

Bhíma I. A.D. 1022-1064.

An inscription at Somanátha shows that soon after Mahmúd was gone Bhímadeva began to build a temple of stone in place of the former temple of brick and wood.

A few years later Bhíma was on bad terms with Dhandhuka the Paramára chief of Ábu, and sent his general Vimala to subdue him. Dhandhuka submitted and made over to Vimala the beautiful Chitrakûṭa peak of Ábu, where, in A.D. 1032 (S. 1088), Vimala built the celebrated Jain temples known as Vimalavasahi still one of the glories of Ábu.[1]

Bhíma had three wives Udayámatí who built a step-well at Aṇahilaváḍa, Bukuládeví, and another. These ladies were the mothers of Karṇa, Kshemarája, and Múlarája. Of the three sons Múlarája, though his mother's name is unknown, was the eldest and the heir-apparent. Of the kindly Múlarája the author of the Prabandhachintámaṇi tells the following tale: In a year of scarcity the Kuṭumbikas or cultivators of Vishopaka and Daṇḍáhi found themselves unable to pay the king his share of the land-produce. Bhímarája sent a minister to inquire and the minister brought before the king all the well-to-do people of the defaulting villages. One day prince Múlarája saw these men talking to one another in alarm. Taking pity on them he pleased the king by his skilful riding. The king asked him to name a boon and the prince begged that the demand on the villagers might be remitted. The boon was granted, the ryots went home in glee, but within three days Múlarája was dead. Next season yielded a bumper harvest, and the people came to present the king with his share for that year as well as with the remitted share for the previous year. Bhímdev declined to receive the arrears. A jury appointed by the king settled that the royal share of the produce for both years should be placed in the king's hands for the erection of a temple called the new Tripurushaprásáda for the spiritual welfare of prince Múlarája.[2]

---

must have been in the crossing of the great desert that he suffered so severely from scarcity of water and forage. Ferishta (Briggs, I. 75) says that many of Mahmúd's troops died raging mad from the intolerable heat and thirst. The historian Muhammad Ufi (A.D. 1200) alleges (Elliot, II. 192) that two Hindus disguised as countrymen offered themselves as guides and led the army three days' march out of the right course, where they were saved only by Mahmúd's miraculous discovery of a pool of sweet water. [This tale of the self-sacrificing Bráhman or priest and the miraculous find of water has gathered round Mahmúd as the latest of myth centres. It is Herodotus' (Book III. 154-158) old Zopyrus tale (Rawlinson's Seventh Monarchy, 318); it is revived in honour of the Great Kushán Kanishka, A.D. 78 (Beruni in Elliot, II. 11), of the Sassanian Firoz A.D. 457-483 (Rawlinson's Seventh Monarchy, 318), and of a certain king of Zábulistán or Ghazni of uncertain date (Elliot II. 170). Similarly the puzzling Dabshilím tale seems to be peculiar neither to Gujarát nor to Mahmúd of Ghazni. It seems a repetition of the tale of Dabshilím the man of the royal race, who, according to the Panchatantra or Fables of Pilpai, was chosen successor of Porus after Alexander the Great's Viceroy had been driven out. [Compare Reinaud's Mémoire Sur l'Inde, 127-128.] The Tabakát-i-Násirí (A.D. 1227) adds (Elliot, II. 475) that the guide devoted his life for the sake of Somanátha and this account is adopted by Ferishta. Briggs' Translation, I. 78.

[1] Vasahi is Prákrit for Vasati that is residence. The word is used to mean a group of temples.

[2] Several later mentions of a *Tripurushaprásáda* show there was only one building of that name. The statement that the great Múlarája I. built a Tripurushaprásáda seems a mistake, due to a confusion with prince Múlarája.

Chapter II.
The Chaulukyas, A.D. 961 - 1242.
Bhíma I. A.D. 1022 - 1064.

Bhíma reigned forty-two years. Both the Prabandhachintámaṇi and the Vichárasreṇi mention Karṇa as his successor. According to the Dvyáśraya Bhíma, wishing to retire to a religious life, offered the succession to Kshemarája. But Kshemarája also was averse from the labour of ruling and it was settled that Karṇa should succeed.

Bhíma died soon after and Kshemarája retired to a holy place on the Sarasvatí named Mundakeśvara not far from Aṇahilaváḍa. Karṇa is said to have granted Dahithalí a neighbouring village to Devaprásáda the son of Kshemarája that he might attend on his father in his religious seclusion. But as the Kumárapálacharita mentions Kshemarája being settled at Dahithalí as a ruler not as an ascetic it seems probable that Dahithalí was granted to Kshemarája for maintenance as villages are still granted to the *bháyás* or brethren of the ruler.

Karṇa, A.D. 1064 - 1094.

Karṇa who came to the throne in A.D. 1064 (S. 1120) had a more peaceful reign than his predecessors. He was able to build charitable public works among them a temple called Karṇa-meru at Aṇahilaváḍa. His only war was an expedition against Ásha Bhil, chief of six lákhs[1] of Bhils residing at Áshápallí the modern village of Asával near Ahmadábád.[2] Ásha was defeated and slain. In consequence of an omen from a local goddess named Kochharva,[3] Karṇa built her a temple in Asával and also built temples to Jayantí Deví and Karṇeśvara Mahádeva. He made a lake called Karṇaságara and founded a city called Karṇávatí which he made his capital.

Karṇa had three ministers Munjála, Sántu, and Udaya. Udaya was a S'rímálí Vániá of Márwár, who had settled in Aṇahilaváḍa and who was originally called Udá. Sántu built a Jain temple called Sántu-vasahi and Udá built at Karṇávatí a large temple called Udaya-varáha, containing seventy-two images of Tirthankars, twenty-four past twenty-four present and twenty-four to come. By different wives Udá had five sons, Áhaḍa or Asthaḍa, Cháhaḍa, Báhaḍa, Ámbada, and Sollá, of whom the last three were half brothers of the first two.[4] Except Sollá, who continued a merchant and became very wealthy, all the sons entered the service of the state and rose to high stations during the reign of Kumárapála.

In late life Karṇa married Miyáṇalladeví daughter of Jayakeśi son of S'ubhakeśi king of the Karṇáṭaka. According to the Dvyáśraya a wandering painter showed Karṇa the portrait of a princess whom he described as daughter of Jayakeśi the Kadamba king[5] of

[1] Meaning a large number of Bhils of whom A'shá was the head.
[2] Forbes' Rás Málá (New Ed.), 79.
[3] Probably a Bhíl goddess. The name does not sound Sanskrit.
[4] In one passage the Prabandhachintámaṇi calls these princes half-brothers of Udaya. Further details show that they were half-brothers of one another and sons of Udaya.
[5] This Jayakeśi is Jayakeśi I. son of Shashṭhadeva (S'uchakeśi) the third of the Goa Kadambas. Jayakeśi's recorded date A.D. 1052 (S. 974) fits well with the time of Karṇa (Fleet's Kánarese Dynasties, 91). The Prabandhachintámaṇi tells the following story of the death of Jayakeśi. Jayakeśi had a favourite parrot whom he

Chapter II.

THE CHAULUKYAS, A.D. 961 - 1242.

Karṇa, A.D. 1064 - 1094.

Chandrapura[1] in the Dakhan, and who he said had taken a vow to marry Karṇa. In token of her wish to marry Karṇa the painter said the princess had sent Karṇa an elephant. Karṇa went to see the present and found on the elephant a beautiful princess who had come so far in the hope of winning him for a husband. According to the Prabandhachintamaṇi Karṇa found the princess ugly and refused to marry her. On this the princess with eight attendants determined to burn themselves on a funeral pyre and Udayámatí Karṇa's mother also declared that if he did not relent she too would be a sacrifice. Under this compulsion Karṇa married the princess but refused to treat her as a wife. The minister Muñjála, learning from a *kañchukí* or palace-servant that the king loved a certain courtezan, contrived that Miyánalladeví should take the woman's place, a device still practised by ministers of native states. Karṇa fell into the snare and the queen became pregnant by him, having secured from the hand of her husband his signet ring as a token which could not be disclaimed. Thus in Karṇa's old age Miyánalladeví became the mother of the illustrious Siddharája Jayasiṃha, who, according to a local tradition quoted by Mr. Forbes, first saw the light at Pálanpur.[2] When three years old the precocious Siddharája climbed and sat upon the throne. This ominous event being brought to the king's notice he consulted his astrologers who advised that from that day Siddharája should be installed as heir-apparent.

The Gujarát chronicles do not record how or when Karṇa died. It appears from a manuscript that he was reigning in A. D. 1089 (S. 1145).[3] The Hammíramahákávya says 'The illustrious Karṇadeva was killed in battle by king Duśśala of S'ákambharí,' and the two appear to have been cotemporaries.[4] The author of the Dvyáśraya says that Karṇa died fixing his thoughts on Vishnu, recommending to Siddharája his cousin Devaprasáda son of Kshemarája. According to the Prabandhachintamaṇi Vichárasreṇí and Sukṛitasankírtana Karṇa died in A.D. 1094 (S. 1150).

Siddharája Jayasingha, A.D. 1094 - 1143.

As, at the time of his father's death, Siddharája was a minor[5] the reins of government must have passed into the hands of his mother Miyánalladeví. That the succession should have been attended with struggle and intrigue is not strange. According to the Dvyás'raya Devaprasáda, the son of Kshemarája burned himself on the funeral pile shortly after the death of Karṇa, an action which was probably the result of some intrigue regarding the succession. Another intrigue

---

one day asked to come out of his cage and dine with him. The parrot said: The cat sitting near you will kill me. The king seeing no cat replied: If any cat kills you I too will die. The parrot left his cage, ate with the king, and was killed by the cat. Jayakesí made ready his funeral pyre, and, in spite of his minister's prayers, taking the dead parrot in his hand laid himself on the funeral pyre and was burned.

[1] Chandrapura is probably Chandávar near Gokarn in North Kánara.

[2] Rás Málá (New Edition), 83.

[3] Kielhorn's Report on Sanskrit Manuscripts for 1881 page 22.

[4] Duśśala was sixth in descent from Vigraharája the enemy of Múlarája from whom Karṇa was fifth in descent.

[5] The date of his installation is given by the author of the Vichárasreṇí as Vikrama S. 1150.

Chapter II.

The Chaulukyas, A.D. 961 - 1242.

Siddharája Jayasingha, A.D. 1094 - 1143.

ended in the death of Madanapála brother of Karṇa's mother queen Udayámatí, at the hands of the minister S'ántu, who along with Muñjála and Udá, helped the queen-mother Miyánalladeví during the regency. Muñjála and Sántu continued in office under Siddharája. Another minister built a famous Jain temple named Mahárájabhuvana in Sidhpur at the time when Siddharája built the Rudramálá. An inscription from a temple near Bhadresar in Kacch dated A.D. 1139 (S. 1195 Áshádha Vad 10, Sunday), in recording grants to Audichya Bráhmans to carry on the worship in an old temple of Udales'vara and in a new temple of Kumárapáles'vara built by Kumárapála son of the great prince Ásapála,[1] notes that Dádáka was then minister of Siddharája. Among his generals the best known was a chief named Jagaddeva (Jag Dev), commonly believed to be a Paramára, many of whose feats of daring are recorded in bardic and popular romances.[2] Though Jag Dev is generally called a Paramára nothing of his family is on record. The author of the Prabandhachintámaṇi describes Jagaddeva as a thrice valiant warrior held in great respect by Siddharája. After Siddharája's death Jagaddeva went to serve king Permádi to whose mother's family he was related.[3] Permádi gave him a chiefship and sent him to attack Málava.

When Siddharája attained manhood his mother prepared to go in great state on pilgrimage to Somanátha. She went with rich offerings as far as Báhuloḍa apparently the large modern village of Bholáda on the Gujarát-Káthiáváḍa frontier about twenty-two miles south-west of Dholká. At this frontier town the Aṇahilaváḍa kings levied a tax on all pilgrims to Somanátha. Many of the pilgrims unable to pay the tax had to return home in tears. Miyánalladeví was so saddened by the woes of the pilgrims that she stopped her pilgrimage and returned home. Siddharája met her on the way and asked her why she had turned back. Miyánalladeví said, I will neither eat nor go to Somanátha until you order the remission of the pilgrim tax. Siddharája called the Bholáda treasurer and found that the levy yielded 72 lákhs a year.[4] In spite of the serious sacrifice Siddharája broke the board authorizing the levy of the tax and pouring water from his hand into his mother's declared that the merit of the remission was hers. The queen went to Somanátha and worshipped the god with gold presenting an elephant and other gifts and handing over her own weight in money.

According to the Prabandhachintámaṇi while Miyánalladeví and Siddharája were on pilgrimage Yasovarman king of Málwa continually harassed the Gurjjara-Maṇḍala. S'ántu who was in charge of the kingdom asked Yas'ovarman on what consideration he would retire.

---

[1] Ásapála and Kumárapála appear to be local chiefs.

[2] Compare Forbes' Rás Málá, I. 118 - 153.

[3] Goa Kádamba inscriptions say that Jaggaddeva was the cousin of the Goa Kadamba king Vijayárka the nephew of Miyánalladeví and call him by courtesy the younger brother of Vijayárka's son Jayakes'i II. He would seem to have been held in esteem by Vijayárka and his son Jayakes'i, to have then gone for some time to Siddharája, and after leaving Siddharája to have transferred his services to Permadi. His being called Paramára may be due to his connection with Permadi. Fleet's Kánarese Dynasties, 91.

[4] Seventy-two a favourite number with Indian authors.

Chapter II.

THE CHAULUKYAS, A.D. 961-1242.

Siddharája Jayasingha, A.D. 1094-1143.

Yaśovarman said he would retire if Siddharája gave up to him the merit of the pilgrimage to Someśvara. Sántu washed his feet and taking water in his hand surrendered to Yaśovarman the merit of Siddharája, on which, according to his promise, Yaśovarman retired. On his return Siddharája asked Sántu what he meant by transferring his sovereign's merit to a rival. Sántu said, 'If you think my giving Yaśovarman your merit has any importance I restore it to you.' This curious story seems to be a Jain fiction probably invented with the object of casting ridicule on the Bráhmanical doctrine of merit. Yaśovarman was not a cotemporary of Siddharája. The Málwa king referred to is probably Yaśovarman's predecessor Naravarman, of whom an inscription dated A.D. 1134 (S. 1190) is recorded.

Under the name Sadharo Jesingh, Siddharája's memory is fresh in Gujarát as its most powerful, most religious, and most charitable ruler. Almost every old work of architectural or antiquarian interest in Gujarát is ascribed to Siddharája. In inscriptions he is styled The great king of kings, The great lord, The great Bhaṭṭáraka, The lord of Avantí, The hero of the three worlds, The conqueror of Barbaraka, The universal ruler Siddha, The illustrious Jayasiṃhadeva. Of these the commonest attributes are Siddhachakravartín the Emperor of Magic and Siddharája the Lord of Magic, titles which seem to claim for the king divine or supernatural powers.[3] In connection with his assumption of these titles the Kumárapálaprabandha, the Dvyáśraya, and the Prabandhachintámaṇi tell curious tales. According to the Dvyáśraya, the king wandering by night had subdued the Bhútas, Sákinís, and other spirits. He had also learnt many *mantras* or charms. From what he saw at night he would call people in the day time and say 'You have such a cause of uneasiness' or 'You have such a comfort.' Seeing that he knew their secrets the people thought that the king knew the hearts of all men and must be the *avatára* of some god. A second story tells how Siddharája helped a Nága prince and princess whom he met by night on the Sarasvatí.[4] According to a third story told in the Kumárapálaprabandha two Yoginís or nymphs came from the Himálayas and asked the king by what mystic powers he justified the use of the title Siddharája. The king agreed to perform some wonders in open court in the presence of the nymphs. With the help of a former minister, Haripála, the king had a dagger prepared whose blade was of sugar and its handle of iron set with jewels. When the king appeared in court to perform the promised wonders a deputation of ambassadors from king Permádi of Kalyánakataka[5] was

1 Prabandhachintámaṇi and Kumárapálacharita.

2 Dr. Kielhorn's Report on Sanskrit Manuscripts for 1881 page 22.

3 The Kumárapálacharita says that the title was assumed on the conquest of Barbaraka. The verse is:

सिद्धो बर्बरकश्चास्य सिद्धराजस्ततोभवत्

that is, by him the demon Barbaraka was vanquished, therefore he became Siddharája The Lord of Magical Power.

4 Ind. Ant. IV. 265.

5 This Permádi may be the Goa Kádamba chief Permádi Śivachitta (A.D. 1147-1175), who was heir-apparent in the time of Siddharája, or the Sinda chief Permádi who was a cotemporary of Siddharája and flourished in A.D. 1144.

Chapter II.

THE CHAULUKYAS, A.D. 961 - 1242.

Siddharája Jayasingha, A.D. 1094 - 1143.

announced. The deputation entered and presented the prepared dagger as a gift from their lord. The king kept the prepared dagger and in its stead sent all round the court a real dagger which was greatly admired. After the real dagger had been seen and returned the king said: I will use this dagger to show my mystic powers, and in its place taking the false dagger ate its sugar blade. When the blade was eaten the minister stopped the king and said Let the Yoginís eat the handle. The king agreed and as the Yoginís failed to eat the handle which was iron the superiority of the king's magic was proved.

A fourth story in the Dvyás'raya tells that when the king was planning an invasion of Málwa a Yoginí came from Ujjain to Patan and said 'O Rája, if you desire great fame, come to Ujjain and humbly entreat Kálika and other Yoginís and make friends with Yas'ovarman the Rája of Ujjain.' The king contemptuously dismissed her, saying, 'If you do not fly hence like a female crow, I will cut off your nose and ears with this sword.'

So also the king's acts of prowess and courage were believed to be due to magical aid. According to the common belief Siddharája did his great acts of heroism by the help of a demon named Bábaro, whom he is said to have subdued by riding on a corpse in a burying ground. The story in the Prabandhachintámaṇi is similar to that told of the father of Harshavardhana who subdued a demon with the help of a Yogí. It is notable that the story had passed into its present form within a hundred years of Siddharája's death. Somes'vara in his Kírtikaumudí says, 'This moon of kings fettered the prince of goblins Barbaraka in a burial-place, and became known among the crowd of kings as Siddharája.' Older records show that the origin of the story, at least of the demon's name, is historical being traceable to one of Siddharája's copperplate attributes Barbaraka-jishṇu that is conqueror of Barbaraka. The Dvyás'rayakosha represents this Barbara as a leader of Rákshasas or Mlechhas, who troubled the Bráhmans at S'rísthala-Siddhapura. Jayasiṃha conquered him and spared his life at the instance of his wife Piṅgaliká. Afterwards Barbara gave valuable presents to Jayasiṃha and 'served him as other Rajputs.'[1] Barbaraka

---

[1] Ind. Ant. IV. 2. Regarding Barbaraka Doctor Bühler remarks in Ind. Ant. VI. 167: 'The Varvarakas are one of the non-Aryan tribes which are settled in great numbers in North Gujárát, Koli, Bhíl, or Mer.' Siddharája's contests with the Barbarakas seem to refer to what Tod (Western India, 173 and 195) describes as the inroads of mountaineers and foresters on the plains of Gujarát during the eleventh and twelfth centuries. To attempt to identify Bhut Barbar or Varvar is hazardous. The name Barbar is of great age and is spread from India to Morocco. Wilson (Works, VII. 176) says: The analogy between Barbaras and barbarians is not in sound only. In all Sanskrit authorities Barbaras are classed with borderers and foreigners and nations not Hindu. According to Sir Henry Rawlinson (Ferrier's Caravan Journies, 223 note) tribes of Berbers are found all over the east. Of the age of the word Canon Rawlinson (Herodotus, IV. 252) writes: Barbar seems to be the local name for the early race of Accad. In India Ptolemy (A.D. 150; McCrindle's Edn. 146) has a town Barbarei on the Indus and the Periplus (A.D. 247; McCrindle's Ed. 108) has a trade-centre Barbarikon on the middle mouth of the Indus. Among Indian writings, in the Ramáyana (Hall in Wilson's Works, VII. 176 Note *) the Barbaras appear between the Tukharas and the Kambojas in the north; in the Mahábhárata (Muir's Sanskrit Texts, I. 481-2) in one list Var-varas are entered between Savaras and Sakas and in another list (Wilson's Works, VII. 176)

seems to be the name of a tribe of non-Áryans whose modern representatives are the Bábariás settled in South Káthiáváḍa in the province still known as Bábariáváḍa.

Chapter II.

The Chaulukyas, A.D. 961-1242.

Siddharája Jayasingha, A.D. 1094-1143.

A Dohad inscription of the time of Siddharája dated A.D. 1140 (S. 1196) says of his frontier wars: 'He threw into prison the lords of Suráshtra and Málwa; he destroyed Sindhurája and other kings; he made the kings of the north bear his commands.' The Suráshtra king referred to is probably a ruler of the Áhír or Chudásamá tribe

---

Barbaras come between Kiratas and Siddhas. Finally (As. Res. XV. 47 footnote) Barbara is the northmost of the Seven Konkanas. The names Barbarei in Ptolemy and Barbarikon in the Periplus look like some local place-name, perhaps Bambhara, altered to a Greek form. The Hindu tribe names, from the sameness in sound as well as from their position on the north-west border of India, suggest the Mongol tribe Juán-Juán or Var-Var, known to the western nations as Avárs, who drove the Little Yuechi out of Balkh in the second half of the fourth century, and, for about a hundred years, ruled to the north and perhaps also to the south of the Hindu Kush. (Specht in Journal Asiatique 1883. II. 390-410; Howorth in Jour. R. A. S. XXI. 721-810.) It seems probable that some of these Var-Vars passed south either before or along with the White Huṇas (A.D. 450-550). Var, under its Mongol plural form Avarti (Howorth, Ditto 722), closely resembles Avartiya one of the two main divisions of the Káthis of Kacch (Mr. Erskine's List in J. Bom. Geo. Soc. II. 59-60 for Aug. 1838). That among the forty-seven clans included under the Avartiyas four (Nos. 30, 35, 42, and 43) are Babariyas, suggests that the Káthis received additions from the Var-Vars at different times and places. Dr. Bühler (Ind. Ant. VI. 186) thinks that the Babaro or Barbar or Var-Var who gave trouble to Siddharája represent some early local non-Aryan tribe. The fact that they are called Rákshasas and Mlecchas and that they stopped the ceremonies at Siddhpur north of Anahilaváḍa seems rather to point to a foreign invasion from the north than to a local uprising of hill tribes. Though no Musalmán invasion of Gujarát during the reign of Siddharája is recorded a Jesalmir legend (Forbes' Rás Málá, 1. 175) tells how Lanja Bijirao the Bhatti prince who married Siddharája's daughter was hailed by his mother-in-law as the bulwark of Anahiláváḍa against the power of the king who grows too strong. This king may be Báhalim the Indian viceroy of the Ghaznavid Bahrám Sháh (A.D. 1116-1157). Báhalim (Elliot, II. 279; Briggs' Ferista, I. 151) collected an army of Arabs, Persians, Afghans, and Khiljis, repaired the fort of Nágor in the province of Sewálik, and committed great devastations in the territories of the independent Indian rulers. He threw off allegiance to Ghazni and advancing to meet Bahrám Sháh near Multán was defeated and slain. Except that they were northerners and that Báhalim's is the only known invasion from the north during Siddharája's reign nothing has been found connecting Barbar and Báhalim. At the same time that the Barbar or Var-Var of the Gujarát writers may have been non-Hindu mercenaries from the north-west frontier whom Siddharája admitted as Hindu subjects is made not unlikely by two incidents preserved by the Muhammadan historians. The Tárikh-i-Soráth (Bayley's Gujarat, 35 Note *) tells how in A.D. 1178 from the defeated army of Shaháb-ud-din Ghori the Turkish Afghán and Moghal women were distributed the higher class to high caste and the commoner to low caste Hindus. Similarly how the better class of male captives were admitted among Chakával and Wadhál Rajputs and the lower among Khánts, Kolis, Bábrias, and Mers. Again about thirty years later (A.D. 1210) when his Turk mercenaries, who were not converted to Islám, revolted against Shamsu-ud-din Altamsh they seized Delhi and built Hindu temples (Elliot, II. 237-239). These cases seem to make it likely that among Báhalim's mercenaries were some un-Islamised North Indian Var-Vars and that they were admitted into Hinduism by Siddharája and as the story states served him as other Rajputs. Some of the new-comers as noted above seem to have merged into the Káthis. Others founded or joined the Babariás who give their name to Babariáváḍa a small division in the south of Káthiáváḍa. Though the tribe is now small the 72 divisions of the Bábariás show that they were once important. One of their leading divisions preserves the early form Var (Káthiáwár Gazetteer, 132-133) and supports their separate northern origin, which is forgotten in the local stories that they are descended from Jetvas and Ahirs and have a Bráhman element in their ancestry. (Tod's Western India, 413; Káthiáwár Gazetteer, 132-123.) Of the Var-Vars in their old seats a somewhat doubtful trace remains in the Barbaris a tribe of Hazáráhs near Herat (Bellew in Imp. and As. Quar. Review Oct. 1891 page 328) and in the Panjáb (Ibbetson's Census, 538) Bhábras a class of Panjáb Jains.

Chapter II.
THE CHAULUKYAS, A.D. 961-1242.
Siddharája Jayasingha, A.D. 1094-1143.

whose head-quarters were at Junágaḍh. According to the Prabandhachintámaṇi Siddharája went in person to subdue Noghan or Navaghani the Áhír ruler of Suráshṭra; he came to Vardhamánapura that is Vadhván and from Vadhván attacked and slew Noghan. Jinaprabhasúri the author of the Tírthakalpa says of Girnár that Jayasiṃha killed the king named Khengár and made one Sajjana his viceroy in Suráshṭra. So many traditions remain regarding wars with Khengár that it seems probable that Siddharája led separate expeditions against more than one king of that name. According to tradition the origin of the war with Khengár was a woman named Ráṇakadeví whom Khengára had married. Ránakadeví was the daughter of a potter of Majevádi village about nine miles north of Junágaḍh, so famous for her beauty that Siddharája determined to marry her. Meanwhile she had accepted an offer from Khengár whose subject she was and had married him. Siddharája enraged at her marriage advanced against Khengár, took him prisoner, and annexed Sorath. That Khengár's kingdom was annexed and Sajjana, mentioned by Jinaprabhasúri, was appointed Viceroy is proved by a Girnár inscription dated A.D. 1120 (S. 1176).

An era called the Siṃha Saṃvatsara connected with the name of Jayasiṃha and beginning with A.D. 1113-1114 (S. 1169-70), occurs in several inscriptions found about Prabhása and South Káthiáváḍa. This era was probably started in that year in honour of this conquest of Khengár and Sorath.[1] The earliest known mention of the Siṃha Saṃvatsara era occurs in a step-well at Mángrol called the Sodhali Váv. The inscription is of the time of Kumárapála and mentions Sahajiga the father of Múlaka the grantor as a member of the bodyguard of the Chálukyas. The inscription states that Sahajiga had several sons able to protect Sauráshṭra, one of whom was Somarája who built the temple of Sahajigeśvara, in the enclosure of the Somanátha temple at Prabhása; another was Múlaka the *náyaka* of Surashṭra, who is recorded to have made grants for the worship of the god by establishing cesses in Mangalapura or Mángrol and other places. The inscription is dated A. D. 1146 (Monday the 13th of the dark half of Ásvín Vikrama S. 1202 and Siṃha S. 32). This inscription supports the view that the Siṃha era was established by Jayasiṃha, since if the era belonged to some other local chief, no Chálukya viceroy would adopt it. The Siṃha era appears to have been kept up in Gujarát so long as Aṇahilapura rule lasted. The well known Verával inscription of the time of Arjuṇadeva is dated Hijri 662, Vikrama S. 1320, Valabhi S. 945, Siṃha S. 151, Sunday the 13th of Ashádha Vadi. This inscription shows that the Siṃha era was in use for a century and a half during the sovereignty of Aṇahilaváḍa in Suráshṭra.

Regarding Sajjana Siddharája's first viceroy in Suráshṭra, the Prabandhachintámaṇi says that finding him worthy the king appointed Sajjana the *daṇḍádhipati* of Suráshṭradeśa. Without consulting his master Sajjana spent three years' revenue in building a stone temple of

[1] Abhayatilaka Gaṇi who revised and completed the Dvyáśraya in Vikrama S. 1312 (A.D. 1256) says, in his twentieth Sarga, that a new era was started by Kumárapála. This would seem to refer to the Siṃha era.

Chapter II.

The Chaulukyas, A.D. 961-1242.

Siddharája Jayasingha, A.D. 1094-1143.

Neminátha on Girnár instead of a wooden temple which he removed. In the fourth year the king sent four officers to bring Sajjana to Aṇahilaváḍa. The king called on Sajjana to pay the revenues of the past three years. In reply Sajjana asked whether the king would prefer the revenue in cash or the merit which had accrued from spending the revenue in building the temple. Preferring the merit the king sanctioned the spending of the revenues on the Tírtha and Sajjana was reappointed governor of Sorath.[1] This stone temple of Sajjana would seem to be the present temple of Neminátha, though many alterations have been made in consequence of Muhammadan sacrilege and a modern enclosure has been added. The inscription of Sajjana which is dated A.D. 1120 (S. 1176) is on the inside to the right in passing to the small south gate. It contains little but the mention of the Sádhu who was Sajjana's constant adviser. On his return from a second pilgrimage to Somanátha Siddharája who was encamped near Raivataka that is Girnár expressed a wish to see Sajjana's temple. But the Bráhmans envious of the Jains persuaded the king that as Girnár was shaped like a *liṅg* it would be sacrilege to climb it. Siddharája respected this objection and worshipped at the foot of the mountain. From Girnár he went to Śatruñjaya. Here too Bráhmans with drawn swords tried to prevent the king ascending the hill. Siddharája went in disguise at night, worshipped the Jain god Ádís'vara with Ganges water, and granted the god twelve neighbouring villages. On the hill he saw so luxuriant a growth of the *śallaki* a plant dear to elephants, that he proposed to make the hill a breeding place for elephants a second Vindhya. He was reminded what damage wild elephants would cause to the holy place and for this reason abandoned his plan.

Siddharája's second and greater war was with Málwa. The cotemporary kings of Málwa were the Paramára ruler Naravarman who flourished from A.D. 1104 to 1133 (S. 1160-1189) and his son and successor Yas'ovarman who ruled up to A.D. 1143 (S. 1199) the year of Siddharája's death. As the names of both these kings occur in different accounts of this war, and, as the war is said to have lasted twelve years, it seems that fighting began in the time of Naravarman and that Siddharája's final victory was gained in the time of Yaśovarman in Siddharája's old age about A.D. 1134 (S. 1190). This view is supported by the local story that his expedition against Yaśovarman was undertaken while Siddharája was building the Sahasraliṅga lake and other religious works. It is not known how the war arose but the statement of the Prabandhachintámaṇi that Siddharája vowed to make a scabbard of Yaśovarman's skin seems to show that Siddharája received grave provocation. Siddharája is said to have left the building of the Sahasraliṅga lake to the masons and architects and himself to have

[1] The Kumárapálacharita states that Sajjana died before the temple was finished, and that the temple was completed by his son Paraśuráma. After the temple was finished Siddharája is said to have come to Somanátha and asked Paraśuráma for the revenues of Sorath. But on seeing the temple on Girnár he was greatly pleased, and on finding that it was called Karṇa-vihára after his father he sanctioned the outlay on the temple.

Chapter II.

THE CHAULUKYAS, A.D. 961-1242.

Siddharája Jayasingha, A.D. 1094-1143.

started for Málwa. The war dragged on and there seemed little hope of victory when news reached Siddharája that the three south gates of Dhárá could be forced. With the help of an elephant an entrance was effected. Yaśovarman was captured and bound with six ropes, and, with his captured enemy as his banner of victory, Siddharája returned to Aṇahilapura. He remembered his vow, but being prevented from carrying it out, he took a little of Yaśovarman's skin and adding other skin to it made a scabbard. The captured king was thenceforward kept in a cage. It was this complete conquest and annexation of Málwa that made Siddharája assume the style of Avantínátha 'Lord of Avantí,' which is mentioned as his *biruḍa* or title in most of the Chaulukya copperplates.[1] Málwa henceforward remained subject to Aṇahilaváḍa. On the return from Málwa an army of Bhíls who tried to block the way were attacked by the minister Sántu and put to flight.

Siddharája's next recorded war is with king Madanavarman the Chandela king of Mahobaka the modern Mahobá in Bundelkhand. Madanavarman, of whom General Cunningham has found numerous inscriptions dating from A.D. 1130 to 1164 (S. 1186-1220),[2] was one of the most famous kings of the Chandela dynasty. An inscription of one of his successors in Kálanjar fort records that Madanavarman 'in an instant defeated the king of Gurjjara, as Krishṇa in former times defeated Kaṃsa,[3] a statement which agrees with the Gujarát accounts of the war between him and Jayasiṃha. In this conflict the Gujarát accounts do not seem to show that Siddharája gained any great victory; he seems to have been contented with a money present. The Kírtikaumudí states that the king of Mahobaka honoured Siddharája as his guest and paid a fine and tribute by way of hospitality. The account in the Kumárapálacharita suggests that Siddharája was compelled to come to terms and make peace. According to the Kírtikaumudí, and this seems likely, Siddharája went from Dhárá to Kálañjara. The account in the Prabandhachintámaṇi is very confused. According to the Kumárapálacharita, on Siddharája's way back from Dhárá at his camp near Patan a bard came to the court and said to the king that his court was as wonderful as the court of Madanavarman. The bard said that Madanavarman was the king of the city of Mahobaka and most clever, wise, liberal, and pleasure-loving. The king sent a courtier to test the truth of the bard's statement. The courtier returned after six months declaring that the bard's account was in no way exaggerated. Hearing this Siddharája at once started against Mahobaka and encamping within sixteen miles of the city sent his minister to summon Madanavarman to surrender. Madanavarman who was enjoying himself took little notice of the minister. This king, he said, is the same who had to fight twelve years with Dhárá; if, as is probable, since he is a *kabádi* or wild king, he wants money, pay him what he wants. The money

---

[1] Ind. Ant. VI. 194ff. Dr. Bühler (Ditto) takes Avantínátha to mean Siddharája's opponent the king of Málwa and not Siddharája himself.

[2] Archæological Survey Report, XXI. 86.

[3] Jour. B. A. Soc. (1848), 319.

was paid. But Siddharája was so struck with Madanavarman's indifference that he would not leave until he had seen him. Madanavarman agreed to receive him. Siddharája went with a large bodyguard to the royal garden which contained a palace and enclosed pleasure-house and was guarded by troops. Only four of Siddharája's guards were allowed to enter. With these four men Siddharája went in, was shown the palace garden and pleasure-houses by Madanavarman, was treated with great hospitality, and on his return to Patan was given a guard of 120 men.

The Dvyás'raya says that after his conquest of Ujjain Siddharája seized and imprisoned the king of a neighbouring country named Sim. We have no other information on this point.

The Dohad inscription dated A.D. 1140 mentions the destruction of Sindhurája that is the king of Sindh and other kings. The Kírtikaumudí also mentions the binding of the lord of Sindhu. Nothing is known regarding the Sindh war. The Kírtikaumudí mentions that after a war with Arṇorája king of Sámbhar Siddharája gave his daughter to Arṇorája. This seems to be a mistake as the war and alliance with Arṇorája belong to Kumárapála's reign.

Siddharája, who like his ancestors was a S'aiva, showed his zeal for the faith by constructing the two grandest works in Gujarát the Rudramahálaya at Siddhpur and the Sahasraliṅga lake at Patan. The Jain chroniclers always try to show that Siddharája was favourably inclined to Jainism. But several of his acts go against this claim and some even show a dislike of the Jains. It is true that the Jain sage Hemáchárya lived with the king, but the king honoured him as a scholar rather than as a Jain. On the occasion of the pilgrimage to Somanátha the king offered Hemáchárya a palanquin, and, as he would not accept the offer but kept on walking, the king blamed him calling him a learned fool with no worldly wisdom. Again on one occasion while returning from Málwa Siddharája encamped at a place called S'rínagara, where the people had decorated their temples with banners in honour of the king. Finding a banner floating over a Jain temple the king asked in anger who had placed it there, as he had forbidden the use of banners on Jain shrines and temples in Gujarát. On being told that it was a very old shrine dating from the time of Bharata, the king ordered that at the end of a year the banner might be replaced. This shows the reverse of a leaning to Jainism. Similarly, according to the Prabandhachintámaṇi, Hemáchárya never dared to speak to the king in favour of Jainism but used to say that all religions were good. This statement is supported by the fact that the opening verses of all works written by Hemáchárya in the time of Siddharája contain no special praise of Jain deities.

So great is Siddharája's fame as a builder that almost every old work in Gujarát is ascribed to him. Tradition gives him the credit of the Dabhoi fort which is of the time of the Vághelá king Víradhavala, A.D. 1220-1260. The Prabandhachintámaṇi gives this old verse regarding Siddharája's public works : 'No one makes a great temple (Rudramahálaya), a great pilgrimage (to Somanátha), a great Ásthána (darbár hall), or a great lake (Sahasraliṅga)

Chapter II.
The Chaulukyas, A.D. 961-1242.
Siddharája Jayasingha, A.D. 1094-1143.

such as Siddharája made.'[1] Of these the Rudramahálaya, though very little is left, from its size and the beauty of its carving, must have been a magnificent work the grandest specimen of the architecture of the Solańki period. The remains of the Sahasralińga lake at Aṇahilapura show that it must have been a work of surprising size and richness well deserving its title of *mahásaraḥ* or great lake. Numerous other public works are ascribed to Siddharája.[2]

At this period it seems that the kings of Gujarát Sámbhar and other districts, seeing the great reputation which his literary tastes had gained for Bhoja of Dhárá used all to keep Pandits. Certain carvings on the pillars of a mosque at the south-west of the modern town of Dhárá show that the building almost as it stands was the Sanskrit school founded by Bhoja. The carvings in question are beautifully cut Sanskrit grammar tables. Other inscriptions in praise of Naravarman show that Bhoja's successors continued to maintain the institution. In the floor of the mosque are many large shining slabs of black marble, the largest as much as seven feet long, all of them covered with inscriptions so badly mutilated that nothing can be made out of them except that they were Sanskrit and Prakrit verses in honour of some prince. On a rough estimate the slabs contain as many as 4000 verses.[3] According to the old saying any one who drank of the Sarasvatí well in Dhárá became a scholar. Sarasvatí's well still exists near the mosque. Its water is good and it is still known as Akkal-kui or the Well of Talent. As in Dhárá so in Ajmir the Aṛhái-dinká Jhopḍá mosque is an old Sanskrit school, recent excavations having brought to light slabs with entire dramas carved on them. So also the Gujarát kings had their Pandits and their halls of learning. Śrípála, Siddharája's poet-laureate, wrote a poetical eulogium or *praśasti* on the Sahasralińga lake. According to the Prabandhachintámaṇi Siddharája gathered numerous Pandits to examine the eulogium. As has already been noticed Siddharája's constant companion was the great scholar and Jain *ácharya* Hemachandra also called Hemácharya, who, under the king's patronage, wrote a treatise on grammar called Siddhahema, and also the well-known Dvyáśrayakosha which was intended to teach both grammar and the history of the Solańkis. Hemachandra came into even greater

---

[1] The original verse is महालयो महायात्रा महास्थानं महासरः यत्कृतं सिद्धराजेन क्रियते तन्न केनाचित् ॥

[2] These, as quoted by Ráo Sáheb Mahípatrám Rúprám in his Sadhara Jesangh, are, the erection of charitable feeding-houses every *yojana* or four miles, of Dabhoi fort, of a *kuṇḍa* or reservoir at Kapadvanj, of the Málavya lake at Dholká, of small temples, of the Rudramahálaya, of the Ráni's step-well, of the Sahasralińga lake, of reservoirs at Sihor, of the fort of Sáelá, of the Daśasahasra or ten thousand temples, of the Muṇa lake at Viramgám, of the *gadhs* or forts of Dadharapur Vadhwán Anantapur and Chubári, of the Sardhár lake, of the *gadhs* of Jhinjhuváḍa, Virpur, Bhádula, Vásingapura, and Thán, of the palaces of Kandola and Sihi Jagapura, of the reservoirs of Dedádrá and Kírtti-stambha and of Jitpur-Anantpura. It is doubtful how many of these were actually Siddharája's works.

[3] One of the best preserved slabs was sent by Sir John Malcolm when Resident of Málwa to the Museum of the B. B. R. A. S., where it still lies. It has verses in twelfth century Prakrit in honour of a king, but nothing historical can be made out of it.

Chapter II.
The Chaulukyas, A.D. 961 - 1242.

prominence in the time of Kumárapála, when he wrote several further works and became closely connected with the state religion. Several stories remain of Siddharája assembling poets, and holding literary and poetic discussions.

Siddharája Jayasingha, A.D. 1094 - 1143.

Record is preserved of a *sabhá* or assembly called by the king to hear discussions between a Śvetámbara Jaina *ácharya* named Bhattáraka Devasúri and a Digambara Jaina *áchárya* named Kumudachandra who had come from the Karnáṭak. Devasúri who was living and preaching in the Jain temple of Arishṭanemi at Karṇávatí,[1] that is the modern Ahmadábád, was there visited by Kumudachandra. Devasúri treated his visitor with little respect telling him to go to Patan and he would follow and hold a religious discussion or *váda*. Kumudachandra being a Digambara or skyclad Jaina went naked to Patan and Siddharája honoured him because he came from his mother's country. Siddharája asked Hemachandra to hold a discussion with Kumudachandra and Hemachandra recommended that Devasúri should be invited as a worthy disputant. At a discussion held before a meeting called by the king Kumudachandra was vanquished, probably because the first principle of his Digambara faith that no woman can attain *nirváṇa*, was insulting to the queen-mother, and the second that no clothes-wearing Jain can gain *mukti* or absorption, was an insult to the Jain ministers. The assembly, like Bráhmanical *sabhás* at the present day, appears to have declined into noise and Siddharája had to interfere and keep order. Devasúri was complimented by the king and taken by one Áhada with great honour to his newly built Jaina temple.[2]

Kumárapála, A.D. 1143 - 1174.

In spite of prayers to Somanátha, of incantations, and of gifts to Bráhmans, Siddharája Jayasiṃha had no son. The throne passed into the line of Tribhuvanapála the great-grandson of Bhímadeva I. (A.D. 1074-62) who was ruling as a feudatory of Siddháraja at his ancestral appanage of Dahithalí. Tribhuvanapála's pedigree is Bhímadeva I.; his son Kshemarája by Bakuládeví a concubine; his son Haripála; his son Tribhuvanapála. By his queen Kásmíradeví Tribhuvanapála had three sons Mahípála, Kírttipála, and Kumárapála, and two daughters Premaladeví and Devaladeví. Premaladeví was married to one of Siddharája's nobles a cavalry general named Kánhada or Kṛishṇadeva: Devaladeví was married to Arṇorája[3] or Anarája

---

[1] See above page 170.

[2] Devasúri was born in S. 1134 (A.D. 1078), took *díkshá* in S. 1152 (A.D. 1096), became a Súri in S. 1174 (A.D. 1118), and died on a Thursday in the dark half of Śrávaṇa S. 1226 (A.D. 1170). His famous disciple Hemachandra was born on the fullmoon of Kártika S. 1145 (A.D. 1089), became an ascetic in S. 1150 (A.D. 1094), and died in S. 1229 (A.D. 1173).

[3] The Prákrit local name was Âno, of which the Sanskritised forms would appear to be Arno, Arnava, A'náka, and A'nalla as given in the Hammíramahákavya. The genealogy of these kings of Śákambhari or Sámbhar is not settled. The Nadol copperplate dated Saṃvat 1218 gives the name of its royal grantor as Alan and of Alan's father as Máharája (Tod's Rajásthán, I. 804), the latter apparently a mistake for Anarája which is the name given in the Dvyáśraya. Alan's date being V. 1218, the date of his father A'na would fit in well with the early part of Kumárapála's reign. The order of the two names Álhana and Ánalla in the Hammíramahákávya would seem to be mistaken and ought to be reversed.

Chapter II.
The Chaulukyas, A.D. 961-1242.
Kumárapalá, A.D. 1143-1174.

king of Śákambhari or Sámbhar, the Analladeva of the Hammiramahákávya. Kumárapála himself was married by his father to one Bhupáladeví. According to the Dvyáśraya, Tribhuvanapála was on good terms with Siddharája serving him and going with him to war. The Kumárapálacharita also states that Kumárapála used to attend the court of Siddharája But from the time he came to feel that he would have no son and that the bastard Kumárapála would succeed him Siddharája became embittered against Kumárapála. According to the Jain chronicles Siddharája was told by the god Somanátha, by the sage Hemachandra, by the goddess Ambiká of Kodinár,[1] and by astrologers that he would have no son and that Kumárapála would be his successor. According to the Kumárapálacharita so bitter did his hate grow that Siddharája planned the death of Tribhuvanapála and his family including Kumárapála. Tribhuvanapála was murdered but Kumárapála escaped. Grieved at this proof of the king's hatred Kumárapála consulted his brother-in-law Krishṇadeva who advised him to leave his family at Dahithalí and go into exile promising to keep him informed of what went on at Aṇahilapura. Kumárapála left in the disguise of a *jaṭádhári* or recluse and escaped the assassins whom the king had ordered to slay him. After some time Kumárapála returned and in spite of his disguise was recognized by the guards. They informed the king who invited all the ascetics in the city to a dinner. Kumárapála came but noticing that the king recognized him in spite of his disguise, he fled. The king sent a trusted officer with a small force in pursuit. Kumárapála persuaded some husbandmen, the chief of whom was Bhímasiṃha, to hide him in a heap of thorns. The pursuers failing to find him returned. At night Kumárapála was let out bleeding from the thorns, and promised the husbandmen that the day would come when their help would be rewarded. He then shaved his topknot or *jaṭá* and while travelling met with a lady named Devaśrí of Udambara village who pitying him took him into her chariot and gave him food. Kumárapála promised to regard her as a sister. He then came to Dahithalí where the royal troops had already arrived. Siddharája sent an army which invested the village leaving Kumárapála without means of escape. He went to a potter named Sajjana or Aliṅga who hid him in the flues of his brick-kiln throwing hay over him. The troops searched the village, failed to find Kumárapála, and retired. The potter then helped Kumárapála from his hiding place and fed him. A former friend named Bosari joined Kumárapála and they went away together Kumárapála commending his family to the care of Sajjana. On the first day they had no food. Next day Bosari went to beg and they together ate the food given to Bosari in a monastery or *maṭh* where they slept. In time they came to Cambay where they called upon Hemácharya and asked him their future. Hemácharya knew and recognized Kumárapála. Kumárapála asked when fate would bless him. Before Hemácharya

[1] Kodinár is a town in Gáikwár territory in South Káthiáváḍa. This temple of Ambiká is noticed as a place of Jain pilgrimage by the sage Jinaprabhasúri in his Tírthakalpa and was a well-known Jain shrine during the Anahilaváḍa period.

Chapter II.

THE CHAULUKYAS, A.D. 961-1242.

Kumárapála, A.D. 1143-1174.

could reply Udayana, one of the king's ministers, came. Hemácharya said to Udayana, 'This is Kumárapála who shall shortly be your king.' Hemácharya also gave Kumárapála a writing stating that he would succeed to the throne. Kumárapála acknowledged his obligations to Hemácharya and promised to follow his advice. Udayana took him to his house and gave him food and clothes. Siddharája came to know of this and sent his soldiers who began to search. Kumárapála returned to Hemácharya who hid him in a cellar covering its door with manuscripts and palm leaves. The soldiers came but failed to search under the manuscripts and returned. Kumárapála acknowledged his obligations to Hemácharya and said he owed him two great debts one for telling him the day on which he would come to the throne; the other for saving his life. Kumárapála left Cambay at midnight, the minister Udayana supplying him with provisions. From Cambay he went to Vaṭapadrapura probably Baroda, where feeling hungry he entered the shop of a Vánia named Katuka and asked for parched gram. The Vánia gave the gram and seeing that Kumárapála had no money accepted his promise of future payment. From Baroda he came to Bhrigukachh or Broach where he saw a soothsayer and asked him his future. The soothsayer, seeing the bird *kali-deví* perched on the temple flagstaff, said 'You will shortly be king.' Kumárapála shaved his matted hair and went from Broach to Ujjain where he met his family. But as here too the royal troops followed him he fled to Kolhápura where he came across a Yogí who foretold his succession to a throne and gave him two spells or *manṭras*. From Kolhápura Kumárapála went to Káñchí or Conjeveram and from there to the city of Kálambapattana.[1] The king of Kálambapattana Pratápasiṃha received him like an elder brother and brought him into his city, built a temple of Śivananda Kumárapáleśvara in his honour, and even issued a coin called a Kumárapála. From Kálambapattana Kumárapála went to Chitrakúṭa or Chitor and from there to Ujjain whence he took his family to Siddhapura going on alone to Aṇahilapura to see his brother-in-law Krishṇadeva. According to the Vichárasreṇí Ṣiddharája died soon after in A.D. 1143 on the 3rd of Kárttika Suddha Saṃvat 1199.

In the dissensions that followed the king's death Kumárapála's interests were well served by his brother-in-law Krishṇadeva. Eventually the names of three candidates, Kumárapála and two others, were laid before the state nobles sitting in council to determine who should be king. Of the three candidates the two others were found wanting, and Kumárapála was chosen and installed according to the Vichárasreṇi on the 4th of Márgaśírsha Śuddha and according to the Kumárapálaprabandha on the 4th of Márgaśírsha Vadhya. At the time of his succession, according to the Prabandhachintámaṇi and the Kumárapálaprabandha, Kumárapála was about fifty years of age.

---

[1] The Kumárapálaprabanda has Kelambapattana and Kolambapattana probably Kolam or Quilon.

Chapter II.

THE CHAULUKYAS, A.D. 961-1242.

Kumárapála, A.D. 1143-1174.

On his accession Kumárapála installed his wife Bhopaladeví his anointed queen or *pattaráni*; appointed Udayana who had befriended him at Cambay minister; Báhaḍa or Vágbhaṭa son of Udayana[1] chief councillor or *mahámátya*; and Alinga second councillor or *mahápradhána*. Áhada or Arabhaṭṭa, apparently another son of Udayana, did not acknowledge Kumárapála and went over to Arṇorája Ánáka or Ano king of Sapádalaksha or the Sámbhar territory who is probably the same as the Analladeva of the Hammíramahákávya.[2]

The potter Sajjana was rewarded with a grant of seven hundred villages near Chitrakúṭa or Chitoḍa fort in Rájputána, and the author of the Prabandhachintámaṇi notices that in his time the descendants of the potter ashamed of their origin called themselves descendants of Sagara. Bhímasiṃha who hid Kumárapála in the thorns was appointed head of the bodyguard; Devaśrí made the sister's mark on the royal forehead at the time of Kumárapála's installation and was granted the village of Devayo;[3] and Katuka the Vániá of Baroda, who had given Kumárapála parched gram was granted the village of Vaṭapadra or Baroda. Bosari Kumárapála's chief companion was given Láṭamaṇḍala, which seems to mean that he was appointed viceroy of Láṭa or South Gujarát.

Kanhada or Kṛishṇadeva Kumárapála's brother-in-law and adviser overvaluing his great services became arrogant and disobedient insulting the king in open court. As remonstrance was of no avail the king had Kṛishṇadeva waylaid and beaten by a band of athletes and taken almost dying to his wife the king's sister. From this time all the state officers were careful to show ready obedience.

The old ministry saw that under so capable and well served a ruler their power was gone. They accordingly planned to slay the king and place their own nominee on the throne. The king heard of the plot: secured the assassins: and employed them in murdering the conspirators. According to the Prabandhachintámaṇi, Áhada or Árabhaṭṭa who had gone over to the Sámbhar king and was in charge of the Sámbhar infantry, bribed the local nobles as a preliminary to a war which he had planned against Kumárapála. He so far succeeded as to bring A'na or Ánáka the Sámbhar king with the whole of his army to the borders of Gujarát to fight Kumárapála.[1] Kumárapála went to meet Ánáka. But, in consequence of intrigues, in the battle that followed the Gujarát army did not obey orders. Kumárapála advanced in front on an elephant, and Báhaḍa trying to climb on Kumárapála's elephant was thrown to the ground and slain. Ánáka was also pierced with arrows and the Sámbhar army was defeated and plundered of its horses.[4]

---

[1] The Kumárapálaprabanda says that Udayana was appointed minister and Vágbhata general. Sollá the youngest son of Udayana did not take part in politics.

[2] Kirtane's Hammíramahákavya, 13.

[3] Dhavalakka or Dholká according to the Kumárapálaprabanda.

[4] According to the Kumárapálacharita Kumárapála's sister who was married to A'na having heard her husband speak slightingly of the kings of Gujarát took offence, resented the language, and bandied words with her husband who beat her. She came to her brother and incited him to make an expedition against her husband.

Kumárapála,
A.D. 1143 - 1174.

The Dvyáśraya, probably by the aid of the author's imagination, gives a fuller account of this war. One fact of importance recorded in the Dvyáśraya is that Ánáka though defeated was not slain, and, to bring hostilities to an end, gave his daughter Jalhaná to Kumárapála in marriage. The Kumárapálacharita calls the Sámbhar king Arṇorája and says that it was Kumárapála who invaded the Sámbhar territory. According to this account Kumárapála went to Chandrávatí near Ábu and taking its Paramára king Vikramasimha with him marched to Śákambhari or Sámbhar and fought Árṇorája who was defeated but not killed. Kumárapála threatened to cut out Arṇorája's tongue but let him go on condition that his people wore a headdress with a tongue on each side. Arṇorája is said to have been confined in a cage for three days and then reinstalled as Kumárapála's feudatory. Vikramasimha of Chandrávatí, who in the battle had sided with Arṇorája, was punished by being disgraced before the assembled seventy-two feudatories at Aṇahilaváḍa and was sent to prison, his throne being given to his nephew Yaśodhavala. After his victory over Arṇorája Kumárapála fought, defeated, and, according to the Kírtikaumudí, beheaded Ballála king of Málwa who had invaded Gujarát. The result of this contest seems to have been to reduce Málwa to its former position of dependence on the Aṇahilaváḍa kings. More than one inscription of Kumárapála's found in the temple of Udayáditya as far north as Udayapura near Bhilsa shows that he conquered the whole of Málwa, as the inscriptions are recorded by one who calls himself Kumárapála's general or *daṇḍanáyaka.*

Another of Kumárapála's recorded victories is over Mallikárjuna said to be king of the Konkan who we know from published lists of the North Konkan Śiláháras flourished about A.D. 1160. The author of the Prabandhachintámaṇi says this war arose from a bard of king Mallikárjuna speaking of him before king Kumárapála as *Rájapitámaha* or grandfather of kings.[3] Kumárapála annoyed at so arrogant a title looked around. Ámbaḍá,[4] one of the sons of Udayana, divining the king's meaning, raised his folded hands to his forehead and expressed his readiness to fight Mallikárjuna. The king sent him with an army which marched to the Konkan without halting. At the crossing of the Kalávini[5] it was met and defeated by Mallikárjuna. Ámbaḍá returned in disgrace and shrouding himself his umbrella and his tents in crape retreated to Aṇahilaváḍa. The king finding Ámbada though humiliated ready to make a second venture gave him a larger and better appointed force. With this army Ámbaḍá again started for the Konkan, crossed the Kalávini, attacked Mallikárjuna, and in a hand-to-hand fight

---

[1] The Dvyáśraya does not say that Kumárapála's sister was married to A'na.

[2] This was a common title of the Siláhára kings. Compare Bombay Gazetteer, XIII. 437 note 1.

[3] Ámbada is his proper name. It is found Sanskritised into Ámrabhaṭa and Ambaka.

[4] This is the Káverí river which flows through Chikhli and Balsár. The name in the text is very like Karabená the name of the same river in the Násik cave inscriptions (Bom. Gaz. XVI. 571) Kalaviní and Karabená being Sanskritised forms of the original Káveri. Perhaps the Kaverí is the Akabarou of the Periplus (A.D. 247).

Chapter II.
The Chaulukyas, A.D. 961-1242.
Kumárapála, A.D. 1143-1174.

climbed his elephant and cut off his head. This head cased in gold with other trophies of the war he presented to the king on his triumphant return to Aṇahilápura. The king was greatly pleased and gave Ámbaḍá the title of *Rájapitámaha*. Of this Mallikárjuna two stone inscriptions have been found one at Chiplún dated A.D. 1156 (Śaka 1078) the other at Bassein dated A.D. 1160 (Śaka 1082). If the story that Mallikárjuna was slain is true the war must have taken place during the two years between A.D. 1160 and 1162 (Śaka 1082, 1084) which latter is the earliest known date of Mallikárjuna's successor Aparáditya.

The Kumárapálacharita also records a war between Kumárapála and Samara king of Suráshṭra or south Káthiáváḍa, the Gujarát army being commanded by Kumárapála's minister Udayana. The Prabandhachintámaṇi gives Sausara as the name of the Suráshṭra king[1]: possibly he was some Gohilvád Mehr chief. Udayana came with the army to Vadhwán, and letting it advance went to Pálitána. While he was worshipping at Pálitána, a mouse carried away the burning wick of the lamp. Reflecting on the risk of fire in a wooden temple Udayana determined to rebuild the temple of stone. In the fight with Sausara the Gujarát army was defeated and Udayana was mortally wounded.[2] Before Udayana died he told his sons that he had meant to repair the temple of Ádíśvara on Śatruñjaya and the Śakuniká Vihára at Broach and also to build steps up the west face of Girnár. His sons Báhaḍa and Ámbaḍá promised to repair the two shrines. Subsequently both shrines were restored, Kumárapála and Hemáchárya and the council of Aṇahilapura attending at the installation of Suvṛittinátha in the Śakuniká Vihára. The Girnár steps were also cut, according to more than one inscription in A.D. 1166 (S. 1222).[3] This war and Udayana's death must have occurred about A.D. 1149 (S. 1205) as the temple of Ádnátha was finished in A.D. 1156-57 (S. 1211). Báhaḍa also established near Satruñjaya a town called Báhaḍapura and adorned it with a temple called Tribhuvanapálavasati.[4] After the fight with Sausara Kumárapála was threatened with another war by Karṇa[5] king of Dáhala or Chedi. Spies informed the king of the

[1] Sausara or Sásar seems the original form from which Samara was Sanskritised. Sásar corresponds with the Mehr name Cháchar.

[2] The Kumárapálacharita says that Samara was defeated and his son placed on the throne.

[3] The translation of the inscription runs: Steps made by the venerable A'mbaka, Samvat 1222. According to the Kumárapálaprabandha the steps were built at a cost of a lákh of *drammas* a *dramma* being of the value of about 5 *annas*. According to the Prabandachintamaṇi an earthquake occurred when the king was at Girnár on his way to Somanátha. The old ascent of Girnár was from the north called *Chhatraśilá* that is the umbrella or overhanging rocks. Hemáchárya said if two persons went up together the *Chhatraśilá* rocks would fall and crush them. So the king ordered A'mrabhaṭṭa to build steps on the west or Junágaḍh face at a cost of 63 *lákhs* of *drammas*.

[4] The site of Báhaḍapura seems to be the ruins close to the east of Pálitána where large quantities of conch shell bangles and pieces of brick and tile have been found.

[5] This would appear to be the Kalachuri king Gayá Karṇa whose inscription is dated 902 of the Chedi era that is A.D. 1152. As the earliest known inscription of Gayá Karṇa's son Narasiṃhadeva is dated A.D. 1157 (Chedi 907) the death of Gayá Karṇa falls between A.D. 1152 and 1157 in the reign of Kumárapála and the story of his being accidentally strangled may be true.

impending invasion as he was starting on a pilgrimage to Somanátha. Next day he was relieved from anxiety by the news that while sleeping on an elephant at night king Karṇa's necklace became entangled in the branch of a banyan tree, and the elephant suddenly running away, the king was strangled.

The Prabandhachintámaṇi records an expedition against Sámbhar which was entrusted to Cháhaḍa a younger brother of Báhaḍa. Though Cháhaḍa was known to be extravagant, the king liked him, and after giving him advice placed him in command. On reaching Sámbhar Cháhaḍa invested the fort of Bábránagar but did not molest the people as on that day 700 brides had to be married.[1] Next day the fort was entered, the city was plundered, and the supremacy of Kumárapála was proclaimed. This Bábránagar has not been identified. There appears to be some confusion and the place may not be in Sámbhar but in Bábariáváda in Káthiáváḍa. Cháhaḍa returned triumphant to Patan. The king expressed himself pleased but blamed Cháhaḍa for his lavish expenditure and conferred on him the title of *Rája-gharatta* the King-grinder.

Though the Gujarát chronicles give no further details an inscription in the name of Kumárapála in a temple at Udepur near Bhilsa dated A.D. 1166 records that on Monday, *Akshaya tritiyá* the 3rd of Vaiśákh Sud (S. 1222), Thakkara Cháhaḍa granted half the village of Sangaváḍa in the Rangáriká district or *bhukti*. Just below this inscription is a second also bearing the name of Kumárapála. The year is lost. But the occasion is said to be an eclipse on Thursday the 15th of Paush Sudi when a gift was made to the god of Udayapura by Yaśodhavala the viceroy of Kumárapála.[2]

---

[1] So many marriages on one day points to the people being either Kaḍva Kunbis or Bharváḍs among whom the custom of holding all marriages on the same day still prevails.

[2] The text of the inscription is:

(1) ······पौषसुदीगुरौ अद्येह श्रीमदण-

(2) हिलपाटके [समस्त] राजावलीविराजितपरमभट्टारकमहा-

(3) [राजाधिराजनिर्जित] साकंभरीभूपालश्रीमदवन्तिनाथश्रीमत्कु

(4) [मारपाल] ······नियुक्तमहामात्यश्रीजसोधव—

(5) ल श्रीकरणादौ समस्तमुद्राव्यापारान्परिपन्थयतीत्येवं

(6) काले [प्रवर्तमाने महाराजा] धिराजश्रीकुमारपालदेवेन विज

(7) ·········श्रीमदुदयपुरो ···रोचकान्वये महाराज—

(8) पुत्र ·········महाराजपुत्रवसन्तपाल एवं अन

(9) ·········लिखिता याञा । अद्य सोमग्रहणपर्वणि

(10) ······लयवने समाहततीर्थोदके स्नात्वा जगद्गु

(11) ····· सुखपुण्यजयवृद्धये उदयपुरकारि

(12) ············कारापित देवश्री················

Lines broken below.

Similar inscriptions of Kumárapála's time and giving his name occur near the ruined town of Kerádu or Kiráṭa-Kúpa near Bálmer in Western Rájputána. The inscriptions show that Kumárapála had another *Amátya* or minister there, and that the kings of the country round Kerádu had been subject to Gujarát since the time of Siddharája Jayasimha. Finally the inscription of Kumárapála found by Colonel Tod in a temple of Brahma on the pinnacle of Chitoḍa fort[1] shows that his conquests extended as far as Mewáḍa.

According to the Kumárapálachintámaṇi Kumárapála married one Padmávatí of Padmapura. The chronicler describes the city as to the west of the Indus. Perhaps the lady belonged to Padmapura a large town in Kashmír. Considering his greatness as a king and conqueror the historical record of Kumárapála is meagre and incomplete. Materials may still come to light which will show his power to have been surprisingly widespread.

Mr. Forbes[2] records the following Bráhmanical tradition of a Mewáḍa queen of Kumárapála, which has probably been intentionally omitted by the Jain chroniclers.

Kumárapála, says the Bráhman tradition, had wedded a Sisodaní Ráni, a daughter of the house of Mewáḍa. At the time that the sword went for her the Sisodaní heard that the Rája had made a vow that his wives should receive initiation into the Jain religion at Hemácharya's convent before entering the palace. The Ráni refused to start for Patan until she was satisfied she would not be called on to visit the Ácharya's convent. Jayadeva Kumárapála's household bard became surety and the queen consented to go to Aṇahilapura. Several days after her arrival Hemácharya said to the Rája 'The Sisodaní Ráni has never come to visit me.' Kumárapála told her she must go. The Ráni refused and fell ill, and the bard's wives went to see her. Hearing her story they disguised her as one of themselves and brought her privately home to their house. At night the bard dug a hole in the wall of the city, and taking the Ráni through the hole started with her for Mewáḍa. When Kumárapála became aware of the Ráni's flight he set off in pursuit with two thousand horse. He came up with the fugitives about fifteen miles from the fort of Idar. The bard said to the Ráni, 'If you can enter Idar you are safe. I have two hundred horse with me. As long as a man of us remains no one shall lay hands on you.' So saying he turned upon his pursuers. But the Ráni's courage failed and she slew herself in the carriage. As the fight went on and the pursuers forced their way to the carriage, the maids cried 'Why struggle more, the Ráni is dead.' Kumárapála and his men returned home.[3]

The Paramára chiefs of Chandrávatí near A'bu were also feudatories of Kumárapála. It has been noted that to punish him for siding with Arṇorája of Sámbhar Kumárapála placed Vikrama Siṃha the Chandrávatí chief in confinement and set Vikrama's

---

[1] Annals of Rájasthán, I. 803.
[2] Rás Málá (New Edition), 154.
[3] Rás Málá (New Edition), 154.

Chapter II.

THE CHAULUKYAS, A.D. 961 - 1242.

Kumárapála, A.D. 1143 - 1174.

nephew Yaśodhavala on his throne. That Kumárapála conquered the chiefs of Sámbhar and Málwa is beyond question. Among his names is the proud title Avantí-nátha Lord of Málwa.

The Kumárapálaprabandha gives the following limits of Kumárapála's sway. The Turushkas or Turks on the north; the heavenly Ganges on the east; the Vindhya mountains on the south; the Sindhu river on the west.[1] Though in tradition Kumárapála's name does not stand so high as a builder as the name of Siddharája Jayasiṃha he carried out several important works. The chief of these was the restoring and rebuilding of the great shrine of Someśvara or Somanátha Patan. According to the Prabandhachintámaṇi when Kumárapála asked Devasúri the teacher of Hemácharya how best to keep his name remembered Devasúri replied: Build a new temple of Somanátha fit to last an age or *yuga*, instead of the wooden one which is ruined by the ocean billows. Kumárapála approved and appointed a building committee or *pañchakula* headed by a Bráhman named Gaṇḍa Bháva Bṛihaspati the state officer at Somanátha. At the instance of Hemácharya the king on hearing the foundations were laid vowed until the temple was finished he would keep apart from women and would take neither flesh nor wine. In proof of his vow he poured a handful of water over Nílakaṇṭha Mahádeva, probably his own royal god. After two years the temple was completed and the flag hoisted. Hemácharya advised the king not to break his vow until he had visited the new temple and paid his obeisance to the god. The king agreed and went to Somanátha, Hemácharya preceding him on foot and promising to come to Somanátha after visiting Satruñjaya and Girnár. On reaching Somanátha the king was received by Gaṇḍa-Bṛihaspati his head local officer and by the building committee, and was taken in state through the town. At the steps of the temple the king bowed his head to the ground. Under the directions of Gaṇḍa-Bṛihaspati he worshipped the god, made gifts of elephants and other costly articles including his own weight in coin, and returned to Aṇahilapura.

It is interesting to know that the present battered sea-shore temple of Somanátha, whose *garbhágára* or shrine has been turned into a mosque and whose spire has been shattered, is the temple of whose building and consecration the above details are preserved. This is shown by the style of the architecture and sculpture which is in complete agreement with the other buildings of the time of Kumárapála.[2]

---

[1] The text is: यः कौबेरीमा तुरुष्कमैन्द्रीमा त्रिदिवापगां
याम्यामा विन्ध्यमा सिन्धुं पश्चिमां यो ह्यसाधयत्

[2] It is also interesting, if there is a foundation of fact to the tale, that this is the temple visited by the Persian poet Saádi (A.D. 1200 - 1230) when he saw the ivory idol of Somanátha whose arms were raised by a hidden priest pulling a cord. According to Saádi on pretence of conversion he was admitted behind the shrine, discovered the cord-puller, threw him into a well, and fled. Compare Journal Royal Asiatic Society Bengal VII.-2 pages 885 - 886. That Saádi ever visited Somanátha is doubtful. No ivory human image can ever have been the chief object of worship at Somanátha.

Chapter II.
The Chaulukyas, A.D. 961-1242.
Kumárapála, A.D. 1143-1174.

Kumárapála's temple seems to have suffered in every subsequent Muhammadan invasion, in Alaf Khan's in A.D. 1300, in Mozaffar's in A.D. 1390, in Mahmúd Begada's about A.D. 1490, and in Muzaffar II.'s about A.D. 1530. Time after time no sooner had the invader passed than the work of repair began afresh. One of the most notable restorations was by Khengár IV. (A.D. 1279-1333) a Chudásamá king of Junágaḍh who is mentioned in two Girnár inscriptions as the repairer of Somanátha after its desecration by Ala-ud-din Khilji. The latest sacrilege, including the turning of the temple into a mosque, was in the time of the Ahmadábád king Muzaffar Sháh II. (A.D. 1511-1535). Since then no attempt has been made to win back the god into his old home.

In the side wall near the door of the little shrine of Bhadrakáli in Patan a broken stone inscription gives interesting details of the temple of Somanátha. Except that the right hand corners of some of the lines are broken, the inscription is clear and well preserved. It is dated A.D. 1169 (Valabhi 850). It records that the temple of the god Somcśa was first of gold built by Soma; next it was of silver built by Rávana; afterwards of wood built by Krishna; and last of stone built by Bhímadeva. The next restoration was through Gaṇḍa-Bṛihaspati under Kumárapála. Of Gaṇḍa-Bṛihaspati it gives these details. He was a Kanyákubja or Kanoj Bráhman of the Pás'upata school, a teacher of the Málwa kings, and a friend of Siddharája Jayasiṃha. He repaired several other temples and founded several other religious buildings in Somanátha. He also repaired the temple of Kedáres'vara in Kumaon on learning that the Khas'a king of that country had allowed it to fall into disrepair. After the time of Kumárapála the descendants of Gaṇḍa-Bṛihaspati remained in religious authority in Somanátha.

Kumárapála made many Jain benefactions.[1] He repaired the temple of Ságala-Vasahiká at Stambha-tírtha or Cambay where Hemácharya received his initiation or *díkshá*. In honour of the lady who gave him barley flour and curds he built a temple called the Karambaka-Vihára in Patan. He also built in Patan a temple called the Mouse or Mushaka-Vihára to free himself from the impurity caused by killing a mouse while digging for treasure. At Dhandhuka Hemácharya's birthplace a temple called the Jholiká-Vihára or cradle temple was built. Besides these Kumárapála is credited with building 1444 temples.

Though Kumárapála was not a learned man, his ministers were men of learning, and he continued the practice of keeping at his court scholars especially Sanskrit poets. Two of his leading Pandits were Rámachandra and Udayachandra both of them Jains. Rámachandra is often mentioned in Gujaráti literature and appears to have been a great scholar. He was the author of a book called the Hundred Accounts or Prabandhas'ata. After Udayana's death Kumárapála's chief minister was Kapardi a man of learning skilled in Sanskrit poetry. And all through his reign his principal adviser

[1] From the Prabandhachintámaṇi and the Kumárapálacharita.

Chapter II.

THE CHAULUKYAS, A.D. 961-1242.

Kumárapála, A.D. 1143-1174.

was Hemachandra or Hemácharya probably the most learned man of his time. Though Hemácharya lived during the reigns both of Siddharája and of Kumárapála, only under Kumárapála did he enjoy political power as the king's companion and religious adviser. What record remains of the early Solankis is chiefly due to Hemachandra.

The Jain life of Hemácharya abounds in wonders. Apart from the magic and mystic elements the chief details are: Cháchiga a Modh Vánia of Dhandhuka[1] in the district of Ardháshṭama had by his wife Páhiní[2] of the Chámuṇḍa *gotra*, a boy named Chángodeva who was born A.D. 1089 (Kartik fullmoon Saṃvat 1145). A Jain priest named Devachandra A'chárya (A.D. 1078-1170; S. 1134-1226) came from Patan to Dhandhuka and when in Dhandhuka went to pay his obeisance at the Modh Vasahiká. While Devachandra was seated Chángodeva came playing with other boys and went and sat beside the *ácharya*. Struck with the boy's audacity and good looks the *ácharya* went with the council of the village to Cháchiga's house. Cháchiga was absent but his wife being a Jain received the *ácharya* with respect. When she heard that her son was wanted by the council, without waiting to consult her husband, she handed the boy to the *ácharya* who carried him off to Karṇávatí and kept him there with the sons of the minister Udayana. Cháchiga, disconsolate at the loss of his son, went in quest of him vowing to eat nothing till the boy was found. He came to Karṇávatí and in an angry mood called on the *ácharya* to restore him his son. Udayana was asked to interfere and at last persuaded Cháchiga to let the boy stay with Devachandra.

In A.D. 1097, when Chángodeva was eight years old Cháchiga celebrated his son's consecration or *díkshá* and gave him the name of Somachandra. As the boy became extremely learned Devachandra changed his name to Hemachandra the Moon of gold. In A.D. 1110 (S. 1166) at the age of 21, his mastery of all the S'ástras and Siddhántas was rewarded by the dignity of Súri or sage. Siddharája was struck with his conversation and honoured him as a man of learning. Hemachandra's knowledge wisdom and tact enabled him to adhere openly to his Jain rules and beliefs though Siddharája's dislike of Jain practices was so great as at times to amount to insult. After one of their quarrels Hemácharya kept away from the king for two or three days. Then the king seeing his humility and his devotion to his faith repented and apologised. The two went together to Somanátha Patan and there Hemácharya paid his obeisance to the *linga* in a way that did not offend his own faith. During Siddharája's reign Hemácharya wrote his well known grammar with aphorisms or *sútras* and commentary or *vṛitti* called Siddha-Hemachandra, a title compounded of the king's name and his own. As the Bráhmans found fault with the absence of any detailed references to the king in the work Hemachandra

[1] The head-quarters of the Dhandhuka sub-division sixty miles south-west of Ahmadábád.

[2] Another reading is Láhiní.

Chapter II.
THE CHAULUKYAS, A.D. 961-1242.
Kumárapála, A.D. 1143-1174.

added one verse at the end of each chapter in praise of the king. During Siddharája's reign he also wrote two other works, the Haimínámamálá "String of Names composed by Hema(chandra)" or Abhidhánachintámaṇi and the Anekárthanámamálá a Collection of words of more than one meaning. He also began the Dvyás'rayakosha[1] or Double Dictionary being both a grammar and a history. In spite of his value to Kumárapála, in the beginning of Kumárapála's reign Hemácharya was not honoured as a spiritual guide and had to remain subordinate to Bráhmans. When Kumárapála asked him what was the most important religious work he could perform Hemácharya advised the restoring of the temple of Somanátha. Still Hemácharya so far won the king to his own faith that till the completion of the temple he succeeded in persuading the king to take the vow of *ahiṁsá* or non-killing which though common to both faiths is a specially Jain observance. Seeing this mark of his ascendancy over the king, the king's family priest and other Bráhmans began to envy and thwart Hemácharya. On the completion of the temple, when the king was starting for Somanátha for the installation ceremony, the Bráhmans told him that Hemácharya did not mean to go with him. Hemácharya who had heard of the plot had already accepted the invitation. He said being a recluse he must go on foot, and that he also wanted to visit Girnár, and from Girnár would join the king at Somanátha. His object was to avoid travelling in a palanquin with the king or suffering a repetition of Siddharája's insult for not accepting a *pálkí*. Soon after reaching Somanátha Kumárapála asked after Hemácharya. The Bráhmans spread a story that he had been drowned, but Hemácharya was careful to appear in the temple as the king reached it. The king saw him, called him, and took him with him to the temple. Some Bráhmans told the king that the Jain priest would not pay any obeisance to Siva, but Hemácharya saluted the god in the following verse in which was nothing contrary to strict Jainism: 'Salutation to him, whether he be Brahma, Vishnu, Hara, or Jina, from whom have fled desires which produce the sprouts of the seed of worldliness.'[2] After this joint visit to Somanátha Hemachandra gained still more ascendancy over the king, who appreciated his calmness of mind and his forbearance. The Bráhmans tried to prevent the growth of his influence, but in the end Hemachandra overcame them. He induced the king to place in the sight of his Bráhmanical family priests an image of S'ántinátha Tírthaṅkara among his family gods. He afterwards persuaded Kumárapála publicly to adopt the Jain faith by going to the hermitage of Hemachandra and giving

---

[1] Prabandhachintamaṇi.

[2] भवबीजाङ्कुरजनना रागाद्याः क्षयमुपागता यस्य ।
ब्रह्मा वा विष्णुर्वा हरो जिनो वा नमस्तस्मै ॥
यत्र तत्र समये यथा तथा योऽसि सोऽस्यभिधया यया तया ।
वीतदोषकलुषः स चेद्भवानेक एव भगवन्नमोऽस्तु ते ॥

numerous presents to Jain ascetics. Finally under his influence Kumárapála put away all Bráhmanical images from his family place of worship. Having gone such lengths Kumárapála began to punish the Bráhmans who insulted Hemachandra. A Bráhman named Vámarás'i, a Pandit at the royal court, who composed a verse insulting Hemachandra, lost his annuity and was reduced to beggary, but on apologising to Hemachandra the annuity was restored. Another Bráhmanical officer named Bháva Brihaspati, who was stationed at Somanátha, was re-called for insulting Hemachandra. But he too on apologising to Hemachandra was restored to Somanátha. Under Hemachandra's influence Kumárapála gave up the use of flesh and wine, ceased to take pleasure in the chase, and by beat of drum forbade throughout his kingdom the taking of animal life. He withdrew their licenses from hunters fowlers and fishermen, and forced them to adopt other callings. To what lengths this dread of life-taking was carried appears from an order that only filtered water was to be given to all animals employed in the royal army. Among the stories told of the king's zeal for life-saving is one of a Bania of Sámbhar who having been caught killing a louse was brought in chains to Aṇahilaváḍa, and had his property confiscated and devoted to the building at Aṇahilaváḍa of a Louse Temple or Yúká-Vihára. According to another story a man of Nador in Márwár was put to death by Kelhana the chief of Nador to appease Kumárapála's wrath at hearing that the man's wife had offered flesh to a field-god or *kshetrapála*. Hemachandra also induced the king to forego the claim of the state to the property of those who died without a son.

Chapter II.

The Chaulukyas, A.D. 961-1244.

Kumárapála, A.D. 1143-1174.

During Kumárapála's reign Hemachandra wrote many well known Sanskrit and Prakrit works on literature and religion. Among these are the Adhyátmopanishad or Yogaśástra a work of 12,000 verses in twelve chapters called Prakáśas, the Trisáshṭhisálákápurushacharitra or lives of sixty-three Jain saints of the Utsarpiní and Avasarpiní ages; the Pariśishṭaparvan, a work of 3500 verses being the life of Jain Sthaviras who flourished after Mahávíra; the Prákṛita S'abdánus'ásana or Prákrit grammar; the Dvyáśraya[1] a Prakrit poem written with the double object of teaching grammar and of giving the history of Kumárapála; the Chhandonuśásana a work of about 6000 verses on prosody; the Lingánuśásana a work on genders; the Deśínámamálá in Prakrit with a commentary a work on local and provincial words; and the Alaṅkárachúḍámaṇi a work on rhetoric. Hemachandra died in A.D. 1172 (S. 1229) at the age of 84. The king greatly mourned his loss and marked his brow with Hemachandra's ashes. Such crowds came to share in the ashes of the pyre that the ground was hollowed into a pit known as the Haima-Khadda or Hema's Pit.

Kumárapála lived to a great age. According to the author of the Prabandhachintámaṇi he was fifty when he succeeded to the

[1] संवत् १२२९ वैशाखशुदि ३ सोमे अद्येह श्रीमदणहिल्लपाटके समस्तराजावलीविराजितमहाराजाधिराजपरमेश्वर अजयपालदेवकल्याणविजयराज्ये तत्पादपद्मोपजीविनि महामात्यश्रीसोमेश्वरे श्रीकरणादौ.

Chapter II.
The Chaulukyas, A.D. 961-1242.
Kumárapála, A.D. 1143-1174.

throne, and after ruling about thirty-one years died in A.D. 1174 (S. 1230). He is said to have died of *lúta* a form of leprosy. Another story given by the Kumárapálaprabandha is that Kumárapála was imprisoned by his nephew and successor Ajayapála. The Kumárapálaprabandha gives the exact length of Kumárapála's reign at 30 years 8 months and 27 days. If the beginning of Kumárapála's reign is placed at the 4th Magsar Sud Saṃvat 1199, the date of the close, taking the year to begin in Kártika, would be Bhádrapada S'uddha Saṃvat 1229. If with Gujarát almanacs the year is taken to begin in Áshádha, the date of the close of the reign would be Bhádrapada of Saṃvat 1230. It is doubtful whether either Saṃvat 1229 or 1230 is the correct year, as an inscription dated Saṃvat 1229 Vaishákha S'uddha 3rd at Udayapura near Bhilsá describes Ajayapála Kumárapála's successor as reigning at Aṇahilapura. This would place Kumárapála's death before the month of Vaishakha 1229 that is in A.D. 1173.[1]

Ajayapála, A.D. 1174-1177.

As Kumárapála had no son he was succeeded by Ajayapála the son of his brother Mahípála.[2] According to the Kumárapálaprabandha Kumárapála desired to give the throne to his daughter's son Pratápamalla, but Ajayapála raised a revolt and got rid of Kumárapála by poison. The Jain chroniclers say nothing of the reign of Ajayapála because he was not a follower of their religion. The author of the Sukṛitasaṅkírtana notices a small silver canopy or pavilion shown in Ajayapála's court as a feudatory's gift from the king of Sapádalaksha[3] or Sewálik. The author of the Kírtikaumudí dismisses Ajayapála with the mere mention of his name, and does not even state his relationship with Kumárapála. According to the Prabandhachintamaṇi Ajayapála destroyed the Jain temples built by his uncle. He showed no favour to Ámbaḍá and Kumárapála's other Jain ministers. Ajayapála seems to have been of a cruel and overbearing temper. He appointed as his minister Kapardi because he was of the Bráhmanical faith.[4] But considering his manners arrogant he ordered him to be thrown into a caldron of boiling oil. On another occasion he ordered the Jain scholar Rámachandra to sit on a red-hot sheet of copper. One of his nobles Ámra-bhaṭa or Ámbaḍá refused to submit to

---

[1] Regarding the remarkable story that not long before their deaths both Hemáchárya and Kumárapála inclined towards if they did not become converts to Islam (Tod's Western India, 184) no fresh information has been obtained. Another curious saying of Tod's (Ditto, 182) also remains doubtful. Kumárapála expelled the tribe of Lár from his kingdom. That this tribe of Lár can have had to do either with Láta or South Gujarát or with the caste of Lád Vánis seems unlikely. The alternative is Pársis from Lar on the Persian Gulf whom Tod (Annals of Rajasthán, I. 235) notices as sending an expedition from Laristhán to Gujarát. In this connection it is worthy of note that Lár remained the seat of a Gueber prince till A.D. 1600 the time of Shah Abas (D'Herbelot Bib. Or. II. 477). A repetition of the Pársi riots (Cambay Gazetteer, VI. 215) may have been the cause of their expulsion from Gujarát.

[2] See the Dvyáśraya. A Patan inscription lying at Verával also calls Ajayapála the brother's son of Kumáraspála.

[3] It is stated in a grant of Bhíma II. dated S. 1283, that Ajayadeva, as he is there called, made the Sapádalaksha or Sámbhar king tributary. Ind. Ant. VI. 199ff.

[4] The Udayapura inscription mentions Someśvara as the minister of Ajayapála in Saṃvat 1229 (A.D. 1173). See above page 193.

Chapter II.
The Chaulukyas, A.D. 961 - 1242.

the king, saying that he would pay obeisance only to Vítarája or Tírthaṅkara as god, to Hemachandra as guide, and to Kumárapála as king. Ajayapála ordered the matter to be settled by a fight. Ambaḍá brought some of his followers to the drum-house near the gate, and in the fight that followed Ámbaḍá was killed. In A.D. 1177 (S. 1233), after a short reign of three years, Ajayapála was slain by a doorkeeper named Vijjaladeva who plunged a dagger into the king's heart.[1]

Múlarája II. A.D. 1177 - 1179.

Ajayapála was succeeded by his son Múlarája II. also called Bála Múlarája as he was only a boy when installed. His mother was Náikídeví the daughter of Paramardi, apparently the Kádamba king Permádi or Siva Chitta who reigned from A.D. 1147 to 1175 (S. 1203 - 1231).[2] The authors of the Kírtikaumudí[3] and the Sukṛitasankírtaṇa say that even in childhood Múlarája II. dispersed the Turushka or Muhammadan army.[4] The Prabandhachintámaṇi states that the king's mother fought at the Gádarárághatta and that her victory was due to a sudden fall of rain. Múlarája II. is said to have died in A.D. 1179 (S. 1235) after a reign of two years.

Múlarája II. was succeeded by Bhíma II. The relationship of the two is not clearly established. Mr. Forbes makes Bhíma the younger brother of Ajayapála. But it appears from the Kírtikaumudí and the Sukṛitasankírtana that Bhíma was the younger brother of Múlarája. The Sukṛitasankírtana after concluding the account of Múlarája,[5] calls Bhíma '*asya bandhu*' 'his brother,' and the Kírtikaumudí, after mentioning the death of Múlarája, says that Bhíma his younger brother '*anujanmásya*' became king.[6]

---

[1] The abuse of Ajayapála is explained if Tod's statement (Western India, 191) that he became a Musalmán is correct.

[2] Fleet's Kánarese Dynasties, 93. [3] Chapter II. Verse 57.

[4] We know much less about this event than its importance deserves, for with the exception of a raid made in A.D. 1197 by one of the Ghorí generals this victory secured Gujarát from any serious Muhammadan attack for more than a century. We learn from various grants made by Bhímadeva II. (Ind. Ant VI. 195, 198, 200, 201) that Múlarája's regular epithet in the *Vaṃśávalí* was "He who overcame in battle the ruler of the Garjjanakas, who are hard to defeat": and Dr. Bühler has pointed out (Ditto, 201) that Garjjanaka is a Sanskritising of the name Ghaznavi. As a matter of fact, however, the leader of the Musalmán army was Muhammad of Ghor, and the battle took place in A.D. 1178 (H. 574). One of the two Muhammadan writers who mentions the invasion (Muhammad 'Ufí, who wrote at Delhi about A.D. 1211) says that Muhammad was at first defeated, but invaded the country a second time two years later "and punished the people for their previous misconduct." But this is only mentioned incidentally as part of an anecdote of Muhammad's equity, and there is some confusion with Muhammad's victory in the second battle of Náráyan (in Jaipur territory) in A.D. 1192, as a better, though slightly later authority, Minháj-us Siráj, speaks of no second expedition to Gujarát led by Muhammad himself. Minháj-us-Siráj's account of the defeat is as follows (Elliott, II. 294): He (Muhammad) conducted his army by way of Uch and Multán towards Nahrwálá. The Rái of Nahrwálá, Bhímdeo, was a minor, but he had a large army and many elephants. In the day of battle the Muhammadans were defeated and the Sultán was compelled to retreat. This happened in the year 574 H. (1178 A.D.)". Further on we read (Elliott, II. 300): "In 593 H. (1197 A.D.) he (Muhammad's general Kutb-ud-din) went towards Nahrwálá, defeated Rái Bhímdeo, and took revenge on the part of the Sultán." As no conquest of the country is spoken of, this expedition was evidently a mere raid. The only inaccuracy in the account is the mention of Bhíma instead of Múlarája as the king who defeated the first invasion.—(A. M. T. J.)

[5] Sarga II. Verse 47. [6] Sarga II. Verse 60.

Chapter II.
THE CHAULUKYAS, A.D. 961-1242.
Bhíma II. A.D. 1179-1242.

Múlarája we know came to the throne as a child. Of Bhíma also the Kírtikaumudí says that he came to the throne while still in his childhood, and this agrees with the statements that he was the younger brother of Múlarája. Bhíma probably came to the throne in A.D. 1178 (S. 1234). There is no doubt he was reigning in A.D. 1179 (S. 1235), as an inscription in the deserted village of Kerálu near Bálmer of Aṇahilaváḍa dated A.D. 1179 (S. 1235) states that it was written 'in the triumphant reign of the illustrious Bhímadeva.'[1] A further proof of his reigning in A.D. 1179 (S. 1235) and of his being a minor at that time is given in the following passage from the Tabakát-i-Násirí: In A.D. 1178 (Hijri 574) the Ráí of Nahrwálá Bhímdeo, was a minor, but he had a large army and many elephants. In the day of battle the Muhammadans were defeated and the Sultán was compelled to retreat.[2] Merutuṅga says that Bhíma reigned from A.D. 1179 (S. 1235) for sixty-three years that is up to A.D. 1242 (S. 1298), and this is borne out by a copperplate of Bhíma which bears date A.D. 1240 (S. 1296[3] Márgha Vadi 14th Sunday[4]).

Bhíma was nicknamed Bholo the Simpleton. The chroniclers of this period mention only the Vághelás and almost pass over Bhíma. The author of the Kírtikaumudí says 'the kingdom of the young ruler was gradually divided among powerful ministers and provincial chiefs'; and according to the Sukṛitasankírtana 'Bhíma felt great anxiety on account of the chiefs who had forcibly eaten away portions of the kingdom.' It appears that during the minority, when the central authority was weak, the kingdom was divided among nobles and feudatories, and that Bhíma proved too weak a ruler to restore the kingly power. Manuscripts and copperplates show that Bhímadeva was ruling at Aṇahilaváḍa in S. 1247, 1251, 1261, 1263, and 1264,[5] and copperplates dated S. 1283, 1888, 1295, and 1296 have also been found. Though Bhíma in name enjoyed a long unbroken reign the verses quoted above show that power rested not with the king but with the nobles. It appears from an inscription that in A.D. 1224 (S. 1280) a Chálukya noble named Jayantasiṃha was supreme at Aṇahilaváḍa though he mentions Bhíma and his predecessors with honour and respect.[6]

It was probably by aiding Bhíma against Jayantasiṃha that the Vághelás rose to power. According to the chroniclers the Vághelás succeeded in the natural course of things. According to the Sukṛitasankírtana Kumárapála appeared to his grandson Bhíma and directed him to appoint as his heir-apparent Víradhavala son of Lavanaprasáda and grandson of Arṇorája the son of Dhavala king of Bhímapallí. Next day in court, in the presence of his nobles, when Lavanaprasáda and Víradhavala entered the king said to

---

[1] The Vichárasreṇi also gives S. 1235 as the beginning of his reign.

[2] Elliot's History of India, II. 294. This event properly belongs to the reign of Múlarája. See above page 195 note 5.

[3] Ind. Ant. VI. 207.

[4] Chapter II. Verse 61.

[5] Kielhorn's and Peterson's Reports on Sanskrit Manuscripts.

[6] Ind. Ant. VI. 197.

Lavanaprasáda: Your father Arṇorája seated me on the throne: you should therefore uphold my power: in return I will name your son Víradhavala my heir-apparent.[1] The author of the Kírtikaumudí notes that Arṇorája son of Dhavala, opposing the revolution against Bhíma, cleared the kingdom of enemies, but at the cost of his own life. The author then describes Lavanaprasáda and Víradhavala as kings. But as he gives no account of their rise to supremacy, it seems probable that they usurped the actual power from Bhíma though till A.D. 1242 (S. 1295) Bhíma continued to be nominal sovereign.

Bhíma's queen was Líládeví the daughter of a Chohán chief named Samarasiṃha.[2]

---

[1] The text is दत्त्वास्मै दोष्यते युवराज्यं राज्यं चिरं कुरु.

[2] The text is चाहू राण that is चाहुमाण राणक. The term Ráṇaka would show him to be a Chohán chief.

CHAPTER III.

THE VÁGHELÁS

(A.D. 1219–1304).

Chapter III.

The Vághelás, A.D. 1219-1304.

Arṇorája, A.D. 1170-1200.

While Bhímadeva II. (A.D. 1178-1241) struggled to maintain his authority in the north, the country between the Sábarmatí and the Narbadá in the south as well as the districts of Dholká and Dhandhuká in the south-west passed to the Vághelás a branch of the Solaṅkis sprung from Ánáka or Arṇorája, the son of the sister of Kumárapála's (A.D. 1143-1173) mother. In return for services to Kumárapála,[1] Ánáka, with the rank of a noble or Sámanta, had received the village of Vyághrapalli or Vághelá, the Tiger's Lair, about ten miles south-west of Aṇahilaváḍa. It is from this village that the dynasty takes its name of Vághela.

Lavaṇaprasáda, A.D. 1200-1233.

Ánáka's son Lavaṇaprasáda, who is mentioned as a minister of Bhímadeva II. (A.D. 1179-1242)[2] held Vághelá and probably Dhavalagadha or Dholká about thirty miles to the south-west. The Kírtikaumudí or Moonlight of Glory, the chief cotemporary chronicle,[3] describes Lavaṇaprasáda as a brave warrior, the slayer of the chief of Nadulá the modern Nándol in Márwár. "In his well-ordered realm, except himself the robber of the glory of hostile kings, robbers were unknown. The ruler of Málava invading the kingdom turned back before the strength of Lavaṇaprasáda. The southern king also when opposed by him gave up the idea of war." The ruler of Málava or Málwa referred to was Sohaḍa or Subhaṭavarman.[4] The southern king was the Devagiri Yádava Singhaṇa II. (A.D. 1209-1247).[5]

Lavaṇaprasáda married Madanarájñí and by her had a son named Víradhavala. As heir apparent Víradhavala, who was also called Víra Vághelá or the Vághelá hero,[6] rose to such distinction as a warrior that in the end Lavaṇaprasáda abdicated in his favour. Probably to reconcile the people to his venturing to oppose his sovereign Bhímadeva, Lavaṇaprasáda gave out that in a dream the Luck of Aṇahilaváḍa

---

[1] Ánáka survived Kumárapála and served also under Bhímadeva II. Seeing the kingdom of his weak sovereign divided among his ministers and chiefs A'náka strove till his death to re-establish the central authority of the Solaṅki dynasty. Káthavate's Kírtikaumudí, xiii.

[2] Rás Málá (New Edition), 200.

[3] Kirtíkaumudí, Bombay Sanskrit Series Number XXV.

[4] Ind. Ant. VI. 188 footnote. According to Merutuṇga a cotemporary chronicler an epigram of Bhíma's minister turned back Subhaṭavarman.

[5] Ind. Ant. VI. 188.

[6] According to one story Madanarájñí left her husband's house taking Víradhavala with her, and went to live with Deva Rája Pattakíla the husband of her deceased sister. On growing up Víradhavala returned to his father's house. Rás Málá (New Edition), 201.

appeared bewailing her home with unlighted shrines, broken walls, and jackal-haunted streets, and called on him to come to her rescue.[1] Though he may have gone to the length of opposing Bhímadeva by force of arms, Lavaṇaprasáda was careful to rule in his sovereign's name. Even after Lavaṇaprasáda's abdication, though his famous minister Vastupála considered it advisable, Víradhavala refused to take the supreme title. It was not until the accession of Víradhavala's son Vísaladeva that the head of the Vághelás took any higher title than Ráṇaka or chieftain. Lavaṇaprasáda's religious adviser or Guru was the poet Someśvara the author of the Kírtikaumudí and of the Vastupálacharita or Life of Vastupála, both being biographical accounts of Vastupála. The leading supporters both of Lavaṇaprasáda and of Víradhavala were their ministers the two Jain brothers Vastupála and Tejaḥpála the famous temple-builders on Ábu, S'atruñjaya, and Girnár. According to one account Tejaḥpála remained at court, while Vastupála went as governor to Stambhatírtha or Cambay where he redressed wrongs and amassed wealth.[2]

One of the chief times of peril in Lavaṇaprasáda's reign was the joint attack of the Devagiri Yádava Singhaṇa or Sinhaṇa from the south and of four Márwár chiefs from the north. Lavaṇaprasáda and his son Víradhavala in joint command marched south to meet Singhaṇa at Broach. While at Broach the Vághelás' position was made still more critical by the desertion of the Godhraha or Godhrá chief to Málwa and of the Láṭa or south Gujarát chief to Singhaṇa. Still Lavaṇaprasáda pressed on, attacked Singhaṇa, and gave him so crushing a defeat, that, though Lavaṇaprasáda had almost at once to turn north to meet the Málwá army, Singhaṇa retired without causing further trouble.[3] Somes'vara gives no reason for Singhaṇa's withdrawal beyond the remark 'Deer do not follow the lion's path even when the lion has left it.' The true reason is supplied by a Manuscript called Forms of Treaties.[4] The details of a treaty between Sinhaṇa and Lavaṇaprasáda under date Samvat 1288 (A.D. 1232) included among the Forms seem to show that the reason why Sinhaṇa did not advance was that Lavaṇaprasáda and his son submitted and concluded an alliance.[5] In this copy of the treaty Siṃhaṇadeva is called the great king of kings or paramount sovereign *Mahárájádhirája*, while Lavaṇaprasáda, Sanskritised into Lavaṇyaprasáda is called a Ràna and a tributary chief *Mahámandales'vara*. The place where the treaty was concluded

---

[1] Dr. Bühler in Ind. Ant. VI. 189.

[2] According to the Kírtikaumudí, Káthavate's Ed. XIV. note 1, under Vastupála low people ceased to earn money by base means; the wicked turned pale; the righteous prospered. All honestly and securely plied their calling. Vastupála put down piracy, and, by building platforms, stopped the mingling of castes in milk shops. He repaired old buildings, planted trees, sank wells, laid out parks, and rebuilt the city. All castes and creeds he treated alike.

[3] Káthavate's Kírtikaumudí, xv.

[4] The use of the date Monday the fullmoon of Vaiśakha, Saṃvat 1288 (A.D. 1232) in the second part of the Forms seems to shew that the work was written in A.D. 1232.

[5] Though the object is to give the form of a treaty of alliance, the author could not have used the names Siṃhana and Lavaṇaprasáda unless such a treaty had been actually concluded between them. Apparently Sinhaṇa's invasion of Gujarát took place but a short time before the book of treaties was compiled. Bhandárkar's Search for Sanskrit Manuscripts (1882-83), 40-41.

Chapter III.
THE VÁGHELÁS, A.D. 1219-1304.
Lavaṇaprasáda, A.D. 1200-1233.

is styled "the victorious camp," and the date is Monday the fullmoon of Vais'ákha in the year Saṃvat 1288 (A.D. 1232). The provisions are that, as before, each of the belligerents should confine himself to his own territory; neither of them should invade the possessions of the other; if a powerful enemy attacked either of them, they should jointly oppose him; if only a hostile general led the attack, troops should be sent against him; and if from the country of either any noble fled into the territory of the other taking with him anything of value he should not be allowed harbourage and all valuables in the refugee's possession should be restored.[1] His good fortune went with Lavaṇaprasáda in his attack on the Márwár chiefs whom he forced to retire. Meanwhile S'ankha[2] who is described as the son of the ruler of Sindh but who seems to have held territory in Broach, raised a claim to Cambay and promised Vastupála Lavaṇaprasáda's governor, that, if Vastupála declared in his favour[3], he would be continued in his government. Vastupála rejected S'ankha's overtures, met him in battle outside of Cambay, and forced him to retire. In honour of Vastupála's victory the people of Cambay held a great festival when Vastupála passed in state through the city to the shrine of the goddess Ekalla Víra outside of the town.[4]

Another of the deeds preserved in the Forms is a royal copperplate grant by Lavaṇaprasáda or Lávaṇyaprasáda of a village, not named, for the worship of Somanátha. Lavaṇaprasáda is described as the illustrious Ráṇaka,[5] the great chief, the local lord or *Mandaleśvara*, the son of the illustrious Ráṇaka Ánalde born in the illustrious pedigree of the Chaulukya dynasty. The grant is noted as executed in the reign of Bhímadeva II.[6] while one Bhábhuya was his great minister. Though Bhímadeva was ruling in A.D. 1232 (Saṃvat 1288) Lavaṇaprasáda apparently had sufficient influence to make grants of villages and otherwise to act as the real ruler of Gujarát. It was apparently immediately after this grant (A.D. 1232?) that Lavaṇaprasáda abdicated in favour of Víradhavala.[7]

Víradhavala, A.D. 1233-1238.

Soon after his accession Víradhavala, accompanied by his minister Tejaḥpála, started on an expedition against his wife's brothers Sángaṇa and Chamuṇḍa the rulers of Vámanasthalí or Vanthalí near Junágaḍh. As in spite of their sister's advice Sángaṇa and Chamuṇḍa refused to pay tribute the siege was pressed. Early in the fight the cry arose 'Víradhavala is slain.' But on his favourite horse Uparavaṭa, Víradhavala put himself at the head of his troops, slew both the brothers, and gained the

---

[1] Bhandárkar's Search for Sanskrit Manuscripts (1882-83), 40.

[2] According to other accounts S'ankha, a Broach chieftain, took up the cause of a certain Sayad or Musalmán merchant with whom Vastupála had quarrelled. In the fight Lunapála a Gola, one of Vastupála's chief supporters, was slain and in his honour Vastupála raised a shrine to the Lord Lunapála. Rás Málá (New Edition), 201-202.

[3] Káthavate's Kírtikaumudí, xv.-xvi.

[4] Kathavate's Kírtikaumudí, xv.-xvi.

[5] The modern Gujaráti Ráṇá.

[6] Bhímadeva's name is preceded by the names of his ten Chaulukya predecessors in the usual order. The attributes of each are given as in published Chaulukya copperplates. Ind. Ant. VI. 180-213.

[7] Bhandárkar's Search for Sanskrit Manuscripts (1882-83), 39.

hoarded treasure of Vanthalí.[1] In an expedition against the chief of Bhadresvara, probably Bhadresar in Kacch, Víradhavala was less successful and was forced to accept the Kacch chief's terms. The chroniclers ascribe this reverse to three Rájput brothers who came to Víradhavala's court and offered their services for 3,00,000 drammas (about £7500). "For 3,00,000 drammas I can raise a thousand men" said Víradhavala, and the brothers withdrew. They went to the court of the Bhadresar chief, stated their terms, and were engaged. The night before the battle the brothers sent to Víradhavala saying 'Keep ready 3000 men, for through a triple bodyguard we will force our way.' The three brothers kept their word. They forced their way to Víradhavala, dismounted him, carried off his favourite steed Uparavaṭa, but since they had been his guests they spared Víradhavala's life.[2]

Another of Víradhavala's expeditions was to East Gujarát. Ghughula, chief of Godraha or Godhrá, plundered the caravans that passed through his territory to the Gujarát ports. When threatened with punishment by Víradhavala, Ghughula in derision sent his overlord a woman's dress and a box of cosmetics. The minister Tejaḥpála, who was ordered to avenge this affront, dispatched some skirmishers ahead to raid the Godhra cattle. Ghughula attacked the raiders and drove them back in such panic that the main body of the army was thrown into disorder. The day was saved by the prowess of Tejaḥpála who in single combat unhorsed Ghughula and made him prisoner. Ghughula escaped the disgrace of the woman's dress and the cosmetic box with which he was decorated by biting his tongue so that he died. The conquest of Ghughula is said to have spread Víradhavala's power to the borders of Maháráshtra.[3] The chroniclers relate another success of Víradhavala's against Muizz-ud-dín apparently the famous Muhammad Gori Sultan Muizz-ud-dín Bahramsháh, the Sultan of Delhi (A.D. 1191-1205)[4] who led an expedition against Gujarát. The chief of Ábu was instructed to let the Musalmán force march south unmolested and when they were through to close the defiles against their return. The Gujarát army met the Musalmáns and the Ábu troops hung on their rear. The Musalmáns fled in confusion and cartloads of heads were brought to Víradhavala in Dholká. The chronicles give the credit of this success to Vastupála. They also credit Vastupála with a stratagem which induced the Sultán to think well of Víradhavala and prevented him taking steps to wipe out the disgrace of his defeat. Hearing that the Sultán's mother, or, according to another story, the Sultán's religious adviser, was going from Cambay to Makka Vastupála ordered his men to attack and plunder the vessels in which the pilgrimage was to be made. On the captain's complaint Vastupála had the pirates arrested and the property restored. So grateful was the owner, whether mother or guide, that Vastupála was taken to Delhi and arranged a friendly treaty between his master and the Sultán.[5]

---

[1] Káthavate's Kírtikaumudí, xxiii.
[2] Káthavate's Kírtikaumudí, xxiii.
[3] Káthavate's Kírtikaumudí, xxiii.-xxiv.
[4] Elliot and Dowson, II. 209.
[5] Káthavate's Kírtikaumudí, xxiv.-xxv.

Chapter III.

THE VÁGHELÁS, A.D. 1219-1304.

Víradhavala, A.D. 1233-1238.

Their lavish expenditure on objects connected with Jain worship make the brothers Vastupála and Tejaḥpála the chief heroes of the Jain chroniclers. They say when the Musalmán trader Sayad was arrested at Cambay his wealth was confiscated. Víradhavala claimed all but the dust which he left to Vastupála. Much of the dust was gold dust and a fire turned to dust more of the Sayad's gold and silver treasure. In this way the bulk of the Sayad's wealth passed to Vastupála. This wealth Vastupála and his brother Tejaḥpála went to bury in Hadálaka in Káthiáváḍa. In digging they chanced to come across a great and unknown treasure. According to the books the burden of their wealth so preyed on the brothers that they ceased to care for food. Finding the cause of her husband Tejaḥpála's anxiety Anupamá said 'Spend your wealth on a hill top. All can see it; no one can carry it away.' According to the chroniclers it was this advice, approved by their mother and by Vastupála's wife Lalitádeví, that led the brothers to adorn the summits of Ábu, Girnár, and S'atruñjaya with magnificent temples.

The S'atruñjaya temple which is dedicated to the twenty-third Tírthaṅkara Neminátha is dated A.D. 1232 (Saṃvat 1288) and has an inscription by Somes'vara, the author of the Kírtikaumudí telling how it was built. The Girnár temple, also dedicated to Neminátha, bears date A.D. 1232 (Saṃvat 1288). The Ábu temple, surpassing the others and almost every building in India in the richness and delicacy of its carving, is dedicated to Neminátha and dated A.D. 1231 (Saṃvat 1287). Such was the liberality of the brothers that to protect them against the cold mountain air each of their masons had a fire near him to warm himself and a hot dinner cooked for him at the close of the day. The finest carvers were paid in silver equal in weight to the dust chiselled out of their carvings.[1]

The author Somes'vara describes how he twice came to the aid of his friend Vastupála. On one occasion he saved Vastupála from a prosecution for peculation. The second occasion was more serious. Simha the maternal uncle of king Vísaladeva whipped the servant of a Jain monastery. Enraged at this insult to his religion Vastupála hired a Rájput who cut off Siṃha's offending hand. The crime was proved and Vastupála was sentenced to death. But according to the Jains the persuasions of Someśvara not only made the king set Vastupála free, but led him to upbraid his uncle for beating the servant of a Jain monastery. Soon after his release Vastupála was seized with fever. Feeling the fever to be mortal he started for Satruñjaya but died on the way. His brother Tejaḥpála and his son Jayantapála burned his body on the holy hill, and over his ashes raised a shrine with the name Svargárohanaprásáda The shrine of the ascent into Heaven.[2]

---

[1] Káthavate's Kírtikaumudí, xx.; J. B. R. A. S. XVIII. Number XLVIII. 28. The Jain writers delight in describing the magnificence of the pilgrimages which Vastupála conducted to the holy places. The details are 4500 carts, 700 palanquins, 1800 camels, 2900 writers, 12,100 white-robed and 1100 naked or sky-clad Jains, 1450 singers, and 3300 bards. Káthavate's Kírtikaumudí, xvi.

[2] Káthavate's Kírtikaumudí, xviii.-xix.

Chapter III.

The Vághelás, A.D. 1219-1304.

In A.D. 1238 six years after his father's withdrawal from power Víradhavala died. One hundred and eighty-two servants passed with their lord through the flames, and such was the devotion that Tejaḥpála had to use force to prevent further sacrifices.[1]

Vísaladeva, A.D. 1243-1261.

Of Víradhavala's two sons, Vírama Vísala and Pratápamalla, Vastupála favoured the second and procured his succession according to one account by forcing the old king to drink poison and preventing by arms the return to Aṇahilavaḍa of the elder brother Vírama who retired for help to Jábálipura (Jabalpur). Besides with his brother's supporters Vísala had to contend with Tribhuvanapála the representative of the Aṇahilaváḍa Solaṅkis. Unlike his father and his grandfather Vísala refused to acknowledge an overlord. By A.D. 1243 he was established as sovereign in Aṇahilaváḍa. A later grant A.D. 1261 (Samvat 1317) from Kaḍi in North Gujarát shows that Aṇahilaváḍa was his capital and his title *Mahárájádhirája* King of Kings. According to his copperplates Vísaladeva was a great warrior, the crusher of the lord of Málwa, a hatchet at the root of the turbulence of Mewáḍ, a volcanic fire to dry up Singhaṇa of Devagiri's ocean of men.[2] Vísaladeva is further described as chosen as a husband by the daughter of Karṇáṭa[3] and as ruling with success and good fortune in Aṇahilaváḍa with the illustrious Nágaḍa as his minister.[4] The bards praise Vísaladeva for lessening the miseries of a three years famine,[5] and state that he built or repaired the fortifications of Vísalanagara in East and of Darbhavatí or Dábhoi in South Gujarát.

Arjuṇadeva, A.D. 1262-1274.

During Vísaladeva's reign Vághela power was established throughout Gujarát. On Vísaladeva's death in A.D. 1261 the succession passed to Arjuṇadeva the son of Vísaladeva's younger brother Pratápamalla.[6] Arjuṇadeva proved a worthy successor and for thirteen years (A.D. 1262-1274; Saṃvat 1318-1331) maintained his supremacy. Two stone inscriptions one from Verával dated A.D. 1264 (Saṃvat 1320) the other from Kacch dated A.D. 1272 (Saṃvat 1328) show that his territory included both Kacch and Káthiáváḍa, and an inscription of his successor Sáraṅgadeva shows that his power passed as far east as Mount Ábu.

The Verával inscription of A.D. 1264 (Saṃvat 1320), which is in the temple of the goddess Harsutá,[7] describes Arjuṇadeva as the king

---

[1] Rás Málá, 202.

[2] Ind. Ant. VI. 191. The word for Mewáḍ is Medapáta the Med or Mher land.

[3] The Karnáta king would probably be Someśvara (A.D. 1252) or his son Narasiṃha III. (A.D. 1254) of the Hoysala Ballálas of Dvárasamudra. Fleet's Kánarese Dynasties, 64, 69.

[4] These details are mentioned in a grant of land in Mándal in Ahmadábád to Bráhmans to fill a drinking fountain, repair temples, and supply offerings. Ind. Ant. VI. 210-213.

[5] Rás Málá (New Ed.), 212. A Jaina Pattávalí or succession list of High-priests notices that the famine lasted for three years from Saṃvat 1315 (A.D. 1259). The text may be translated as follows: Vikrama Saṃvat 1315, three years' famine the king (being) Vísaladeva. Bhandarkar's Search for Sanskrit Manuscripts for 1883-84, 15, 323.

[6] See Ep. Ind. I.

[7] The inscription was first noticed by Colonel Tod: Rajasthán, I. 705: Western India, 506.

Chapter III.
THE VÁGHELÁS, A.D. 1219-1304.
Arjuṇadeva, A.D. 1262-1274.

of kings, the emperor (*chakravartin*) of the illustrious Chaulukya race, who is a thorn in the heart of the hostile king Niḥsankamalla, the supreme lord, the supreme ruler, who is adorned by a long line of ancestral kings, who resides in the famous Aṇahillapáṭaka. The grant allots certain income from houses and shops in Somanátha Patan to a mosque built by Piroz a Muhammadan shipowner of Ormuz which is then mentioned as being under the sway of Amír Rukn-ud-dín.[1] The grant also provides for the expenses of certain religious festivals to be celebrated by the Shiite sailors of Somanátha Patan, and lays down that under the management of the Musalmán community of Somanátha any surplus is to be made over to the holy districts of Makka and Madina. The grant is written in bad Sanskrit and contains several Arabic Persian and Gujaráti words. Its chief interest is that it is dated in four eras, "in 662 of the Prophet Muhammad who is described as the teacher of the sailors, who live near the holy lord of the Universe that is Somanátha; in 1320 of the great king Vikrama; in 945 of the famous Valabhi; and in 151 of the illustrious Siṃha." The date is given in these four different eras, because the Muhammadan is the donor's era, the Saṃvat the era of the country, the Valabhi of the province, and the Siṃha of the locality.[2] The Kacch inscription is at the village of Rav about sixty miles east of Bhúj. It is engraved on a memorial slab at the corner of the courtyard wall of an old temple and bears date A.D. 1272 (Saṃvat 1328). It describes Arjuṇadeva as the great king of kings, the supreme ruler, the supreme lord. It mentions the illustrious Máladeva as his chief minister and records the building of a step-well in the village of Rav.[3]

Sáraṅgadeva, A.D. 1275-1296.

Arjuṇadeva was succeeded by his son Sáraṅgadeva. According to the Vichárasreṇí Sáraṅgadeva ruled for twenty-two years from A.D. 1274 to 1296 (Saṃvat 1331-1353). Inscriptions of the reign of Sáraṅgadeva have been found in Kacch and at Ábu. The Kacch inscription is on a *pália* or memorial slab now at the village of Khokhar near Kanthkot which was brought there from the holy village of Bhadresar about thirty-five miles north-east of Mándvi. It bears date A.D. 1275 (Saṃvat 1332) and describes Sáraṅgadeva as the great king of kings, the supreme ruler, the supreme lord ruling at Aṇahillapáṭaka with the illustrious Máladeva as his chief minister.[4] The Ábu inscription dated A.D. 1294 (Saṃvat 1350) in the temple of Vastupála regulates certain dues payable to the Jain temple and mentions Sáraṅgadeva as sovereign of Aṇahillapáṭaka and as having for vassal Vísaladeva ruler of the old capital of Chandrávati about twelve miles south of Mount Ábu.[5] A third inscription dated A.D.

---

[1] This is not Sultán Rukn-ud-dín of the slave kings, who ruled from A.D. 1234 to A.D. 1235. Elliot and Dowson, II.

[2] All four dates tally. The middle of A.D. 1264 (Saṃvat 1320) falls in Hijra 662. As the Valabhi era begins in A.D. 318-319 and the Siṃha era in A.D. 1113, 945 of Valabhi and 151 of Siṃha tally with A.D. 1264.

[3] Bombay Government Selections CLII. New Series, 71.

[4] From an unpublished copy in the possession of Ráo Sáheb Dalpatram Pranjiwan Khakhar, late Educational Inspector, Kacch. Only the upper six lines of the inscription are preserved.

[5] Asiatic Researches, XVI. 311; Rás Malá, 213.

1287 (Samvat 1343), originally from Somanátha, is now at Cintra in Portugal. It records the pilgrimages and religious benefactions of one Tripurántaka, a follower of the Nakulís'á Pás'upata sect, in the reign of Sárangadeva, whose genealogy is given. A manuscript found in Ahmadábád is described as having been finished on Sunday the 3rd of the dark fortnight of Jyeshṭha in the Samvat year 1350, in the triumphant reign of Sárangadeva the great king of kings, while his victorious army was encamped near Ás'ápalli (Ahmadábád).[1]

Karṇadeva, A.D. 1296 - 1304.

Sárangadeva's successor Karṇadeva ruled for eight years A.D. 1296 - 1304 (Samvat 1352 - 1360). Under this weak ruler, who was known as Ghelo or the Insane, Gujarát passed into Musalmán hands. In A.D. 1297 Alaf Khán the brother of the Emperor Ala-u-dín Khilji (A.D. 1296 - 1317) with Nasrat Khán led an expedition against Gujarát. They laid waste the country and occupied Aṇahilaváḍa. Leaving his wives, children, elephants, and baggage Karṇadeva fled to Ramadeva the Yádava chief of Devagiri.[2] All his wealth fell to his conquerors. Among the wives of Karṇadeva who were made captive was a famous beauty named Kauládeví, who was carried to the harem of the Sultán. In the plunder of Cambay Nasrat Khán took a merchant's slave Malik Káfur who shortly after became the Emperor's chief favourite. From Cambay the Muhammadans passed to Káthiáváḍa and destroyed the temple of Somanátha. In 1304 Alaf Khán's term of office as governor of Gujarát was renewed. According to the Mirát-i-Ahmadí after the renewal of his appointment, from white marble pillars taken from many Jain temples, Alaf Khán constructed at Anahilaváḍa the Jáma Masjid or general mosque.

In A.D. 1306 the Cambay slave Káfur who had already risen to be Sultán Ala-u-dín's chief favourite was invested with the title of Malik Naib and placed in command of an army sent to subdue the Dakhan. Alaf Khán, the governor of Gujarát, was ordered to help Malik Káfur in his arrangements. At the same time Kauládeví persuaded the Emperor to issue orders that her daughter Devaladeví should be sent to her to Delhi. Devaladeví was then with her father the unfortunate Karṇadeva in hiding in Báglán in Násik. Malik Káfur sent a messenger desiring Karṇadeva to give up his daughter. Karṇadeva refused and Alaf Khán was ordered to lead his army to the Báglán hills and capture the princess. While for two months he succeeded in keeping the Muhammadan army at bay, Karṇadeva received and accepted an offer for the hand of Devaladeví from the Devagiri Yadava chief S'ankaradeva. On her way to Devagiri near Elura Devaladeví's escort was attacked by a party of Alaf Khán's troops, and the lady seized and sent to Delhi where she was married to prince Khizar Khán.

---

[1] Professor Bhandarkar's Report for 1883-84, 17 - 18.

[2] The bardic story is that king Karṇa had two Nágar Bráhman ministers Mádhava and Kes'ava. He slew Kes'ava and took Mádhava's wife from her husband. In revenge Mádhava went to Delhi and brought the Muhammadans. After the Muhammadan conquest Mádhava presented Ala-u-dín with 360 horses. In return Mádhava was appointed civil minister with Aláf Khán as military governor commanding a lákh of horsemen, 1500 elephants, 20,000 foot soldiers and having with him forty-five officers entitled to use kettledrums. Rás Málá, 214.

Chapter III.
The Vághelás, A.D. 1219-1304.

Nothing more is known of Karṇadeva who appears to have died a fugitive.

Though the main cities and all central Gujarát passed under Musalmán rule a branch of the Vághelás continued to hold much of the country to the west of the Sábarmatí, while other branches maintained their independence in the rugged land beyond Ambá Bhawání between Vírpur on the Mahí and Posiná at the northmost verge of Gujarát.[1]

GENEALOGY OF THE VÁGHELÁS.

Dhavala,
A.D. 1160
Married Kumárapála's Aunt.
|
Arṇorája,
A.D. 1170
Founder of Vághela.
|
Lavaṇaprasáda,
A.D. 1200
Chief of Dholká.
|
Víradhavala,
A.D. 1233-1238
Chief of Dholká.
|
Vísaladeva,
A.D. 1243-1261
King of Aṇahilaváḍa.
|
Arjuṇadeva,
A.D. 1262-1274.
|
Sáraṅgadeva,
A.D. 1274-1295.
|
Karṇadeva or Ghelo,
A.D. 1296-1304.

---

[1] Rás Málá, 222. The Jhálás were firmly fixed in the plains between the Lesser Ran of Kacch and the Gulf of Cambay. The Koli branches of these clans with other tribes of pure or of adulterated aboriginal descent, spread over the Chunvál near Viramgám and appeared in many remote and inaccessible tracts of hill or forest. On the east, under the protection of a line of Rájput princes, the banner of the goddess Káli floated from the hill of Pávágad; while in the west the descendants of Khengár held their famous fortress of Junágaḍh from within its walls controlling much of the peninsula over which they had maintained undisputed sway. Chiefs of Junágaḍh origin were scattered over the rest of the peninsula among whom were the Gohils of Gogo and Píram, and of the sea-washed province which from them derived its name of Gohilvád.

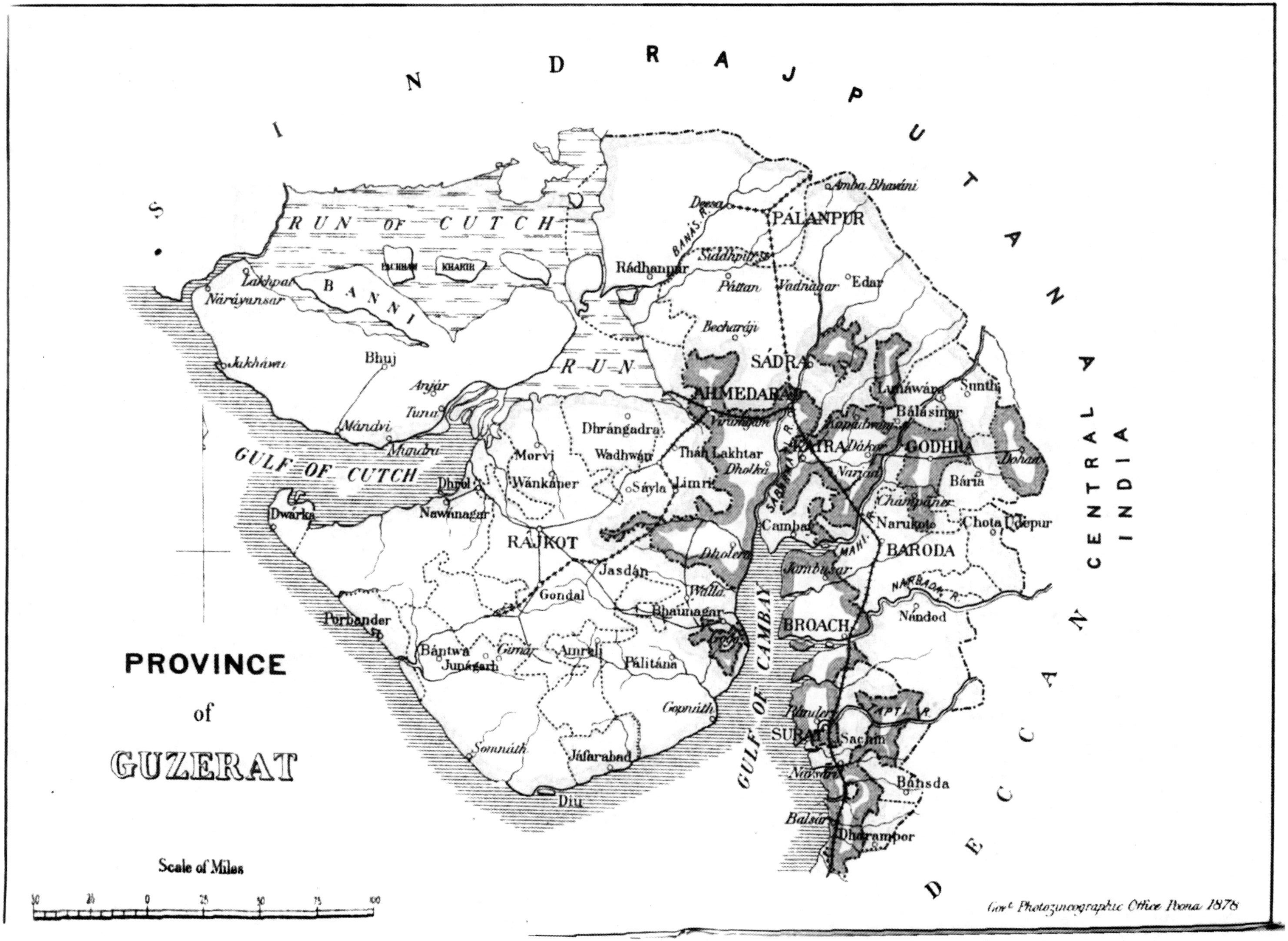
I N D R A J P U T A N A
CENTRAL INDIA
D E C C A N
S .
RUN OF CUTCH
BANNI
RUN
GULF OF CUTCH
GULF OF CAMBAY
Lakhpat
Náráyansar
Jakháwu
Bhuj
Anjár
Tuna
Mándvi
Mundra
Dhrol
Nawánagar
Dwárka
Porbander
Bántwa
Junágarh
Girnár
Amreli
Pálitána
Gopnáth
Somnáth
Jáfarabad
Diu
Morvi
Wánkáner
Dhrángadra
Wadhwán
Sáyla
Limri
RAJKOT
Jasdán
Gondal
Bhaunagar
Walla
Dholera
Dholka
Thán
Lakhtar
Viramgám
AHMEDABAD
SÁDRA
Rádhanpur
Deesa
BANÁS R.
Siddhpur
Páttan
Becharáji
Vadnagar
PÁLANPUR
Amba Bhawáni
Edar
Lunáwára
Sunth
Bálásinor
Kapadwanj
KAIRA
Dákor
Nariád
GODHRA
Dohad
Bária
Chámpáner
Narukote
Chota Udepur
Cambay
SABARMATI R.
MAHI R.
BARODA
Jambusar
NARBADA R.
Nándod
BROACH
Rander
SURAT
Sachin
TAPTI R.
Nausári
Bansda
Balsár
Dharampor
PROVINCE
of
GUZERAT
Scale of Miles
50 25 0 25 50 75 100
Govt. Photozincographic Office Poona 1878

PART II.

MUSALMÁN GUJARÁT.

A.D. 1297-1760.

This history of Musalmán Gujarát is based on translations of the Mirăt-i-Sikandari (A.D. 1611) and of the Mirăt-i-Ahmedi (A.D. 1756) by the late Colonel J. W. Watson. Since Colonel Watson's death in 1889 the translations have been revised and the account enriched by additions from the Persian texts of Farishtah and of the two Mirăts by Mr. Fazl Lutfulláh Farídi of Surat. A careful comparison has also been made with other extracts in Elliot's History of India and in Bayley's History of Gujarát.

MUSALMÁN GUJARÁT.

A.D. 1297 - 1760.

INTRODUCTION.

Introduction.

MUSALMÁN GUJARÁT, A.D. 1297 - 1760.

MUHAMMADAN rule in Gujarát lasted from the conquest of the province by the Dehli emperor Alá-ud-din Khilji (A.D. 1295 - 1315), shortly before the close of the thirteenth century A.D., to the final defeat of the Mughal viceroy Momin Khán by the Maráthás and the loss of the city of Áhmedábád at the end of February 1758.

This whole term of Musalmán ascendancy, stretching over slightly more than four and a half centuries, may conveniently be divided into three parts. The First, the rule of the early sovereigns of Dehli, lasting a few years more than a century, or, more strictly from A.D. 1297 to A.D. 1403; the Second, the rule of the Áhmedábád kings, a term of nearly a century and three-quarters, from A.D. 1403 to A.D. 1573; the Third, the rule of the Mughal Emperors, when, for little less than two hundred years, A.D. 1573 - 1760, Gujarát was administered by viceroys of the court of Dehli.

Territorial Limits.

In the course of these 450 years the limits of Gujarát varied greatly. In the fourteenth century the territory nominally under the control of the Musalmán governors of Pátan (Aṇahiláváḍa) extended southwards from Jhálor, about fifty miles north of Mount Abu, to the neighbourhood of Bombay, and in breadth from the line of the Málwa and Khándesh hills to the western shores of peninsular Gujarát.[1] The earlier kings of Áhmedábád (A.D. 1403 - 1450), content with establishing their power on a firm footing, did not greatly extend the limits of their kingdom. Afterwards, during the latter part of the fifteenth and the beginning of the sixteenth centuries (A.D. 1450 - 1530), the dominions of the Áhmedábád kings gradually spread till they included large tracts to the east and north-east formerly in the possession of the rulers of Khándesh and Málwa. Still later, during the years of misrule between A.D. 1530 and A.D. 1573, the west of Khándesh and the north of the Konkan ceased to form part of the kingdom of Gujarát. Finally, under the arrangements introduced by the emperor Akbar in A.D. 1583, more lands were restored to Málwa and Khándesh. With the exception of Jhálor and Sirohi on the north, Dungarpur and Bánsváda on the north-east, and Alirájpur on

[1] The first notice of the exercise of sovereignty by the Musalmán rulers of Gujarát over lands further south than the neighbourhood of Surat is in A.D. 1428, when king Áhmed I. (A.D. 1412 - 1443) contested with the Dakhan sovereign the possession of Máhim (north latitude 19° 40′; east longitude 72° 47′). As no record remains of a Musalmán conquest of the coast as far south as Danda Rájapuri or Janjira, about fifty miles south of Bombay, it seems probable that the North Konkan fell to the Musalmans in A.D. 1297 as part of the recognised territories of the lords of Anahilapura (Pátan). Rás Mála, I. 350. One earlier reference may be noted. In A.D. 1422 among the leading men slain in the battle of Sárangpur, about fifty miles north-east of Ujjain in Central India, was Sávant chief of Danda Rájapuri that is Janjíra. Mirát-i-Sikandari (Persian Text), 40, and Farishtah (Persian Text), II. 468.

Introduction.

MUSALMÁN GUJARÁT, A.D. 1297 - 1760.

Sorath.

the east, since handed to Rájputána and Central India, the limits of Gujarát remain almost as they were laid down by Akbar.

Though, under the Musalmáns, peninsular Gujarát did not bear the name of Káthiáváḍa, it was then, as at present, considered part of the province of Gujarát. During the early years of Musalmán rule, the peninsula, together with a small portion of the adjoining mainland, was known as Sorath, a shortened form of Saurâshtra, the name originally applied by the Hindus to a long stretch of sea-coast between the banks of the Indus and Daman.[1] Towards the close of the sixteenth century the official use of the word Sorath was confined to a portion, though by much the largest part, of the peninsula. At the same time, the name Sorath seems then, and for long after, to have been commonly applied to the whole peninsula. For the author of the Mirăt-i-Áhmedi, writing as late as the middle of the eighteenth century (A.D. 1756 : A.H. 1170), speaks of Sorath as divided into five districts or *zilláhs*, Hálár, Káthiáváḍa, Gohilváḍa, Bábriáváḍa, and Jetváḍa, and notices that though Navánagar was considered a separate district, its tribute was included in the revenue derived from Sorath.[2] In another passage the same writer thus defines Saurâshtra :

> Saurâshtra or Sorath comprehends the Sarkár of Sorath the Sarkár of Islámnagar or Navánagar and the Sarkár of Kachh or Bhujnagar. It also includes several *zillahs* or districts, Naiyad which they call Jatwár, Hálár or Navánagar and its vicinity, Káthiáváḍa, Gohilváḍa, Bábriáváḍa, Chorvár, Panchál, Okhagir in the neighbourhood of Jagat otherwise called Dwarka, Prabhás Khetr or Pátan Somnáth and its neighbourhood, Nághír also called Sálgogha, and the Nalkántha.[3]

---

[1] The details of Akbar's settlement in A.D. 1583 show Sorath with sixty-three subdivisions and Navánagar (Islámnagar) with seventeen. Similarly in the A'in-i-Akbari (A.D. 1590) Sorath with its nine divisions includes the whole peninsula except Jháláváḍa in the north, which was then part of Áhmedábád. Gladwin, II. 64 and 66 - 71.

[2] Bird's History of Gujarát, 418.

[3] Naiyad is the present Naiyadkántha about ten miles south-west of Rádhanpur containing Jatvár and Varáhi in the west near the Ran and spreading east to Sami and Munjpur thirty to forty miles south-west of Pátan. Hálár is in the north-west of the peninsula ; Káthiáváḍa in the centre ; Gohilváḍa in the south-east ; Bábriáváḍa south-west of Gohilvaḍa ; Chorár or Chorvár north-west of Virával ; Panchál in the north-east centre ; Okhágir or Okhamandal in the extreme west. Nalkántha is the hollow between Káthiáváḍa and the mainland. Besides these names the author of the Mirăt-i-Áhmedi gives one more district in Sorath and others in Gujarát. The name he gives in Sorath is Nágher or Nághír which he says is also called Sálgogah. Sálgogah is apparently Siálbet and its neighbourhood, as Kodinár, Mádhúpúr, Chingaria, and Páta in south Káthiáváḍa are still locally known as Nágher, a tract famous for its fruitfulness. The Mirăt-i-Áhmedi contains the following additional local names: For Kadi thirty-five miles north-west of Áhmedábád, Dandái ; for Dholka twenty-five miles south-west of Áhmedábád, Práth-Nagri ; for Cambay, Támbánagri ; for Vírangám forty miles north-west of Áhmedábád, Jháláwár ; for Múnjpur twenty-two miles south-east of Rádhanpur and some of the country between it and Pátan, Párpas ; for the tract ten miles south-east of Rádhanpur to the neighbourhood of Pátan, Kákrez ; for the town of Rádhanpur in the Pálanpur Political Superintendency and its neighbourhood, Vágaḍh ; for the town of Pálanpur and its neighbourhood up to Dísa and Dántiváda, Dhándár ; for Bálásinor forty-two miles east of Áhmedábád with a part of Kapadvanj in the Kaira district, Masálwaḍa ; for Baroda, Párkher ; for the subdivision of Jambúsar in the Broach district fifteen miles north-west of Broach city, Kánam ; for Alimohan that is Chota Udepur and the rough lands east of Godhra, Pálwára.

Introduction.

MUSALMÁN GUJARÁT A.D. 1297-1760.

Káthiáváḍa.

The present Sorath stretches no further than the limits of Júnágaḍh, Bántwa, and a few smaller holdings.

The name Káthiáváḍa is of recent origin. It was not until after the establishment of Musalmán power in Gujarát that any portion of the peninsula came to bear the name of the tribe of Káthis. Even as late as the middle of the eighteenth century, the name Káthiáváḍa was applied only to one of the sub-divisions of the peninsula. In the disorders which prevailed during the latter part of the eighteenth century, the Káthis made themselves conspicuous. As it was from the hardy horsemen of this tribe that the tribute-exacting Maráthás met with the fiercest resistance, they came to speak of the whole peninsula as the land of the Káthis. This use was adopted by the early British officers and has since continued.

UNDER THE KINGS, 1403-1573.

Under the Áhmedábád kings, as it still is under British rule, Gujarát was divided politically into two main parts; one, called the *khálsah* or crown domain administered directly by the central authority; the other, on payment of tribute in service or in money, left under the control of its former rulers. The amount of tribute paid by the different chiefs depended, not on the value of their territory, but on the terms granted to them when they agreed to become feudatories of the kings of Áhmedábád. Under the Gujarát Sultáns this tribute was occasionally collected by military expeditions headed by the king in person and called *mulkgíri* or country-seizing circuits.

States.

The internal management of the feudatory states was unaffected by their payment of tribute. Justice was administered and the revenue collected in the same way as under the Anahilapur kings. The revenue consisted, as before, of a share of the crops received in kind, supplemented by the levy of special cesses, trade, and transit dues. The chief's share of the crops differed according to the locality; it rarely exceeded one-third of the produce, it rarely fell short of one-sixth. From some parts the chief's share was realised directly from the cultivator by agents called *mantris*; from other parts the collection was through superior landowners.[1]

Districts.

The Áhmedábád kings divided the portion of their territory which was under their direct authority into districts or *sarkárs*. These districts were administered in one of two ways. They were either assigned to nobles in support of a contingent of troops, or they were set apart as crown domains and managed by paid officers.

Crown Lands.

The officers placed in charge of districts set apart as crown domains were called *muktiă*.[2] Their chief duties were to preserve the peace and to collect the revenue. For the maintenance of order, a body of soldiers from the army head-quarters at Áhmedábád was detached for service in each of these divisions, and placed under the command of the district governor. At the same time, in addition to the presence of this detachment of regular troops, every district contained certain

[1] Rás Mála, I. 241.

[2] Maktaă and *iktáă*, the district administered by a *muktiă*, come from the Arabic root *kataă*, he cut, in allusion to the public revenue or the lands cut and apportioned for the pay of the officers and their establishments.

Introduction. UNDER THE KINGS, A.D. 1403-1573.

fortified outposts called *thánás*, varying in number according to the character of the country and the temper of the people. These posts were in charge of officers called *thánadárs* subordinate to the district governor. They were garrisoned by bodies of local soldiery, for whose maintenance, in addition to money payments, a small assignment of land was set apart in the neighbourhood of the post. On the arrival of the tribute-collecting army the governors of the districts through which it passed were expected to join the main body with their local contingents. At other times the district governors had little control over the feudatory chiefs in the neighbourhood of their charge.

Fiscal.

For fiscal purposes each district or *sarkár* was distributed among a certain number of sub-divisions or *parganáhs*, each under a paid official styled *ámil* or *tahsildár*. These sub-divisional officers realised the state demand, nominally one-half of the produce, by the help of the headmen of the villages under their charge. In the sharehold and simple villages of North Gujarát these village headmen were styled *patels* or according to Musalmán writers *mukaddams* and in the simple villages of the south they were known as *desáis*. They arranged for the final distribution of the total demand in joint villages among the shareholders, and in simple villages from the individual cultivators.[1] The sub-divisional officer presented a statement of the accounts of the villages in his sub-division to the district officer, whose record of the revenue of his whole district was in turn forwarded to the head revenue officer at court. As a check on the internal management of his charge, and especially to help him in the work of collecting the revenue, with each district governor was associated an accountant. Further that each of these officers might be the greater check on the other, king Áhmed I. (A.D. 1412-1443) enforced the rule that when the governor was chosen from among the royal slaves the accountant should be a free man, and that when the accountant was a slave the district governor should be chosen from some other class. This practise was maintained till the end of the reign of Muzaffar Sháh (A.D. 1511-1525), when, according to the Mirăt-i-Áhmedi, the army became much increased, and the ministers, condensing the details of revenue, farmed it on contract, so that many parts formerly yielding one rupee now produced ten, and many others seven eight or nine, and in no place was there a less increase than from ten to twenty per cent. Many other changes occurred at the same time, and the spirit of innovation creeping into the administration the wholesome system of checking the accounts was given up and mutiny and confusion spread over Gujarát.[2]

Assigned Lands.

The second class of directly governed districts were the lands assigned to nobles for the maintenance of contingents of troops. As in other parts of India, it would seem that at first these assignments were for specified sums equal to the pay of the contingent. When such assignments were of long standing, and were large enough to swallow the whole revenue of a district, it was natural to simplify the

---

[1] Further particulars regarding these village headmen are given below.
[2] Bird's History of Gujarát, 192; Mirăt-i-Sikandari, Persian Text, 44.

Introduction.

UNDER THE KINGS, A.D. 1403-1573.

Assigned Lands.

arrangement by transferring the collection of the revenue and the whole management of the district to the military leader of the contingent. So long as the central power was strong, precautions were doubtless taken to prevent the holder of the grant from unduly rackrenting his district and appropriating to himself more than the pay of the troops, or from exercising any powers not vested in the local governors of districts included within the crown domains. As in other parts of India, those stipulations were probably enforced by the appointment of certain civil officers directly from the government to inspect the whole of the noble's proceedings, as well in managing his troops as in administering his lands.[1] The decline of the king's power freed the nobles from all check or control in the management of their lands. And when, in A.D. 1536, the practice of farming was introduced into the crown domains, it would seem to have been adopted by the military leaders in their lands, and to have been continued till the annexation of Gujarát by the emperor Akbar in A.D. 1573.

UNDER THE MUGHALS, A.D. 1573-1760.

Administration.

It was the policy of Akbar rather to improve the existing system than to introduce a new form of government. After to some extent contracting the limits of Gujarát he constituted it a province or *súbah* of the empire, appointing to its government an officer of the highest rank with the title of *súbahdár* or viceroy. As was the case under the Ahmedábád kings, the province continued to be divided into territories managed by feudatory chiefs, and districts administered by officers appointed either by the court of Dehli or by the local viceroy. The head-quarters of the army remained at Ahmedábád, and detachments were told off and placed under the orders of the officers in charge of the directly administered divisions. These district governors, as before, belonged to two classes, paid officers responsible for the management of the crown domains and military leaders in possession of lands assigned to them in pay of their contingent of troops. The governors of the crown domains, who were now known as *faujdárs* or commanders, had, in addition to the command of the regular troops, the control of the outposts maintained within the limits of their charge. Like their predecessors they accompanied the viceroy in his yearly circuit for the collection of tribute.

Crown Lands.

As a check on the military governors and to help them in collecting the revenue, the distinct class of account officers formerly established by king Ahmed I. (A.D. 1412-1443) was again introduced. The head of this branch of the administration was an officer, second in rank to the viceroy alone, appointed direct from the court of Dehli with the title of *diván*. Besides acting as collector-general of the revenues of the province, this officer was also the head of its civil administration. His title *diván* is generally translated minister. And though the word minister does not express the functions of the office, which corresponded more nearly with those of a chief secretary, it represents with sufficient accuracy the relation in which the holder of the office of *diván* generally stood to the viceroy.

[1] Elphistone's History, 76.

Introduction.

UNDER THE MUGHALS, A.D. 1573-1760.

Revenue Officials.

For its revenue administration each district or group of districts had its revenue officials called *amíns* who corresponded to the collector of modern times. There were also *amíns* in the customs department separate from those whose function was to control and administer the land revenue. Beneath the *amín* came the *ámil*[1] who carried on the actual collection of the land revenue or customs in each district or *parganáh*, and below the *ámil* were the *fáils*, *mushrifs*, or *kárkúns* that is the revenue clerks. The *ámil* corresponded to the modern *mámlatdár*, both terms meaning him who carries on the *amal* or revenue management. In the leading ports the *ámil* of the customs was called *mutasaddi* that is civil officer.

Village Officers.

The *ámil* or *mámlatdár* dealt directly with the village officials, namely with the *mukaddam* or headman, the *patwári* or lease manager, the *kánúngo* or accountant, and the *havúldár* or grain-yard guardian. The *havúldár* superintended the separation of the government share of the produce; apportioned to the classes subject to forced labour their respective turns of duty; and exercised a general police superintendence by means of subordinates called *pasáitás* or *vartaniás*. In ports under the *mutasaddi* was a harbour-master or *sháh-bandar*.

Desáis.

Crown sub-divisions had, in addition, the important class called *desáis*. The *desái's* duty appears at first to have been to collect the *salámi* or tribute due by the smaller chiefs, landholders, and *vántadárs* or sharers. For this, in Akbar's time, the *desái* received a remuneration of 2½ per cent on the sum collected. Under the first viceroy Mírza Azíz Kokaltásh (A.D. 1573-1575) this percentage was reduced to one-half of its former amount, and in later times this one-half was again reduced by one-half. Though the Muhammadan historians give no reason for so sweeping a reduction, the cause seems to have been the inability of the *desáis* to collect the tribute without the aid of a military force. Under the new system the *desái* seems merely to have kept the accounts of the tribute due, and the records both of the amount which should be levied as tribute and of other customary rights of the crown. In later times the *desáis* were to a great extent superseded by the district accountants or *majmudárs*, and many *desáis*, especially in south Gujarát, seem to have sunk to *patels*.

Land Tax.

Up to the viceroyalty of Mírza Ísá Tarkhán (A.D. 1642-1644), the land tax appears to have been levied from the cultivator in a fixed sum, but he was also subject to numerous other imposts. Land grants in *wazífah* carried with them an hereditary title and special exemption from all levies except the land tax. The levy in kind appears to have ceased before the close of Mughal rule. In place of a levy in kind each village paid a fixed sum or *jama* through the district accountant or *majmudár* who had taken the place of the *desái*. As in many cases the *jama* really meant the lump sum at which the crown villages were assessed and farmed to the chiefs and *patels*, on the collapse of the empire many villages thus farmed to chiefs and landlords were

[1] In Márwár and in the north and north-east this official was styled *tahsildár* and in the Dakhan *kamávisdár*.

Introduction. Under the Mughals, A.D. 1573-1760.

retained by them with the connivance of the *mujmudárs desáis* and others.

Justice.

The administration of justice seems to have been very complete. In each *kasbah* or town *kázis*, endowed with glebe lands in addition to a permanent salary, adjudicated disputes among Muhammadans according to the laws of Islám. Disputes between Muhammadans and unbelievers, or amongst unbelievers, were decided by the department called the *sadárat*, the local judge being termed a *sadr*. The decisions of the local *kázis* and *sadrs* were subject to revision by the *kázi* or *sadr* of the *súbah* who resided at Ahmedábád. And as a last resort the Ahmedábád decisions were subject to appeal to the *Kázi-ul-Kuzzát* and the *Sadr-ûs-Sudûr* at the capital.

Fiscal.

The revenue appears to have been classed under four main heads: 1. The *Khazánah-i-A'mirah* or imperial treasury which comprehended the land tax received from the crown *parganáhs* or districts, the tribute, the five per cent customs dues from infidels, the import dues on stuffs, and the *sáyer* or land customs including transit dues, slave market dues, and miscellaneous taxes. 2. The treasury of arrears into which were paid government claims in arrear either from the *ámils* or from the farmers of land revenue; *takávi* advances due by the *raiyats*; and tribute levied by the presence of a military force. 3. The treasury of charitable endowments. Into this treasury was paid the 2½ per cent levied as customs dues from Muhammadans.[1] The pay of the religious classes was defrayed from this treasury. 4. The treasury, into which the *jaziah* or capitation tax levied from *zimmís* or infidels who acknowledged Muhammadan rule, was paid. The proceeds were expended in charity and public works. After the death of the emperor Farrukhsiyar (A.D. 1713-1719), this source of revenue was abolished. The arrangements introduced by Akbar in the end of the sixteenth century remained in force till the death of Aurangzíb in A.D. 1707. Then trouble and perplexity daily increased, till in A.D. 1724-25, Hamid Khán usurped the government lands, and, seeking to get rid of the servants and assignments, gradually obtained possession of the records of the registry office. The keepers of the records were scattered, and yearly revenue statements ceased to be received from the districts.[2]

Assigned Lands.

Akbar continued the system of assigning lands to military leaders in payment of their contingents of troops. Immediately after the annexation in A.D. 1573, almost the whole country was divided among the great nobles.[3] Except that the revenues of certain tracts were

---

[1] *Zakát*, literally purification or cleansing, is the name of a tax levied from Muslims for charitable purposes or religious uses. In the endowments-treasury the customs dues from Muslims at 2½ per cent (the technical 1 in 40) as contrasted with the five per cent levied from infidels (the technical 2 in 40) were entered. Hence in these accounts *zakát* corresponds with customs dues, and is divisible into two kinds *khushki zakát* or land customs and *tari zakát* or sea customs.

[2] Bird's History of Gujarát, 93. Though under the Mughal viceroys the state demand was at first realized in grain, at the last the custom was to assess each sub-division, and probably each village, at a fixed sum or *jama*. The total amount for the sub-division was collected by an officer called *mujmudár*, literally keeper of collections, the village headmen, *patels* or *mukáddums*, being responsible each for his own village.

[3] Bird's History of Gujarát, 325.

Introduction.

UNDER THE MUGHALS, A.D. 1573-1760.

Assigned Lands.

set aside for the imperial exchequer the directly governed districts passed into the hands of military leaders who employed their own agents to collect the revenue. During the seventeenth century the practice of submitting a yearly record of their revenues, and the power of the viceroy to bring them to account for misgovernment, exercised a check on the management of the military leaders. And during this time a yearly surplus revenue of £600,000 (Rs. 60,00,000) from the assigned and crown lands was on an average forwarded from Gujarát to Dehli. In the eighteenth century the decay of the viceroy's authority was accompanied by the gradually increased power of the military leaders in possession of assigned districts, till finally, as in the case of the Nawábs of Broach and Surat, they openly claimed the position of independent rulers.[1]

Minor Offices.

Of both leading and minor officials the Mirăt-i-Ahmedi supplies the following additional details. The highest officer who was appointed under the seal of the minister of the empire was the provincial *diván* or minister. He had charge of the fiscal affairs of the province and of the revenues of the *khálsa* or crown lands, and was in some matters independent of the viceroy. Besides his personal salary he had 150 *sawárs* for two provincial *thánás* Arjanpur and Khambália. Under the *diván* the chief officers were the *píshkár diván* his first assistant, who was appointed under imperial orders by the patent of the *diván*, the *daroghah* or head of the office, and the *sharf* or *mushrif* and *tehwildár* of the *daftar khánáhs*, who presided over the accounts with *munshis* and *muharrirs* or secretaries and writers. The *kázis*, both town and city, with the sanction of the emperor were appointed by the chief law officer of the empire through the chief law officer of the province. They were lodged by the state, paid partly in cash partly in land, and kept up a certain number of troopers. In the *kázi's* courts *wakils* or pleaders and *muftís* or law officers drew 8 as. to Re. 1 a day. Newly converted Musalmáns also drew 8 as. a day. The city censor or *muhtasib* had the supervision of morals and of weights and measures. He was paid in cash and land, and was expected to keep up sixty troopers. The news-writer, who was sometimes also *bakhshi* or military paymaster, had a large staff of news-writers called *wákiáh-nigár* who worked in the district courts and offices as well as in the city courts. He received his news-reports every evening and embodied them in a letter which was sent to court by camel post. A second staff of news-writers called *sawáníhnigár* reported rumours. A third set were the *harkárás* on the viceroy's staff. Postal *chaukis* or stations extended from Ahmedábád to the Ajmír frontier, each with men and horse ready to carry the imperial post which reached Sháh Jehánábád or Dehli in seven days. A line of posts also ran south through Broach to the Dakhan. The *faujdárs* or military police, who were sometimes commanders of a thousand and held estates, controlled both the city and the district police. The *kotwál* or head of the city night-watch was appointed by the viceroy. He had fifty troopers and a hundred foot. In the treasury department were the *amín* or chief, the *dároghah*, the

---

[1] Bird's History of Gujarát, 341.

Introduction.

UNDER THE MUGHALS, A.D. 1573-1760.

mushrif, the treasurer, and five messengers. In the medical department were a Yúnáni or Greek school and a Hindu physician, two under-physicians on eight and ten annas a day, and a surgeon. The yearly grant for food and medicine amounted to Rs. 2000.[1]

Land Tenures.

Besides the class of vernacular terms that belong to the administration of the province, certain technical words connected with the tenure of land are of frequent occurrence in this history. For each of these, in addition to the English equivalent which as far as possible has been given in the text, some explanation seems necessary. During the period to which this history refers, the superior holders of the land of the province belonged to two main classes, those whose claims dated from before the Musalmán conquest and those whose interest in the land was based on a Musalmán grant. By the Musalmán historians, landholders of the first class, who were all Hindus, are called *zamíndárs*, while landholders of the second class, Musalmáns as a rule, are spoken of as *jágírdárs*. Though the term *zamíndár* was used to include the whole body of superior Hindu landholders, in practice a marked distinction was drawn between the almost independent chief, who still enjoyed his Hindu title of *rája, rával, ráv*, or *jám*, and the petty claimant to a share in a government village, who in a Hindu state would have been known as a *garásiá*.[2]

Hereditary Hindu Landholders.

The larger landholders, who had succeeded in avoiding complete subjection, were, as noticed above, liable only for the payment of a certain fixed sum, the collection of which by the central power in later times usually required the presence of a military force. With regard to the settlement of the claims of the smaller landholders of the superior class, whose estates fell within the limits of the directly administered districts, no steps seem to have been taken till the reign of Áhmed Sháh I. (A.D. 1411-1443). About the year A.D. 1420 the peace of his kingdom was so broken by agrarian disturbances, that Áhmed Sháh agreed, on condition of their paying tribute and performing military service, to re-grant to the landholders of the *zamíndár* class as hereditary possessions a one-fourth share of their former village lands. The portion so set apart was called *vánta* or share, and the remainder, retained as state land, was called *talpat*. This agreement continued till, in the year A.D. 1545, during the reign of Mahmúd Sháh II. (A.D. 1536-1553), an attempt was made to annex these private shares to the crown. This measure caused much discontent and disorder. It was reversed by the emperor Akbar who, as part of the settlement of the province in A.D. 1583, restored their one-fourth share to the landholders, and, except that the Maráthás

[1] Mirát-i-Áhmedi Persian Text page 115.

[2] The title *rája* is applicable to the head of a family only. The payment of tribute to the Mughals or Maráthás does not affect the right to use this title. *Rána* and *ráv* seem to be of the same dignity as *rája*. *Rával* is of lower rank. The sons of *rájás*, *ránás*, *rávs*, and *rávals* are called *kuvars* and their sons *thákurs*. The younger sons of *thákurs* became *bhumiás* that is landowners or *garásiás*, that is owners of *garás* or a mouthful. *Jám* is the title of the chiefs of the Jádeja tribe both of the elder branch in Kachh and of the younger branch in Navánagar, or Little Kachh in Káthiáváda. Rás Mála, II. 277.

Introduction.

UNDER THE MUGHALS, A.D. 1573-1760.

afterwards levied an additional quit-rent from these lands, the arrangements then introduced have since continued in force.[1]

Levies.

During the decay of Musalmán rule in Gujarát in the first half of the eighteenth century, shareholders of the *garásia* class in government villages, who were always ready to increase their power by force, levied many irregular exactions from their more peaceful neighbours, the cultivators or inferior landholders. These levies are known as *vol* that is a forced contribution or *pál* that is protection. All have this peculiar characteristic that they were paid by the cultivators of crown lands to petty marauders to purchase immunity from their attacks. They in no case partook of the nature of dues imposed by a settled government on its own subjects. *Tora garás*, more correctly *toda garás*, is another levy which had its origin in eighteenth century disorder. It was usually a readymoney payment taken from villages which, though at the time crown or *khálsa*, had formerly belonged to the *garásia* who exacted the levy. Besides a readymoney payment contributions in kind were sometimes exacted.

Service Lands.

The second class of superior landholders were those whose title was based on a Musalmán grant. Such grants were either assignments of large tracts of land to the viceroy, district-governors, and nobles, to support the dignity of their position and maintain a contingent of troops, or they were allotments on a smaller scale granted in reward for some special service. Land granted with these objects was called *jágír*, and the holder of the land *jágírdár*. In theory, on the death of the original grantee, such possessions were strictly resumable; in practice they tended to become hereditary. No regular payments were required from holders of *jágírs*. Only under the name of *peshkash* occasional contributions were demanded. These occasional contributions generally consisted of such presents as a horse, an elephant, or some other article of value. They had more of the nature of a freewill offering than of an enforced tribute. Under the Musalmáns contributions of this kind were the only payments exacted from proprietors of the *jágírdár* class. But the Maráthás, in addition to contributions, imposed on *jágírdárs* a regular tribute, similar to that paid by the representatives of the original class of superior Hindu landholders.

Under Musalmán rule great part of Gujarát was always in the hands of *jágírdárs*. So powerful were they that on two occasions under the Ahmedábád kings, in A.D. 1554 and A.D. 1572, the leading

---

[1] Under the Maráthás the title *zamíndár* was bestowed on the farmers of the land revenue, and this practice was adopted by the earlier English writers on Gujarát. In consequence of this change small landholders of the superior class, in directly administered districts, came again to be called by their original Hindu name of *garásia*. Mr. Elphinstone (History, 79 and note 13) includes under the term *zamíndár*: (1) half-subdued chieftains, (2) independent governors of districts, and (3) farmers of revenue. He also notices that until Aurangzíb's time such chiefs as enjoyed some degree of independence were alone called *zamíndárs*. But in Colonel Walker's time, A.D. 1805, at least in Gujarát (Bombay Government Selections, XXXIX. 25) the term *zamíndár* included *desáis*, *majmudárs* (district accountants), *patels*, and *taláti*s (village clerks).

Introduction.

Condition of Gujarát, A.D. 1297-1760.

nobles distributed among themselves the entire area of the kingdom.[1] Again, during the eighteenth century, when Mughal rule was on the decline, the *jágírdárs* by degrees won for themselves positions of almost complete independence.[2]

The changes in the extent of territory and in the form of administration illustrate the effect of the government on the condition of the people during the different periods of Musalmán rule. The following summary of the leading characteristics of each of the main divisions of the four-and-a-half centuries of Musalmán ascendancy may serve as an introduction to the detailed narrative of events.

Under the Early Viceroys, 1297-1403.

On conquering Gujarát in A.D. 1297 the Musalmáns found the country in disorder. The last kings of Aṇahilapur or Pátan, suffering under the defects of an incomplete title, held even their crown lands with no firmness of grasp, and had allowed the outlying territory to slip almost entirely from their control. Several of the larger and more distant rulers had resumed their independence. The Bhíls and Kolis of the hills, forests, and rough river banks were in revolt. And stranger chiefs, driven south by the Musalmán conquests in Upper India, had robbed the central power of much territory.[3] The records of the early Musalmán governors (A.D. 1297-1391) show suspicion on the side of the Dehli court and disloyalty on the part of more than one viceroy, much confusion throughout the province, and little in the way of government beyond the exercise of military force. At the same time, in spite of wars and rebellions, the country, in parts at least, seems to

---

[1] Details of A.D. 1571 given in the Mirăt-i-Ahmedi show that the chief nobles were bound to furnish cavalry contingents varying from 4000 to 25,000 horse, and held lands estimated to yield yearly revenues of £160,000 to £1,620,000. Bird's Gujarát, 109-127.

[2] According to the European travellers in India during the seventeenth century, provincial governors, and probably to some extent all large holders of service lands, employed various methods for adding to the profits which the assigned lands were meant to yield them. Of these devices two seem to have been specially common, the practice of supporting a body of horse smaller than the number agreed for, and the practice of purveyance that is of levying supplies without payment. Sir Thomas Roe, from A.D. 1615 to 1618 English ambassador at the court of the emperor Jehángír, gives the following details of these irregular practices: 'The Pátan (that is Patna in Bengal) viceroy's government was estimated at 5000 horse, the yearly pay of each trooper being £20 (Rs. 200), of which he kept only 1500, being allowed the surplus as dead pay. On one occasion this governor wished to present me with 100 loaves of the finest sugar, as white as snow, each loaf weighing fifty pounds. On my declining, he said, 'You refuse these loaves, thinking I am poor; but being made in my government the sugar costs me nothing, as it comes to me gratis.' Sir Thomas Roe in Kerr's Voyages, IX. 282-284. The same writer, the best qualified of the English travellers of that time to form a correct opinion, thus describes the administration of the Musalmán governors of the seventeenth century: 'They practise every kind of tyranny against the natives under their jurisdiction, oppressing them with continual exactions, and are exceedingly averse from any way being opened by which the king may be informed of their infamous proceedings. They grind the people under their government to extract money from them, often hanging men up by the heels to make them confess that they are rich, or to ransom themselves from faults merely imputed with a view to fleece them.' Sir Thomas Roe in Kerr's Voyages, IX. 338.

[3] Of these settlements the principal was that of the Ráthod chief who in the thirteenth century established himself at Ídar, now one of the states of the Mahi Kántha. In the thirteenth century also, Gohils from the north and Sodha Parmárs and Káthis from Sindh entered Gujarát. Rás Mála, II. 269.

Introduction.

CONDITION OF GUJARÁT, A.D. 1297-1760.

Under the Kings, 1403-1573.

have been well cultivated, and trade and manufactures to have been flourishing.[1]

The period of the rule of the Áhmedábád kings (A.D. 1403-1573) contains two divisions, one lasting from A.D. 1403 to A.D. 1530, on the whole a time of strong government and of growing power and prosperity; the other the forty-three years from A.D. 1530 to the conquest of the province by the emperor Akbar in A.D. 1573, a time of disorder and misrule. In A.D. 1403 when Gujarát separated from Dehli the new king held but a narrow strip of plain. On the north were the independent chiefs of Sirohi and Jhálor, from whom he occasionally levied contributions. On the east the Rája of Ídar, another Rájput prince, was in possession of the western skirts of the hills and forests, and the rest of that tract was held by the mountain tribes of Bhils and Kolis. On the west the peninsula was in the hands of nine or ten Hindu tribes, probably tributary, but by no means obedient.[2] In the midst of so unsettled and warlike a population, all the efforts of Muzaffar I., the founder of the dynasty, were spent in establishing his power. It was not until the reign of his successor Áhmed I. (A.D. 1412-1443) that steps were taken to settle the different classes of the people in positions of permanent order. About the year A.D. 1420 two important measures were introduced. Of these one assigned lands for the support of the troops, and the other recognised the rights of the superior class of Hindu landholders to a portion of the village lands they had formerly held. The effect of these changes was to establish order throughout the districts directly under the authority of the crown. And though, in the territories subject to feudatory chiefs, the presence of an armed force was still required to give effect to the king's claims for tribute, his increasing power and wealth made efforts at independence more hopeless, and gradually secured the subjection of the greater number of his vassals. During the latter part of the fifteenth and the first quarter of the sixteenth century the power of the Áhmedábád kings was at its height. At that time their dominions included twenty-five divisions or *sarkárs*. Among nine of these namely Pátan, Áhmedábád, Sûnth, Godhra, Chámpáner, Baroda, Broach, Nándod or Rájpípla, and Surat the central plain was distributed. In addition in the north were four divisions, Sirohi, Jhálor, Jodhpur, and Nágor now in south-west and central Rájputána; in the north-east two, Dûngarpur and Bánsváda, now in the extreme

---

[1] Gujarát of about the year A.D. 1300 is thus described: 'The air of Gujarát is healthy, and the earth picturesque; the vineyards bring forth blue grapes twice a year, and the strength of the soil is such that the cotton plants spread their branches like willow and plane trees, and yield produce for several years successively. Besides Cambay, the most celebrated of the cities of Hind in population and wealth, there are 70,000 towns and villages, all populous, and the people abounding in wealth and luxuries.' Elliot's History of India, III. 31, 32, and 43. Marco Polo, about A.D. 1292, says: 'In Gujarát there grows much pepper and ginger and indigo. They have also a great deal of cotton. Their cotton trees are of very great size, growing full six paces high, and attaining to an age of twenty years.' Yule's Edition, II. 328. The cotton referred to was probably the variety known as *devkapás* Gossypium religiosum or peruvianum, which grows from ten to fifteen feet high, and bears for several years. Royle, 149-150.

[2] Elphinstone's History, 762.

Introduction.

CONDITION OF GUJARÁT, A.D. 1297-1760.

Under the Kings, 1403-1573.

south of Rájputána; in the east and south-east three, Nandurbár now in Khándesh, Mulher or Báglán now in Násik, and Rám Nagar or Dharampur now in Surat; in the south four, Dandá-Rájapuri or Janjira, Bombay, Bassein, and Daman now in the Konkan; in the west two, Sorath and Navánagar now in Káthiáváda; and Kachh in the north-west. Besides the revenues of these districts, tribute was received from the rulers of Áhmednagar, Burhánpur, Berár, Golkonda, and Bijápur, and customs dues from twenty-five ports on the western coast of India and from twenty-six foreign marts, some of them in India and others in the Persian Gulf and along the Arabian coast.[1] The total revenue from these three sources is said in prosperous times to have amounted to a yearly sum of £11,460,000 (Rs. 11,46,00,000). Of this total amount the territorial revenue from the twenty-five districts yielded £5,840,000 (Rs. 5,84,00,000), or slightly more than one-half. Of the remaining £5,620,000 (Rs. 5,62,00,000) about one-fifth part was derived from the Dakhan tribute and the rest from customs-dues.[2]

The buildings at Áhmedábád, and the ruins of Chámpáner and Mehmúdábád, prove how much wealth was at the command of the sovereign and his nobles, while the accounts of travellers seem to show that the private expenditure of the rulers was not greater than the kingdom was well able to bear. The Portuguese traveller Duarte Barbosa, who was in Gujarát between A.D. 1511 and A.D. 1514, found the capital Chámpáner a great city, in a very fertile country of abundant provisions, with many cows sheep and goats and plenty of fruit, so that it was full of all things.[3] Áhmedábád was still larger, very rich and well

---

[1] Bird's History of Gujarát, 110, 129, and 130.

[2] The passage from the Mirăt i-Áhmedi, Bird 109, is: 'A sum of 25 *lákhs* of *húns* and one *kror* of *ibrahims*, that were two parts greater, being altogether nearly equal to 5 *krors* and 62 *lákhs* of rupees, was collected from the Dakhan tribute and the customs of the European and Arab ports.' The word *hún*, from an old Karnátak word for gold, is the Musalmán name for the coin known among Hindus as *varáha* or the wild-boar coin, and among the Portuguese as the *pagoda* or temple coin. Prinsep Ind. Ant. Thomas' Ed. II. U. T. 18. The old specimens of this coin weigh either 60 grains the *máda* or half pagoda, or 120 grains the *hún* or full pagoda. Thomas, Chron. Pat. Ks. II. 224, note. The star pagoda, in which English accounts at Madras were formerly kept, weighs 52·56 grains, and was commonly valued at 8s. or Rs. 4 (Prinsep as above). At this rate in the present sum the 25 *lákhs* of *húns* would equal one *kror* (100 *lákhs*) of rupees. The *ibráhimi*, 'two parts greater than the *hún*,' would seem to be a gold coin, perhaps a variety of the Persian *ashrafi* (worth about 9s. English. Marsden, N. O. 455). Taking the two parts of a *hún* as *fánams* or sixteenths, this would give the *ibráhimi* a value of Rs. 4¼, and make a total customs revenue of 425 *lákhs* of rupees. This statement of the revenues of the kingdom is, according to the author of the Mirăt-i-Áhmedi, taken from such times as the power of the Gujarát kings continued to increase. The total revenue of the twenty-five districts (£5,840,000) is the amount recovered in the year A.D. 1571. But the receipts under the head of Tribute must have been compiled from accounts of earlier years. For, as will be seen below, the neighbouring kings ceased to pay tribute after the end of the reign of Bahádur (A.D. 1536). Similarly the customs revenues entered as received from Daman and other places must have been taken from the accounts of some year previous to A.D. 1560.

[3] The remains at Chámpáner in the British district of the Panch Maháls are well known. Of Mehmúdábád, the town of that name in the district of Kaira, eighteen miles south of Áhmedábád, a few ruins only are left. In A.D. 1590 this city is said to have contained many grand edifices surrounded with a wall eleven miles (7 *kos*) square with at every ¾ mile (½ *kos*) a pleasure house, and an enclosure for deer and other game. (Áin-i-Ákbari: Gladwin, II. 64.) The Mirăt-i-Áhmedi makes no special reference to the sovereign's share of the revenue. The greater part of the £5,620,000 derived from

Introduction.

CONDITION OF GUJARÁT, A.D. 1297-1760.

Under the Kings, 1403-1573.

supplied, embellished with good streets and squares, with houses of stone and cement. It was not from the interior districts of the province that the Áhmedábád kings derived the chief part of their wealth, but from those lying along the coast, which were enriched by manufactures and commerce.[1] So it was that along the shores of the gulf of Cambay and southward as far as Bombay the limit of the Gujarát kingdom, besides many small sea-ports, Barbosa chooses out for special mention twelve 'towns of commerce, very rich and of great trade.' Among these was Diu, off the south coast of Káthiáváḍa, yielding so large a revenue to the king as to be 'a marvel and amazement.' And chief of all Cambay, in a goodly, fertile, and pretty country full of abundant provisions; with rich merchants and men of great prosperity; with craftsmen and mechanics of subtle workmanship in cotton, silk, ivory, silver, and precious stones; the people well dressed, leading luxurious lives, much given to pleasure and amusement.[2]

The thirty-eight years between the defeat of king Bahádur by the emperor Humáyún in A.D. 1535 and the annexation of Gujarát by Akbar in A.D. 1573 was a time of confusion. Abroad, the superiority of Gujarát over the neighbouring powers was lost, and the limits of the kingdom shrank; at home, after the attempted confiscation (A.D. 1545) of their shares in village lands the disaffection of the superior landowners became general, and the court, beyond the narrow limits of the crown domains, ceased to exercise substantial control over

---

tribute and customs would probably go to the king, besides the lands specially set apart as crown domains, which in A.D. 1571 were returned as yielding a yearly revenue of £900,000 (900,000,000 *tankás*). This would bring the total income of the crown to a little more than 6¼ millions sterling.

[1] So Sikandar Lodi emperor of Dehli, A.D. 1488-1517, is reported to have said: 'The magnificence of the kings of Dehli rests on wheat and barley; the magnificence of the kings of Gujarát rests on coral and pearls.' Bird, 132.

[2] The twelve Gujarát ports mentioned by Barbosa are: On the south coast of the peninsula, two: Patenixi (Pátan-Somnáth, now Verával), very rich and of great trade; Surati-Mangalor (Mangrul), a town of commerce, and Diu. On the shores of the gulf of Cambay four: Gogari (Gogha), a large town; Barbesy (Broach); Guandári or Gandar (Gandhár), a very good town; and Cambay. On the western coast five: Ravel (Ránder), a rich place; Surat, a city of very great trade; Denvy (Gandevi), a place of great trade; Baxay (Bassein), a good seaport in which much goods are exchanged; and Tanamayambu (Thána-Máhim), a town of great Moorish mosques, but of little trade. (Stanley's Barbosa, 59-68). The only one of these ports whose identification seems doubtful is Ravel, described by Barbosa (page 67) as a pretty town of the Moors on a good river, twenty leagues south of Gandhár. This agrees with the position of Ránder on the Tápti, nearly opposite Surat, which appears in Al Birúni (A.D. 1030) as Ráhanur one of the capitals of south Gujarát and is mentioned under the name Ránir, both in the Áin-i-Akbari (A.D. 1590) and in the Mirăt-i-Áhmedi for the year A.D. 1571, as a place of trade, 'in ancient times a great city.' In his description of the wealth of Cambay, Barbosa is supported by the other European travellers of the fifteenth and early sixteenth centuries. According to Nicolo de Conti (A.D. 1420-1444), the town, including its suburbs, was twelve miles in circuit abounding in spikenard, lac, indigo, myrobalans, and silk. Athanasius Nikotin (A.D. 1468-1474) found it a manufacturing place for every sort of goods as long gowns damasks and blankets; and Varthema (A.D. 1503-1508) says it abounds in grain and very good fruits, supplying Africa Arabia and India with silk and cotton stuffs; it is impossible to describe its excellence.' Barbosa's account of Áhmedábád is borne out by the statement in the Áin-i-Akbari (Gladwin, II. 63) that the whole number of the suburbs (*purás*) of the city was 360, and in the Mirăt-i-Áhmedi, that it once contained 380 suburbs each of considerable size, containing good buildings and markets filled with everything valuable and rare, so that each was almost a city. Bird, 311.

Introduction.

CONDITION OF GUJARÁT, A.D. 1297-1760

either its chief nobles or the more turbulent classes. In spite of these forty years of disorder, the province retained so much of its former prosperity, that the boast of the local historians that in A.D. 1573 Gujarát was in every respect allowed to be the finest country in Hindustán is supported by the details shortly afterwards (A.D. 1590) given by Abul Fazl in the Áin-i-Akbari. The high road from Pátan to Baroda was throughout its length of 150 miles (100 *kos*) lined on both sides with mango trees; the fields were bounded with hedges; and such was the abundance of mango and other fruit trees that the whole country seemed a garden. The people were well housed in dwellings with walls of brick and mortar and with tiled roofs; many of them rode in carriages drawn by oxen: the province was famous for its painters, carvers, inlayers, and other craftsmen.[1]

Under the Mughals, 1573-1760.

Like the period of the rule of the Áhmedábád kings, the period of Mughal rule contains two divisions, a time of good government lasting from A.D. 1573 to A.D. 1700, and a time of disorder from A.D. 1700 to A.D. 1760. Under the arrangements introduced by the emperor Akbar in A.D. 1583, the area of the province was considerably curtailed. Of its twenty-five districts nine were restored to the states from which the vigour of the Áhmedábád kings had wrested them; Jálor and Jodhpur were transferred to Rájputána; Nágor to Ajmír; Mulher and Nandurbár to Khándesh; Bombay, Bassein, and Daman were allowed to remain under the Portuguese; and Danda-Rájápuri (Jinjira) was made over to the Nizámsháhi (A.D. 1490-1595) rulers of the Dakhan Ahmednagar. Of the remaining sixteen, Sirohi, Dungarpur, and Bánsváda now in Rájputána, Kachh, Sûnth in Rewa Kántha, and Rámnagar (Dharampur) in Surat were, on the payment of tribute, allowed to continue in the hands of their Hindu rulers. The ten remaining districts were administered directly by imperial officers. But as the revenues of the district of Surat had been separately assigned to its revenue officer or *mutasaddi*, only nine districts with 184 sub-divisions or *parganáhs* were entered in the collections from the viceroy of Gujarát. These nine districts were in continental Gujarát, Pátan with seventeen sub-divisions, Áhmedábád with thirty-three, Godhra with eleven, Chámpáner with thirteen, Baroda with four, Broach with fourteen, and Rájpipla (Nándod) with twelve. In the peninsula were Sorath with sixty-two and Navánagar with seventeen sub-divisions. This lessening of area seems to have been accompanied by even more than a corresponding reduction in the state demand. Instead of £5,840,050 (Rs.5,84,00,500), the revenue recovered in A.D. 1571, two years before the province was annexed, under the arrangement introduced by the emperor Akbar, the total amount, including the receipts from Surat and the tribute of the six feudatory

[1] Gladwin's Áin-i-Akbari, II. 62-63. Compare Terry (Voyage, 80, 181) in 1615: Gujarát a very goodly large and exceeding rich province with, besides its most spacious populous and rich capital Áhmedábád, four fair cities Cambay Baroda Broach and Surat with great trade to the Red Sea, Achin, and other places. At the same time (Ditto, 179-180) though the villages stood very thick, the houses were generally very poor and base, all set close together some with earthen walls and flat roofs, most of them cottages miserably poor little and base set up with sticks rather than timber.

Introduction.

CONDITION OF GUJARÁT, A.D. 1297-1760.

Under the Mughals, 1573-1760.

districts, is returned at £1,999,113 (Rs. 1,99,91,130) or little more than one-third part of what was formerly collected.[1]

According to the Mirát-i-Áhmedi this revenue of £1,999,113 (Rs. 1,99,91,130) continued to be realised as late as the reign of Muhammad Sháh (A.D. 1719-1748). But within the next twelve years (A.D. 1748-1762) the whole revenue had fallen to £1,235,000 (Rs. 1,23,50,000). Of £1,999,113 (Rs. 1,99,91,130), the total amount levied by Akbar on the annexation of the province, £520,501 (Rs. 52,05,010), or a little more than a quarter, were set apart for imperial use and royal expense; £55,000 (Rs. 5,50,000) were assigned for the support of the viceroy and the personal estates of the nobles, and the remainder was settled for the pay of other officers of rank and court officials. Nearly £30,000 (Rs. 3,00,000) were given away as rewards and pensions to religious orders and establishments.[2]

---

[1] The decrease in the Mughal collections from Gujarát compared with the revenues of the Áhmedábád kings may have been due to Akbar's moderation. It may also have been due to a decline in prosperity. Compare Roe's (1617) account of Toda about fifty miles south-east of Ajmír. It was the best and most populous country Roe had seen in India. The district was level with fertile soil abounding in corn cotton and cattle and the villages were so numerous and near together as hardly to exceed a *kos* from each other. The town was the best built Roe had seen in India tiled two-storied houses good enough for decent shopkeepers. It had been the residence of a Rájput Rája before the conquests of Akbar Sháh and stood at the foot of a good and strong rock about which were many excellent works of hewn stone, well cut, with many tanks arched over with well-turned vaults and large and deep descents to them. Near it was a beautiful grove two miles long and a quarter of a mile broad all planted with mangoes tamarinds and other fruit trees, divided by shady walks and interspersed with little temples and idol altars with many fountains wells and summer houses of carved stone curiously arched so that a poor banished Englishman might have been content to dwell there. This observation may serve universally for the whole country that ruin and devastation operate everywhere. For since the property of all has become vested in the king no person takes care of anything so that in every place the spoil and devastations of war appear and nowhere is anything repaired. Roe in Kerr's Voyages, IX. 320-321.

[2] Bird's History of Gujarát. Another detailed statement of the revenue of Gujarát given in the Mirát-i-Áhmedi, apparently for the time when the author wrote (A.D. 1760) gives: Revenue from crown lands £2,107,518; tribute-paying divisions or *sarkárs* £12,700; Mahi Kántha tribute £178,741; Watrak Kántha tribute £159,768; and Sábar Kantha tribute £121,151; in all £2,579,878: adding to this £20,000 for Kachh, £40,000 for Dungarpur, and £5000 for Sirohi, gives a grand total of £2,644,878. According to a statement given by Bird in a note at page 108 of his History, the revenue of Gujarát under Jehángir (A.D. 1605-1627) averaged £1,250,000; under Aurangzíb (A.D. 1658-1707) £1,519,622; and under Muhammad Sháh (A.D. 1719-1748) £1,218,360. In this passage the revenue under the emperor Akbar (A.D. 1556-1605) is given at £66,845. This total is taken from Gladwin's Áin-i-Akbari. But at vol. II. page 73 of that work there would seem to be some miscalculation; for while the total number of *dáms* ($\frac{1}{40}$th of a rupee) is 43,68,02,301, the conversion into rupees is Rs. 10,96,123 instead of Rs. 1,09,20,057½. The corresponding returns given by Mr. Thomas (Rev. of the Mog. Emp. page 52) are under Akbar, A.D. 1594, £1,092,412; under Sháh Jahán, A.D. 1648, £1,325,000; and under Aurangzíb, A.D. 1658 £2,173,220, A.D. 1663-1666 £1,339,500, A.D. 1697 £2,330,500, and A.D. 1707 £1,519,623. The varieties in the currency employed in different parts of the accounts cause some confusion in calculating the Gujarát revenue. Under the Áhmedábád kings the accounts were kept in *tánkás* or $\frac{1}{100}$ of rupees, while under the Mughals *dáms* or $\frac{1}{40}$th of a rupee took the place of *tankás*. The revenues from Surat Baroda Broach and other districts south of the Máhi were returned in *changízis*, a coin varying in value from something over ⅔rds of a rupee to slightly less than ¾; the revenues from Rádhanpur and Morvi were entered in *mahmúdis*, a coin nearly identical in value with the *changízi*, while, as noticed above, the tribute and customs dues are returned in a gold currency, the tribute in *huns* of about 8s. (Rs. 4) and the customs in *ibráhímís* of 9s. (Rs. 4½).

Introduction.

CONDITION OF GUJARÁT, A.D. 1297-1760.

Under the Mughals, 1573-1760.

Besides lightening the state demand the emperor Akbar introduced three improvements: (1) The survey of the land; (2) The payment of the headmen or *mukaddams* of government villages; and (3) The restoration to small superior landholders of the share they formerly enjoyed in the lands of government villages. The survey which was entrusted to Rája Todar Mal, the revenue minister of the empire, was completed in A.D. 1575. The operations were confined to a small portion of the whole area of the province. Besides the six tributary districts which were unaffected by the measure, Godhra in the east, the western peninsula, and a large portion of the central strip of directly governed lands were excluded, so that of the 184 sub-divisions only 64 were surveyed. In A.D. 1575, of 7,261,849 acres (12,360,594 *bighás*), the whole area measured, 4,920,818 acres (8,374,498 *bighás*) or about two-thirds were found to be fit for cultivation, and the remainder was waste. In those parts of the directly governed districts where the land was not measured the existing method of determining the government share of the produce either by selecting a portion of the field while the crop was still standing, or by dividing the grain heap at harvest time, was continued. In surveyed districts the amount paid was determined by the area and character of the land under cultivation. Payment was made either in grain or in money, according to the instructions issued to the revenue-collectors, 'that when it would not prove oppressive the value of the grain should be taken in ready money at the market price.'[1] The chief change in the revenue management was that, instead of each year calculating the government share from the character of the crop, an uniform demand was fixed to run for a term of ten years.

Another important effect of this survey was to extend to cultivators in simple villages the proprietary interest in the soil formerly enjoyed only by the shareholders of joint villages. By this change the power of the military nobles to make undue exactions from the cultivators in their assigned lands was to some extent checked. It was, perhaps, also an indirect effect of this more definite settlement of the crown demand that the revenue agents of government and of the holders of assigned lands, finding that the revenues could be realised without their help, refused to allow to the heads of villages certain revenue dues which, in return for their services, they had hitherto enjoyed. Accordingly, in A.D. 1589-90, these heads of villages appealed to government and Akbar decided that in assigned districts as well as in the crown domains from the collections of government lands two-and-a-half per cent should be set apart as a perquisite for men of this class.[2]

---

[1] Áin-i-Akbari (Gladwin), I. 305. The Áin-i-Akbari mentions four ways of calculating the state share in an unsurveyed field: (1) to measure the land with the crops standing and make an estimate; (2) to reap the crops, collect the grain in barns, and divide it according to agreement; (3) to divide the field as soon as the seed is sown; and (4) to gather the grain into heaps on the field and divide it there.

[2] The men to whom this 2½ per cent was granted are referred to in the Mirăt-i-Áhmedi as *desáis*. Whatever doubt may attach to the precise meaning of the term *desái* it seems clear that it was as village headmen that the *desáis* petitioned for and received this grant. These *desáis* were the heads of villages with whom, as noticed above, the government agent for collecting the revenue dealt, and who, agreeing for the

Introduction.
CONDITION OF GUJARÁT, A.D. 1297-1760.
Under the Mughals, 1573-1760.

When the heads of villages laid their own private grievance before government, they also brought to its notice that the Koli and Rájput landowners, whose shares in government villages had been resumed by the crown in A.D. 1545, had since that time continued in a state of discontent and revolt and were then causing the ruin of the subjects and a deficiency in the government collections. An inquiry was instituted, and, to satisfy the claims of landowners of this class, it was agreed that, on furnishing good security for their conduct and receiving the government mark on their contingent of cavalry, they should again be put in possession of a one-fourth share of the land of government villages. While the province was managed agreeably to these regulations, says the author of the Mirăt-i-Áhmedi, its prosperity continued to increase.[1]

Though these measures did much to check internal disorder, Gujarát, for several years after it came under Mughal control, continued disturbed by insurrections among the nobles, and so imperfectly protected from the attacks of foreign enemies that between the years A.D. 1573 and 1609 each of its three richest cities, Áhmedábád Cambay and Surat, was in turn taken and plundered.[2] During the rest

---

whole village contribution, themselves carried out the details of allotment and collection from the individual cultivators. In the sharehold villages north of the Narbada, the headman who would be entitled to this 2½ per cent was the representative of the body of village shareholders. South of the Narbada, in villages originally colonised by officers of the state, the representatives of these officers would enjoy the 2½ per cent. In south Gujarát the *desdis* or heads of villages also acted as district hereditary revenue officers; but it was not as district hereditary revenue officers, but as heads of villages, that they received from Akbar this 2½ per cent assignment. In north Gujarát there were *desdis* who were only district revenue officers. These men would seem to have received no part of Akbar's grant in 1589-90, for as late as A.D. 1706 the emperor Aurangzíb, having occasion to make inquiries into the position of the *desdis*, found that hitherto they had been supported by cesses and illegal exactions, and ordered that a stop should be put to all such exactions, and a fixed assignment of 2½ per cent on the revenues of the villages under their charge should be allowed them. It does not appear whether the Surat *desdis* succeeded in obtaining Aurangzíb's grant of 2½ per cent as district revenue officers in addition to Akbar's (A.D. 1589) assignment of 2½ per cent as heads of villages.

[1] Bird's History of Gujarát, 409.

[2] Áhmedábád (A.D. 1583) by Muzaffar Sháh the last king of Gujarát; Cambay (A.D. 1573) by Muhammad Husain Mirza; and Surat (A.D. 1609) by Malik Ambar the famous general of the king of Áhmednagar. In such unsettled times it is not surprising that the European travellers of the late sixteenth and early seventeenth centuries, between Áhmedábád and Cambay found native merchants marching in large weekly caravans which rested at night within a space barricaded by carts. (Kerr, IX. 127 and 201.) The English merchants, on their way from one factory to another, were accompanied by an escort, and, in spite of their guard, were on more than one occasion attacked by large bands of Rájputs. (Kerr, IX. 127, 187, 201, 203.) As regards the state of the different parts of the province, Nicholas Ufflet, who went from Agra to Surat about 1610, describes the north, from Jhálor to Áhmedábád, as throughout the whole way a sandy and woody country, full of thievish beastly men, and savage beasts such as lions and tigers; from Áhmedabád to Cambay the road was through sands and woods much infested by thieves; from Cambay to Broach it was a woody and dangerous journey; but from Broach to Surat the country was goodly, fertile, and full of villages, abounding in wild date trees. (Kerr, VIII. 303.) Passing from the mouth of the Tápti to Surat Mr. Copland (24th Dec. 1613) was delighted to see at the same time the goodliest spring and harvest he had ever seen. 'Often of two adjoining fields, one was as green as a fine meadow, and the other waving yellow like gold and ready to be cut down, and all along the roads were many goodly villages.' (Kerr, IX. 119.) At that time the state of north-east Gujarát was very different. Terry, 1617 (Voyage, 404), describes the passage of nineteen days from Mándu near Dhár to Áhmedabád as short journeys in

of the seventeenth century, though the country was from time to time disturbed by Koli and Rájput risings, and towards the end of the century suffered much from the raids of the Maráthás, the viceroys were, on the whole, able to maintain their authority, repressing the outbreaks of the disorderly classes, and enforcing the imperial claims for tribute on the more independent feudatory chiefs. Throughout the greater part of the seventeenth century the general state of the province seems to have been prosperous. Its cities were the wonder of European travellers. Surat, which only since the transfer of Gujarát to the Mughal empire had risen to hold a place among its chief centres of trade, was, in A.D. 1664, when taken by Shiváji, rich enough to supply him with plunder in treasure and precious stones worth a million sterling [1]; and at that time Cambay is said to have been beyond comparison greater than Surat, and Áhmedábád much richer and more populous than either.[2]

From the beginning of the eighteenth century disorder increased. Unable to rely for support on the imperial court, the viceroys failed to maintain order among the leading nobles, or to enforce their tribute from the more powerful feudatories. And while the small Koli and Rájput landholders, freed from the control of a strong central power, were destroying the military posts, taking possession of the state share of village lands, and levying dues from their more peaceful neighbours, the burden of the Marátha tribute was year by year growing heavier. During the last ten years of Musalmán rule so entirely did the viceroy's authority forsake him, that, according to the author of the Mirăt-i-Áhmedi, when the great landholders refused to pay their tribute, the viceroy had no power to enforce payment. And so faithless had the great landowners become that the viceroy could not pass the city gate without an escort.[3]

---

a wilderness where a way had to be cut and made even and the great space required for the Mughal's camp rid and made plain by grubbing up trees and bushes. And between Cambay and Áhmedábád De la Valle, A.D. 1623 (Travels, Haklyt Ed. I. 92), resolved to go with the káfila since the insecurity of the ways did not allow him to go alone. Still at that time Gujarát as a whole (see above page 220 note 2) was an exceeding rich province, a description which twenty years later (1638) is borne out by Mandelslo (Travels, French Edition, 56): No province in India is more fertile; none yields more fruit or victuals. With the boast of the author of the Mirăt-i-Áhmedi (A.D. 1756) that Gujarát was the richest province in India compare Kháfi Khán's (A.D. 1719) remark (Elliot, VII. 530): This rich province which no other province in India can equal.

[1] Orme's Historical Fragments, 12.

[2] The following are some of the notices of Áhmedábád and Cambay by the European travellers of the seventeenth century: Cambay, 1598, trade so great that if he had not seen it he would not have believed it possible (Cæsar Frederick); 1623, indifferent large with sufficiently spacious suburbs and a great concourse of vessels (De la Valle, Haklyt Edition, I. 66-67); 1638, beyond comparison larger than Surat (Mandelslo, 101-108); 1663-1671, twice as big as Surat (Baldæus in Churchill, III. 506). Áhmedábád, 1598, a very great city and populous (Cæsar Frederick); 1623, competently large with great suburbs, a goodly and great city, with large fair and straight but sadly dusty streets (De la Valle, Haklyt Edition, I. 95); 1627, large and beautiful with many broad and comely streets, a rich and uniform bazár, and shops redundant with gums perfumes spices silks cottons and calicoes (Herbert's Travels, 3rd Edition, 66); 1638, great manufactures, satin and velvet, silk and cotton (Mandelslo, 80); 1695, the greatest city in India, nothing inferior to Venice for rich silks and gold stuffs (Gemelli Careri in Churchill, IV. 188).

[3] Bird, 411.

Introduction.

CONDITION OF GUJARÁT, A.D. 1297 - 1760.

Self-governed Zamíndárs.

The above summary contains frequent references to three classes of *zamíndárs*: (1) The *zamíndárs* of the self-governed states; (2) The greater *zamíndárs* of the crown districts; and (3) The lesser *zamíndárs* of the crown districts.

In the case of the *zamíndárs* of self-governed states the principle was military service and no tribute. The author of the Mirăt-i-Áhmedi says that finally the *zamíndárs* of the self-governed states ceased to do service. In spite of this statement it seems probable that some of this class served almost until the complete collapse of the empire, and that tribute was rarely levied from them by an armed force. In the Mirăt-i-Áhmedi account of the office of *súbahdár* or *názim súbah* the following passage occurs: When occasion arose the *názims* used to take with their armies the contingents of the Ránás of Udepur-Dúngarpur and Bánsváda, which were always permanently posted outside their official residences (in Áhmedábád). This shows that these great *zamíndárs* had official residences at the capital, where probably their contingents were posted under *vakíls* or agents. It therefore seems probable that their tribute too would be paid through their representatives at the capital and that a military force was seldom sent against them. Accordingly notices of military expeditions in the tributary *sarkárs* are rare though they were of constant occurrence in the crown districts.

Crown Zamíndárs.

The position of the *zamíndárs* of the *khálsa* or crown districts was very different from that of the *zamíndárs* of self-governed territories. The *khálsa zamíndárs* had been deprived of the greater portion of their ancestral estates which were administered by the viceregal revenue establishment. In some instances their capitals had been annexed. Even if not annexed the capital was the seat of a *faujdár* who possessed the authority and encroached daily on the rights and privileges of the chieftain. The principal chiefs in this position were those of Rájpípla and Ídar in Gujarát and the Jám of Navánagar in Káthiáváḍa. Of the three, Rájpipla had been deprived of his capital Nándod and of all the fertile districts, and was reduced to a barren sovereignty over rocks hills and Bhíls at Rájpípla. Ídar had suffered similar treatment and the capital was the seat of a Muhammadan *faujdár*. Navánagar, which had hitherto been a tributary *sarkár*, was during the reign of Aurangzíb made a crown district. But after Aurangzíb's death the Jám returned to his capital and again resumed his tributary relations.

Smaller Zamíndárs.

The lesser holders, including *grásiás wántádárs* and others, had suffered similar deprivation of lands and were subject to much encroachment from the government officials. Throughout the empire widespread discontent prevailed among subordinate holders of this description as well as among all the *zamíndárs* of the crown districts, so that the successes of Shiváji in the Dakhan found ardent sympathisers even in Gujarát. When the *zamíndárs* saw that this Hindu rebel was strong enough to pillage Surat they began to hope that a day of deliverance was near. The death of Aurangzíb (A.D. 1707) was the signal for these restless spirits to bestir themselves. When the Maráthás began regular inroads they were hailed as deliverers from the yoke

Introduction.

CONDITION OF GUJARÁT, A.D. 1297-1760.

of the Mughal. The Rájpípla chief afforded them shelter and a passage through his country. The encouragement to anarchy given by some of the Rájput viceroys who were anxious to emancipate themselves from the central control further enabled many chieftains *girásiás* and others to absorb large portions of the crown domains, and even to recover their ancient capitals. Finally disaffected Muhammadan *faujdárs* succeeded in building up estates out of the possessions of the crown and founding the families which most of the present Muhammadan chieftains of Gujarát represent.

Marátha Ascendancy, 1760-1802.

When the imperial power had been usurped by the Marátha leaders, the chiefs who had just shaken off the more powerful Mughal yoke were by no means disposed tamely to submit to Marátha domination. Every chief resisted the levy of tribute and Momin Khán reconquered Ahmedábád. In this struggle the Maráthás laboured under the disadvantage of dissensions between the Peshwa and the Gáikwár. They were also unaware of the actual extent of the old imperial domain and were ignorant of the amount of tribute formerly levied. They found that the *faujdárs*, who, in return for Marátha aid in enabling them to absorb the crown *parganáhs*, had agreed to pay tribute, now joined the *zamíndárs* in resisting Marátha demands, while with few exceptions the *desáis* and *majmudárs* either openly allied themselves with the *zamíndárs* or were by force or fraud deprived of their records.

Gáikwár Saved by British Alliance, 1802.

So serious were the obstacles to the collection of the Marátha tribute that, had it not been for the British alliance in A.D. 1802, there seems little doubt that the Gáikwár would have been unable to enforce his demands in his more distant possessions. The British alliance checked the disintegration of the Gáikwár's power, and the permanent settlement of the tribute early in this century enabled that chief to collect a large revenue at a comparatively trifling cost. Not only were rebels like Malhárráo and Kánoji suppressed, but powerful servants like Vithalráv Deváji, who without doubt would have asserted their independence, were confirmed in their allegiance and the rich possessions they had acquired became part of the Gáikwár's dominions.

Power of Chiefs.

It must not be supposed that while the larger chiefs were busy absorbing whole *parganáhs* the lesser chiefs were more backward. They too annexed villages and even Mughal posts or *thánáhs*, while *wántádárs* or sharers absorbed the *talpat* or state portion, and, under the name of *tora garás*,[1] daring spirits imposed certain rights over crown villages once their ancient possessions, or, under the name of *pál* or *vol*, enforced from neighbouring villages payments to secure immunity from pillage. Even in the Baroda district of the thirteen Mughal posts only ten now belong to the Gáikwár, two having been conquered by *girásiás* and one having fallen under Broach. In Sauráshtra except Ránpur and Gogha and those in the Amreli district, not a single Mughal post is in the possession either of the British Government or of the

[1] The usual explanation of *toda garás* is the word *toda* meaning the beam-end above each house door. The sense being that it was a levy exacted from every house in the village. A more likely derivation is *toda* a heap or money-bag with the sense of a ready-money levy. *Toda* differed from *vol* in being exacted from the *garás* or land once the property of the levier's ancestors.

Introduction.

CONDITION OF GUJARÁT, A.D. 1297-1802.

Gáikwár. A reference to the Mughal posts in other parts of Gujarát shows that the same result followed the collapse of Musalmán power.

Power of Local Chiefs.

Since the introduction of Musalmán rule in A.D. 1297 each successive government has been subverted by the ambition of the nobles and the disaffection of the chiefs. It was thus that the Gujarát Sultáns rendered themselves independent of Dehli. It was thus that the Sultán's territories became divided among the nobles, whose dissensions reduced the province to Akbar's authority. It was thus that the chiefs and local governors, conniving at Marátha inroads, subverted Mughal rule. Finally it was thus that the Gáikwár lost his hold of his possessions and was rescued from ruin solely by the power of the British.

CHAPTER I.

EARLY MUSALMÁN GOVERNORS.

A.D. 1297-1403.

Chapter I.

Early Musalmán Governors.

Ala-ud-din Khilji Emperor, 1295-1315.

ULUGH KHÁN, 1297-1317.

EXCEPT the great expedition of Mahmúd Ghaznawi against Somnáth in A.D. 1024[1]; the defeat of Muhammad Muiz-ud-dín or Shaháb-ud-dín Ghori by Bhím Dev II. of Anahiláváda about A.D. 1178[2]; and the avenging sack of Anahiláváda and defeat of Bhím by Kutb-ud-dín Eibak in A.D. 1194, until the reign of Alá-ud-dín Khilji in A.D. 1295-1315, Gujarát remained free from Muhammadan interference.[3] In A.D. 1297, Ulugh Khán, general of Alá-ud-dín and Nasrat Khán Wazír were sent against Anahiláváda. They took the city expelling Karan Wághela, usually called *Ghelo* The Mad, who took refuge at Devgadh with Rámdeva the Yádav sovereign of the north Dakhan.[4] They next seized Khambát (the modern Cambay), and, after appointing a local governor, returned to Dehli. From this time Gujarát remained under Muhammadan power, and Ulugh Khán, a man of great energy, by repeated expeditions consolidated the conquest and established Muhammadan rule. The Kánaddeva Rása says that he plundered Somnáth, and there is no doubt that he conquered Jhálor (the ancient Jhálindar) from the Songarha Chohháns.[5] After Ulugh Khán had governed Gujarát for about twenty years, at the instigation of Malik Káfur, he was recalled and put to death by the emperor Alá-ud-dín.[6]

AIN-UL-MULK Governor, 1318.

Ulugh Khán's departure shook Muhammadan power in Gujarát, and Kamál-ud-dín, whom Mubárak Khilji sent to quell the disturbances, was slain in battle. Sedition spread till Ain-ul-Mulk Multáni arrived

---

[1] Somnáth (north latitude 20° 55'; east longitude 70° 23'), the temple of Mahádev 'Lord of the Moon,' near the southern extremity of the peninsula of Káthiáváda.

[2] Anahiláváda (north latitude 23° 48'; east longitude 72° 2'), Nehrwála or Pátan, on the south bank of the Saraswati river, sixty-five miles north-east of Ahmedábád, was from A.D. 746 to A.D. 1298 the capital of the Rájput dynasties of Gujarát. As a result of Muhammad Ghori's defeat the Tárikh-i-Sorath (Burgess, 112-113) states that the Turkish Afghán and Mughal prisoners, according to the rule of the Kurán (XXIV. 25) were distributed, the wicked women to the wicked men and the good women to the good men. Of the male prisoners the better class after having their heads shaved were enrolled among the Chakáwal and Wadhel tribes of Rájputs. The lower class were allotted to the Kolis, Khánts, Bábriás, and Mers. All were allowed to keep their wedding and funeral ceremonies and to remain aloof from other classes.

[3] The Mirát-i-Áhmedi gives an account of an expedition by one Alifkhán a noble of Sultán Sanjar's against Anahiláváda in A.D. 1257. He is said to have built the large stone mosque without the city. Alifkhán returned unsuccessful, but not without levying tribute.

[4] Devgadh near Daulatabad in the Dakhan, about ten miles north-west of Aurangábád (north latitude 19° 57'; east longitude 75° 18'). The Mirát-i-Áhmedi has Devgadh Chandah, which is in the Central Provinces.

[5] Jhálor (north latitude 25° 23'; east longitude 72° 40') in the Rájput state of Jodhpur, seventy miles south-west by south from the city of Jodhpur.

[6] Bayley (Gujarát, 39 note) shows strong ground for holding that, though Gujarát was conquered by Ulugh Khán a brother of Alá-ud-dín, its first governor was not Ulugh Khán but Álp Khán a brother-in-law of Alá-ud-dín. According to this account Ulugh Khán died in A.D. 1299 and Álp Khán at Malik Káfúr's instigation was killed in A.D. 1315. Ziá Barni (Elliot, III. 169) supports this account.

Chapter I.
Early Musalmán Governors.
Ain-ul-Mulk Governor, 1318.
Order Established, 1318.

with a powerful army, defeated the rebels and restored order. He was succeeded by Zafar Khán, who after completing the subjection of the country was recalled, and his place supplied by Hisám-ud-dín Parmár.[1] This officer, showing treasonable intentions, was imprisoned and succeeded by Malik Wájid-ud-dín Kuraishi, who was afterwards ennobled by the title of Táj or Sadr-ul-Mulk. Khusraw Khán Parmár was then appointed governor, but it is not clear whether he ever joined his appointment. The next governor to whom reference is made is Táj-ul-Mulk, who about A.D. 1320, was, for the second time, chosen as governor by Sultán Ghiás-ud-dín Tughlak. He was succeeded by Malik Mukbil, who held the titles of Khán Jahán and Náib-i-Mukhtár, and who was appointed by Sultán Muhammad Tughlak, A.D. 1325-1351. Subsequently the same emperor granted the government of Gujarát to Áhmad Ayáz, Malik Mukbil continuing to act as his deputy. Afterwards when Áhmad Ayáz, who received the title of Khwájah Jahán, proceeded as governor to Gujarát, Malik Mukbil acted as his minister. And about A.D. 1338, when Khwájah Jahán was sent against the emperor's nephew Karshásp and the Rája of Kampila[2] who had sheltered him, Malik Mukbil succeeded to the post of governor. On one occasion between Baroda and Dabhoi Malik Mukbil, who was escorting treasure and a caravan of merchants to Dehli, was plundered by some bands of the Amíráni Sadah or Captains of Hundreds freelances and freebooters, most of them New Musalmáns or Mughal converts, and the rest Turk and Afghán adventurers. This success emboldened these banditti and for several years they caused loss and confusion in Gujarát. At last, about A.D. 1346, being joined by certain Muhammadan nobles and Hindu chieftains, they broke into open rebellion and defeated one Áziz, who was appointed by the emperor to march against them. In the following year, A.D. 1347, Muhammad Tughlak, advancing in person, defeated the rebels, and sacked the towns of Cambay and Surat. During the same campaign he drove the Gohil chief Mokheráji out of his stronghold on Piram Island near Gogha on the Gulf of Cambay, and then, landing his forces, after a stubborn conflict, defeated the Gohils, killing Mokheráji and capturing Gogha. Afterwards Muhammad Tughlak left for Daulatábád in the Dakhan, and in his absence the chiefs and nobles under Malik Túghán, a leader of the Amíráni Sadah, again rebelled, and, obtaining possession of Pátan, imprisoned Muizz-ud-dín the viceroy. The insurgents then plundered Cambay, and afterwards laid siege to Broach. Muhammad Tughlak at once marched for Gujarát and relieved Broach, Malik Túghán retreating to Cambay, whither he was followed by Malik Yúsuf, whom the emperor sent in pursuit of him. In the battle that ensued near Cambay, Malik Yúsuf was defeated and slain, and

Muhammad Tughlak Emperor, 1325-1351.
Táj-ul-Mulk Governor, 1320.

The Emperor Quells an Insurrection, 1347.

[1] According to Ziá Barni (Elliot, III. 218) Hisám-ud-dín was the mother's brother, according to others he was the brother of Hasan afterwards Khusraw Khán Parmár the favourite of Mubárak Sháh. On coming to Gujarát Hisám-ud-dín collected his Parmár kindred and revolted, but the nobles joining against him seized him and sent him to Dehli. To their disgust Mubárak in his infatuation for Hisám-ud-dín's nephew or brother, after slapping Hisám-ud-dín on the face set him at liberty.

[2] In the Karnátak, probably on the Tungabhadra near Vijayanagar. Briggs' Muhammadan Power in India, I. 418 and 428. Briggs speaks of two Kampilás one on the Ganges and the other on the Tungbhadra near Bijánagar.

Chapter I. Early Musalmán Governors.

Muhammad Tughlak Emperor, 1325-1351.

all the prisoners, both of this engagement and those who had been previously captured, were put to death by Malik Túghán. Among the prisoners was Muîzz-ud-dín, the governor of Gujarát. Muhammad Tughlak now marched to Cambay in person, whence Malik Túghán retreated to Pátan, pursued by the emperor, who was forced by stress of weather to halt at Asáwal.[1] Eventually the emperor came up with Malik Túghán near Kadi and gained a complete victory, Malik Túghán fleeing to Thatha in Sindh. To establish order throughout Gujarát Muhammad Tughlak marched against Girnár,[2] reduced the fortress,[3] and levied tribute from the chief named Khengár. He then went to Kachh, and after subduing that country returned to Sorath. At Gondal he contracted a fever, and before he was entirely recovered, he advanced through Kachh into Sindh with the view of subduing the Sumra chief of Thatha, who had sheltered Malik Túghán. Before reaching Thatha he succumbed to the fever, and died in the spring of A.D. 1351. Shortly before his death he appointed Nizám-ul-Mulk to the government of Gujarát.

Táj-ul-Mulk Governor, 1320.

Subdues Girnár and Kachh, 1350.

Firuz Tughlak Emperor, 1351-1388.

In A.D. 1351, Fírúz Túghlak succeeded Muhammad Tughlak on the throne of Dehli. Shortly after his accession the emperor marched to Sindh and sent a force against Malik Túghán. About A.D. 1360 he again advanced to Sindh against Jám Bábunia. From Sindh he proceeded to Gujarát, where he stayed for some months. Next year, on leaving for Sindh for the third time, he bestowed the government of Gujarát on Zafar Khán in place of Nizám-ul-Mulk. On Zafar Khán's death, in A.D. 1373 according to Farishtah and A.D. 1371 according to the Mirăt-i-Ahmedi, he was succeeded by his son Daryá Khán who appears to have governed by a deputy named Shams-ud-dín Anwar Khán. In A.D. 1376, besides presents of elephants horses and other valuables, one Shams-ud-dín Dámghání offered a considerable advance on the usual collections from Gujarát. As Daryá Khán would not agree to pay this sum he was displaced and Shams-ud-dín Dámghání was appointed governor. Finding himself unable to pay the stipulated amount this officer rebelled and withheld the revenue. Fírúz Tughlak sent an army against him, and by the aid of the chieftains and people, whom he had greatly oppressed, Shams-ud-dín was slain. The government of the province was then entrusted to Farhat-ul-Mulk Rásti Khán. In about A.D. 1388, a noble named Sikandar Khán was sent to supersede Farhat-ul-Mulk, but was defeated and slain by him. As the emperor Fírúz Túghlak died shortly after no notice was taken of Farhat-ul-Mulk's conduct and in the short reign of Fírúz's successor Ghiás-ud-dín Tughlak, no change was made in the government of Gujarát. During the brief rule of Abu Bakr, Farhat-ul-Mulk continued

Zafar Khan Governor, 1371.

Farhat-ul-Mulk Governor, 1376-1391.

---

[1] Asáwal (north latitude 23° 0'; east longitude 72° 36'), a town of some size, afterwards, A.D. 1413, made the capital of the Musalmán kings of Gujarát and called Ahmedábád.

[2] Girnár (north latitude 21° 30'; east longitude 70° 42'), in the Sorath sub-division of the peninsula of Káthiáváda.

[3] Both the Mirăt-i-Ahmedi and the Táríkh-i-Fírúz Sháhi say that the fortress was taken. The Úparkot or citadel of Junágadh, in the plain about two miles west of Mount Girnár, is probably meant.

Chapter I.
Early Musalmán Governors.

undisturbed. But in A.D. 1391, on the accession of Násír-ud-dín Muhammad Tughlak II., a noble of the name of Zafar Khán was appointed governor of Gujarát, and despatched with an army to recall or, if necessary, expel Farhat-ul-Mulk.

Muhammad Tughlak II. Emperor, 1391-1393.

This Zafar Khán was the son of Wajíh-ul-Mulk, of the Tánk tribe of Rájputs who claim to be of Suryavansi descent and together with the Gurjjaras appear from very early times to have inhabited the plains of the Punjáb. Of Wajíh-ul-Mulk's rise to power at the Dehli court the following story is told. Before he sat on the throne of Dehli, Fíráz Tughlak, when hunting in the Punjáb, lost his way and came to a village near Thánesar, held by chieftains of the Tánk tribe. He was hospitably entertained by two brothers of the chief's family named Sáháran and Sádhu, and became enamoured of their beautiful sister. When his hosts learned who the stranger was, they gave him their sister in marriage and followed his fortunes. Afterwards Fírúz persuading them to embrace Islám, conferred on Saháran the title of Wajíh-ul-Mulk, and on Sádhu the title of Shamshír Khán. Finally, in A.D. 1351, when Fírúz Tughlak ascended the throne, he made Shamshír Khán and Zafar Khán, the son of Wajíh-ul-Mulk, his cup-bearers, and raised them to the rank of nobles.

Zafar Khán Governor, 1391-1403.

In A.D. 1391, on being appointed viceroy, Zafar Khán marched without delay for Gujarát. In passing Nágor[1] he was met by a deputation from Cambay, complaining of the tyranny of Rásti Khán. Consoling them, he proceeded to Pátan, the seat of government, and thence marched against Rásti Khán. The armies met near the village of Khambhoi,[2] a dependency of Pátan, and Farhat-ul-Mulk Rásti Khán was slain and his army defeated. To commemorate the victory, Zafar Khán founded a village on the battle-field, which he named Jítpur (the city of victory), and then, starting for Cambay, redressed the grievances of the people.

Battle of Jitpur; Farhat-ul-Mulk Slain, 1391.

Zafar Khán Attacks Ídar, 1393.

Zafar Khán's first warlike expedition was against the Ráv of Ídar,[3] who, in A.D. 1393, had refused to pay the customary tribute, and this chief he humbled. The contemporary histories seem to show that the previous governors had recovered tribute from all or most of the chiefs of Gujarát except from the Ráv of Júnágadh[4] and the Rája of Rájpípla,[5] who had retained their independence. Zafar Khán now planned an expedition against the celebrated Hindu shrine of Somnáth, but, hearing that Ádil Khán of Ásír-Burhánpur had invaded Sultánpur and Nandurbár,[6] he moved his troops in that direction, and Ádil Khán retired to Ásír.[7]

---

[1] Nágor (north latitude 27° 10; east longitude 73° 50'), in the Ráthod state of Jodhpur, eighty miles north-east of Jodhpur city.

[2] The Tabakát-i-Ákbari has Khánpur or Kánpur. The place is Khambhoi about twenty miles west of Pátan.

[3] Ídar is the principal state of the Mahi Kántha. The town of Ídar is in north latitude 23° 50' and east longitude 73° 3'.

[4] Junágadh in the Sorath sub-division of Káthiáváda. This is Briggs' Rái of Jehrend. Junágadh was formerly called Jirangad, both names meaning ancient fortress.

[5] Rájpípla is in the Rewa Kántha division of Gujarát.

[6] Sultánpur and Nandurbár now form part of the British district of Khándesh.

[7] Ásír, now Ásírgad (north latitude 21° 26'; east longitude 76° 26'), beyond the north-eastern frontier of Khándesh.

Chapter I.

Early Musalmán Governors.

ZAFAR KHÁN Governor, 1391-1403.

Exacts Tribute from Junágadh, 1394.

In A.D. 1394, he marched against the Ráv of Júnágadh and exacted tribute. Afterwards, proceeding to Somnáth, he destroyed the temple, built an Assembly Mosque, introduced Islám, left Musalmán law officers, and established a *thána* or post in the city of Pátan Somnáth or Deva Pátan. He now heard that the Hindus of Mándu[1] were oppressing the Muslims, and, accordingly, marching thither, he beleaguered that fortress for a year, but failing to take it contented himself with accepting the excuses of the Rája. From Mándu he performed a pilgrimage to Ajmír.[2] Here he proceeded against the chiefs of Sámbhar and Dandwána, and then attacking the Rájputs of Delváda and Jháláváda,[3] he defeated them, and returned to Pátan in A.D. 1396. About this time his son Tátár Khán, leaving his baggage in the fort of Pánipat,[4] made an attempt on Dehli. But Ikbál Khán took the fort of Pánipat, captured Tátár Khán's baggage, and forced him to withdraw to Gujarát. In A.D. 1397, with the view of reducing Ídar, Zafar Khán besieged the fort, laying waste the neighbouring country. Before he had taken the fort Zafar Khán received news of Timúr's conquests, and concluding a peace with the Ídar Rája, returned to Pátan.[5] In A.D. 1398, bearing that the Somnáth people claimed independence, Zafar Khán led an army against them, defeated them, and established Islám on a firm footing.

Lays Siege to Ídar Fort, 1397.

Establishes Islám at Somnáth, 1398.

---

[1] Mándu (north latitude 22° 20′; east longitude 75° 27′), one of the most famous forts in India, the capital of the Pathán dynasty of Málwa, A.D. 1404-1561, stands on the crest of the Vindhyás about twenty-five miles south of Dhár. During a considerable part of the fifteenth century Mándu was either directly or indirectly under Gujarát. An account of Mándu is given in the Appendix.

[2] Ajmír (north latitude 26° 29; east longitude 74° 43′), the chief town of the district of the same name to which Sámbhar and Dandwána belong.

[3] Delváda and Jhálváda are somewhat difficult. The context suggests either Jhálor in Márwár or Jhálává‍da in the extreme south-east of Rajputána south of Kotah. The combination Delváda and Jhálává‍da seems to favour Káthiáváda since there is a Delváda in the south of the peninsula near Diu and a Jhálává‍da in the north-east. But the Delváda of the text can hardly be near Diu. It apparently is Delváda near Eklingji about twenty miles north of Udepur. The account of Áhmed Sháh's expedition to the same place in A.D. 1431 (below page 239) confirms this identification.

[4] Pánipat (north latitude 29° 23′; east longitude 77° 2′), seventy-eight miles north of Dehli.

[5] Farishtah (II. 355) calls the Ídar chief Ranbal.

CHAPTER II.

A'HMEDA'BA'D KINGS.

A.D. 1403-1573.

Chapter II.
Ahmedábád Kings.
A.D. 1403-1573.

The rule of the Áhmedábád kings extends over 170 years and includes the names of fifteen sovereigns. The period may conveniently be divided into two parts. The first, lasting for a little more than a century and a quarter, when, under strong rulers, Gujarát rose to consequence among the kingdoms of Western India; the second, from A.D. 1536 to A.D. 1573, an evil time when the sovereigns were minors and the wealth and supremacy of Gujarát were wasted by the rivalry of its nobles.

The date on which Zafar Khán openly threw off his allegiance to Dehli is doubtful. Farishtah says he had the Friday prayer or *khutbah* repeated in his name after his successful campaign against Jhálávâda and Delváḍa in A.D. 1396. According to the Mirât-i-Sikandari he maintained a nominal allegiance till A.D. 1403 when he formally invested his son Tátár Khán with the sovereignty of Gujarát, under the title of Násir-ud-dín Muhammad Sháh.

Muhammad I.
1403-1404.

On ascending the throne in A.D. 1403, Muhammad Sháh made Asáwal his capital, and, after humbling the chief of Nándoḍ or Nádot in Rájpipla, marched against Dehli by way of Pátan. On his way to Pátan the king sickened and died. His body was brought back to Pátan, and the expedition against Dehli came to nothing. It seems probable that this is a courtly version of the tale; the fact being that in A.D. 1403 Tátár Khán imprisoned his father at Asáwal, and assumed the title of Muhammad Sháh, and that Tátár Khán's death was caused by poison administered in the interest, if not at the suggestion, of his father Zafar Khán.[1]

Zafar Khán reigns as Muzaffar.
1407-1419.

After the death of Muhammad Sháh, Zafar Khán asked his own younger brother Shams Khán Dandáni to carry on the government, but he refused. Zafar Khán accordingly sent Shams Khán Dandáni to Nágor in place of Jalál Khán Khokhar, and in A.D. 1407-8, at Bírpur, at the request of the nobles and chief men of the country, himself formally mounted the throne and assumed the title of Muzaffar Sháh. At this time Alp Khán, son of Diláwar Khán of Málwa, was rumoured to have poisoned his father and ascended the throne with the title of Sultán Hushang Ghori. On hearing this Muzaffar Sháh marched against

---

[1] Compare Farishtah, II. 355-356. After his death Muhammad was known as Khudáigán-i-Shahíd, Our Lord the Martyr, according to the custom of the Sultáns of Dehli, all of whom had three names, their family name, their throne name, and their after-death name whose letters contain the date of the monarch's decease. Thus the emperor Akbar's after-death title is 'Arsh Áshiáni, The Holder of the Heavenly Throne; the emperor Jehángír's is Jannat Makáni, The Dweller in Heaven; the emperor Sháh Jehán's is Firdaus Makáni, He Whose Home is Paradise; and the emperor Aurangzib's is Khuld Makáni, The Occupier of the Eternal Residence. Similarly the after-death title of Muzaffar Sháh, Tátár Khán's father, is Khudáigán-i-Kabir, The Great Lord.

Muzaffar. 1407-1419.

Hushang and besieged him in Dhár.[1] On reducing Dhár Muzaffar handed Hushang to the charge of his brother Shams Khán, on whom he conferred the title of Nasrat Khán. Hushang remained a year in confinement, and Músa Khán one of his relations usurped his authority. On hearing this, Hushang begged to be released, and Muzaffar Sháh not only agreed to his prayer, but sent his grandson Áhmed Khán with an army to reinstate him. This expedition was successful; the fortress of Mándu was taken and the usurper Músa Khán was put to flight. Áhmed Khán returned to Gujarát in A.D. 1409-10. Meanwhile Muzaffar advancing towards Dehli to aid Sultán Mahmúd (A.D. 1393-1413), prevented an intended attack on that city by Sultán Ibráhím of Jaunpúr. On his return to Gujarát Muzaffar led, or more probably despatched, an unsuccessful expedition against Kambhkot.[2] In the following year (A.D. 1410-11), to quell a rising among the Kolis near Asával, Muzaffar placed his grandson Áhmed Khán in command of an army. Áhmed Khán camped outside of Pátan. He convened an assembly of learned men and asked them whether a son was not bound to exact retribution from his father's murderer. The assembly stated in writing that a son was bound to exact retribution. Armed with this decision, Áhmed suddenly entered the city, overpowered his grandfather, and forced him to drink poison. The old Khán said: 'Why so hasty, my boy. A little patience and power would have come to you of itself.' He advised Áhmed to kill the evil counsellors of murder and to drink no wine. Remorse so embittered Áhmed's after-life that he was never known to laugh.

Ahmed I. 1411-1441.

On his grandfather's death, Áhmed succeeded with the title of Násir-ud-dunya Wad-dín Abúl fateh Áhmed Sháh. Shortly after Áhmed Sháh's accession, his cousin Moid-ud-dín Fírúz Khán, governor of Baroda, allying himself with Hisám or Nizám-ul-Mulk Bhandári and other nobles, collected an army at Nadiád in Kaira, and, laying claim to the crown, defeated the king's followers. Jívandás, one of the insurgents, proposed to march upon Pátan, but as the others refused a dispute arose in which Jívandás was slain, and the rest sought and obtained Áhmed Sháh's forgiveness. Moid-ud-dín Fírúz Khán went to Cambay and was there joined by Masti Khán, son of Muzaffar Sháh, who was governor of Surat: on the king's advance they fled from Cambay to Broach, to which fort Ahmed Sháh laid siege. As soon as the king arrived, Moid-ud-dín's army went over to the king, and Masti Khán also submitted. After a few days Áhmed Sháh sent for and forgave Moid-ud-dín, and returned to Asáwal victorious and triumphant.

Builds Áhmedábád, 1413.

In the following year (A.D. 1413-14)[3] Áhmed Sháh defeated Ása Bhíl, chief of Asáwal, and, finding the site of that town suitable for his capital, he changed its name to Áhmedábád, and busied himself

[1] Dhár (north latitude 22° 35'; east longitude 75° 20'), the capital of the state of Dhár thirty-three miles west of Mhow in Central India.

[2] The Tabakát-i-Akbári has Kanthkot a dependency of Kachh. This is probably correct.

[3] The date is doubtful: Farishtah (II. 630) gives A.D. 1412, the Áín-i-Akbári (Blochman's Edition, I. 507) A.D. 1411.

Chapter II.
Áhmedábád Kings, A.D. 1403-1573.
Ahmed I. 1411-1441.
Defeats the Ídar Chief, 1414.

in enlarging and fortifying the city.[1] During this year Moid-ud-dín Fírúz Khán and Masti Khán again revolted, and, joining the Ídar Rája, took shelter in that fortress. A force under Fateh Khán was despatched against the rebels, and finally Fírúz Khán and the Ídar Rája were forced to flee by way of Kherálu a town in the district of Kadi. Moid-ud-dín now persuaded Rukn Khán governor of Modása, fifty miles north of Áhmedábád, to join. They united their forces with those of Badri-úlá, Masti Khán, and Ranmal Rája of Ídar and encamped at Rangpura an Ídar village about five miles from Modása and began to strengthen Modása and dig a ditch round it. The Sultán camped before the fort and offered favourable terms. The besieged bent on treachery asked the Sultán to send Nizám-ul-Mulk the minister and certain other great nobles. The Sultán agreed, and the besieged imprisoned the envoys. After a three days' siege Modása fell. Badri-úlá and Rukn Khán were slain, and Fírúz Khán and the Rája of Ídar fled. The imprisoned nobles were released unharmed. The Rája seeing that all hope of success was gone, made his peace with the king by surrendering to him the elephants horses and other baggage of Moid-ud-dín Fírúz Khán and Masti Khán, who now fled to Nágor, where they were sheltered by Shams Khán Dandáni. Áhmed Sháh after levying the stipulated tribute departed. Moid-ud-dín Fírúz Khán was afterwards slain in the war between Shams Khán and Rána Mokal of Chitor.

Suppresses a Revolt, 1414.

In A.D. 1414-15 Uthmán Áhmed and Sheikh Malik, in command at Pátan, and Suleimán Afghán called Ázam Khán, and Ísa Sálár rebelled, and wrote secretly to Sultán Hushang of Málwa, inviting him to invade Gujarát, and promising to seat him on the throne and expel Áhmed Sháh. They were joined in their rebellion by Jhála Satarsálji[2] of Pátdi and other chiefs of Gujarát. Áhmed Sháh despatched Latíf Khán and Nizám-ul-Mulk against Sheikh Malik and his associates, while he sent Imád-ul-Mulk aginst Sultán Hushang, who retired, and Imád-ul-Mulk, after plundering Málwa, returned to Gujarát. Latíf Khán, pressing in hot pursuit of Satarsál and Sheikh Malik, drove them to Sorath. The king returned with joyful heart to Áhmedábád.

Spread of Islám, 1414.

Though, with their first possession of the country, A.D. 1297-1318, the Muhammadans had introduced their faith from Pátan to Broach, the rest of the province long remained unconverted. By degrees, through the efforts of the Áhmedábád kings, the power of Islám became more directly felt in all parts of the province. Many districts, till then all but independent, accepted the Musalmán faith at the hands of Áhmed Sháh, and agreed to the payment of a regular tribute. In A.D. 1414 he led an army against the Ráv of Júnágadh and defeated him. The Ráv retired to the hill fortress of Girnár. Áhmed Sháh, though unable to capture the hill, gained the fortified citadel of Júnágadh. Finding further resistance vain, the chief tendered his submission, and Júnágadh was admitted among the tributary states.

---

[1] Four Áhmeds who had never missed the afternoon prayer helped to build Áhmedábád: Saint Sheikh Áhmed Khattu, Sultán Áhmed, Sheikh Áhmed, and Mulla Áhmed. Compare Bombay Gazetteer, IV. 249 note 5.

[2] Called in the Tabakát-i-Akbári the Rája of Mandal.

Ahmed I.
1411-1441.

Áhmed I. Quells a Second Revolt, 1416.

This example was followed by the greater number of the Sorath chiefs, who, for the time, resigned their independence. Sayad Ábûl Khair and Sayad Kásim were left to collect the tribute, and Áhmed Sháh returned to Áhmedábád. Next year he marched against Sidhpur,[1] and in A.D. 1415 advanced from Sidhpur to Dhár in Málwa. At this time the most powerful feudatories were the Ráv of Junágaḍh, the Rával of Chámpáner,[2] the Rája of Nándoḍ, the Ráv of Ídar, and the Rája of Jhálávâḍa. Trimbakdás of Chámpáner, Púnja of Ídar, Siri of Nándoḍ, and Mándlik of Jhálávâḍa, alarmed at the activity of Áhmed Sháh and his zeal for Islám, instigated Sultán Hushang of Málwa to invade Gujarát. Áhmed Sháh promptly marched to Modása,[3] forced Sultán Hushang of Málwa to retire, and broke up the conspiracy, reproving and pardoning the chiefs concerned. About the same time the Sorath chiefs withheld their tribute, but the patience and unwearied activity of the king overcame all opposition. When at Modása Áhmed heard that, by the treachery of the son of the governor, Násír of Asír and Gheirát or Ghazni Khán of Málwa had seized the fort of Thálner in Sirpur in Khándesh, and, with the aid of the chief of Nándoḍ, were marching against Sultánpur and Nandurbár. Áhmed sent an expedition against Nasír of Asír under Malik Mahmúd Barki or Turki. When the Malik reached Nándoḍ he found that Gheirat Khán had fled to Málwa and that Nasír had retired to Thálner. The Malik advanced, besieged and took Thálner, capturing Nasír whom Áhmed forgave and dignified with the title of Khán.[4]

Expedition against Málwa, 1417.

After quelling these rebellions Áhmed Sháh despatched Nizám-ul-Mulk to punish the Rája of Mandal near Viramgám, and himself marched to Málwa against Sultán Hushang, whom he defeated, capturing his treasure and elephants. In A.D. 1418, in accordance with his policy of separately engaging his enemies, Áhmed Sháh marched to chastise Trimbakdás of Chámpáner, and though unable to take the fortress he laid waste the surrounding country. In A.D. 1419 he ravaged the lands round Sankheda[5] and built a fort there and a mosque within the fort; he also built a wall round the town of Mángni,[6] and then marched upon Mándu. On the way ambassadors from Sultán Hushang met him suing for peace, and Áhmed Sháh, returning towards Chámpáner, again laid waste the surrounding country. During the following year (A.D. 1420) he remained in Áhmedábád bringing his own dominions into thorough subjection by establishing fortified posts and by humbling the chiefs and destroying their strongholds. Among other works he built the forts of Dohad[7] on the

Attacks Chámpáner, 1418.

---

[1] Sidhpur (north latitude 23°50′; east longitude 72° 20′), on the Sarasvati, fifty-eight miles north of Áhmedábád.

[2] Chámpáner (north latitude 22° 30′; east longitude 73° 30′), in the British district of the Panch Mahâls, from A.D. 1483 to A.D. 1560 the chief city of Gujarát, now in ruins.

[3] Modása (north latitude 23° 27′; east longitude 73° 21′), fifty miles north east of Áhmedábád.

[4] Mirát-i-Sikandari Persian Text, 34, 35; Farishtah, II. 363, 364.

[5] Sankheda is on the left bank of the Or river about twenty miles south-east of Baroda.

[6] Mángni Mákani or Mánki, famous for its witches, eight miles east of Sankheda. Mr. J. Pollen, I.C.S., LL.D. Compare Bom. Gov. Rec. N. S. XXIII. 98.

[7] Dohad (north latitude 22° 50′; east longitude 74° 15′), seventy-seven miles north-east of Baroda, now the chief town of the sub-division of the same name in the British district of the Panch Mahâls. Mr. J. Pollen, I.C.S., LL.D.

Chapter II.
Áhmedábád Kings, A.D. 1403-1573.
Ahmed I. 1411-1441.
War with Málwa, 1422.

Málwa frontier and of Jítpur in Lúnáváda.[1] In A.D. 1421 he repaired the fort in the town of Kahreth, otherwise called Meimún in Lúnáváda, which had been built by Ulugh Khán Sanjar in the reign of Sultán Alá-ud-dín (A.D. 1295-1315) and changed the name to Sultánpur. He next advanced against Málwa and took the fort of Mesar. After an unsuccessful siege of Mándu he went to Ujjain.[2] From Ujjain he returned to Mándu, and failing to capture Mándu, he marched against Sárangpur.[3] Sultán Hushang sent ambassadors and concluded a peace. In spite of the agreement, while Ahmed Sháh was returning to Gujarát, Sultán Hushang made a night attack on his army and caused much havoc. Áhmed Sháh, collecting what men he could, waited till dawn and then fell on and defeated the Málwa troops, who were busy plundering. Sultán Hushang took shelter in the fort of Sárangpur to which Ahmed Sháh again laid siege. Failing to take the fort Áhmed retreated towards Gujarát, closely followed by Sultán Hushang, who was eager to wipe out his former defeat. On Hushang's approach, Áhmed Sháh, halting his troops, joined battle and repulsing Hushang returned to Áhmedábád.

Defeats the Ídar Chief, 1425.

In A.D. 1425 Áhmed Sháh led an army against Ídar, defeating the force brought to meet him and driving their leader to the hills. Ídar was always a troublesome neighbour to the Áhmedábád kings and one difficult to subdue, for when his country was threatened, the chief could retire to his hills, where he could not easily be followed. As a permanent check on his movements, Áhmed Sháh, in A.D. 1427, built the fort of Ahmednagar,[4] on the banks of the Háthmati, eighteen miles south-west of Ídar. In the following year the Ídar chief, Ráv Púnja, attacked a foraging party and carried off one of the royal elephants. He was pursued into the hills and brought to bay in a narrow pathway at the edge of a steep ravine. Púnja was driving back his pursuers when the keeper of the Sultán's elephant urged his animal against the Ráv's horse. The horse swerving lost his foothold and rolling down the ravine destroyed himself and his rider.[5]

During the two following years Áhmed Sháh abstained from foreign conquests, devoting himself to improving his dominions and to working out a system of paying his troops. The method he finally adopted was payment half in money and half in land. This arrangement attached the men to the country, and, while keeping them dependent on the state, enabled them to be free from debt. Further to keep his officials in check he arranged that the treasurer should be one of the king's slaves while the actual paymaster was a native of the particular locality. He also appointed *ámils* that is subdivisional revenue officers. After Ráv Púnja's death Áhmed Sháh marched upon Ídar, and did not return until Ráv Púnja's son agreed to pay an annual tribute of £300 (Rs. 3000). In the following year, according to Farishtah (II. 369) in spite of the young chief's promise

---

[1] Jítpur about twelve miles north-east of Bálásinor.

[2] Ujjain (north latitude 23° 10′; east longitude 75° 47′), at different times the capital of Málwa. [3] Sárangpur about fifty miles north-east of Ujjain.

[4] Ahmednagar (north latitude 23° 34′; east longitude 73° 1′) in the native state of Ídar. [5] Mirát-i-Sikandari Persian Text, 43.

Chapter II.

Áhmedábád Kings, A.D. 1403-1573.

Ahmed I. 1411-1441.

to pay tribute, Áhmed Sháh attacked Ídar, took the fort, and built an assembly mosque. Fearing that their turn would come next the chief of Jhálaváda and Kánha apparently chief of Dungarpur fled to Nasír Khán of Asír. Nasír Khán gave Kánha a letter to Áhmed Sháh Báhmani, to whose son Alá-ud-dín Násír's daughter was married, and having detached part of his own troops to help Kánha they plundered and laid waste some villages of Nandurbár and Sultánpur. Sultán Áhmed sent his eldest son Muhammad Khán with Mukarrabul Mulk and others to meet the Dakhánis who were repulsed with considerable loss. On this Sultán Áhmed Báhmani, under Kadr Khán Dakhani, sent his eldest son Alá-ud-dín and his second son Khán Jehán against the Gujarátis. Kadr Khán marched to Daulatábád and joining Nasír Khán and the Gujarát rebels fought a great battle near the pass of Mánek Púj, six miles south of Nándgaon in Násik. The confederates were defeated with great slaughter. The Dakhan princes fled to Daulatábad and Kánha and Nasír Khán to Kalanda near Chálisgaum in south Khándesh.

Recovers Máhim, 1429;

In the same year (A.D. 1429), on the death of Kutub Khán the Gujarát governor of the island of Máhim, now the north part of the island of Bombay,[1] Áhmed Sháh Báhmani smarting under his defeats, ordered Hasan Izzat, otherwise called Malik-ut-Tujjár, to the Konkan and by the Malik's activity the North Konkan passed to the Dakhanis. On the news of this disaster Áhmed Sháh sent his youngest son Zafar Khán, with an army under Malik Iftikhár Khán, to retake Máhim. A fleet, collected from Diu Gogha and Cambay sailed to the Konkan, attacked Thána[2] by sea and land, captured it, and regained possession of Máhim. In A.D. 1431 Áhmed Sháh advanced upon Chámpáner, and Áhmed Sháh Bahmani, anxious to retrieve his defeat at Máhim, marched an army into Báglán[3] and laid it waste. This news brought Áhmed Sháh back to Nandurbár. Destroying Nándod he passed to Tambol, a fort in Báglán which Áhmed Sháh Báhmani was besieging, defeated the besiegers and relieved the fort. He then went to Thána, repaired the fort, and returned to Gujarát by way of Sultánpur and Nandurbár. In A.D. 1432, after contracting his son Fateh Khán in marriage with the daughter of the Rái of Máhim to the north of Bassein Áhmed Sháh marched towards Nágor, and exacted tribute and presents from the Rával of Dúngarpur.[4] From Dúngarpur he went to Mewár, enforcing his

and Báglán, 1431.

[1] There are two Máhims on the North Konkan coast, one about twenty-two miles north of Bassein (north latitude 19° 40′; east longitude 72° 47′), and the other in the northern extremity of the island of Bombay (north latitude 19° 2′; east longitude 72° 54′). The southern Máhim, to which Farishtah (II. 370-371) is careful to apply the term *jazirah* or island, is the town referred to in the text. The northern Máhim, now known as Kelva Máhim, was, as is noted in the text, the head-quarters of a Hindu chief.

[2] Thána (north latitude 19° 11′; east longitude 73° 6′), the head-quarters of the British district of that name, about twenty-four miles north-by-east of Bombay, was from the tenth to the sixteenth century A.D. the chief city in the Northern Konkan.

[3] Báglán, now called Satána, is the northern sub-division of the British district of Násik. In A.D. 1590 the chief commanded 8000 cavalry and 5000 infantry. The country was famous for fruit. Áin-i-Akbári (Gladwin), II. 73. The chief, a Ráthod, was converted to Islám by Aurangzíb (A.D. 1656-1707).

[4] Dúngarpur (north latitude 23° 50′; east longitude 73° 50′) in Rájputána, 150 miles north-west of Mhow.

Chapter II.
Áhmedábád Kings, A.D. 1403-1573.
Ahmed I. 1411-1441.

claims on Búndi and Kota, two Hára Rájput states in south-east Rájputána. He then entered the Delváda country, levelling temples and destroying the palace of Rána Mokalsingh, the chief of Chitor. Thence he invaded Nágor in the country of the Ráthods, who submitted to him. After this he returned to Gujarát, and during the next few years was warring principally in Málwa, where, according to Farishtah, his army suffered greatly from pestilence and famine. Áhmed died in A.D. 1441 in the fifty-third year of his life and the thirty-third of his reign and was buried in the mausoleum in the Mánek Chauk in Áhmedábád. His after-death title is Khûdaigán-i-Maghfûr the Forgiven Lord in token that, according to his merciful promise, Allah the pitiful, moved by the prayer of forty believers, had spread his forgiveness over the crime of Áhmed's youth, a crime bewailed by a lifelong remorse.

Sultán Áhmed is still a name of power among Gujarát Musalmáns. He is not more honoured for his bravery, skill, and success as a war leader than for his piety and his justice. His piety showed itself in his respect for three great religious teachers Sheikh Rukn-ud-dín the representative of Sheikh Moín-ud-dín the great Khwájah of Ajmír, Sheikh Áhmed Khattu who is buried at Sarkhej five miles west of Áhmedábád, and the Bukháran Sheikh Burhán-ud-dín known as Kutbi Álam the father of the more famous Sháh Álam. Of Áhmed's justice two instances are recorded. Sitting in the window of his palace watching the Sábarmati in flood Áhmed saw a large earthen jar float by. The jar was opened and the body of a murdered man was found wrapped in a blanket. The potters were called and one said the jar was his and had been sold to the headman of a neighbouring village. On inquiry the headman was proved to have murdered a grain merchant and was hanged. The second case was the murder of a poor man by Áhmed's son-in-law. The Kázi found the relations of the deceased willing to accept a blood fine and when the fine was paid released the prince. Áhmed hearing of his son-in-law's release said in the case of the rich fine is no punishment and ordered his son-in-law to be hanged.[1]

Muhammad II. 1441-1452.

Áhmed Sháh was succeeded by his generous pleasure-loving son Muhammad Sháh, Ghiás-ud-dunya Wad-dín, also styled Zarbaksh the Gold Giver. In A.D. 1445 Muhammad marched against Bír Rái of Ídar, but on that chief agreeing to give him his daughter in marriage, he confirmed him in the possession of his state. His next expedition was against Kánha Rái of Dúngarpur, who took refuge in the hills, but afterwards returned, and paying tribute, was given charge of his country. Muhammad married Bíbi Mughli, daughter of Jám Júna of Thatha in Sindh. She bore a son, Fateh Khán, who was afterwards Sultán Mahmúd Begada. In A.D. 1450, Muhammad marched upon Chámpáner, and took the lower fortress. Gangadás of Chámpáner had a strong ally in Sultán Mahmúd Khilji, the ruler of Málwa, and on his approach Muhammad Sháh retired to Godhra,[2] and Mahmúd

[1] Mirát-i-Sikandari Persian Text, 45, 46.

[2] Godhra (north latitude 22° 45′; east longitude 73° 36′), the chief town of the subdivision of that name in the British district of the Panch Mahâls. The Mirât-i-Sikandari (Persian Text, 49) gives, probably rightly, Kothra a village of Sáunli or Savli about twenty miles north of Baroda.

Chapter II.
Áhmedábád Kings, A.D. 1403 - 1573.

Khilji continued his march upon Gujarát at the head of 80,000 horse. Muhammad Sháh was preparing to fly to Diu, when the nobles, disgusted at his cowardice, caused him to be poisoned. Muhammad Sháh's after-death title is Khúdáigán-i-Karím the Gracious Lord.

Kutb-ud-dín, 1451 - 1459.
War with Málwa, 1451.

In A.D. 1451 the nobles placed Muhammad's son Jalál Khán on the throne with the title of Kutb-ud-dín. Meanwhile Sultán Mahmúd of Málwa had laid siege to Sultánpur.[1] Málik Alá-ud-dín bin Sohráb Kutb-ud-dín's commander surrendered the fort, and was sent with honour to Málwa and appointed governor of Mándu. Sultán Mahmúd, marching to Sársa-Pálri, summoned Broach, then commanded by Sídi Marján on behalf of Gujarát. The Sídi refused, and fearing delay, the Málwa Sultán after plundering Baroda proceeded to Nadiád, whose Bráhmans astonished him by their bravery in killing a mad elephant. Kutb-ud-dín Sháh now advancing met Sultán Mahmúd at Kapadvanj,[2] where, after a doubtful fight of some hours, he defeated Sultán Mahmúd, though during the battle that prince was able to penetrate to Kutb-ud-dín's camp and carry off his crown and jewelled girdle. The Mirăt-i-Sikandari ascribes Kutb-ud-dín's victory in great measure to the gallantry of certain inhabitants of Dholka[3] called Darwáziyahs. Muzaffar Khán, who is said to have incited the Málwa Sultán to invade Gujarát, was captured and beheaded, and his head was hung up at the gate of Kapadvanj. On his return from Kapadvanj Kutb-ud-dín built the magnificent Hauzi Kutb or Kánkariya Tank about a mile to the south of Áhmedábád. According to the Mirăt-i-Sikandari (Persian Text, 50 - 57) this war between Málwa and Gujarát was controlled by the spiritual power of certain holy teachers. The war was brought on by the prayers of Sheikh Kamál Málwi, whose shrine is in Áhmedábád behind Khudáwand Khán's mosque near Sháh-i-Alam's tomb, who favoured Málwa. Kutb-ud-dín's cause was aided by the blessing of Kutbi Álam who sent his son the famous Sháh Álam time after time to persuade Kamál to be loyal to Gujarát. At last Kamál produced a writing said to be from heaven giving the victory to Málwa. The young Sháh Álam tore this charter to shreds, and, as no evil befel him, Kamál saw that his spiritual power paled before Sháh Álam and fell back dead. Sháh Álam against his will accompanied Kutb-ud-dín some marches on his advance to Kapadvanj. Before leaving the army Sháh Álam blessed a mean camp elephant and ordered him to destroy the famous Málwa champion elephant known as the Butcher. He also, against his wish for he knew the future, at the Sultán's request bound his own sword round Kutb-ud-dín's waist. In the battle the commissariat elephant ripped the Butcher and some years later Kutb-ud-dín by accident gashed his knee with the saint's sword and died.

Battle of Kapadvanj, 1454.

---

[1] Sultánpur (north latitude 21° 43′; east longitude 74° 40′), in the north of the Sháháda sub-division of the British district of Khándesh, till A.D. 1804 a place of consequence and the head-quarters of a large district.

[2] Kapadvanj (north latitude 23° 2′; east longitude 73° 9′), the chief town of the subdivision of that name in the British district of Kaira.

[3] Dholka (north latitude 22° 42′; east longitude 72° 25′), the chief town of the subdivision of that name in the British district of Áhmedábád.

Chapter II.
Ahmedábád Kings,
A.D. 1403 - 1573.

Kutb-ud-dín,
1454-1459.
War with Nágor,
1454 - 1459.

In the same year Sultán Mahmúd Khilji attempted to conquer Nágor then held by Fíruz Khán, a cousin of the Ahmedábád Sultán. Kutb-ud-dín Sháh despatched an army under the command of Sayad Atáulláh, and, as it drew near Sámbhar,[1] the Málwa Sultán retired and shortly after Fíruz Khán died. Kúmbha Rána of Chitor[2] now began interfering in the Nágor succession on behalf of Shams Khán, who had been dispossessed by his brother Mujáhid Khán, and expelled Mujáhid. But as Shams Khán refused to dismantle the fortifications of Nágor, the Chitor chief collected an army to capture Nágor, while Shams Khán repaired to Kutb-ud-dín Sháh for aid and gave that sovereign his daughter in marriage. Upon this Kutb-ud-dín sent Rái Anupchand Mánek and Malik Gadái with an army to Nágor to repulse the Rána of Chitor. In a battle near Nágor the Gujarát troops were defeated, and the Rána after laying waste the neighbourhood of that city, returned to Chitor. In A.D. 1455-56, to avenge this raid, Kutb-ud-dín Sháh marched against Chitor. On his way the Devra Rája of Sirohi[3] attended Kutb-ud-dín Sháh's camp, praying him to restore the fortress of Ábu,[4] part of the ancestral domain of Sirohi, which the Rána of Chitor had wrested from his house. The king ordered one of his generals, Malik Shaâbán, to take possession of Ábu and restore it to the Devra chieftain, while he himself continued to advance against Kumbhámer. Malik Shaâbán was entangled in the defiles near Ábu, and defeated with great slaughter, and shortly after Kutb-ud-dín Sháh, making a truce with Chitor, retired to his own country. On his return the Málwa sovereign proposed that they should unite against Chitor, conquer the Rána's territories, and divide them equally between them. Kutb-ud-dín agreed and in A.D. 1456-57 marched against the Rána by way of Ábu, which fortress he captured and handed to the Devra Rája.[5] Next, advancing upon Kumbhalmer, he plundered the country round, and then turned towards Chitor. On his way to Chitor, he was met by the Rána, and a battle was fought, after which the Rána fell back on his capital, and was there besieged by the Gujarát army. The siege was not pressed, and, on the Rána agreeing to pay tribute and not to harass Nágor, Kutb-ud-dín withdrew to Gujarát, where he gave himself up to licentious excess. Meanwhile, the Rána by ceding Mandisor[6] to Málwa, came to terms with the Sultán of Mándu, and within three months attacked Nágor. Kutb-ud-dín Sháh, though so overcome with drink as to be unable to sit his horse, mustered his troops and started in a palanquin. As soon as the Rána heard that the Gujárat army was in motion he retired, and the king returned to Ahmedábád. In A.D. 1458, he again led an army by way of Sirohi

War with Chitor,
1455 - 1459.

[1] Sámbhar (north latitude 26° 53′; east longitude 75° 18′), a town in the province of Ajmír, about fifty-one miles north-north-east from the city of Ajmír.

[2] Chitor (north latitude 24° 52′; east longitude 74° 4′), for several centuries before A.D. 1567 the capital of the principality of Udepur.

[3] Sirohi (north latitude 24° 59′; east longitude 72° 56′), the capital of the principality of the same name in the province of Ajmír.

[4] Ábu (north latitude 24° 45′; east longitude 72° 49′) in the state of Sirohi.

[5] The Rája is called Krishna Kishan or Kánh Devra. Ábu is still held by the Sirohi Devrás.

[6] Mandisor (north latitude 24° 4′; east longitude 75° 9′), the chief town of a large district of the same name in the province of Málwa.

and Kumbhalmer against Chitor, and laid waste the country. Soon after his return, according to one account by an accidental sword wound, according to another account poisoned by his wife, Kutb-ud-dín died in May A.D. 1459 after a reign of seven years and seven days. He was brave with a sternness of nature, which, under the influence of wine, amounted to fierceness. His after-death title is Sultán-i-Ghází the Warrior King.

Chapter II.

Áhmedábád Kings, A.D. 1403-1573.

Mahmu'd I. (Begada), 1459-1513.

On the death of Kutb-ud-dín Sháh, the nobles raised to the throne his uncle Dáúd, son of Áhmed Sháh. But as Dáúd appointed low-born men to high offices and committed other foolish acts, he was deposed, and in A.D. 1459 his half-brother Fateh Khán the son of Muhammad Sháh, son of Áhmed Sháh by Bíbi Mughli a daughter of Jám Júna of Thatha in Sindh, was seated on the throne at the age of little more than thirteen with the title of Mahmúd Sháh.

The close connection of Fateh Khán with the saintly Sháh Álam is a favourite topic with Gujarát historians. According to the Mirăt-i-Sikandari (Persian Text, 66-70) of his two daughters Jám Júna intended Bíbi Mughli the more beautiful for the Saint and Bíbi Mirghi the less comely for the Sultán. By bribing the Jám's envoys the king secured the prettier sister. The enraged Saint was consoled by his father who said: My son, to you will come both the cow and the calf. After Muhammad II.'s death, fear of Kutb-ud-dín's designs against the young Fateh Khán forced Bíbi Mughli to seek safety with her sister, and on her sister's death she married the Saint. Kutb-ud-dín made several attempts to seize Fateh Khán. But by the power of the Saint when Kutb-ud-dín attempted to seize him, Fateh Khán in body as well as in dress became a girl. According to one account Kutb-ud-dín met his death in an attempt to carry off Fateh Khán. As he rode into the Saint's quarter Death in the form of a mad camel met the king. The king struck at the phantom, and his sword cleaving the air gashed his knee. This was the Saint's sword, which against his will, for he knew it would be the death of the king, Kutb-ud-dín forced Sháh Álam to bind round him before the battle of Kapadvanj.

Defeats a Conspiracy, 1459.

The death of his uncle, the late Sultán Dáúd, who had become a religious devotee, relieved Fateh Khán of one source of danger. Shortly after certain of the nobles including Seiful Mulk, Kabír-ud-dín Sultáni surnamed Akd-ul-Mulk, Burhán-ul-Mulk and Hisám-ul-Mulk represented to the Sultán that the minister Shaâbán Imád-ul-Mulk contemplated treason and wished to set his son on the throne. Having seized and imprisoned the minister in the Bhadra citadel and set five hundred of their trusted retainers as guards over him, the rebels retired to their homes. At nightfall Abdulláh, the chief of the elephant stables, going to the young Sultán represented to him that the nobles who had imprisoned Imád-ul-Mulk were the real traitors and had determined to place Habíb Khán, an uncle of the Sultán's, on the throne. The Sultán consulting his mother and some of his faithful friends ordered Abdulláh at daybreak to equip all his elephants in full armour and draw them up in the square before the Bhadra. He then seated himself on the throne and in a voice of feigned anger ordered one of the courtiers to bring out Shaâbán Imád-ul-Mulk, that he might wreak his vengeance

Chapter II.
Áhmedábád Kings, A.D. 1403-1573.
Mahmu'd I. (Begada), 1459-1513.

upon him. As these orders were not obeyed the Sultán rose, and walking up the Bhadra called: "Bring out Shaâbán!" The guards brought forth Imád-ul-Mulk, and the Sultán ordered his fetters to be broken. Some of the nobles' retainers made their submission to the Sultán, others fled and hid themselves. In the morning, hearing what had happened, the refractory nobles marched against the Sultán. Many advised the Sultán to cross the Sábarmati by the postern gate and retire from the city, and, after collecting an army, to march against the nobles. Giving no ear to these counsels the young Sultán ordered Abdulláh to charge the advancing nobles with his six hundred elephants. The charge dispersed the malcontents who fled and either hid themselves in the city or betook themselves to the country. Some were killed, some were trampled by the Sultán's orders under the elephants' feet, and one was pardoned.[1] His religious ardour, his love of justice, his bravery, and his wise measures entitle Mahmúd to the highest place among the Gujarát kings. One of the measures which the Mirăt-i-Sikandari specially notices is his continuance of land grants to the son of the holder, and in cases where there was no male issue of half the grant to the daughter. His firm policy of never ousting the landholder except for proved oppression or exaction was productive of such prosperity that the revenue increased two three and in some cases tenfold. The roads were safe from freebooters and trade was secure. A rule forbidding soldiers to borrow money at interest is favourably noticed.

Improves the Soldiery, 1459-1461.

A special officer was appointed to make advances to needy soldiers with the power to recover from their pay in fixed instalments.[2] Mahmúd also devoted much attention to the culture of fruit trees.[3] In A.D. 1461, or A.D. 1462 according to Farishtah, Nizám Sháh Báhmani (A.D. 1461-1463), king of the Dakhan, whose country had been invaded by Sultán Mahmúd Khilji of Málwa, applied for help to the Gujarát king.

Helps the King of the Dakhan, 1461.

Mahmúd Sháh at once started to Nizám Sháh's aid, and on his way receiving another equally pressing letter from the Dakhan sovereign, and being joined by the Bahmani general Khwájáh Jehán Gáwán, he

---

[1] Persian Text, Mirăt-i-Sikandari, 75-76.

[2] The Portuguese merchant and traveller Barbosa (A.D. 1511-1514) gives the following details of Mahmúd Begada's cavalry: The Moors and Gentiles of this kingdom are bold riders, mounted on horses bred in the country, for it has a wonderful quantity. They ride on small saddles and use whips. Their arms are very thick round shields edged with silk; each man has two swords, a dagger, and a Turkish bow with very good arrows. Some of them carry maces, and many of them coats-of-mail, and others tunics quilted with cotton. The horses have housings and steel headpieces, and so they fight very well and are light in their movements. The Moorish horsemen are white and of many countries, Turks and Mamelukes, military slaves from Georgia Circassia and Mingrelia, Arabs Persians Khorásánis Turkomans, men from the great kingdom of Dehli, and others born in the country itself. Their pay is good, and they receive it regularly. They are well dressed with very rich stuffs of gold silk cotton and goat's wool, and all wear caps on their heads, and their clothes long, such as morisco shirts and drawers, and leggings to the knee of good thick leather worked with gold knots and embroidery, and their swords richly ornamented with gold and silver are borne in their girdles or in the hands of their pages. Their women are very white and pretty: also very richly decked out. They live well and spend much money. Stanley's Barbosa, 55-56.

[3] Mahmúd's favourite trees were the mango *ámbo* Mangifera indica, *rāen* Mimusops hexandra, *jámbu* Eugenia jambolana, *gúlar* Ficus glomerata, tamarind *ámli* Tamarindus indica, and the shrubby phyllanthus *áonla* Emblica officinalis.

Chapter II. Áhmedábád Kings, A.D. 1403-1573.

Mahmu'd I. (Begada), 1459-1513.

pushed on with all speed by way of Burhánpur.[1] When Sultán Mahmúd Khilji heard of his approach, he retired to his own country by way of Gondwána,[2] from thirst and from the attacks of the Gonds, losing 5000 to 6000 men. The king of Gujarát, after receiving the thanks of the Dakhan sovereign, returned to his own dominions. In A.D. 1462 Sultán Mahmúd Khilji made another incursion into the Dakhan at the head of 90,000 horse, plundering and laying waste the country as far as Daulatábád. Again the Dakhan sovereign applied for help to Mahmúd Sháh, and on hearing of Mahmúd's advance the Málwa Sultán retired a second time to his own dominions. Mahmúd Sháh now wrote to the Málwa Sultán to desist from harassing the Dakhan, threatening, in case of refusal, to march at once upon Mándu. His next expedition was against the pirate zamíndárs of the hill fort of Barûr and the bandar of Dûn or Dahánu, whose fort he took, and after imposing an annual tribute allowed the chief to continue to hold his hundred villages.[3]

Expedition against Junágadh, 1467.

Mahmúd Sháh next turned his thoughts to the conquest of the mountain citadel of Girnár in central Káthiáváḍa.[4] In A.D. 1467 he made an attack on the fort of Júnágaḍh, and receiving the submission of Ráv Mandlik, the local ruler, returned to his capital. In the following year, hearing that the Júnágaḍh chief continued to visit his idol temple in state with a golden umbrella and other ensigns of royalty, Mahmúd despatched an army to Júnágaḍh, and the chief sent the obnoxious umbrella to the king, accompanied by fitting presents. In A.D. 1469 Mahmúd once more sent an army to ravage Sorath, with the intention of finally conquering both Júnágaḍh and Girnár. While Mahmúd was on the march the Ráv Mandlik suddenly joined him, and asking why the Sultán was so bent on his destruction when he had committed no fault, agreed to do whatever Mahmúd might command. The king replied there is no fault like infidelity, and ordered the Ráv to embrace Islám. The chief, now thoroughly alarmed, fled by night and made his way into Girnár. In A.D. 1472-73 after a siege of nearly two years, forced by the failure of his stores, he quitted the fort and handing the keys to the king, repeated after him the Muhammadan profession of faith. Though the Ráv's life was spared Sorath from this date became a crown possession, and was governed by an officer appointed by the king and stationed at Júnágaḍh. At the close of the war Mahmúd Sháh repaired the fort Jehánpanáh, the present outer or town wall of Júnágaḍh, and, charmed with the beauty of the neighbourhood, settled sayads and learned men at Júnágaḍh and other towns

Capture of Girnar, 1472.

---

[1] Burhánpur (north latitude 21° 18′; east longitude 76° 20′), under the Musalmáns the capital of Khándesh, now within the limits of the Berárs.

[2] Gondwána, a large hilly tract lying between north latitude 19° 50′ and 24° 30′ and east longitude 77° 33′ and 87° 20′.

[3] The Mirăt-i-Sikandari (Persian Text, page 89) gives the hill fort of Bárudar. The Persian *r* may be a miswritten *g* and the *d* a mistake for *w* that is Baguwar or Baguwarah. The seaport Dûn may be Dungri hill six miles from the coast. But Dûn for Dáhánu a well-known port in north Thána is perhaps more likely. Farishtah (Briggs, IV. 51) gives Bavur for Baru and Dura for Dûn. Compare Tabakát-i-Akbari in Bayley's Gujarát, page 178 note 2.

[4] Girnár the diadem of Káthiáváḍa. See above page 231 note 2.

Chapter II.

Áhmedábád Kings, A.D. 1403-1573

Mahmu'd I. (Begada). 1459-1513.

Disturbances in Chámpáner, 1472.

in Sorath. He induced the nobles to build houses, himself raised a palace and made the new city his capital under the name of Mustafábad and enforced his claims as overlord on all the neighbouring chiefs. It is true that in the times of Ahmed Sháh these chieftains, including even the Júnágadh Ráv himself, had paid tribute. But Mahmúd established Ahmedábád rule so firmly that the duty of collecting the tribute was entrusted to an officer permanently settled in the country. The author of the Mirât-i-Sikandari dilates on the dense woods round Júnágadh, full of mango, *ráen, jámbu, gúlar, ámli,* and *áonla*[1] trees, and notes that this forest tract was inhabited by a wild race of men called Khánts.[2]

During Mahmúd Sháh's prolonged absence from his capital, Malik Jamál-ud-dín was appointed governor of Ahmedábád, with the title of Muháfiz Khán that is Care-taker. At this time Jesingh, son of Gangádás the chief of Chámpáner, harassed the country round Pavágad. The king appointed Bahá-ul-Mulk, who had the title of Imád-ul-Mulk, to the command of Sankheda; Malik Sárang Kiwám-ul-Mulk to the command of Godhra; and Táj Khán bin Sálár to the command of Norkha and Dákhna on the Mahi. In consequence of these precautions Jesingh abstained from rebellion. At this time the Ráv Mandlik received the title of Khán Jahán, and lands were bestowed on him, while the golden idols, which had been taken from the Júnágadh temples, were broken and distributed among the soldiers.

Conquest of Kachh.

Mahmúd Sháh's next expedition was against the turbulent inhabitants of the confines of Sindh. These were Jádejás, though they are described as Rájputs of the Sumra and Sodha tribes.[3] They appear to have readily submitted, and to have voluntarily sent men to Júnágadh to be instructed in Islám and to settle in Gujarát. Shortly afterwards they again became troublesome, and the king advancing into Kachh completely defeated them. About this time a learned man, Mulla Mahmúd Samarkandi, on his way from the Dakhan to Central Asia, complained to the king that he had been robbed by the pirates of Jagat or Dwárka.[4] On hearing of this outrage Mahmúd Sháh marched to Jagat, took the fort, and destroyed the idol temples. The pirates, in the first instance, retired to the island of Shankhodára or Bet, but from this, too, after a stout resistance they were driven with great slaughter. The king built a mosque at Jagat, entrusted the government to Farhat-ul-Mulk, and himself returned to Júnágadh. Before this Dwárka had never been conquered. Bhím, the Rája of Dwarka, was sent to Muháfiz Khán, the governor of Ahmedábád, with orders that he was to be hewn in pieces and a piece fastened to every gate of the city. After settling the affairs of Sorath, the king turned

Jagat Destroyed.

[1] Mangifera indica, Mimusops hexandra, Eugenia jambolana, Ficus glomerata, Tamarindus indica, and Emblica officinalis.

[2] Khánts are still found chiefly in Soráth. See Bombay Gazetteer, VIII. 142.

[3] The Tabakát-i-Akbari says they were Játs. Sir H. Elliot (History of India, I. 496) represents the Sumrás to be Agnikula Rájputs of the Parmára stock. The Jádejás had been ruling in Kachh since A.D. 1350-1365.

[4] Dwárka (north latitude 22° 15'; east longitude 69°), on the north-western shore of Káthiáváda, famous for its temple of Krishna.

Chapter II. Áhmedábád Kings, A.D. 1403-1573. Mahmu'd (Begada) 1459-1513.

his face towards Áhmedábád. On the way hearing that a fleet of Malabár craft were annoying the Gujarát ports, he marched to Gogha, equipped a fleet to oppose the pirates, and stopping at Cambay returned to Áhmedábád.

Conspiracy, 1480.

In A.D. 1480, when Mahmúd Sháh was at Júnágadh, Khudáwand Khán and others, who were weary of the king's constant warfare, incited his eldest son Áhmed to assume royal power. But Imád-ul-Mulk, by refusing to join, upset their plans, and on the king's return the conspiracy was stamped out. In the previous year (A.D. 1479) Mahmúd Sháh sent an army to ravage Chámpáner, which he was determined to conquer. About this time, hearing that the neighbourhood was infested with robbers, he founded the city of Mehmúdábád on the banks of the Vátrak, about eighteen miles south of Áhmedábád. In A.D. 1482 there was a partial famine in Gujarát, and the Chámpáner country being exempt from scarcity the commandant of Morámli or Rasúlábad, a post in the Gáekwár's Sáonli district on the Chámpáner frontier, made several forays across the border. In return the chief attacked the commandant and defeated him, killing most of his men and capturing two elephants and several horses. On hearing this Mahmúd Sháh set out for Baroda with a powerful army. When Mahmúd reached Baroda the Rával of Chámpáner, becoming alarmed, sent ambassadors and sued for forgiveness. The king rejected his overtures, saying: 'Except the sword and the dagger no message shall pass between me and you.'[1] The Rával made preparations for a determined resistance, and sent messengers to summon Ghiás-ud-dín Khilji of Málwa to his aid. To prevent this junction Mahmúd Sháh entrusted the siege to his nobles and marched to Dohad, on which Sultán Ghiás-ud-dín withdrew to Mándu. On his return from Dohad the Sultán began building a Jáma Mosque at Chámpáner to show that he would not leave the place till he had taken the hill-fort of Pávágad. After the siege had lasted more than twenty months (April 1483 – December 1484), the Musalmáns noticed that for an hour or two in the morning most of the Rájputs were off duty bathing and dressing. A morning assault was planned and the first gate carried. Then Malik Ayáz Sultáni finding a practicable breach passed through with some of his men and took the great gate. The Rával and his Rájputs, throwing their women children and valuables into a huge fire, rushed out in a fierce but unavailing charge.[2]

War against Chámpáner, 1482-1484.

Capture of Pávágad, 1484.

The Rával and his minister Dúngarshi fell wounded into the conqueror's hands, and, on refusing to embrace Islám, were put to death. The Rával's son, who was entrusted to Seif-ul-Mulk, and instructed by him in the Muhammadan religion, afterwards, in the reign of Muzaffar Sháh (A.D. 1523-1526), was ennobled by the title of Nizám-ul-Mulk. On the capture of Pávágad in A.D. 1484, Mahmúd Sháh built a wall round the town of Chámpáner, and made it his capital under the name of Muhammadábád. Under Mahmúd's orders the neigh-

[1] The Tabakát-i-Akbari has 'To-morrow the sword of adamant shall answer your message.'

[2] Farishtah, II. 396-397.

Chapter II.

Áhmedábád Kings, A.D. 1403 - 1573.

Mahmu'd (Begada), 1459-1513.

bourhood became stocked with mangoes, pomegranates, figs, grapes, sugarcane, plantains, oranges, custard apples, *khirnis* or *raens* (Mimusops indica or hexandra), jackfruit, and cocoapalms, as well as with roses, chrysanthemums, jasmins, *champás*, and sweet pandanus. A sandal grove near Chámpáner is said to have had trees large enough to help the Musalmán nobles to build their mansions. At the instance of the Sultán a Khurásáni beautified one of the gardens with fountains and cascades. A Gujaráti named Hálur learning the principle improved on his master's design in a garden about four miles west of Chámpáner, which in his honour still bears the name Hálol.[1]

In Mahmúd's reign an instance is mentioned of the form of compensation known as *valtar*. Some merchants bringing horses and other goods for sale from Irák and Khurásán were plundered in Sirohi limits. The king caused them to give in writing the price of their horses and stuffs, and paying them from his own treasury recovered the amount from the Rája of Sirohi.

In A.D. 1494-95 Mahmúd went against Bahádur Khán Gíláni, a vassal of the Bahmanis, who from Goa and Dábhol[2] had so harassed the Gujarát harbours that, from the failure of the supply of betelnut, coriander seed had to be eaten with betel leaves. The Bahmani Sultán, fearing the consequences to himself, marched against Bahádur Khán, and, capturing him alive, struck off his head, and sent it to the Gujarát monarch, who returned to his own country. In A.D. 1499-1500, hearing that Násir-ud-dín of Málwa had killed his father Ghiás-ud-dín and seated himself on the throne, the Sultán prepared to advance against him, but was appeased by Násir-ud-dín's humble attitude. The next seven years passed without any warlike expedition. In A.D. 1507, near Daman on his way to Cheul, Mahmúd heard of the victory gained at Cheul over the Portuguese by the Gujarát squadron under Malik Ayáz Sultáni, in concert with the Turkish fleet.[3] In A.D. 1508 Mahmúd succeeded in placing his nephew Mirán Muhammad Adil Khán Fárúki on the throne of Ásir-Burhánpur. From 1508 Mahmúd remained at his capital till his death in December A.D. 1513 at the age of sixty-seven years and three months, after a reign of fifty-four years and one month. Mahmúd was buried at Sarkhej,[4] and received

The Khándesh Succession, 1508.

---

[1] Mirăt-i-Sikandari, 112-114.

[2] Dábhol (north latitude 17° 34'; east longitude 73° 16'), on the north bank of the river Váshishti (called Halewacko and Kalewacko by the early navigators. See Badger's Varthema, page 114 note 1) in the British district of Ratnágiri. About this time, according to Athanasius Nikitin (A.D. 1468-1474), Dábhol was the great meeting place for all nations living along the coast of India and Ethiopia. In A.D. 1501 it was taken by the Portuguese. Between A.D. 1626 and 1630 an English factory was established here, but by the end of the century trade had left Dábhol and has never returned.

[3] Cheul, now Revdanda (north latitude 18° 33'; east longitude 72° 59'), from about A.D. 1500 to 1650 a place of much trade.

[4] Mahmúd Begada greatly impressed travellers, whose strange tales of him made the king well-known in Europe. Varthema (1503-1508) thus describes his manner of living: 'The king has constantly 20,000 horsemen. In the morning when he rises there come to his palace 50 elephants, on each of which a man sits astride, and the said elephants do reverence to the king, and, except this, they have nothing else to do. When the

Chapter II.
Áhmedábád Kings, A.D. 1403-1573.
Mahmu'd (Begada), 1459-1513.

the after-death title of Khúdáigán-i-Halím or the Meek Lord. Immediately before his death Sultán Mahmúd was informed that Sháh Ismáil Safawi of Persia had sent him a friendly embassy headed by Yádgár Beg Kazil-básh. As the Kazil-báshes were known to be Shiáhs the Sultán, who was a staunch Sunni, prayed that he might not be forced to see a Shíah's face during his last days. His prayer was heard. He died before the Persian embassy entered the city.[1] During the last days of Sultán Mahmúd, Sayad Muhammad of Jaunpur, who claimed to be the Mahdi or Messiah, came from Jaunpur and lodged in Tájkhán Sálár's mosque near the Jamálpur gate of Áhmedábád. His sermons drew crowds, and were so persuasive that he gained a large body of followers, who believed his eloquence to be due to *hál* or inspiration. Mahmúd's ministers persuaded him not to see the Jaunpur preacher.

---

king eats, fifty or sixty kinds of instruments, drums trumpets flageolets and fifes play, and the elephants again do him reverence. As for the king himself, his mustachios under his nose are so long that he ties them over his head as a woman would tie her tresses, and he has a white beard that reaches to his girdle. As to his food, every day he eats poison (Hudibras' Prince whose 'daily food was asp and basilisk and toad'), not that he fills his stomach with it, but he eats a certain quantity, so that when he wishes to destroy any great person he makes him come before him stripped and naked, and then eats certain fruits which are called *chofole* (*jáiphal*, nutmeg), like a muscatel nut. He also eats certain leaves called *tamboli* (*pán* or betel leaf) like the leaves of a sour orange, and with these he eats lime of oyster shells. When he has chewed this well he spurts it out on the person he wishes to kill, and so in the space of half an hour the victim falls to the ground dead. The Sultán has also three or four thousand women, and every night that he sleeps with one, she is found dead in the morning.' Barbosa (A.D. 1511) goes further (Stanley's Trans. 57), saying that so soaked was the king with poison that if a fly settled on his hand it swelled and immediately fell dead. This was the result of his early training. For, on Varthema's companion asking how it was that the king could eat poison in this manner, certain merchants, who were older than the Sultán, answered that his father had fed him upon poison from his childhood. (Badger's Varthema, 110.) Of the origin of Mahmúd's surname Begada two explanations are given: (1) 'From his mustachios being large and twisted like a bullock's horn, such a bullock being called Begado; (2) that the word comes from the Gujaráti *be*, two, and *gad*, a fort, the people giving him this title in honour of his capture of Júnágadh (A.D. 1472) and Chámpáner (A.D. 1484).' (Bird's History of Gujarát, 202; Mirát-i-Ahmedi Persian Text, 74.) Varthema's account of the poison-eating is probably an exaggeration of the Sultán's habit of opium-eating to which from his infancy he was addicted. The Mirát-i-Sikandari (Persian Text, 751) speaks of the great physical power of Mahmúd and of his wonderful appetite. Mahmúd's daily food weighed forty *sers* the ser being 15 *bahlulis* a little over half a pound. He used to eat about three pounds (5 *sers*) of parched gram to dessert. For breakfast, after his morning prayer, Mahmúd used to consume a cupfull of pure Makkah honey with a second cupfull of clarified butter and fifty small plantains called *sohan kelas*. At night they set by his bed two plates of *sambúsás* or minced mutton sausages. In the morning Mahmúd seeing the empty plates used to give thanks: 'Oh Allah,' he said, 'hadst thou not given this unworthy slave rule over Gujarát, who could have filled his stomach.' His virile powers were as unusual as his appetite. The only woman who could bear his embraces unharmed was a powerful Abyssinian girl who was his great favourite. Of the wealth and weapons kept in store the Mirát-i-Sikandari gives the following details regarding the great expedition against Júnágadh (Persian Text, 94): The Sultán ordered the treasurer to send with the army gold coins worth five *krors*, 1700 Egyptian Allemand Moorish and Khurásáni swords with gold handles weighing $2\frac{1}{2}$ to 3 pounds (4-5 *sers*), 1700 daggers and poignards with gold handles weighing 1 to $1\frac{1}{2}$ pounds (2-3 *sers*), and 2000 Arab and Turki horses with gold-embroidered housings. All this treasure of coin and weapons the Sultán spent in presents to his army (Ditto, 94-95).

[1] Ferishtah, II. 404. The Mirát-i-Sikandari (Persian Text, 148, 149) calls the Persian ambassador Ibráhím Khán.

Chapter II.
Ahmedábád Kings, A.D. 1403-1573.
Mahmu'd (Begada), 1459-1513.

Mahmúd Begada's court was adorned by several pious and high-minded nobles. In life they vied with one another in generous acts; and after death, according to the Persian poet Urfi, they left their traces in the characters and carvings of stone walls and marble piles. First among these nobles the Mirát-i-Sikandari (Persian Text, 132, 142) mentions Dáwar-ul-Mulk, whose god-fearing administration made his estates so prosperous that they were coveted by princes of the blood. As Thánadár of Amron in north Káthiáváda, he spread the light of Islám from Morvi to Bhúj, and after his death his fame as a spirit-ruling guardian drew hosts of sick and possessed to his shrine near Morvi. The second was Malik Ayáz, governor of Diu, who built the strong fortress afterwards reconstructed by the Portuguese. He also built a tower on an under-water rock, and from the tower drew a massive iron chain across the mouth of the harbour. A substantial bridge over the creek, that runs through the island of Diu, was afterwards destroyed by the Portuguese. The third was Khudáwand Khán Âlim, the founder of Âlímpura a suburb to the south of Áhmedábád, adorned with a mosque of sandstone and marble. He introduced the cultivation of melons figs and sugarcane into Gujarát from Bijápur. The fourth was Imád-ul-Mulk Âsas who founded Ísanpur, a suburb between Sháh Alam's suburb of Islámpur and Batwa, and planted along the road-groves of *khirnis* and mangoes. The fifth was Tájkhán Sálár, so loved of his peers that after his death none of them would accept his title. The sixth was Malik Sárang Kiwám-ul-Mulk, a Rájput by birth, the founder of the suburb of Sárangpur and its mosque to the east of Áhmedábád. The seventh and eighth were the Khurásáni brothers Aâzam and Moâzzam, who built a cistern, a mosque, and a tomb between Áhmedábád and Sarkhej.

Besides Khalíl Khán, who succeeded him, Mahmúd had three sons: Muhammad Kála, Ápá Khán, and Áhmed Khán. Kála, son of Ráni Rúp Manjhri died during his father's lifetime as did his mother, who was buried in Mának Chauk in Áhmedábád in the building known as the Ráni's Hazíra. The second son Ápá Khán was caught trespassing in a noble's *harim*, and was ordered by the Sultán to be poisoned. The third son was the Áhmed Khán whom Khudáwand Khán sought to raise to the throne during Sultán Mahmúd's lifetime.

Muzaffar II. 1513-1526.

Muhammad was succeeded by Khalil Khán, the son of Ráni Hírábái the daughter of a Rájput chieftain named Nágá Rána who lived on the bank of the Mahi. On ascending the throne, at the age of twenty-seven, Khalíl adopted the title of Muzaffar Sháh. For some time before his father's death, Prince Khalíl Khán had been living at Baroda and shortly after his accession he visited that neighbourhood, and founded a town which he named Daulatábád. In A.D. 1514 Ráv Bhím, the son of Ráv Bhán of Ídar, defeated Ain-ul-Mulk, governor of Pátan, who was coming to Áhmedábád to pay his respects to the king. This officer had turned aside to punish the Ráv for some disturbance he had created, but failing in his purpose, was himself defeated. On the approach of Muzaffar Sháh, Ídar was abandoned by the Ráv, who made his peace with difficulty and only by agreeing to pay a heavy tribute. Meanwhile the king marched to Godhra, and so to Málwa by way of Dohad, whose fort he caused to be repaired, and soon after went on to Dhár.

Expedition against Ídar, 1514.

Chapter II.
Áhmedábád Kings, A.D. 1403-1573.
Muzaffar II. 1513-1526.

After a short stay in Málwa, thinking it mean to take advantage of the distracted condition of Mahmúd of Málwa, who was at war with his nobles, Muzaffar returned to Muhammadábád (Chámpáner). At this time Ráimal, nephew of the late Ráv Bhím of Ídar, expelled the Ráv's son Bhármal by the aid of his father-in-law Rána Sánga of Chitor, and succeeded to the chieftainship of Ídar. The king was displeased at the interference of the Rána, and directed Nizám Khán, the governor of Ahmednagar, to expel Ráimal and reinstate Bhármal. Nizám Khán took Ídar and gave it to Bhármal. Ráimal betook himself to the hills where Nizám Khán incautiously pursuing and engaging him lost many men. When the rains were over the Sultán visited Ídar. Shortly after, Nizám Khán, the governor of Ahmednagar, fell sick and was called to court. He left Ídar in charge of Zahír-ul-Mulk at the head of a hundred horse. Ráimal made a sudden raid on Ídar and killed Zahír-ul-Mulk and twenty-seven of his men. On hearing of this reverse Sultán Muzaffar ordered Nizám Khán to destroy Bíjápur.[1] In A.D. 1517, the nobles of Málwa besought Muzaffar's interference, alleging that the Hindu minister Medáni Rái was planning to depose the Málwa Sultán, Mahmúd Khilji, and usurp the throne. Muzaffar Sháh promised to come to their help, and shortly after Sultán Mahmúd Khilji, escaping from the surveillance of Medáni Rái, himself sought the aid of the Gujarát monarch. In A.D. 1518 Muzaffar Sháh marched by Godhra into Málwa, and on his arrival at Dhár, that town was evacuated by Medáni Rái. The Gujarát king next besieged Mándu and Medáni Rái summoned the Chitor Rána to his aid. When the Rána had reached Sárangpur, Muzaffar Sháh detaching a force caused the Rána to retire, while the Gujarát soldiers exerted themselves so strenuously that they captured Mándu, recovering the girdle which Kutb-ud-dín had lost at the battle of Kapadvanj. This conquest virtually placed Málwa in Muzaffar's power, but he honourably restored the kingdom to Sultán Mahmúd Khilji, and, withdrawing to Gujarát, proceeded to Muhammadábad. In A.D. 1519, news was received of the defeat and capture of Sultán Mahmúd Khilji by the Rána of Chitor. Muzaffar Sháh sent a force to protect Mándu. But the Rána, who distinguished himself by releasing the Sultán of Málwa and keeping his son in his stead as a hostage, enjoyed continued good fortune. Some time before these events a *bhát* or bard in the presence of Nizám Khán, the governor of Ídar, boasted that the Rána of Chitor would never fail to help Rána Ráimal of Ídar. The angry governor said 'Whose dog is Rána Sánga to help Ráimal while we are here.' Nizám Khán called a dog Sánga, chained him in the fort, and dared the Rána to carry him away. His successes enabled Sánga to answer the challenge. In consequence of dissensions at head-quarters Nizám Khán withdrew to Ahmednagar leaving a small garrison in Ídar. When Rána Sánga appeared before Ídar the garrison resisted but were slain to a man. The Rána advanced to Ahmednagar and severely defeated Nizám Khán who withdrew to Ahmedábád, while the Rána plundered Vishálnagar.[2] In A.D. 1521, Malik Ayáz Sultáni, the governor of

Disturbances in Málwa, 1517.

Capture of Mándu, 1518.

War with Chitor, 1519.

---

[1] Farishtah, II. 408.
[2] Mirăt-i-Sikandari, 166-167; Farishtah, II. 411.

Chapter II.
Ahmedábád Kings.
A.D. 1403-1573.
Muzaffar II.
1513-1526.
The Rána of Chitor Submits,
1521.

Sorath, was sent with a large and carefully equipped force to revenge this inroad. Dissensions between Malik Ayáz and the Gujárat nobles prevented this expedition doing more than burn and despoil both Dungarpur and Bánsváda. Muzaffar Sháh, greatly displeased with the result, was preparing to march against Chitor, when he was dissuaded by a submissive embassy from that chief, who sent his son to Ahmedábád with valuable presents for the king. Shortly afterwards, on the death of Malik Ayáz, Muzaffar Sháh confirmed his elder son Malik Is-hák in his father's rank and possessions. Malik Is-hák remained in Sorath which was confirmed as his *jágir*. In the following year the Sultán went about his dominions strengthening his frontier posts, especially the fort of Modása, which he rebuilt. About A.D. 1524 prince Báhádur Khán, ostensibly dissatisfied with the smallness of his estates but really to remove himself from the jealousy of his brother Sikandar who being appointed heir-apparent was seeking his life, left Gujárat and withdrew to Hindustán. King Muzaffar, after formally appointing his son Sikándar Khán his heir, died at Ahmedábád in A.D. 1526, after a reign of fourteen years and nine months. Muzaffar was buried in the shrine of Sheikh Ahmed Khattu at Sarkhej near his father's grave. He was the most learned and one of the most pious of the Ahmedábád Sultáns. So extreme an abstainer was he that not only during his whole life did he eschew intoxicating drugs and liquor but he never again rode a favourite horse because the horse was cured by a draught of wine. He was an accomplished musician, a finished horseman, a practised swordsman, and withal so modest and humble in his dress and temper that observing once to a favourite page how simple and yet graceful his own turban was the boy laughed: 'Ay, if the turbans of Mullahs and Bohoras are graceful, then is your Majesty's.' The Sultán said 'I should have been proud to have my turban likened to a Mullah's, why compare it with the headdress of a schismatic Bohora.' Muzaffar was careful never to pain the feelings of those around him. He suspected Kiwám-ul-Mulk who was in charge of his drinking water but contented himself with breathing over the water one of the verses of the Kurâân which make poison harmless.[1] During his reign cultivation increased so much in Jhálávála that it became necessary to reserve certain waste land for pasture. In 1526 the rains held off so long that famine began to rage. The Sultán exclaimed, 'Oh Allah! If thou scourgest the country for the sins of its king take his life and spare thy creatures.' The prayer was heard and the soul of the guardian Sultán passed in a flood of gracious rain.[2]

Dies,
1526.

Sikandar,
1526.

Mahmu'd II.
1526.

After Sikandar Sháh had been in power a few months he was murdered by Imád-ul-Mulk Khush Kadam, who seated a younger brother of Sikandar's, named Násir Khán, on the throne with the title of Mahmúd II. and governed on his behalf. The only event of Sikandar's reign was the destruction of an army sent against his brother

[1] The verse supposed to possess the highest virtue against poison is the last verse of Chap. cvi. of the Kurâán. . . . . Serve the Lord of this House who supplieth them with food against hunger and maketh them free from fear.

[2] Mirât-i-Sikandari (Pers. Manuscript), 174, 175, 194.

Chapter II.

Áhmedábád Kings, A.D. 1403-1573.

Baha'dur, 1527-1536.

Latíf Khán who was helped by Rána Bhím of Munga.[1] The nobles deserted Imád-ul-Mulk's cause, and prince Báhádur Khán, returning to Gujarát from Hindustán, was joined by many supporters prominent among whom was Táj Khán, proprietor of Dhandhuka. Bahádur marched at once on Chámpáner, captured and executed Imád-ul-Mulk and poisoning Násir Khán ascended the throne in A.D. 1527 with the title of Bahádur Sháh. His brother Latíf Khán, aided by Rája Bhím of the Kohistan or hill land of Pál,[2] now asserted his claim to the throne. He was defeated, and fell wounded into the hands of the Gujarát army and died of his wounds and was buried at Hálol. Rája Bhím was slain. As Bhím's successor Ráisingh plundered Dohad, a large force was sent againt him, commanded by Táj Khán, who laid waste Ráisingh's country and dismantled his forts. Soon after Bahádur Sháh visited Cambay, and found that Malik Is-hák the governor of Sorath had, in the interests of the Portuguese, attempted to seize Diu but had been repulsed by the Gujarát admiral Mahmúd Áka. The Sultán entrusted Diu to Kiwám-ul-Mulk and Júnágadh to Mujáhid Khán Bhíkan and returned to Áhmedábád. In 1527 he enforced tribute from Ídar and the neighbouring country. During one of his numerous expeditions he went to hunt in Nándod and received the homage of the Rája. As the Portuguese were endeavouring to establish themselves on the coast of Sorath, and, if possible, to obtain Diu, the king was constantly at Cambay Diu and Gogha to frustrate their attempts, and he now directed the construction of the fortress of Broach. At this time Muhammad Khán, ruler of Asír and Burhánpur, requested Bahádur's aid on behalf of Imád-ul-Mulk, ruler of Berár. Bahádur Sháh started at once and at Nandurhár was joined by Muhammad Khán Asíri, and thence proceeded to Burhánpur, where he was met by Imád Sháh from Gávalgad. After certain successes he made peace between Burhán Nizám Sháh and Imád Sháh Gávali, and returned to Gujarát. Jám Fírúz the ruler of Tatha in Sindh now sought refuge with Bahádur Sháh from the oppression either of the Ghoris or of the

Portuguese Intrigues, 1526.

Khándesh Affairs, 1528.

---

[1] Both the Mirát-i-Sikandari (287) and Farishtah (II. 419) place Munga in Nandurbár-Sultánpur. The further reference to Rána Bhím of Pál seems to apply to the same man as the Rána Bhím of Munga. Munga may then be Mohangad that is Chota Udepur.

[2] Mirát-i-Sikandari Persian Text, 225-226: Farishtah, II. 425-428. The Gujarát Musalmán historians give a somewhat vague application to the word Pál which means a bank or step downwards to the plain. In the Mirát-i-Áhmedi (Páhlanpur Edition, page 168) Pálvaráh, whose climate is proverbially bad, includes Godhra Ali Mohan and Rájpípla that is the rough eastern fringe of the plain land of Gujarát from the Mahi to the Tapti. As the Raja of Nándod or Rájpípla was the leading chief south of Ídar Colonel Watson took references to the Rája of Pál to apply to the Rája of Rájpípla. An examination of the passages in which the name Pál occurs seems to show that the hill country to the east rather than to the south of Pávágad or Chámpáner is meant. In A.D. 1527 Latíf Khán the rival of Bahádur Sháh after joining the Rája Bhím in his *kohistan* or highlands of Pál when wounded is taken into Hálol. The same passage contains a reference to the Rája of Nándod as some one distinct from the Rája of Pál. In A.D. 1531 Ráisingh of Pál tried to rescue Mahmúd Khilji on his way from Mándu in Málwa to Chámpáner. In A.D. 1551 Násir Khán fled to Chámpáner and died in the Pál hills. These references seem to agree in allotting Pál to the hills of Bária and of Mohan or Chhota Udepur. This identification is in accord with the local use of Pál. Mr. Pollen, I.C.S., LL.D., Political Agent, Rewa Kántha, writes (8th Jan. 1895): Bhíls Kolis and traders all apply the word Pál to the Bária Pál which besides Bária takes in Sanjeli and the Navánagar-Saliát uplands in Godhra.

Chapter II.
Áhmedábád Kings, A.D. 1403-1573.
Bahádur, 1527-1536.

Mughals and was hospitably received. In A.D. 1528 Bahádur made an expedition into the Dakhan which ended in a battle at Daulatábád. The issue of this battle seems to have been unfavourable as hardly any reference to the campaign remains. Next year (A.D. 1529) at the request of Jaâfar or Khizr Khán, son of Imád Sháh Gávali, who was sent to Gujarát to solicit Bahádur's help, he again marched for the Dakhan. As he passed through Muler Biharji the Rája of Báglán gave him his daughter in marriage and in return received the title of Bahr Khán. From Báglán Bahr Khán was told off to ravage Cheul which by this time had fallen into the hands of the Portuguese. Bahádur himself advanced to Ahmednagar, took the fort and destroyed many of the buildings. Purandhar also was sacked of its stores of gold.[1] From Ahmednagar Bahádur Sháh passed to Burhánpur, and there his general Kaisar Khán gained a victory over the united forces of Nizám Sháh, Malik Beríd, and Ain-ul-Mulk. After having the public sermon read in his name both in Ahmednagar and in Burhánpur Bahádur returned to Gujarát and for some time refrained from interfering in the affairs of the Dakhan.

Turks at Diu, 1526-1530.

Between A.D. 1526 and 1530 certain Turks under one Mústafa came to Gujarát, traders according to one account according to another part of a Turkish fleet expected to act against the Portuguese. Diu was assigned them as a place of residence and the command of the island was granted to Malik Túghán, son of Malik Ayáz, the former governor. In A.D. 1530 the king marched to Nágor, and gave an audience both to Prathiráj Rája of Dúngarpur and to the ambassadors from Rána Ratansi of Chitor. The Rána's ambassadors complained of encroachments on Chitor by Mahmúd of Málwa. Mahmúd promised to appear before Bahádur to explain the alleged encroachments. Bahádur waited. At last as Mahmúd failed to attend Bahádur said he would go and meet Mahmúd. He invested Mándu and received with favour certain deserters from Mahmúd's army. The fortress fell and Sultán Mahmúd and his seven sons were captured. The success of the siege was due to Bahádur's personal prowess. He scaled an almost inaccessible height and sweeping down from it with a handful of men took the fort, a feat which for daring and dash is described as unsurpassed in the history of Musalmán Gujarát.[2] After passing the rainy season at Mándu Bahádur Sháh went to Burhánpur to visit his nephew Mirán Muhammad Shah. At Burhánpur Bahádur under the influence of the great priest-statesman Sháh Táhir, was reconciled with Burhán Nizám and gave him the royal canopy he had taken from Málwa. Bahádur offered Sháh Táhir the post of minister. Sháh Táhir declined saying he must make a pilgrimage to Makkah. He retired to Ahmednagar and there converted Burhán Nizám Sháh to the Shíâh faith.[3] In the same year, hearing that Mánsingji, Rája of

Capture of Mándu, 1530.

[1] Purandhar about twenty miles south by east of Poona, one of the greatest of Dakhan hill forts.

[2] Mirăt-i-Sikandari, 238, 239; Farishtah, II. 430. According to the Mirăt-i-Sikandari (239) the Sultán enquired on which side was the loftiest height. They told him that in the direction of Songad-Chitauri the hill was extremely high. These details show that the cliff scaled by Bahádur was in the extreme south-west of Mándu where a high nearly isolated point stretches out from the main plateau. For details see Appendix II. Mándu.

[3] Mirăt-i-Sikandari, 241-242; Farishtah, II. 432.

Chapter II.

Áhmedábád Kings, A.D. 1403-1573.

Baha'dur, 1527-1536.

Halvad,[1] had killed the commandant of Dasáda Bahádur despatched Khán Khánán against him. Víramgám and Mándal were reft from the Jhála chieftains, and ever after formed part of the crown dominions. When Sultán Mahmúd Khilji and his sons were being conveyed to the fortress of Chámpáner, Ráisingh, Rája of Pál, endeavoured to rescue them. The attempt failed, and the prisoners were put to death by their guards. In A.D. 1531, on Bahádur's return from Burhánpur to Dhár, hearing that Silehdi the Rájput chief of Ráisin in east Málwa kept in captivity certain Muhammadan women who had belonged to the *harím* of Sultán Násir-ud-dín of Málwa, Bahádur marched against him and forced him to surrender and embrace Islám. The chief secretly sent to the Rána of Chitor for aid and delayed handing over Ráisin. On learning this Bahádur despatched a force to keep Chitor in check and pressed the siege. At his own request, Silehdi was sent to persuade the garrison to surrender. But their reproaches stung him so sharply, that, joining with them, and after burning their women and children, they sallied forth sword in hand and were all slain. Ráisin fell into Bahádur's hands, and this district together with those of Bhílsa and Chanderi were entrusted to the government of Sultán Alam Lodhi. The king now went to Gondwána to hunt elephants, and, after capturing many, employed his army in reducing Gágraun and other minor fortresses.[2] In A.D. 1532 he advanced against Chitor, but raised the siege on receiving an enormous ransom. Shortly afterwards his troops took the strong fort of Rantanbhur.[3] About this time on receipt of news that the Portuguese were usurping authority the Sultán repaired to Diu. Before he arrived the Portuguese had taken to flight, leaving behind them an enormous gun which the Sultán ordered to be dragged to Chámpáner.

Quarrel with Humáyún, 1532.

Before A.D. 1532 was over Bahádur Sháh quarrelled with Humáyún, emperor of Delhi. The original ground of quarrel was that Bahádur Sháh had sheltered Sultán Muhammad Zamán Mírza the grandson of a daughter of the emperor Bábar (A.D. 1482-1530). Humáyún's anger was increased by an insolent answer from the Gujarát king. Without considering that he had provoked a powerful enemy, Bahádur Sháh again laid siege to Chitor, and though he heard that Humáyún had arrived at Gwálior, he would not desist from the siege. In March 1535 Chitor fell into the hands of the Gujarát king but near Mandasúr his army was shortly afterwards routed by Humáyún. According to one account, the failure of the Gujarát army was due to Bahádur and his nobles being spell-bound by looking at a heap of salt and some cloth soaked in indigo which were mysteriously left before Bahádur's tent by an unknown elephant. The usual and probably true explanation is that Rúmi Khán the Turk, head of the Gujarát artillery, betrayed Bahádur's interest.[4] Still though Rúmi Khán's treachery may have had a share in Bahádur's defeat it seems probable that in valour, discipline, and tactics the Gujarát army was

Fall of Chitor, 1535.

[1] Halvad is a former capital of the chief of Dhrángadhra in Káthiávála.
[2] Gágraun in Central India about seventy miles north-east of Ujjain.
[3] Rantanbhúr about seventy-five miles south by east of Jaipur.
[4] Mirát-i-Sikandari Persian Text, 266, 268; Farishtah, II. 439.

Chapter II.
Áhmedábád Kings,
A.D. 1403-1573.

Bahádur,
1527-1536.
Mughal Conquest of Gujarát,
1535.
Are Driven Out,
1536.
The Portuguese at Diu,
1536.

inferior to the Mughals. Bahádur Sháh, unaccustomed to defeat, lost heart and fled to Mándu, which fortress was speedily taken by Humáyún. From Mándu the king fled to Chámpáner, and finally took refuge in Diu. Chámpáner fell to Humáyún, and the whole of Gujarát, except Sorath, came under his rule. At this time Sher Sháh Súr revolted, in Bihár and Jaunpur, and Humáyún returned to Agra to oppose him leaving his brother Hindál Mírza in Áhmedábád, Kásam Beg in Broach, and Yádgár Násir Mírza in Pátan. As soon as Humáyún departed, the country rose against the Mughals, and his old nobles requested the king to join them. Bahádur joined them, and, defeating the Mughals at Kaníj near Mahmúdábád, expelled them from Gujarát. During Humáyún's time of success Bahádur Sháh, being forced to court the Portuguese, had granted them leave to erect a factory in Diu. Instead of a factory the Portuguese built a fort. When he recovered his kingdom, Bahádur, repenting of his alliance with the Portuguese, went to Sorath to persuade an army of Portuguese, whom he had asked to come to his assistance, to return to Goa. When the Portuguese arrived at Diu five or six thousand strong the Sultán hoping to get rid of them by stratagem, repaired to Diu and endeavoured to get the viceroy into his power. The viceroy excused himself, and in return invited the king to visit his ship. Bahádur agreed, and on his way back was attacked and slain, in the thirty-first year of his life and the eleventh of his reign. According to the author of the Mirăt-i-Sikandari the reason of Bahádur's assassination was that a paper from him to the kings of the Dakhan, inviting them to join him in an alliance against the Portuguese, had fallen into the hands of the Portuguese viceroy. Whatever may have been the provocation or the intention, the result seems to show that while both sides had treacherous designs neither party was able to carry out his original plan, and the end was unpremeditated, hurried on by mutual suspicions.[1] Up to the defeat of Sultán Bahádur by Humáyún, the power of Gujarát was at its height. Cadets of noble Rájput houses, Prithiraj, the nephew of Rána Sánga of Chitor, and Narsingh Deva the cousin of the Rája of Gwálior, were proud to enrol themselves as the Sultán's vassals. The Rája of Baglána readily gave Bahádur Sháh his daughter. Jám Fírúz of Tatha in Sindh and the sons of Bahlúl Lodhi were suppliants at his court. Málwa was a dependency of Gujarát and the Nizám Sháhis of Ahmednagar and Nasírkhan of Burhánpur acknowledged him as overlord, while the Fárúkis of Khándesh were dependent on Bahádur's constant help.[2]

Death of Bahádur,
1536.

Muhammad II. (Ásíri),
1536.

On the death of king Bahádur in A.D. 1536, the nobles of Gujarát invited his sister's son Muhammad Sháh Ásíri to succeed him. Muhammad Sháh died shortly after his accession, and the nobles conferred the crown on Mahmúd Khán, son of Latíf Khán, brother of Bahádur Sháh, and he ascended the throne in A.D. 1536, when only eleven years of age. The government of the country was carried on by Darya Khán and Imád-ul-Mulk, who kept the king under

[1] A detailed account of the death of Sultán Bahádur is given in the Appendix.
[2] Mirăt-i-Sikandari Persian Text, 233. Compare Farishtah, II. 427.

Chapter II.

Ahmedábád Kings, A.D. 1403-1573.

Mahmu'd II. 1536-1554.

strict surveillance. Darya Khán resolved to overthrow Imád-ul-Mulk and acquire supreme power. With this object he obtained an order from the king, whom, on the pretence of a hunting expedition, he removed from Áhmedábád, directing Imád-ul-Mulk to retire to his estates in Jhálává*d*a. Six months later, taking the Sultán with him, Darya Khán led an army into Jhálává*d*a, and defeating Imád-ul-Mulk in a battle at Pátri, fifty two miles west of Áhmedábád, pursued him to Burhánpur, and there defeated Imád-ul-Mulk's ally the ruler of Khándesh and forced Imád-ul-Mulk to fly to Málwa.[1] After this success Darya Khán became absorbed in pleasure, and resigned the management of the kingdom to Álam Khán Lodhi. The king, dissembling his dissatisfaction at the way he was treated, pretended to take no interest in affairs of state. Álam Khán Lodhi, seeing the carelessness of Darya Khán, began to entertain ambitious designs, and retiring to his estate of Dhandhúka invited the king to join him. Mahmúd Sháh, believing him to be in earnest, contrived to escape from surveillance and joined Álam Khán. On discovering the king's flight, Darya Khán raised to the throne a descendant of Áhmed Sháh by the title of Muzaffar Sháh, and striking coin in his name set out with an army towards Dhandhúka. Álam Khán and the king met him at Dhúr in Dholka, and a battle was fought in which Mahmúd and Álam Khán were defeated. The king fled to Ránpur, and thence to Páliád, while Álam Khán fled to Sádra. Darya Khán occupied Dhandhuka; but his men, dissatisfied at being placed in opposition to the king, rapidly deserted, some joining Álam Khan and some Mahmúd Sháh. Soon after the king joined Álam Khan and marched on Ahmedábád, whither Darya Khán had preceded them. The citizens closed the gates against Darya Khán, but he forced an entry by way of the Burhánpur wicket. Hearing of the king's approach Darya Khán fled to Mubárak Sháh at Burhánpur, leaving his family and treasure in the fortress of Chámpáner.

Escapes from Control.

The king entered Áhmedábád, and soon after captured Chámpáner. Álam Khán now obtained the recall of Imád-ul-Mulk, who received a grant of Broach and the port of Surat. Shortly afterwards Mahmúd Sháh began to show favour to men of low degree, especially to one Charji, a birdcatcher, whom he ennobled by the title of Muháfiz Khán. Charji counselled Mahmúd to put to death Sultán Alá-ud-dín Lodhi and Shujáát Khán, two of the principal nobles; and the king, without consulting his ministers, caused these men to be executed. The nobles joining together besieged Mahmúd Sháh in his palace, and demanded that Muháfiz Khán should be surrendered to them, but the king refused to give him up. The nobles then demanded an audience, and this the king granted, Muháfiz Khán, though warned of his danger, being foolishly present. On entering the royal presence Álam Khán signalled to his followers to slay Muháfiz, and he was killed in spite of the king's remonstrances. Mahmúd then attempted to kill himself, but was prevented and placed under guard, and the chief nobles took it in turn to watch him. Strife soon arose between Álam Khán and Mujáhid

Chooses Evil Favourites.

[1] Mirát-i-Sikandari, Persian Text, 292.

Chapter II.
Áhmedábád Kings, A.D. 1403-1573.
Mahmu'd II. 1536-1554.
Quarrels among the Nobles.

Khán and his brother, and the two latter nobles contrived the king's escape and sacked the houses of Álam Khán and his followers. Álam Khán escaped to Pethápur in the Mahi Kántha. He then joined Darya Khán, whom he called from the Dakhan, and obtained help in money from Imád-ul-Mulk of Surat and from Álp Khán of Dholka. Imád-ul-Mulk wrote to the Sultán asking forgiveness for the rebels. But before the Sultán, who was mercifully disposed, could grant them pardon, Álam Khán and Darya Khán again committed themselves by acts of open revolt. The Sultán displeased with the part Imád-ul-Mulk had taken in the rising summoned him to Champáner where, with the Sultán's connivance, his camp was given over to pillage. The Sultán disclaimed all knowledge of this attack and at Imád-ul-Mulk's request allowed him to go on pilgrimage to Makkah. In A.D. 1545 as he was preparing to start for Makkah Imád-ul-Mulk was killed. He was succeeded in Surat by Khudáwand Khán Rúmi, who had held Surat under him, and who, in spite of Portuguese opposition and intrigue, had five years before completed the building of Surat Castle.[1] Meanwhile Álam Khán and Darya Khán were driven from Gujarát and forced to take shelter with the sovereign of Dehli. The king now appointed as his own minister Afzal Khán, the minister of the late Bahádur Sháh, and though Afzal Khán lived in retirement, his counsel was taken on measures of importance. Other great nobles were Sayad Mubárak, Fateh Khán Baloch, and Abdul Karím Khán, who received the title of Ítimád Khán, and was so entirely in the Sultán's confidence that he was admitted to the harem. Mahmúd now consulted Ásif Khán as to the propriety of conquering Málwa. Ásif Khán advised him rather to deprive the Rájput chiefs and proprietors of their *wántas* or hereditary lands. The attempt to follow this advice stirred to resistance the chief men of Ídar, Sirohi, Dúngarpur, Bánsváda, Lúnáváda, Rájpípla, Dohad, and the banks of the Mahi. The king strengthened his line of outposts, establishing one at Sirohi and another at Ídar, besides fresh posts in other places. At the same time he began to persecute the Hindus, allowing them to be killed on the slightest pretence, branding Rájputs and Kolis, forcing them to wear a red rag on the right sleeve, forbidding them to ride in Áhmedábád, and punishing the celebration of Holi and Diwáli.[2] In A.D. 1554 Burhán, a servant of the king's, conceived the idea of killing him and reigning in his stead. He accordingly gave his master an intoxicating drug, and when he was overcome with sleep stabbed him to the heart. Then summoning the principal nobles in the king's name, he put to death Ásaf Khán the prime minister and twelve others, and endeavoured to have himself accepted as Sultán. No one aided him; even his

Disturbances, 1545.

Death of Mahmúd, 1554.

---

[1] A poet of the time, Mulla Muhammad of Astarábád, enshrined the date H. 947 (A.D. 1540) in the words:

SADD BUWAD BAR SÍNAH-O-JÁNAI FIRANGÍ ÍN BINÁI.

'May this fabric press like a pillar on the breast and the life of the Frank.

Farishtah, II. 447. The letter values that make 947 are: *S*=60, *d*=4, *b*=2, *w*=6, *d*=4, *b*=2, *r*=200, *s*=60, *y*=10, *n*=50, *h*=5, *w*=6, *j*=3, *a*=1, *n*=50, *f*=80, *r*=200, *n*=50, *g*=20, *y*=10, *a*=1, *y*=10, *n*=50, *b*=2, *n*=50, *a*=1, *y*=10, Total 947.

[2] Mirát-i-Sikandari, Persian Text, 326-27.

Chapter II.

Áhmedábád Kings, A.D. 1403 - 1573.

Mahmu'd II. 1536 - 1554.

accomplices deserted him. Imád-ul-Mulk Rumi,[1] Ulugh Khán, and others joined to oppose him, and when marching against them he was cut down by Shirwán Khán. Mahmúd's persecutions had raised such bitter hate among the Hindus, that they regarded Burhán as a saviour, and after Burhan's death are said to have made a stone image of him and worshipped it.[2] Mahmúd moved his capital from Áhmedábád to Mehmudábád, eighteen miles south of Áhmedábád where he built a palace and enclosed a deer park. At each corner of the park he raised a palace the stone walls and ceilings of which were ornamented with beautiful and precious gold traceries and arabesques.[3] His strict regard for public morals led him to forbid Muhammadan women visiting saints' tombs as the practice gave rise to irregularities. He died at the age of twenty-eight after a reign of eighteen years.

Ahmed II. 1554 - 1561. Ítimád Khán Regent.

On the death of Burhán, the nobles elected as sovereign a descendant of the stock of Áhmed Sháh of the name of Áhmed Khán, and proclaimed him king by the title of Áhmed Sháh II. At the same time they agreed that, as the king was young, Ítimád Khán should carry on the government and they further divided the country among themselves, each one undertaking to protect the frontiers and preserve the public peace. Mubárak Sháh of Khándesh, considering this a good opportunity, preferred a claim to the crown and marched to the frontier. An army led by the chief Gujarát nobles and accompanied by the young king met the invaders at the village of Ránpur Kotriá in Broach, the Gujarát army encamping on the north bank and the Khándesh army on the south bank of the Narbada. Násir-ul-Mulk, one of the Gujarát nobles, taking certain of his friends into his confidence, determined to remain neutral till the battle was over and then to fall on the exhausted troops and possess himself of both kingdoms. Sayad Mubárak, a descendant of the saint Sháhi Álam, who led the van of the Gujarát army, becoming aware of Násir-ul-Mulk's design opened communications with Mubárak Sháh of Khándesh and induced him to withdraw.[4] Násir-ul-Mulk, who still aspired to supreme power, gaining several nobles to his side near Baroda, surprised and defeated the forces of Ítimád Khán and Sayad Mubárak. The Sayad withdrew to his estate of Kapadvanj and he was joined by Ítimád Khán, while Násir-ul-Mulk, taking Sultán Áhmed with him to Áhmedábád, assumed the entire government of the country. After a short time he assembled an army and marched against Sayad Mubárak and Ítimád Khán encamping at Kamand, the village now called Od Kámod, ten miles north-east of Áhmedábád at the head of 50,000 horse. Ítimád feared to attack so

[1] This Imád-ul-Mulk is different from the Imád-ul-Mulk mentioned above (page 258) as receiving a grant of Broach and Surat. The latter had before this retired to Surat, and was killed there in A.D. 1545. (Bird, 266.) Imád-ul-Mulk II. who attacked Burhán, was originally called Malik Arslán (Bird, 272). He is also called the leader of the Turks and Rúmi. This Imád-ul-Mulk Rúmi, who was the father of Changíz Khán, was ultimately killed in A.D. 1560 at Surat by his own son-in-law Khudáwand or Ikhtiyár Khán.

[2] Mirăt-i-Sikandari, Persian Text, 326-27.

[3] This seems to be the palace referred to in the Tabákát-i-Akbari (Sir Henry Elliot's History of India, V. 369): After his second settlement of Gujarát (A.D. 1573, H. 981) Akbar left Áhmedábád for Mehmudábád and rested in the lofty and fine palace of Sultán Mahmúd of Gujarát.

[4] Mirăt-i-Sikandari, Persian Text, 332.

Chapter II. Áhmedábád Kings, A.D. 1403-1573. Ahmed II. 1554-1561.

strong a force. But Sayad Mubárak, who knew of the defection of Ulugh Khán and Imád-ul-Mulk, surprised Násir-ul-Mulk's army at night. During the confusion Ulugh Khán and Imád-ul-Mulk, disgusted with the assumption of Násir-ul-Mulk, deserted him and bringing the young Sultán with them joined Sayad Mubárak and Ítimád Khán. Násir-ul-Mulk was forced to fly, and after a short time died in the mountains of Pál.[1] Ikhtiyár-ul-Mulk, Fateh Khán Balúch, and Hasan Khán Dakhani now set up another king, a descendant of Áhmed, named Sháhu. A battle was fought near Mehmúdábád in which Sháhu and his supporters were defeated and Hasan Khán Dakhani was slain. Before the battle Fateh Khán Balúch had been induced to forsake Sháhu, and Ikhtiyár-ul-Mulk, taking Sháhu with him, fled. The nobles now divided Gujarát into the following shares :

Partition of the Province.

Áhmed Sháh for Private Purse ...	Áhmedábád and the Daskrohi sub-division.
Ítimád Khán and Party	Kadi, Jhálaváda, Pitlád, Nadiád, Bhil, Rádhanpur, Sami, Múnjpur, Godhra, and Sorath.
Sayad Mubárak and Party ...	Pátan and Cambay, with its Chorási or 84 villages, Dholka, Gogha, and Dhandhúka. Chámpáner, Sarnál, Bálásinor, and Kapadvanj.
Imád-ul-Mulk Rúmi and Party ...	Broach, Baroda, and Surat as far as the Sultánpur-Nandurbár frontier.
Nobles under Ítimád Khán ...	Modása and surrounding districts.

Of these shares Ítimád Khán bestowed the country of Sorath on Tátár Khán Ghori; the districts of Rádhanpur, Sami, and Múnjpur on Fateh Khán Baluch; Nadiád on Malik-ush-Shark, and some of the dependencies of Jhálávaḍa on Álaf Khán Habshi. Sayad Mubárak conferred the territory of Pátan on Músa Khán and Sher Khán Fuládi, Imád-ul-Mulk Rúmi bestowed the district of Baroda on Álaf Khán Habshi and the port of Surat on his wife's brother Khudáwand Khán Rúmi.

Dissensions.

About this time (A.D. 1552) Álam Khán returned, and, through the influence of Sayad Mubárak, was allowed to remain. The Sayad gave him and Ázam Humáyun Chámpáner, and Ítimád Khán gave Godhra to Álp Khán Khatri, a follower of Álam Khán. Álam Khán and Ítimád Khán shortly after expelled Álaf Khán Habshi from Jhálávaḍa, and he fled to Imád-ul-Mulk Rúmi at Broach, and at his intercession Álaf Khán received the Bhíl district. Álam Khán's success tempted him to try and get rid of Ítimád Khán and govern in his stead. Ítimád Khán, discovering his intention, made him leave the city and live in his own house in the Asáwal suburb. Álam Khán now made overtures to Imád-ul-Mulk Rúmi and became very friendly with him. 'One day Álam Khán proposed to get rid of Ítimád Khán;

[1] For Pál compare note 2 page 253.

but seeing that Imád-ul Mulk Rúmi did not take to his proposal, he next endeavoured to ruin Sayad Mubárak. But when the Gujarát army marched against him the Sayad made peace, and Álam Khán's intrigues being apparent, he was attacked and compelled to fly. He now went to Berár and sought aid of Mubárak Sháh, who marched an army towards the Gujarát frontier. The Gujarát nobles, taking Áhmed Sháh with them, advanced to oppose him, and he retired. Álam Khán now repaired to Sher Khán Fauládi at Pátan, and they together seized Ítimád Khán's district of Kadi, but, through the exertions of Ikhtiyár-ul-Mulk, Álam Khán was slain and Sher Khán forced to retire to Pátan. Imád-ul-Mulk Rúmi and Ítimád Khán now carried on the government, but dissension springing up between them, Ítimád Khán fled to Mubárak Sháh in Khándesh, and induced him to lead an army against Gujarát. The nobles, fearing this combination, made peaceful overtures and it was eventually settled that the lands of Sultánpur and Nandurbár should be given to Mubárak Sháh, and that Ítimád Khán should be restored to his former position. Since this date the districts of Sultánpur and Nandurbár have been permanently severed from Gujarát and have formed a part of Khándesh, to which province they now belong. Áhmed Sháh, finding himself more strictly guarded than ever, contrived to flee to Sayad Mubárak at Sayadpur, who, though vexed at his coming, would not refuse him shelter. At this time Háji Khán, a Dehli noble, on his way from Chitor to help Humáyún, passed through Gujarát with a well equipped force, and arrived at Pátan. The Gujarát nobles, especially Ítimád Khán and Imád-ul-Mulk Rúmi, conceiving that he came at the Sayad's invitation, and that the flight of the king was part of the plot, determined to crush the Sayad ere Háji Khán could join him, and on their march to Sayadpur meeting Sayad Mubárak near Mehmúdábád defeated him. The Sayad fell and was buried on the field of battle. His estates were resumed, though eventually Dholka was restored to his son Sayad Mírán.

Sultánpur and Nandurbár handed to Khándesh, 1560.

Defeat and Death of Sayad Mubárak.

The army and the two protectors returned to Áhmedábád. Dissensions again sprang up between them, and Imád-ul-Mulk Rúmi summoned to his aid his son Changíz Khán from Broach, while Ítimád Khán sent for Tátár Khán Ghori from Sorath. Tátár Khán arrived first and Ítimád Khán further strengthened by contingents from the Fauládis of Pátan and Fateh Khán Balúch from Rádhanpur ordered Imád-ul-Mulk Rúmi to return to his estate; and he, seeing it would be useless for him to contend against so overwhelming a force, retired to his possessions at Broach. Shortly after, having marched against Surat at the request of the inhabitants who were wearied of the tyranny of Khudáwand Khán, he was decoyed by that chief to an entertainment and was there assassinated. His son Changíz Khán marched against Surat to take vengeance for his father's death, and, finding the fortress too strong for him, summoned to his aid the Portuguese, to whom, as the price of their assistance, he surrendered the districts of Daman and Sanján.[1] The Portuguese, bringing a strong

Death of Imád-ul-Mulk Rúmi.

Daman District ceded to the Portuguese, 1550.

[1] The fort of Daman was taken by the Portuguese in A.D. 1530, and, according to Portuguese accounts (Faria y Souza in Kerr's Voyages, VI. 413) the country round was

Chapter II.

Áhmedábád Kings, A.D. 1403-1573.

Ahmed II. 1554-1561.

fleet up the Tápti, cut off the supplies, and Khudáwand Khán was forced to surrender, and was slain by Changíz Khán in revenge for his father's death. Shortly afterwards Changíz Khán quarrelled with Jhujhár Khán Habshi of Baroda because the Habshi had installed his nephew, son of Alif Khán Habshi, without consulting Changíz. Jhujhár and his nephew being defeated fled to Ítimád Khán, who allotted them a grant of land. At this time Fateh Khán Balúch, the proprietor of Rádhanpur and Sami, was Ítimád Khán's chief supporter, and with his assistance Ítimád Khán marched to besiege Changíz Khán in Broach. Tátár Khán Ghori and other nobles, fearing lest Ítimád Khán should become too powerful, endeavoured to make peace. As their efforts failed, Tátár Khán wrote to the Fauládis to attack Fateh Khán Balúch. They did so, and Fateh Khán, after being defeated near Rádhanpur, took refuge in the fort of Fatehkot or Dhúlkot, which is close to the town. Ítimád Khán raised the siege of Broach and came to Áhmedábád, where he busied himself in checking the intrigues of king Áhmed, who was doing all in his power to become independent. Finally, in A.D. 1560-61, at the instigation of Wajíh-ul-Mulk and Razí-ul-Mulk Ítimád Khán caused Áhmed II. to be assassinated. The murder took place in the house of Wajíh-ul-Mulk. The Sultán's body was thrown on the sands of the Sábarmati and the story circulated that the Sultán had been killed by robbers. Áhmed's nominal reign had lasted about eight years.

Assassinated, 1560.

Muzaffar III. 1561-1572. A Minor.

Ítimád Khán then raised to the throne a youth, whom he styled Muzaffar Sháh III., and who, he asserted, was a posthumous son of Mahmúd Sháh,[1] and then marched towards Pátan to take his revenge on the Fauládis for their attack on Fateh Khán Balúch. The nobles unwilling to crush the Fauládis, fearing lest their turn might come next, entered into secret correspondence with them, and withdrew when battle was joined. The nobles were now independent in their respective *jágirs*, in which according to the Tabakát-i-Akbari they allowed no interference though still owning nominal allegiance to the throne.[2] Ítimád Khán, forced to return unsuccessful to Áhmedábád, with a view of again attacking the Fauládis, summoned Tátár Káhán Ghori from Júnágadh. The nobles remained aloof, and even Tátár

---

annexed by them in 1558. According to a statement in Bird's History, 128, the districts surrendered by Changíz Khán contained 700 towns (villages) yielding a yearly revenue of £430,000 (Rs. 43,00,000). Sanján, since known as St. John's Head (north latitude 20° 13'; east longitude 72° 47'), between Daman and Bassein, seems to be one of the two Sindáns, the other being in Kachh, mentioned by the ninth to twelfth century Arab geographers. According to Ídrísi (Jaubert's Edition, 172) the mainland Sindán was a great town with a large import and export trade and well peopled with rich warlike and industrious inhabitants. Ídrísi's (Elliot, I. 85) notice of an island of the same name to the east is perhaps a confused reference to the Kachh Sindán which is generally supposed to be the Sindán of the Arab geographers. In A.D. 842, Sindán then a city of some size, is mentioned by Al-Biláduri (Reinaud's Fragments, 216-217) as having been taken by a Musalmán slave Fazl son of Máhán. This Fazl is related to have sent an elephant from Sindán to the Khalífah Al Maamún the Abbási (A.D. 813-833) and to have built an Assembly Mosque at Sindán. (Al-Biláduri in Elliot, I. 129.)

[1] According to Abul Fazl (Akbarnáma, III. 404; Elliot, V. 730) Muzaffar was a base-born boy of the name of Nathu.

[2] Tabákat-i-Akbari in Elliot's India, V. 339 note 2.

Chapter II.

Áhmedábád Kings. A.D. 1403-1573.

Muzaffar III. 1561-1572.

Ítimád Khán and the Fauládis.

Khán Ghori made excuses, which so exasperated Ítimád Khán that he sought to slay him. Tátár Khán escaped to Sorath, and there openly sided with the Fauládis. Sayad Mírán also left Áhmedábád for his estate at Dholka, and joining Tátár Khán at Ránpur they both went over to the Fauládis at Pátan. Meanwhile Ítimád Khán, again collecting an army, marched once more towards Pátan. He was met by the Fauládis near the village of Jhotáná, about thirty miles south of Pátan, where he was defeated and compelled to return to Áhmedábád. Sayad Mírán now intervened and made peace. Ítimád Khán still thirsting for revenge on the Fauládis, invited Changíz Khán, son of Imád-ul-Mulk Rúmi, to the capital, and by courteous treatment induced him to join in another expedition against the Fauládis. Like the other nobles Changíz Khán was lukewarm; and as Músa Khán Fauládi died while Ítimád Khán was marching on Pátan, Changíz Khán assigned this as a reason for not proceeding further, averring that it was not fit to war with people in misfortune. Ítimád Khán perforce returned to Áhmedábád.

The Mírzás, 1571.

Though Ítimád Khán had disgusted the nobles, both by causing the assassination of Áhmed Sháh and by his enmity with the Fauládis, as he had charge of Muzaffar Sháh and possession of the capital, the government of the country was in his hands. At this time the Mírzás,[1] who were the sons of Sultán Hussain of Khurásán, quarrelling with Jalál-ul-dín Muhammad Akbar, entered Gujarát, and joined Changíz Khán. Changíz Khán now proposed to Sher Khán Fauládi that they should expel I'timád Khán and divide Gujarát between them, the capital and the country south of the Sábarmati falling to the share of Changíz Khán, and that to the north to Sher Khán Fauládi. Sher Khán agreed, and Changíz Khán joining him they marched on Áhmedábád. Sayad Mírán induced Sher Khán to stay in Kadi. But Changíz Khán refused to listen to him, and a battle was fought between him, Ítimád Khán, and the Sayad on the right bank of the Khári about eight miles south of Áhmedábád. Ítimád Khán was defeated, and fled with the king to Modása, while Changíz Khán took possession of the capital. Sher Khán Fauládi now advanced to the Sábarmati, and, after dividing the province as had been agreed, Sher Khán retired to Kadi. Ítimád Khán entreated Mírán Muhammad Sháh, king of Khándesh, to march to his aid, and Changíz Khán invited Ítimád Khán to return. He came to Mehmudábád, where hearing that Muhammad Sháh had sustained a defeat and retired to his own country, he took Muzaffar Sháh with him and returned through Modása to Dungarpur. Changíz Khán remained in Áhmedábád, and Sher Khán withdrew to Kadi. After this success all the chief nobles of Gujarát, including the Habshis, joined Changíz Khán, who was now at the zenith of his power, and began to think of subduing Sher Khán Fauládi,

They Defeat Ítimád Khán.

[1] These Mírzás were the great grandsons of a Muhammad Sultán Mírza, the ruler of Khurásán, who, on being driven out of his dominions, sought refuge in India. This prince and his family on the ground of their common descent from Taimúr, were entertained first by Bábar (A.D. 1526-1531), and afterwards by Humáyún (A.D. 1531-1556). Before this quarrel Akbar had treated the Mírzás with great honour. Elliot's History, VI. 122.

Chapter II. Áhmedábád Kings, A.D. 1403-1573. Muzaffar III. 1561-1572. Death of Changíz Khán.

who on his part was anxious and fearful. At this time Bijli Khán a Habshi eunuch who was offended with Changíz Khán, because he had resumed the grant of Cambay, persuaded A'líf Khán and Jhujhár Khán Habshi that Changíz Khán had determined to kill them. The Habshi Kháns, resolving to be beforehand, invited Changíz Khán, with whom they were intimate, to play a game of *chaugán* or polo.[1] Changíz agreed and when near the Farhat-ul-Mulk mosque, between the Bhadar and the Three Gates, A'líf Khán, after making Jhujhár Khán a signal, attracted Changíz Khán's notice to the horse on which he was riding saying it was the best of the last batch imported from the Persian Gulf. As Changíz Khán turned to look at the horse, Jhujhár Khán cut him down. The Habshis now plundered Changíz Khán's house, while the Mírzás, mounting, went south and took possession of Broach, Baroda, and Chámpáner. Sher Khán advanced from Kadi, and ordered the Habshis to hand him over A'hmedábád. While treating with him the Habshis secretly summoned Ítimád Khán, who, returning with Muzaffar Sháh, entered the city. It was arranged that Ítimád Khán should take the place of Changíz Khán, and that the division of Gujarát between Changíz Khán and Sher Khán should be maintained. Ítimád Khán found the Habshis so domineering that he withdrew from public affairs. Afterwards A'laf Khán and Jhujhár Khán, quarrelling over the division of Changíz Khán's property, A'laf Khán left A'hmedábád and joined Sher Khán, who, advancing from Kadi, laid siege to A'hmedábád. Ítimád Khán now sought aid from the Mírzás, and Mírza Ibráhím Husain marched from Broach and harassed Sher Khán's army with his Mughal archers.

Ítimád Khán and the Emperor Akbar, 1572.

At the same time Ítimád Khán turned for help to the emperor Akbar, who, glad of any pretext for driving the Mírzás from their place of refuge in Gujarát, was not slow in availing himself of Ítimád Khán's proposal. Early in July 1572 he started for A'hmedabad, and with his arrival in the province, the history of Gujarát as a separate kingdom comes to an end.

---

[1] The modern game of polo. Lane in his translation of the Thousand and One Nights (I. 76, 1883 Edition) calls it the golf-stick, but the nature of the game described there does not in any way differ from polo. *Chaugán* is the Persian and *As-súljan-wal-kurah* the Arabic name for the game.

CHAPTER III.

MUGHAL VICEROYS.

A.D. 1573-1758.

Chapter III. Mughal Viceroys.

Akbar Emperor, 1573-1605.

To the nobles thus fighting among themselves, news was brought that the emperor Akbar was at Dísa. Ibráhím Husain Mírza returned to Broach and the army of the Fauládis dispersed. From Dísa the imperial troops advanced to Pátan and thence to Jhotána thirty miles south of Pátan. Sultán Muzaffar, who had separated from the Fauládis, fell into the hands of the emperor, who granted him his life but placed him under charge of one of his nobles named Karam Áli.[1] When the imperial army reached Kadi, Itimád Khán, Ikhtiyár Khán, Álaf Khán, and Jhujhár Khán met Akbar and Sayad Hámid also was honoured with an audience at Hájipur.[2] The emperor imprisoned Álaf Khán and Jhujhár Khán Habshi and encouraged the other Gujarát nobles. Ikhtiyár-ul-Mulk now fled to Lunáváḍa, and the emperor, fearing that others of the Gujarát nobles might follow his example, sent Ítimád Khán to Cambay and placed him under the charge of Shahbáz Khán Kambo.[3] From Áhmedábád Akbar advanced to Cambay. At this time Ibráhím Mírza held Baroda, Muhammad Husain Mírza held Surat, and Sháh Mírza held Chámpáner. On leaving Cambay to expel the Mírzas, Akbar appointed Mírza Ázíz Kokaltash his first viceroy of Gujarát. At Baroda Akbar heard that Ibráhím Mírza had treacherously killed Rustam Khán Rúmi, who was Changíz Khán's governor of Broach. The emperor recalled the detachment he had sent against Surat, and overtaking the Mírza at Sarnál or Thásra on the right bank of the Mahi about twenty-three miles north-east of Naḍiád, after a bloody conflict routed him. The Mírza fled by Ahmednagar to Sirohi, and Akbar rejoined his camp at Baroda. The emperor now sent a force under Sháh Kuli Khán to invest the fort of Surat, and following in person pitched his camp at Gopi Tálao, a suburb of that city. After an obstinate defence of one month and seventeen days, the garrison under Hamzabán, a slave of Humáyún's who had joined the Mírzás, surrendered. Hamzabán was in treaty with the Portuguese. Under his invitation a large party of Portuguese came to

---

[1] The emperor Akbar took Muzaffar Sháh with him to Agra, and settled on him the districts of Sárangpur and Ujjain in Málwa with a revenue of Rs. 20,00,000 (50 *lákhs* of *tankás*) (Elliot, V. 353). When Mun'im Khán Khán Khánán was going to Bengal, the emperor made Muzaffar over to him. Mun'im Khán gave his daughter Sháhzádah Khánam in marriage to Muzaffar, but shortly afterwards having reason to suspect him imprisoned him, whence Muzaffar finding an opportunity fled to Gujarát in A.D. 1581 (H. 989) according to Farishtah (II. 460), 1583 according to the Mirát-i-Sikandari.

[2] Both the Tabakát-i-Akbari (Elliot, V. 342) and Farishtah (I. 491) name four other nobles Mír Abu Turáb, Sayad Áhmed Bhukhári, Malik Ashraf, and Wajíh-ul-Mulk. The Sayad Áhmed of these two writers is a misprint for the Sayad Hámid of the text.

[3] Mirát-i-Sikandari, 415; Tabakát-i Akbari in Elliot, V. 343.

Chapter III.

Mughal Viceroys.

Akbar Emperor, 1573-1605.

Akbar captures Broach and Surat, and advances to A'hmedábád, 1573.

Surat during the siege, but seeing the strength of the imperial army, represented themselves as ambassadors and besought the honour of an interview.[1] While at Surat the emperor received from Bihár or Vihárji the Rája of Baglána, Sharfuddín Husain Mírza whom the Rája had captured.[2] After the capture of Surat, the emperor ordered the great Suleimáni cannon which had been brought by the Turks with the view of destroying the Portuguese forts and left by them in Surat, to be taken to A'gra. Surat was placed in the charge of Kalíj Khán. The emperor now advanced to A'hmedábád, where the mother of Changíz Khán came and demanded justice on Jhujhár Khán for having wantonly slain her son. As her complaint was just, the emperor ordered Jhujhár Khán to be thrown under the feet of an elephant. Muhammad Khán, son of Sher Khán Fauládi, who had fled to the Ídar hills, now returned and took the city of Pátan, besieging the imperial governor, Sayad A'hmed Khán Bárha, in the citadel. At this time Mírza Muhammad Husain was at Ránpúr near Dhandhuka. When Sher Khán Fauládi, who had taken refuge in Sorath, heard of Muhammad Khán's return to Pátan, he met Mírza Muhammad Husain, and uniting their forces they joined Muhammad Khán at Pátan. The viceroy Mírza Âzíz Kokaltásh with other nobles marched against them, and after a hard-fought battle, in which several of the imperial nobles were slain, Mírza Âzíz Kokaltásh was victorious. Sher Khán again took refuge in Sorath, and his son fled for safety to the Ídar hills, while the Mírza withdrew to the Khándesh frontier. As the conquest of Gujarát was completed, Akbar returned to Agra.

From A.D. 1573, the date of its annexation as a province of the empire, to A.D. 1758, the year of the final capture of A'hmedábád by the Maráthás, Gujarát remained under the government of officers appointed by the court of Dehli. Like the rule of the A'hmedábád kings, this term of 184 years falls into two periods: the first of 134 years from A.D. 1573 to the death of Aurangzíb in A.D. 1707, a time on the whole of public order and strong government; the second from A.D. 1707 to A.D. 1758, fifty-one years of declining power and growing disorder.

SECTION I.—A.D. 1573-1707.

Mirza Âzíz First Viceroy, 1573-1575.

Before leaving Gujarát Akbar placed the charge of the province in the hands of Mírza Âzíz Kokaltásh.[3] At the same time the emperor rewarded his supporters by grants of land, assigning A'hmedábád with Pitlád and several other districts to the viceroy Mírza Azíz, Pátan to the Khán-i-Kalán Mír Muhammad Khán, and Baroda to Nawáb Aurang Khán. Broach was given to Kutb-ud-dín Muhammad, and Dholka Khánpur and Sami were confirmed to Sayad Hámíd and Sayad Mahmúd Bukhári. As soon as the emperor was gone Ikhtiyár-ul-

[1] These details of the Surat expedition are taken from the Tabákát-i-Akbari in Elliot, V. 343-346 and Abúl Fazl's Akbar-námah in Elliot, VI. 42.

[2] The emperor Jehángír in his Diary (Tuzuk-i-Jehángíri, Persian Text, Sir Sayad Ahmed's Edition, page 196) says that Biharji or Viharji was the hereditary title of the chiefs of Báglán. The personal name of the Baglan Bihárji of his time was Partáp.

[3] According to the A'ín-i-Akbari (Blochmann, I. 325) the province of Gujarát over which the Kokaltásh was placed did not pass further south than the river Mahi.

Chapter III.

Mughal Viceroys.

Akbar Emperor, 1573-1605.

Mírza Âzíz First Viceroy, 1573-1575.

Mulk and Muhammad Khán, son of Sher Khán, who had taken shelter in the Ídar hills, issued forth, and the viceroy marched to Ahmednagar to hold them in check. Mírza Muhammad Husain advancing rapidly from the Nandurbár frontier, took the fort of Broach, and went thence to Cambay which he found abandoned by its governor Husain Khán Karkaráh, while he himself marched to Ahmednagar and Ídar against Ikhtyár-ul-Mulk. The viceroy ordered Sayad Hámíd Bukhári, Nawáb Naurang Khán, and others to join Kutb-ud-dín Muhammad Khán. They went and laid siege to Cambay, but Mírza Muhammad managed to evacuate the town and join Ikhtiyár-ul-Mulk and Muhammad Khán. After several unsuccessful attempts to scatter the enemy the viceroy retired to Áhmedábád, and the rebels laid siege to the city. Kutb-ud-dín Khán, Sayad Mírán, and others of the imperial party succeeded in entering the city and joining the garrison. After the siege had lasted two months, Akbar, making his famous 600 mile (400 *kos*) march in nine days from Agra, arrived before Áhmedábád, and, at once engaging the enemy, totally defeated them with the loss of two of their leaders Mírza Muhammad Husain and Ikhtiyár-ul-Mulk.

Insurrection Quelled by Akbar, 1573.

On the day before the battle Akbar consulting a Hazára Afghán versed in drawing omens from sheeps' shoulder-blades, was told that victory was certain, but that it would be won at the cost of the life of one of his nobles. Seif Khán, brother of Zein Khán Koka, coming in prayed that he should be chosen to receive the crown of martyrdom. At the end of the day the only leading noble that was killed was Seif Khán.[1]

After only eleven days' stay, Akbar again entrusting the government of Gujarát to Mírza Âzíz Koka, returned to Agra. Mírza Âzíz Koka did not long continue viceroy. In A.D. 1575, in consequence of some dispute with the emperor, he retired into private life. On his resignation Akbar conferred the post of viceroy on Mírza Khán, son of Behrám Khán, who afterwards rose to the high rank of Khán Khánán or chief of the nobles. As this was Mírza Khán's first service, and as he was still a youth, he was ordered to follow the advice of the deputy viceroy, Wazír Khán, in whose hands the administration of the province remained during the two following years. Soon after the insurrection of 1573 was suppressed the emperor sent Rája Todar Mal to make a survey settlement of the province. In A.D. 1575 after the survey was completed Wajíh-ul-Mulk Gujaráti was appointed *díwán* or minister. Some historians say that in A.D. 1576 Wazír Khán relieved Mírza Âzíz Koka as viceroy, but according to the Mirăt-i-

Mírza Khán Second Viceroy, 1575-1577.

Survey by Rája Todar Mal.

[1] Tuzuki Jehángíri or Jehangír's Memoirs, Pers. Text, Sayad Áhmed Khán's Edition page 20. For Akbar's march compare Tabakát-i-Akbari in Elliot, V. 365 and Blochman's Áin-i-Akbari, I. 325 and note. The Mirát-i-Áhmedi (Pers. Text, 131) records these further details: When starting from his last camp Akbar began to mount his horse on the day of the battle that took place near Áhmedábád. The royal steed unable to bear the weight of the hero laden with the spirit of victory sat down. Rája Bhagwándás Kachwáhah ran up to the rather embarrassed emperor and offered him his congratulations saying: This, your Majesty, is the surest sign of victory. There are also two further signs: the wind blows from our back and the kites and vultures accompany our host.

Chpater III.
Mughal Viceroys.
Akbar Emperor, 1573-1605.
Mírza Khán Second Viceroy, 1575-1577.

Áhmedi Mirza Khán held office with Wazír Khán as his deputy. One Prágdás, a Hindu, succeeded Wajíh-ul-Mulk as *díwán*. Troops were sent to reduce the Nándod and Ídar districts, and the fort of Sirohi was captured by Tarsu Khán, the military governor of Pátan. Afterwards, through the intervention of Pahár Khán Jálori, the Sirohi Rája, at an interview with Rája Todar Mal, presented £6000 (Rs. 12,000) and other articles and was allowed to serve the provincial governor of Gujarát with 1500 horse.

During Wazír Khán's administration Muzaffar Husain Mírza, son of Ibráhím Husain Mírza, raised an insurrection in Gujarát. This Mírza Muzaffar was as an infant carried to the Dakhan from Surat shortly before its investment by Akbar. He lived peacefully till under the influence of an ambitious retainer Mihr Ali by name, he gathered an army of adventurers and entered Nandurbár. Wazír Khán distrusting his troops shut himself in a fortress, and wrote to Rája Todar Mal, who was in Pátan settling revenue affairs. The Mírza defeated the imperial forces in Nandurbár and failing to get possession of Cambay marched straight to Áhmedábád. On the advance of Rája Todar Mal the Mírza fell back on Dholka. The Rája and the Khán pursuing defeated him, and he retired to Júnágadh. The Rája then withdrew, but the Mírza again advanced and besieged him in Áhmedábád. In an attempt to escalade the city wall Mihr Ali was killed. Muzaffar Mírza withdrew to Khándesh and the insurrection came to an end.

Shaháb-ud-dín Third Viceroy, 1577-1583.

In the end of A.D. 1577, as Wazír Khán's management was not successful, the post of viceroy was conferred upon Shaháb-ud-dín Áhmed Khán, the governor of Málwa. Shaháb-ud-dín's first step was to create new military posts and strengthen the old ones. At this time Fateh Khán Shirwáni, the commander of Amín Khán Ghori's army, quarrelled with his chief, and, coming to Shaháb-ud-dín, offered to capture the fort of Júnágadh. Shaháb-ud-dín entertained his proposal, and sent his nephew Mírza Khán and 4000 horse with him.

Sends a Force against Júnágadh.

When the troops crossed the Sorath frontier, they were met by envoys from Amín Khán, agreeing, in his name, to pay tribute and surrender the country, provided he were permitted to retain the fortress of Júnágadh and were allotted a sufficient grant of land. Mírza Khán rejected these proposals and continued his march against Júnágadh. Amín Khán made a vigorous resistance and applied for aid to the Jám of Navánagar. At this juncture Fateh Khán died, and Mírza Khán went and besieged Mángrúl. The Jám's minister Isá now joined Amín Khán with 4000 horse, and he, quitting Júnágadh, marched to Mángrúl.[2] On their approach Mírza Khán retired to the town of

[1] Tabakát-i-Akbari in Elliot, V. 405.

[2] Mángrúl (north latitude 21° 8'; east longitude 70° 10'), a seaport on the south coast of Káthiáváda, about twenty miles west of Somnáth. This town, which is supposed to be the Monoglossum emporium of Ptolemy (A.D. 150) (see Bird, 115), is spelt Mánglúr by the Muhammadan historians. Barbosa (A.D. 1511-1514), under the name of Suratimangaler, calls it a 'very good port where many ships from Malabár touch for horses, wheat, rice, cotton goods, and vegetables.' In A.D. 1531 the city was taken by the Portuguese general Sylveira with a vast booty and a great number of prisoners (Churchill's Travels, III. 529). It is incidentally mentioned in the Áin-i-Akbari (A.D. 1590). In A.D. 1638 Mandelslo describes it as famous for its linen cloth, and in A.D. 1700 it is mentioned by Hamilton (New Account, I. 136) as a place of trade.

Chapter III.

Mughal Viceroys.

Akbar Emperor, 1573-1605.

Shaháb-ud-dín Third Viceroy, 1577-1583.

Kodinár[1] followed by Amín Khán. Here a pitched battle was fought, and Mírza Khán was defeated with the loss of his baggage. Many of his men were slain, and he himself, being wounded, escaped with difficulty to Áhmedábád. Shaháb-ud-dín, who had meanwhile been giving his attention to revenue matters, and to the more correct measurement of the lands of the province, was rudely recalled from these peaceful occupations by his nephew's defeat. At the same time news was brought of the escape of the former king, Muzaffar Khán, who, eluding the vigilance of the imperial servants, appeared in Gujarát in A.D. 1583. Muzaffar remained for some time in the Rájpípla country, and thence came to one Lúna or Lúmbha Káthi, at the village of Khiri in the district of Sardhár in Sorath.

Ítimád Khán Gujaráti Fourth Viceroy, 1583-4.

Before he could march against Muzaffar, Shaháb-ud-dín was recalled, and in A.D. 1583 or 1584[2] I'timád Khán Gujaráti was appointed viceroy. At this time a party of 700 or 800 Mughals, called Wazír Khánis, separating from Shaháb-ud-dín, remained behind in hope of being entertained by the new viceroy. As Ítimád Khán declared that he was unable to take them into his service, they went off in a body and joined Muzaffar at Khíri, and he with them and three or four thousand Káthi horse marched at once on Áhmedábád. On hearing this Ítimád Khán, leaving his son Sher Khán in Áhmedábád, followed Shaháb-ud-dín to Kadi, and entreated him to return. Shaháb-ud-dín at first affected indifference telling Ítimád that as he had given over charge he had no more interest in the province. After two days he consented to return if Ítimád stated in writing that the country was on the verge of being lost and that Ítimád being unable to hold it was obliged to relinquish charge to Shaháb-ud-dín. Ítimád Khán made the required statement and Shaháb-ud-dín returned with him.[3] Meanwhile Muzaffar Sháh reached Áhmedábád, which was weakly defended, and in A.D. 1583, after a brief struggle, took possession of the city. While the siege of Áhmedábád was in progress Shaháb-ud-dín and I'timád Khán were returning, and were within a few miles of the city, when news of its capture reached them. They continued their advance, but had barely arrived at Áhmedábád when Muzaffar Sháh totally defeated them taking all their baggage. Seeing the issue of the fight, most of their army went over to Muzaffar Sháh, and the viceroy and Shaháb-ud-dín with a few men fled to Pátan. Kutb-ud-dín Muhammad Khán Atkah, one of the imperial commanders, who was on the Khándesh frontier, now advanced by forced marches to Baroda. Muzaffar marched against him with a large army, recently strengthened by the union of the army of Sayad Daulát ruler of Cambay. Kutb-ud-dín threw himself into Baroda, and, in spite of the treachery of his troops, defended the city for some time. At last, on Muzaffar's assurance that his life should be spared Kutb-ud-dín repaired to the enemies' camp to treat for peace. On his arrival he was treated with respect, but next day was treacherously put to death. The fort of Broach was also at this

Muzaffar captures Áhmedábád, 1583.

[1] This has been rendered by Bird, 353, 'the mountain of Dínár,' as if Koh Dínár.
[2] H. 992 (1584 A.C.) according to the Tabakat-i-Akbari (Elliot, V. 428).
[3] Mirät-i-Sikandári, 422. Compare Blochman's Áin-i-Akbari, I. 386.

Chapter III.
Mughal Viceroys.
Akbar Emperor, 1573-1605.
Mírza Abdur-Rahím Khán (Khán Khánán) Fifth Viceroy 1583-1587.
Defeat of Muzaffar, 1584.

time traitorously surrendered to Muzaffar by the slaves of the mother of Naurang Khán, fief-holder of the district.

On learning of the Gujarát insurrection the emperor, at the close of A.D. 1583, conferred the government of the province on Mírza Abdúr-Rahím Khán, son of Behrám Khán, who had formerly (A.D. 1575) acted as viceroy. Muzaffar, who was still at Broach, hearing of the advance of the new viceroy with a large army, returned rapidly to Áhmedábád, and in A.D. 1584 fought a pitched battle with Mírza Abdur-Rahím Khán between Sirkhej and Sháh Bhíkan's tomb.[1] In this engagement Muzaffar was entirely defeated, and fled to Cambay pursued by Mírza Abdúr-Rahím Khán. Muzaffar now hearing that Mírza Abdur-Rahím Khán had been joined by Naurang Khán and other nobles with the imperial army from Málwa, quitted Cambay, and made for his old place of shelter in Rájpípla. Finding no rest in Rájpípla, after fighting and losing another battle in the Rájpipla hills, he fled first to Pátan and then to Ídar, and afterwards again repaired to Lúmbha Káthi in Khiri. In reward for these two victories, the emperor bestowed on Mírza Abdúr-Rahím Khán the title of Khán Khánán. Broach now submitted, and Muzaffar sought shelter with Amín Khán Ghori at Júnágadh, by whom he was allotted the waste town of Gondal as a residence. Muzaffar made one more attempt to establish his power. He advanced to Morvi, and thence made a raid on Rádhanpúr and plundered that town, but was soon compelled to return to Káthiáváda and seek safety in flight. Amín Khán, seeing that his cause was hopeless, on pretence of aiding him, induced Muzaf-

---

[1] Mirăt-i-Sikandari, 426; Farishtah, I. 503; Elliot, V. 434. In honour of this victory the Khán Khánán built, on the site of the battle, a palace and garden enclosing all with a high wall. This which he named Jítpur the City of Victory was one of the chief ornaments of Áhmedábád. In November 1613 the English merchant Wittington writes (Kerr's Voyages, IX. 127): A *kos* from Sarkhej is a pleasant house with a large garden all round on the banks of the river which Chon-Chin-Naw (Khán Khánán) built in honour of a great victory over the last king of Gujarát. No person inhabits the house. Two years later (1615) another English merchant Dodsworth (Kerr, IX. 203) describes the field of Victory as strongly walled all round with brick about 1½ miles in circuit all planted with fruit trees and delightfully watered having a costly house called by a name signifying Victory in which Khán Khánán for some time resided. In 1618, the emperor Jehángír (Memoirs Persian Text, 210-213) on his way to Sarkhej visited the Khán-i-Khánán's Bághi Fateh or Garden of Victory which he had built at a cost of two *lákhs* of rupees ornamenting the garden with buildings and surrounding it with a wall. The natives he notices call it Fateh-Wádi. In 1626 the English traveller Herbert (Travels, 66) writes: Two miles nearer Áhmedábád than Sirkhej are the curious gardens and palace of Khán Khánán where he defeated the last of the Cambay kings and in memory built a stately house and spacious gardens the view whereof worthily attracts the traveller. Mandelslo writing in 1638 is still louder in praise of Tschietbág the Garden of Victory. It is the largest and most beautiful garden in all India because of its splendid buildings and abundance of fine fruits. Its site is one of the pleasantest in the world on the border of a great tank having on the water side many pavilions and a high wall on the side of Áhmedábád. The lodge and the caravanserai are worthy of the prince who built them. The garden has many fruit trees oranges, citrons, pomegranates, dates, almonds, mulberries, tamarinds, mangoes, and cocoanuts so closely planted that all walking in the garden is under most pleasing shade (Mandelslo's Travels, French Ed. 111-112). When (A.D. 1750) the Mirăt-i-Áhmedi was written several of the buildings and the remains of the summer house were still to be seen (Bird's History of Gujarát, 375). A few traces of the buildings known as Fateh Bádi or Victory Garden remains (1879). (Áhmedábád Gazetteer, 292.)

Akbar Emperor, 1583-1605.

Mírza Abdur-Rahím Khán (Khán Khánán) Fifth Viceroy, 1583-1587.

far to give him about £10,000.[1] When he had obtained the money, on one pretext or another, Amín Khán withheld the promised aid. The Khán Khánán now marched an army into Sorath against Muzaffar. The Jám of Navánagar and Amín Khán sent their envoys to meet the viceroy, declaring that they had not sheltered Muzaffar, and that he was leading an outlaw's life, entirely unaided by them. The viceroy agreed not to molest them, on condition that they withheld aid and shelter from Muzaffar, and himself marched against him. When he reached Upleta, about fifteen miles north-west of the fortress of Júnágadh, the viceroy heard that Muzaffar had sought shelter in the Barda hills in the south-west corner of the peninsula. Advancing to the hills, he halted his main force outside of the rough country and sent skirmishing parties to examine the hills. Muzaffar had already passed through Navánagar and across Gujarát to Dánta in the Mahi Kántha. Here he was once more defeated by the Parántej garrison, and a third time took refuge in Rájpípla. The viceroy now marched on Navánagar to punish the Jám. The Jám sent in his submission, and the viceroy taking from him, by way of fine, an elephant and some valuable horses, returned to Ahmedábád. He next sent a detachment against Ghazni Khán of Jhálor who had favoured Muzaffar. Ghazni Khán submitted, and no further steps were taken against him.

Ismáíl Kuli Khán Sixth Viceroy, 1587.

Mírza Áziz Kokaltásh Seventh Viceroy, 1588-1592.

Muzaffar seeks Refuge in Káthiaváda.

In A.D. 1587 the Khán Khánán was recalled and his place supplied by Ismáil Kuli Khán. Ismáíl's government lasted only for a few months, when he was superseded by Mírza Ázíz Kokaltásh, who was a second time appointed viceroy. In A.D. 1591, Muzaffar again returned to Sorath. The viceroy, hearing that he had been joined by the Jám, the Kachh chief, and Daulat Khán Ghori the son of Amín Khán, marched with a large army towards Sorath, and, halting at Víramgám, sent forward a detachment under Naurang Khán, Sayad Kásim, and other officers. Advancing as far as Morvi,[2] Naurang Khán entered into negotiations with the Jám, who, however, refused to accede to the demands of the imperial commander. On this the viceroy joined Naurang Khán with the bulk of his army, and after a short delay marched on Navánagar. On his way, at the village of Dhokar near Navánagar, Muzaffar and the Jám opposed him, and an obstinate battle in which the imperialists were nearly worsted, ended in Muzaffar's defeat. The son and minister of the Jám were slain, and Muzaffar, the Jám, and Daulat Khán who was wounded, fled to the fortress of Júnágadh. The viceroy now advanced and plundered Navánagar, and remaining there sent Naurang Khán, Sayad Kásím, and Gújar Khán against Júnágadh. The day the army arrived before the fortress Daulat Khán died of his wounds. Still the fortress held out, and though the viceroy joined them the siege made little progress as the imperial troops were in great straits for grain. The viceroy returned to Ahmedábád, and after seven or eight months again marched against Júnágadh. The Jám, who was still a fugitive, sent envoys

Is attacked by the Imperial Army.

[1] Two *lákhs* of *mahmúdis*. The *mahmúdi* varied in value from about one-third to one-half of a rupee. See Introduction page 222 note 2.

[2] Morvi (north latitude 29° 48'; east longitude 70° 50'), a town in Káthiáváda, about twenty-one miles south of Kachh.

Chapter III.
Mughal Viceroys.
Akbar Emperor, 1583-1605.
Mírza Áziz Kokaltash Seventh Viceroy, 1587.
Muzaffar Flies to Kachh.

and promised to aid the viceroy if his country were restored to him. The viceroy assented on condition that, during the operations against Júnágadh, the Jám should furnish his army with grain. The Jám agreed to provide grain, and after a siege of three months the garrison surrendered.

News was next received that Muzaffar had taken refuge at Jagat.[1] The viceroy at once sent Naurang Khán and others with an army in pursuit. On reaching Jagat it was found that Muzaffar had already left for a village owned by a Rájput named Sewa Wádhel. Without halting Naurang Khán started in pursuit, nearly surprising Muzaffar, who escaping on horseback with a few followers, crossed to Kachh. Sewa Wádhel covering Muzaffar's retreat was surprised before he could put to sea and fought gallantly with the imperial forces till he was slain. Naurang Khán then came to Arámra, a village belonging to Singrám Wádhel, Rája of Jagat, and after frustrating a scheme devised by that chief to entrap a body of the troops on board ship under pretence of pursuing Muzaffar's family, led his men back to Júnágadh. The viceroy, hearing in what direction Muzaffar had fled, marched to Morvi, where the Jám of Navánagar came and paid his respects. At the same time the Kachh chief, who is called Khengár by Farishtah and in the Mirăt-i-Áhmedi and Bhára in the Mirăt-i-Sikandri, sent a message that if the viceroy would refrain from invading his country and would give him his ancestral district of Morvi and supply him with a detachment of troops, he would point out where Muzaffar was concealed. The Khán-i-Ázam agreed to these terms and the chief captured Muzaffar and handed him to the force sent to secure him. The detachment, strictly guarding the prisoner, were marching rapidly towards Morvi, when, on reaching Dhrol, about thirty miles east of Jámnagar, under pretence of obeying a call of nature, Muzaffar withdrew and cut his throat with a razor, so that he died. This happened in A.D. 1591-92. The viceroy sent Muzaffar's head to court, and though he was now recalled by the emperor, he delayed on pretence of wishing to humble the Portuguese. His real object was to make a pilgrimage to Makkah, and in A.D. 1592, after obtaining the necessary permission from the Portuguese, he started from Verával.[2] During this viceroyalty an imperial *farmán* ordered that the state share of the produce should be one-half and the other half should be left to the cultivator and further that from each half five per cent should be deducted for the village headmen. All other taxes were declared illegal, and it was provided that when lands or houses were sold, half the government demand should be realized from the seller and half from the buyer.

Commits Suicide, 1591-92.

Sultán Murád Baksh Eighth Viceroy, 1592-1600.

The emperor, who was much vexed to hear of the departure of the viceroy, appointed prince Sultán Murád Bakhsh in his stead with as his minister Muhammad Sádikkhán one of the great nobles. In A.D. 1593-94 Mírza Ázíz Kokaltásh returned from his pilgrimage and

[1] Jagat (north latitude 22° 15'; east longitude 69° 1'), the site of the temple of Dwárka, at the western extremity of the peninsula of Káthiáváda.

[2] Verával (north latitude 20° 55'; east longitude 70° 21'), on the south-west coast of Káthiáváda. On the south-east point of Verával bay stood the city of Dev or Mungi Pátan and within its walls the temple of Somanátha.

Chapter III. Mughal Viceroys. Akbar Emperor, 1583-1605. Mírza Âzíz Kokaltásh Ninth Viceroy, 1600-1606.

repaired to court, and next year on prince Murád Bakhsh going to the Dakhan, Súrajsingh was appointed his deputy. In A.D. 1594-95 Bahádur, son of the late Muzaffar Sháh, excited a rebellion, but was defeated by Súrajsingh. In A.D. 1600, owing to the death of Sultán Murád, Mírza Âzíz Kokaltásh was a third time appointed viceroy of Gujarát, and he sent Shams-ud-dín Husain as his deputy to Ahmedábád. Further changes were made in A.D. 1602 when Mírza Âzíz sent his eldest son Shádmán as deputy; his second son Khurram as governor of Junágadh; and Sayad Báyázid as minister. Khurram was afterwards relieved of the charge of Sorath and Júnágadh by his brother Abdulláh.

Jehángír Emperor, 1605-1627.

In A.D. 1605 Núr-ud-dín Muhammad Jehángír ascended the imperial throne. Shortly after his accession the emperor published a decree remitting certain taxes, and also in cases of robbery fixing the responsibility on the landowners of the place where the robbery was committed. The decree also renewed Akbar's decree forbidding soldiers billetting themselves forcibly in cultivators' houses. Finally it directed that dispensaries and hospital wards should be opened in all large towns. In the early days of Jehángír's reign disturbance was caused in the neighbourhood of Ahmedábád by Bahádur a son of Muzaffar Sháh. Jehángír despatched Patrdás Rája Vikramájit as viceroy of Gujarát to put down the rising. The Rája's arrival at Ahmedabád restored order. Some of the rebel officers submitting were reinstated in their commands; the rest fled to the hills.[1] On the Rája's return Jehángír appointed Kalíj Khán to be viceroy of Gujarát; but Kalíj Khán never joined his charge, allowing Mírza Âzíz Kokaltásh to act in his place. In A.D. 1606, on the transfer of Mírza Âzíz to the Láhor viceroyalty, Sayad Murtaza Khán Bukhári, who had recently been ennobled in consequence of crushing the rebellion under Jehángír's son Khusráo, was entrusted with the charge of Gujarát, Sayad Báyázíd being continued as minister. Sayad Murtaza, who is said to have further ingratiated himself with the emperor by the present of a magnificent ruby, appears to have been more of a scholar than a governor. His only notable acts were the repair of the fort of Kadi[2] and the populating of the Bukhára quarter of Ahmedábád. During his tenure of power disturbances broke out, and Rái Gopináth, son of Rája Todar Mal, with Rája Sursingh of Jodhpur, were sent to Gujarát by way of Málwa Surat and Baroda. They overcame and imprisoned Kalián, chief of Belpár,[3] but were defeated by the Mándwa[4] chieftain, and withdrew to Ahmedábád. Rái Gopináth, obtaining reinforcements, returned to Mándwa and succeeded in capturing the chief. He then marched against the rebellious Kolis of the Kánkrej, and took prisoner their

Kalíj Khán Tenth Viceroy, 1606.

Sayad Murtaza Eleventh Viceroy, 1606-1609.

---

[1] Jehángír's Memoirs, Persian Text, 23; Blochman's Aín-i-Akbari, I. 470. Bahádur died about A.D. 1614: Jehángír's Memoirs, 134.

[2] Now belonging to His Highness the Gáikwár about twenty-seven miles north-west of Ahmedábád.

[3] Belpár, belonging to the Thákor of Umeta in the Rewa Kántha.

[4] This Mándwa is probably the Mándwa under His Highness the Gáikwár in his district of Atarsumba, but it may be Mándwa on the Narbada in the Rewa Kántha. Atarsumba is about ten miles west of Kapadvanj in the British district of Kaira.

Chapter III.
Mughal Viceroys.

leader, whom, on promising not to stir up future rebellions, he afterwards restored to liberty.

Jehangir Emperor, 1605-1607.

The first connection of the English with Gujarát dates from Sayad Murtaza's viceroyalty. In A.D. 1608 he allowed Captain Hawkins to sell goods in Surat.

Mírza Âzíz Kokaltash Twelfth Viceroy, 1609-1611.

In A.D. 1609 the Khán-i-Âzam Mírza Âzíz Kokaltásh was for the fourth time appointed viceroy of Gujarát. He was allowed to remain at court and send his son Jehángír Kuli Khán as his deputy with Mohandás Díván and Masûd Beg Hamadáni.[1] This was the beginning of government by deputy, a custom which in later times was so injurious to imperial interests.

Sack of Surat by Malik Âmbar, 1609.

In 1609 Malik Âmbar, chief minister of Nizám Sháh's court and governor of Daulatábád, invaded Gujarát at the head of 50,000 horse, and after plundering both the Surat and Baroda districts retired as quickly as he came. To prevent such raids a body of 25,000 men was posted at Rámnagar[2] on the Dakhan frontier, and remained there for four years. The details of the contingents of this force are :

The Viceroy of Áhmedábád	4000	Men.
The Nobles of his Court	5000	„
The Chiefs of Sáler and Mulher (Báglán) ...	3000	„
The Son of the Kachh Chief	2500	„
The Chief of Navánagar	2500	„
The Chief of Ídar	2000	„
The Chief of Dúngarpúr } Now under the Hilly Tracts Agency, Rájputána.	2000	„
The Chief of Bánsvada }	2000	„
The Chief of Rámnagar (Dharampur)	1000	„
The Chief of Rájipípla	1000	„
The Chief of Áli (Álirájpur under the Bhopáwar Agency)	300	„
The Chief of Mohan (a former capital of the state of Chhota Udepur in the Rewa Kántha) ...	350	„
Total ...	25,650	Men.

Abdulláh Khán Fírúz Jang Thirteenth Viceroy, 1611-1616.

In A.D. 1611 Abdulláh Khán Bahádur Fírúz Jang was appointed thirteenth viceroy of Gujarát, with Ghiás-ud-dín as his minister, under orders to proceed to the Dakhan to avenge the recent inroad.[3] The viceroy marched to the Dakhan but returned without effecting anything. In A.D. 1616, he was again, in company with prince Sháh

[1] Jehángír's Memoirs, Persian Text, 75.

[2] Now belonging to the Rája of Dharampur, east of the British district of Surat.

[3] In this year (A.D. 1611) the English East India Company sent vessels to trade with Surat. The Portuguese made an armed resistance, but were defeated. The Mughal commander, who was not sorry to see the Portuguese beaten, gave the English a warm reception, and in A.D. 1612-13 a factory was opened in Surat by the English, and in A.D. 1614 a fleet was kept in the Tápti under Captain Downton to protect the factory. In A.D. 1615, Sir Thomas Roe came as ambassador to the emperor Jehángír, and obtained permission to establish factories, not only at Surat but also at Broach Cambay and Gogha. The factory at Gogha seems to have been established in A.D. 1613. The emperor Jehángír notes in his memoirs (Persian Text, 105) that Mukarrab Khán, viceroy from A.D. 1616-1618, regardless of cost had bought from the English at Gogha a turkey a lemur and other curiosities. On his return from Jehángír's camp at Áhmedábád in January 1618 Roe obtained valuable concessions from the viceroy. The governor of Surat was to lend ships to the English, the resident English might carry arms, build a house, practise their religion, and settle their disputes. Kerr's Voyages, IX. 253. The Dutch closely followed the English at Surat and were established there in A.D. 1618.

Chapter III.

Mughal Viceroys.

Jeha'ngir Emperor, 1605-1627.

MUKARRAB KHÁN Fourteenth Viceroy, 1616.

Elephant-hunting in the Panch Mahals, 1616.

Jehán, directed to move against Ahmednagar. This second expedition was successful. The country was humbled, and, except Malik Ambar, most of the nobles submitted to the emperor. During this viceroy's term of office an imperial decree was issued forbidding nobles on the frontiers and in distant provinces to affix their seals to any communications addressed to imperial servants.

In A.D. 1616 on their return to Dehli, Mukarrab Khán, a surgeon who had risen to notice by curing the emperor Akbar and was ennobled by Jehángír, and who, since A.D. 1608, had been in charge of Surat or of Cambay, was appointed fourteenth viceroy of Gujarát, with Muhammad Safi as his minister. In the following year (A.D. 1617) the emperor Jehángír came to Gujarát to hunt wild elephants in the Dohad forests. But owing to the density of the forest only twelve were captured. Early in A.D. 1618 he visited Cambay which he notes only vessels of small draught could reach and where he ordered a gold and silver *tanka* twenty times heavier than the gold *mohar* to be minted. From Cambay after a stay of ten days he went to Áhmedábád and received the Rája of Ídar. As the climate of Áhmedábád disagreed with him Jehángír retired to the banks of the Mahi.[1] Here the Jám of Navánagar came to pay homage, and presented fifty Kachh horses, a hundred gold *mohars*, and a hundred rupees, and received a dress of honour. The emperor now returned to Áhmedábád, where he was visited by Rái Bhára of Kachh, who presented 100 Kachh horses 100 *ashrafis*[2] and 2000 rupees. The Rái, who was ninety years of age,

---

1 At first Jehángír, who reached Áhmedábád in the hot weather (March A.D. 1618), contented himself with abusing its sandy streets, calling the city the 'abode of dust' *gardábád*. After an attack of fever his dislike grew stronger, and he was uncertain whether the 'home of the simoom' *samumistán*, the 'place of sickness' *bímáristán*, the 'thorn brake' *zakumdár*, or 'hell' *jahánnamábád*, was its most fitting name. Even the last title did not satisfy his dislike. In derision he adds the verse, 'Oh essence of all goodnesses by what name shall I call thee.' Elliot's History of India, VI. 358; Jehángír's Memoirs Persian Text, 231. Of the old buildings of Áhmedábád, the emperor (Memoirs, Persian Text, 208-210) speaks of the Kánkariya tank and its island garden and of the royal palaces in the Bhadar as having nearly gone to ruin within the last fifty years. He notes that his Bakhshi had repaired the Kánkariya tank and that the viceroy Mukarrab Khán had partly restored the Bhadar palaces against his arrival. The emperor was disappointed with the capital. After the accounts he had heard it seemed rather poor with its narrow streets, its shops with ignoble fronts, and its dust, though to greet the emperor as he came on elephant-back scattering gold the city and its population had put on their holiday dress. The emperor speaks (Memoirs, Persian Text page 211) of having met some of the great men of Gujarát. Chief among these was Sayad Muhammad Bukhári the representative of Sháhi Álam and the sons of Sháh Wajih-ud-dín of Áhmedábád. They came as far as Cambay to meet the emperor. After his arrival in the capital Jehángír with great kindness informally visited the house and garden of Sikandar Gujaráti the author of the Mirât-i-Sikandari, to pick some of the author's famous figs off the trees. Jehángír speaks of the historian as a man of a refined literary style well versed in all matters of Gujarát history, who six or seven years since had entered his (the imperial) service (Memoirs, 207-211). On the occasion of celebrating Sháh Jehán's twenty-seventh birthday at Áhmedábád Jehángír records having granted the territory from Mándu to Cambay as the estate of his son Sháh Jehán (Prince Khurram). Memoirs, Persian Text, 210-211. Before leaving Gujarát the emperor ordered the expulsion of the Sevadas or Jain priests, because of a prophecy unfavourable to him made by Mán Sing Sewda (Memoirs, Persian Text, 217).

2 This was probably the gold *ashrafi* or seraph of which Hawkins (1609-1611) says, 'Serraffins Ekberi, which be ten rupees a-piece.' Thomas Chron. Pat. Kings of Dehli, 425.

Chapter III.
Mughal Viceroys.
Jehángír Emperor, 1605 - 1627.

had never paid his respects to any emperor. Jehángír, much pleased with the greatest of Gujarát Zamíndars, who, in spite of his ninety years was hale and in full possession of all his senses, gave him his own horse, a male and female elephant, a dagger, a sword with diamond-mounted hilt, and four rings of different coloured precious stones. As he still suffered from the climate, the emperor set out to return to Ágra, and just at that time (A.D. 1618-19) he heard of the birth of a grandson, afterwards the famous Abúl Muzaffar Muhiyy-ud-dín Muhammad Aurangzíb who was born at Dohad in Gujarát.[1] In honour of this event Sháh Jehán held a great festival at Ujjain.

Prince Sháh Jehán Fifteenth Viceroy, 1618 - 1622.

Before the emperor started for Ágra, he appointed prince Sháh Jehán fifteenth viceroy of Gujarát in the place of Mukarrab Khán whose general inefficiency and churlish treatment of the European traders he did not approve. Muhammad Safi was continued as minister. As Sháh Jehán preferred remaining at Ujjain he chose Rustam Khán as his deputy; but the emperor, disapproving of this choice, selected Rája Vikramájit in Rustam Khán's stead. Shortly after, in A.D. 1622-23, Sháh Jehán rebelled, and in one of the battles which took place Rája Vikramájit was killed. Sháh Jehán, during his viceroyalty, built the Sháhi Bágh and the royal baths in the Bhadar at Áhmedábád. After the death of Vikramájit, his brother succeeded as deputy viceroy. While Sháh Jehán was still in rebellion, the emperor appointed Sultán Dáwar Baksh the son of prince Khusrao, sixteenth viceroy of Gujarát, Muhammad Safi being retained in his post of minister. Sháh Jehán, who was then at Mándu in Málwa, appointed on his part Abdulláh Khán Bahádur Fírúz Jang viceroy and a *khájahsara* or eunuch of Abdulláh Khán his minister. Sultán Dáwar Baksh, the emperor's nominee, was accompanied by Khán-i-Ázam Mírza Âzíz Kokaltásh to instruct him in the management of affairs. Prince Sháh Jehán had directed his minister to carry away all the treasure; but Muhammad Safi, who appears to have been a man of great ability, at once imprisoned the prince's partisans in Áhmedábád, and, among others, captured the eunuch of Abdulláh Khán. When this news reached the prince at Mándu, he sent Abdulláh Khán Bahádur with an army to Gujarát by way of Baroda. Muhammad Safi Khán met and defeated him, and forced him to fly and rejoin the prince at Mándu. For his gallant conduct Muhammad Safi received the title of Saif Khán, with an increase in his monthly pay from £70 to £300 (Rs. 700 - 3000) and the command of 3000 horse. Meanwhile Sultán Dáwar Baksh, with the Khán-i-Ázam, arrived and assumed the charge of the government, but the Khán-i-Ázam died soon after in A.D. 1624, and was buried at Sarkhej. Sultán Dáwar Baksh was

Sháh Jehán Rebels, 1622 - 1623.
Builds the Sháhi Bágh at Áhmedábád.
Sultán Dáwar Baksh Sixteenth Viceroy, 1622 - 1624.

1 The peaked masonry tomb over Aurangzíb's after-birth with its mosque, enclosure, and intact endowment is one of the curiosities of Dohad. In a letter to his eldest son Muhammad Muâzzam then (A.D. 1704) viceroy of Gujarát the aged Aurangzíb writes: My son of exalted rank, the town of Dohad, one of the dependencies of Gujarát, is the birth-place of this sinner. Please to consider a regard for the inhabitants of that town incumbent on you, and continue in office its decrepid old Faujdár. In regard to that old man listen not to the whisperings of those suffering from the disease of self-interest: "Verily they have a sickness in their hearts and Allah addeth to their ailments" (Letters of the Emperor Aurangzíb: Persian Text, Cawnpur Edition, Letter 31.)

Chapter III.

Mughal Viceroys.

re-called, and Khán Jehán was appointed deputy viceroy with Yúsuf Khán as his minister. On his arrival at Áhmedábád, prince Sháh Jehán employed Khán Jehán in his own service, and sent him as his ambassador to the emperor. Saif Khán, who acted for him, may be called the seventeenth viceroy, as indeed he had been the governing spirit for the last eight or ten years. He held the post of viceroy of Gujarát until the death of the emperor in A.D. 1627.

SAIF KHÁN Seventeenth Viceroy, 1624 - 1627.

On the death of the emperor Jehángir, his son Abul Muzaffar Shaháb-ud-dín Sháh Jehán ascended the throne. Remembering Saif Khán's hostility he at once caused him to be imprisoned, and appointed Sher Khán Túar eighteenth viceroy with Khwájah Hayát as his minister. When the emperor was near Surat, he appointed Mír Shamsuddín to be governor of Surat castle. In A.D. 1627, Sháh Jehán on his way to Dehli visited Áhmedábád and encamped outside of the city near the Kánkariya lake. Sher Khán was advanced to the command of 5000 men, and received an increase of salary and other gifts. At the same time Khán Jehán was appointed his minister, and Mírza Ísa Tarkhán was made viceroy of Thatta in Sindh. In A.D. 1628 Khwájah Abúl Hasan was sent to conquer the country of Násik and Sangamner which he ravaged, and returned after taking the fort of Chándoḍ and levying tribute from the chief of Báglán. In A.D. 1630, Jamál Khán Karáwal came to the Gujarát-Khándesh frontier and captured 130 elephants in the Sultánpur forests, seventy of which valued at a lákh of rupees were sent to Dehli. In A.D. 1631-32 Gujarát was wasted by the famine known as the *Satiásio Kál* or '87 famine. So severe was the scarcity that according to the Bádsháh Náma, rank sold for a cake, life was offered for a loaf, the flesh of a son was preferred to his love. The emperor opened soup kitchens and alms-houses at Surat and Áhmedábád and ordered Rs. 5000 to be distributed.[1]

Shah Jehán Emperor, 1627 - 1658.

SHER KHÁN TÚAR Eighteenth Viceroy, 1627 - 1632.

Famine, 1631-32.

Sher Khán was re-called in A.D. 1632, but died ere he could be relieved by Islám Khán, the nineteenth viceroy of Gujarát, along with whom Khwájah Jehán was chosen minister. Islám Khán's monthly salary was £400 (Rs. 4000), and his command was raised from 5000 to 6000. In A.D. 1632, Khwájah Jehán went on pilgrimage to Makkah, and was succeeded as minister by Ágha Afzal with the title of Afzal Khán. Afzal Khán was soon appointed commander of Baroda, and Riáyat Khán succeeded him as minister. The post of viceroy of Gujarát appears to have been granted to whichever of the nobles of the court was in a position to make the most valuable presents to the emperor. Government became lax, the Kolis of the Kánkrej committed excesses, and the Jám of Navánagar withheld his tribute. At this time Bákar Khán presented the emperor with golden and jewelled ornaments to the value of Rs. 2,00,000 and was appointed viceroy, Riáyat Khán being continued as minister. In A.D. 1633 Sipáhdar Khán was appointed viceroy, and presented the emperor with costly embroidered velvet tents with golden posts worthy to hold the famous *Takhti-Táús* or Peacock Throne which was just completed at a cost of one *kror* of rupees. Riáyat Khán was continued as minister.

ISLÁM KHÁN Nineteenth Viceroy, 1632.

Disorder, 1632.

BÁKAR KHÁN Twentieth Viceroy, 1632.

SIPÁHDÁR KHÁN Twenty-first Viceroy, 1633.

[1] Elliot, VII. 24.

Chapter III.

Mughal Viceroys.

Sháh Jehán Emperor, 1627-1658.

SAIF KHÁN Twenty-second Viceroy, 1633-1635.

ÁZAM KHÁN Twenty-third Viceroy, 1635-1642.

In A.D. 1635 Saif Khán was appointed twenty-second viceroy, with Riáyat Khán as minister. During Saif Khán's tenure of power Mírza Ísa Tarkhán received a grant[1] of the province of Sorath, which had fallen waste through the laxity of its governors. Before he had been in power for more than a year Saif Khán was recalled. As he was preparing to start, he died at Áhmedábád and was buried in Sháhi Alám's shrine to which he had added the dome over the tomb and the mosque to the north of the enclosure.

At the end of A.D. 1635 Ázam Khán was appointed twenty-third viceroy, with Riáyat Khán in the first instance, and afterwards with Mír Muhammad Sábir, as minister. The men who had recently been allowed to act as viceroys had shown themselves unfit to keep in order the rebellious chiefs and predatory tribes of Gujarát. For this reason the emperor's choice fell upon Ázam Khán, a man of ability, who perceived the danger of the existing state of affairs, and saw that to restore the province to order, firm, even severe, measures were required. When Ázam Khán reached Sidhpur, the merchants complained bitterly of the outrages of one Kánji, a Chúnvália Koli, who had been especially daring in plundering merchandise and committing highway robberies. Ázam Khán, anxious to start with a show of vigour, before proceeding to Áhmedábád, marched against Kánji, who fled to the village of Bhádar in the Kherálu district of Kadi, sixty miles north-east of Áhmedábád. Ázam Khán pursued him so hotly that Kánji surrendered, handed over his plunder, and gave security not only that he would not again commit robberies, but that he would pay an annual tribute of £1000 (Rs. 10,000). Ázam Khán then built two fortified posts in the Koli country, naming one Ázamábád after himself, and the other Khalílábád after his son. He next marched to Káthiáváda[2] and subdued the Káthis, who were continually ravaging the country near Dhandhúka, and to check them erected a fortified post called Sháhpúr, on the opposite side of the river to Chuda-Ránpur. Ágha Fázil known as Fázil Khán, who had at one time held the post of minister, and had, in A.D. 1636, been appointed governor of Baroda, was now selected to command the special cavalry composing the bodyguard of prince Muhammad Aurangzíb. At the same time Sayad Ilahdád was appointed governor of Surat fort, Ísa Tarkhán remaining at Júnágadh. In A.D. 1637, Mír Muhammad Sábir was chosen minister in place of Riáyat Khán, and in A.D. 1638 Muîz-zul-Mulk was re-appointed to the command of Surat fort. Shortly after Ázam Khán's daughter was sent to Dehli, and espoused to the emperor's son Muhammad Shujá Bahádur. In A.D. 1639, Ázam Khán, who for his love of building was known as Udhai or the Whiteant, devoted his attention to establishing fortified posts to check rebellion and robbery in the country of the Kolis and the Káthis. So complete were his arrangements that people could travel safely all over Jhálávada,

Punishes the Kolis,

Subdues the Káthis.

[1] The words used in the text is *tuyúl*. In meaning it does not differ from *jágír*.

[2] This is one of the first mentions in history of peninsular Gujarát as Káthiáváda, or as anything other than Sorath or Sauráshtra. The district referred to was probably united to the eastern possessions of the Khachar Káthis and Panchál.

Chapter III.

Mughal Viceroys.

Sháh Jehán Emperor, 1627-1658.

Ázam Khán Twenty-third Viceroy, 1635-1642.

Revolt of the Jam of Navánagar, 1640.

Káthiáváda, Navánagar, and Kachh. The Jám, who of late years had been accustomed to do much as he pleased, resented these arrangements, and in A.D. 1640 withheld his tribute, and set up a mint to coin *koris*.[1] When Ázam Khán heard of this, he marched with an army against Navánagar, and, on arriving about three miles from the city, he sent the Jám a peremptory order to pay the arrears of tribute and to close his mint, ordering him, if any disturbance occurred in that part of the country, at once to send his son to the viceroy to learn his will. He further ordered the Jám to dismiss to their own countries all refugees from other parts of Gujarát. The Jám being unable to cope with Ázam Khán, acceded to these terms; and Ázam Khán, receiving the arrears of tribute, returned to Áhmedábád. As Ázam Khán's stern and somewhat rough rule made him unpopular, Sayad Jálál Bukhári whose estates were being deserted from fear of him brought the matter to the emperor's notice.

Ísa Tarkhán Twenty-fourth Viceroy, 1642-1644.

In consequence in A.D. 1642 the emperor recalled Ázam Khán and appointed in his place Mírza Ísa Tarkhán, then governor of Sorath, twenty-fourth viceroy of Gujarát. And as it was feared that in anger at being re-called Ázam Khán might oppress some of those who had complained against him, this order was written by the emperor with his own hand. Thanks to Ázam Khán's firm rule, the new viceroy found the province in good order, and was able to devote his attention to financial reforms, among them the introduction of the share, *bhágvatái*, system of levying land revenue in kind. When Mírza I'sa Tarkhán was raised to be viceroy of Gujarát, he appointed his son Ináyat-ulláh to be governor of Júnágadh, and Muiz-zul-Mulk to fill the post of minister. During the viceroyalty of Mírza Ísa Sayad Jalál Bukhári a descendant of Saint Sháhi Álam was appointed to the high post of Sadr-us-Sudúr or chief law officer for the whole of India. This was a time of prosperity especially in Surat, whose port dues which were settled on the Pádsháh Begam had risen from two and a half to five lákhs. Mírza Ísa Tarkhán's term of power was brief. In A.D. 1644 the emperor appointed prince Muhammad Aurangzíb to the charge of Gujarát, Muiz-zul-Mulk being ordered by the emperor to continue to act as his minister. An event of interest in the next year (A.D. 1645) is the capture of seventy-three elephants in the forests of Dohad and Chámpáner.[2]

---

[1] The author of the Mirát-i-Áhmedi says that in his time, A.D. 1746-1762, these Navánagar *koris* were current even in Áhmedábád, two *koris* and two-thirds being equal to one imperial rupee. They were also called *jámis*. The Mirát-i-Áhmedi (Persian Text, 225) calls them *mahmúdis*. The legend on the reverse was the name of the Gujarát Sultán Muzaffar and on the obverse in Gujaráti the name of the Jám. Usually two *mahmúdis* and sometimes three went to the imperial rupee. The author says that in Áhmedábád up to his day (A.C. 1756) the account for *ghi* clarified butter was made in *mahmúdis*. When the order for melting the *mahmúdis* was passed a mint was established at Júnágadh but was afterwards closed to suit the merchants from Diu and other parts who transmitted their specie to Áhmedábád.

[2] The traveller Mandelslo, who was in Áhmedábád in 1638, says: No prince in Europe has so fine a court as the governor of Gujarát. Of none are the public appearances so magnificent. He never goes out without a great number of gentlemen and guards on foot and horse. Before him march many elephants with housings of brocade and velvet, standards, drums, trumpets, and cymbals. In his palace he is served like a king and suffers no one to appear before him unless he has asked an audience. (Travels, French

Chapter III.

Mughal Viceroys.

Shah Jehan Emperor, 1627-1658.

PRINCE MUHAMMAD AURANGZÍB Twenty-fifth Viceroy, 1644-1646.

Prince Aurangzíb's rule in Gujarát was marked by religious disputes. In 1644 a quarrel between Hindus and Musálmans ended in the prince ordering a newly built (1638) temple of Chintáman near Saraspur, a suburb of Ahmedábád, above a mile and a half east of the city, to be desecrated by slaughtering a cow in it. He then turned the building into a mosque, but the emperor ordered its restoration to the Hindus. In another case both of the contending parties were Musalmáns, the orthodox believers, aided by the military under the prince's orders, who was enraged at Sayad Ráju one of his followers joining the heretics, attacking and slaughtering the representatives of the Mahdawiyeh sect in Ahmedábád. Sayad Ráju's spirit, under the name of Rájú Shahíd or Rájú the martyr, is still worshipped as a disease-scaring guardian by the Pinjárás and Mansúris and Dúdhwálas of Ahmedábád.[1] In consequence of the part he had taken in promoting these disturbances, prince Aurangzíb was relieved and Sháistah Khán appointed twenty-sixth viceroy of Gujarát. In the following year Muiz-zul-Mulk, who had till then acted as minister, was recalled, and his place supplied by Háfiz Muhammad Násir. At the same time the governorship of Surat and Cambay was given to Ali Akbar of Ispahán. This Ali Akbar was a Persian horse merchant who brought to Agra seven horses of pure Arabian breed. For six of these Sháh Jehán paid Rs. 25,000. The seventh a bay so pleased the emperor that he paid Rs. 15,000 for it, named it the Priceless Ruby, and considered it the gem of the imperial stud. In A.D. 1646 Ali Akbar was assassinated by a Hindu and Muiz-zul-Mulk succeeded him as governor of Surat and Cambay. As Sháistah Khán failed to control the Gujarát Kolis, in A.D. 1648 prince Muhammad Dárá Shikoh was chosen viceroy, with Ghairat Khán as his deputy and Háfiz Muhammad Násir as minister, while Sháistah Khán was sent to Málwa to relieve Sháh Nawáz Khán. While Dárá Shikoh was viceroy an ambassador landed at Surat from the court of the Turkish Sultán Muhammad IV. (A.D. 1648-1687).[2] In A.D. 1651, Mír Yahyá was appointed minister in place of Háfiz Muhammad Násir, and in A.D. 1652 prince Dárá was sent to Kandahár. On

SHÁISTAH KHÁN Twenty-sixth Viceroy, 1646-1648.

PRINCE MUHAMMAD DÁRÁ SHIKOH Twenty-seventh Viceroy, 1648-1652.

Edition, 151.) Of the general system of government he says: The viceroy is absolute. It is true he summons leading lords of the country to deliberate on judgments and important matters. But they are called to ascertain their views not to adopt them. On the one hand the king often changes his governors that they may not grow overpowerful. On the other hand the governors knowing they may be recalled at any time take immense sums from the rich merchants especially from the merchants of Ahmedábád against whom false charges are brought with the view of forcing them to pay. As the governor is both civil and criminal judge if the merchants did not temper his greed they would be ruined beyond remedy. (Ditto, 150.) The frequent changes of viceroys in Gujarát is explained by Terry, 1615-17 (Voyage to East Indies, 364): To prevent them from becoming popular the king usually removes his viceroys after one year sending them to a new government remote from the old one. Terry adds a curious note: When the king sends any one to a place of government they never cut their hair till they return into his presence as if they desired not to appear beautiful except in the king's sight. As soon as he sees them the king bids them cut their hair (Ditto, 365). It does not seem to have been cheating to keep up fewer horse than the number named. Terry (Voyage to East Indies, 391) says: He who hath the pay of five or six thousand must always have one thousand or more in readiness according to the king's need of them, and so in proportion all the rest.

[1] Mirát-i-Ahmedi Persian Text, II. 46-47. Pinjárás are cotton teasers, Mansúris are Pinjárás who worship Mansúr a tenth century (3rd century *Hijrah*) saint.

[2] Mirát-i-Ahmedi Persian Text, 237.

the transfer of the prince Sháistah Khán became viceroy for the second time, with Mír Yahyá as minister and Sultán Yár governor of Baroda with the title of Himmat Khán. Mírza Ísa Tarkhán was summoned to court from his charge of Sorath and his son Muhammad Sálih was appointed his successor. In A.D. 1653 an ill-advised imperial order reducing the pay of the troopers, as well as of the better class of horsemen who brought with them a certain number of followers, created much discontent. During this year several changes of governors were made. Muhammad Násir was sent to Surat, Himmat Khán to Dholka, the governor of Dholka to Baroda, Kutb-ud-dín to Júnágadh, Sayad Sheikhan son-in-law of Sayad Diler Khán to Tharád under Pátan, and Jagmál, the holder of Sánand, to Dholka. In the same year Sháistah Khán made an expedition against the Chunvália Kolis, who, since Ázam Khán's time (A.D. 1642), had been ravaging Víramgám, Dholka, and Kadi, and raiding even as far as the villages round Áhmedábád.

Chapter III. Mughal Viceroys. Sháh Jehán Emperor, 1627-1658. SHÁISTAH KHÁN Twenty-eighth Viceroy, 1652-1654.

In spite of Sháistah Khán's success in restoring order the emperor in A.D. 1654 appointed in his place prince Muhammad Murád Bakhsh twenty-ninth viceroy of Gujarát. Diánat Khán, and immediately after him Rehmat Khán, was appointed minister in place of Mír Yahyá. Mujáhid Khán Jhálori relieved Mír Shams-ud-dín as governor of Pátan and Godhra was entrusted to Sayad Hasan, son of Sayad Diler Khán, and its revenues assigned to him. When prince Murád Bakhsh reached Jhábua[1] on his way to Áhmedábád, the chief presented him with £1500 (Rs. 15,000) as tribute; and when he reached Ahmedábád, Kánji, the notorious leader of the Chunvália Kolis, surrendered through Sayad Sheikhan, and promised to remain quiet and pay a yearly tribute of £1000 (Rs. 10,000). Dildost, son of Sarfaráz Khán, was appointed to the charge of the post of Bíjápur under Pátan; while Sayad Sheikhan was made governor of Sádra and Píplod, and Sayad Áli paymaster, with the title of Radawi Khán. Many other changes were made at the same time, the prince receiving a grant of the district of Júnágadh. One Pírjí, a Bohora, said to have been one of the richest merchants of Surat, is noted as sending the emperor four Arab horses and prince Murád as presenting the emperor with eighteen of the famous Gujarát bullocks. During the viceroyalty of Dárá Shikoh sums of Rs. 1,00,000 to Rs. 2,00,000 used to be spent on articles in demand in Arabia. The articles were sent under some trustworthy officer and the proceeds applied to charitable purposes in the sacred cities.

PRINCE MURÁD BAKHSH Twenty-ninth Viceroy, 1654-1657.

At the end of A.D. 1657, on the receipt of news that Sháh Jehán was dangerously ill prince Murád Bakhsh proclaimed himself emperor by the title of Murawwaj-ud-dín and ordered the reading of the Friday sermon and the striking of coin in his own name.[2] His next step was to put to death the minister Áli Naki, and direct his men to seize the fort of Surat then held by his sister the Begam Sáhibah and to take possession of the property of the Begam. He imprisoned Abdul-Latíf, son of Islám Khán, an old servant of the empire. Dárá Shikoh representing Murád's conduct to the emperor obtained an order to

Murád proclaims himself Emperor, 1657.

[1] Jhábua, now under the Bhopáwar Agency.
[2] Mirát-i-Áhmedi Persian Text, 249.

Chapter III.

Mughal Viceroys.

Sháh Jehán Emperor, 1627-1658.

Kásam Khán Thirtieth Viceroy, 1657-1659.

Victory of Murád and Aurangzíb.

transfer him to the governorship of the Berárs. Murád Bakhsh borrowing £55,000 (5½ *lákhs* of rupees) from the sons of Sántidás Jauhari, £4000 (Rs. 40,000) from Ravidás partner of Sántidás, and £8800 (Rs. 88,000) from Sánmal and others, raised an army and arranged to meet his brother prince Aurangzíb, and with him march against the Mahárája Jasvatsingh of Jodhpur and Kásam Khán, whom Sháh Jehán had appointed viceroys of Málwa and Gujarát, and had ordered to meet at Ujjain and march against the princes. Murád Bakhsh and Aurangzíb, uniting their forces early in A.D. 1658, fought an obstinate battle with Jasvantsingh, in which they were victorious, and entered Ujjain in triumph. From Ujjain prince Murád Bakhsh wrote Muâtamid Khán his eunuch an order allotting to Mánikchand £15,000 (Rs. 1,50,000) from the revenues of Surat, £10,000 (Rs. 1,00,000) from Cambay, £10,000 (Rs. 1,00,00) from Pitlád, £7500 (Rs. 75,000) from Dholka, £5000 (Rs. 50,000) from Broach, £4500 (Rs. 45,000) from Víramgám, and £3000 (Rs. 30,000) from the salt works, in all £55,000 (5½ *lákhs* of rupees). Further sums of £4000 (Rs. 40,000) are mentioned as due to Ravidás partner of Sántidás, and £8800 (Rs. 88,000) to Sánmal and others. From Ujjain the princes advanced on Agra. At Dholpúr they fought a still more obstinate battle with the imperial forces commanded by prince Dárá Shikoh and after a long and doubtful contest were victorious. Prince Dárá Shikoh fled to Dehli, and the princes advanced and took possession of Agra. After confining his father, Aurangzíb marched for Mathura, and having no further use of Murád, he there seized and imprisoned him. From Mathura, Aurangzíb went to Dehli from which Dará Shikoh had meanwhile retired to Láhor.

Aurangzíb confines Murád, 1658.

Aurangzíb Emperor, 1658-1707.

Sháh Nawáz Khán Safávi Thirty-first Viceroy, 1659.

In A.D. 1658, while his father was still alive, Aurangzíb assumed the imperial titles and ascended the throne. In A.D. 1659 he appointed Sháh Nawáz Khán Safávi thirty-first viceroy of Gujarát, with Rahmat Khán as minister. On this occasion Sántidás received a decree directing that the provincial officials should settle his accounts and Kutb-ud-dín Kheshgi was appointed to Sorath. Sháh Nawáz Khán was the father-in-law of both Aurangzíb and Murád Bakhsh. Shortly after his appointment, while Murád's wife was paying a visit to her father, prince Dárá Shikoh leaving Kachh, where he had been hospitably received by the Ráv, made a sudden descent on Gujarát. The viceroy, won over by the entreaties of his daughter who saw in the success of Dárá a hope of release for her husband, joined the prince who entered Ahmedábád. After raising funds from Surat and Ahmedábád he collected an army of 22,000 horse and appointing Sayad Ahmed deputy viceroy, marched towards Ajmír, once more to try his chance of empire. He was defeated and fled to Ahmedábád, where Sardár Khán, who had confined Sayad Ahmed, closed the gates of the city in his face. The unhappy prince retired to Kachh, but finding no support fled to Sindh, where he was treacherously seized and handed to his brother by the chief of Jún. The emperor Aurangzíb, forgiving Jasvantsingh his opposition at Ujjain, conferred on him the government of Gujarát, and in the place of Rahmat Khán appointed Makramat Khán to act as minister. Sardár

Prince Dárá Rebels, 1659.

Is Defeated, 1659.

Jasvantsingh Thirty-second Viceroy, 1659-1662.

Aurangzib Emperor, 1658-1707.

Jasvantsingh Thirty-second Viceroy, 1659-1662.

Khán was thanked for his loyal conduct and made governor of Broach. Praise was also given to Sher and Ábid of the Bábi family. Presents were bestowed on Kutb-ud-dín, governor of Sorath, and, shortly after, for his refusal to help prince Dárá, Tamáchi chief of Kachh was rewarded. These measures removed all signs of disaffection at the accession of Aurangzíb. A decree was issued directing Rahmat Khán the minister to forbid the cultivation of the bhang plant. *Mohtasibs* or censors were appointed to prevent the drinking of wine or the use of intoxicating drugs and preparations. On the formal installation of Aurangzíb in A.D. 1658-59 the Ahmedábád Kázi was ordered to read the sermon in his name. The Kázi objected that Sháh Jehán was alive. Sheikh Abdul Wahháb, a Sunni Bohora of Pattan, whom on account of his learning and intelligence Aurangzíb had made Kázi of his camp, contended that the weakness and age of Sháh Jehán made a successor necessary. The Bohora prevailed and the sermon was read in Aurangzíb's name.

Jasvantsinghji sent against Shiváji, 1662.

In A.D. 1662 Jasvantsingh received orders to march to the Dakhan and join prince Muâzzam against Shiváji the Marátha leader; and Kutb-ud-dín, governor of Sorath, was directed to act for him in his absence. In this year Mahábat Khán was appointed thirty-third viceroy of Gujárat, and Sardár Khán, the governor of Broach, was sent to Ídar to suppress disturbances. About A.D. 1664 Ranmalji or Satarsála Jám of Navánagar died, leaving by a Ráhthod mother a child named Lákha whom the late chief's brother Ráisinghji with the aid of the Ráv of Kachh and other Jádejás, set aside and himself mounted the throne. Malik Ísa, a servant of the family, took Lákha to Ahmedábád and invoked the aid of the viceroy. Kutb-ub-dín marching on Navánagar, defeated and slew Ráisingh, took possession of Navánagar, and annexed the territory, changing the name of the city into Islámnagar. Ráisingh's son, Tamáchi, then an infant, escaped and was sheltered in Kachh. In the same year (A.D. 1664) a Balúch personating Dárá Shikoh, was joined by many Kolis, and disturbed the peace of the Chúnvál, now a portion of the Ahmedábád collectorate north of Víramgám. With the aid of Sherkhán Bábi, Mahábat Khán quelled these disturbances, and established two new military posts, one at Gájna under Cambay and one at Belpár under Petlád.

Mahábat Khán Thirty-third Viceroy, 1662-1668.

Capture of Navánagar (Islámnagar), 1664.

In this year an imperial decree was received requiring the discontinuance of the following abuses: The charging of blackmail by executive subordinates; A tax on private individuals on their cutting their own trees; Forced purchases by state servants; The levy by local officers of a tax on persons starting certain crafts; The levy of a tax on laden carts and on cattle for sale; The closing of Hindu shops on the Jain *Pachusan* and at the monthly elevenths or *Ekádasi*; Forced labour; The exclusive purchase of new grain by revenue officers; The exclusive sale by officers of the vegetables and other produce of their gardens; A tax on the slaughtering of cattle in addition to that on their sale; Payments to the Ahmednagar Kolis to prevent Musalmáns praying in the Ahmednagar mosque; The re-opening of certain Hindu temples; The aggressive conduct and obscenity practised during the Holi and Diváli holidays; The sale by Hindus of toy horses and elephants

Chapter III.

Mughal Viceroys.

Aurangzib Emperor, 1658-1707.

MAHÁBAT KHÁN Thirty-third Viceroy, 1662-1668.

during Musalmán holidays; The exclusive sale of rice by certain rich Banias; The exclusive purchase by Imperial officers of roses for the manufacture of rosewater; The mixed gatherings of men and women at Musalmán shrines; The setting up of *nezas* or holy hands and the sitting of harlots on roadsides or in markets; The charging by revenue officers of scarcity rates; The special tax in Parántij, Modasa, Vadnagar, Bisnápur, and Hársol on Musalmán owners of mango trees; The levy of duty both at Surat and Ahmedábád from English and Dutch merchants.[1]

Shívaji Plunders Surat, 1664.

In the same year (A.D. 1664) Shíváji made a rapid descent on Surat, then undefended by walls, and, by plundering the city, created great alarm over the whole province. The viceroy Mahábat Khán marched to Surat with the following chiefs and officers: Jagmál, proprietor of Sánand; the governor of Dholka; Shádimal, chief of Ídar; Sayad Hasan Khán, governor of Ídar; Muhammad Abid with 200 superior landholders of the district of Kadi; the Rája of Dúngarpur; Sabalsingh Rája of Wadhwán and other chiefs of Jhálávádh; Lál Kalián chief of Mándva in the Gáikwár's dominions near Atarsumba; the chief of Elol under Ahmednagar in the Mahi Kántha Agency; Prathiráj of Haldarvás; and the chief of Belpár. Before the viceroy's army arrived at Surat Shíváji had carried off his plunder to his head-quarters at Ráygad.[2] After remaining three months at Surat levying tribute from the superior landholders, the viceroy returned to Ahmedábád, and Ináyat Khán, the revenue collector of Surat, built a wall round the town for its protection. About this time Kutb-ud-dín Khán, governor of Sorath, was sent with an army to aid the Mahárája Jasvantsingh in the Dakhan and Sardár Khán was appointed in his place. In A.D. 1666 the Maráthás again attacked and plundered Surat, and in the same year the deposed emperor Sháh Jehán died. Aurangzíb attempted to induce the English to supply him with European artillerymen and engineers. The request was evaded. In this year the viceroy, Mahábat Khán, in place of the old iron coins, introduced a copper coinage into Gujarát. Sardár Khán, the governor of Júnágadh, was put in charge of Islámnagar (Navánagar) and 500 additional horsemen were placed under him. Special checks by branding and inspection were introduced to prevent nobles and others keeping less than their proper contingent of horse. In the same year the cultivator who paid the rent was acknowledged to be the owner of the land and a system of strengtheners or *takáwi* after due security was introduced.

Copper Coinage Introduced, 1668.

KHÁN JEHÁN Thirty-fourth Viceroy, 1668-1671.

In A.D. 1668, Bahádur Khán Khán Jehán, who had formerly been viceroy of Alláhábád, was appointed viceroy of Gujarát, with Háji Shafi Khán, and afterwards Khwájah Muhammad Háshim, as his ministers. Khán Jehán joined his government in A.D. 1669, and in A.D. 1670 Shíváji again plundered Surat. In A.D. 1670 Shíváji made

[1] Mirát-i-Ahmedi, Persian Text, 274, 279.

[2] Ráygad (north latitude 18° 14'; east longitude 73° 30'), the name given in A.D. 1662 to Rairi, a hill fortress in the Mahád sub-division of the Kolába collectorate. Shívaji took the place and made it his capital in A.D. 1662.

Chapter III.

Mughal Viceroys.

Aurangzib Emperor, 1658-1707.

Khán Jehán Thirty-fourth Viceroy, 1668-1671.

Sídi Yákút the Mughal Admiral, 1670.

an attempt on Janjira,[1] the residence and stronghold of the Sídi or Abyssinian admirals of Bíjápur. Sídi Yákút the commander of Janjira applied for aid to the governor of Surat. On his offering to become a vassal of the emperor and place his fleet at the emperor's disposal, Sídi Yákút received the title of Yákút Khán, and a yearly subsidy of £15,000 (Rs. 1,50,000) payable from the port of Surat. About the same time Sayad Diler Khán, who had accompanied Mahárája Jasvantsingh to the Dakhan, was recalled by the viceroy Khán Jehán and appointed governor of Sorath in place of Sardár Khán, who was sent to Ídar. Sayad Haidar, in charge of the military post of Haidarábád, about twenty-four miles south of Áhmedábád, reported that he had put down the rebellion but recommended that a small fort should be built. In A.D. 1670 the emperor summoned Diler Khán to discuss Dakhan affairs, and sent him to the seat of war, replacing him in the government of Sorath by Sardár Khán.

Mahárája Jasvantsingh Thirty-fifth Viceroy, 1671-1674.

In A.D. 1671, Bahádur Khán Khán Jehán was sent as viceroy to the Dakhan. He was relieved by the Mahárája Jasvantsingh, who, as viceroy, received an assignment of the districts of Dhandhúka and Pitlád. In A.D. 1673 through the intercession of the viceroy, Jám Tamáchi, the son of Ráisingh, on condition of serving the viceroy and of keeping order was restored to Navánagar, and twenty-five villages were granted to certain dependent Jádeja Rajputs. So long as the emperor Aurangzíb lived the city of Navanagar (Islámnagar) remained in the hands of a Musalmán noble, the Jám residing at Khambhália, a town about thirty miles south-west of the head-quarters of the state. In A.D. 1707, on Aurangzíb's death, the Jám was allowed to return to Navánagar where he built a strong fort. Similarly so long as Aurangzíb lived, the Jám forbore to work the pearl fisheries in the Gulf of Kachh, but afterwards again made use of this source of revenue. Early in 1674 an order issued forbidding the levy from Musalmáns of *rahádari* or transit dues, of taxes on fish vegetables grass firewood and other forest produce, on Muhammadan artisans, and many other miscellaneous dues. The officer in charge of Morví, which was then an imperial district, was ordered to strive to increase its population and revenue, and the chief of Porbandar, also an imperial district, on condition of service and of protecting the port was allowed a fourth share of its revenue. Much discontent was caused by enforcing an imperial order confiscating all *wazífah* land, that is all land held on religious tenure by Hindus.

Muhammad Amín Khán Umdat-ul-Mulk Thirty-sixth Viceroy, 1674-1683.

About the close of the year A.D. 1674, Mahárája Jasvantsinghji was relieved and sent to Kábul, and Muhammad Amín Khán Umdat-ul-Mulk, who had just been defeated at Kábul, was appointed thirty-sixth viceroy of Gujarát, receiving an assignment of the districts of Pátan and Víramgám. Among the military posts mentioned in the Mirát-i-Áhmedi is that of Sádra or Sháhdarah the present head-quarters of the Mahi Kántha Agency, also called Islámábád,[2] which was under the

---

[1] Janjira (north latitude 17° 59′ to 18° 32′) that is *Jazírah* the Island, on the western coast, about forty-four miles south of Bombay.

[2] Another post of Islámábád was at Punádra in the *parganah* of Ázamábád on the Wátrak about twenty-one miles east-south-east of Áhmedábád. Ázamábád was built

Chapter III.
Mughal Viceroys.
Aurangzib Emperor, 1658-1707.
MUHAMMAD AMÍN KHÁN UMDAT-UL-MULK Thirty-sixth Viceroy, 1674-1683.
Increased Power of the Bábi Family.

command of Sayad Kamál, son of Sayad Kámil. The Bábi family were now rising into importance. Muhammad Muzaffar, son of Sher Khán Bábi, was governor of Kadi, and Muhammad Mubáriz, another son of Sher Bábi, was in charge of one of the posts under Kadi. Kamál Khán Jhálori, who had been removed from the government of Pálanpur and replaced by Muhammad Fateh, was now restored to his former post. About the same time, at the representation of Mulla Hasan Gujaráti, twenty-one villages were taken from Bijápur and Kadi and Pátan and formed into the separate division of Visalnagar. In A.D. 1676, the fort of Júnágadh was put into repair, and Sheikh Nizám-ud-dín Ahmed, minister of Gujarát, was sent to Málwa, and was succeeded by Muhammad Sharíf. The Kánkrej Kolis were again rebellious, and Muhammad Amín Khán Umdat-ul-Mulk went against them and remained four months in their country, subduing them and enforcing tribute. In the end of A.D. 1678, the viceroy paid his respects to the emperor at Ajmír. The emperor forbade the fining of Musalmán officials as contrary to the Muhammadan law and directed that if guilty of any fault they should be imprisoned or degraded from office, but not fined. An order was also given to change the name of the new Visalnagar district to Rasúlnagar.

Revolt of Ídar, 1679.

At this time (A.D. 1679) the emperor was doing his utmost to crush both the Rána of Udepur and the Ráthods of Márwár. While the emperor was at Chitor, Bhímsing the Rána's youngest son raided into Gujarát plundering Vadnagar Visalnagar and other towns and villages. The chief of Ídar, thinking the opportunity favourable for regaining his independence, expelled the Muhammadan garrison from Ídar and established himself in his capital. Muhammad Amín Khán sent Muhammad Bahlol Khán Shirwáni who with the help of the Kasbatis of Parántij re-took Ídar, and the chief pursued by Bahlol Khán fled to the hills, where he died in a cave from want of his usual dose of opium to which he was much addicted. His body was found by a woodcutter who brought the head to Bahlol Khán. The head was recognized by the chief's widow, who from that day put on mourning. Muhammad Bahlol Khán was much praised, and was appointed to the charge of Ídar, and at the same time the minister Muhammad Sharíf was succeeded by Abdúl Latíf.[1]

To this time belongs an imperial decree imposing the *jazyah* or head tax on all subjects not professing the Muhammadan faith, and another regulating the levy from Musalmáns of the *zakát* or poor rate.[2] In 1681 a severe famine led to riots in Ahmedábád. As the

---

by Ázam Khán during his viceroyalty (A.D. 1635-1642) and at his request by permission of the emperor Sháh Jehán was erected into a *parganah*. For the pay of the garrison twelve villages were attached from the neighbouring *parganahs* of Bahyal and Kapadvanj.

[1] The Mirăt-i-Áhmedi (Persian Text, 311) adds that Bahlol's following of *Kasbátis* was so poorly equipped that he had to mount many of them, for whom he could not find horses, on bullocks. The sense of security in the mind of the Ídar chief bred by contempt at the sight of this motley crowd was the chief cause of Bahlol's success.

[2] The *zakát* or purification is the tax required by law to be given annually to the poor. It is levied on camels, oxen, buffaloes, sheep, goats, horses, asses, mules, and gold or silver whether in money or ornaments or vessels. The tax is not levied on any

viceroy Muhammad Amín was returning in state from the Íd prayers Abu Bakr an A'hmedábád Sheikh instigated the people to throw stones and dust. The viceroy's bodyguard attacked the mob, but owing to the viceroy's forbearance no serious results followed. On hearing of the riot the emperor ordered the city to be put under martial law. The more politic viceroy contented himself by inviting Sheikh Abu Bakr and others to a banquet. After dinner he gave a piece of a poisoned watermelon to Abu Bakr, who died and the riot with him. In A.D. 1683 Muhammad Amín the viceroy died. According to the Mirăt-i-A'hmedi, Muhammad Amín was one of the best of Gujarát governors. The emperor Aurangzíb used to say 'No viceroy of mine keeps order like Amín Khán.'

Chapter III.
Moghal Viceroys.
Aurangzib Emperor, 1658-1707.

Mukhtár Khán Thirty-seventh Viceroy, 1683-1684.

Amín Khán was succeeded by Mukhtár Khán as thirty-seventh viceroy, Abdul Latíf continuing to hold the office of minister. Fresh orders were passed forbidding import dues on merchandise, fruit, grass, firewood, and similar produce entering A'hmedábád. In 1682 a decree was received ordering pauper prisoners to be provided with rations and dress at the cost of the state. In 1683 the Sábarmáti rose so high that the water reached as far as the *Tín Darwázah* or Triple Gateway in the west of A'hmedábád city. In consequence of disturbances in Sorath the viceroy called on the minister to advance funds for an expedition. The minister refused to make advances without special orders from the emperor. On a reference to court the minister was directed to make advances in emergent cases. In A.D. 1684, at the request of the inhabitants of that city Abdúr Rahmán Krori, the governor of Deva Pátan, was removed and in his place Muhammad Sayad chose Sardár Khán as governor of Sorath. In the following year on the death of Sardár Khán at Thatha in Sindh, where he had gone as viceroy, he was, in the first instance, succeeded in the government of Sorath by Sayad Muhammad Khán. Not long after Sorath was assigned as a personal estate to the emperor's second son prince Muhammad A'zam Sháh Bahádur and during the prince's absence Sháhwardi Khán was sent to manage its affairs. In A.D. 1684 a famine in Gujarát raised the price of grain in A'hmedábád to such a degree that Sheikh Muhy-ud-dín, the son of the Kázi and regulator of prices, was mobbed.

Famine, 1684.

Shujáat Khán (Kártalab Khán) Thirty-eighth Viceroy, 1684-1703.

On the death of the viceroy in 1684 prince Muhammad A'zam Sháh was nominated to succeed him with Kártalab Khán, governor of Sorath, as his deputy. Before the prince took charge Kártalab Khán was raised to the post of viceroy, and Muhammad Táhir appointed minister. In addition to his command as viceroy of Gujarát, Kártalab Khán was afterwards placed in charge of Jodhpur. In this rearrangement besides his previous personal estate, the district of Petlád was assigned to prince Muhammad A'zam Sháh, and Sher Afghan Khán, son of Sháhwardi Khán, was appointed governor of Sorath. In A.D.

one who owns less than a minimum of five camels, thirty oxen, forty-five sheep, five horses, two hundred *dirhems* or twenty *dinárs*. The proportion to income is generally one-fortieth; the amount may be paid either in kind or in money. Compare Stanley Lane Poole's Arabian Society in the Middle Ages, 14.

Chapter III.
Mughal Viceroys.
Aurangzib Emperor, 1658-1707.
SHUJÁÂT KHÁN (KÁRTALAB KHÁN) Thirty-eighth Viceroy, 1684-1703.
He Quells a Mutiny, 1689.

1687, Sher Afghan Khán was relieved by Bahlol Shirwáni, but in the following year was restored to his command. In A.D. 1689, on the news of the death of its governor Ináyat Khán, Kártalab Khán started to settle the affairs of Jodhpur. As soon as he left Ahmedábád, a rumour spread that a new viceroy was coming, and the troops, with whom as well as with the people of Gujarát Kártalab was most popular, grew mutinous. On hearing of this disturbance Kártalab Khán at once returned to Ahmedábád and quelled the mutiny. His firmness so pleased the emperor that he gave him the title of Shujaât Khán, and placed the governor of Jodhpur under his orders. Shujaât Khán now proceeded to Jodhpur, where Durgádás Ráthod, who had incited prince Abkar to rebellion, and Ajítsingh, the son of Mahárája Jasvantsingh, were causing disturbance. Finding that a strong resident governor was required to keep the insurgents in check, Shujaât Khán appointed Kázim Beg Muhammad Amín, a brave and resolute soldier, to be his deputy and returned to Ahmedábád. During this viceroyalty the pay of the leader or *jamádár* of a troop of fifty horse was fixed at £10 (Rs. 100); of a *do-aspah* or two-horse trooper at £6 (Rs. 60); and of an *ek-aspah* or one-horse trooper at £3 (Rs. 30) a month. An imperial order was also issued directing the levy on merchandise to be taken at the place and time of sale instead of the time and place of purchase. As this change caused loss to the revenue the old system was again adopted. In A.D. 1690 the minister Amánat Khán, with the title of Ítimád Khán, was made military governor of Surat, and Sayad Muhsín was chosen minister in his place. To prevent the peons of great officials extorting fees and dues officials were forbidden to entertain peons without payment.

Revolt of Matiás and Momnás, 1691.

In the following year (A.D. 1691) an attempt on the part of the emperor to suppress a body of Musalmán sectarians led to a somewhat serious insurrection. Sayad Sháhji was the religious preceptor of the Matiás of Khándesh and the Momnás of Gujarát, two classes of converted Hindus closely allied to the Khojás of Káthiáváḍa, all of them being followers of Sayad Imám-ud-dín an Ismâilíáh missionary who came to Gujarát during the reign of Mahmúd Begada (A.D. 1459-1513). Hearing that his followers paid obeisance to their veiled spiritual guide by kissing his toe, the emperor ordered the guide to be sent to court to be examined before the religious doctors. Afraid of the result of this examination, the Sayad committed suicide and was buried at Karamtah nine miles south of Ahmedábád. The loss of their leader so enraged his followers that, collecting from all sides, they marched against Broach, seized the fort, and slew the governor. The insurgents held the fort of Broach against the governor of Baroda who was sent to punish them, and for a time successfully resisted the efforts of his successor Nazar Âli Khán. At last, at an unguarded spot, some of the besiegers stole over the city wall and opening the gates admitted their companions. The Momnás were defeated and almost all slain as they sought death either by the sword or by drowning to merit their saint's favour in the next world.

Disturbances in Káthiáváḍa, 1692;

In A.D. 1692 Shujáât Khán, during his tribute-gathering campaign in Jhálávaḍa and Sorath, stormed the fort of Thán, the head-quarters

Chapter III. Mughal Viceroys.

Aurangzib Emperor, 1658-1707.

SHUJÁÁT KHÁN (KÁRTALAB KHÁN) Thirty-eighth Viceroy, 1684-1703.

of the plundering Káthis and after destroying the fort returned to A'hmedábád. Shujáât Khán was one of the ablest of Gujarát viceroys. He gave so much of his attention to the management of Jodhpur, that he used to spend about six months of every year in Márwár. He beautified A'hmedábád by building the college and mosque still known by his name near the Lál Gate. In A.D. 1642 two hundred cart-loads of marble were received from the ancient buildings at Pátan and the deputy governor Safdar Khán Bábi wrote that if a thousand cart-loads more were required they could be supplied from the same source. At this time the emperor ordered that Sheikh Akram-ud-dín, the local tax-collector, should levy the head tax from the Hindus of Pálanpur and Jhálor. The viceroy deputed Muhammad Mujáhid, son of Kamál Khán Jhálori, governor of Pálanpur to help in collecting. As Durgádás Ráthod was again stirring tumults and sedition in Márwár, the viceroy went to Jodhpur, and by confirming their estates to the chief vassals and landholders and guaranteeing other public measures on condition of service, persuaded them to abandon their alliance with Durgádás against whom he sent his deputy Kázim Beg, who expelled him from Márwár. After appointing Kunvár Muhkamsingh, governor of Mertha in Márwár, Shujáât Khán returned to A'hmedábád. In A.D. 1693, at the request of Sher Afghan Khán, governor of Sorath, the walls of the fort of Jagat were restored. In this year the viceroy went to Jhálávaḍa to exact tribute. On his return to A'hmedábád Safdar Khán Bábi, governor of Pátan, wrote to the viceroy, and at his request the forts of Kambhoi and Sámprah were repaired. The viceroy now went to Jodhpúr and from that returned to A'hmedábád. A circumstance in connection with a sum of Rs. 7000 spent on the repairs of forts illustrates the close imperial supervision of provincial accounts. The item having come to imperial notice from the provincial disbursement sheets was disallowed as unfair and ordered to be refunded under the rule that such charges were to be met out of their incomes by the local governors and military deputy governors. Imperial officers were also from time to time deputed to collect from the books of the *desái's* statements of provincial disbursements and receipts for periods of ten years that they might render an independent check. In this year the emperor hearing that Ajítsingh and Durgádás were again contemplating rebellion ordered the viceroy to Jodhpur. Muhammad Mubáriz Bábi was at the same time appointed deputy governor of Vadnagar, and an order was issued that the revenue of Pátan should be paid to Shujáât Khán instead of as formerly into the imperial treasury. In this year also Safdar Khán Bábi, governor of Pátan, was succeeded by Mubáriz Khán Bábi. Not long afterwards under imperial orders the viceroy directed Muhammad Mubáriz Bábi to destroy the Vadnagar temple of Hateshwar-Mahádev the Nágar Bráhmans' special guardian.

Disturbances in Márwár.

In A.D. 1696, Muhammad Bahlol Shírwáni, governor of Baroda, died, and his place was supplied by Muhammad Beg Khán. During this year the viceroy again went to Jodhpúr and remained there for some months. In A.D. 1697 Buláki Beg the mace-bearer arrived from the imperial court to settle disputes connected with the Navánagar succes-

Chapter III.
Mughal Viceroys.
Aurangzib Emperor, 1658-1707.
Shujáát Khán (Kártalab Khán) Thirty-eighth Viceroy, 1684-1703.
Durgádás Ráthod reconciled to the Emperor, 1697.

sion, and to inquire into complaints made by the inhabitants of Sorath. In 1696 an imperial circular was addressed to all officers in charge of districts ordering them to show no respect or consideration for royalty in their efforts to capture or kill the rebel prince Akbar. About the same time Durgádás Ráthod, in whose charge were the son and daughter of prince Akbar, made an application to Shujáât Khán, proposing a truce, and saying that he wished personally to hand the children to their grandfather. Shujaât Khán agreed and Durgádás restored Akbar's children to the emperor. Aurangzíb finding the children able to repeat the whole Kurâán was much pleased with Durgádas, and made peace with him, assigning him as a personal estate the lands of Mertha in Jodhpur, and afterwards adding to this the grant of Dhandhúka and other districts of Gujarát. In consequence of a failure of crops the price of grain rose so high that the government share of the produce was brought to Áhmedábád and sold in public to the poor and needy. About this time Muhammad Mubáriz Bábi was killed by a Koli who shot him with an arrow while he was sacking the village of Sámprah.[1] Safdar Khán Bábi was appointed deputy governor of Pátan in his stead.

In the same year it was reported to the emperor that the money-changers and capitalists of Áhmedábád in making payments passed money short of weight to poor men and in receiving charged an exchange of two to three *tankás* the rupee. The Súbah and minister were ordered to stop the currency of rupees more than two *surkhs* short.[2]

Scarcity, 1698.

In A.D. 1698, on the death of Ítimád Khán, his son Muhammad Muhsín was made minister, and he was ordered to hand the district of Mertha to Durgádás Ráthod. Among other changes Muhammad Muním was raised to the command of the fort of Jodhpur and Khwájáh Abdul Hamíd was appointed minister. Owing to a second failure of rain 1698 was a year of much scarcity in Márwár and north Gujarát. The accounts of this year notice a petition addressed to the viceroy by a Sinor Bráhman, praying that he might not be seized as a carrier or labourer.[3] In connection with some revenue and civil affairs, a difference of opinion arose between Shujáât Khán and Safdar Khán Bábi, deputy governor of Pátan. Safdar Khán resigned, and, until a successor was appointed, Muhammad Bahlol Shírwáni was directed to administer the Pátan district. In the same year the emperor bestowed the government of Sorath on Muhammad Beg Khán. In A.D. 1699 Durgádás Ráthod obtained from the emperor not only a pardon for Ajítsingh, son of the late Mahárája Jasvantsingh, but procured him

---

[1] This Sámprah according to the Mirăt-i-Áhmedi, Persian Text, II. 327, was a small police post or *thána* in Parganah Bahyal twenty miles north-east of Áhmedábád. It is now in the Gaekwár's territory. Bahyal was under Pátan, so in the text the place is described as under Pátan.

[2] The *surkh* or little black-dotted red seed of the Abrus precatorius is called *ghúngchi* in Hindi and cock's-eye, *chashmi-i-khurús*, in Persian. As a weight the seed is known as a *rati* 96 going to the *tola*. It is used in weighing precious stones. Blochmann's Áín-i-Akbari, I. 16 note 1 and Mirăt-i-Áhmedi Persian Text, 366.

[3] Sinor in Baroda territory on the right bank of the Narbada about thirty miles south of Baroda.

Chapter III.

Mughal Viceroys.

Aurangzib Emperor, 1658-1707.

SHUJÂÂT KHÁN KÁRTALAB KHÁN) Thirty-eighth Viceroy, 1684-1703.

an assignment of lands in, as well as the official charge of, the districts of Jhálor and Sáchor in Marwár. Mujáhid Khán Jhálori, who as representing a family of landholders dating as far back as the Gujarát Sultáns, had held Jhálor and Sáchor, now received in their stead the lands in Pálanpur and Dísa which his descendants still hold. In this year also (A.D. 1699) Amánat Khán, governor of Surat, died, and the Maráthás making a raid into the province, Shujáât Khán sent Nazar Ali Khán to drive them out. About this time an imperial order arrived, addressed to the provincial *díwán* directing him to purchase 1000 horses for the government at the average rate of £20 (Rs. 200).

In A.D. 1700 on the death of Fírúz Khán Mewáti, deputy governor of Jodhpúr, the viceroy appointed in his place Muhammad Záhid from Víramgám. Rája Ajitsingh of Márwár was now ordered to repair to court, and as he delayed, a *mohsal* or speed fine was imposed upon him in agreement with Shujáât Khán's directions. About this time an order came to Kamál Khán Jhálori for the despatch to the emperor of some of the Pálanpur *chítáhs* or hunting leopards which are still in demand in other parts of India. In the same year the manager of Dhandhúka on behalf of Durgádás Ráthod, asked the viceroy for aid against the Káthis, who were plundering that district. The viceroy ordered Muhammad Beg, governor of Sorath, to march against them. At this time Shujáât Khán despatched Nazar Ali Khán with a large force to join the imperial camp which was then at Panhála in Kolhápur. Shujáât Khán, who had so long and ably filled the office of viceroy in a most critical time, died in A.D. 1703. In his place prince Muhammad Aâzam Shah, who was then at Dhár in Málwa, was appointed thirty-ninth viceroy of Gujarát, as well as governor of Ajmír and Jodhpur; and until his arrival the minister Khwájáh Abdul Hamíd Khán was ordered to administer the province. Owing to the recall of the late governor's troops from many of the posts disorders broke out in the Pátan districts and the Kolis plundered the country and made the roads impassable.

PRINCE MUHAMMAD AÂZAM Thirty-ninth Viceroy, 1703-1705.

On his way from the Dakhan to Ahmedábád, the chief of Jhábua, a state now under the Bhopáwar Agency, paid his respects to the new viceroy and presented him with a tribute of £1600 (Rs. 16,000). Among other arrangements the prince sent to Jodhpur Jáfar Kuli, son of Kázim Beg, as deputy governor, and appointed Durgádás Ráthod governor of Pátan. Shortly after, on suspicion of his tampering with the Ráthod Rajputs, an order came from the emperor to summon Durgádás to the prince's court at Ahmedábád, and there confine him or slay him.[1] Safdar Khán Bábi, who, in displeasure with Shujáât Khán had retired to Málwa, returned and offered to slay or capture Durgádás, who was accordingly invited to the prince's court at Ahmedábád. Durgádás came and pitched his camp at the village of Báreja on the Sábarmati near Ahmedábád. On the day Durgádás was to present himself, the prince, on pretence of a hunt, had ordered the attendance of a strong detachment of the army.

Intrigue against Durgadas Rathod, 1703.

---

[1] Mirât-i-Áhmedi, Persian Text, 372.

Chapter III.
Mughal Viceroys.
Aurangzib Emperor, 1658-1707.
PRINCE MUHAMMAD AÂZAM Thirty-ninth Viceroy, 1703-1705.
Durgádás Ráthod Escapes.

When all was ready and Safdar Khán Bábi and his sons appeared mailed and gauntleted the prince sent for Durgádás. As this day was an eleventh or *agiáras* Durgádás had put off waiting on the prince until the fast was over. Growing suspicious of the number of messengers from the prince, he burned his tents and fled. Safdar Khán Bábi was sent in pursuit. He was overtaking Durgádás when Durgádás' grandson praying his grandfather to make good his escape, stayed behind with a band of followers, charged the pursuers, and after a gallant combat, he and his Rájputs were slain. The grandson of Durgádás was killed in a hand-to-hand fight with Salábat Khán, the son of Safdar Khán Bábi. Emerald rings are to this day worn by youths of the Bábi families of North Gujarát in memory of the emerald earrings which adorned the young Rájput and were afterwards worn by Salábat as trophies of this fight. Meanwhile Durgádás had reached Unjáh-Unáwa, forty miles east of Pátan, and from Unjáh made his way to Pátan. From Pátan, taking his family with him, he retired to Tharád, and from that to Márwár, where he was afterwards joined by Ajítsingh of Márwár, whom the emperor opposed on the ground of illegitimacy. The imperial troops followed and took possession of Pátan, putting to death the head of the city police.

In his old age the emperor Aurangzíb became more and more strict in religious matters. In 1702 an imperial order forbad the making of almanacs as contrary to the Muhammadan law. Hindus were also forbidden to keep Muhammadan servants.

Surat, 1700-1703.

About this time (A.D. 1700) news arrived that the Maráthás with a force of 10,000 horse were threatening Surat from the foot of the Kására pass and the confines of Sultánpur and Nandurbár. The viceroy despatched a body of troops to guard Surat against their incursions. Disputes between the government and the Portuguese were also injuring the trade of the province. In A.D. 1701 the viceroy received an order from Court directing him to destroy the temple of Somnáth beyond possibility of repair. The despatch adds that a similar order had been issued at the beginning of Aurangzíb's reign. In A.D. 1703, at the request of the merchants of Gujarát, with the view of inducing the Portuguese to let ships from Surat pass unmolested and release some Musalmáns who had been imprisoned on their way back from Makkah, orders were issued that certain confiscated Portuguese merchandise should be restored to its owners. An imperial order was also received to encourage the art of brocade weaving in Ahmedábád. In A.D. 1704, Safdar Khán Bábi was raised to be governor of Bijápur, about fifty miles north-east of Ahmedábád. Sarandáz Khán was at the same time appointed to Sorath instead of Muhammad Beg Khán, who was placed in charge of the lands round Ahmedábád. As the Maráthás once more threatened Surat, Mustafa Kuli, governor of Broach, was sent with 1000 horse to defend the city.

Certain passages in Aurangzíb's letters to prince Aâzam when (A.D. 1703-1705) viceroy of Gujarát, show how keen and shrewd an interest the aged emperor maintained in the government of his viceroys. In Letter 19 he writes to prince Aâzam: To take the government of Sorath

Chapter III.

Mughal Viceroys.

Aurangzib Emperor, 1658-1707.

PRINCE MUHAMMAD AÂZAM Thirty-ninth Viceroy, 1703-1705.

from Fateh Jang Khán Bábi and give it to your chamberlain's brother is to break a sound glass vessel with your own hands. These Bábis have been time out of mind a respected race in Gujarát and are well versed in the arts of war. There is no sense in giving the management of Sorath to anyone but to a Bábi. Sorath is a place which commanders of five thousand like Hasan Álikhán and Safshikan Khán have with difficulty administered. If your officers follow the principles laid down by the late Shujáât Khán, it will be well. If they do not, the province of Gujarát is such that if order is broken in one or two places, it will not soon be restored. For the rest you are your own master. I say not, do this or do that; look that the end is good, and do that which is easiest. In another passage (Letter 37 to the same prince Áâzam) Aurangzíb writes: You who are a well intentioned man, why do you not retaliate on oppressors? Over Hájipúr Aminpúr and other posts where atrocities occur every day, and at Kapadvanj where the Kolis rob the highways up to the posts, you have made your chamberlain and artillery superintendent your commandant. He entrusted his powers to his carrion-eating and fraudulent relatives. Owing to his influence the oppressed cannot come to you . . . You ought to give the command to one of the Gujarátis like Safdar Khán Bábi or one of the sons of Bahlúl Shírwáni who have earned reputations during the administration of the late Shujáât Khán and who are popular with the people. Else I tell you plainly that on the Day of Justice we shall be caught for neglecting to punish the oppressions of our servants.

IBRÁHÍM KHÁN Fortieth Viceroy, 1705.

In A.D. 1705, as the climate of Gujarát did not agree with prince Aâzam, Ibráhím Khán, viceroy of Kashmír, was appointed fortieth viceroy of Gujarát, and his son Zabardast Khán, viceroy of Láhor, was appointed to the government of Ajmír and Jodhpur. Prince Aâzam at once went to Burhánpur in Khándesh, handing charge of Gujarát to the minister Abdúl Hamíd Khán until the new viceroy should arrive. Durgádás Ráthod now asked for and received pardon. Abdúl Hamíd Khán was ordered to restore the lands formerly granted to Durgádás, and Durgádás was directed to act under Abdúl Hamíd's orders. In A.D. 1705 the emperor learned that Khánji, a successor of Kutb the high priest of the Ismáília Bohorás, had sent out twelve missionaries to win people to his faith, and that his followers had subscribed Rs. 1,14,000 to relieve those of their number who were imprisoned. The emperor ordered that the twelve missionaries should be secured and sent to him and appointed Sunni Mullás to preach in their villages and bring the Bohoras' children to the Sunni form of faith.

The Maráthás enter Gujarát.

About this time (A.D. 1705) the Maráthás, who had long been hovering on the south-east frontiers of the province, bursting into south Gujarát with an army 15,000 strong, under the leadership of Dhanáji Jádhav, defeated the local forces and laid the country waste. Abdúl Hamíd Khán, who was then in charge of the province, ordered all governors of districts and officers in charge of posts to collect their men and advance to Surat. Between Nazar Áli Khán and Safdar Khán Bábi, the officers in command of this

Chapter III.
Mughal Viceroys.
Aurangzib Emperor, 1658-1707.
Ibrahím Khán Fortieth Viceroy, 1705.

army, an unfortunate jealousy prevailed. Not knowing where the Maráthás were to be found, they halted on the Narbada near the Bába Piárah ford. Here they remained for a month and a half, the leaders contenting themselves with sending out spies to search for the enemy. At last, hearing of the approach of the Maráthás, they sent to head-quarters asking for artillery and other reinforcements. In reply, Abdúl Hamíd Khán, a man of hasty temper, upbraided them for their inactivity and for allowing so much time to pass without making their way to Surat. Orders were accordingly at once issued for an advance, and the army next halted at Ratanpúr in Rájpípla.

Battle of Ratanpúr. Defeat of the Musalmáns, 1705.

Here, apparently from the jealousy of the commanders, the different chiefs pitched their camps at some distance from each other. Finding the enemy's forces thus scattered, the Maráthás, under the command of Dhanáji Jádhav, lost no time in advancing against them. First attacking the camp of Safdar Khán Bábi, they defeated his troops, killed his son, and took prisoner the chief himself. Only a few of his men, with his nephew Muhammad Aâzam, escaped to the camp of Nazar Áli Khán. Next, the Maráthás attacked the army under Muhammad Purdil Khán Shirwáni; and it also they defeated. Of the Musalmán army those who were not slain, drowned in the Narbada, or captured, reached Broach in miserable plight, where they were relieved by Akbar Áli Khán. Nazar Áli Khán burned his tents and surrendered to the Maráthás, by whom he was well treated.

Battle of the Bába Piárah Ford. Second Defeat of the Musalmáns, 1705.

The Maráthás now heard that Abdúl Hamíd Khán was coming with an army to oppose them. Thinking he would not risk a battle, they went to the Bába Piárah ford, and there crossed the Narbada. That very day Abdúl Hamíd Khán, with Muhammad Sher and Muhammad Salábat, sons of Safdar Khán Bábi, and others came to the spot where the Maráthás were encamped. All night long they were harassed by the Maráthás, and next morning found the enemy ready for a general attack. The Muhammadans, weary with watching, dispirited from the defeats of Safdar Khán, and inferior in number to their assailants, were repulsed and surrounded. The two sons of Safdar Khán Bábi, and two other nobles, seeing that the day was lost, cut their way through the enemy and escaped, Abdúl Hamíd Khán, Nazar Áli Khán, and many others were taken prisoners. The Maráthás plundered the Muhammadan camp, declared their right to tribute, levied sums from the adjacent towns and villages and extorted heavy ransoms which in the case of Abdúl Hamíd Khán was fixed at as large a sum as £30,000 (Rs. 3 *lákhs*).

Koli Disturbances.

The Kolis, seeing the disorganized state of Gujarát, began ravaging the country, and plundered Baroda for two days. At Áhmedábád Muhammad Beg Khán, who had been appointed governor of Sorath, was recalled to defend the capital. When the news of the defeat at Bába Piárah reached Dehli, the emperor despatched prince Muhammad Bidár Bakht with a large army to drive out the invaders. Before this force reached Gujarát the Maráthás had retired.

Prince Muhammad Bídár Bakht Forty-first Viceroy, 1705-1706.

Prince Muhammad Bídár Bakht arrived in A.D. 1705 as forty-first viceroy, and appointed Amánat Khán governor of the ports of Surat and Cambay. News was now received that Ajítsingh of Jodhpur and Verisálji of Rájpípla were about to rebel, and the prince took

Aurangzib Emperor, 1658-1707.

Prince Muhammad Bídár Bakht Forty-first Viceroy, 1705-1706.

measures to check their plans. About this time the emperor, hearing that an attack had been made on the Muhammadan post at Dwárka, ordered the temple to be levelled to the ground. It seems doubtful whether this order was carried out. Nazar A'li Khán, who had formerly enjoyed a grant of Halvad in Jhálává̤da, had been driven out by Chandrasingh, chief of Vánkáner; but, on condition of his expelling Chandrasingh, these lands were again granted to him. Kamál Khán Jhálori, leaving under his son Fírúz Khán at Pálanpur a body of men for the defence of his charge, advanced to A'hmedábád to guard the city from Marátha attack. He petitioned that according to Gujarát custom his troops should receive rations so long as they were employed on imperial service. To this request the emperor agreed and issued orders to the provincial minister. Shortly after Durgádás Ráthod took advantage of the general confusion to rejoin Ajítsingh, and an army was sent to Tharád against them. Ajítsingh was at first forced to retire. Finally he succeeded in defeating Kunvar Muhkamsingh, and marching on Jodhpur recovered it from Jaâfar Kuli, son of Kázím Beg. Durgádás meanwhile had taken shelter with the Kolis. At the head of a band of robbers, meeting Sháh Kúli the son of Kázím Beg on his way to join his appointment as deputy governor of Pátan, Durgádás attacked and killed him. And soon after at Chaniár in the Chunvál, laying in wait for Maâsúm Kúli, the governor of Víramgám, he routed his escort, Maâsúm Kúli escaping with difficulty. On condition of being appointed governor of Pátan Safdar Khán Bábi now offered to kill or capture Durgádás. His offer was accepted, and as from this time Durgádás is no more heard of, it seems probable that Safdar Khán succeeded in killing him. As the disturbed state of the province seemed to require a change of government Ibráhím Khán, who had been appointed viceroy in the previous year, was ordered to join his post. This order he reluctantly obeyed in A.D. 1706.

Durgádás Ráthod again in Rebellion.

Ibráhím Khán Forty-second Viceroy, 1706.

SECTION II.—Fifty Years of Disorder, 1707-1757.

The Maráthás advance to A'hmedábád and levy Tribute, 1707.

With the death of the emperor Aurangzíb, early in A.D. 1707, the period of strong government which had latterly from year to year been growing weaker came to an end. As soon as Aurangzíb's death was known, the Maráthás under Báláji Vishvanáth burst into east Gujarát, marching by Jhábua and Godhra, where they were ineffectually opposed by the governor Murád Baksh. From Godhra they went to and plundered the town of Mahuda in Kaira, and proposed marching on A'hmedábád by way of Na̤diád. The viceroy prepared to resist them, and, enlisting special troops, camped outside of the city near the Kánkariya lake. Of the warlike population on the north bank of the Sábarmati opposite A'hmedábád nearly eight thousand Musalmán horse and three thousand foot together with four thousand Rájpúts and Kolis in three days gathered at the Kánkariya camp. The viceroy was also joined by Abdúl Hádi Pandemal the viceroy's minister, Abdúl Hamíd Khán provincial minister, Muhammad Beg Khán, Nazar A'li Khán, Safdar Khán Bábi, and several other deputy governors with their retinues and artillery. Though strong in numbers the practised eye of the viceroy failed to find in the host that

Chapter III.
Mughal Viceroys.
Baha'dur Sha'h I. Emperor, 1707-1712.
Ibráhím Khán Forty-second Viceroy, 1706.

firmness and unity of purpose which could alone ensure victory over the Marátha hordes. The Maráthás did much mischief, plundering as far as Batva, only four-and-a-half miles from the viceroy's camp. The author of the Mirát-i-Áhmedi, whose father was an actor in these scenes, describes the panic in the capital of Gujarát which since its capture by Muzaffar in A.D. 1583 had been free from the horrors of war. Crowds of scared and terror-stricken men women and children laden with as much of their property as they could carry were pressing from the suburbs into the city. In the city the streets were crowded with squatters. The cries of parents bereft of children, added to the din and turmoil of the soldiery, was like the horror of the Day of Resurrection. The dejected faces of the soldiers beaten in the late engagements added to the general gloom. The viceroy, thoroughly alarmed, concluded a treaty with Báláji, and on receiving a tribute of £21,000 (Rs. 2,10,000) the Maráthás withdrew. Meanwhile, in the contest between the princes for the throne of Dehli, prince Muhammad Áâzam Sháh was defeated and slain, and prince Muhammad Muâzzam Sháh mounted the throne with the title of Bahádur Sháh. Ibráhím Khán was confirmed in the post of viceroy of Gujarát, but, fearing that the emperor might be displeased at his concession of tribute to the Maráthás, he went to Dehli to explain his conduct, and there resigned office.

Gházi-ud-dín Forty-third Viceroy, 1708-1710.

In A.D. 1708, in consequence of Ibráhím Khán's resignation, Gházi-ud-dín Khán Bahádur Fírúz Jang was appointed forty-third viceroy of Gujarát. The leaning of the new emperor towards Shíâh tenets and his order to insert in the Friday sermon the words the lawful successor of the Prophet after the name of 'Ali, the fourth Khalífah, besides giving general dissatisfaction, caused a small disturbance in Áhmedábád. On the first Friday on which the sermon was read the Túráni or Turk soldiers publicly called on the preacher to desist on pain of death. The preacher disregarding their threats on the next Friday was pulled down from the pulpit by the Túránis and brained with a mace. In the same year (A.D. 1708), hearing that the representative of Sháhi Álam had a copy of a Kurâan written by the Imám Áli Taki son of Músa Razá (A.C. 810-829), the emperor expressed a wish to obtain a sight of it, and the viceroy sent it to him at Mándu in charge of Sayad Ákíl and Salábat Khán Bábi. In A.D. 1709, Shariât Khán, brother of Abdúl Hamíd Khán, was appointed minister in place of his brother, who obtained the office of chief Kázi. Much treasure was sent to the imperial camp by order of the emperor. Ajítsingh of Márwár now rebelled and recovered Jodhpur. As the emperor wished to visit Ajmír the viceroy of Gujarát was directed to join him with his army. At this time the pay of a horseman is said to have been £3 8s. (Rs. 34) and of a footman 8s. (Rs. 4) a month. During his administration Fírúz Jang introduced the practice, which his successors continued, of levying taxes on grain piece-goods and garden produce on his own account, the viceroy's men by degrees getting into their hands the whole power of collecting. In A.D. 1710, when on tour exacting tribute, the viceroy fell ill at Dánta and was brought to Áhmedábád, where he died. As Fírúz Jang had not submitted

Chapter III.

Mughal Viceroys.

Baha'dur Sha'h I. Emperor, 1707-1712.

GHÁZI-UD-DÍN Forty-third Viceroy, 1708-1710.

satisfactory accounts, his property was confiscated, and in A.D. 1711 Amánat Khán, governor of Surat, was appointed deputy viceroy with the title of Shahámat Khán. When Shahámat Khán was levying tribute from the Kadi and Bijápur districts, he heard that a Marátha force had advanced to the Bába Piárah ford on the Narbada. He at once marched to oppose them, summoning Sayad Áhmed Gíláni, governor of Sorath, to his assistance. When he reached Ankleshvar, the Maráthás met him, and a battle was fought in which the Maráthás were defeated. Shahámat Khán then proceeded to Surat, and, after providing for its safety returned to Áhmedábád. In spite of their reverse at Ankleshvar the Maráthás from this time began to make yearly raids into Gujarát.

Jeha'nda'r Sha'h Emperor, 1712-1713.

A'SIF-UD-DAULAH Forty-fourth Viceroy, 1712-13.

In A.D. 1712, the emperor died, and was succeeded by his son Abúl Fateh Muîzz-ud-dín Jehándár Sháh, and Ásif-ud-daulah Asad Khán Bahádur was appointed forty-fourth viceroy of Gujarát. As Muhammad Beg Khán, who was then at Kharkol, was a favourite of the new viceroy and through his interest was appointed deputy, he went to Áhmedábád, and Shahámat Khán was transferred to Málwa as viceroy. In the meantime Muhammad Beg Khán was appointed governor of Surat, and Sarbuland Khán Bahádur was sent to Áhmedábád as deputy viceroy. On his way to Gujarát, Sarbuland Khán was robbed in the Ságbára wilds to the east of Rájpípla. On his arrival he promptly marched against the rebellious Kolis of the Chunvál and subdued them. At the end of the year, as Farrukhsiyar son of Ázím-us-Shán, second son of the late emperor, was marching with a large army on the capital, Sarbuland Khán returned to Dehli.

Farrukhsiyar Emperor, 1713-1719.

This expedition of Farrukhsiyar was successful. He put Jehándár Sháh to death and mounted the throne in A.D. 1713. As he had been raised to the throne mainly by the aid of Sayads Husain Áli and Abdullah Khán, the new emperor fell under the power of these nobles. Husain Áli was sent against Ajítsingh of Márwár, and concluded a treaty with that chief, whereby Ajítsingh engaged to send his son to court and to give his daughter to the emperor in marriage: and the marriage was solemnised in A.D. 1715. In A.D. 1714, shortly after this treaty was concluded, Ajítsingh sent his son Abheysingh to court, and on him in place of one Sayad Áhmed Gíláni was conferred the post of governor of Sorath. Abheysingh remained at court and sent his deputy Káyath Fatehsingh to Júnágadh. Abdúl Hamíd Khán was appointed revenue officer of Surat. After some time he resigned his Surat office and went to court, where on being made superintendent of the shrine of Sheikh Ahmed Khattú he returned to Áhmedábád. In A.D. 1713 Muhtarim Khán was appointed to succeed him in Surat.

SHAHÁMAT KHÁN Forty-fifth Viceroy, 1713.

Early in A.D. 1714, Shahámat Khán, who had been appointed forty-fifth viceroy of Gujarát, was superseded by Dáud Khán Panni as forty-sixth viceroy. The reckless courage of Dáud Khán Panni was renowned throughout India. His memory survives in the tales and proverbs of the Dakhan. On giving battle he used to show his contempt for his enemies by wearing nothing stronger than a muslin jerkin. So stern was his discipline that none of his Afghán soldiers dared to touch a leaf of the standing crops where they were encamped. When at

Chapter III.

Mughal Viceroys.

Farrukhsiyar Emperor, 1713-1719.

Dáud Khán Panni Forty-sixth Viceroy, 1714-15.

Religious Riots in Áhmedábád, 1714.

Áhmedábád he was either engaged in scattering the Kolis or in coursing with greyhounds. He preferred life under canvas on the Sábarmati sands to the viceregal surroundings of the Bhadar Palace. His civil work he used to trust to Dakhan Bráhmans and Pandits. He was much devoted to the use of bhang. Until Dáud Khán's arrival Abdúl Hamíd Khán was appointed viceroy and took charge of the province from Shahámat Khán. At this time, on the security of Rája Muhkamsingh of Nágor, a sum of £5000 (Rs. 50,000) was granted to the brother of Durgádás Ráthod. In A.D. 1714 in Áhmedábád Harirám, the agent of Madan Gopál a successful North Indian banker, who came to Áhmedábád as treasurer with Fírúz Jang, while celebrating the Holi with his friends, seized a Musalmán gentleman and handled him with great roughness. Aggrieved with this treatment the Musalmán complained to a preacher of much eloquence and influence, Mulla Muhammad Ali. The preacher took the Muslim to the Assembly Mosque and sent for Mulla Abdúl Âzíz the chief or leading member of the Sunni Bohora community. He answered the call with a strong party of his men, and on his way was joined by numbers of Musalmáns both soldiers and citizens. With cries of 'Dín' 'Dín' they went to the mosque and carried off the insulted man and the priest and the Bohra leader to the house of the Kázi Khair-ul-láh. The Kázi closed his doors against the crowd who returned abusing him to the Jewellers' quarter pillaging and killing as they went. They next swarmed towards Madan Gopál's Haveli in the Jewellers' quarters. But the Nagarsheth Kapúrchand Bhansáli closed its strong gates and with his Musalmán soldiers met the swarm with firearms. The viceroy who was camped at the Sháhi Bágh sent soldiers and under the influence of the leading citizens of both classes the disturbance was quelled. When the particulars of the riots were known in the imperial camp the Hindus, clamouring against Mulla Muhammad Áli and Sheikh Abdúl Âzíz Gujaráti, struck business and closed their shops. The emperor ordered mace-bearers to proceed to Gujarát and bring the Musalmán ringleaders together with the Hindu Nagarsheth Kapurchand Bhansáli. Some Bohoras at the imperial camp, sending advance news to Áhmedábád, the Mullah and the Bohora Sheth and after him the Bhansáli started for the imperial camp. On reaching the camp the Mulla, who was very impressive and eloquent, preached a sermon in the Assembly Mosque and his fame reaching the emperor he was called to court and asked to preach. He and the Sheth were now able to explain their case to the emperor and the Bhansáli was imprisoned. It is said that the Bhansáli made the Mulla the medium of his release and that he and the Bohora returned to Gujarát while the Mulla remained in honour at court till he died. About the same time a great flood in the Sábarmati did much damage.

Abdúl Hamíd Khán was now chosen governor of Sorath in place of Abheysingh, and Momin Khán was appointed from Dehli, governor of Surat, and was at the same time placed in charge of Baroda, Broach, Dholka, Petlad, and Nadiád. Dáud Khán the viceroy now went into Káthiáváda and Navánagar to collect tribute, and on his return to Áhmedábád, married the daughter of the chief of Halvad in the

Farrukhsiyar Emperor, 1713-1719.

DÁUD KHAN PANNI Forty-sixth Viceroy, 1714-15.

Jhálávâḍa sub-division of Káthiáváḍa. It is related that this lady, who was with child, on hearing of Dáud Khán's death cut open her womb and saved the child at the sacrifice of her own life.[1] Dáud Khán, though an excellent soldier and strict disciplinarian failed to distinguish himself as a civil administrator. He introduced Dakhani *pandits* into official posts, who levied a fee called *chithyáman* from landholders and took taxes from the holdings of Sayads and otherwise made themselves unpopular.

Further Riots in Áhmedábád, 1715.

About this time Momín Khán, governor of Surat, arrived in Gujarát, and placing his deputies in Petlád, Dholka, Baroda, and Naḍiád, went himself to Surat in A.D. 1715. Here he was opposed by the commandant of the fort, Zia Khán, who was obliged to give way, his subordinate, Sayad Kásim, being defeated by Fidá-ud-dín Khán. At this time much ill-feeling was caused by the plunder by Muhammadan troops of the shops of some Hindu merchants in A'hmedábád. On this account, and for other reasons, Dáud Khán was recalled, and Ghazni Khán Jhálori was directed to act in his place until the arrival of a new viceroy. In this year, A.D. 1715, the Mahárája Ajítsingh was appointed forty-seventh viceroy of Gujarát, and his son Kunvar Abheysingh was appointed governor of Sorath. Ajítsingh sent Vajeráj Bhandári to act as his deputy until his arrival, and Fatehsingh Káyath was chosen deputy governor of Sorath. Perhaps one of the most remarkable appointments of this time was that of Haidar Kúli Khán to be minister as well as military commandant of Baroda, Nándod, Arhar-Mátar in the district[2] of Kaira, and of the ports of Surat and Cambay. Haidar Kúli chose an officer to act for him as minister, and after appointing deputies in his different charges himself went to Surat.

MAHÁRÁJA AJÍTSINGH Forty-seventh Viceroy, 1715-16.

The Mahárája Ajítsingh, on reaching A'hmedábád, appointed Ghazni Khán Jhálori governor of Pálanpur and Jawán Mard Khán Bábi governor of Rádhanpur.[3] During this year an imperial order conferred on Haidar Kúli Khán, Sorath and Gohilváḍ or south-east Káthiáváḍa[4] then in charge of Fatehsingh, the viceroy's deputy.[5] On receiving this order Haidar sent Sayad Âkil as his deputy, and that officer went to Jambúsar, and, collecting men, set out to join his appointment. He

[1] Mirăt-i-A'hmedi, Persian Text, 427-434.

[2] Arhar-Mátar is according to the Mirăt-i-A'hmedi (Persian Text, II. 126) the present Kaira sub-division of Mátar. The Mirăt-i-A'hmedi places it twenty miles south-west of A'hmedábád. It is four miles south-west of Kaira.

[3] In the beginning of Ajítsingh's administration the Sacrifice Íd of the Musalmáns very nearly ended in a riot. An overzealous police officer belonging to the Kalúpúr section of A'hmedábád, hoping to please the Hindu viceroy, by force deprived some of the Sunni Bohorás of that quarter of a cow which they had purchased for the sacrifice. The Bohorás in a mass appealed to the Kázi who not succeeding in his representation to the viceroy was obliged to allay the popular excitement by publicly sacrificing a cow after the Íd prayers. Mirăt-i-A'hmedi Royal Asiatic Society MS., I. 567-568.

[4] This is the first known mention of Gohilváḍa, the Gohils country, as a separate district.

[5] During the governorship of Haidar Kúli at Surat the Mirăt-i-A'hmedi (Royal Asiatic Society MS., I. 567-568) notices the death of Mulla Abdul Ghafúr the founder of the wealthy family of the Mullás of Surat. Haidar Kúli confiscated Abdul Ghafúr's property representing to the emperor that the Mulla died issueless. But the Mulla's son Abdúl Hye proceeding to Dehli not only obtained from the emperor an order of restitution of property but the title of chief of merchants, Umda-tut-Tujjár, and an elephant.

Chapter III.

Mughal Viceroys.

Farrukhsiyar Emperor, 1713-1719.

MAHÁRÁJA AJÍTSINGH Forty-seventh Viceroy, 1715-16.

Disagreement between the Viceroy and Haidar Kúli Khán, 1715.

first camped at Loliánah, where the province of Sorath begins, and from Loliánah marched against Pálitána and plundered the town. The viceroy, who was by no means well disposed to Haidar Kúli Khán, sent a message that if any injury was done in Sorath he would take vengeance on the aggressors; and as neither Ajítsingh nor Haidar Kúli Khán was of a vary compliant temper, civil war was on the point of breaking out. By the help of Salábat Khán Bábi, the deputy in Gohilváḍa, matters were arranged, and Sayad Âkil returned from Sorath. Haidar was anxious to send Salábat Khán as deputy to Sorath. But as Salábat demanded too high a salary, Raza Kúli, brother of the late governor of Baroda, was chosen. When this officer, with his brother MaâsúmKúli, reached Amreli Fatehsingh, the viceroy's deputy, evacuated Júnágaḍh. After this Haidar Kúli Khán, in company with Kázím Beg, governor of Baroda, marched against and defeated the chief of Munjpúr, now under Rádhanpúr, who had refused to pay the usual tribute. The viceroy went to Sorath to collect the imperial revenue, and, owing to his excessive demands, met with armed resistance from the Jám of Navánagar. Finally, the matter of tribute was settled, and after visiting the shrine of Dwárka, the viceroy returned to A'hmedábád.

KHÁN DAURÁN NASRAT JANG BAHÁDUR Forty-eighth Viceroy, 1716-1719.

In A.D. 1716, while the viceroy was at Dwárka, in consequence of numerous complaints against Ajítsingh and his Márwári followers, the emperor sent Samsám-ud-daulah Khán Daurán Nasrat Jang Bahádur as forty-eighth viceroy of Gujarát. As it was expected that Ajítsingh would not give up his government without a contest, an army was prepared to compel him to leave. On the arrival of the army Ajítsingh marched straight on A'hmedábád and encamped at Sarkhej, but Nahar Khán persuaded him to retire to Jodhpur without giving battle. In A.D. 1717, after the departure of Ajítsingh, Haidar Kúli Khan, who had been appointed deputy viceroy, leaving Surat set out for A'hmedábád. When Haidar arrived at Petlád, some of the A'hmedábád nobles, among whom was Safdar Khán Bábi, went out to meet him. A dispute arose between one of Haidar's water carriers and a water-carrier in the army of the Bábi, which increased to a serious affray, which from the camp followers spread to the soldiers and officers, and the Bábi's baggage was plundered. Safdar Khán took serious offence, and returning to A'hmedábád collected his kinsmen and followers and marched against Haidar Kúli Khán. In a battle fought on the following day Safdar Khán was defeated. The other Bábis escaped to Pálanpur, and Safdar Khán, who in the first instance had fled to Atarsumba, joined his party at Pálanpur. Muhammad Fírúz Jhálori, governor of Pálanpur, with the title of Ghazni Khán, afterwards succeeded in reconciling the Bábis and Haidar Kúli Khán. A.D. 1719 was a year of great famine. Abdúl Hamíd Khán, who had filled so many appointments in Gujarát, went to court, and was made governor of Sorath. Haidar Kúli Khán now marched against the Mahi Kolis. In the meantime news was received of the appointment of a new viceroy, and Ghazni Khán, governor of Pálanpur, was ordered to stay at A'hmedábád for the defence of the city.

Famine, 1719.

Chapter III.
Mughal Viceroys.

Muhammad Sháh Emperor, 1721-1748.

Mahárája Ajítsingh Forty-ninth Viceroy, 1719-1721.

Early in A.D. 1719, the emperor Farrúkhsiyar was deposed and put to death by the Sayads; and a prince named Rafíá-ud-Daraját, a grandson of the emperor, was raised to the throne. Rafíá-ud-Daraját was put to death by the Sayads after a reign of three months, and his brother Rafíá-ud-daulah, who succeeded him, also died after a few days' reign. The Sayads then raised to the throne prince Raushan Akhtar with the title of Muhammad Sháh. After the murder of Farrúkhsiyar, the most powerful vassal in the neighbourhood of Delhi was Ajítsingh of Márwár. To win him to their side the Sayads granted him the viceroyalty of Gujarát, and Míhr A'li Khán was appointed to act for him until his arrival, while Muhammad Bahádur Bábi, son of Salábat Muhammad Khán Bábi, was placed in charge of the police of the district immediately round A'hmedábád. Shortly after, through the influence of the Mahárája Ajítsingh, Náhir Khán superseded Míhr A'li Khán as deputy viceroy. Náhir Khán was also appointed to the charge of Dholka Dohad and Petlád, and made superintendent of customs. About this time the head tax was repealed, and orders were issued that its levy in Gujarát should cease.

Píláji Gáikwár at Songad, 1719.

In the same year, A.D. 1719, Píláji Gáikwár marched on Surat with a large army and defeated the imperial troops commanded by Sayad Âkil and Muhammad Panáh, the latter commander being taken prisoner and forced to pay a heavy ransom. Píláji, finding Gujarát an easy prey, made frequent incursions, and taking Songaḍ in the extreme south-east established himself there. Míhr A'li Khán, who had been acting for Náhir Khán, marched against and subdued the Kolis, who were committing piracy in the Mahi estuary. From this year Mughal rule in Gujarát was doomed. Píláji Gáikwár was established at Songaḍ, and in the anarchy that ensued, the great Gujarát houses of the Bábis and Jhálorís, as well as the newly arrived Momín Khán, turned their thoughts to independence. Ajítsingh so hated Muhammadan rule that he secretly favoured the Maráthás, and strove to establish his own authority over such portions of Gujarát as bordered on Márwár. In after years, Sarbuland Khán made a vigorous attempt to reassert imperial dominion, but the seeds of dissolution were sown and efforts at recovery were vain.

Decay of Imperial Power, 1720.

In A.D. 1720, Ajítsingh the viceroy sent Anopsingh Bhandári to Gujarát as his deputy. In this year Nizám-ul-Mulk, viceroy of Ujjain, was superseded by Sayad Diláwar Khán. While Diláwar Khán was yet on the Málwa frontiers the Nizám desirous of possessing himself of the Dakhan and its resources retired to Burhánpur pursued by Sayad Diláwar Khán, who giving battle was killed, the Nizám retiring to Aurangábád in the Dakhan. A'lam A'li Khán, deputy viceroy of the Dakhan, was directed to march against him, while from north Gujarát Anopsingh Bhandári was ordered to send 10,000 horse to Surat, and Náhir Khán, the deputy viceroy, was instructed to proceed thither in person. The Nizám and A'lam A'li Khán met near Bálápur in the Berárs and a battle was fought in which the Nizám was successful and A'lam Khán was slain. At this time Anopsingh Bhandári committed many oppressive acts, of which the

Chapter III.

Mughal Viceroys.

Muhammad Sha'h Emperor, 1721-1748.

chief was the murder of Kapurchand Bhansáli, the leading merchant of A'hmedábád. The cause of Kapúrchand's murder was that he had hired a number of armed retainers who used to oppose the Bhandári's orders and set free people unjustly imprisoned by him. To remove this meddler from his way the Bhandári got him assassinated. In A.D. 1721, Nizám-ul-Mulk was appointed prime minister of the empire, Abdúl Hamíd Khán was recalled from Sorath, and in his stead Asad Kuli Khán, with the title of Amir-ul-Umara, was appointed governor of Sorath and sent Muhammad Sharíf Khán into Sorath as his deputy.

Nizám-ul-Mulk Prime Minister, of the Empire, 1721.

Haidar Kúli Khán Fiftieth Viceroy, 1721-22.

In A.D. 1721, in conjunction with Muhammad Amín and Saádat Khán, Haidar Kúli Khán freed the emperor from the tyranny of the Sayads, and was rewarded with the title of Muîz-ud-daulah Haidar Kúli Khán Bahádur Zafar Jang and the viceroyalty of Gujarát. He obtained the appointment of minister for his brother Jaâfar Kúli Khán. Maîsúm Kúli Khán was dignified by the title of Shujáât Khán Bahádur and appointed deputy viceroy. As soon as this change was notified, the people of A'hmedábád, who were discontented with the rule of Anopsingh, attacked his palace, the Bhadar, and he escaped with difficulty. In consequence of the enmity between Haidar Kúli Khán and the Márwáris, Shujaât Khán, the deputy viceroy, attacked the house of Náhir Khán who had been Ajítsingh's minister, and forced him to pay £10,000 (Rs. 1 *lákh*) and leave the city. Shujáât Khán next interfered with the lands of Safdar Khán Bábi, the deputy governor of Godhra, and his brothers. On one of the brothers repairing to Dehli and remonstrating, Haidar Kúli, who, above all things, was a Muhammadan and anxious to strengthen himself with the Muhammadan nobility of Gujarát, restored their lands to the Bábis. In consequence of this decision ill-feeling sprung up between Shujáât Khán and the Bábis, and when Shujáât Khán went to exact tribute he forced Muhammad Khán Bábi, governor of Kaira, to pay a special fine of £1000 (Rs. 10,000). Shortly after one of the viceroy's officers, Kásím A'li Khán, while employed against the Kolis of that part of the country, was killed at Pethápur. Shujáât Khán advanced, and revenged Kásím A'li's death by burning the town. Next, he passed into Sorath, and after exacting tribute, crossed to Kachh. The chief opposed him, and in the fight that followed was beaten and forced to pay about £22,500 (Rs. 2¼ *lákhs*).[1] In A.D. 1721, a Sayad was sent to Sorath as deputy governor in place of Muhammad Sharíf, and Haidar Kúli was appointed governor of Kadi, the Chúnvál, and Halvad (called Muhammadnagar), and put in charge of Tharád, Arjanpur, Bhámnárli, Pethápur, and Kherálu in place of Vakhatsingh, son of the Mahárája Ajítsingh.

Disorder in A'hmedábád, 1721.

Leaves Dehli for Gujarát, 1722.

Early in A.D. 1722, Nizám-ul-Mulk took up the office of prime minister of the empire, to which he had been appointed in the previous year. Strenuous efforts were made to embroil him with Haidar Kúli

---

[1] The sum is 6,75,000 *mahmúdis*. Like the *changízi* (see above page 222 note 2) the *mahmúdi* seems to have varied in value from one-third to one-half of a rupee.

Chapter III.

Mughal Viceroys.

Muhammad Sha'h Emperor, 1721-1748.

Haidar Kúli Khán Fiftieth Viceroy, 1721-22.

Khán, as the Nizám's austerity and craft were a source of not less anxiety to the Dehli court than Haidar Kúli's more daring and restless ambition. Haidar Kúli Khán, unable to contend with the Nizám, left Dehli and retired to Gujarát. On his way the villagers of Dabháli opposed him killing one of his chief men named Alif Beg Khán. Haidar burned the village and put all the people to death, a severity which caused such terror that throughout his rule no difficulty was experienced in realizing tribute or in keeping the roads safe. About this time, among other changes, Muhammad Bahádúr, son of Salábat Khán Bábi, was placed in charge of Sádra and Vírpur, with the title of Sher Khán. Shortly after his arrival the viceroy marched against and subdued the rebellious Kolis of the Chunvál, appointing Rustam A'li Khán his governor there. Then, returning to A'hmedábád, he took up his residence in the Bhadra. There is little doubt that at this time Haidar Kúli aimed at bringing all Gujarát under his rule. He seized the imperial horses which passed through A'hmedábád on their way to Dehli, and confiscated many estates and gave them to his own men. On his way to enforce tribute from the Dungarpúr chiefs, he levied £8000 (Rs. 80,000) from Lunáváda. Through the mediation of the Udepúr Rána, and as he agreed to pay a tribute of £10,000 (1 *lákh* of rupees), the Rával of Dungarpur escaped. Haidar Kúli next proceeded to Bijápur, north of A'hmedábád, but hearing that the emperor was displeased at his assumption of the power of giving and changing grants of land, he returned to A'hmedábád and restored several estates which he had confiscated. The court continued to distrust him, and at the close of A.D. 1722 appointed Jumlat-ul-Mulk Nizám-ul-Mulk fifty-first viceroy.

Shows Signs of Independence and is Recalled, 1722.

Nizám-ul-Mulk Fifty-first Viceroy, 1722.

Haidar Kúli Khán, finding himself no match for the Nizám, was induced to retire quietly, and accordingly left Gujarát by way of Dungarpur. Shujáát Khán and Rustam A'li Khán accompanied him as far as Dungarpúr, and then returned to A'hmedábád. In the meantime the Nizám had reached Ujjain, and thence directed Safdar Khán Bábi to carry on the government till he should arrive, appointing at the same time his uncle Hámid Khán as deputy viceroy and Fidwi Khán as minister. Subsequently the Nizám came to Gujarát and chose officers of his own for places of trust, the chief of whom was Momín Khán, who was appointed governor of Surat. The Nizám then returned to Dehli, but, after a short time, disgusted with his treatment at court, he retired to the Dakhan, where, making Haidarábad his capital, he gradually began to act as an independent ruler. Meanwhile in Gujarát dissensions sprang up between Hámid Khán and other officers, but matters were arranged without any outbreak of hostility. Tribute was exacted from the chiefs on the banks of the Vátrak and from Modhera an unruly Koli village was burned down, and garrisons were placed in the Koli country. In A.D. 1723 Rustam A'li Khán and Shujáát Khán were ordered from Dehli to march on Jodhpur, which they captured and plundered, and then returned to A'hmedábád.

Hámid Khán Deputy Viceroy; Momín Khán Governor of Surat, 1722.

Increase of Marátha Power, 1723.

In A.D. 1723 Piláji Gáikwár, who had been long hovering on the frontier, marched on Surat and was opposed by Momín Khán, whom he defeated. After levying contributions from the surrounding country,

Chapter III.

Mughal Viceroys.

Muhammad Shah Emperor, 1721-1748.

Sarbuland Khán Fifty-second Viceroy, 1723-1730.

he returned to his head-quarters at Songad, and from this overran a considerable portion of the Surat territory, building several forts in the Rájpípla country. At the same time Kántáji Kadam Bánde, invading Gujarát from the side of Dohad, began to levy fixed contributions. Though before this occasional demands had often been made, A.D. 1723 was the first year in which the Maráthás imposed a regular tribute on Gujarát. Momín Khán was now appointed provincial minister, and Rustam Áli Khán succeeded him as revenue officer of Surat, and, as the Nizám had gone to the Dakhan without the emperor's leave, Mubáriz-ul-Mulk Sarbuland Khán Bahádur Diláwar Jang was appointed fifty-second viceroy of Gujarát. He selected Shujáât Khán as his deputy, and made other arrangements for the government of the province. Hámid Khán, uncle and deputy of the Nizám, prepared to oppose Shujáât Khán, but through the intervention of Bábis Salábat Khán, Safdar Khán, and Jawán Mard Khán, Hámid Khán evacuated the Bhadra, and withdrew to Dohad. Shujáât Khán now went to collect tribute, leaving Ibráhím Kúli Khán at Áhmedábád, while Rámrái was posted at Mahudba in Kaira, with orders to watch the movements of Hámid Khán. As the viceroy was in need of money, he farmed to one Jívan Jugal the districts of Jambúsar, Makbúlábad or Ámod about twenty-two miles north of Broach, Dholka, and Broach. In A.D. 1724, he came to Áhmedábád with Áli Muhammad Khán father of the author of the Mirát-i-Áhmedi, as his private minister.

Appoints Shujáât Khán his Deputy.

Nizám-ul-Mulk and Sarbuland Khán.

Rustam Áli, governor of Surat, having succeeded twice or thrice in defeating the Maráthás under Píláji Gáikwár, now offered, in conjunction with his brother Shujáât Khán, that if 20,000 men were placed under their orders, they would march against the Nizám. The emperor accepted this offer, allowing Rustam Áli to draw on the Surat treasury to the extent of £20,000 (Rs. 2 *lákhs*). Rustam Áli accordingly, with the aid of Áhmed Kúli his brother's son, equipped an army. In the meantime the Nizám was not idle. He promised to Kántáji Kadam Bánde a one-fourth share of the revenue of Gujarát, provided he should be able, in concert with Hámid Khán, to re-conquer the province from Mubáriz-ul-Mulk. Shujáât Khán, who was now at Kadi, instead of following the advice of his minister and carefully watching Hámid Khán's movements from Kapadvani, went to a distant part of the province. Hámid Khán seeing his opportunity, united his forces with those of Kántáji Kadam, and marched to Kapadvanj. Shujáât Khán hearing of this, advanced towards Áhmedabád and encamped at Dabhora under Bahyal, eighteen miles east of Áhmedábád and thence proceeded to Mota Medra, about six miles east of the capital. When he came so near Áhmedábád, many of his soldiers went without leave into the city to visit their families. The Maráthás attacked his rear guard, and his men giving way took to flight. Hámid Khán seeing that Shujáât Khán had but a small force, marched between him and the capital. A battle was fought, in which Shujáât Khán was slain, and his two sons Hasan Kúli and Mustafa Kúli were taken prisoners. Shujáât Khán's head was cut off and sent to Safdar Khán Bábi, to be sent to Ibráhím Kúli his son, who was doing duty as commandant at Áhmedábád. Hámid Khán took up his quarters in

Sarbuland Khán's Deputy Defeated, 1724.

Chapter III.

Mughal Viceroys.

Muhammad Sha'h Emperor, 1721-1748.

SARBULAND KHÁN Fifty-second Viceroy, 1723-1730.

the Sháhi Bágh, and got possession of all A'hmedábád except the city. Hámid Khán now sent a message to the emperor, that the Maráthás had been successful in defeating Shujáât Khán and conquering Gujarát, but that he had defended A'hmedábád against them. The emperor sent him a dress of honour, but after a few days discovered that Hámid's message was false. The Maráthás now marched through the country, collecting their *chauth* or one-fourth and their *sardeshmukhi* or one-tenth shares of the revenue. Kántáji went to Víramgám and besieged the town, but on the promise of one of the chief inhabitants to raise a sum of £35,000 (Rs. 3½ *lákhs*) the Maráthás retired. Hámid Khán who was now independent began to bestow lands and districts many of which remained with the grantees and were never recovered by future governors. Ibráhím Kúli, son of Shujáât Khán, in revenge for his father's death, determined to assassinate Hámid Khán. The attempt failed. Hámid Khán escaped and Ibráhím Kúli was slain.

The Maráthás engaged as Allies.

Rustam A'li Khán, governor of Surat, in the hope of being revenged on Hámid Khán, invited the aid of Píláji Gáikwár, and it was agreed that they should meet on the north bank of the Narbada. Píláji promised to aid Rustam Khán, and the allied armies, crossing the Mahi, encamped at Aras in the plain between Anand and the Mahi. Hámid Khán, accompanied by Mír Nathu, Muhammad Salábat Rohila, and Kántáji Kadam, marched to oppose Rustam Khán. Hámid Khán also entered into secret negotiations with Píláji Gáikwár, who resolved to remain neutral and side with the conqueror. A battle was fought, in which, though Pílaji took no part, Hámid Khán was defeated and put to flight, and Mír Nathu was killed. After the fight Rustam A'li remained on the field of battle and liberated his nephews, plundering Hámid Khán's camp. Píláji plundered Rustam A'li's camp and then moved off, while Kántáji carried away what was left in the camp of Hámid Khán. Hámid Khán reproached Kántáji for his inactivity; but he pleaded in excuse that he was watching the mode of warfare amongst Muhammadans, and promised to attack Rustam A'li shortly. Now, as the Maráthás really desired to ruin Rustam A'li, who was their bitter foe, they after a few days surrounded him and cut off his supplies. Rustam A'li stood a blockade of eight days, and then forced his way through his enemies and went to Nápád, about fourteen miles west of the Vásad railway station in the Anand sub-division of the Kaira district, and thence through Kalamsar to Nápa or Nába under Petlád. The Maráthás still pursuing Rustam A'li retired to Vasu under Petlád, ten miles east of Nadiad and about twenty-five miles south of A'hmedábád, where he gave battle, and by a furious charge broke the Máratha line. The Maráthás rallied, and Rustam A'li and his men were defeated, Rustam A'li being slain and his nephews again taken prisoners. Rustam was buried on the field of battle and his head sent to A'hmedábád.

Battle of Arás. Hamid Khán defeated by Rustam A'li, 1723.

Maráthás join Hámid Khán against Rustam A'li.

Hámid Khán returned to A'hmedábád with the Maráthás, who saw that their only means of effecting a permanent footing in the province was by supporting him. Hámid Khán then assigned a one-fourth share of the revenue of the territory north of the Mahi to Kántáji, and to Píláji a corresponding interest in the territory south of the Mahi,

Chapter III.

Mughal Viceroys.

Muhammad Shah Emperor, 1721-1748.

SARBULAND KHÁN Fifty-second Viceroy, 1723-1730.

Mubáriz-ul-Mulk sent against the Maráthás, 1725.

including Surat and Baroda. After this Hámid Khán acted tyrannically. He extorted large sums from the rich, and poisoned the two sons of Shujáât Khán. When the news of Kántáji's and Piláji's success reached the Dakhan, Trimbakráv Dhábáde, son of Khanderáv Senápati, came with a large army and laid siege to Cambay. While the siege was being pressed a quarrel among the Marátha leaders culminated in strife and bloodshed. Trimbakráv Senápati was wounded and the Marátha army had to disperse and retire.[1] Salábat Khán, leaving Áhmedábád, went to Víramgám, and after some time, placing his nephew at Víramgám, he went into Gohilváḍa. When the news of the defeat and death of Rustam Áli reached Dehli, the emperor ordered Mubáriz-ul-Mulk to take a strong army and proceed in person to Gujarát and expel Hámid Khán and the Maráthás. Mubáriz-ul-Mulk marched on Gujarát with a large army, assisted by Maháraja Abheysingh of Jodhpur, Chatarsingh Rája of Narwar in Bundelkhand, Gandrapsingh, and the Maháràna of Udepur. On his arrival at Ajmír Mubáriz-ul-Mulk was received by his private minister Áli Muhammad Khán, who afterwards joined Jawán Mard Khán Bábi in Rádhanpur, and united their troops with those under Mubáriz-ul-Mulk. At that time Salábat Khán was removed from his government, and Safdar Khán Bábi died. In obedience to the imperial order, Mubáriz-ul-Mulk marched from Ajmír and came to the Gujarát frontier. On his approach Hámid Khán returned to Áhmedábád. He placed Rúpsingh and Sardár Muhammad Ghorni in charge of the city and himself withdrew to Mehmúdábád. Mubáriz-ul-Mulk now sent Sheikh Alíyár in advance with an army against Áhmedábád. When Sheikh Alíyár arrived before the city, Muhammad Ghorni, who was dissatisfied with Hámid Khán for bringing in the Maráthás, persuaded Rúpsingh to fly. In the meantime Mubáriz-ul-Mulk with the main body of his forces reached Sidhpur.

Hámid Khán and other Maráthás Retire.

Hámid Khán, accompanied by a detachment of Marátha horse, now returned to Áhmedábád; but Muhammad Ghorni closed the gates, and would not suffer him to enter the city. Mubáriz-ul-Mulk marched to Mesána. About this time Áli Muhammad Khán, the father of the author of the Mirăt-i-Áhmedi, who was now with Mubáriz-ul-Mulk at Mesána, advised him to conciliate the influential Muhammadan family of Bábi. Under his advice, Salábat Muhammad Khán Bábi was appointed governor of Víramgám, and Jawán Mard Khán governor of Pátan. Shortly afterwards Murlidhardás, the Gujaráti minister of Hámid Khán, deserted his master's declining cause.

Mubáriz-ul-Mulk enters Áhmedábád, 1725.

When Kantáji heard that Mubáriz-ul-Mulk had arrived at Pethápur, only eighteen miles from Áhmedábád, he retired to Mehmúdábád. Before the close of A.D. 1725, Mubáriz-ul-Mulk reached Áhmedábád, where he was well received by the officials and merchants.

---

[1] See note 1 page 312. The author of the Mirăt-i-Áhmedi (Persian Text Royal Asiatic Society's Library Edition, I. 658) says Trimbakrav was slain. This seems an oversight as in another passage (Ditto, 738-739, see below page 312) he states that Trimbakrav was killed in 1731. The latter statement is in agreement with Grant Duff (History of the Maráthás, I. 364).

Chapter III.

Mughal Viceroys.

Muhammad Sháh Emperor, 1721-1748.

SARBULAND KHÁN Fifty-second Viceroy, 1723-1730.

Defeat of the Maráthás at Sojitra and Kapadvanj, 1725.

Hámid Khán and Kantáji, who had by this time reached the banks of the Mahi, were now joined by Píláji Gáikwár. The Marátha leaders, seeing that the only way to preserve their footing in the province was to espouse the cause of Hámid Khán, united their forces with his, and prepared to march on A'hmedábád. Mubáriz-ul-Mulk deputed his son Khánahzád Khán with an army to oppose them, and made several appointments, among other changes raising A'li Muhammad Khán to the post of minister. Khánahzád Khán met the Maráthás near Sojítra, about ten miles north-west of Petlád, and defeated them, pursuing them as far as the Mahi. Then, returning, he was reinforced by his brother Sháh Nawáz Khán, and marched against the Maráthás, who were encamped at Kapadvanj. Another battle was fought, and the Maráthás were again defeated and pursued as far as the hills of A'li-Mohan now Chota Udepur in the extreme east of the province. Khánahzád Khán now appointed Hasan-ud-dín governor of Baroda, Broach, Jambúsar, and Makbulábád. Meanwhile Antáji Bháskar, a Marátha noble, entering Gujarát from the side of Ídar, laid siege to the town of Vadnagar, which, according to the old Gujarát proverb, with Umreth in the Kaira district, are the two golden feathers of the kingdom of Gujarát. Vadnagar was inhabited by wealthy Bráhmans of the Nágar caste who prayed Mubáriz-ul-Mulk to march to their relief; but as both his sons were in pursuit of the other Marátha bands defeated at Kapadvanj, the viceroy had no troops to spare from the A'hmedábád garrison. The Nágars accordingly, seeing no prospect of help, paid a sum of £40,000 (Rs. 4 *lákhs*) and Antáji Bháskar retired. Kantáji and Píláji, encouraged by this raid of Antáji's, entered Gujarát from different quarters. Kántáji again laid siege to Vadnagar. The Nágars, unable to pay the contribution demanded, leaving their property fled and Kántáji in his attempts to unearth the buried treasure burned down the town. Shortly afterwards Umreth in the Kaira district suffered a similar fate at the hands of Kántáji. In one of his raids Píláji Gáikwár advancing as far as Baroda was met by Khánahzád Khán, the son of the viceroy. Distrusting the issue of a battle Píláji fled to Cambay, and from Cambay withdrew to Sorath. For these services the emperor raised Khánahzád Khán to the rank of a noble, with the title Ghálib Jang. About this time A'li Muhammad Khán was dismissed from the post of minister, and in his stead first Muhammad Sayad Beg and afterwards Muhammad Sulaimán were appointed. Not long afterwards A'li Muhammad Khán was again entrusted with a command and raised to be governor of Dholka.

Marátha Expedition against Vadnagar, 1725.

Mubáriz-ul-Mulk pays the Marátha Tribute, 1726.

The Maráthás retired to the Dakhan, but, returning in A.D. 1726, compelled Mubáriz-ul-Mulk to confirm his predecessor's grants in their favour. The emperor refused to acknowledge any cessions of revenue to the Maráthás; and the viceroy, hard pressed for money, unable to obtain support from the court and receiving little help from his impoverished districts, was forced to impose fresh taxes on the citizens of A'hmedábád, and at the same time to send an army to collect their tribute from the Mahi chiefs. As part of the agreement between Mubáriz-ul-Mulk and the Marátha chiefs Píláji was to receive a share in the

Chapter III.

Mughal Viceroys.

Muhammad Sha'h Emperor. 1721-1748.

SARBULAND KHÁN Fifty-second Viceroy, 1723-1730.

revenue of the districts south of the Mahi. But Peshwa Bájiráv Balál, to whom, as agent of his rival Khanderáv Dábháde, Píláji was obnoxious, sent Udáji Pavár to drive Píláji away. In this Udáji was successful, and defeating Píláji forced him to seek the aid of Kántáji. Kántáji, perceiving that if the Peshwa became supreme his own independence would suffer, joined Píláji, and marching together upon Baroda they endeavoured, but without success, to prevent the Musalmán governor Sadr-ud-dín Khán from entering the city. About this time want of funds forced Mubáriz ul-Mulk to sell the greater part of the Dholka district to different landholders.

Alliance with the Peshwa, 1727.

In the following year, A.D. 1727, Bájiráv Peshwa began to negotiate with Mubáriz-ul-Mulk, undertaking that if the one-fourth and one-tenth shares in the revenue of the province were guaranteed to him, he would protect Gujarát from other invaders. Though he did not consent to these proposals, the viceroy so far accepted the alliance of the Peshwa as to allow the governor of Baroda to aid Udáji Pavár against Píláji. Píláji and Kántáji outmanœuvred Udáji and prevented him from effecting a junction with the governor of Baroda, who in the end was forced to abandon both that city and the stronghold of Dabhoi, while Udáji retired to Málwa. Píláji Gáikwár now obtained possession of Baroda. Mubáriz-ul-Mulk, still sorely pressed for funds, marched into Sorath to exact tribute. On reaching Víramgám, Salábat Muhammad Khán Bábi, on behalf of the Jám of Navánagar, presented the viceroy with £10,000 (Rs. 1 *lákh*), and for this service was rewarded with the gift of an elephant. Mubáriz-ul-Mulk then marched against Chháya, the capital of the chief of Porbandar in the south-west of Káthiáváda. This chief, by putting to sea, hoped to escape the payment of tribute. But on hearing that the viceroy proposed to annex his territory and appoint an officer to govern it, he returned and agreed to pay a tribute of £4000 (Rs. 40,000).[1] On his way back to A'hmedábád, Mubáriz-ul-Mulk passed through Halvad in Jháláváda, and there married the daughter of Jhála Pratápsingh, the chief of that district, whom he accordingly exempted from the payment of tribute. About this time the viceroy received orders from the emperor to restore certain land which he had confiscated, and as he neglected to obey, certain estates of his in the Panjáb were resumed. In the meantime Krishnáji, foster son of Kántáji, made a sudden attack upon Chámpáner and captured that fortress, and from that time Kántáji's agents remained permanently in Gujarát to collect his share of the tribute.

Píláji Gáikwár obtains Baroda and Dabhoi, 1727.

Capture of Chámpáner by the Maráthás, 1728.

In A.D. 1728 the minister Momín Khán died, and in his place the emperor selected Momín Khán's brother Abd-ul-Ghani Khán. About this time Asad A'li, governor of Júnágadh, also died, and on his death-bed appointed Salábat Muhammad Khán Bábi deputy governor of that fortress. Salábat Muhammad Khán sent his son Sher Khán Bábi to act on his behalf. When the emperor heard of the death of Asad A'li, he appointed Ghulám Muhy-ud din Khán, son of the late Asad A'li, governor. Ghulám Muhy-ud-din did not proceed to Júnágadh but continued Sher Khán Bábi as his deputy. Mubáriz-ul-Mulk, now

[1] The amount was 1,25,000 *mahmúdis*.

Chapter III.

Mughal Viceroys.

Muhammad Sha'h Emperor, 1721-1748.

SARBULAND KHÁN Fifty-second Viceroy, 1723-1730.

Grant of Tribute to the Peshwa, 1729.

perceiving that neither Píláji nor Kántáji afforded any protection to Gujarát, but rather pillaged it, closed with the offers of Bájiráv Peshwa, and in A.D. 1729 formally granted to him the one-fourth and one-tenth shares of the revenue of the province. The Peshwa accordingly sent his brother Chimnájiráv to collect the tribute. Chimnáji plundered Dholka and the country near Chámpáner, while Mubáriz-ul-Mulk exacted tribute from the chiefs on the banks of the Vátrak. Kántáji now entered Gujarát and prepared for war in case Chimnáji and the viceroy should unite against him. His movements were not interfered with, and after collecting his share of the tribute, he retired to Sorath. The viceroy now marched against the Kolis, and after destroying many of them together with their wives and children, returned to Áhmedábád by way of Modasa and Ahmednagar. Ghulám Muhy-ud-dín Khán, governor of Júnágadh, who had not yet proceeded to his command, appointed a second deputy. Through the influence of the viceroy this appointment was not confirmed, and instead Sher Khán Bábi, son of Salábat Muhammad Khán, was placed in charge of that fortress.

Mulla Muhammad A'li raises a Disturbance at Surat, 1729.

In Surat the year A.D. 1729 was marked by a severe flood in the Tápti and by a somewhat serious local disturbance. The chief cause of the disturbance was Mulla Muhammad A'li, a rich Musalmán trader of Surat. This man who, as Ûmda-tut-tujjár or chief of the merchants, had already a special rank in the city, was tempted to take advantage of the disorders of the time to raise himself to the position of an independent ruler. With this object he chose as his head-quarters the island of Píram in the Gulf of Cambay, near the port of Gogha, and there spent considerable sums in strengthening the island and tempting settlers to place themselves under his protection. As Píram was not popular Mulla Muhammad fixed on the village of Athva, on the left bank of the Tápti, about twelve miles from its mouth. Here he began to build a fort, but was ordered to desist by Sohráb Khán, the governor of Surat, from which city the proposed stronghold was only three miles distant. Mulla Muhammad so far from obeying, persuaded Beglar-Beg Khán the commander of the fort of Surat to side with him. Accordingly, next day, Beglar-Beg Khán bombarded the governor Sohráb Khán's residence, proclaiming that his own brother Teghbeg Khán was appointed governor of Surat. In the end Mulla Muhammad A'li induced the chief merchants of the city to pray for the removal of Sohráb who pending receipt of orders from the emperor was made to hand over his official residence in the city to Teg-Beg Khán.

Nadiád given in Farm, 1729.

In the same year, A.D. 1729, Jawán Mard Khán Bábi was chosen governor of Petlád, A'li Muhammad Khán was made collector of Áhmedábád, and A'li Muhammad's son, the author of the Mirăt-i-Áhmedi and his brother were appointed governor and superintendent of the customs of that district. A'li Muhammad Khán shortly resigned and was succeeded by Rú-ín Khán. At this time Jawán Mard Khán Bábi, while punishing the Kolis of Bálor, probably Bhátod about fifteen miles east of Broach, was killed by a man of that tribe, and in revenge for his death the town of Bálor was plundered. On the death of Jawán Mard Khán, at the request of Salábat Muhammad Khán Bábi, his eldest son Kamál-ud-dín Khán Bábi received the districts of

Chapter III.
Mughal Viceroys.
Muhammad Shah Emperor, 1721-1748.
Sarbuland Khan Fifty-second Viceroy, 1723-1730.

Sami and Munjpur and the title of Jawán Mard Khán. At the same time the second son, Muhammad Anwar, with the title of Safdar Khán, was appointed to the government of Rádhanpur. The viceroy now went to Nadiád, where Rái Kishandás, agent of Jawán Mard Khán, received the district of Petlád in farm. From Nadiád Mubáriz-ul-Mulk went to collect tribute from Sardársingh, the chief of Bhádarva in the Rewa Kántha about fifteen miles north of Baroda, on the banks of the Mahi, who, after some fighting, agreed to pay a sum of £2000 (Rs. 20,000). On his way back to A'hmedábád the viceroy levied tribute from the chief of Úmeta, fifteen miles west of Baroda. As Rái Kishandás failed to pay the sum agreed on for the farm of Petlád, an order was issued for his imprisonment. To save himself from the indignity he committed suicide.

Athva Fort, 1730.

When Kántáji returned from Sorath he camped at Sánand, and his advanced guard carried off some of the viceroy's elephants which were grazing there. Men were sent in pursuit, but in vain, and the Maráthás escaped. Meanwhile, at Surat, Mulla Muhammad A'li continued to build the fort at Athva. At last his accomplice, Beglar-Beg Khán the commander of the Surat fort, began to perceive that if the Athva fort were completed the Mulla would be in a position to obstruct the trade of the port of Surat. He consequently ordered him to stop building. In spite of this the Mulla succeeded in persuading Sohráb Khán to allow him to go on with his fort promising in return to get him confirmed as governor of Surat. Sohráb Khán agreed, and the fort was completed, and Sohráb Khán was duly appointed governor. As the fort was immediately below Surat the revenue of Surat was greatly diminished, and Sohráb Khán, when it was too late, saw his mistake.

The Viceroy in Káthiáváda and Kachh, 1730.

In A.D. 1730 Mubáriz-ul-Mulk went into Gohilváda in south-east Káthiáváda and levied tribute from Bhávsingh, chief of Síhor; thence he proceeded to Mádhupur, a town under Porbandar, and laid it waste. While engaged at Mádhupur, Momín Khán, son-in-law of the late Momín Khán, owing to some misunderstanding with the viceroy suddenly set out for A'hmedábád and from A'hmedábád proceeded to A'gra. The viceroy now marched in the direction of Kachh and refusing the offer of a yearly tribute of about £33,000 (10,00,000 *máhmúdis*), advanced against Bhúj. He experienced great difficulty in crossing the Ran, and as the Ráo had cut off all supplies, and as at the same time news arrived of disturbances in A'hmedábád, he was obliged, after a month and a half, to retire to Rádhanpur. The author of the Mirăt-i-A'hmedi was ordered to suppress the A'hmedábád riots, which had arisen out of the levy of some fresh taxes, and was invested with the title of Hasan Muhammad Khán. In this year Udaikaran, Desái of Víramgám, was murdered by a Kasbáti[1] of that town named A'li, and Salábat Muhammad Khán Bábi, who was sent to investigate this murder, died on his way at Páldi, a village on the right bank of the Sábarmati, opposite to A'hmedábád.

Riots at A'hmedábád.

Mahárája Abheysingh Fifty-third Viceroy, 1730-1733.

News was now (A.D. 1730) received that Mahárája Abheysingh of Jodhpur had been appointed viceroy and had reached Pálanpur.

[1] Kasbátis are the descendants of the Musalman garrisons of some towns of north Gujarát. The Kasbátis of Víramgám were originally Tánk Rájputs.

Chapter III.
Mughal Viceroys.
Muhammad Sha'h Emperor, 1721-1748.
MAHÁRÁJA ABHEYSINGH Fifty-third Viceroy, 1730-1733.
Mubáriz-ul-Mulk Resists the New Viceroy.

The friends of order endeavoured to arrange a peaceable transfer between the Maháraja and the late viceroy, but Mubáriz-ul-Mulk determined to try the chances of war, and prepared for resistance. At this time Mír Ismaíl, deputy of Ghulám Muhy-ud-dín Khán, arrived and took charge of the government of Júnágadh from Sher Khán Bábi. Mahárája Abheysingh, after making various appointments, set out with his brother Vakhatsingh and 20,000 men to take over the government of Gujarát. When he reached Pálanpur and saw that Mubáriz-ul-Mulk was determined on resistance, he sent an order to Sardár Muhammad Ghorni appointing him his minister and directing him to take possession of the city of A'hmedábád and drive out the late viceroy. As Sardár Muhammad was not strong enough to carry out these orders he awaited the Mahárája's arrival. When the Mahárája reached Sidhpur he was joined by Safdar Khán Bábi and Jawán Mard Khán Bábi from Rádhanpur. They then advanced together to Adálaj, distant only about eight miles from the capital, their army increasing daily. Mubáriz-ul-Mulk was already encamped between Adálaj and the city, and on the approach of the Mahára'ja a battle was fought in which the Mahárája was defeated. Abheysingh changed his position, and another and bloodier engagement took place, in which both sides tried to kill the opposing commander. But as both Mubáriz-ul-Mulk and the Mahárája fought disguised as common soldiers, neither party succeeded. At first the Mahárája who had the advantage in position repulsed the enemy, but Muba'riz-ul-Mulk fought so desperately in the river-bed that the Ráthods gave way. They rallied and made one more desperate charge, but were met, repulsed, and finally pursued as far as Sarkhej. The Mahárája, who had not expected so determined an opposition, now sent Momin Khán and Amarsingh to negotiate wtih Mubáriz-ul-Mulk, who was still determined to resist to the uttermost. It was finally agreed that Mubáriz-ul-Mulk should receive a sum of £10,000 (Rs. 1 *lákh*) and should surrender A'hmedábád to the Mahárája. Mubáriz-ul-Mulk accordingly quitted the city and left for A'gra by way of Udepur.

Battle of Adálaj; the Mahárája defeated by Mubáriz-ul-Mulk, 1730.

Mubáriz-ul-Mulk Retires.

Government of Abheysingh.

The Mahárája entering A'hmedábád, appointed Ratansingh Bhandári his deputy, and placed Fidá-ud-din Khán, cousin of Momín Khán, in charge of the city police. Shortly afterwards Karímdád Khán Jhálori, governor of Pálanpur, who had accompanied the Mahárája into Gujarát, died. After the death of Salábat Muhammad Khán Bábi, his son, Sher Khán Bábi, was dismissed from the government of Junágadh. He retired to his estate of Gogha, and when the Mahárája arrived in A'hmedábád he paid his respects, presenting the viceroy with an elephant and some horses. The Mahárája confirmed the lands assigned to his father, and reported his action to the emperor. Momín Khán was made ruler of Cambay, and Fidá-ud-dín Khán, his cousin, was made governor of the lands near that city, the revenue of which had been assigned to the Mahárája. So great was the fear of the Maráthás, that Mustafíd Khán, the governor elect of Surat, instead of proceeding direct by land, went to Cambay. From Cambay he moved to Broach, and from Broach entered into negotiations with Píláji Gáikwár, promising, if allowed to retain

Momín Khán Ruler of Cambay, 1730.

Chapter III.
Mughal Viceroys.
Muhammad Sháh Emperor, 1721-1748.
MAHÁRÁJA ABHEYSINGH Fifty-third Viceroy, 1730-1733.

possession of Surat, to pay Píláji the one-fourth share of its revenues. Píláji agreed, but Sohráb Khán, who was still in possession of Surat, refused to hand it over to Mustafíd Khán. In this year also Vakhatsingh, brother of the Mahárája Abheysingh, was appointed governor of Pátan, and sent a deputy to act for him. About the same time Mír Fakhr-ud-dín, a follower of the late viceroy Mubáriz-ul-Mulk, leaving him secretly, came to Ahmedábád, and in an interview with the Mahárája obtained for himself the post of deputy governor of Júnágadh. When he proceeded to take up his appointment he was opposed by Mír Ismáil, and was killed in a battle fought near Amreli in central Káthiáváda. Muhammad Pahár, son of Karímdád Khán Jhálori, was appointed governor of Pálanpúr in succession to his father, and Jawán Mard Khán was sent to Vadnagar.

The Peshwa and Viceroy against Piláji Gáikwár, 1731.

In the following year, A.D. 1731, Bájiráv Peshwa, entering Gujarát at the head of an army, advanced against Baroda, then in the possession of Píláji Gáikwár. Afterwards, at the invitation of the Mahárája, he visited Ahmedábád and had a meeting with the viceroy in the Sháhi Bágh. At this meeting it was agreed that Bájiráv should assist Ázmatulláh, the governor of Baroda, in taking possession of that town and in expelling Píláji Gáikwár. By this arrangement the viceroy hoped by playing off the Peshwa against Píláji, to succeed in getting rid of the latter, while the Peshwa intended that if Píláji was forced to give up Baroda, he himself should gain possession of that city. Accordingly the Peshwa, together with an army from the viceroy, marched on Baroda. They had scarcely laid siege to the city when the Peshwa heard that Nizám-ul-Mulk was advancing on Gujarát against him. Abandoning all operations against Baroda, the Peshwa withdrew, with all speed, to the Dakhan. On his way he encountered the army of Trimbakráv Senápati, who, together with Piláji Kántáji and Udáji Pavár, had united to resist the pretensions of the Peshwa in Gujarát, and were also secretly leagued with the Nizám. An engagement was fought in which the Peshwa was victorious and Trimbakráv was slain.[1] The Peshwa at once pushed on to the Dakhan, contriving to avoid the Nizám, though his baggage was plundered by that chief, who had camped at Ghala Kámrej, on the river Tápti, about ten miles above Surat.

The Peshwa Withdraws.

Defeats his Opponents.

Abdúlláh Beg appointed the Nizám's Deputy at Broach.

During these changes the city of Broach, which on account of the strength of its fort the Maráthás had failed to take, was governed by Abdúlláh Beg, an officer originally appointed to that command by Mubáriz-ul-Mulk. Dissatisfied that the government of Gujarát should be in the hands of Abheysingh, Abdúlláh Beg, in A.D. 1731, entered into negotiations with the Nizám, offering to hold Broach as the Nizám's deputy. Nizám-ul-Mulk agreed, appointed Abdúlláh his deputy, and ennobled him with the title of Nek Álam Khán. About the same time Vakhatsingh, brother of the viceroy, withdrew to his chiefship of Nágor in Jodhpur, and Ázmat-ulláh went to Ágra. After his safe arrival in the Dakhan Bájiráv Peshwa entered into an agreement

[1] See note on page 306.

Muhammad Sha'h Emperor, 1721-1748.
MAHÁRÁJA ABHEYSINGH Fifty-third Viceroy, 1730-1733.

with the Nizám under the terms of which the grants of Dholka, Broach, Jambusar, and Makbúlábád were continued to the Nizám. Momin Khán received the farm of Petlád, and Kántáji was confirmed in the share he had acquired of the revenues of Gujarát. In A.D. 1732 the paymaster, Amánatdár Khán, died, and was succeeded by Ghulám Hasan Khán, who sent Mujáhid-ud-dín Khán to act as his deputy. Through the influence of Mulla Muhammad Ali, Sohráb A'li was now confirmed as governor of Surat, and Mustafíd Khán was obliged to return to A'hmedábád.

The Viceroy procures the Death of Piláji Gaikwár, 1732;

Píláji Gáikwár as the agent of the deceased Khanderáv Dábháde Senápati, as the owner of the fort of Songad, and as the ally of the Bhíls and Kolis, was naturally a thorn in the side of the viceroy Abheysingh. The recent acquisition of the town of Baroda and of the strong fortress of Dabhoi had made Piláji still more formidable. Under these circumstances, Abheysing, who had long wished to recover Baroda and Dabhoi determined to assassinate Piláji, and this was effected by a Márvádi at the holy village of Dákor. The Maráthás slew the assassin and withdrew across the Mahi, burning the body of Piláji at the village of Sánoli or Sáonli, fourteen miles north of Baroda. They then evacuated the district of Baroda, retiring to the fortress of Dabhoi. On hearing of the death of Píláji the viceroy immediately advanced against the Maráthás, and, after taking possession of Baroda, laid siege to Dabhoi. He failed to capture this fortress, and as the rainy season had set in and provisions were scarce, he was obliged to retire. He then went to Baroda, and after placing Sher Khán Bábi in charge of the city, returned to A'hmedábád. In this year, A.D. 1732, Gujarát was wasted by famine.

and takes Bároda.

Famine, 1732.

Affairs at Surat, 1732.

Meanwhile at Surat Múlla Muhammad Ali of Athva was again the cause of disturbance. Resisting with force the demand of a sum of £10,000 (Rs. 1 *lákh*) by Sohráb Khán, the governor of Surat, he succeeded in driving Sohráb Khán out of the city, and the government of Surat was then usurped by Teghbeg Khán, a brother of Beglar-Beg Khán. The success of the Múlla against Soráb Khán made him so forgetful of his position that he arrogated to himself all the emblems of the governor's office and wrote to the emperor asking a patent of the governorship of Surat in the name of his son Múlla Fakhr-ud-dín. The messengers bearing these communications were intercepted at Broach by the partisans of Teghbeg, who determined to remove this powerful cause of anxiety. Teghbeg Khán, inviting Muhammad Ali to an entertainment, placed him in confinement, and after keeping him in prison for two years, in A.D. 1734 put him to death. Teghbeg also took possession of the fort of Athva, and plundered it. Sohráb Khán, seeing that he could not recover Surat, went with Sayad Wali to Gogha, where his relatives lived, and from that, proceeding to Bhávnagar settled there. When the emperor heard what had happened, he appointed Momín Khán to Surat and Teghbeg Khán to Cambay. Momín Khán sent Sayad Núrullah to act for him, but he was defeated by Teghbeg Khán, who afterwards contrived, in A.D. 1733, to be formally appointed governor of Surat with the title of Bahádur.

Teghbeg Khán Governor of Surát.

Chapter III.

Mughal Viceroys.

Muhammad Sháh Emperor, 1721-1748.

Mahárája Abheysingh Fifty-third Viceroy, 1730-1733.

When Umábái, widow of Khanderáv Senápati, heard of the assassination of Píláji Gáikwár, she determined to avenge his death. Collecting an army and taking with her Kántáji Kadam and Dámáji Gáikwár, son of Píláji, she marched upon Áhmedábád. As the Maráthás failed to do more than slay a Rájput leader named Jívaráj they came to terms. In the end it was agreed that in addition to the one-fourth and the one-tenth shares of the revenue a sum of £8000 (Rs. 80,000) should be paid from the Áhmedábád treasury, Jawán Mard Khán being kept as a hostage till the payments were made. For his services on this occasion Jawán Mard Khán was made governor of Vírамgám. During this year an imperial order appointed Khushálchand Sheth, son of Sántidás, Nagar Sheth or chief merchant of Áhmedábád. The Maráthás plundered Rasúlábád a mile south of Áhmedábád and its excellent library was pillaged. Umábái now marched upon Baroda, and the governor, Sher Khán Bábi, prepared to oppose the Maráthás. But Umábái, sending a message to Sher Khán, explained that she had just concluded a peace with the Mahárája, and was suffered to pass unmolested. The emperor, satisfied with the arrangements made by the Mahárája, presented him with a dress of honour. In this year the Mahárája went to court by way of Jodhpur, and appointed Ratansingh Bhandári as his deputy, and the author of the Mirăt-i-Áhmedi as news recorder. In the same year, A.D. 1733, Ghulám Muhy-ud-dín Khán, governor of Júnágadh died, and his son Mír Hazabr Khán was selected to fill his place.

Ratansingh Bhandári Deputy Viceroy, 1733-1737.

The Maráthás Return.

Meanwhile as the Maráthás had not received their rights, Jádoji Dábháde, son of Umábái, returned to Gujarát. Peace was concluded on the former basis, and Jádoji marched into Sorath to exact tribute. In this year the Kolis of the Chúnvál and Kánkrej committed many excesses, and a Rájput noble was robbed in the Pátan district. In the meantime Sohráb Khán, the former governor of Surat, who had been kindly received by Bhávsinghji the chief of Sihor, began to raise a following and was appointed collector of arrears in Sorath. He chose Sayad Núrullah as his deputy, and sent him to recover the revenue for the current year.

Contest for the government of Gogha.

On the death of Salábat Khán Bábi, though the Mahárája had endeavoured to get Sher Khán Bábi appointed in place of his father, Gogha had been granted to Burhán-ul-Mulk, who chose Sohráb Khán as his deputy. At this time Sher Khán Bábi was at Baroda, and his younger brother, though he resisted, was compelled to leave Gogha. The deputy governor of Sorath complained to the governor of the oppressive conduct of Sohráb Khán. But Burhán-ul-Mulk supported Sohráb and having obtained for himself the government of Sorath, sent Sohráb Khán as his deputy to Júnágadh. In A.D. 1734, Ratansingh Bhandári, the deputy viceroy, who held in hatred Bhávsingh, son of Udaikaran, the hereditary officer of Vírамgám, persuaded Jawán-Mard Khán to imprison him and send him to Áhmedábád. Jawan-Mard Khán went so far as to arrest Bhávsingh, but was forced by his supporters to release him.

Disturbance at Vírамgám, 1734.

Baroda recovered by the Maráthás, 1734.

In this year Sher Khán Bábi, governor of Baroda, went to visit his lands at Bálásinor, leaving Muhammad Sarbáz in command at Baroda,

Muhammad Sha'h Emperor, 1721-1748.

Ratansingh Bhandári Deputy Viceroy in charge, 1733-1737.

Máhadáji Gáikwár, brother of Píláji, who then held Jambúsar, sending to Songad to Dámáji for aid, marched on Baroda with a strong force. The garrison made a brave defence, and Sher Khán hearing of the attack at Bálásinor, called for aid from Ratansingh Bhandári, the deputy viceroy, who directed Momín Khán, the governor of Cambay, to join Sher Khán and drive back the Maráthás. Sher Khán started at once for Baroda. But Máhadaji leaving a sufficient force before the town pushed on with the bulk of his army to meet Sher Khán, and, though he and his men fought bravely, defeated him, and then returned to Baroda, Sher Khán retiring to Bálásinor. Momín Khán, who arrived after Sher Khán's defeat, did not deem it prudent to engage the Maráthás, and retired to Cambay. In the meantime the garrison of Baroda, hopeless of succour, surrendered the town, and since that day Baroda has continued to be the head-quarters of the Gáikwár family.

Change of Governor at Víramgám.

Since Jawán Mard Khán's capture of Bhávsingh of Víramgám he had become much disliked. For this reason Ratansingh Bhandári, the deputy viceroy, transferred him to Kadi and Bijápur, and in his place appointed Sher Khán Bábi, whose father Muhammad Salábát Khán Bábi had been a popular governor of Víramgám. At this time Dhanrúp Bhandári, governor of Petlád, died, and the farm of the districts of Nadiád, Arhar-Mátar, Petlád, and Mahudha was given to Momín Khán. Mulla Muhammad A'li managed to write letters from his confinement at Surat to the Nizám; and as that chief was now not far from Surat, he wrote urgently to Teghbeg Khán to release him. Teghbeg Khán put the Mulla to death, and bribing the Nizám's messenger, gave out that he had died of joy at his release. Khushálchand, the chief of the merchants of Ahmedábád, having had a difference with Ratansingh, was forced to leave the city, and sought shelter at Cambay and afterwards at Júnágadh. Jawán Mard Khán, who was of an ambitious temperament, now conceived the design of conquering Ídar from Anandsingh and Ráisingh, brothers of the Maháraja Abheysingh. He accordingly marched upon Ídar, taking with him as allies Aghráji Koli of Katosan and Koli Amra of Elol Kánrah. In this strait Anandsingh and Ráisingh sought the aid of Malhárráv Holkár and Ránoji Sindia, who were at this time in Málwa. The Marátha chiefs at once marched to the help of Ídar, and Jawán Mard Khán, disbelieving the report of Marátha aid, continued to advance until he found himself opposed by an overwhelming force. Negotiations were entered into, and Jawán Mard Khán agreed to pay a sum of £17,500 (Rs. 1,75,000). Of the total amount £2500 (Rs. 25,000) were paid at once, and Zorávar Khán, brother of Jawán Mard Khán, and Ajabsingh, agent of Aghráji Koli, were kept as hostages until the balance should be paid. In this year Teghbeg Khán of Surat caused a wealthy merchant named Ahmed Chalabi to be assassinated, and confiscated his property. He also caused a fanatic named Sayad A'li to be put to death by certain Afgháns, as he considered that he might excite sedition.

Jawán Mard Khán fails in an attempt on Ídar.

Rivalry of Ratansingh Bhandári and Sohráb Khán, 1735.

In the following year (A.D. 1735) Dholka was assigned to Ratansingh Bhandári, and through the influence of Burhán-ul-Mulk, Sohráb

Chapter III.
Mughal Viceroys.
Muhammad Shah Emperor, 1721-1748.
Ratansingh Bhandári Deputy Viceroy in charge, 1733-1737.
Battle of Dholi. Defeat and Death of Sohráb Khán, 1735.

Khán was appointed governor of Víramgám. Ratansingh resented this, and eventually Víramgám was conferred on the Maháraja Abheysingh. When this order reached Sohráb Khán, he forwarded it to Burhán-ul-Mulk, and in consequence of Burhán-ul-Mulk's remonstrances, the arrangements were changed and Sohráb Khán appointed governor. Upon this Sohráb Khán, leaving Sádak Ali as his deputy in Junágaḍh, marched for Víramgám; while Ratansingh Bhandári, hearing of Sohráb Khán's approach, summoned Momín Khán and others to his assistance, and with his own army proceeded to Dholka and plundered Koth. From Koth he advanced and pitched at Harálah, about ten miles from Sohráb Khán's camp, and here he was joined by Momín Khán and others whom he had summoned to support him. After the union of these forces he marched to Dholi, six miles from Dhandhuka, at which place Sohráb Khán was then encamped. Ratansingh Bhandári now proposed that peace should be concluded, and that Sohráb Khán should enjoy Víramgám until final orders were passed by the emperor. Safdar Khán Bábi and others went to Sohráb Khán and endeavoured to bring him to consent to these terms; but he would not listen, and on both sides preparations were made for battle. During the following night Ratansingh Bhandári planned an attack on Sohráb Khán's camp. The surprise was complete. Sohráb Khán's troops fled, and himself, mortally wounded, shortly afterwards died. By the death of Sohráb Khán the family of Kázím Beg Khán became extinct. He was buried at Sihor in Káthiáváḍa.

Rivalry between Ratansingh Bhandári and Momín Khán, 1735.

After this success a single horseman attacked and wounded Ratansingh Bhandári in two places. The horseman was at once slain, but no one was able to recognize him. Ratansingh, who in two months had recovered from his injuries, now determined to attack Momín Khán, as that officer in the recent struggle had taken part with Sohráb Khán. Momín Khán hearing of Ratansingh's intentions, withdrew to Cambay. In the course of this year, on the expiry of the period of the farm of Mahudha, Arhar-Mátar, and Naḍiád, these districts were transferred from Momín Khán to Safdár Khán Bábi. Kaliánchand, a man of low origin, was appointed to Víramgám in place of Sher Khán Bábi, and instead of Sohráb Khán, Muhsin Khán Khálvi was made deputy governor of Sorath.

Maráthá Affairs.
Dámáji Gáikwár and Kántaji, 1735.
Battle of Ánand-Mogri. Defeat of Kántáji.

About this time Dámáji Gáikwár, who had been chosen by Umábái as her representative in Gujarát, appointed Rangoji to act as his agent. Kántáji being dissatisfied with this arrangement, in which his rights were ignored, marched into Gujarát. Rangoji met him, and a battle was fought at Ánand-Mogri, twenty-five miles south-east of Kaira, in which Kántáji was defeated and his son killed. In consequence of this reverse Kántáji retired to Petlád. Momin Khán, who with his army was drawn up near Petlád to oppose Rangoji, was compelled to retire to Cambay, where peace was concluded on condition that Dámáji should receive the one-fourth share of the revenues of the country north of the Mahi. As the districts where these battles were fought were held in farm by Safdar Khán Bábi, he suffered much loss, and consequently retired to Rádhanpur. Rangoji was joined by Dámáji Gáikwár, and these two leaders went together to Dholka. While they

Muhammad Sha'h Emperor, 1721-1748.

Ratansingh Bhandári Deputy Viceroy in charge, 1733-1737.

The Maráthás help Bhávsingh to expel the Víramgám Kasbátis.

were there, Bhávsingh of Víramgám invited them to that town, both on account of the annoyance he suffered from the Márvádis and that he might take vengeance on the Kasbátis for the murder of his father Udaikaran. He accordingly treacherously admitted the Maráthás and slew Daulat Muhammad Tánk, brother of the murderer of his father, and expelled the rest of the Kasbátis, while Kalián, the Márvádi administrator, was permitted to go to Áhmedábád. Leaving Rangoji at Víramgám, Dámáji marched into Sorath to levy tribute from the chiefs, and after collecting a portion of his dues, returned to the Dakhan. In the following year (A.D. 1736) Rangoji advanced as far as Bávla near Dholka wasting the country. Ratansingh Bhandári, the deputy viceroy, marched against him, and forced him to retire to Víramgám. Ratansingh pursued the Maráthás to Víramgám, attacked and defeated them capturing their baggage, but failed to prevent them taking shelter in the town. About this time some Marátha horse who were at Sarnál, otherwise called Thásra, joined the Kolis of those parts, advanced with them against Kapadvanj and without any serious resistance succeeded in capturing the town. Meanwhile though Ratansingh had summoned Momín Khán to his aid, he delayed coming, as he began to scheme independence at Cambay.

The Gáikwár and Peshwa Plunder the Country.

Ratansingh Bhandári heard that Pratápráv, brother of Dámáji, and Deváji Tákpar were advancing on Áhmedábád with 10,000 horse. At first he thought this a device to draw him from Víramgám, to whose walls his mines had reached. On ascertaining from trusty spies that the report was true, he raised the siege of Víramgám, returned rapidly to Áhmedábád, and pushing forward to meet Pratápráv, exacted tribute from the chiefs on the banks of the Vátrak. As Pratápráv drew near, the governor of the Bhíl district retired before him, and he continuing his advance, passed through Valad and Pethápur, and so by way of Chhála reached Dholka. Here, through Muhammad Ismáil, the governor of Dholka, he demanded from the Bhandári his share of the revenue. Afterwards, leaving 2000 horse in Dholka, he went to Dhandhúka. In the meantime Kántáji, who was a follower of Bájiráv Peshwa, joining with Malhárráv Holkar, advanced upon Ídar, and coming against Dánta, plundered that town. Some Nágar Bráhmans of the town of Vadnagar, who were settled in Dánta, tried to escape to the hills, but were intercepted and pillaged. The Maráthás then proceeded to Vadnagar and plundered the town. From Vadnagar they went as far as Pálanpur, where Pahár Khán Jhálori, being unable to oppose them, agreed to pay a tribute of £10,000 (Rs. 1 *lákh*). Kántáji and Malhárráv Holkar then marched into Márwár, while Pratápráv and Rangoji crossed over from Dhandhuka into Káthiávada and Gohilváda. About this time Muhammad Pahár Khán Jhálori was appointed deputy governor of Pátan on behalf of Vakhatsingh. As no settlement of his demands on the revenues of Dholka had yet been made, Pratápráv returned to that town and sent Narhar Pandit to receive the tribute due to him. Afterwards proceeding to Baroda with Rangoji they were summoned to Sorath by Dámáji to assist him. Sher Khán Bábi, who up to his time had been at Kaira, now came to Áhmedábád, and as the deputy viceroy

Chapter III.

Mughal Viceroys.

Muhammad Sháh Emperor, 1721-1748.

was displeased with Momin Khán's conduct when Víramgám was besieged, he appointed Sher Khán his own deputy at Petlád, Arhar-Mátar, and Nadiád. Afterwards on Momín Khán's remonstrance Subháchand Márvádi was appointed to examine the accounts and receive the revenue in place of Sher Khán. In A.D. 1737 Dámáji's brother Pratápráv, returning to his country after exacting tribute from the chiefs of Sorath, died of small-pox at Kánkar near Dholka. Momín Khán seeing that Sher Khán had not yet left Kaira, collected some men and came to Petlád, while Sher Khán went to Dehgám and awaited the departure of Rangoji. Ratansingh Bhandári made preparations to help Sher Khán and Momín Khán returned to Cambay.

Momín Khán Fifty-fourth Viceroy, 1737.

At this time as the Mahárája Abheysingh was not in favour at court, Momín Khán was appointed fifty-fourth viceroy. As he was unable to effect anything by himself he persuaded Jawán Mard Khán Bábi to join him by a promise of the government of Pátan and directed him to proceed and take up that appointment. Now the Jháloris were allies of the Ráthods, and Pahár Khán Jhálori, then in command of Pátan, opposed Jawán Mard Khán, but was finally obliged to vacate Pátan. Momín Khán, who had not hitherto produced the order appointing him viceroy, now made it public and began to act as viceroy with the title of Najm-ud-dauláh Momín Khán Bahádur Firúz Jang, and in A.D. 1737 sent a copy of this order to Abdúl Husain Khán, the deputy minister, and to Mustafíd Khán, who held the office of Kázi.

Sher Khán Bábi, wishing to remain neutral, retired to Bálásinor and Momín Khán summoned Rangoji, who was in the neighbourhood of Cambay, to his assistance. Rangoji agreed to aid him in expelling the Márvádis, on condition that, if successful, he should be granted one-half of the produce of Gujarát except the city of Áhmedábád, the lands in the neighbourhood of the city, and the port of Cambay. This disastrous alliance with the Maráthás gave the last blow to Mughal power in Gujarát, which otherwise might have lingered for at least a quarter of a century. Momín Khán lived to repent his conduct.

When Ratansingh Bhandári heard of the appointment of Momín Khán to be viceroy he wrote to Mahárája Abheysingh for orders. Meanwhile he sent Muhammadan officials to Cambay to persuade Momín Khán to take no further steps until a reply should be received to the reference Momín Khán had made to Ágra. The reply of the Mahárája was that Ratansingh should resist Momín Khán if he could. Ratansingh prepared to defend Áhmedábád while Momín Khán collecting an army, camped at the Náransar lake.

From the Náransar lake where Momín Khán remained encamped for one and a half months collecting his partisans he advanced to Sojitra, where he was joined by Jawán Mard Khán Bábi; and proceeding together they came to Vasu under Petlád, about twenty-six miles from Áhmedábád, and from Vasu to Kaira, about eighteen miles from the capital. At Kaira they encamped on the banks of the Vátrak, where, owing to the incessant rain, they were forced to remain for about a month. When the rain abated and the rivers were fordable, Momín Khán, moving to Áhmedábád, encamped in front of the city on the Kánkariya tank and prepared for a siege. About the same time Momín Khán's manager, Vajerám, whom he had sent to Songad to solicit Dámáji to march in person to his assistance, arrived and informed him that Dámáji would join him shortly. Zoráwar Khán, who had been left at the Marátha camp as security for the payment of the tribute, was recalled, and instead the district of Parántij was formally assigned to the Maráthás in payment of their demands. Some of the Maháraja's guns, which were being sent to A'hmedábád by his agents at Surat through Cambay for facility of transit, were about this time captured by a party of Momín Khán's men. When Ratansingh Bhandári wrote to the Maháraja of Momín Khán's advance on A'hmedábád, the Maháraja was much displeased, and went from the emperor's presence in anger. The nobles fearing the consequences, recalled him, and persuaded the emperor to re-appoint him viceroy of Gujarát.

Chapter III.

Mughal Viceroys.

Muhammad Sha'h Emperor, 1721-1748.

MOMÍN KHÁN Fifty-fourth Viceroy, 1737.

Lays Siege to A'hmedábád.

Momín Khán was secretly enjoined to disregard the Maháraja's appointment and persevere in expelling the Ráthods, and was assured of the emperor's approbation of this line of conduct. He therefore continued to prosecute the siege with vigour. In the meantime another order was received from the imperial court, confirming the reappointment of the Maháraja and appointing Fidá-ud-dín Khán to guard the city with 500 men, directing also that Momín Khán should return to Cambay. It was further stated that, as Ratansingh Bhandári had acted oppressively, some other person should be appointed deputy to fill his place, and that in the meantime a Rájput noble, named Abhaikaran, was to carry on the government. Shortly before this Muhammad Bákir Khán, son of Muátamid Khán, joined Momín Khán from Surat, while Sádik Ali Khán and his nephew reinforced him from Junágadh. When Momín Khán was informed of the purport of the imperial order he agreed to return to Cambay, provided Ratansingh Bhandári would quit the city, hand over charge to Abhaikaran, and admit Fidá-ud-dín Khán and his men into the city.

MAHÁRÁJA ABHEYSINGH Fifty-fifth Viceroy, 1737.

Momin Khán continues the Siege of A'hmedábád.

Ratansingh Bhandári determined not to leave the city, and prepared to defend himself to the last. Dámáji Gáikwár now joined Momín Khán from Songad. Momín Khán met Dámáji at I'sanpur, three miles from A'hmedábád, and made great show of friendship, calling him his brother. When Ratansingh Bhandári heard of the arrangements made between Dámáji and Momín Khán, he sent a message to Dámáji saying, 'Momín Khán has promised Rangoji half of the revenues of Gujarát excepting the city of Ahmedábád, the lands immediately round it, and Cambay. If you will join me, I will give you half of everything not excepting the city nor Cambay, and will send to your camp some of my chief landholders as security if you agree.' Dámáji showed this to Momín Khán, and asked him what he proposed to do. Momín Khán now perforce agreed to do the same; but instead of Cambay offered to make over to the Maráthás the whole district of Víramgám. Dámáji, accepting these terms, ceased to negotiate with Ratansingh. He then went on pilgrimage to Dúdesar, and returning in the same year, A.D. 1738, he and Rangoji began active operations against A'hmedábád. Their bombardment did so much

Defence of the City by Ratansingh Bhandári.

Chapter III.

Mughal Viceroys.

Muhammad Sha'h Emperor, 1721-1748.

Mahárája Abheysingh Fifty-fifth Viceroy, 1737.

damage to the city that Momín Khán repented having called them to his aid, and foresaw that if the Maráthás once gained any portion of the city it would be no easy matter to drive them out. Momín Khán now sent the writer of the Mirăt-i-A'hmedi to Ratansingh Bhandári, in hopes that he might withdraw peaceably, but Ratansingh refused to listen to any terms. After some time the Musalmáns under Kázim A'li Khán and others, and the Maráthás under Báburáv endeavoured to take the city by storm, but after a bloody contest were forced to retire. Next day Ratansingh, seeing that he could not long hold the city, entered into a negotiation with Momín Khán, and, on receiving a sum of money for his expenses, and on being allowed to retire with the honours of war, left the city.

Momín Khán captures A'hmedábád, 1738.

Momín Khán entered A'hmedábád. On the capture of the city, in accordance with Momín Khán's engagement, half of it was handed to the Maráthás. Momín Khán sent news of what had taken place to the emperor, and appointed Fidá-ud-dín Khán his deputy. Dámáji, who in the meantime had been to Sorath, now returned and was met by Rangoji, who accompanied him as far as the banks of the Mahi, whence Rangoji proceeded to Dholka. After spending a few days at Dholka, Rangoji returned to A'hmedábád and took charge of his share of the city, which comprised the Ráikhar, Khánjehán, and Jamálpur quarters as far as the Astoria and Ráipur gates. The city was thus equally divided, and the Astoria and Raipur gates were guarded by the Maráthás. At that time the inhabitants of A'hmedábád were chiefly Muhammadans, and the Maráthás, accustomed to extortion, attempting to oppress them, they rose against the strangers, and after a severe affray expelled the greater part of them from the city. Momín Khán, though secretly pleased, affected ignorance and sent Fidá-ud-dín Khán to reassure Rangoji. This with some difficulty he succeeded in doing and Rangoji remained in the city. Jawán Mard Khán was sent to Pátan, and, instead of Parántij, the district of Kherálu was granted to Zoráwar Khán Bábi.

Momín Khán Fifty-sixth Viceroy, 1738-1743.

Prosperity of A'hmedábád, 1738.

With the cessation of Marátha oppression, A'hmedábád began to recover its splendour and opulence. The emperor was much pleased with Momín Khán, and, raising his rank, presented him with a dress of honour, a sword, and other articles of value. At the close of the rainy season Momín Khán went to levy tribute from the chiefs on the banks of the Sábarmati, and Rangoji was asked to accompany him. They marched to Adálaj whence Fidá-ud-dín Khán, the deputy viceroy, returned to the city accompanied by Rámáji as deputy of Rangoji. Jawán Mard Khán and Sher Khán Bábi now joined the viceroy's camp, and, about the same time Hathising, chief of Pethápur, paid a visit to the viceroy and settled his tribute. From Adálaj they advanced to Mánsa, and were met by the Mánsa chief. From Mánsa they proceeded to Kadi, and from Kadi to Bijápur. After Momín Khán left the people of A'hmedábád were badly treated, and Rangoji, leaving his brother Akoji in camp, returned to the capital, whence he marched towards Víramgám and Sorath. Momín Khán went from Bijápur to Ídar, and there levied tribute from the chiefs of Mohanpur and Ranásan.

Chapter III.

Mughal Viceroys.

Muhammad Sha'h Emperor, 1721-1748.

Momín Khán Fifty-sixth Viceroy, 1738-1743.

The Viceroy collects Tribute, 1738.

When Momín Khán arrived at Ídar, A'nandsingh and Ráisingh, brothers of Mahárája Abheysingh, went to him and paid the tribute of Mohanpur and Ranásan as being within the limits of the Ídar territory. The matter was amicably settled, and the two brothers accompanied the viceroy as far as the Ídar frontier, when A'nandsingh returned to Ídar, and Ráisingh, at Momín Khán's request, remained with him, Momín Khán undertaking to pay the expenses of his men. Prathiráj, the chief of Mánsa, agreed to pay £2300 (Rs. 23,000) and the chief of Varsoda £1000 (Rs. 10,000) as tribute. At this time Sher Muhammad Khán Bábi was appointed to succeed Mír Dost A'li as deputy governor of Sorath. The Maráthás, who had attempted to deprive some of the Rasúlábád and Batwa Sayads of their land, were attacked by the Muhammadan population, and a few men were wounded on either side. Momín Khán, receiving tribute from various chiefs, had now reached Pálanpur, and Páhar Khán Jhálori, the governor of that place, was introduced to the viceroy by Sher Khán Bábi. As news was now received that Deváji Tákpar was advancing through the Baroda districts, Momín Khán marched towards A'hmedábád, dismissing Pahár Khán Jhálori on the Pálanpur frontier. Jawán Mard Khán Bábi, appointing his brother Safdar Khán Bábi as his deputy at Pátan, pushed forward in advance for A'hmedábád. Mámúr Khán, who had been chosen by Mír Huzabr A'li as his deputy in Sorath, now arrived and complained to Momín Khán regarding Sher Khán Bábi's appointment. Momín Khán said that, as neither had assumed charge of their duties, they should await final orders from the emperor. He then advanced to Hájipur, and thence encamped on the side of the city near Bahrámpur and occupied himself in strengthening the city defences. From that camp he proceeded to Ísanpur four miles south of A'hmedábád on his way to levy tribute from the Koli chiefs of the banks of the Vátrak. After this he proceeded to Kúlej on the Vátrak and levied tribute from the Koli chiefs of that neighbourhood. Hearing that Dámáji had left Songad, and crossing the Mahi had gone to A'rás, Momín Khán struck his camp and returned to the city, while Dámáji going to Dholka marched from that to Sorath. Momin Khán now permitted Sher Khán to return to his lands in Gogha, whence he proceeded to Júnágaḍh and took charge of the office of deputy governor.

Sher Khán Bábi Deputy Governor of Sorath, 1738.

In A.D. 1738, Mír Huzabr Khán, the governor of Sorath, died, and as Sher Khán had occupied Júnágaḍh, and taken into his employ all the troops of Mir Dost A'li, Mámúr Khán was obliged to resign his pretensions and return. The emperor now appointed Himmat A'li Khán, nephew of Momín Khán, governor of Sorath, and he wrote to his uncle to choose a fitting deputy. Momín Khán, as the Marátha incursions into Sorath increased yearly, and as Sher Khán Bábi was a man able to hold his own with them, suffered him to remain as deputy. When Dámáji returned to Víramgám, after levying tribute from the chiefs of Sorath, he was obliged to march against Kánji Koli, the chief of Chhaniár in the Chúnvál. As he could not prevail against them he was forced to call on Momín Khán for aid. Momín Khán sent Fidá-ud-dín Khán at the head of a well-equipped army. On their approach the

Chapter III.

Mughal Viceroys.

Muhammad Sháh Emperor, 1721-1748.

Momín Khán Fifty-sixth Viceroy, 1738-1743.

Kolis fled, and the village was burned, and Fidá-ud-dín Khán returned to the capital. Dámáji, leaving Rangoji as his deputy, returned to Songad. In this year, A.D. 1738, Hindustán was invaded by the great Persian Nádir Sháh, Dehli sacked, and the emperor made prisoner. Except that coin was struck in Nádir's name, the collapse of Mughal power caused little change in Gujarát.

The Deputy Viceroy collects Tribute, 1739.

In A.D. 1739 Fidá-ud-dín Khán was sent to levy tribute from the chiefs on the banks of the Sábarmati, and, accompanied by Jawán Mard Khán Bábi and Rája Ráisingh of Ídar, marched to Charárah. As the village of Pánmul under Bijápur had been assigned to the author of the Mirát-i-Ahmedi, he accompanied Fidá-ud-dín Khán, who marched to Ahmednagar, and demanded tribute from Jítsingh of Mohanpur and Ranásan. Jítsingh resisted and a doubtful battle was fought. Next day Fidá-ud-dín Khán changed his position and again attacked Jítsingh, who being defeated agreed to pay £1000 (Rs. 10,000). They then went to Ídar, where they were hospitably received by Rája Ráising, who presented the leaders with horses. From Ídar they proceeded to Vadnagar, which was under Jawán Mard Khán, who also received them courteously and presented horses. The army then marched to Visalnagar. On the arrival of the troops at Visalnagar, Jawán Mard Khán requested Fidá-ud-dín Khán to subdue Jámáji the Koli chief of Thara-Jámpur in the Kánkrej, who was then at Bálísana under Pátan and who was continually plundering the country. Fidá-ud-dín Khán marched to Bálísána, but Jámáji fled to Thara-Jámpur without risking a battle and the Muhammadans plundered Thara-Jámpur. From Bálísána Fidá-ud-dín marched to Kadi, and allowing Jawán Mard Khán to return to Pátan proceeded to Ahmedábád.

At Ahmedábád disputes between Rangoji and Momín Khán regarding the government of the city were frequent. In one serious disturbance Momín Khán was worsted and forced to sue for peace and grant Rangoji his half share both in the government and revenue, which, since the affray in A.D. 1738, Momín Khán had withheld. A formal agreement was drawn up but did not long remain in force. About this time Momín Khán's nephew Muhammad Momín Khán Bakhshi received a patent granting him the title of Nazar Ali Khán. The year A.D. 1739 was marked by a disastrous flood in the Sábarmati. In this year also the Maráthás under Chimnáji Apa achieved the memorable success of taking the fort of Bassein from the Portuguese.

Capture of Bassein by the Maráthás, 1739.

Tribute Expedition, 1740.

In A.D. 1740 on his return from Sorath, Dámáji Gáikwár took Rangoji to the Dakhan and appointed Malhárráv Khúni his deputy at Ahmedábád. Fidá-ud-dín Khán met the new deputy at Ísanpur and escorted him to the city. Shortly after Fidá-ud-dín Khán and Nazar Ali Khán started to collect tribute, and Jawán Mard Khán sent his brother Zoráwar Khán Bábi to accompany them. They advanced against Dábhora under Bahyal eighteen miles east of Ahmedábád in the Bhil district and fought with the chief, who agreed to pay tribute. Thence they went to Atarsumba, where the Kolis after a vain attempt to carry off their cannon agreed to pay tribute. The force then proceeded to Mándva and levied a contribution from the Mándva chief. They next went to Kapadvanj, and passing

Chapter III.

Mughal Viceroys.

Muhammad Sha'h Emperor, 1721-1748.

Momín Khán Fifty-sixth Viceroy, 1738-1743.

through Bálásinor reached Vírpur under Lunáváda. Here, from Sultánsingh, agent of the Lunáváda chief, they received two horses and £300 (Rs. 3000) as tribute. While at Lunáváda an order of recall came from Momín Khán, who intimated that Malhárráv Khúni had laid up large stores of grain and contemplated war. Fidá-ud-dín Khán at once pushed forward through Bálásinor and Kapadvanj, advancing rapidly towards the capital. On the way he received a second despatch from Momín Khán saying that, as the risk of war had for the present passed, they should advance to Petlád, where they would find Malhárrav Khúni and settle with him about the revenue accounts. They continued their march, and in two days reached Kaira, being joined on the way by Muhammad Kúli Khán, who was charged with messages from Momín Khán. At Kaira they found Muhammad Husain, nephew of Fidá-ud-dín Khán who had been sent with a force to Mahudha. As Malhárráv Khúni was at Pinj near Kaira, Fidá-ud-dín Khán expressed a wish to meet him, and it was agreed that both sides should go to the Petlád district and there settle the disputed collections. Shortly after they met and arrangements were in progress when the Kolis of the Bhíl district rebelled and Abdúl Husain Khán and Vajerám were sent against them. After burning two or three villages this detachment rejoined the main body, and not long after all returned to Ahmedábád. During A.D. 1740 Bájiráv Peshwa died.

The Viceroy at Cambay, 1741.

In A.D. 1741 Momín Khán went to Cambay, and while residing at Ghiáspur near that city received information that Dámáji had again appointed Rangoji his deputy in place of Malharráv Khúni, and shortly after Rangoji arrived at Petlád. At this time Momín Khán turned his attention to the falling off in the customs revenue of Cambay and appointed Ismáil Muhammad collector of customs. As he was anxious to clear some misunderstanding between Rangoji and himself, Momín Khán set out to visit Rangoji and assure him of his good wishes. At this time Bhávsingh of Vírамgám, who found the Maráthás even more troublesome than the Muhammadans, as soon as he heard of Malhárráv's recall, suddenly attacked the fort of Vírамgám and with the aid of some Arabs and Rohillás expelled the Marátha garrison and prepared to hold the fort on his own account. Shortly after Rangoji demanded that a tower in Ahmedábád, which had been raised a story by Momín Khán so as to command the residence of the Marátha deputy at the Jamálpur gate, should be reduced to its original height. At the same time he suggested that Momín Khán and he, uniting their forces, should advance and expel Bhávsingh from Vírамgám. Momín Khán agreed to both proposals. The addition to the tower was pulled down, and Momín Khán and Rangoji, marching against Vírамgám, laid siege to the town. Bhávsingh made a gallant defence, and Momín Khán, who was not sorry to see the Maráthás in difficulties, after a time left them and marched to Kadi and Bijápur to levy tribute. Rangoji continued the siege, and as Bhávsingh saw that even without Momín Khán the Marátha army was sufficient to reduce the place, he agreed to surrender Vírамgám, provided the fort of Pátdi and its dependent villages were granted

Bhávsingh surrenders Vírамgám and receives Pátdi.

Chapter III. Mughal Viceroys. Muhammad Sháh Emperor, 1721-1748. Momín Khán Fifty-sixth Viceroy, 1738-1743.

to him. Rangoji agreed, and thus the Maráthás again obtained possession of Víramgám, while Bhávsingh acquired Pátdi,[1] a property which his descendants hold to this day.

Siege of Broach by the Maráthás, 1741.

When Momín Khán arrived at Mánsa, about twenty-six miles north-west of Áhmedábád, hearing that Dámáji had crossed the Mahi with 10,000 men, he at once returned to the capital. Dámáji arrived at Mánsa and besieged it. The chiefs and Kolis defended the place bravely for about a month, when it fell into Dámáji's hands, who not only cleared the prickly-pear stockade which surrounded it, but also burned the town. From Mánsa Dámáji marched to Sorath. On his return he laid siege to Broach, a fort which, from its natural strength as well as from its favourable position on the Narbada, it had been the constant ambition both of Dámáji and of his father Píláji to capture. On the approach of Dámáji, Nek Álam Khán, who held the place in the interests of the Nizám, prepared to defend the fort, and wrote to the Nizám for aid. In reply the Nizám warned Dámáji not to attack his possessions. On receiving this letter Dámáji raised the siege and returned to Songad. It seems probable that concessions were made to tempt Dámáji to retire from Broach, and that the Gáikwár's share in the Broach customs dates from this siege.

Battle of Dholka, Defeat of the Maráthás, 1741.

In A.D. 1741 in a battle between Káim Kúli Khán, governor of Dholka, and Rangoji's deputy, the Maráthás were defeated. Momín Khán, at the request of Rangoji, made peace between them. Fidá-ud-dín Khán, who had recently been raised in rank with the title of Bahádur, starting to collect tribute burned down the refractory Koli village of Dabhora, and placing a post there, passed to Sátumba, Bálásinor, and Thásra. After the battle at Dholka, the building by Rangoji of the fort of Borsad, caused renewed fighting between the Muhammadans and Maráthás of Dholka. At the request of Muhammad Hádi Khán, governor of Dholka, Fidá-ud-dín Khán, passing through Mahudha to Petlád pushed forward to help him. In the meantime a battle was fought, in which the Maráthás under Malhárráv attacked Muhammad Hádi Khán, and after a short contest withdrew. Next day the Muhammadans, strengthened by the arrival of Fidá-ud-dín Khán, besieged Sojitra. A letter was written to Rangoji, asking the meaning of the attack, and he replied excusing himself and attributing it to the ignorance of Malhárráv. Muhammad Hádi Khán and the author of the Mirăt-i-Áhmedi eventually met Rangoji at Borsad, and settled that he and Fidá-ud-dín Khán should come together and arrange matters. But Rangoji in his heart intended to fight and wrote to his deputy Rámáji at Áhmedábád to be ready for war. Malhárráv now joined Rangoji at Borsad. At this time many misunderstandings and several fights between the Maráthás and the Muhammadans were appeased by Momín Khán and Rangoji, who, in spite of the ill-feeling among their subordinates and a certain distrust of each other's designs, appear throughout to have maintained a warm

Contests between the Musalmáns and Maráthás.

[1] Pátdi (north latitude 23° 10′; east longitude 71° 44′), at the south-east angle of the Ran of Cutch, fifty-two miles west of Áhmedábád.

Chapter III.

Mughal Viceroys.

Muhammad Sha'h Emperor, 1721-1748.

MOMÍN KHÁN Fifty-sixth Viceroy, 1738-1743.

mutual regard. Dámáji from his stronghold at Songad was too much occupied in Dakhan politics to give much attention to Gujarát. Rangoji, on the other hand, gained so much influence with the Gujarát chiefs, that at one time he succeeded in engaging Sajansingh Hazári in his service, and also induced Rája Ráisingh of Ídar to join him. But Momín Khán detached Ráisingh from this alliance, by placing him in charge of the post of Amaliára and granting him the districts of Modása, Meghrej, Ahmednagar, Parántij, and Harsol. Moreover the customary Gujarát sum at first sent daily by Rangoji to Rája Ráisingh for the expenses of his troops had begun to fall into arrears. Rája Ráisingh made his peace with Momín Khán through the mediation of Nazar A'li Khán, Momín Khán's nephew, who appears to have been one of the leading spirits of the time.

Disturbance at Áhmedábád, 1742.

In A.D. 1742 in another fight between the Maráthás and Muhammadans in A'hmedábád, the Muhammadans gained a slight advantage. After this Rangoji left the city, appointing as before Rámáji as his deputy, and joining Jagjíwan Pavár went to Borsad, where he had built a fort. At this time one Jívandás came with authority from the Nizám to act as collector of Dholka, part of the lands assigned to the Nizám as a personal grant, but failed to enforce his position. Shortly after this Rája A'nandsing of Ídar was killed, and his brother Ráising, taking leave, went to Ídar to settle matters. Momín Khán had his patent increased to the personal rank of commander of 6000 with a contingent of 6000 cavalry. He received a dress of honour, a jewelled turban, a plume, six pieces of cloth, an elephant, the order of Máhi-marátib,[1] and the title of Najm-ud-daulah Momín Khán Bahádur Diláwar Jang. Differences again broke out between Momín Khán and Rangoji, and again matters were settled by a friendly meeting between the two chiefs at Borsad, where Rangoji had taken up his residence. Momín Khán now went to Petlád, and from that to Cambay, where he was taken ill, but after six weeks came to Vasu, where Rangoji visited him. Here though again unwell he went to Dholka, and shortly afterwards he and Rangoji marched upon Límbdi, which at this time is mentioned as under Víramgám. While before Límbdi, Rangoji was summoned by Dámáji to help him against Bápu Náik, and at once started to his assistance. Momín Khán now marched into Gohilváḍa, and proceeded by Loliána to Gogha, then under the charge of a resident deputy of Sher Khán Bábi. Here he received tribute from the chief of Sihor, and from that, marching into Hálár, went against Navánagar. The Jám resisted for twenty days, and eventually, on his agreeing to pay £5000 (Rs. 50,000) as tribute, Momín Khán returned to A'hmedabád. During his absence in spite of stubborn resistance Nazar A'li Khán and Vajerám had collected tribute from the Koli chiefs. Rangoji, who had now left Dámáji, joined battle with Bápu Náik ere he crossed the Mahi, and Bápu Náik turned back. Rangoji therefore remained at Borsad, but hearing that Momín Khán's illness had become serious, he went once or twice to A'hmedábád to visit him.

The Viceroy collects Tribute in Káthiávaḍa.

[1] The Máhi-marátib was a banner having the likeness of a fish at its top.

Chapter III.

Mughal Viceroys.

Muhammad Sha'h Emperor, 1721-1748.

Death of Momín Khán, 1743.

Fidá-ud-dín acts as Viceroy, 1743.

In A.D. 1743 Momín Khán died. His wife, fearing lest Fidá-ud-dín Khán and Muftakhir Khán, Momín Khan's son, would deprive her of her estate, sought the protection of Rangoji. In the meantime Fidá-ud-dín Khán and Muftakhir Khán received an imperial order to carry on the government until a new viceroy should be appointed. At this time a man named Ánandrám, who had been disgraced by Momín Khán, went over to Rangoji and incited him to murder Fidá-ud-dín Khán and Muftakhir Khán. Rangoji with this intention invited them both to his house, but his heart failed him, and shortly afterwards Fidá-ud-dín Khán went to Cambay. Rangoji now determined at all hazards to assassinate Muftakhir Khán. With this object he took Muftakhir Khán's associates, Vajerám and Káim Kúli Khán, into his confidence. Muftakhir Khán accidentally heard of his designs, and remained on his guard. As Rangoji had failed to carry out his promise to raise Sher Khán Bábi to the post of deputy viceroy, Sher Khán advanced to Dholka and began plundering some Cambay villages. Rangoji, after another futile attempt to assassinate Muftakhir Khán, sent for his deputy Rámáji, who was then in the neighbourhood, and prepared to fight. Muftakhir Khán, on his part, summoned Fidá-ud-dín Khán from Cambay, and in a few days they succeeded in uniting their forces. Sher Khán Bábi deserting the cause of Rangoji, the Maráthás were worsted and Rangoji's house was besieged. Rangoji, being hard pressed, agreed to give up Ánandrám and to surrender both Borsad and Vírangám, Sher Khán Bábi becoming his security. In this way Fidá-ud-dín Khán became sole master of Gujarát.

Muftakhir Khán Defeats the Maráthás.

Dámáji Gáikwár Returns to Gujarát.

Shortly after Dámáji Gáikwár returned from Sátára and came to Cambay. In the meantime Rangoji, who had been living with Sher Khán Bábi, his security, contrived, with the connivance of Sher Khán, to escape together with his family. Fidá-ud-dín Khán was so greatly enraged with Sher Khán for this treachery, that Sher Khán leaving Áhmedábád on pretence of hunting, escaped to Bálásinor, where his wife joined him. Fidá-ud-dín Khán put Ánandrám to death, while Rangoji through the aid of Sher Khán Bábi's wife, made good his escape to Borsad. Fidá-ud-dín Khán had set out to collect tribute, when news arrived that Khanderáv Gáikwár, brother of Dámáji, had crossed the Mahi and joining Rangoji had laid siege to Petlád. On hearing this, Fidá-ud-din at once returned to Áhmedábád, and sent Valabhdás Kotwál to Khanderáv to complain of the misconduct of Rangoji.

Abdúl Ázíz Khán of Junnar, Viceroy (by a forged order).

After the death of Momín Khán, Jawán Mard Khán Bábi was the greatest noble in Gujarát. He began to aspire to power, and Fidá-ud-dín, who was not good in the field, had thoughts of appointing him as a deputy. While matters were in this state, and Jawán Mard Khán was already laying claim to the revenue of the district round Áhmedábád, an order was received appointing Abdúl Ázíz Khán the commander of Junnar, near Poona, to be viceroy of Gujarát. This order was forged by Abdúl Ázíz Khán in Jawán Mard Khán's interests, whom he appointed his deputy. Though Fidá-ud-dín Khán doubted the genuineness of the order, he was not powerful enough to remove Jawán Mard Khán, who accordingly proclaimed himself deputy viceroy. At this time the troops, clamorous on account of arrears,

Mutiny of the Troops.

Chapter III.

Mughal Viceroys.

Muhammad Sha'h Emperor, 1721-1748.

placed both Fidá-ud-dín Khán and Muftakhir Khán under confinement. Jawán Mard Khán assumed charge of the city and stationed his own men on guard. While Fidá-ud-dín Khán and Muftakir Khán were in confinement, Khanderáv Gáikwár sent them a message that if they would cause the fort of Petlád to be surrendered to him, he would help them. To this they returned no answer. Fidá-ud-dín Khán now entreated Jawán Mard Khán to interfere between him and his troops. Jawán Mard Khán accordingly persuaded the mutineers to release Fidá-ud-dín Khán, who eventually escaped from the city and went to A'gra.

Maráthás Capture Petlád.

Meanwhile Rangoji continued to press the siege of Petlád and the commander, A'gha Muhammad Husain, after in vain appealing for help to Jawán Mard Khán, was forced to surrender. Rangoji demolished the fort of Petlád and marched upon A'hmedábád. As he approached the city Jawán Mard Khán sent the writer of the Mirăt-i-A'hmedi and Ajabsingh to negotiate with Rangoji, who demanded all his former rights and possessions.

Muftakhir Khán Fifty-seventh Viceroy, 1743-44.

Appoints Jawán Mard Khán his Deputy.

News had now reached Dehli that a false viceroy was governing Gujarát, and accordingly Muftakhir Khán was chosen fifty-seventh viceroy, the order explaining that Abdúl A'zíz had never been appointed viceroy, and directing Jawán Mard Khán to withdraw from the conduct of affairs. Muftakhir Khán was perplexed how to act. He succeeded in persuading his troops that he would be able to pay them their arrears, and he sent a copy of the order to Jawán Mard Khán; and, as he dared not displace him, he informed Jawán Mard Khán that he had appointed him as his deputy, and that he himself would shortly leave A'hmedábád. Jawán Mard Khán, so far from obeying, ordered Muftakhir Khán's house to be surrounded. Eventually Muftakhir Khán, leaving the city, joined Rangojii, and then retired to Cambay.

The Maráthás in A'hmedábád.

Khanderáv Gáikwár returned, and, with the view of enforcing his claims, uniting with Rangoji, marched to Banjar, about five miles south of A'hmedábád. Jawán Mard Khán issuing from the city camped near the Kánkariya lake. Narhar Pandit and Krishnáji on behalf of the Marátha leaders were sent to Jawán Mard Khán to demand their former rights and possessions. Jawán at first refused, but in the end gave way and the Maráthás appointed Dádu Morár deputy of the city. Sher Khán Bábi now returned to Bálásinor. Khanderáv and Kánáji then went to Dholka, Rangoji to Petlád, and Khanderáv Gáikwár to Sorath. Fidá-ud-dín Khán requested Rangoji to help Muftakhir Khán; he replied that he was willing to help him, but had no money. Rangoji then accompanied Fidá-ud-dín Khán to Cambay, where Muftakhir Khán was. Negotiations were entered into, and the Kháns tried to collect £10,000 (Rs. 1 *lákh*) which Rangoji asked for to enable him to make military preparations to aid them. They raised £8000 (Rs. 80,000) with great difficulty and admitted Rangoji's Náib to a share in the administration. Rangoji withdrew to Borsad with the £8000 (Rs. 80,000) under the pretext that when the remaining £2000 (Rs. 20,000) were paid he would take action. Fidá-ud-dín Khán, annoyed at Rangoji's conduct, went to reside at Dhowan, a village belonging to Jálam Jália Koli.

Chapter III.

Mughal Viceroys.

Muhammad Shah Emperor, 1721-1748.

MUFTAKHIR KHÁN Fifty-seventh Viceroy, 1743-44.

Battle of Kím Kathodra. Defeat and Death of Abdúl Áziz Khán, 1744.

In A.D. 1744 Jawán Mard Khán, after appointing one of his brothers, Zoráwar Khán, his deputy at Pátan, and keeping his other brother Safdar Khán at Áhmedábád, advanced from the city to Kadi to collect tribute. His next step was to invite Abdúl Áziz Khán, the commander of Junnar, near Poona, to join him in Gujarát. Abdul Áziz accordingly set out from Junnar, taking with him Fatehyáb Khán, commander of the fort of Mulher in Báglan and Rustamráv Marátha. Directing his march in the first instance to Surat he was there watched in the interests of Dámáji Gáikwár, by Deváji Tákpar, the lieutenant of that chief, who, seeing that on leaving Surat, Abdúl Áziz continued to advance to Áhmedábád, pursued him to Kím Kathodra, about fifteen miles north-west of Surat, and there attacked him. In the engagement Deváji Tákpar, who had gained over Rustamráv Marátha, one of the leading men in Abdúl Áziz's army, was victorious. Abdúl Áziz Khán retired, but was so closely followed by the Maráthás, that at Pánoli he was forced to leave his elephant, and, mounting a horse, fled with all speed towards Broach. On reaching the Narbada he failed to find any boats, and, as his pursuers were close upon him, putting his horse at the water, he tried to swim the river; but, sticking fast in the mud, he was overtaken and slain by the Maráthás.

FAKHR-UD-DAULAH Fifty-eighth Viceroy, 1744-1748.

On hearing of the death of Abdúl Áziz, Jawán Mard Khán thought of joining Muftakhir Khán. Ere he could carry this plan into effect, the emperor receiving, it is said, a present of £20,000 (Rs. 2 *lákhs*) for the nomination, appointed Fakhr-ud-daulah Fakhr-ud-dín Khán Shujáât Jang Bahádur fifty-eighth viceroy of Gujarát. The new viceroy forwarded a blank paper to a banker of his acquaintance named Sitárám, asking him to enter in it the name of a fitting deputy. Sitárám filled in the name of Jawán Mard Khán, and Fakhr-ud-daulah was proclaimed viceroy. About this time Safdar Khán Bábi, after levying tribute from the Sábarmati chiefs, returned to Áhmedábád, and Khanderáv Gáikwár, as he passed from Sorath to Songad, appointed Rangoji his deputy. On being appointed deputy Rangoji sent Krishnáji instead of Morár Náik as his deputy to Áhmedábád, and himself proceeded to Arhar-Mátar on the Vátrak, and from that moved to Kaira to visit Jawán Mard Khán, with whom he established friendly relations. In the same year Áli Muhammad Khán, superintendent of customs, died, and in his place the author of the Mirát-i-Áhmedi was appointed. In this year, too, Pahár Khán Jhálori died, and his uncle, Muhammad Bahádur, was appointed governor of Pálanpur in his stead.

Jawán Mard Khán Bábi, Deputy Viceroy.

Khanderáv Gáikwár called to Sátára.

About this time Umábái, widow of Khanderáv Dábháde, summoned Khanderáv Gáikwár to help her in her attempt to lessen the power of the Peshwa. As Dámáji Gáikwár could not be spared from the Dakhan Khanderáv was appointed his deputy in Gujarát, and he chose one Rámchandra to represent him at Áhmedábád. When Fakhr-ud-daulah advanced to join his appointment as viceroy he was received at Bálásinor with much respect by Sher Khán Bábi. Jawán Mard Khán Bábi, on the other hand, determining to resist Fakhr-ud-daulah to the utmost of his power, summoned Gangádhar with a body of Marátha horse from Petlád, and posting them at Ísanpur, about ten miles south-west of the city, himself leaving the fortifications of Áhmedábád, encamped at

Chapter III.

Mughal Viceroys.

Muhammad Sháh Emperor, 1721-1748.

Fakhr-ud-daulah Fifty-eighth Viceroy, 1744-1748.

Asárva, about a mile and a half from the walls. During his progress towards the capital the new viceroy was joined by Ráisinghji of Ídar at Kapadvanj, and, advancing together, they arrived at Bhilpur, eighteen miles east of Áhmedábád. On their approach Jawán Mard Khán sent Safdar Khán and Gangádar to oppose them, and the two armies met about six miles from the capital. After some fighting Fakhr-ud daulah succeeded in forcing his way to the suburb of Rájpura, and next day continuing to drive back the enemy occupied the suburb of Bahrámpura and began the actual siege of the city. At this point affairs took a turn. Fakhr-ud-daulah was wounded and returned to his camp, while Jawán Mard Khán succeeded in winning over to his side Sher Khán Bábi and Ráisinghji of Ídar, two of the viceroy's chief supporters. The Mirát-i-Áhmedi especially notes that Rája Ráisingh asked for money to pay his troops but Fakhr-ud-daulah, not knowing that this rule had long been a dead letter, said that as he held a district on service tenure, it was not proper for him to ask for a money aid when on imperial service. Next day Fakhr-ud-daulah was surrounded by Safdar Khán Bábi and the Maráthás, and himself one wife and some children were taken prisoners, while another of his wives and his son, who had managed to escape to Sidhpur, were captured and brought back to Áhmedábád.

Defeat and capture of the Viceroy by Jawán Mard Khán Bábi.

After this Khanderáv Gáikwár returned to Gujarát to receive his share of the spoil taken from Fakhr-ud-daulah. Reaching Borsad, he took Rangoji with him as far as Áhmedábád, where he met Jawán Mard Khán, and obtained from Rangoji his share of the tribute. Khanderáv was not satisfied with Rangoji's accounts, and appointing a fresh deputy, he attached Rangoji's property, and before leaving Áhmedábád for Sorath, put him in confinement at Borsad. He also confined Fakhr-ud-daulah in the Ghiáspur outpost on the bank of the river Mahi. Meanwhile in consequence of some misunderstanding between Jawán Mard Khán Bábi and his brother Safdar Khán, the latter retired to Udepur, and Jawán Mard Khán went to Visalnagar then in the hands of his brother Zoráwar Khán. From Visalnagar, Jawán Mard Khán proceeded to Rádhanpur, and meeting his brother Safdar Khán, they became reconciled, and returned together to Áhmedábád. Khanderáv Gáikwár, who had in the meantime returned from Sorath, encamping at Dholka appointed Trimbakráv Pandit as his deputy at Áhmedábád in place of Moro Pandit. On hearing that Rangoji had been thrown into confinement, Umábái sent for him, and he along with Khanderáv Gáikwár repaired to the Dakhan.

Rangoji Disgraced by Khanderáv Gáikwár.

Shortly afterwards Punáji Vithal, in concert with Trimbak Pandit, being dissatisfied with Jawán Mard Khán, began to intrigue with Fakhr-ud-daulah. In the meantime Umábái had appointed Rangoji as her deputy, and, as he was a staunch friend of Jawán Mard Khán, he expelled Trimbakráv from Áhmedábád, and himself collected the Marátha share of the city revenues. Upon this Punáji Vithal sent Gangádhar and Krishnáji with an army, and they, expelling the Muhammadan officers from the districts from which the Maráthás levied the one-fourth share of the revenue, took the management of them into their own hands. Rangoji now asked Sher Khán Bábi to help him. Sher

Punáji Vithal and Fakhr-ud-daulah oppose Rangoji and Jawán Mard Khán.

Chapter III.

Mughal Viceroys.

Muhammad Sha'h Emperor, 1721-1748.

FAKHR-UD-DAULAH Fifty-eighth Viceroy, 1744-1748.

Khán agreed; but as he had not funds to pay his troops, he delayed, and afterwards plundered Mahudha and Naḍiád. As Rangoji failed to join him, Sher Khán proceeded by himself to Kapadvanj, and from Kapadvanj marched against the Marátha camp, with which Fakhr-ud-daulah was then associated. On the night after his arrival, the Maráthás made an attack on Sher Khán's camp, in which many men on both sides were slain. Next morning the battle was renewed, but on Sher Khán suggesting certain terms the fighting ceased. That very night, hearing that Rangoji had reached Bálásinor, Sher Khán stole off towards Kapadvanj. Punáji and Fakhr-ud-daulah followed in pursuit but failed to prevent Rangoji and Sher Khán from joining their forces.

Siege of Kapadvanj by Fakhr-ud-daulah, 1746.

In A.D. 1746 a battle was fought in the neighbourhood of the town of Kapadvanj in which Sher Khán was wounded. He was forced to take shelter with Rangoji in Kapadvanj, while Fakhr-ud-daulah, Gangádhar, and Krishnáji laid siege to that town. At this time the Lunáváḍa chief asked Malhárráv Holkar on his way back from his yearly raid into Málwa, to join him in attacking Virpur. Holkar agreed and Virpur was plundered. Rangoji, hearing of the arrival of Holkar, begged him to come to his aid, and on promise of receiving a sum of £20,000 (Rs. 2 *lákhs*) and two elephants, Holkar consented. Gangádhar, Krishnáji, and Fakhr-ud-daulah, hearing of the approach of Holkar, raised the siege of Kapadvanj, and marching to Dholka expelled the governor of that district. Shortly afterwards on a summons from Dámáji and Khanderáv Gáikwár Rangoji retired to Baroda. Meanwhile Fakhr-ud-daulah, Krishnáji, and Gangádhar advanced to Jetalpur in the Daskroi sub-division of A'hmedábád and, taking possession of it, expelled A'mbar Habshi, the deputy of Jawán Mard Khán. Dámáji and Khanderáv Gáikwár passed from Baroda to Vasu, where they were met by Krishnáji and Gangádhar, whom Dámáji censured for aiding Fakhr-ud-daulah. On this occasion Dámáji bestowed the districts of Baroda Naḍiád and Borsad on his brother Khanderáv, an action which for ever removed any ill feeling on the part of Khanderáv. Then, proceeding to Goklej, Dámáji had an interview with Jawán Mard Khán. From Goklej he sent Kánoji Tákpar with Fakhr-ud-daulah to Sorath, and himself returned to Songaḍ. As Borsad had been given to Khanderáv, Rangoji fixed on Umreth as his residence.

At the approach of Holkar the Siege is raised.

In this year, A.D. 1746, Teghbeg Khán, governor of Surat, died, and was succeeded by his brother Safdar Muhammad Khán, who, in acknowledgment of a present of seven horses, received from the emperor the title of Bahádur. At this time Tálib A'li Khán died, and the writer of the Mirăt-i-A'hmedi was appointed minister by the emperor. In A.D. 1747 Rangoji returned to A'hmedábád, and Jawăn Mard Khán had an interview with him a few miles from the city. Shortly after this the Kolis of Mehmúdábád and Mahudha rebelled, but the revolt was speedily crushed by Sháhbáz Rohilla.

Momin Khán II. Governor of Cambay, 1748.

During this year Najm Khán, governor of Cambay, died. Muftakhir Khán, son of Najm-ud-daulah Momín Khán I., who had also received the title of Momín Khán, informed the emperor of Najm

Chapter III.

Mughal Viceroys.

Muhammad Sháh Emperor, 1721-1748.

Fakhr-ud-daulah Fifty-eighth Viceroy, 1744-1748.

Khán's death, and himself assumed the office of governor in which in A.D. 1748 he was confirmed. On hearing of the death of Najm Khán, on pretence of condoling with the family of the late governor, Fidá-ud-dín Khán marched to Cambay, but as he was not allowed to enter the town he retired. He afterwards went to Umreth and lived with Rangoji. Kánoji Tákpar, who had gone with Fakhr-ud-daulah into Sorath, now laid siege to and took the town of Vanthali. As it was nearly time for the Maráthás to return to their country, Kánoji and Fakhr-ud-daulah, retiring to Dholka, expelled Muhammad Jánbáz, the deputy governor. Rangoji, who had at this time a dispute with Jawán Mard Khán regarding his share of tribute, now came and joined them, and their combined forces marched upon Sánand, where, after plundering the town, they encamped. It was now time for Kánoji to withdraw to the Dakhan. Rangoji and Fakhr-ud-daulah, remaining behind to collect tribute from the neighbouring districts, marched to Ísanpur, where they were opposed by Jawán Mard Khán. On this occasion both Jawán Mard Khán and Fakhr-ud-daulah sought the alliance of Rája Ráisingh of Ídar. But, as he offered more favourable terms, Rája Ráisingh determined to join Fakhr-ud-daulah. Sher Khán Bábi also joined Fakhr-ud-daulah, who, thus reinforced, laid siege to Áhmedábád. While these events were passing at Áhmedábád, Hariba, an adopted son of Khanderáv Gáikwár, at that time in possession of the fort of Borsad, began to plunder Rangoji's villages under Petlád, and, attacking his deputy, defeated and killed him. On this Rangoji withdrew from Áhmedábád, attacked and captured the fort of Borsad, and forced Hariba to leave the country. Jawán Mard Khán now sent for Janárdhan Pandit, Khanderáv's deputy at Nadiád, and, in place of Rangoji's representative, appointed him to manage the Marátha share of Áhmedábád.

Increased Strength of Fakhr-ud-daulah's Party.

Dissensions among the Maráthás.

Surat Affairs, 1748.

During these years important changes had taken place in the government of Surat. In A.D. 1734, when Mulla Muhammad Áli, the chief of the merchants and builder of the Athva fort, was killed in prison by Teghbeg Khán, the Nizám sent Sayad Miththan to revenge his death. Sayad Miththan was forced to return unsuccessful. After Teghbeg Khán's death Sayad Miththan again came to Surat and lived there with his brother Sayad Achchan, who held the office of paymaster. Sayad Miththan tried to get the government of the town into his hands, but, again failing, committed suicide. His brother Sayad Achchan then attacked and took the citadel, expelling the commander; and for several days war was waged between him and the governor Safdar Muhammad Khán with doubtful success. At last Sayad Achchan called to his aid Malhárráv, the deputy at Baroda, and their combined forces took possession of the whole city. During the sack of the city Malhárráv was killed and the entire management of affairs fell into the hands of Sayad Achchan. Safdar Muhammad Khán, the late governor, though obliged to leave the city, was determined not to give up Surat without a struggle, and raising some men opened fire on the fort. Sayad Achchan now begged the Arab Turk English Dutch and Portuguese merchants to aid him. A deed addressed to the emperor and the Nizám, begging that Sayad Achchan should be appointed

Chapter III. Mughal Viceroys. Muhammad Sháh Emperor, 1721-1748. FAKHR-UD-DAULAH Fifty-eighth Viceroy, 1744-1748.

governor, was signed by all the merchants except by Mr. Lamb the English chief, and though he at first refused, he was in the end persuaded by the other merchants to sign. The merchants then assisted Sayad Achchan, and Safdar Muhammad Khán retired to Sindh.

Mulla Fakhr-ud-din Escapes to Bombay.

Meanwhile, on account of some enmity between Mulla Fakhr-ud-dín, the son of Mulla Muhammad Áli, chief of the merchants, and Sayad Achchan, the Mulla was thrown into prison. Mr. Lamb went to Sayad Achchan, and remonstrating with him suggested that the Mulla should be sent for. Sayad Achchan agreed, but on the way Mr. Lamb carried off Mulla Fakhr-ud-dín to the English factory, and afterwards sent him to Bombay in disguise. In the meantime Kedárji Gáikwár, a cousin of Dámáji's, whom, with Malhárrav, Sayad Achchan had asked to his help, arrived at Surat, and though Sayad Achchan had been successful without his aid, Kedárji demanded the £30,000 (Rs. 3 *lákhs*) which had been promised him. As the Sayad was not in a position to resist Kedárji's demands, and as he had no ready money to give him, he made over to him a third of the revenues of Surat until the amount should be paid. As before this another third of the revenues of Surat had been assigned to Háfiz Masûud Khán, the deputy of Yákut Khán of Janjira, the emoluments of the governor of Surat were reduced to one-third of the entire revenue and this was divided between the Mutasaddi and Bakhshi.

Cession of Surat Revenue to the Gáikwár, 1747.

Famine, 1747.

In this year (A.D. 1747, S. 1803) there was a severe shock of earthquake and a great famine which caused many deaths. In the following year Jawán Mard Khán endeavoured to recapture Jetalpur, but failed. About the same time Umábái died, and Dámáji's brother Khanderáv, who was on good terms with Ambika wife of Báburáv Senápati, the guardian of Umábái's son, procured his own appointment as deputy of his brother Dámáji in Gujarát. On being appointed deputy Khanderáv at once marched against Rangoji to recover Borsad, which, as above mentioned, Rangoji had taken from Haríba. Their forces were joined by two detachments, one from Momín Khán under the command of Ágha Muhammad Husain, the other from Jawán Mard Khán commanded by Janárdhan Pandit. The combined army besieged Borsad. After a five months' siege Borsad was taken, and Rangoji was imprisoned by Khanderáv. On the fall of Borsad Sher Khán Bábi and Rája Ráisingh of Ídar, who were allies of Rangoji, returned to Bálásinor and Ídar; Fakhr-ud-daulah was sent to Petlád and Fidá-ud-dín Khán, leaving Umreth, took shelter with Jetha, the chief of Atarsumba.

Maráthá Dissensions.

Fall of Borsad.

MAHÁRÁJA VAKHATSINGH Fifty-ninth Viceroy, 1748.

In this year the emperor Muhammad Sháh died and was succeeded by his son Ahmed Sháh (A.D. 1748-1754). Shortly after Ahmed's accession Mahárája Vakhatsingh, brother of Mahárája Abheysingh, was appointed fifty-ninth viceroy of Gujarát. When he learned what was the state of the province, he pleaded that his presence would be more useful in his own dominions, and never took up his appointment of viceroy. Vakhatsingh was the last viceroy of Gujarát nominated by the imperial court, for although by the aid of the Maráthás Fakhr-ud-daulah was of importance in the province, he had never been able

Chapter III.

Mughal Viceroys.

Ahmed Sha'h Emperor, 1748-1754.

MAHÁRÁJA VAKHATSINGH Fifty-ninth Viceroy, 1748.

to establish himself as viceroy. In this year also occurred the death of Khushálchand Sheth, the chief merchant of Áhmedábád.

Khanderáv Gáikwár appointed Rághavshankar his deputy at Áhmedábád, and Safdar Khán Bábi issued from Áhmedábád with an army to levy tribute from the chiefs on the banks of the Sábarmati. When Fakhr-ud-daulah, the former viceroy, heard of the appointment of Maháraja Vakhatsingh, seeing no chance of any benefit from a longer stay in Gujarát, he retired to Dehli. In A.D. 1748 Ásif Jáh, Nizám-ul-Mulk, died at an advanced age, leaving six sons and a disputed succession.

Disorder Spreads.

About the same time Bálájiráv Peshwa, who was jealous of the power of the Gáikwár, sent a body of troops, and freed Rangoji from the hands of Khanderáv Gaikwár. During these years adventurers, in different parts of the country, taking advantage of the decay of the central power, endeavoured to establish themselves in independence. Of these attempts the most formidable was the revolt of one of the Pátan Kasbátis who established his power so firmly in Pátan that Jawán Mard Khán found it necessary to proceed in person to reduce him. Shortly afterwards Jawán Mard Khán deemed it advisable to recall his brothers Safdar Khán and Zoráwár Khán, who were then at Únja under Pátan, and took them with him to Áhmedábád. Fidá-ud-dín Khán who had been residing at Atarsumba now asked permission to return to Áhmedábád, but as Jawán Mard Khán did not approve of this suggestion, Fidá-ud-dín departed to Broach and there took up his residence. Janárdhan Pandit marched to Kaira and the Bhíl district to levy tribute, and Khanderáv appointed Shevakrám his deputy.

SURAT AFFAIRS. A.D. 1750.

Sayad Achchan Unpopular.

In the meantime at Surat, Sayad Achchan endeavoured to consolidate his rule, and with this view tried to expel Háfiz Masûud Habshí, and prevent him again entering the city. But his plans failed, and he was obliged to make excuses for his conduct. Sayad Achchan then oppressed other influential persons, until eventually the Habshí and others joining, attacked him in the citadel. Except Mr. Lamb, who considered himself bound by the deed signed in A.D. 1747 in favour of Sayad Achchan, all the merchants of Surat joined the assailants.

Safdar Muhammad brought back by the Dutch.

Among the chief opponents of Sayad Achchan were the Dutch, who sending ships brought back Safdar Muhammad Khán from Thatta, and established him as governor of Surat. The English factory was next besieged, and, though a stout resistance was made, the guards were bribed, and the factory plundered.

Sayad Achchan Retires.

In A.D. 1750 Sayad Achchan, surrendering the citadel to the Habshí, withdrew first to Bombay and then to Poona, to Bálájiráv Peshwa. Shortly afterwards, in consequence of the censure passed upon him by the Bombay Government for his support of Sayad Achchan, Mr. Lamb committed suicide. Wearied by these continual contests for power, the merchants of Surat asked Rája Raghunathdás, minister to the Nizám, to choose them a governor. Rája Raghunáthdás accordingly nominated his own nephew, Rája Harprasád, to be governor, and the writer of the Mirãt-i-Áhmedi to be his deputy. But before Rája Harprasád could join his appointment at Surat, both he and his father were slain in battle.

Chapter III.
Mughal Viceroys.
Ahmed Sha'h Emperor, 1748-1754.
Jawán Mard Khán and the Peshwa, 1750.

In the same year, A.D. 1750, occurred the deaths of Rája Ráisingh of Ídar, of Safdar Khán Bábi of Bálásinor, and of Fidá-ud-dín Khán, who had for some time been settled at Broach. Jawán Mard Khán, who, seeing that they were inclined to become permanent residents in Gujarát, was always opposed to the Gáikwár's power, now entered into negotiations with Bálájiráv Peshwa. He chose Patel Sukhdev to collect the Marátha revenue and asked the Peshwa to help him in expelling Dámáji's agents. The Peshwa, being now engaged in war in the Dakhan with Salábat Jang Bahádur, son of the late Nizám, was unable to send Jawán Mard Khán any assistance. Towards the close of the year Jawán Mard Khán started from A'hmedábád to collect tribute from the Sábarmati chiefs. Returning early in A.D. 1751, at the request of Jetha Patel a subordinate of Bhávsingh Desái, he proceeded to Banod or Vanod under Víramgám and reduced the village. A'li Muhammad Khán, the author of the Mirát-i-A'hmedi, who about this time was raised in rank with the title of Bahádur, states that owing to the Marátha inroads most of the districts had passed entirely into their possession; in others according to agreements with Jawán Mard Khán they held a half share. Consequently in spite of new taxes, the entire remaining income of the province was only four *lákhs* of rupees, and it was impossible to maintain the military posts or control the rebellious Kolis.

The Peshwa and Gáikwár, 1751.

It was in this year (A.D. 1751) that the Peshwa, decoying Dámájiráv into his power, imprisoned him and forced him to surrender half of his rights and conquests in Gujarát. Taking advantage of the absence of the Gáikwár and his army in the Dakhan, Jawán Mard Khán marched into Sorath. He first visited Gogha, and then levying tribute in Gohilváḍa advanced into Káthiáváḍa and marched against Navánagar, and, after collecting a contribution from the Jám, returned to A'hmedábád. In the following year (A.D. 1752), as soon as the news reached Gujarát that the Maráthás' share in the province had been divided between the Peshwa and Gáikwár, Momín Khán, who was always quarrelling with the Gáikwár's agent, sending Varajlál his steward to Bálájiráv Peshwa begged him to include Cambay in his share and send his agent in place of the Gáikwár's agent. Bálájiráv agreed, and from that time an agent of the Peshwa was established at Cambay. In the same year Raghunáthráv, brother of the Peshwa, entering Gujarát took possession of the Rewa and Mahi Kántha districts and marched on Surat. Shiaji Dhangar was appointed in Shevakrám's place as Dámáji's deputy, and Krishnáji came to collect the Peshwa's share.

Broach Independent, 1752.

Up to this time the city of Broach had remained part of the Nizám's personal estate, managed by Abdúllah Beg, whom, with the title of Nek A'lam Khán, A'sif Jáh the late Nizám-ul-Mulk had chosen his deputy. On the death of Abdúllah Beg in A.D. 1752 the emperor appointed his son to succeed him with the same title as his father, while he gave to another son, named Mughal Beg, the title of Khertalab Khán. During the contests for succession that followed upon the death of the Nizám in A.D. 1752, no attempt was made to enforce the Nizám's claims on the lands of Broach; and for the future, except for the share of the revenue paid to the Maráthás, the governors of Broach were practically independent.

Chapter III.

Mughal Viceroys.

Ahmed Sha'h Emperor, 1748-1754.

Pándurang Pandit Repulsed at Ahmedábád, 1752.

The Peshwa now sent Pándurang Pandit to levy tribute from his share of Gujarát, and that officer crossing the Mahi marched upon Cambay. Momín Khán prepared to oppose him, but the Pandit made friendly overtures, and eventually Momín Khán not only paid the sum of £700 (Rs. 7000) for grass and grain for the Pandit's troops, but also lent him four small cannon. Pándurang Pandit then marched upon Ahmedábád, and encamping near the Kánkariya lake laid siege to the city which was defended by Jawán Mard Khán. During the siege Pándurang Pandit, sending some troops, ravaged Níkol, part of the lands of Ali Muhammad Khán Bahádur, the author of the Mirăt-i-Ahmedi. Meanwhile, as the operations against Ahmedábád made no progress, Pándurang Pandit made offers of peace. These Jawán Mard Khán accepted, and on receiving from Jawán Mard Khán the present of a mare and a small sum of money under the name of entertainment, the Marátha leader withdrew to Sorath.

Marátha Invasion.

About this time the Peshwa released Dámáji Gáikwár on his promise to help the Peshwa's brother Raghunáthráv, who was shortly afterwards despatched with an army to complete the conquest of Gujarát. Meanwhile Jawán Mard Khán's anxiety regarding the Maráthás was for a time removed by the departure of Pándurang Pandit. And, as the harvest season had arrived, he with his brother Zoráwar Khán Bábi, leaving Muhammad Mubáriz Sherwáni behind as his deputy, set out from Ahmedábád to levy tribute from the chiefs of the Sábar Kántha. Certain well informed persons, who had heard of Raghunáthráv's preparations for invading Gujarát, begged Jawán Mard Khán not to leave the city but to depute his brother Zoráwar Khán Bábi to collect the tribute. Jawán Mard Khán, not believing their reports, said that he would not go more than from forty-five to sixty miles from the city, and that, should the necessity of any more distant excursion arise, he would entrust it to his brother. Jáwan Mard Khán then marched from the city, levying tribute until he arrived on the Pálanpur frontier about seventy-five miles north of Ahmedábád. Here meeting Muhammad Bahádur Jhálori, the governor of Pálanpur, Jawán Mard Khán was foolishly induced to join him in plundering the fertile districts of Sirohi, till at last he was not less than 150 miles from his head-quarters. Meanwhile Raghunáthráv, joining Dámáji Gáikwár, entered suddenly by an unusual route into Gujarát, and news reached Ahmedábád that the Maráthás had crossed the Narbada. On this the townspeople sent messenger after messenger to recall Jawán Mard Khán, and building up the gateways prepared for defence, while the inhabitants of the suburbs, leaving their houses, crowded with their families into the city for protection. Raghunáthráv, hearing that Jawán Mard Khán and his army were absent from the city, pressed on by forced marches, and crossing the river Mahi despatched an advance corps under Vithal Sukhdev. Kosáji, proprietor of Nadiád, at Dámáji Gáikwár's invitation also marched towards Ahmedábád, plundering Mehmúdábád Khokhri, only three miles from the city. In the meantime Vithal Sukhdev reached Kaira, and taking with him the chief man of that place, Muhammad Daurán, son of Muhammad Bábi, continued his march. He was shortly joined by Raghunáthráv, and the combined forces now proceeded to Ahmedábád and encamped by the Kánkariya

Chapter III.
Mughal Viceroys.
Ahmed Sháh Emperor, 1748-1754.

lake. Next day Raghunáthráv moved his camp to near the tomb of Hazrat Sháh Bhíkan,[1] on the bank of the Sábarmati to the south-west of the city. Raghunáthráv now proceeded to invest the city, distributing his thirty to forty thousand horse into three divisions. The operations against the north of the city were entrusted to Dámáji Gáikwár; those on the east to Gopál Hari; while the troops on the south and west were under the personal command of Raghunáthráv and his officers.

Return of Jawán Mard Khán.

After leaving Sirohi Jawán Mard Khán had gone westwards to Tharád and Váv, so that the first messengers failed to find him. One of the later messengers, Mándan by name, who had not left Áhmedábád until the arrival of Raghunáthráv at the Kánkariya lake, made his way to Váv and Tharád, and told Jawán Mard Khán what had happened. Jawán Mard Khán set out by forced marches for Rádhanpur, and leaving his family and the bulk of his army at Pátan, he pushed on with 200 picked horsemen to Kadi and from that to Áhmedábád, contriving to enter the city by night. The presence of Jawán Mard Khán raised the spirits of the besieged, and the defence was conducted with ardour. In spite of their watchfulness, a party of about 700 Maráthás under cover of night succeeded in scaling the walls and entering the city. Ere they could do any mischief they were discovered and driven out of the town with much slaughter. The bulk of the besieging army, which had advanced in hopes that this party would succeed in opening one of the city gates, were forced to retire disappointed. Raghunáthráv now made proposals for peace, but Jawán Mard Khán did not think it consistent with his honour to accept them. On his refusal, the Marátha general redoubled his efforts and sprung several mines, but owing to the thickness of the city walls no practicable breach was effected. Jawán Mard Khán now expelled the Marátha deputies, and continuing to defend the city with much gallantry contrived at night to introduce into the town by detachments a great portion of his army from Pátan. At length, embarrassed by want of provisions and the clamour of his troops for pay, he extorted £5000 (Rs. 50,000) from the official classes. As Jawán Mard was known to have an ample supply of money of his own this untimely meanness caused great discontent. The official classes who were the

He enters Áhmedábád.

Gallant Defence of the City.

[1] Of the death at the age of nine years of this son of Saint Sháh-i-Álam the Mirăt-i-Áhmedi (Printed Persian Text, II. 26) gives the following details: Malik Seif-ud-dín, the daughter's son of Sultán Áhmed I., had a son who he believed was born to him by the prayer of Saint Sháh-i-Álam. This boy who was about nine years old died. Malik Seif-ud-dín ran to Sháh-i-Álam, who used then to live at Asáwal, two or three miles east of Áhmedábád, and in a transport of grief and rage said to the Saint: 'Is this the way you deceive people? Surely you obtained me the gift of that boy to live and not to die? This I suppose is how you will keep your promise of mediating for our sinful souls before Alláh also?' The Saint could give no reply and retired to his inner apartments. The stricken father went to the Saint's son Sháh Bhíkan, who, going in to his father, entreated him to restore the Malik's boy to life. The Saint asked his son 'Are you prepared to die for the boy?' Sháh Bhíkan said 'I am ready.' The Saint, going into an inner room, spread his skirts before Alláh crying 'Rájanji,' a pet name by which the Saint used to address Alláh, meaning Dear King or Lord, 'Rájanji, here is a goat for a goat; take thou this one and return the other.' Lamentations in the Saint's harem showed that half of the prayer was granted and the Malik on returning to his house found the other half fulfilled.

Chapter III. Mughal Viceroys. Ahmed Sha'h Emperor, 1748-1754. Jawán Mard Khán Surrenders.

repository of all real power murmured against his rule and openly advocated the surrender of the city, and Jawán Mard Khán, much against his will, was forced to enter into negotiations with Raghunáthráv.

Raghunáthráv was so little hopeful of taking A'hmedábád that he had determined, should the siege last a month longer, to depart on condition of receiving the one-fourth share of the revenue and a safe conduct. Had Jawán Mard Khán only disbursed his own money to pay the troops, and encouraged instead of disheartening the official class, he need never have lost the city. At last to Raghunáthráv's relief, Jawán Mard Khán was reduced to treat for peace through Vithal Sukhdev. It was arranged that the Maráthás should give Jawán Mard Khán the sum of £10,000 (Rs. 1 *lákh*) to pay his troops, besides presenting him with an elephant and other articles of value. It was at the same time agreed that the garrison should leave the city with all the honours of war. And that, for himself and his brothers, Jawán Mard Khán should receive, free from any Marátha claim, the districts of Pátan, Vadnagar, Sami, Munjpur, Visalnagar, Tharád, Kherálu, and Rádhanpur with Tervada and Bijápur. It was further agreed that one of Jawán Mard Khán's brothers should always serve the Maráthás with 300 horse and 500 foot, the expenses of the force being paid by the Maráthás. It was also stipulated that neither the Peshwa's army nor his deputy's, nor that of any commander should enter Jawán Mard Khán's territory, and that in A'hmedábád no Marátha official should put up at any of the Khán Bahádur's mansions, new or old, or at any of those belonging to his brothers followers or servants. Finally that the estates of other members of the family, namely Kaira, Kasba Mátar and Bánsa Mahudha, which belonged to Muhammad Khán, Khán Daurán, and A'bid Khán were not to be meddled with, nor were encroachments to be allowed on the lands of Káyam Kúli Khán or of Zoráwar Khán. This agreement was signed and sealed by Raghunáthráv, with Dámáji Gáikwár (half sharer), Malhárráv Holkar, Jye A'pa Sindhia, Rámchandar Vithal Sukhdev, Sakhárám Bhagvant, and Mádhavráv Gopálráv as securities. The treaty was then delivered to Jawán Mard Khán, and he and his garrison, marching out with the honours of war, the Maráthás took possession of A'hmedábád on April 2nd, 1753.

The Maráthás take Possession, 1753.

Collect Tribute.

On leaving A'hmedábád Jawán Mard Khán retired to Pátan. At A'hmedábád Raghunáthráv with Dámáji arranged for the government of the city, appointing Shripatráv his deputy. He then marched into Jhálávada to levy tribute from the Limbdi and Wadhwán chiefs; and was so far successful that Harbhamji of Limbdi agreed to pay an annual tribute of £4000 (Rs. 40,000). As the rainy season was drawing near Raghunáthráv returned to Dholka, while Patel Vithal Sukhdev forced Muhammad Bahádur, the governor of Pálanpur, to consent to a payment of £11,500 (Rs. 1,15,000). From Dholka Raghunáthráv went to Tárápur, about twelve miles north of Cambay, and compelled Momín Khán to submit to an annual payment of £1000 (Rs. 10,000). At the same time A'li Muhammad Khán Bahádur, the author of the Mirăt-i-A'hmedi, was appointed collector of customs, and his former grants were confirmed and he was allowed to retain

Chapter III.
Mughal Viceroys.
Ahmed Shah Emperor, 1748-1754.
Mughal Coinage Ceases.

his villages of Sayadpur and Kûjádh close to Áhmedábád, as well as the village of Pánmûl in Bijápur. Dámáji Gáikwár, after levying tribute in the Vátrak Kántha, went to Kapadvanj, which he took from Sher Khán Bábi. From Kapadvanj he passed to Nadiád and appointed Shevakrái to collect his half share of the revenue of Gujarát. In the Áhmedábád mint, coin ceased to be struck in the emperor's name and the suburbs of the city which had been deserted during the siege were not again inhabited. The Kolis commenced a system of depredation, and their outrages were so daring that women and children were sometimes carried off and sold as slaves. After the rains were over (A.D. 1754) Shetuji, commander of the Áhmedábád garrison, and Shankarji, governor of Vírangám, were sent to collect tribute from Sorath. Though the imperial power was sunk so low, the emperor was allowed to confer the post of Kázi of the city on Kázi Rûkn-ul-Hak Khán who arrived at Áhmedábád and assumed office. At the close of the year Shripatráv, who was anxious to acquire Cambay, marched against Momín Khán. After two doubtful battles in which the Maráthás gained no advantage, it was agreed that Momín Khán should pay a sum of £700 (Rs. 7000), and Shripatráv departed from Áhmedábád early in A.D. 1754. When the Kolis heard of the ill success of the Maráthás at Cambay, they revolted and Rághoshankar was sent to subdue them. In an engagement near Luhára in Bahyal in His Highness the Gáikwár's territory about eighteen miles east of Áhmedábád, Rághoshankar scattered the Kolis, but they again collected and forced the Maráthás to retire. At this time Shetuji and Shankarji returned from Sorath, where they had performed the pilgrimage to Dwárka. Shetuji was sent to the Bhíl district against the Kolis. He was unsuccessful, and was so ashamed of his failure that he returned to the Dakhan and Dandu Dátátri was appointed in his place.

Failure of an Attempt on Cambay, 1753.

The Kolis.

In this year died Nek Álam Khán II. governor of Broach. He was succeeded by his brother Khertalab Khán who expelled his nephew Hámid Beg, son of Nek Álam Khán. Hámid Beg took refuge in Surat. At Bálásinor a dispute arose between Sher Khán Bábi and a body of Arab mercenaries who took possession of a hill, but in the end came to terms. With the Peshwa's permission his deputy Bhagvantráv marched on Cambay. But Varajlál, Momín Khán's steward, who was then at Poona, sent word to his master, who prepared himself against any emergency. When Bhagvantráv arrived at Cambay he showed no hostile intentions and was well received by Momín Khán. Subsequently a letter from Bhagvantráv to Sálim Jamádár at Áhmedábád ordering him to march against Cambay fell into Momín Khán's hands. He at once surrounded Bhagvantráv's house and made him prisoner. When the Peshwa heard that Bhagvantráv had been captured, he ordered Ganesh Ápa, governor of Jambusar, as well as the governors of Vírangám, Dhandhuka, and other places to march at once upon Cambay. They went and besieged the town for three months, but without success. Eventually Shripatráv, the Peshwa's deputy, sent the author of the Mirăt-i-Áhmedi to negotiate, and it was agreed that Bhagvantráv should be released and that no alteration should be made in the position of Momín Khán. Shortly afterwards Shripatráv was recalled by the Peshwa and his place supplied by an

Maráthás Attack Cambay, 1754.

Chapter III.

Mughal Viceroys.

officer of the name of Rágho. About this time Khertalab Khán, governor of Broach, died, and quarrels arose regarding the succession. Ultimately Hamid Beg, nephew of Khertalab Khán, obtained the post, and he afterwards received an imperial order confirming him as governor, and bestowing on him the title of Neknám Khán Bahádur.

A'lamgir II. Emperor, 1754-1759.

At Dehli, during A.D. 1754, the emperor A'hmed Sháh was deposed, and Âzíz-ud-dín, son of Jahándár Sháh, was raised to the throne with the title of A'lamgír II. After his release Bhagvantráv established himself in the Cambay fort of Nápád and not long after began to attack Momín Khán's villages. After several doubtful engagements peace was concluded on Momín Khán paying £1000 (Rs. 10,000) on account of the usual share of the Maráthás which he had withheld. This arrangement was made through the mediation of Tukáji, the steward of Sadáshiv Dámodar, who had come to Gujarát with an army and orders to help Bhagvantráv. As Momín Khán had no ready money Tukáji offered himself as security and Bhagvantráv and Tukáji withdrew to the Dakhan. Momín Khán's soldiery now clamoured for pay. As he was not in a position to meet their demands he sent a body of men against some villages to the west belonging to Limbdi and plundered them, dividing the booty among his troops. In the following year, A.D. 1755, Momín Khán went to Gogha, a port which, though at one time subordinate to Cambay, had fallen into the hands of Sher Khán Bábi, and was now in the possession of the Peshwa's officers. Gogha fell and leaving a garrison of 100 Arabs under Ibráhím Kúli Khán, Momín Khán returned to Cambay, levying tribute. He then sent the bulk of his army under the command of Muhammad Zamán Khán, son of Fidá-ud-dín Khán, and Varajlál his own steward, to plunder and collect money in Gohilváḍa and Káthiáváḍa. Here they remained until their arrears were paid off, and then returned to Cambay. After this Momín Khán plundered several Petlád villages and finally, in concert with the Kolis of Dhowan, attacked Jambusar and carried off much booty. Momín Khán next marched against Borsad, and was on the point of taking the fort when Sayáji, son of Dámáji Gáikwár, who lived at Baroda, hearing of Momín Khán's success, came rapidly with a small body of men to the relief of the fort and surprised the besiegers. The Muhammadan troops soon recovered from the effects of the surprise, and Sayáji fearing to engage them with so small a force retired. On Sayáji's departure Momín Khán raised the siege of Borsad and returned to Cambay.

Contest with Momín Khán Renewed, 1754.

Momín Khán takes Gogha, 1755.

Momín Khán recovers A'hmedábád, 17th Oct. 1756.

In the year A.D. 1756 the rains were very heavy, and the walls of A'hmedábád fell in many places. Momín Khán, hearing of this as well as of the discontent of the inhabitants, resolved to capture the city. He sent spies to ascertain the strength of the garrison and set about making allies of the chief men in the province and enlisting troops. About this time Rághoji, the Marátha deputy, was assassinated by a Rohilla. As soon as Momín Khán heard of Rághoji's death he sent his nephew, Muhammad Zamán Khán, with some men in advance, and afterwards himself at the close of the year, A.D. 1756, marched from Cambay and camped on the Vátrak. From this camp they moved to Kaira, and from Kaira to A'hmedábád. After one or two fights in

Chapter III. Mughal Viceroys. A'lamgir II. Emperor, 1754-1759.

the suburbs the Muhammadans, finding their way through the breaches in the walls, opened the gates and entered the town. The Kolis commenced plundering, and a hand-to-hand fight ensued, in which the Maráthás were worsted and were eventually expelled from the city. The Kolis attempted to plunder the Dutch factory, but met with a spirited resistance, and when Shambhúrám, a Nágar Bráhman, one of Momín Khán's chief supporters, heard it he ordered the Kolis to cease attacking the factory and consoled the Dutch.

Jawán Mard Khán allies himself with the Maráthás.

In the meantime Jawán Mard Khán, who had been invited by the Maráthás to their assistance, set out from Pátan, and when he arrived at Pethápur and Mánsa he heard of the capture of A'hmedábád. On reaching Kalol he was joined by Harbhamrám, governor of Kadi. They resolved to send Zoráwar Khán Bábi to recall Sadáshiv Dámodar, and to await his arrival at Víramgám. Shevakrám, the Gáikwár's deputy, had taken refuge at Dholka. Momín Khán himself now advanced, and entering A'hmedábád on the 17th October 1756, appointed Shambhúrám his deputy. Sadáshiv Dámodar now joined Jawán Mard Khán at Víramgám, and at Jawán Mard Khán's advice it was resolved, before taking further steps, to write to the Peshwa for aid. Jawán Mard Khán, although he held large service estates, charged the Maráthás £150 (Rs. 1500) a day for his troops. Jawán Mard Khán and the Maráthás then advanced to Sánand and Jitalpur, and thence marched towards Cambay. On their way they were met, and, after several combats, defeated by a detachment of Momín Khán's army. Momín Khán sent troops to overrun Kadi, but Harbhamrám, the governor of Kadi, defeated the force, and captured their guns. When the emperor heard of the capture of Gogha, he sent a sword as a present to Momín Khán; and when the news of the capture of A'hmedábád reached A'gra, Momín Khán received many compliments. Bálájirav Peshwa on the other hand was greatly enraged at these reverses. He at once sent off Sadáshiv Rámchandra to Gujarát as his deputy, and Dámáji and Khanderáv Gáikwár also accompanied him with their forces. Momín Khán refusing to give up A'hmedábád, prepared for defence. Sadáshiv Rámchandra, Dámáji and Khanderáv Gáikwár advanced, and, crossing the Mahi, reached Kaira. Here they were met by Jawán Mard Khán and the rest of the Marátha forces in Gujarát, and the combined army advancing against the capital camped by the Kánkariya lake.

Maráthás Invest A'hmedábád, 1756.

The Maráthás now regularly invested the city, but Momín Khán, aided by Shambhúrám, made a vigorous defence. Up to this time Jawán Mard Khán was receiving £150 (Rs. 1500) daily for the pay of his own and his brother's troops. Sadáshiv Rámchandra, considering the number of the troops too small for so large a payment, reduced the amount and retained the men in his own service. After a month's siege, Momín Khán's troops began to clamour for pay, but Shambhúrám, by collecting the sum of £10,000 (Rs. 1 *lákh*) from the inhabitants of the town managed for the time to appease their demands. When they again became urgent for pay, Shambhúrám diverted their thoughts by a general sally from all the gates at night. On this occasion many men were slain on both sides, and many of the inhabitants deserted the town. The copper vessels of such of the townspeople as had fled

Chapter III.

Mughal Viceroys.

A'lamgir II. Emperor, 1754-1759.

were melted and coined into money and given to the soldiery. In this state of affairs an order arrived from the imperial court bestowing on Momín Khán a dress of honour and the title of Bahádur. Although the imperial power had for years been merely a name Momín Khán asked and obtained permission from the besiegers to leave the city and meet the bearers of the order. The Maráthás redoubled their efforts. Still though the besiegers were successful in intercepting supplies of grain the garrison fought gallantly in defence of the town.

Ráv of Ídar helps Momín Khán, 1757.

At this juncture, in A.D. 1757, Rája Shivsingh of Ídar, son of the late Anandsingh, who was friendly to Momín Khán, sent Sajánsingh Hazári with a force to assist the besieged. On their way to A'hmedábád, Harbhamrám with a body of Maráthás attacked this detachment, while Momín Khán sent to their aid Muhammad Lál Rohilla and others, and a doubtful battle was fought. Shortly afterwards Sadáshiv Rámchandar made an attempt on the fort of Kálikot. The fort was successfully defended by Jamádár Núr Muhammad, and the Maráthás were repulsed. The Maráthás endeavoured in vain to persuade Shambhúrám to desert Momín Khán, and though the garrison were often endangered by the faithlessness of the Kolis and other causes, they remained staunch. Momín Khán, though frequently in difficulties owing to want of funds to pay his soldiery, continued to defend the town. The Maráthás next tried to seduce some of Momín Khan's officers, but in this they also failed, and in a sally Shambhúrám attacked the camp of Sadáshiv Ramchandar, and burning his tents all but captured the chief himself.

Successful Sally under Shambhurám.

Negotiations for Peace.

When the siege was at this stage, Hassan Kúli Khán Bahádur, viceroy of Oudh, relinquishing worldly affairs and dividing his property among his nephews, set out to perform a pilgrimage to Makkah. Before he started Shuja-úd-daulah, the Nawáb of Lucknow, requested him on his way to visit Bálájiráv, and endeavour to come to some settlement of A'hmedábád affairs. Accordingly, adopting the name of Sháh Núr, and assuming the dress of an ascetic, Hassan Kúli made his way to Poona, and appearing before the Peshwa offered to make peace at A'hmedábád. Sháh Núr with much difficulty persuaded the Peshwa to allow Momín Khán to retain Cambay and Gogha without any Marátha share, and to grant him a *lákh* of rupees for the payment of his troops, on condition that he should surrender A'hmedábád. He obtained letters from the Peshwa addressed to Sadáshiv Rámchandra to this effect, and set out with them for A'hmedábád. When he arrived Sadáshiv Rámchandra was unwilling to accede to the terms, as the A'hmedábád garrison were reduced to great straits. Sháh Núr persuaded him at last to agree, provided Momín Khán would surrender without delay. Accordingly Sháh Núr entered the city and endeavoured to persuade Momín Khán. Momín Khán demanded in addition a few Petlád villages, and to this the Maráthás refused their consent. Sháh Núr left in disgust. Before many days Momín Khán was forced to make overtures for peace. After discussions with Dámáji Gáikwár, it was agreed that Momín Khán should surrender the city, receive £10,000 (Rs. 1 *lákh*) to pay his soldiery, and be allowed to retain Cambay as heretofore, that is to say that the Peshwa should, as

Chapter III.
Mughal Viceroys.
A'lamgir II. Emperor, 1754-1759.

formerly, enjoy half the revenues. In addition to this Momin Khán had to promise to pay the Maráthás a yearly tribute of £1000 (Rs. 10,000) and to give up all claims on the town of Gogha and hand over Shambhúrám to the Maráthás. It was also arranged that the £3500 (Rs. 35,000) worth of *ashrafis* which he had taken through Jamádár Sálim should be deducted from the £10,000 (Rs. 1 *lákh*). Momín Khán surrendered the town on February 27th, 1758.

Marátha Arrangements in A'hmedábád.

Sadáshiv Rámchandar and Dámáji Gáikwár entered the city and undertook its management on behalf of the Maráthás. Of the other chiefs who were engaged in prosecuting the siege, Sadáshiv Dámodar returned to the Dakhan and Jawán Mard Khán receiving some presents from Sadáshiv Rámchandar departed for Pátan after having had a meeting with Dámáji Gáikwár at a village a few miles from the capital. Shambhurám, the Nágar Bráhman, who had so zealously supported Momín Khán, when he saw that further assistance was useless, tried to escape, but was taken prisoner and sent in chains to Baroda. Sadáshiv Rámchandar, on taking charge of the city, had interviews with the principal officials, among whom was the author of the Mirăt-i-A'hmedi, and, receiving them graciously, confirmed most of them in their offices. Then, after chosing Náro Pandit, brother of Pándurang Pandit, to be his deputy in A'hmedábád, he started on an expedition to collect tribute in Jhálává̧da and Sorath. On receiving the government of the city the Marátha generals ordered new coin bearing the mark of an elephant goad to be struck in the A'hmedábád mint. Sayájiráv Gáikwár remained in A'hmedábád on behalf of his father Dámáji, and shortly afterwards went towards Kapadvanj to collect tribute. Thence at his father's request he proceeded to Sorath to arrange for the payment of the Gáikwár's share of the revenues of that district. On his return to Cambay Momín Khán was much harassed by his troops for arrears of pay. The timely arrival of his steward Varajlál with the Peshwa's contribution of £10,000 (Rs. 1 *lákh*) enabled him to satisfy their demands.

New Coins.

Momín Khán at Cambay.

Momín Khán now began to oppress and extort money from his own followers, and is said to have instigated the murder of his steward Varajlál. Sadáshiv Rámchandar went from Porbandar to Júnágadh, where he was joined by Sayájiráv Gáikwár. At Júnágadh Sher Khán Bábi presented Sadáshiv Rámchandra and Siyájiráv with horses and they spoke of the necessity of admitting a Marátha deputy into Júnágadh. Nothing was settled as the Maráthás were forced to return to A'hmedábád. In accordance with orders from the Peshwa, Shambhurám and his sons, who were still in confinement, were sent to Poona. Dámáji Gáikwár was also summoned to Poona, but he did not go. In this year Ráo Lakhpat of Kachh presented Kachh horses and Gujarát bullocks to the emperor, and in return received the title of Mírza Rája.

Expedition from Kachh against Sindh, 1758.

About this time the Ráo of Kachh, who planned an expedition against Sindh, solicited aid both from Dámáji Gáikwár and Sadáshiv Rámchandar to enable him to conquer Thatta, and, as he agreed to pay expenses, Sadáshiv sent Ranchordás, and Dámáji sent Shevakrám to help him. In this year also Neknám Khán, governor of Broach, received the title of Bahádur and other honours. In A.D. 1758, Sadáshiv Rámchandar advanced to Kaira and after settling accounts

Chapter III.

Mughal Viceroys.

A'lamgir II. Emperor, 1754-1759.

with Dámáji's agent proceeded against Cambay. Momín Khán, who was about to visit the Peshwa at Poona, remained to defend the town, but was forced to pay arrears of tribute amounting to £2000 (Rs. 20,000). In this year Sher Khán Bábi died at Júnágadh, and the nobles of his court seated his son Muhammad Mahábat Khán in his place.

The Maráthás levy Tribute.

Shortly after at the invitation of the Peshwa, Dámáji Gáikwár went to Poona, and sent his son Sayájiráv into Sorath. After his success at Cambay Sadáshiv Rámchandra levied tribute from the chiefs of Umeta, and then returned. On his way back, on account of the opposition caused by Sardár Muhammad Khán son of Sher Khán Bábi, the chief of Bálásinor, Sadáshiv Rámchandar besieged Bálásinor and forced the chief to pay £3000 (Rs. 30,000). Next marching against Lunáváda, he compelled the chief Dípsingh to pay £5000 (Rs. 50,000). Sadáshiv then went to Visalnagar and so to Pálanpur, where Muhammad Khán Bahádur Jhálori resisted him; but after a month's siege he agreed to pay a tribute of £3500 (Rs. 35,000). Passing south from Pálanpur, Sadáshiv went to Únja-Unáva, and from that to Katosan where he levied £1000 (Rs. 10,000) from the chief Shuja, and then proceeded to Límbdi.

SURAT AFFAIRS, 1758.

During A.D. 1758 important changes took place in Surat. In the early part of the year Sayad Muîn-ud-dín, otherwise called Sayad Achchan, visited the Peshwa at Poona, and received from him the appointment of governor of Surat. Sayad Achchan then set out for his charge, and as he was aided by a body of Marátha troops under the command of Muzaffar Khán Gárdi and had also secured the support of Neknám Khán, the governor of Broach, he succeeded after some resistance in expelling Ali Nawáz Khán, son of the late Safdar Muhammad Khán, and establishing himself in the government. During the recent troubles, the English factory had been plundered and two of their clerks murdered by Ahmed Khán Habshi, commandant of the fort. The English therefore determined to drive out the Habshi and themselves assume the government of the castle. With this object men-of-war were despatched from Bombay to the help of Mr. Spencer, the chief of the English factory, and the castle was taken in March A.D. 1759, and Mr. Spencer appointed governor. The Peshwa appears to have consented to this conquest. The Marátha troops aided and made a demonstration without the city, and a Marátha man-of-war which had been stationed at Bassein, came to assist the English. A Mr. Glass appears to have been appointed *kiledár* under Governor Spencer.

The English take command of Surat, 1759.

Momín Khán Visits Poona, 1759.

Shortly afterwards Momín Khán, by the advice of Sayad Husain, an agent of the Peshwa, contracted friendship with the English through Mr. Erskine, the chief of the English factory at Cambay. Momín Khán then asked Mr. Erskine to obtain permission for him to go to Poona by Bombay. Leave being granted, Momín Khán set out for Surat, and was there received by Mr. Spencer. From Surat he sailed for Bombay, where the governor, Mr. Bourchier, treating him with much courtesy, informed the Peshwa of his arrival. The Peshwa sending permission for his further advance to Poona, Momín Khán took leave of Mr. Bourchier and proceeded to Poona.

Chapter III.

Mughal Viceroys.

Álamgir II. Emperor, 1754-1759.

Sadáshiv Rámchandra Peshwa's Viceroy, 1760.

The Maráthás in Káthiáváḍa, 1759.

From Limbḍi, to which point his tribute tour has been traced, Sadáshiv Rámchandra advanced against Dhrángadhra, when the chief who was at Halvad sent an army against him. The Maráthás, informed of the chief's design, detaching a force, attacked Halvad at night, and breaching the walls forced open the gates. The chief retired to his palace, which was fortified, and there defended himself, but was at last forced to surrender, and was detained a prisoner until he should pay a sum of £12,000 (Rs. 1,20,000). The neighbouring chiefs, impressed with the fate of Halvad, paid tribute without opposition. Sadáshiv Rámchandra now went to Júnágaḍh, but ere he could commence operations against the fortress, the rainy season drew near, and returning to Áhmedábád he prepared to depart for Poona. Sayáji Gáikwár, who was also in Sorath collecting tribute, amongst other places besieged Kundla, and levying from that town a tribute of £7500 (Rs. 75,000) returned to the capital. During this time Khanderáv Gáikwár had been levying tribute from the Kolis, and after visiting the Bhíl district went to Bijápur, Ídar, Kadi, Dholka, and Naḍiád. The chief of Halvad on paying his £12,000 (Rs. 1,20,000) was allowed to depart, and Dípsingh of Lunáváḍa, who was also a prisoner, was sent to Lunáváḍa and there released after paying his tribute. On receiving the news of the capture of the Surat fort by the English the emperor issued an order, in the name of the governor of Bombay, confirming the command of the fort to the English instead of to the Habshis of Janjira, appointing the Honourable East India Company admirals of the imperial fleet, and at the same time discontinuing the yearly payment of £2000 (Rs. 20,000) formerly made to the Habshi on this account. When in the course of the following year, A.D. 1760, this imperial order reached Surat, Mr. Spencer and other chief men of the city went outside of the walls to meet and escort the bearers of the despatch. Sadáshiv Rámchandra was appointed viceroy of Áhmedábád on behalf of the Peshwa. Bhagvantráv now conquered Bálásinor from Sardár Muhammad Khán Bábi, and then marching to Sorath, collected the Peshwa's share of the tribute of that province, according to the scale of the previous year. Sayáji Gáikwár, when Bhagvantráv had returned, set out to Sorath to levy the Gáikwár's share of the tribute. He was accompanied by Harbhamrám whom Dámáji Gáikwár had specially sent from his own court to act as Kámdár to Sayáji. When Sadáshiv Rámchandra reported to the Peshwa the conquest of Bálásinor by Bhagvantráv he was highly pleased, and gave Bhagvantráv a dress of honour and allowed him to keep the elephant which he had captured at Lunáváḍa; and passed a patent bestowing Bálásinor upon him. Momín Khán, after making firm promises to the Peshwa never to depart from the terms of the treaty he had made with the Maráthás, left Poona and came to Bombay, where he was courteously entertained by the Governor, and despatched by boat to Surat. From Surat he passed to Cambay by land through Broach. Sayáji Gáikwár had returned to Áhmedábad from Sorath in bad health, and his uncle Khánderáv Gáikwár, who had been vainly endeavouring to subdue the Kolis of Lúhára, came to Áhmedábád and took Sáyáji Gáikwár to Naḍiád. In 1761 Sadáshiv Rámchandra was displaced as viceroy of Gujarát by

Chapter III.

Mughal Viceroys.

A'lamgir II. Emperor, 1754-1759.

A'pa Ganesh Viceroy, 1761.

A'pa Ganesh. This officer acted in a friendly manner to Momín Khán, and marching to Cambay, he fixed the Marátha share of the revenues of that place for that year at £8400 (Rs. 84,000), and then went to A'hmedábád by way of Dákor. Narbherám collected this year the Gáikwár's share of the tribute of Sorath and Sayáji Gáikwár went to Baroda. On his return to A'hmedábád at the end of the year, Sayáji sacked and burned the Koli village of Lúhára in Bahyal about eighteen miles east of A'hmedábád. Jawán Mard Khán now issued from Pátan and levied small contributions from the holdings in Vágad, as far as Anjár in Kachh. From Vágad he proceeded to Sorath, and in concert with Muhammad Mahábat Khán of Júnágadh and Muhammad Muzáffar Khán Bábi, between whom he made peace, he levied tribute in Sorath as far as Loliyána, and returned to Pátan.

Pánipat, 1761.

While their power and plunderings were thus prospering in Gujarát the crushing ruin of Pánipat (A.D. 1761) fell on the Maráthás. Taking advantage of the confusion that followed, the Dehli court despatched instructions to the chief Musalmán nobles of Gujarát, directing Momín Khán, Jáwan Mard Khán, and the governor of Broach to join in driving the Maráthás out of the province. In consequence of this despatch Sardár Muhammad Khán Bábi, defeating the Marátha garrison, regained Bálásinor, while the governor of Broach, with the aid of Momín Khán, succeeded in winning back Jambúsar. A'pa Ganesh, the Peshwa's viceroy, remonstrated with Momín Khán for this breach of faith. In reply his envoy was shown the despatch received from Dehli, and was made the bearer of a message, that before it was too late, it would be wisdom for the Maráthás to abandon Gujarát. Things were in this state when Dámáji Gáikwár, wisely forgetting his quarrels with the Peshwa, marched to the aid of Sadashiv with a large army. Advancing against Cambay he attacked and defeated Momín Khán, plundering one of his villages. But the Maráthás were too weak to follow up this success, or exact severer punishment from the Musalmán confederates. A'pa Ganesh invited Sardár Muhammad Khán Bábi to Kaira, and on condition of the payment of tribute, agreed to allow him to keep possession of Bálásinor. Subsequently Damáji's energy enabled him to enlarge the power and possessions of the Gáikwár's house, besides acquisitions from other chiefs, recovering the districts of Visalnagar, Kherálu, Vadnagar, Bijápur, and Pátan from Jawán Mard Khán. After the death of the great Dámáji, the importance of the Gáikwár's power sensibly diminished. Had it not been for their alliance with the British, the feeble hands of Sayájiráv I. (A.D. 1771-1778) would probably have been the last to hold the emblem of Gáikwár rule. If in the zenith of Gáikwár power Momín Khán could reconquer, and for so long successfully defend A'hmedábad, what might not have been possible in its decline?

APPENDIX I.

The Death of Sulta'n Baha'dur, A.D. 1526-1536.[1]

Appendix I.

The Death of Sultán Bahádur, A.D. 1526-1536.

Colonel Briggs (Muhammadan Power in India, IV. 132) gives the following summary of the events which led to the fatal meeting of Sultán Bahádur and the Portuguese viceroy Nono da Cunha in the beginning of 1536-37:

When in 1529 Nono daCunha came as viceroy to India he held instructions to make himself master of the island of Diu. In the following year a great expedition, consisting of 400 vessels and 15,600 men, met in Bombay and sailed to the Káthiáváda coast. After vigorous assaults it was repulsed off Diu on the 17th February 1531. From that day the Portuguese made ceaseless efforts to obtain a footing on the island of Diu. In 1531 besides harrying the sea trade of Gujarát the Portuguese sacked the towns of Tárápur, Balsár, and Surat, and, to give colour to their pretensions, received under their protection Chánd Khán an illegitimate brother of Bahádur. In 1532, under James de Silveira, the Portuguese burned the south Káthiáváda ports of Pattan-Somnáth, Mangrul, Talája, and Muzaffarábád, killing many of the people and carrying off 4000 as slaves. Shortly after the Portuguese took and destroyed Bassein in Thána obtaining 400 cannon and much ammunition. They also burned Daman, Thána, and Bombay. "All this" says the Portuguese historian "they did to straiten Diu and to oblige the king of Gujarát to consent to their raising a fort on the island of Diu." When Bahádur was engaged with the Mughals (A.D. 1532-1534) the Portuguese Governor General deputed an embassy to wait on Humáyún to endeavour to obtain from him the cession of Diu, hoping by this action to work indirectly on the fears of Bahádur. At last in 1534 Bahádur consented to a peace by which he agreed to cede the town of Bassein to Portugal; not to construct ships of war in his ports; and not to combine with Turkish fleets against Portugal.

Permission was also given to the Portuguese to build in Diu. In consideration of these terms the Portuguese agreed to furnish Bahádur with 500 Europeans of whom fifty were men of note. According to the Portuguese historian it was solely because of this Portuguese help that Bahádur succeeded in driving the Mughals out of Gujarát. Bahádur's cession of land in Diu to the Portuguese was for the purpose of building a mercantile factory. From the moment Bahádur discovered they had raised formidable fortifications, especially when by the withdrawal of the Mughals he no longer had any motive for keeping on terms with them, he resolved to wrest the fort out of the hands of the Portuguese. On the plea of separating the natives from the Europeans, Bahádur instructed his governor of Diu to build a wall with a rampart capable of being mounted with guns. But as this created much dispute and ill-will the rampart was given up. Bahádur next attempted to seize Emanuel de Souza the captain of Diu fort. With this object he invited DeSouza to his camp. DeSouza was warned but determined to accept Bahádur's invitation. He went attended by only one servant, an act of courage which

[1] See above page 256. The Portuguese details have been obtained through the kindness of Dr. Gerson DaCunha.

Appendix I.

The Death of Sultán Bahádur, A.D. 1526 - 1536.

Bahádur so greatly admired that he treated him with honour and allowed him to return in safety. Bahádur next schemed to secure DeSouza in the fort by surprise. With this end he began to pay the Portuguese officers visits at all hours. But DeSouza was always on his guard and Bahádur's surprise visits failed to give him an opportunity. In 1536 DeSouza wrote to the viceroy complaining of the bad feeling of the Gujarát Moors towards the Portuguese in Diu and of the efforts of the king to drive them out of the fort. In consequence of DeSouza's letter Nono daCunha the viceroy arrived at Diu early in 1536-7. Bahádur went to visit the viceroy on board the viceroy's ship. On his return he was attacked and leaping into the water was killed by a blow on the head and sank.

Of the unplanned and confused circumstances in which the brave Bahádur met his death four Musalmán and four Portuguese versions remain. The author of the Mirăt-i-Sikandari (Persian Text, 280 - 281) states that the Portuguese, who offered their help to Bahádur in the days of his defeat by the emperor Humáyún, obtained from him the grant of land at Diu, and on this land built a fort. After the re-establishment of his power the Sultán, who had no longer any need of their help, kept constantly planning some means of ousting the Portuguese from Diu. With this object Bahádur came to Diu and opened negotiations with the Portuguese viceroy, hoping in the end to get the viceroy into his power. The viceroy knowing that Bahádur regretted the concessions he had made to them was too wary to place himself in Bahádur's hands. To inspire confidence Bahádur, with five or six of his nobles all unarmed, paid the viceroy a visit on board his ship. Suspecting foul play from the behaviour of the Portuguese the king rose to retire, but the Portuguese pressed upon him on all sides. He had nearly reached his boat when one of the Portuguese struck him a blow with a sword, killed him, and threw his body overboard.

The same author gives a second version which he says is more generally received and is probably more accurate. According to this account the Portuguese had come to know that Bahádur had invited the Sultáns of the Dakhan to co-operate with him in driving the Portuguese from the Gujarát, Konkan, and Dakhan ports. That the Portuguese viceroy had come with 150 ships and had anchored at Diu off the chain bastion. That Sultán Bahádur not suspecting that the Portuguese were aware of his insincerity went in a barge to see the fleet, and when he got in the midst of their ships, the Portuguese surrounded his barge and killed him with lances.

According to Farishtah (II. 442, 443, Pers. Text) on the invasion of Gujarát by the emperor Humáyún, Sultán Bahádur had asked help of the Portuguese. When his power was re-established, Bahádur, hearing of the arrival of between five and six thousand Portuguese at Diu, feared they would take possession of that port. He therefore hastened to Diu from Júnágadh. The Portuguese who were aware that Humáyún had withdrawn and that Bahádur had re-established his power, preferred to attempt to gain Diu by stratagem rather than by force. Bahádur asked the viceroy to visit him. The viceroy feigned sickness and Bahádur with the object of proving his goodwill offered to visit the viceroy on board his ship. On leaving the viceroy's ship to enter his own barge the Portuguese suddenly moved their vessel and Bahádur fell overboard. While in the water a Portuguese struck the king with a lance and killed him.

Appendix I.

THE DEATH OF SULTÁN BAHÁDUR, A.D. 1526 - 1536.

Abul Fazl's account A.D. 1590 (Akbarnámah in Elliot, VI. 18) seems more natural and in better keeping with Bahádur's impetuous vigour and bravery than either the Gujarát or Farishtah's narratives. The Portuguese chief was apprehensive that as the Sultán was no longer in want of assistance he meditated treachery. So he sent to inform the Sultán that he had come as requested, but that he was ill and unable to go on shore, so that the interview must be deferred till he got better. The Sultán, quitting the royal road of safety, embarked on the 12th February 1536 (3rd Ramazan H. 943) with a small escort to visit the viceroy on board the viceroy's ship. As soon as Bahádur reached the vessel he found the viceroy's sickness was a pretence and regretted that he had come. He at once sought to return. But the Portuguese were unwilling that such a prey should escape them and hoped that by keeping him prisoner they might get more ports. The viceroy came forward and asked the Sultán to stay a little and examine some curiosities he had to present. The Sultán replied that the curiosities might be sent after him and turned quickly towards his own boat. A European *kázi* or priest placed himself in the Sultán's way and bade him stop. The Sultán, in exasperation, drew his sword and cleft the priest in twain. He then leaped into his own boat. The Portuguese vessels drew round the Sultán's boat and a fight began. The Sultán and Rúmi Khán threw themselves into the water. A friend among the Portuguese stretched a hand to Rúmi Khán and saved him: the Sultán was drowned in the waves.

Of the four Portuguese versions of Bahádur's death the first appears in Correa's (A.D. 1512 - 1550) Lendas Da Asia, A.D. 1497 to 1550; the second in DeBarros' (died A.D. 1570) Decadas, A.D. 1497 to 1539; the third in Do Couto's (died A.D. 1600 ?) continuation of DeBarros, A.D. 1529 to 1600; and the fourth in Faria-e-Souza's (died A.D. 1650) Portuguese Asia to A.D. 1640. A fifth reference to Bahádur's death will be found in Castaneda's Historia which extends to A.D. 1538.

As Correa was in India from A.D. 1512 till his death in Goa in A.D. 1550, and as his narrative which was never published till A.D. 1856-64 has the highest reputation for accuracy of detail his version carries special weight. According to Correa (Lendas Da Asia, Vol. III. Chap. XCV.) during the monsoon of 1536, Nono DaCunha the viceroy received by land a letter from Manoel deSouza the captain of Diu fort, telling him of the discontent of the Gujarát Moors with king Bahádur for allowing the Portuguese to build a fort at Diu. In consequence of this information early in the fair season Nono daCunha sailed from Goa in his own galleon accompanied by about ten small vessels *fustas* and *katurs* under the command of Antonio deSylveira. Nono reached Diu about the end of December. King Bahádur was glad that the viceroy should come to Diu almost alone since it seemed to show he was not aware of Bahádur's designs against the Portuguese. When Bahádur arrived at Diu he sent a message to the viceroy inviting him to come ashore to meet him as he had important business to transact. The king's messenger found the viceroy ill in bed, and brought back a message that the viceroy would come ashore to meet the king in the evening. Immediately after the king's messenger left, Manoel deSouza, the captain of Diu fort, came on board to see the viceroy. The viceroy told Manoel to go and thank the king and to return his visit. The king expressed his grief at the viceroy's illness and proposed to start at once to see him. He went to his barge and rowed straight to the viceroy's

Appendix I.

THE DEATH OF SULTÁN BAHÁDUR, A.D. 1526 - 1536.

galleon. The king had with him, besides the interpreter St. Jago, seven men and two pages one carrying a sword and the other a bow. The captain of the fort and some other officers in their own barges followed the king. Bahádur, who was the first to arrive, came so speedily that the viceroy had hardly time to make preparations to receive him. He put on heavy clothes to show he was suffering from ague and ordered all the officers to be well armed. When Bahádur came on board he saw the men busy with their weapons but showed no signs that he suspected foul play. He went straight to the viceroy's cabin. The viceroy tried to get up but Bahádur prevented him, asked how he was, and returned at once to the deck. As Bahádur stood on the deck the captain of the fort boarded the galleon, and, as he passed to the cabin to see the viceroy, Bahádur laughingly upbraided him with being behind time. Then without taking leave of the viceroy Bahádur went to his barge. When the viceroy learned that the king had left he told the captain to follow the king and to take him to the fort and keep him there till the viceroy saw him. The captain rowed after the king who was already well ahead. He called to the king asking him to wait. The king waited. When the captain came close to the king's barge he asked the king to come into his vessel. But the interpreter without referring to the king replied that the captain should come into the king's barge. DeSouza ordered his boat alongside. His barge struck the king's barge and DeSouza who was standing on the poop tripped and fell into the water. The rowers of the royal barge picked him out and placed him near the king who laughed at his wet clothes. Other Portuguese barges whose officers thought the Moors were fighting with the captain began to gather. The first to arrive was Antonio Cardoza. When Cardoza came up the interpreter told the king to make for land with all speed as the Portuguese seemed to be coming to seize and kill him. The king gave the order to make for the shore. He also told the page to shoot the hollow arrow whose whistling noise was a danger signal. When the Moors in the king's barge heard the whistle they attacked Manoel deSouza, who fell dead into the sea. Then Diogo de Mesquita, D'Almeida, and Antonio Correa forced their way on to the king's barge. When the king saw them he unsheathed his sword and the page shot an arrow and killed Antonio Cardoza, who fell overboard and was drowned. D'Almeida was killed by a sword-cut from a Moor called Tiger and Tiger was killed by Correa. At that moment Diogo de Mesquita gave the king a slight sword-cut and the king jumped into the sea. After the king, the interpreter and Rúmi Khán, two Moors, and all the rowers leapt into the water. The Portuguese barges surrounded them and the men struck at the three swimmers with lances and oars. The king twice cried aloud 'I am Sultán Bahádur,' hoping that some one would help him. A man who did not know that he was the king struck Bahádur on the head with a club. The blow was fatal and Bahádur sank. The second version is given by Barros (A.D. 1560) in his Decadas da Asia, Vol. V. page 357 of the 1707 edition. The third version by Do Couto (A.D. 1600) in his continuation of Barros' Decadas, and the fourth by Faria-e-Souza (A.D. 1650) in his Portuguese Asia are in the main taken from De Barros. The following details are from Steevens' (A.D. 1697) translation of Faria given in Briggs' Muhammadan Power in India, IV. 135-138.

Bahádur king of Cambay, who had recovered his kingdom solely by the assistance of the Portuguese, now studied their ruin, and repenting of the leave he had granted to build a fort at Diu endeavoured to

Appendix I.

THE DEATH OF SULTÁN BAHÁDUR, A.D. 1526-1536.

take it and to kill the commander and the garrison. Nono da Cunha the Portuguese viceroy understood his designs and prepared to prevent them. Emanuel deSouza who commanded at Diu was warned by a Moor that the king would send for him by a certain Moor and kill him. DeSouza determined to go, and, when sent for, appeared with only one servant. Admiring DeSouza's courage the king treated him honourably and allowed him to return in safety. The king's mother tried to dissuade her son from plotting against DeSouza but to no effect. To remove suspicion Bahádur began to pay the Portuguese officers visits at unseasonable hours, but was ever received by DeSouza on his guard. Meanwhile, on the 9th January 1536, Nono daCunha the Portuguese viceroy set out from Goa for Diu with 300 sail. When he put in at Cheul he found Nizám-ul-Mulk who pretended he had come to divert his women at sea but really with designs on that place. When Nono reached Diu the king was hunting in the mountains and Nono apprised him of his arrival. The king sent for him by a Portuguese apostate of the name of John de St. Jago called Firangi Khán, but Nono daCunha pleaded illness. The king pretending great friendship came to Diu accompanied by Emanuel deSouza, who had brought the last message from DaCunha. At Diu the king went on board the viceroy's ship and for a time they discoursed. The king was troubled at a page whispering something to DaCunha, but as DaCunha took no notice his suspicions were allayed. The message was from DeSouza, stating that the captains whom he had summoned were awaiting orders to secure or kill the king. DaCunha thought it strange that DeSouza had not killed the king while he was in his power in the fort; and DeSouza thought it strange that DaCunha did not now seize the king when he was in his power in the ship. DaCunha directed all the officers to escort the king to the palace and then accompany DeSouza to the fort, where DaCunha intended to seize the king when he came to visit him. The king on his part had resolved to seize DaCunha at a dinner to which he had invited him and send him in a cage to the Great Turk. De Souza who was going to invite the king to the fort after DaCunha had entered it, came up with the king's barge and delivered his invitation through Rúmi Khán. Rúmi Khán warned the king not to accept it. The king disregarding this warning invited DeSouza into his barge. While stepping into the king's barge DeSouza fell overboard, but was picked up by officers who carried him to the king. At this time three Portuguese barges came up and some of the officers seeing DeSouza hastily enter the king's barge drew close to the king's barge. The king remembering Rúmi Khán's warning ordered Emanuel deSouza to be killed. James deMesquita understanding the order flew at and wounded the king. An affray followed and four Portuguese and seven of the king's men were killed. The king tried to get away in a boat but a cannon shot killed three of his rowers and he was stopped. He next attempted to escape by swimming, but being in danger of drowning discovered himself by crying for help. A Portuguese held out an oar to him; but others struck him fatal blows, so that he sank.

The conclusion to be drawn from these four Musalmán and four Portuguese versions is that on either side the leader hoped by some future treachery to seize the person of the other; and that mutual suspicion turned into a fatal affray a meeting which both parties intended should pass peacefully and lull the other into a false and favourable security.

APPENDIX II.

THE HILL FORT OF MA'NDU.

PART I.—DESCRIPTION.

Appendix II.

THE HILL FORT OF MÁNDU.

DESCRIPTION.

MÁNDU, about twenty-three miles south of Dhár in Central India, is a wide waving hill-top, part of the great wall of the Vindhyan range. The hill-top is three to four miles from north to south and four to five miles from east to west. On the north, the east, and the west, Mándu is islanded from the main plateau of Málwa by valleys and ravines that circle round to its southern face, which stands 1200 feet out of the Nímár plain. The area of the hill-top is over 12,000 English acres, and, so broken is its outline, that the encircling wall is said to have a length of between thirty-seven and thirty-eight miles. Its height, 1950 feet above the sea, secures for the hill-top at all seasons the boon of fresh and cool air.

About twenty miles south of Dhár the level cultivated plateau breaks into woody glades and uplands. Two miles further the plain is cleft by two great ravines, which from their deeper and broader southern mouths 700 to 800 feet below the Dhár plateau, as they wind northwards, narrow and rise, till, to the north of Mándu hill, they shallow into a woody dip or valley about 300 yards broad and 200 feet below the south crest of Málwa. From the south crest of the Málwa plateau, across the tree tops of this wild valley, stand the cliffs of the island Mándu, their crests crowned by the great Dehli gateway and its long lofty line of flanking walls. At the foot of the sudden dip into the valley the Âlamgír or World-Guarding Gate stands sentinel.[1] Beyond the gateway, among wild reaches of rock and forest, a noble causeway with high domed tombs on either hand fills the lowest dip of the valley. From the south end of the causeway the road winds up to a second gateway, and beyond the second gateway between side walls climbs till at the crest of the slope it passes through the ruined but still lofty and beautiful Dehli or northern gateway, one of the earliest works of Diláwar Khán (A.D. 1400), the founder of Musalmán Mándu.

Close inside of the Dehli gate, on the right or west, stands the handsome Hindola Palace. The name Hindola, which is probably the title of the builder, is explained by the people as the Swingcot palace, because, like the sides of the cage of a swinging cot, the walls of the hall bulge

---

[1] The following Persian verses are carved on the Âlamgír gateway:

In the time of A'lamgi'r Aurangzi'b (A.D. 1658 - 1707), the ruler of the World,
This gate resembling the skies in altitude was built anew.
In the year A.H. 1079 (A.D. 1668) the work of renewal was begun and completed
By the endeavour of the exalted Kha'n Muhammad Beg Kha'n.
From the accession of this Emperor of the World Aurangzi'b.
This was the eleventh year by way of writing and history.

Appendix II.

THE HILL FORT OF MÁNDU.

Description.

below and narrow towards the top. Its great baronial hall and hanging windows give the Hindola palace a special merit and interest, and an air of lordly wealth and luxury still clings to the tree-covered ruins which stretch west to large underground cisterns and hot weather retreats. About a quarter of a mile south stand the notable group of the Jaház Mehel or Ship palace on the west, and the Tapela Mehel or Caldron palace on the south, with their rows of lofty pointed arches below deep stone caves, their heavy windowless upper stories, and their massive arched and domed roof chambers. These palaces are not more handsomely built than finely set. The massive ship-like length of the Jaház Mehel lies between two large tree-girt ponds, and the Tapela, across a beautiful foreground of water and ruin, looks east into the mass of tangled bush and tree which once formed part of the 130 acres of the Lál Bágh or Royal Gardens.

The flat palace roofs command the whole 12,000 acres of Mándu hill, north to the knolls and broken uplands beyond the great ravine-moat and south across the waving hill-top with its miles of glades and ridges, its scattered villages hamlets and tombs, and its gleaming groves of mangoes, *khirnis*, banyans, *mhowras*, and *pipals*. In the middle distance, out from the tree-tops, stand the lofty domes of Hoshang's tomb and of the great Jámá mosque. Further south lies the tree-girt hollow of the Ságar Taláv or Sea Lake, and beyond the Ságar lake a woody plateau rises about 200 feet to the southern crest, where, clear against the sky, stand the airy cupolas of the pavilion of Rúp Mati, the beautiful wife of Báz Bahádur (A.D. 1551-1561), the last Sultán of Málwa. Finally to the west, from the end of the Rúp Mati heights, rises even higher the bare nearly isolated shoulder of Songad, the citadel or inner fort of Mándu, the scene of the Gujarát Bahádur's (A.D. 1531) daring and successful surprise. This fair hill-top, beautiful from its tangled wildness and scattered ruins, is a strange contrast to Mándu, the capital of a warlike independent dynasty. During the palmy days of the fifteenth century, of the 12,000 acres of the Mándu hill-top, 560 were fields, 370 were gardens, 200 were wells, 780 were lakes and ponds, 100 were bazár roads, 1500 were dwellings, 200 were rest-houses, 260 were baths, 470 were mosques, and 334 were palaces. These allotments crowded out the wild to a narrow pittance of 1560 acres of knolls and ridges.

From the Jaház Mehel the road winds through fields and woods, gemmed with peafowl and droll with monkeys, among scattered palaces mosques and tombs, some shapely some in heaps, about a mile south to the walled enclosure of the lofty domed tomb of the establisher of Mándu's greatness, Hoshang Sháh Ghori (A.D. 1405-1432). Though the badly-fitted joinings of the marble slabs of the tomb walls are a notable contrast to the finish of the later Mughal buildings, Hoshang's tomb, in its massive simplicity and dim-lighted roughness, is a solemn and suitable resting-place for a great Pathán warrior. Along the west of the tomb enclosure runs a handsome flat-roofed colonnade. The pillars, which near the base are four-sided, pass through an eight-sided and a sixteen-sided belt into a round upper shaft. The round shaft ends in a square under-capital, each face of which is filled by a group of leafage in outline the same as the favourite Hindu *Singh-múkh* or horned face. Over the entwined leafy horns of this moulding, stone brackets support heavy stone beams, all Hindu in pattern.[1] Close to the east of Hoshang's tomb is Hoshang's

---

[1] Mr. Fergusson (Indian Architecture, page 543) says: "The pillars appear to have been taken from a Jain building." But the refinement on the square capital of each pillar of the Hindu *Singh-múkh* or horned face into a group of leaves of the same

Appendix II.
THE HILL FORT OF MÁNDU.
DESCRIPTION.

Jámá Masjid or Great Mosque, built of blocks of red limestone. Hoshang's mosque is approached from the east through a massive domed gateway and across a quadrangle enclosed on the east north and south by wrecked colonnades of pointed arches. The west is filled by the great pointed arches of the mosque in fair repair. On the roof of the mosque from a thick undergrowth of domelets rise three lofty domes.[1]

In front of the gateway of the Great Mosque, in the centre of a masonry plinth about three feet high, stands an iron pillar about a foot in diameter at the base and twenty feet high. Close to the east of the gateway is the site of Mehmúd's (A.D. 1442) Tower of Victory, traces of which remained as late as A.D. 1840. About fifty yards further east are the ruins of a great building called the Ashrafi Mehel, said to have been a Musalmán college. To the north-east a banner marks a temple and the local state offices. South the road passes between the two lines of small houses and huts that make modern Mándu. Beyond the village, among ruins and huge swollen baobab stems, the road winds south along a downward slope to the richly-wooded lowland, where stretches to the west the wide coolness of the Ságar Taláv or Sea lake. Its broad surface covering 600 acres is green with fanlike lotus leaves, reeds, and water-grasses. Its banks are rough with brakes of tangled bush from which, in uncramped stateliness, rise lofty *mhauras*, mangoes, *kirnis*, and *pipals*. To the east round a smaller tank, whose banks are crowned by splendid mangoes and tamarinds, stand the domes of several handsome tombs. Of some

---

outline shows that the pillars were specially carved for use in a Muslim building. The porch on the north side of the tomb enclosure is described (Ditto, page 543) as composed of pillars avowedly re-erected from a Jain building. This note of Mr. Fergusson's must have gone astray, as the north porch of Hoshang's tomb enclosure is in the plain massive pointed arch and square-shafted style of the tomb and of the great mosque. Mr. Fergusson's note apparently belongs to the second and smaller Jámá Masjid, about a hundred yards east of the Sea or *Sagár* lake, the pillars of whose colonnade and porch are still enlivened by rows of the lucky face of the Hindu old horny.

[1] Hoshang's great mosque has the following much damaged Persian inscription:

> The mosque of exalted construction, the temple of heavenly altitude,
> Whose every thick pillar is a copy of the (pillars of the) Sacred Temple (the Temple of Makkah).
> On account of the greatness of its dignity, like the pigeons of the Temple of Makkah,
> Sacred angels of high degree are always engaged in hovering around it,
> The result of the events born of the merciless revolution of the skies.
> When the sun of his life came as far as the balcony (i. e. was ready to set).
> A'asam Huma'yu'n (that is Malik Mughi's) said . . .
> The administration of the country, the construction of buildings, and the driving back of enemies
> Are things which I leave you (the son of A'asam Huma'yu'n) as parting advice with great earnestness.
> The personification of the kindness of Providence, the Sulta'n A'la'-ud-di'n (Mehmu'd I. A.D.1436-1469), who is
> The outcome of the refulgence of the Faith, and the satisfier of the wants of the people.
> In the year A.H.858 (A.D.1454).
> In the words of the above parting advice, finished the construction of this building.

Appendix II.

THE HILL FORT OF MÁNDU.

DESCRIPTION.

of these domes the black masses are brightened by belts of brilliant pale and deep-blue enamel. To the north of this overflow-pool a long black wall is the back of the smaller Jámá or congregation mosque, badly ruined, but of special interest, as each of its numerous pillars shows the uninjured Hindu *Singh-mu'kh* or horned face. By a rough piece of constructive skill the original cross corners of the end cupolas have been worked into vaulted Musalmán domes.[1]

From the Sea Lake, about a mile across the waving richly-wooded plain, bounded by the southern height of the plateau, the path leads to the sacred Rewa Kund or Narbada Pool, a small shady pond lined with rich masonry, and its west side enriched by the ruins of a handsome Bath or Hammám Khánah. From the north-east corner of the Rewa Pool a broad flight of easy stairs leads thirty or forty feet up the slope on whose top stands the palace of Báz Bahádur (A.D. 1551-1561) the last independent chief of Mándu.[2] The broad easy flight of steps ends in a lofty arched gateway through which a roomy hall or passage gives entrance into a courtyard with a central masonry cistern and an enclosing double colonnade, which on the right opens into an arched balcony overlooking the Rewa Kund and garden. Within this courtyard is a second court enclosed on three sides by an arched gallery. The roof of the colonnades, which are reached by flights of easy steps, are shaded by arched pavilions topped by cupolas brightened by belts of blue enamel.

---

[1] This Jámá Mosque has the following Persian inscription dated H. 835 (A.D. 1431):

> With good omens, at a happy time, and in a lucky and well-started year,
> On the 4th of the month of Alla'h (Ramasa'n) on the great day of Friday,
> In the year 835 and six months from the Hijrah (A.D. 1431)
> Counted according to the revolution of the moon in the Arabian manner.
> This Islamic mosque was founded in this world,
> The top of whose dome rubs its head against the green canopy of Heaven.
> The construction of this high mosque was due to Mughi's-ud-di'n-wad-dunya (Malik Mughi's), the father of Mehmu'd I. of Ma'lwa (A.D. 1436-1469), the redresser of temporal and spiritual wrongs.
> Ulugh (brave), A'asam (great), Huma'yu'n (august), the Kha'n of the seven climes and the nine countries.
> By the hands of his enterprise this so great mosque was founded,
> That some call it the House of Peace, others style it the Kaa'bah.
> This good building was completed on the last of the month of Shawwa'l (A.H. 835, A.D. 1431).
> May the merit of this good act be inserted in the scroll of the Kha'n's actions!
> In this centre may the praises of the sermon read (in the name) of Mehmu'd Sha'h
> Be everlasting, so long as mountains stand on the earth and stars in the firmament.

[2] The following Persian inscription carved on the entrance arch shows that though it may have been repaired by Báz Bahádur, the building of the palace was fifty years earlier (H. 914, A.D. 1508):

> "In the time of the Sulta'n of Nations, the most just and great, and the most knowing and munificent Kha'ka'n Na'sir Sha'h Khilji (A.D. 1500 - 1512). Written by Yu'suf, the year (H. 914) (A.D. 1508)."

Appendix II.

THE HILL FORT OF MÁNDU.

Description.

To the south of Báz Baháduŕs Palace a winding path climbs the steep slope of the southern rim of Mándu to the massive pillared cupolas of Rúp Mati's palace, which, clear against the sky, are the most notable ornament of the hill-top. From a ground floor of heavy masonry walls and arched gateways stairs lead to a flat masonry terrace. At the north and south ends of the terrace stand massive heavy-eaved pavilions, whose square pillars and pointed arches support lofty deep-grooved domes. The south pavilion on the crest of the Vindhyan cliff commands a long stretch of the south face of Mándu with its guardian wall crowning the heights and hollows of the hill-top. Twelve hundred feet below spreads the dim hazy Nímár plain brightened eastwards by the gleaming coil of the Narbada. The north pavilion, through the clear fresh air of the hill-top, looks over the entire stretch of Mándu from the high shoulder of Songad in the extreme south-west across rolling tree-brightened fields, past the domes, the tangled bush, and the broad gray of the Sea Lake, to the five-domed cluster of Hoshang's mosque and tomb, on, across a sea of green tree tops, to the domed roof-chambers of the Jaház and Tapela palaces, through the Dehli gateway, and, beyond the deep cleft of the northern ravine, to the bare level and the low ranges of the Málwa plain.

From the Rewa Pool a path, along the foot of the southern height among noble solitary *mhauras* and *khirnis*, across fields and past small clusters of huts, guides to a flight of steps which lead down to a deep shady rock-cut dell where a Muhammadan chamber with great open arched front looks out across a fountained courtyard and sloping scalloped water table to the wild western slopes of Mándu. This is Nílkanth, where the emperor Akbar lodged in A.D. 1574, and which Jehángír visited in A.D. 1617.[1]

From the top of the steps that lead to the dell the hill stretches west bare and stony to the Songad or Tárápúr gateway on the narrow neck beyond which rises the broad shoulder of Songad, the lofty south-west limit of the Mándu hill-top.[2]

PART II.—HISTORY.[3]

History.

The Málwa Sultáns, A.D. 1400-1570.

The history of Mándu belongs to two main sections, before and after the overthrow by the emperor Akbar in A.D. 1563 of the independent power of the Sultáns of Málwa.

SECTION I.—THE MÁLWA SULTÁNS, A.D. 1400-1570.

Of early Hindu Mándu, which is said to date from A.D. 313, nothing is known.[4] Hind spire stones are built into the Hindola palace walls; and the pillars of the lesser Jámá mosque, about a hundred yards from the east end of the sea or Ságar Lake, are Hindu apparently Jain. Of these local Hind chiefs almost nothing is known except that their fort was

---

[1] Translations of its two much-admired Persian inscriptions are given below pages 370-371.

[2] On the Tárápúr gateway a Persian inscription of the reign of the emperor Akbar (A.D. 1556-1605) states that the royal road that passed through this gateway was repaired by Táhir Muhammad Hasan Imád-ud-dín.

[3] The Persian references and extracts in this section are contributed by Khán Sáheb Fazl-ul-láh Lutfullah Faridi of Surat.

[4] Sir John Malcolm in Eastwick's Handbook of the Panjáb, 119. This reference has not been traced. Farishtah (Elliot, VI. 563) says Mándu was built by Anand Dev of the Bais tribe, who was a contemporary of Khusrao Parwíz the Sassanian (A.D. 591-621).

Appendix II.
THE HILL FORT OF MÁNDU.
HISTORY.
The Málwa Sultáns, A.D. 1400-1570.

taken and their power brought to an end by Sultán Shams-ud-dín Altamsh about A.D. 1234.[1] Dhár, not Mándu, was at that time the capital. It seems doubtful whether Mándu ever enjoyed the position of a capital till the end of the fourteenth century. In A.D. 1401, in the ruin that followed Timúr's (A.D. 1398-1400) conquest of Northern India, a Pathán from the country of Ghor, Diláwar Khán Ghori (A.D. 1387-1405), at the suggestion of his son Alp Khán, assumed the white canopy and scarlet pavilion of royalty.[2] Though Dhár was Diláwar's head-quarters he sometimes stayed for months at a time at Mándu,[3] strengthening the defences and adorning the hill with buildings, as he always entertained the desire of making Mándu his capital.[4] Three available inscriptions of Diláwar

---

[1] The date is uncertain. Compare Elphinstone's History, 323; Briggs' Farishtah, I. 210-211; Tabakát-i-Násiri in Elliot, II. 328. The conquest of Mándu in A.D. 1227 is not Mandu in Málwa as Elphinstone and Briggs supposed, but Mandúr in the Siwálik Hills. See Elliot, Vol. II. page 325 Note 1. The Persian text of Farishtah (I. 115), though by mistake calling it Mándu (not Mándu), notes that it was the Mandu in the Siwálik hills. The poetical date-script also terms it Biládi-Siwálik or the Siwálik countries. The date of the conquest of the Siwálik Mándu by Altamsh is given by Farishtah (Ditto) as A.H. 624 (A.D. 1226). The conquest of Málwa by Altamsh, the taking by him of Bhilsah and Ujjain, and the destruction of the temple of Maha Káli and of the statue or image of Bikramajit are given as occurring in A.H. 631 (A.D. 1233). The Mirát-i-Sikandari (Persian Text, 13) notices an expedition made in A.D. 1395 by Zafar Khán (Muzaffar I. of Gujarát) against a Hindu chief of Mándu, who, it was reported, was oppressing the Musalmáns. A siege of more than twelve months failed to capture the fort.

[2] Briggs' Farishtah, IV. 170.

[3] Briggs' Farishtah, IV. 168. According to the Wákiát-i-Mushtáki (Elliot, IV. 553) Diláwar Khán, or as the writer calls him Amín Sháh, through the good offices of a merchant whom he had refrained from plundering obtained the grant of Mándu, which was entirely desolate. The king sent a robe and a horse, and Amín gave up walking and took to riding. He made his friends ride, enlisted horsemen, and promoted the cultivation of the country (Elliot, IV. 552). Farishtah (Pers. Text, II. 460-61) states that when Sultán Muhammad, the son of Fírúz Tughlak, made Khwajah Sarwar his chief minister with the title of Khwajah Jehán, and gave Zafar Khán the viceroyalty of Gujarát and Khizr Khán that of Multán, he sent Diláwar Khán to be governor of Málwa. In another passage Farishtah (II. 461) states that one of Diláwar's grandfathers, Sultán Shaháb-ud-dín, came from Ghor and took service in the court of the Dehli Sultáns. His son rose to be an *Amír*, and his grandson Diláwar Khán, in the time of Sultán Fírúz, became a leading nobleman, and in the reign of Muhammad, son of Fírúz, obtained Málwa in fief. When the power of the Tughlaks went to ruin Diláwar assumed the royal emblems of the umbrella and the red-tent.

[4] Diláwar Khán Ghori, whose original name was Husein, was one of the grandsons of Sultán Shaháb-ud-dín Muhammad bin Sám. He was one of the nobles of Muhammad, the son of Fírúz Tughlak, who after the death of that monarch, settled in and asserted his power over Málwa. (Pers. Text Faristah, II. 460). The emperor Jehángír (who calls him Âmíd Sháh Ghorí) attributes to him the construction of the fort of Dhár. He says (Memoirs Pers. Text, 201-202): Dhár is one of the oldest cities of India. Rája Bhoj, one of the famous ancient Hindu kings, lived in this city. From his time up to this a thousand years have passed. Dhár was also the capital of the Muhammadan rulers of Málwa. When Sultán Muhammad Tughlak (A.D. 1325) was on his way to the conquest of the Dakhan he built a cut-stone fort on a raised site. Its outline is very elegant and beautiful, but the space inside is empty of buildings. Âmíd Sháh Ghori, known as Diláwar Khán, who in the days of Sultán Muhammad the son of Sultán Fírúz, king of Dehli, gained the independent rule of Málwa, built outside this fort an assembly mosque, which has in front of it fixed in the ground a four-cornered iron column about four feet round. When Sultán Bahádur of Gujarát took Málwa (A.D. 1530-31) he wished to carry this column to Gujarát. In digging it up the pillar fell and broke in two, one piece measuring twenty-two feet the other thirteen feet. As it was lying here uncared-for I (Jehángír) ordered the big piece to be carried to Ágra to be put up in the courtyard of the shrine of him whose abode is the heavenly throne (Akbar), to be utilised as a lamp post. The mosque has two gates. In

Appendix II.

THE HILL FORT OF MÁNDU.

HISTORY.

The Málwa Sultáns, A.D. 1400-1570.

Khán (A.D. 1387-1405) seem to show that he built an assembly mosque near the Ship Palace, a mosque near the Dehli Gate, and a gate at the entrance to Songaḍh, the south-west corner and citadel of Mándu, afterwards known as the Tárápúr Gate.

In A.D. 1398 Alp Khán, son of Diláwar Khán, annoyed with his father for entertaining as his overlord at Dhár Mehmúd Tughlak, the refugee monarch of Dehli, withdrew to Mándu. He stayed in Mándu for three years, laying, according to Farishtah, the foundation of the famous fortress of solid masonry which was the strongest fortification in that part of the world.[1] On his father's death in A.D. 1405 Alp Khán took the title of Sultán Hoshang, and moved the capital to Mándu. The rumour that Hoshang had poisoned his father gave Diláwar's brother in arms, Muzaffar Sháh of Gujarát (A.D. 1399-1411), an excuse for an expedition against Hoshang.[2] Hoshang was defeated at Dhár, made prisoner, and carried to Gujarát, and Muzaffar's brother Nasrat was appointed in his place. Nasrat failed to gain the goodwill either of the people or of the army of Málwa, and was forced to retire from Dhár and take refuge in Mándu. In consequence of this failure in A.D. 1408, at Hoshang's request Muzaffar set Hoshang free after a year's confinement, and deputed his grandson Ahmed to take Hoshang to Málwa and establish Hoshang's power.[3] With Ahmed's help Hoshang took Dhár and shortly after secured the fort of Mándu. Hoshang (A.D. 1405-1431) made Mándu his capital and spread his power on all sides except towards Gujarát.[4] Shortly after the death of Muzaffar I. and the accession of Ahmed, when (A.D. 1414) Ahmed was quelling the disturbances raised by his cousins, Hoshang, instead of helping Ahmed as requested, marched towards Gujarát and created a diversion in favour of the rebels by sending two of his nobles to attack Broach. They were soon expelled by Ahmed Sháh. Shortly after Hoshang marched to the help of the chief of Jhálávâḍa in Káthiáváḍa,

---

front of the arch of one gate they have fixed a stone tablet engraved with a prose passage to the effect that Áhmíd Sháh Ghori in the year. H. 808 (A.D. 1405) laid the foundation of this mosque. On the other arch they have written a poetic inscription of which the following verses are a part:

> The liege lord of the world.
> The star of the sphere of glory.
> The stay of the people.
> The sun of the zenith of perfection.
> The bulwark of the law of the Prophet, A'mi'd Sha'h Da'u'd.
> The possessor of amiable qualities, the pride of Ghor.
> Dila'war Kha'n, the helper and defender of the Prophet's faith.
> The chosen instrument of the exalted Lord, who in the city of
> Dha'r constructed the assembly mosque
> In a happy and auspicious moment on a day of lucky omen.
> Of the date 808 years have passed (A.D. 1405)
> When this fabric of Hope was completed.

[1] Briggs' Farishtah, IV. 169.

[2] When fellow-nobles in the court of the Tughlak Sultán, Zafar Khán (Sultán Muzaffar of Gujarát) and Diláwar Khán bound themselves under an oath to be brothers in arms. Farishtah, Pers. Text II. 462.

[3] Briggs' Farishtah, IV. 173; Elphinstone's History, 678.

[4] Though their temples were turned into mosques the Jains continued to prosper under the Ghoris. At Deogarh in Lalitpura in Jhánsi in the North-West Provinces an inscription of Samvat 1481, that is of A.D. 1424, records the dedication of two Jaina images by a Jain priest named Holi during the reign of Sháh Alambhaka of Mandapapura, that is of Sháh Alp Khán of Mándu that is Sultán Hoshang Ghori. Archæological Survey of India, New Series, II. 120.

Appendix II.

THE HILL FORT OF MÁNDU.

HISTORY.

The Málwa Sultáns, A.D. 1400-1570.

and ravaged eastern and central Gujarát.[1] To punish Hoshang for these acts of ingratitude, between A.D. 1418 and 1422, Ahmed twice besieged Mándu, and though he failed to take the fort his retirement had to be purchased, and both as regards success and fair-dealing the honours of the campaign remained with Ahmed.[2] In A.D. 1421 Hoshang went disguised as a horse-dealer to Jájnagar (now Jájpur) in Cuttack in Orissa. He took with him a number of cream-coloured horses, of which he had heard the Rája was very fond. His object was to barter these horses and other goods for the famous war elephants of Jájnagar. An accident in the camp of the disguised merchants led to a fight, in which the Rája was taken prisoner and Hoshang was able to secure 150 elephants to fight the Gujarát Sultán.[3] During Hoshang's absence at Jájnagar Ahmed pressed the siege of Mándu so hard that the garrison would have surrendered had Hoshang not succeeded in finding his way into the fort through the south or Tárápur Gate.[4] For ten years after the Gujarát campaign, by the help of his minister Malik Mughís of the Khilji family and of his minister's son Mehmúd Khán, Málwa prospered and Hoshang's power was extended. Hoshang enriched his capital with buildings, among them the Great Mosque and his own tomb, both of which he left unfinished. Hoshang's minister Malik Mughís (who received the title of Ulugh Aâzam Humáyún Khán) appears to have built the assembly mosque near the Ságar Lake in Hoshang's life-time, A.D. 1431. Another of his buildings must have been a mint, as copper coins remain bearing Hoshang's name, and Mándu Shádiábád as the place of mintage.[5] In A.D. 1432, at Hoshangábád, on the left bank of the Narbada, about 120 miles east of Mándu, Hoshang, who was suffering from diabetes, took greatly to heart the fall of a ruby out of his crown. He said: A few days before the death of Fírúz Tughlak a jewel dropped from his crown. Hoshang ordered that he should be taken to Mándu. Before he had gone many miles the king died. His nobles carried the body to the Madrasah or college in Shádiábád or Mándu, and buried him in the college on the ninth day of Zil Hajjah, the twelfth month of A.H. 838 = A.D. 1434. The year of Hoshang's death is to be found in the letters

Ah Sha'h Hoshang na mund: Alas, Sháh Hoshang stayed not.[6]

On Hoshang's death his son Ghazni Khán, with the title of Sultán Muhammad Ghori, succeeded. Malik Mughís, his father's minister, and the minister's son Mehmúd were maintained in power. In three years

---

[1] Farishtah, Pers. Text II. 464-65.

[2] Briggs' Farishtah, IV. 176, 178, 180, 181, 183.

[3] Farishtah, Pers. Text II. 466-67.

[4] Briggs' Farishtah, IV. 180. In connection with the Tárápúr Gate Farishtah says (Pers. Text, II. 468): The fort of Mándu is built on the top of a mountain, and the line of its fortification is about twenty-eight miles in length. In place of a moat it is surrounded by a deep chasm, so that it is impossible to use missiles against it. Within the fort water and provisions are abundant and it includes land enough to grow grain for the garrison. The extent of its walls makes it impossible for an army to invest it. Most of the villages near it are too small to furnish supplies to a besieging force. The south or Tárápúr gate is exceedingly difficult of access. A horseman can hardly approach it. From whichever side the fort may be attempted, most difficult heights have to be scaled. The long distances and intervening hills prevent the watchers of the besieging force communicating with each other. The gate on the side of Delhi is of easier access than the other gates.

[5] It follows that Farishtah (Briggs, IV. 196) is mistaken in stating that Hoshang's son Muhammad gave Mándu the name of Shádiábád, the Abode of Joy.

[6] Farishtah, Pers. Text II. 472-475. It seems to follow that from the first the monument to Hoshang in Hoshangábád was an empty tomb. Compare Briggs' Farishtah, IV. 180-190.

Appendix II.

THE HILL FORT OF MÁNDU.

HISTORY.

The Málwa Sultáns, A.D. 1400-1570.

(A.D. 1433-1436), as Sultán Muhammad proved dissipated cruel and suspicions, Mehmúd, the minister's son, procured his death by poison. Mehmúd Khilji then asked his father to accept the succession, but his father declined, saying that Mehmúd was fitter to be king. In A.D. 1436 Mehmúd was accordingly crowned with the royal tiara of Hoshang.[1] He conferred on his father the honour of being attended by mace-bearers carrying gold and silver sticks, who, when the Khán mounted or went out, had, like the mace-bearers of independent monarchs, the privilege of repeating the *Bismillah* 'In the name of the compassionate and merciful Alláh.'[2] He gave his father royal honours, the white canopy and the silver quiver, and to his title of Malik Ashraf Khán Jehán he added among others Amír-ul-Umara and Aâzam Humáyún.[3] Mehmúd quelled a revolt among his nobles. An outbreak of plague in the Gujarát camp relieved him from a contest with Ahmed Sháh.[4] In A.D. 1439 Mehmúd repaired the palace of Sultán Hoshang and opened the mosque built in commemoration of that monarch which Farishtah describes as a splendid edifice with 208 columns.[5] About the same time Mehmúd completed Hoshang's tomb which Hoshang had left unfinished. On the completion of this building Hoshang's remains seem to have been moved into it from their first resting-place in the college. In A.D. 1441 Mehmúd built a

---

[1] The following more detailed, but also more confused, story is told in the Wákiát-i-Mushtáki (Elliot, IV. 552-54): A man named Mehmúd, son of Mughís Khilji, came to Hoshang and entered his service. He was a treacherous man, who secretly aspired to the throne. He became minister, and gave his daughter in marriage to the king. [Farishtah, Pers. Text II. 474, says: "Malik Mughís gave his daughter (Mehmúd's sister) in marriage, not to Hoshang, but to Hoshang's son Muhammad Shah."] His father Malik Mughís, coming to know of his son's ambitious designs, informed the king of them. Hereupon Mehmúd feigned illness, and to deceive the king's physicians shut himself in a dark room and drank the blood of a newly killed goat. When the physicians came Mehmúd rose hastily, threw up the blood into a basin, and tossing back his head rolled on the floor as if in pain. The physicians called for a light. When they saw that what Mehmúd bad spat up was blood they were satisfied of his sickness, and told the king that Mehmúd had not long to live. The king refrained from killing a dying man. This strange story seems to be an embellishment of a passage in Farishtah (Pers. Text, II. 477). When Khán Jehán, that is Malik Mughís the father of Mehmúd, was ordered by Sultán Muhammad to take the field against the Rájput rebels of Nadoti (Hároti?) many of the old nobles of Málwa went with him. In their absence the party hostile to the Khiljis represented to Sultán Muhammad that Mehmúd Khilji was plotting his death. On hearing that the Sultán was enraged against him Mehmúd secluded himself from the Court on pretence of illness. At the same time he worked secretly and bribed Sultán Muhammad's cup-bearer to poison his master. On the death of Sultán Muhammad the party of nobles opposed to Mehmúd, concealing the fact of Muhammad's death, sent word that Muhammad had ordered him immediately to the palace, as he wanted to send him on an embassy to Gujarát. Mehmúd, who knew that the Sultán was dead, returned word to the nobles that he had vowed a life-long seclusion as the sweeper of the shrine of his patron Sultán Hoshang, but that if the nobles came to him and convinced him that the good of his country depended on his going to Gujarát he was ready to go and see Sultán Muhammad. The nobles were caught in their own trap. They went to Mehmúd and were secured and imprisoned by him.

[2] Farishtah, Pers. Text II. 480.

[3] Briggs' Farishtah, IV. 196. These titles mean: The Chief of Nobles, the Great, the August.

[4] It is related that one of the pious men in the camp of Sultán Ahmed of Gujarát had a warning dream, in which the Prophet (on whom be peace) appeared to him and said: "The calamity of (spirit of) pestilence is coming down from the skies. Tell Sultán Ahmed to leave this country." This warning was told to Sultán Ahmed, but he disregarded it, and within three days pestilence raged in his camp. Farishtah Pers. Text, II. 484.

[5] Briggs' Farishtah, IV. 205, gives 230 minarets and 360 arches. This must have been an addition in the Text used by Briggs. These details do not apply to the building. The Persian text of Farishtah, II. 485, mentions 208 columns or pillars (*duyast o hasht ustuwánah*). No reference is made either to minarets or to arches.

Appendix II.

THE HILL FORT OF MÁNDU.

HISTORY.

The Málwa Sultáns, A.D. 1400-1570.

garden with a dome and palaces[1] and a mosque at Naâlchah about three miles north of the Dehli Gate of Mándu, a pleasing well-watered spot where the plateau of Málwa breaks into glades and knolls.[2] In A.D. 1443 in honour of his victory over Rána Kúmbha of Chitor, Mehmúd built a beautiful column of victory,[3] seven storeys high, and a college in front of the mosque of Hoshang Ghori. Facing the east entrance to the Great Mosque stands a paved ramp crowned by a confused ruin. As late as A.D. 1843 this ruin is described as a square marble chamber. Each face of the chamber had three arches, the centre arch in two of the faces being a door. Above the arches the wall was of yellow stone faced with marble. Inside the chamber the square corners were cut off by arches. No roof or other trace of superstructure remained.[4] This chamber seems to be the basement of the column of victory which was raised in A.D. 1443 by Mehmúd I. (A.D. 1432-1469) in honour of his victory over Rána Kúmbha of Chitor.[5] Mehmúd's column has the special interest of being, if not the original, at least the cause of the building of Kúmbha Rána's still uninjured Victory Pillar, which was completed in A.D. 1454 at a cost of £900,000 in honour of his defeat of Mehmúd.[6] That the Mándu Column of Victory was a famous work is shown by Abul Fazl's reference to it in A.D. 1590 as an eight-storeyed minaret.[7] Farishtah, about twenty years later (A.D. 1610), calls it a beautiful Victory Pillar seven storeys high.[8] The emperor Jehángír (A.D. 1605-1627) gives the following account of Mehmúd's Tower of Victory[9]: This day, the 29th of the month *Tir*, corresponding to July-August of A.D. 1617, about the close of the day, with the ladies of the palace, I went out to see the *Haft Manzar* or Seven Storeys, literally Seven Prospects. This building is one of the structures of the old rulers of Málwa, that is of Sultán Mehmúd Khilji. It has seven storeys, and on each storey there are four porticos, and in each portico are four windows. The height of this tower is about 163 feet and its circumference 150 feet. From the surface of the ground to the top of the seventh storey there are one hundred and seventy-one steps." Sir Thomas Herbert, the traveller, in A.D. 1626 describes it from hearsay, or at least at second-hand, as a tower 170 steps high, supported by massive pillars and adorned with gates and windows very observable. It was built, he adds, by Khán Jehán, who there lies buried.[10]

---

1 Farishtah, Pers. Text II. 487.

2 Briggs' Farishtah, IV. 207. Malcolm's Central India, I. 32. In A.D. 1817 Sir John Malcolm (Central India, I. 32 Note) fitted up one of Mehmúd's palaces as a hot-weather residence.

3 Of the siege of Kumbhalmer a curious incident is recorded by Farishtah (Pers. Text, II. 485). He says that a temple outside the town destroyed by Mehmúd had a marble idol in the form of a goat. The Sultán ordered the idol to be ground into lime and sold to the Rájputs as betel-leaf lime, so that the Hindus might eat their god. The idol was perhaps a ram, not a goat. The temple would then have been a Sun-temple and the ram, the carrier or *váhana* of the Sun, would have occupied in the porch a position similar to that held by the bull in a Mahádeva temple.

4 Ruins of Mándu, 13.

5 In the end of A.H. 846 (A.D. 1442) Mehmúd built a seven-storeyed tower and a college opposite the Jámá Mosque of Hoshang Sháh. Briggs' Farishtah, IV. 210; Persian Text, II. 488.

6 Compare Briggs' Farishtah, IV 323.

7 Gladwin's Áin-i-Akbari, II. 41.

8 Briggs' Farishtah, IV. 210; Farishtah, Persian Text II. 488.

9 Memoirs of the emperor Jehángír (Pers. Text) Sir Sayad Áhmed's Edition, page 188, eleventh year of Jehángír, A.D. 1617.

10 Herbert's Khán Jehan is doubtless Mehmúd's father the minister Malik Mughís, Khán Jehán Aâzam Humáyún. It cannot be Khán Jehán Pír Muhammad, Akbar's general, who after only a few months' residence was slain in Mándu in A.D. 1561; nor can it be Jehángír's great Afghán general, Khán Jehán Lodi (A.D. 1600-1630), as he

Appendix II.

THE HILL FORT OF MÁNDU.

HISTORY.

The Málwa Sultáns, A.D. 1400-1570.

Two years later (A.D. 1445) Mehmúd built at Mándu, and endowed with the revenues of several villages a large *Shifa Khánah* or Hospital, with wards and attendants for all classes and separate apartments for maniacs. He placed in charge of it his own physician Mauláns Fazlulláh.[1] He also built a college to the east of the Jámá mosque, of which traces remain.[2]

In A.D. 1453, though defeated, Mehmúd brought back from Gujarát the jewelled waistbelt of Gujarát, which in a daring charge he had taken from the tent of the Gujarát king Kutb-ud-dín Sháh.[3] In A.D. 1441 Mehmúd's father died at Mandisor. Mehmúd felt the loss so keenly that he tore his hair like one bereft of reason.[4] After his father's death Mehmúd made his son Ghiás-ud-dín minister, and conferred the command of the army and the title of Aâzam Humáyún on his kinsman Táj Khán. In A.D. 1469, after a reign of thirty-four years (A.D. 1436-1469) of untiring energy and activity Mehmúd died. Farishtah says of him: "His tent was his home: the field of battle his resting-place. He was polite, brave, just, and learned. His Hindu and Musalmán subjects were happy and friendly. He guarded his lands from invaders. He made good his loss to any one who suffered from robbery in his dominions, recovering the amount from the village in whose lands the robbery had taken place, a system which worked so well that theft and robbery became almost unknown. Finally, by a systematic effort he freed the country from the dread of wild beasts.[5]

In A.D. 1469 Mehmúd was succeeded by his son and minister Ghiás-ud-dín, to whose skill as a soldier much of Mehmúd's success had been due. On his accession Ghiás-ud-dín made his son Abdul Kádir Prime Minister and heir-apparent, and gave him the title of Násir-ud-dín. He called his nobles, and in their presence handed his sword to Násir-ud-dín, saying: "I have passed thirty-four years in ceaseless fighting. I now devote my life to rest and enjoyment."[6] Ghiás-ud-dín, who never left Mándu during the whole thirty years of his reign (A.D. 1469-1499), is said to have completed the Jaház Mehel or Ship Palace,[7] and the widespread buildings

---

was not in Mándu until A.D. 1628, that is more than a year after Herbert left India. Compare Herbert's Travels, 107-118; Elliot, VI. 249-323, VII. 7, 8, and 21; and Blochman's Áín-i-Akbari, 503-506.

[1] Briggs' Farishtah, IV. 214.

[2] Ruins of Mándu, 13. Farishtah has three mentions of colleges. One (Pers. Text. II. 475) as the place where the body of Hoshang was carried, probably that prayers might be said over it. In another passage in the reign of Mehmúd I. (Pers. Text, II. 480) he states that Mehmúd built colleges in his territories which became the envy of Shiráz and Samarkand. In a third passage he mentions a college (page 488) near the Victory Tower.

[3] Briggs' Farishtah, IV. 217. A different but almost incredible account of the capture of the royal belt is given in the Mirát-i-Sikandari, Pers. Text, 159: When Sultán Kutb-ud-dín, son of Sultán Muhammad, defeated Sultán Mehmúd Khilji at the battle of Kapadvanj, there was such a slaughter as could not be exceeded. By chance, in the heat of the fray, which resembled the Day of Judgment, the wardrobe-keeper of Sultán Kutb-ud-dín, in whose charge was the jewelled belt, was by the restiveness of his horse carried into the ranks of the enemy. The animal there became so violent that the wardrobe-keeper fell off and was captured by the enemy, and the jewelled belt was taken from him and given to Sultán Mehmúd of Málwa. The author adds: This jewelled waistband was in the Málwa treasury at the time the fortress of Mándu was taken by the strength of the arm of Sultán Muzaffar (A.D. 1531). Sultán Mehmúd sent this belt together with a fitting sword and horse to Sultán Muzaffar by the hands of his son.

[4] Briggs' Farishtah, IV. 209.

[5] Briggs' Farishtah, IV. 234-235; Pers. Text, II. 503.

[6] Briggs' Farishtah, IV. 236. [7] Ruins of Mándu, 6.

which surround it. It seems probable that the Tapela Palace close to the south-east of the Ship palace and the lake and royal gardens immediately to the north and north-east of the Tapela palace were part of Ghiás-ud-dín's pleasure-houses and grounds. The scale of the ruins behind the Hindola or Swingcot palace to the north, and their connection with the out-buildings to the west of the Jaház Mehel, suggest that they also belonged to the palaces and women's quarters of the pleasure-loving Ghiás-ud-dín.

Of the surprising size and fantastic arrangements of Ghiás-ud-dín's pleasure city, the true Mándu Shádiábád or Abode of Joy, curious details have been preserved. This Abode of Pleasure was a city not a palace. It contained 15,000 inhabitants, all of them women, none either old or plain-featured, and each trained to some profession or craft. Among them were the whole officers of a court, besides courtiers, teachers, musicians, dancers, prayer-readers, embroiderers, and followers of all crafts and callings. Whenever the king heard of a beautiful girl he never rested till he obtained her. This city of women had its two regiments of guards, the Archers and the Carabineers, each 500 strong, its soldiers dressed like men in a distinguishing uniform. The archers were beautiful young Turkí damsels, all armed with bows and arrows: the carabineers were Abyssinian maidens, each carrying a carbine. Attached to the palace and city was a deer park, where the Lord of Leisure used to hunt with his favourites. Each dweller in the city of women received her daily dole of grain and coppers, and besides the women were many pensioners, mice parrots and pigeons, who also received the same dole as their owners. So evenly just was Ghiás-ud-dín in the matter of his allowances, that the prettiest of his favourites received the same allowance as the roughest carabineer.[1]

The Lord of the City of Pleasure was deeply religious. Whenever he was amusing himself two of his companions held in front of him a cloth to remind him of his shroud. A thousand *Háfizahs*, that is women who knew the Kuráán by heart, constantly repeated its holy verses, and, under the orders of the king, whenever he changed his raiment the *Háfizahs* blew on his body from head to foot with their prayer-hallowed breath.[2] None of the five daily prayers passed unprayed. If at any of the hours of prayer the king was asleep he was sprinkled with water, and when water failed to arouse him, he was dragged out of bed. Even when dragged out of bed by his servants the king never uttered an improper or querulous word.

So keen was his sense of justice that when one of his courtiers pretending he had purchased her, brought to him a maiden of ideal beauty, and her relations, not knowing she had been given to the king, came to complain, though they gladly resigned her, the king grieved over his unconscious wrong. Besides paying compensation he mourned long and truly, and ordered that no more inmates should be brought to his palace.[3] So great was the king's charity that every night below his pillow he placed a bag containing some thousand gold-mohurs, and before evening all were distributed to the deserving. So religious was the king that he paid 50,000 *tankas* for each of the four feet of the ass of Christ. A man came bringing a fifth hoof, and one of the courtiers said: "My Lord, an ass has four feet. I never heard that it had five, unless perhaps the ass of Christ had five." "Who knows," the king replied, "it may be that this

[1] Farishtah Pers. Text, II. 504-505.
[2] Farishtah Pers. Text, II. 505.
[3] Farishtah Pers. Text, II. 507.

Appendix II.

THE HILL FORT OF MÁNDU.

HISTORY.

The Málwa Sultáns, A.D. 1400-1570.

last man has told the truth, and one of the others was wrong. See that he is paid." So sober was the king that he would neither look upon nor hear of intoxicants or stimulants. A potion that had cost 100,000 *tankas* was brought to him. Among the 300 ingredients one was nutmeg. The king directed the potion to be thrown into a drain. His favourite horse fell sick. The king ordered it to have medicine, and the horse recovered. "What medicine was given the horse?" asked the king. "The medicine ordered by the physicians" replied his servants. Fearing that in this medicine there might be an intoxicant, the king commanded that the horse should be taken out of the stables and turned loose into the forest.[1]

The king's spirit of peace steeped the land, which, like its ruler, after thirty years of fighting yearned for rest. For fourteen years neither inward malcontent nor foreign foe broke the quiet. In A.D. 1482 Bahlol Lodi advanced from Dehli to subdue Málwa. The talk of Mándu was Bahlol's approach, but no whisper of it passed into the charmed City of Women. At last the son-minister forced his way into the king's presence. At the news of pressing danger his soldier-spirit awoke in Ghiás-ud-dín. His orders for meeting the invaders were so prompt and well-planned that the king of Dehli paid a ransom and withdrew. A second rest of fifteen years ended in the son-minister once more forcing his way into the Presence. In A.D. 1500 the son presented his father, now an aged man of eighty, with a cup of sherbet and told him to drink The king, whose armlet of bezoar stone had already twice made poison harmless, drew the stone from his arm. He thanked the Almighty for granting him, unworthy, the happiest life that had ever fallen to the lot of man. He prayed that the sin of his death might not be laid to his son's charge, drank the poison, and died.[2]

Ghiás-ud-dín can hardly have shut himself off so completely from state affairs as the story-tellers make out. He seems to have been the first of the Málwa kings who minted gold. He also introduced new titles and ornaments, which implies an interest in his coinage.[3] Farishtah says that

---

[1] Wákiát-i-Mushtáki in Elliot, IV. 554-556. Probably these are stock tales. The Gujarát historians give Muzaffar and Muhammad the Gold-giver (A.D. 1441-1451) credit for the horse scrupulosity. See Mirát-i-Sikandari Pers. Text, 178.

[2] Briggs' Farishtah, IV. 236-239; Wákiát-i-Jehángíri in Elliot, VI. 349-350; Wákiát-i-Mushtáki in Elliot, IV. 551-55; Malcolm's Central India, I. 35-36. The Mirát-i-Sikandari (Pers. Text, 160) has the following notice of Ghiás-ud-dín: The Sultáns of Mándu had reached such a pitch of luxury and ease that it is impossible to imagine aught exceeding it. Among them Sultán Ghiás-ud-dín was so famous for his luxurious habits, that at present (A.D. 1611) if any one exceeds in luxury and pleasure, they say he is a second Ghiás-ud-dín. The orders of the Sultán were that no event of a painful nature or one in which there was any touch of sadness should be related to him. They say that during his entire reign news of a sad nature was only twice conveyed to him: once when his son-in-law died and once when his daughter was brought before him clothed in white. On this occasion the Sultán is related to have simply said: "Perhaps her husband is dead." This he said because the custom of the people of India is that when the husband of a woman dies she gives up wearing coloured clothes. The second occasion was when the army of Sultán Bahlol Lodi plundered several of the districts of Chanderi. Though it was necessary to report this to the Sultán, his ministers were unable to communicate it to him. They therefore asked a band of actors (*bhánds*) to assume the dress of Afgháns, and mentioning the districts to represent them as being pillaged and laid waste. Sultán Ghiás-ud-dín exclaimed in surprise: "But is the governor of Chanderi dead that he does not avenge upon the Afgháns the ruin of his country!"

[3] Compare Catalogue of Indian Coins, The Mahomedan States, pages LIV. LV. and 118-121.

Ghiás-ud-dín used to come out every day for an hour from his *harím*, sit on the throne and receive the salutations of his nobles and subjects, and give orders in all weighty matters of state. He used to entrust all minor affairs to his ministers; but in all grave matters he was so anxious not to shirk his responsibility as a ruler, that he had given strict orders that all such communications should be made to him at whatever time they came through a particular female officer appointed to receive his orders.[1]

According to most accounts Násir-ud-dín was led to poison his father by an attempt of his younger brother Shujáât Khán, supported if not organised by some of Ghiás-ud-dín's favourite wives to oust Násir-ud-dín from the succession.[2] In the struggle Násir-ud-dín triumphed and was crowned at Mándu in A.D. 1500.[3] The new king left Mándu to put down a revolt. On his return to Mándu he devoted himself to debauchery and to hunting down and murdering his brother's adherents. He subjected his mother Khurshíd Ráni to great indignities and torture to force from her information regarding his father's concealed treasures.[4] In a fit of drunkenness he fell into a reservoir. He was pulled out by four of his female slaves. He awoke with a headache, and discovering what his slaves had done put them to death with his own hand.[5] Some time after in A.D. 1512, he again fell into the reservoir, and there he was left till he was dead.[6] Násir-ud-dín was fond of building. His palace at Akbarpúr in the Nímar plain about twenty miles south of Mándu was splendid and greatly admired.[7] And at Mándu besides his sepulchre[8] which the emperor Jehángír (A.D. 1617) mentions,[9] an

---

[1] Farishtah Pers. Text, II. 507.

[2] Farishtah (Pers. Text, II. 508) detailing how Násir-ud-dín came to power, says: There was a difference between Násir-ud-dín and his brother Alá-ud-dín. The mother of these princes, Khurshíd Ráni, who was the daughter of the Hindu chief of Bágláua, had taken Alá-ud-dín the younger brother's side. After killing his father Násir-ud-dín ordered his mother to be dragged out of the *harim* and Alá-ud-dín and his children to be slaughtered like lambs.

[3] Briggs' Farishtah, IV. 238-239. Farishtah holds that Násir-ud-dín's murder of his father is not proved. He adds (Pers. Text, II. 515) that Násir-ud-dín was at Dhár where he had gone to quell the rebellion of the nobles when the news of Ghiás-ud-dín's death reached him. He argues that as a parricide cannot flourish more than a year after his father's murder, and as Násir-ud-dín ruled for years after that event, he could not have killed his father.

[4] Farishtah Pers. Text, II. 516.

[5] Briggs' Farishtah, IV. 243. The emperor Jehángír (Memoirs Pers. Text, 181) says that Násir-ud-dín had a disease which made him feel so hot that he used to sit for hours in water.

[6] Wákiát-i-Jehángíri in Elliot, VI. 350. Farishtah (Pers. Text, II. 517-18) says that Násir-ud-dín died of a burning-fever he had contracted by hard drinking and other evil habits, that he showed keen penitence before his death, and bequeathed his kingdom to his third son Mehmúd. The emperor Jehángír (Memoirs Pers. Text, 181) confirms the account of the Wákiát as to the manner of Násir-ud-dín's death.

[7] Briggs' Farishtah, IV. 243.

[8] The emperor Jehángír thus describes (Memoirs Pers. Text, 181) his visit to Násir-ud-dín's grave. It is related that when during his reign Sher Khán Afghán Súr (A.D. 1540-1555) visited Násir-ud-dín's grave he ordered his attendants to flagellate the parricide's tomb: When I visited the sepulchre I kicked his grave and ordered those with me to do the same. Not satisfied with this I ordered his bones to be dug out and burned and the ashes to be thrown into the Narbada.

[9] Wákiát-i-Jehángíri in Elliot, VI. 350. The emperor Jehángír (Memoirs Pers. Text, 202) refers to the well-known bridge and water-palace about three miles north of Ujjain as the work of Násir-ud-dín. He says: On Sunday I reached Saádulpur near Ujjain. In this village is a river house with a bridge on which are alcoves both built by Násir-ud-dín Khilji (A.D. 1500-1512). Though the bridge is not specially praiseworthy the water-courses and cisterns connected with it have a certain merit.

Appendix II.
THE HILL FORT OF MÁNDU.
HISTORY.
The Málwa Sultáns, A.D. 1400-1570.

inscription shows that the palace now known by the name of Báz Bahádur was built by Násir-ud-dín.

Násir-ud-dín was succeeded by his younger son (Mehmúd A.D. 1512-1530), who, with the title of Mehmúd the Second, was crowned with great pomp at Mándu. Seven hundred elephants in gold-embroidered velvet housings adorned the procession.[1] Shortly after his accession Mehmúd II. was driven out of Mándu by the revolt of the commandant Muháfiz Khán, but was restored by the skill and courage of Medáni Rái his Rájput commander-in-chief.[2] A still more dangerous combination by Muzaffar II. (A.D. 1511-1526) of Gujarát and Sikandar Sháh Lodi (A.D. 1488-1516) of Dehli, was baffled by the foresight and energy of the same Rájput general. Mehmúd, feeling that his power had passed to the Hindus, tried to disband the Rájputs and assassinate Medáni Rái. Failing in both attempts Mehmúd fled from Mándu to Gujarát, where he was well received by Sultán Muzaffar (A.D. 1511-1526).[3] They advanced together against Mándu, and in A.D. 1519, after a close siege of several months, took the fort by assault. The Rájput garrison, who are said to have lost 19,000 men, fought to the last, consecrating the close of their defence by a general *javar* or fire-sacrifice. Sultán Mehmúd entered Mándu close after the storming party, and while Mehmúd established his authority in Mándu, Muzaffar withdrew to Dhár. When order was restored Mehmúd sent this message to Muzaffar at Dhár: "Mándu is a splendid fort. You should come and see it." "May Mándu," Muzaffar replied, "bring good fortune to Sultán Mehmúd. He is the master of the fort. For the sake of the Lord I came to his help. On Friday I will go to the fortress, and having had the sermon read in Mehmúd's name will return." On Muzaffar's arrival in Mándu Mehmúd gave a great entertainment;[4] and Muzaffar

---

[1] Briggs' Farishtah, IV. 246.

[2] Briggs' Farishtah, IV. 247-249. Malcolm's (Central India, I. 38) writes the Rájput's name Maderay. The Mirát-i-Sikandari (Persian Text, 149-155), gives the form Medáni Rai, the Lord of the Battlefield, a title which the author says (page 149) Mehmúd conferred on the Rájput in acknowledgment of his prowess.

[3] The Mirát-i-Sikandari (Pers. Text, 154) gives the following details of Mehmúd's flight: Sultán Mehmúd, on pretence of hunting left Mándu and remained hunting for several days. The Hindus, whom Medáni Rái had placed on guard over him, slept after the fatigue of the chase. Only some of the more trusted guards remained. Among them was a Rájput named Krishna, a Málwa *zamíndár* who was attached to the Sultán. Mehmúd said to Krishna: "Can you find me two horses and show me the way to Gujarát that I may get aid from Sultán Muzaffar to punish these rascals? If you can, do so at once, and, Alláh willing, you shall be handsomely rewarded." Krishna brought two horses from the Sultán's stables. Mehmúd rode on one and seated his dearest of wives, Ráni Kannya Kuar, on the other. Krishna marched in front. In half the night and one day they reached the Gujarát frontier.

[4] Tárikh-i-Sher Sháhi in Elliot, IV. 386. The Mirát-i-Sikandari (Pers. Text, 160) gives the following details of the banquet: Sultán Mehmúd showed great hospitality and humility. After the banquet as he led the Sultán over the palaces, they came to a mansion in the centre of which was a four-cornered building like the Kaábah, carved and gilded, and round it were many apartments. When Sultán Muzaffar placed his foot within the threshold of that building the thousand beauties of Sultán Mehmúd's *harím*, magnificently apparelled and jewelled, all at once opened the doors of thier chambers and burst into view like húris and fairies. When Muzaffar's eyes fell on their charms he bowed his head and said: "To see other than one's own *harím* is sinful." Sultán Mehmúd replied: "These are mine, and therefore your's, seeing that I am the slave purchased by your Majesty's kindness." Muzaffar said: "They are more suitable for you. May you have joy in them. Let them retire." At a signal from Sultán Mehmúd the ladies vanished.

Appendix II.

THE HILL FORT OF MÁNDU.

HISTORY.

The Málwa Sultáns, A.D. 1400-1570.

retired to Gujarát leaving a force of 3000 Gujarátis to help to guard the hill.[1] Immediately after Muzaffar's departure, as Sultán Mehmúd was anxious to recover Chanderi and Gágraun, which still remained in the possession of Medáni Rái and his supporters, he marched against them. Rána Sánga of Chitor came to Medáni's aid and a great battle was fought.[2] Mehmúd's hastiness led him to attack when his men were weary and the Rajputs were fresh. In spite of the greatest bravery on the part of himself and of his officers the Musalmán army was defeated, and Mehmúd, weakened by loss of blood, was made prisoner. Rána Sánga had Mehmúd's wounds dressed, sent him to Chitor, and on his recovery released him.[3]

Sultán Bahádur of Gujarát, A.D. 1526-1534.

In A.D. 1526, by giving protection to his outlawed brother Chánd Khán and to Razí-ul-Mulk, a refugee Gujarát noble, Mehmúd brought on himself the wrath of Bahádur Sháh of Gujarát (A.D. 1526-1536). The offended Bahádur did not act hastily. He wrote to Mehmúd asking him to come to his camp and settle their quarrels. He waited on the Gujarát frontier at Karji Ghát, east of Bánswara, until at last satisfied that Mehmúd did not wish for a peaceful settlement he advanced on Mándu. Meanwhile Mehmúd had repaired the walls of Mándu, which soon after was invested by Bahádur. The siege was proceeding in regular course by mines and batteries, and the garrison, though overtaxed, were still loyal and in heart, when in the dim light of morning Mehmúd suddenly found the Gujarát flag waving on the battlements. According to the Mirăt-i-Sikandari[4] Bahádur annoyed by the slow progress of the siege asked his spies where was the highest ground near Mándu. The spies said: Towards Songad-Chitor the hill is extremely high. With a few followers the Sultán scaled Songad, and rushing down the slope burst through the wall and took the fort (May 20th, 1526).[5] Mehmúd surrendered. Near Dohad, on his way to his prison at Chámpánír, an attempt was made to rescue Mehmúd, and to prevent their escape he and some of his sons were slain and buried on the bank of the Dohad tank.[6] Bahádur spent the rainy season (June-October 1526) in Mándu, and Málwa was incorporated with Gujarát.

The Emperor Humáyún, A.D. 1534-1535.

Mándu remained under Gujarát, till in A.D. 1534, after Bahádur's defeat by Humáyún at Mandasor, Bahádur retired to Mándu. Humáyun followed. At night 200 of Humáyún's soldiers went to the back of the fortress, according to Farishtah the south-west height of Songad[7] by which Bahádur had surprised Mehmúd's garrison, scaled the walls by ladders and ropes, opened the gate, and let others in. Mallu Khán, the commandant of the batteries, a native of Málwa, who afterwards gained the title of Kádir Sháh, went to Bahádur and wakened him. Bahádur rushed out with four or five attendants. He was joined by about twenty more, and reaching the gate at the top of the *maidán*, apparently the Tárápúr gate by which Humáyún's men had entered, cut through 200 of Humáyún's troops and went off with Mallu Khán to the fort of Songad,

---

[1] Briggs' Farishtah, IV. 250-263.

[2] Farishtah Pers. Text. II. 527. According to the Mirăt-i-Sikandari (Pers. Text, 161) Mehmúd marched against Gágraun first, and slew Hemkaran, a partisan of Medáni Rái, in a hand-to-hand fight. On this the Rána and Medáni Rái joined their forces against Mehmúd.

[3] Briggs' Farishtah, IV. 262-263.

[4] Persian Edition, 239.

[5] Briggs' Farishtah, IV. 267-68. Sultán Bahádur apparently surprised the party in charge of the Tárápúr or Southern Gate.

[6] Briggs' Farishtah, IV. 269; Mirăt-i-Ahmedi, Persian Text, I. 76.

[7] Briggs' Farishtah, II. 77.

Appendix II.

THE HILL FORT OF MÁNDU.

HISTORY.

The Málwa Sultáns, A.D. 1400-1570.

the citadel of Mándu. While two of Bahádur's chiefs, Sadr Khán and Sultán Álam Lodi, threw themselves into Songad, Bahádur himself let his horses down the cliff by ropes and after a thousand difficulties made his way to Chámpánír.[1] On the day after Bahádur's escape Sadr Khán and Sultán Álam Lodi came out of Songad and surrendered to Humáyún.[2]

In the following year (A.D. 1535) the combined news of Sher Sháh's revolt in Bengal, and of the defeat of his officers at Broach and Cambay, forced Humáyún to retire from Gujarát. As he preferred its climate he withdrew, not to Agra but to Mándu.[3] From Mándu, as fortune was against him in Bengal, Humáyún went (A.D. 1535-36) to Agra.

Local Musalmán Chiefs, A.D. 1536-1542.

On Humáyún's departure three chiefs attempted to establish themselves at Mándu: Bhúpat Rái, the ruler of Bíjágar, sixty miles south of Mándu; Mallu Khán or Kádir Sháh, a former commandant of Mándu; and Mírán Muhammad Fárúki from Burhánpur.[4] Of these three Mallu Khán was successful. In A.D. 1536, when Humáyún fled from Sher Sháh to Persia, Mallu spread his power from Mándu to Ujjain Sárangpúr and Rantambhor, assumed the title of Kádir Sháh Málwi, and made Mándu his capital. Some time after Sher Sháh, who was now supreme, wrote to Mallu Kádir Sháh ordering him to co-operate in expelling the Mughals. Kádir Sháh resenting this assumption of overlordship, addressed Sher Sháh as an inferior. When Sher Sháh received Mallu's order he folded it and placed it in the scabbard of his poniard to keep the indignity fresh in his mind. Alláh willing, he said, we shall ask an explanation for this in person.[5] In A.D. 1542 (H. 949) as Kádir Sháh failed to act with Kutb Khán, who had been sent to establish Sher Sháh's overlordship in Málwa, Sher Sháh advanced from Gwalior towards Mándu with the object of punishing Kádir Sháh.[6] As he knew he could not stand against Sher Sháh Kádir Sháh went to Sárangpúr to do homage. Though on arrival Kádir Sháh was well received, his kingdom was given to Shujáát Khán, one of Sher Sháh's chief followers, and himself placed in Shujáát Khán's keeping.[7] Suspicious of what might be in store for

Sher Sháh Súr, A.D. 1542-1545.

---

[1] Abul Fazl's Akbar Námah in Elliot, VI. 14; Briggs' Farishtah, II. 77.

[2] Abul Fazl's Akbar Námah in Elliot, V. 192.

[3] Abul Fazl's Akbar Námah in Elliot, VI. 15; Briggs' Farishtah, II. 80-81.

[4] Abul Fazl's Akbar Námah in Elliot, VI. 18. According to Farishtah (Pers. Text, II. 532) Mallu, the son of Mallu, was a native of Málwa and a Khilji slave noble. Mallu received his title of Kádir Sháh from Sultán Mehmúd III. of Gujarát (A.D. 1536-1544) at the recommendation of his minister Imád-ul-Mulk who was a great friend of Mallu. Mirăt-i-Sikandari, Persian Text, 298.

[5] Farishtah Pers. Text, II. 532.

[6] Tárikh-i-Sher Sháh in Elliot, IV. 391; Briggs' Farishtah, IV. 271-72.

[7] Farishtah (Pers. Text, 533-34) refers to the following circumstance as the cause of Kádir Sháh's suspicion. On his way to Sher Sháh's darbár at Ujjain Kádir saw some Mughal prisoners in chains making a road. One of the prisoners seeing him began to sing:

Mard mí bín darín ahwál o fikri khishtan mí kun!
In this plight thou seest me to-day,
Thine own turn is not far away.

When Kádir Sháh escaped, Sher Sháh on hearing of his flight exclaimed:

Bá má chi kard dídí
Mallú Ghulám-i-gídí.
Thus he treats us with scorn,
Mallu the slave base born.

To this one of Sher Sháh's men replied:

Kaul-i-Rasúl bar hakk
Lá khaira fil abídi.
The words of the Prophet are true
No good can a slave ever do.

Appendix II.

THE HILL FORT OF MÁNDU.

HISTORY.

The Málwa Sultáns, A.D. 1400-1570.

him Kádir Sháh fled to Gujarát. Sher Sháh was so much annoyed at Shujáât Khán's remissness in not preventing Kádir Sháh's escape that he transferred the command at Dhár and Mándu from Shujáât Khán to Háji Khán and Junaid Khán. Shortly after Kádir Sháh brought a force from Gujarát and attacked Mándu. Shujáât came to Háji Khán's help and routed Kádir Sháh under the walls of Mándu. In reward Sher Sháh made him ruler of the whole country of Mándu.[1] Shujáât Khán established his head-quarters at Mándu with 10,000 horse and 7000 matchlockmen.

Salím Sháh Súr, A.D. 1545-1553.

During the reign of Sher Sháh's successor Salím Sháh (A.D. 1545-1553), Shujáât was forced to leave Málwa and seek shelter in Dúngarpúr. Selím pardoned Shujáât, but divided Málwa among other nobles. Shujáât remained in Hindustán till in A.D. 1553, on the accession of Salím's successor, Ádili, he recovered Málwa, and in A.D. 1554, on the decay of Ádili's power, assumed independence.[2] He died almost immediately after, and was succeeded by his eldest son Malik Báyazíd.[3] Shujáât Khán was a great builder. Besides his chief works at Shujáwalpúr near Ujjain, he left many memorials in different parts of Málwa.[4] So far none of the remains at Mándu are known to have been erected during the rule of Shujáât Khán.

Báz Bahádur, A.D. 1555-1570.

On the death of his father Malik Báyazíd killed his brother Daulat Khán, and was crowned in A.D. 1555 with the title of Báz Bahádur. He attacked the Gonds, but met with so crushing a defeat that he foreswore fighting.[5] He gave himself to enjoyment and become famous as a musician,[6] and for his poetic love of Rúp Mani or Rúp Mati, who according to one account was a wise and beautiful courtezan of Saháranpúr in Northern India, and according to another was the daughter of a Nímar Rájput, the master of the town of Dharampuri.[7] In A.D. 1560 Pír Muhammad, a general of Akbar's, afterwards ennobled as Khán Jehán, defeated Báz Bahádur, drove him out of Mándu, and made the hill his own head-quarters.[8] In the following year (A.D. 1561), by the help of the Berár chief, Pír Muhammad was slain and Báz Bahádur reinstated. On news of this defeat (A.D. 1562) Akbar sent Abdulláh Khán Uzbak with almost unlimited power to reconquer the province. Abdulláh was successful, but, as he showed signs of assuming independence, Akbar moved against him and he fled to Gujarát.[9] Akbar remained in Mándu during the greater part of the following rains (A.D. 1563), examining with interest the buildings erected by the Khilji kings.[10] At Mándu Akbar married the daughter of Mírán Mubárak Khán of Khándesh.[11] When Akbar left (August 1564) he appointed Karra Bahádur Khán governor of Mándu and returned to Ágra.[12] In A.D. 1568 the Mírzás, Akbar's cousins, flying from Gujarát attacked

---

[1] Táríkh-i-Sher Sháhi in Elliot, IV. 397.

[2] Táríkh-i-Alfi in Elliott, V. 168; Elphinstone's India, 402-403.

[3] Táríkh-i-Alfi in Elliot, V. 168.

[4] Briggs' Farishtah, IV. 276.

[5] When Báz Bahádur attacked the Gonds their chief was dead, and his widow, Ráni Durgávati, was ruling in his place. The Ráni led the Gonds against the invaders, and hemming them in one of the passes, inflicted on them such a defeat that Báz Bahádur fled from the field leaving his baggage and camp in her hands. Farishtah Pers. Text, II. 538.

[6] According to Farishtah (Pers. Text, II. 538) Báz Bahádur was already an adept in music.

[7] Malcolm's Central India, I. 89; Ruins of Mándu, 30.

[8] Briggs' Farishtah, II. 210.

[9] Blochman's Áin-i-Akbari, 321.

[10] Briggs' Farishtah, IV. 211.

[11] Briggs' Farishtah, IV. 216.

[12] Tabakát-i-Akbari in Elliot, V. 291.

Ujjain. From Ujjain they retreated to Mándu and failing to make any impression on the fort withdrew to Gujarát.[1] The Mirzás' failure was due to the ability of Akbar's general, Háji Muhammad Khán, to whom Akbar granted the province of Mándu.[2] At the same time (A.D. 1568) the command of Mándu hill was entrusted to Sháh Budágh Khán, who continued commandant of the fort till his death many years later. During his command, in a picturesque spot overlooking a well-watered ravine in the south of Mándu, between the Ságar Lake and the Tárápur Gateway, Budágh Khán built a pleasure-house, which he named, or rather perhaps which he continued to call Nílkanth or Blue Throat. This lodge is interesting from the following inscriptions, which show that the emperor Akbar more than once rested within its walls.[3]

The inscription on the small north arch of Nílkanth, dated A.D. 1574, runs:

> **(Call it not waste) to spend your life in water and earth (*i.e.* in building).**
> **If perchance a man of mind for a moment makes your house his lodging.**
> **Written by Sha'h Buda'gh Kha'n in the year A.H. 982-87.**[4]

The inscription on the great southern arch of Nílkanth, dated A.D. 1574, runs:

> **This pleasant building was completed in the reign of the great Sulta'n, the most munificent and just Kha'ka'n, the Lord of the countries of Arabia and Persia,[5] the shadow of God on the two earths, the ruler of the sea and of the land, the exalter of the standards of those who war on the side of God, Abul Fatah Jala'l-ud-di'n Muhammad Akbar, the warrior king, may his dominion and his kingdom be everlasting.**
> **Written by Fari'du'n Husein, son of Ha'tim-al-Wardi, in the year A.H. 982.**[6]

The inscription on the right wall of Nílkanth, dated A.D. 1591-92, runs:

> **In the year A.H. 1000, when on his way to the conquest of the Dakhan, the slaves of the Exalted Lord of the Earth, the holder of the sky-like Throne, the shadow of Alla'h (the Emperor Akbar), passed by this place.**
>
> **That time wastes your home cease, Soul, to complain,**
> **Who will not scorn a complainer so vain.**
> **From the story of others this wisdom derive,**
> **Ere naught of thyself but stories survive.**

The inscription on the left wall of Nílkanth, dated A.D. 1600, runs:

> **The (Lord of the mighty Presence) shadow of Alla'h, the Emperor Akbar, after the conquest of the Dakhan and**

---

[1] Tabakát-i-Akbari in Elliot, V. 330-31. [2] Blochman's Áín-i-Akbari, 375.

[3] The emperor Jehángír thus describes (Memoirs Pers. Text, 372) a visit to this building: On the third day of Amardád (July 1617) with the palace ladies I set out to see Nílkanth, which is one of the pleasantest places in Mándu fort. Sháh Budágh Khán, who was one of the trusted nobles of my august father, built this very pleasing and joy-giving lodge during the time he held this province in fief (A.D. 1572-1577). I remained at Nílkanth till about an hour after nightfall and then returned to my state quarters.

[4] An officer who distinguished himself under Humáyún, one of Akbar's commanders of Three Thousand, long governor of Mándu, where he died. Blochman's Áín-i-Akbari, 372.

[5] When opposed to Árab the word Ájam signifies all countries except Arabia, and in a narrow sense, Persia. The meaning of the word Ájam is dumbness, the Arabs so glorying in the richness of their own tongue as to hold all other countries and nations dumb.

[6] The stones on which this inscription is carved have been wrongly arranged by some restorer. Those with the latter portion of the inscription come first and those with the beginning come last. Múnshi Abdur Rahím of Dhár.

Appendix II.

THE HILL FORT OF MÁNDU.

HISTORY.

The Mughals, A.D. 1570-1720.

Da'ndes (Kha'ndesh) in the year A.H. 1009 set out for Hind (Northern India).

May the name of the writer last for ever!

At dawn and at eve I have watched an owl sitting
On the lofty wall-top of Shirwa'n Sha'h's Tomb.[1]
The owl's plaintive hooting convey'd me this warning
"Here pomp, wealth, and greatness lie dumb."

In A.D. 1573, with the rest of Málwa, Akbar handed Mándu to Muzaffar III. the dethroned ruler of Gujarát. It seems doubtful if Muzaffar ever visited his new territory.[2] On his second defeat in A.D. 1562 Báz Bahádur retired to Gondwána, where he remained, his power gradually waning, till in A.D. 1570 he paid homage to the emperor and received the command of 2000 horse.[3] His decoration of the Rewa Pool, of the palace close by, which though built by Násir-ud-dín Khilji (A.D. 1500-1512) was probably repaired by Báz Bahádur, and of Rúp Mati's pavilion on the crest of the southern ridge make Báz Bahádur one of the chief beautifiers of Mándu. According to Farishtah (Pers. Text, II. 538-39) in 1562, when Báz Bahádur went out to meet Akbar's general, Adham Khán Atkah, he placed Rúp Mati and his other singers in Sárangpúr under a party of his men with orders to kill the women in case of a reverse. On hearing of Báz Bahádur's defeat the soldiers hastily sabred as many of the women as they could and fled. Among the women left for dead was Rúp Mati, who, though dangerously wounded, was not killed. When Adham Atkah entered Sárangpúr his first care was to enquire what had become of Rúp Mati. On hearing of her condition he had her wound attended to by the best surgeons, promising her, as a help to her cure, a speedy union with her beloved. On her recovery Rúp Mati claimed the general's promise. He prevaricated and pressed his own suit. Rúp Mati temporised. One night the impatient Turk sent her a message asking her to come to him. Rúp Mati to gain time invited him to her own pavilion which she said was specially adorned to be the abode of love. Next night the Atkah went to her house in disguise. Her women directed him to Rúp Mati's couch. Adham found her robed and garlanded, but cold in death. Rúp Mati was buried on an island in a lake at Ujjain, and there, according to the Áín-i-Akbari, Báz Bahádur when he died was laid beside her.[4]

SECTION II.—MUGHALS (A.D. 1570-1720) AND MARÁTHÁS (A.D. 1720-1820).

About A.D. 1590 Akbar's historian, the great Abul Fazl, described Mándu as a large city whose fortress is twenty-four miles (twelve *kos*) in circuit. He notices that besides in the centre of the hill where stands an eight-storeyed minaret, the city had many monuments of ancient magnificence, among them the tombs of the Khilji Sultáns. And that from the dome which is over the sepulchre of Sultán Mehmúd, the son of Hoshang (this should be the sepulchre of Hoshang built by his successor Sultán Mehmúd) water drops in the height of summer to the astonishment of the ignorant. But, he adds, men of understanding know how to account for the water-drops.[5] Abul Fazl further notices that on Mándu Hill is found a species of tamarind whose fruit is as big as the cocoanut, the pulp of

---

[1] The maternal uncle of Naushirwán (A.D. 586-635) the Sássánian, Shirwán Sháh was ruler of a district on Mount Caucasus. Al Masüdi, Arabic Text Prairies d'Or, II. 4, and Rauzat-us-Safa, Persian Text, I. 259.

[2] Blochman's A'ín-i-Akbari, 353.

[3] Briggs' Farishtah, IV. 279.

[4] Blochman's A'ín-i-Akbari, 429.

[5] Gladwin's A'ín-i-Akbari, II. 41.

Appendix II.

THE HILL FORT OF MÁNDU.

HISTORY.

The Mughals, A.D. 1570-1720.

which is very white. This is the African baobab or Adansonia digitata, known in Hindustáni as *goramli* or white tamarind, whose great fruit is about the size of a cocoanut. Its monster baobabs are still a feature of Mándu. Some among them look old enough to have been yielding fruit 300 years ago. Finally Abul Fazl refers to Mándu as one of twenty-eight towns where Akbar's copper coins were struck.[1] About twenty years later (A.D. 1610) the historian Farishtah[2] thus describes the hill. The fort of Mándu is a work of solid masonry deemed to be one of the strongest fortifications in that part of the world. It is built on an insulated mountain thirty-eight miles in circumference.[3] The place of a ditch round the fortification is supplied by a natural ravine so deep that it seems impossible to take the fort by regular approaches. Within the fort is abundance of water and forage, but the area is not large enough to grow a sufficient store of grain. The hill cannot be invested. The easiest access is from the north by the Dehli Gate. The south road with an entrance by the Tárápúr Gate is so steep that cavalry can with difficulty be led up. Like Abul Fazl Farishtah notices that, except during the rains, water constantly oozes from between the chinks in the masonry of the dome of Sultán Hoshang's tomb. He says the natives of India attribute this dropping to universal veneration for Sultán Hoshang, for whose death, they say, the very stones shed tears.

Except that copper coins continued to be minted and that it was nominally one of the four capitals of the empire, during the emperor Akbar's reign Mándu was practically deserted. The only traces of Akbar's presence on the hill are in two of the five inscriptions already quoted from the Nílkanth pleasure-house, dated A.D. 1591 and A.D. 1600.

After about fifty years of almost complete neglect the emperor Jehángír, during a few months in A.D. 1617, enabled Mándu once more to justify its title of Shádiábád, the Abode of Joy. Early in March A.D. 1617, in the eleventh year of his reign, the emperor Jehángír after spending four months in travelling the 189 miles from Ajmír by way of Ujjain, arrived at Nâalchah on the main land close to the north of Mándu. The emperor notices that most of the forty-six marches into which the 189 miles were divided ended on the bank of some lake stream or great river in green grass and woody landscape, brightened by poppy fields. We came, he writes, enjoying the beauty of the country and shooting, never weary, as if we were moving from one garden to another.

Of the country round Naâlchah Jehángír says:[4] What can be written worthy of the beauty and the pleasantness of Naâlchah. The neighbourhood is full of mango trees. The whole country is one unbroken and restful evergreen. Owing to its beauty I remained there three days. I granted the place to Kamál Khán, taking it from Keshava Márú, and I changed its name to Kamálpúr. I had frequent meetings with some of the wise men of the *jogis*, many of whom had assembled here. Naâlchah is one of the best places in Málwa. It has an extensive growth of vines, and among its mango groves and vineyards wander streamlets of water. I arrived at a time when, contrary to the northern climes, the vines were in blossom and fruit, and so great was the vintage that the meanest boor could eat grapes to his fill. The poppy was also in flower, and its fields delighted the eye with their many-coloured beauty.

---

[1] Blochman's Áín-i-Akbari, 31.
[2] Briggs' Farishtah, IV. 169, 181, 190.
[3] Nineteen *kos*, taking the *kos* to be two miles.
[4] The emperor Jehángír's Memoirs, Pers. Text, Sir Sayad Ahmed's Edition, 173-203.

Appendix II.

THE HILL FORT OF MÁNDU.

HISTORY.

The Mughals, A.D. 1570-1720.

Of the emperor's entrance into Mándu the Memoirs have the following note: On Monday the 23rd of Ispandád, the last month of the Persian year, that is according to Sir Thomas Roe's account on the 6th of March 1617, when one quarter of the day had passed, I mounted my elephant, and, in good fortune and under kindly influences, made my happy entry into the fort of Mándu. About an hour (three *ghadis*) later I entered the quarters which had been prepared to receive me. During my passage across the hill-top I scattered Rs. 1500. Before my arrival Abdul Karím the engineer had been sent by me to repair the buildings of the former kings of Mándu. While my fortunate standards were at Ajmír Abdul Karím repaired such of the old Mándu buildings as were fit to be repaired and built others anew. On the whole he had provided quarters for me, the like of which have probably never been built in any other place. Three *lakhs* of rupees were spent on these repairs and buildings. I wish it had been possible to construct buildings like these in all cities likely to be visited by royalty. This fortress, he continues, stands on the top of a hill about thirty-six miles (18 *kos*) in circumference. They say that before the days of Rája Bikramájit a king was reigning over these parts who name was Jaisingh Deva. In his time a man went to the forest to cut grass. When he brought the grass back he found that the blade of his sickle had turned yellow. The grasscutter in his surprise went to Mándan, an ironsmith. Mándan knew that the sickle was gold. He had heard that in those parts was to be found the philosopher's stone, whose touch turns iron and copper into gold. He told the grasscutter to lead him to the place where the sickle had turned yellow, and there he found the philosopher's stone. The smith presented this treasure to his king. The king amassed untold wealth, part of which he spent in building Mándu fortress which he completed in twelve years. At the request of the smith on most of the stones in the walls a mark was cut in the form of an anvil. Towards the close of his life, when king Jaisingh Deva withdrew his heart from the world, he called many Bráhmans together on the bank of the Narbada close to Mándu. He gave each Bráhman a share of his wealth. And to the Bráhman in whom he had the greatest faith he gave the philosopher's stone. Enraged at the gift of a paltry stone the Bráhman threw it into the Narbada, and there the philosopher's stone still lies. The emperor continues: On the 20th of *Farwardín*, five weeks after my arrival (11th April 1617) in reward for his services in repairing the buildings of Mándu, I conferred on my engineer Abdul Karím the command of 1200 horse, with the title of Maámúr Khán.

Mándu had for the emperor the strong attraction of abundance of game. Among numerous entries of *nílgái* or blue-bull shooting the following occur: On the 4th of the first month of *Farwardín* (16th) March the watchmen of the chase brought word that they had marked down a lion near the Ságar Lake, which is a construction of the ancient rulers of Mándu. I mounted and proceeded towards the lake. When the lion broke cover he attacked and wounded ten or twelve of the *Ahidís*[1] and other men of my retinue. In the end I brought him down with three gun shots and saved God's creatures from his evil. On the 22nd of the same month (April 3rd, 1617) the watchmen brought news of a tiger. I mounted forthwith and despatched him with three bullets. On the 7th of *Ardí Bihisht* (April 18th, 1617) the watchmen brought word that they had marked down four tigers. At one in the afternoon I started for the

[1] Literally single-men. The Ahadís were a corps of men who stood immediately under the emperor's orders. Blochman's Áín-i-Akbari, 20 note 1.

Appendix II.
THE HILL FORT OF MÁNDU.
HISTORY.
The Mughals, A.D. 1570-1720.

place with Núr Jehán Begam. Núr Jehán asked my leave to shoot the tigers with her gun. I said "Be it so." In a trice she killed these four tigers with six bullets. I had never seen such shooting. To shoot from the back of an elephant from within a closed *howdah* and bring down with six bullets four wild beasts without giving them an opportunity of moving or springing is wonderful. In acknowledgment of this capital marksmanship I ordered a thousand *ashrafis* (Rs. 4500) to be scattered [1] over Núr Jehán and granted her a pair of ruby wristlets worth a lákh of rupees.[2]

Of the mangoes of Mándu Jehángir says: In these days many mangoes have come into my fruit stores from the Dakhan, Burhánpur, Gujarát, and the districts of Málwa. This country is famous for its mangoes. There are few places the mangoes of which can rival those of this country in richness of flavour, in sweetness, in freedom from fibre, and in size.[3]

The rains set in with unusual severity. Rain fell for forty days continuously. With the rain were severe thunderstorms accompanied by lightning which injured some of the old buildings.[4] His account of the beauty of the hill in July, when clear sunshine followed the forty days of rain, is one of the pleasantest passages in Jehángír's Memoirs: What words of mine can describe the beauty of the grass and of the wild flowers! They clothe each hill and dale, each slope and plain. I know of no place so pleasant in climate and so pretty in scenery as Mándu in the rainy season. This month of July which is one of the months of the hot season, the sun being in Leo, one cannot sleep within the house without a coverlet, and during the day there is no need for a fan. What I have noticed is but a small part of the many beauties of Mándu. Two things I have seen here which I had seen nowhere in India. One of them is the tree of the wild plantain which grows all over the hill top, the other is the nest of the *mamolah* or wagtail. Till now no bird-catcher could tell its nest. It so happened that in the building where I lodged we found a wagtail's nest with two young ones.

The following additional entries in the Memoirs belong to Jehángír's stay at Mándu. Among the presents submitted by Mahábat Khán, who received the honour of kissing the ground at Mándu, Jehángír describes a ruby weighing eleven *miskáls*.[5] He says: This ruby was brought to Ajmír last year by a Frankish jeweller who wanted two lákhs of rupees for it. Mahábat Khán bought it at Burhánpur for one lákh of rupees.[6]

On the 1st of *Tír*, the fourth month of the Persian year (15th May 1617), the Hindu chiefs of the neighbourhood came to pay their

---

[1] This scattering of gold silver or copper coin, called in Arabic and Persian *nisár*, is a common form of offering. The influence of the evil eye or other baneful influence is believed to be transferred from the person over whom the coin is scattered to the coin and through the coin to him who takes it.

[2] This feat of Núr Jehán's drew from one of the Court poets the couplet:

Núr Jehán gar chih ba súrat zanast
Dar safi Mardán zani sher afkanast.
Núr Jehán the tiger-slayer's woman
Ranks with men as the tiger-slaying woman.

Sherafkan, that is tiger-slayer, was the title of Núr Jehán's first husband Ali-Kuli Istajlu.

[3] Tuzuk-i-Jehángíri Pers. Text, 187.

[4] Tuzuk-i-Jehángíri Pers. Text, 189.

[5] The *miskál* which was used in weighing gold was equal in weight to ninety-six barleycorns. Blochman's Áín-i-Akbari, 36.

[6] Tuzuk-i-Jehángíri Pers. Text, 195.

Appendix II.

The Hill Fort of Mándu.

History.

The Mughals, A.D. 1570-1720.

respects and present their tribute. The Hindu chief of Jítpúr in the neighbourhood of Mándu, through his evil fortune, did not come to kiss the threshold.[1] For this reason I ordered Fidáíkhán to pillage the Jítpúr country at the head of thirteen officers and four or five hundred matchlockmen. On the approach of Fidáíkhán the chief fled. He is now reported to regret his past conduct and to intend to come to Court and make his submission. On the 9th of *Yúr*, the sixth month of the Persian calendar (late July, A.D. 1617), I heard that while raiding the lands of the chief of Jítpúr, Rúh-ul-láh, the brother of Fidáíkhán, was slain with a lance in the village where the chief's wives and children were in hiding. The village was burned, and the women and daughters of the rebel chief were taken captives.[2]

The beautiful surroundings of the Ságar lake offered to the elegant taste of Núr Jehán a fitting opportunity for honouring the Shab-i-Barát or Night of Jubilee with special illuminations. The emperor describes the result in these words: On the evening of Thursday the 19th of *Amardád*, the fifth month of the Persian year (early July, A.D. 1617), I went with the ladies of the palace to see the buildings and palaces on the Ságar lake which were built by the old kings of Mándu. The 26th of *Amardád* (about mid-July) was the Shab-i-Barát holiday. I ordered a jubilee or assembly of joy to be held on the occasion in one of the palaces occupied by Núr Jehán Begam in the midst of the big lake. The nobles and others were invited to attend this party which was organized by the Begam, and I ordered the cup and other intoxicants with various fruits and minced meats to be given to all who wished them. It was a wonderful gathering. As evening set in the lanterns and lamps gleaming along the banks of the lake made an illumination such as never had been seen. The countless lights with which the palaces and buildings were ablaze shining on the lake made the whole surface of the water appear to be on fire.[3]

The Memoirs continue: On Sunday the 9th of *Yúr*, the sixth Persian month (late July), I went with the ladies of the palace to the quarters of Ásaf Khán, Núr Jehán's brother, the second son of Mirza Ghiás Beg. I found Ásaf Khán lodged in a glen of great beauty surrounded by other little vales and dells with waterfalls and running streamlets and green and shady mango groves. In one of these dells were from two to three hundred sweet pandanus or *kewda* trees. I passed a very happy day in this spot and got up a wine party with some of my lords-in-waiting, giving them bumpers of wine.[4] Two months later (early September) Jehángír has the following entry[5] regarding a visit from his eldest son and heir prince Khurram, afterwards the emperor Shah Jehán, who had lately brought the war in the Dakhan to a successful close. On the 8th of the month of *Máh* (H. 1026: according to Roe September 2nd, 1617), my son of exalted name obtained the good fortune of waiting upon me in the fort of Mándu after three-quarters and one *ghadi* of the day had passed, that is about half an hour after sunrise. He had been absent fifteen months and eleven days. After he had performed the ceremonies of kissing the ground and the *kurnish* or prostration, I called him up to my bay window or *jharokah*. In a transport of affection I could not restrain myself from getting up and taking him into my arms. The more

---

[1] Tuzuk-i-Jehángíri Pers. Text, 195.
[2] Tuzuk-i-Jehángíri Pers. Text, 192-194.
[3] Tuzuk-i-Jehángíri Pers. Text, 190.
[4] Tuzuk-i-Jehángíri Pers. Text, 192.
[5] Tuzuk-i-Jehángíri Pers. Text, 194-5.

Appendix II.

THE HILL FORT OF MÁNDU.

HISTORY.

The Mughals, A.D. 1570-1720.

I increased the measure of affection and honours the more humility and respect did he show. I called him near me and made him sit by me. He submitted a thousand *ashrafis* (= Rs. 4500) and a thousand rupees as a gift or *nazar* and the same amount as sacrifice or *nisár*. As there was not time for me to inspect all his presents he produced the elephant Sarnák, the best of the elephants of Ádil Khán of Bijápur. He also gave me a case full of the rarest precious stones. I ordered the military paymasters to make presents to his nobles according to their rank. The first to come was Khán Jehán, whom I allowed the honour of kissing my feet. For his victory over the Rána of Chitor I had before granted to my fortunate child Kurram the rank of a commander of 20,000 with 10,000 horse. Now for his service in the Dakhan I made him a commander of 30,000 and 20,000 horse with the title of Sháh Jehán. I also ordered that henceforward he should enjoy the privilege of sitting on a stool near my throne, an honour which did not exist and is the first of its kind granted to anyone in my family. I further granted him a special dress. To do him honour I came down from the window and with my own hand scattered over his head as sacrifice a trayfull of precious stones as well as a large trayfull of gold.

Jehángír's last Mándu entry is this: On the night of Friday in the month of *Abán* (October 24th, 1617) in all happiness and good fortune I marched from Mándu and halted on the bank of the lake at Naálchah.

Jehángír's stay at Mándu is referred to by more than one English traveller. In March 1617, the Rev. Edward Terry, chaplain to the Right Honourable Sir T. Roe Lord Ambassador to the Great Mughal, came to Mándu from Burhánpúr in east Khándesh.[1] Terry crossed a broad river, the Narbada, at a great town called Anchabarpur (Akbarpur)[2] in the Nímár plain not far south of Mándu hill. The way up, probably by the Bhairav pass a few miles east of Mándu, seemed to Terry exceeding long. The ascent was very difficult, taking the carriages, apparently meaning coaches and wagons, two whole days.[3] Terry found the hill of Mándu stuck round with fair trees that kept their distance so, one from and below the other, that there was much delight in beholding them from either the bottom or the top of the hill. From one side only was the ascent not very high and steep. The top was flat plain and spacious with vast and

---

[1] A Voyage to East India, 181. Terry gives April 1616, but Roe seems correct in saying March 1617. Compare Wákiát-i-Jehángíri in Elliot, VI. 351.

[2] Akbarpur lies between Dharampuri and Waisar. Malcolm's Central India, I. 81 note.

[3] Carriages may have the old meaning of things carried, that is baggage. The time taken favours the view that wagons or carts were forced up the hill. For the early seventeenth century use of carriages in its modern sense compare Terry (Voyage, 161). Of our wagons drawn with oxen . . . . and other carriages we made a ring every night; also Dodsworth (1614), who describes a band of Rajpúts near Baroda cutting off two of his carriages (Kerr's Voyages, IX. 203); and Roe (1616), who journeyed from Ajmír to Mándu with twenty camels four carts and two coaches (Kerr, IX. 308). Terry's carriages seem to be Roe's coaches, to which Dela Valle (A.D. 1623) Haklyt's Edition, I. 21) refers as much like the Indian chariots described by Strabo (B.C. 50) covered with crimson silk fringed with yellow about the roof and the curtains. Compare Idrísi (A.D. 1100-1150, but probably from Al Istakhiri, A.D. 960: Elliot, I. 87). In all Nahrwala or north Gujarát the only mode of carrying either passengers or goods is in chariots drawn by oxen with harness and traces under the control of a driver. When in 1616 Jehángír left Ajmír for Mándu the English carriage presented to him by the English ambassador Sir Thomas Roe was allotted to the Sultánah Núr Jehán Begam. It was driven by an English coachman. Jehángír followed in the coach his own men had made in imitation of the English coach. Corryat (1615, Crudities III., Letters from India, unpaged) calls the English chariot a gallant coach of 150 pounds price.

Appendix II.

THE HILL FORT OF MÁNDU.

HISTORY.

The Mughals, A.D. 1570-1720.

far-stretching woods in which were lions tigers and other beasts of prey and many wild elephants. Terry passed through Mándu a few days' march across a plain and level country, apparently towards Dhár, where he met the Lord Ambassador Sir Thomas Roe, who had summoned Terry from Surat to be his chaplain. Sir Thomas Roe was then marching from Ajmír to Mándu with the Court of the emperor Jehángír, whom Terry calls the Great King.

On the 3rd of March, says Roe, the Mughal was to have entered Mándu. But all had to wait for the good hour fixed by the astrologers. From the 6th of March, when he entered Mándu, till the 24th of October, the emperor Jehángír, with Sir Thomas Roe in attendance, remained at Mándu.[1] According to Roe before the Mughal visited Mándu the hill was not much inhabited, having more ruins by far than standing houses.[2] But the moving city that accompanied the emperor soon overflowed the hill-top. According to Roe Jehángír's own encampment was walled round half a mile in circuit in the form of a fortress, with high screens or curtains of coarse stuff, somewhat like Aras hangings, red on the outside, the inside divided into compartments with a variety of figures. This enclosure had a handsome gateway and the circuit was formed into various coins and bulwarks. The posts that supported the curtains were all surmounted with brass tops.[3] Besides the emperor's encampment were the noblemen's quarters, each at an appointed distance from the king's tents, very handsome, some having their tents green, others white, others of mixed colours. The whole composed the most curious and magnificent sight Roe had ever beheld.[4] The hour taken by Jehángír in passing from the Dehli Gate to his own quarters, the two English miles from Roe's lodge which was not far from the Dehli Gate to Jehángír's palace, and other reasons noted below make it almost certain that the Mughal's encampment and the camps of the leading nobles were on the open slopes to the south of the Sea Lake between Báz Bahádur's palace on the east and Songad on the west. And that the palace at Mándu from which Jehángír wrote was the building now known as Báz Bahádur's palace.[5] A few months before it reached Mándu the imperial camp had turned the whole valley of Ajmír into a magnificent city,[6] and a few weeks before reaching Mándu at Thoda, about fifty miles south-east of Ajmír, the camp formed a settlement not less in circuit than twenty English miles, equalling in size almost any town in Europe.[7] In the middle of the encampment were all sorts of shops so regularly disposed that all persons knew where to go for everything.

The demands of so great a city overtaxed the powers of the deserted Mándu. The scarcity of water soon became so pressing that the poor were commanded to leave and all horses and cattle were ordered off the hill.[8] Of the scarcity of water the English traveller Corryat, who was then a guest of Sir Thomas Roe, writes: On the first day one of my Lord's people, Master Herbert, brother to Sir Edward Herbert, found a fountain which, if he had not done, he would have had to send ten course

---

[1] Kerr's Voyages, IX. 335; Wákiát-i-Jehángíri in Elliot, VI. 377.

[2] Roe writing from Ajmír in the previous year (29th August 1616) describes Mándu as a castle on a hill, where there is no town and no buildings. Kerr, IX. 267.

[3] Roe in Kerr's Travels, IX. 313.

[4] Roe in Kerr's Travels, IX. 314.

[5] Compare Wákiát-i-Jehángíri in Elliot, VI. 377.

[6] Roe in Kerr's Travels, IX. 314.

[7] Roe in Kerr's Travels, IX. 321.

[8] Roe in Kerr's Travels, IX. 335.

Appendix II.
THE HILL FORT OF MÁNDU.
HISTORY.
The Mughals, A.D. 1570-1720.

(*kos*) every day for water to a river called Narbada that falleth into the Bay of Cambye near Broach. The custom being such that whatsoever fountain or tank is found by any great man in time of drought he shall keep it proper to his without interruption. The day after one of the king's Hadis (*Ahádis*) finding the same and striving for it was taken by my Lord's people and bound.[1] Corryat adds: During the time of the great drought two Moor nobles daily sent ten camels to the Narbada and distributed the water to the poor, which was so dear they sold a little skin for 8 pies (one penny).[2]

Terry notices that among the piles of buildings that held their heads above ruin were not a few unfrequented mosques or Muhammadan churches. Though the people who attended the king were marvellously straitened for room to put their most excellent horses, none would use the churches as stables, even though they were forsaken and out of use. This abstinence seems to have been voluntary, as Roe's servants, who were sent in advance, took possession of a fair court with walled enclosure in which was a goodly temple and a tomb. It was the best in the whole circuit of Mándu, the only drawback being that it was two miles from the king's house.[3] The air was wholesome and the prospect was pleasant, as it was on the edge of the hill.[4] The emperor, perhaps referring rather to the south of the hill, which from the elaborate building and repairs carried out in advance by Abdul Karím seems to have been called the New City, gives a less deserted impression of Mándu. He writes (24th March 1617): Many buildings and relics of the old kings are still standing, for as yet decay has not fallen upon the city. On the 24th I rode to see the royal edifices. First I visited the Jámá Masjid built by Sultán Hoshang Ghori. It is a very lofty building and erected entirely of hewn stone. Although it has been standing 180 years it looks as if built to-day. Then I visited the sepulchres of the kings and rulers of the Khilji dynasty, among which is the sepulchre of the eternally cursed Násir-ud-din.[5] Sher Sháh to show his horror of Násir-ud-dín, the father-slayer, ordered his people to beat Násir-ud-dín's tomb with sticks. Jehángir also kicked the grave. Then he ordered the tomb to be opened and the remains to be taken out and burnt. Finally, fearing the remains might pollute the eternal light, he ordered the ashes to be thrown into the Narbada.[6]

The pleasant outlying position of Roe's lodge proved to be open to the objection that out of the vast wilderness wild beasts often came, seldom returning without a sheep, a goat, or a kid. One evening a great lion leapt over the stone wall that encompassed the yard and snapt up the Lord Ambassador's little white neat shock, that is as Roe explains a small Irish mastiff, which ran out barking at the lion. Out of the ruins of the mosque and tomb Roe built a lodge,[7] and here he passed the rains with his "family," including besides his secretary, chaplain, and cook twenty-three Englishmen and about sixty native servants, and during part of the time the sturdy half-crazed traveller Tom Coryate or Corryat.[8] They had

---

[1] Corryat's Crudities, III. Extracts (unpaged). This Master Herbert was Thomas, brother of Sir Edward Herbert, the first Lord Herbert. It seems probable that this Thomas supplied his cousin Sir Thomas Herbert who was travelling in India and Persia in A.D. 1627 with his account of Mándu. See below pages 381-382.

[2] Corryat's Crudities, III. Extracts (unpaged).

[3] Terry's Voyage, 183; Roe in Kerr, IX. 335.

[4] Roe in Kerr, IX. 335.

[5] Wákiát-i-Jehángiri in Elliot, VI. 349.

[6] Wákiát-i-Jehángiri in Elliot, VI. 350.

[7] Terry's Voyage, 228.

[8] Terry's Voyage, 69.

Appendix II.

THE HILL FORT OF MÁNDU.

HISTORY.

The Mughals, A.D. 1570-1720.

their flock of sheep and goats, all necessaries belonging to the kitchen and everything else required for bodily use including bedding and all things pertaining thereto.[1] Among the necessaries were tables[2] and chairs, since the Ambassador refused to adopt the Mughal practice of sitting cross-legged on mats "like taylors on their shopboards." Roe's diet was dressed by an English and an Indian cook and was served on plate by waiters in red taffata cloaks guarded with green taffata. The chaplain wore a long black cassock, and the Lord Ambassador wore English habits made as light and cool as possible.[3]

On the 12th of March, a few days after they were settled at Mándu, came the festival of the Persian New Year. Jehángir held a great reception seated on a throne of gold bespangled with rubies emeralds and turquoises. The hall was adorned with pictures of the King and Queen of England, the Princess Elizabeth, Sir Thomas Smith and others, with beautiful Persian hangings. On one side, on a little stage, was a couple of women singers. The king commanded that Sir T. Roe should come up and stand beside him on the steps of the throne where stood on one side the Persian Ambassador and on the other the old king of Kandahár with whom Sir T. Roe ranked. The king called the Persian Ambassador and gave him some stones and a young elephant. The Ambassador knelt and knocked his head against the steps of the throne to thank him.[4] From time to time during Terry's stay at Mándu, the Mughal, with his stout daring Persian and Tartarian horsemen and some grandees, went out to take young wild elephants in the great woods that environed Mándu. The elephants were caught in strong toils prepared for the purpose and were manned and made fit for service. In these hunts the king and his men also pursued lions and other wild beasts on horseback, killing some of them with their bows carbines and lances.[5]

The first of September was Jehángír's birthday. The king, says Corryat,[6] was forty-five years old, of middle height, corpulent, of a seemly composition of body, and of an olive coloured skin. Roe went to pay his respects and was conducted apparently to Báz Bahádur's Gardens to the east of the Rewa Pool. This tangled orchard was then a beautiful garden with a great square pond or tank set all round with trees and flowers and in the middle of the garden a pavilion or pleasure-house under which hung the scales in which the king was to be weighed.[7] The scales were of beaten gold set with many small stones as rubies and turquoises. They were hung by chains of gold, large and massive, but strengthened by silken ropes. The beam and tressels from which the scales hung were covered with thin plates of gold. All round were the nobles of the court seated on rich carpets waiting for the king. He came laden with diamonds rubies pearls and other precious vanities, making a great and glorious show. His swords targets and throne were corresponding in riches and splendour. His head neck breast and arms above the elbows and at the wrist were decked with chains of precious stones, and every finger had two or three rich rings. His legs were as it were fettered with chains of diamonds and rubies as large as walnuts and amazing pearls. He got into the scales crouching or sitting on his legs like a woman. To counterpoise his weight bags said to contain Rs. 9000 in

[1] Terry's Voyage, 183. [2] Terry's Voyage, 186, 198. [3] Terry's Voyage, 198, 205.
[4] Roe in Kerr's Voyages, IX. 337; Pinkerton's Voyages, VIII. 35.
[5] Terry's Voyage, 403. [6] Corryat's Crudities, III. Letter 2. Extracts unpaged.
[7] Roe in Kerr's Voyages, IX. 343.

Appendix II.

THE HILL FORT OF MÁNDU.

HISTORY.

The Mughals, A.D. 1570-1720.

silver were changed six times. After this he was weighed against bags containing gold jewels and precious stones. Then against cloth of gold, silk stuffs, cotton goods, spices, and all commodities. Last of all against meal, butter, and corn. Except the silver, which was reserved for the poor, all was said to be distributed to Baniahs (that is Bráhmans).[1] After he was weighed Jehángír ascended the throne and had basons of nuts almonds and spices of all sorts given him. These the king threw about, and his great men scrambled prostrate on their bellies. Roe thought it not decent that he should scramble. And the king seeing that he stood aloof reached him a bason almost full and poured the contents into his cloak.[2] Terry adds: The physicians noted the king's weight and spoke flatteringly of it. Then the Mughal drank to his nobles in his royal wine and the nobles pledged his health. The king drank also to the Lord Ambassador, whom he always treated with special consideration, and presented him with the cup of gold curiously enamelled and crusted with rubies turkesses and emeralds.[3]

Of prince Khurram's visit Roe writes: A month later (October 2nd) the proud prince Khurram, afterwards the emperor Sháh Jehán (A.D. 1626-1657), returned from his glorious success in the Dakhan, accompanied by all the great men, in wondrous triumph.[4] A week later (October 9th), hearing that the emperor was to pass near his lodging on his way to take the air at the Narbada, in accordance with the rule that the masters of all houses near which the king passes must make him a present, Roe took horse to meet the king. He offered the king an Atlas neatly bound, saying he presented the king with the whole world. The king was pleased. In return he praised Roe's lodge, which he had built out of the ruins of the temple and the ancient tomb, and which was one of the best lodges in the camp.[5] Jehángír left Mándu on the 24th October. On the 30th when Roe started the hill was entirely deserted.[6]

Terry mentions only two buildings at Mándu. One was the house of the Mughal, apparently Báz Bahádur's palace, which he describes as large and stately, built of excellent stone, well squared and put together, taking up a large compass of ground. He adds: We could never see how it was contrived within, as the king's wives and women were there.[7] The only other building to which Terry refers, he calls "The Grot." Of the grot, which is almost certainly the pleasure-house Nílkanth, whose Persian inscriptions have been quoted above, Terry gives the following details: To the Mughal's house, at a small distance from it, belonged a very curious grot. In the building of the grot a way was made into a

---

[1] Roe in Kerr's Travels, IX. 340-343. [2] Roe in Kerr's Travels, IX. 344.

[3] Terry's Voyage, 377. Terry's details seem not to agree with Roe's who states (Kerr's Voyages, IX. 344 and Pinkerton's Voyages, VIII. 37): I was invited to the drinking, but desired to be excused because there was no avoiding drinking, and their liquors are so hot that they burn out a man's very bowels. Perhaps the invitation Roe declined was to a private drinking party after the public weighing was over.

[4] Roe in Kerr's Voyage, IX. 347; Elphinstone's History, 494. Kerr (IX. 347) gives September 2 but October 2 is right. Compare Pinkerton's Voyages, VIII. 39.

[5] Ruins of Mándu, 57. As the emperor must have passed out by the Dehli Gate, and as Roe's lodge was two miles from Báz Bahádur's palace, the lodge cannot have been far from the Dehli Gate. It is disappointing that, of his many genial gossipy entries Jehángír does not devote one to Roe. The only reference to Roe's visit is the indirect entry (Wákiát-i-Jehángíri in Elliot, VI. 347) that Jehángír gave one of his nobles a coach, apparently a copy of the English coach, with which, to Jehángír's delight, Roe had presented him.

[6] Roe in Kerr's Voyages, IX. 353. [7] Terry's Voyage, 180.

firm rock which showed itself on the side of the hill canopied over with part of that rock. It was a place that had much beauty in it by reason of the curious workmanship bestowed on it and much pleasure by reason of its coolness.[1] Besides the fountain this grot has still one of the charmingly cool and murmuring scallopped rillstones where, as Terry says, water runs down a broad stone table with many hollows like to scallop shells, in its passage over the hollows making so pretty a murmur as helps to tie the senses with the bonds of sleep.

Sháh Jehán seems to have been pleased with Mándu. He returned in A.D. 1621 and stayed at Mándu till he marched north against his father in A.D. 1622.[2] In March A.D. 1623, Sháh Jehán came out of Mándu with 20,000 horse, many elephants, and powerful artillery, intending to fight his brother Sháh Parwíz.[3] After the failure of this expedition Sháh Jehán retired to Mándu.[4] At this time (A.D. 1623) the Italian traveller Dela Valle ranks Mándu with Agra Lábor and Ahmedábád, as the four capitals, each endowed with an imperial palace and court.[5] Five years later the great general Khán Jehán Lodi besieged Mándu, but apparently without success.[6] Khán Jehán Lodi's siege of Mándu is interesting in connection with a description of Mándu in Herbert's Travels. Herbert, who was in Gujarát in A.D. 1626, says Mándu is seated at the side of a declining hill (apparently Herbert refers to the slope from the southern crest northwards to Ságar Lake and the Grot or Nílkanth) in which both for ornament and defence is a castle which is strong in being encompassed with a defensive wall of nearly five miles (probably *kos* that is ten miles): the whole, he adds, heretofore had fifteen miles circuit. But the city later built is of less time yet fresher beauty, whether you behold the temples (in one of which are entombed four kings), palaces or fortresses, especially that tower which is elevated 170 steps, supported by massive pillars and adorned with gates and windows very observable. It was built by Khán Jehán, who there lies buried. The confusedness of these details shows that Herbert obtained them second-hand, probably from Corryat's Master Herbert on Sir T. Roe's staff.[7] The new city of fresher

---

[1] Terry's Voyage, 181.
[2] Wákiát-i-Jehángíri in Elliot, VI. 383.
[3] Wákiát-i-Jehángíri in Elliot, VI. 387.
[4] Elphinstone's History, 496-97. Compare Dela Valle (Haklyt Edition, I. 177) writing in A.D. 1622, Sultán Khurram after his defeat by Jehángír retired to Mándu.
[5] Dela Valle's Travels, Haklyt Edition, I. 97.
[6] Elphinstone's History, 507.
[7] Herbert's Travels, 81. Corryat's Master Herbert was as already noticed named like the traveller Thomas. The two Thomases were distant relations, both being fourth in descent from Sir Richard Herbert of Colebroke, who lived about the middle of the fifteenth century. A further connection between the two families is the copy of complimentary verses "To my cousin Sir Thomas Herbert," signed Ch. Herbert, in the 1634 and 1665 editions of Herbert's Travels, which are naturally, though somewhat doubtfully, ascribed to Charles Herbert, a brother of our Master Thomas. It is therefore probable that after his return to England Sir Thomas Herbert obtained the Mándu details from Master Thomas who was himself a writer, the author of several poems and pamphlets. Corryat's tale how, during the water-famine at Mándu, Master Herbert annexed a spring or cistern, and then bound a servant of the Great King who attempted to share in its use, shows admirable courage and resolution on the part of Master Thomas, then a youth of twenty years. The details of Thomas in his brother Lord Herbert's autobiography give additional interest to the hero of Corryat's tale of a Tank. Master Thomas was born in A.D. 1597. In 1610, when a page to Sir Edward Cecil and a boy of thirteen, in the German War especially in the siege of Juliers fifteen miles north-east of Aix-la-Chapelle, Master Thomas showed such forwardness as no man in that great army surpassed. On his voyage to India in 1617, in a fight with a great Portuguese carrack,

Appendix II.

THE HILL FORT OF MÁNDU.

HISTORY.

beauty is probably a reference to the buildings raised and repaired by Abdul Karím against Jehangír's coming, among which the chief seems to have been the palace now known by the name of Báz Bahádur. The tower of 170 steps is Mehmúd Khilji's Tower of Victory, erected in A.D. 1443, the Khán Jehán being Mehmúd's father, the great minister Khán Jehán Aâzam Humáyún.

The Maráthás, A.D. 1720-1820.

In A.D. 1658 a Rája Shívráj was commandant of Mándu.[1] No reference has been traced to any imperial visit to Mándu during Aurangzib's reign. But that great monarch has left an example of his watchful care in the rebuilding of the Âlamgír or Aurangzib Gate, which guards the approach to the stone-crossing of the great northern ravine and bears an inscription of A.D. 1668, the eleventh year of Âlamgír's reign. In spite of this additional safeguard thirty years later (A.D. 1696) Mándu was taken and the standard of Udáji Pavár was planted on the battlement.[2] The Maráthás soon withdrew and Málwa again passed under an imperial governor. In A.D. 1708 the Shia-loving emperor Bahádur Sháh I. (A.D. 1707-1712) visited Mándu, and there received from Ahmedábád a copy of the Kurâán written by Imám Âli Taki, son of Imám Músa Raza (A.D. 810-829), seventh in descent from Âli, the famous son-in-law of the Prophet, the first of Musalmán mystics. In A.D. 1717 Ásaph Jáh Nizám-ul-Mulk was appointed governor of Málwa and continued to manage the province by deputy till A.D. 1721. In A.D. 1722 Rája Girdhar Bahádur, a Nágar Bráhman, was made governor and remained in charge till in A.D. 1724 he was attacked and defeated by Chimnáji Pandit and Udáji Pavár.[3] Rája Girdhar was succeeded by his relation Dia Bahádur, whose successful government ended in A.D. 1732, when through the secret help of the local chiefs Malhárao Holkar led an army up the Bhairav pass, a few miles east of Mándu, and at Tirellah, between Amjhera and Dhár, defeated and slew Dia Bahádur. As neither the next governor Muhammad Khán Bangash nor his successor Rája Jai Singh of Jaipúr were able to oust the Maráthás, their success was admitted in A.D. 1734 by the appointment of Peshwa Bájiráo (A.D. 1720-1740) to be governor of Málwa. On his appointment (A.D. 1734) the Peshwa chose Anand Ráo Pavár as his deputy. Anand Ráo shortly after settled at Dhár, and since A.D. 1734 Mándu has continued part of the territory of the Pavárs of Dhar.[4] In A.D. 1805 Mándu sheltered the heroic Mína Bái during the birth-time of her son Rámchundra Ráo Pavár, whose state was saved from the clutches of

---

Captain Joseph, in command of Herbert's ship *Globe*, was killed. Thomas took Joseph's place, forced the carrack aground, and so riddled her with shot that she never floated again. To his brother's visit to India Lord Herbert refers as a year spent with the merchants who went from Surat to the Great Mughal. After his return to England Master Thomas distinguished himself at Algiers, capturing a vessel worth £1800. In 1622, when Master Thomas was in command of one of the ships sent to fetch Prince Charles (afterwards King Charles I.) from Spain, during the return voyage certain Low Countrymen and Dunkirkers, that is Dutch and Spanish vessels, offended the Prince's dignity by fighting in his presence without his leave. The Prince ordered the fighting ships to be separated; whereupon Master Thomas, with some other ships got betwixt the fighters on either side, and shot so long that both Low Countrymen and Dunkirkers were glad to desist. Afterwards at divers times Thomas fought with great courage and success with divers men in single fight, sometimes hurting and disarming his adversary, sometimes driving him away. The end of Master Thomas was sad. Finding his proofs of himself undervalued he retired into a private and melancholy life, and after living in this sullen humour for many years, he died about 1642 and was buried in London in St. Martin's near Charing Cross.

[1] Khafi Khán in Elliot, VII. 218.

[2] Malcolm's Central India, I. 64.

[3] Malcolm's Central India, I. 78.

[4] Malcolm's Central India, I. 100.

Appendix II.

THE HILL FORT OF MÁNDU.

HISTORY.

Notices, A.D. 1820 - 1895.

Holkar and Sindhia by the establishment of British overlordship in A.D. 1817.[1]

In A.D. 1820 Sir John Malcolm[2] describes the hill-top as a place of religious resort occupied by some mendicants. The holy places on the hill are the shrine of Hoshang Ghori. whose guardian spirit still scares barrenness and other disease fiends[3] and the Rewa or Narbada Pool, whose holy water, according to common belief, prevents the dreaded return of the spirit of the Hindu whose ashes are strewn on its surface, or, in the refined phrase of the Bráhman, enables the dead to lose self in the ocean of being.[4] In A.D. 1820 the Jámá Mosque, Hoshang's tomb, and the palaces of Báz Bahádur were still fine remains, though surrounded with jungle and fast crumbling to pieces.[5] In A.D. 1827 Colonel Briggs says[6]: Perhaps no part of India so abounds with tigers as the neighbourhood of the once famous city of Mándu. The capital now deserted by man is overgrown by forest and from being the seat of luxury, elegance, and wealth, it has become the abode of wild beasts and is resorted to by the few Europeans in that quarter for the pleasure of destroying them. Instances have been known of tigers being so bold as to carry off troopers riding in the ranks of their regiments. Twelve years later (A.D. 1839) Mr. Fergusson[7] found the hill a vast uninhabited jungle, the rank vegetation tearing the buildings of the city to pieces and obscuring them so that they could hardly be seen.[8] Between A.D. 1842 and 1852 tigers are described as prowling among the regal rooms, the half-savage marauding Bhíl as eating his meal and feeding his cattle in the cloisters of its sanctuaries and the insidious *pípal* as levelling to the earth the magnificent remains.[9] So favourite a tiger retreat was the Jaház Palace that it was dangerous to venture into it unarmed. Close to the very huts of the poor central village, near the Jámá Mosque, cattle were frequently seized by tigers. In the south tigers came nightly to drink at the Ságar lake. Huge bonfires had to be burnt to prevent them attacking the houses.[10] In A.D. 1883 Captain Eastwick wrote: At Mándu the traveller will require some armed men, as tigers are very numerous and dangerous. He will do well not to have any dogs with him, as the panthers will take them even from under his bed.[11] If this was true of Mándu in A.D. 1883—and is not as seems likely the repetition of an old-world tale—the last ten years have wrought notable changes. Through the interest His Highness Sir Anand Ráo Pavár, K.C.S.I., C.I.E., the present Mahárája of Dhár takes in the old capital of his state, travelling in Mándu is now as safe and easier than in many, perhaps than in most, outlying districts. A phæton can drive across the northern ravine-moat through the three gateways and along the hill-top, at least as far south as the Sea Lake. Large stretches of the level are cleared and tilled, and herds of cattle graze free from the dread of wild beasts. The leading buildings have been saved from their ruinous tree-growth, the underwood has been cleared, the marauding Bhíl has settled to tillage, the tiger, even the panther, is nearly

[1] Malcolm's Central India, I. 106.
[2] Central India, II. 503.
[3] Ruins of Mándu, 43 : March 1852 page 34.
[4] Ruins of Mándu, 43 : March 1852 page 34.
[5] Malcolm's Central India, II. 503.
[6] Briggs' Farishtah, IV. 235 note *.
[7] Indian Architecture, 54?.
[8] Ruins of Mándu, 9.
[9] Ruins of Mándu, 9.
[10] Ruins of Mándu, 13, 25, 35. Some of these extracts seem to belong to a Bombay Subaltern, who was at Mándu about A.D. 1842, and some to Captain Claudius Harris, who visited the hill in April 1852. Compare Ruins of Mándu, 34.
[11] Murray's Handbook of the Panjáb, 118.

Appendix II.

THE HILL FORT OF MÁNDU.

HISTORY.

Notices, A.D. 1820-1895.

as rare as the wild elephant, and finally its old wholesomeness has returned to the air of the hill-top.

This sketch notices only the main events and the main buildings. Even about the main buildings much is still doubtful. Many inscriptions, some in the puzzling interlaced *Tughra* character, have still to be read. They may bring to light traces of the Mándu kings and of the Mughal emperors, whose connection with Mándu, so far as the buildings are concerned, is still a blank. The ruins are so many and so widespread that weeks are wanted to ensure their complete examination. It may be hoped that at no distant date Major Delasseau, the Political Agent of Dhár, whose opportunities are not more special than his knowledge, may be able to prepare a complete description of the hill and of its many ruins and writings.

MARÁTHA HISTORY

OF

GUJARÁT:

A.D. 1760-1819.

BY

J. A. BAINES Esquire, C.S.I.,

LATE OF H. M.'s BOMBAY CIVIL SERVICE.

[*Contributed in 1879.*]

HISTORY OF GUJARAT.

MARÁTHA PERIOD.

A.D. 1760-1819.

The Maráthás, A.D. 1760-1819.

It will be evident from what has been related in the Musalmán portion of this history that long before 1760, the Maráthás had a firm foothold in Gujarát, and were able to dictate to the local chiefs the policy of the Dakhan Court. Long before 1819 too, Marátha influence was on the wane before the rising fortunes of the British. Between these two dates however is comprised the whole or nearly the whole of the period during which the Maráthás were virtually paramount in Gujarát. From each of these two dates the political history took a new departure, and on this account they serve respectively to denote the starting point and terminus of Marátha supremacy. Most of what took place before 1760 is so interwoven with the interests and intrigues of the Muhammadan delegates of the court of Dehli that it has been fully described in the history of the Musalmán Period. It is however necessary, in order to trace the growth of Marátha power, to briefly set forth in a continuous narrative the events in which this race was principally concerned, adding such as transpired independently of Musalmán politics. This task is rendered easier by the very nature of Marátha policy, which has left little to be recorded of its action in Gujarát beyond the deeds and fortunes of its initiators and their adherents.

The connection of the Maráthás with Gujarát can be divided by the chronicler into the following periods. First, the time of predatory inroads from 1664 to 1743, before the leaders of these expeditions had permanently established themselves within the province. Secondly, what may be termed the mercenary period, when the Maráthás partly by independent action, but far more by a course of judicious interference in the quarrels of the Muhammadan officials and by loans of troops, had acquired considerable territorial advantages. Towards the end of this period, as has been already seen, their aid was usually sufficient to ensure the success of the side which had managed to secure it, and at last the capital itself was claimed and held by them. Then came the time of domination, from 1760 to 1801, during which period the Gáikwár influence was occasionally greater than that of the Peshwa. From 1802, internal dissensions at the courts of Poona and Baroda weakened the hold the Maráthás had on the province, and the paramount power had to all intents and purposes passed over to the British long before the downfall of Bájiráv Peshwa and the final annexation of his rights and territory in 1819.

THE MARÁTHÁS, A.D. 1760-1819.

Shortly after, when the Gáikwár made over to the British the work of collecting the tribute from Káthiáváḍa, Marátha supremacy came to an end.

Śiváji's First Inroad, 1664.

The first Marátha force that made its appearance in Gujarát was led there early in 1664 by Śiváji. This leader was at the time engaged in a warfare with the Mughals, which, however desultory, required him to keep up a much larger force than could be supported out of the revenues of his dominions. He therefore looked to plunder to supply the deficiency, and Surat, then the richest town of Western India, was marked down by him as an easy prey. His mode of attack was cautious. He first sent one Bahirji Náik to spy out the country and report the chances of a rich booty, whilst he himself moved a force up to Junnar on pretence of visiting some forts in that direction recently acquired by one of his subordinates. On receiving a favourable report from Bahirji, Śiváji gave out that he was going to perform religious ceremonies at Násik, and taking with him 4000 picked horsemen, he marched suddenly down the Gháts and through the Dáng jungles, and appeared before Surat. There he found an insignificant garrison, so he rested outside the city six days whilst his men plundered at their leisure. On hearing of the tardy approach of a relieving force sent by the governor of Ahmedábád, Śiváji beat a retreat with all his booty to the stronghold of Ráygad. By the time the reinforcement reached Surat, the only trace of the invaders was the emptied coffers of the inhabitants. About the same time, or shortly after, the fleet which Śiváji had equipped at Alibág about two years before came up to the mouth of the gulf of Cambay and carried off one or two Mughal ships which were conveying to Makka large numbers of pilgrims with their rich oblations.[1]

Śiváji's Second Attack, 1670.

This insult to the Muhammadan religion was enough to incense the bigoted Aurangzeb, apart from the additional offences of the sack of Surat and the assumption in 1665 of royal insignia by Śiváji. He therefore sent an expedition to the Dakhan strong enough to keep the Maráthás for some time away from Gujarát. One of Śiváji's officers, however, seems to have attacked a part of the Surat district in 1666, and to have got off safely with his spoils. In 1670, Śiváji again descended upon that city with about 15,000 men. The only serious resistance he experienced was, as before, from the English factors. He plundered the town for three days, and only left on receiving some information about the Mughals' movements in the Dakhan, which made him fear lest he should be intercepted on his way back to the country about the Gháts.

1671.

Śiváji left a claim for twelve lákhs of rupees to be paid as a guarantee against future expeditions. It is possible, however, that as he does not appear to have taken any immediate steps to recover this sum, the demand was made only in accordance with Marátha policy,

[1] Surat was known as Báb-ul-makkah or the Gate of Makka on account of its being the starting place of the ships annually conveying the Muhammadan pilgrims of India to the shrine of their Prophet.

The Maráthás, A.D. 1760 - 1819.

which looked upon a country once overrun as tributary, and assumed a right to exercise paramount authority over it by virtue of the completed act of a successful invasion. In 1671 the Marátha fleet was ordered to sail up the gulf and plunder Broach, and it is probable that Śiváji intended at the same time to levy tribute from Surat, but the whole expedition was countermanded before the ships sailed.

The conduct of the military authorities in Gujarát with regard to this expedition of 1670 was such as to render it highly probable that the Mughal leaders were in complicity with the Maráthás in order to gain the favour and support of their leader. Shortly before Śiváji's arrival there had been a large garrison in Surat, apparently kept there by the governor, who suspected that some attempt on the town would soon be made. This garrison was withdrawn before Śiváji's attack, and almost immediately after his departure 5000 men were sent back again. The commanders of the Mughal army in the Dakhan were Jasvant Singh the Ráhtor chief of Jodhpur and prince Muazzam. Jasvant Singh had been viceroy of Gujarát from A.D. 1659 to 1662, and in A.D. 1671 shortly after Śiváji's second expedition was re-appointed to that post for three years. He had, moreover, been accused of taking bribes from Śiváji during the operations in the Dakhan. Prince Muazzam, again, had every reason for wishing to secure to himself so powerful an ally as Śiváji in the struggle for the imperial crown that took place, as a rule, at every succession. Aurangzeb, reasoning from his own experiences as a son, refused to allow a possible heir to his throne to become powerful at court; and accordingly sent him against Śiváji with an army quite inadequate for such operations. It is therefore not unreasonable to suppose that if there had not been some previous understanding between Śiváji and the Mughal leaders, the troops that were known to be within easy reach of Surat would have been found strong and numerous enough either to have repulsed him altogether or at least to have prevented the three days' sack of the city.

Sáler Taken, 1672.

In A.D. 1672 Śiváji took some of the small forts to the south of Surat, such as Párnera and Bagváda, now in the Párdi sub-division of the Surat district, whilst Moro Trimal got possession of the large fort of Sáler in Báglán, which guarded one of the most frequented passes from the Dakhan into Gujarát. The Maráthás were thus able to command the routes along which their expeditions could most conveniently be despatched.

The Narbada Crossed, 1675.

No further incursion was made till 1675, in which year a Marátha force first crossed the Narbada. On the resumption of hostilities between Siváji and the Mughals, Hasáji Mohite, who had been made Senápati, with the title of Hambirráv, marched up the North Konkan, and divided his army into two forces near Surat. One portion plundered towards Burhánpur, the other commanded by himself plundered the Broach district. Ten years later a successful expedition was made against Broach itself, either preconcerted or

THE MARÁTHÁS, A.D. 1760-1819.

actually led by a younger son of Aurangzeb, who had taken refuge with the Maráthás. Broach was plundered, and the booty safely carried off before the local force could get near the invaders. Gujarát was now left free from inroad for some fourteen years, probably because the attention of the Marátha leaders was concentrated on their quarrels in the Dakhan.

Raids by Dábhâde, 1699.

In A.D. 1699 Rám Rája appointed one of his most trusted officers, Khanderáv Dábháde, to collect in Báglán the *chauth* [1] and *sardeshmukhi* imposts which had by that time become regularly instituted. This chief, whose name was afterwards so intimately connected with Gujarát, not only collected all that was due to his master from the village officers in Báglán, but also made an incursion into the Surat
1700-1704. districts on his own account. Between 1700 and 1704 Khanderáv attempted two expeditions, but was foiled by the vigilance of the
1705. Mughal authorities. In 1705, however, he made a raid on a large scale and got safely across the Narbada, where he defeated two Muhammadan detachments sent against him, and got back to Sáler
1706-1711. with his booty. Khanderáv now kept bodies of troops constantly hovering on the outskirts of Gujarát and along the road to Burhánpur. He himself led several expeditions into the Ahmedábád territory, and is said to have once got as far as Sorath in the peninsula, where however he was repelled by the Musalmán governor. In 1711, again he was severely defeated by the Mughals near Anklesvar in the Broach district, and had to withdraw to the borders of Khándesh.

1713.

In 1713 some treasure was being conveyed from Surat to Aurangábád escorted by a large force under Muhammad Tabrízí. The party was attacked in the jungles east of Surat and the treasure carried off. Just before this, Sarbuland Khán, the deputy viceroy, on his way to take up his office at Ahmedábád, was attacked and robbed in the wilds of Ságbára on the north bank of the Tápti. As Khanderáv had a short while previous to these occurrences taken up his position near Nándod [2] in the Rájpipla territory, it is probably to him or to his subordinates that these raids are to be attributed. He managed by a system of outposts to cut off communication between Surat and Burhánpur, except for those who had paid him a fee for safe conduct. If this charge was evaded or resisted, he appropriated one-fourth of the property that the traveller was conveying up country.

Dábháde, 1716.

As the Burhánpur road was one of those most frequented by both pilgrims and merchants, the Dehli authorities were obliged, in 1716, to organize an expedition against Dábháde. The leader of the force was one Zulfikar Beg, an officer inexperienced in Marátha warfare. Dábháde found little difficulty in decoying him into a mountainous country, and there completely defeated him with the usual Marátha accompaniment of plunder.

[1] *Sardeshmukhi* or ten per cent on the revenue. The *chauth* was nominally one-fourth, but both these claims were fluctuating in their proportions to the total revenue.

[2] Now the capital of the Rája of Rájpipla.

The Maráthás, A.D. 1760-1819.

Dábhāde Senápati.

Finding himself once more in the Dakhan, Khanderáv Dábháde took the opportunity of rejoining the court at Sátára, from which he had long been absent. He was lucky enough to arrive just as the Senápati Manáji Morár had failed on an important expedition and was consequently in disgrace. Rája Sháhu, pleased with Khanderáv's recent success against the Delhi troops, divested Manáji of the title of Senápati, and bestowed it upon the more fortunate leader.

The Peshwa's Negotiations, 1717.

Khanderáv remained away from Gujarát for three years, accompanying, meanwhile, Bálaji Vishvanáth the Peshwa to Dehli, where the latter was engaged in negotiations for the confirmation of the Marátha rights to *chauth* and other tribute from certain districts in the Dakhan.

It is evident that at this time there was no definite claim to tribute from Gujarát on the part of the Marátha government; for in spite of the intrigues of Báláji and the weakness of the court party at Delhi no concessions were obtained with regard to it, although the Marátha dues from other parts of the country were fully ratified. The grounds on which Báláji demanded the tribute from Gujarát were that Sháhu would thereby gain the right to restrain the excesses of Marátha freebooters from the frontier and would guarantee the whole country against irregular pillage. The argument was a curious one, considering that the most troublesome and notorious freebooter of the whole tribe was at the elbow of the envoy, who was so strenuously pleading for the right to suppress him. It is probable that Báláji foresaw that Khanderáv's newly acquired rank would take him for a time from Báglán to the court, so that meanwhile an arrangement could be made to prevent the growth of any powerful chief in the Gujarát direction who might interfere with the plans of the central government. The Marátha statesman was as anxious to ensure the subordination of distant feudatories as the Mughals to secure the freedom of the Ghát roads to the coast.

In the redistribution of authority carried out about this time by Báláji Vishvanáth, the responsibility of collecting the Marátha dues[1] from Gujarát and Báglán was assigned to Khanderáv as Senápáti or commander-in-chief; but as these dues were not yet settled, at least as regards the country below the Gháts, Khanderáv seems to have remained with the Peshwa in the field.

Dámáji Gáikwár, 1720.

At the battle of Bálápur, fought against the Nizám-ul-Mulk, one of the officers of Khanderáv, by name Dámáji Gáikwár, so distinguished himself that the Senápati brought his conduct prominently to the notice of Rája Sháhu. The latter promoted Dámáji to be second in command to Khanderáv with the title of Shamsher Bahádur, which had been formerly borne by one of the Atole family in 1692. This is the first mention of the present ruling family of Baroda. Before many months both Khanderáv and Dámáji died. The former was succeeded by his son Trimbakráv, on whom his father's title was conferred. Piláji, nephew of Dámáji, was confirmed in his uncle's

[1] *Chauth* and *Sardeshmukhi* as settled in 1699.

The Maráthás, A.D. 1760-1819.

honours and retired to Gujarát. As soon as he could collect a sufficiently strong force, he attacked the Surat district and defeated the Musalmán commander close to the city itself. After extorting from him a handsome sum as ransom, Piláji returned eastwards. He selected Songad,[1] a fort about fifty miles east of Surat, as his headquarters, and from thence made continual excursions against the neighbouring towns. He once attacked Surat, but although he defeated the Mughal leader, he seems to have contented himself with contributions levied from the adjacent country, and not to have entered the town. Piláji soon obtained possession of some strongholds in the Rájpipla country between Nándod and Ságbára, which he fortified, as Khanderáv Dábháde had formerly done. Here he resided as representative of the Senápati, whose family had removed for a while to the Dakhan. The tribute collected from Báglán and Gujarát was supposed to be transmitted by Piláji to the royal treasury through the Peshwa; but there is no record of these dues having been levied with any regularity or even fixed at any special amount. Whilst Trimbakráv was taking an active part in the affairs of his royal patron in the Dakhan, Piláji occupied himself in sedulously cultivating the goodwill of the border tribes surrounding his residence in Gujarát.

1723.

Marátha Tribute, 1723.

The year 1723 is noteworthy as being the date of the first imposition of the regular Marátha demand of one-fourth, *chauth*, and one-tenth, *sardeshmukhi*, of the revenue of Gujarát. Whilst Piláji was directing his attacks against Surat and the south of the province another of Rája Sháhu's officers, who had been sent up towards Málwa, entered Gujarát by the north-east, and after ravaging the country round Dohad,[2] settled a fixed tribute on the district.

Kantáji Kadam.

This officer, Kantáji Kadam Bánde, was soon after engaged by one of the parties struggling for the viceroyalty of Ahmedábád to bring his cavalry into the province and take part in the civil war. The leader of the opposite party, Rustam Ali, enlisted the services of Piláji Gáikwár. The Nizám-ul-Mulk, whose influence in the Dakhan was very great, managed to detach Piláji from Rustam Ali's side. This was the easier, as Rustam had already defeated Piláji more than once in attacks by the latter against Surat, of which district Rustam was governor. There are two different accounts[3] of what took place when the rival forces came into action, but both show clearly that the Marátha leaders acted on both sides with utter disregard of their agreements and looked only to plundering the Muhammadan camps whilst the soldiers were engaged in battle. After the defeat of Rustam, the two Marátha chiefs joined forces and proceeded to levy *chauth*, of which the Mughal deputy had granted Piláji a share equal to that of his first ally Kantáji.

Marátha Dissensions, 1725.

This division led to quarrels and at last to an open rupture between the two Marátha leaders, which was only patched up by the

---

1 On the western skirts of the Dáng forests.

2 Now in the British districts of the Panch Maháls.

3 The Muhammadan account is given in the Musalmán portion of this history. Grant Duff's description differs considerably.

THE MARÁTHÁS, A.D. 1760-1819.

grant of the *chauth* north of the Mahi river to Kantáji and of that to the south to Piláji. The chief ground of quarrel seems to have been the relative position of the Gáikwár as agent for the Senápati, who had a right to collect all dues from Gujarát, and of Kantáji, who claimed superior rank as holding his commission direct from Rája Shâhu. On hearing of this dispute and the consequent partition of the Marátha tribute, Trimbakrav Dábháde himself hastened up to Cambay with an army, but effected nothing, and seems to have retired, leaving Piláji to look after his interests at Ahmedábád. Both the latter, however, and Kantáji soon after withdrew from Gujarát, but were within a short period encouraged to return by the success of a raid made by another leader, Antáji Bháskar, on the north-east district. They both joined Hamid Khán in his resistance to the new viceroy, but received several checks from the Muhammadan army, and after plundering again returned to their strongholds for the rainy season.

The Peshwa, 1726.

Next year they returned for the tribute and plundered as usual. The Peshwa Bájiráv then opened for the first time direct negotiations with the viceroy of Gujarát. The rapid increase of the authority of the Bráhman ministers at the Rája's court in the Dakhan had aroused the jealousy of the Marátha nobles, amongst whom Trimbakráv Dábháde was one of the most influential. Bájiráv, being fully aware of the fact, and having by this time acquired from the Rája the power of acting with foreign powers independently of the throne, determined to undermine Trimbakráv's authority in Gujarát by aiming at the rights said to have been formally granted to him by Hamid Khán over the country south of the Mahi. He therefore applied to the viceroy for a confirmation of the right to levy *chauth* and *sardeshmukhi* over the whole country, on condition that he would protect it from the inroads of Kantáji, Piláji, and other irresponsible freebooters. The viceroy had still some resources left at his disposal and was in hopes that his repeated applications to Dehli for assistance would soon meet with a favourable answer. He declined therefore to accede to Bájiráv's proposals at once, on the grounds that the court at Dehli had repudiated the concessions made to Piláji and Kantáji by his predecessor's deputy. As however the depredations on the frontier caused serious injury both to the revenues and the people, he allowed the Peshwa to send a feudatory, Udáji Pavár, chief of Dhár, through the Mughal territories to operate against Piláji. The latter, who was fully aware of these negotiations, persuaded Kantáji to join him in expelling the agents of the Peshwa party, as it was clear that if Piláji's forces were scattered the way would be open for Udáji to attack Kantáji himself. The two then proceeded to Baroda and after a while drove back Udáji, and occupied Baroda and Dabhoi. Here Piláji remained, and next year Kantáji succeeded in taking Chámpáner, thus advancing his posts nearer the centre of the province. With such an advantage gained these two chiefs instituted raids still more frequently than before. In these straits, and finding himself utterly neglected by the emperor, the viceroy re-opened negotiations with the Peshwa, who lost no time in sending his

Cession of Tribute, 1728.

THE MARÁTHÁS, A.D. 1760-1819.

Cession of Tribute, 1728.

brother Chimnáji A'ppa with an army through Gujarát. Petlad and Dholka were plundered, but Kantáji was left undisturbed, so he took this opportunity of marching to Sorath, where he remained for some time extorting tribute. The viceroy agreed formally to cede the *sardesmukhi* of the whole revenue, land and customs (with the exception of the port of Surat and the districts attached to it) and the *chauth* of the same district, with five per cent on the revenue from the city of Ahmedábád. Special clauses were inserted in the grant of *chauth* to suit the convenience of both the Peshwa and the viceroy. The latter stipulated that as few collectors as possible should be kept by the Maráthás in the districts under tribute, and that no extra demands beyond the one-fourth should be made. He also insisted that the percentage should be calculated on the actual collections and not on the *kamál* or highest sum recorded as having been collected.[1] The Maráthás were also to support the imperial authority and to keep up a body of horse. The Peshwa agreed (probably at his own request) to prevent all Marátha subjects from joining disaffected chiefs, or other turbulent characters, thus receiving the right to suppress Kantáji and Piláji, as well as the Bhils and Kolis with whom the latter was on such friendly terms.

After this agreement was executed, Bájiráv made over part of the *sardeshmukhi* to the Dábháde, as well as the *mokása* or three-fourths of the *svaráj* as settled by Báláji Vishvanáth. The consideration as set forth in the preamble of this agreement was the great improvement effected by the Marátha rulers as regards the wealth and tranquillity of the Dakhan provinces. This was inserted either to give the transaction the appearance of having been executed on the part of the emperor (for otherwise the viceroy had no concern in the state of the Dakhan), or simply as an expression of gratitude on the part of this special viceroy towards the Maráthás who had just brought to terms the Nizám-ul-Mulk, his former rival and enemy. It is even probable that it was merely intended, as usual with such preambles, to veil the forced nature of the treaty.

The hostile movements of the Pratinidhi in the Southern Marátha Country induced the Peshwa to return to the Dakhan. Kantáji returned from Sorath to Chámpáner, plundering part of the viceroy's camp on his way. Trimbakráv Dábháde, jealous of the interference of the Peshwa in the affairs of Gujarát, began to intrigue with other chiefs to overturn the power of the Bráhman ministers.

Coalition against the Peshwa, 1730.

As soon as Nizám-ul-Mulk became aware of this discontent on the part of Trimbakráv, of whose power he was well informed, he proposed to assist him by an attack on the Peshwa from the east, whilst the Maráthás operated in another direction. Trimbakráv was successful in his overtures with Piláji Gáikwár, the Bánde, the Pavárs, and a few other chiefs resident in Khándesh or the north Dakhan. The troops sent by them to join his standard soon amounted

[1] The Marátha practice was to base their demands on the standard or *tankha* assessment (which was seldom if ever collected), so that by this means they evaded all possibility of claims against them for over-collections.

THE MARATHÁS, A.D. 1760-1819.

to 35,000 men, who were collected in Gujarát. He then gave out that he was bent on rescuing the Marátha Rája from the thraldom in which he was being kept by the Bráhmans. The Peshwa, who had discovered the intercourse between Trimbakráv and the Nizám, proclaimed this treason on the part of the Dábháde as a royal officer, and stated that the malcontents were only planning the partition of the inheritance of Shiváji between the Rája of Kolhápur and themselves. As soon as he found the Nizám's troops were on the march, he collected his picked men and advanced on the Dábháde in Gujarát.

Defeat of the Allies, 1731.

The Peshwa's army was inferior in numbers but consisted of better trained men. He closed at once with the allies near Dabhoi, and easily defeated the undisciplined forces of the Pavárs and Bánde. The Dábháde's army, however, had more experience of regular warfare and made a stand. But a stray shot killed Trimbakráv as he was endeavouring to rally the forces of his allies, and as usual in such engagements, the loss of the leader disheartened the army. Utter confusion ensued, in which many of the nobles fell, others ran away, and the Peshwa, without the necessity of pushing further his advantage, made good his retreat to the Dakhan. The Nizám, who was in pursuit, only managed to capture some of the baggage with the rear guard as it was crossing the Tápti near Surat.[1]

Safe again in the Dakhan, the Peshwa at once began negotiations with both the Nizám and the adherents of Trimbakráv Dábháde. He recognized the rights of the former to some possessions in Gujarát independent of the viceroy of Ahmedábád, and agreed to further his designs of severing the Dakhan from the possessions of the emperor. He conciliated the Dábháde family by establishing at Poona an annual distribution of food and presents to Bráhmans such as had formerly been the practice in the native village of Khanderáv.[2] This institution was known as Dakshiná.

Bájiráv acquiesced also in the general tendency amongst Maráthás of all offices to become hereditary, and conferred the title of Senápati on Yeshvantráv the minor son of the deceased Trimbakráv. The widow Umábái became guardian, and Piláji Gáikwár deputy or *mutálik* in Gujarát. This latter appointment seems to have been made by the Peshwa and not by the Dábháde, for Piláji received at the same time a new title, namely that of *Sená Khás Khel* or commander of the special band or perhaps the household brigade. He was also bound on behalf of the Senápati to respect the Peshwa's rights in Málwa and Gujarát, and to pay half the collections from the territory he administered to the royal treasury through the minister. A provision was also inserted with regard to future acquisitions. This reciprocal agreement was executed at the special command of the Marátha Rája Sháhu, who had not yet quite abrogated his authority in favour of the Peshwa. Piláji after these negotiations retired to Gujarát.

---

[1] At Gala about twelve miles above Surat in the territory of the Gáikwár.
[2] Tálegaon in the north-west of Poona, now a station on the railway to Bombay.

THE MARÁTHÁS, A.D. 1760 - 1819.

Assassination of Piláji Gáikwár, 1732.

His influence amongst the Bhils and other troublesome races dwelling in the wild parts of the eastern frontier made Piláji an object of hatred and fear to the Mughal viceroy, who had him assassinated by one of his adherents whilst the latter was pretending to whisper some important and confidential news in Piláji's ear. This event took place at Dákor in the Kaira district. The followers of the Gáikwár slew the assassin and retired south of the Mahi. They were driven by the Mughals out of Baroda, but continued to hold Dabhoi. Dámáji Gáikwár, son of Piláji, was at this time prowling round Surat watching for an opportunity of interfering in the disturbed affairs of that town. One of the candidates for the governorship had offered him one-fourth the revenue of the city for his assistance, but the expedition was deferred on account of the appointment of a rival by the emperor. Dámáji therefore was preparing to act on his own account independently of his ally. The news of his father's assassination, however, took him northwards. He found that the Desái of Pádra near Baroda had stirred up the Bhils and Kolis to revolt, in order to give the relations of Piláji a chance of striking a blow at the murderers of their deceased leader.

1733.

Umábái Dábháde, too, bent on the same errand, moved down the Gháts with an army. The Maráthás were bought off, however, by the viceroy and peace was restored for a while.

Gáikwárs Secure Baroda, 1734.

In this year also Jádoji, a younger son of Trimbakráv, made an expedition to collect tribute through Gujarát as far as Sorath. Next year Mádhavráv Gáikwár, brother of Piláji, obtained possession of Baroda during the absence of Sher Khán Bábi the governor. Since that date this town has been the capital of the Gáikwár family. Sindia and Holkar soon afterwards joined the chief of Ídar against the Musalmán deputy, and extorted from the latter a considerable sum as ransom.

The Marátha Deputy Governor, 1736.

Umábái had recognized Dámáji as her agent in succession to Piláji; but as she required Dámáji in the Dakhan the latter had been obliged to leave in his turn a *locum tenens* in Gujarát. There ensued quarrels between this deputy, named Rangoji, and Kantaji Kadam which brought Dámáji back again, and after obtaining from the Muhammadan viceroy, who had espoused the cause of Kantáji, a grant of one-fourth the revenues of the country north of the Mahi he went as usual to Sorath. Kantáji Kadam, who as a partisan of the Peshwa was hostile to the Senápati, harassed the country within reach of his frontier. Dámáji, meanwhile, had again proceeded to the Dakhan, where Umábái was intriguing against the Peshwa and required all the help she could obtain to further the ambitious schemes she was devising in the name of her half-witted son. His deputy Rangoji, by demanding a heavy price for his aid at a time when an aspirant to the viceroyalty of Ahmedábád was in distress, managed to secure for the Maráthás half the revenue of Gujarát with certain exceptions.

Ahmedábád Riots, 1738.

Dámáji then moved into Gujarát again, and on his way to join Rangoji extorted Rs. 7000 from the English at Surat as a guarantee against plundering them. The events of this year have been detailed in full in the history of the Musalmán Period. After getting possession of a great part of the city of Ahmedábád the Maráthás, by their oppressive rule, excited a rising amongst the Musalmán inhabitants. Similar quarrels and subsequent reconciliations took place between 1739 and 1741, the Musalmáns distrusting the Maráthás, yet not daring to attempt to oust them. Dámáji, on his way back from one of his Sorath expeditions, laid siege to Broach, which was held by a Muhammadan officer direct from the viceroy of the Dakhan.[1] As the latter personage was still regarded by the Marátha chiefs as a possible ally against the Peshwa, Dámáji at once obeyed the request of the Nizám to raise the siege, but probably obtained a promise of future concessions such as he had acquired at Surat.

1739.

1741.

Rangoji in the absence of Dámáji took up his residence in Borsad. There he fell into several disputes with the Muhammadan officials, in the course of one of which he was taken prisoner, but escaped the next year (1743). Meanwhile Dámáji had joined with Rághoji Bhonslé in attacking the Peshwa. Whilst Rághoji was preparing his army in the east, Dámáji made a feint against Málwa, which had the desired effect of withdrawing a large portion of the ministerial army. The Gaikwár's troops retreated without giving battle, but to prevent any future junction between Dámáji and the Bhonslé party in Berár, Báláji Peshwa confirmed the Pavár family in their claims to Dhár, which had never been acknowledged as their territory since the defection of the Pavárs to the Dábháde party in 1731. It is worth remarking that though the rank of Senápati had apparently been made hereditary in the Dábháde family (for the owner of the title was quite unfit for the command of an army), the Ghorpadé family applied at this time to have it restored to them on the ground that it once had been held by one of their house. The Peshwa, however, managed to secure their alliance by a grant of land, and their claims to the chief command of the army seem to have been waived.

1742.

For the next two years the Marátha force in Gujarát under Rangoji and Deváji Tákpar was employed by the Musalmáns in their quarrels regarding the viceroyalty. The Marátha practice of appointing deputies gives rise to some confusion as to the negotiations that took place about this time between the Gáikwár's party and the rival candidates for the office of subhedár. For instance, Umábái Dábháde had appointed the Gáikwár family as her agents-in-chief, but the principal members of that house were absent in the Dakhan. Dámáji Gáikwár had appointed Rangoji, who in his turn left one Krishnáji in charge of the Marátha share of the city of Ahmedábád. On the departure, however, of Dámáji from Gujarát, Umábái left Rámáji as her agent. Rámáji, who seems to have

1743-44.

[1] Broach was constituted part of the Nizám's personal estate on his resigning the viceroyalty in 1722.

been employed previously by Dámáji, followed the example of his predecesors and placed one Rámchandra in charge at Ahmedábád. There does not appear to have been any direct agent of the Peshwa in Gujarát at this time.

1745. On Khanderáv Gáikwár's return from the Dakhan he demanded the acounts of the tribute from Rangoji, and not being satisfied with this agent confined him in Borsad and appointed one Trimbakráv in his place. Umábái caused Rangoji to be set at liberty and sent to her in the Dakhan, after which she reappointed him her agent. He expelled Trimbakráv from Ahmedábád, but was attacked by Krishnáji and Gangádhar, two other late deputies. Dámáji and Khanderáv were obliged at last to come to Gujarát and summon all these deputies to their presence. A private arrangement was concluded under which Khanderáv was allowed by Dámáji to keep Naḍiád and Borsad as a private estate and to act as the Gáikwár's deputy at Baroda. Rangoji was to live at Umreth when not on active service. Gangádhar and Krishnáji were censured and forbidden to engage in any independent alliances with the Muhammadan leaders.

1746. After this Dámáji sent a general named Kánoji Tákpar to collect the Sorath tribute whilst he himself retired to Songad.

Rangoji returned to Ahmedábád, and not long after began to quarrel with the viceroy about the Marátha share in the revenue of the city ceded in 1728.

The Gáikwár in Surat, 1747.

In A.D. 1747 Kedárji Gáikwár, cousin of Dámáji, was asked by Syed Achchan, an aspirant to the governorship of Surat, to assist him in maintaining possession of that city. Before Kedárji could reach Surat the disputes as to the succession had been settled by negotiations, and the aid of Marátha troops was no longer required. Kedárji, however, finding himself in a position to dictate terms, demanded three lákhs of rupees for the aid that he was prepared to give, and as the Surat treasury could not afford to pay this sum in cash, one-third of the revenues of Surat was promised to the Gáikwár.

1748. Rangoji meanwhile attacked Haribá, an adopted son of Khanderáv Gáikwár, and recovered from him the town and fort of Borsad, which had been seized during the time that Rangoji had been occupied with his disputes in Ahmedábád. Khanderáv and Dámáji both turned against him and captured the fort after a long siege. Rangoji was then again imprisoned, and not released until the next year when the Peshwa sent a body of troops into Gujarát. In 1748 Umábái, widow of Trimbakráv Dábháde, died, leaving one Báburáv guardian of Yeshvántráv her son. Partly through the solicitations of Khanderáv, who had private influence with the Dábhádes, partly from the fact of previous possession, Dámáji was confirmed as deputy of the Maráthás in Gujarát. He there began to collect an army as quickly as possible, in order to co-operate with Raghunáth Bhonslé against the Peshwa, in answer to an appeal by Sakvárbái, widow of Sháhu, to support the throne against the ministers, and to secure the succession of Sambháji to the Sátára kingdom. The Peshwa, aware of Dámáji's ill-will towards himself, did his best to foment disturbances in Gujarát and to extend his own influence there so as to keep Dámáji away from the Dakhan.

THE MARÁTHÁS, A.D. 1760-1819.

1750.

The Peshwa accordingly entered into some negotiations with Jawán Mard Khán, then in power at Ahmedábád, but was unable to lend substantial aid in Gujarát against Dámáji's agents, as the whole Marátha power was required in the Dakhan to operate against the son of the late Nizám-ul-Mulk.

Dámáji Gáikwár Arrested, 1751.

Next year Dámáji, at the request of Tárábái, guardian of Rám Rája, ascended the Salpi ghát with a strong force, defeated the Peshwa's army, and advanced as far as Sátára. From this position he was forced to retire, and whilst in treaty with the Peshwa was treacherously seized by the latter and put into prison. Báláji at once demanded arrears of tribute, but Dámáji declined to agree to any payment, on the ground that he was no independent chief but only the agent of the Senápati. He therefore refused to bind his principal or himself on account of what was due from his principal. Báláji then imprisoned all the members of the Gáikwár and Dábháde family that were at that time in the Dakhan.

The Peshwa and Surat.

The state of Surat was at this time such as to afford a good opportunity to the Peshwa to obtain a footing there independently of the English or of Dámáji. He had recently had dealings with the former in the expeditions against Ángria of Kolába, and as the merchants had found him one of the most stable and powerful rulers of the country, they were willing to treat with him for the future security of their buildings and goods in Surat. Taking advantage of Dámáji's confinement, Báláji sent Ragunáthráv to Gujarát. This leader, afterwards so well known as Rághoba, took possession of a few *tálukas* in the north-east of the province, but was recalled to the Dakhan before he could approach Surat. Jawán Mard Khán also took advantage of Dámáji's absence to make an expedition into Sorath and Káthiáváda where the Gáikwár family had now established themselves permanently.

Release of Dámáji, 1752.

The news of these two expeditions made Dámáji very eager to return to his province; and as he had full information as to Báláji's plans with regard to Gujarát, he bribed freely, and in order to regain his liberty consented to much harsher terms than he would otherwise have done. He agreed to maintain an army for defence and collection purposes in Gujarát, as well as to furnish a contingent to the Peshwa's army in the Dakhan, and to contribute towards the support of the Rája, now in reality a state-prisoner dependent upon the wishes of his minister. The Gáikwár was also to furnish the tribute due on account of the Dábháde family, whom the Peshwa was apparently trying to oust from the administration altogether. After deducting the necessary expenses of collection and defence, half the surplus revenue was to be handed over to the Peshwa. Even after acceding to all these proposals, the Gáikwár was not at once released. The Peshwa protracted the negotiations, as he had

THE MARÁTHÁS, A.D. 1760-1819.

to contend against a factious court party in whose counsels he knew Dámáji would play a leading part when once set at liberty. At last, however, after agreeing to a final request that he would assist Raghunáthráv against Surat, Dámáji was allowed to go. There was at this time one Pándurang Pant levying tribute on behalf of the Peshwa in Cambay and Ahmedábád. The Nawáb of Cambay, not having any reason to like or trust his neighbour the Gáikwár, had persuaded the Peshwa at the time the partition of the Marátha rights over Gujarát was being settled at Poona, to take Cambay into his share of the province. The Nawáb bought off the agent of his ally with a present of guns and cash. The ruler of Ahmedábád also came to terms with the Maráthás, so Pándurang was at liberty to go and see if he could find equal good fortune in Sorath.

Capture of Ahmedábád, 1753.

Dámáji now came back with a fresh army, which was soon reinforced by Raghunáthráv. They marched towards Ahmedábád, and Jawán Mard Khán was too late to intercept them before they invested the capital. He managed, however, by a bold movement to enter the town, but after a long siege was obliged to capitulate and march out with the honours of war. The Maráthás conferred on him an estate in the north-west of Gujarát, which, however, was recovered by them some time afterwards.

After taking possession of Ahmedábád in April 1753, Raghunáthráv went to Sorath, and on his return extorted a large sum as tribute from the Nawáb of Cambay. He left a deputy in Ahmedá-

1754. bád, who marched against the same chief again in 1754, but on this occasion he could levy no tribute. As the Nawáb had firmly established himself and considerably enlarged his dominions, the Peshwa's deputy marched against him in person a second time, but was defeated and taken prisoner. The nominee of Raghunáthráv procured his release, and the Peshwa's deputy continued to demand

1755. arrears of tribute for his master till he obtained an agreement to pay at a future date. He then retired to the Dakhan, and the Nawáb, taking advantage of the lull to strengthen his army, captured Ahmedábád from the Marátha garrison and established himself in the city. After a while Dámáji and Khanderáv Gáikwár, with an agent sent direct by the Peshwa, arrived before the town

1757. and commenced a siege. It was not until April 1757 that the Maráthás again entered the city. The Nawáb surrendered after the Maráthás had fully ratified the conditions he himself had proposed.

1758. Sayájiráv, son of Dámáji, remained in Ahmedábád on behalf of his father, and the Peshwa's agent Sadáshiv put in a deputy in his turn and went himself to Surat. Here he was soon joined by Sayáji, who had to arrange the shares of the tribute in accordance with the partition treaty of 1751. Next year a body of Marátha troops was sent to the aid of the Ráv of Kachh, who was engaged in an expedition against Thatta in Sindh. Sadáshiv lent the Nawáb of Cambay some money on the part of the Peshwa to enable him to liquidate the arrears of pay due to his army, but a year afterwards the Marátha army appeared at the town gates with a demand for two years' arrears of tribute in full, amounting to Rs. 20,000. The Nawáb managed to raise this sum, and the Maráthás moved south. Dámáji was at this time in Poona.

1759. The Peshwa had supported Syed Achchan of Surat with the view of putting him under an obligation so as to secure some future advantages, and this year lent him some troops as a bodyguard. The Nawáb of Cambay, who was also indebted to the ministerial party, left his dominions to pay a visit to the Peshwa at Poona. Khanderáv meanwhile plundered Lunáváḍa and Ídar, whilst Sayájiráv was similarly engaged in Soráth.

1761. Dámáji Gáikwár accompanied the Peshwa to Delhi, and was one of the few Marátha leaders that escaped after the defeat at Pánipat. On his return to Gujarát he successfully opposed an expedition by the Nawáb of Cambay against Bálásinor and re-took the estates of Jawán Mard Khán. He also strengthened his position in Sorath and Káthiáváḍa against the Peshwa's party.

1761. The Peshwa, being hard pressed by his rival the Nizám, began in this year to make overtures to the East India Company's officers in Bombay, with a view to getting the aid of European artillery and gunners. He at first offered to give up a valuable tract of land in Jámbusar. But the English would accept no territory but the island of Sálsette, the town of Bassein, and the small islands in the harbour of Bombay. These the Marátha government declined to give up, so negotiations were broken off.

1762. Next year Raghunáthráv, as guardian of the son of Báláji, named Mádhavráv, who was still a minor, conferred the title of Senápati on one of the Jádhav family who had formerly borne it. The administration of Gujarát, however, which had always accompanied the title when held by the Dábháde family, was left practically in the hands of Dámáji, and no mention of any transfer of it was made at the time Jádhav was appointed commander-in-chief. Discontented with the empty honour thus conferred, Rámchandra, the new Senápati, joined the Nizám's party, and on account of this defection the Peshwa, two years afterwards, cancelled the appointment and restored the office to the Ghorpade family, one of whose members had held it long before. This put an end to the connection of Gujarát with the chief military dignity of the Marátha state.

Intrigues of Rághoba, 1768. After Mádhavráv Báláji came of age he had constantly to be on this guard against the plots of his uncle Raghunáthráv, who had refused to accept the share in the government offered him by the young Peshwa. Raghunáthráv, perhaps instigated by his wife, had no doubt great hopes of obtaining a share in the whole power of the administration, and suspecting Mádhavráv to be aware of his designs, looked upon all the overtures made by the latter as intended in some way or other to entrap him. He therefore collected an army of some 15,000 men in Báglán and Násik, and hoping to be joined on his way by Jánoji Bhonslé, advanced towards Poona. In his army was Govindráv, son of Dámáji Gáikwár, with a detachment of his father's troops. The Peshwa, without giving Jánoji time to effect

The Maráthás, A.D. 1760-1819.

a junction with Raghunáthráv, even if he had been prepared to do so, defeated his uncle's army at Dhorap, a fort in the Ajunta range, and carried off Rághobá and Govindráv to Poona, where they were placed in confinement.

Death of Dámáji Gáikwár, 1768.

Not long after this action Dámáji died. He had brought the fortunes of the Gáikwár house to the highest pitch they ever reached and not long after his death the family influence began to decline. It was his personal authority alone that was able to counteract the usual tendency of quasi-independent Marátha states towards disintegration, especially when they are at a distance from the central power. Khanderáv and Sayájiráv had shown frequent signs of insubordination (as for instance in their espousal of the cause of Rangoji) and a desire to establish themselves in an independant position, but the sagacity of Dámáji foresaw the advantage such a partition would give an enemy like the Peshwa, and his tact enabled him to preserve unity in his family, at least in resistance to what he showed them to be their common foe.

Disputed Succession.

The quarrel for the succession that arose on Dámáj's death was the first step towards the breaking up of the Gáikwár's power. Dámaji had three wives. By the first he had Govindráv, who however was born after Sayájiráv, the son by the second wife. His sons by the third wife were Mánáji and Fatesingh. Govindráv was in confinement at Poona near the court, and therefore in a position to offer conditions for the confirmation of his rights without loss of time.

In the Hindu law current amongst Maráthás, there are to be found precedents in favour of the heirship of either Govindráv or Sayájiráv. Some authorities support the rights of the son of the first wife whether he be the eldest or not, others again regard simply the age of the claimants, deciding in favour of the first born, of whatever wife he may be the son. Rámráv Shástri, the celebrated adviser of Mádhavráv Peshwa, is said to have expressed an opinion in favour of the rights of Sayájiráv: Govindráv, however, was on the spot where his influence could be used most extensively. Sayáji, moreover, was an idiot and a puppet in the hands of his half brother Fatesingh. Govindráv applied at once for investiture with the title of Sená-Khas-Khel. A payment of 50½ lákhs of rupees to the Peshwa on account of arrears of tribute and a fine for his conduct in taking part with Rághobá was a strong argument in his favour, and when he agreed to a tribute previously demanded from his father of Rs. 7,79,000 yearly and to maintain a peace contingent at Poona of 3000 horse, to be increased by a thousand more in time of war, there could be little doubt as to the legitimacy of his claim, and he was duly invested with his father's title and estate.

1771.

For reasons not apparent Sayáji's claims were not brought forward till nearly two years later. Govindráv had never been allowed to join his charge in Gujarát, so that he could exercise no interference in that direction, and the court affairs in the Dakhan left perhaps little time for the disposal of Sayájiráv's application, even if it had been made. Sayáji had entrusted his interests to Fatesingh, a man

THE MARÁTHÁS, A.D. 1760-1819.

of considerable ability, who came at once to Poona to get a reversal of the recognition of Govindráv. The Peshwa was glad to have this opportunity of undoing so much of Dámáji's work and dividing the Gáikwár family against itself, so using the verdict of Rám Shástri as his weapon, he cancelled the former grant in favour of Govindráv, and appointed Sayájiráv with Fatesingh as his *mutálik* or deputy. The latter, by agreeing to pay an extra sum of 6½ lákhs of rupees annually, got permission to retain the Poona contingent of Gáikwár horse in Gujarát, on the pretext that Govindráv would probably attack his brothers on the earliest opportunity. Thus, whatever happened, all went to the profit of the Peshwa's party and to the injury of the tax-paying Gujarát ryot.

1773.

Fatesingh retired in triumph to Baroda, and opened negotiations with the English in Surat, as he had been endeavouring to do for a year past without success. In January 1773, however, he succeeded in getting an agreement from the Chief for Affairs of the British Nation in Surat, that his share in the revenues of the town of Broach, which had been taken by storm in 1772 by the English, should not be affected by the change of masters. In the same year Náráyanráv Peshwa was murdered, and Rághobá was invested by the titular king at Sátára with the ministerial robe of honour. Govindráv Gáikwár, still in Poona, reminded the new Peshwa of the good offices of the Gáikwár family at Dhorap and elsewhere, and found means of getting reinstated as Sená-Khás-Khel. In 1774 he set out for Gujarát, and collecting a fair number of adherents on his way, he attacked Fatesingh. After various engagements of little importance, the latter found himself shut into the city of Baroda, which was invested by Govindráv in January 1775.

1774.

Rághobá Peshwa, 1774.

In the meantime Rághobá had been driven from power by the intrigues of Bráhmans of a different class from that to which he belonged, headed by the afterwards well-known Nána Phadnis. The ex-Peshwa first betook himself towards Málwa, where he hoped to be joined or at least assisted by Holkar and Sindia. As soon however as he got together some scattered forces he marched down the Tápti and opened negotiations with the English through Mr. Gambier, the chief at Surat. The Bombay Government at once demanded the cession of Bassein, Sálsette, and the adjacent islands. Rághobá refused, partly, in all probability, on account of the pride felt by the Marátha soldiery in their achievements before Bassein at the time of the great siege. He however offered valuable territory in Gujarát, yielding a revenue of about eleven lákhs, and to pay six lákhs down and 1½ lákhs monthly for the maintenance of a European contingent with artillery. The English at Bombay were debating whether this offer should not be accepted when news reached them that the Portuguese were about to organise an expedition to re-take Bassein. Negotiations with Rághobá were hastily broken off and a small force sent to forestall the rival Europeans. Before the end of 1774, both Thána and Versova fort in Sálsette had been taken.

Rághobá in Gujarát, 1775.

Rághobá now heard that Sindia and Holkar had been bought over by the ministerial party and would not come to his assistance.

THE MARÁTHÁS, A.D. 1760-1819.

Quickly moving his force down the river he reached Baroda in January 1775 with 10,000 horse and 400 foot. He joined Govindráv in investing that town, but sent meanwhile an agent to re-open the discussion of his proposals in the Bombay Council. This agent was captured by a party of Fatesingh's horse whilst he was out on an expedition near Párnera on behalf of Govindráv. On his release he repaired to Surat and took steps to get a treaty of alliance signed as soon as possible.

Rághobá Defeated.

The ministerial army of 30,000 men under Haripant Phadke entered Gujarát and obliged Govindráv and Rághobá to raise the siege of Baroda and to retire towards the Mahi. Fatesingh's force then joined Haripant. An attack on all sides was made (Feb. 17th). Rághobá, who was in the centre, was first charged, and before Govindráv and Khanderáv Gáikwár could come to his assistance his best officers were wounded, some of his Arab mercenaries refused to fight as large arrears of pay were due to them, and he was defeated on both flanks. He fled to Cambay with only 1000 horse; whilst the two Gáikwárs and Manáji Sindia (Phadke) led the rest of the scattered army to Kapadvanj, where it was again set in order. The Nawáb of Cambay, fearing lest the Marátha army should come in pursuit, shut the town gates on the fugitive and refused to give him shelter.

Reaches Surat.

Mr. Malet, chief of the English residents, who had been informed of the negotiations in progress between his Government and Rághobá, contrived to get the ex-Peshwa conveyed privately to Bhávnagar and from thence by boat to Surat. Here he arrived on February 23rd.

Treaty of Surat, 1775.

The stipulations of the treaty negotiated by Narotamdás, agent of Rághobá, and the Bombay Government were: The English to provide a force of 3000 men, of which 800 were to be Europeans and 1700 natives, together with a due proportion of artillery. In return for this Rághobá, still recognized as Peshwa, was to cede in perpetuity Sálsette, Bassein and the islands, Jámbusar, and Olpád. He also made over an assignment of Rs. 75,000 out of the revenues of Anklesvar, the remaining portion of which district, together with A'mod, Hánsot, and Balsár was placed under British management as security for the monthly contribution of 1½ lákhs for the support of the troops in his service. He also promised to procure the cession of the Gáikwár's share in the revenues of Broach. Sundry other provisions (dealing with different parts of the Marátha dominions) were inserted, Rághobá being treated throughout as the representative of the Marátha kingdom. This treaty was signed on March 6th, 1775, at Surat, but on the previous day there had been a debate in the Council at Bombay as to the propriety of continuing to support Rághobá, as the news from Gujarát made the British authorities doubtful whether the contingent they had already sent to Surat was enough to ensure success.

Colonel Keating in Gujarát.

Just before the treaty was drawn up, at the end of February Lieut.-Colonel Keating had been despatched in command of 350 European infantry 800 sepoys 80 European artillerymen and 60 gun lascars with others, in all about 1500 men, ready for active service. This force landed at Surat four days after Rághobá had arrived from Bhávnagar.

Before receiving this token of the intention of the British to support Rágliobá, the Nawáb had treated the latter simply as a fugitive, but upon finding that the Bombay Government had determined to make the ex-Peshwa their ally, he paid the customary visits and offered presents as to a superior.

Keating Sails with Rághobá for Cambay.

When the news reached Surat that Govindráv's troops and the rest had been reorganized at Kapadvanj, it was determined to effect a junction with them by landing Colonel Keating's detachment at Cambay and from thence marching north.

Rághobá in Cambay, 1775.

Considerable delay occurred in carrying out the first part of this proposal. First of all Rághobá detained the army at Dumas[1] whilst he paid a visit of ceremony to the frequented temple of Bhimpor in the neighbourhood. Then again, the convoy met with contrary winds the whole way up the gulf, and it was not till March 17th that the contingent landed. The Nawáb, accompanied by the British Resident, paid a visit of ceremony and presented *nazaránás* to Rághobá as a sort of atonement for his previous discourtesy and neglect. The Maráthás, however, knowing that this change of tone was entirely due to the presence and alliance of the Europeans, paid much more attention to the latter than to the Muhammadans.

Govindráv Gáikwár's Army.

The British contingent encamped at a place called Náráyan-Sarovar, just north of the town. Here they waited until the reinforcement from Bombay arrived, bringing the whole force up to the complement stipulated for in the treaty. Rághobá's army under Govindráv Gáikwár was reported to be moving southwards, and Colonel Keating agreed to let it pass the Sábarmati river before joining it. Meanwhile the enemy, said to number 40,000 infantry and 12,000 cavalry, marched north to intercept Govindráv. The latter, however, by forced marches succeeded in crossing the Sábarmati before the arrival of the ministerial army, and encamped a few miles north-east of Cambay at a place called Darmaj or Dara. Here Colonel Keating joined him about the middle of April.

Govindráv's army consisted of about 8000 fighting men and nearly 18,000 camp followers. These latter were chiefly Pindháris who used to attach themselves to the camp of one of the Marátha chiefs, on condition of surrendering to him half their plunder. Each chief had his separate encampment, where he exercised independent authority over his own troops, although bound to general obedience to the commander-in-chief of the whole army. The confusion of this arrangement is described by an eye-witness as utterly destructive of all military discipline. To add to the cumbrousness of such an expedition, most of the Pindháris brought their wives and children with them, the cooking pots and plunder being carried on bullocks and ponies, of which there were altogether nearly 200,000 attached to the troops. In every camp there was a regular

[1] At the mouth of the Tápti, now belonging to the little Muhammadan state of Sachin.

THE MARÁTHÁS, A.D. 1760-1819.

bazár where cash payment or barter passed equally current, so that a premium was thus placed on the pilfering of small articles by the Pindháris, whose stipulations as to plunder were confined neither to friend nor enemy.

Advance of the Combined Forces.

When all needful preparations had been made, the army, accompanied by a battery of ten guns, besides mortars and howitzers, all of which were manned by Europeans, moved out against the enemy. The latter slowly retreated, burning the crops and forage and destroying the water-supply on its way. On the 20th April the first engagement took place at Usámli, resulting in the repulse of the ministerial troops. On May 1st a similar skirmish on the banks of the Vátrak drove the ministerialists into Kaira. From this post they were driven after a series of slight engagements with the army of Rághobá, which crossed the river at Mátar. Fatesingh now received a reinforcement of 10,000 horse under Khanderáv Gáikwár, but to counterbalance this aid, Sindia and Holkar from some unexplained cause, connected probably with intrigues at Poona, withdrew from further co-operation with him. Colonel Keating was unable to follow up the advantages he had gained owing to the large proportion of cavalry in the enemy's army. He therefore continued his march southwards, after persuading Rághoba to spend the monsoon in Poona, where he would be on the spot to counteract intrigues, instead of at Ahmedábád, as had been at first proposed.

On May 8th the army reached Nadiád, after repulsing on the road two attacks by the enemy's cavalry. This result was obtained chiefly by means of the European light artillery. Nadiád belonged at this time to Khanderáv Gáikwár, and to punish his defection to Fatesingh, Rághobá inflicted a fine of 60,000 rupees on the town. The amount was assessed on the several castes in proportion to their reputed means of payment. The Bháts, a peculiar people of whom more hereafter, objected to being assessed, and slaughtered each other in public: so that the guilt of their blood might fall on the oppressor. The Bráhmans, who also claimed exemption from all taxation, more astutely brought two old women of their caste into the market place and there murdered them. Having made this protest, both castes paid their contributions. Rághobá injudiciously wasted seven days over the collection of this fine, and in the end only levied 40,000 rupees.

Defeat of Fatesingh, 1775.

On May 14th the march was resumed, under the usual skirmishing onslaughts of the ministerial party. At Arás, where Rághobá had been defeated shortly before, he was in imminent danger of a second and still more serious discomfiture. An order mistaken by a British company, and the want of discipline on the part of Rághobá's cavalry nearly led to a total defeat with great slaughter. The European infantry and artillery, however, turned the fortunes of the day. The troops of Fatesingh were allowed to approach in pursuit to within a few yards of the batteries, all the guns of which then opened on them with grape, the infantry meanwhile plying their small arms along the whole line. Fatesingh was obliged to withdraw his diminished forces and the army of Rághobá received no further molesta-

THE MARÁTHÁS, A.D. 1760-1819.

tions from him on its way to the Mahi. Colonel Keating then ordered a general move to Broach, where he arrived safely on 27th May, after a troublesome march through the robber-infested country between the Dhádhar river and Ámod.

The Ministerial General Retreats.

Here they remained until June 8th, when Colonel Keating was about to move south again. Luckily, as it turned out for him, the nearest ford was impassable and he had to march to one higher up at a place variously called Bába Piára or Báva Pir. On his way thither he heard that Haripant, the ministerial commander-in-chief, was halting on the north bank by the ford; he therefore pushed on to make an attack on the rear, but owing partly to timely information received and partly to the confusion caused by the irrepressibility of Rághobá's cavalry, Haripant had time to withdraw all his force except some bagage and ammunition, which, with a few guns, he was forced in the hurry of his passage across the river to leave behind. Colonel Keating then marched fourteen miles north from the ford and halted before proceeding to Dabhoi, a town belonging to Fatesingh. The general ignorance of tactics and want of discipline in the native army had determined Colonel Keating not to lead his force as far as Poona, but to spend the monsoon near Baroda.

Colonel Keating at Dabhoi, 1775.

Rághobá detached one of his generals, Amir Khán, in pursuit of Ganeshpant, whom Hari Pant had left as his deputy in Gujarát. Ganeshpant with a detachment of the ministerial army had separated from Hari at the Bába Piára ford and found his way through the wild country on the north of the Tápti towards Ahmedábád. He was finally caught by Amir Khán.

Dabhoi was at this time in charge of a Bráhman governor, who submitted on the approach of Rághobá's army. Colonel Keating quartered his force in the town, but Rághobá, after exacting a levy of three lákhs of rupees, encamped at Bhilápur on the Dhádhar, ten miles from Dabhoi. Here he began to negotiate with Fatesingh in Baroda through the mediation of Colonel Keating. Fatesingh was all the more ready to come to definite terms of agreement, as he knew that Govindráv was on the watch to recover Baroda.

Rághobá and the Gáikwárs.

It is not certain what the terms proposed and agreed to really were. The only record of them is a copy sent in 1802 to the Resident at Poona by Governor Duncan. According to this document Govindráv was to lose his pension and to occupy the same position as before the accession of Rághobá. Khanderáv was to revert to the situation in which he had been placed by Dámáji. The provision of the treaty of the 6th March regarding the Gáikwár's claims on Broach was ratified, and as a reward for the mediation of the Bombay Government, the Gáikwár ceded to the British in perpetuity the sub-divisions of Chikhli and Variáv near Surat and Koral on the Narbada. Before this treaty could be concluded, Colonel Keating received orders to withdraw his contingent into British territory and to leave Rághobá to manage for himself. This change of policy was due to the disapproval by the Supreme Government of the treaty of 6th March, which they alleged had been made inconsistently with the negotiations then being carried on with the ruling powers at Poona as well as with the authority of the Calcutta Government. The treaty was therefore declared to be invalid and the troops in the field were ordered by the Supreme Government to be withdrawn at once into British garrisons. A special envoy, Colonel Upton, was sent from Bengal to negotiate a treaty with the Ministers in accordance with the views current in Calcutta.

Withdrawal of the British Contingent.

As soon as the roads were open Colonel Keating moved towards Surat, but at the solicitation of Rághobá he disobeyed his orders so far as to encamp at Kadod, about twenty miles east of Surat, but not in British territory. Here he awaited the results of the overtures of Colonel Upton. This envoy remained at Poona from the 28th December 1775 till the 1st March 1776, on which date he signed the treaty of Purandhar, in which the office only and not the name of the Peshwa is mentioned. By this compact the Peshwa ceded all claims on the revenue of Broach together with land in the neighbourhood of that town to the British. He also paid twelve lákhs of rupees in compensation for the expenses of the war. Sálsette was to be either retained by the English or restored in exchange for territory yielding three lákhs of rupees annually. The cessions made by Fatesingh Gáikwár were to be restored to him if the Peshwa's Government could prove that he had no right to make them without due authorization from Poona. The treaty of the 6th March was declared null and void. Rághobá was to disband his army and take a pension. If he resisted, the English were to give him no assistance. If he agreed to the terms proposed, he was to live at Kopargaon[1] on the Godávari with an ample pension. When he received information as to the terms of the new treaty, he at once declined to accept the pension, and, as he could not understand the position of the Bombay Government with regard to that at Calcutta, he proceeded to offer still more favourable terms for further assistance.

Negotiations at Poona.

Rághobá at Surat, 1776.

Rághobá was at Mándvi[2] on the Tápti when he was finally given to understand that the British could no longer aid him. He thereupon took refuge in Surat with two hundred followers. The rest of his army which had been ordered to disperse, gathered round Surat, on pretence of waiting for the payment of the arrears due to them. As their attitude was suspicious, and there were rumours of an expedition having started from Poona under Haripant to subdue them, the Bombay Government garrisoned Surat and Broach with all the forces it could spare.

Colonel Upton meanwhile offered Rághobá, on behalf of the ministers, a larger pension with liberty of residing at Benáres. This also was declined, and the ex-Peshwa fled to Bombay, where he lived on a monthly pension allotted him by the Government.

---

[1] Now in the Ahmednagar district.

[2] In the Surat district ome thirty miles east of the city.

On 20th August 1776, a despatch of the Court of Directors arrived confirming the treaty of the 6th March 1775. At first the Bombay Government were inclined to take this as authorizing the retention of all the territory ceded, but on further deliberation it was decided that as the treaty of Purandhar had been ratified by the Supreme Government subsequent to the signing of the despatch, which was dated 5th April 1776, it was evident that the Court of Directors did not mean to uphold the previous engagement more than temporarily, or until the final treaty had been concluded.

Negotiations at Poona, 1777.

At the end of 1776, a Bombay officer was sent in place of Colonel Upton to be a resident envoy at Poona for the carrying out of the provisions of the treaty. Mr. Mostyn was the person selected, and he arrived in Poona in March 1777. He soon found that the ministers had little intention of adhering to the treaty, so he at once took up the question that he thought it most important to the Bombay Government to have settled, namely the relations of the Peshwa's Court with Fatesingh Gáikwár as regards the cessions of territory. The ministers asserted that the Gáikwárs merely administered Gujarát on the part of the Peshwa and were entirely dependent upon the Poona government, so that they could conclude no agreement with foreign states except with its approbation. Fatesingh did not deny the dependence, but evaded the question of his right to make direct treaties and claimed the restitution of the cessions on the ground that Raghunáthráv had failed to perform his part of the stipulations. The point was discussed for some time, and at last the question of dependence seems to have been let drop, for in February 1778 Fatesingh paid up the arrears of tribute, made the usual presents to the ministers and their favourites, and was again invested with the title of Sená-Khás-Khel.

In October a despatch from the Court of Directors reached the Governments of Bengal and Bombay, disapproving of the treaty of Purandhar, but ratifying it on the principle of *factum valet*. It was suggested, however, that in case of evasion on the part of the ministers, a fresh treaty should be concluded with Rághobá on the lines of that of 1775.

Fresh Alliance with Rághobá, 1778.

In November 1778 it was rumoured that the ministers in Poona were intriguing with the French, so the Bombay Government took this opportunity of entering into a treaty with Rághobá, who was still in Bombay. He confirmed the grants of 1775, and as security for the pay of the British contingent that was to help in placing him on the Peshwa's throne in Poona, he agreed to assign the revenues of Balsár and the remainder of Anklesvar, as he had done before. He stipulated, however, that his own agents should collect the dues from these districts, and that the British should take charge of them only in case of the full sum due not being paid and then merely as a temporary measure.

The Convention of Bhadgaon, 1779.

On the 22nd November 1778 the force moved out of Bombay, and by dint of mismanagement and internal dissension the campaign was brought to an end by the convention of the 16th January 1779.

THE MARÁTHÁS, A.D. 1760 - 1879.

Under this agreement all possessions in Gujarát acquired since the time of Mádhavráv Peshwa were to be restored by the British, together with Sálsette, Uran, and other islands. Rághobá was to be made over to Sindia's charge, and a separate treaty assigned to Sindia the sovereignty of Broach.

Negotiation with the Gáikwár.

The Council at Bombay disavowed the convention and were inclined to adhere only to the clause allotting Broach to Sindia. Mr. Hornby proposed to the Supreme Government an alliance with Fatesingh, engaging to free him from dependence on the Poona Government and to reconcile the disputants within the Gáikwár family itself. After the arrival of General Goddard with reinforcements from Bengal the Governor General approved of the alliance proposed with Fatesingh as head of the Baroda state, but specially declined to admit any participation or support in the family disputes. The British were to conquer for themselves the Peshwa's share of Gujarát, if they were able to do so.

Rághobá Escapes from Sindia, 1779.

Rághobá, meanwhile, who had been given over to Sindia to be conveyed to Bundelkhand, escaped with the connivance of his custodian and fled to Broach. This was evidently a move calculated by Sindia to bring on hostilities between Nána Phadnis, the head of the ministerial party, and the English. General Goddard, who was conducting the negotiations with Poona on the part both of the Supreme Government and of the Government of Bombay, received Rághobá on June 12th, but evaded any proposals for a direct alliance. At the end of the rains of the same year, information was received by the English that a coalition against them had been formed by the Maráthás, the Nizám, and Hyder Ali of Mysor. The rumour was partially confirmed by the demand by Nána Phadnis for the cession of Sálsette and the person of Rághobá as preliminaries to any treaty. No answer was given, but reinforcements were called for and the overtures with Fatesingh pushed forward. This chief prevaricated about the terms of the treaty and evidently did not like to enter into any special engagement that might perhaps bring down upon him the Poona army. General Goddard therefore advanced on 1st January 1780 against Dabhoi, which was garrisoned by the Peshwa's troops from the Dakhan, whilst the English in Broach expelled the Marátha officers from their posts and re-took possession of Anklesvar, Hánsot, and Amod. On January 20th Dabhoi was evacuated by the Maráthás and occupied by General Goddard. Fatesingh now showed himself willing to enter into the proposed treaty, and on the 26th January 1780 signed an offensive and defensive alliance.

League against the English, 1780.

Treaty with Fatesingh Gáikwár.

In the re-opening of hostilities there was no mention of Rághobá, but the ground given was simply the non-fulfilment on the part of the Peshwa of his treaty engagement. Rághobá remained under English supervision in the enjoyment of a large allowance. Dabhoi was occupied by an English civil officer with a detachment of irregulars, and General Goddard moved towards Ahmedábád.

THE MARÁTHÁS, A.D. 1760-1819.

By the treaty of 1780 the Peshwa was to be excluded from Gujarát. To avoid confusion in collection, the district north of the Mahi was to belong entirely to the share of the Gáikwár. The English were to enjoy the whole district south of the Tápti, together with the Gáikwár share in the revenue of Surat. In return for the support the English were to give him in withholding tribute from the Peshwa, Fatesing ceded Sinor on the Narbada and the Gáikwár's villages round Broach. These cessions, however, were not to have effect until Fatesingh was in possession of Ahmedábád. The contingent of 3000 horse was to be still furnished by the Gáikwár government.

General Goddard takes Ahmedábád, 1780.

As soon as these conditions were agreed upon, General Goddard went with his own army and the contingent furnished by Fatesingh to Ahmedábád. After encamping before it for five days, he took the city by storm on 15th February 1780.

Operations against Sindia and Holkar.

Sindia and Holkar had combined their forces against the English and were marching up Gujarát, plundering on their way. They were opposed by General Goddard, who marched across the Mahi early in March. The allies turned off towards Chámpáner without risking a pitched battle on the plain. Sindia at once opened negotiations with the view of wasting time during the fair season. His first proposal was that Rághobá should be sent to Jhánsi, where Sindia had allotted him an estate, and that Bájiráv, Rághobá's son, should be appointed *diván* or manager of the Peshwa Madhávráv, who was a minor. Bájiráv himself was under age, so Sindia was, of course, to assume temporarily the reins of government.

Goddard at once refused to force Rághobá to take any course other than the one he should select of his own free will; for Sindia did not appear to be aware that the English were now at war with the ministers on their own account and not as allies of an ex-Peshwa. Negotiations were broken off and Sindia and Holkar dislodged from place after place without any decisive engagement being fought. General Goddard was preparing monsoon quarters for his army, when he heard that a division of a Marátha force which had been plundering the Konkan in order to cut off supplies from Bombay had attacked parts of the Surat Athávisi. He detached some troops under Lieut. Welsh and sent them to the south, whilst he remained himself on the Narbada. Lieut. Welsh drove back the marauders and took possession of the forts of Párnera, Indargad, and Bagváda.

After the monsoon of 1780, General Goddard went to besiege Bassein, leaving Major Forbes in charge of the Gujarát army. This officer posted one body of troops at Ahmedábád for the protection of Fatesingh, another at Surat, and a third at Broach. Two battalions of Bengal infantry were sent to Sinor and some few men to Dabhoi.

1781.

An attack was made by Sindia on the newly acquired district of Sinor, but Major Forbes successfully resisted it and Sindia's position with regard to his own dominions was now such as to prevent him from sending more expeditions against Gujarát.

The military necessities of other parts of India were such as to induce General Goddard to apply to Fatesingh for an increase to

The Maráthás, A.D. 1760-1819.

his contingent, in accordance with the treaty of 1780. After some personal communications with this Chief in Gujarát, General Goddard was able to arrange with the Gáikwár for the defence of part of that province and thus set free some European troops for service elsewhere.

Treaty of Sálbai, 1782.

No further attack was made in this direction during the continuance of the war which came to an end on 17th May 1782. The treaty of Sálbai between an envoy of the Governor General on one side and Mahádáji Sindia as plenipotentiary for the Peshwa and minister of Poona on the other, replaced the Marátha territory in Gujarát exactly where it was on the outbreak of hostilities against Rághobá in 1775. It was, however, specially stipulated that no demand for arrears of tribute during the late hostilities should be made against the Gáikwár, a clause that led to misunderstandings many years later. The town of Broach was given over to Sindia in accordance with the secret negotiation of 1779 and the votes of the Bengal and Bombay Councils. The territory round Broach yielding a revenue of three lákhs of rupees, ceded by the Peshwa, was likewise returned. Rághobá was granted a pension of 25,000 rupees a month and allowed to select his own place of residence. He went to Kopargaon and there died a few months after the conclusion of the treaty of Sálbai. Thus came to an end one of the chief sources of disturbance to the Poona government. For the next six years no event of any political importance took place in Gujarát, which province was left almost entirely to the administration of the Gáikwár family.

Death of Fatesingh, 1789.

In 1789, however, Fatesingh died, leaving Sayájiráv without a guardian. Mánáji, a younger brother, at once seized the reins of government and began the usual sort of negotiations to secure his recognition by the Poona government. He paid a nazarána of 3,13,000 rupees and agreed to pay up thirty-six lákhs of rupees as arrears, though it is not clear on what account, unless that sum had accrued since the treaty of Sálbai, or was part of the long standing account left open by Dámáji in 1753. Mánáji, however, was not allowed to succeed to the post of guardian without opposition. Govindráv Gáikwár was living at Poona, and, though he had himself little influence with the Peshwa's immediate adherents, he had managed to secure the then powerful Sindia on his side. This chief, since his recognition as plenipotentiary at the treaty of Sálbai, had been gradually making good his position with the Peshwa and his favourites as well as with the leading Marátha nobles, so as to be able to successfully oppose Nána Phadnis when the time came for a coalition of the outlying chiefs against the ministerial party. Govindráv offered his son Ánandráv as husband for the daughter of Sindia, a proposal which it is not probable that he ever intended to carry out. A grant of three lákhs of rupees was also promised, in return for which Sindia allowed his garrison in Broach to assist Govindráv's illegitimate son Kánhoji to reach Baroda. Mánáji applied to the Bombay Government on the grounds that the steps taken by Govindráv were contrary to the provisions of the treaty of 1780. As however this treaty had been abrogated by the later agreement at Sálbai, the Bombay Government declined to interfere. Mánáji's agents at Poona contrived to get Nána Phadnis to propose a compromise, to which however Govindráv, at the instigation probably of Sindia, declined to accede. Before any decision was reached Mánáji died.

The Maráthás, A.D. 1760-1819.

1793.

Nána detained Govindráv in Poona till he had agreed to hold by former stipulations and to cede to the Peshwa the Gáikwár's share in the districts south of the Tápti together with his share of the Surat customs. To this the Government of Bombay demurred as an infraction of the provision of the Sálbai treaty whereby the integrity of the Gáikwár's possessions was assured. Nána Phadnis at once withdrew his proposals. Govindráv at last joined his brother at Baroda on 19th December, and took up the office of regent.

Ába Shelukar Deputy Governor of Gujarát, 1796.

For two years Gujarát remained quiet. In 1796 Bájiráv, son of Rághobá, suceeded to the Peshwa's dignity and at once appointed his younger brother, ten years of age, governor of Gujarát. In accordance with Marátha custom a deputy was sent to take charge of the province, one Ába Shelukar, and he too seems to have administered vicariously, for next year (1797) we find him amongst those taken prisoners with Nána Phadnis when that minister was treacherously seized by Daulatrav Sindia in the Dakhan. Ába was released on promising to pay ten lákhs of rupees as ransom. He then joined his appointment as subhedár in order to take measures to get together the money he required.

1797.

Disputes between Ába and Govindráv Gáikwár.

Bájiráv Peshwa was anxious to embroil Ába with Govindráv, whom he knew to be favourable to Nána Phadnis and too powerful to be allowed to acquire influence beyond the reach of head-quarter supervision. A cause of quarrel soon arose. Daulatráv pressed Ába for part payment of the above ten lákhs, and the latter being unable to squeeze enough out of his own territory, forced contributions from some of the villages administered by the Gáikwár. Govindráv at once took up arms against him and applied for aid to the English Agent at Surat. In this city Governor Jonathan Duncan had just assumed chief authority in accordance with an agreement between the English and the Nawáb. Duncan was anxious to secure for his government the land round Surat and the Gáikwár's share in the *chauth* of the town and district. Govindráv, when this demand was made, referred the Governor to Poona, knowing that under the treaty of Sálbai the British Government had no more right to acquire a share of the Gáikwár territory than the Poona authorities had when they made a somewhat similar demand in 1793, which was withdrawn as stated above. Before the reference could be made, Ába was penned up by Govindráv's own army in Ahmedábád and forced to surrender that city. He was kept in confinement for more than seven years.

1798.

Gujarát farmed to the Gáikwár, 1799.

In the same year (1799) the Peshwa, apparently without formally revoking the appointment of his brother Chimnáji as Subhedár, gave Govindráv a farm for five years of his whole rights in Gujarát, at the rate of five lákhs of rupees a year. These rights included shares in the Káthiáváḍa and Sorath tribute, the revenue of Petlád, Nápád, Ránpur, Dhandhuka, and Gogha, together with rights to certain customs dues in Cambay and a share in the revenue of the city of Ahmedábád.

THE MARÁTHÁS, A.D. 1760-1819.

Govindráv unfortunately died a month before this farm was formally made over by the Peshwa.

Ánandráv Gáikwár, 1800.

As had happened at the death of Dámáji, so again now, the heir Ánandráv was all but an idiot and quite incapable of managing his affairs. The disputes as to the guardianship again set the whole state in confusion. Kánhoji, a son of Govindráv by a Rájputni princess of Dharampor, who had been the first agent of his father in Baroda in 1793, had been put in prison for refusing to give place to Govindráv when the latter at length joined him at Baroda. At the death of Govindráv, Kánhoji managed to obtain his liberty and to secure the ascendancy in the counsels of his weak-minded elder brother. He assumed, in fact, the whole government. His arrogant conduct in this new position excited the Arab guard against him and he was again thrown into confinement. His mother Gajrábái, who was a refugee in Surat, endeavoured to get assistance from the English there, and at the same time made overtures to Malhár, son of Khanderáv Gáikwár, who had formerly been one of Govindráv's bitterest opponents.

1800.

Meanwhile the administration of the Gáikwár's affairs passed into the hands of Rávji and Bábáji Áppa, two brothers who had been brought to Baroda in 1793 by Govindráv himself Rávji took charge of the civil work, whilst Bábáji undertook the military duties, which at that time consisted in great measure in collecting the revenue by show of force. These two ministers, on hearing of the proceedings of Gajrábái, outbid her for the aid of the Bombay Government. In addition to the cessions formerly offered by Govindráv, they were willing to give up Chikhli also. Matters were precipitated by the successes of Malhárav in the field. Rávji offered to subsidize five European battalions, and Governor Duncan took upon himself the responsibility of sending an auxiliary force of 1600 men under Major Walker to act with the troops of Rávji and Bábáji north of Ahmedábád. Reinforcements were afterwards sent up, but the campaign was not closed till April 1802, when the fort of Kadi had been taken by storm. Malhárav surrendered and a residence in Nadiad was assigned him with a liberal pension out of the revenues of that subdivision. The fort of Sankheda, which had been held by Ganpatráv Gáikwár for his cousin Malhárav, was soon after this reduced and the country for a time pacified.

The British aid Govindráv's Party.

In March Rávji had an interview at Cambay with Governor Duncan, which was followed on June 6th by a definite treaty, of which the groundwork had been previously sketched in anticipation of the reduction of the revolted Gáikwárs. Two thousand men, besides artillery, were to be subsidized and a *jáidád* or assignment for their payment was made on the revenue of Dholka and the part of Nadiád not assigned to Malhárráv. Chikhli was given to the British in reward for their aid in storming Kadi, and Residents were to be appointed reciprocally. A large sum of money was borrowed by Rávji, partly from Bombay partly from Baroda bankers, to pay off the arrears due to about 7000 Arab mercenaries, who had usurped a great deal of objectionable influence in civil affairs at the Gáikwár's

The British and the Gáikwár, 1800.

capital. Major Walker was appointed Resident and proceeded to Baroda on 8th June.

The Gáikwár's Minister Rávji.

On the same day was signed a secret compact assuring Rávji of the support of the British Government and awarding him a village out of the territory ceded by the treaty of June 6th. It was deemed advisable by the British Government to have at the Baroda court some leading personage who might, in the present state of the relations between Bombay and Poona, further the designs of the former government in preventing a recurrence of the coalition of Marátha powers. Rávji was sure of his reward if he served British interests, whilst in case of the reorganization of a Marátha confederacy the state he was administering would probably play but a very subordinate part in subsequent events.

Treaty of Bassein, 31st Dec. 1802.

The treaty of June 6th was disapproved by the Court of Directors as being in direct contravention of the treaty of Sálbai. Before, however, any orders had been issued by the Home authorities to restore to the Gáikwár the territory he had ceded, the Peshwa, out of regard for whom the treaty had been disavowed, was a fugitive before the army of Holkar, and by December had ratified these very concessions at the treaty of Bassein. By this treaty the Peshwa virtually placed his independence in the hands of the British. He ceded his share of Surat, thus giving them sole control over that district. In payment of the subsidiary force required he handed over territory in Gujarát, the revenue of which amounted to 12,28,000 rupees, and finally he constituted the British Government arbiter in the disputes between his government and that of Baroda. The grants made by the Gáikwár for the support of the subsidiary force amounted in 1802 to 7,80,000 rupees.

Arabs Disbanded.

Major Walker attempted to negotiate with the Arab guard, but the greater part of them flew to arms and released Kánhoji Gáikwár. The latter then tried to collect an army near Baroda, and succeeded in obtaining possession of the person of A'nandráv the titular ruler. The British force then took Baroda by storm, after which most of the Arabs submitted, except a few who joined Kánhoji. The rest took the arrears due to them and left the country. Kánhoji was not subdued till February 1803. Malhárráv meanwhile had broken out in rebellion in Káthiávada and was plundering the Marátha possessions there. Bábáji A'ppáji and a young officer named Vithal Deváji (or Divánji) led the operations against him; and to the latter belongs the honour of having captured this troublesome member of the ruling family. The estate of Nadiád, which had been assigned to Madhavráo by Govindráv, was resumed by Rávji A'ppáji and made over in its entirety to the British Government. A treaty, supplementary to that of 1802, was drawn up guaranteeing this cession as well as the *inám* or free gift of the fort and district of Kaira, "out of gratitude for the support given in the recent troubles to the Gáikwár's honour and for assistance in securing the good of the State."

Malhárráv in Revolt, 1803.

THE MARÁTHÁS, A.D. 1760-1819.

Contingent Strengthened, 1803.

Very soon after this agreement Rávji applied for an addition to the subsidiary force, in payment of which he assigned Mátar Mahudha and the customs of Kim-Kathodra, a station about seventeen miles north of Surat. His reason for strengthening the subsidiary force appears to have been that owing to the reduction of the Arabs, his own force was not enough to guard even the frontier, and that a great part of that duty fell on the European contingent, which was numerically insufficient for service on so extended a scale. This was the last public act of note on the part of Rávji A'ppa, who died in July 1803, after adopting one Sitárám to succeed to his estate.

Death of Rávji, 1803.

War with Sindia.

Whilst these arrangements were being carried out at Baroda, Bájiráv Peshwa, chafing at the dependence to which his straits of the previous winter had reduced him with regard to the English, was actively propagating dissension between Sindia and the Calcutta Government. Not long after, the war that had been some time imminent broke out, and a contingent of 7352 men from Gujarát was ordered to the field. In August or September Broach and Pávágad[1] both fell to the British.

The Revenue Collecting Force.

Under the treaty of Sirjé Anjangaon in December 1803, both Pávágad and Dohad were restored to Sindia, but Broach remained British. By this means one of the rising Marátha powers was extruded from the centre to the outlying portion of the province. The employment of all the British contingent against Sindia's possessions in Gujarát precluded Major Walker from furnishing any portion of the army that was annually sent to collect the tribute in Káthiávaḍa. Rávji A'ppáji had expressly stipulated that some part of the contingent might be so used when it could be spared from its main duties. The Supreme Government agreed to the proposal when made by Governor Duncan, on the grounds of the advantage both to the Gáikwár and the tributaries of employing on this disagreeable duty a strong and well-disciplined force. Already some of the tributaries had made overtures to Major Walker with a view to obtaining British protection against powerful neighbours. Governor Duncan was in favour of accepting the duty of protection and also of helping the Gáikwar's commander in his expeditions through the peninsula on these grounds. Firstly, the officer in command could exercise a certain supervision over the collections in which the British as part assignees had a direct interest. Secondly, a way could thus be opened for the acquisition of a port on the coast from which the intrigues, supposed to be carried on by agents from the Isle of France, could be watched and counteracted. From such a point, too, the views of the Bombay Government as regards Kachh could be promoted. Thirdly, the commandant could take steps to improve the system of forcible collections, and towards abolishing the barbarous features of this rude method of levying tribute. He could also, perhaps, suggest some system by which the advantages of all three parties concerned would be better secured than by reliance on the uncertainty of temporary expeditions. The fourth and last

[1] A celebrated hill fort south of Chámpáner in the Panch Mahals district.

THE MARÁTHÁS, A.D. 1760-1819.

reason given savours strongly of the Marátha policy of the time, of which the leading maxim was *Divide et impera.* It was represented that Bábáji, who had successfully collected the tribute during 1802-03 and whose subordinate and companion Vithal Deváji was a person of similar energy and capability, might possibly acquire too great influence if left in a quasi-independent command at such a distance from the Court. It was politic, then, to join with the force under his command a strong foreign body, thus dividing both the power and the responsibility. The war with Sindia caused these proposals to fall into abeyance for some time.

Renewal of Farm, 1804.

Meanwhile the Resident at Poona was doing his best to secure for the Gáikwár a further lease for ten years of the farm of the Peshwa's dominions in Gujarát, so that the inconveniences of dual government might be avoided. In October 1804 a ten years' farm was granted in the name of Bhagvantráv Gáikwár at an annual rate of 4½ lákhs of rupees.

The British and the Gáikwár, 1805.

This grant led to the consolidation of all previous engagements into a single treaty, which was signed in April 1805. Previous agreements were confirmed and the whole brought into consonance with the treaty of Bassein.. Districts yielding 11,70,000 rupees per annum were made over for the support of the subsidiary force, and arrangements were also made for the repayment of the cash loan advanced by the British Government in 1802, when the liquidation of the arrears due to the Arabs was a matter of urgent political necessity. The British contingent was to be available in part for service in Káthiáváḍa, whenever the British Government thought such an employment of it advisable.

Finally, the British Government was constituted arbiter in all disputes of the Gáikwár, not alone with foreign powers, but also in the adjustment of his financial transactions with the Peshwa his paramount power. These transactions, which ranged back from the capture of Dámáji in 1751, had never been the subject of a formal investigation, and were by this time complicated by the numerous engagements with third parties into which both governments had been obliged to enter at their various moments of distress. Bájiráv, who was apparently intriguing for a Marátha coalition against his new protectors, was careful not to bring before the notice of the chiefs, whose esteem he wished to gain, a provision which exhibited him as in any way dependent upon the arbitration of a foreign power. He therefore granted the farm for ten years to the Gáikwár, as much by way of remanding for a time the proposed inquiries and settlement of their respective claims as for the purpose of diverting the attention of the British to the administration of this new appanage, whilst leaving him free scope for his intrigues in the Dakhan. He used, moreover, every pretext to defer the consideration of the Gáikwár question until he could make use of his claims to further his own designs. His success in preventing a discussion of these transactions is apparent by the fact that in the financial statement of the Gáikwár's affairs made by Colonel Walker in 1804, no mention of the Poona demand is to be found.

The Maráthás, A.D. 1760 - 1819.

No important event took place during the next year or two. Bábáji relinquished the command of the force in Káthiáváḍa in favour of Vithalráv Deváji, whilst he himself took part in the civil administration at Baroda. The Resident, too, seems to have been likewise engaged in internal matters and in securing the country against an invasion by Kánhoji, now a fugitive at the court of Holkar.

1807.

In 1807 the Resident made over A'ba Shelukar, late Sar Subhedár of the Peshwa, to the British Government, by whom he could be prevented from engaging in fresh conspiracies. After this Colonel Walker was at last enabled to leave Baroda in order to assist in the settlement of the Káthiáváḍa tribute question, an object he had long had in view, but which the necessity for his continuous presence at the Gáikwár's capital had hitherto prevented him from undertaking.

Káthiáváḍa Tribute.

The changes with regard to the collection of the tribute from the chiefs of Káthiáváḍa that were carried out in 1807 deserve a special description. Firstly, they placed the relations of the tributary to the paramount power on quite a new basis. Secondly, by them the British influence over both parties concerned was much increased and the connection between the governments of Bombay and Baroda drawn closer. Thirdly, they were subsequently, as will be seen hereafter, the subject of much discussion and delay in the settlement of the questions at issue between the Peshwa and the Gáikwár. And lastly, their effect was most beneficial to both the chiefs and their subjects in removing the uncertainty that had hitherto pervaded the whole revenue administration of Káthiáváḍa.

Before entering on the details of the settlement itself, some description is necessary of the social and political state of the peninsula at the time the changes were introduced.

State of Káthiáváḍa, 1807.

The greater part of the population of Káthiáváḍa consisted of two classes, chiefs and cultivators, called Bhumiás and ryots. The power of the chief ranged from the headship of a single village up to absolute jurisdiction over several score. The ryots were usually tenants long resident in the province. The chiefs were in almost every case foreigners, invaders from the north and north-east; Muhammadan adventurers from the court of Ahmedábád; Káthis animated by the love of plunder and cattle-lifting; and Miánás and Vághelás who had settled on the coast on account of the facilities it afforded for their favourite pursuits of wrecking and piracy. More numerous than any others were the Rajputs, driven south by the disturbed state of their native kingdoms or by the restless spirit of military adventure to be found in a class where one profession alone is honourable. There is a certain uniformity in the building up of all these chieftainships. A powerful leader, with a sufficient band of followers, oppressed his weaker neighbours till they were glad to come to terms and place themselves under his protection, so as both to escape themselves and to take their chance of sharing in the plunder of others. It frequently happened in the growth of one of these states that the *bháyád* or relations of the chief (who are sure to be numerous in a polygamous society) were influential enough to assume, in their turn, a partial independence and to claim recogni-

State of Káthiáváda, 1807.

tion as a separate state. As a rule, however, they continued to unite with the head of the family against external foes, and only disagreed as to domestic administration. It is also noticeable that though so addicted to the profession of arms, the Rajputs cannot be called a military race; they possess few of the true military virtues; hence the slowness of their advance, and their failure in competition with perhaps less courageous though more compact and pliable races. In Káthiáváda fortified strongholds, formidable enough to an army moving rapidly without siege trains, arose in all directions, and even villages were surrounded by a high mud wall as a protection against cattle-lifters.

The groundwork of these states being itself so unstable, their relations with each other were conducted on no principle but the law of the stronger. General distrust reigned throughout. Each chief well knew that his neighbours had won their position as he had won his own by the gradual absorption of the weaker, and that they were ready enough whenever opportunity offered to subject his dominions to the same process. The administration of his territory consisted merely in levying, within certain limits sanctioned by long usage, as much revenue as would suffice to maintain himself and his forces in their position with regard to the surrounding states. When a foreign enemy appeared there was no co-operation amongst the local chiefs in resistance. It was a point of honour not to yield except to a superior force. Each chief, therefore, resisted the demands made upon him until he considered that he had done enough to satisfy the family conscience and then, agreeing to the terms proposed, he allowed the wave of extortion to pass on and deluge the domains of his neighbour. It should be remembered that the peninsula had never been subjugated, though overrun times innumerable. The evil of invasion was thus transitory. To a chief the mere payment of tribute tended in no wise to derogate from his independence. In his capacity of military freebooter he acknowledged the principle as just. His country had been won by the sword and was retained by the sword and not by acquiescence in the payment of tribute, so that if he could avoid this extortion he was justified in doing so. If he weakened his state in resisting foreigners, he knew that his neighbours would certainly take advantage of the favourable juncture and annex his territory. It was his policy therefore, after resistance up to a certain point, to succumb.

The Revenue Raid System.

Owing to this local peculiarity and to the general want of union in the province, both the Mughals and Maráthás found it advantageous to follow a system of successive expeditions rather than to incur the expense of permanently occupying the peninsula with an army which would necessarily have to be a large one. There is every reason to believe that in adopting the raid system the Musalmáns were only pursuing the practice of their predecessors, who used to take tribute from Jodhpur to Dwárka.

Some of the subhedárs of Ahmedábád divided their tributary district into three circuits of collection and personally undertook the

THE MARÁTHÁS, A.D. 1760-1819.

The Revenue Raid System.

charge of one each year. This was the *mulakgiri* Land-raiding system. Besides this chief expedition, there was the smaller one of the Bábi of Junágadh and the still more minute operations of the Rával of Bhávnagar against some of his weaker neighbours. The great Ahmedábád expedition had long been an annual grievance and was conducted with some show of system and under special rules called the *Raj-ul-Mulak*. Three of these rules are of importance, and seem to have been generally acquiesced in before the great incursions of Bábáji and Vithalráv at the beginning of the nineteenth century. The first was that the paramount power (by which was meant the foreign government which was strong enough to enforce tribute from all the chiefs) had authority to interfere in cases of dismemberment, or in proceedings tending to the depreciation of the revenue or to the dismemberment of any tributary state. It was again an acknowledged rule that whilst the mulakgiri expedition of the paramount power was in motion no other army should be in the field throughout the whole province. The third provision was not so well established, but it appears to have been understood that the tribute from each state should be regulated by some standard of former date. In practice, however, the measure of the Marátha demand was simply the power to enforce payment.

It is worthy of remark that about the beginning of this century the resistance to the collection of tribute was stronger towards the west than in the east and south of the province. In the Mahi Kántha the lawlessness of the Koli chiefs, who had established themselves in the ravines and on the hills, necessitated the employment of a military force for collections. In the neighbourhood of Bijápur and Kadi, the chiefs would not pay tribute except under the compulsion of a siege or raid, but the mulakgiri system only reached its full development west of Dholka.

From these explanatory remarks the system and practice of the Maráthás can be clearly understood.

The Maráthás in Sorath.

The Maráthás found their way to Sorath very early in their Gujarát career. The first raid probably took place about 1711, when the Muhammadans were occupied near Ahmedábád. After this incursions were frequent, and under Dámáji Gáikwár became, as has been seen above, annual. This leader did more. He took to wife a daughter of the Gohil chief of the small state of Láthi in east central Káthiáváda, whose dowry in land gave him the standpoint he sought in the heart of the peninsula. He managed also to secure his position in what are known as the Amreli Mahâls, probably under the force of circumstances similar to those which caused the weaker Rajputs to gravitate towards the stronger of their own tribe. His expedition through the peninsula, generally as near the time of harvest as possible, was made regularly every year as soon as he had amassed a sufficient number of troops on the mainland to admit of a force being detached for mulakgiri. The object of these inroads was plunder, not conquest; the leaders would readily have entered into negotiations for the payment of the tribute had the chieftains been disposed to treat otherwise than after defeat. The expenses

THE MARÁTHÁS, A.D. 1760-1819.

The Maráthás in Sorath.

of such an army were heavy, and the more so as the time during which it would be in the field was quite indefinite, and dependent entirely upon the amount of resistance offered. In more than one instance the Marátha leaders, who usually had no artillery for a siege, were obliged to regularly beleaguer a town. Early in this century the town of Mália successfully defended itself against a remarkably well equipped force under Bábáji, and the Junágadh state was usually avoided by the Maráthás as much as possible on account of the time it would take to reduce its army to terms.

It is not on record that the mulakgiri force habitually devastated the country over which it passed, or caused much greater hardships to the ryots than are inseparable from the passage of an army in the field. There are, however, well authenticated stories of the depredations and damage committed during these expeditions. A village is said to have been deserted by order of the *bhumia* in order that the timber of its houses might furnish fuel for the Marátha army on its march. Tortures were doubtless inflicted on men supposed to be well off, who were suspected to have hidden their property. A Marátha army was usually, if not always, ill disciplined, as is proved by the testimony of Mr. Forbes, an eye witness of the campaigns of 1775.[1] From the same writer it is learned what an immense proportion the camp followers bore to the actual combatants. If this were the case in a real campaign against a formidable and active enemy, it is likely that the irresponsible element was still larger in an expedition like this of mulakgiri, where the enemy was insignificant and the country at the mercy of the invaders. It is probable therefore that the troops have been credited with misconduct that should in point of fact be attributed to these Pindháris. In after years, when the expeditions were conducted systematically, villages on the line of march were always allowed the alternative of entertaining a pioneer or two as a sort of guarantee. If no *bandhári* of this sort were accepted, the army occupied the place. In many cases the demands for supplies made by these pioneers were so exorbitant that the villagers preferred to compound in turn with them also for their absence. Another method by which a chieftain might avoid the necessity of the army's passing through his territories was by sending to the commander of the expedition an envoy empowered to treat for the amount of tribute and to execute a provisional guarantee for its future liquidation. This deed was destroyed on the subsequent confirmation by the chief himself of the agreement for the sum fixed.

Securities.

This habit of taking securities in all engagements was so prevalent in all parts of the province, and played so prominent a part in the financial administration of the Gáikwár's home and tributary domains, that its main features are worth describing.

It is a well known characteristic of Hindu dealings that no transaction is carried on by two parties alone if a third can possibly be dragged in. This practice no doubt originated in the former insecure

[1] Oriental Memoirs.

THE MARATHÁS, A.D. 1760-1819.

Securities.

state of society when no man considered himself safe in person or property from government on the one hand and his neighbour on the other. With classes like Kolis and predatory Rajputs, the feeling is intelligible enough, and from these it spread into other branches of the society. To such a pitch was distrust carried in the early part of the nineteenth century, that the Gáikwár himself could find no one to enter into a contract with him without the guarantee of one of his own subjects. The consequences of this practice and the power it threw into the hands of the Arab mercenaries, who were the principal securities for the public debts, are matters that touch the history of the Baroda State rather than that of the province. The chiefs in their dealings employed a special sort of security which owed its validity not to political consideration like that of the Arab Jamádárs but entirely to its religious and traditional character.

Bháts and Chárans, 1807.

A society of the military type like the Rajput has a tendency towards caste and privilege. Without a leader the warlike instincts of the tribe would not carry them beyond petty robberies; whilst with a leader they can achieve greater exploits of valour and destruction. The successful chief then is idolized, and after a certain stage the privileges of the chieftainship become hereditary. Once this system is established, the celebration of ancestors follows, and when circumstances are favourable to the perpetuation of the hereditary position, the genealogy of the chief is a matter of the highest importance, and the person entrusted with the record of this is vested with peculiar sanctity. It is the genealogist's duty to enter in the record, not only the direct line but the names of the more distant relations of the chief by whom he is retained, and also to be the continual chanter of the glorious deeds of their common ancestors. He is therefore a referee of the highest authority in questions of pedigree or of the partition of inheritance. An injury to his person might entail the loss of the pedigree of the ruling family (especially as many of the bards kept no written record) and thus produce a misfortune which would be felt by the whole tribe. The chief, being a warrior, must take his chance in the field with the rest, but the person of the genealogist was sacred and inviolable. Amongst the Rajputs the greatest reverence was paid to purity of pedigree, and each principal family had its Bhát to record births and deaths amongst its members and to stimulate pride in their lineage by the recital of the wars and exploits of their ancestors.

These Bháts necessarily multiplied beyond the number of the families that could entertain them, so that many took to banking and some to cultivation. Surrounded as they were by the social system of the Hindus, it was not long before they became differentiated into a distinct caste, and the inviolability of their persons, formerly due only to respect for the pedigree, was now extended to the whole tribe, even though a large proportion of it performed none of the duties of genealogists. Similar to the Bháts in many respects, notably in that of sacredness of person, were the Chárans, numerous in Káthiáváḍa, where they had founded villages and lived as ordinary

The Maráthás, A.D. 1760-1819.

Bháts and Cháraus, 1807.

cultivators. This tribe also claimed divine origin like the race whose annals they had the privilege of recording. It is said that Rája Todar Mal, the celebrated minister of the Dehli empire, was the first to introduce the practice of taking these Bháts as securities for the Rajputs. The assertion is possibly true, but rests merely on tradition, and after ages usually find some great man as a sponsor for all such innovations. It is clear however that for many years before 1807 no dealings of Kolis or Rajputs with the state or with each other took place without the security of a Bhát being taken. This practice seems to have been as prevalent on the mainland as in the peninsula, the Kolis having doubtless borrowed it from their Rajput neighbours after the Bháts had become a separate caste.

Under this system the Bháts acquired considerable wealth, as they usually demanded a percentage on the amount for which they became security. There are instances in which they presumed upon the strength of their engagements and sacred character to bully or dictate to their employer. Such was the case of the Rával of Bhávnagar in 1808, which is also interesting in another way, as showing how the spirit of industry and commerce tends to sap the old observances which have their roots in superstition. This chief engaged in trade, fostered merchants, and increased his revenue. When his security, a Bhát, got troublesome and interfering, he applied to the power to whom he paid tribute to have the old security bond cancelled and a fresh one taken on his own personal responsibility. In doing this he seems to have been prompted by nothing but his appreciation of the modern code of commercial honour.

To return to the *mulakgiri*. The tribute for which preliminary security had been taken seems to have fluctuated from year to year, but always with reference to a fixed standard. It was one of the Marátha rules never to recede from a former demand lest they should be thereby setting up a precedent for future years. They preferred to secure a year or two's arrears at the full rate to the payment of all the arrears due at a reduced rate.

British Intervention.

In spite of this fiction of a settled *jama* or tribute, the Maráthás, when they had a sufficient force at their back, invariably demanded a larger sum, the excess being called *khará-ját* or extra distinct from the actual tribute. This ingenious plan of increasing the collections originated, it is said, with Shivrám Gárdi, and was carried out scrupulously by both Bábáji and Vithalráv in their tours. In fact during the last few years of the old system Vithalráv had so good a force with him that the extra demand formed a large proportion of the whole tribute collected and had been paid only under strong protest. The British had not long been established in Ránpur, Gogha, and Dhandhuka before a few petty chiefs of Gohilvád and Sorath applied to the Resident at Baroda for protection against the mulakgiri of the Nawáb of Júnágadh and the Rával of Bhávnagar, offering to cede the sovereignty of their states to the British on condition that certain rights and privileges were preserved to the chiefs and their families. The conditions they named were not such as were likely to meet with the approval of the British Government, and do

THE MARÁTHÁS, A.D. 1760-1819.

British Intervention.

not seem to have received much consideration. The proposals had, however, the effect of drawing the attention of the Bombay Government towards the state of Káthiáváḍa, and permission to aid the mulakgiri of the Gáikwár by detaching a few companies of British troops was accorded by the Supreme Government. The outbreak of hostilities with Sindia led to the whole question as to the best means of collecting the tribute being for a time deferred. The internal disputes of some of the more turbulent states, a few years afterwards, gave the Resident an opportunity of sending an envoy to one or two courts to see how matters stood, and to open a way for a settlement in conjunction with the Gáikwár. Affairs at Baroda, as mentioned above (page 416), detained the Resident there till 1807, in which year he joined Vithalráv's army with a British contingent, at a place in the Morvi state.

Settlement of 1807.

Before treating directly with the chiefs a circular was sent round to all of them both by the Gáikwár's agent and by Colonel Walker the Resident, containing the basis of the proposals with regard to the tribute about to be submitted to them. The position of the British Government throughout this negotiation is not clearly defined. Vithalráv in his circular mentions indeed that a British force was with his own, but urges the chiefs to come to a settlement entirely with the government he represented. Colonel Walker's note was longer, more explicit, and conciliatory, but at the same time assumes a tone of protection and superiority. The replies of the chiefs were various, and, as a rule, seem to show that they regarded the British Government as the chief mover in these negotiations. They were probably aware of the position in which the engagements of the Gáikwár had placed him with reference to the British, and for some years had had the latter as their neighbours in the east of the peninsula. They were therefore not able at once to take in the whole scope of the action of the British Government in the tribute question.

Many seemed to take the note as a preliminary to a mulakgiri on the part of the East India Company. The Rája of Mália, who had just been causing disturbances in the dominions of all his neighbours, had repulsed Bábáji and permitted the self-immolation of a Bhát rather than fulfil an engagement, openly proposed a joint expedition across the Ran to plunder Kachh and Sindh. From the inquiries made by the Resident and from information gathered from the Gáikwár's accounts, it was anticipated that separate engagements need only be entered into with the twenty-nine chiefs to whom the circular invitation had been issued, provided that the rights and interests of subordinate members of the Bháyád were clearly defined in the agreement. When, however, these rights came to be investigated in the light of the peculiar rules of Rajput inheritance, it was found that no less than one hundred and fifty-three persons had a claim to settle independently of each other for their tribute. This greatly prolonged the settlement, but at last the agreements were all framed on one principle. The amount settled was determined by a close scrutiny of the collections of past years, and Colonel Walker found it advisable to make great

THE MARÁTHÁS, A.D. 1760-1819.

reductions in the item of extras or *kharáját*, for which the later Gáekwár collectors had such predilection. The engagements were of the following nature.

Settlement of 1807. *Financial.*

First, the chief bound himself his heirs and successors to pay at Baroda each year the tribute fixed in perpetuity in 1807. He also procured a counter security for this payment who engaged himself in this capacity for ten years. The Honourable Company's government had then to become security on the part of the Gáikwár for the fixity of the tribute demanded. This participation of the British in the engagement was insisted upon by the chiefs, and in all probability Colonel Walker was not averse from admitting it. Having thus arranged for the payment of the tribute and guaranteed the amount to be demanded, it was proposed to take measures to prevent internal quarrels between the chiefs themselves. The object of a fixed settlement was simply to remove the necessity for overrunning the country from time to time with an irregular army and to protect the chiefs against extortion. It was found that if the army of the paramount power were removed, all means of keeping order in the province would be lost, and the internecine feuds of the chiefs would soon destroy the good effects of the permanent settlement by materially altering the then existing position of the weaker feudatories and rendering them unable to pay the tribute. It was also the wish of the British Government to bring about such a state of things in Káthiáváda that the presence of an army to control the chiefs would be wholly uncalled-for and that the chiefs themselves would co-operate to keep order and maintain the permanent settlement.

Political.

A second agreement therefore was called for from each signatory state of the nature of a security for good and peaceful conduct. The counter security to this was usually that of another chief. This bond was perpetual. On the execution of both these engagements the chief received a *parvána* or guarantee that the Gáikwár government would not take from him more than the tribute agreed upon, and to this deed the countersignature of the Resident on behalf of the British Government was affixed. This guarantee, like the promise of the chief himself, was apparently given in perpetuity. It will be noted that the amount of tribute was fixed permanently, but that it was considered advisable to renew the security every ten years. It is also remarkable that, except in the *failzámin* or bond for good behaviour, the name of the Peshwa's government, the rights of which over the tribute had only been temporarily alienated, does not appear. The total amount of the tribute thus settled was Rs. 9,79,882.

By means of these engagements the relations of the tributaries to their paramount power were made a matter of contract, instead of as heretofore a series of uncertain and arbitrary exactions dependent upon the respective means of coercion and resistance.

Peshwa's Share in Káthiáváḍa.

Seven years of the lease granted to the Gáikwár in 1804 by the Peshwa still remained unexpired and during at least six of these

THE MARÁTHÁS, A.D. 1760 - 1819.

Peshwa's Share in Káthiávád̤a.

the arrangements that had been made about the Káthiávád̤a tribute do not seem to have been officially communicated to the Peshwa's government. It was not until 1815, when the Resident at Poona was trying to procure the renewal of the lease for the Gáikwár, that an account of the settlement was drawn up in a draft agreement which the Resident submitted to Bájiráv. In this draft the curious mistake was made of mentioning the settlement instead of only the security bond as decennial. The Peshwa, whose policy was to protract negotiations, submitted in his turn a second draft which he said he was willing to sign. In this he seized at once on the supposition that the tribute was fixed only for ten years and stipulated for an increase at the expiration of that period. He also demanded that certain extra collections should be refunded by the Gáikwár, and assumed the British Government to have become security for the tribute owed by the chiefs to his own government.

It was evident that no accord would be reached on the lines of either of these draft agreements as they stood. Before others were prepared, Gangádhar Shástri had been murdered and the treaty of June 1817 was a completed act, leaving further negotiations unnecessary.

Later Arrangements.

Meanwhile the tribute since the expiry of the farm of 1804 had been collected by a joint British and Gáikwár expedition, for it was found that partly from their own disputes and partly owing to the instigation of the agents of Bájiráv, the chiefs were little disposed to act up to the engagements of 1807, either with respect to tribute or good conduct. The Peshwa, whose interference in the affairs of the peninsula had been constantly discouraged, declined to trouble himself to collect the tribute, the responsibility of which he asserted rested entirely upon the British and Gáikwár governments. He subsequently ceded the tribute to the British Government on account of military expenses. After his fall in 1819 his territories, including the rights in Gujarát, fell to the British Government, and in 1820 the Gáikwár arranged that the whole of the Káthiávád̤a tribute, except that due from the districts directly subordinate to Baroda, should be collected by the agency of the British.

The Mahi Kántha.

Turning to the events on the mainland, we find that soon after Colonel Walker's return from the Káthiávád̤a expedition, he introduced the Káthiávád̤a tribute system into the Mahi Kántha, in spite of the opposition of Sitárám Rávji and the anti-English party in the Darbár.

Supplementary Treaty, 1808.

The territory ceded for the payment of the British contingent in 1805 was found to yield less revenue than had been anticipated, so in 1808 a treaty supplementary to the consolidating one of 1805 was drawn up, allotting additional assignments amounting to about 1,76,168 rupees to the British. This revenue was derived partly from alienated villages in Nadiád, Mahudha, Dholka, Mátar, and near the Ranjar Ghát. The *ghásdána* or tribute of Bhávnagar was also made over by this agreement. With regard to this latter

THE MARATHAS, A.D. 1760-1819.

acquisition, it is to be noticed that the agreement is drawn up in the name of the Honourable Company alone, and not in that of the British Government on account of A'nandráv Gáikwár. It also differs from other engagements of a similar nature in containing a provision against the contingency of future irregular demands being made by the Peshwa's army. The reason for this distinction is evidently that the Bhávnagar contribution was not part of the Káthiáváḍa revenue farmed to the Gáikwár by Bájiráv, and was thus not divisible on the expiration of the lease. The right to this tribute rested with the British by virtue of the previous cession of Gogha, of which sub-division the fifty nine villages of the Bhávnagar Bháyád formed part.

Okhámandal, 1809.

Next year the Okhámandal chiefs, who had not come under the settlement of 1807, were driven to engage not to continue their piratical depredations along the coast, and to admit one Sundarji Shivji as Resident on behalf of the British Government. The Gáikwár government then, too, seems to have become their counter security, an arrangement which led to misunderstandings a short while afterwards.

Disturbances in Káthiáváḍa, 1811.

In 1811, some disturbances in Navánagar and Junágaḍh and symptoms of discontent in Okhámandal took the Resident from Baroda into the peninsula with part of the British contingent.

The Jám of Navánagar had got involved in pecuniary transactions with the Ráv of Kachh, and the British Government had mediated with a view of arranging for the repayment by gradual instalments. The Jám, however, repudiated all the engagements of 1807 both as regards the debt and the tribute, ejected the Gáikwár's agent from his dominions, and prepared for war. He also began to incite the neighbouring chiefs to join in sweeping out the paramount power from the whole of Káthiáváḍa. It was not till after a considerable show of force that he laid down his arms and came to terms. Captain Carnac, the Resident, got him to submit the Kachh claims to the arbitration of the English Government, and after fixing them at Rs. 4,33,830, Captain Carnac made an arrangement similar to that originally intended.

There remained the question of a disputed succession in Junágaḍh. Bahádur Khán, son of a slave girl, was put forward in opposition to a younger aspirant, Salábat Khán, reputed to be the son of a lady of the Rádhanpur house. The Baroda government with the concurrence of the Resident had admitted the claims of the latter. On a report, however, by the Assistant Resident in Káthiáváḍa. Captain Carnac was induced to alter his opinion and to support Bahádur Khán, on the grounds that Salábat Khán was a spurious child, and that Bahádur was ready to make concessions of value to the Gáikwár government. The Bombay Council, however, disavowed all countenance of the claims of Bahádur Khán, and the matter was let drop.

1812.

In the year 1812 the Gáikwár had paid off the pecuniary loan borrowed in 1803 from the British Government, but there still

The Maráthás, A.D. 1760-1819.

remained the debts for which that government had become *bhandári* or security in place of the ejected *jamádárs* of the Arab force. These claims could not be paid off for at least two years longer, so that for that period the Resident was ordered to maintain the same close supervision of Baroda affairs as heretofore.

1813-14.

The next two years were spent chiefly in discussions with the Poona government about the old claims by the Peshwa on the Gáikwár's estate. There is no doubt that at the time of his death, Dámáji had not paid up nearly all that he had bound himself in 1753 to pay. On the other hand there had been at least six intermediate compacts between the Peshwa and various members of the Gáikwár family. Amongst others was that of 1768 fixing the arrears of the previous three years, that of 1778 and of 1781, by the tenth clause of which Fatehsingh was excused payment of arrears for the time during which he was engaged in hostilities against Rághobá. Then came the agreement with Govindráv in 1797, to which a sort of debit and credit account is appended.

Peshwa Intrigue in Baroda, 1814.

The Peshwa had been content, for reasons that have been shown above, to let these claims lie dormant during the currency of the ten years' farm. But, as the question of the renewal of this agreement became imminent, he gradually opened more frequent communications with the Baroda council, using these claims as a pretext for sounding the disposition of the chief officials and ascertaining their feelings especially towards the British Government. When the negotiations for the settlement of these claims were fairly set on foot, he used every possible means to protract them till he had finally decided what he should do in 1814, when the Ahmedábád farm expired.

It was easy for Bájiráv to discover who were the malcontents at the Baroda Court. Sitárám, the adopted son of Rávji Áppáji, having been found both incompetent and untrustworthy in the management of affairs, had been practically removed from any post of influence in the council, and was moreover chafing at the refusal of the British Government to recognize him in the same way as they had done his father. He had also been superseded as Suba of Káthiáváda by Vithalráv Deváji. Under these circumstances, and finding that he had the support of a large number of the older court party against the authority of the Resident and of his native agent, he either himself opened communications with Bájiráv or readily listened to the counsels sent to him direct from Poona. Before long, agents were sent to the Peshwa's Court by Takhtbái, wife of Ánandráv, with instructions, it is supposed, to thwart all the proposals and designs of Gangádhar Shástri, who had been recently sent as envoy by the Gáikwár council of administration. The chief obstacle to the settlement of the Peshwa's claims was the counter-demand made by the Baroda government on account of Broach, which had been disposed of without the Gáikwár's consent, and also on account of the damage caused by the inroads of Ába Shelukar, when accredited agent of Bájiráv in Gujarát.

There is no need to detail here the events that took place in Poona during these negotiations. On the expiration of the farm in 1814,

Peshwa Intrigue in Baroda, 1814.

Bájiráv appointed Trimbakji Dengle Sarsuba of Ahmedábád. The latter, however, did not leave Poona, where his presence was indispensable to his master, but sent agents with instructions rather of a political than of a fiscal nature. He himself undertook the task of disposing of Gangádhar Shástri, whom he caused to be assassinated at Pandharpur in July 1815.

Meanwhile the Jám of Navánagar had died leaving a disputed succession. The chief's Khavás or family slaves, instigated probably by agents from Ahmedábád, began to usurp the government, and the whole question was submitted by the Darbár to the Peshwa as being lord paramount. The Ahmedábád commander sent a body of two hundred cavalry to Navánagar, but before they could arrive, the Khavás' revolt had been quelled by a British force detached from the contingent. They therefore dispersed through the province inciting discontent and revolt amongst the Játs and Káthis. In Kaira they instigated a tribe of Kolis to attack the British lines by night. Sitárám Rávji's adherents also collected a force at Dhár, a state well-known for lending itself for such purposes, and kept the frontier in confusion. Severe measures at Poona and Baroda soon put an end to this state of things, and at last Trimbakji Dengle was surrendered to the British Government to answer for his share in the murder of Gangádhar Shástri. The discussion of the Gáikwár's debts, however, was carried on all through the year at Poona, whilst Bájiráv was maturing his then vacillating plans for extirpating the British from the west of India.

Okhámandal ceded to the Gáikwár.

In 1816 the chiefs of Okhámandal again betook themselves to piracy. Their territory was occupied by a British force. It will be remembered that in 1809 the Gáikwár's government had become counter security for these chiefs, but owing to the distance of the district from a military post, the Baroda authorities found themselves unable to spare troops enough to put a check on the misconduct of their tributaries. In A.D. 1816, at the time of occupation, the Bombay Government informed the Baroda administration that they had no wish to permanently establish themselves at so distant a spot, which contained, moreover, a much frequented shrine of Hindu worship, and that they were willing to put the Gáikwár in possession if he would engage to keep up a sufficient force in the district to protect the neighbouring ports and shores from the pirates and wreckers that infested the island of Dwárká and the adjoining mainland. The Bombay Government made a point of asserting on this occasion, in opposition apparently to some proposal by the Baroda Darbár, that they could not admit that the mere fact of having become security or counter-security gave any preferential right to the possession of the country. Finally, the Gáikwár government agreed to the condition proposed, and the district was made over to them.

British Aid at Junágadh.

In the same year (A.D. 1816) British aid was invoked by the Nawáb of Junágadh who was oppressed by a too powerful minister, backed by the Arab mercenaries. After a settlement of this dispute had been satisfactorily brought about, the Nawáb, in gratitude, waived his rights to tribute over the territories recently ceded to

The Maráthás, A.D. 1760-1819.

the British in the peninsula, where his family had formerly great influence and considerable property. The escape of Trimbakji Dengle from Thána, and the subsequent attempts of the Peshwa to prevent the re-capture of his favourite and to re-unite the Marátha confederacy, led to the execution of a fresh treaty on June 13th, 1817, in accordance with the orders of the Supreme Government.

Treaty of Poona, 1817.

It was intended to bind the Peshwa in such a way that he could never again enjoy the ascendancy amongst the Marátha chiefs to which he aspired. The Resident at Poona took this opportunity of also putting an end to the discussions about the mutual claims on each other by the Poona and Baroda governments. The Peshwa agreed to abandon all claims on any territory in possession of the Gáikwár and to accept an annual payment of four lákhs of rupees in satisfaction of all previous debts. The farm of Gujarát was made perpetual to the Gáikwár on the payment of four and a half lákhs annually, but the Káthiáváda tribute was made over to the British Government in liquidation of military expenses. The latter Government, by this treaty, also entered into possession of the Peshwa's revenue in Gujarát, except that of Ulpád, which had been assigned to a favourite officer. All the Peshwa's rights north of the Narbada were also ceded.

Treaty with the Gáikwár, 1817-18.

These conditions necessitated a readjustment of the agreements with the Gáikwár. On November 1817, a definitive treaty, afterwards supplemented by one of November 1818, was executed between the Baroda and British Governments. The force furnished by the former state was found inefficient and the employment of a larger body of British troops was therefore necessary. To pay for these the Gáikwár ceded his share in the fort of Ahmedábád and the districts immediately surrounding that city.[1] He also made over some districts near Surat, and the town of Umreth in Kaira with the whole of the rights acquired by the perpetual farm of Ahmedábád. The British remitted the *mughlái* or dues taken by the Nawábs of Surat on the Gáikwár's possessions near that city. Okhámandal having now been pacified, was also given up to the Gáikwár, but revolted four months afterwards and was not again subdued for a considerable time.

1819.

At the final settlement of the dominions of the late Peshwa in 1819, the whole of his rights in Gujarát passed in sovereignty to the British, who remitted the four lákhs due from the Gáikwár in composition of arrears claimed by Bájiráv. The next year a special inquiry was made into the respective shares of the Peshwa and Baroda governments in the Káthiáváda tribute and in the extra allowance levied by the Gáikwár called *ghás-dána* allowance. In the course of this inquiry so many abuses of power and instances of extortion on the part of the Gáikwár's officers were brought to light, that the Bombay Government on these grounds, and on account also of the general deterioration in the province since the

1820.

---

[1] Known as Daskroi.

THE MARÁTHÁS, A.D. 1760-1819.

Close of Marátha Supremacy, 1819.

Gáikwár's troops were stationed there, prevailed upon Sayájiráv, who had now succeeded to the throne, to let the duty of collection be undertaken and superintended by a British officer stationed in Káthiáváda, who should, however, employ the Gáikwár's troops on occasions of necessity. A similar arrangement was made with regard to the Mahi Kántha, where the effects of the settlement of 1811 had been much weakened by the disorderly conduct of the Gáikwár's troops stationed there. The administration of nearly the whole of the province passed into the hands of the British and the period of Marátha ascendancy came to an end.

General Review.

It remains to review generally the nature and characteristics of the Marátha connection with Gujarát, the chief events in which have been chronicled above. The most prominent feature has already been indicated at the beginning of this section and is apparent throughout the whole narrative. It is, in fact, the small space in history occupied during this period by the people, compared with the share appropriated to the actions of the government and its delegates. The reasons for this are as easily seen as the fact itself. From first to last the Marátha interests in Gujarát were, except at one or two special junctures, simply pecuniary ones. In comparison with other countries within reach of Marátha arms, Gujarát has always had a very large proportion of inhabitants engaged in commerce and manufacturing industries. It was the object of Śiváji to get as much booty as he could and carry it away then and there; hence the commercial classes and manufacturers presented the most favourable opportunities for pillage, and the agriculturists were at first only mulcted in forage and provisions. Rapidity of action was another of Śiváji's aims, so not only were his visits short and their effects transitory, but all his booty consisted of property that could be carried away by his horsemen. No women or followers accompanied his expeditions, no prisoners were made excepting the few who could afford to pay a heavy ransom. Torture was resorted to only when the captive was suspected of having concealed his treasure. Cows women and cultivators were, according to Śiváji's system, exempted from capture. Assignments on revenue were seldom made by him for fear of weakening his own authority. Subsequently the Marátha demands became more regular and assumed the form of a certain proportion of the revenue. The *sar-deshmukhi* and *chauth* were supposed to be calculated on the standard assessment so as to avoid subsequent claims as tribute or over-collection. In reality, however, they consisted of a fixed share in actual collections together with whatever extras the officer in charge could manage to extort, and which were, of course, kept undefined in any agreement. The expeditions, too, moved more leisurely and in greater force. The passes and roads in their rear were protected by their own comrades, so that the booty could be brought to the Dakhan in carts, and more bulky property therefore was removed than in former times. The times, too, when the demands were likely to be made were known to the headmen of the district and village, so that the cultivators could be pressed beforehand to furnish their share of the contributions. The extortion by this means passed from the commercial classes down to the agriculturists, the latter having also the burden of supporting a larger and more cumbrous army for a longer period.

When the power of the Dábháde and his deputy the Gáikwár was fairly established, a regular system of administration was introduced. It will be remembered that by the treaty of 1729 as few Marátha officers were to be employed as possible beyond those necessary to collect the Dábháde's share of the revenue. In consequence, however, of the internal struggles of the Muhammadan chiefs, this minimum quota grew to be a large establishment, with the usual accompaniment of alienations and assignments for the support of the officers and their religious institutions which the weakness of the central power had allowed to become customary. The Dábháde himself was non-resident and his deputy usually being too valuable an assistant to be spared from the arena of Dakhan politics, the collection was left to subdeputies and their subordinates, who in turn delegated a great part of their duties to village officers and even to strangers. The Dábhádes, who were throughout more interested in the Dakhan than in Gujarát, had, no doubt, an idea of raising up a power in the latter province in opposition to the administration of the Peshwa, which was conducted purely by Bráhman agency. It was soon evident, however, that all that could be done politically with Gujarát was to make it a treasury for the support of schemes that had to be carried out in the Dakhan.

The fertility of the soil and the facilities the country afforded for commerce and manufactures both tended to make it unlikely to become a field for recruiting. The inhabitants of the towns had fixed and lucrative occupations; the cultivators were mostly of a class which on account of the fertility of their land neither Muhammadan nor Marátha had been able to impoverish. The Maráthás had still to seek for soldiers in the rugged and barren country on the Gháts and in the Konkan, where the people could only look for a hand-to-mouth existence if they remained at home. The warlike tribes of Gujarát were, as has been already seen, too proud by birth and position to engage themselves to fight for any but their own race and interest. The aboriginal races were not likely to prove effective allies even if they had been willing to move from their own woods and fortresses. None of the Marátha governors of Gujárat seem to have consistently attempted to weld the various interests subordinate to them into a cohesion and unity that they might have made politically useful against the Poona influence. All that they endeavoured to do was to draw from their charge as much revenue as possible and to keep out interlopers. To the taxpayer the result was the same, whether his district was invaded by Kantáji or Piláji. If one anticipated the other in carrying off the harvest, the ryot still had to pay the latter for ejecting the intruder. The only resistance to be feared by the Maráthás was that, not of the cultivators, but of their own race or of the Rajput Girásiás. These latter were treated in all districts as mere robbers, probably because the class which bears that name near Rájpipla where the Maráthás first came in contact with it subsists usually on blackmail. In the north, however, the Girásiás were land-owners of great influence and fixed residence, not likely to be conciliated by the knowledge that the invaders of their country classed them along with Bhils and Kolis as *mehvásis* or outlaws.

In order to relieve the chief officials of direct responsibility for the revenue, the Gáikwár towards the last quarter of the eighteenth century if not before, introduced the system of letting out each revenue sub-division in farm for from one to five years at a fixed annual rate. The farmer was as often as not an absentee, but the supervision and administration were never entrusted to any one but a Marátha Bráhman. The revenue for the year was settled by an inspection of the accounts of previous years and the crops of each village. The amount was taken in kind, but the actual distribution of the whole on individual cultivators was left to the headman, who was in most cases made responsible for the assessment imposed on his village.

The frequent passages of hostile armies and other causes had left much culturable land a desert. In order to restore the population and induce colonists to settle and cultivate in such spots, leases on favourable terms were granted to desáis, who administered the land as they pleased, and were directly responsible to the head revenue authority of the sub-division for the annual rent. The patels and other village officials also made use of their position with reference to the foreign supervisors in appropriating large tracts of waste land to their own uses. The *kamávísdár* or farmer for the time being, was interested only in recouping himself for the amout he had agreed to pay the Marátha government, together with a margin for bribes paid to underlings at head-quarters for good offices with regard to the farm. He was ready, therefore, to make use of any agency in collecting his revenue that he found effective, and which saved the cost of a personal establishment. In many parts of the country there were hereditary village headmen accustomed to the duty of extorting money from unwilling ryots. In other places, such for instance as Dholka, it had been customary for certain Muhammadans called Kasbátis, to become responsible for the revenue of certain villages in return for a discount on the *jama* or amount collected (*manoti*). These *manotidárs* were found so useful by the Marátha officials that they gradually acquired an hereditary position and claimed proprietary rights in the villages for which they had been formerly mere agents for collection. They also acted as *desáis* or colonists, and succeeded in getting their leases of certain tracts renewed long after they had ceased to actively improve the land, which had in fact been all brought under regular cultivation.

Such was the agency employed in administering the revenue. The *kamávísdár* was also the dispenser of justice both civil and criminal. As his object was to make money and not to improve the condition of his charge, his punishments consisted chiefly in fines, and most offences could be paid for. No record of trials was

The Maráthás, A.D. 1760-1819.

General Review.

kept except a memorandum of the amount passed at each decision to the credit of the farmer. In civil suits sometimes one-fourth of the amount in dispute was assigned as costs and appropriated by the court. The Girásiás in their own territory exercised somewhat similar jurisdiction, but grave crimes with violence were apparently left to the party injured or his relations to decide after the manner of the offence. Arbitration, too, was a frequent mode of deciding differences of both civil and criminal nature, but the *kamávísdár* or *girásiá* usually managed that the State should not be a loser by such a method of settlement.

The whole system indicates clearly enough the slight hold the Maráthás had on the province and their desire to make the most out of it for the furtherance of court intrigues or political ends above the Ghâts. There is nothing to show that they contemplated a permanent colonization of the country until the British Government undertook the task of dividing the Marátha nation by the establishment of a powerful and independent court at Baroda.

The home of the Maráthás was always the Dakhan, and for many years after they had effected a lodgment in Gujarát, their army regularly returned for the rainy season to the country from whence they originally came. Their leaders were encouraged to be as much as possible near the court by the Dábháde, or the regent on the one side and by the Peshwa on the other: the former on account of their weight with the army and the Marátha chiefs, the latter in order that their influence in a distant dependency might not grow beyond what prudence recommended or might be counteracted if its tendency to increase became manifest. For similar reasons no force was allowed to be maintained in Gujarát sufficient to consolidate the Marátha acquisitions there into a manageable whole. Dámáji Gáikwár, had he lived, would undoubtedly have done much towards this end by means of his personal influence; but, as it happened, the thin crust of Marátha domination rapidly disappeared before it either was assimilated into the system of the province or hardened over it. A military occupation of a large and civilised district at a distance from the mother-country, and prevented by the jealousy of the central authority and the short-sightedness of those in charge of its exploitation, from either conforming itself to the elements it found already established, or absorbing the vital forces of the government it dispossessed, a system without the breath of life, without elasticity, without the capacity of self-direction, imposed bodily upon a foreign people, without even the care of preparing a foundation, such seems to have been the Marátha government, containing within itself all that was necessary to ensure a precarious, but while it lasted, an oppressive existence.

GUJARÁT DISTURBANCES,

1857-1859.

BY

L. R. ASHBURNER Esq., C.S.I.,

LATE OF H. M.'s BOMBAY CIVIL SERVICE.

[CONTRIBUTED MAY 1880.]

GUJARÁT DISTURBANCES,

1857-1859.

Gujarát Disturbances, 1857-1859.

The Red Salt Scare, 1857.

Very soon after the outbreak of the mutinies in the North-West of India in May 1857, an uneasy feeling began to prevail in the Bombay Presidency, especially in Gujarát. The story of the greased cartridges had been industriously repeated and found credulous listeners in every village. A similar incident occurred in Gujarát. A consignment of salt from the Ran of Kachh having been carried in bags which had previously held red ochre (*sindur*) had become discoloured. This was observed at Sádra in the Mahi Kántha as the salt was in transit to Rajputána, and a report was at once spread that the salt had been defiled with cow's blood. It was believed in Ahmedábád and throughout Gujarát that this was a device of the British Government to destroy the caste of the people as a preliminary to their forcible conversion to Christianity.

The Passing of the Pariah Dog.

About the time that the cakes or *chapátis* were being circulated throughout the North-West of India, a common pariah dog was passed from village to village in the Panch Mahals and eastern Gujarát. It was never ascertained who first set the dog in motion, but it came from the Central India frontier with a basket of food which was given to the village dogs, and a similar supply with the dog was forwarded to the next village. When pestilence or other calamity threatens an Indian village, it is the custom to take a goat or a buffalo to the boundary and drive it into the lands of the adjoining village, in the hope that it will avert evil from the community. A similar belief prevailed among the Jews. There is no reason to suppose that this movement of the dog in Gujarát was a signal of revolt or had any deeper political significance than a vague feeling that troublous times were approaching. Still it was by many regarded as an evil omen and created considerable alarm.[1]

---

[1] The rite of passing cakes from village to village or of passing a dog from village to village is in such complete accord with magical and religious rites practised all over India that it seems hardly possible to accept either as meaningless or as accidental the passing of cakes and of a dog from one part of the country to another on the brink of the Mutinies. Knowing how suitable such a rite is to the state of feeling as well as to the phase of belief prevalent among the plotters of rebellion in Northern India it seems difficult to suppose that the passing of the cakes and the passing of the dog were not both sacramental; that is designed to spread over the country a spirit which had by religious or magical rites been housed in the dog and in the cakes. The cake-spirit, like the sugar-spirit of the Thags, was doubtless Káli, the fierce longing for unbridled cruelty, which worked on the partaker of the Thag sugar with such power that he entered with zest and without remorse on any scheme however cowardly and cruel. Like the Thags those who ate the Mutiny cakes would by partaking become of one spirit, the spirit of the indwelling Káli, and, in that spirit would be ready to support and to take part in any scheme of blood which the leaders of Mutiny might devise and start. Similarly by religious rites the Central India dog, possibly the dog of Báiza Bái of Gwalior (See Text page 437), had been made the home of some fierce war-spirit, apparently of the dog-formed Khandoba the Marátha Sword God and Dog of War. The inspired dog and the inspired dogs-meat were passed through the land in the confidence that through them the spirit of unrest would pervade every village of Gujarát. Since the Mutinies, by the

Gujarát Disturbances, 1857-1859.

Gold Hoarding.

Although Gujarát was apparently tranquil in the hot season of 1857, those who were most familiar with native opinion were aware of the existence of very serious discontent, and indications of the storm which lowered on the horizon were not wanting. When disturbances are impending natives invariably convert their savings into gold, because gold is more portable and more easily concealed than silver. A sudden and unusual demand for gold in the markets, especially by the native troops, had been observed. This fall of the political barometer should never be disregarded. It indicates the approach of a storm with great certainty.

Seditious Native Press.

The native press, which had been merely disloyal, now assumed an attitude of decided hostility. Every paper contained the most exaggerated accounts of the massacre of Europeans in the North-West Provinces, and absurd rumours were circulated of the approach of a combined Russian and Persian army, which, it was said, had reached Attok and would shortly invade Hindustán. It is much to be regretted that the measures which were found necessary in 1880 for the suppression of seditious publications were not enforced in 1857. Had this been done much evil would have been averted. The native mind would not have become familiar with the spectacle of the British Government held up to the execration and contempt of its subjects and the vilest motives attributed to every public measure.

Maulvi Saráj-ud-din.

The native press was not the only source of sedition. The fall of the British Government was openly predicted in every masjid, and in Ahmedábád a Maulvi named Saráj-ud-din became especially prominent by preaching a *jehád* in the Jáma Masjid to audiences of native officers and *savárs* of the Gujarát Horse and troops from the

---

magic of letters, Káli has passed from the wafer into the leaflet, and the paid political propagandist has taken the place of Khandoba's pariah dog.

The correctness of the view suggested above is supported if not established by certain passages in Kaye's Sepoy War, I. 632-642. Chuni says; 'The circulating of cakes was supposed to foretell disturbance and to imply an invitation to the people to unite for some secret purpose.' According to the king of Delhi's physician (page 636) some charm attached to the cakes. The people thought they were made by some adept in the secret arts to keep unpolluted the religion of the country. Another authority (page 637) says; 'The first circulation of the cakes was on the authority of a pandit who said the people would rise in rebellion if cakes were sent round and that the person in whose name the cakes were sent would rule India.' The secret comes out in Sitarám Báwá's evidence (pages 646-648); 'The cakes in question were a charm or *jádu* which originated with Dása Báwa the *guru* or teacher of Nána Sáheb. Dása told Nána Sáheb he would make a charm and as far as the magic cakes should be carried so far should the people be on his side. He then took lotusseed-dough called *makána* and made an idol of it. He reduced the idol to very small pills and having made an immense number of cakes he put a pillet in each and said that as far as the cakes were carried so far would the people determine to throw off the Company's yoke.' With this making of a cake as a sacramental home of Durga or Káli compare the Buddhist of Tibet offering in a human skull to the Máhárání or Queen, that is to Durga or Káli, a sacramental cake made of black-goat's fat, wine, dough, and butter. (Waddell's Buddhism in Tibet, 365.). As to the effect of sharing in Durga's mutiny cakes compare the statement of the Thag Faringia (Sleeman's Ramaseeana, page 216); The sugar sacrament, *gur-tapávant*, changes our nature. Let a man once taste the sacramental sugar and he will remain a Thag however skilful a craftsman, however well-to-do. The Urdu proverb says *Tapauni-ki-dhaunika gur jisne kháyá wuh waisá huá* Who eats the sugar of the sacramental Vase as he is so he remains. The Thags are tools in the hand of the god they have eaten. (Compare Ramaseeana, 76.)—J. M. C.

GUJARÁT DISTURBANCES, 1857-1859.

Ahmedábád cantonment. The Maulvi was expelled from Ahmedábád and found his way to Baroda, where he was afterwards arrested; but the impunity he so long enjoyed brought great discredit upon Government, for it was very naturally supposed that a government which tamely submitted to be publicly reviled was too weak to resent the indignity. Oriental races are so accustomed to violent measures that they seldom appreciate moderation or forbearance. The generation that had known and suffered from the anarchy of the Peshwa had passed away. The seditious language of the native press and the masjid was addressed to a population too ignorant to understand the latent power of the British Government.

Apparent Weakness of British Rule.

In 1857 the immense continent of Hindustán was governed by what appeared to the people to be a few Englishmen unsupported by troops, for they knew that the native army was not to be depended on, and the European troops were so few that they were only seen in the larger military cantonments. It must have seemed an easy task to dispose of such a handful of men, and it probably never occurred to those who took part in the insurrection that the overthrow of the British Government would involve more serious operations than the capture or murder of the Europeans who governed the country so easily. They could not perceive that England would never submit to a defeat, and that the handful of men who ruled India were supported by the whole power of the nation. The plotters had no very definite ideas for the future. The Musalmáns regarded the subversion of a government of Káfirs as a triumph of Islám, and both Muslims and Hindus looked forward to a period of anarchy during which they might indulge that appetite for plunder which had been restrained for so many years. The descendants of the feudal aristocracy of the Peshwa are an ignorant and improvident race deeply involved in debt. They could not fail to see that under the operation of our laws their estates were rapidly passing into the possession of the more intelligent mercantile classes, and they hoped to recover their position in the revolution that was about to ensue.

Administrative Defects.

A great change had taken place in the character of the administration. The civilians of the school of Duncan, Malcolm, and Mountstuart Elphinstone, though not deeply learned in the law, were accomplished earnest men, sufficiently acquainted with the unalterable principles of right and wrong to administer substantial justice to a simple people who had not yet learnt the art of lying. The people asked for justice rather than law. They were satisfied with the justice they obtained from the able and upright men who ruled this country during the first half of this century. The writings and official reports of the officers of that period indicate a knowledge of native customs and feelings and a sympathy with the people that is unknown in the present day, for knowledge and sympathy cannot be acquired except by a long and familiar residence amongst the people which is now becoming every year more impossible. When the overland route rendered communication with England more easy and frequent, a reaction set in against patriarchal administration. Concubinage with native women, which had been common, was now declared vulgar, if not immoral; and the

GUJARÁT DISTURBANCES, 1857-1859.

The Courts Disliked.

relations between Europeans and Natives soon became less cordial than they had been during the early period of British rule. About this time a considerable immigration of lawyers appeared in India. These briefless gentlemen, envious of the official monopoly of the Civil Service, raised an outcry that justice was being administered by men who had not acquired that knowledge of law which the formality of eating a certain number of dinners at the Temple was supposed to guarantee. They worked the press so industriously to this cry, that in the course of a few years they had succeeded in impressing their views on the Court of Directors in London and on the less intelligent members of the Civil Service in India.

Unfortunately the Sadar Court was then presided over by a succession of feeble old gentlemen who had not sufficient force of character to resist this selfish agitation, and by way of refuting the charge of ignorance of law devoted themselves to the study of those petty technicalities which have so often brought the administration of justice into contempt, and which the progress of law reform has not even now removed from the law of England. In 1827, Mountstuart Elphinstone had enacted a Civil and Criminal Code which was still the substantive law of the land. It was simple and admirably suited to the people, but justice was administered according to the spirit rather than the letter of the law. A district officer would have incurred severe censure if his decisions were found to be inequitable, however they might have been supported by the letter of the law. The national character for even-handed justice had made the English name respected throughout India and far across the steppes of Central Asia. But the demoralizing example of the Sadar Adálat soon extended to the lower grades of the service. The Civil Service was afflicted with the foolishness which, we are told, precedes ruin. Its members diligently searched their law-books for precedents and cases, and rejoiced exceedingly if they could show their knowledge of law by reversing the decision of a lower Court on some long-forgotten ruling of the Courts of Westminster. The first effect of this evil was to fill the courts with corrupt and unprincipled *vakils* who perverted the course of justice by perjury, forgery, and fraud of every description. Litigation increased enormously, no cause was too rotten, no claim too fraudulent to deprive it of the chance of success. The grossest injustice was committed in the name of the law, and though the Civil Service was above all suspicion of corruption, the evil could hardly have been greater if the Judges had been corrupt. This state of affairs gave rise to great discontent, for the administration of justice fell almost entirely into the hands of the *vakils*. When men quarrelled they no longer said, "I'll beat or I'll kill you," but "I'll pay a *vakil* Rs. 50 to ruin you," and too often this was no mere idle threat.

The Inám Commission.

The operations of the Inám Commission and of the Survey Department were also a fruitful cause of alarm and discontent. Many of the estates of the more influential Jághírdárs had been acquired by fraud or violence during the period of anarchy which preceded the fall of the Peshwa. The Patels and Deshmukhs had also appropriated large areas of lands and had made grants of villages to temples and assignments of revenue to Bráhmans, religious mendicants, and dancing

GUJARÁT DISTURBANCES, 1857-1859.

The Inám Commission.

girls. The Peshwa had never recognized these alienations as any limitation of his rights, for he farmed his revenues, and so long as a large sum was paid into his treasury by the farmers it was immaterial to him how much land was alienated. But when the Survey Department revealed the fact that nearly a fourth part of the fertile province of Gujarát was unauthorizedly enjoyed by these parasites; and that in other districts the proportion of alienations was nearly equally large, a due regard for the public interests demanded that there should be an investigation into the title on which the lands were held rent-free. It became the duty of the Inám Commission to make this inquiry, and though a very small portion of land was resumed or rather assessed to the land revenue and the rules for the continuation of cash allowances were extremely liberal, they could hardly be expected to give satisfaction to those who had so long enjoyed immunity from any share of the public burdens. The Bráhmans and the priesthood of every sect deeply resented the scrutiny of the Inám Commission and excited an intensely fanatical spirit by representing the inquiry as a sacrilegious attack on their religious endowments and a departure from the principle of neutrality and toleration which had been the policy of Government from a very early period.

The Army Disloyal.

Notwithstanding all these elements of danger there would probably have been no revolt if the army had remained loyal. Fortunately the Bombay army was composed of a great variety of races, Musalmáns of the Shia and Sunni sects, Maráthás of the Dakhan and Konkan, Parváris, Pardeshis, and a few Jews and Christians. Little community of sentiment could exist in so heterogeneous a force, and to this circumstance we may trace the failure of each mutinous outbreak in the regiments of the Bombay army. Many of its regiments had, however, recruited extensively in the North-West Provinces which were then the centre of the political cyclone, and it was soon discovered that seditious overtures were being made to them not only by their brethren in the regiments which had already mutinied, but by discontented persons of higher rank. The most important of these was a clever woman known as the Báiza Bái. She was the daughter of a Dakhan Sardár named Sirji Ráo Ghátke, and had been married in early life to His Highness Dowlat Ráo Sindia the Mahárája of Gwálior. On his death she had been allowed to adopt Jankoji Ráo as heir to the *gádi*, and during his minority she had been appointed by the British Government Regent of the Gwalior state. In this position the Bái had accumulated great wealth. She had deposited £370,000 (37 lákhs of rupees) for safe custody in the treasury at Benares, and it was known that she had other resources at Gwalior. Her avarice and ambition were insatiable. She sent emissaries to all the Marátha chiefs and Thákors in Western India calling on them to take up arms and restore the empire of Shiváji. She appealed to the troops, urging them to emulate the deeds of their comrades in the Bengal army who had already nearly exterminated the Europeans in the North-West, and warned them that if they did not now strike in defence of their religion they would shortly be converted to Christianity and made to drink the blood of the sacred cow.

Báiza Bái of Gwálior.

Pársi Riot in Broach, June 1857.

In May and June 1857 our troops were fighting before Delhi, only just holding their own, and making little impression on the walls

GUJARÁT DISTURBANCES, 1857-1859.

Pársi Riot in Broach, June 1857.

of the city which were strongly held by the mutinous regiments. Gujarát was still tranquil. It is true there had been a riot in Broach originating in a long-standing feud between the Pársis and Musalmáns of that town, but it had no political significance and had been promptly suppressed. The ringleaders were arrested, tried, and sentenced to be hanged for the murder of a Pársi, but there is no reason to suppose that this disturbance had any immediate connection with the outbreak in the North-West. It was probably only a coincidence, but the violence of the rioters was no doubt encouraged by the weakness of our position in Gujarát, and the exaggerated rumours which reached them of the massacre of our countrymen.

Mutiny at Mhow, July 1857.

On July 1st, 1857, the 23rd Bengal Native Infantry and the 1st Bengal Cavalry stationed at Mhow mutinied and murdered Colonel Platt, Captain Fagan, Captain Harris, and a number of European subordinates of the Telegraph Department. The troops of His Highness Holkar fraternized with the mutineers, attacked the Residency, and after a desultory fight drove out Colonel Durand the Resident, who took refuge in Bhopál with the surviving Europeans of Indor. Information of the mutiny at Mhow soon reached Ahmedábád, and treasonable negotiations were at once opened for a simultaneous rising of the Gujarát Horse and of the troops in the cantonment; but they could not agree to combined operations. The Maráthás hoped for the restoration of the dynasty of the Peshwa, while the Pardeshis looked towards Dehli where their brethren were already in arms, without any very definite comprehension of what they were fighting for, but with some vague idea that they would establish a Musalmán *Ráj* on the throne of the Great Mughal.

Mutiny at Ahmedábád, July 1857.

On July 9th, 1857, seven *savárs* of the Gujarát Horse raised a green flag in their regimental lines in Ahmedábád and attempted to seize the quarter guard in which the ammunition was stored; but the guard made some slight show of resistance, and finding the regiment did not join them the mutineers left the lines in the direction of Sarkhej. They were followed by the Adjutant, Lieutenant Pym, with twelve *savárs*, and Captain Taylor, the commandant, joined them soon after with three men of the Koli Corps, whom he had met on the Dholka road. The *savárs* were overtaken near the village of Tájpor, and having taken up a strong position between three survey boundary-marks opened fire on their officers and the Kolis, the *savárs* standing aloof. After many shots had been exchanged without result, Captain Taylor advanced to parley, and while endeavouring to reason with his men was shot through the body. The Kolis now re-opened fire and having shot two of the *savárs* the rest laid down their arms. They were tried under Act XIV. of 1857 and hanged. The *savárs* who followed Lieutenant Pym passively declined to act against their comrades, and if the Kolis had not been present the mutineers would have escaped. Captain Taylor's wound was severe; the bullet passed through his body, but he eventually recovered. The execution of the *savárs* had a good effect on the troops, but it became evident that a serious struggle was impending, and Lord Elphinstone, who was then at the head of the Bombay Government, took all the precautions that were possible under the circumstances.

Gujarát Disturbances, 1857-1859.

Mr. Ashburner's Force.

Mr. Ashburner, Assistant Magistrate of Kaira, was ordered to raise a force of 200 Foot and 30 Horse for the protection of his districts, and Husain Khán Battangi, a Musalmán gentleman of Ahmedábád, was authorized to enlist 2000 of the dangerous classes. It was not expected that this Ahmedábád force would add to our fighting strength, but the employment of the rabble of Ahmedábád on good pay kept them out of mischief till the crisis was passed. Mr. Ashburner's small force was composed of Rajputs, Makránis, and Kolis. They were a very useful body of men and were afterwards drafted into the Kaira Police of which they formed the nucleus. It was this force that suppressed the rising of the Thákors on the Mahi, which will be described below.

Genl. Roberts.

General Roberts, a very able soldier, commanded the Northern Division at this time. He fully realized the critical position of affairs in Gujarát. He was aware that the troops were on the verge of mutiny, that the Thákors were sharpening their swords and enlisting men, and that no relief could be expected till after the rains. But he was not the man to despond or to shirk the responsibility now thrown upon him. He proved equal to the occasion and met each emergency as it arose with the calm determination of a brave man.

Rising at Amjera

And in the Panch Mahals, July 1857.

When the troops at Mhow mutinied, the Rája of Amjera took up arms and attacked Captain Hutchinson the Political Agent of Bhopáwar. He fled and was sheltered by the Rája of Jábwa. At the same time (July 1857) the Musalmán Kanungus or accountants and Zamindárs of the Panch Mahals revolted, laid siege to the fort of Dohad, and threatened the Kaira district. Captain Buckle, the Political Agent, Rewa Kántha, marched from Baroda with two guns under Captain Sheppee, R. A., and two companies of the 8th Regiment Native Infantry, to relieve Dohad, while Major Andrews, with a wing of the 7th Regiment, two guns under Captain Saulez, R. A., and 100 Sabres of the Gujarát Horse, marched on Thásra to support Mr. Ashburner and act generally under his orders. On the approach of Captain Buckle's force the insurgents abandoned the siege, and Captain Hutchinson soon after re-established his authority in Bhopáwar by the aid of the Málwa Bhil Corps which remained loyal. He arrested the Rája of Amjera and hanged him.

Mutinies at Abu and Erinpur, 1857.

On the 5th August the Jodhpur Legion stationed at Abu mutinied. They made a feeble attack on the barracks of H. M. 33rd Regiment and Captain Hall's bungalow, into which they fired a volley of musketry, but were repulsed, leaving one of their men on the ground badly wounded. The fog was so dense that it was impossible to use firearms effectively. Mr. Lawrence of the Civil Service was the only person wounded. A party of the 17th Bombay Native Infantry who were on duty at Ábu, were suspected of complicity with the Jodhpur Legion and were disarmed. The head-quarters of the Legion mutinied at Erinpur on the same day as the attack at Ábu; they made the Adjutant, Lieutenant Conolly, prisoner and plundered the treasury.

Gujarát Disturbances, 1857-1859.

Disturbance at Ahmedábád, 14th Sept. 1857.

An incident occurred early in September which had an important influence on events. The two Native regiments quartered at Ahmedábád were the 2nd Regiment of Grenadiers and the 7th Native Infantry. The Grenadiers were chiefly Pardeshis from Oudh, while the majority of the 7th Regiment were Maráthás. As is often the case, an enmity sprang up between the two regiments. One night Captain Muter of the 2nd Grenadiers was visiting the guards as officer of the day. On approaching the quarter guard of the 7th Regiment, the sentry demanded the password which Captain Muter could not give. The sentry very properly refused to let him pass. Captain Muter returned to his lines, called out a party of Grenadiers, and made the sentry a prisoner. Next morning General Roberts put Captain Muter under arrest and released the sentry. This incident intensified the ill-feeling between the two regiments, and prevented their combination when the Grenadiers mutinied a few days later. It had been arranged that the two Native Regiments and the Golandauz artillery should mutiny at the same time, but there was mutual distrust between them, and the Native officers of the artillery had stipulated that they should make a show of resistance in order to let it appear that they had been overpowered by a superior force. About midnight on the 14th September 1857 the Grenadiers turned out and fell in on their parade ground armed and loaded. The guns were also brought out and loaded on their own parade ground. A Native officer of the Grenadiers was sent with a party to take possession of the guns in accordance with the preconcerted agreement, but the Subhedár of the Artillery threatened to fire on them, and the Native officer expecting that the guns would be given up without resistance, thought he had been betrayed, and retreated with his party, who threw away their arms as they ran across the parade ground. The Grenadiers were under arms on the parade waiting for the guns, when seeing the disorder in which the party was retreating from the Artillery lines, they also were seized with a panic and broke up in confusion. Then for the first time the Native officers reported to Colonel Grimes that there had been a slight disturbance in the lines. The mere accident that the Native officer detached to take the guns had not been informed of the show of resistance he was to expect from the Artillery, probably averted the massacre of every European in Gujarát. Twenty-one loaded muskets were found on the parade ground, and though the whole regiment was guilty it was decided to try the owners of those muskets by court martial. They were sentenced to death. As it was doubtful if the Native troops would permit the execution it was considered prudent to await the arrival of the 89th Regiment under Colonel Ferryman and Captain Hatch's battery of Artillery. They had been landed at Gogha during the monsoon with great difficulty, and were compelled to make a wide detour to the north owing to the flooded state of the country. On their arrival the executions were carried out; five of the mutineers were blown from guns, three were shot with musketry, and the rest were hanged in the presence of the whole of the troops. They

GUJARÁT DISTURBANCES, 1857 - 1859.

met their death with a gentlemanly calmness which won the respect of all who were present.

Rádhanpur Disloyal.

The example thus made, together with the presence of the European troops in Gujarát, restored our prestige and gave us time to attend to affairs on our frontier. The whole country was in a very disturbed state. On the fall of Delhi on September 28th, 1857, a treasonable correspondence was found between the Nawáb of Rádhanpur in Gujarát and the Emperor of Delhi, which deeply implicated the Nawáb. He and his ministers had forwarded *nazránás* of gold *mohars* to Delhi and asked for orders from the Emperor, offering to attack the British cantonments at Disa and Ahmedábád. The Nawáb had been on the most friendly terms with Captain Black the Political Agent, and had been considered perfectly loyal. Preparations were made to depose him for this treacherous conduct. We were then so strong in Gujarát that his estate could have been seized without the least difficulty, but he was considered too contemptible an enemy and his treason was pardoned.

Arab Outbreak at Sunth.

Lieutenant Alban, with a party of Gujarát Horse, was now sent to settle affairs in Sunth, a petty state in the Rewa Kántha. Mustapha Khán, at the head of a turbulent body of Arabs, had made the Rája a prisoner in his own palace with a view to extort arrears of pay and other claims. Lieutenant Alban's orders were to disarm the Arabs. After some negotiations Mustapha Khán waited on Lieutenant Alban. He was attended by the whole of his armed followers with the matches of their matchlocks alight, thinking no doubt to intimidate Lieutenant Alban. On entering the tent Lieutenant Alban disarmed him, but imprudently placed his sword on the table. While they were conversing Mustapha Khán seized his sword and Lieutenant Alban immediately shot him with a revolver. The Arabs who crowded round the tent now opened fire on Alban and his men, but they were soon overpowered. Mustapha Khán, four Arabs, and one *savár* of the Gujarát Horse were killed.

Disturbance in Lunáváḍa.

Lieutenant Alban, with a party of the 7th Native Infantry under Lieutenant Cunningham then proceeded to Páli. A few months before one Surajmal, a claimant of the Lúnáváḍa *gádi*, had attacked the Rája of Lúnáváḍa, but was repulsed with severe loss and had since been harboured in the village of Páli. On the approach of Alban's force, it was attacked by Surajmal's Rájputs and the village was accordingly burnt. Order was then restored in the Panch Mahála, and it was not again disturbed till Tátia Topi entered the Mahála.

Conspiracy at Disa.

In October 1857 a conspiracy was discovered between the Thákor of Samda near Disa and some Native officers of the 2nd Cavalry and 12th Regiment Native Infantry to attack and plunder the camp at Disa and to murder the officers; but the evidence was not very clear, and before the trial could take place the amnesty had been published under which the suspected men were released. The peace of Northern Gujarát was much disturbed at this time by the Thákor of Rova, who plundered the Pálanpur and Sirohi

Gujarát Disturbances, 1857-1859.

Conspiracy at Baroda.

villages at the head of 500 men, and the Thákor of Mandeta was also in arms but was held in check by a detachment of the 89th Regiment and a squadron of cavalry at Ahmednagar near Idar.[1] The two Thákors were acting in concert with some influential conspirators at Baroda of whom Malhár Ráo Gáikwár *alias* Dáda Sáheb was the chief. It was this man who afterwards became Gáikwár of Baroda and was deposed for the attempt to murder Colonel Phayre by poison.

Want of Combination.

It is very remarkable that the sepoy war did not produce one man who showed any capacity for command. Every native regiment was in a state of mutiny and a large proportion of the civil population was ripe for revolt. If only one honest man had been found who could have secured the confidence and support of his fellow-countrymen, the fertile province of Gujarát would have been at his mercy; but amongst natives conflicting interests and mutual distrust make combination most difficult. In India a conspirator's first impulse is to betray his associates lest they should anticipate him. The failure of every mutinous outbreak in Gujarát was due to this moral defect. This trait may be traced throughout the history of the war and should be studied by those who advocate the independence of India, and the capacity of the native for self-government. It is an apt illustration of native inability to organize combined operations that the most formidable conspiracy for the subversion of our power should have been delayed till October 1857. By this time the arrival of Her Majesty's 89th Regiment and a battery of European artillery at Ahmedábád had rendered a successful revolt impossible. The mutinies of the Gujarát Horse and Grenadiers had been promptly suppressed and severely punished. The termination of the monsoon had opened the ports and reinforcements were daily expected. Had the outbreak occurred simultaneously with the mutiny of the Gujarát Horse, the Artillery, and the Second Grenadiers, Gujarát must have been lost for a time and every European would have been murdered.

Marátha Conspiracy.

For many years Govindráo *alias* Bápu Gáikwár, a half brother of His Highness the Gáikwár, had resided near the Sháhibág at Ahmedábád. He had been deported from Baroda for intriguing against his brother and had been treated as a political refugee. This man with Malhárráo, another brother of His Highness the Gáikwár, Bháu Sáheb Pawár, and a Sardár who called himself the Bhonsla Rája, also related to His Highness by marriage, conceived the design to murder the Europeans in Baroda Ahmedábád and Kaira and establish a government in the name of the Rája of Sátára. To Bápu Gáikwár was entrusted the task of tampering with the troops in Ahmedábád, and frequent meetings of the Native officers were held at his house every night. The Bhonsla Rája, with a man named Jhaveri Nálchand, was deputed to the Kaira district to secure the aid of the Thákors of Umeta, Bhádarva, Kera, and Dáima, and of the Patels of Ánand and Partábpur.

[1] Rova in the south-east corner of Sirohi: Mandeta in Ídar in the Máhi Kántha. P. FitzGerald Esq. Political Agent Máhi Kántha.

GUJARÁT DISTURBANCES, 1857 - 1859.

Marátha Conspiracy.

These landholders assured Bápu of their support and the Thákor of Umeta mounted some iron guns and put his fort in a state of defence. An agent named Maganlál was sent into the Gáikwár's Kadi Pargana, where he enlisted a body of 2000 foot and 150 horse, which he encamped near the village of Lodra. The followers of the Kaira Thákors assembled in the strong country on the banks of the Mahi near the village of Partábpur with a detachment and advanced to the Chauk Taláv within five miles of Baroda. The massacre at Baroda was fixed for the night of October 16th. The native troops in Baroda had been tampered with and had promised in the event of their being called out that they would fire blank ammunition only.

Gathering at Partábpur,

The Thákors had been encamped at Partábpur for several days, but owing partly to the sympathy of the people and partly to the terror which they inspired, no report was made to any British officers till the 15th October, when Mr. Ashburner, who was encamped at Thásra, marched to attack them with his new levies and a party of the Kaira police. There was, as usual, disunion in the ranks of the insurgents; they had no leaders they could depend upon, and they dispersed on hearing of the approach of Ashburner's force without firing a shot. Ninety-nine men who had taken refuge in the ravines of the Mahi were captured and a commission under Act XIV. of 1857 was issued to Mr. Ashburner and Captain Buckle, the Political Agent in the Rewa Kántha, to try them. Ten of the ringleaders were found guilty of treason and blown from guns at Kanvári, nine were transported for life, and the remainder were pardoned. The turbulent villages of Partábpur and Angar in Kaira were destroyed and the inhabitants removed to more accessible ground in the open country. Their strong position in the ravines of the Mahi river had on several occasions enabled the people of Purtábpur and Angar to set Government at defiance, and this was considered a favourable opportunity of making an example of them and breaking up their stronghold.

And at Lodra.

In the meantime information of the gathering at Lodra had reached Major Agar, the Superintendent of Police, Ahmedábád. He marched to attack them with the Koli Corps and a squadron of the Gujarát Horse. Maganlál fled to the north after a slight skirmish in which two men were killed and four wounded, and was captured a few days afterwards by the *Thándár* of Sammu with eleven followers. They were tried by General Roberts and Mr. Hadow, the Collector of Ahmedábád, under Act XIV. of 1857. Three of them were blown from guns at Waizápur, three were hanged, and the rest were transported for life.

It is much to be regretted that Malhárráo Gáikwár and the Bhonsla Rája were allowed to escape punishment. There was very clear evidence of the guilt of the Bhonsla Rája, but His Highness the Gáikwár interceded for him, and Sir Richmond Shakespeare, the Resident, weakly consented that his life should be spared on condition that he should be imprisoned for life at Baroda, a sentence which, it is hardly necessary to say, was never carried out.

GUJARÁT DISTURBANCES, 1857-1859.

Partial Disarming.

On the suppression of this abortive insurrection it was determined to disarm Gujarát, and in January 1858 strong detachments of the 72nd Highlanders and of Her Majesty's 86th Regiment with the 8th Regiment Native Infantry, two guns under Captain Conybere, and a squadron of Gujarát Horse were placed at the disposal of Mr. Ashburner to carry out this measure. His Highness the Gáikwár had consented to a simultaneous disarmament of his country, but he evaded the performance of his promise. In the Kaira district and in the Jambusar táluka of Broach the disarmament was very strictly enforced; every male adult of the fighting classes was required to produce an arm of some kind. The town of Ahmedábád was relieved of 20,000 arms in the first two days, but the Highlanders and 86th Regiment were required for operations in Rajputána, and after their departure from Gujarát it was deemed prudent to postpone this very unpopular measure.

Náikda Revolt, Oct. 1858.

After these events Gujarát remained tranquil for nearly a year till, in October 1858, the Náikda Bhils of Nárukot revolted under Rupa and Keval Náiks, and a few months later Tátia Topi's scattered force being hard-pressed by Colonel Park's column, plundered several villages of the Panch Mahálṣ during its rapid march through that district.

Tátia Topi, 1858.

In 1858, after his defeat at Gwálior, at the close of the mutinies in Northern India, Tátia Topi moved rapidly towards the Dakhan. The chiefs of Jamkhandi and Nárgund had been in treasonable correspondence with the rebel chiefs in the North-West and had invoked their aid. It is more than probable that if Tátia Topi had entered the Dakhan in force, there would have been a general insurrection of the Marátha population. Tátia's march to the Dakhan soon assumed the character of a flight. He was closely pressed by two columns under Generals Somerset and Mitchell, and a very compact and enterprizing little field force commanded by Colonel Park. Colonel Park's own regiment, the 72nd Highlanders, many of the men mounted on camels, formed the main fighting power of this force. His indefatigable energy in the pursuit of the enemy allowed them no rest, and eventually brought them to bay at Chhota Udepur. Fearing to face the open country of Berár with such an uncompromising enemy in pursuit, Tátia recrossed the Narbada at Chikalda and marched towards Baroda. He had, by means of an agent named Ganpatráo, for some time been in communication with the Bháu Sáheb Pavár, a brother-in-law of His Highness the Gáikwár, and had been led to expect aid from the Baroda Sardárs and the Thákors of the Kaira and Rewa Kántha districts. Immediately it became known that Tátia had crossed the Narbada, troops were put in motion from Kaira, Ahmedábád, and Disa for the protection of the eastern frontier of Gujarát. Captain Thatcher, who had succeeded to the command of the irregular levies raised by Mr. Ashburner in Kaira, was ordered to hold Sankheda with the irregulars and two of the Gáikwár's guns. He was afterwards reinforced by Captain Collier's detachment of the 7th Regiment N. I., which fell back from Chhota Udepur on the approach of the enemy.

GUJARÁT DISTURBANCES, 1857-1859.

Tátia Topi's Defeat at Chhota Udepur, Dec. 1858.

Tátia Topi at this time commanded a formidable force composed of fragments of many mutinous Bengal regiments. He had also been joined by a mixed rabble of Villáyatis, Rohillás, and Rájputs, who followed his fortune in hopes of plunder. Ferozsha Nawáb of Kamona and a Marátha Sardar who was known as the Ráo Sáheb, held subordinate commands. Each fighting man was followed by one or more ponies laden with plunder which greatly impeded their movements. It was chiefly owing to this that Colonel Park was enabled to overtake the rebels and to force them into action. On reaching Chhota Udepur the troops of the Rája fraternised with the enemy, and Captain Collier having evacuated the town, Tátia Topi was allowed to occupy it without opposition. He had intended to halt at Chhota Udepur to recruit his men and to develop his intrigues with the Baroda Sardárs, but Park gave him no respite. On the 1st December 1858, he fell upon Tátia's rebel force and defeated it with great slaughter, his own loss being trifling. After this defeat there was great confusion in the ranks of the insurgents. Tátia Topi abandoned his army and did not rejoin it till it had reached the forest lands of Párona. Discipline which had always been lax, was now entirely thrown aside. The muster roll of one of Tátia's cavalry regiments was picked up and showed that out of a strength of 300 sabres only sixteen were present for duty. The rebel force separated into two bodies, one doubled back and plundered Park's baggage which had fallen far to the rear, the other under Ferozsha entered the Panch Mahals and looted Báriya, Jhálod, Limdi, and other villages; Godhra being covered by Muter's force was not attacked. Park's force was so disabled by the plunder of its baggage and by long continued forced marches, that it was compelled to halt at Chhota Udepur, but General Somerset took up the pursuit and rapidly drove Tátia from the Panch Mahals. He fled in the direction of Salumba. The Thákor of that place was in arms, and Tátia no doubt expected support from him, but the Thákor was too cautious to join what was then evidently a hopeless cause. On reaching Nargad on the 20th February 1859, Ferozsha made overtures of surrender, and a week later 300 cavalry and a mixed force of 1500 men under Zahur Ali and the Maulvi Vazir Khán laid down their arms to General Mitchell. They were admitted to the benefit of the amnesty. The remnant of Tátia's force fled to the north-east.

Náikda Disturbance, 1858.

In October 1858, instigated by the intrigues of the Bháu Sáheb Pavár, the Sankheda Náikdás, a very wild forest tribe, took up arms under Rupa and Keval Náiks, and after having plundered the outpost, *thána*, at Nárukot, attacked a detachment of the 8th Regiment N. I. under Captain Bates at Jámbughoda. They were repulsed with considerable loss after a desultory fight during the greater part of two days. On the arrest of Ganpatráo, the Bháu Sáheb's agent, this troublesome insurrection would probably have collapsed, but the Naikdás were joined by a number of Villayatis, matchlock-men, the fragments of Tátia's broken force, who encouraged them to hold out. They occupied the very strong country between Chámpáner and Nárukot, and kept up a harassing warfare, plundering the villages as far north as Godhra.

GUJARÁT DISTURBANCES, 1857-1859.

Náikda Disturbance, 1858.

A field force commanded by the Political Agent of the Rewa Kántha, Colonel Wallace, was employed against the Náikdás during the cold weather of 1858, and in one of the frequent skirmishes with the insurgents Captain Hayward of the 17th Regiment N. I. was severely wounded by a matchlock bullet on the 28th January 1859. The only success obtained by the Náikdás was the surprise of Hassan Ali's company of Hussein Khán's levy. The Subhedár had been ordered to protect the labourers who were employed in opening the pass near the village of Sivrájpur, but the duty was very distasteful to him, and his son deserted with twenty-four men on the march to Sivrájpur. They were suddenly attacked by a mixed force of Makránis and Náikdás. Seven men including the Subhedár were killed and eleven wounded without any loss to the enemy. The Subhedár neglected to protect his camp by the most ordinary precautions and his men appear to have behaved badly. They fled without firing a shot directly they were attacked. But little progress had been made in pacifying the Náikdás till Captain Richard Bonner was employed to raise and organize a corps composed chiefly of Bhils with their head-quarters at Dohad in the Panch Maháls. Captain Bonner's untiring energy and moral influence soon reduced the Náikdás to submission. Rupa Náik laid down his arms and accepted the amnesty of the 10th March 1859, and Keval Náik followed his example soon after.

Wágher Outbreak, 1859.

In July 1859 the Wághers of Okhámandal, a mahál in Káthiáváḍa belonging to His Highness the Gáikwár, suddenly seized and plundered Dwárka, Barvála, and Bet. They were led by a Wágher chief named Toda Manik, who alleged that he had been compelled to take up arms by the oppression of the Gáikwár's *kámdárs*; but it is probable that he was encouraged to throw off allegiance by the weakness of the Baroda administration and the belief that he would have to deal with the troops of the Darbár only. He soon found he was in error. Major Christie with 200 sabres of the Gujarát Horse and a wing of the 17th Regiment Native Infantry from Rájkot marched to Mandána on the Ran to cut off the communication between Okhámandal and the Káthiáváḍa peninsula. The cantonment of Rájkot was reinforced from Ahmedábád by six guns of Aytoun's battery, a wing of the 33rd Regiment and a detachment of the 14th Regiment Native Infantry under Captain Hall, and a naval and military force was at the same time prepared in Bombay for the recovery of Bet and Dwárka as soon as the close of the monsoon should render naval operations on the western coast possible.

Expedition against Bet, 1859.

On the 29th September 1859, the following force embarked in the transports *South Ramilies* and *Empress of India,* towed by Her Majesty's steam-ships *Zenobia* and *Victoria,* and followed by the frigate *Firoz,* the gunboat *Clyde,* and the schooner *Constance*:

Her Majesty's 28th Regiment	500 Men.
Her Majesty's 6th Regiment Native Infantry ...	600 „
Marine Battalion	200 „
Royal Artillery	60 „
Sappers and Miners	90 „

The expedition was under the command of Colonel Donovan

Gujarát Disturbances, 1857-1859.

Expedition against Bet, 1859.

of Her Majesty's 28th Regiment, but it was intended that on arrival at Bet, Colonel Scobie should command the combined naval and military force. Colonel Scobie marched from Rájkot early in October with the wings of Her Majesty's 33rd Regiment and 17th Native Infantry, the 12th Light Field Battery and detachments of the 14th Native Infantry and Gujarát Horse. Had Colonel Donovan waited for this force he might have effectually invested the fort of Bet, which is situated on an island, and exterminated the rebels; but he was too anxious to distinguish himself before he could be relieved of command. He arrived off Bet on the 4th October 1859, and at sunrise that morning the steam-ships *Firoz*, *Zenobia*, *Clyde*, and *Constance* took up their positions off the fort of Bet and opened fire with shot and shell at 950 yards. The fort replied feebly with a few small guns. Shells effectually scorched the fort and temples occupied by the enemy, but the shot made little impression on the wall which was here thirty feet thick. The bombardment continued throughout the day and at intervals during the night. Next morning Dewa Chabasni, the Wágher chief in command of the fort, opened negotiations for surrender, but he would not consent to the unconditional surrender which was demanded, and after an interval of half an hour the artillery fire was resumed and preparations were made to disembark the troops. They landed under a heavy musketry fire from the fort and adjacent buildings, and an attempt was made to escalade. The ladders were placed against the wall but the storming party of Her Majesty's 28th Regiment and 6th Regiment Native Infantry were repulsed with heavy loss. Captain McCormack of Her Majesty's 28th Regiment, Ensign Willaume of the 6th Regiment, and ten European soldiers were killed; and Captain Glasspoole, Lieutenant Grant of the 6th Native Infantry, and thirty-seven men of the 28th Regiment were wounded, many of them severely. One sepoy of the Marine Battalion was killed and five wounded.

Bet Fort Taken.

During the night which succeeded this disastrous attack the Wághers evacuated the fort. They reached the mainland, taking with them their women the children and the plunder of the temple, but Dewa Chabasni, the Wágher chief, had been killed the previous day. Considering the large and well-equipped force at Colonel Donovan's disposal and the facilities which the insular position of Bet afforded to a blockading force, the escape of the Wághers almost with impunity, encumbered with women and plunder, did not enhance Colonel Donovan's military reputation. Captain D. Nasmyth, R. E., Field Engineer of the Okhámandal Force, was directed to destroy the fort of Bet and carried out his instructions most effectually. Some of the Hindu temples nearest the walls were severely shaken by the explosion of the mines, and a great outcry was raised of the desecration of the temples; but if Hindus will convert their temples into fortified enclosures, they must take the consequence when they are occupied by the enemies of the British Government.

Lieutenant Charles Goodfellow, R. E., greatly distinguished himself on this occasion. He earned the Victoria Cross by carrying

GUJARÁT DISTURBANCES, 1857 - 1859.

off a wounded man of Her Majesty's 28th Regiment under a very heavy fire. Treasure valued at 3½ lákhs of rupees was taken on board the *Firoz* for safe custody. It was eventually restored to the Pujáris of the temples, but most of the temples had been carefully plundered bythe Wághers before the entry of the British force.

Dwarka Fort Taken.

Many of the fugitives from Bet took refuge in Dwárka, and Colonel Donovan's force having re-embarked proceeded to Dwárka to await the arrival of Colonel Scobie's small brigade. Scobie's force did not reach Dwárka till October 20th. The Naval Brigade under Lieutenant Sedley with sixteen officers and 110 men had already landed under very heavy matchlock fire, and thrown up a slight breastwork of loose stone within 150 yards of the walls. A field piece from the *Zenobia* and afterwards a thirty-two pounder were placed in position in this work. The successful result of the siege was mainly due to the determined bravery of this small naval force. They repulsed repeated sorties from the fort and inflicted severe losses on the enemy. As soon as the stores and ammunition could be landed, Colonel Donovan took up a position to the north-east of the fort, Colonel Scobie to the south-east, and Captain Hall occupied an intermediate position with detachments of Her Majesty's 33rd Regiment, the 14th Native Infantry, and Gujarát Horse under Lieutenant Pym. The garrison made several determined attempts to break through Captain Hall's position, but they were on each occasion driven back with loss.

The first battery opened fire on the northern face of the fort on October 28th, while the *Zenobia* and the *Firoz* poured a well-directed fire of shells on the houses and temples which sheltered the enemy towards the sea. The shells did immense execution and relieved the attack on the Naval Brigade which continued to hold its position with the greatest gallantry though several times surrounded by the enemy. On the night of the 31st October the garrison evacuated the fort and cut its way through a picket of Her Majesty's 28th Regiment, wounding Ensign Hunter and four men. A detachment under Colonel Christie followed the fugitives next morning and overtook them near Vasatri. A skirmish ensued, but they escaped without much loss and took refuge in the Barda hill. They continued to disturb the peace of Káthiávada for several years. In one of the desultory skirmishes which followed, Lieutenants LaTouche and Hebbert were killed.

Rising in Nagar Párkar.

While these events were in progress, Karranji Hati the Rána of Nagar Párkar on the Sindh frontier of Gujarát, took up arms at the head of a band of Sodhás, plundered the treasury and telegraph office at Nagar Párkar, and released the prisoners in the jail. Colonel Evans commanded the field force which was employed against him for many months without any very definite results. The country is a desert and the Sodhás avoided a collision with the troops. The Rána eventually submitted and peace was restored.

APPENDIX III.

BHINMÁL.

Appendix III.
BHINMÁL.
Description.

BHINMAL,[1] North Latitude 24° 42′ East Longitude 72° 4′, the historical Shrimál, the capital of the Gurjjaras from about the sixth to the ninth century, lies about fifty miles west of Ábu hill. The site of the city is in a wide plain about fifteen miles west of the last outlier of the Ábu range. To the east, between the hills and Bhinmál, except a few widely-separated village sites, the plain is chiefly a grazing ground with brakes of thorn and cassia bushes overtopped by standards of the camel-loved *pilu* Salvadora persica. To the south, the west, and the north the plain is smooth and bare passing westwards into sand. From the level of the plain stand out a few isolated blocks of hill, 500 to 800 feet high, of which one peak, about a mile west of the city, is crowned by the shrine of Chámunda the Śrí or Luck of Bhinmál. From a distance the present Bhinmál shows few traces of being the site of an ancient capital. Its 1500 houses cover the gentle slope of an artificial mound, the level of their roofs broken by the spires of four Jain temples and by the ruined state office at the south end of the mound. Closer at hand the number and size of the old stone-stripped tank and fortification mounds and the large areas honeycombed by diggers for bricks show that the site of the present Bhinmál was once the centre of a great and widespread city. Of its fortifications, which, as late as A.D. 1611, the English merchant Nicholas Ufflet, in a journey from Jhálor to Ahmedábád, describes as enclosing a circuit of thirty-six miles (24 *kos*) containing many fine tanks going to ruin, almost no trace remains.[2] The names of some of the old gates are remembered, Surya in the north-east, Śrí Lakshmí in the south-east, Sanchor in the west, and Jhálor in the north. Sites are pointed out

---

[1] The translations of the inscriptions and the bulk of the history are the work of Mr. A. M. T. Jackson of the Indian Civil Service.

[2] Finch in Kerr's Voyages, VIII. 301. Thirty years later the traveller Tavernier (Ball's Edition, II. 87) has: Bargant (Wangam in Jodhpur?) to Bimál 15 *kos*: Bimál to Modra 15 *kos*. Of Jhálor Ufflet has left the following description. Jhálor is a castle on the top of a steep mountain three *kos* in ascent by a fair stone causeway broad enough for two men. At the end of the first *kos* is a gate and a place of guard where the causeway is enclosed on both sides with walls. At the end of the second *kos* is a double gate strongly fortified; and at the third *kos* is the castle which is entered by three successive gates. The first is very strongly plated with iron, the second not so strong with places above for throwing down melted lead or boiling oil, and the third is thickly beset with iron spikes. Between each of these gates are spacious places of arms and at the inner gate is a strong portcullis. A bowshot within the castle is a splendid pagoda, built by the founders of the castle and ancestors of Ghazni (Gidney) Khán who were Gentiles. He turned Muhammadan and deprived his elder brother of this castle by the following stratagem. Having invited him and his women to a banquet which his brother requited by a similar entertainment he substituted chosen soldiers well armed instead of women, sending them two and two in a *dhuli* or litter who getting in by this device gained possession of the gates and held the place for the Great Mughal to whom it now (A.D. 1611) appertains being one of the strongest situated forts in the world. About half a *kos* within the gate is a goodly square tank cut out of the solid rock said to be fifty fathoms deep and full of excellent water. Quoted by Finch in Kerr's Voyages, VIII. 300-301.

Appendix III.

BHINMÁL.

Description.

as old gateways five to six miles to the east and south-east of the present town, and, though their distance and isolation make it hard to believe that these ruined mounds were more than outworks, Ufflet's testimony seems to establish the correctness of the local memory.[1] Besides these outlying gateways traces remain round the foot of the present Bhinmál mound of a smaller and later wall. To the east and south the line of fortification has been so cleared of masonry and is so confused with the lines of tank banks, which perhaps were worked into the scheme of defence, that all accurate local knowledge of their position has passed. The Gujarát gate in the south of the town though ruined is well marked. From the Gujarát gateway a line of mounds may be traced south and then west to the ruins of Pipalduara perhaps the western gateway. The wall seems then to have turned east crossing the watercourse and passing inside that is along the east bank of the watercourse north to the south-west corner of the Jaikop or Yaksha lake. From this corner it ran east along the south bank of Jaikop to the Jhálor or north gate which still remains in fair preservation its pointed arch showing it to be of Musalmán or late (17th-18th century) Ráhtor construction. From the Jhálor gate the foundations of the wall may be traced east to the Kanaksen or Karáda tank. The area to the east of the town from the Karáda tank to the Gujarát gate has been so quarried for brick to build the present Bhinmál that no sign remains of a line of fortifications running from the Karáda tank in the east to the Gujarát gate in the south.

The site of the present town the probable centre of the old city, is a mound stretching for about three-quarters of a mile north and south and swelling twenty to thirty feet out of the plain. On almost all sides its outskirts are protected by well made thorn fences enclosing either garden land or the pens and folds of Rabáris and Bhíls. The streets are narrow and winding. The dwellings are of three classes, the flat mud-roofed houses of the Mahájans or traders and of the better-to-do Bráhmans and craftsmen with canopied doors and fronts plastered with white clay: Second the tiled sloping-roofed sheds of the bulk of the craftsmen and gardeners and of the better-off Rabáris and Bhíls: and Third the thatched bee-hive huts of the bulk of the Rabáris and Bhíls and of some of the poorer craftsmen and husbandmen. Especially to the north-west and west the houses are skirted by a broad belt of garden land. In other parts patches of watered crops are separated by the bare banks of old tanks or by stretches of plain covered with thorn and cassia bushes or roughened by the heaps of old buildings honey-combed by shafts sunk by searchers for bricks. Besides the four spired temples to Párasnáth the only outstanding building is the old *kacheri* or state office a mass of ruins which tops the steep south end of the city mound.

People.

Of the 1400 inhabited houses of Bhinmál the details are: Mahájans 475, chiefly Oswál Vánis of many subdivisions; Shrimáli Bráhmans, 200; Shevaks 35, Maga Bráhmans worshippers of the sun and priests to Oswáls; Sonárs, 80; Bándháras or Calico-printers, 35; Kásáras or Brass-smiths 4, Ghánchis or Oilpressers, 30; Mális or Gardeners, 25; Káthias or Woodworkers, 12; Bháts 120 including 80 Gunas or Grain-carriers,

[1] The names of these gateways are Surajpul about six miles (4 *kos*) east of Bhinmál near Khánpur at the site of a temple of Mahádev; Sávidár about six miles (4 *kos*) to the south near a temple of Hanumán; Dharanidhar near Vandar about six miles (4 *kos*) west of Bhinmál at the site of a large well; Kishanbivao about six miles (4 *kos*) to the north near Nartan at the site of a large well and stones. Rattan Lal Pandit.

Appendix III.

Bhinmál.

People.

and 40 Rájbhats or Bráhm Bháts, Genealogists[1]; Kumbhárs or Potters, 12; Musalmán Potters, 4; Rebbárisor Herdsmen, 70[2]; Shádhs Beggars, 10; Shámis Aliks Beggars, 10; Kotwál and Panjára Musalmáns, 15; Lohárs or Blacksmiths, 3; Darjis or Tailors, 12; Nais or Barbers, 7; Bhumiás that is Solanki Jágirdárs, 15[3]; Kavás Bhumiás servants, 12; Játs Cultivators, 2; Deshantris or Saturday Oilbeggars, 1; Achárayas or Funeral Bráhmans, 1; Dholis Drumbeaters, 12; Pátrias or Professionals that is Dancing Girls, 80[4]; Turki Vohorás that is Memons, 2; Vishayati Musalmán Padlock-makers, 1; Rangrez or Dyers, 2; Mochis or Shoemakers, 30; Karias or Salávats that is Masons, 6; Churigars Musalmán Ivory bangle-makers, 2; Jatiyas[5] or Tanners, 17; Khátiks or Butchers working as tanners, 1; Sargaras, Bhil messengers, 1; Bhils, 120; Tirgars or Arrow-makers, 5; Gorádas priests to Bombias leather-workers, 2; Bombias literally Weavers now Leather-workers, 40; Wághria Castrator, 1; Mirásis Musalmán Drummers, 8; Mehtars or Sweepers, 1.

Objects.

In the Town

Inside of the town the objects of interest are few. The four temples of Párasnáth are either modern or altered by modern repairs. A rest-house to the south of a temple of Barági or Varáha the Boar in the east of the town has white marble pillars with inscriptions of the eleventh and thirteenth centuries which show that the pillars have been brought from the ruined temple of the sun or Jag Svámi Lord of the World on the mound about eighty yards east of the south or modern Gujarát gate. In the west of the town, close to the wall of the enclosure of the old Mahálakshmi temple, is a portion of a white marble pillar with an

---

[1] The Shrimáli Bráhm-Bháts are of the following subdivisions: Dhondaleshvar, Hár, Hera, Loh, Poeshsha, Pitalia, and Varing. They say Shrimál is their original home.

[2] The local explanation of Reh-bári is liver out of the way. Their subdivisions are; Ál, Barod, Bougaro, Dagalla, Gansor, Gengala, Kalotra, Karamtha, Nangu, Panna, Pramára, Roj. All are strong dark full-bearded men.

[3] The importance of Bhinmál as a centre of population is shown not only by the Shrimáli Bráhmans and Vánis who are spread all over Gujarát, but by the Porwárs a class of Vánis now unrepresented in their native town who are said to take their name from a suburb of Bhinmál. Oswáls, almost all of whom are Shrávaks or followers of the Jain religion, have practically spread from Bhinmál. The origin of the name Osvál is (Trans. Roy. As. Soc. III. 337) from Osi the Mother or Luck of Osianagar an ancient town and still a place of pilgrimage about eighteen miles north of Jodhpur. The Oswáls were originally Rajputs of several classes including Pawárs but mainly Solaṅkis and so apparently (Tod's Western India, 209) of Gurjjara origin. Equally of Gurjjara origin are the Shrimáli Vánis who hold a specially high place among Western Indian Jains. The care taken by the Jains to secure foreign conquerors within their fold is notable. The Tirthankar is a Rája who by piety and other virtues attained *moksha* or absorption. The fifty-four worshipfuls *uttama-purushas*, the twenty-four *tirthankars*, the twelve *chakravartis*, the nine *báladevas*, and the nine *vásudevas* are Rájás, most of them great conquerors (Trans. Royal Asiatic Society, III. 338-341). The local story is that the Solaṅkis were called to help the people of Shrimál to resist the Songara Rajputs of Jhálor who took Bhinmál about A.D. 1290. Before that the Shrimális and Solaṅkis were enemies. This tradition of hostility is interesting as it may go back to A.D. 740 when Múlarája Solaṅki transferred the seat of power from Bhinmál to Anahilaváda Pátan. (See Below page 469.) A class who trace to Bhinmál are the Pitals or Kálbis of Márwár (Márwár Castes, 41). They claim descent from Rajput men and Bráhman women. In support of the tradition the women still keep separate neither eating with nor using the same vessels as their husbands.

[4] These dancing girls hold land. They are said to have been brought by the Songara Rajputs, who according to the local account retreating from Ala-ud-din Khilji (A.D. 1290) took Bhinmál from the Shrimáli Bráhmans.

[5] The Jatiyas all Hindus of the three subdivisions Baletta, Sunkaria, and Talvaria came from Mándu near Dhár in Central India. The name is locally derived from *jatukarta* a skin.

Appendix III.
BHINMÁL.
Objects.

inscription dated S. 1342 (A.D. 1286) which apparently has been brought from the same ruined sun temple. In the *kacheri* ruins at the south end of the mound the only object of interest is a small shrine to Máta with two snakes supporting her seat and above in modern characters the words Nágáne the *kuldevi* or tribe guardian of the Ráhtors.

Surroundings.

The chief object of interest at Bhinmál is the ruined temple of the Sun on a mound close to the south of the town. Of this temple and its inscriptions details are given below. About fifty yards west of the Sun temple are the remains of a gateway known as the Gujarát gateway. This modern name and the presence near it of blocks of the white quartz-marble of the Sun temple make it probable that the gateway is not older than Musalmán or eighteenth century Ráhtor times. Close to the west of the gate is Khári Báva the Salt Well an old step and water-bag well with many old stones mixed with brick work. About a hundred yards south of the Gujarát gate, in a brick-walled enclosure about sixteen yards by eight and nine feet high topped by a shield parapet, is the shrine of Mahádeva Naulákheshwar. An inscription dated S. 1800 (A.D. 1744) states that the enclosure marks the site of an old temple to Naulákheshwar. About fifty yards east of the Naulákheshwar shrine is a large brick enclosure about seventy-five yards square with walls about twelve feet high and a pointed-arched gateway in the Moslim wave-edged style. On entering, to the left, is a plinth with a large Hanumán and further to the left in domed shrines are a Ganpati and a Máta. A few paces south is Brahma's Pool or Brahmakhund with steep steps on the west and north, a rough stone and brick wall to the east, and a circular well to the south. The pool walls and steps have been repaired by stones taken from Hindu temples or from former decorations of the pool on some of which are old figures of Matás in good repair. The story is that Som, according to one account the builder of the Sun temple according to another account a restorer of Shrimál, wandering in search of a cure for leprosy, came to the south gate of Shrimál. Som's dog which was suffering from mange disappeared and soon after appeared sound and clean. The king traced the dog's footmarks to the Brahmakhund, bathed in it, and was cured. As a thank-offering he surrounded the pool with masonry walls. To the south of the pool, to the right, are an underground *ling* sacred to Patáleshwar the lord of the Under World and south of the *ling* a small domed shrine of Chandi Devi. To the left, at the east side of a small brick enclosure, is a snake-canopied *ling* known as Chandeshwar hung about with strings of *rudráksh* Elæocarpus ganitrus beads.[1] In front of Chandeshwar's shrine is a small inscribed stone with at its top a cow and calf recording a land grant to Shrimáli Bráhmans. About forty yards north-east of the Brahmakhund a large straggling heap of brick and earth, now known as Lakshamíthala or Lakshmí's settlement, is said to be the site of a temple to Lakshmí built, according to the local

[1] According to a local story there was a hermitage of Jangams near the temple of Jagamdeva the Sun-God and a hermitage of Bharatis near Chandeshvar's shrine. In a fight between the rival ascetics many were slain and the knowledge where their treasure was stored passed away. When repairs were made in A.D. 1814 (S. 1870) the Bharati hermitage was cleared. Two large earthen pots were found one of which still stands at the door of Chandeshvar's temple. These pots contained the treasure of the Bharatis. In A.D. 1814 nothing but white dust was found. Most of the dust was thrown away till a Jain ascetic came and examined the white dust. The ascetic called for an iron rod, heated the rod, sprinkled it with the white dust, and the iron became gold.

Appendix III.

BHINMÁL.

Objects.

Surroundings.

legend, by a Bráhman to whom in return for his devotedness Lakshmí had given great wealth. The hollow to the south-east is known as the Khandália pool. About fifty yards south-east at the end of a small enclosure is a shrine and cistern of Jageshwar, said to be called after a certain Jag who in return for the gift of a son built the temple. Several old carved and dressed stones are built into the walls of this temple. About seventy-five yards further south-east a large area rough with heaps of brick is said to be the site of an old Vidhya-Sála or Sanskrit College. This college is mentioned in the local Mahátmya as a famous place of learning the resort of scholars from distant lands.[1] The local account states that as the Bhils grew too powerful the Bráhmans were unable to live in the college and retired to Dholka in north Gujarát.

The slope and skirts of the town beyond the thorn-fenced enclosures of Bhils and Rabáris lie in heaps honeycombed with holes hollowed by searchers for bricks. Beyond this fringe of fenced enclosures from a half to a whole mile from the city are the bare white banks of pools and tanks some for size worthy to be called lakes. Of these, working from the south northwards, the three chief are the Nimbáli or Narmukhsarovar, the Goni or Gayakund, and the Talbi or Trambaksarovar. The Nimbáli tank, about 300 yards south-east of the college site, is a large area opening eastwards whence it draws its supply of water and enclosed with high bare banks scattered with bricks along the south-west and north. The lake is said to be named Nimbali after a Váni to whom Mahádeva granted a son and for whom Mahádeva formed the hollow of the lake by ploughing it with his thunderbolt. About half a mile north-east of Nimbáli a horseshoe bank fifteen to thirty feet high, except to the open east, is the remains of the Goni lake. Lines of stone along the foot of the north-west and north-east banks shew that portions at least of these sides were once lined with masonry. A trace of steps remains at a place known as the Gau Ghát or Cowgate. The lake is said to have been named Goni after a Bráhman whose parents being eaten by a Rákshas went to hell. For their benefit Goni devoted his life to the worship of Vishnu and built a temple and lake. In reward Vishnu gave to the water of the lake the merit or cleansing virtue of the water of Gáya. In the foreground a row of small *chatris* or pavilions marks the burying ground of the Mahajan or high Hindu community of Bhinmál. Behind the pavilions are the bare banks of the Talbi lake. At the west end is the Bombáro well and near the south-west is the shrine of Trímbakeshvar Mahádev. This lake is said to have been made in connection with a great sacrifice or *yag*, that is *yajna*, held by Bráhmans to induce or to compel the god Trimbakeshwar to slay the demon Tripurásur. Beginning close to the south of Talbi lake and stretching north-west towards the city is the Karádá Sarovar or Karádá lake said to have been built by Kanaksen or Kanishka the great founder of the Skythian era (A.D. 78). On the western bank of the lake stands an open air *liṅg* of Karaiteshwar.[2] At the south end of the Karádá

---

[1] According to Alberuni (A.D. 1030) the Brahmasiddhánta was composed by Brahmagupta the son of Jishnu from the town of Bhillamála between Multán and Ánhilwára. Sachau's Translation, I. 153. Another light of the college was the Sanskrit poet Magha, the son of Srimáli parents, who is said to have lived in the time of Bhoj Rája of Ujjain (A.D. 1010-1040). Márwár Castes, 68.

[2] The local account explains the origin of the name Kanak which also means gold by the story of a Bhil who was drowned on the waxing fifth of Bhádarwa. The Bhil's wife who was with him failing to drown herself prepared a funeral pyre. Mahádeva pleased with the woman's devotion restored her husband to life and made his body shine like gold. As a thankoffering the Bhil enlarged the tank and built a shrine to Kirait Mahádeva.

Appendix III.
BHINMÁL.
Objects.
Surroundings.

lake, which stretches close to the fenced enclosures round the city, are the remains of a modern bastion and of a wall which runs north-west to the Jhálor gate. Beyond the site of the bastion is an enclosure and shrine of Maheshwar Mahádev. To the north and north-west of the Karait sea lie four large tanks. Of these the most eastern, about 300 yards north-west of Karádá, is Brahmasarovar a large area fed from the north and with high broken banks. Next, about 500 yards north-west, lies the far-stretching Vánkund or Forest Pool open to the north-east. About 800 yards west is Gautam's tank which holds water throughout the year. The banks of brick and *kánkar* form nearly a complete circle except at the feeding channels in the east and south. In the centre of the lake is an islet on which are the white-stone foundations (18' × 12') of Gautam's hermitage. On the bank above the east feeding-channel is an image of Hanumán and on the east side of the southern channel at the foot of the bank is a white inscribed stone with letters so worn that nothing but the date S. 1106 (A.D. 1049) has been made out. Of the balls of *kankar* or nodular limestone which are piled into the bank of the tank those which are pierced with holes are lucky and are kept to guard wooden partitions against the attacks of insects. The last and westmost of the north row of tanks is the Jaikop properly Jakshkop that is the Yaksha's Pool about 600 yards south-west of the Gautam tank and close to the north-west of the town.[1] This tank holds water throughout the year and supplies most of the town's demand. Along the south bank of the Jaikop, where are tombs a shrine to Bhairav and a ruined mosque, the line of the later city walls used to run. At the south-east corner of the tank are three square masonry plinths each with a headstone carved with the figure of a man or woman. One of the plinths which is adorned with a pillared canopy has a stone carved with a man on horseback and a standing woman in memory of a Tehsildar of Bhinmál of recent date (S. 1869; A.D. 1812) whose wife became *Sati*. About 200 yards south-east is a row of white *pália* or memorial slabs of which the third from the south end of the row is dated S. 1245 (A.D. 1186). On the south-east bank is the shrine of Nimghoria Bhairav at which Shrávaks as well as other Hindus worship. In the centre of the shrine is a leaning pillar about five feet high with four fronts, Hanumán on the east, a standing Snake on the south, a Sakti on the west, and Bhairav on the north. To the south of the pillar, about a foot out of the ground rises a five-faced *ling* or pillar-home of the god one facing each quarter of the heaven and one uncarved facing the sky. Close to a well within the circuit of the lake near the south-east corner is a stone inscribed with letters which are too worn to be read. At the east end of the north bank under a *pilu* Salvadora persica tree is a massive seated figure still worshipped and still dignified though the features have been broken off, and the left lower arm and leg and both feet have disappeared. This is believed to be the image of the Yaksha king who made the tank. Details are given Below pages 456-458. To the west of the seated statue are the marks of the foundations of a temple, shrine hall and outer hall, which is believed to have originally been the shrine of Yaksh. About a hundred yards west, under a pillared canopy of white quartz, are two Musalmán

---

1 The local explanation of the name Yaksha's Pool is that Rávana went to Abaka the city of the great Yaksha Kuvera god of wealth and stole Pushpak Kuvera's *vimán* or carrier. Kuvera in sorrow asked his father what he should do to recover his carrier. The father said Worship in Shrimál. Kuvera came to Shrimál and worshipped Brahma who appeared to him and said: When Rámchandra destroys Ravana he will bring back Pushpak.

Appendix III.

BHINMÁL.

Objects.

Surroundings.

graves in honour of Ghazni Khán and Hamál Khán who were killed about 400 years ago at Jhálor fighting for Shrimál. In obedience to their dying request their Bháts brought the champions' bodies to Yaksh's tank. The white quartz, the shape of the pillars, and an inscription on one of them dated S. 1333 (A.D. 1276), go to show that the stones have been brought from the Sun temple to the south of the town. To the north of the canopy is a large step-well the Dadeli Well separated into an outer and an inner section by a row of Hindu pillars supporting flat architraves. Some of the stones have figures of goddesses and in a niche is an old goddess' image. The upper part of the well and the parapet are of recent brick work. On a low mound about 150 yards to the north is the shrine of Nilkanth Máhádev, with, about a hundred paces to the south-east, a fine old step-well. The lake was fed from the south-west corner where is a silt trap built of stones in many cases taken from old temples and carved with the *chaitya* or horse-shoe ornament. Some of the stones have apparently been brought from the great white quartz Sun temple. Several of them have a few letters of the fourteenth century character apparently the names of masons or carvers. Some of the blocks are of a rich red sandstone which is said to be found only in the Rupe quarries eight miles south of Bhinmál.

On the right, about half a mile south of the south-west corner of the Jaikop lake, is a ruined heap hid among trees called the Pipal Duára or Gateway perhaps the remains of the western Gateway which may have formed part of the later line of fortifications which can be traced running south along the inner bank of the Jaikop feeding channel. About a mile south of the Pipal Duára are the bare banks of the large lake Bansarovar the Desert Sea. To the north-west north and north-east its great earthen banks remain stripped of their masonry gradually sloping to the west and south the direction of its supply of water. The island in the centre is Lakhára. This lake was made by Gauri or Párvati when she came from Sunda hill to slay the female demon Uttamiyár. When Párvati killed the demon she piled over her body Shri's hill which she had brought with her to form a burial mound. At the same time Párvati scooped the tank, and crowned Shri's hill with a tower-like temple. This hill, where lives the Śrí or Luck of Shrimál, rises 500 feet out of the plain about a mile west of the town. It is approached from the south by a flight of unhewn stones roughly laid as steps. The hill-top is smoothed into a level pavement of brick and cement. The pavement is supported on the east side by a lofty bastion-like wall. It is surrounded by a parapet about two feet high. On the platform two shrines face eastwards. To the left or south is the main temple of Lakshmí and to the right or north the smaller shrine of Suṇḍa Máta. The main shrine has a porch with pillars and shield frieze of white quartz limestone apparently spoils of the great Sun Temple. Three or four bells hang from the roof of the porch and some loose white stones apparently also from the Sun temple are scattered about. In the west wall of the main shrine facing east is the image of the Guardian of Bhinmál covered with red paint and gold leaf. The only trace of ornament on the outside of Lakshmí's shrine is in the north-face portion of a belt of the horse-shoe or *chaitya* pattern and a disc perhaps the disc of the Sun. The smaller shrine of Suṇḍa Máta to the right or north is square and flat-roofed. The ceiling is partly made of carved stones apparently prepared for, perhaps formerly the centre slabs of domes. The door posts and lintels are of white quartz marble. On the right door post are two short inscriptions of A.D. 1612 and 1664 (S. 1669 and 1691). A second pillar bears the date A.D. 1543

Appendix III.

BHINMÁL.

Objects.

Surroundings.

(S. 1600). The roof is supported by four square central pillars which with eight wall pilasters form four shallow domes with lotus carved roof-stones from some other or some older temple. In a recess in the west wall, surmounted with a stone carved in the *chaitya* or horse-shoe pattern, is the Trident or *Trisula* of Sunḍa Máta the only object of worship.

From the hill-top the mound of Bhinmál hardly seems to stand out of the general level. The mound seems hidden in trees. Only in the south gleam the white pillars of the Sun Temple and to the north rise the high mound of the old offices, and still further north the spires of the four temples of Parasnáth. Beyond the town to the south and west spread green gardens fenced with dry thorn hedges. Outside of the garden enclosures to the south-east south and south-west run the lofty bare banks of dry lakes confused in places with the lines of old fortifications. To the north-west and north shine the waters of the Jaikop and Gautam tanks. Westwards the plain, dark with thorn brake and green with acacias, stretches to the horizon. On other sides the sea-like level of the plain is broken by groups of hills the Borta range along the north and north-east and to the east the handsomer Ratanágar, Thur, and Ram Sen rising southwards to the lofty clear-cut ranges of Doḍala and Sunḍa.

Only two objects of interest in Bhinmál require special description, the massive broken statue of the Jaksha or Yaksha on the north bank of the Jaikop lake, and the temple to Jagsvámi the Sun at the south-east entrance to the city.

Jaikop.

On the north bank of the Jaikop or Yaksha Lake,[1] leaning against the stem of a *pilu* or *júl* Salvidora persica tree, is a massive stone about 4′ high by 2′ 6″ broad and 1′ thick. The block is carved with considerable skill into the seated figure of a king. The figure is greatly damaged by the blows of a mace. The nose and mouth are broken off, half of the right hand and the whole of the left hand and leg are gone and the feet and almost the whole of the seat or throne have disappeared. The figure is seated on a narrow lion-supported throne or *sinhásan* the right hand resting on the right knee and holding a round ball of stone about six inches in diameter. The left foot was drawn back like the right foot and the left hand apparently lay on the left knee, but, as no trace remains except the fracture on the side of the stone the position of the left hand and of the left leg is uncertain. The head is massive. The hair falls about

[1] No local tradition throws light on the reason why this figure is called a Yaksha. The holding a head in his hand suggests that he may have been a guardian Bhairav in some Buddhist temple and so remembered as a guardian or Yaksha. Or he may have been supposed to be a statue of the builder of the temple and so have been called a Yaksha since that word was used for a race of skilful architects and craftsmen. Troyer's Rajataraṅginí, I. 369. In the Vrijji temples in Tirhut which Buddhist accounts make older than Buddhism the objects of worship were ancestral spirits who were called Yakshas. If the Buddhist legends of Śaka settlements in Tirhut during Gautama's lifetime (A.D. 540) have any historical value these Vrijjis were Śakas. As (J. As. Ser. VI. Tom. II. page 310) Yaka is a Mongol form of Śaka the ancestral guardians would be Śakas. Compare in Eastern Siberia the Turki tribe called Yakuts by the Russians and Sokhas by themselves, Ency. Brit. XXIV. 725. This would explain why the mythic Yaksha was a guardian, a builder, and a white horseman. It would explain why the name Yaksha was given to the Baktrian Greeks who built stupas and conquered India for Aśoka (J. As. Ser. VII. Vol. VI. page 170; Heeley in Indian Antiquary, IV. 101). It further explains how the name came to be applied to the Yuechi or Kusháns who like the Yavanas were guardians white horsemen and builders. In Sindh and Kachh the word Yaksha seems to belong to the white Syrian horsemen who formed the strength of Muhammad Kásim's army, A.D. 712. (Tod's Western India, 197; Reinaud's Fragments, 191; Briggs' Farishtah, IV. 404-409).

Appendix III.
BHINMÁL.
Objects.
Jaikop.

two feet from the crown of the head in four long lines of curls on to the shoulders, and, over the curls, or what seems more likely the curled wig, is a diadem or *mukut* with a central spike and two upright side ornaments connected by two round bands. The face is broken flat. It seems to have been clean shaved or at least beardless. A heavy ring hangs from each ear. A stiff collar-like band encircles the neck and strings of beads or plates hang on the chest too worn to be distinguished. On both arms are upper armlets, a centre lion-face still showing clear on the left armlet. On the right hand is a bracelet composed of two outer bands and a central row of beads. A light belt encircles the waist. Lower down are the *kandora* or hip girdle and the *kopul* or *dhotar* knot.[1] In spite of its featureless face and its broken hands and feet the figure has considerable dignity. The head is well set and the curls and diadem are an effective ornament. The chest and the full rounded belly are carved with skill. The main fault in proportion, the overshortened lower arm and leg and the narrowness of the throne, are due to the want of depth in the stone. The chief details of interest are the figure's head-dress and the ball of stone in its right hand. The head-dress seems to be a wig with a row of crisp round curls across the brow and four lines of long curls hanging down to the shoulders and crisp curls on the top of the head. The *mukut* or diadem has three upright faces, a front face over the nose and side faces over the ears joined together by two rounded bands. At first sight the stone ball in the right hand seems a cocoanut which the king might hold in dedicating the lake. Examination shows on the left side of the ball an outstanding semicircle very like a human ear. Also that above the ear are three rolls as if turban folds. And that the right ear may be hid either by the end of the turban drawn under the chin or by the fingers of the half-closed hand. That the front of the ball has been wilfully smashed further supports the view that it was its human features that drew upon it the Muslim mace. The local Bráhmans contend that the ball is either a round sweetmeat or a handful of mud held in the right hand of the king during the dedication service. But Tappa a Bráhm-Bhát, a man of curiously correct information, was urgent that the stone ball is a human head. Tappa gives the following tale to explain why the king should hold a human head in his hand. An evil spirit called Satka had been wasting the Bráhmans by carrying off the head of each bridegroom so soon as a wedding ceremony was completed. The king vowed that by the help of his goddess Chamunda he would put a stop to this evil. The marriage of a hundred Bráhman couples was arranged for one night. The king sat by. So long as the king remained awake the demon dared not appear. When the hundredth marriage was being performed the king gave way to sleep. Satka dashed in and carried off the last bridegroom's head. The girl-bride awoke the king and said I will curse you. You watched for the others, for me you did not watch. The king said to his Luck Chamunda, What shall I do. Chamunda said Ride after Satka. The king rode after Satka. He overtook her fourteen miles out of Shrimál and killed her. But before her

[1] The measurements are: Height 4'; head round the brow to behind the ear the back of the head not being cut free, 2' 6"; height of head-dress, 8"; length of face, 10"; length of ringlets or wig curls from the crown of the head, 2'; breadth of face, 9"; across the shoulders, 2' 3"; throat to waistband, 1'; waistband to loose hip-belt or *kandora*, 1' 3"; right shoulder to elbow, 1'; elbow to wrist, 9"; head in the right hand 5" high 7" across top; hip to broken knee, 1'; knee to ankle, 1' 5"; foot broken off. Left shoulder to broken upper arm, 8"; left leg broken off leaving a fracture which shows it was drawn back like the right leg.

Appendix III. BHINMÁL. Objects. *Jaikop.*

death Satka had eaten the bridegroom's head. What is to be done the king asked Chamunda. Trust me said his guardian. The king rode back to Shrimál. As he was entering the city the goddess pointed out to him a gardener or Máli and said Off with his head. The king obeyed. The goddess caught the falling head, stuck it to the bridegroom's neck, and the bridegroom came to life. Thus, ends the tale, the local Bráhmans are known as Shrimális that is men with gardeners' heads. This meaning-making pun and the likeness of the stone-ball to a human head may be the origin of this story. On the other hand the story may be older than the image and may be the reason why the king is shown holding a human head in his hand. On the whole it seems likely that the story was made to explain the image and that the image is a Bhairav holding the head of a human sacrifice and acting as gatekeeper or guardian of some Buddhist or Sun-worshipping temple.[1] The appearance of the figure, its massive well-proportioned and dignified pose, and the long wiglike curls, like the bag wig on the figure of Chánd on the south-west or marriage compartment of the great Elephanta Cave, make it probable that this statue is the oldest relic of Shrimál, belonging like the Elephanta wigged figures to the sixth or early seventh century the probable date of the founding or refounding of the city by the Gurjjarás.[2] According to the local story the image stands about twenty paces east of the temple where it was originally enshrined and worshipped. The lie of the ground and traces of foundations seem to show about fifty paces west of the present image the sites of an entrance porch, a central hall or *mandap*, and a western shrine. The surface of what seemed the site of the shrine was dug about two feet deep on the chance that the base of the throne might still be in site. Nothing was found but loose brickwork. Mutilated as he is the Yaksha is still worshipped. His high day is the *A'shad* (July-August) fullmoon when as rain-mediator between them and Indra the villagers lay in front of him *gugri* that is wheat boiled in water and milk, butter, flour, molasses, and sugar.

---

[1] The Jains call the guardian figures at Sánchi Bhairavas. Massey's Sánchi, pages 7 and 25. Bhairava is revered as a guardian by the Buddhists of Nipál and Tibet. Compare Burgess' Bauddha Rock Temples, page 96. A connection between Bhairav and the Sun is shown by the practice among Ajmir Gujar women of wearing round the neck a medal of Bhairava before marriage and of the Sun after marriage.

[2] The Egyptians Romans and Parthians are the three chief wig-wearers. Some of the Parthian kings (B.C. 250 - A.D. 240) had elaborate hair like peruques and frizzled beards. In Trajan's time (A.D. 133), fashions changed so quickly that Roman statues were hairless and provided with wigs. Gobineau Histoire Des Perses, II. 530. Compare Wagner's Manners, 69. The number of wigs in the Elephanta sculptures, probably of the sixth or early seventh century, is notable. In the panel of Śiva and Párvati in Kailas are several figures with curly wigs. Burgess' Elephanta, page 33; in the marriage panel one figure has his hair curled like a barrister's wig, Ditto 31; in the Ardhanarishwara compartment Garuda and two other figures have wigs, Ditto 22; the dwarf demon on which one of the guardians of the Trimurti leans has a wig, Ditto 14-15; finally in the west wing wigged figures uphold the throne, Ditto 47. Gandharvas in the Bráhmanic Rávan cave at Elura probably of the seventh century have curly wigs: Fergusson and Burgess, 435. Wigged images also occur in some of the Elura Buddhist caves of the sixth or seventh centuries: Ditto, 370-371. In Ajanta caves I. II. and XXXIV. of the sixth and seventh centuries are cherubs and grotesques with large wigs. Among the Bágh carvings and paintings of the sixth or seventh century are a king with baggy hair if not a wig and small human heads with full wigs: MS. Notes. Finally at the Chandi Sewa temple in Java of about the seventh century the janitor and other figures have large full-bottomed wigs curled all over. Indian Ant. for Aug. 1876, 240-241. On the other hand except the curly haired or Astrakan-capped music boys in Sánchi no trace of wigs seems to occur in the Bhilsa Sánchi or Bhárut sculptures between the third century after and the third century before the Christian era. Compare Cunningham's Bharut and Bhilsa; Massey's Sánchi; Fergusson's Tree and Serpent Worship.

BHINMÁL
(S'RIMÁL)

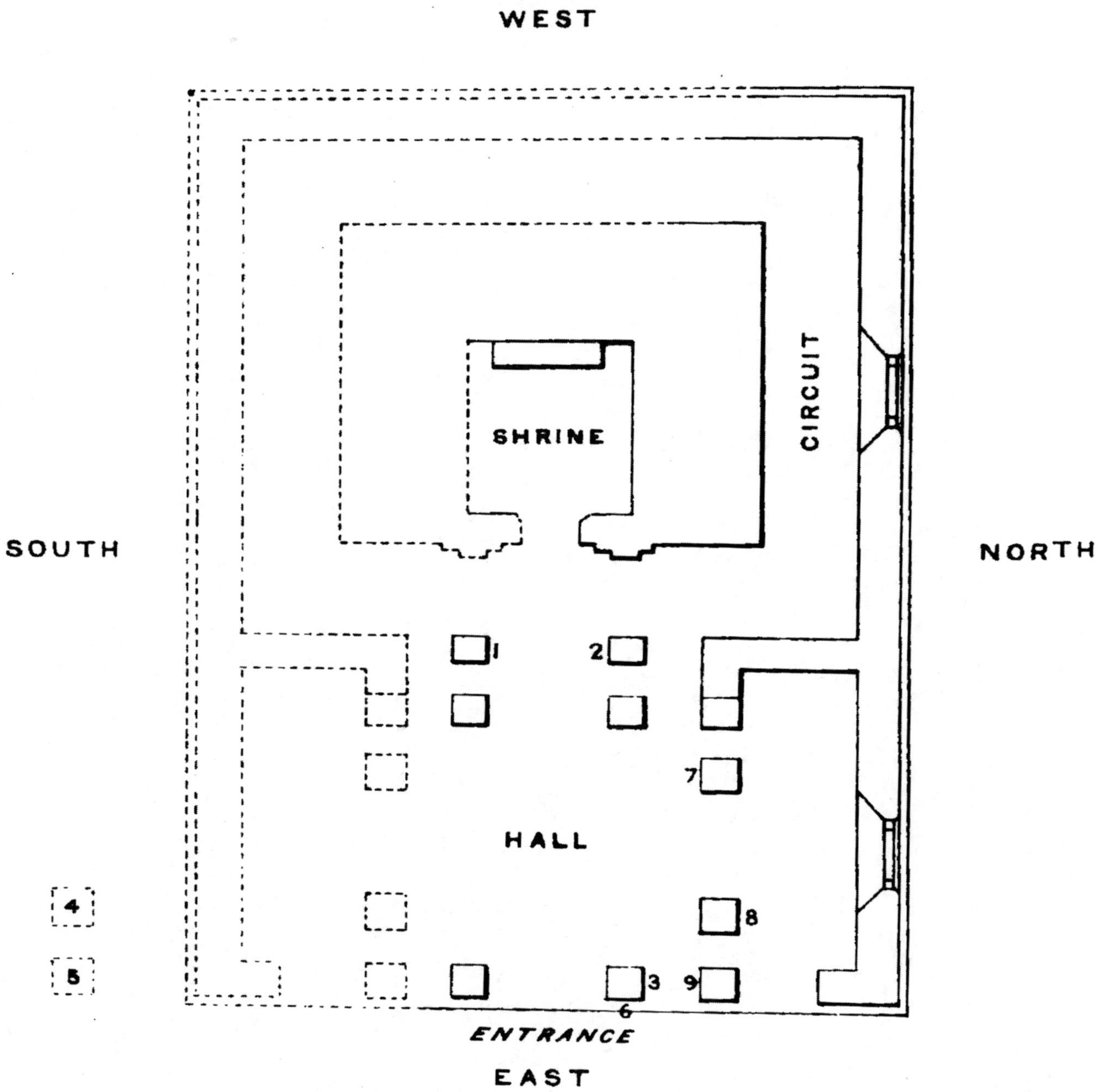

TEMPLE OF JAG SVÁMI
THE SUN
(Ruined)

Scale of Feet

B. 1746

Drawn and Photozincographed
Govt Photozinco: Office, Poona 1896

Appendix III.

BHINMÁL.

Sun Temple.

The second and main object of interest is the ruined Sun temple in the south of the town on a brick mound about eighty yards east of the remains of the Gujarát gateway. The brick mound which is crowned by the white marble pillars and the massive laterite ruins of the temple of Jagsvámi Lord of the World has been so dug into that its true form and size cannot be determined. The size of many of the bricks 1' 16" × 1' × 3" suggests that the mound is older even than the massive laterite masonry of the shrine. And that here as at Multán about the sixth century during the supremacy of the sun-worshipping White Húnas a temple of the Sun was raised on the ruins of a Buddhist temple or relic mound. Still except the doubtful evidence of the size of the bricks nothing has been found to support the theory that the Sun temple stands on an earlier Buddhist ruin. The apparent present dimensions of the mound are 42' broad 60' long and 20' high. Of the temple the north side and north-west corner are fairly complete The east entrance to the hall, the south pillars of the hall, and with them the hall dome and the outer wall of the temple round the south and west of the shrine have disappeared. A confused heap of bricks on the top of the shrine and of the entrance from the hall to the shrine is all that is left of the spire and upper buildings. The materials used are of three kinds. The pillars of the hall are of a white quartzlike marble; the masonry of the shrine walls and of the passage round the north of the shrine is of a reddish yellow laterite, and the interior of the spire and apparently some other roof buildings are of brick. Beginning from the original east entrance the ground has been cut away so close to the temple and so many of the pillars have fallen that almost no trace of the entrance is left. The first masonry, entering from the east, are the two eastern pillars of the hall dome and to the north of this central pair the pillar that supported the north-eastern corner of the dome. Except the lowest rim, on the east side, all trace of the dome and of the roof over the dome are gone. The centre of the hall is open to the sky. The south side is even more ruined than the east side. The whole outer wall has fallen and been removed. The south-east corner the two south pillars of the dome and the south-west corner pillars are gone. The north side is better preserved. The masonry that rounds off the corners from which the dome sprung remains and along the rim of the north face runs a belt of finely carved female figures. The north-east corner pillar, the two north pillars of the dome, and the north-west corner pillar all remain. Outside of the pillars runs a passage about four feet broad and eleven feet high, and, beyond the passage, stands the north wall of the temple with an outstanding deep-eaved window balcony with white marble seats and backs and massive pillars whose six feet shafts are in three sections square eightsided and round and on whose double-disc capitals rest brackets which support a shallow cross-cornered dome. At its west end the north passage is ornamented with a rich *gokla* or recess 3½ broad with side pillars 3¼ feet high. On the west side of the dome the central pair of dome pillars and as has been noticed the north corner pillar remain. About three feet west of the west pair of dome pillars a second pair support the domed entrance to the shrine. The richly carved side pillars, a goddess with fly-flap bearers, and the lintel of the shrine door remain but the bare square chamber of the shrine is open to the sky. To the south of the shrine the entire basis of the south side of the spire, the outer circling or *pradakshana* passage and the outer wall of the temple have disappeared. The north side is much less ruinous. There remain

Appendix III.

BHINMÁL.

Sun Temple.

the massive blocks of yellow and red trap which formed the basis of the spire built in horizontal bands of deep-cut cushions and in the centre of the north wall a niche with outstanding pillared frame, the circling passage with walls of plain trap and roof of single slabs laid across and the outer wall of the temple with bracket capitaled pillars and a central deep-eaved and pillared hanging window of white marble. The circling passage and the outer wall of the temple end at the north-west corner. Of the western outer wall all trace is gone. The pillars of the temple are massive and handsome with pleasantly broken outline, a pedestal, a square, an eightsided band, a sixteensided band, a round belt, a narrow band of horned faces, the capital a pair of discs, and above the discs outstanding brackets each ending in a crouching four-armed male or female human figure upholding the roof. The six central dome pillars resemble the rest except that instead of the sixteensided band the inner face is carved into an urn from whose mouth overhang rich leafy festoons and which stand on a roll of cloth or a ring of cane such as women set between the head and the waterpot.[1] On the roof piles of bricks show that besides the spire some building rose over the central dome and eastern entrance but of its structure nothing can now be traced.

History.

According to a local legend this temple of the Sun was built by Yayati the son of king Nahush[2] of the Chandravansi or Moon stock. Yayati came to Shrimál accompanied by his two queens Sharmistha and Devyani, and began to perform severe austerities at one of the places sacred to Surya the Sun. Surya was so pleased by the fervour of Yayati's devotion that he appeared before him and asked Yayati to name a boon. Yayati said May I with god-like vision see thee in thy true form. The Sun granted this wish and told Yayati to name a second boon. Yayati said I am weary of ruling and of the pleasures of life. My one wish is that for the good of Shrimálpur you may be present here in your true form. The Sun agreed. An image was set up in the Sun's true form (apparently meaning in a human form) and a Hariya Bráhman was set over it.[3] The God said Call me Jagat-Svámi the Lord of the World for I am its only protector. According to a local Bráhman account the original image of the Sun was of wood and is still preserved in Lakshmi's temple at Pátan in North Gujarát.[4] Another account makes the builder of the temple Shripunj or Jagsom. According to one legend Jagsom's true name was Kanak who came from Kashmír. According to the Bráhm Bhát Tappa Jagsom was a king of Kashmír of the Jamáwal tribe who established himself in Bhinmál about 500 years before Kumarápála. As Kumarápála's date is A.D. 1186, Jagsom's date would be A.D. 680.

[1] The ten feet of the pillars are thus divided: pedestal 2′, square block 2′, eight-sided belt 18″, sixteensided belt 18″, round band 2′, horned face belt 6″, double disc capital 6″.

[2] This according to another account is Násik town.

[3] Hariya Bráhman is said to mean a descendant of Hariyaji, a well known Bráhman of Shrimál, so rich that he gave every member of his caste a present of brass vessels.

[4] This tradition seems correct. In the temple of Lakshmi near the Tripolia or Triple gateway in Pátan are two standing images of *chámpa* Michelia champaca wood one a man the other a woman black and dressed. The male image which is about three feet high and thirteen inches across the shoulders is of the Sun Jagat Shám that is Jagat Svámi the World Lord: the female image, about 2′ 6″ high and 9″ across the shoulders is Ranadevi or Randel the Sun's wife. Neither image has any writing. They are believed to be about 1000 years old and to have been secretly brought from Bhinmál by Shrimál Bráhmans about A.D. 1400. Ráo Bahádur Himatlál Dharajlál. Compare (Rajputána Gazetteer, II. 282) in the temple of Bálárikh at Bálmer about a hundred miles south-west of Jodhpur a wooden image of the sun.

Appendix III.

BHINMÁL.

Sun Temple.

According to the common local story Jagsom was tormented by the presence of a live snake in his belly. When Jagsom halted at the south gate of Bhinmál in the course of a pilgrimage from Káshmír to Dwárka, he fell asleep and the snake came out at his mouth. At the same time a snake issued from a hole close to the city gate and said to the king's belly snake 'You should depart and cease to afflict the king.' 'There is a fine treasure in your hole' said the belly snake. 'How would you like to leave it? Why then ask me to leave my home?' The gate snake said 'If any servant of the king is near let him hearken. If some leaves of the *kir* Capparis aphylla tree are plucked and mixed with the flowers of a creeper that grows under it and boiled and given to the king the snake inside him will be killed.' 'If any servant of the king is near' retorted the king's snake 'let him hearken. If boiling oil is poured down the hole of the gate-snake the snake will perish and great treasure will be found.' A clever Kayasth of the king's retinue was near and took notes. He found the *kir* tree and the creeper growing under it: he prepared the medicine and gave it to the king. The writhing of the snake caused the king so much agony that he ordered the Kayasth to be killed. Presently the king became sick and the dead snake was thrown up through the king's mouth. The king mourned for the dead Kayasth. So clever a man, he said, must have made other good notes. They examined the Kayasth's note book, poured the boiling oil down the hole, killed the gate-snake, and found the treasure. To appease the Kayasths and the two snakes lákhs were spent in feeding Bráhmans. With the rest a magnificent temple was built to the Sun and an image duly enshrined. Nine upper stories were afterwards added by Vishvakarma.

Legends.

The legends of Bhinmál are collected in the Shrímál Mahátmya of the Skanda Purána a work supposed to be about 400 years old. According to the Mahátmya the city has been known by a different name in each of the chief cycles or Yugs. In the Satyayug it was Shrimál, in the Tretayug Ratanmál, in the Dwáparyug Pushpamal, and in the Káliyug Bhinmál. In the Satyayug Shrimál or Shrinagar had 84 Chaudis; 336 Kshetrapáls; 27 Varáhas; 101 Suryás; 51 Mátás; 21 Brehispatis; 300 to 11,000 Lingas; 88,000 Rushis; 999 Wells and Tanks; and $3\frac{1}{4}$ krors of *tirthas* or holy places. At first the plain of Bhinmál was sea and Bhraghurishi called on Surya and the sun dried the water and made it land. Then Braghu started a hermitage and the saints Kashyáp, Atri, Baradwaj, Gautam, Jámdagni, Vishvamitra, and Vashista came from Ábu to interview Braghu. Gautam was pleased with the land to the north of Braghu's hermitage and prayed Trimbakeshwar that the place might combine the holiness of all holy places and that he and his wife Ahilya might live there in happiness. The God granted the sage's prayer. A lake was formed and in the centre an island was raised on which Gautam built his hermitage the foundations of which may still be seen. The channel which feeds Gautam's lake from the north-east was cut by an ascetic Bráhman named Yajanasila and in the channel a stone is set with writing none of which but the date S. 1117 (A.D. 1060) is legible. Some years after Gautam had settled at Shrimál a daughter named Lakshmí was born in the house of the sage Braghu. When the girl came of age Braghu consulted Naradji about a husband. When Naradji saw Lakshmí, he said; This girl can be the wife of no one but of Vishnu. Naradji went to Vishnu and said that in consequence of the curse of Durvasarashi Lakshmí could not be born anywhere except in Braghu's house and that Vishnu ought to marry her. Vishnu agreed. After the

Appendix III.

BHINMÁL.

Legends.

marriage the bride and bridegroom bathed together in the holy Trimbak pond about half a mile east of Gautam's island. The holy water cleared the veil of forgetfulness and Lakshmí remembered her former life. The *devtas* or guardians came to worship her. They asked her what she would wish. Lakshmí replied; May the country be decked with the houses of Bráhmans as the sky is decked with their carriers the stars. Bhagwán that is Vishnu, pleased with this wish, sent messengers to fetch Bráhmans and called Vishvakarma the divine architect to build a town. Vishvakarma built the town. He received golden bangles and a garland of gold lotus flowers and the promise that his work would meet with the praise of men and that his descendants would rule the art of building. This town said the Gods has been decked as it were with the garlands or *mála* of Śrí or Lakshmí. So it shall be called Shrimála. When the houses were ready Bráhmans began to gather from all parts.[1] When the Bráhmans were gathered Lakshmí asked Vishnu to which among the Bráhmans worship was first due. The Bráhmans agreed that Gautam's claim was the highest. The Bráhmans from Sindh objected and withdrew in anger. Then Vishnu and Lakshmí made presents of clothes money and jewels to the Bráhmans and they, because they had settled in the town of Shrimál, came to be known as Shrimáli Bráhmans.

The angry Sindh Bráhmans in their own country worshipped the Sea. And at their request Samudra sent the demon Sarika to ruin Shrimál. Sarika carried off the marriageable Bráhman girls. And the Bráhmans finding no one to protect them withdrew to Ábu. Shrimál became waste and the dwellings ruins.[2] When Shrimál had long lain waste a king named Shripunj, according to one account suffering from worms according to another account stricken with leprosy, came to the Brahmakund to the south of the city and was cleansed.[3] Thankful at heart Shripunj collected Bráhmans and restored Shrimála and at the Brahmakund built a temple of Chandish Mahádev. When they heard that the Shrimál Bráhmans had returned to their old city and were prospering the

---

[1] The details are: From Kausika 500, from the Ganges 10,000, from Gaya 500, from Kálinjar 700, from Mahendra 300, from Kundad 1000, from Veni 500, from Surpárak 808, from Gokarn 1000, from Godávari 108, from Prabhás 122, from the hill Ujjayan or Girnár 115, from the Narbada 110, from Gometi 79, and from Nandivardhan 1000.

[2] According to one account (Márwár Castes, 61) these Sindh Bráhmans are represented by the present Pushkar Bráhmans. In proof the Pushkars are said to worship Sarika as Untadevi riding on a camel. This must be a mistake. The Pushkars are almost certainly Gujars.

[3] Details are given above under Objects. The local legends confuse Shripunj and Jagsom. It seems probable that Jagsom was not the name of a king but is a contraction of Jagatsvámi the title of the Sun. This Shripunj, or at least the restorer or founder of Shrimál, is also called Kanak, who according to some accounts came from the east and according to others came from Kashmír. Kanak is said also to have founded a town Kankávati near the site of the present village of Chhakla about eleven miles (7 *kos*) east of Bhinmál. This recollection of Kanak or Kanaksen is perhaps a trace of the possession of Márwár and north Gujarát by the generals or successors of the great Kushán or Śaka emperor Kanak or Kanishka the founder of the Śaka era of A.D. 78. According to the local Bhats this Kanak was of the Janghrabal caste and the Pradiya branch. This caste is said still to hold 300 villages in Kashmír. According to local accounts the Shrimáli Bráhmans, and the Dewala and Devra Rajputs all came from Kashmir with Kanak. Tod (Western India, 213) notices that the Annals of Mewar all trace to Kanaksen of the Sun race whose invasion is put at A.D. 100. As the Shrimalis and most of the present Rajput chiefs are of the Gujar stock which entered India about A.D. 450 this tracing to Kanishka is a case of the Hindu law that the conqueror assimilates the traditions of the conquered that with the tradition he may bind to his own family the Śrí or Luck of his predecessors.

Appendix III.
BHINMÁL.
Legends.

Bráhmans of Sindh once more sent Sarika to carry away their marriageable daughters. One girl as she was being haled away called on her house goddess and Sarika was spell-bound to the spot. King Shripunj came up and was about to slay Sarika with an arrow when Sarika said Do not kill me. Make some provision for my food and I will henceforth guard your Bráhmans. The king asked her what she required. Sarika said Let your Bráhmans at their weddings give a dinner in my honour and let them also marry their daughters in unwashed clothes. If they follow these two rules I will protect them. The king agreed and gave Sarika leave to go. Sárika could not move. While the king wondered the home-goddess of the maiden appeared and told the king she had stopped the fiend. Truly said the king you are the rightful guardian. But Sarika is not ill disposed let her go. On this Sarika fled to Sindh. And in her honour the people both of Shrimál and of Jodhpur still marry their daughters in unwashed clothes.[1] The Bráhman girls whom Sarika had carried off had been placed in charge of the snake Kankal lord of the under world. The Bráhmans found this out and Kankal agreed to restore the girls if the Bráhmans would worship snakes or *nágs* at the beginning of their *shrádh* or after-death ceremonies. Since that time the Shrimális set up the image of a Nág when they perform death rites. Other legends relating to the building of the Jagsvámi or Sun temple, to the temple of Chandish Mahadev near the Brahmakund,[2] and to the making of the Jaikop lake are given above. The dates preserved by local tradition are S. 222 (A.D. 166) the building of the first temple of the Sun; S. 265 (A.D. 209) a destructive attack on the city; S. 494 (A.D. 438) a second sack by a Rákshasa; S. 700 (A.D. 644) a re-building; S. 900 (A.D. 844) a third destruction; S. 955 (A.D. 899) a new restoration followed by a period of prosperity which lasted till the beginning of the fourteenth century.

Caste Legends.

That Shrimál was once the capital of the Gurjjaras seems to explain the local saying that Jagatsen the son of the builder of the Sun temple gave Shrimál to Gujarat Bráhmans where Gujarát is a natural alteration of the forgotten Gurjjaras or Gurjjara Bráhmans. That Shrimál was once a centre of population is shown by the Shrimáli subdivisions of the Bráhman and Váni castes who are widely scattered over north Gujarát and Káthiáváda. Most Shrimáli Vánis are Shrávaks. It seems probable that their history closely resembles the history of the Osvál Shrávaks or Jains who take their name from the ancient city of Osia about fifteen miles south of Jodhpur to which they still go to pay vows. The bulk of these Osvál Vánis, who are Jains by religion, were Solanki Rajputs before their change of faith which according to Jain records took place about A.D. 743 (S. 800).[3] The present Bhinmál

---

[1] According to a local tradition the people in despair at the ravages of Sarika turned for help to Devi. The goddess said: Kill buffaloes, eat their flesh, and wear their hides and Sarika will not touch you. The people obeyed and were saved. Since then a dough buffalo has taken the place of the flesh buffalo and unwashed cloth of the bleeding hide. Another version sounds like a reminiscence of the Tartar origin of Krishna. The goddess Khamangiri persuaded the Lord Krishna to celebrate his marriage clad in the raw hide of a cow. In the present era unwashed cloth has taken the place of leather. MS. Note from Mr. Ratan Lall Pandit.

[2] The tradition recorded by Tod (Western India, 209) that the Gurjjaras are descended from the Solankis of Anahilaváda, taken with the evidence noted in the section on History that the Chávadás or Chápas and the Parihâras are also Gurjjaras makes it probable that the Chohâns are of the same origin and therefore that the whole of the Agnikulas were northern conquerors who adopting Hinduism were given a place among Rajputs or Kshatriyás.

[3] Epigraphia Indica, II. 40-41.

Appendix III.

BHINMÁL.

Caste Legends.

bards claim the Osváls as originally people of Shrimál. Lakshmí they say when she was being married to Vishnu at Shrimál looked into her bosom and the Jariya goldsmiths came forth: she looked north and the Oswáls appeared, east and from her look were born the Porwáls.[1] From her lucky necklace of flowers sprang the Shrimáli Bráhmans. According to other accounts the Shrimáli Bráhmans and Vánis were of Kashmír origin of the Jamawála caste and were brought to south Márwár by Jag Som by which name apparently Kanaksen that is the Kushán or Kshatrapa (A.D. 78-250) dynasty is meant. They say that in S. 759 (A.D. 703) Bugra an Arab laid the country waste and that from fear of him the Shrimáli Bráhmans and Vánis fled south. Another account giving the date A.D. 744 (S. 800) says the assailants were Songara Rajputs. The Shrimális were brought back to Bhinmál by Abhai Singh Ráhtor when viceroy of Gujarát in A.D. 1694 (S. 1750).

The memory of the Gurjjaras, who they say are descended from Garab Rishi, lingers among the Bháts or bards of Shrimál. They say the Gurjjaras moved from Shrimál to Pushkar about ten miles north-west of Ajmír and there dug the great lake. They are aware that Gurjjaras have a very sacred burning ground at Pushkar or Pokarn and also that the Savitri or wife of Brahma at Pokarn was a Gurjjara maiden.

But as the leading Gurjjarás have dropped their tribe name in becoming Kshatriyás or Rajputs the bards naturally do not know of the Gurjjaras as a ruling race. The ordinary Gurjjara they say is the same as the Rehbári; the Bad or High Gujjars to whom Krishna belonged are Rajputs. The bards further say that the Sompuras who live near Poshkar (Pokarn north of Ajmír) and are the best builders who alone know the names of all ornamental patterns are of Gurjjara descent and of Shrimál origin. They do not admit that the Chávadás were Gurjjarás. In their opinion Chávadás are the same as Bhárods and came north into Márwár from Dánta in Jhálávada in north-east Káthiávada. The Choháns they say came from Sámbhar to Ajmír, from Ajmir to Delhi, from Delhi to Nágor north of Jodhpur, from Nágor to Jodhpur, from Jodhpur to Bhadgaon thirty miles south of Bhinmál, and from Bhadgaon to Sirohi. According to a local Jaghirdár of the Devra caste the Chohâns' original seat was at Jhálor forty miles north of Shrimál. They say that in the eighteenth century the Solankis came north from Pátan in north Gujarát to Hiyu in Pálanpur where they have still a settlement, and that from Hiyu they went to Bhinmál.

In connection with the Sun temple and the traces of sun worship among the Jains, whose *gurus* or religious guides have a sun face which they say was given them by the Rána of Chitor, the existence in Bhinmál of so many (thirty-five) houses of Shevaks is interesting. These Shevaks are the religious dependents of the Oswál Shrávaks. They are strange highnosed hatchet-faced men with long lank hair and long beards and whiskers. They were originally Magha Bráhmans and still are Vaishnavas worshipping the sun. They know that their story is told in the Námagranth of the Surya Purána. The Bhinmál Shevaks know of sixteen

[1] According to Katta, a Bráhma-Bhát of remarkable intelligence, the Osvals include Rajputs of a large number of tribes, Aadas, Bhatis, Boránas, Buruds, Chováns, Gehlots, Gohils, Jadavs, Makvánás, Mohils, Parmars, Ráhtors, Shálas, Tilars. They are said to have been converted to the Jain religion in Osianagara in Samvat Bia Varsh 22 that is in A.D. 165.

Appendix III.

BHINMÁL.

Caste Legends.

branches or *sakas* but remember the names of ten only: Aboti, Bhinmála, Devira, Hirgota, Kuwara, Lalár, Mahtariya, Mundiara, Saparwála, and Shánda. The story of these Maghás in the Surya and Bhavishya Puránas, how they were brought by Garuda from the land of the Śakas and were fire and sun worshippers, gives these Shevaks a special interest. The Devalás are believed to have come from Kashmír with Jog Svámi who is said to have been a Yaksh of the Rákshas division of Parihár Rajputs. The other division of Parihárs were *girásias* of Ábu who in virtue of the fire baptism of the Agnikund became Kshatriyás. The Devalás are supposed to get their name because they built Jag Som's temple at Bhinmál. The Devra Rájputs whose head is the Sirohi chief and who according to the bards are of Chohán descent, came at the same time and marry with the Devalás. With this origin from Kanaksen it is natural to associate the Devras and Devalás with the Devaputras of the Samudragupta (A.D. 370-395) inscription. Of Húṇa or of Jávla, the tribe name of the great Húṇa conquerors Toromana and Mihirakula (A.D. 450-530), few signs have been traced. The Jaghirdár of Devala knows the name Húṇa. They are a Rákshasa people he says. He mentions Honots or Sonots who may be a trace of Húṇas, and Húṇáls in Káthiáváḍa and a Huṇi subdivision among the Kunbis of Márwár. Jávla he does not know as a caste name.

History.

The historical interest of Shrimál centres in the fact that it was long the capital of the main branch of the great northern race of Gurjjaras. It is well known that many mentions of the Gurjjaras and their country in inscriptions and historical works refer to the Chaulukya or Solanki kingdom of Anahilaváḍa (A.D. 961-1242) or to its successor the Vághelá principality (A.D. 1219-1304). But the name Gurjjara occurs also in many documents older than the tenth century and has been most variously and inconsistently explained. Some take the name to denote the Chávaḍás of Anahilaváḍa (A.D. 746-942), some the Gurjjaras of Broach (A.D. 580-808) and some, among them Dr. Bhagvánlál Indráji, even the Valabhis (A.D. 509-766), but not one of these identifications can be made to apply to all cases. As regards the Valabhis even if they were of Gurjjara origin they are not known to have at any time called themselves Gurjjaras or to have been known by that name to their neighbours. The identification with the Gurjjaras of Broach is at first sight more plausible, as they admitted their Gurjjara origin as late as the middle of the seventh century, but there are strong reasons against the identification of the Broach branch as the leading family of Gurjjaras. Pulakeśi II. in his Aihole inscription of A.D. 634 (S. 556)[1] claims to have subdued by his prowess the Láṭas Málavas and Gurjjaras, which shows that the land of the Gurjjaras was distinct from Láṭa, the province in which Broach stood. Similarly Hiuen Tsiang (c. 640 A.D.) speaks of the kingdom of Broach by the name of the city and not as Gurjjara or the Gurjjara country. In the following century the historians of the Arab raids[2] notice Barus (Broach) separately from Jurz or Gurjjara, and the Chálukya grant of 490 that is of A.D. 738-739 mentions the Gurjjaras after the Chávoṭakas (Chávaḍás) and the Mauryas (of Chitor) as the last of the kingdoms attacked by the Arab army. Later instances occur of a distinction between Láṭa and Gurjjara, but it seems unnecessary to quote them as the Gurjjara kingdom of Broach probably did not survive the Ráshtrakúṭa conquest of south Gujarát (A.D. 750-760).

The evidence that the name Gurjjara was not confined to the Chávaḍás

[1] Indian Antiquary, VIII. 237. [2] Elliot, I. 432.

Appendix III.
BHINMÁL.
History.

is not less abundant. It will not be disputed that references of earlier date than the foundation of Anahilaváḍa (A.D. 746) cannot apply to the Chávaḍá kingdom, and further we find the Chálukya grant of A.D. 738-739 expressly distinguishing between the Chávaḍás and the Gurjjaras and calling the former by their tribal name Chávoṭaka. It might be supposed that as the power of the Chávaḍás increased, they became known as the rulers of the Gurjjara country; and it must be admitted that some of the references to Gurjjaras in the Ráshṭrakúṭa grants are vague enough to apply to the Chávaḍás. Still, if it can be shown that others of these references cannot possibly apply to the Chávaḍás, and if we assume, as we must, that the name of Gurjjara was used with the slightest consistency, it will follow that the ninth and tenth century references to the Gurjjaras do not apply to the Chávaḍá kingdom of Anahilaváḍa.

The Van-Dindori and Rádhanpur plates of the great Ráshṭrakúṭa Govinda III.[1] state that Govinda's father Dhruva (c. 780-800 A.D.) "quickly caused Vatsarája, intoxicated with the goddess of the sovereignty of Gauḍa that he had acquired with ease, to enter upon the path of misfortune in the centre of Maru" and took away from him the two umbrellas of Gauḍa. A comparison of this statement with that in the Baroda grant of Karka II.[2] which is dated A.D. 812-813, to the effect that Karka made his arm "the door-bar of the country of the lord of the Gurjjaras, who had become evilly inflamed by conquering the lord of Gauḍa and the lord of Vanga" makes it highly probable that Vatsarája was king of the Gurjjaras at the end of the eighth century. As no such name occurs in the Chávaḍá lists, it follows that the Gurjjaras referred to in the inscriptions of about A.D. 800 were not Chávaḍás.

It is also possible to show that more than a century later the Chávaḍás were distinct from the Gurjjaras. The Kánarese poet Pampa, writing in A. D. 941,[3] states that the father of his patron Arikesari vanquished Mahipála king of the Gurjjaras, who may be identified with the Mahipála who is named as overlord in the grant of Dharaṇivaráha of Wadhwán,[4] dated A.D. 914. As no Mahipála occurs in the Chávaḍá lists, the Gurjjara kingdom must be sought elsewhere than at Anahilaváḍa. Since the Gurjjaras of the eighth and ninth century inscriptions cannot be identified either with the Valabhis, the Broach Gurjjaras, or the Anahiláváḍa Chávaḍás, they must represent some other family of rulers. A suitable dynasty seems to be supplied by Hiuen Tsiang's kingdom of Kiú-che-lo or Gurjjara, the capital of which he calls Pi-lo-mo-lo.[5] The French translators took Pi-lo-mo-lo to be Bálmer in Rajputána. But Dr. Bühler following the late Colonel Watson, identifies it, no doubt rightly, with Bhinmál or Bhilmál.[6]

---

1 Indian Antiquary, XI. 156 and VI. 59.
2 Indian Antiquary, XII. 156.
3 Jour. R. A. S. XIV. 19ff.
4 Indian Antiquary, XII. 190 and XVIII. 91.
5 Beal's Buddhist Records, II. 270.
6 Indian Antiquary, VI. 63. That the name Bhilmál should have come into use while the Gurjjaras were still in the height of their power is strange. The explanation may perhaps be that Bhilmál may mean the Gurjjara's town the name Bhil or bowman being given to the Gurjjaras on account of their skill as archers. So Chápa the original name of the Chávaḍás is Sanskritised into Chapoṭkaṭas the strong bowmen. So also, perhaps, the Chápa or Chaura who gave its name to Chápanir or Chámpaner was according to the local story a Bhil. Several tribes of Mewár Bhils are well enough made to suggest that in their case Bhil may mean Gurjjara. This is specially the case with the Lauriyah Bhils of Nerwer, the finest of the race, whose name further suggests an origin in the Gurjjara division of Lor. Compare Malcolm's Trans. Bombay As. Soc. I. 71.

A short sketch of the history of the Gurjjaras, so far as it can be pieced together from contemporary sources, may help to show the probability of these identifications. The Gurjjaras apparently entered India in the fifth century A.D. The earliest notice of them occurs in the Śri Harshacharita, a work of the early seventh century, in which during the early years of the seventh century Prabhâkaravardhana the father of Śrí Harsha of Magadha (A.D. 606-641) is said to have conquered the king of Gandhára, the Húnas, the king of Sindh, the Gurjjaras, the Láṭas, and the king of Málava.[1] The date of their settlement at Bhinmál is unknown, but as their king was recognised as a Kshatriya in Hiuen Tsiang's time (c. 640 A.D.) it probably was not later than A.D. 550. Towards the end of the sixth century (c. 585) they seem to have conquered northern Gujarát and Broach and to have forced the Valabhis (A.D. 509-766) to acknowledge their supremacy. (See Above page 465.) They took very kindly to Indian culture, for in A.D. 628 the astronomer Brahmagupta wrote his Siddhánta at Bhinmál under king Vyághramukha, who, he states, belonged to the Śrí Chápa dynasty.[2] This valuable statement not only gives the name of the Gurjjara royal house but at the same time proves the Gurjjara origin of the Chápoṭkaṭas or Chávoṭakas, that is the Chávaḍás of later times. This Vyághramukha is probably the same as the Gurjjara king whom in his inscription of S. 556 (A.D. 634) Pulakeśi II. claims to have subdued.[3] A few years later (c. 640 A.D.) Hiuen Tsiang describes the king (probably Vyághramukha's successor) as a devout Buddhist and just twenty years of age. The country was populous and wealthy, but Buddhists were few and unbelievers many. The Gurjjaras did not long retain their southern conquests. In Hiuen Tsiang's time both Kaira (Kie-cha) and Vadnagar (Ánandapura) belonged to Málava, while the Broach chiefs probably submitted to the Chálukyas. No further reference to the Bhinmál kingdom has been traced until after the Arab conquest of Sindh when (A.D. 724-750) the Khalifa's governor Junaid sent his plundering bands into all the neighbouring countries and attacked among other places Márwád (Márwár), Maliba (Málwa), Barus (Broach), Uzain (Ujjain), Al Bailamán (Bhilmál ?), and Jurz (Gurjjara).[4] As noticed above the contemporary Chálukya plate of A.D. 738-9 also mentions Gurjjara as one of the kingdoms attacked. After these events the Arabs seem to have confined themselves to raiding the coast towns of Káthiáváḍa without attacking inland states such as Bhinmál. Immediately after the Arab raids ceased the Gurjjaras had to meet a new enemy the Ráshṭrakúṭas who after supplanting the Chálukyas in the Dakhan turned their attention northwards. Dantidurga in his Samangad grant of A.D. 753-4[5] speaks of ploughing the banks of the Mahí and the Revá (Narbada), and in his Elura inscription[6] of conquering among other countries Málava Láṭa and Tanka.[7] A few years later (A.D. 757-58) a branch of the main Rashṭrakúṭa line established its independence in Láṭa in the person of Kakka.

---

[1] The Madhuban Grant : Epigraphia Indica, I. 67.

[2] Reinaud, Mémoire Sur L'Inde, 337, in quoting this reference through Alberuni (A.D. 1031) writes Pohlmal between Multán and Anhalwara.

[3] Indian Antiquary, VIII. 237.

[4] Elliot, I. 440-41.

[5] Indian Antiquary, XI. 109.

[6] Arch. Surv. West. India, X. 91.

[7] Tanka may be the northern half of the Broach District. Traces of the name seem to remain in the two Tankáriás, one Sitpore Tankária in north Broach and the other in Ámod. The name seems also to survive in the better known Tankári the port of Jambusar on the Dhádhar. This Tankári is the second port in the district of Broach and was formerly the emporium for the trade with Málwa. Bombay Gazetteer, II. 113-569.

Appendix III.
BHINMÁL.
History.

The next notice of the Gurjjaras occurs in the Rádhanpur and Van-Dindori grants of Govinda III.[1] who states that his father Dhruva (c. 780-800 A.D.) caused "Vatsarája, intoxicated with the goddess of the sovereignty of Gauda that he had acquired with ease, to enter upon the path of misfortune in the centre of Maru" and took from him the two white umbrellas of Gauda. As already stated, a comparison with the Baroda grant of Karka II.[2] shows that this Vatsarája was a Gurjjara king and that he had made extensive conquests in Upper India as far east as Bengal. Now it is notable that the genealogies of two of the most important Agnikula races, the Paramáras and the Chauháns, go back to this very time (c. 800 A.D.)[3]. Taking this fact in connection with the prevalence of the surnames Pavár and Chaván among Gujars in such remote provinces as the Panjáb and Khándesh, it seems obvious that these two tribes and therefore also the two other Agnikula races, the Parihárs and Solaṅkis are, if not of Gurjjara origin, at all events members of the great horde of northern invaders whom the Gurjjaras led. The agreement between this theory and the Agnikula legends of Ábu need only be pointed out to be admitted. The origin of the modern Rajput races has always been one of the puzzles of Indian history. This suggestion seems to offer at least a partial solution.

The Rádhanpur grant (A.D. 807-8) further states that when the Gurjjara saw Govinda III. approaching, he fled in fear to some unknown hiding-place. This probably means no more than that Vatsarája did not oppose Govinda in his march to the Vindhyas. The next reference is in the Baroda grant of Karka II. of Gujarát who boasts that his father Indra (c. 810 A.D.) alone caused the leader of the Gurjjara lords to flee. Karka adds that he himself, for the purpose of protecting Málava, "who had been struck down," made his arm the door-bar of the country of Gurjjareśvara, who "had become evilly inflamed" by the conquest of Gauḍa and Vanga.[4] It is difficult to avoid supposing that we have here a reference to the Paramára conquest of Málwa and that Karka checked the southward march of the victorious army. For some years no further mention has been traced of the Gurjjaras. But in A.D. 851 the Arab merchant Sulaiman states[5] that the king of Juzr was one of the kings "around" the Balhará, that is the Ráshṭrakúṭa, and that he was very hostile to the Musalmáns, which is not surprising, considering how his kingdom was exposed to the Arab raids from Sindh. Dhruva III. of Broach, in his Bagumrá grant of A.D. 867[6] speaks of "the host of the powerful Gurjjaras" as one of the dangerous enemies he had to fear. About A.D. 890 a Gurjjara chief named Alakhána ceded Takkadesa in the Panjáb to Śankaravarmman of Kashmír.[7] But as Alakhána was a vassal of Lalliya, the Śáhi of Ohind near Swát, this event did not affect the Bhínmál empire. To about A.D. 900 belongs the notice of the Ráshṭrakúṭa Krishna II. in the Deoli and Navsári grants[8] where he is stated to have frightened the Gurjjaras, destroyed the pride of Láṭa, and deprived the coast people of sleep. His fights with the Gurjjaras are compared to the storms of the rainy season, implying that while the relations of the two empires continued hostile, neither was able to gain any decisive advantage over the other. To this same period belongs Ibn Khurdádba's (A.D. 912) statement[9] that the king of Juzr was the fourth

---

[1] Indian Antiquary, VI. 59 and XI. 156. [2] Indian Antiquary, XII. 156.
[3] See the Udaipur *praśasti* in Ep. Ind. I. and the Harsha Inscription in ditto.
[4] See the Baroda grant of A.D. 812-13. Indian Antiquary, XII. 156.
[5] Elliot, I. 4. [6] Indian Antiquary, XII. 179. [7] Rajataraṅginí, 149.
[8] B. B. R. A. Soc, Jourl. XVIII. 239. [9] Elliot, I. 13.

Appendix III.
BHINMÁL.
History.

in rank of the kings of India and that the Tátariya *dirhams* were used in his country. In connection with the latter point it is worth noting that the *pattávali* of the Upakeśagaccha[1] gives a story which distinctly connects the origin of the Gadhia coinage with Bhínmál.[2] The grant of Dharaṇivaráha, the Chápa chief of Vadhván, dated A.D. 914[3] gives us the name of his overlord Mahipála, who, as already pointed out, must be identified with the Mahipála who was defeated by the Karnátak king Narasiṁha.[4] The fact that Vadhván was a Chápa dependency implies that Anahilaváḍa was one also. We may in fact conclude that throughout the Chávaḍá period Anahilaváḍa was a mere feudatory of Bhínmál, a fact which would account for the obscurities and contradictions of Chávaḍá history.

The Deoli grant of the Ráshṭrakúṭa Krishṇa III. which is dated A.D. 940[5] describes the king's victories in the south as causing the hope of Kálanjara and Chitrakúṭa to drop away from the heart of the Gurjjara. At this time Kalinjar belonged to the Kalachuris of Central India and Chitrakúṭa or Chitoḍ to the Gehlots of Mewáḍ and the phrase used by Krishṇa implies that the Gurjjara chief had his eye on these two famous fortresses and had perhaps already besieged them unsuccessfully. In either case this notice is evidence of the great and far-reaching power of the Gurjjaras. Masudi (A.D. 915) notices that the king of Juzr was frequently at war with the Balhara (Ráshṭrakúṭa) and that he had a large army and many horses and camels.

A Chandel stone inscription from Khajuráho describes Yaśovarmman and Lakshavarmman as successful in war against Gauḍas, Khaśas, Kosalas, Kásmíras, Maithilas, Málavas, Chedis, Kurus, and Gurjjaras.[6] And soon after about A.D. 953 during the reign of Bhímasena a migration of 18,000 Gurjjaras from Bhínmál is recorded.[7] The memory of this movement remains in the traditions of the Gujars of Khándesh into which they passed with their carts in large numbers by way of Málwa.[8] An important result of this abandonment of Bhínmál was the transfer of overlordship from Bhínmál to Anahilaváḍa whose first Chálukya or Solaṅki king Múlarája (A.D. 961-996) is, about A.D. 990, described as being accompanied by the chief of Bhinmál as a subordinate ally in his war with Graharipu (see Above page 451). The Gurjjara or Bhinmál empire seems to have broken into several sections of which the three leading portions were the Chauháns of Sámbhar, the Paramáras of Málwa, and the Solaṅkis of Anahilaváḍa.

The inscriptions which follow throw a certain amount of light on the history of Bhinmál during and after the Solaṅki period. The two earliest

---

[1] Indian Antiquary, XIX. 233.

[2] According to Cunningham (Ancient Geography, 313) the coins called Tátariya *dirhams* stretch from the fifth and sixth to the eleventh century. They are frequently found in Kábul probably of the ninth century. In the tenth century Ibn Haukal (A.D. 977) found them current in Gandhara and the Panjáb where the Boar coin has since ousted them. They are rare in Central India east of the Arávali range. They are not uncommon in Rajputána or Gujarát and were once so plentiful in Sindh, that in A.D. 725 the Sindh treasury had eighteen million Tatariya dirhams. (See Dowson in Elliot's History, I. 3.) They are the rude silver pieces generally known as Indo-Sassanian because they combine Indian letters with Sassanian types. A worn fire temple is the supposed Ass-head which has given rise to the name Gadiya Paisa or Ass money.

[3] Indian Antiquary, XII. 190 and XVIII. 91.

[4] Jour. R. A. S. XIV. 19.

[5] B. B. R. A. S. Jourl. XVIII. 239.

[6] Kielhorn in Epig. Indica, I. 122.

[7] Hœrnle in Ind. Antiq. XIX. 233.

[8] Details given in Khándesh Gazetteer, XII. 39.

Appendix III.
BHINMÁL.
History.

in date (Nos. 1 and 2) which are probably of the tenth century, give no historical details. Nos. 3 and 4 show that between A.D. 1057 and 1067 Bhinmál was ruled by the Mahárájádhirája Krishnarája of the Paramára race. This is a valuable confirmation of Rájput tradition, according to which[1] the Paramára Rája of A'bu was followed by the prince of Śrímála, when he aided Múlarája against Grahatipu (c. 990 A.D.) and the Paramáras remained paramount in this region until the beginning of the thirteenth century.[2] The title of Mahárájádhirája meant much less at this period than it meant before the Valabhi kings had cheapened it. Still it shows that Krishnarája's rank was considerably higher than that of a mere feudatory chieftain. Inscription No. 3 gives the names of Krishnarája's father Dhaṁdhuka and of his grandfather Devarája. The first of these two names occurs in the main line of A'bu as the successor of Dhúmarája the first Paramára sovereign.[3] According to Rajput tradition the Paramáras were at one time supreme in Marásthalí and held all the nine castles of the Waste. But in the historical period their chief possessions in Márwád lay about A'bu and Chandrávati, though we have a glimpse of another branch maintaining itself at Kerálu near Bádmer.[4] The Paramára chiefs of A'bu are constantly referred to in the Solaṅki annals, and during the golden age of the Solaṅki monarchy (A.D. 1094-1174) they were the vassals of that power, and their Bhinmál branch, if it was ever a distinct chiefship, probably followed the fortunes of the main line, though the Bhinmál inscriptions give us no facts for this long period. The next item of information is given by Inscription 5, which is dated in the Saṁvat year 1239 (A.D. 1183) in the reign of the Maháraul Śrí Jayatasíha-deva. This name is of special interest, as it can hardly be doubted that we have here to do with that "Jaitsí Parmár" of A'bu whose daughter's beauty caused the fatal feud between "Bhíma Solaṅki" of Anahilaváda and Prithiráj Chohán of Delhi.[5] The title of Maháraul is to be noted as indicating the decline of the family from the great days of Krishnarája.

Towards the end of the thirteenth century the old world was falling to pieces, and the Paramáras lost one after another nearly all their ancient possessions to the Chohána of Nádol. Bhinmál must have fallen about A.D. 1200 or a few years before, for Inscription No. 6 is dated Saṁvat 1262 (A.D. 1206) in the reign of the Mahárájádhirája Śrí Udayasiṁhadêva, who, as we learn from Inscription 12, was the son of the Maháraul Śrí Samarasiṁhadeva, of the Chohán race. The sudden rise of the son to greatness is implied in the difference of title and it may be inferred that Udayasiṁha himself was the conqueror of Bhinmál, though the capture of Ábu is ascribed by Forbes to a chief named Lúniga.[6]

Inscriptions Nos. 6 to 8 being dated in the reign of Udayasiṁha, show that he lived to at least the year A.D. 1249 and therefore reigned at least forty-three years. He is also referred to in the Inscription No. 10, dated A.D. 1274, but in a way that does not necessarily imply that he was still alive, as the record only speaks of an endowment for his spiritual benefit, made by a person who was perhaps an old retainer. His name also occurs in the genealogy in No. 12. His reign was apparently a prosperous one but no historical facts beyond those already noted are known about him.

---

[1] Rás Málá, 44. [2] Rás Málá, 210ff. [3] Rás Málá, 211.
[4] Śrí Bhaunagar Prá. I. No. 30 of the list of Sanskrit Inscriptions dated Saṁ. 1218.
[5] Śrí Rás Málá, 161ff. [6] Rás Málá, 211.

Inscription No. 12 shows that Udayasiṁha had a son named Váhadhasiṁha, who, as he is given no royal title, probably died before his father. Udayasiṁha's successor, or at all events the next king in whose reign grants are dated, was Cáciga, who is given the title of Maháraul in Inscriptions 11 (A.D. 1277) and 12 (A.D. 1278).[1] His relationship to Udayasiṁha does not clearly appear, but he was probably either an elder brother or an uncle of the Cámuṇḍa for whose benefit the gift recorded in Inscription 12 was made and who seems to be a grandson of Udayasiṁha. Cáciga appears to be the Mahámandaleśvara Cáciga of Inscription 15 in the Bháunagar State Collection (Bháu. Prá. I. list page 5) which is stated to bear the date Saṁvat 1332 (A.D. 1276) and to be engraved on a pillar in the temple of Pársvanátha at Ratanpur near Jódhpur. It is clear that he was tributary to some greater power though it is not easy to say who his suzerain was. At this period Márwár was in a state of chaos under the increasing pressure of the Ráthods. Only five years after Cáciga's last date (A.D. 1278) we meet with the name of a new ruler, the Maháraul ori Sámvatasiṁha. He is mentioned in Inscriptions 13 (A.D. 1283) 14 (A.D. 1286) and 15 (A.D. 1289) and also in 44 of the Bháunagar Collection (A.D. 1296 Bháu. Prá. I. list page 13) from a Jain temple at Juná. He is not stated to have belonged to the same family as the previous rulers, but he bears the family title of Maháraul, and it may be inferred with probability that he was a son of Cáciga. He reigned for at least thirteen years (A.D. 1283 - 1296). It must have been about A.D. 1300 or a little later, that the Chóháns were deprived of Bhinmál by the Ráthods and the line of Udayasiṁha died out.[2]

Inscriptions.

The Jagsvámi temple has the honour of supplying fifteen of eighteen unmodern inscriptions found at Bhinmál. Of the fifteen inscriptions belonging to Jagsvámi's temple nine are in place and six have been removed to other buildings. Of the six which have been moved five are in Báráji's rest-house in the east and one is in the enclosure of Mahálakshámi's temple in the south of the town. Of the three remaining inscriptions of one (No. 3) the date S. 1106 (A.D. 1043) is alone legible. Of the letters on the two others, one in the bed and the other on the north bank of the Jaikop lake, no portion can be read. Arranged according to date the sixteen inscriptions of which any portion has been read come in the following order :

I.—(S. 950 - 1050 ; A.D. 900 - 1000. No. 1 of Plan.) On the left hand side of the eastern face of the broken architrave of the porch of the shrine of Jagsvâmi. The letters show the inscription to be of about the tenth century :

Śrí Jagasvâmidêvasya vâsare
on the day of Śrí Jagasvâmi.*

* Read S'rí Jagatsvâmi.

II.—(S. 950 - 1050 ; A.D. 900 - 1000. No. 2 of Plan.) On the south face of the eightsided section of the northern pillar of the shrine porch in the temple of Jagsvâmi. Wrongly described in Bhâvanagara prâcîna-śodhasaṅgraha I. under No. 46 of the State Collection, as referring to a man called Vasuṁdhara and dated Vi. S. 1330. As the letters show, the inscription is of about the tenth century. It consists of a single

[1] Inscriptions 9 and 10 are not dated in any king's reign.
[2] Compare Tod's Rajasthán, I.

Appendix III.
BHINMÁL.
Inscriptions.

complete verse :

1. Vasumdharî-kârî-
2. tâu dvâu stambhâv ê-
3. -tâu manôharâu
4. svapituḥ Santaka-
5. sârthê satatam
6. punyavṛiddhayê ॥

These two lovely pillars Vasumdharî had made for her father Santaka's sake for increase of merit for ever.

III.—(S. 1106; A.D. 1049. Not on Plan.) On the east side of the southern water channel into Gautama's lake three-quarters of a mile north of the town. Except the date nothing can be deciphered.

IV.—(S. 1117; A.D. 1060. Not on Plan.) On the lower part of a pillar in the dharmaśálá east of the temple of Bârâji on the east of the town. Prose :

1. Om Namaḥ sûryâya | yasyôdayâstasamayêsuramakuṭa-nispṛi-
2. shṭa-caraṇa-kamalô s pi | kurutê s jalim Trinetraḥ sa jayati dhâmnâ nidhi
3. Sûryaḥ | Samvat 1117 (A.D. 1057) Mâgha Sudi 6 Ravâu Śrî Śrîmâle Paramâravamś
4. dbhavo Mahârâjâdhîrâjâ Srî Krishṇarâjaḥ Srî Dhamdhu-kasutaḥ Śrîmad Dêvarâ-
5. -ja-pauttraḥ tasmin kshitîśê vijayini | vartamâna-varsha-vârika-Dharkuṭa-
6. jâti-Kiriṇâdityô Jêla-sutô Dêda-Harir Mâdhava-sutô Dhamdha-nâkô Dha-
7. raṇacaṇḍa-sutas tathâ Thâkhâṭa-jâti Dharaṇâdityaḥ Sar-vadêva-sutaḥ | amî-
8. bhiścaturbhis tathâ Vânyêna Dharkuṭa-jâtyâ Dhamdhakêna Jêlasutêna nija-ku-
9. -la-maṇḍanêna dêva-guru-vrâhmaṇa-suśrûshâ-parêṇa Ravi-caraṇa-yuga-dhyânâ-
10. -vishṭena samsârasyânityatâm(n)irîkshya râjâno râjapu-trâmśca vrâhmaṇân (ma-)
11. -hâjana-paurâṇiśca tathâ lokân Saura-dharmê pravarttâyya dravyâṇi me . . . (ni)
12. -tya-tejo-nidheḥ Śrî Jagatsvâmi-dêvasya deva-bhavana-jîrṇoddhâ . . . .
13. (kâ)râpitam bhavanasyopari svarṇṇa-kalasam vrâhmaṇena para-(ma-dhâ-)
14. -rmmikeṇa Jêjâkêna nija-dravyeṇa kâritam iti || Sam 1
15. Jyeshṭha Su di 8 somê râtrâu ghaṭikâ 8 pala 25 asmin la-
16. (g)nê sarvakarma nishpâdya kalasam dhvajam ca dayapi-tam iti ||
17. (Ta)thâ purâtanavṛittêna pari devasyâsya Râjñâ Śrî Krishṇa-râjêna Śrî-
18. . . . (pu-)rîya-maṇḍalê grâmam prativa° drâ. 20 Sacaliyâ-grâmê kshêtram êkam
19. . . . . . . trâyâ râjabhôgât tu drôṇa . . . . . . sati kâ . .
20. . . . || Râmasî Pômarapi kâ . . . . . . prativa° drâ. 1 . . . . . .
21. . . . . vijñapya camdanena kârâpitam iti || Tathâ âlav. . . .
22. . . . ya pra da . . . likhitam kada . . . .
23. . . . . .kâya . . . . .

Appendix III.

BHINMAL.
Inscriptions.

Translation.

1 - 3. Oṁ ! Reverence to the Sun ! Victorious is that sun, the storehouse of brightness, at whose rising and setting the three-eyed (Śiva), even though (his own) lotus feet are touched by the diadems of the gods, folds his hands (in adoration).

3 - 5. On Sunday the 6th of the light half of Mâgha, the year 1113, at holy Śrîmâla the Mahârâjâdhirâja Śrî Kṛishṇarâja son of Śrî Dhaṁdhuka and grandson of the glorious Devarâja, of the Paramâra race—in his victorious reign.

6 - 7. Kiriṇâditya, Jêla's son, of the Dharkuṭa family, (being office-holder) in his turn for the current year, Dada Hari son of Mâdhava, Dhaṁdhanaka son of Dharaṇacaṇḍa and Dharaṇâditya son of Sarvadeva of the Thâkhâṭa race.

8 - 12. By these four and by the Vâṇî (?) Dhaṁdhaka son of Jêla of the Dharkuṭa race, the ornament of his family, strict in obedience to the gods, to his teachers and to Brâhmaṇas, and full of devotion to the feet of Ravi (the Sun), observing the perishableness of this world, and urging kings Kshatriyas Brâhmaṇas merchants and townsfolk to worship the sun, repairs were done to the temple of the god Śrî Jagatsvâmi, the everlasting store of light.

13. The kalaśa of gold above the temple the very righteous Brâhmaṇa Jêjâka had made at his own charges. In the year 1 . . . .

15. on Monday the 8th of the light half of Jyêshṭha, in the 25th pala of the 3rd ghaṭikâ of night—at this moment

16. all the work being finished the kalaśa and banner were set up (?)

17. and after the ancient manner by the king Śrî Krishṇarâja . . . . of this complaint . . . .

18. a village in the Śrî . . . . purîya district, yearly 20 drammas. In Sacaliyâ village a field

19. . . . . But from the king's share (of the crop) a drôṇa . . . .

20. . . . . yearly 1 dramma . . . .

21. . . . . by order was caused to be made by Caṃdana || and . . .

22. . . . . written . . . .

23. . . . . . . kâya.

V.—(S. 1123 ; A.D. 1066. No. 3 of Plan.) On the north face of the upper square section of the more northerly of the two pillars that support the eastern side of the dome of the temple of Jagsvâmi. Entirely in prose :

1. Oṁ. Saṁvat 1123, Jyêshṭha Vadi 12 Śanâu || adyêha Śrî Śrîmâlê Mahârâjâdhirâja-Śrî Krishṇarâ-

2. ja-râjyê Dêvaśrîcaṇḍîśa-Mahâdêva-dharmâdhikâra-cêṭakaparama Pâśupatâcârya-Śrî Jâvalasyê . . . . | Sauva-

3. -rṇika Jasaṇâśâ | Śrêshthi Caṁdanâ Kiraṇâdityâ Stharâ varttamâna-varsha-vârika-Joga-candra . . . . .

4. Gugâ navâi . . . . lôkê ca êka . . matîbhûtvâ . . . . Śrîmâlîya Vrâ-

5. hmaṇa Vâhaṭêna . . . . Śrî Caṁdîśa . . . . dramma . . . .

6 - 13. Badly damaged ; only a few letters legible here and there.

Appendix III.

BHINMÁL.
Inscriptions.

Translation.

1 - 2. Ôṁ! On Saturday the 12th of the dark half of Jyêshṭha Saṁvat 1123—on this day at holy Śrîmâla, in the reign of the Mahârâjâdhirâja Śrî Kṛishṇarâja—of Śrî Jâvala, the servant of the offices of religion to the god Śrî Caṃḍîśa Mahâdêva, the supreme teacher of the Pâśupatas . . . .

3. The goldsmith Jasaṇâśâ, the seṭh Caṁdanâ, Kiraṇâditya, Stharâ, Jogacaṁdra the office-holder in turn for the current year

4 - 5. Gugâ . . . . and in the world . . being of one mind . . . . by Vâhaṭa the Śrîmâlî Brâhmaṇa . . . . . . Śrî Caṁdîśa . . . . *drammas* . . . .

VI.—(S. 1239; A.D. 1183. No. 4 of Plan.) On the upper face of the eightsided section of the fallen pillar on the south side of the dome of the temple of Jagsvâmi. Entirely in prose:

1. Saṁ. 1239 Âśvina Vadi 10 Vudhê
2. Adyêha Śrî Śrîmâle Mahârâja-
3. -putra Śrî Jayatastha-dêva-râjyê ||
4. Guhilo Pramahidâsuta-tra° arava-
5. sâka Vahiyaṇa Vâlâka-dêvâya
6. drava dra. 1 tathâ bhâryâ Mâlhaṇadê-
7. ḍî kṛita dra. 1 yê kêऽpi pa ati bhava
8. ṁti teshâṁ pratidra° vi 1 labhyâ yaḥko(s)
9. pi catra-pâlô bhavati tena varshân(u-)
10. -varsha(ṁ) dinê dêvâya dâtavyaṁ ||

Translation.

1. In the year 1239 (1183 A.D.) on Wednesday the tenth of the dark half of Âśvina

2 - 3. On this day here in holy Śrîmâla in the reign of his majesty Śrî Jayatastha the Mahâraul.

4 - 6. Aravasâka Vahiyaṇa the Guhila, the Tra°,* son of Pramahidâ (gave) to Vâlâka-dêva one *dramma* in cash.

6 - 7. And (his) wife Mâlhaṇa-dêḍî (dêvî) (gave) one *dramma*. Whosoever are , by them for each *dramma* one *vi* is to be received. Whosoever

9. is the ruler by him every

10. year on the day it is to be given to the god.

* Evidently the name of his office, but the abbreviation is not intelligible.

VII.—(S. 1262; A.D. 1206. No. 5 of Plan.) On the upper face of the lower square section of the fallen pillar which is one of the pair of three dome pillars. Prose:

1. ° || Oṁ. Namaḥ Suryâyaḥ || Yasyodayâstasamayê suramakuṭa-nispṛi-
2. shṭa-caraṇa-kamaloऽpi kurutê ऽṁjali(ṁ) trinêtra(ḥ) sajayati dhâmnâṁ niddhi(ḥ) sûryaḥ||
3. Saṁvat 1262 varshê adyêha Śrî Śrîmâle Mahârâjâdhirâja Śrî Uda-
4. -yasîṁha-dêva-kalyâṇa-vijaya-râjyê maha° Âsvapasî-prabhṛiti-paṁca-kula-
5. pratipattâu || Kâyastha-jâtîya-Vâlamyânvayê maha° Yaśôpâlaśrêyô ऽrthaṁvê (cê?)-
6. -ṭaka-Vîlhâkêna Śrî Jayasvâmi-dêvîya-bhâṁḍâgârê kshêpita dra. 40 catvari(ṁ).

7. Śat Âśvina mâsê yâtr(ôtsavê ?) Âśvina śudi 13 , ...
1 Âgni cayê.
8. Mâlâyâ pushpamû dra. 4 aguru dra. . . . .
9. -dra. 4 pramadâ kulasya dra. 1 êvaṁ dra. 12 dvâdaśa-drammâ âcaṁdrârkaṁ prativarshaṁ dêvêna kârâpa
10. nîyâ ‖ tathâ śrêyârthaṁ Madrakêna(?) dêva bhâṁḍâgârê kshipita dra. 15 paṁcadaśa drammâ Mâgha-
11. -vadi 6 dinê balinibaṁdhê(?) gôdhûma sê 2 pâkâ ghṛita palî 9 naivêdya 32 aṁga-
12. -bhôgô prativarshaṁ âcaṁdrârkaṁ yâvat dêvêna karaṇîyaḥ.. dinê Âhaḍasvâ-
13. -mi-suhâlaṁ/ Bhadrasvâmi-suhâlaṁ/ Acaṁdrârkavat âpanîya(ṁ) likhitaṁ pâ° Bâṁdhavada su(tê)-
14. -na Câṁḍapasâkêna hînâksharam adhikâksharaṁ pramâṇaṁ ‖ .

Translation.

1 - 2. Oṁ. Reverence to the Sun ! Victorious is that sun, the storehouse of brightness, at whose rising and setting the three-eyed (Śiva) folds his hands (in adoration), even though his lotus feet are touched by the diadems of the gods.

3 - 5. In the Saṁvat year 1262 (1206 A.D.), on this day here in holy Śrîmâla, in the prosperous and victorious reign of his majesty the Mahârâjâdhirâja Śrî Udayasiṁha in the term of office of the *panch* (consisting of) Âśvapasî &c.

5 - 7. For the (spiritual) benefit of Yaśôpâla in the Vâlamya family of the Kâyastha caste, dra. 40, forty *drammas* were deposited by Vîlhâka the Veṭaka (or Cêṭaka) in the treasury of the god Śrî Jayasvâmi.

7. At the yâtrâ festival in the month of Âśvina, on the 13th of the light half of Âśvina . . . . . . 1, at the building of the fire-(altar).

8. . . . . . . for flowers for the garland dra. 4, aloewood dra. . . .

9. 4 *drammas*, for the band of singing women one *dramma* : thus dra. 12, twelve *drammas* (in all) are to be applied yearly by the god so long as sun and moon endure.

10. So also the dra. 15, fifteen *drammas* deposited in the treasury of the god by Madraka(?) for (spiritual) benefit.

11 - 12. On the sixth of the dark half of Mâgha in the fixed ritual of the *bali*, wheat one *ser*, ... *ghi* nine *palis*, the *naivêdya* . . . . 32, the *angabhôga* is to be performed yearly by the god so long as sun and moon endure.

12 - 13. On the . . . . day the *suhâla* of Âhaḍasvâmi and the *suhâla* of Bhadrasvâmi is to be given so long as sun and moon endure.

13 - 14. Written by the *pâ°* Caṁḍapasâka son of Bâṁdhavada. * The letter less or the letter more . . . . . . of authority.

* *i. e.* "Errors excepted."

VIII.—(S. 1274 ; A.D. 1218. Not in Plan.) In Bârâji's rest-house on the west face of the third right hand pillar. Prose :

1. Saṁvat 1274 varshê Bhâdrapada sudi 9 Śukrê dyêha Śrî-Śrîmâ-
2. -lê Mahârâjâdhirâja Śrî Udaya-siṁha-dêva-kalyâṇa-vijaya-râjyê Sa°.
3. Dêpâlaprabhṛiti-paṁcakulạ pratipattâu . . . .

Appendix III.

BHINMAL.

Inscriptions.

4\. . . . . . Srî Udayastha . . . . . . Śrîdêva Jagasvâmi-naivêdyê . .

5\. . . . . . dina . . nityadêya lô 2 dvân.

6\. }
7\. } Illegible.
8\. }

Translation.

1\. In the Saṁvat year 1274 (1218 A.D.) on Friday the 9th of the bright half of Bhâdrapada—on this day here in holy Śrîmâla,

2\. in the prosperous and victorious reign of his majesty the Mahârâjâdhirâja Śrî Udayasiṁha, in

3\. the term of office of the panch (consisting of) Sa° Dêpâla and others . . . . .

4\. . . . Śrî Udayastha . . . . . in the *naivedya* of Śrîdêva Jagasvâmi . . . .

5\. . . . . . day . . . to be given regularly 2 two lô° (?).

IX.—(S. 1305; A.D. 1249. Not in Plan.) On the south face of the fifth right pillar on the right hand of Bârâji's rest-house. Prose:

1\. Ôṁ Namaḥ Sûryâyaḥ || yasyodayâstasa-

2\. -mayê Sura-makuṭa-nieprishṭa-caraṇa-

3\. -kamalo ऽ pi kurutê ऽ ṁjaliṁ Trinetra sa

4\. jayati dhâmnâ(ṁ) nidhi(ḥ) Suryaḥ || Saṁ. 1305 va-

5\. -rshê adyêha Śrî Śrîmâlê Mahârâjâdhirâjaśrî (Uda-)

6\. -ya-siha-dêva-kalyâṇa-vijaya-râjyê maha° Gaja(si-)

7\. -ha-prabhṛiti paṁca(kûla-pratipattâu) . . . . . ṇadêvî . . .

8\. vâha . . . Śrî Jagasvâmidêvîyabhâṇḍâgâre kshêpita dra. 50 paṁcâ (śaddrammâ â-)

9\. -Śvina-yâtrâyâṁ Âśvina śudi (4) dinê divasa-bali . .

10\. . . . . (gô-)

11\. -dhûma sê 2 . . ghṛita ka 8 . . . . mugа pâ 2 ghṛita ka 2.

12\. }
13\. }
14\. } Illegible.
15\. }

Translation.

1-4\. Ôṁ. Reverence to the Sun! Victorious is that sun, the storehouse of brightness, at whose rising and setting the three-eyed (Śiva) folds his hands (in adoration), even though his feet are touched by the diadems of the gods.

4-7\. In the year Saṁ. 1305 (1249 A.D.), on this day here in holy Śrîmâla in the prosperous and victorious reign of his majesty the Mahârâjâdhirâja Śrî Udayasiha, in the term of office of the *panch* (consisting of) Maha° Gajasiha and others . . . . . . ṇadêvî.

8\. Vâha . . . . . dra. 50 fifty *drammas* deposited in the treasury of the god Śrî Jagasvâmi.

9\. At the Âśvina festival on the 4th day of the light half of Âśvina the day's *bali*.

10\. . . . .

11. Wheat sers 2 .. ghi *karshas* (8) ..... *mung* pâ 2, ghi *karshas* 2.

12-15. Illegible.

X.—(S. 1320; A.D. 1264. No. 6 of Plan.) On the east face of the lower square section of the more northerly of the east pair of dome pillars of Jagsvâmi's temple. First thirteen lines in verse, the rest in prose. No. 49 of the Bhâunagar State Collection (Bhâu. Prâ. I.)

1. Ôm namo Vighnarâjâya namo devâya bhâsvate | namo ऽ nanta-sva-
2. rûpâya Harayê Cakrapâṇayê || namaḥ ŚivâyaSomâya namaḥ para-
3. ma-Vrahmaṇê | Iti paṁcanamaskârâḥ sarvapâpapraṇâ-śakâḥ || sarva-maṁ-
4. gala-maṁgalyâḥ sarva-saukhya-pradâyakâḥ | sarvârtha-siddhi-saṁpannâḥ saṁ-
5. -tu mê hṛidi sarvadâ || Iti jantur japan nityaṁ nityam âśrayatê sukhaṁ | ta-
6. -smâd asmin japê puṇyê ratir astu sadaiva mê || Iti dhyâ-naikanishṭhâtmâ-
7. Kâyastho naigamânvayê | Ṛishir âsît purâ Saḍhunamdano naṁdanaḥ satâin ||
8. Śrikrishṇa-Kṛishṇa-Govinda-pranidhâna-parâyanaḥ | Pautras tasyâjani Srîmâ-
9. -n Saḍhḍhalo Valaṇâṁgajaḥ || Sadaiva datta-mishṭânna-toshitâneka-vâḍavaḥ |
10. Ahâra-prasaro yasya pâṇiḥ padmâlayâlayaḥ || paropakâra-vratinâm vaishṇa
11. vadharmasêvinâṁ || yêna janmâtmanaścakrê sâdhuvâda-vibhûshitaṁ || tataḥ parama-
12. -dharmmâtmâ sadâ viśadamânasaḥ || dêvîdatta-varaḥ Śrîmân Subhaṭo ऽ bhût tadaṁgabhûḥ |
13. Câgneyas tasya Kêdâra-pukaḥ Kânhaḍo ऽ bhavat | Mahâ-dêvasuto yasya bhrârau Râ-
14. -ma. Âsalô || Têna Śrîkêdâraputraka Kânhaḍêna svaśrêyasê Saṁ 1320 va-
15. -rshê Mâgha Śu di 9 navamîdinê prativarshaṁ balini-mittaṁ Śrî Jayasvâmi-dê-
16. vîya-bhâṇḍâgârê kshêpita dra.50 paṁcâśan drammâḥ || bali-nibaṁdhê godhûma sê 1½
17. ghrita ka 6 naivêdyê mâ ¼ muga mâ ⅜ ghṛita ka ½ Âbôtî dra ¼ + 2
18. Vyâsa lô 2 pushpakuṁkumâguru-mûlyê dra. 2 patra-pûga-mû dra | pramadâkula
19. dra. 1 Êvaṁ prativarshaṁ dêvakîyabhâṇḍâgârât shaḍ drammâ vyayê dêvêna kârâ
20. pyaṃ || Iyaṁ praśastir Maha° Subhaṭêna bhaṇitâ | Dhruva-Nâgvala-suta-Dêdâ-
21. -kêna likhitâ || sûtra° Gôgâ Suta-Bhîmasîhênôtkîrṇâ || कृ || कृ ||

Translation.

1. "Oṁ. Reverence to the lord of obstacles (Gaṇeśa), reverence to the brilliant god (the Sun), reverence to him of ever-lasting nature,
2. To Hari, wielder of the discus. Reverence to Śiva (and) to Sôma, reverence

Appendix III
BHINMÁL.
Inscriptions.

3-5. to the highest Brahma. May these five reverences which destroy all sin, the most auspicious of all auspicious (sayings), which grant all happiness, attended with the accomplishment of all objects, be ever in my heart."

5-6. The creature that constantly murmurs (these words) resorts to everlasting happiness. Therefore may I for ever take pleasure in this holy murmur.

6-7. There was formerly in the Naigama family a Kâyastha, Rishi son of Sadhu, the delight of the good, whose mind was solely intent upon (the above) meditation.

7-9. (He was) devoted to meditation on (the names) Śrî Krishṇa, Krishṇa, and Govinda. To him was born a grandson, the glorious Saḍhḍhala son of Valaṇa, who constantly satisfied numerous Brâhmaṇas with gifts of sweet food,

10. whose hand was not stretched out to steal, who was the home of Lakshmî for the followers of the Vaishṇava religion, who are vowed to doing good to others,

11-12. who adorned his life with the discussions of saints. From him there was the glorious Subhaṭa, the very righteous, whose mind was ever clear, and to whom Dêvî granted a boon. Born of his body

13-14. was Câgneya. His (grandson) was Kânhaḍa son of Kêdâra or Mahâdêva and his (Kânhaḍa's) two brothers were Râma and Âsala.

14-16. By this Kânhaḍa, son of Kêdâra for his own benefit, fifty *drammas*, dra. 50, were deposited in the treasury of Śrî Jayasvâmidêva for a yearly *bali*, on the ninth (9) of the light half of Mâgha, in the Saṁvat year 1320 (1264 A.D.)

16-18. In the *Bali* endowment wheat $1\frac{1}{2}$ seers, ghî 6 *karshas*, in the *naivêdya* 1 measure, *mung* $\frac{3}{4}$ measure, ghî $\frac{1}{2}$ *karsha*, Âbôti (?) $\frac{1}{4}$ *dramma*+2, Bhaṭa *lô* (?), for the price of flowers turmeric and aloe wood one *dramma*, for the price of leaves and betelnut one *dramma*, for the band of singing women one *dramma*.

19. So let six *drammas* be expended every year by the god from his treasury.

20-21. This *praśasti* was spoken (composed) by the Maha-(ttara?) Subhaṭa. It was written by Dêdâka, son of Nâgvala the Dhruva. It is engraved by the carpenter Bhîmasêna son of Gôgâ.

XI.—(S. 1330; A.D. 1264. No. 7 of Plan.) On the south face of the lower square section of the western side of the north pair of dome pillars. First $11\frac{1}{2}$ lines and lines 21 22 and half of 23 in verse, the rest in prose. No. 47 of the Bhâunagar State Collection. (Bhâu. Prâ. I. list page 14):

1. Namaḥ Śrî Vighnarâjâya namo dêvâya bhâsvatê namo . . .
2. Paramâna(ṁ) dadâyinô cakrapâṇayê | Kâyastha-vaṁśa prasavaḥ purâsît.
3. Śrî Sâḍha-nâmâ purushaḥ purâṇaḥ | Rishi . . . .
4. }
5. } Damaged and illegible.
6. }
7. . . . . dharmârtha . . . vigâha-
8. -mânô ânaṁdakâraḥ . . . . 5 janishṭa sâ
9. nuḥ Subhaṭa . . . . saubhâgya-sampal-lalitâ-

10. -bhidhânâ | trivarga-sâram tanaya-svarûpam .... sajjanâgryam Râjâdhi.
11. Râjôdaya-siha-deva-niḥśreyasê Śrî Subhaṭêna têna | dêvasya kośê ....
12. ..... mkshêpitam ..... || Têncaiva Maha° Subhaṭêna-sva śrê-
13. -yasê Saṁvat 1330 varshê Âśvina śu di 4 caturthîdinê divasa *bali-*
14. -pûjâ-prêkshaṇîyakârtha(ṁ) dêva Srî Jayasvâmi-bhâṇḍâ-gârê dra 50 paṁ-
15. -câśan drammâ nikshêpitâḥ || Tathâ Śrîkaraṇê Maha° Gajasthaprabhṛiti-
16. -paṁcakulaṁ upârâdhayita(-yati) | Balidinê varshanibaṁ-dhê kârâpita dra. 4 catu-
17. -ro drammâḥ prativarshaṁ svîya pastalâ bhâvya ... paṁ-cakulêna dâtâvyâḥ
18. Vali-nivaṁdhê gôdhûma sê 2 ghṛita ka 8 muga mâ | côshâṁ mâ ½ ghṛita ka ½ vyâ-
19. -sa-nirvâpa I Abôtî nirvâpa I Kuṁkumâguru dra. 2 pushpa dra. 2 patrapûga dra. 2.
20. Pramadâkula dra 2 êvam êtat prativarsham âcaṁdrârkkaṁ dêvêna kârâpyaṁ ||
21. Śrîsatya-ratna-pura-lâṭa-hradâdhikârî, Śrîmâladeśavahikâ-dhikṛi |
22. -to dhurînaḥ | vyâsêna caṇḍahariṇâ vidushâṁ varêṇa yo ...
dhyâpitaḥ sa vi-
23. -dadhê Subhataḥ praśastiṁ || Dhru° Dêdâkêna likhitâ sûtra° Gôshasthê-
24. -na utkirṇâ || ॐ ||

Translation.

1 - 2. Reverence to the Lord of Obstacles (Gaṇeśa). Reverence to the shining god. Reverence . . . to (Vishnu) the holder of the discus who bestows supreme happiness.

2 - 3. There was formerly an ancient man named Śrî Sâdha born of the Kâyastha race. Ṛishi ......

4 - 6. Illegible.

7 - 9. .... for righteousness .... entering ..... giving pleasure .... there was born a son Subhaṭa—

9 - 10. ... (a wife) Lalitâ by name, rich in excellence ... the summing-up of the three objects of human effort (religious merit, wealth, and pleasure) in the form of a son ..... the chief of the virtuous—

11. By that Śrî Subhaṭa for the spiritual benefit of the king of kings his majesty Udayastha in the treasury of the god .... deposited ......

12 - 15. By that same Maha° Subhaṭa for his own (spiritual) benefit in the Saṁvat year 1330 (1274 A.D.) on the fourth day of the bright half of Âśvina, for the day's *bali*, worship and *darśana* dra. 50, fifty *drammas* were deposited in the treasury of the god Śrî Jayasvâmi.

15 - 17. And he serves (propitiates?) the *paṁca* consisting of Maha° Gajastha and the rest at Śrî Karaṇa. On the *bali* day the four (4) *drammas* given for the *bali* endowment are to paid every year by the *paṁca* from their own ....

Appendix III.

BHINMAL.

Inscriptions.

18-20. In the *bali* endowment wheat *sê* 2, ghî *ka(rshas)* 8, *mung.* one measure, *côsha* ½ measure, ghî *ka(rsha)* ½, the Bhat's dole 1, the Abôtî's dole 1, turmeric and aloe-wood *dra.* 2, flowers *dra.* 2, leaves and betelnut *dra.* 2, the band of singing women *dra.* 2 : so is this to be given yearly by the god so long as sun and moon endure.

21-23. Subhaṭa, the officer of Srî Satyapura Ratnapura and Lâṭa-hrada, the chief set over the *vahikas* of the Śrîmâla country, who was taught by Canḍa Hari the purâṇik, best of the learned, composed the *praśasti.*

24. Written by Dêdâka the Dhruva and engraved by Gôshastha the carpenter.

XII.—(S. 1333; A.D. 1277. Not in Plan.) On the north bank of Jaikop lake on a fallen pillar to the west of Ghazni Khán's tomb. Lines 1-4 and half of line 5 and lines 18-22 (and perhaps 23 and 24) in verse, the rest in prose. No. 52 of the Bhâunagar State Collection (Bhâu. Prâ. I. list pages 15-16) :

1. Yaḥ purâtra mahâsthânê Śrîmâlê susamâgataḥ | sa deva(ḥ) Śrî
2. Mahâvîra . . . . bhayatrâtâ (?) prajñâ.
3. Yaṁ śaraṇaṁ gatâḥ | tasya Vîrajinêṁdrasya prajârthaṁ śâsanaṁ navaṁ || 2 Pâ-
4. -râpaddha-mahâgacchê puṇya-puṇya-svabhâvinâ(?) Śrî pûrṇacaṁdra-sûri-
5. ṇâ prasâdâl likhyatê yathâ || svasti Saṁvat 1333 varshê || Âśvi-
6. -na śu di 14 Sômê | adyêha Śrî Śrîmâlê Mahârâjakula Śrî Ca(?)
7. -ciga-dêva-kalyâṇa-vijayi-râjyê tanniyukta-maha° Gajastha-
8. -prabhṛiti-paṁcakula-pratipattâu Śrî Śrimâla-dêśa-vahikâdhikritêna
9. Naigamânvaya-kâyastha-mahattama-Subhaṭêna tathâ(ve ?) cêṭaka Karmasthê-
10. -na svaârêyasê Âśvinamâsîya-yâtrâ-mahôtsavê Âśvina Śu di 14 ca-
11. -turdaśî-dinê Śrî Mahâvîradêvâya prativarshaṁ paṁcôpacâra-pûjânimi-
12. -ttaṁ Śrîkaraṇîyapaṁcakulaṁ sêlahatha-ḍâsî-narapâla-varakti-pûrvasaṁbô-
13. -dhya-talapa-dêhala-sahaḍî-pada-ma . . . . hala-sahaḍî
14. da 5 saptaviśôpakôpê paṁcadrammâ samâ sêlahathâ--bhâvyê âṭha
15. drâ°. ma dra. 8 ashṭâu dramma : || ubhayaṁ saptaviśôpakôpêna trayôdaśa dra-
16. -mmâ âcaṁdrârkkaṁ dêvadâyê kârâpitâḥ || varttamâna-paṁca-kulêna va-
17. -rttamâna-sêlahathêna dêvadâyê kṛitam idaṁ svaśrêyasê pâlanîyaṁ ||
18. Yasmân paṁcakulô sarvô maṅtavyam iti sarvadâ | tasya tasya tadâ śrêyo
19. Yasya yasya yadâ padaṁ || || Śrîsatya-ratna-pura-Lâṭa-hradâdhikârî Śrî-
20. -mâla-dêśa-vahikâdhikṛito dhurîṇaḥ | vyâsêna Caṇḍahariṇâ vidushâṁ va-
21. -rêṇa yodhyâpitaḥ sa vidadhê Subhaṭaḥ praśastiṁ || ठ || Iyaṁ Gôgânujâtê-

22. (-na) sûtradhârêṇa dhîmatâ | utkîrṇâ Bhîmasthêna śâsanâkshara-mâlikâ |
23. . . sanam idaṁ maṭhapatimahendragoshṭika Âcaṁdra-pratipattâu || ठ ||
24. . . vasasamaya. . . . . (li) khitaṁ têna dhîmatâ | yo vâcayati puṇyâ-
25. . . . sata . . . . tî || ठ || ma(ṁ)gala-sadâśrṭh || śivamastu saṁp.

Translation.

1. The god Srî Mahâvîra who formerly came in(to) this great town Śrîmâla . . . . . in whom the wise protected from fear take refuge—a new ordinance is written as follows for the people's sake through the favour of that Vîra, chief of the Jinas by Srî Pûrṇacandra Sûri, whose nature is most holy.

5-9. Good luck! In the Saṁvat year 1333 (1277 A.D.), on Monday the 14th of the light half of Âśvina—on this day here in holy Śrîmâla in the prosperous and victorious reign of his majesty Śrî Caciga the Mahâraul, in the term of office of the *panch* (consisting of) Maha° Gajastha and others, appointed by him.

9-11. By Subhaṭa the leading Kâyastha, of the Naigama family, the officer in authority over the Vahikas of the Śrîmâla country, and by Karmastha the Cêṭaka (servant) (or vêṭaka), for their own (spiritual) benefit, at the great festival of the jatrâ of the month of Âśvina on the fourteenth day 14 of the light half of Âśvina, for the worship (consisting of) the five services yearly to the god Śrî Mahâvîra.

12-15. [These four lines seem to be made up chiefly of Prâkṛit words which I am unable to translate. They specify two sums, one of 5 and the other of 8 drammas.]

15-17. Both, with the twenty-seventh *upakopa* (?), the 13 *drammas* have been given in religious endowment. This which has been made as a religious endowment is to be maintained by the *paṁca* and by the *Sêlahatha* (?) officiating (from time to time) for their own (spiritual) benefit.

18-19. Because every *paṁca* is always to be honoured, the benefit (of maintaining the endowment) belongs to whomsoever at any time (holds) the office.

19-22. Subhaṭa, the officer of Śrîsatyapura Ratnapura and Lâṭahrada, the chief set over the *vahikas* of the Śrîmâla country, who was taught by Caṇḍahari the purâṇik, the best of the learned, composed the *praśasti*. The series of letters of this grant was engraved by the wise carpenter Bhîmastha the son of Gôga.

23-25. This grant was written by that wise one . . . at the time . . . . . in the term of office of the Abbot Mahêndra and the committeeman Âcaṁdra (?) . . who causes to speak . . . . . . Good luck! Bliss for ever! May it be auspicious . . . Finis.

XIII.—(S. 1334; A.D. 1278. No. 8 in Plan.) On the north face of the lower square section of the eastern of the north pair of dome pillars. All in prose:

1. Oṁ namaḥ Sûryâyaḥ || yasyôdayâstasamayê suramukuṭa-nispṛishṭa-caraṇa-

Appendix III.

BHINMAL. Inscriptions.

2. kamalo ऽ pi kurutê ऽ ṁjaliṁ trinêtra sajayati dhâmnâ(ṁ) nidhi(ḥ) sûryaḥ || | Saṁvat 1334.

3. Varshê Âśvina va di 8 adyêha S'rî Srîmâlê Mahârâjakula-Srî-Câciga-Kalyâna-vija-

4. -yá-râjyê tanniyukta-maha° . . . (si)ha-prabhṛiti-paṁcakula-pratipattâu | êvaṁ kâlê pravarttamânê

5. Câhumânânvayê Mahârâja(ku)la Śrî Samarasihâtmaja-Mahârâjâdhirâja-Śrî Udaya||

6. Sihadêvâṁgaja-S'rî Vâhaḍhasiha . . . . Śri Câmuṇḍa-râja-deva-śrêyasê maha°

7. Dêdâkêna . . . . . . Śrî Jagasvâmidêvîya bhâṇḍâgâre . . . bali . . . .

8. . . . dra. 100 śataṁ drammâ nikshêpitâ Âśvina-yâtrâyâ(ṁ) Âśvinâ vadi 8 ashṭamî-dinê divasa-bali ta-

9. -thâ aṁgabhôga . . . prêkshaṇika . . . . . . Śrîdêvîya-bhâṁḍâgârât kârâpaṇîya | bali-nibaṁdhê

10. gôdhûma sê 3 ghṛita ka 1 (naivêdyê) . . . . . côshâ(ṁ) mâ 2, muga sê ½, ghṛita ka ½ vyâsanirvâpa 1 Âbôṭt.

11. -nirvâpa 1 kuṁkumâguru-mûly(ê) dra. 2 tathâ pushpa-mûlyê dra. 2 (?) tathâ patrapûga-mûlyê dra. 2 pramadâ-kulê mûlyê dra. 2 ê-

12. -vaṁ êtat Vyâsa-Âbôṭika-śrêshṭi-goshṭika- . . kula-pramadâ-kula prabhritinâṁ varshaṁ varshaṁ pratî â-

13. caṁdrârka-yâvat tathâ . . . . . . itî kârâpaṇîya śrî-dêvêna kârâpaṇîya | pari kênâpi na karaṇî-

14. -yâ | likhitaṁ dhru° Nâgula-suta-Dêdâkêna . . . . . . hînâ-ksharam adhikâksharaṁ vâ sarvaṁ pramâṇa-

15. -miti || maṁgalaṁ sadâ śrîḥ || (sûtradhârêṇa ?) Nânâ-suta Dêpâla Saṁ 33 varshê Caitra va di 15 . . . . . . saha.

16. Maṇasihêna (?) . . . . . ||

Translation.

1-2. Ôṁ. Reverence to the Sun ! Victorious is that sun, the storehouse of brightness, at whose rising and setting the three-eyed (Śiva), even though (his own) lotus feet are touched by the diadems of the gods, folds his hands (in adoration).

2-4. In the *Saṁvat* year 1334 (1278 A.D.) on the 8th of the dark half of Âśvina—on this day here in holy Śrîmâla in the prosperous and victorious reign of his majesty the Mahâraul Śrî Câciga, in the term of office of the *paṁca* (consisting of) the Maha° . . . . Sîha and the rest, appointed by him—at this time

5-6. for the (spiritual) benefit of his majesty Śrî Câmuṇḍa-râja . . . . (son of) Śri-Vâhaḍhasiha the son of his majesty Śrî Udayasiha the Mahârâjâdhirâja, (who was) the son of his majesty the Mahâraul Śrî Samarasiha in the Câhumâna race

7. By the Maha° Dêdâka . . . . in the treasury of the god Śrî Jagasvâmi . . . . *bali* . . .

8. *dra.* 100, one hundred *drammas*, were deposited. At the Âśvina yâtrâ the day's *bali* on the eighth 8 of the dark half of Âśvina

Appendix III.

BHINMÁL.
Inscriptions.

9. and the *aṁgabhoga* . . *darśana*. . . to be expended from the treasury of the god. In the endowment of the *bali*

10-11. Wheat *sê*. 3: ghi *ka(rshas)* 1: in the *naivêdya* . . Côsha measures 2, munga *sê*. ⅔, ghi *ka(rsha)* ½, the Bhat's dole 1, the Âbôṭṭ's dole 1, for buying turmeric and aloe wood *dra*. 2, and for buying flowers *dra*. 2 (?), and for buying leaves and betel *dra*. 2, for the band of singing women *dra*. 2.

12-13. Thus this for the Bhat's, Âbôṭṭs, Committeemen, . . . , band of singing women &c. every year so long as sun and moon (endure) is so . . . . to be expended, is to be expended by the god. Interruption (?) is to be made by no one.

14. Written by Dêdâka son of Nâgula the *dhruva* . . . . the letter less or the letter more—all is of (no ?) authority.

15. Good luck ! Bliss for ever. By the carpenter Dêpâla son of Nânâ, on the 15th of the dark half of Çaitra in the year 33 . . .

16. By Maṛasiha (?) . . . .

XIV.—(S. 1339 ; A.D. 1283. Not on Plan.) In Báráji's rest-house on the south face of the first right pillar. Prose. No. 51 of the Bhâunagar State Collection (Bhâu. Prâ. I. list page 5) :

1. Ôṁ namaḥ Sûryâyaḥ || yasyôdayâstasamayê sura-mukuṭa-nispṛishṭa-caraṇa-

2. -kamalô pi | kurutê 'ṁjaliṁ trinêtra sa jayati dhâmnâṁ nidhiḥ sûryaḥ || saṁva

3. t. 1339 varshê Âśvina Su di | śanâv adyêha Srî Srîmâlê Mahârâja kula-Śrîsâmva-

4. -tastha-dêva-kalyâṇa-vîjaya-râjyê tanniyukta-mahâ° stha prabhṛiti-paṁcakûla-

5. pratipattau Srî Jâvâlipurât atrâyâta-Guhilô -Ru-

6. -drapâla-suta-sâha° Sahajapâlêna âtmaśrêyasê pitṛimâtṛiśrê-yasê bali-pujâ-

7. aṁga bhôga pratyaṁ(gaṁ) Srî Jayasvâmi-dêvâya Sûryadê-vâya bhâṁdâgârê (k)shêpita dra. 20 viṁ

8. śati drammâ || Svîya-Jâyakâsarahi Rudrâmârga-samîpe Kathara-pânâ-

9. âbhidhâna-kshêtra | êka pradattaḥ | dêvâya dinê pûjâ nimi(t) aṁ Sâha° Saha-

10. -ja-pâla-bhâryâ âtma-śrêyasê mâtâ-pitṛôśrêyasê bhaṁḍâgâre (k)shêpita-

11. dra. 10 dasa-drammâ . . . . : . . . . drammâ Asvi-

12. -na-yâtrâyâṁ Âśvina-śu-di | dinê divasa-bali-pujâ bhâṁḍâgârât Srîdêvê-

13. -na kârâpantyâ | vali-nivaṁdhê gôdhuma sê 2 ghṛita ka 8 naivêdyê côshâ(ṁ) pâ 2 mu-

14. -ga ghṛita ka ½ aṁgabhôgê patra-puga

15. pratyaṁ(gaṁ) dra. | Vyâsanirvâpa . . . . pôtî-nirvâpa | pramadâ-kula dra. 2 êtat saṁrva Srîdêvîya . . . .

Appendix III.

BHINMÁL.
Inscriptions.

16. kosa dra. . . . . pramadâkulêna . . . . âcamdrâ-kâlaṁ yâva
17. -t. . . . . nirvâpanîyaṁ ı kârâpanîyaṁ. . . . . nâgula-sutêna maha° Dê-
18. -dâkêna . . . .] Guhilô Sâha° Rudrapâla-suta-sôḍha° Harisihê na (Srîdê-)
19. -vîya-sthitaka dra. 4 • Sahajapâla-suta-sâ sthita-
20. -ka dra 4. . . . .
21-23. Illegible.

Translation.

1-2. Ôṁ. Reverence to the Sun ! Victorious is that sun, the storehouse of brightness, at whose rising and setting the three-eyed (Śiva), even though (his own) lotus feet are touched by the diadems of the gods, folds his hands (in adoration).

3-5. On Saturday the first of the light half of Âśvina in the year 1339 (1283 A.D.) on this day here in holy Śrîmâla, in the prosperous and victorious reign of his majesty the Mahâraul Srî Sâmvatastha, in the term of office of the *pamca* (consisting of) the maha° . . . . stha and the rest, appointed by him.

5-8. Dra. 20, twenty drammas, were deposited in the treasury for the sun-god Srî Jagasvâmi by Sâha° Sahajapâla son of Rudrapâla the Guhila, who came here from Srî Jávâlipura, for every part of the *bali*, the worship, and the *amgabhoga*, for his own (spiritual) benefit and for the benefit of his father and mother.

8-9. . . . . near the Rudrâ road 1 one field was given called Kathara-pânâ

9-11. To the god on . . . . day for worship, the wife of Sâha° Sahajapâla for her own benefit and for the benefit of her father and mother. . . . . deposited *dra.* 10, ten *drammas*. . . . .

11-12. *Drammas* in the Âśvina *Yâtrâ* on the first day of the light half of Âśvina are to be expended by the god from the treasury (for) the day's *bali*, worship. . . . .

13-17. In the *bali* endowment wheat *sê* 2. . . . . *ghi ka(rshas)* 8 : in the *nâivêdya côsha* pâ 2 mung . . . . . *ghi ka(rsha)* ½ : in the *amgabhôga* for every part of the leaves and betel dra. 1, the Bhat's dole . . . . , (the Âb)ôṭî's dole 1, the band of singing women dra. 2 ; all this the god's treasury *dra*. . . . . by the band of singing women . . . . so long as sun and moon endure . . . . is to be doled out, is to be expended.

17-20. By the Maha° Dêdâka son of Nâgula . . . . By Sôḍha° Harisiha son of Sâha° Rudrapâla the Guhila, four *sthitaka drammas* of the god . . . . By Sâ . . . . son of Sahajapâla . . . . *sthitaka drammas* 4. . . . .

21-23. Illegible.

XV.—(S. 1342 ; A.D. 1286. Not in Plan.) In the ground close to the wall on the right in entering the enclosure of old Mahâlakshmí's temple Prose. No. 50 of the Bhâunagar State Collection (Bhâu. Prâ. I. page 15.)

Appendix III.
BHINMÂL.
Inscriptions.

1. Ôṁ. Namaḥ Sûryâyaḥ || Yasyôdayâstasamayê sura-ma-
2. -kuṭa-nisprishṭa-caraṇa kamalô pi kurutê ऽ ṁjaliṁ trinêtra saja-
3. -yati dhâmnâṁ nidhiḥ sûryaḥ || Saṁvat 1342 (1286 A.D.) Âśvina vadi 10 Ra-
4. -vâvadyêha Śrî Śrîmâlê Mahârâjakula Śrî Śâmvatastha dê-
5. -va-kalyâṇa-vijaya-râjyê tanniyukta-maha° Pândyâ-prabhṛiti-paṁca-
6. -kula pratipattâu | Śâsanâksharâṇi praya(c)chati yathâ | Râṭhô-ḍa-
7. -jâtîya-Ûtisvatîha-pâutra Vâgasasuta Sîla° Alhaṇasthê-
8. -na âtmîya-mâtâ-pitrô śrêyasê svaśrêyasê Śrî Jagasvâmi-dê-
9. -vâya Âśvinê yâtrâyâṁ daśamîdinê divasa-bali-pûjâ prê-
10. -kshaṇîkâdi aṁga-bhôga-nimi(t)taṁ sêlahathâbhâvya-
11. -t Śrî kârâpita âcaṁdrârkayâvat pradatta dra. 4½.
12. Śrîdêvîya-kôṭa(ṭ)ṭ.
13. Âcaṁdrârkaṁ yaḥ kôpi Sêlahathô bhavati têna varshaṁ varshaṁ prati pâ-
14. -laniyaṁ ca | vahubhir vasudhâ bhuktâ râjabhi Sagarâdibhi yasya
15. yasya yadâ bhûmî tasya tasya tadâ phalaṁ || 1 Aśvina vadi 10 va-
16. -li-nibaṁdhê gôdhûma sê ghṛita ka 12 naivêdyê côshâṁ pâ 4.
17. mugâṁ mâ 1 ghṛita ka ½ Vyâsanirvâpa 1 Abôṭṭnirvâpa 1 kuṁkuma
18. kastûrî-pratyaṁ(gaṁ) dra. 4 pushpa-pratyaṁ(gaṁ) dra. 4 pramadâkula-pratyaṁ(gaṁ) dra. 4 patra-pû-
19. ga-pratyaṁ(gaṁ) dra. 4 êtat sarvaṁ varshaṁ 2 prati Śrî-dêvîya bhâṁḍâgârât
20. Varttâpakai kârâpanîyaṁ || maṁgalaṁ sadâśrîḥ || likhitaṁ Dhruva
21. Nâgula-suta-dhru° Dêdâkêna Utkîrṇṇâ sûtra° Bhîmasthêna||.

Translation.

1 - 3. Ôṁ. Reverence to the Sun ! Victorious is that sun, the storehouse of brightness, at whose rising and setting the three-eyed (Śiva), even though (his own) lotus feet are touched by the diadems of the gods, folds his hands (in adoration).

3 - 6. Saṁvat 1342 on Sunday the 10th of the dark half of Âśvina, on this day here in holy Śrîmâla, in the prosperous and victorious reign of his majesty the Maharâul Śrî Sâmvatastha-dêva, in the term of office of the *paṁca* (consisting of) Maha° Pândyâ and the rest, appointed by him, he sets forth the writing of the grant as follows.

6 - 11. By Sîla° Alhaṇastha son of Vâgasa and grandson of Ûtisvâtîha of the Râṭhôḍa race, for the benefit of his own mother and father and for his own benefit, 4½ *drammas* (were) given to the god Śrî Jagasvâmi, for the day's *bali*, the worship, the *darśana* &c., and the *aṁgabhôga* on the 10th day at the Âśvina yâtrâ . . . . so long as sun and moon (endure) . . . .

12 - 14. The god's treasure house . . . . . whosoever is Sêlahatha, by him every year it is to be maintained also. .

Appendix III.
BHINMÁL.
Inscriptions.

14 - 15. The earth has been enjoyed by many kings, beginning with Sagara. Whosesoever the earth is at any time, his is also the fruit thereof.

15 - 16. In the endowment of the *bali* for the 10th of the dark half of Âśvina wheat *sê* . . . . ghi *ka*(*rshas*) 12 : in the *naivedya côsha pâ* 4.

17 - 19. Mung *mâ* 1, ghi *ka* ½, the Bhat's dole 1, the Âbôṭî's dole 1, for turmeric and musk each dra. 4, for flowers each dra. 4, for the band of singing women each dra. 4, for leaves and betel each dra. 4.

19 - 21. All this is to be expended yearly from the god's treasury . . . . Good luck ! Bliss for ever. Written by Dhru° Dêdâka son of Dhruva Nâgula. Engraved by Bhîmasiha the carpenter.

XVI.—(S. 1345 ; A.D. 1289. No. 9 of Plan.) On the south face of the lower square section of the north-east corner pillar of the dome. The first thirteen lines are in verse, the rest in prose. No. 48 of the Bhâunagar State Collection (Bhâu. Prâ. I. list page 14) :-

1. Svargâpavargasukhadaṁ paramâtmarûpaṁ dhṛisayaṁti yaṁ sukṛitinô hṛidi sa-
2. -rvadâiva tasmâi namaj-janahitâya surâsurêṁdra saṁstûyamâna-caritâya
3. namaḥ Śivâya || 1 Ślâghyaḥ satâm sukṛitî sakṛitî manushyôs mânyô maha-
4. -ttama-guṇâi Subhataḥ sa êva | yaścâ jagattrayaguruṁ girijâdhinâthaṁ devaṁ
5. namasyati natô S nudinaṁ mahêśa || 2 Sômô S si nâtha natimattara-kâiravê-
6. -shu puṇya-Prabhâsa-sarasi sthitim âśritêshu | tasmâ . . . . . . mahâbdhi-
7. -tîrê Śrî Sômanâtha iti siddhigataṁ smarâmi || 3 Puṇyaiḥ Prabhâsaśaśi-bhûsha-
8. -ṇa-Kardamâla-pâpa-pramôcana-runârtti-vimôcanâdyaih | êtâiḥ Ka-
9. -pardi-kṛita-sat-tithibhiḥ pradhânais tîrthâir alaṁ kṛitam idaṁ hṛidayaṁ mamâstu ||
10. 4 Êtasya puṇya-payasô jaladhês tathâsya Sârasvata-nivahasyata.
11. Da° || Ôṁ namaḥ Sûryâyaḥ Jaj(j)yôti prasarati tarâm lôka kṛityâya ni-
12. -tyam | yannâmôktaṁ sakalakalushaṁ yâti pâraṁ payodhê | sarvasyâtmâ sugati-
13. -surathô -dhvâṁta-mâtaṁga-siṁgha | drishṭa-sûryô nava(bha) si bhagavâu sarvasyântyaṁka-
14. -rôti || Saṁvat 1345 varshê Mâgha Vadi 2 Sômê S dyêha Srî 2 mâlô mahârâja-
15. -kula-Śrî Sâmvata-siṁgha-dêva-kalyâṇa-vijaya-râjyê tanniyukta-maha° chaṁhâ-
16. -prabhṛiti-paṁcakula-pratipatâu êvaṁkâle pravarttamâne Śrî-Jâvâlipuravâstavya-
17. Puskaraṇisthânîya-yajur-vêda pâthakâya | Padamalasyagôtrâya | Vrâhma° na-
18. -vaghana-vaṁśotpannâdhyava° Vâlhapâutra | Jyôti° Mâdhava-pratidâuhitrâ Jyô°

19. Tilaka-dâuhitra-Soḍhala-putra-mâtu-Pûnala-suta | Vrâhma° Vâgaḍa saṁsârasyâ
20. Asâratâṁ jñâtvâ | Śrî Jagasvâmina | Śrîsûryasya mûrttô prâsâdê sâuvarṇṇaka-
21. -laśârôpita | jâtasradhâ dêvaṁ sampûjya samasta-dêva-lôka-Vrahma-lôka-pra-
22. -tyaksham | Vaṁśadvayôdharaṇa-samaksham | Âtmanaśca Âcaṁdrârkayâvat sûrya-prasâda-prâ-
23. -pta-tyarthaṁ | prativarshaṁ | pûjâṁ Śrî Jagasvâmi-dêva-bhâṁḍâgârê nikshipita | râukma-vî
24. sâna-prî-dra. 200 dvâu Śatâni Amîshâm drammânâm vyâjapadât A'svina-yâtrâyâṁ Aśvi-
25. -na vadi || dinê divasa-vali kâyôvali nivaṁdhê gôdhûma sê . 4 pakvê ghriṭa ||
26. ka 16 nâivêdyê côshâṁ mâ 1 muga mâ 1½ ghṛita ka | vîdakê patra 8 pûga 2 aṁga-
27. -bhôga-pratya° dra. 4 pushpa pratya° dra. 6 patrapûga-pratya° dra. 4 vyâsa-nirvâpa-Âbôṭî-nirvâ-
28. -pa-nivaṁdhê côshâṁ sê ¼ muga pâ 3 ghṛita ka 1 dakshiṇâ lô 2 pramadâkula dra. 4 êta-
29. -t sarvaṁ prativarshaṁ âcaṁdrârka-yâvat Śrîdevasya bhâṁḍâgârât vêcantyam kârâpa-
30. -nîyaṁ ca | subhaṁ bhavatu sarvadâ | Jyoti° Sûguda-sutêna Caṁdrâdityêna samakshaṁ li-
31. -khitaṁ Kava° Nâgula sutêna Dêdâkêna utkîrṇṇâ Sûtra° Nâná-suta-Dêpâlê-
32. -na || maṁgalaṁ sadâ Śrîḥ.

Translation.

1 - 3. Reverence to that Śiva ! the benefactor of those who bow to him, whose actions are praised by the leaders of gods and demons, who gives the happiness of heaven and of salvation, whose form is the supreme soul, whom the wise ever lay hold upon in (their) heart.

3 - 5. Oh Mahêśa, whosoever bowing daily does reverence to the god who is *guru* of the three worlds, the lord of the mountain's daughter (Pârvatî), that man is worthy of praise from the righteous, fortunate, wise, to be honoured for most excellent virtues, a true hero.

5 - 7. Oh Lord thou art the moon among the bending lotuses that have found their place in the holy pool of Prabhâsa : therefore I make mention (of thee) famous by the name of Sômanâtha on the seashore . . . .

7 - 9. May this heart of mine be adorned by these holy chief *tîrthas*, Prabhâsa, the moon's ornament, the Lotus (pool), the Release from Sin, the Release from Debt and Suffering &c., whose lucky days have been fixed by Kapardi (Śiva).

10. Of this pool of pure water and . . . . of Sarasvatî.
. . . . .

11. Da° Oṁ ! Reverence to the Sun, whose light ever reaches far for the work of mankind, at the mention of whose name all sin goes beyond the ocean : the soul of all, whose path and whose car are good, a lion to the trumpeting elephants (of darkness) : When the Lord Sun is seen in the sky, he makes the last (?) . . of all.

Appendix III.

BHINMÁL.

Inscriptions.

14-16. On Monday the second of the dark half of Mâgha in the Saṁvat year 1345 (1289 A.D.), on this day here in holy Śrîmâla, in the prosperous and victorious reign of his majesty the Mahâraul Śrî Sâmvata Siṁgha, in the term of office of the *paṁca* (consisting of) the Maha° Châmhâ and the rest, appointed by him.

16-21. At this time to (*read* by) Vâgaḍa the Brâhmaṇa son of Sôḍhala and grandson of Adhyava° Vâlhâ, of the Navaghana family, of the Padamala gôtra, student of the Yajurvêda, of the town of Puskariṇi and living in Śrî Jâvâlipura, son of his mother Pûnala, and daughter's son of Tilaka the Jôshî, and granddaughter's son of Mâdhava the Jôshî—recognizing the impermanence of this world, a golden *kalaśa* was set up on the palace . . . of the Sun Jagasvâmi.

21-24. (By him) worshipping the god in faith, before the world of the gods and the world of Brahma, for the purpose (?) of saving his ancestors in both lines, and himself, to gain the favour of the Sun so long as sun and moon (endure), (for) worship every year, 200 *Vîsalaprî drammas* in gold were deposited in the treasury of the god Śrî Jagasvâmi.

24-28. Out of the interest of these *drammas*, in the endowment of the day's *bali* and the *kâyôvali* on the 11th of the dark half of Âśvina at the Âśvina festival, wheat *sê* 4, ghî *ka(rshas)* 16: in the Nâivêdya côsha measure 1, mung *pâ*. 1½, ghî *ka(rsha)* 1, for *pânsupârî* leaves 8, betel 2: for the Aṁgabhôga severally dra. 4, for flowers severally *dra*. 6, for leaves and betel severally *dra*. 4 : in the endowment of the Bhat's dole and the Abôṭî's dole, *côsha* sê. ½, mung *pâ*. 3, ghî *ka(rsha)* 1, dakshiṇâ *lô* 2, the band of singing women *dra*. 4.

29-32. All this is to be separated and expended from the treasury of the god every year so long as sun and moon (endure). May it always be auspicious. Written by Dêdâka son of Kava° Nâgula for Caṁdrâditya son of Jyoti° Sûgada. Engraved by Dêpâla son of Nânâ the carpenter. Good luck! Bliss for ever!

APPENDIX IV.

JAVA AND CAMBODIA.

Appendix IV.

Java.

An incident redeems the early history of Gujarát from provincial narrowness and raises its ruling tribes to a place among the greater conquerors and colonisers. This incident is the tradition that during the sixth and seventh centuries fleets from the coasts of Sindh and Gujarát formed settlements in Java and in Cambodia. The Java legend is that about A.D. 603 Hindus led by Bhruvijáya Savelachála the son of Kasamachitra or Bálya Achá king of Kujrát or Gujarát settled on the west coast of the island.[1] The details of the settlement recorded by Sir Stamford Raffles[2] are that Kasamachitra, ruler of Gujarát, the tenth in descent from Arjun, was warned of the coming destruction of his kingdom. He accordingly started his son Bhruvijáya Savelachála with 5000 followers, among whom were cultivators artisans warriors physicians and writers, in six large and a hundred small vessels for Java. After a voyage of four months the fleet touched at an island they took to be Java. Finding their mistake the pilots put to sea and finally reached Matarem in the island of Java. The prince built the town of Mendang Kumulan. He sent to his father for more men. A reinforcement of 2000 arrived among them carvers in stone and in brass. An extensive commerce sprang up with Gujarát and other countries. The bay of Matarem was filled with stranger vessels and temples were built both at the capital, afterwards known as Brambanum, and, during the reign of Bhruvijáya's grandson Ardivijáya that is about A.D. 660, at Boro Buddor in Kedu.[3] The remark that an ancestor of the immigrant prince had changed the name of his kingdom to Gujarát is held by Lassen to prove that the tradition is modern. Instead of telling against the truth of the tradition this note is a strong argument in its favour. One of the earliest mentions of the name Gujarát for south Márwár is Hiuen Tsiang's (A.D. 630) Kiu-che-lo or Gurjjara. As when Hiuen Tsiang wrote the Gurjjara chief of Bhinmál, fifty miles west of Ábu, already ranked as a Kshatriya his family had probably been for some time established perhaps as far back as A.D. 490 a date by which the Mihira or Gurjjara conquest of Valabhi and north Gujarát was completed.[4] The

---

[1] Sir Stamford Raffles' Java, II. 83. From Java Hindus passed to near Banjar Massin in Borneo probably the most eastern of Hindu settlements (Jour. R. A. Soc. IV. 185). Temples of superior workmanship with Hindu figures also occur at Waahoo 400 miles from the coast. Dalton's Diaks of Borneo Jour. Asiatique (N. S.) VII. 153. An instance may be quoted from the extreme west of Hindu influence. In 1873 an Indian architect was found building a palace at Gondar in Abyssinia. Keith Johnson's Africa, 269.

[2] Raffles' Java, II. 65-85. Compare Lassen's Indische Alterthumskunde, II. 10, 40; IV. 460.

[3] Raffles' Java, II. 87.

[4] Compare Tod's Annals of Rájasthán (Third Reprint), I. 87. The thirty-nine Chohán successions, working back from about A.D. 1200 with an average reign of eighteen years, lead to A.D. 498.

Appendix IV.
JAVA.

details of the help received from Gujarát after the prince's arrival show that the parent state had weathered the storm which threatened to destroy it. This agrees with the position of the Bhinmál Gurjjaras at the opening of the seventh century, when, in spite of their defeat by Prabhákaravardhana (A.D. 600-606) the father of Śrí Harsha (A.D. 606-641) of Magadha, they maintained their power at Broach and at Valabhi as well as at Bhinmál.[1] The close relations between the Gurjjaras and the great seafaring Mihiras or Meds make it likely that the captains and pilots who guided the fleets to Java belonged to the Med tribe. Perhaps it was in their honour that the new Java capital received the name Mendan, as, at a later period it was called Brambanum or the town of Bráhmans. The fact that the Gurjjaras of Broach were sun-worshippers not Buddhists causes no difficulty since the Bhilmál Gurjjaras whom Hiuen Tsiang visited in A.D. 630 were Buddhists and since at Valabhi Buddhism Shaivism and sun-worship seem to have secured the equal patronage of the state.

Besides of Gujarát and its king the traditions of both Java and Cambodia contain references to Hastinagara or Hastinapura, to Taxila, and to Rumadesa.[2] With regard to these names and also with regard to Gandhára

---

[1] Compare Note on Bhinmál page 467.

[2] According to Cunningham (Ancient Geography, 43 and Beal's Buddhist Records, I. 109 note 92) the site of **Hastinagara** or the eight cities is on the Swát river eighteen miles north of Peshávar. In Vedic and early Mahábhárata times Hastinapura was the capital of Gandhára (Hewitt Jour. Roy. As. Soc. XXI. 217). In the seventh century it was called Pushkalávatí. (Beal's Buddhist Records, I. 109.) **Taxila**, the capital of the country east of the Indus, was situated about forty miles east of Attok at Sháhderi near Kálaka-sarai (Cunningham's Ancient Geography, 105). According to Cunningham (Ditto 109), Taxila continued a great city from the time of Alexander till the fifth century after Christ. It was then laid waste apparently by the great White Húna conqueror Mihirakula (A.D. 500-550). A hundred years later when Hiuen Tsiang visited it the country was under Kashmir, the royal family were extinct, and the nobles were struggling for power (Beal's Buddhist Records, I. 136). **Rumadesa.** References to Rumadesa occur in the traditions of Siam and Cambodia as well as in those of Java. Fleets of Rúm are also noted in the traditions of Bengal and Orissa as attacking the coast (Fergusson's Architecture, III. 640). Coupling the mention of Rúm with the tradition that the Cambodian temples were the work of Alexander the Great Colonel Yule (Ency. Brit. Article Cambodia) takes Rúm in its Musalmán sense of Greece or Asia Minor. The variety of references suggested to Fergusson (Architecture, III. 640) that these exploits are a vague memory of Roman commerce in the Bay of Bengal. But the Roman rule was that no fleet should pass east of Ceylon (Reinaud Jour. As. Ser. VI. Tom. I. page 322). This rule may occasionally have been departed from as in A.D. 166 when the emperor Marcus Aurelius sent an ambassador by sea to China. Still it seems unlikely that Roman commerce in the Bay of Bengal was ever active enough to gain a place as settler and coloniser in the traditions of Java and Cambodia. It was with the west not with the east of India that the relations of Rome were close and important. From the time of Mark Antony to the time of Justinian, that is from about B.C. 30 to A.D. 550, their political importance as allies against the Parthians and Sassanians and their commercial importance as controllers of one of the main trade routes between the east and the west made the friendship of the Kushans or Śakas who held the Indus valley and Baktria a matter of the highest importance to Rome. How close was the friendship is shown in A.D. 60 by the Roman General Corbulo escorting the Hyrkanian ambassadors up the Indus and through the territories of the Kusháns or Indo-Skythians on their return from their embassy to Rome. (Compare Rawlinson's Parthia, 271.) The close connection is shown by the accurate details of the Indus valley and Baktria recorded by Ptolemy (A.D. 166) and about a hundred years later (A.D. 247) by the author of the Periplus and by the special value of the gifts which the Periplus notices were set apart for the rulers of Sindh. One result of this long continued alliance was the gaining by the Kushán and other rulers of Peshawar and the Panjáb of a knowledge of Roman coinage astronomy and architecture. Certain Afghán or Baktrian coins bear the word Roma apparently the name of some Afghán city. In spite of this there seems no

and to Cambodía, all of which places are in the north-west of India, the question arises whether the occurrence of these names implies an historical connection with Kábul Pesháwar and the west Panjáb or whether they are mere local applications and assumptions by foreign settlers and converts of names known in the Bráhman and Buddhist writings of India.[1] That elaborate applications of names mentioned in the Mahábhárata to places in Java have been made in the Java version of the Mahábharáta is shown by Raffles.[2] Still it is to be noticed that the places mentioned above, Kamboja or Kábul, Gandhara or Pesháwar, Taxila or the west Panjáb, and Rumadesa apparently the south Panjáb are not, like Ayodhya the capital of Siam or like *Intha-patha-puri* that is Indraprastha or Dehli the later capital of Cambodia,[3] the names of places which either by their special fame or by their geographical position would naturally be chosen as their original home by settlers or converts in Java and Cambodia. Fair ground can therefore be claimed for the presumption that the leading position given to Kamboja, Gandhára, Taxila, and Rumadesa in Javan and Cambodian legends and place-names is a trace of an actual and direct historical connection between the north-west of India and the Malay Archipelago. This presumption gains probability by the argument from the architectural remains of the three countries which in certain peculiar features show so marked a resemblance both in design and in detail as in the judgment of Mr. Fergusson to establish a strong and direct connection.[4] A third argument in favour of a Gujarát strain in Java are the traditions of settlements and expeditions by the rulers of Málwa which are still current in south Márwár.[5] Further a proverb

---

reason to suppose that Rome attempted to overlord the north-west of India still less that any local ruler was permitted to make use of the great name of Rome. It seems possible that certain notices of the fleets of Rúm in the Bay of Bengal refer to the fleets of the Arab Al-Rami that is Lambri or north-west Sumatra apparently the Romania of the Chaldean breviary of the Malabár Coast. (Yule's Cathay, I. lxxxix. note and Marco Polo, II. 243.)

[1] Compare Fergusson's Architecture, III. 640; Yule in Ency. Brit. Cambodia.

[2] Java, I. 411. Compare Fergusson's Architecture, III. 640.

[3] See Yule in Jour. Roy. As. Soc. (N. S.), I. 356; Fergusson's Architecture, III. 631.

[4] Of the Java remains Mr. Fergusson writes (Architecture, III. 644-648): The style and character of the sculptures of the great temple of Boro Buddor are nearly identical with those of the later caves of Ajanta, on the Western Gháts, and in Salsette. The resemblance in style is almost equally close with the buildings of Takht-i-Bahi in Gandhára (Ditto, 647). Again (page 637) he says: The Hindu immigrants into Java came from the west coast of India. They came from the valley of the Indus not from the valley of the Ganges. Once more, in describing No. XXVI. of the Ajanta caves Messrs. Fergusson and Burgess (Rock-cut Temples, 345 note 1) write: The execution of these figures is so nearly the same as in the Boro Buddor temple in Java that both must have been the work of the same artists during the latter half of the seventh century or somewhat later. The Buddhists were not in Java in the fifth century. They must have begun to go soon after since there is a considerable local element in the Boro Buddor.

[5] Traditions of expeditions by sea to Java remain in Márwár. In April 1895 a bard at Bhinmál related how Bhojrája of Ujjain in anger with his son Chandraban drove him away. The son went to a Gujarát or Káthiáváda port obtained ships and sailed to Java. He took with him as his Bráhman the son of a Magh Pandit. A second tale tells how Vikram the redresser of evils in a dream saw a Javanese woman weeping, because by an enemy's curse her son had been turned into stone. Vikram sailed to Java found the woman and removed the curse. According to a third legend Chandraván the grandson of Vir Pramár saw a beautiful woman in a dream. He travelled everywhere in search of her. At last a Rishi told him the girl lived in Java. He started by sea and after many dangers and wonders found the dream-girl in Java. The people of Bhinmál are familiar with the Gujarát proverb referred to below Who goes to Java comes not back. MS. Notes, March 1895.

Appendix IV.

JAVA.

still well known both in Márwár and in Gujarát runs:

Je jae Jáve te kadi nahi áve
A've to sáth pidhi baithke khdve.

Who to Java roam ne'er come home.
If they return, through seven lives
Seated at ease their wealth survives.[1]

Once more the connection with Gujarát is supported by the detail in the Java account which makes Laut Mira the starting point for the colonising fleet. This Sir S. Raffles supposed to be the Red Sea but the Mihiras' or Meds' sea may be suggested as it seems to correspond to the somewhat doubtful Arab name Baharimad (sea of the Meds?) for a town in western India sacked by Junaid. Against this evidence two considerations have been urged[2]: (*a*) The great length of the voyage from Gujarát to Java compared with the passage to Java from the east coast of India; (*b*) That no people in India have known enough of navigation to send a fleet fit to make a conquest. As regards the length of the voyage it is to be remembered that though Sumatra is more favourably placed for being colonised from Bengal Orissa and the mouths of the Godávari and Krishna, in the case either of Java or of Cambodia the distance from the Sindh and Káthiáváda ports is not much greater and the navigation is in some respects both safer and simpler than from the coasts of Orissa and Bengal. In reply to the second objection that no class of Hindus have shown sufficient skill and enterprise at sea to justify the belief that they could transport armies of settlers from Gujarát to Java, the answer is that the assumption is erroneous. Though the bulk of Hindus have at all times been averse from a seafaring life yet there are notable exceptions. During the last two thousand years the record of the Gujarát coast shows a genius for seafaring fit to ensure the successful planting of north-west India in the Malay Archipelago.[3]

---

[1] Another version is:

Je jáe Jáve te phari na áve
Jo phari áve to paryn parya khdve
Etalu dhan ldve.

Who go to Java stay for aye.
If they return they feast and play
Such stores of wealth their risks repay.

[2] Compare Crawford (A.D. 1820) in As. Res. XIII. 157 and Lassen Ind. Alt. II. 1043.

[3] The following details summarise the available evidence of Gujarát Hindu enterprise by sea. According to the Greek writers, though it is difficult to accept their statements as free from exaggeration, when, in B.C. 325, Alexander passed down the Indus the river showed no trace of any trade by sea. If at that time sea trade at the mouth of the Indus was so scanty as to escape notice it seems fair to suppose that Alexander's ship-building and fleet gave a start to deep-sea sailing which the constant succession of strong and vigorous northern tribes which entered and ruled Western India during the centuries before and after the Christian era continued to develope.* According to Vincent (Periplus, I. 25, 35, 254) in the time of Agatharcides (B.C. 200) the ports of Arabia and Ceylon were entirely in the hands of the people of Gujarát. During the second century after Christ, when, under the great Rudradáman (A.D. 143-158), the Sinh or Kshatrapa dynasty of Kathiavada was at the height of its power, Indians of Tientço, that is Sindhu, brought presents by sea to China (Journal Royal Asiatic Society for January 1896 page 9). In A.D. 166 (perhaps the same as the preceding) the Roman emperor Marcus Aurelius sent by sea to China ambassadors with ivory rhinoceros' horn and other articles apparently the produce of Western India (DeGuignes' Huns, I. [Part I.] 32). In the third century A.D. 247 the Periplus (McCrindle, 17, 52, 64, 96, 109)

* Alexander built his own boats on the Indus. (McCrindle's Alexander, 77.) He carried (pages 93 and 131) these boats to the Hydaspes: on the Jhelum (134 note 1) where he found some country boats he built a flotilla of gallies with thirty oars: he made dockyards (pages 156-157), his crews were Phoenikians, Cyprians, Karians, and Egyptians.

notices large Hindu ships in the east African Arab and Persian ports and Hindu settlements on the north coast of Sokotra. About a century later occurs the doubtful reference (Wilford in Asiatic Researches, IX. 224) to the Diveni or pirates of Diu who had to send hostages to Constantine the Great (A.D. 320 - 340) one of whom was Theophilus afterwards a Christian bishop. Though it seems probable that the Kshatrapas (A.D. 70 - 400) ruled by sea as well as by land fresh seafaring energy seems to have marked the arrival on the Sindh and Káthiáváḍ coasts of the Juan-Juan or Avars (A.D. 390 - 450) and of the White Húṇas (A.D. 450 - 550). During the fifth and sixth centuries the ports of Sindh and Gujarát appear among the chief centres of naval enterprise in the east. How the sea ruled the religion of the newcomers is shown by the fame which gathered round the new or revised gods Śiva the Poseidon of Somnáth and Krishna the Apollo or St. Nicholas of Dwarka. (Compare Tod's Annals of Rájasthán, I. 525.) In the fifth century (Yule's Cathay, I. lxxviii.) according to Hamza of Ispahán, at Hira near Kufa on the Euphrates the ships of India and China were constantly moored. In the early sixth century (A.D. 518 - 519) a Persian ambassador went by sea to China (Ditto, I. lxxiv.) About the same time (A.D. 526) Cosmas (Ditto, I. clxxviii.) describes Sindhu or Debal and Orhota that is Soratha or Verával as leading places of trade with Ceylon. In the sixth century, apparently driven out by the White Húṇas and the Mihiras, the Jats from the Indus and Kachh occupied the islands in the Bahrein gulf, and perhaps manned the fleet with which about A.D. 570 Naushiraván the great Sassanian (A.D. 531 - 574) is said to have invaded the lower Indus and perhaps Ceylon.* About the same time (Fergusson Architecture, III. 612) Amrávati at the Krishna mouth was superseded as the port for the Golden Chersonese by the direct voyage from Gujarát and the west coast of India. In A.D. 630 Hiuen Tsiang (Beal's Buddhist Records, II. 269) describes the people of Suráshtra as deriving their livelihood from the sea, engaging in commerce, and exchanging commodities. He further notices that in the chief cities of Persia Hindus were settled enjoying the full practice of their religion (Reinaud's Abulfeda, ccclxxxv.) That the Jat not the Arab was the moving spirit in the early (A.D. 637 - 770) Muhammadan sea raids against the Gujarát and Konkan coasts is made probable by the fact that these seafaring ventures began not in Arabia but in the Jat-settled shores of the Persian Gulf, that for more than fifty years the Arab heads of the state forbad them, and that in the Mediterranean where they had no Jat element the Arab was powerless at sea. (Compare Elliot, I. 416,417.) That during the seventh and eighth centuries when the chief migrations by sea from Gujarát to Java and Cambodia seem to have taken place, Chinese fleets visited Diu (Yule's Cathay, lxxix.), and that in A.D. 759 Arabs and Persians besieged Canton and pillaged the storehouses going and returning by sea (DeGuignes' Huns, I. [Pt. II.] 503) suggest that the Jats were pilots as well as pirates.† On the Sindh Kachh and Gujarát coasts besides the Jats several of the new-come northern tribes showed notable energy at sea. It is to be remembered that as detailed in the Statistical Account of Thána (Bombay Gazetteer, XIII. Part II. 433) this remarkable outburst of sea enterprise may have been due not only to the vigour of the new-come northerners but to the fact that some of them, perhaps the famous iron-working Turks (A.D. 580 - 680), brought with them the knowledge of the magnet, and that the local Bráhman, with religious skill and secrecy, shaped the bar into a divine fish-machine or *machiyantra*, which, floating in a basin of oil, he consulted in some private quarter of the ship and when the stars were hid guided the pilot in what direction to steer. Among new seafaring classes were, on the Makran and Sindh

* Reinaud's Mémoire Sur L'Inde, 125. The statement that Naushiraván received Karáchi from the king of Seringdip (Elliot's History, I. 407 : Tabari, II. 221) throws doubt on this expedition to Ceylon. At the close of the sixth century Karáchi or Diul Sindhi cannot have been in the gift of the king of Ceylon. It was in the possession of the Sáharái kings of Aror in Upper Sindh perhaps of Sháhi Tegin Devaja shortened to Shahindev. (Compare Cunningham Oriental Congress, I. 243.) According to Garrez (J. As. Ser. VI. Tom. XIII. 182 note 2) this Serendip is Surandeb that is Syria and Antioch places which Naushiraván is known to have taken. Several other references that seem to imply a close connection between Gujarát and Ceylon are equally doubtful. In the Mahábhárata (A.D. 100 - 300?) the Sinhalas bring *vaidúryas* (rubies?) elephants' housings and heaps of pearls. The meaning of Sainhalaka in Samudragupta's inscription (A.D. 395) Early Gujarát History page 64 and note 5 is uncertain. Neither Mihirakula's (A.D. 530) nor Lalitáditya's (A.D. 700) conquest of Ceylon can be historical. In A.D. 1005 when Abul Fatha the Carmatian ruler of Multán was attacked by Mahmud of Ghazni he retired to Ceylon. (Reinaud's Mémoire, 225). When Somnáth was taken (A.D. 1025) the people embarked for Ceylon (Ditto, 270).

† Compare at a later period (A.D. 1342) Ibn Batuta's great ship sailing from Kandahár (Gandhár north of Broach) to China with its guard of Abyssinians as a defence against pirates. Reinaud's Abulfeda, clxxv.

Appendix IV.

Java.

east coast of India and that Bengal Orissa and Masulipatam had a large

---

coasts the Bodhas Kerks and Meds and along the shores of Kachh and Káthiáváda the closely connected Meds and Gurjjaras. In the seventh and eighth centuries the Gurjjaras, chiefly of the Chápa or Chávadá clan, both in Dwárka and Somnáth and also inland, rose to power, a change which, as already noticed, may explain the efforts of the Jats to settle along the Persian Gulf and the Red Sea. About A.D. 740 the Chápas or Chávadás, who had for a century and a half been in command in Dwárka and Somnáth, established themselves at Anahilaváda Pattan. According to their tradition king Vanarája (A.D. 720-780) and his successor Yogarája (A.D. 806-841) made great efforts to put down piracy. Yogarája's sons plundered some Bengal or Bot ships which stress of weather forced into Veraval. The king said 'My sons with labour we were raising ourselves to be Chávadás of princely rank; your greed throws us back on our old nickname of Choras or thieves.' Yogarája refused to be comforted and mounted the funeral pyre. Dr. Bhagvanlál's History, 154. This tale seems to be a parable. Yogarája's efforts to put down piracy seem to have driven large bodies of Jats from the Gujarát coasts. In A.D. 834-35, according to Ibn Alathyr (A.D. 834), a fleet manned by Djaths or Jats made a descent on the Tigris. The whole strength of the Khiláfat had to be set in motion to stop them. Those who fell into the hands of the Moslems were sent to Anararbe on the borders of the Greek empire (Reinaud's Fragments, 201-2). As in the legend, the Chavadá king's sons, that is the Chauras Mers and Gurjjaras, proved not less dangerous pirates than the Jats whom they had driven out.* About fifty years later, in A.D. 892, Al-Biláduri describes as pirates who scoured the seas the Meds and the people of Saurashtra that is Devpatan or Somnáth who were Choras or Gurjjaras.† Biláduri (Reinaud Sur L'Inde, 169) further notices that the Jats and other Indians had formed the same type of settlement in Persia which the Persians and Arabs had formed in India. During the ninth and tenth centuries the Gujarát kingdom which had been established in Java was at the height of its power. (Ditto, Abulfeda, ccclxxxviii.) Early in the tenth century (A.D. 915-930) Masudi (Yule's Marco Polo, II. 344; Elliot, I. 65) describes Sokotra as a noted haunt of the Indian corsairs called Bawárij which chase Arab ships bound for India and China. The merchant fleets of the early tenth century were not Arab alone. The Chauras of Anahilaváda sent fleets to Bhot and Chin (Rás Mála, I. 11). Nor were Mers and Chauras the only pirates. Towards the end of the tenth century (A.D. 980) Grahári the Chudásama, known in story as Graharipu the Ahir of Sorath and Girnár, so passed and repassed the ocean that no one was safe (Ditto, I. 11). In the eleventh century (A.D. 1021) Alberuni (Sachau, II. 104) notes that the Bawárij, who take their name from their boats called *behra* or *bira*, were Meds a seafaring people of Kachh and of Somnáth a great place of call for merchants trading between Sofala in east Africa and China. About the same time (A.D. 1025) when they despaired of withstanding Máhmud of Ghazni the defenders of Somnáth prepared to escape by sea,‡ and after his victory Mahmud is said to have planned an expedition by sea to conquer Ceylon (Tod's Rajasthán, I. 108). In the twelfth century Idrisi (A.D. 1135) notices that Tatariya dirhams, that is the Gupta (A.D. 319-500) and White Húṇa (A.D. 500-580) coinage of Sindh and Gujarát, were in use both in Madagascar and in the Malaya islands (Reinaud's Mémoires, 236), and that the merchants of Java could understand the people of Madagascar (Ditto, Abulfeda, cdxxii).¶ With the decline of the power of Anahiláváda (A.D. 1250-1300) its fleet ceased to keep order at sea. In A.D. 1290 Marco Polo (Yule's Ed. II. 325, 328, 341) found the people of Gujarát the most desperate

* As an example of the readiness with which an inland race of northerners conquer seamanship compare the Franks of the Pontus who about A.D. 279 passed in a few years from the Pontus to the Mediterranean ports and leaving behind them Malta the limit of Greek voyages sailed through Gibraltar to the Baltic. Gibbon, I. 404-405.

† Reinaud's Mémoire Sur L'Inde, 200. The traders of Chorwár, that is of the old Chaura or Chápa country near Virával and Mangrul, are now known in Bombay as Chápadias. The received explanation of Chápadia is the roofed men it is said in derisive allusion to their large and heavy headdress. But as the Porbandar headdress is neither specially large nor ungraceful the common explanation can be hardly more than a pun. This suggests that the name Chápadia is a trace of the early Chápa tribe of Gurjjaras who also gave their name to Chápanir. Tod's (Western India, 250, 256) description of the Chauras race with traditions of having come from the Red Sea and as a nautical Arabia is the result of taking for Sokotra Sankodwára that is Bet to the north of Dwárka.

‡ According to Abulfeda A.D. 1334 (Reinaud's Abulfeda, ccexlix.) some of the besieged fled to Ceylon. Farishtah (Briggs' Muhammadan Powers, I. 75) records that after the fall of Somnáth Mahmud intended to fit out a fleet to conquer Ceylon and Pegu. According to Bird (Mirát-i-Ahmedi, 146) Ceylon or Sirandip remained a dependency of Somnáth till A.D. 1290 when the king Vijayabáhu became independent.

¶ The common element in the two languages may have been the result of Gujarát settlements in Madagascar as well as in Java and Cambodia. This is however doubtful as the common element may be either Arabic or Polynesian.

share in colonising both Java and Cambodia cannot be doubted.[1]

---

pirates in existence. More than a hundred corsair vessels went forth every year taking their wives and children with them and staying out the whole summer. They joined in fleets of twenty to thirty and made a sea cordon five or six miles apart. Sokotra was infested by multitudes of Hindu pirates who encamped there and put up their plunder to sale. Ibn Batuta (in Elliot, I. 344 - 345) fifty years later makes the same complaint. Musalmán ascendancy had driven Rájput chiefs to the coast and turned them into pirates. The most notable addition was the Gohils who under Mokheráji Gohil, from his castle on Piram island, ruled the sea till his power was broken by Muhammad Tughlak in A.D. 1345 (Rás Mala, I. 318). Before their overthrow by the Muhammadans what large vessels the Rájput sailors of Gujarát managed is shown by Friar Oderic, who about A.D. 1321 (Stevenson in Kerr's Voyages, XVIII. 324) crossed the Indian ocean in a ship that carried 700 people. How far the Rajputs went is shown by the mention in A.D. 1270 (Yule's Cathay, 57 in Howorth's Mongols, I. 247) of ships sailing between Sumena or Somnáth and China. Till the arrival of the Portuguese (A.D. 1500 - 1508) the Ahmedábád Sultáns maintained their position as lords of the sea.* In the fifteenth century Java appears in the state list of foreign bandars which paid tribute (Bird's Gujarát, 131), the tribute probably being a cess or ship tax paid by Gujarát traders with Java in return for the protection of the royal navy.† In east Africa, in A.D. 1498 (J. As. Soc. of Bengal, V. 784) Vasco da Gama found sailors from Cambay and other parts of India who guided themselves by the help of the stars in the north and south and had nautical instruments of their own. In A.D. 1510 Albuquerque found a strong Hindu element in Java and Malacca. Sumatra was ruled by Parameshwara a Hindu whose son by a Chinese mother was called Rajput (Commentaries, II. 63; III. 73 - 79). After the rule of the sea had passed to the European, Gujarát Hindus continued to show marked courage and skill as merchants seamen and pirates. In the seventeenth century the French traveller Mandelslo (A.D. 1638, Travels 101, 108) found Achin in north Sumatra a great centre of trade with Gujarát. During the seventeenth and eighteenth centuries the Sanganians or Sangar Rajputs of Mándvi in Kachh and of Navánagar in north Káthiáváḍa were much dreaded. In A.D. 1750 Grose describes the small cruisers of the Sanganians troubling boats going to the Persian Gulf, though they seldom attacked large ships. Between A.D. 1803 and 1808 (Low's Indian Navy, I. 274) pirates from Bet established themselves in the ruined temple at Somnáth. In 1820, when the English took Bet and Dwarka from the Wághels, among the pirates besides Wághels were Badhels a branch of Rahtors, Bhattis, Khárwás, Lohánás, Makwánás, Rahtors, and Wagharis. A trace of the Chauras remained in the neighbouring chief of Aramra.‡ Nor had the old love of seafaring deserted the Káthiáváda chiefs. In the beginning of the present century (A.D. 1823) Tod (Western India, 452; compare Rás Mála, I. 245) tells how with Biji Singh of Bhávnagar his port was his grand hobby and shipbuilding his chief interest and pleasure; also how Ráo Ghor of Kachh (A.D. 1760 - 1778) built equipped and manned a ship at Mándvi which without European or other outside assistance safely made the voyage to England and back to the Malabar Coast where arriving during the south-west monsoon the vessel seems to have been wrecked.§

[1] Crawford (A.D. 1820) held that all Hindu influence in Java came from Kalinga or north-east Madras. Fergusson (Ind. Arch. 103, Ed. 1876) says: The splendid remains at Amrávati show that from the mouths of the Krishna and Godávari the Buddhist of north and north-west India colonised Pegu, Cambodia, and eventually the Island of Java. Compare Tavernier (A.D. 1666: Ball's Translation, I. 174.) Masulipatam is the

---

* When in A.D. 1535 he secured Bahádur's splendid jewelled belt Humayun said These are the trappings of the lord of the sea. Bayley's Gujarát, 386.

† Compare in Bombay Public Diary 10, pages 197 - 207 of 1736-37, the revenue headings Surat and Cambay with entries of two per cent on all goods imported and exported from either of these places by traders under the Honourable Company's protection.

‡ These Badhels seem to be Hamilton's (A.D. 1720) Warels of Chance (New Account, I. 141). This Chance is Chách near Diu apparently the place from which the Bhátiás get their Bombay name of Cháchiás. Towards the close of the eighteenth century Bhátiás from Chách seem to have formed a pirate settlement near Dahánu on the Thána coast. Major Price (Memoirs of a Field Officer, 322) notes (A.D. 1792 June) the cautionary speed with which in travelling from Surat to Bombay by land they passed Dáhánu through the Chánsiáh jungle the district of a piratical community of that name.

§ According to Sir A. Burnes (Jl. Bombay Geog. Soc. VI. (1835) 27, 28) the special skill of the people of Kachh in navigation and ship-building was due to a young Rajput of Kachh, Rámsingh Málani, who about a century earlier had gone to Holland and learned those arts. See Bombay Gazetteer, V. 116 note 2.

Appendix IV.

JAVA.

Reasons have been given in support of the settlement in Java of large bodies of men from the north-west coasts of India and evidence has been offered to show that the objections taken to such a migration have little practical force. It remains to consider the time and the conditions of the Gujarát conquest and settlement of Java and Cambodia. The Javan date S. 525 that is A.D. 603 may be accepted as marking some central event in a process which continued for at least half a century before and after the beginning of the seventh century. Reasons have been given for holding that neither the commercial nor the political ascendancy of Rome makes it probable that to Rome the Rúm of the legends refers. The notable Roman element in the architecture of Java and Cambodia may suggest that the memory of great Roman builders kept for Rome a place in the local legends. But the Roman element seems not to have come direct into the buildings of Java or Cambodia; as at Amrávati at the Krishna mouth, the classic characteristics came by way of the Panjáb (Táhia) only, in the case of Java, not by the personal taste and study of a prince, but as an incident of conquest and settlement.[1] Who then was the ruler of Rúm near Taxila, who led a great settlement of Hindus from the Panjáb to Java. Names in appearance like Rome, occur in north-west India. None are of enough importance to explain the prince's title.[2] There remains the word *raum* or *rum* applied to salt land in the south Panjáb, in Márwár, and in north Sindh.[3] The great battle of Kárur, about sixty miles south-east of Multán, in which apparently about A.D. 530 Yaśodharmman of Málwa defeated the famous White Húṇa conqueror Mihirakula (A.D. 500 - 550) is described as fought in the land of Rúm.[4] This great White Húṇa defeat is apparently the origin of the legend of the prince of Rúm who retired by sea to Java. At the time of the battle of Kárur the south Panjáb, together with the north of Sindh, was under the Sábaráis of Aror in north Sindh, whose coins show them to have been not only White Húṇas, but of the same Jávla family which the great conquerors Toramáṇa

---

only place in the Bay of Bengal from which vessels sail eastwards for Bengal, Arrakan, Pegu, Siam, Sumatra, Cochin China, and the Manillas and west to Hormuz, Makha, and Madagascar. Inscriptions (Indian Antiquary, V. 314 ; VI. 356) bear out the correctness of the connection between the Kalinga coast and Java which Java legends have preserved. As explained in Dr. Bhandarkar's interesting article on the eastern passage of the Śakas (Jour. B. B. R. A. S. XVII.) certain inscriptions also show a Magadhi element which may have reached Java from Sumatra and Sumatra from the coast either of Bengal or of Orissa. Later information tends to increase the east and south Indian share. Compare Notices et Extraits des Manuscripts de la Bibliotheque Nationale Vol. XXVII. (Partie II) 2 Fasicule page 350.

[1] Compare Hiuen Tsiang in Beal's Buddhist Records, II. 222 note 102. *Táhia* may be Tochara that is Baktria, but the Panjab seems more likely. Compare Beal's Life of Hiuen Tsiang, 136 note 2.

[2] Idrísi A.D. 1135 (Elliot, I. 92) has a Romala a middling town on the borders of the desert between Multán and Seistán. Cunningham (Ancient Geog. 252) has a Romaka Bazaar near where the Nára the old Indus enters the Ran of Kachh.

[3] Cunningham's Num. Chron. 3rd Ser. VIII. 241. The Mahábhárata Romakas (Wilson's Works, VII. 176 : Cunningham's Anc. Geog. 187) may have taken their name from one of these salt stretches. Ibn Khurdádbah (A.D. 912) mentions Rumala (Elliot, I. 14, 87, 92, 93) as one of the countries of Sindh. In connection with the town Romala Al Idrísi A.D. 1153 (Elliot, I. 74, 93) has a district three days' journey from Kalbata.

[4] Cunningham's Numismatic Chronicle 3rd Ser. VIII. 236. The date of Kárur is uncertain. Fergussor (Arch. III. 746) puts it at A.D. 544. It was apparently earlier as in an inscription of A.D. 532 Yaśodharmman king of Málwa claims to hold lands which were never held by either Guptas or Húṇas. Cunningham Num. Chron. 3rd Ser. VIII. 236. Compare History Text, 76,77.

and Mibirakula adorned. So close a connection with Mihirakula makes it probable that the chief in charge of the north of the Aror dominions shared in the defeat and disgrace of Kárur. Seeing that the power of the Sáharáis of Aror spread as far south as the Káthiáváḍa ports of Somnáth and Diu, and probably also of Diul at the Indus mouth, if the defeated chief of the south Panjáb was unable or unwilling to remain as a vassal to his conqueror, no serious difficulty would stand in the way of his passage to the seaboard of Aror or of his finding in Diu and other Sindh and Gujarát ports sufficient transport to convey him and his followers by sea to Java.[1] This then may be the chief whom the Cambodian story names Phra Tong or Thom apparently Great Lord that is Mahárája.[2]

The success of the Javan enterprise would tempt others to follow especially as during the latter half of the sixth and almost the whole of the seventh centuries, the state of North India favoured migration. Their defeats by Sassanians and Turks between A.D. 550 and 600 would close to the White Húṇas the way of retreat northwards by either the Indus or the Kábul valleys. If hard pressed the alternative was a retreat to Kashmir or an advance south or east to the sea. When, in the early years of the seventh century (A.D. 600-606), Prabhákaravardhana the father of Śrí Harsha of Magadha (A.D. 610-642) defeated the king of Gandhára, the Húṇas, the king of Sindh, the Gurjjaras, the Láṭas, and the king of Malava,[3] and when, about twenty years later, further defeats were inflicted by Śrí Harsha himself numbers of refugees would gather to the Gujarát ports eager to escape further attack and to share the prosperity of Java. It is worthy of note that the details of Prabhákaravardhana's conquests explain how Gandhára and Láṭa are both mentioned in the Java legends; how northerners from the Panjáb were able to pass to the coast; how the Márwár stories give the king of Málwa a share in the migrations; how the fleets may have started from any Sindh or Gujarát port; and how with emigrants may have sailed artists and sculptors acquainted both with the monasteries and stupas of the Kábul valley and Peshâwar and with the carvings of the Ajanta caves. During the second half of the seventh century the advance of the Turks from the north and of the Arabs both by sea (A.D 637) and through Persia (A.D. 650-660);[4] the conquering progress of a Chinese army from Magadha to Bamian in A.D. 645-650[5]; the overthrow (A.D. 642) of

[1] Jour. As. Soc. Bl. VII. (Plate I.) 298; Burnes' Bokhára, III. 76; Elliot's History, I. 405. Diu which is specially mentioned as a Sáharái port was during the seventh and eighth centuries a place of call for China ships. Yule's Cathay, I. lxxix.

[2] Phra like the Panjáb Porus of the embassy to Augustus in B.C. 30 (though this Porus may be so called merely because he ruled the lands of Alexander's Porus) may seem to be the favourite Parthian name Phraates. But no instance of the name Phraates is noted among White Húṇa chiefs and the use of Phra as in Phra Bot or Lord Buddha seems ground for holding that the Phra Thong of the Cambodia legend means Great Lord.

[3] Epigraphia Indica, I. 67.

[4] In A.D. 637 raiders attacked Thána from Oman and Broach and Sindh from Bahrein. Reinaud's Mémoire Sur L'Inde, 170, 176.

[5] The passage of a Chinese army from Magadha to the Gandhára river about A.D. 650 seems beyond question. The emperor sent an ambassador Ouang-h-wuentse to Śrí Harsha. Before Ouang-h-wuentse arrived Śrí Harsha was dead (died A.D. 642), and his place taken by an usurping minister (Se)na-fu-ti) Alana-chun. The usurper drove off the envoy, who retired to Tibet then under the great Songbtsan. With help from Tibet and from the Rája of Nepál Ouang returned, defeated Alana, and pursued him to the Gandhára river (Khien-to-wei). The passage was forced, the army captured, the king queen and king's sons were led prisoners to China, and 580 cities surrendered, the magistrates proclaimed the victory in the temple of the ancients and the emperor raised Ouang to the rank of Tch'ao-san-ta-fore. Journal Asiatique Ser.

Appendix IV.

JAVA.

the Buddhist Sáharáis by their usurping Bráhmanist minister Chach and his persecution of the Jats must have resulted in a fairly constant movement of northern Indians southwards from the ports of Sindh and Gujarát.[1] In the leading migrations though fear may have moved the followers, enterprise and tidings of Java's prosperity would stir the leaders. The same longing that tempted Alexander to put to sea from the Indus mouth; Trajan (A.D. 116) from the mouth of the Tigris; and Mahmúd of Ghazni from Somnáth must have drawn Śaka Húṇa and Gurjjara chiefs to lead their men south to the land of rubies and of gold.[2]

Of the appearance and condition of the Hindus who settled in Java during the seventh and eighth centuries the Arab travellers Sulaimán A.D. 850 and Masúdi A.D. 915 have left the following details. The people near the volcanoes have white skins pierced ears and shaved heads: their religion is both Bráhmanic and Buddhist; their trade is in the costliest articles camphor aloes cloves and sandalwood.[3]

CAMBODIA.

CAMBODIA.

The close connection between Java and Cambodia, the alternate supremacy of Cambodia in Java and of Java in Cambodia, the likelihood of settlers passing from Java to Cambodia explain, to a considerable extent, why the traditions and the buildings of Java and Cambodia should point to a common origin in north-west India. The question remains: Do the people and buildings of Cambodia contain a distinct north Hindu element which worked its way south and east not by sea but by land across the Himalayas and Tibet and down the valley of the Yang-tse-kiang to Yunnan and Angkor. Whether the name Cambodia[4] proves an actual raçe or historical connection with Kamboja or the Kábul valley is a point

IV. Tom. X. pages 81-121. The translator thinks the whole war was in the east of India and that the mention of the Gandhára river is a mistake. The correctness of this view is doubtful. It is to be remembered that this was a time of the widest spread of Chinese power. They held Balk and probably Bamian. Yule's Cathay, I. lxviii. Compare Julien in Jour. As. Soc. Ser. IV. Tom. X. 289-291.

[1] Regarding these disturbances see Beal's Life of Hiuen Tsiang, 155; Max Müller's India, 286. The Arab writers (A.D. 713) notice to what a degraded state Chach had reduced the Jats. In comparing the relative importance of the western and eastern Indian strains in Java it is to be remembered that the western element has been overlaid by a late Bengal and Kalinga layer of fugitives from the Tibetan conquest of Bengal in the eighth century, the Babu with the Gurkha at his heels, and during the ninth and later centuries by bands of Buddhists withdrawing from a land where their religion was no longer honoured.

[2] In A.D. 116 after the capture of Babylon and Ctesiphon Hadrian sailed down the Tigris and the Persian Gulf, embarked on the waters of the South Sea, made inquiries about India and regretted he was too old to get there. Rawlinson's Ancient Monarchies, VI. 313.

[3] Reinaud's Abulfeda, ccexc.

[4] The origin of the name Kámboja seems to be Kámbojápura an old name of Kábul preserved almost in its present form in Ptolemy's (A.D. 160) Kaboura. The word is doubtfully connected with the Achæmenian Kambyses (B.C. 529-521) the Kambujiya of the Behistun inscription. In the fifth of the Aśoka edicts (B.C. 240) Kámboja holds the middle distance between Gandhára or Peshávar and Yona or Baktria. According to Yáska, whose uncertain date varies from B.C. 500 to B.C. 200, the Kámbojas spoke Sanskrit (Muir's Sanskrit Texts, II. 355 note 145). In the last battle of the Mahábhárata, A.D. 100 to 300 (Jl. Roy. As. Soc. [1842] VII. 139-140), apparently from near Bamian the Kambojas ranked as Mlechchhas with Śakas Daradas and Húṇas. One account (Fergusson, III. 665) places the original site of the Kambojas in the country round Taxila east of the Indus. This is probably incorrect. A trace of the Kambojas in their original seat seems to remain in the Kaumojas of the Hindu Kush.

Appendix IV.

CAMBODIA.

on which authorities disagree. Sir H. Yule held that the connection was purely literary and that as in the case of Inthapatha-puri or Indraprastha (Dehli) the later capital of Cambodia and of Ayodhya or Oudh the capital of Assam no connection existed beyond the application to a new settlement of ancient worshipful Indian place-names. The objection to applying this rule to Cambodia is that except to immigrants from the Kábul valley the name is of too distant and also of too scanty a reputation to be chosen in preference to places in the nearer and holier lands of Tirhut and Magadha. For this reason, and because the view is supported by the notable connection between the two styles of architecture, it seems advisable to accept Mr. Fergusson's decision that the name Cambodia was given to a portion of Cochin-China by immigrants from Kamboja that is from the Kábul valley. Traces remain of more than one migration from India to Indo-China. The earliest is the mythic account of the conversion of Indo-China to Buddhism before the time of Aśoka (B C. 240). A migration in the first century A.D. of Yavanas or Śakas, from Tamluk or Ratnávate on the Hugli, is in agreement with the large number of Indian place-names recorded by Ptolemy (A.D. 160).[1] Of this migration Hiuen Tsiang's name Yavana (Yen-mo-na) for Cambodia may be a trace.[2] A Śaka invasion further explains Pausanias' (A.D. 170) name Sakæa for Cochin-China and his description of the people as Skythians mixed with Indians.[3] During the fifth and sixth centuries a fresh migration seems to have set in. Cambodia was divided into shore and inland and the name Cambose applied to both.[4] Chinese records notice an embassy from the king of Cambodia in A.D. 617.[5] Among the deciphered Cambodian inscriptions a considerable share belong to a Bráhmanic dynasty whose local initial date is in the early years of the seventh century,[6] and one of whose kings Somaśarmman (A.D. 610) is recorded to have held daily Mahábhárata readings in the temples.[7] Of a fresh wave of Buddhists, who seem to have belonged to the northern branch, the earliest deciphered inscription is A.D. 953 (S. 875) that is about 350 years later.[8] Meanwhile, though, so far as information goes, the new capital of Angkor on the north bank of lake Tale Sap about 200 miles up the Mekong river was not founded till A.D. 1078 (S. 1000),[9] the neighbourhood of the holy lake was already sacred and the series of temples of which the Nakhonwat or Nága's Shrine[10] is one of the latest and finest examples, was begun at least as early as A.D. 825 (S. 750), and

---

[1] See Hunter's Orissa, I. 310.

[2] Yavana to the south-west of Siam. Beal's Life of Hiuen Tsiang, xxxii.

[3] Quoted in Bunbury's Ancient Geography, II. 659. Bunbury suggests that Pausanias may have gained his information from Marcus Aurelius' (A.D. 166) ambassador to China.

[4] Jour. Bengal Soc. VII. (I.) 317.

[5] Remusat Nouveaux Melanges Asiatiques, I. 77 in Jour. Asiatique Series, VI. Tom. XIX. page 199 note 1; Fergusson's Architecture, III. 678.

[6] Barth in Journal Asiatique Ser. VI. Tom. XIX. page 150.

[7] Barth in Journal Asiatique, X. 57.

[8] Barth in Jour. As. Ser. VI. Tom. XIX. page 190; Journal Royal Asiatic Society, XIV. (1882) cii.

[9] Barth in Journal Asiatique Ser. VI. Tom. XIX. pages 181, 186.

[10] Mr. Fergusson (Architecture page 666) and Colonel Yule (Ency. Brit. Cambodia) accept the local Buddhist rendering of Nakhonwat as the City Settlement. Against this it is to be noted (Ditto ditto) that *nagara* city corrupts locally into Angkor. Nagara therefore can hardly also be the origin of the local Nakhon. Further as the local Buddhists claim the temple for Buddha they were bound to find in Nakhon some source other than its original meaning of Snake. The change finds a close parallel in the Nága that is snake or Skythian now Nágara or city Bráhman of Gujarát.

Appendix IV.
CAMBODIA.

Nakhonwat itself seems to have been completed and was being embellished in A.D. 950 (S. 875).[1] During the ninth and tenth centuries by conquest and otherwise considerable interchange took place between Java and Cambodia.[2] As many of the inscriptions are written in two Indian characters a northern and a southern[3] two migrations by sea seem to have taken place one from the Orissa and Masulipatam coasts and the other, with the same legend of the prince of Rúm land, from the ports of Sindh and Gujarát.[4] The question remains how far there is trace of such a distinct migration as would explain the close resemblance noted by Fergusson between the architecture of Kashmir and Cambodia as well as the northern element which Fergusson recognises in the religion and art of Cambodia.[5] The people by whom this Panjáb and Kashmir influence may have been introduced from the north are the people who still call themselves Khmers to whose skill as builders the magnificence of Cambodian temples lakes and bridges is apparently due.[6] Of these people, who, by the beginning of the eleventh century had already given their name to the whole of Cambodia, Alberuni (A.D. 1031) says: The Kumairs are whitish of short stature and Turk-like build. They follow the religion of the Hindus and have the practice of piercing their ears.[7] It will be noticed that so far as information is available the apparent holiness of the neighbourhood of Angkor had lasted for at least 250 years before A.D. 1078 when it was chosen as a capital. This point is in agreement with Mr. Fergusson's view that the details of Nakhonwat and other temples of that series show that the builders came neither by sea nor down the Ganges valley but by way of Kashmir and the back of the Himalayas.[8] Though the evidence is incomplete and to some extent speculative the following considerations suggest a route and a medium through which the Roman and Greek elements in the early (A.D. 100-500) architecture of the Kábul valley and Peshawar may have been carried inland to Cambodia. It may perhaps be accepted that the Ephthalites or White Húṇas and a share of the Kedarites, that is of the later Little Yuechi from Gandhára the Peshawar country, retreated to Kashmir before the father of Srí Harsha (A.D. 590-606) and afterwards (A.D. 606-642) before Śrí Harsha himself.[9] Further it seems fair to assume that from

---

[1] Barth in Journal Asiatique Ser. VI. Tom. XIX. 190.

[2] Yule's Marco Polo, II. 108; Reinaud's Abulfeda, cdxvi.

[3] Barth in Journal Asiatique Ser. VI. Tom. XIX. 174.

[4] Mr. Fergusson at first suggested the fourth century as the period of migration to Cambodia. He afterwards came to the conclusion that the settlers must have been much the same as the Gujarát conquerors of Java. Architecture, III. 665 - 678.

[5] Fergusson Architecture, 665. Compare Tree and Serpent Worship, 49, 50. The people of Cambodia seem Indian serpent worshippers: they seem to have come from Taxila.

[6] The name Khmer has been adopted as the technical term for the early literature and arts of the peninsula. Compare Barth J. As. Ser. VI. Tom. XIX. 193; Renan in ditto page 75 note 3 and Ser. VII. Tom. VIII. page 68; Yule in Encyclopædia Britanica Art. Cambodia. The resemblance of Cambodian and Kábul valley work recalls the praise by Chinese writers of the Han (B.C. 206 - A.D. 24) and Wei (A.D. 386 - 556) dynasties of the craftsmen of Kipin, that is Kophene or Kamboja the Kábul valley, whose skill was not less remarkable in sculpturing and chiselling stone than in working gold silver copper and tin into vases and other articles. Specht in Journal Asiatique, II. (1883), 333 and note 3. A ninth century inscription mentions the architect Achyuta son of Ráma of Kámboja. Epigraphia Indica, I. 243.

[7] Reinaud's Abulfeda, cdxxi.; Sachau's Alberuni, I. 210.

[8] Fergusson's Architecture, III. 666.

[9] For the joint Kedarite-Ephthalite rule in Kashmir see Cunningham's Ninth Oriental Congress, I. 231-2. The sameness of names, if not an identity of rulers, shows how close was the union between the Ephthalites and the Kedarites. The coins preserve one difference depicting the Yuechi or Kedarite ruler with bushy and the White Húṇa or Ephthalite ruler with cropped hair.

Kashmir they moved into Tibet and were the western Turks by whose aid in the second half of the seventh century Srongbtsan or Srongdzan-gambo (A.D. 640-698), the founder of Tibetan power and civilization, overran the Tarim valley and western China.[1] During the first years of the eighth century (A.D. 703) a revolt in Nepal and the country of the Bráhmans was crushed by Srongdzan's successor Donsrong,[2] and the supremacy of Tibet was so firmly established in Bengal that, for over 200 years, the Bay of Bengal was known as the sea of Tibet.[3] In A.D. 709 a Chinese advance across the Pamirs is said to have been checked by the great Arab soldier Kotieba the comrade of Muhammad Kasim of Sindh.[4] But according to Chinese records this reverse was wiped out in A.D. 713 by the defeat of the joint Arab and Tibet armies.[5] In the following years, aided by disorders in China, Tibet conquered east to Hosi on the upper Hoangho and in A.D. 729 ceased to acknowledge the overlordship of China. Though about A.D. 750 he was for a time crippled by China's allies the Shado Turks the chief of Tibet spread his power so far down the Yangtsekiang valley that in A.D. 787 the emperor of China, the king of Yunnan to the east of Burma, certain Indian chiefs, and the Arabs joined in a treaty against Tibet. As under the great Thisrong (A.D. 803-845) and his successor Thi-tsong-ti (A.D. 878-901) the power of Tibet increased it seems probable that during the ninth century they overran and settled in Yunnan.[6] That among the Tibetans who passed south-east into Yunnan were Kedarites and White Húnas is supported by the fact that about A.D. 1290, according both to Marco Polo and to Rashid-ud-din, the common name of Yunnan was Kárájang whose capital was Yachi and whose people spoke a special language.[7] The name Kárájang was Mongol meaning Black People and was used to distinguish the mass of the inhabitants from certain fair tribes who were known as Chaganjang or Whites. That the ruler of Kárájang was of Hindu origin is shown by his title Mahara or Mahárája. That the Hindu element came from the Kábul valley is shown by its Hindu name of Kandhar that is Gandhára or Peshávar, a name still in use as Gandálarit (Gandhára-rashtra) the Burmese for Yunnan.[8] The strange confusion which Rashid-ud-din makes between the surroundings of Yunnan and of Peshávar is perhaps due to the fact that in his time the connection between the two places was still known and admitted.[9] A further trace

---

[1] About A.D. 700 Urumtsi Kashgar Khoten and Kuche in the Tarim valley became Tibetan for a few years. Parker's Thousand Years of the Tartars, 243. In A.D. 691 the western Turks who for some years had been declining and divided were broken by the great eastern Turk conqueror Mercho. The following passage from Masúdi (Prairies D'Or, I. 289) supports the establishment of White Húna or Mihira power in Tibet. The sons of Amúr (a general phrase for Turks) mixed with the people of India. They founded a kingdom in Tibet the capital of which they called Med.

[2] Encyclopædia Britannica Articles Tibet and Turkestan.

[3] Both Ibn Haukal and Al Istakhri (A.D. 950) call the Bay of Bengal the sea of Tibet. Compare Reinaud's Abulfeda, ccclviii.; Encyclopædia Britannica Article Tibet page 345. [4] Yule's Cathay, I. lxxxi. [5] Ency. Brit. China, 646.

[6] Thisrong besides spreading the power of Tibet (he was important enough to join with Mámún the son of the great Harun-ar-Rashid (A.D. 788-809) in a league against the Hindus) brought many learned Hindus into Tibet, had Sanskrit books translated, settled Lamaism, and built many temples. It is remarkable that (so far as inscriptions are read) the series of Nakhonwat temples was begun during Thisrong's reign (A.D. 803-845). [7] Yule's Marco Polo, II. 39-42; J. R. A. Soc. I. 355.

[8] Yule Jour. R. A. Soc. (N. S.) I. 356.

[9] Compare Yule in Jour. R. A. S. (N. S.) I. 355. Kandahar in south-west Afghanistán is another example of the Kedarite or Little Yuechi fondness for giving to their colonies the name of their parent country.

Appendix IV.

CAMBODIA.

of stranger whites like the Chaganjang of Yunnan occurs south-east in the Anin or Honli whose name suggests the Húṇas and whose fondness for silver ornaments at once distinguishes them from their neighbours and connects them with India.[1] Even though these traces may be accepted as confirming a possible migration of Húṇas and Kedaras to Yunnan and Anin a considerable gap remains between Anin and Angkor. Three local Cambodian considerations go some way to fill this gap. The first is that unlike the Siamese and Cochin Chinese the Khmers are a strong well made race with very little trace of the Mongoloid, with a language devoid of the intonations of other Indo-Chinese dialects, and with the hair worn cropped except the top-knot. The second point is that the Khmers claim a northern origin; and the third that important architectural remains similar to Nakhonwat are found within Siam limits about sixty miles north of Angkor.[2] One further point has to be considered: How far is an origin from White Húṇas and Kedáras in agreement with the Nága phase of Cambodian worship. Hiuen Tsiang's details of the Tarim Oxus and Swát valleys contain nothing so remarkable as the apparent increase of Dragon worship. In those countries dragons are rarely mentioned by Fa Hian in A.D. 400: dragons seem to have had somewhat more importance in the eyes of Sung-Yun in A.D. 520; and to Hiuen Tsiang, the champion of the Maháyána or Broadway, dragons are everywhere explaining all misfortunes earthquakes storms and diseases. Buddhism may be the state religion but the secret of luck lies in pleasing the Dragon.[3]

---

[1] Compare Yule's Marco Polo, II. 82-84.

[2] Yule in Ency. Brit. Art. Cambodia, 724, 725, 726.

[3] Fa Hian (A.D. 400) about fifty miles north-west of Kanauj found a dragon chapel (Beal's Buddhist Records, I. 40) of which a white eared dragon was the patron. The dragon, he notes, gives seasonable showers and keeps off all plagues and calamities. At the end of the rains the dragon turns into a little white-eared serpent and the priests feed him. At the deserted Kapilavastu in Tirhut Fa Hian was shown a tank and in it a dragon who, he says, constantly guards and protects a tower to Buddha and worships there night and morning (Ditto, I. 50).

Sung-Yun (A.D. 519) notices (Beal's Buddhist Records, I. 69) in Swát (Udyána) a tank and a temple with fifty priests called the temple of the Nága Rája because the Nága supplies it with funds. In another passage (Ditto, 92) he notices that in a narrow land on the border of Posse (Fars) a dragon had taken his residence and was stopping the rain and piling the snow. Hiuen Tsiang (Ditto, I. 20) notes that in Kucha, north of the Tarim river east of the Bolor mountains, the Shen horses are half dragon horses and the Shen men half-dragon men. In Aksu, 150 miles west of Kucha, fierce dragons molest travellers with storms of flying sand and gravel (Ditto, 25); the hot lake or Johai, 100 miles north-east of Aksu, is jointly inhabited by dragons and fish; scaly monsters rise to the surface and travellers pray to them (Ditto, 26). An Arhat (page 63) prays that he may become a Nágarája. He becomes a Nágarája, kills the real Nágarája, takes his palace, attaches the Nágas to him, and raises winds and tempests; Kanishka comes against him and the Arhat takes the form of a Bráhman and knocks down Kanishka's towers. A great merit-flame bursts from Kanishka's shoulders and the Bráhman Nágarája apologises. His evil and passionate spirit, the fruit of evil deeds in a former birth, had made the Arhat pray to be a Nágarája. If clouds gathered the monks knew that the Nágarája meant mischief. The convent gong was beaten and the Nágarája pacified (or scared) Ditto, 64-66. Nágas were powerful brutes, cloud-riding wind-driving water-walking brutes, still only brutes. The account of the Nága or dragon of Jelalábád (in Kambojia) is excellent. In Buddha's time the dragon had been Buddha's milkman. He lost his temper, laid flowers at the Dragon's cave, prayed he might become a dragon, and leaped over the cliff. He laid the country waste and did so much harm that Tathágata (or Buddha) converted him. The Nága asked Buddha to take his cave. Buddha said No. I will leave my shadow. If you get angry look at my shadow and it will quiet you (Ditto,

This apparent increased importance of dragon or Nága worship in north-west India during the fifth and sixth centuries may have been due partly to the decline of the earlier Buddhism partly to the genial wonder-loving temper of Hiuen Tsiang. Still so marked an increase makes it probable that with some of the great fifth and sixth century conquerors of Baktria Kábul and the Panjáb, of whom a trace may remain in the snake-

---

94). Another typical dragon is Apalála of the Swát river (Ditto, 68). In the time of Kaśyapa Buddha Apalála was a weaver of spells named Gangi. Gangi's spells kept the dragons quiet and saved the crops. But the people were thankless and paid no tithes. May I be born a dragon, cursed Gangi, poisonous and ruinous. He was born the dragon of the Swát valley, Apalála, who belched forth a salt stream and burned the crops. The ruin of the fair and pious valley of Swát reached Śakya's (Buddha's) ears. He passed to Mangala and beat the mountain side with Indra's mace. Apalála came forth was lectured and converted. He agreed to do no more mischief on condition that once in twelve years he might ruin the crops. (Ditto, 122.) In a lake about seven miles west of Takshaśilá, a spot dear to the exiled Kambojan, lived Elápatra the Nágarája, a Bhikshu or ascetic who in a former life had destroyed a tree. When the crops wanted rain or fair weather, the Shamans or medicine-men led the people to pray at Elápatra's tank (page 137). In Kashmir, perhaps the place of halt of the Kambojan in his conquests eastwards, in old times the country was a dragon lake.* Madhyantika drove out the waters but left one small part as a house for the Nága king (I. 150). What sense have these tales? In a hilly land where the people live in valleys the river is at once the most whimsical and the most dangerous force. Few seasons pass in which the river does not either damage with its floods or with its failure and at times glaciers and landslips stop the entire flow and the valley is ruined. So great and so strange an evil as the complete drying of a river must be the result of some one's will, of some one's temper. The Dragon is angry he wants a sacrifice. Again the river ponds into a lake, the lake tops the earth bank and rushes in a flood wasting as only a dragon can waste. For generations after so awful a proof of power all doubts regarding dragons are dead. (Compare Drew's Cashmere and Jummoo, 414-421.) In India the Chinese dragon turns into a cobra. In China the cobra is unknown: in India than the cobra no power is more dreaded. How can the mighty unwieldy dragon be the little silent cobra. How not? Can the dragon be worshipful if he is unable to change his shape. To the spirit not to the form is worship due. Again the worshipped dragon becomes the guardian. The great earth Bodhisattva transforms himself into a Nágarája and dwells in lake Anavatapta whose flow of cool water enriches the world (Buddhist Records, II. 11). In a fane in Swát Buddha takes the form of a dragon and the people live on him (125). A pestilence wasted Swát. Buddha becomes the serpent Suma, all who taste his flesh are healed of the plague (126). A Nága maiden, who for her sins has been born in serpent shape and lives in a pool, loves Buddha who was then a Śakya chief. Buddha's merit regains for the girl her lost human form. He goes into the pool slays the girl's snake-kin and marries her. Not even by marriage with the S'akya is her serpent spirit driven out of the maiden. At night from her head issues a nine-crested Nága. S'akya strikes off the nine crests and ever since that blow the royal family has suffered from headaches (132). This last tale shows how Buddhism works on the coarser and fiercer tribes who accept its teaching. The converts rise to be men though a snake-head may peep out to show that not all of the old leaven is dead. In other stories Buddha as the sacramental snake shows the moral advance in Buddhism from fiend to guardian worship. The rest of the tales illustrate the corresponding intellectual progress from force worship to man, that is mind, worship. The water force sometimes kindly and enriching sometimes fierce and wasting becomes a Bodhisattva always kindly though his goodwill may have to give way to the rage of evil powers. So Bráhmanism turns Náráyana the sea into Śiva or Somnáth the sea ruler. In this as in other phases religion passes from the worship of the forces of Nature to which in his beginnings man has to bow to the worship of Man or conscious Mind whose growth in skill and in knowledge has made him the Lord of the forces. These higher ideals are to a great extent a veneer. The Buddhist evangelist may dry the lake; he is careful to leave a pool for the Nágarája. In times of trouble among the fierce struggles of pioneers and settlers the spirit of Buddha withdraws and leaves the empty shrine to the earlier and the more immortal spirit of Force, the Nágarája who has lived on in the pool which for the sake of peace Buddha refrained from drying.

* Kashmir has still a trace of Gandhára. Compare (Ency. Brit. Art. Kashmir page 13: The races of Kashmir are Gandháras, Khasás, and Daradas.

Appendix IV.
CAMBODIA.

worshipping Nágas and Takkas of the Kamaon and Garhwal hills, the Dragon was the chief object of worship. Temple remains show that the seventh and eighth century rulers of Kashmir, with a knowledge of classic architecture probably brought from beyond the Indus were Nága worshippers.[1] The fact that the ninth century revision of religion in Tibet came mainly from Kashmir and that among the eighteen chief gods of the reformed faith the great Serpent had a place favours the view that through Tibet passed the scheme and the classic details of the Kashmir Nága temples which in greater wealth and splendour are repeated in the Nakhonwat of Angkor in Cambodia.[2] It is true that the dedication of the great temple to Nága worship before the Siamese priests filled it with statues of Buddha is questioned both by Lieut. Garnier and by Sir H. Yule.[3] In spite of this objection and though some of the series have been Buddhist from the first, it is difficult to refuse acceptance to Mr. Fergusson's conclusions that in the great Nákhon, all traces of Buddhism are additions. The local conditions and the worshipful Tale Sap lake favour this conclusion. What holier dragon site can be imagined than the great lake Tale Sap, 100 miles by 30, joined to the river Mekong by a huge natural channel which of itself empties the lake in the dry season and refills it during the rains giving a water harvest of fish as well as a land harvest of grain. What more typical work of the dragon as guardian water lord. Again not far off betwen Angkor and Yunnán was the head-quarters of the dragon as the unsquared fiend. In Carrajan ten days west of the city of Yachi Marco Polo (A.D. 1200) found a land of snakes and great serpents ten paces in length with very great heads, eyes bigger than a loaf of bread, mouths garnished with pointed teeth able to swallow a man whole, two fore-legs with claws for feet and bodies equal in bulk to a great cask. He adds: 'These serpents devour the cubs of lions and bears without the sire and dam being able to prevent it. Indeed if they catch the big ones they devour them too: no one can make any resistance. Every man and beast stands in fear and trembling of them.' Even in these fiend dragons was the sacramental guardian element. The gall from their inside healed the bite of a mad dog, delivered a woman in hard labour, and cured itch or it might be worse. Moreover, he concludes, the flesh of these serpents is excellent eating and toothsome.[4]

---

[1] Mr. Fergusson (Architecture, 219) places the Káshmir temples between A.D. 600 and 1200 and allots Mártand the greatest to about A.D. 750. The classical element, he says, cannot be mistaken. The shafts are fluted Grecian Doric probably taken from the Gandhára monasteries of the fourth and fifth centuries. Fergusson was satisfied (Ditto, 289) that the religion of the builders of the Káshmir temples was Nága worship. In Cambodia the Bráhman remains were like those of Java (Ditto, 667). But the connection between the Nakhonwat series and the Káshmir temples was unmistakeable (Ditto, 297, 665). Naga worship was the object of both (Ditto, 677-679). Imperfect information forced Fergusson to date the Nakhonwat not earlier than the thirteenth century (Ditto, 660, 679). The evidence of the inscriptions which (J. As. Ser. VI. Tom. XIX. page 190) brings back the date of this the latest of a long series of temples to the ninth and tenth centuries adds greatly to the probability of some direct connection between the builders of the Mártand shrine in Káshmir and of the great Nakhonwat temple at Angkor.

[2] Ency. Brit. Art. Tibet, 344.

[3] Ency. Brit. Art. Cambodia.

[4] Yule's Marco Polo, II. 45, 47.

APPENDIX V.

ARAB REFERENCES.[1]

Appendix V.

ARAB REFERENCES, A.D. 851-1350.

THE earliest Arab reference to Gujarát is by the merchant Sulaimán[2] A.D. 851 (A.H. 237). Other Arab accounts follow up to A.D. 1263, a period of over four centuries. Sulaimán describes Jurz or Gujarát as bordering on the kingdom of the Balhára (A.D. 743-974) and as forming a tongue of land, rich in horses and camels and said to have "mines of gold and silver, exchanges being carried on by means of these metals in dust."

Al Biláduri[3] (A.D. 892) states that the first Islámic expedition to India was the one despatched against *Táná*[4] (Thána) by Usmán, son of Al-Ási the Thakafi, who in the fifteenth year of the Hijrah (A.D. 636) was appointed governor of Bahrein and Umán (the Persian Gulf) by the second Khalífah Umar, the son of Khattáb. On the return of the expedition, in reply to his governor's despatch, the Khalífah Umar is said to have written:[5] "Oh brother of Thakif, thou hast placed the worm in the wood, but by Alláh, had any of my men been slain, I would have taken an equal number from thy tribe." In spite of this threat Usmán's brother Hakam, who was deputed by the governor to the charge of Bahrein, despatched a force to Bárúz[6] (Broach). Al Biláduri does not record the result of this expedition, but

---

[1] Contributed by Khán Sáheb Fazlulláh Lutfulláh Farídi of Surat.

[2] This account which is in two parts is named Silsilát-ut-Tawárikh, that is the Chain of History. The first part was written in A.D. 851-52 by Sulaimán and has the advantage of being the work of a traveller who himself knew the countries he describes. The second part was written by Abu Zeid-al-Hasan of Siráf on the Persian Gulf about sixty years after Sulaimán's account. Though Abu Zeid never visited India, he made it his business to read and question travellers who had been in India. Abul Hasan-el-Masúdi (A.D. 915-943) who met him at Basrah is said to have imparted to and derived much information from Abu Zeid. Sir Henry Elliot's History of India, I. 2.

[3] Ahmed bin Yahyá, surnamed Abu Jáafar and called Biláduri or Bilásuri from his addiction to the electuary of the Malacca bean (*bilazur* بلاذر) or anacardium, lived about the middle of the ninth century of the Christian era at the court of Al-Mutawakkil the Abbási, as an instructor to one of the royal princes. He died A.H. 279 (A.D. 892-93). His work is styled the Futúh-ul-Buldán The Conquest of Countries. He did not visit Sindh, but was in personal communication with men who had travelled far and wide.

[4] Sir Henry Elliot's History of India, I. 115-116.

[5] The reason of Umar's dislike for India is described by Al Masúdi (Murúj Arabic Text, Cairo Edition, III. 166-171), to have originated from the description of the country by a philosopher to whom Umar had referred on the first spread of Islám in his reign. The philosopher said: India is a distant and remote land peopled by rebellious infidels. Immediately after the battle of Kadesiah (A.D. 636) when sending out Utbah, his first governor to the newly-founded camp-town of Basrah Umar is reported to have said: I am sending thee to the land of Al-Hind (India) as governor. Remember it is a field of the fields of the enemy. The third Khalífah Usmán (A.D. 643-655) ordered his governor of Irák to depute a special officer to visit India and wait upon the Khalífah to report his opinion of that country. His report of India was not encouraging. He said: Its water is scarce, its fruits are poor, and its robbers bold. If the troops sent there are few they will be slain; if many they will starve. (Al-Biláduri in Elliot, I. 116.)

[6] Sir H. Elliot's History of India, I. 116.

Appendix V.

ARAB REFERENCES, A.D. 651 - 1350.

mentions a more successful one to Debal at the mouth of the Indus sent by Hakam under the command of his brother Mughaira. On the death of his uncle Al-Hajjáj (A.D. 714; H. 95) Muhammad the son of Kasim the Arab conqueror of Sindh, is said to have made peace with the inhabitants of Surast or Káthiáváḍ with whom he states the people of Bátia[1] that is Bet to the north of Dwárka were then at war. Al Biláduri describes the Bátia men as Meds seafarers and pirates. In the reign of Hishám (A.D. 724) Junnaid, son of Abdur Rahmán Al Murri, who was appointed to the frontier of Sindh is stated to have conquered Jurz (Gujarát) and Bárús (Broach).[2] A more permanent result followed a great expedition from Mansúrah in Sindh. This result was the overthrow, from which it never recovered, of the great seaport and capital of Vala or Valabhi.[3] Al Biláduri's next mention[4] of Gujarát is in connection with the conquest of Sindán in Kachh and the founding there of a Jámá mosque by Fazl, son of Mahán in the reign of the Abbási Khalífah Al Mámún (A.D. 813-833) the son of the famous Hárún-ur-Rashíd. After Fazl's death his son Muhammad sailed with sixty vessels against the Meds of Hind, captured Máli[5] apparently Mália in north Káthiáváḍ after a great slaughter of the Meds and returned to Sindán.

The dissension between Muhammad and his brother Mahán, who in Muhammad's absence had usurped his authority at Sindán, re-established the power of the Hindus. The Hindus however, adds Al Biláduri, spared the assembly mosque in which for long the Musalmáns used to offer their Friday prayers.[6] Ibni Khurdádbah (A.D. 912; H. 300) erroneously enumerates Bárúh and Sindán (Broach and Sindán) as cities of Sindh.[7] The king of Juzr he describes as the fourth Indian sovereign. According to Al Masúdi[8] (A.D. 915) the country of the Balháras or Ráshtrakútas (A.D. 743-974), which is also called the country of Kumkar (Konkan), is open on one side to the attacks of the king of Juzr (Gujarát) a prince owning many horses and camels and troops who does not think any king on earth equal to him except the king of Bábal (Babylon). He prides himself and holds himself high above all other kings and owns many elephants, but hates Musalmáns. His country is on a tongue of land, and there are gold and silver mines in it, in which trade is carried on. Al Istakhri[9] (H. 340; A.D. 951) gives an itinerary in which he shows the distance between

---

1 Sir H. Elliot (Hist. of India) transliterates this as *Básia*. But neither *Básea* nor his other supposition (Note 4 Ditto) *Budha* seem to have any sense. The original is probably *Bátiah*, a form in which other Arab historians and geographers also allude to *Baet*, the residence of the notorious *Bawárij* who are referred to a little farther on as seafarers and pirates. Ditto, I. 123.

2 This important expedition extended to Ujjain. Details Above page 109 and also under Bhinmál. Raids by sea from Sindh were repeated in A.D. 758, 760, 755, and perhaps A.D. 830. Reinaud's Fragments, 212. See Above Bhagvánlál's Early History page 96 note 3.

3 Details Above pages 94-96.

4 Sir Henry Elliot's History of India, I. 129.

5 Sir Henry Elliot (History of India, I. 129) calls it Kállari though (Ditto note 3) he says the text has Máli.

6 Sir H. Elliot's History of India, I. 129.

7 Ibni Khurdádbah a Musalmán of Magian descent as his name signifies, died H. 300 (A.D. 912). He held high office under the Abbási Khalífahs at Baghdád (Elliot's History of India, I. 13).

8 Abul Hasan Al Masudi, a native of Baghdád, who visited India about A.D. 915 and wrote his "Meadows of Gold" (Murúj-uz-zahab) about A.D. 950-51 and died A.D. 956 in Egypt. (Sir Henry Elliot's History of India, I. 23-25.)

9 Abu Is-hák Al Istakhri, a native (as his cognomen signifies) of Persepolis who flourished about the middle of the tenth century and wrote his Book of Climes (Kitábul Akálím) about A.H. 340 (A.D. 951). Elliot's History of India, I. 26.

Mansurah and Kámhal[1] (Anhilwára) to be eight days' journey; from Kámhal to Kambáya (Cambay) four days; from Kambáya to the sea about two *farasangs* that is between seven and eight miles[2]; from Kambáya to Surabáya[3] perhaps Surabára the Surat river mouth which is half a *farasang* (between 1½ and two miles) from the sea, about four days. He places five days between Surabáya (Surat) and Sindán (St. John near Daman) and a like distance between Sindán and Saimur (Chewal or Cheul) thirty miles south of Bombay. Ibni Haukal[4] (H. 366; A.D. 976) enumerates[5] (Fámhal)[6] (Anhilwára), Kambáya (Cambay), Surbárah (Surat), Sindán (Daman), and Saimur (Cheul) as cities of Al Hind (India), as opposed to As Sindh or the Indus valley. From Kambáya to Saimur, he writes, is the land of the Balhára, which is in the possession of several kings.[7] Ibni Haukal describes the land between Kámhal (Anhilwára) and Kambáya (Cambay), and Bánia three days' journey from Mansúrah as desert,[8] and between Kambáya and Saimúr as thickly covered with villages. Al Bírúni,[9] in his famous Indica about A.D. 1030-31 writes: From Kanauj, travelling south-west you come to Ási, a distance of eighteen *farsakhs*[10] that is of seventy two miles; to *Sahiva* 17 *farsakhs* or sixty-eight miles; to Chandra 18 *farsakhs* or seventy-two miles; to Rajauri fifteen *farsakhs* or sixty miles; and to Nárána (near Jaipur) the former capital of Gujarát, 18 *farsakhs* or seventy-two miles. Nárána he adds was destroyed and the capital transferred to another town on the frontier. From Nárána at a distance of 60 *farsakhs* or 240 miles south-west lies Anhilwára, and thence to Somnáth on the sea is fifty *farsakhs* or 200 miles. From Anhilwára, passing south is Lárdes with its capitals Bihruch (Broach) and Rahánjur[11] (Rándir) forty-two *farsakhs* (168

---

[1] See Appendix A. Volume I. Sir Henry Elliot's History of India.

[2] Elliot's History of India, 394, where Sir Henry Elliot calculates a *parsang* or *farsang* (Arabic *farsakh*) to be 3½ miles. Al Bírúni, however, counts four *kroh* or miles to a *farsakh*. Sachau's Al Bírúni Arabic Text, chapter 18 page 97.

[3] Sir Henry Elliot (History of India, I. 403) locates Surabáya somewhere near Surat. The mouth of the Tápti is still known in Surat as the Bára.

[4] Ibni Haukal (Muhammad Abul Kásim) a native of Baghdád, left that city in H. 331 (A.D. 943), returned to it H. 358 (A.D. 968), and finished his work about H. 366 (A.D. 976). Sir Henry Elliot's History of India, I. 31.

[5] Elliot, I. 34.

[6] Sir Henry Elliot (History of India, I. 363) correctly takes Fámhal to be a misreading for Anhal that is Anhilwára. Al Bírúni (A.D. 970-1039) uses the name Anhilwára without any Arab peculiarity of transliteration or pronunciation. Sachau's Arabic Text, 100. Al Idrísi (end of the eleventh century) styles Anhilwára "Nahrwára" (Elliot, I. 84) an equally well known name.

[7] Sir Henry Elliot's History of India, I. 34.

[8] M. Gildemeister's Latin translation of Ibni Haukal's Ashkál-ul-Bilád (Sir Henry Elliot's History of India, I. 39).

[9] Abu Rihán Al Bírúni was a native of Balkh in Central Asia. He accompanied Mahmúd of Ghazni to India in his expeditions and acquired an accurate knowledge of Sanskrit. His acquaintance with this language and Greek and his love of enquiry and research together with his fairness and impartiality, make his Indica a most valuable contribution to our information on India in the end of the tenth and beginning of the eleventh centuries. He finished his work after the death of his patron in A.D. 1030-31. See Sachau's Preface to the Arabic Text of the Indica, ix.

[10] Al Bírúni makes his *farsakh* of four miles. Sachau's Arabic Text, 97.

[11] Sir Henry Elliot's translation and transliteration of Rahanjúr (History of India, I. 61) are, be it said with all respect to the memory of that great scholar, inaccurate. He cannot make anything of the word (note 3) while in the Arabic Text of Sachau (page 100) the first letter is a plain ر = *r* and not د = *d*. From the context also the ancient town of Rándir seems to be meant. It is plainly written (رهنجور) Rahanjúr and is very likely the copyist's mistake for the very similar form رهندور or Ráhandúr.

Appendix V.

ARAB REFERENCES, A.D. 851-1350.

miles). These he states are on the shore of the sea to the east of Tána (the modern Thána).[1] After describing the coast of Makrán till it reaches Debal[2] (Karáchi or Thatta) Abu Rihán comes to the coast of Kachh[3] and Somnáth, the population of which he calls the Bawárij because, he says, they commit their piratical depredations in boats called Baira.[4] He gives the distance[5] between Debal (Karáchi or Thatta) and Kachh the country that yields *mukl* (gum or myrrh)[6] and *bádrúd* (balm) as six *farsakhs* (24 miles); to Somnáth (from Debal) fourteen (56 miles); to Kambáya thirty (120 miles); to Asáwal the site of Ahmedábád (from Cambay) two days' journey; to Bahrúj (Broach) (from Debal)[7] thirty, to Sindán or St. John (from Debal) fifty; to Subára (Sopára) from Sindán six[8]; to Tána (from Sopára) five. Rashíd-ud-dín in his translation (A.D. 1310) of Al Bíruni (A.D. 970-1031) states[9] that beyond Gujarát are Konkan and Tána. He calls Tánah the chief town of the Konkans and mentions the forest of the Dángs as the habitat of the *sharva* an animal resembling the buffalo, but larger than a rhinoceros, with a small trunk and two big horns with which it attacks and destroys the elephant. Al Idrísi,[10] writing about the end of the eleventh century but with tenth century materials, places[11] in the seventh section of the second climate, the Gujarát towns of Mámhal (Anhilwára), Kambáya (Cambay), Subára (apparently Surabára or Surat), Sindán[12] (Sanján in Thána), and Saimúr (Chewal or Cheul). He adds, probably quoting from Al Jauhari (A.D. 950), that Nahrwára is governed by a great prince who bears the title of Balhára who owns the whole country from Nahrwára to Saimúr. He ranks the king of Juzr fourth among Indian potentates. The country from Debal to Kambáya (Karáchi to Cambay) he describes[13] as "nothing but a marine strand without habitations and almost without water, and impassable for travellers."[14] The situation of Mámhal (Anhilwára) he gives as between Sindh and Hind. He notices the Meds as Mánds[15] grazing their flocks to within a short distance of

---

[1] Sachau's Arabic Text of Al Bírúni, 98 and Sir Henry Elliot's History of India, I. 61.

[2] Elphinstone's History of India, Book V. Chapter I. 263 Note 25 (John Murray's 1849 Edition) on the authority of Captain MacMurdo and Captain Alexander Burnes inclines to the opinion that Debal was somewhere near the site of the modern Karáchi.

[3] Sir Henry Elliot's History of India, I. 65. Sachau's Text of Al Bíruni, chapter 18 page 102.

[4] Al Biláduri uses the word Barija for a strong built war vessel. Sir Henry Elliot derives the word from the Arabic and gives an interesting note on the subject in his Appendix I. 539. The word is still used in Hindustani as *beda* (بیڑا) to signify a boat or bark. [5] Sachau's Arabic Text, 102.

[6] According to Richardson (Arabic Dictionary voce مقل myrrh) though rendered gum by all translators. According to the *Makhzan* the word *mukl* (Urdu *gughal*) is Balsamodendron and Bádrud the corruption of *Barus* (Urdu *biroza*) is balsam or bezoar. [7] Sachau's Arabic Text page 99 chapter 18.

[8] After giving the distances in days or journeys the Text (page 102 Sachau's Text of Al Bírúni) does not particularise the distances of the places that follow in journeys or *farsakhs*. [9] Elliot's History of India, I. 67.

[10] Abu Abdallah Muhammad Al Idrísi, a native of Ceuta in Morocco and descended from the royal family of the Idrísis of that country, settled at the court of Roger II. of Sicily, where and at whose desire he wrote his book The Nuzhat-ul-Mushtak or The Seeker's Delight. Elliot's History of India, I. 74. Almost all Al Idrísi's special information regarding Sindh and Western India is from Al-Jauhari governor of Khurásán (A.D. 892-999), whose knowledge of Sindh and the Indus valley is unusually complete and accurate. Compare Reinaud's Abulfeda, lxiii.

[11] Sir Henry Elliot's History of India, I. 77.

[12] Bombay Gazetteer, II. 69.

[13] Elliot's History of India, I. 78.

[14] Elliot's History of India, I. 79.

[15] Elliot's History of India, I. 79.

Mámhal (Anhilwára). He speaks of Mámhal, Kambáya, Subára (probably Surabára or Surat), Sindán, and Saimúr as countries of Hind (India) touching upon Sindh.[1] He describes Mámhal as a frontier town, numbered by some among the cities of Sindh, and he classifies Aubkin, Mánd, Kulámmali (Quilon),[2] and Sindán (Sandhán in Kachh) as maritime islands. Among the numerous towns of India are Mámhal (Anhilwára), Kambáya (Cambay), Subára, Asáwal (Ahmedábád), Janáwal (Chunvál), Sindán, Saimúr, Jandur[4] (Rándir), Sandur (apparently a repetition of Rándir), and Rúmála (perhaps the south Panjáb).[5] He speaks of Kalbata, Augasht, Nahrwára (Anhilwára), and Lahawar (Lahori Bandar) as in the desert[6] of Kambáya. Of the three Subára (Surabára or Surat), Sindán (the Thána Sanján), and Saimúr (Cheul), he says Saimúr alone belongs to the Balhára, whose kingdom, he adds, is large, well-peopled, commercial, and fertile. Near Subára (apparently Surabára) he locates small islands which he styles Bára where, he adds, cocoanuts and the costus grow.[7] East of Sindán, due to a confusion between Sandhán in Kachh and Sanján in Thána, he places another island bearing the same name as the port and under the same government as the mainland, highly cultivated and producing the cocoa palm the bamboo and the cane. Five miles by sea from Kulámmali lies another island called Máli, an elevated plateau, but not hilly, and covered with vegetation. The mention of the pepper vine suggests that Al Idrísi has wandered to the Malabár Coast. In the eighth section of the second clime Al Idrísi places Barúh (Broach), Sandápúr (apparently Goa), Tána (Thána), Kandárina (Gandhár, north of Broach), Jirbátan a town mentioned by Al Idrísi as the nearest in a voyage from Ceylon to the continent of India on that continent. It is described as a populous town on a river supplying rice and grain to Ceylon,[8] Kalkáyan, Luluwa, Kanja, and Samandirún, and in the interior Dulaka (Dholka), Janwál (Chunvál or Viramgám), and Nahrwár (Anhilwára).[9] Opposite the sea-port of Barúh (Broach), Al Idrísi places an island called Mullán, producing large quantities of pepper. Al Idrísi describes the port of Barúh (Broach) as accessible to ships from China and Sindh. The distance from Barúh to Saimúr he puts at two days journey, and that between Barúh and Nahrwara (Anhilwára) at eight days through a flat country travelled over in wheeled carriages drawn by oxen, which he adds furnished the only mode for the conveyance also of merchandise. He locates the towns of Dulaka and Hanawal

---

[1] Elliot's History of India, I. 84.

[2] The details of Kulámmali given by Al Kazwíni (A.D. 1263 - 1275) seem to show it is Quilon on the Malabár Coast. When a ruler died his successor was always chosen from China.

[3] Elliot (I. 363-364) on the authority of Al Istakhri thinks that all the names Ámhal, Fámhal, Kámhal, and Mámhal are faulty readings of Anhal (Anhil)wára owing to irregularity in the position or absence of diacritical points.

[4] This is probably Rander, a very natural Arab corruption. Instance Al Birúni's Ranjhur. See page 507 note 11 and page 520.

[5] Rumála is mentioned at pages 14, 87, 92 and 93 volume I. of Elliot. It is first mentioned (page 14) by Ibni Khurdádbah (A.D. 912) as one of the countries of Sindh. It is next mentioned by Al Idrisi (end of the eleventh century according to Elliot, I. 74) as one of the places of the eighth section describing the coast of India, but is mentioned along with Nahrwára, Kandhár, and Kalbata (?). At page 92 (Ditto) the same writer (Idrisi) says that Kalbata and Rúmála are on the borders of the desert which separates Múltán from Sijistán. Again at page 93 (Ditto) Idrísi gives the distance between Kalbata and Rumála as a distance of three days.

[6] Elliot's History of India, I. 84.

[7] Sir H. Elliot's History of India, I. 85.

[8] Elliot, I. 90 - 93.

[9] Elliot's History of India, I. 89.

Appendix V.

ARAB REFERENCES, A.D. 851-1350.

or Janáwal (Chunwál or Jháláwar) with Asáwal (Ahmedábád) between Báruh and Nahrwára. He represents all three of these towns to be centres of a considerable trade, and among their products mentions the bamboo and the cocoanut. From Báruh to Sandábúr (that is Goa), a commercial town with fine houses and rich bazárs situated on a great gulf where ships cast anchor, the distance along the coast given by Al Idrísi is four-days. Al Kazwíni[1] writing about the middle of the thirteenth century A.D. 1263-1275, but mainly from information of the tenth century notes Saimúr (Cheul) "a city of Hind near the confines of Sindh" with its handsome people of Turkish extraction worshippers of fire having their own fire-temples. Al Kazwíni (A.D. 1230) dwells at length on the wonders of Somnáth and its temple. He calls it a celebrated city of India situated on the shore of the sea and washed by its waves. Among its wonders is Somnáth, an idol hung in space resting on nothing. In Somnáth he says Hindus assemble by the ten thousand at lunar eclipses, believing that the souls of men meet there after separation from the body and that at the will of the idol they are re-born into other animals. The two centuries since its destruction by the idol-breaker of Ghaznah had restored Somnáth to its ancient prosperity. He concludes his account of Somnáth by telling how Mahmúd ascertained that the chief idol was of iron and its canopy a loadstone and how by removing one of the walls the idol fell to the ground.

Rivers.

Regarding the rivers and streams of Gujarát the Arab writers are almost completely silent. The first reference to rivers is in Al Masúdi (A.D. 944) who in an oddly puzzled passage says:[2] "On the Lárwi Sea (Cambay and Cheul) great rivers run from the south whilst all the rivers of the world except the Nile of the Egypt, the Mehrán (Indus) of Sindh, and a few others flow from the north." Al Bírúní (A.D. 970-1030) states that between the drainage areas of the Sarsut and the Ganges is the valley of the river Narmaza[3] which comes from the eastern mountains and flows south-west till it falls into the sea near Bahrúch about 180 miles (60 *yojanas*) east of Somnáth. Another river the Sarsut (Sarasvati) he rightly describes as falling into the sea an arrowshot to the east of Somnáth.[4] He further mentions the Tábi (Tapti) from the Vindu or Vindhya hills and the Támbra Barani or copper-coloured, apparently also the Tápti, as coming from Málwa. In addition he refers to the Máhindri or Máhi and the Sarusa apparently

---

[1] Zakariah Ibni Muhammad Al Kazwíni, a native of Kazwín (Kasbin) in Persia, wrote his Asár-ul-Bilád or "Signs or Monuments of Countries" about A.H. 661 (A.D. 1263) compiling it chiefly from the writings of Al Istakhri (A.D. 951) and Ibni Haukal (A.D. 976). He also frequently quotes Misár bin Muhalhil, a traveller who (A.D. 942) visited India and China. Sir Henry Elliot's History of India, I. 94.

[2] Barbier De Meynard's Text of Al Masúdi's Les Prairies D'Or, I. 382.

[3] Sir Henry Elliot misreads *Tamraz* for Al Bírúni's Arabic form of *Narmaza*. He says: It comes from the city of Tamraz and the eastern hills; it has a south-easterly course till it falls into the sea near Báhruch about 60 *yojanas* to the east of Somnáth. The literal translation of the text of Al Bírúni (see Sachau's Al Bírúni's India, 130) is that given above. It is hard to believe that the accurate Al Bírúni while in one place (see Sachau's Text, 99) giving the name of the Narbada faultlessly, should in another place fall into the error of tracing it from *Tirmiz* a city of Central Asia. A comparison of Elliot's version with the text sets the difficulty at rest. Compare Sir Henry Elliot's History of India, I. 49 and note 3 ditto and Sachau's Arabic Text of Al Bírúni, 130 chapter 25.

[4] Compare Sachau's Al Bírúni with Sir Henry Elliot, I. 49, who is silent as to the distance.

Appendix V.

ARAB REFERENCES, A.D. 851-1350.

Sarasvati perhaps meant for the Sábarmati. Al Idrísi (A.D. 1100) is the only other Arab writer who names any of the Gujarát rivers. As usual he is confused, describing Dulka (Dholka) as standing on the bank of a river flowing into the sea which forms an estuary or gulf on the east of which stands the town of Bárúh (Broach).[1]

The Arab writers record the following details of twenty-two leading towns:

Towns. *Anahalváda.*

Anahalva'da (ÁMHAL, FÁMHAL, KÁMHAL, KÁMUHUL, MÁMHUL, NAHLWÁRA, NAHRWÁLA). Al Istakhri (H. 340; A.D. 951) mentions Ámhal Fámhal and Kámhal, Ibni Haukal (A.D. 976) Fámhal Kámhal and Kámuhal, and Al Idrísi (end of the eleventh century) Mámhul. That these are perversions of one name and that this town stood on the border of 'Hind' or Gujarát (in contradistinction to Sindh) the position given to each by the Arab geographers[2] places beyond question. Al Istakhri (A.D. 951) alone calls the place by the name of Ámhal which he mentions[3] as one of the chief cities of 'Hind.' Later he gives the name of *Fámhal* to a place forming the northern border of "*Hind*", as all beyond it as far as Makrán belongs to Sindh. Again a little later[4] he describes Kámhal as a town eight days from Mansúrah and four days from Kambáya, thus making Kámhal the first Gujarát town on the road from Mansúrah about seventy miles north of Haidarábád in Sindh to Gujarát. Ibni Haukal (A.D. 968-976) in his Ashkál-ul-Bilád gives Fámhal in his text and Kámhal in his map[5] and again while referring[6] to the desert between Makrán and Fámhal as the home of the Meds, he styles it Kámhal. Once more he refers to Fámhal as a strong and great city, containing a Jámá or Assembly Mosque; a little later[7] he calls it Kámuhul and places it eight days from Mansúrah and four from Kambáya. He afterwards contradicts himself by making Mansúrah two days' journey from 'Kámuhul,' but this is an obvious error.[8] Al Bírúni (A.D. 970-1039) notices Anhilwára and does not recognize any other form.[9] Al Idrísi (end of the eleventh century) adopts no form but Mámhal referring to it as one of the towns of the second climate[10] on the confines of a desert between Sindh and "Hind" (India or Gujarát) the home of the sheep-grazing and horse and camel-breeding Meds,[11] as a place numbered by some among the cities of Hind (Gujarát) by others as one of the cities of Sindh situated at the extremity of the desert which stretches between Kambáya, Debal, and Bánia.[12] Again he describes Mámhal as a town of moderate importance on the route "from Sindh to India," a place of little trade, producing small quantities of fruit but numerous flocks, nine days from Mansúrah through Bánia and five from Kambáya.[13] Al Idrísi (quoting from tenth century

[1] See Ahmedábád Gazetteer, IV. 338; also Elliot's History of India, I. 356-357.
[2] See Appendix Elliot's History of India, I. 363.
[3] Al Istakhri in Elliot (History of India), I. 27.
[4] Al Istakhri in Elliot (History of India), I. 30.
[5] Ibni Haukal in Elliot (History of India), I. 32-34.
[6] Ibni Haukal in Elliot (History of India), I. 34-38.
[7] Ibni Haukal in Elliot (History of India), I. 39.
[8] Ibni Haukal in Elliot (History of India), I. 40.
[9] Al Bírúni in Elliot (History of India), I. 61.
[10] Al Idrísi in Elliot (History of India), I. 77.
[11] Al Idrísi in Elliot (History of India), I. 79.
[12] Bánia seems to be a copyist's error for Bazána or Náráyana. The distances agree and the fact that to this day the neighbourhood of Jaipur is noted for its flocks of sheep bears additional testimony to the correctness of the supposition.
[13] Al Idrísi in Elliot's History of India, I. 84.

Appendix V.

ARAB REFERENCES, A.D. 851 - 1350.

Towns.

Anahalvada.

materials) also notices Nahrwára as eight days' journey from Báréh (Broách) across a flat country a place governed by a prince having the title of the Balhára, a prince with numerous troops and elephants, a place frequented by large numbers of Musalmáns who go there on business.[1] It is remarkable that though Vanarája (A.D. 720 - 780?) founded Anhilwára as early as about A.D. 750 no Arab geographer refers to the capital under any of the many forms into which its name was twisted before Al Istakhri in A.D. 951. At first Anhilwára may have been a small place but before the tenth century it ought to have been large enough to attract the notice of Ibni Khurdádbah (A.D. 912) and Al Masúdi (A.D. 915). In the eleventh century the Musalmán historians of Mahmúd's reign are profuse in their references to Anhilwára. According to Farishtah[2] after the capture of Anhilwára and the destruction of Somnáth (H. 414; A.D. 1025) Mahmúd was anxious to make Anhilwára his capital especially as it had mines of gold and as Singaldip (Ceylon) rich in rubies was one of its dependencies. Mahmúd was dissuaded from the project by his ministers.[3] But two mosques in the town of Pattan remain to show Mahmúd's fondness for the city. The next Muhammadan reference to Anhilwára is by Núr-ud-dín Muhammad U'fi, who lived in the reign of Shams-ud-dín Altamsh (A.D. 1211).[4] In his Romance of History U'fi refers to Anhilwára as the capital of that Jai Ráj, who on receiving the complaint of a poor Musalmán preacher of Cambay, whose mosque the Hindus instigated the fire-worshippers of the place to destroy, left the capital alone on a fleet dromedary and returning after personal enquiry at Cambay summoned the complainant and ordered the chief men of the infidels to be punished and the Musalmán mosque to be rebuilt at their expense.[5]

The Jámi-ûl-Hikáyát of Muhammad U'fi alludes[6] to the defeat of Sultán Shaháb-ud-dín or Muhammad bin Sám, usually styled Muhammad Ghori, at the hands of Múlarája II. of Anahilaváda in A.D. 1178. And the Tájul Maásir[7] describes how in A.D. 1297 the Musalmáns under Kutb-ud-dín Aibak retrieved the honour of their arms by the defeat of Karan and his flight from Anhilwára. This account refers to Gujarát as "a country full of rivers and a separate region of the world." It also notices that Sultán Násir-ud-dín Kabáchah (A.D. 1246 - 1266) deputed his general Kháskhán from Debal to attack Nahrwála and that Kháskhán brought back many captives and much spoil. After the conquest of Gujarát, in A.D. 1300 Sultán Alá-ud-dín Khilji despatched Ulughkhán (that is the Great Khán commonly styled Alfkhán) to destroy the idol-temple of Somnáth. This was done and the largest idol was sent to Alá-ud-dín.[8]

Chief Towns.

Asáwal.

Asáwal. Abú Rihán Al Birúni is the first (A.D. 970 - 1039) of Arab geographers to mention Asáwal the site of Ahmedábád which he correctly

[1] Al Idrísi in Elliot's History of India, I. 9. The Balháras or Ráshṭrakúṭas lost their power in A.D. 974. The only explanation of Idrísi's (A.D. 1100) Balharas at Anhilwára is that Idrísi is quoting from Al Birúni A.D. 950.

[2] Farishtah Persian Text Lithographed Bombay Edition, I. 57.

[3] Farishtah Persian Text Lithographed Bombay Edition, IV. 48. The Rauzat-us-Safa states that it was at Somnáth the Ghaznavide wanted to fix his capital (IV. 42 Persian Text, Lakhnau Edition). Anahilaváḍa seems more likely.

[4] Sir Henry Elliot's History of India, II. 155.

[5] The Jámi-ûl-Hikáyát in Elliot (History of India), II. 162.

[6] Elliot's History of India, II. 200.

[7] Elliot's History of India, II. 229-30.

[8] Sir Henry Elliot's History of India, III. 74.

Appendix V.

ARAB REFERENCES, A.D. 851 - 1350.

Chief Towns.

Asáwal.

places two days journey from Cambay.[1] The next notice is along with Khábirún (probably Kávi on the left mouth of the Máhi) and near Hanáwal or Janáwal, apparently Chunvál or Viramgám, by Al Idrísi (end of the eleventh century) as a town, populous, commercial, rich, industrious, and productive of useful articles.[2] He likens Asáwal "both in size and condition" to Dhulaka both being places of good trade.[3] In the early fourteenth century (A.D.1325) Ziá-ud-dín Barni refers to Asáwal as the place where Sultán Muhammad Tughlak (A.D.1325-1351) had to pass a month in the height of the rains owing to the evil condition to which his horses were reduced in marching and countermarching in pursuit of the rebel Tághi. In the beginning of the fifteenth century (A.D. 1403-4) the Tárikh-i-Mubárak Sháhi notices Asáwal as the place where Tátárkhán the son of Zafarkhán had basely seized and confined his own father.[4] The Mirát-i-Sikandari also speaks[5] of Asáwal (A.D. 1403) but with the more courtly remark that it was the place where Zafarkhán the grandfather of Sultán Ahmad the founder of Ahmedábád, retired into private life after placing his son Tátárkhán on the throne.[6] The Mirát-i-Sikandari states that the city of Ahmedábád was built[7] in the immediate vicinity of Asáwal. The present village of Asarwa is, under a slightly changed name, probably what remains of the old town.

Ahmedábád.

Barda.

Barda. See VALABHI.

Capital and Port Towns.

Broach.

Broach (BÁHRU'J, BÁRU'H, BÁRU'S) is one of the places first attacked by the Muslim Arabs. In the fifteenth year of the Hijrah (A.D. 636) the Khalífah Umar appointed Usmán son of Abdul Ási to Bahrein. Usmán sent Hakam to Bahrein and Hakam despatched a fleet to Báráúz (or Broach).[8] Al Biláduri (A.D. 892-93) speaks of Junnaid the son of Abdur Rahmán Al Murri on his appointment to the frontier of Sindh in the Khiláfat of Hishám bin Abdal Malik (A.D. 724-743) sending an expedition by land against Bárús (Broach) .... and overrunning Jurz[9] (Gujarát). Ibni Khurdádbah (A.D. 912) enumerates Báráh among the countries of Sindh.[10] Broach is next noticed[11] by Al Bírúni (A.D. 970-1039) as standing near the estuary of the river Narbada, as 120 miles (30 *parasangs*) from Debal, and as being with Rahanjur (Ránder) the capital of Lárdes. In describing the coasts of the Persian Gulf and the Indian Ocean Al Masúdi (A.C. 915-944) speaks of Broach as بروص *Barús* adding from which come the famous lance shafts called *Bárúsi*.[12] Al Idrísi (A.D. 1100) mentions[13] Bárúh as a large town well-built of brick and plaster, the inhabitants rich, engaged in trade and ready to enter upon speculations and distant expeditions, a port for vessels coming from China and Sindh, being two days' journey from Saimúr (Cheul) and eight days from Nahrwára Anhilwára Pattan. In the fourteenth century (A.D. 1325) Broach is described as in the flames of the insurrection

---

1 Sachau's Text, 102.
2 Al Idrísi in Elliot (History of India), I. 87.
3 Al Idrísi in Elliot (History of India), I. 88.
4 Elliot's History of India, III. 260.
5 Bayley's Gujarát, 81.
6 Elliot's History of India, IV. 39; History of Gujarát, 81.
7 Bayley's Gujarát, 90.
8 Al Biláduri (A.D. 892) in Elliot's History of India, I. 116.
9 Al Biláduri (A.D. 892) in Elliot's History of India, I. 126. Details of this far-stretching affliction of Sindh, Kachh, the Chávadás, Chitor, Bhínmál, and Ujjain are given above, History 109.
10 Ibni Khurdádbah in Elliot (History of India), I. 14.
11 Al Bírúni in Elliot (History of India, I. 49-66), and Sachau's Arabic Text, 100.
12 Barbier DeMeynard's Arabic Text of Les Prairies D'Or, I. 239.
13 Al Idrísi in Elliot (History of India), I. 87.

Appendix V.

ARAB REFERENCES, A.D. 851-1350.

caused by the foreign *amírs* or nobles of the hot-tempered and impolitic Muhammad bin Tughlak (A.D. 1325-1351) who visited it in person to quell their revolt. Ziáuddín Barni the famous annalist of his reign and the author of the Tárikh-i-Fírúz Sháhi speaks of his deputation to Broach by Malik Kabír the future Sultán Fírúz Sháh with a letter to the Sultán.[1]

Port or Coast Towns.

Cambay.

Cambay (KAMBÁYA, KAMBÁYAT, KAMBÁYAH, KHAMBÁIT.) According to Al Istakhri (A.D. 951) Kambáya formed the north boundary of the land of the Balhárás.[2] Al Istakhri describes it as four days from Kámhal (Anhilwára) sixteen miles (4 *farsangs*) from the sea and four days from Surabáya probably Surabára or the mouth of the Tápti a term which is still in use.[3] Al Masúdi (A.D. 915) in speaking[4] of the ebb and flow of the ocean mentions Kambáya. He notices that Kambáya was famous in Baghdád, as it still is famous in Gujarát, for its shoes. These shoes, he says, were made in Kambáya and the towns about it like Sindán (Sanján in Thána) and Sufáráh (Supára). He notices that when he visited Kambáya in H. 303 (A.D. 913-14) the city was ruled by a Bráhman of the name of Bănia, on behalf of the Balhára, lord of Mánkir (Málkhet). He states that this Bánia was kind to and held friendly discussions with stranger Musalmáns and people of other faiths. He gives a pleasing picture of Cambay, on a gulf far broader than the estuaries of the Nile, the Euphrates, or the Tigris whose shores were covered with villages, estates, and gardens wooded and stocked with palm and date groves full of peacocks parrots and other Indian birds. Between Kambáya and the sea from which this gulf branches was two days' journey. When, says Al Masúdi, the waters ebb from the gulf stretches of sands come to view. One day I saw a dog on one of these desert-like stretches of sand The tide began to pour up the gulf and the dog hearing it ran for his life to the shore. but the rush was too rapid. The waters overtook and drowned him. Al Masúdi speaks of an emerald known as the Makkan emerald being carried from Kambáya by Aden to Makkah where it found a market.[5] Ibni Haukal (A.D. 968-996) names Kambáya among the cities of Hind.[6] In his time there were Jámá or assembly mosques in Kambáya, where the precepts of Islám were openly taught. Among the productions of Kambáya he gives mangoes cocoanuts lemons and rice in great plenty and some honey but no date trees.[7] He makes Kambáya four miles (one *farasang*) from the sea and four (that is four days' journey) from Subára apparently Surabára that is Surat. The distance to Kámuhul or Anhilwára by some mistake is shown as four *farsangs* instead of four days' journey.[8] Al Bírúni (A.D. 970-1031) places Kambáya within the large country of Gujarát (120 miles)[9] (30 *farsakhs*) from Debal (Karáchi). He says the men of Kambáya receive tribute from the chiefs of the island of Kís or Kísh (probably Kich-Makrán).[10] Al Idrísi (A.D. 1100) places Kambáya with other Gujarát cities in the second

---

[1] Elliot's History of India, III. 256-260.
[2] Al Istakhri in Elliot (History of India), I. 27.
[3] Al Istakhri in Elliot (History of India), I. 30.
[4] Prairies D'Or (Barbier DeMeynard's Arabic Text), I. 253-54.
[5] Prairies D'Or (Arabic Text), III. 47.
[6] Ibni Haukal in Elliot (History of India), I. 34.
[7] Ibni Haukal in Elliot (History of India), I. 38.
[8] Ibni Haukal in Elliot (History of India), I. 39.
[9] Rashíd-ud-dín from Al Bírúni in Elliot's History of India, I. 66 and Sachau's Arabic Text, chapter 18 pages 99-102.
[10] Sir Henry Elliot's History of India, I. 67.

Port or Coast Towns.

Cambay.

climate.[1] He says it is a pretty and well known naval station, second among the towns of Gujarát.[2] It stands at the end of a bay three miles from the sea where vessels can enter and cast anchor. It is well supplied with water and has a fine fortress built by the Government to prevent the inroads of the pirates of Kísh (Makrán). From Kambáya to the island of Aubkin (Píram) is two and a half days' sail and from Aubkin to Debal (or Karáchi) two days more. The country is fertile in wheat and rice and its mountains yield the bamboo. Its inhabitants are idolators. In his *Tazjiyat-ul-Amsár*, Abdullah Wassáf[3] in A.D. 1300 (H. 699) writes: "Gujarát which is commonly called Kambáyat contains 70,000 villages and towns all populous and the people abounding in wealth and luxuries. In the course of the four seasons seventy different species of beautiful flowers bloom. The purity of the air is so great that the picture of an animal drawn with the pen is lifelike. Many plants and herbs grow wild. Even in winter the ground is full of tulips (poppies). The air is healthy, the climate a perpetual spring. The moisture of the dew of itself suffices for the cold season crops. Then comes the summer harvest which is dependent on the rain. The vineyards bring forth blue grapes twice a year."

The trade in horses from the Persian isles and coast and from Katíf, Láhsa, Bahrein, and Hurmuz was so great that during the reign of Atábak Abu Bakr[4] (A.D. 1154-1189) 10,000 horses worth 2,20,000 *dínárs*[5] (Rs. 1,10,00,000) were imported into Cambay and the ports of Malabár. These enormous sums were not paid out of the government treasuries but from the endowments of Hindu temples and from taxes on the courtezans attached to them. The same author mentions the conquest[6] of Gujarát and the plunder of Kambáyat by Malik Muíz-ud-dín (called by Farishtah Alf and by Barni U'lugh meaning the great Khán.) The Táríkh-i-Fírúz Sháhi states that Nasrat Khán and not U'lugh Khán took and plundered Cambay and notices that in Cambay Nasrat Khán purchased Káfúr Hazár Dínári (the thousand Dínár Káfur), the future favourite minister and famous general of Alá-ud-dín. About fifty years later the hot-headed Muhammad bin Tughlak (A.D. 1325-1351) was in Cambay quelling an insurrection and collecting the arrears of Cambay revenue.[7]

---

[1] Sir Henry Elliot's History of India, I. 77.

[2] Sir Henry Elliot's History of India, I. 84. [3] Tazjiyat-ul-Amsar in Elliot, III. 32.

[4] Saâdi's patron mentioned by him in his Garden of Roses.

[5] The word *dínár* is from the Latin *denarius* (a silver coin worth 10 oz. of brass) through the Greek *δηναρυον*. It is a Kuráanic word, the ancient Arabic equivalent being مثقال *mithkál*. The dínár sequin or ducat varied in value in different times. In Abu Hanífah's (the greatest of the four Sunni Jurisconsults') time (A.D. 749) its value ranged from 10 to 12 dirhams. Then from 20 to 25 dirhams or drachmas. As a weight it represented a drachma and a half. Though generally fluctuating, its value may be assessed at 9s. or 10 francs to half a sovereign. For an elaborate article on the Dínár see Yule's Cathay, II. 439; Burton's Alf Leilah, I. 32. The word Dirham is used in Arabic in the sense of "silver" (vulg. siller) the Greek *δραχμη* and the drachuma of Plautus. This silver piece was 9¾d. and as a weight 66½ grains. Sir Henry Elliot does not speak more at length of the *dínár* and the *dirham* than to say (History of India, I. 461) that they were introduced in Sindh in the reign of Abdul Malik (A.D. 685) and Elliot, VIII. 31) that the *dínár* was a Rúm and the *dirham* a Persian coin. The value of the *dínár* in modern Indian currency may be said to be Rs. 5 and that of the *dirham* nearly annas 4.

[6] Wassáf gives the date of this event as A.C. 1298, but the Tárikh-i-Alái of Amír Khusrao places it at A.C. 1300. See Elliot's History of India, III. 43 and 74.

[7] Elliot's History of India, III. 256-57.

Appendix V.

ARAB REFERENCES, A.D. 851-1350.

Port or Coast Towns.

Cheul.

Cheul (SAIMU'R). Al Masúdi (A.D. 943) is the first Arab geographer to mention *Saimúr.*[1] He says: On the coast as in Saimúr Subára and Tána the *Laríyyah* language is spoken. In describing Saimúr Al Masúdi states[2] that at the time of his visit (H. 304; A.D. 914) the ruler on behalf of the Balhára was Jhánjha (this is the fifth Siláhára A.D. 916). Nearly ten thousand Musalmáns were settled in Saimúr including some (called Bayásirah) born in the land of Arab parents and others from *Síráf* and Persian Gulf, Basrah, Baghdád, and other towns. A certain Músa bin Is-hák was appointed Raís or ruler[3] by the Balhára or Valabhi, that is the reigning Ráshṭrakúṭa Indra Nityaṁvarsha to adjudicate Muhammadan disputes according to Musalmán law and customs. He describes[4] at length the ceremony of self-destruction by a *Besar*[5] youth (a Hindu by religion) to gain a better state in his future life, his scalping himself and putting fire on his head, his cutting out a piece of his heart and sending it to a friend as a souvenir.

Al Istákhri (A.D. 951) mentions Saimúr as one of the cities of Hind, makes it the southern end of the Balhára kingdom with Kambáya as the northern,[6] and places it at a distance of five days from Sindán (the Thána Sanján) and fifteen days from *Sarandíb* or Ceylon.[7] Ibni Haukal (A.D. 968) notices Saimúr as one of the cities of Hind known to him and mentions the sea of Fárs (or the Indian Ocean) as stretching from Saimúr on the east to Tíz or Makrán.[8] He states[9] that the country between Saimúr and Támhal (Anhilawára) belongs to Hind. He makes[10] the distance between Subára (probably Surabára or Swat), Sindán, and Saimúr five days each and between Saimúr and Sarandib (Ceylon) fifteen days. Al Bírúni (A.D. 1020) says:[11] "Then you enter the land of Lárán in which is Saimúr also called *Jaimúr* or *Chaimúr.*" Al Idrísi (end of the eleventh century) mentions Saimúr as one of the towns of the second climate.[12] He describes it as large and well-built, five days from Sindán and among its products notes cocoanut trees in abundance, henna (Lawsonia inermis), and on its mountains many aromatic plants.[13] His remark that Saimúr formed a part of the vast, fertile, well-peopled and commercial kingdom of the Balhárás must be taken from the work of Al-Jauharí (A.D. 950).

Al Kazwíni (A.D. 1236) quoting Misáar bin Muhalhil (A.D. 942) describes Saimúr as one of the cities of Hind near the confines of Sind,[14] whose people born of Turkish and Indian parents are very beautiful. It was a flourishing trade centre with a mixed population of Jews, Firewor-

---

1 Al Masúdi in Elliot (History of India), I. 24. 3 Prairies D'Or, II. 85.

2 He was called a Hairam or Hairamah in the language of the country. Al Masúdi's Murúj Arabic Text Cairo Edition, II. 56.

4 Al Masúdi's Murúj Arabic Text Cairo Edition, II. 56-57.

5 One born in India of an Arab father and an Indian mother probably from the Gujaráti word *Ádh-besra* meaning mixed blood. This seems the origin of the Bais Rajpút. The performer in the case in the text was a Hindu. Al Masúdi (Murúj Arabic Text II. 57 Cairo Edition) says that the singular of Bayásirah is Besar.

6 Al Istakhri in Elliot (History of India), I. 27.

7 Al Istakhri in Elliot (History of India), I. 30.

8 Ibni Haukal in Elliot (History of India), I. 33-34.

9 Ibni Haukal in Elliot (History of India), I. 38.

10 Ibni Haukal in Elliot (History of India), I. 38.

11 Al Bírúni Sachau's Arabic Text, 102; Elliot's History of India, I. 39, 66.

12 Al Idrísi in Elliot (History of India), I. 77.

13 Al Idrísi in Elliot (History of India), I. 77, 85.

14 Al Kazwíni in Elliot (History of India), I. 97.

Appendix V.

ARAB REFERENCES, A.D. 851-1350.

shippers, Christians, and Musalmáns.[1] The merchandise of the Turks (probably of the Indo-Afghán frontier) was conveyed thither and the best of aloes were exported and called *Saimúri* after its name. The temple of Saimúr was on an eminence with idols of turquoise and *baidjadak* or ruby. In the city were many mosques churches synagogues and fire-temples.

Chief Towns. *Dholka.*

Dholka (DU'LAKA). Al Idrísi (end of the eleventh century) places Dúlaka and another town he calls Hanáwal that is Chunwal or Junawal perhaps Jháláwár between Barúh (Broach) and Nahrwára. He describes Dúlaka as on the banks of a river (the Sábarmati) which flows into the sea, which forms an estuary or gulf on the west (east) of which stands the town of Bárúh. Both these towns, he adds, stand at the foot of a chain of mountains which lie to the north and which are called *Undarun* apparently Vindhya. The *kana* (bamboo) grows here as well as a few cocoanut trees.[2]

Goa.

Goa. See SINDÁBUR.

Gondal.

Gondal (KONDAL). Ziá-ud-dín Barni in his Tárikh-i-Fíruz Sháhi states[3] that Sultán Muhammad Tughlak spent (A.D. 1349) his third rainy season in Gujarát in Kondal (Gondal). Here the Sultán assembled his forces before starting on his fatal march to Sindh.

Capitals. *Kachh.*

Kachh. Al Bírúni (A.D. 970-1031) is the only Arab writer who refers to Kachh. He calls Kachh[4] with Somnáth the head-quarters of the country of the Bawárij or Medh pirates. Speaking of the Indus he notices[5] that one of its branches which reaches the borders of Kachh is known as Sind Ságar. In a third passage he refers[6] to Kachh as the land of the *mukl* or balsamodendron and of *bádrúd* or bezoar. It was twenty-four miles (6 *farsangs*) from Debal (Karáchi). According to the Tárikh-i-Maásúmi[7] when (A.D. 1069) the sovereignty of Sindh passed from the descendants of Mahmúd of Ghazni to the Sumras, Singhar, the grandson of Sumra (A.D. 1069)[8] extended his sway from Kachh to Nasarpúr[9] near Sindh Haidarábád and Khafíf the son of Singhar consolidated his power and made Kachh a Sumra dependency.[10] Dúda the grandson of Khafíf quelled a threatened Sumra rising by proceeding to Kachh and chastising the Sammas.[11] On the fall of the Sumras the Cháuras became masters of Kachh from whose hands the country passed to those of the Sammas. Ground down under the iron sway of the Sumras a number of Sammas fled from Sindh and entered Kachh where they were kindly received by the Chauras who gave them land to cultivate. After acquainting themselves with the country and the resources of its rulers the Samma immigrants who seem to have increased in numbers and strengthened themselves by union, obtained possession by stratagem but not without heroism of the chief fortress of Kachh.[12] This fort now in ruins

[1] Though Al Kazwíni wrote in the thirteenth century, he derives his information of India from Misáar bin Muhalhil, who visited India about A.D. 942. Elliot (History of India), I. 94.

[2] Al Idrísi in Elliot (History of India), I. 87.

[3] Tárikh-i-Fírúz Sháhi by Ziá Barni (Elliot's History of India), III. 264-65.

[4] Rashíd-ud-dín (A.D. 1310) from Al Birúni in Elliot's History of India, I. 65.

[5] Rashíd-ud-dín (A.D. 1310) from Al Birúni in Elliot's History of India, I. 49.

[6] Rashíd-ud-dín (A.D. 1310) from Al Birúni in Elliot's History of India, I. 66.

[7] Written A.D. 1600 (Elliot, I. 213).

[8] Tarikh-i-Maásumi in Elliot, I. 16.

[9] Tuhfatul Kirám in Elliot, I. 344.

[10] Tarikh-i-Maásumi in Elliot, I. 217.

[11] Tárikh-i-Maásumi in Elliot, I. 218.

[12] Tárikh-i-Tábiri (Elliot's History of India), I. 267-68.

Appendix V.

ARAB REFERENCES, A.D. 851 - 1350.

was the fort of Gúntri.[1] The Tárikh-i-Táhiri states that up to the time the history was written (A.D. 1621)[2] the country was in the possession of the Sammas, both the Ráis Bhára and Jám Sihta of great and little Kachh in his time being of Samma descent.

Capitals. *Kaira.*

Kaira (KARRA). One mention of Karra apparently Kaira or Kheda occurs in Ziánddín Barni's[3] account of Muhammad Tughlak's (A.D. 1325) pursuit of his rebellious Gujarát noble Tághi. He speaks of Muhammad's detention for a month at Asáwal during the rains and his overtaking and dispersing Tághi's forces at Karra. From Karra the rebels fled in disorder to Nahrwára (Anhilwára). Several of Tághi's supporters sought and were refused shelter by the Rána of Mándal that is Patri near Viramgám.

Chief Towns. *Kábirún.*

Ka'biru'n. Al Idrísi (end of the eleventh century) mentions Kábirún and Asáwal as towns of the same 'section' both of them populous, commercial, rich, and producing useful articles. He adds that at the time he wrote the Musalmáns had made their way into the greater portion of these countries and conquered them. Kábirún like the Akabarou of the Periplus (A.D. 240) is perhaps a town on the Káveri river in south Gujarát.

Kambay.

Kambay. See CAMBAY.

Kanauj.

Kanauj. Al Masûdi[4] (A.D. 956) is the first Arab traveller who gives an account of Kanauj. He says:[5] The kingdom of the Baûûra king of Kanauj extends about a hundred and twenty square *parasangs* of Sindh, each *parasang* being equal to eight miles of this country. This king has four armies according to the four quarters of the world. Each of them numbers 700,000 or 900,000. The army of the north wars against the prince of Multán and with his Musalmán subjects on the frontier. The army of the south fights against the Balhára king of Mánkír. The other two armies march to meet enemies in every direction. Ibni Haukal (A.D. 968-976) says[6] that from the sea of Fárs to the country of Kanauj is three months journey. Rashíd-ud-dín from Al Bírúni (A.D. 970-1039) places[7] Kanauj south of the Himálayás and states[8] that the Jamna falls into the Ganga below Kanauj which is situated on the west of the river (Ganga). The chief portion of Hind included in the "second climate" is called the central land or Madhya Desh. He adds that the Persians call it Kanauj. It was the capital of the great, haughty, and proud despots of India. He praises the former magnificence of Kanauj, which he says being now deserted by its ruler has fallen into neglect and ruin, and the city of Bári, three days' journey from Kanauj on the eastern

---

[1] Journal Asiatic Society of Bengal for February 1838, 102.

[2] Sir Henry Elliot's History of India, I. 268.

[3] Tárikh-i-Fírúz Sháhi in Elliot, II. 260.

[4] In his Arabic Text of the Murúj (Prairies D'Or, Cairo Edition) Al Masûdi writes the name of the Kanauj king as Farwarah. (If the *F* stands for *P* and the *w* for *m*, as is quite possible in Arab writing, then this can be Parmárah the Arab plural for Parmár.) At volume I. page 240 the word Farwarah is twice used. Once: "And the king of Kanauj, of the kings of Sindh (India) is Farwarah." Again at the same page (240): "And Farwarah he who is king of Kanauj is opposed to Balhara." Then at page 241: Farwarah is again used in the beginning of the account quoted by Elliot in I. 23.

[5] Elliot's History of India, I. 23. In the Cairo Edition of the Arabic Text of Al Masúdi's Murúj (Prairies D'Or) vol. I. page 241 is the original of this account.

[6] Elliot's History of India, I. 33.

[7] Elliot's History of India, I. 45.

[8] Elliot's History of India, I. 49.

Chief Towns. *Kanauj.*

side of the Ganges being now the capital. Kanauj was celebrated for its descendants of the Pándavas as Máhura (Mathra) is on account of Bás Dev (Krishna). Al Idrisí, end of the eleventh century, speaks[1] of Kanauj in connection with a river port town of the name of Samandár "a large town, commercial and rich, where there are large profits to be made and which is dependent" on the rule of the Kanauj king. Samandár, he says, stands on a river coming from Kashmír. To the north of Samandár at seven days is, he says, the city of Inner Kashmír under the rule of Kanauj. The Chách Námah (an Arabic history of great antiqnity written before A.D. 753, translated into Persian in the time of Sultán Násiruddín Kabáchah) (A.D. 1216) says[2] that when Chách (A.D. 631-670) advanced against Akham Lohána of Brahmanábád that the Lohána wrote to ask the help of "the king of Hindustán," that is Kanauj, at that time Satbán son of Rásal, but that Akham died before his answer came.

Kol.

Kol. Ibni Khurdádbah (A.D. 912) has Kol seventy-two miles (18 *farsakhs*) from Sanján in Kachh.[3] And the Táj-ul-Máásir[4] relates how in A.D. 1194 Kutbuddín advanced to Kol and took the fort.

Málkhet.

Málkhet (*Mánkír*). Al Masúdi (A.D. 943) is the first Arab writer to mention *Mánkír* that is Mányákheta now Málkhet about sixty miles south-east of Sholápúr. In relating the extinction of the great Brahma-born dynasty of India Al Masúdi states[5] that at the time the city of Mánkír, the great centre of India, submitted to the kings called the *Balháras* who in his time were still ruling at Mánkír.[6]

Al Masúdi correctly describes the position of Málkhet as eighty Sindh or eight-mile *farsakhs* that is six hundred and forty miles from the sea in a mountainous country. Again he notices that the language spoken in Mánkír was Kiriya,[7] called from Karah or Kanara the district where it was spoken. The current coin was the *Tártariyeh dirham* (each weighing a dirham and a half)[8] on which was impressed the date of the ruler's reign. He describes the country of the Balháras as stretching from the Kamkar (or Konkan) in the south or south-west north to the frontiers of the king of Juzr (Gujarát), "a monarch rich in men horses and camels." Al Istakhri (A.D. 951) describes Mánkír as the dwelling of the wide-ruling Balhára. Ibni Haukal (A.D. 968-976) repeats almost to the letter the information given by Al Istakhri. The destruction of Málkhet (Mánya Kheta) by the western Chálukya king Tailappa in A.D. 972 explains why none of the writers after Ibni Haukal mentions Mánkír.

---

[1] Elliot, I. 90. [2] Elliot's History of India, I. 147.

[3] Sir Henry Elliot's History of India, I. 15.

[4] Táj-ul-Máásir in Sir Henry Elliot's History of India, II. 222. 'After staying some time at Dehli he (Kutb-ud-dín) marched in A.D. 1194 (H. 590) towards Kol and Banáras passing the Jumna which from its exceeding purity resembled a mirror.' It would seem to place Kol near Banáras.

[5] Al Masúdi's Prairies D'Or (Arabic Text), I. 162.

[6] Al Masúdi in Elliot (History of India), I. 19, 20, 21 and Prairies D'Or, I. 178.

[7] Al Masúdi Arabic Text Prairies D'Or, (I. 381); Al Masúdi in Elliot (History of India), I. 24.

[8] That is an Arab dirhem and a half. Al Istakhri in Elliot (History of India), I. 27. These *Tártariyya* dirhems are mentioned by almost all Arab writers. Al Idrísi says they were current in Mansúrah in Sindh and in the Malay archipelago. See Elliot, I. 3 note 4. According to *Sulaimán* (A.C. 851) the Tártariya dirham weighed "a dirhem and a half of the coinage of the king." Elliot, I. 3. Al Masúdi (Prairies D'Or, I. 382) calls these "Tátiriyyah" dirhams, giving them the same weight as that given by *Sulaimán* to the Tártariyah dirhams. *Ibni Haukal* calls it the Titari dirhem and makes its weight equal to "a dirham and a third" (Elliot, I. 85).

Appendix V.

ARAB REFERENCES, A.D. 851 - 1350.

Chief Towns.

Mándal.

Ma'ndal. Ibni Khurdádbah (A.D. 912) enumerates Mándal (in Viramgám) with Rúmla,[1] Kuli, and Báruh as countries of Sindh. During the Khilafat of Hishám the son of Abdul Malik (A.D. 724 - 743) Junnaid son of Abdur Rahman-al-Murri was appointed to the frontier of Sindh. According to Al Biláduri (A.D. 892) Junnaid sent his officers to Mándal,[2] Dahnaj perhaps Kamlej, and Báhrús (Broach).

Náràna.

Na'ra'na. In his Indica Al Biruni (A.D. 970-1031) notices Náràna near Jaipur as the ancient capital of Gujarát. He says that its correct name is Bazánah but that "it is known to our people (the Arabs) as Nárain." He places it eighty miles (20 *farsakhs*) south-west of Kanauj, and adds that when it was destroyed the inhabitants removed to and founded another city.[3] Abú Ríhán makes Náràna the starting point of three itineraries to the south the south-west and the west. Al Bírúni's details suffice to place this centre in the neighbourhood of the modern Jaipúr and to identify it with Náráyan the capital of Bairat of Matsya which according to Farishtah[4] Mahmúd of Ghazni took in A.D. 1022 (H. 412).

Rándler.

Ra'nder (RÁHANJIR OR RAHANJU'R). Al Bírúni (A.D. 1031) gives[5] Ráhanjúr and Báhrúj (Broach) as the capitals of Lar Desh or south Gujarát. Elliot (Note 3. I. 61) writes the word Damanhúr or Dahanhúr but the reading given by Sachau in his Arabic text of Al Bírúni (page 100 chapter 18) is plainly Rahanjúr (رہنجور) and the place intended is without doubt Ránder on the right bank of the Tápti opposite Surat. In his list of Indian towns Al Idrísi (end of the eleventh century) seems to refer[6] to it under the forms Jandúr and Sandúr.

Sanján.

Sanja'n (SINDÁN). The two Sanjáns, one in Kachh the other in Thána, complicate the references to Sindán. Sindán in Kachh was one of the earliest gains of Islám in India. Al Biláduri[7] (A.D. 892) speaks of Fazl, the son of Máhán, in the reign of the greatest of the Abbási Khalífáhs Al-Mámún (A.D. 813 - 833), taking Sindán and sending Al Mámún the rare present of "an elephant and the longest and largest *sáj* or turban or teak spar ever seen." Fazl built an assembly mosque that was spared by the Hindus on their recapture of the town. Ibni Khurdádbah (A.D. 912) includes this Kachh Sindán with Broach and other places in Gujarát among the cities of Sindh. In his itinerary starting from Bakkar, he places Sindán seventy-two miles[8] (18 *farsakhs*) from Kol. Al Masúdi (A.D. 915 - 944) states that Indian emeralds from (the Kachh) Sindán and the neighbourhood of Kambáyat (Cambay) approached those of the first water in the intensity of their green and in brilliance. As they found a market in Makkah they were called Makkan emeralds.[9] Al Istakhri (A.D. 951) under cities of Hind places the Konkan Sindán five days from *Surabáya* (Surabára or Surat) and as many from *Saimúr*[10]

---

1 Kumlah is *rauma* salt land. There is a Rúm near Karúr about sixty miles south-east of Multán. Al Idrísi (A.D. 1135) has a Rumálah three days from Kalbata the salt range. Elliot, I. 92.

2 Probably Okhámandal. See Appendix vol. I. page 390 Elliot's History of India.

3 Sachau's Arabic Text of Al Bírúni's Indica, 99.

4 Persian Text Bombay Edition of 1832, I. 53.

5 Sachau's Arabic Text of Al Biruni, 100.

6 Elliot's History of India, I. 84.

7 Al Biláduri in Elliot (History of India), I. 129. The word *sáj* in the Arabic text means besides a teak-spar (which seems to be an improbable present to be sent to a Khalífáh), a large black or green turban or sash.

8 Ibni Khurdadbha in Elliot (History of India), I. 14 and 15.

9 De Meynard's Arabic Text of Les Prairies D'Or, III. 47-48.

10 Al Istakhri in Elliot (History of India), I. 27 and 30.

Appendix V.

ARAB REFERENCES, A.D. 851 - 1350.

(Cheval). Ibni Haukal (A.D. 968) mentions (the Kachh) Sindán among the cities of Hind, which have a large Musalmán population and a Jámá Masjid[1] or assembly mosque. Al Bírúni (A.D. 970 - 1031)[2] in his itinerary from Debal in Sindh places the Kokan 200 miles (50 *farsakhs*) from that port and between Broach and Supára. At the end of the eleventh century probably the Kachh Sindán was a large commercial town rich both in exports and imports with an intelligent and warlike, industrious, and rich population. Al Idrísi gives the situation of the Konkan Sindán as a mile and a half from the sea and five days from Saimúr (Cheval).[3] Apparently Abul Fida[4] (A.D. 1324) confused Sindán with Sindábúr or Goa which Ibni Batúta (A.D. 1340) rightly describes as an island.[5]

Port or Coast Towns. *Sindábúr or Sindápúr.*

Sinda'bu'r or Sinda'pu'r. Al Masúdi (A.D. 943) places *Sindápúr* he writes it Sindábúra or Goa in the country of the Bughara (Balhára) in India.[6] Al Bírúni (A.D. 1021) places Sindápúr or Sindábúr that is Goa as the first of coast towns in Malabár the next being Fáknúr.[7] Al Idrísi (end of the eleventh century) describes Sindábúr as a commercial town with fine buildings and rich bazaars in a great gulf where ships cast anchor, four days along the coast[8] from Thána.

Somnáth.

Somna'th. Al Bírúni (A.D. 970-1031) is the first of the Arab writers to notice Somnáth. He calls Somnáth and Kachh the capital of the Bawárij pirates who commit their depredations in boats called *baira*.[9] He places Somnáth (14 *farsakhs*) fifty-six miles from Debal or Karáchi 200 miles (50 *farsakhs*) from Anhilwára and 180 miles (60 *yojanas*) from Broach. He notes that the river Sarsút falls into the sea an arrow-shot from the town. He speaks of Somnáth as an important place of Hindu worship and as a centre of pilgrimage from all parts of India. He tells of votaries and pilgrims performing the last stage of their journey crawling on their sides or on their ankles, never touching the sacred ground with the soles of their feet, even progressing on their heads.[10] Al Bírúni gives[11] the legendary origin of the Somnáth idol: how the moon loved the daughters of Prajápati; how his surpassing love for one of them the fair Rohini kindled the jealousy of her slighted sisters; how their angry sire punished the partiality of the moon by pronouncing a curse which caused the pallor of leprosy to overspread his face; how the penitent moon sued for forgiveness to the saint and how the saint unable to recall his curse showed him the way of salvation by the worship of the *Lingam*; how he set up and called the Moon-Lord a stone which[12] for ages had lain on the sea shore less than three miles to the west of the mouth of the Sarasvati, and to the east of the site of the golden castle of *Barwi* (Verával) the residence of Básudeo and near the scene of his death and of the destruction of his people the Yádavas. The waxing and the waning of the moon caused the flood that hid the *Lingam* and the ebb that showed it and proved that the Moon was its servant who bathed it regularly. Al Bírúni notices[13] that in his time the castellated walls and other fortifications round the temple were not more than a hundred

---

1 Ibni Haukal in Elliot (History of India), I. 34 and 38.
2 Al Bírúni in Elliot, I. 66. 3 Al Idrísi in Elliot, I. 77 - 85.
4 Sir Henry Elliot's History of India, I. 403 Appendix.
5 Lee's Ibni Batuta, 166. 6 Al Masúdi in Elliot (History of India), I. 21.
7 Rashid-ud-dín from Al Bírúni in Elliot, I. 68. 8 Al Idrísi in Elliot, I. 89.
9 Sir Henry Elliot's History of India, I. 65; Sachau's Arabic Text of Al Bírúni, 102.
10 Elliot's History of India, I. 67.
11 Sachau's Text of Al Bírúni, 252. 12 Sachau's Arabic Text, 253.
13 Sachau's Arabic Text, 253 chapter 58.

Appendix V.

ARAB REFERENCES, A.D. 851 - 1350.

Port or Coast Towns. *Somna'th.*

years old. Al Bírúni represents the upper part of the *Liṅgam* as hung with massive and bejewelled gold chains. These chains together with the upper half of the idol were, he observes, carried away by the Emir[1] Mahmúd to Ghazna, where a part of the idol was used to form one of the steps of the Assembly Mosque and the other part was left to lie with *Chakra Swám*, the Thánesar idol, in the *maidán* or hippodrome of Mahmúd's capital. Somnáth, says Al Bírúni,[2] was the greatest of the *Liṅgams* worshipped in India where in the countries to the south-west of Sindh the worship of these emblems abounds. A jar of Ganges water and a basket of Kashmir flowers were brought daily to Somnáth. Its worshippers believed the stone to possess the power of curing all diseases, and the mariners and the wanderers over the deep between Sofála and China addressed their prayers to it as their patron deity.[3] Ibni Asír[4] (A.D. 1121) gives a detailed account of the temple of Somnáth and its ancient grandeur. He says Somnáth was the greatest of all the idols of Hind. Pilgrims by the hundred thousand met at the temple especially at the times of eclipses and believed that the ebb and flow of the tide was the homage paid by the sea to the god. Everything of the most precious was brought to Somnáth and the temple was endowed with more than 10,000 villages. Jewels of incalculable value were stored in the temple and to wash the idol water from the sacred stream of the Ganga was brought every day over a distance of two hundred *farsangs* (1200 miles). A thousand Bráhmans were on duty every day in the temple, three hundred and fifty singers and dancers performed before the image, and three hundred barbers shaved the pilgrims who intended to pay their devotions at the shrine. Every one of these servants had a settled allowance. The temple of Somnáth was built upon fifty pillars of teakwood covered with lead. The idol, which did not appear to be sculptured,[5] stood three cubits out of the ground and had a girth of three cubits. The idol was by itself in a dark chamber lighted by most exquisitely jewelled chandeliers. Near the idol was a chain of gold to which bells were hung weighing 200 *mans*. The chain was shaken at certain intervals during the night that the bells might rouse fresh parties of worshipping Bráhmans. The treasury containing many gold and silver idols, with doors hung with curtains set with valuable jewels, was near the chamber of the idol. The worth of what was found in the temple exceeded two millions of *dínárs* (Rs. 1,00,00,000). According to Ibni Asír Mahmúd reached Somnáth on a Thursday in the middle of *Zilkaáda* H. 414 (A.D. December 1023). On the approach of Mahmúd Bhím the ruler of Anhilvád fled abandoning his capital and took refuge in a fort to prepare for war. From Anhilvád Mahmúd started for Somnáth taking several forts with images which, Ibni Asír says, were the heralds

---

[1] It appears that at the time of his expedition to Somnáth Mahmúd had not adopted the title of Sultán.

[2] Sachau's Arabic Text, 253 chapter 58. [3] Sachau's Text, 253 chapter 58.

[4] The Táríkh-i-Kámil. Ibni Asír (A.D. 1160 - 1232) is a voluminous and reliable historian. Ibni Khallikán, the author of the famous biographical dictionary, knew and respected Asír always alluding to him as "our Sheikh." See Elliot, II. 245.

[5] From the term 'sculptured' it would seem the idol was of stone. It is curious how Ibni Asír states a little further that a part of the idol was "burned by Mahmúd." See Elliot, II. 471. The Tárikh-i-Alfi says (Elliot, II. 471) that the idol was cut of solid stone. It however represents it as hollow and containing jewels, in repeating the somewhat hackneyed words of Mahmúd when breaking the idol regardless of the handsome offer of the Bráhmans, and finding it full of jewels.

Appendix V.
ARAB REFERENCES, A.D. 851-1350.
Port or Coast Towns.
Somnath.

or chamberlains of Somnáth. Resuming his march he crossed a desert with little water. Here he was encountered by an army of 20,000 fighting men under chiefs who had determined not to submit to the invader. These forces were defeated and put to flight by a detachment sent against them by Mahmúd. Mahmúd himself marched to Dabalwárah a place said by Ibni Asír to be two days journey from Somnáth. When he reached Somnáth Mahmúd beheld a strong fortress whose base was washed by the waves of the sea. The assault began on the next day Friday. During nearly two days of hard fighting the invaders seemed doomed to defeat. On the third the Musalmáns drove the Hindus from the town to the temple. A terrible carnage took place at the temple-gate. Those of the defenders that survived took themselves to the sea in boats but were overtaken and some slain and the rest drowned.[1]

Supára.

Supa'ra (SUBÁRÁ, SUFÁRA, OR SURBÁRÁH.)—The references to Subárá are doubtful as some seem to belong to Surabára the Tápti mouth and others to Sopára six miles north of Bassein. The first Arab reference to Subára belongs to Sopára. Al Masúdi's (A.C. 915)[2] reference is that in *Saimúr* (Cheval), *Subára* (Sopára), and *Tána* (Thána) the people speak the Láriyáh language, so called from the sea which washes the coast. On this coast Al Istakhri (A.D. 951)[3] refers to *Subára* that is apparently to Surabára or Surat a city of Hind, four days from Kambáyah (Cambay).[4]

Ibni Haukal (A.D. 968-976) mentions[5] *Surbárah* apparently the Tápti mouth or Surat as one of the cities of Hind four *farsakhs*, correctly days, from *Kambáyah* and two miles (half *farsakh*) from the sea. From Surbára to *Sindán*, perhaps the Kachh Sanján, he makes ten days. Al Birúni (A.D. 970-1031) makes *Subára* perhaps the Thána Sopára six days' journey from *Debal*[6] (perhaps Diu). Al Idrísi (A.D. 1100) mentions Subára apparently Sopára as a town in the second climate, a mile and a half from the sea and five days (an excessive allowance) from Sindán. It was a populous busy town, one of the entrepôts of India and a pearl fishery. Near *Subára* he places Bára, a small island with a growth of cactus and cocoanut trees.[7]

Surábára.

Sura'ba'ra. See SUPÁRA.

Capitals.
Thána.

Tha'na (TÁNA).—That Thána was known to the Arabs in pre-Islám times is shown by one of the first Musalmán expeditions to the coast of India being directed against it. As early as the reign of the second Khalífah Umar Ibnal Khattáb (A.D. 634-643; H. 13-23) mention is made[8] of Usmán, Umar's governor of Umán (the Persian Gulf) and Bahrein,

---

[1] The Rauzat-us-Safa (Lithgd. Edition, IV. 48) speaks of Mahmúd's project of making Somnáth his capital and not Anhilwára as stated by Farishtah (I. 57, Original Persian Text). The Rauzát-us-Safa says that when Mahmúd had conquered Somnáth he wished to fix his residence there for some years as the country was very large and had a great many advantages including mines of pure gold and rubies brought from Sarandíb or Ceylon which he represents as a dependency of Gujarát. At last he yielded to his minister's advice and agreed to return to Khurásán.

[2] Prairies D'Or (DeMeynard's Arabic Text, I. 381; also Al Masúdi in Elliot (History of India, I. 24). [3] Al Istakhri in Elliot (History of India), I. 27.

[4] Al Istakhri in Elliot (History of India), I. 30.

[5] Ibni Haukal in Elliot (History of India), I. 34, 39.

[6] Thus in Sachau's Arabic Text page 102, but Elliot (I. 66) spells the word Sufára in his translation. It might have assumed that form in coming from the Arabic through Rashíd-ud-dín's Persian version from which Sir Henry Elliot derives his account.

[7] Al Idrísi in Elliot (History of India), I. 77 and 85.

[8] Al Bilázuri in Elliot, I. 116.

Appendix V.

ARAB REFERENCES, A.D. 851-1350.

Capitals.

Thána.

sending a successful expedition against Thána. Al Masúdi (A.D. 943) refers to Thána on the shore of the Lárwi sea or Indian Ocean, as one of the coast towns in which the Lárwi language is spoken.[1] Al Bírúni (A.D. 970-1031) gives[2] the distance from *Mahrat Desh* (the Marátha country) to the Konkan "with its capital Tána on the sea-shore" as 100 miles (25 *farsakhs*) and locates the *Lár Desh* (south Gujarát) capitals of *Báhrúj* and *Bahanjur* (Broach and Ránder) to the east of Thána. He places Thána with Somnáth Konkan and Kambáya in Gujarát and notices that from Thána the Lár country begins. Al Idrísi (end of the eleventh century) describes[3] Thána as a pretty town upon a great gulf where vessels anchor and from where they set sail. He gives the distance from Sindábur (or Goa) to Thána as four days' sail. From the neighbourhood of Thána he says the *kana* or bamboo and the *tabáshír* or bamboo pith are transported to the east and west.[4]

Vála or Valabhi.

Bara'da (PORBANDAR).—Of the Arab attacks on the great sea-port Vala or Valabhi, twenty miles west of Bhávnagar, during the eighth and ninth centuries details are given Above pages 94-96. The manner of writing the name of the city attacked leaves it doubtful whether Balaba that is Valabhi or Baráda near Porbandar is meant. But the importance of the town destroyed and the agreement in dates with other accounts leaves little doubt that the reference is to Valabhi.[5]

In the fourth year of his reign about A.D. 758 the Khalífah Jaáfar-al-Mansúr[6] (A.D. 754-775) the second ruler of the house of Abbás appointed Hishám governor of Sindh. Hishám despatched a fleet to the coast of Barádah, which may generally be read Balabha, under the command of Amru bin Jamál Taghlabi. Tabari (A.D. 838-932) and Ibni Asir (A.D. 1160-1232)[7] state that another expedition was sent to this coast in A.H. 160 (A.D. 776) in which though the Arabs succeeded in taking the town, disease thinned the ranks of the party stationed to garrison the port. A thousand of them died, and the remaining troops while returning to their country were shipwrecked on the coast of Persia. This he adds deterred

[1] Barbier DeMeynard's Text of Masúdi's Prairies D'Or, I. 330 and 381.

[2] Sachau's Arabic Text of Al Bírúni, chapters 18, 99, 102 and Elliot's History of India, I. 60-61, 66-67.

[3] Al Idrísi in Elliot, I-89.

[4] Al Idrísi says the real *tabáshír* is extracted from the root of the reed called *sharki*. *Sarki* is Gujaráti for reed. It is generally applied to the reeds growing on river banks used by the poor for thatching their cottages. *Tabáshír* is a drug obtained from the pith of the bamboo and prescribed by Indian physicians as a cooling drink good for fever.

[5] The name *Barádah* برادة in Arabic orthography bears a close resemblance to برابه *Barâbah*, بارلبه *Bárlabah*, برلبه *Barlabah*, all three being the forms or nearly the forms in which the word ولبه *Walabah* or ولبي *Walabi* would be written by an Arab, supposing the diacritical points to be, as they often are, omitted. Besides as Barádah the word has been read and miswritten نارند *Nárand* or *Bárand* and بارد *Bárad* or *Barid*. In the *shikastah* or broken hand *Nárand* or *Bárand* بارند would closely resemble بارلبه *Bárlabah* or *Báradah* بارده. Al Bilázuri in Elliot's History of India I. 127, writes the word *Nárand* or *Bárand*. Sir Henry Elliot (History, I. 444) reads the word Barada and would identify the place with the Barda hills inland from Porbandar in south-west Káthiáváḍ. The objection to this is that the word used by the Arab writers was the name of a town as well as of a coast tract, while the name of Barda is applied solely to a range of hills. On the other hand Balaba the coast and town meets all requirements.

[6] Reigned A.D. 754-775.

[7] Sir Henry Elliot's History of India, II. 246 and Frag. Arabes 3, 120, 212; Weil's Geschichte der Chalifen, II. 115.

Appendix V.

ARAB REFERENCES, A.D. 851-1350.

Capitals. *Vala or Valabhi.*

Al Mahdi[1] (A.D. 775-785) the succeeding Khalífah from extending the eastern limits of his empire. Besides against Balaba the Sindhi Arabs sent a fleet against Kandhár apparently, though somewhat doubtfully,[2] the town of that name to the north of Broach where they destroyed a temple or *budd* and built a mosque. Al Bírúni[3] (A.D. 1030) writing of the Valabhi era describes the city of Balabah بلبه as nearly thirty *jauzhans* (*yojanas*) that is ninety miles to the south of Anhilvára In another passage[4] he describes how the Bánia Ránka sued for and obtained the aid of an Arab fleet from the Arab lord of Mansúrah (built A.D. 750) for the destruction of Balaba. A land grant by a Valabhi chief remains as late as A.D. 766. For this reason and as the invaders of that expedition fled panic-struck by sickness Valabhi seems to have continued as a place of consequence if the expedition of A.D. 830 against Bala king of the east refers to the final attack on Valabhi an identification which is supported by a Jain authority which places the final overthrow of Valabhi at 888 Samvat that is A.D. 830.[5]

Kings.

Of the rulers of Gujarát between A.D. 850 and A.D. 1250 the only dynasty which impressed the Arabs was the Balháras of Málkhet or Mányakheta (A.D. 630-972) sixty miles south-east of Sholápúr. From about A.D. 736 to about A.D. 978, at first through a more or less independent local branch and afterwards (A.D. 914) direct the Ráshtrakútas continued overlords of most of Gujarát. The Arabs knew the Ráshtrakútas by their title *Vallabha* or Beloved in the case of Govind III. (A.D. 803-814), Prithvivallabha Beloved by the Earth, and of his successor the long beloved Amoghavarsha Vallabhaskanda, the Beloved of Śiva. Al Masúdi (A.D. 915-944) said : Bálárái is a name which he who follows takes. So entirely did the Arabs believe in the overlordship of the Ráshtrakútas in Gujarát that Al Idrísi (A.D. 1100, but probably quoting Al Jauhari A.D. 950) describes Nehrwalla as the capital of the Balarás. Until Dr. Bhándárkar discovered its origin in Vallabha, the ease with which meanings could be tortured out of the word and in Gujarát its apparent connection with the Valabhi kings (A.D. 509-770) made the word Balarái a cause of matchless confusion.

The merchant Sulaimán (A.D. 851) ranks the Balhára, the lord of Mánkír, as the fourth of the great rulers of the world. Every prince in India even in his own land paid him homage. He was the owner of many elephants and of great wealth. He refrained from wine and paid his troops and servants regularly. Their favour to Arabs was famous. Abu Zaid[6] (A.D. 913) says that though the Indian kings acknowledge the supremacy of no one, yet the Balháras or Ráshtrakútas by virtue of the title Balhára are kings of kings. Ibni Khurdádbah (A.D. 912) describes the Balháras as the greatest of Indian kings being as the name imports the king of kings. Al Masúdi (A.D. 915) described Balhára as a dynastic name which he who followed took. Though he introduces two other potentates the king of Jurz and the Baûra or Parmár king of Kanauj fighting with each other and with the Balhára he makes the Balhára, the lord of the Mánkír or the great centre, the greatest king

---

[1] Sir Henry Elliot's History of India, I. 444.

[2] Sir Henry Elliot (History of India, I. 445) identifies Kandhár with Kandadár in north-west Káthiavád.

[3] Sachau's Original Text, 205.

[4] Sachau's Original Text, 17-94.

[5] Details Above in Dr. Bhagvanlál's History, 96 note 3.

[6] Elliot's History of India, I. 7.

Appendix V.

ARAB REFERENCES, A.D. 851-1350.

Kings.

of India[1] to whom the kings of India bow in their prayers and whose emissaries they honour. He notices that the Balhára favours and honours Musalmáns and allows them to have mosques and assembly mosques. When Al Masúdi was in Cambay the town was ruled by Bánia, the deputy of the Balhára. Al Istakhri (A.D. 951) describes the land from Kambáyah to Saimúr (Cheul) as the land of the Balhára of Mánkír. In the Konkan were many Musalmáns over whom the Balhára appointed no one but a Musalmán to rule. Ibni Haukal (A.D. 970) describes the Balhára as holding sway over a land in which are several Indian kings.[2] Al Idrísi (A.D. 1100 but quoting Al Jauhari A.D. 950) agrees with Ibni Khurdádbah that Balhára is a title meaning King of Kings. He says the title is hereditary in this country, where when a king ascends the throne he takes the name of his predecessor and transmits it to his heirs.[3]

Condition.

That the Arabs found the Ráshtrakúṭas kind and liberal rulers there is ample evidence. In their territories property was secure,[4] theft or robbery was unknown, commerce was encouraged, foreigners were treated with consideration and respect. The Arabs especially were honoured not only with a marked and delicate regard, but magistrates from among themselves were appointed to adjudicate their disputes according to the Musalmán law.

The Gurjjaras.

The ruler next in importance to the Balhára was the Jurz that is the Gurjjara king. It is remarkable, though natural, that the Arabs should preserve the true name of the rulers of Anhilváḍa which the three tribe or dynastic names Chápa or Chaura (A.D. 720-956), Solanki or Cáulukya (A.D. 961-1242), and Vághela (A.D. 1240-1290) should so long have concealed. Sulaimán (A.D. 851) notices that the Jurz king hated Musalmáns while the Balhára king loved Musalmáns. He may not have known what excellent reasons the Gurjjaras had for hating the Arab raiders from sea and from Sindh. Nor would it strike him that the main reason why the Balhára fostered the Moslem was the hope of Arab help in his struggles with the Gurjjaras.

Jurz.

According to the merchant Sulaimán[5] (A.D. 851) the kingdom next after the Balhára's was that of Jurz the Gurjjara king whose territories "consisted of a tongue of land." The king of Jurz maintained a large force: his cavalry was the best in India. He was unfriendly to the Arabs. His territories were very rich and abounded in horses and camels. In his realms exchanges were carried on in silver and gold dust of which metals mines were said to be worked.

The king of Jurz was at war with the Balháras as well as with the neighbouring kingdom of Táfak or the Panjáb. The details given under Bhínmál page 468 show that Sulaimán's tongue of land, by which he apparently meant either Káthiáváḍ or Gujarát was an imperfect idea of the extent of Gurjjara rule. At the beginning of the tenth century A.D. 916 Sulaimán's editor Abu Zaid describes Kanauj as a large country

---

[1] Elliot's History of India, I. 22, 24, 25. [2] Elliot's History of India, I. 34.

[3] Elliot's History of India, I. 86.

[4] Al Masúdi Les Prairies D'Or, II. chapter 18 page 85.

[5] Giving an account of the diviners and jugglers of India Abu Zaid says: These observations are especially applicable to Kanauj, a large country forming the empire of Jurz. Abu Zaid in Elliot's History of India, I. 10. References given in the History of Bhínmál show that the Gurjjara power spread not only to Kanauj but to Bengal.

forming the empire of Jurz,[1] a description which the Gurjjara Vatsarája's success in Bengal about a century before shows not to be impossible. Ibni Khurdádbah (A.D. 912) ranks the king of Juzr as fourth in importance among Indian kings. According to him "the Tátariya dirhams were in use in the Juzr kingdom." Al Masúdi (A.D. 943) speaks of the Konkan country of the Balhára as on one side exposed to the attacks of the king of Juzr a monarch rich in men horses and camels. He speaks of the Juzr kingdom bordering on Táfán apparently the Panjáb and Táfán as bounded by Rahma[2] apparently Burma and Sumátra. Ibni Haukal (A.D. 968-976) notices that several kingdoms existed, including the domain of the Śiláháras of the north Konkan within the land of the Balhára between Kambáyah and Saimúr.[3] Al Bírúni (A.D. 970-1031) uses not Juzr, but Gujarát.[4] Beyond that is to the south of Gujarát he places Konkan and Tána. In Al Bírúni's time Náráyan near Jaipúr, the former capital of Gujarát, had been taken and the inhabitants removed to a town on the frontier.[5] Al Idrísi (end of the eleventh century really from tenth century materials) ranks the king of Juzr as the fourth and the king of Sáfán or Táfan as the second in greatness to the Balhára.[6] In another passage in a list of titular sovereigns Al Idrísi enters the names of Sáfir (Táfán) Hazr (Jazr-Juzr) and Dumi (Rahmi).[7] By the side of Juzr was Táfak (doubtfully the Panjáb) a small state producing the whitest and most beautiful women in India; the king having few soldiers; living at peace with his neighbours and like the Balháras highly esteeming the Arabs.[8] Ibni Khurdádbah (A.D. 912) calls Tában the king next in eminence to the Balhára.[9] Al Masúdi (A.D. 943) calls Táfak the ruler of a mountainous country like Kashmír[10] with small forces living on friendly terms with neighbouring sovereigns and well disposed to the Moslims.[11] Al Idrísi (end of eleventh century but materials of the tenth century) notices Sáfán (Táfán) as the principality that ranks next to the Konkan that is to the Ráshtrakúṭas.

Appendix V. ARAB REFERENCES, A.D. 851-1350. Kings. *Jurz.*

Rahma or **Ruhmi**, according to the merchant Sulaimán (A.D. 851) borders the land of the Balháras, the Juzr, and Táfán. The king who was not much respected was at war with both the Juzr and the Balhára. He had the most numerous army in India and a following of 50,000 elephants when he took the field. Suláimán notices a cotton fabric made in Rahma, so delicate that a dress of it could pass through a signet-ring. The medium of exchange was *cowries* Cypræa moneta shell money. The country produced gold silver and aloes and the whisk of the *samara* or *yák* Bos poëphagus the bushy-tailed ox. Ibni Khurdádbáh[12] (A.D. 912) places Rahmi as the sixth kingdom. He apparently identified it with Al Rahmi or north Sumátra as he notes that between it and the other kingdoms communication is kept up by ships. He notices that the ruler had five thousand elephants and that cotton cloth and aloes probably the well-known Kumári

Rahma or Ruhmi.

---

1 Ibni Khurdádbah in Elliot's History of India, I. 13.
2 Al Masúdi in Elliot (History of India), I. 25.
3 Ibni Haukal in Elliot (History of India), I. 34.
4 Al Bírúni in Elliot (History of India), I. 67.
5 Al Bírúni in Elliot (History of India), I. 59.
6 Al Idrísi in Elliot (History of India), I. 76.
7 Al Idrísi in Elliot (History of India), I. 86.
8 The merchant Sulaimán (851 A.D.) in Elliot's History of India, I. 5.
9 Ibni Khurdádbah in Elliot (History of India), I. 13.
10 Al Masúdi in Elliot (History of India), I. 23.
11 Al Masúdi in Elliot (History of India), I. 25.
12 Ibni Khurdádbah in Elliot's History of India, I. 14.

Appendix V.

ARAB REFERENCES, A.D. 851-1350.

Kings.

Rahma or Ruhmi.

or Cambodian aloes, were the staple produce. Al Masúdi (A.D. 943) after stating that former accounts of Rahma's[1] elephants troops and horses were probably exaggerated, adds that the kingdom of Rahma extends both along the sea and the continent and that it is bounded by an inland state called Káman (probably Kámarup that is Assam). He describes the inhabitants as fair and handsome and notices that both men and women had their ears pierced. This description of the people still more the extension of the country both along the sea and along the continent suggests that Masúdi's Al Rahmi is a combination of Burma which by dropping the B he has mixed with Al Rahma. Lane identifies Rahmi[2] with Sumátra on the authority of an Account of India and China by two Muhammadan Travellers of the Ninth Century. This identification is supported by Al Masúdi's[3] mention of Rámi as one of the islands of the Java group. the kingdom of the Indian Mihráj. The absence of reference to Bengal in these accounts agrees with the view that during the ninth century Bengal was under Tibet.

Products.

In the middle of the ninth century mines of gold and silver are said to be worked in Gujarát.[4] Abu Zaid (A.D. 916) represents pearls as in great demand. The Tártáriyah, or according to Al Masúdi the Táhiriyah *dínars* of Sindh, fluctuating[5] in price from one and a half to three and a fraction of the Baghdád *dínars*, were the current coin in the Gujarát ports. Emeralds also were imported from Egypt mounted as seals.[6]

Ibni Khurdádbah[7] (A.D. 912) mentions teakwood and the bamboo as products of Sindán that is the Konkan Sanjan.[8] Al Masúdi (A.D. 943) notes that at the great fair of Multán the people of Sindh and Hind offered Kumar that is Cambodian aloe-wood of the purest quality worth twenty *dínars* a *man*.[9] Among other articles of trade he mentions an inferior emerald exported from Cambay and Saimúr to Makkah,[10] the lance shafts of Broach,[11] the shoes of Cambay,[12] and the white and handsome maidens of Táfan[13] who were in great demand in Arab countries. Ibni Haukal (A.D 968-976) states that the country comprising Fámbal, Sindán, Saimúr, and Kambáyah produced mangoes cocoanuts lemons and rice in abundance. That honey could be had in great quantities, but no date palms were to be found.[14]

Al Bírúni (A.D. 1031) notices that its import of horses from Mekran and the islands of the Persian Gulf was a leading portion of Cambay trade.[15] According to Al Idrísi (A.D. 1100) the people of Mámhal[16] (Anhilwára) had many horses and camels.[17] One of the peculiarities of

---

1 Al Masúdi in History of India by Sir Henry Elliot, I. 25.
2 Lane's Notes on his Translation of the Alf Leilah, III. 80.
3 Al Masúdi's Murúj (Arabic Text Cairo Edition, I. 221).
4 The merchant Sulaimán (Elliot's History of India), I. 4 and 5.
5 See page 519 note 8.
6 Sir Henry Elliot's History of India, I. 11.
7 Ibni Khurdádbah in Elliot's History of India, I. 14.
8 Ibni Khurdádbah in Elliot's History of India, I. 15.
9 Al Masúdi (Elliot's History of India), I. 23.
10 Barbier De Meynard's Arabic Text of Les Prairies D'Or, III. 47-48.
11 Barbier De Meynard's Arabic Text of Les Prairies D'Or, I. 239.
12 Barbier De Meynard's Arabic Text of Les Prairies D'Or, I. 253.
13 Barbier De Meynard's Arabic Text of Les Prairies D'Or, I. 384.
14 Ibni Haukal (Ashkál-ul-Bilád) and Elliot's History of India, I. 39.
15 Elliot's History of India, III. 33.
16 Mámhal is by some numbered among the cities of India. Al Idrísi in Elliot, I. 84.
17 Al Idrísi in Elliot, I. 79.

Appendix V.

ARAB REFERENCES, A.D. 851-1350.

Products.

the Nahrwála country was that all journeys were made and all merchandise was carried in bullock waggons. Kambáyah was rich in wheat and rice and its mountains yielded the Indian *kaná* or bamboo. At Subára[1] (Sopára) they fished for pearls and Bára a small island close to Subára produced the cocoanut and the costus. Sindán according to Al Idrísi produced the cocoa palm, the ratan, and the bamboo. Saimúr had many cocoa palms, much henna (Lawsonia inermis), and a number of aromatic plants.[2] The hills of Thána yielded the bamboo and *tabáshír*[3] or bamboo pith. From Saimúr according to Al Kazwíni (A.D. 1236, but from tenth century materials) came aloes. Rashíd-ud-dín (A.D. 1310) states that in Kambáyah, Somnáth, Kankan, and Tána the vines yield twice a year and such is the strength of the soil that cotton-plants grow like willow or plane trees and yield produce for ten years. He refers to the betel leaf, to which he and other Arab writers and physicians ascribe strange virtues as the produce of the whole country of Malabár. The exports from the Gujarát coasts are said to be sugar (the staple product of Málwa), *bádrúd* that is bezoar, and *haldi* that is turmeric.[4]

According to Ibni Haukal (A.D. 170) from Kambáya to Saimúr the villages lay close to one another and much land was under cultivation.[5] At the end[6] of the eleventh century trade was brisk merchandise from every country finding its way to the ports of Gujarát whose local products were in turn exported all over the east.[7] The Ráshtrakúta dominion was vast, well-peopled, commercial, and fertile.[8] The people lived mostly on a vegetable diet, rice peas beans haricots and lentils being their daily food.[9] Al Idrísi speaks of certain Hindus eating animals whose deaths had been caused by falls or by being gored,[10] but Al Masúdi states that the higher classes who wore the "baldric like yellow thread" (the Janoi) abstained from flesh. According to Ibni Haukal (A.D. 968-970) the ordinary dress of the kings of Hind was trousers and a tunic.[11] He also notices that between Kambáyah and Saimúr the Muslims and infidels wear the same cool fine muslin dress and let their beards grow in the same fashion.[12] During the tenth century on high days the Balhára wore a crown of gold and a dress of rich stuff. The attendant women were richly clad, wearing rings of gold and silver upon their feet and hands and having their hair in curls.[13] At the close of the Hindu period (A.D. 1300) Rashíd-ud-dín describes Gujarát as a flourishing country with no less than 80,000 villages and hamlets the people happy the soil rich growing in the four seasons seventy varieties of flowers. Two harvests repaid the husbandman, the earlier crop refreshed by the dew of the cold season the late crop enriched by a certain rainfall.[14]

Review.

In their intercourse with Western India nothing struck the Arabs more than the toleration shown to their religion both by chief and peoples.

---

1 Al Idrísi in Elliot, I. 85. 2 Al Idrísi in Elliot's History of India, I. 85.
3 Al Idrísi in Elliot's History of India, I. 85.
4 Rashíd-ud-dín in Elliot's History of India, I. 67 - 68.
5 Ibni Haukal (A.D. 968) in Elliot, I. 39.
6 Al Idrísi (A.D. 968) in Elliot, I. 84 and 87.
7 Al Idrísi speaking of Cambay in Elliot's History of India, I. 84.
8 Al Idrísi in Elliot, I. 85. 9 Al Idrísi in Elliot, I. 88.
10 Al Masúdi in Elliot's History of India, I. 9.
11 Ibni Haukal in Elliot, I. 35. 12 Ibni Haukal in Elliot, I. 39.
13 Al Idrísi in Elliot's History of India, I. 88.
14 Rashíd-ud-dín (A.D. 1310) in Elliot's History of India, I. 67. The passage seems to be a quotation from Al Bírúni (A.D. 1031).

Appendix V.

ARAB REFERENCES, A.D. 851 - 1350.

Review.

This was specially marked in the Ráshṭrakúṭa towns where besides free use of mosques and Jámá mosques. Musalmán magistrates or kázis were appointed to settle disputes among Musalmáns according to their own laws.[1] Toleration was not peculiar to the Balháras. Al Bírúni records[2] that in the ninth century (A.D. 581), when the Hindus recovered Sindán (Sanján in Kachh) they spared the assembly mosque where long after the Faithful congregated on Fridays praying for their Khalífah without hindrance. In the Balhára country so strongly did the people believe in the power of Islám or which is perhaps more likely so courteous were they that they said that our king enjoys a long life and long reign is solely due to the favour shown by him to the Musalmáns. So far as the merchant Sulaimán saw in the ninth century the chief religion in Gujarát was Buddhism. He notices that the principles of the religion of China were brought from India and that the Chinese ascribe to the Indians the introduction of Buddhas into their country. Of religious beliefs metempsychoses or re-birth and of religious practices widow-burning or *satti* and self-torture seem to have struck him most.[3] As a rule the dead were burned.[4] Sulaimán represents the people of Gujarát as steady abstemious and sober abstaining from wine as well as from vinegar, 'not' he adds 'from religious motives but from their disdain of it.' Among their sovereigns the desire of conquest was seldom the cause of war.[5] Abu Zaid (A.D. 916) describes the Bráhmans as Hindus devoted to religion and science. Among Bráhmans were poets who lived at kings' courts, astronomers, philosophers, diviners, and drawers of omens from the flight of crows.[6] He adds: So sure are the people that after death they shall return to life upon the earth, that when a person grows old "he begs some one of his family to throw him into the fire or to drown him."[7] In Abu Zaid's time (A.D. 916) the Hindus did not seclude their women. Even the wives of the kings used to mix freely with men and attend courts and places of public resort unveiled.[8] According to Ibni Khurdádbah (A.D. 912) India has forty-two religious sects "part of whom believe in God and his Prophet (on whom be peace) and part who deny his mission."[9] Ibni Khurdádbah (A.D. 912) describes the Hindus as divided into seven classes. Of these the first are Thákarias [10] or Thákurs men of high caste from whom kings are chosen and to whom men of the other classes render homage, the second are the Baráhmas[11] who abstain from wine and fermented liquors; the third are the Katariya or Kshatrias who drink not more than three cups of wine; the fourth are the Sudaria or Shudras husbandmen by profession; the fifth are the Baisura or Vaish artificers and domestics; the sixth Sandalias or Chandala menials; and the seventh the 'Lahúd,' whose women adorn themselves and whose men are fond of amusements and games of skill. Both among the people and the kings of Gujarát[12] wine

---

1 Ibni Haukal in Elliot's History of India, I. 34-38, also Al Kazwíni, I. 97.

2 Sir Henry Elliot's History of India, I. 29.

3 The merchant Sulaimán in Elliot's History of India, I. 7.

4 The merchant Sulaimán in Elliot's History of India, I. 6.

5 The merchant Sulaimán in Elliot's History of India, I. 7.

6 Abu Zaid in Elliot's History of India, I. 10.

7 Abu Zaid in Elliot's History of India, I. 9-10.

8 Abu Zaid in Elliot's History of India, I. 11.

9 Ibni Khurdádbah in Elliot, I. 17.

10 See Elliot, I. 76, where Al Idrísi calls the first class '*Sákariá*' the word being a transliteration of the Arabic Thákariyah or Thákurs.

11 The Arabic plural of the word Barahman.

12 Ibni Khurdádbah in Elliot's History of India, I. 13-17.

was "unlawful and lawful" that is it was not used though no religious rule forbad its use. According to Al Masúdi (A.D. 943) a general opinion prevailed that India was the earliest home of order and wisdom. The Indians chose as their king the great Bráhma who ruled them for 366 years. His descendants retain the name of Bráhman and are honoured as the most illustrious caste. They abstain from the flesh of animals.[1] Hindu kings cannot succeed before the age of forty nor do they appear in public except on certain occasions for the conduct of state affairs. Royalty and all the high offices of state[2] are limited to the descendants of one family. The Hindus strongly disapprove of the use of wine both in themselves and in others not from any religious objection but on account of its intoxicating and reason-clouding qualities.[3] Al Bírúni (A.D. 970-1031) quoted by Rashíd-ud-dín (A.D. 1310) states that the people of Gujarát are idolators and notices the great penance-pilgrimages to Somnáth details of which have already been given.[4] Al Idrísi (end of the eleventh century) closely follows Ibni Khurdádbah's (A.D. 912) division of the people of India. The chief exception is that he represents[5] the second class, the Bráhmans, as wearing the skins of tigers and going about staff in hand collecting crowds and from morn till eve proclaiming to their hearers the glory and power of God. He makes out that the Kastariás or Kshatriyas are able to drink three *ratl* (a *ratl* being one pound troy) of wine and are allowed to marry Bráhman women. The Sabdaliya or Chandal women, he says, are noted for beauty. Of the forty-two sects he enumerates worshippers of trees and adorers of serpents, which they keep in stables and feed as well as they can, deeming it to be a meritorious work. He says that the inhabitants of Kambáya are Buddhists (idolators)[6] and that the Balhára also worships the idol Buddha.[7] The Indians, says Al Idrísi[8] (end of the eleventh century) are naturally inclined to justice and in their actions never depart from it. Their reputation for good faith, honesty, and fidelity to their engagements brings strangers flocking to their country and aids its prosperity. In illustration of the peaceable disposition of the Hindus, he quotes the ancient practice of *duhái* or conjuring in the name of the king, a rite which is still in vogue in some native states. When a man has a rightful claim he draws a circle on the ground and asks his debtor to step into the circle in the name of the king. The debtor never fails to step in nor does he ever leave the circle without paying his debts. Al Idrísi describes the people of Nahrwára as having so high a respect for oxen that when an ox dies they bury it. "When enfeebled by age or if unable to work they provide their oxen with food without exacting any return."[9]

---

[1] Text Les Prairies D'Or, I. 149-154 and Elliot's History of India, I. 19.
[2] Arabic Text Les Prairies D'Or, I. 149-154, and Elliot's History of India, I. 20.
[3] Al Masúdi's Prairies D'Or, I. 169, and Elliot's History of India. I. 20.
[4] Rashíd-ud-dín from Al Bírúni in Elliot's History of India, I. 67-68.
[5] Al Idrísi in Elliot (History of India), I. 76.
[6] Al Idrísi in Elliot (History of India), I. 85.
[7] Al Idrísi in Elliot (History of India), I. 87.
[8] Sir Henry Elliot's History of India, I. 88.
[9] Al Idrísi in Elliot (History of India), I. 88.

APPENDIX VI.

WESTERN INDIA AS KNOWN TO THE GREEKS AND ROMANS.

Appendix VI.

EARLY GREEKS AND ROMANS.

Ktêsias.

He'rodotos and **Hekataios**, the earliest Greek writers who make mention of India, give no information in regard to Western India in particular.

Kte'sias (c. 400 B.C.) learnt in Persia that a race of Pygmies lived in India in the neighbourhood of the silver mines, which Lassen places near Udaipur (Mewar). From the description of these Pygmies (Phôtios. Bibl. LXXII. 11-12) it is evident that they represent the Bhíls. Ktêsias also mentions (Phótios. Bibl. LXXII. 8) that there is a place in an uninhabited region fifteen days from Mount Sardous, where they venerate the sun and moon and where for thirty-five days in each year the sun remits his heat for the comfort of his worshippers. This place must apparently have been somewhere in Marwar, and perhaps Mount Âbu is the place referred to.

Alexander.

Alexander (B.C. 326-25) did not reach Gujarát, and his companions have nothing to tell of this part of the country. It is otherwise with

Megasthenês.

Megasthene's (c. 300 B.C.) who resided with Candragupta as the ambassador of Seleukos Nikator and wrote an account of India in four books, of which considerable fragments are preserved, chiefly by Strabo, Pliny, and Arrian. His general account of the manners of the Indians relates chiefly to those of northern India, of whom he had personal knowledge. But he also gave a geographical description of India, for Arrian informs us (Ind. VII) that he gave the total number of Indian tribes as 118, and Pliny (VI. 17ff) does in fact enumerate about 90, to whom may be added some seven or eight more mentioned by Arrian. It is true that Pliny does not distinctly state that he takes his geographical details from Megasthenês, and that he quotes Seneca as having written a book on India. But Seneca also (Pliny, VI. 17) gave the number of the tribes as 118 in which he must have followed Megasthenês. Further, Pliny says (*ibid*) that accounts of the military forces of each nation were given by writers such as Megasthenês and Dionysius who stayed with Indian kings: and as he does not mention Dionysius in his list of authorities for his Book VI., it follows that it was from Megasthenês that he drew his accounts of the forces of the Gangaridæ, Modogalinga, Andaræ, Prasi, Megallæ, Asmagi, Oratæ, Suaratarataæ, Automula, Charmæ, and Pandæ (VI. 19), names which, as will be shown below, betray a knowledge of all parts of India. It is a fair inference that the remaining names mentioned by Pliny were taken by him from Megasthenês, perhaps through the medium of Seneca's work. The corruption of Pliny's text

---

1 Contributed by Mr. A. M. T. Jackson, M.A., I.C.S.

and the fact that Mégasthenês learnt the tribal names in their Prakrit forms, make it extremely difficult to identify many of the races referred to.

That part of Pliny's account of India which may with some certainty be traced back to Megasthenês begins with a statement of the stages of the royal road from the Hypasis (Biás) to Palibothra (Patna) (Nat. Hist. VI. 17). The next chapter gives an account of the Ganges and its tributaries and mentions the Gangaridæ of Kalinga with their capital Pertalis as the most distant nation on its banks. In the 19th chapter, after an account of the forces of the Gangaridæ, Pliny gives a list of thirteen tribes, of which the only ones that can be said to be satisfactorily identified are Modogalinga (the three Calingas: Caldwell Drav. Gr.), Molindæ (compare Mount Mâlindya of Varâha Mihira Br. S. XIV.), and Thalutæ (McCrindle reads Taluctæ and identifies with the Tâmraliptakas of Tamluk on the lower Ganges). He next mentions the Andaræ (Andhras of Telingana) with thirty cities 100,000 foot 2000 horse and 1000 elephants. He then digresses to speak of the Dardæ (Dards of the Upper Indus) as rich in gold and the Setæ (of Mêwâr, Lassen) in silver, and next introduces the Prasi (Prâcyas) of Palibothra (Pâtaliputra) as the most famous and powerful of all the tribes, having 600,000 foot 30,000 horse and 8000 elephants. Inland from these he names the Monsædes (Munda of Singbhúm) and Suari (Śavaras of Central India) among whom is Mount Maleus (Mâhendra Male ?). Then after some account of the Iomanes (Yamunâ) running between Methora (Mathurâ) and Chrysobora (McCrindle reads Carisobora, Arrian Ind. VIII. Kleisobora = Krishnapura ?) he turns to the Indus, of some of whose nineteen tributaries he gives some account in chapter 20. He then digresses to give an account of the coast of India, starting from the mouth of the Ganges, whence to Point Calingon (Point Godâvari) and the city of Dandaguda (Cunningham's Râja Mahendri, but more probably the Dhanakaṭaka or Dhenukâkaṭa of the Western cave inscriptions) he reckons 625 miles. The distance thence to Tropina (Tirupanatara near Kochin according to Burgess) is 1225 miles. Next at a distance of 750 miles is the cape of Perimula, where is the most famous mart of India. Further on in the same chapter is mentioned a city named Automula on the sea shore among the Arabastræ (or Salabastræ and Oratæ, McCrindle) a noble mart where five rivers together flow into the sea. There can hardly be a doubt that the two places are the same, the two names being taken from different authorities, and that the place meant is Chemula or Cheul (Ptolemy's Simulla) the five rivers being those that flow into Bombay Harbour northward of Cheul. The distance from Perimula to the Island of Patala in the Indus is 620 miles. Pliny next enumerates as hill tribes between the Indus and Jamna, shut in a ring of mountains and deserts for a space of 625 miles, the Cæsi (the Kekioi of Arr. Ind. IV. and Kêkayas of the Purâṇas, about the head waters of the Sutlej), the Cetriboni of the woods (. . . . . Vana ?), the Megallæ (Mêkalas) with 500 elephants and unknown numbers of horse and foot, the Chrysei (Karûsha) Parasangæ (Pâraśava, corrupted by the likeness of its first three syllables to the word παρασαγγα), the Asmagi (Aśmaka of Varâha Mihira) with 30,000 foot 300 elephants and 800 horse. These are shut in by the Indus and surrounded by a circle of mountains and deserts for 625 miles. Next come the Dari and Suræ and then deserts again for 187 miles. Whether these are or are not correctly identified with the Dhars and Saurs of Sindh, they must be placed somewhere to the north of the Ran. Below them come five kingless tribes living in the hills along the sea-

Appendix VI.
EARLY GREEKS AND ROMANS.
Megasthenês.

coast—the Maltecoræ, Singhæ, Marohæ, Rarungæ, and Moruni—none of whom are satisfactorily identified, but who may be placed in Kachh. Next follow the Nareæ. enclosed by Mount Capitalia (Âbu) the highest mountain in India, on the other side of which are mines of gold and silver. The identification of Capitalia with Âbu is probable enough, but the name given to the mountain must be connected with the Kapishṭhala of the *Purâṇas*, who have given their name to one of the recensions of the Yajur Veda, though Kaithal, their modern representative, lies far away from Âbu in the Karnâl district of the Panjâb, and Arrian places his καμβισθολοι (Ind. IV) about the head waters of the Hydraôtês (Râvi). After Capitalia and the Nareæ come the Oratæ with but ten elephants but numerous infantry. These must be the Aparântakas of the inscriptions and *purâṇas*, Megasthenês having learnt the name in a Prakṛit form (Avarâta, Orâta). The name of the next tribe, who have no elephants but horse and foot only, is commonly read Suarataratæ (Nobbe) but the preferable reading is Varetatæ (McCrindle) which when corrected to Varelatæ represents Varalatta, the sixth of the seven Konkans in the purâṇic lists (Wilson As. Res. XV. 47), which occupied the centre of the Thána district and the country of the wild tribe of the Varlîs. Next are the Odonbæores, whose name is connected with the *udumbara* Ficus glomerata tree, and who are not the Audumbari Sâlvas of Pâṇini (IV. i. 173) but must be placed in Southern Thána. Next come the Arabastræ Oratæ (so read for Arabastræ Thorace of Nobbe, and Salabastræ Horatæ of McCrindle) or Arabastra division of the Oratæ or Koṅkaṇîs. Arabastra may be connected with the Ârava of Varâha-Mihira's South-Western Division (Br. S. XIV. 17) where they are mentioned along with Barbara (the seventh or northernmost Koṅkaṇ). This tribe had a fine city in a marsh infested by crocodiles and also the great mart of Automula (Cheul) at the confluence of five rivers, and the king had 1600 elephants 150,000 foot and 5000 horse, and must therefore have held a large part of the Dakhan as well as of the sea coast. Next to this kingdom is that of the Charmæ, whose forces are small, and next to them the Pandæ (Pâṇḍya of Travancor) with 300 cities 150,000 foot and 500 elephants. Next follows a list of thirteen tribes, some of which St. Martin has identified with modern Rajput tribes about the Indus because the last name of the thirteen is Orostræ, " who reach to the island of Patala " and may be confidently identified with the Sâurâshṭra of Kâthiâvâda. We must however assume that Megasthenês after naming the tribes of the west coast enumerates the inland tribes of the Dakhan until he arrives at the point from which he started. But the only identification that seems plausible is that of the Derangæ with the Telingas or Telugus. Next to the Orostræ follows a list of tribes on the east of the Indus from south to north—the Mathoæ (compare Mânthava, a Bâhîka town Pân. IV. ii. 117), Bolingæ (Bhâulingi, a Sâlva tribe Pân. IV. i. 173), Gallitalutæ (perhaps a corruption of Tâilakhali, another Sâlva tribe, *ib.*), Dimuri, Megari, Ardabæ, Mesæ (Matsya of Jaipur ?), Abi, Suri, (v. l. Abhis Uri), Silæ, and then deserts for 250 miles. Next come three more tribes and then again deserts, then four or five (according to the reading) more tribes, and the Asini whose capital is Bucephala (Jalâlpur) (Cunningham Anc. Geog. 177). Megasthenês then gives two mountain tribes and ten beyond the Indus including the Orsi (Uraśâ) Taxilæ (Takshaśilâ) and Peucolitæ (people of Pushkâlavatî). Of the work of Dêïmachos, who went on an embassy to Allitrochadês (Bindusâra) son of Candragupta, nothing is known except that it was in two books and was reckoned the most untrustworthy of all accounts of India (Strabo, II. i. 9).

Appendix VI.

EARLY GREEKS AND ROMANS.

Ptolemy II.

Ptolemy II. Philadelphos (died 247 B.C.) interested himself in the trade with India and opened a caravan road from Koptos on the Nile to Berenikê on the Red Sea (Strabo, XVII. i. 45) and for centuries the Indian trade resorted either to this port or to the neighbouring Myos Hormos. He also sent to India (apparently to Aśoka) an envoy named Dionysius, who is said by Pliny (VI. 17) to have written an account of things Indian of which no certain fragments appear to remain. But we know from the fragments of

Agatharkhides.

Agatharkhides (born c. 250 A.D.) who wrote in old age an account of the Red Sea of which we have considerable extracts in Diodôros (III. 12 - 48) and Phôtios (Müller's Geogr. Gr. Min. I. 111ff), states that in his time the Indian trade with Potana (Patala) was in the hands of the Sabæans of Yemen. (Müller, I. 191.) In fact it was not until the voyages of Eudoxos (see below) that any direct trade sprang up between India and Egypt. The mention of Patala as the mart resorted to by the Arabs shows that we are still in Pliny's first period (see below).

The Baktrian Greeks.

The Baktrian Greeks extended their power into India after the fall of the Mâurya empire (c. 180 B.C.) their leader being Dêmêtrios son of Euthydêmos, whose conquests are referred to by Justin (XLI. 6) and Strabo (XI. ii. 1). But the most extensive conquests to the east and south were made by Menandros (c. 110 B.C.) who advanced to the Jumna and conquered the whole coast from Pattalênê (lower Sindh) to the kingdoms of Saraostos (Surâshṭra) and Sigertis (Pliny's Sigerus ?) (Strabo, XI. ii. 1). These statements of Strabo are confirmed by the author of the Periplus (c. 250 A.D.) who says that in his time *drakhmai* with Greek inscriptions of Menandros and Apollodotos were still current at Barygaza (Per. 47). Apollodotos is now generally thought to have been the successor of Menandros (c. 100 B.C.) (Brit. Museum Cat. of Bactrian Coins page xxxiii.). Plutarch (Reip. Ger. Princ.) tells us that Menandros' rule was so mild, that on his death his towns disputed the possession of his ashes and finally divided them.

Eudoxos of Cyzicus.

Eudoxos of Cyzicus (c. 117 B.C.) made in company with others two very successful voyages to India, in the first of which the company were guided by an Indian who had been shipwrecked on the Egyptian coast. Strabo (II. iii. 4), in quoting the story of his doings from Poseidônios, lays more stress upon his attempt to circumnavigate Africa than upon these two Indian voyages, but they are of very great importance as the beginnings of the direct trade with India.

Eratokthenês.

The Geographers down to Ptolemy drew their knowledge of India almost entirely from the works of Megasthenês and of the companions of Alexander. Among them Eratosthenês (c. 275 - 194 B.C.), the founder of scientific geography, deserves mention as having first given wide currency to the notion that the width of India from west to east was greater than its length from north to south, an error which lies at the root of Ptolemy's distortion of the map. Eratosthenês' critic Hipparkhos (c. 130 B.C.) on this point followed the more correct account of Megasthenês, and is otherwise notable as the first to make use of astronomy for the determination of the geographical position of places.

Strabo.

Strabo (c. 63 B.C. - 23 A.D.) drew his knowledge of India, like his predecessors, chiefly from Megasthenês and from Alexander's followers, but adds (XV. i. 72) on the authority of Nikolaos of Damascus (tutor to the children of Antony and Cleopatra, and envoy of Herod) (an account of three Indian envoys from a certain king Pôros to Augustus (*ob.* A.D. 14),

Appendix VI.

EARLY GREEKS AND ROMANS.

Strabo.

who brought presents consisting of an armless man, snakes, a huge turtle and a large partridge, with a letter in Greek written on parchment offering free passage and traffic through his dominions to the emperor's subjects. With these envoys came a certain Zarmanokhêgas (Sramanâcârya, Lassen) from Bargosê (Broach, the earliest mention of the name) who afterwards burnt himself at Athens, "according to the ancestral custom of the Indians." The fact that the embassy came from Broach and passed through Antioch shows that they took the route by the Persian Gulf, which long remained one of the chief lines of trade (Per. chap. 36). If the embassy was not a purely commercial speculation on the part of merchants of Broach, it is hard to see how king Pôros, who had 600 under-kings, can be other than the Indo-Skythian Kozolakadaphes, who held Pôros' old kingdom as well as much other territory in North-West India. This if correct would show that as early as the beginning of our era the Indo-Skythian power reached as far south as Broach. The fact that the embassy took the Persian Gulf route and that their object was to open commercial relations with the Roman empire seems to show that at this period there was no direct trade between Broach and the Egyptian ports of the Red Sea. Strabo however mentions that in his time Arabian and Indian wares were carried on camels from Myos Hormos (near Râs Abu Somer) on the Red Sea to Koptos on the Nile (XVII. i. 45 and XVI. iv. 24) and dilates upon the increase of the Indian trade since the days of the Ptolemies when not so many as twenty ships dared pass through the Red Sea "to peer out of the Straits," whereas in his time whole fleets of as many as 120 vessels voyaged to India and the headlands of Ethiopia from Myos Hormos (II. v. 12 and XV. i. 13). It would seem that we have here to do with Pliny's second period of Indian trade, when Sigerus (probably Janjira) was the goal of the Egyptian shipmasters (see below). Strabo learnt these particulars during his stay in Egypt with Aelius Gallus, but they were unknown to his contemporary Diodôros who drew his account of India entirely from Megasthenês (Diod. II. 31-42) and had no knowledge of the East beyond the stories told by Jamboulos a person of uncertain date of an island in the Indian Archipelago (Bali, according to Lassen) (Diod. II. 57-60). Pomponius Mela (A.D. 43) also had no recent information as regards India.

Pliny.

Pliny (A.D. 23-79) who published his Natural History in A.D. 77 gives a fairly full account of India, chiefly drawn from Megasthenês (see above). He also gives two valuable pieces of contemporary information:

(i) An account of Ceylon (Taprobanê) to which a freedman of Annius Plocamus, farmer of the Red Sea tribute, was carried by stress of weather in the reign of Claudius (A.D. 41-54). On his return the king sent to the emperor four envoys, headed by one Rachias (VI. 22).

(ii) An account of the voyage from Alexandria to India by a course which had only lately been made known (VI. 23). Pliny divides the history of navigation from the time of Nearchus to his own age into three periods:

(*a*) the period of sailing from Syagrus (Râs Fartak) in Arabia to Patalê (Indus delta) by the south-west wind called Hippalus, 1332 miles;

(*b*) the period of sailing from Syagrus (Râs Fartak) to Sigerus (*Ptol.* Milizêgyris, *Peripl.* Melizeigara, probably Janjíra, and perhaps the same as Strabo's Sigertis);

(*c*) the modern period, when traffic went on from Alexandria to Koptos up the Nile, and thence by camels across the desert to Berenice (in Foul Bay), 257 miles. Thence the merchants start in the middle of

Appendix VI.

EARLY GREEKS AND ROMANS.

Pliny.

summer before the rising of the dogstar and in thirty days reach Okelis (Ghalla) or Cane (Hisn Ghorab), the former port being most frequented by the Indian trade. From Okelis it is a forty days' voyage to Muziris (Muyyiri, Kranganur) which is dangerous on account of the neighbouring pirates of Nitrias (Mangalor) and inconvenient by reason of the distance of the roads from the shore. Another better port is Becare (Kallada, Yule) belonging to the tribe Neacyndon (*Ptol.* Melkynda, *Peripl.* Nelkynda) of the kingdom of Pandion (Pâṇḍya) whose capital is Modura (Madura). Here pepper is brought in canoes from Cottonara (Kaḍattanâḍu). The ships return to the Red Sea in December or January.

It is clear that the modern improvement in navigation on which Pliny lays so much stress consisted, not in making use of the monsoon wind, but in striking straight across the Indian ocean to the Malabar coast. The fact that the ships which took this course carried a guard of archers in Pliny's time, but not in that of the Periplus, is another indication that the direct route to Malabar was new and unfamiliar in the first century A.D. The name Hippalus given to the monsoon wind will be discussed below in dealing with the Periplus.

Dionysios Periêgêtês.

Dionysios Perie'ge'te's who has lately been proved to have written under Hadrian (A.D. 117-138) (Christ's Griech, Litteratur Gesch, page 507) gives a very superficial description of India but has a valuable notice of the Southern Skythians who live along the river Indus to the east of the Gedrôsoi (l. 1087-88).

Klaudios Ptolemaios.

Klaudios Ptolemaios of Alexandria lived according to Suidas under Marcus Aurelius Antoninus (A.D. 161-180). He compiled his account of India as part of a geographical description of the then known world, and drew much of his materials from Marinos of Tyre, whose work is lost, but who must have written about A.D. 130. Ptolemy (or Marinos before him) had a very wide knowledge of India, drawn partly from the relations of shipmasters and traders and partly from Indian lists similar to those of the *Purânas* but drawn up in Prâkṛit. He seems to have made little if any use of Megasthenês and the companions of Alexander. But his map of India is distorted by the erroneous idea, which he took from Eratosthenês, that the width of India from west to east greatly exceeded its length from north to south. Ptolemy begins his description of India with the first chapter of his seventh book, which deals with India within the Ganges. He gives first the names of rivers, countries, towns, and capes along the whole coast of India from the westernmost mouth of the Indus to the easternmost mouth of the Ganges. He next mentions in detail the mountains and the rivers with their tributaries, and then proceeds to enumerate the various nations of India and the cities belonging to each, beginning with the north-west and working southwards: and he finally gives a list of the islands lying off the coast. In dealing with his account of western India it will be convenient to notice together the cities of each nation which he mentions separately under the heads of coast and inland towns.

He gives the name of Indo-Skythia to the whole country on both sides of the lower course of the Indus from its junction with the Koa (Kábul river), and gives its three divisions as Patalênê (lower Sindh) Abiria (read Sabiria, that is Sauvîra or upper Sindh and Multan) and Surastrênê (Surâshṭra or Kâthiâvâda). We have seen that Dionysios knew the southern Skythians of the Indus, and we shall meet with them again in the Periplus (chapter 38ff).

Appendix VI.

EARLY GREEKS AND ROMANS.

Klaudios Ptolemaios.

He enumerates seven mouths of the Indus, but the river is so constantly changing its course that it is hopeless to expect to identify all the names given by him (Sagapa. Sinthôn, Khariphron, Sapara, Sabalaessa. and Lônibare) with the existing channels. Only it may be noted that Sinthôn preserves the Indian name of the river (Sindhu) and that the easternmost mouth (Lônibare) probably represents both the present Korî or Launî and the Lûnî river of Mârwâr, a fact which goes some way to explain why Ptolemy had no idea of the existence of Kachh, though he knows the Ran as the gulf of Kanthi. Hence he misplaces Surastrênê (Surâshtra or Kâthiâvâḍa) in the Indus delta instead of south of the Ran. Ptolemy enumerates a group of five towns in the north-western part of Indo-Skythia (Kohat, Bannu, and Dera Ismail Khân) of which Cunningham (Anc. Geog. pages 84ff) has identified Banagara with Bannu, and Andrapana with Daraban, while the sites of Artoarta, Sabana, and Kodrana are unknown. Ptolemy next gives a list of twelve towns along the western bank of the Indus to the sea. Of these Embolima has been identified by Cunningham (Anc. Geog. page 52) with Amb sixty miles above Attok, and Pasipêda is identified by St. Martin with the Besmaid of the Arab geographers and placed near Mithankot at the junction of the Chenab with the Indus. Sousikana, which comes next in the list to Pasipêda, is generally thought to be a corruption of Mousikanos, and is placed by the latest authority (General Haig, *The Indus Delta Country*, page 130) in Bahawalpur, though Cunningham (Anc. Geog. page 257) puts it at Alor, which is somewhat more in accordance with Ptolemy's distances. Kôlaka the most southerly town of the list, cannot well be the Krôkala of Arrian (Karâchi) as McCrindle supposes, for Ptolemy puts it nearly a degree north of the western mouth of the Indus.

The two great towns of the delta which Ptolemy next mentions, are placed by General Haig, Patala at a point thirty-five miles south-east of Haidarâbâd (*op. cit.* page 19) and Barbarei near Shâh Bandar (*op. cit.* page 31). Barbarei is mentioned again in the Periplus (chapter 38) under the name of Barbarikon. Ptolemy gives the names of nine towns on the left bank of the Indus from the confluence to the sea, but very few of them can be satisfactorily identified. Panasa can only be Osanpur (St. Martin) on Fluellen's principles. Boudaia must represent the Budhîya of the Arabs, though it is on the wrong side of the river (see Haig, *op. cit.* page 57ff). Naagramma may with Yule be placed at Naushahro. Kamigara cannot be Aror (McCrindle), if that place represents Sousikana. Binagara is commonly thought to be a corrupt reading of Minnagara (compare Periplus chapter 38). Haig (*op. cit.* page 32 note 47) refers to the Tuhfatu'l Kirâm as mentioning a Minnagar in pargana Shâhdâdpur (north-east of Haidarâbâd). Parabali, Sydros, and Epitausa have not been identified, but must be looked for either in Haidarâbâd or in Thar and Pârkar. Xoana may with Yule be identified with Siwana in the bend of the Lûnî and gives another indication that Ptolemy confounded the Lûnî with the eastern mouth of the Indus.

On the coast of Surastrênê (Kâthiâvâḍa) Ptolemy mentions, first, the island of Barakê (Dvârakâ Bêt): then the city Bardaxêma which must be Porbandar (Yule), in front of the Barada hills: then the village of Surastra, which perhaps represents Verâval, though it is placed too far north. Surastra cannot well be Junâgad (Lassen) which is not on the coast and in Ptolemy's time was not a village, but a city, though it is certainly strange that Ptolemy does not anywhere mention it. Further south Ptolemy places the mart of Monoglôsson (Mangrol). The eastern boundary of the coast of Indo-Skythia seems to have been the mouth of the Môphis (Mahî). Ptolemy's account of Indo-Skythia may be completed by mentioning the list of places which he puts to the east of the Indus (*i. e.* the Lûnî) and at some distance from it.

These are: Xodrakê, which has not been identified, but which must be placed somewhere in Mewâr, perhaps at the old city of Pûr, seventy-two miles north-east of Udaipur, or possibly at the old city of Ahar, two miles from Udaipur itself (Tod's Râjasthân, I. 677-78).

Sarbana, which is marked in Ptolemy's map at the head-waters of the Mahî in the Apokopa mountains (Aravallis), must be identified with Sarwan about ten miles north-west of Ratlâm. There is also a place called Sarwanio close to Nimach, which Ptolemy may have confused with Sarwan.

Auxoamis, which St. Martin identifies with Sûmî, and Yule with Ajmir, but neither place suits the distance and direction from Sarwan. If Ptolemy, as above suggested, confused Sarwan and Sarwanio, Auxoamis may be Ahar near Udaipur, Pûr being then Xodrakê: otherwise Auxoamis may be I'dar. The question can only be settled by more exact knowledge of the age of Ahar and of I'dar. Orbadarou may provisionally with Yule be placed at Âbu.

Asinda must be looked for near Sidhpur, though it cannot with St. Martin be identified with that place. Perhaps Vadnagar (formerly Ânandapura and a very old town) may be its modern representative.

Theophila may be Devaliya (Yule) or Thân (Burgess) in north-east Kâthiâvâḍa.

Astakapra is admitted to be Hastakavapra or Hâthab near Bhávnagar (Bühler).

Larikê is described by Ptolemy next after Indo-Skythia on his way down the West Coast. The northern limit of its coast was the mouth of the river Môphis (Mahî). Its name is the Lâṭa of *purâṇas* and inscriptions. Ptolemy mentions as on its coast the village of Pakidarê, which may be a misreading for Kâpidarê and represent Kâvî (Kâpikâ of inscriptions) a holy place just south of the Mahî. Next comes Cape Maleô, which Ptolemy both in his text and in his map includes in Larikê, though there is no prominent headland in a suitable position on the east side of the Gulf of Cambay. As he puts it $2\frac{1}{4}$ degrees west of Broach, it may probably be identified with Gôpnâth Point in Kâthiâvâḍa on the other side of the gulf (the Pâpikê of the Periplus), his name for it surviving in the neighbouring shoals known as the Malai banks. It is in agreement with this that Ptolemy puts the mouth of the river Namados (Narmadâ) to the north of Cape Maleô. South of the river is Kamanê which may be identified with the Kamanijja or Karmaṇêya of inscriptions, that is with Kamlej on the Taptî above Surat. It has been supposed to be the Kammôni of the Periplus (chapter 43), which was the village opposite to the reef called Hêrônê on the right (east) of the gulf of Barygaza: but it is perhaps best to separate the two and to identify Kammôni with Kim, north of Olpâd. The next town mentioned is Nousaripa, which should probably be read Nousarika, being the Navasârikâ of inscriptions and the modern Nausâri. The most southerly town of Larikê is Poulipoula, which has been identified with Phulpâdâ or old Surat, but is too far south. Bilimora is perhaps the most likely position for it, though the names do not correspond (unless Pouli is the Dravidian *Puli* or *poli* = a tiger, afterwards replaced by *Bili* = a cat). Ptolemy begins his list of the inland cities of Larikê with Agrinagara, which may with Yule be identified with

Appendix VI.

EARLY GREEKS AND ROMANS.

Klaudios Ptolemaios.

Âgar, thirty-five miles north-east of Ujjain, and the Âkara of inscriptions. The next town is Siripalla, which has not been identified, but should be looked for about thirty miles to the south-east of Agar, not far from Shâhjahânpur. The modern name would probably be Shirol. Bammogoura must be identified, not with Pawangad (Yule), but with Hiuen Tsiang's "city of the Brâhmans" (Beal, Si-yu-ki, II. 262), 200 *li* (about 33 miles) to the north-west of the capital of Mâlava in his time. The distance and direction bring us nearly to Jaora. Sazantiou and Zerogerei have not been satisfactorily identified but may provisionally be placed at Ratlâm and Badnawar respectively, or Zêrogerei may be Dhâr as Yule suggested. Ozênê the capital of Tiastanês is Ujjain the capital of the Kshatrapa Cashṭana who reigned c. 130 A.D. His kingdom included Western Mâlwâ, West Khandesh, and the whole of Gujárat south of the Mahi. His grandson Rudradâman (A.D. 150) tells us in his Girnâr inscription (I. A. VII. 259) that his own kingdom included also Mârwâr Sindh and the lower Panjâb. Next to Ujjain Ptolemy mentions Minnagara, which must have been somewhere near Mânpur. Then we come to Tiatoura or Chândor (Yule) on the ridge which separates Khandesh from the valley of the Godâvari, and finally on that river itself Nasika the modern Nâsik. It is very doubtful whether Nâsik at any time formed part of the dominions of Cashṭana, since we know from the inscriptions in the Nâsik caves that the Kshatrapas were driven out of that part of the country by Gautamîputra Śâtakarṇi, the father of Ptolemy's contemporary Pulumâyi. Ptolemy probably found Nâsik mentioned in one of his lists as on a road leading from Ujjain southwards and he concluded that they belonged to the same kingdom.

Ariakê of the Sadinoi included the coast of the Konkan as far south as Baltipatna (near Mahâd) and the Deccan between the Godâvari and the Krishṇa. The name occurs in Varâha Mihira's Bṛihat Samhitâ XIV. in the form Âryaka. The tribal name Sadinoi is less easy to explain. The suggested connection with the word *Sâdhana* as meaning an agent (Lassen) and its application to the Kshatrapas of Gujarat, are not tenable. The only authority for this meaning of *Sâdhana* is Wilson's Sanskrit Dictionary, and at this time it is certain that Ariakê belonged, not to the Kshatrapas of Gujarat, but to the Śâtakarṇis of Paithan on the Godâvari. Bhândârkar's identification of the Sadinoi with Varâha Mihira's Śântikas seems also somewhat unsatisfactory. Ptolemy's name may possibly be a corruption of Śâtakarṇi or Śâtavâhana. The coast towns of this region were Soupara (Supârâ near Bassein), south of which Ptolemy places the river Goaris (Vaitaraṇî), Dounga (perhaps Dugaḍ ten miles north of Bhiwndi) south of which is the Bênda river (Bhiwndî Creek), Simylla, a mart and a cape, the Automula and Perimula of Pliny and the modern Cheul (Chemula); Milizêgyris an island, the same as the Melizêigara of the Periplus and (probably) as the Sigerus of Pliny and the modern Janjîra; Hippokoura, either Ghodegâon or Kudâ (Yule) in Kolâbâ district; Baltipatna, probably the Palaipatmai of the Periplus and the same as Pâl near Mahâd.

The inland dominions of the Sadinoi were much more extensive than their coast line. Ptolemy gives two lists of cities, one of those lying to the west (*i. e.* north) of the Bênda, whose course in the Deccan represents the Bhîmâ river, and the other of those between the Bênda and the Pseudostomos (here the Mâlprabhâ and Krishṇa or possibly the Tungabhadra with its tributaries). The most easterly towns in the first list, Malippala and Sarisabis, are not satisfactorily identified, but must be looked for in the Nizâm's country to the south-east of Haidarâbâd, Next comes Tagara mentioned in the Periplus (chapter 51) as ten days east from Paithan, and therefore about the latitude of Kulbarga, with which it is identified by Yule. The distance and direction make its identification with Deogir (Wilford and others), Junnar (Bhagwanlâl), or Kolhâpur (Fleet) impossible. The best suggestion hitherto made is that it is Dârur or Dhârur (Bhândârkar), but Dârur in the Bhîr district is too far north, so Dhârur fifty miles west of Haidarâbâd must be taken as the most likely site. Next to Tagara Ptolemy mentions Baithana, which is the Paithana of the Periplus and the modern Paithan on the Godâvari. It is called by our author the capital of Siroptolemaios, who is the Śrî-Pulumâyi of the Nâsik cave inscriptions. Next to Baithana comes Deopali, which may safely be identified with the modern Deoli in the suburbs of Ahmadnagar. Gamaliba, the next stage, must be placed somewhere on the line between Ahmednagar and Junnar, which latter ancient town is to be identified with Ptolemy's Omênogara, although this name is not easy to explain.

The second list of towns in Ariakê begins with Nagarouris (Nagarapurî) which probably represents Poona which even then must have been a place of importance, being at the head of the great road down the Bhorghat. Tabasô (compare Varâha Mihira's Tâpasâśrâmâḥ and Ptolemy's own Tabasoi) may be the holy city of Pandharpur. Indê has retained its ancient name (Indî in the north of the Bijapur district). Next follows Tiripangalida (Tikota in the Kurundwâd State ?) and then Hippokoura, the capital of Baleokuros. Dr. Bhândârkar has identified this king with the Vilivâyakûra of coins found in the Kolhâpur state. His capital may possibly be Hippargi in the Sindgi taluka of the Bîjâpur district. Soubouttou, the next town on Ptolemy's list, is not identifiable, but the name which follows, Sirimalaga, must be Sirnâl in the Bîjâpur taluka of the same district.

Kalligeris may be identified not with Kaṇhagiri (McCrindle) but with Galgali at the crossing of the Krishṇa, and Modogoulla is not Mûdgal (McCrindle) but Mudhol on the Ghâtprabhâ. Petirgala should probably read Penengala, and would then represent the old town of Panangala or Hongal in the Dhârvâḍ district. The last name on the list is Banaouasei, which is Vanavâsî, about ten miles from Sirsi in Kanara, a very old town where a separate branch of the Śâtakarṇis once ruled.

The Pirate Coast is the next division of Western India described by Ptolemy, who mentions five sea-ports but only two inland cities. It is clear that the pirates were hemmed in on the land side by the dominions of the Śâtakarṇis, and that they held but little territory above the ghâts, though their capital Mousopallê was in that region. The places on the coast from north to south were Mandagara, the Mandagara of the Periplus (chapter 53) which has been satisfactorily identified with Mandangaḍ to the south of the Bânkot creek.

Byzantion, which, as Dr. Bhândârkar first pointed out, is the Vaijayantî of inscriptions may be placed either at Chiplun or at Dabhol at the mouth of the Vâsishthî river. Chiplun is the only town of great antiquity in this part of the Koṅkaṇ, and if it is not Vaijayantî Ptolemy has passed over it altogether. The similarity of the names has suggested the identification of Byzantion with Jaygaḍ (Bhândârkar) or Vijayadrug (Vincent), but both these places are comparatively modern. There are indeed no very ancient towns in the Koṅkaṇ between Saṅgamêshvar and the Sâvantvâḍi border.

Khersonêsos is generally admitted to be the peninsula of Goa.

Appendix VI.

EARLY GREEKS AND ROMANS.

Klaudios Ptolemaios.

Armagara is placed a little to the north of the river Nanagounâ and may be represented by Cape Ramas in Portuguese territory.

The river Nanagouna here is generally supposed to be the Kâlinadi, though in its upper course it seems to represent the Taptî, and a confusion with the Nânâ pass led Ptolemy to bring it into connection with the rivers Goaris and Bênda (Campbell).

Nitra, the southernmost mart on the pirate coast, is the Nitrias of Pliny, and has been satisfactorily identified by Yule with Mangalor on the Nêtravatî.

The inland cities of the Pirates are Olokhoira and Mousopallê the capital, both of which must be sought for in the rugged country about the sources of the Krishṇa and may provisionally be identified with the ancient towns of Karâḍ and Karvîr (Kolhápur) respectively. To complete Ptolemy's account of this coast it is only necessary to mention the islands of Heptanêsia (Burnt Islands ?) Trikadiba and Peperinê. We are not here concerned with his account of the rest of India.

Bardesanês.

Bardesane's met at Babylon certain envoys sent from India to the emperor Antoninus Pius (A.D. 154-181) and received from Damadamis and Sandanês, who were of their number, accounts of the customs of the Brâhmans and of a rock temple containing a statue of Śiva in the Ardhanârî form. Lassen (III. 62 and 348) connects Sandanês with the Sadinoi and places the temple in Western India, but neither of these conclusions is necessary. The object of the embassy is unknown.

Periplus.

The Periplus of the Erythrean Sea, formerly though wrongly attributed to Arrian (150 A.D.), is an account of the Egyptian trade with East Africa and India, written by a merchant of Alexandria for the use of his fellows. It is preserved in a single manuscript which in some places is very corrupt. The age of this work has been much disputed : the chief views as to this matter are,

(i) that the Periplus was written before Pliny and made use of by him (Vincent, Schwanbeck, and Glaser). The arguments of Vincent and Schwanbeck are refuted by Müller (Geogr. Gr. Min. I. xcviii) Glaser's case is (Ausland 1891, page 45) that the Malikhas of the Periplus is Malchos III. of Nabathæa (A.D. 49-71), that the Periplus knows Meroê as capital of Ethiopia, while at the time of Nero's expedition to East Africa (A.D. 68), it had almost vanished, and lastly that the author of the Periplus is Basilis or Basilês, whom Pliny names as an authority for his Book VI. It may be replied that Malikhas is the title Malik and may have been applied to any Arab Sheikh (Reinaud): that the Periplus does not with certainty mention Meroê at all: and that Basilis whether or not a contemporary of Ptolemy Philadelphos was at any rate earlier than Agatharkhidês (c. 200 B.C.), who quotes him (Geog. Gr. Min. I. 156) ;

(ii) that the Periplus was written at the same time as Pliny's work, but neither used the other (Salmasius). This view is refuted by Müller (*op. cit.* page 155) ;

(iii) that the Periplus was written after 161 A.D. (Dodwell); Müller has shown (*ibid*) that Dodwell's arguments are inconclusive ;

(iv) the received view that the Periplus was written between A.D. 80 and A.D. 89 (Müller) ;

(v) that the Periplus was written about the middle of the third century (Reinaud Mém. de l'Ac. des Inscr. XXIV. Pt. ii. translated in I. A. VIII. pages 330ff).

Appendix VI.

EARLY GREEKS AND ROMANS.

Periplus.

The only choice lies between the view of Müller and that of Reinaud. Müller argues for a date between A.D. 80 and A.D. 89, because the Periplus knows no more than Pliny of India beyond the Ganges, whereas Ptolemy's knowledge is much greater: because the Periplus calls Ceylon Palaisimoundou, which is to Ptolemy (VII. iv. 1) an old name: because the Nabathæan kingdom, which was destroyed A.D. 105, was still in existence at the time of the Periplus: because the Periplus account of Hippalos shows it to be later than Pliny: and because the Periplus mentions king Zôskalês, who must be the Za Hakalê of the Abyssinian lists who reigned A.D. 77-89. It may be replied that the Periplus is not a geography of Eastern Asia, but a guide book for traders with certain ports only: that Ptolemy must have found in his lists three names for Ceylon, Taprobanê, Palaisimoundou, and Salikê, and that he has wrongly separated Palai from Simoundou, taking it to mean "formerly" and therefore entered Simoundou as the old and Salikê as the modern name,* whereas all three names were in use together: that the Nabathæan king Malikhas was simply the Sheikh of the tribe (Reinaud), and points to no definite date: that the Periplus' account of Hippalos is certainly later than Pliny: and that the Zôskalês of the Periplus is the Za Sâgal or Za Asgal of the Abyssinian lists, who reigned A.D. 246-47 (Reinaud).

It follows that Reinaud's date for the Periplus (A.D. 250) is the only one consistent with the facts and especially with the Indian facts. As will appear below, the growth of the Hippalos legend since Pliny's time, the rival Parthians in Sindh, the mention of Mambaros and the supplanting of Ozênê by Minnagara as his capital since Ptolemy's time, the independence of Baktria, and the notices of Saraganês and Sandanês, are all points strongly in favour of Reinaud's date.

In the time of the Periplus the ships carrying on the Indian trade started from Myos Hormos (near Ras Abu Somer) or Berenikê (in Foul Bay) and sailed down the Red Sea to Mouza (Musa twenty-five miles north of Mokhâ), and thence to the watering place Okêlis (Ghalla) at the Straits. They then followed the Arabian coast as far as Kanê (Hisn Ghurâb in Hadramaut) passing on the way Eudaimôn Arabia (Aden) once a great mart for Indian traders, but lately destroyed by king Elisar (Müller's conjecture for ΚΑΙΣΑΡ of the MS.) From Kanê the routes to India diverge, some ships sailing to the Indus and on to Barygaza, and others direct to the ports of Limyrikê (Malabár Coast). There was also another route to Limyrikê, starting from Arômata (Cape Guardafui). In all three voyages the ships made use of the monsoon, starting from Egypt in July. The monsoon was called Hippalos, according to the Periplus (chapter 57), after the navigator who first discovered the direct course across the sea, and it has been inferred from Pliny's words (VI. 23) that this pilot lived in the middle of the first century A.D. But Pliny's own account shows that, as we should expect, the progress from a coasting to a direct voyage was a gradual one, with several intermediate stages, in all of which the monsoon was more or less made use of. There was therefore no reason for naming the wind from the pilot who merely made the last step. Further though Pliny knows Hippalus as the local name of the monsoon wind in the eastern seas, he says nothing of its having been the name of the inventor of the direct course. The inference seems to be that Hippalos the pilot is the child of a seaman's yarn arising out of the local name of

---

* We learn from Pliny (VI. 22) that Palaisimoundou was the name of a town and a river in Ceylon, whence the name was extended to the whole island.

Appendix VI.
EARLY GREEKS AND ROMANS.
Periplus.

the monsoon wind, and that his presence in the Periplus and not in Pliny shows that the former writer is much later than the latter.

The merchant bound for Skythia (Sindh) before he reaches land, which lies low to the northward, meets the white water from the river Sinthos (Indus) and water snakes (chapter 38). The river has seven mouths, small and marshy all but the middle one, on which is the port of Barbarikon (Shâhbandar, Haig, page 31) whence the merchants' wares are carried up by river to the capital Minnagar (near Shâhdâdpur. Haig, page 32), which is ruled by Parthians who constantly expel one another (chapter 39). These contending Parthians must have been the remnant of the Karên Pahlavs who joined with the Kushâns to attack Ardeshir Pâpakân (Journ. As. [1866] VII. 134). The imports are clothing, flowered cottons, topazes, coral, storax, frankincense, glass vessels, silver plate, specie, and wine: and the exports costus (spice), bdellium (gum), yellow dye, spikenard, emeralds, sapphires, furs from Tibet, cottons, silk thread, and indigo. The list of imports shows that the people of Skythia were a civilised race and by no means wild nomads.

The Periplus next (chapter 40) gives an accurate account of the Ran (Eirinon) which in those days was probably below sea level (Haig, page 22, Burnes' Travels into Bokhara, III. 309ff), and was already divided into the Great and the Little. Both were marshy shallows even out of sight of land and therefore dangerous to navigators. The Ran was then as now bounded fo. south and west by seven islands, and the headland Barakê (Dvâraka) a place of special danger of whose neighbourhood ships were warned by meeting with great black water-snakes.

The next chapter (41) describes the gulf of Barygaza (gulf of Cambay) and the adjoining land, but the passage has been much mangled by the copyist of our only MS. and more still by the guesses of editors. According to the simplest correction (ἤπροστης Ἀριακης χώρα) our author says that next after Barakê (Dvâraka) follows the gulf of Barygaza and the country towards Ariakê, being the beginning of the kingdom of Mambaros and of all India. Mambaros may possibly be a corruption of Makhatrapos or some similar Greek form of Mahâkshatrapa, the title of the so-called "Sâh Kings" who ruled here at this period (A.D. 250). According to the reading of the MS. the author goes on to say that "the inland part of this country bordering on the Ibêria (read Sabiria = Sauvira) district of Skythia is called . . . . (the name, perhaps Maru, has dropped out of the text), and the sea-coast Syrastrênê (Surâshṭra)." The country abounded then as now in cattle, corn, rice, cotton and coarse cotton cloth, and the people were tall and dark. The capital of the country was Minnagara whence much cotton was brought down to Barygaza. This Minnagara is perhaps the city of that name placed by Ptolemy near Mânpur in the Vindhyas, but it has with more probability been identified with Junâgad (Bhagvânlâl) which was once called Manipura (Kath. Gaz. 487). Our author states that in this part of the country were to be found old temples, ruined camps and large wells, relics (he says) of Alexander's march, but more probably the work of Menandros and Apollodotos. This statement certainly points to Kâthiâvâda rather than to Mânpur. The voyage along this coast from Barbarikon to the headland of Pâpikê (Gopnâth) near Astakapra (Hâthab) and opposite to Barygaza (Broach) was one of 3000 stadia = 300 miles, which is roughly correct. The next chapter (42) describes the northern part of the gulf of Cambay as 300 stadia wide and running northward to the river Maïs (Mahi). Ships bound for Barygaza steer first northward past the island

Appendix VI.

EARLY GREEKS AND ROMANS.

Periplus.

Baiônes (Peram) and then eastward towards the mouth of the Namnadios (Narmadâ) the river of Broach. The navigation (chapter 43) is difficult by reason of rocks and shoals such as Hêrônê (perhaps named from some wreck) opposite the village of Kammôni (Kim) on the eastern shore and by reason of the current on the western near Pâpiké (perhaps a sailor's name meaning Unlucky). Hence the government sends out fishermen in long boats called Trappaga or Kotumba (Kotia) to meet the ships (chapter 44) and pilot them into Barygaza, 300 stadia up the river, by towing and taking advantage of the tides. In this connection our author gives a graphic description of the Bore in the Narbadâ (chapter 45) and of the dangers to which strange ships are exposed thereby (chapter 46).

Inland from Barygaza (that is, from the whole kingdom, which, as we have seen, bordered on Sauvîra or Multân) lay (chapter 47) the Aratrioi (Arattas of the Mahâbhârata and Purânas, who lived in the Panjâb), the Arakhôsioi (people of eastern Afghanistan), Gandaraioi (Gandhâra of N.-W. Panjâb), Proklais (near Peshâwar), and beyond them the Baktrianoi (of Balkh) a most warlike race, governed by their own independent sovereigns. These last are probably the Kushâns who, when the Parthian empire fell to pieces in the second quarter of the third century, joined the Karên Pahlavs in attacking Ardeshir. It was from these parts, says our author, that Alexander marched into India as far as the Ganges—an interesting glimpse of the growth of the Alexander legend since the days of Arrian (A.D. 150). Our author found old *drakhmai* of Menandros and Apollodotos still current in Barygaza.

Eastward in the same kingdom (chapter 48) is the city of Ozênê, which was formerly the capital, whence onyxes, porcelain, muslins, and cottons are brought to Barygaza. From the country beyond Proklais came costus, bdellium, and spikenard of three kinds, the Kattybourine, the Patropapigic, and the Kabalitic (this last from Kábul).

We learn incidentally that besides the regular Egyptian trade Barygaza had commercial relations with Mouza in Arabia (chapter 21) with the East African coast (chapter 14) and with Apologos (Obollah) at the head of the Persian Gulf and with Omana on its eastern shore (chapter 36). The imports of Barygaza were wine, bronze, tin and lead, coral and gold stone (topaz?), cloth of all sorts, variegated sashes (like the horrible Berlin wool comforters of modern days), storax, sweet clover, white glass, gum sandarac, stibium for the eyes, and gold and silver coin, and unguents. Besides, there were imported for the king costly silver plate, musical instruments (musical boxes are still favoured by Indian royalty), handsome girls for the harem (these are the famous Yavanî handmaids of the Indian drama), high-class wine, apparel and choice unguents, a list which shows that these monarchs lived in considerable luxury. The exports of Barygaza were spikenard, costus, bdellium, ivory, onyxes, porcelain, box-thorn, cottons, silk, silk thread, long pepper (chillies), and other wares from the coast ports.

From Barygaza our author rightly says (chapter 50) that the coast trends southward and the country is called Dakhinabadês (Dakshinâpatha): much of the inland country is waste and infested by wild beasts, while populous tribes inhabit other regions as far as the Ganges. The chief towns in Dakhinabadês (chapter 51) are Paithana (Paithan) twenty days journey south of Barygaza and Tagara (Dhârur) a very large city ten days east of Paithana. From Paithana come onyxes, and from Tagara cottons muslins and other local wares from the (east) coast.

Appendix VI.

EARLY GREEKS AND ROMANS.

Periplus.

The smaller ports south of Barygaza are Akabarou (perhaps the Khabirun of Mahomedan writers and the modern Kâvêrî the river of Nâusâri) Souppara (Supârâ near Bassein) and Kalliena, which was made a mart by the elder Saraganês, but much injured when Sandanês became its master, for from his time Greek vessels visiting the port are sent under guard to Barygaza. This interesting statement is one of the clearest indications of the date of the Periplus. As Bhândârkar has shown, the elder Saraganês implies also a younger, who can be no other than Yajñaśrî Śâtakarṇi (A.D. 140), and the Periplus must be later than his time. The Sandanês of the text must have been a ruler of Gujarát and may be identified with the Kshatrapa Saṅghadâman (A.D. 224).

South of Kalliena (chapter 53) were Sêmylla (Chaul) Mandagora (Mandangaḍ) Palaipatmai (Pâl near Mahâd) Melizeigara (probably Janjîra) and Byzantion (Chiplun). The words which follow probably give another name of Byzantion "which was formerly also called Turannosboas," the name Toparon being a misunderstanding (Müller, Geogr. Gr. Min. I. 296). South of this are the islands of Sêsekreienai (Burnt Islands), Aigidioi (Angediva), Kaineitai (Island of St. George) near the Khersonêsos (Goa), and Leukê (Laccadives ?) all pirate haunts. Next comes Limyrikê (the Tamil country) the first marts of which are Naoura (Cannanor or Tellichery, rather than Honávar, which is too far north) and Tyndis (Kaḍaluṇḍi near Bepur) and south of these Muziris (Kranganur) and Nelkynda (Kallaḍa). Tyndis and Muziris were subject to Kêprobotras (Keralaputra that is the Cera king) and Nelkynda to Pandion (the Pâṇḍya king of Madura). Muziris was a very prosperous mart trading with Ariakê (North Konkan) as well as Egypt. Nelkynda was up a river 120 stadia from the sea, ships taking in cargo at the village of Bekarê at the mouth of the river. Our author gives an interesting account of the trade at these ports and further south as well as on the east coast, but we are not concerned with this part of his work.

Markianos.

Markianos of Hîrakleia about the year 400 A.D. is the leading geographer of the period following Ptolemy, but his work consisted chiefly in corrections of Ptolemy's distances taken from an obscure geographer named Prôtagoras. He adds no new facts to Ptolemy's account of western India.

Stephanos.

Stephanos of Byzantium wrote about 450 A.D. (or at any rate later than Markianos, whom he quotes) a huge geographical dictionary of which we have an epitome by one Hermolaos. The Indian names he gives are chiefly taken from Hekataios, Arrianos, and especially from a poem called Bassarika on the exploits of Dionysos, by a certain Dionysos. But his geography is far from accurate: he calls Barakê (Dvârakâ) an island, and Barygaza (Broach) a city, of Gedrôsia. Among the cities he names are Argantê (quoted from Hekataios), Barygaza (Broach), Boukephala (Jalâlpur), Byzantion (Chiplun), Gêreia, Gorgippia, Darsania famous for woven cloths, Dionysopolis (Nysa ?), Kathia (Multan ?), Kaspapyros and Kaspeiros (Kaśmîr), Margana, Massaka (in Swât), Nysa, Palimbothra (Pâtaliputra), Panaioura near the Indus, Patala (thirty-five miles south-east of Haidarâbâd, Sindh), Rhodoê, Rhôganê, Rhôn in Gandarikê, Saneia, Sesindion, Sinda on the great gulf (perhaps Ptolemy's Asinda, Vaḍnagar), Sôlimna, and Taxila. He also names a number of tribes, of whom none but the Orbitai (Makrân) the Pandai (Pâṇḍya) Bôlingæ (Bhâulingi Sâlvas) and possibly the Salangoi (Sâlaṅkâyana) belong to the western coast..

Appendix VI.

EARLY GREEKS AND ROMANS.

Kosmas.

Kosmas Indikopleustes, shipman and monk, who wrote his Topographia Christiana between A.D. 530 and 550, is the last of the ancient writers who shows independent knowledge of India. He says that Sindu (Sindh), is where India begins, the Indus being the boundary between it and Persia. The chief ports of India are Sindu (Debal), which exports musk and nard: Orrhotha (Surâshtra that is Verâval) which had a king of its own: Kalliana (Kalyân) a great port exporting brass, and sîsam (blackwood) logs and cloth having a king of its own and a community of Christians under a Persian bishop: Sibor which also had a king of its own and therefore cannot be Supârâ, which is too close to Kalliana, but must be Goa, the Sindabur of the Arabs: Parti, Mangaruth (Mangalor), Salopatana, Nalopatana, and Pudopatana which are the five marts of Malê the pepper country (Malabâr), where also there are many Christians. Five days' sail south of Malê lay Sieledība or Taprobanê (Ceylon), divided into two kingdoms in one of which is found the hyacinth-stone. The island has many temples, and a church of Persian Christians, and is much resorted to by ships from India Persia and Ethiopia dealing in silk, aloewood, cloves, sandalwood, &c. On the east coast of India is Marallo (Morava opposite Ceylon) whence conch-shells are exported: Then Kaber (Kaveripatam or Pegu. Yule's Cathay Introd. page clxxviii.) which exports Alabandinum; further on is the clove country and furthest of all Tzinista (China) which produces the silk. In India further up the country, that is further north, are the White Ounoi or Hûnas who have a king named Gollas (Mihirakula of inscriptions) who goes forth to war with 1000 elephants and many horsemen and tyrannises over India, exacting tribute from the people. His army is said to be so vast as once to have drunk dry the ditch surrounding a besieged city and marched in dryshod.

In his book XI. Kosmas gives some account of the wild beasts of India, but this part of his work does not require notice here.

This is the last glimpse we get of India before the Arabs cut off the old line of communication with the Empire by the conquest of Egypt A.D. 641-2).

INDEX.